The Four
Masterworks of
the Ming Novel
Ssu ta ch'i-shu

The Four Masterworks of the Ming Novel

Ssu ta ch'i-shu

四大奇書

ANDREW
H. PLAKS

PRINCETON
UNIVERSITY
PRESS

Copyright ©1987 by Princeton
University Press

Published by Princeton University Press,
41 William Street, Princeton, New Jersey
08540

In the United Kingdom: Princeton
University Press, Guildford, Surrey

All Rights Reserved

Library of Congress Cataloging in
Publication Data will be found on the last
printed page of this book

ISBN 0-691-06708-2

Publication of this book has been aided by
a grant from the Lacy Lockert Fund of
Princeton University Press.

This book has been composed in
Palatino by Asco Trade Typesetting Ltd.,
Hong Kong

Clothbound editions of Princeton
University Press books are printed on
acid-free paper, and binding materials are
chosen for strength and durability.

Printed in the United States of America
by Princeton University Press, Princeton,
New Jersey

Designed by Laury A. Egan

Contents

Since this is a rather large book, I would like to state at the outset what I aim to accomplish. Basically, this is a set of four separate studies of what are known in Chinese as "the four extraordinary books" (*ssu ta ch'i-shu* 四大奇書), to which I have found it unavoidable to attach a dull translation: "the four masterworks of Ming fiction." These studies can stand or fall independently as critical readings of the respective texts. But this book also has something of an argument to it, which I will try to set forth here as simply as possible before making any further claims on the reader's time.

First, my readings of these "amazing books" are based on the conviction that they yield the most meaningful interpretations when viewed not simply as compendia of popular narrative materials, but as reflections of the cultural values and intellectual concerns of the sophisticated literary circles of the late Ming period. I believe that the fullest recensions of each of these novels were composed by and for the same sort of people who gave us the startlingly original achievements of Ming "literati painting" and the gems of the contemporary "literati stage," which is why I speak of them with the somewhat pretentious, and perhaps misleading term "literati novels."

Once this assumption has been made, my argument must take several particular directions. First, I attempt to show that the appearance of these four works in their most mature forms marks the emergence of a new genre of Chinese prose fiction. I believe that the range of structural and rhetorical features shared by these texts, for all their differences in subject matter and style, demonstrates a strong generic consciousness on the part of their authors—despite the fact that there has never been any label for this genre much more precise than "the four extraordinary books," which I have modified for the title of this study. In order to support my contention that this genre took on its recognizable shape only around the sixteenth century, I have found it necessary to go into a time-consuming review of the current evidence regarding the textual history and authorship of each work. This sort of background study is not my primary concern, and I claim no original contributions in this area. I simply try to synthesize the state of the field in order to show the remarkable contributions of the sixteenth-century recensions to the generation of each masterwork, and to bring out the radical transformation that has been effected in each case on the prior tradition of narrative sources. This, of course, is not to deny the importance of the popular sources and antecedent narrative materials that feed into the development of each of these texts; it is merely to insist that the new bottles, in this case, may be more significant than the old wine.

To put it another way, I wish to suggest that each of the major texts under study here represents not just the most elaborate reworking of the respective narrative traditions, but actually a thoroughgoing process of revision of these materials, one governed primarily by ironic treatment of the prior sources and popular images. In my understanding, the crucial role of ironic rhetoric in the development of the Ming novel, as in the case of the slightly later European novel form, is a double-edged tool. On the one hand, it produces texts that are primarily concerned with the undercutting or deflation of popular images and sympathies. But at the same time, it also carries with it the necessary implication of some sort of positive projection of meaning, even if this amounts to nothing more than the debris of a crumbling system of values. In my very tentative gropings toward the range of meanings thus projected in these four ironic masterpieces, I try as far as possible to locate the ideas I see reflected in them on the map of Ming intellectual history. In doing so, I place special emphasis on what I describe as an essentially "Confucian" orientation of these novels—this in spite of the fact that the didactic schemes actually presented in the texts, meager as they are, seem to be couched entirely in Buddhist or Taoist terms of discourse. I attempt to justify this approach in my concluding essay. In the meantime, however, I would like to state that the apparent contradiction here is far less important than it may seem, since what we are always dealing with in this context is the syncretic vision at the heart of late Ming thought, a view of life that is much richer for its infusion of Buddhist and Taoist sensibilities, but never gets away from the Confucian bedrock of the literary training and values of the age.

My insistence on an ironic reading of these books betrays the fact that I come to them from the perspective of comparative literature methodology, and in particular from recent theories of the novel in Western criticism. This I freely acknowledge. I hope this approach to the Chinese texts will not only lend more substance to the common application of the term "novel" to such works (a problem I have tried to deal with elsewhere), but at the same time may broaden the definition of this term to take in examples of parallel literary developments in non-Western traditions. In any event, the "masterworks" under study here are of a stature that requires no justification in fashionable critical terms.

There is, however, another side to my treatment of the great Ming novels that does require a bit of an apology. I must confess that I feel some hesitation about attempting to impose my own critical readings on the masterpieces of a cultural heritage that is not my own birthright. But any such reservations are rendered trivial by the gracious hospitality I have always encountered on the part of Chinese friends and colleagues toward an outsider's interpretations of the Chinese literary monuments. This generosity of spirit can only be appreciated when it is compared to the corresponding treatment that might be expected in virtually any other cultural sphere by a foreign scholar who would dare to tread on the sacred ground of literary patrimony.

Beyond this, there is another reason I believe the interpretations offered here are less alien than they may appear. This is because I draw my principal inspiration and guidance from the traditional Chinese commentators, whose critical readings accompanied many of the best late Ming and early Ch'ing editions of these novels. Because of the excesses and idiosyncrasies of these critics, their insights have often been barred from the serious study of the Ming novel in recent times. But I believe the systematic use of these materials can be justified on at least two points. First, though their critical stabs are often off the mark, their ratio of hits to misses can still compare favorably enough with the record of some of our modern critics. More to the point, these commentaries provide us with the possibility of reconstructing, for better or for worse, what these books may have meant to their immediate audiences, the literati readers of the sixteenth and seventeenth centuries.

My debt to the early Chinese critics is matched by my debt to twentieth-century Chinese literary scholarship, both to the giants of the past generation who put the great vernacular novels into the curriculum of serious learning, and to the many more recent scholars in China who are turning out a virtual flood of valuable new critical materials. Closer to home, my study is obviously deeply indebted to the work of C. T. Hsia, Patrick Hanan, Liu Ts'un-yan, André Lévy, and others, who have essentially established the field of serious criticism of the classical Chinese novel in the West.

More specific debts of gratitude are due to a number of friends and colleagues who have helped to shape the present manuscript in its various stages of preparation. First, I wish to express my appreciation to Professors Frederick W. Mote, Yu-kung Kao, James T. C. Liu, Hai-t'ao T'ang, and my other teachers and colleagues at Princeton, not only for a lifetime of guidance—this debt is too far-reaching to turn into a few choice phrases— but also for their patience with my endless requests for advice and information regarding this book over the past ten years. I owe a similar debt to David T. Roy of the University of Chicago for his characteristically thorough reading and correction of several of my draft chapters, and, more generally, for teaching so many of us how to read the Chinese novel. Dr. Wang Ch'iu-kuei has also provided extremely helpful comments on a few chapters, as have Professors Anthony C. Yu, Y. W. Ma, Chang Ching-erh and others. The first chapter in this book could not have been written without the assistance of Professor Hsü Shuo-fang of Hang-chou University, who, as a Luce Fellow at Princeton during the 1983–84 academic year, helped me run a series of graduate seminars on Chia-ching and Wan-li literature. I am also deeply indebted to Professor Wu Hsiao-ling of Beijing, for generously sharing with me his vast knowledge and literary resources; and for writing the characters that grace the cover of this volume. Other parts of the manuscript have been read and commented upon by Willard Peterson, James Geiss, David Rolston, and others too numerous to mention. I also want to express here my profound gratitude and affection toward the students with whom I have worked on these texts through all this period. Most of the insights presented in this volume, such as they are, are the unacknowledged contributions of the participants in a series of seminars devoted to reading the major novels. In addition, I want to thank my student assistants Tam King-fai and Deborah Porter for their valuable assistance during the final stages of the preparation of this manuscript.

This is the time and place to express my gratitude to a number of organizations that have provided generous financial support over the years. These include the National Endowment for the Humanities, whose study fellowship in 1976–77 enabled me to spend a year reading Ming and Ch'ing commentary editions of the novels in various libraries around the world, at which time the outlines of this study were conceived; and the Committee for Studies of Chinese Civilization of the American Council of Learned Societies, which made possible a semester on leave in 1980 to write up the first drafts of this book, before it began to grow to its present proportions. I should also thank the Committee on Scholarly Communication with the People's Republic of China for supporting a study program in China for several months in 1984–85, which, while not actually connected to the four masterworks project, still afforded many opportunities for additional research and personal contacts that have proven invaluable in making my final revisions on this book. I also want to express my appreciation to the Committee on Research in the Humanities of Princeton for their generous provision of typing funds, and to the Program in East Asian Studies for kindly granting my repeated requests for summer research assistance year after year.

Over the years, I have received gracious assistance from a number of libraries and special collections of Chinese books around the world. In addition to the East Asian libraries at Harvard, Columbia, Chicago, and other universities in this country, as well as the Library of Congress in Washington, I have benefited from the cooperation of the British Library, School of Oriental and African Studies, and Cambridge Library in England; the Bibliothèque nationale, Institut des hautes études chinoises, and École des langues orientales in Paris; the Vatican Library in Rome; the Oriental Institute of the Soviet Academy of Sciences in Leningrad; the Naikaku Bunko, Tōyō Bunko, National Diet Library, Seikadō and Sonkeikaku Collections, and the various Tokyo University Chinese collections in Japan; the National Central Library and Palace Museum Library in Taiwan; and the Peking Library, Peking University Library, Metropolitan Library, Institute of Literature of the Chinese Academy of Social Sciences, Tientsin Library, and Shanghai Library in China—to name just the most important. The principal research, however, has been conducted in the Gest Oriental Library at Princeton, which, under the far-seeing guidance of curator Diane Perushek and past curators, and with the expert assistance of Dr. Chou Min-chih, has put together one of the most complete collections available of microfilms and secondary materials on the Ming and Ch'ing novel. In addition, I want to thank the administrative staff of the Department of East Asian Studies here at Princeton for their helpful assistance in so many of the phases of this labor, particularly the retyping of many pages of this manuscript. Finally, I wish to express my appreciation to the editors of Princeton University Press, especially R. Miriam Brokaw, who first encouraged me to submit my sprawling manuscript; Lois Krieger, who has made some sense out of my stylistic anarchy; and Margaret Case, who has seen the book through to final publication.

Princeton, New Jersey
June 1986

Reader's Note

The romanization system adhered to in this study is modified Wade-Giles, with the following exception: for the e/o sound ㄜ, I use *o* after initial *k, h, l,* and without initial, but *e* in all other combinations (*k'e, te, t'e, che, ch'e, je, she, tse, ts'e, se.* The umlaut on *yüan* is omitted when referrring to the Yuan dynasty.

Capitalization is used for the first word in all romanized titles, plus all proper nouns occurring in titles (personal names, place-names, book titles). In Chinese romanization, hyphens are used to connect compound terms, as well as combinations that seem to me to form lexical units. In Japanese romanization, compound words are spelled together without hyphenation.

Chinese characters are provided for names, titles, and important terms at the first appearance only. They have been omitted in the footnotes if they appear later in the text or in the bibliography.

The Four
Masterworks of
the Ming Novel

Ssu ta ch'i-shu

CHAPTER 1

The Literati Novel:
Historical Background

During the hundred-odd years from the Hung-chih 弘治 period (1488–1505) until about halfway through the Wan-li 萬曆 reign (1573–1619)—a span of time that roughly corresponds to the sixteenth century by Western reckoning, four of the most beloved works of traditional Chinese fiction came into circulation in their most fully developed forms. These four texts —the *San-kuo chih t'ung-su yen-i* 三國志通俗演義, *Chung-i shui-hu chuan* 忠義水滸傳, *Hsi-yu chi* 西遊記 and *Chin P'ing Mei tz'u-hua* 金瓶梅詞話 — are, with certain later modifications, essentially the same books as those that are known by those titles and read today.[1] As we shall see in the detailed analysis of each of these works that comprises the substance of this study, none of these sixteenth-century editions is an entirely original literary creation. Rather, each represents the culmination of a long prior and subsequent history of source materials, antecedent narratives, and alternate recensions. Yet my principal thesis here will be that in each case the sixteenth-century text we have represents the most significant phase of this

[1] For the dates and identification of these editions, see bibliographical notes at the end of this book (hereafter referred to as b.n.) Each of these editions was superseded by revised commentary editions in the seventeenth century. The *San-kuo chih t'ung-su yen-i* was replaced by Mao Tsung-kang's *Ti-i ts'ai-tzu shu*; *Chung-i shui-hu chuan* was truncated and revised by Chin Sheng-t'an to produce *Ti-wu ts'ai-tzu shu Shui-hu chuan*; the *Chin P'ing Mei tz'u-hua* was reissued by Chang Chu-p'o as *Ti-i ch'i-shu* in a new edition based on the Ch'ung-chen period *Hsin-k'e hsiu-hsiang p'i-p'ing Chin P'ing Mei*; and what is generally taken to be the earliest complete edition of *Hsi-yu chi*, the 1592 Shih-te t'ang edition, was eclipsed by Wang Hsiang-hsü's *Hsi-yu cheng-tao shu* by the K'ang-hsi period.

process of evolution, the one that puts the final stamp on the process and raises the respective narrative materials to the level of self-conscious artistic constructs. With this in mind, my discussions here will proceed on the supposition that it is these particular editions we should subject to the most thorough critical scrutiny and interpretation, while leaving the other versions of these narratives as simply documents in the historical development of Chinese fiction.

Once these four recensions were in place, they immediately came to function as models for the subsequent development of full-length *hsiao-shuo* 小說 fiction, what is today commonly called the traditional Chinese "novel." In fact, I could go one step further and state that it was precisely these texts that defined and shaped the generic outlines of the serious novel form in Ming and Ch'ing China.[2] This crucial position of the four works as fountainheads of the genre is somewhat obscured by their very preeminence, since few if any other examples of the genre come close to their level of richness and sophistication. And so they stand apart as a class among themselves, a special set of masterworks that was not equaled for nearly 150 years, when they were joined by *Ju-lin wai-shih* 儒林外史 and *Hung-lou meng* 紅樓夢 to form the so-called "six classic novels."[3]

Even before the addition of the latter two masterworks in the eighteenth century, however, the special status of the earlier four was granted due recognition. For example, Li Chih 李贄 listed *Shui-hu chuan* among what he called the "five great literary texts" (*wu ta pu wen-chang* 五大部文章), as did Chin Sheng-t'an 金聖歎 within his list of the "six works of genius" (*liu ts'ai-tzu shu* 六才子書).[4] By the early Ch'ing, book publishers were

---

[2] I have presented this argument in full in an article entitled "Full-Length *Hsiao-shuo* and the Western Novel," pp. 163–76.

[3] The term for the "six classic novels" (*ku-tien hsiao-shuo* 古典小說) is a neologism of twentieth-century scholarship. It was used as early as 1958 in Liu Hsiu-yeh's *Ku-tien hsiao-shuo hsi-ch'ü ts'ung-k'ao*, and seems to have come into common use under the influence of C. T. Hsia's *The Classic Chinese Novel*. I am not sure at what point during the Ch'ing or Republican periods this became a fixed critical category, but the view that these six works constitute a special class is reflected in a wide variety of critical writings on the novel.

[4] Li Chih's list of five preeminent masterpieces is reported in a late Ming *pi-chi* work by Chou Hui entitled *Chin-ling so-shih*, *chüan* 1, p. 5b. His other choices are *Shih Chi*, the poetry of Tu Fu and Su Shih, plus the writings of Li Meng-yang. Chin Sheng-t'an's "six works of genius" form the basis for a set of commentary editions, only some of which were apparently completed. These are described in *Hsin-ch'ou chi-wen*, p. 15b (1263). See Teng Chih-ch'eng, "Sung-k'an hsiao-chi," no. 2 (下), p. 132; and Richard G. Irwin, *The Evolution of a Chinese Novel*, p. 89. The other five "works of genius" are the *Li-sao*, *Shih Chi*, the book of Chuang Tzu, Tu Fu's poetry, and *Hsi-hsiang chi*. Cf. Chin's other commentaries on great literary texts, reprinted in *Ch'ang-ching t'ang ts'ai-tzu shu hui pien*, *Chin Sheng-t'an ch'i-shu shih-pa chung*, and other places. The most notable examples of novels labeled *ts'ai-tzu shu* or *ch'i-shu* are Mao Tsung-kang's *Ti-i ts'ai-tzu ch'i-shu* 第一才子奇書 (also *Ssu ta ch'i-shu ti-i chung* 第一種), *Hsi-yu cheng-tao ch'i-shu*, and Chang Chu-p'o's edition of *Chin P'ing Mei*, issued

regularly advertising editions of the four novels as "masterworks" (ch'i-shu 奇書), and even when the same terms came to be applied fairly indiscriminately to lesser works, they continued to carry the implication that the original four set the standard against which all comparable works must be measured. Eventually the expression "four masterworks" (ssu ta ch'i-shu 四大奇書) became something of a set term. I am not certain precisely when this expression was coined, but at least as early as the seventeenth century it was used by Liu T'ing-chi in his *Tsai-yüan tsa-chih*, as well as in a preface to a commentary edition of *San-kuo chih yen-i* attributed to Li Yü 李漁 (which ascribes the coining of the term to Feng Meng-lung 馮夢龍), among other places.[5] By the Ch'ien-lung 乾隆 period, it appears to have been used as the title of a set of the four novels reportedly issued in the name of the same Chieh-tzu yüan 芥子園 publishing house originally associated with Li Yü, and since that time it has come down to us as a fairly common designation.[6]

In proposing that it is these sixteenth-century editions of the four masterworks, rather than their earlier or later forms, that deserve the primary credit for transforming their respective narrative and textual traditions into literary monuments, I will have to pursue several lines of argumentation. First, I will review the evidence to attempt to show, in each chapter, that these particular recensions represent a significant advance over their hypothetical or extant antecedents. Next, I will provide a thorough structural and rhetorical analysis of the texts to demonstrate the degree of intricacy and artistic sophistication that goes into their composi-

---

under the title *Ti-i ch'i-shu* 第一奇書. A number of reprints of the Chang Chu-p'o text bear the title *Ssu ta ch'i-shu ti-ssu chung* (copies in Gest Oriental Library, Princeton; Tokyo University Library; and elsewhere). Other examples of editions of novels and plays laying claim to *ch'i-shu* or *ts'ai-tzu shu* status include minor works such as *Yü Chiao Li* 玉嬌梨 (*ti-san ts'ai-tzu shu*), *P'ing Shan Leng Yan* 平山冷燕 (*ti-ssu ts'ai-tzu shu*), *P'i-p'a chi* 琵琶記 (*ti-ch'i ts'ai-tzu shu*), *Pai-kuei chih* 白圭志 (*ti-pa ts'ai-tzu shu*), and *P'ing-kuei chuan* 平鬼傳 (*ti-chiu ts'ai-tzu shu*). Cf. also *Nü-hsien wai shih ch'i-shu* 女仙外史奇書, *Han Sung ch'i-shu* 漢宋奇書, and other examples.

[5] See Liu T'ing-chi, *Tsai-yüan tsa-chih*, pp. 24a–25a. On the *Li Li-weng p'ing-yüeh San-kuo chih yen-i*, see b.n. I.4 for additional details. A preface and *fan-li* introduction to *Hsü Chin P'ing Mei* (reprinted in *Han-pen Chung-kuo t'ung-su hsiao-shuo ts'ung-k'an* 罕本中國通俗小說叢刊 series; Taipei: T'ien-i, 1975) speaks of the "three masterworks" 三大奇書: *Shui-hu chuan*, *Hsi-yu chi*, and *Chin P'ing Mei*. See also the Hsien-chai lao-jen 閑齋老人 preface to *Ju-lin wai-shih* for a similar usage.

[6] The Ch'ien-lung set of the four novels is described by Chao Ts'ung in *Chung-kuo ssu ta hsiao-shuo chih yen-chiu*, p. 126. (The "four masterworks" in Chao's study are *San-kuo*, *Shui-hu*, *Hsi-yu chi* and *Hung-lou meng*.) A book fitting this description is listed in the Kyoto University Library catalogue. The designation *ssu ta ch'i-shu* is accepted as a fixed term in much contemporary scholarship on the Ming-Ch'ing novel. See, for example, Kuo Chen-i, *Chung-kuo hsiao-shuo shih*, pp. 185ff.; T'an Cheng-pi, *Chung-kuo hsiao-shuo fa-ta shih*, pp. 294ff.; and Shionoya On, *Shina bungaku gairon kōwa*, pp. 466ff.

tion. Once this groundwork has been set down, I will then turn to an extensive close reading and interpretation of the works, trying to relate this interpretation to some of the specific intellectual currents of the time.

Before I plunge into this task, however, it may be helpful to place these discussions in a broader context by speculating as far as possible on the question of why it was precisely at this moment in history that full-length Chinese narrative fiction reached this degree of maturity. There is obviously no reason, other than convenience, to cling to the imported time frame of the century—any more than that the conventional Chinese periodization by reign periods, for that matter, must necessarily mark out significant chunks of cultural history. One could just as well opt for a looser designation of the period in question as simply "late Ming," or, alternatively, one could narrow that focus to particular generations, as has recently been suggested.[7] On the other hand, one might prefer to look beyond the border of the Ming-Ch'ing transition to the swath of cultural history from, say, 1500 to 1750 as a more meaningful frame of reference. Nevertheless, I will attempt to show in this introductory chapter that the period within and around the hundred years from 1500 to 1600, which sits astride the circulation of the four masterworks, happens to take in marked developments in a wide variety of fields, so that in this case at least the unlikely division of this "century" may prove to be a useful tool of periodization after all.

Broadly speaking, an overview of Ming history begins with the impressive achievements of the founding generation, whose political and military successes were accompanied by cultural and literary accomplishments of the first order, followed by a period of retrenchment during much of the fifteenth century. Then the pace begins to pick up again in the final decades of that century, bringing us into a period of remarkable flowering right up to the generation of the fall of the dynasty. Of course, one might well assume that this apparent slackening of the rate of achievement in the fifteenth century is nothing more than an optical illusion, attributable to the shifting sands of reputation and taste and the selective preservation of evidence. But there is a widespread perception, on the part of both observers of that time and modern historians, that fresh winds were blowing in practically every field of endeavor for much of the sixteenth century, so that even certain trends that had been gradually taking shape over a much longer period of time now take on the aspect of striking new develop-

---

[7] See, for example, Willard Peterson, "Ming Periodization," pp. 7–8. Peterson designates the years from 1457 to 1521 as a transition period overlapping what he sees as a time of "contraction and consolidation" from 1449 to 1501, followed by a period of "expansion and change" for most of the sixteenth century (1502–82), up to the turning point of the demise of Chang Chü-cheng in 1582.

ments.[8] In the following pages, I will review some of the scholarly opinion on these historical trends, with an eye toward those points that can later be brought to bear on my interpretations of the four masterworks themselves.

First, let us consider the political climate of the period, as manifest in the court intrigues and military affairs that make up the central focus of most traditional and modern historical accounts of the dynasty. In terms of the overall span of the Ming state, what we are talking about is roughly the last half of the dynasty, which reached its arithmetical midpoint around the year 1500. The scenario of a dynamic revival of creativity at this point, gradually giving way to internal contradictions that leave the state more vulnerable than ever to challenges from within and without, is an over-simplified picture that readily conforms not only to the restoration phase of traditional dynastic cycle theories, but also to certain models in modern political theory regarding the rise and fall of empires.[9] When we come to look for the specific factors responsible for this failed "restoration," how-ever, the situation, as expected, turns out to be far more complex.

On the surface, these hundred years were, relatively speaking, an age of peace and security. To be sure, the nominally swollen forces of the paper military establishment were kept busy dealing with a variety of external enemies. Chief among these were the Mongols to the north, who had been pushed back into the steppe in the earlier campaigns of the dynasty's founder and the Yung-lo 永樂 emperor but never entirely subdued (as witnessed in the T'u-mu debacle 土木之變 in 1449),[10] and the coastal pirates (wo-k'ou 倭寇), who preyed upon the southeastern littoral and succeeded in occupying sizable chunks of inland territory.[11] Both of these fronts remained "hot" for much of the century. The steppe forces continued their harassment and scored some notable victories, most spectacularly

[8] See, for example, Cheng Chen-to, *Chung-kuo wen-hsüeh yen-chiu hsin pien*, pp. 509f. Cf. James Geiss's characterization of the period 1522−84 as one of "precarious stability," in his "Peking under the Ming," p. 215. See also Matteo Ricci's optimistic assessment of the state of the Chinese empire at this point, in *China in the Sixteenth Century*, p. 45.

[9] See, for example, Mark Elvin, *The Pattern of the Chinese Past*, pp. 17−22; and Ray Huang, "Fiscal Administration during the Ming Dynasty," p. 125. For the "theory of empires," I have in mind studies by Weber, Wittfogel, Parsons, and others, such as those collected in S. N. Eisenstadt's *The Decline of Empires*, as well as in his *The Political Systems of Empires*.

[10] For the causes and repercussions of the T'u-mu incident, see Frederick W. Mote, "The T'u-mu Incident of 1449," pp. 243−72; Tilemann Grimm, "Cheng-t'ung," pp. 322ff.; and James Geiss, "The Chia-ching Reign," pp. 466ff., 471ff. The subject is also the central focus of chaps. 59 ad 60 in Ku Ying-t'ai, *Ming-shih chi-shih pen-mo*, pp. 624−51.

[11] On the wo-k'ou pirates, see Geiss, "Chia-ching," pp. 490f., 495ff.; and the following studies: So Kwan-wai, *Japanese Pirates in Ming China during the Sixteenth Century*; John E. Wills, Jr., "Maritime China from Wang Chih to Shih Lang," pp. 210−15; Ray Huang, "Fiscal Administration," p. 111; Roland C. Higgins, "Piracy and Coastal Defense in the Ming Period"; and Charles Hucker, "Hu Tsung-hsien's Campaign against Hsü Hai, 1556," pp. 273−307. The topic is also treated in detail in *Ming-shih chi-shih pen-mo*, chap. 55.

when a Mongol raiding party reached the gates of Peking in 1550; in the other direction, the *wo-k'ou* depredations managed to tie up some of the best government commanders for decades. Still, the Ming military some-how managed to keep an unsteady grip on the situation, showing con-siderable staying power in spite of the serious deterioration of its logistic base due to the erosion of its fiscal and command structure.[12]

Even late in the century, the government was still able to field credible enough forces to stage what came to be called, with a certain measure of poetic license, the "three great campaigns," although in doing so it also depleted the imperial treasuries beyond recovery.[13] By late Wan-li, the hindsight of history clearly bears witness to the rising power of the new military threat in the northeast; but through the 1620s and 1630s the handwriting was not yet on the wall. Thus, between the T'u-mu debacle, which marked the midpoint of the fifteenth century, and the Manchu conquest halfway through the seventeenth, the Ming forces were able to hold their own with little sense of a global crisis.[14] The same may be said with respect to internal security, since, after the suppression of the Chu Ch'en-hao 朱宸豪 (Ning-wang 寧王) rebellion of 1519—20, no serious military challenge of national proportions—other than local mutinies, riots, and other disturbances—threatened the state for a good hundred years, right up to the final decades of the dynasty.[15]

Something more on the order of a "crisis" does appear, however, on the home front. The series of critical issues that rocked the court and paralyzed the administration for extended periods of time were in many instances largely matters of individual rivalries and the normal political intrigues of government officials fighting for professional and personal survival. But in the bitter wrangling over certain issues, the endemic infighting comes out as a testing of the limits of institutional power in the Ming polity.

To be sure, few of the broader issues underlying these specific areas of

[12] Ray Huang traces the breakdown of the logistic base of the late Ming military establishment in "Fiscal Administration," p. 110. See also Ho Ping-ti, *The Ladder of Success in Imperial China*, pp. 60ff.; Elvin, *Pattern*, pp. 91—110, esp. 100f.; James P. Geiss, "Peking," pp. 99f., 121ff. Cf. the various types of mutinies and insurrections described in *Ming-shih chi-shih pen-mo*, chaps. 53, 57, 58.

[13] For detailed discussions of the "three campaigns," see *Ming-shih chi-shih pen-mo*, chaps. 62 (pp. 670—82), 63 (683—91), 64 (691—98). See also Ray Huang, "The Lung-ch'ing and Wan-li Reigns," pp. 563—74; and Charles Hucker, "Chu I-chün," pp. 335f.

[14] On the rise of Manchu power in the northeast, see *Ming shih*, "Shen-tsung pen-chi" 神宗本紀 vol. 2, *chüan* 21, pp. 291ff.; Ray Huang, "Wan-li," pp. 574—84; and Hucker, "Chu I-chün," p. 336f.

[15] For the background of the Ning-wang rebellion, see Meng Sen, *Ming-tai shih*, pp. 210—14; *Ming-shih chi-shih pen-mo*, chap. 47 (pp. 479—92); and James Geiss, "The Cheng-te Reign," pp. 423ff.

contention were actually new. Such problems as factionalism based on regional, generational, and ideological ties; succession disputes threatening the continuity of dynastic rule; delegation of excessive authority to eunuch officers loyal directly to the throne; battles over institutional jurisdiction between the "outer court" and the "inner court," or between censorial and ministerial control—these problems had perennially plagued many of China's dynastic regimes. Yet it is precisely in this period that some of the same issues begin to take on the dimensions of what has been described as a full-blown "constitutional crisis." [16]

It is significant that both the Chia-ching 嘉靖 (1522–66) and the Wan-li emperors, whose uncommonly long reigns stretch over the greater part of the century, were self-willed and stubborn men, and in this they follow in the footsteps of the Cheng-te 正德 emperor (1506–21), whose escapades were already legendary by this time.[17] Each of the these two rulers went through earlier phases in which they attempted to assert their independence as rulers and break away from the stranglehold of entrenched political forces, only to eventually withdraw fom the arena of court politics entirely for unconscionably long periods of time, leaving the exercise of statecraft in the hands of self-serving power brokers.

This range of radical swings, from willful personal control to cynical disregard, reflects the basic contradictions in the system: between theoretically absolute and in fact often brutal despotism on the one hand—most concretely manifested in the corporal punishment meted out in full court—and a kind of laissez-faire attitude in certain areas of government policy.[18]

[16] The jurisdictional friction between the inner and outer court is discussed by Hucker in *The Traditional Chinese State in Ming Times*, pp. 52ff. See also Tilemann Grimm, "Das Neiko der Ming-Zeit," pp. 139–77. For a nearly contemporary description of this problem, see Shen Te-fu's *Wan-li yeh-huo pien, chüan* 7 (pp. 180ff.), 8 (206ff.), 9 (227ff.). James Geiss provides a useful evaluation of the weakness of the system in "Peking," pp. 211ff. The idea of a constitutional crisis is suggested by Ray Huang in *1587: A Year of No Significance*, pp. 30, 75, 83, 112, 114, passim. See also his *Taxation and Government Finance in Sixteenth-Century Ming China*.

[17] See James Geiss, "Cheng-te," and his "Peking," pp. 213f. Ray Huang evaluates the Cheng-te legacy in *1587*, pp. 95–102. See Meng Sen, *Ming-tai shih*, pp. 194ff., on the "moral lapses" (*shih-tao* 失道) of the Chia-ching emperor. Ray Huang provides an excellent portrait of the Wan-li emperor and his shortcomings in *1587*, pp. 1–41. Meng Sen divides the Wan-li reign into three phases: a period in which the youthful monarch was "overwhelmed" by the influence of Chang Chü-cheng (*ch'ung-yu* 沖幼), pp. 268–80; one of "intoxication with power" (*tsui-meng* 醉夢), pp. 280–98; and one of "disintegration" (*chüeh-lieh* 決裂), pp. 298–303. Geiss describes the neglect and extravagance of Wan-li rule in "Peking," pp. 201ff.

[18] The view of the Ming state as "oriental despotism" is evaluated by W. T. deBary in "Chinese Despotism and Confucian Ideals," pp. 153–203. See also Hucker, *Traditional State*, esp. pp. 40–60; and James B. Parsons, "The Ming Dynasty Bureaucracy: Aspects of Background Forces," pp. 175–227. Parsons takes the Cheng-te and Chia-ching reigns together as

It is probably not very accurate to credit either of these reigns with "benign neglect," as one scholar has suggested, since they were not really all that benign.[19] But the institutional neglect was very palpable, most obviously in such matters as fiscal irresponsibility, failure to make appointments to administrative posts, and cultivation of special interest groups at the expense of alienating large numbers of scholar-officials.

This breakdown in the system worked in two contradictory directions. On the one hand, it gave rise to much confusion and demoralization; on the other, it also led to the opening of certain windows of opportunity for the exercise of individual initiative. For the most part these cracks in the system were filled by the assertive action of a small number of strongmen, numbering among them constructive statesmen such as Hsia Yen 夏言 and Chang Chü-cheng 張居正 and obstructionist politicians such as Yen Sung 嚴嵩. They also allowed a chain of powerful eunuchs leading from Liu Chin 劉瑾 to Feng Pao 馮保 and later Wei Chung-hsien 魏忠賢 to wield significant power over the administration at certain points.[20] For the bulk of those in official service, however, the simultaneous presentation of both possibilities for concerted action, in conformity with the imperatives of Confucian ideology, and the all-too-real prospect of the terrifying consequences of a wrong move or alliance, resulted in a rather heady atmosphere—going beyond the earlier forms of bureaucratic resistance in the direction of something as close to political consciousness as was perhaps possible within the imperial order.[21] To say that the gradual relaxation of central

---

his "Period IV" (1506–66), followed by a period composed of the Lung-ch'ing and Wan-li reigns (1567–1620). See also Frederic Wakeman, Jr., Price of Autonomy," pp. 39f.

[19] The terms "laissez faire" and "benign neglect" are suggested by K. T. Wu in "Ming Printing and Printers," p. 258.

[20] For the careers of Liu Chin, Hsia Yen, Yen Sung, Chang Chü-cheng, and others, see Dictionary of Ming Biography (hereafter DMB), pp. 941ff., 527ff., 1586ff., 53ff. The Ming-shih chi-shih pen-mo devotes an entire chapter to the period of Yen Sung's ascendancy (chap. 54, pp. 564–84). See also Geiss, "Chia-ching," pp. 483ff. The contributions of Chang Chü-cheng are analyzed by Chu Tung-jun in Chang Chü-cheng ta chuan; Robert B. Crawford, "Chang Chü-cheng's Confucian Legalism," pp. 367–413; and Huang, "Wan-li," pp. 518–30. See also Chi Wen-fu Wan-Ming ssu-hsiang shih-lun, pp. 48–57. On the abuses of eunuch power in the Ming, see Hucker, Traditional State, pp. 55ff.; Wakeman, "Price of Autonomy," p. 40; and Robert B. Crawford, "Eunuch Power in the Ming Dynasty," pp. 115–48, esp. 137ff.; etc. The Yeh-huo pien also raises this issue in chüan 6, pp. 153ff.

[21] The idea of an emerging political consciousness is presented in somewhat overstated form in Thomas A. Metzger, Escape from Predicament. See critiques of Metzger's positions in a special issue of Journal of Asian Studies, 39, no. 2 (February 1980): 237–90. A more cogent formulation of the same sense of frustration is provided by Wakeman, in "Price of Autonomy," esp. pp. 39f., 44; and by Shimada Kenji in Chūgoku ni okeru kindai shii no zasetsu, pp. 271ff. See also Huang, "Wan-li," pp. 511ff., 544ff., 550ff.; and deBary, Self and Society in Ming Thought, pp. 6f. Julia Ching suggests in her To Acquire Wisdom, p. xxi, that the shock of the purge of Fang Hsiao-ju in 1402 never fully wore off for later Ming officials.

authority after the crushing autocracy of the Hung-wu 洪武 and Yung-lo reigns, and before the final traumas of repression and Manchu conquest, may have contributed to an unleashing of creative energies would of course be an oversimplification, but not without a measure of truth. At the least, this may help to account for the age of cultural flowering that gets under way after the slump of the mid-fifteenth century and picks up speed around the turn of the sixteenth.

Some of the clearest instances of such a phenomenon can be observed in the principal disputes dominating court politics during the Chia-ching and Wan-li reigns. The various rites controversies that embroiled the Chia-ching court, like the succession issue in Wan-li, were questions not only of theoretical import but also with immediate practical ramifications. Even such initially minor incidents as the Li Fu-ta 李福達 case in Chia-ching or the "three great cases" of late Wan-li start as specific disputes but eventually lead to an across-the-board polarization of the court and the administration, resulting in deep schisms along partisan lines.[22] Once again, there is nothing new about factional disputes in the history of Chinese imperial politics. But the degree to which these issues now forced the realignment of the entire government bureaucracy, the rhetorical brutality of the polemics, as well as the appearance of certain new methods of applying political pressure—from the spectacle of a public demonstration of courtiers kneeling en masse in the palace courtyard, to strikes and later gentry-organized urban riots—significantly raise the stakes of the political game.[23]

One of best examples of this heightened degree of political belligerence is the case of Lo Yü-jen 雒于仁, whose well-known memorial denouncing

[22] For further background on the rites controversies and the Li Fu-ta case that rocked the Chia-ching court, see Geiss, "Chia-ching," pp. 443ff., 453–61; Carney T. Fisher, "The Great Ritual Controversy in Ming China," pp. 93ff.; and Meng Sen, *Ming-tai shih*, pp. 218–36. The controversies are covered in the *Ming-shih chi-shih pen-mo*, chaps. 50 (pp. 508–45) and 56 (pp. 607–11); and in *Yeh-huo pien*, pp. 35f., 39–46. The succession issue in Wan-li is the focus of chap. 67 (pp. 736–48) in *Ming-shih chi-shih pen-mo*, as well as several sections in the *Yeh-huo pien* (pp. 62, 98), and in Liu Jo-yü, *Cho chung chih, chüan* 1. See also Hucker, "Chu I-chün," p. 331; and Huang, *1587*, pp. 83–88. On the "three great cases" initiated in late Wan-li and spilling over into Ch'ung-chen, see *Ming-shih chi-shih pen-mo*, chap. 68, pp. 748–71; Huang, "Wan-li," pp. 554ff.; and Hucker, "Chu I-chün," pp. 332f.

[23] The incident of the courtiers' "demonstration" is described by James Geiss in "Chia-ching," pp. 448f., and is the subject of fictionalized narration in *Ming-shih t'ung-su yen-i*, in *Li-ch'ao t'ung-su yen-i*, chap. 57. On the phenomenon of labor strikes and mutinies, see Yuan Tsing, "Urban Riots and Disturbances," pp. 277–320, esp. 280ff., 285–93. For a general treatment of the phenomenon of bureaucratic resistance, see David Nivison, "Protest against Convention and Conventions of Protest," pp. 137–201. Lo Jung-pang discusses the kinds of leverage wielded by the court officials in "Policy Formulation and Decision-making on Issues Respecting Peace and War," pp. 41–72, esp. 69ff.

his sovereign's violation of the "four vices of excess" (*ssu t'an* 四貪) sounds as shockingly blunt to the modern ear as it must have in 1590.[24] The fact that Lo was not simply obliterated, but managed to get away with his mad gesture, demonstrates the subtle power of the political forces at work in his time. The same may be said of other leading examples of self-righteous defiance, including the desperate martyrdom of Yang Chi-sheng 楊繼盛 (1516—55), the more circumspect resistance activities of Ku Hsien-ch'eng 顧憲成 (1550—1612), even the quixotic gestures of Hai Jui 海瑞.[25]

The gradual shift into the political arena of such burgeoning academic and literary associations as the Tung-lin Academy 東林書院 and later the Fu She 復社 is but the logical conclusion of these tendencies. Although it is certainly true, as has often been pointed out, that these groups were in no way equivalent to political parties in the modern sense, still they are closer to organized interest groups than the sort of factions to which the term *tang* 黨 conventionally refers.[26] In any event, I will attempt here to relate this new spirit of partisanship, especially its more militant aspects, to the disputatious spirit that spills over into the area of literary polemics. And in fact, there is often a direct correlation between the literary and the political alignments in this period. I will even suggest that this new critical attitude may be one of the factors responsible for the refinement of ironic vision

[24] Lo's memorial is recorded in Hsia Hsieh, *Ming t'ung-chien*, vol. 3, *chüan* 69, pp. 2696ff.; and in fuller form in *Wan-li ti-ch'ao*, 1: 468—74. See David T. Roy, "The Case for T'ang Hsien-tsu's Authorship of the *Chin P'ing Mei*," pp. 2—11 and n. 134. See also Huang, *1587*, pp. 223—29, where the entire interview of Shen Shih-hsing with the emperor is reproduced. The scandal also elicits comment by Shen Te-fu in *Yeh-huo pien*, p. 64, as well as by the contemporary observer Liu Jo-yü in his *Cho chung chih*, *chüan* 1, p. 11b, and *chüan* 5, p. 3a. See also fictionalized treatment in the *Ming-shih yen-i*, chap. 75.

[25] See relevant biographies in DMB, pp. 1503ff., 736ff., 474ff. The affair of Hai Jui is discussed by Ku Chieh-kang 顧頡剛 in "A Study of Literary Persecution during the Ming," pp. 272ff.; in Huang, *1587*, pp. 130—55; and in Joanna Handlin, *Action in Late Ming Thought*. Hai Jui is also the subject of fictionalized treatment in the *Ming-shih yen-i*, chap. 67; and in the novels *Hai-kung ta hung-p'ao ch'üan-chuan* 海公大紅袍全傳 and *Hai-kung hsiao hung-p'ao ch'üan-chuan* 海公小紅袍全傳. Ku Chieh-kang's "Literary Persecution" also provides a number of additional examples.

[26] The large number of studies on the Tung-lin group and other academic and political factions includes Hsieh Kuo-chen's *Ming-Ch'ing chih chi tang-she yün-tung k'ao*; Heinrich Busch, "The Tung-lin shu-yüan and Its Political and Philosophical Significance," pp. 1—163; Tilemann Grimm, "Intellectual Groups in Fifteenth and Sixteenth Century Kiangsi: A Study of Regionalism in Forming Elites" (unpublished paper), and his *Erziehung und Politik im Konfuzianischen China der Ming-Zeit*, pp. 108—38; Hou Wai-lu, *Chung-kuo ssu-hsiang t'ung-shih*, 4B: 1096—1120; Jung Chao-tsu, *Ming-tai ssu-hsiang shih*, pp. 284—314; William S. Atwell, "From Education to Politics," pp. 333—68; Wakeman, "Price of Autonomy," pp. 39, 41ff., 45f., 50f.; and Nivison, "Protest against Convention." See also Huang, "Wan-li," pp. 532—50; and Hucker, "Chu I-chün," pp. 328—30. The *Ming-shih chi-shih pen-mo* also devotes a chapter to this topic (chap. 66, pp. 713—36), as does the *Ming-shih yen-i* (chap. 88).

and expression, which provides a crucial element in the development of the rhetorical conventions of the literati novel form.[27]

While these vexed controversies were raging at court and sending shock waves as far as the provincial yamens and academies, great changes were also beginning to be felt in the economic and social spheres. There is a widespread scholarly consensus that the entire Ming economic structure was entering a new phase of development by around the Hung-chih period, beyond the simple fact that the economy showed a sharp upturn at this point after the slump of the mid-fifteenth century.[28] Regardless of whether we think of these changes as evidence of "sprouts of capitalism" or incipient modernization, we witness in this period a shift from the timeless agrarian basis of the imperial order to something closer to a money economy, with increasingly varied modes of production and distribution. Such factors as the switch to cash crops, the development of cottage crafts such as spinning, weaving, and porcelain manufacturing to the level of highly organized local industries, the expansion of marketing networks, and the general increase in personal wealth and luxury, particularly in the great cities of the lower Yangtze, have been cited by a number of scholars as far-reaching changes under way during the sixteenth century.[29]

The striking convergence of all these factors comes at a time when the population of China increased two or threefold within the space of a hundred years.[30] This may be seen as the cause or the effect of these

[27] On the crucial significance of irony in the aesthetics of the novel form, see Chapter 6, below.

[28] The economic upswing of the late fifteenth century is attested to by a wide range of scholars, including Ray Huang, "Fiscal Administration," p. 110, who notes the "phenomenal strides" made by the Chinese economy between 1505 and 1590; and Ho Ping-ti, Ladder, p. 284, who speaks of "steady development"; Evelyn Rawski, "Economic and Social Foundations of Ming and Ch'ing Culture," p. 6ff.; William S. Atwell, "Time and Money," pp. 20f.; Mark Elvin, Pattern, pp. 203f., who notes an economic decline from 1300 to 1500, followed by renewed vigor after 1500; Richard Shek, "Religion and Society in Late Ming"; and many others.

[29] The rise of a money economy and the switch to cash crops are described by Evelyn Rawski, "Economic and Social Foundations," pp. 2ff., and in her Agricultural Change and the Peasant Economy of South China; Yuan Tsing, "Continuities and Discontinuities in Chinese Agriculture," pp. 35–51; James Geiss, "Peking," p. 143; Ray Huang, "Fiscal Administration," pp. 110ff.; Mark Elvin, Pattern, pp. 212, 268ff.; and Ho Ping-ti, Studies on the Population of China, 1368–1953, pp. 196ff.

[30] On the demographic changes in the sixteenth century, see Ho Ping-ti, Studies on Population, pp. 262ff.; and Michel Cartier, "Nouvelles données sur la démographie chinoise à l'époque des Ming 1368–1644," among a number of other specialized studies. On the development of specific urban areas as population centers, see Michael Marmé, "Population and Possibility in Ming Suzhou," pp. 29–64; Christian F. Murck, "Chu Yün-ming and Cultural Commitment in Suchou," pp. 24ff.; Frederick W. Mote, "A Millennium of Chinese Urban History," pp. 35–65; and his "The Transformation of Nanking, 1350–1400," pp. 101–53;

economic shifts, but either way, the demographic changes are reflected in an increasing abandonment of small landholdings, caused in part by the unequal tax burdens of the outmoded fiscal structure. The attempt to counterbalance this movement by relying more and more on commutation of land taxes to silver only reinforced the trend, especially after the adoption of the "single-whip" method 一條鞭法 of taxation on a national scale in 1581.[31] This, in turn, led to increased dependence on the importation of silver bullion, first from Japan and later from the New World channeled through the Manila trade, resulting in a well-documented scourge of inflation, with many of the political ills and social dislocations that go with that. In fact, one recent scholar has argued that it may be possible to arrive at a fairly precise economic periodization of the late Ming based on the volume of silver in circulation alone.[32]

Another consequence of the transformation of the Ming economy to a silver base is the drawing of China into the emerging sixteenth-century world trade network, carrying with this such corollary phenomena as maritime expeditions, overseas colonization, rising demand for imported goods, and even the first stirrings of renewed interest in foreign ideas.[33] The obvious parallels here to the convergence of similar factors in the Age of Discovery in late Renaissance Europe are perhaps easy to dismiss as misleading. But the connection between these expanding horizons in political and economic life and the rise of the novel in both Europe and China as a major form of literary expression provides very fertile ground for comparative speculation, a subject to which I will return shortly.

Even more far-reaching are the consequences of social changes under way in this period, under the pressure of the surge in population mentioned

---

G. W. Skinner, *The City in Late Imperial China*, pp. 3–31, esp. 26ff.; Albert Chan, S. J., "Peking at the Time of the Wan-li Emperor," pp. 119–48; and James Geiss, "*Peking*," pp. 14ff.

[31] The abandonment of small landholdings and subsequent loss of tax revenues is described in Shek, "Religion and Society," pp. 29f, 31ff.; Elvin, *Pattern*, pp. 35ff.; Huang, "Fiscal Administration," pp. 73–128; and Geiss, "Chia-ching," pp. 485–88. See also Liang Fang-chung, *The Single Whip Method of Taxation in China*; Ho Ping-ti, *Studies on Population*, p. 210; and Amano Motosuke, "Ming Agriculture," etc.

[32] The great increase in circulation of silver has been documented by William Atwell in several articles: "Time and Money," "International Bullion Flows and the Chinese Economy, 1550–1650," and "Notes on Silver, Foreign Trade, and the Late Ming Economy." See also Geiss, "Peking," pp. 143–59; and Elvin, *Pattern*, p. 222. Earlier accounts of this phenomenon occur in *Ming-shih chi-shih pen-mo*, chap. 65, pp. 699–712; *Yeh-huo pien*, chüan 2, pp. 69f.; and in Matteo Ricci, *China in the Sixteenth Century*, pp. 14f.

[33] See articles by Atwell (see n. 32) and Geiss, "Chia-ching," pp. 491ff., 495ff.; Elvin, *Pattern*, pp. 218–22ff.; and Mote, "Yuan and Ming," in *Food in Chinese Culture*, p. 195. The example of colonization by Chinese in the Philippines is treated by Ray Huang in "Wan-li," pp. 560–62.

earlier—sustained by, among other things, the widespread introduction of New World crops at this juncture.[34] The sheer press of numbers, added to improvements in internal transportation networks, the abandonment of small landholdings, the first signs of a landless labor force employed in manufacturing, and the release of large numbers of military personnel due to fiscal inadequacies—all lead to a degree of horizontal demographic mobility going far beyond anything observed before.[35]

Perhaps the most important set of factors in this increased mobility, however, lies in the area of education. The imperial examination system, with its own network of schools as the central avenue of training and recruitment, was a longstanding institution; but certain new administrative practices in the awarding of degrees and the fixing of regional quotas rendered the system of government schools established by the dynastic founder inadequate by this time, and this led to the restoration of private academies as the premier educational institutions of the realm.[36] At the same time, we witness a ballooning of the numbers of first-degree licentiates, as attested by a number of recent studies, to an extent far beyond the general spread of literacy in this period.[37] This latter phenomenon had an undeniable effect on the broadening of the audience for printed fiction. But it is still the scholar-official class, with its own sense of identity and mission, along with its special aesthetic pretensions, that forms the social basis for the emergence of the sophisticated novel genre in the sixteenth century.[38]

[34] For further information on the introduction of New World crops see Mote, "Yuan and Ming," pp. 195–98; Ho Ping-ti, Studies on Population, pp. 169f., 184ff.; Amano Motosuke, "Ming Agriculture," passim; and Dwight H. Perkins, Agricultural Development in China, 1368–1968, esp. pp. 47ff.

[35] Among the many studies of the factors involved in this demographic mobility, the most important include Ho Ping-ti, Ladder of Success, esp. pp. 53ff., 62ff., 67ff., 264ff.; Ray Huang, "Fiscal Administration," p. 125; Amano Motosuke, "Ming Agriculture," passim; Evelyn Rawski, Agricultural Change, pp. 205f.; and James Geiss, "Peking," pp. 173ff.

[36] The rapid growth of private academies in this period is treated in John Meskill, "Academies and Politics in the Ming Dynasty," pp. 149–74. Tilemann Grimm, Erziehung und Politik, speaks of a "new class" of intellectuals produced by these academies (see also his "Ming Educational Intendants," pp. 129–47); Ho Ping-ti, Ladder, pp. 17, 32, 168ff., 194ff., 261; Evelyn Rawski, "Economic and Social Foundations," pp. 10–17; and Frederic Wakeman, "Price of Autonomy," pp. 43f.

[37] On the quotas and regional distribution of degree earners, see especially Ho Ping-ti, Ladder, pp. 20, 32ff., 46f., 172ff., 261; Frederic Wakeman, "Price of Autonomy," p. 38; Michel Cartier, "Démographie," p. 1358; and James Parsons, "Ming Dynasty Bureaucracy," pp. 181ff.

[38] The spread of printed literature is attested to by Evelyn Rawski in her Education and Popular Literature in Ch'ing China, pp. 6, 11f.; Tadao Sakai, "Confucianism and Popular Educational Works," pp. 331–66; and Richard Shek, "Religion and Society," pp. 41ff.

Within this context, it is perhaps more significant than is generally acknowledged that the consolidation of the *pa-ku* 八股 form for examination essays has been pegged to the end of the fifteenth century, according to some, the year 1487. Although the institution of the examination essay based on classical exegesis had progressed from legend to actual practice as early as the T'ang, and was reinstituted and refined in the Sung, and again in Yuan and early Ming, it was only at this later point that the *pa-ku* took on its precise formal requirements and then came to symbolize, for better or for worse, the Ming ladder of success.[39] At the same time, it also came to be accepted as an important genre of literary prose in its own right, as I will discuss below.

This is not the place to present a thorough review of Ming economic and social history. But it is worth enumerating some of these factors here because practically every one of them suggests the same constellation of processes: things that in the European context are described with such terms as mercantilism, urbanization, and the rise of bourgeois culture, which have been associated with the rise of the novel form in Europe a century or two later.[40] In considering the Ming novel, I will attempt to refute the common view that this genre is primarily an outgrowth of the popular tradition, relating it instead to patterns of composition, critical theories, and prevailing intellectual trends more characteristic of the literati milieu. But it is fairly certain that the consolidation of a new mimetic narrative mode at precisely this time cannot be unrelated to the changes taking place in the contemporary political, economic, and social reality reflected directly or indirectly in the works themselves.[41]

At this point, however, one might still ask what connection there may have been between these various social and economic factors, assuming they are in fact an accurate representation of the state of the times, and the emergence of a sophisticated genre of vernacular fiction. The key to my argument, therefore—though perhaps the most debatable point of all—is whether or not all this horizontal mobility of economic and social oppor-

---

[39] For a review of the history of the examination essay in general and the *pa-ku* form in particular, see Sung P'ei-wei, *Ming wen-hsüeh shih* pp. 204–33; Ch'ien Chi-po, *Ming-tai wen-hsüeh*, pp. 105–16; Chou Tso-jen, *Chung-kuo hsin wen-hsüeh ti yüan-liu*, pp. 41–56, 85–91; Shimada Kenji, *Zasetsu*, pp. 281ff.; and Tu Ching-i, "The Chinese Examination Essay," pp. 393–406. See also *Yeh-huo pien, chüan* 14–16 (pp.367–427). The year 1487 is reportedly the first time in which the precise *pa-ku* form was prescribed; see Ku Yen-wu, *Jih-chih lu chi-shih, chüan* 16, pp. 389f. See Huang Yün-mei, *Ming-shih k'ao-cheng*, p. 169.

[40] The connection between these historical trends and the rise of the European novel is frequently associated with the thesis of Ian Watt's *The Rise of the Novel*, although actually Watt's argument is not so narrow or unequivocal.

[41] This, at least, is reflected in the focus on less exalted characters and quotidian narrative details in much of the vernacular fiction of the sixteenth and seventeenth centuries.

tunity translated into a corresponding mobility of consciousness.[42] My own conviction, based on readings in a wide spectrum of the literature of the period, is that this is indeed the case, that certain windows were opening up precisely in this period that directly contribute to and help account for the maturation of the novel form.

It is enough to recall in this context that the career of Wang Shou-jen 王守仁 (Wang Yang-ming 王陽明, 1472–1529) falls precisely within the first few decades of the sixteenth century, with the ripples it aroused spreading quickly throughout the empire until they came to dominate the intellectual scene for much of the next hundred years.[43] The suggestion that the thought of Wang Yang-ming marks a revolutionary new beginning is a commonplace of Ming intellectual history, but it still needs to be qualified to some extent.[44] On the one hand, the teachings of Wang Yang-ming were of course not invented out of whole cloth, but fall squarely within the universe of Neo-Confucian discourse. It is not simply that Wang's ideas regarding the cultivation of the mind grow directly out of the philosophy of mind pioneered by Lu Chiu-yüan 陸九淵 (Lu Hsiang-shan 陸象山, 1139–93)—and for that matter the bulk of his basic teachings conform to, more than they diverge from, the central tenets of Ch'eng-

[42] What I have in mind here is a concept such as that of "psychic mobility," used, for example, by Daniel Lerner in *The Passing of a Traditional Society*, pp. 49–52, to describe the crucial role of expanding mental horizons in the genesis of the great Western revolutions. Shimada Kenji says similar things about the rise of "bourgeois consciousness" in this period in *Zasetu*, pp. 254ff., 288ff. See also Araki Kengo, *Mindai shisō kenkyū*, pp. 120–26. Ho Ping-ti seems to be saying as much when he speaks of "nouveaux riches" in *Ladder*, pp. 154ff.

[43] For general reviews of the life and thought of Wang Yang-ming, see Wing-tsit Chan, *Instructions for Practical Living and Other Neo-Confucian Writings by Wang Yang-ming*, pp. xxiff.; Julia Ching, *To Acquire Wisdom*, pp. xxiif., 24ff.; Tu Wei-ming, *Neo-Confucian Thought in Action*; Araki Kengo, *Mindai shisō*, pp. 51–99; Hou Wai-lu, *Ssu-hsiang t'ung-shih*, pp. 875–82; and Jung Chao-tsu, *Ssu-hsiang shih*, pp. 71–81. On post–Wang Yang-ming developments during the sixteenth century, especially the rise of the T'ai-chou School, see Hou Wai-lu, *Ssu-hsiang t'ung-shih*, pp. 958–1095; Jung Chao-tsu, *Ssu-hsiang shih*, pp. 110–82, 206–69; Araki Kengo, *Mindai shisō*, pp. 100–148; Chi Wen-fu, *Wan-Ming ssu-hsiang*, pp. 1–47; Shimada Kenji, *Zasetsu*, pp. 94–177; and W. T. deBary, *Self and Society*, articles by T'ang Chün-i, Takehiko Okada, and deBary. See also Yü Ying-shih, "Ts'ung Sung Ming ju-hsüeh ti fa-chan lun Ch'ing-tai ssu-hsiang shih," pp. 19–42.

[44] The revolutionary nature of Wang Yang-ming's thought is stressed by Wing-tsit Chan in his Introduction to *Instructions*, pp. xixff. ("a complete spiritual revolution"). Similar views are expressed by Ch'ien Mu in *Kuo-hsüeh kai-lun*, chap. 8, p. 44; and by Chi Wen-fu, *Wan-Ming ssu-hsiang*, p. 3. Edward Ch'ien claims that Wang Yang-ming "restructured" Neo-Confucianism in his review of Metzger's *Escape from Predicament*, in *JAS* 39, no. 2 (February 1980): 237. See Wakeman, "Price of Autonomy," p. 46, for the influence of Wang Yang-ming's thought on Ku Hsien-ch'eng. Huang Tsung-hsi's *Ming-ju hsüeh-an* (Taipei: Shih-chieh, 1961), pp. 380f, gives a backhanded acknowledgment of the pivotal position of Wang Yang-ming, as does a review of the stages of Ming classical scholarship at the beginning of the *Ssu-k'u ch'üan-shu tsung-mu t'i-yao*, p. 1.

Chu 程朱 learning.[45] They also fall in line with the succession of more proximate intellectual developments within Neo-Confucian thought of the earlier generations of the Ming, owing a considerable debt to figures such as Ch'en Hsien-chang 陳獻章, Chan Jo-shui 湛若水, and even to more orthodox thinkers such as Hu Chü-jen 胡居仁 and Wu Yü-pi 吳與弼.[46] One could easily argue that the elevation of Wang Yang-ming to the status of an epoch-making culture hero reflects no small measure of hindsight; or perhaps it can be chalked up to the image of Wang as a model Confucian official.[47] On the other hand, what we call "Wang Yang-ming thought" may simply be a convenient rubric to describe ideas and trends long in the incubation and nurtured in a number of minds in addition to his. But that does not change the fact that during much of the period in question Wang Yang-ming was perceived to have played a pivotal role in intellectual life. Although it is true that certain of his teachings are very much in the mainstream, others, especially his insistence on the autonomy of individual moral consciousness (liang-chih 良知), and his rethinking of the relation of theoretical cognition to concrete realization (chih-hsing ho-i 知行合一), open up new paths of conceptualization.[48] Whether or not one

[45] The continuities and discontinuities between Wang Yang-ming's ideas and Ch'eng-Chu teachings are brought out in Julia Ching, *To Acquire Wisdom*, pp. 75–103, 171–77; Wing-tsit Chan, *Instructions*, pp. xxxiff., xxxviiif.; Metzger, *Escape from Predicament*, pp. 70ff., 134–60; Tu Wei-ming, *Thought in Action*, pp. 153–72; Araki Kengo, *Mindai shisō*, pp. 150–54; Shimada Kenji, *Zasetsu*, pp. 19–24; and Takehiko Okada, "Wang Chi and the Rise of Existentialism," pp. 123ff.

[46] Wang's debt to early Ming Confucianism is explored by Wing-tsit Chan in "The Ch'eng-Chu School of Early Ming," pp. 29–51; David Gedalecia, "Evolution and Synthesis in Neo-Confucianism," pp. 91–102, esp. 94–97; Jen Yu-wen, "Ch'en Hsien-chang's Philosophy of the Natural," pp. 53–92; Jung Chao-tsu, *Ssu-hsiang shih*, pp. 18–23ff., 34ff., 51ff.; Araki Kengo, *Mindai shisō*, pp. 51ff., 71–80, 292–328; Helmut Wilhelm, "On Ming Orthodoxy," pp. 1–26; and W. T. deBary, Introduction to *The Unfolding of Neo-Confucianism*, pp. 21f. See also T'ang Chün-i, "The Development of the Concept of Moral Mind from Wang Yang-ming to Wang Chi," and his *Chung-kuo che-hsüeh yüan-lun*, pp. 202–54, 354–60; and Julia Ching, *To Acquire Wisdom*, pp. 12ff.

[47] See Ho Ping-ti, *Ladder*, p. 198.

[48] The concept of liang-chih is defined and discussed in Julia Ching, *To Acquire Wisdom*, pp. 107–24, 177ff.; Jung Chao-tsu, *Ssu-hsiang shih*, pp. 87–93; T'ang Chün-i, "Moral Mind," pp. 97ff., 108ff., 298–311, 320–48, 360–65; his *Chung-kuo che-hsüeh yüan-lun*, pp. 320–38; and his "Liu Tsung-chou's Doctrine of Moral Mind and Practice and His Critique of Wang Yang-ming," pp. 305–32; Hou Wai-lu, *Ssu-hsiang t'ung-shih*, pp. 882–967; Chi Wen-fu, *Wan-Ming ssu-hsiang*, pp. 3ff.; Shimada Kenji, *Zasetsu*, pp. 45f., 73f.; and Irene Bloom, "Wang Yang-ming, Lo Ch'in-shun, and Concepts of Personal Identity in Ming Neo-Confucianism," pp. 268ff., 274f. For the concept of chih-hsing ho-i, see Julia Ching, *To Acquire Wisdom*, pp. 66–69; Wing-tsit Chan, *Instructions*, pp. xxxivf.; Jung Chao-tsu, *Ssu-hsiang shih*, pp. 202–6; Tu Wei-ming, *Thought in Action*, pp. 147–53, 172–76; Metzger, *Escape from Predicament*, pp. 78ff.; A. S. Cua, *The Unity of Knowledge and Action*; and Ronald G. Dimberg, "The Sage and Society," pp. 20ff.

judges these ideas to be entirely original in themselves, we certainly can say that the extreme positions later espoused by Wang Chi 王畿, Wang Ken 王艮, Ho Hsin-yin 何心隱, and other thinkers associated with the "T'ai-chou 泰州 School" would never have been possible without the groundwork laid down by Wang Yang-ming.[49]

In my discussions of the interpretation of the four masterworks, I will have frequent occasion to speak about their reflection of a revised understanding of certain key concepts of basic Four Books Neo-Confucian thought, with special emphasis on the terms of hsin-hsüeh 心學 occasionally involved in the texts (or brought into the discussion of commentators).[50] It would be a bit facile to say that Wang Yang-ming's attempt to bring sagehood down to the common man may find expression in the more down-to-earth characters of colloquial fiction, or that his insistence on concrete realization of abstract truths may lend epistemological support to the medium of mimetic narrative.[51] But on a more subtle level, such things as the new exploration of the substance of individual desire, or the reappraisal of the significance and consequences of moral action, have a very special relevance to the intellectual underpinnings of the novel. This latter phenomenon is, no doubt, related to the widely observed sixteenth-century interest in the evaluation of personal behavior, taking on a variety of forms, from the so-called "morality books" (shan-shu 善書) and "registers of good and evil" (kung-kuo ko 功過格) to instances of traumatic public confession.[52] This heightened sense of commitment to the rigorous evaluation of individual moral behavior lends perhaps an even greater urgency to the dilemma of these few generations of intellectuals, imbued with Neo-

---

[49] On the excessive tendencies of the T'ai-chou School, see Chi Wen-fu, Wan-Ming ssu-hsiang, pp. 55–77; Araki Kengo, Mindai shisō, pp. 100–107; and his "Confucianism and Buddhism in the Late Ming," pp. 48ff.; Julia Ching, To Acquire Wisdom, pp. 185ff,; T'ang Chün-i, Chung-kuo che-hsüeh yüan-lun, pp. 366–91, 422–45; and his "Liu Tsung-chou," pp. 305–31; Hou Wai-lu, Ssu-hsiang t'ung-shih, pp. 958–1002; Shimada Kenji, Zasetsu, pp. 94–177, 178–254, 258f.; W. T. deBary, "Individualism and Humanitarianism in Late Ming Thought," pp. 157ff., 171ff.; and his Introduction to Self and Society, pp. 1–3; Okada Takehiko, "Wang Chi," pp. 121–44; Edward Ch'ien, "Chiao Hung and the Revolt against Ch'eng-Chu Orthodoxy," p. 272; and Frederic Wakeman, "Price of Autonomy," pp. 46f.

[50] For some very explicit examples in comments on Hsi-yu chi, see below, Chapter 3, notes 163, 164, etc.

[51] For an argument of this sort in the history of Western narrative, see Erich Auerbach, Mimesis.

[52] On the shan-shu, kung-kuo ko, etc., see deBary "Individualism and Humanitarianism," pp. 175f.; Tadao Sakai, "Popular Educational Works," pp. 341ff.; and Richard Shek, "Religion and Society," p. 65. The phenomenon of confessions is treated in Rodney L. Taylor, "The Centered Self," pp. 266–84; Wu Pei-yi, "Self-examination and Confession of Sins in Traditional China," pp. 5–38; Chou Chih-wen, T'ai-chou hsüeh-p'ai tui wan-Ming wen-hsüeh feng-ch'i ti ying-hsiang.

Confucian values of noble service, yet confronting the impasse of late
Ming political life. It also gives an edge to the defensiveness that characterizes the heated polemics and debates of the period, in which the participants often seem to be struggling just to put their names on the intellectual
map.[53]

At the heart of these philosophical debates is the redefinition of the
crucial issue of self-cultivation, in line with the new focus on the autonomy
of the self and the revalorization of individual desire. The familiar ring of
these terms to our modern ears reminds us that the issue of the realization
of the individual self is also central to the intellectual assumptions of
post-Renaissance, bourgeois culture underlying the emergence of the novel
in eighteenth-century Europe. Here, however, the specific Chinese understanding of the concept of self-cultivation—as a means of bridging the
gap between the abstract self in isolation and the physical self within
its interpersonal context—marks it as a characteristically Neo-Confucian
concern.[54]

While recognizing the essentially Confucian intellectual orientation of
the sixteenth-century literati, we may also note here that the same period
marks something of a renascence in Buddhist, and to a lesser extent Taoist,
thought as well. This resurgence is partly the result of notable court
patronage, first by the Chia-ching emperor, whose flirtation with Taoist
luminaries and especially his infatuation with Taoist liturgical poetry
(ch'ing-tz'u 青詞) are bywords for his misrule;[55] then by the Wan-li emperor,
whose Buddhist leanings under the influence of his devout mother led to
what has been described as a pendulum swing of Buddhist restoration.[56]

[53] On the "dilemma" of Ming-Ch'ing intellectuals, see Wakeman, "Price of Autonomy,"
p. 37ff.; and Metzger, *Escape from Predicament*, pp. 42ff.

[54] Cf. deBary's discussion of "Neo-Confucian interiority," in his Introduction to *Unfolding*,
pp. 18ff.; and his discussions of the "Ming Experience of the Self," in his Introduction to *Self
and Society*, and his "Individualism and Humanitarianism," esp. pp. 150ff. Edward Ch'ien's
critique of Metzger acknowledges a "new view of the self" developing in this period.
See also Irene Bloom, "Concepts of Personal Identity"; Tu Wei-ming, "Ultimate Self-
transformation as a Communal Act," pp. 237–46; and Shimada Kenji, *Zasetsu*, pp. 178f.,
271ff.

[55] On the patronage of Taoism during the Chia-ching period, see Geiss, "Chia-ching,"
pp. 479–82; Wu Han, "Chin P'ing Mei ti chu-tso shih-tai chi ch'i she-hui pei-ching"; and
Miyakawa Hisayuki, "Min no Kasei jidai no dōkyō," pp. 631–43. See also Liu Ts'un-yan,
"Taoist Self-cultivation in Ming Thought," pp. 291–330, and his "Ming-ju yü tao-chiao,"
pp. 233–71, also published as "The Penetration of Taoism into the Ming Neo-Confucian
Elite," pp. 31–102; Judith Berling, "Paths of Convergence," pp. 123–47. A section is devoted
to this subject in the *Ming-shih chi-shih pen-mo*, as well as in *Yeh-huo pien, chüan* 2, p. 59.

[56] On the revival of Buddhism in the Wan-li period, see Wu Han, "Chin P'ing Mei ti chu-
tso," pp. 24ff.

But it is probably more meaningful to credit this phenomenon to the impact of a small number of impressive monks, most notably Chu-hung 袾宏, Te-ch'ing 德清, Chih-hsü 智旭, and Ta-kuan 達觀, about whom a considerable number of studies have been published in recent years.[57] Significantly, these alternating movements of Buddhist and Taoist influence do not seem to have elevated any particular sects to a dominant position, although the Ch'an school does stand out as a factor in intellectual developments, due to the ease with which its teachings could be harmonized with the predominant *hsin-hsüeh* strains in Confucian thought.[58]

This common philosophical ground shared with the more accommodating strains of Buddhism and Taoism is most widely referred to as the "unification of the three teachings" (*san-chiao ho-i* 三教合一).[59] In outlines of Ming intellectual history this syncretic tendency is generally treated as at best a passing fashion, and at worst a hodgepodge of unsophisticated popular notions. But as an aspect of the intellectual background of the sixteenth-century novel it may be isolated as perhaps the central factor.[60]

The perception of common ground shared by the three schools is of course not a fresh discovery on the part of the sixteenth-century thinkers.

[57] Specific studies on Buddhist figures include Yü Chün-fang (Kristin Yü Greenblatt), "Chu-hung and Lay Buddhism in the Late Ming," pp. 93–140, and her more recent unpublished paper "Some Ming Buddhists' Responses to Neo-Confucianism"; Leon Hurvitz, "Chu-hung's One Mind of Pure Land and Ch'an Buddhism," pp. 451–81; Araki Kengo, "Confucianism and Buddhism," esp. pp. 54ff., and his *Mindai shisō*, pp. 284f., 336ff., 354ff.; Wu Pei-yi, "The Spiritual Autobiography of Te-ch'ing," pp. 67–92, and his "Self-examination and Confession," pp. 19f., 24ff.; and Hsü Sung-peng, "The Life and Thought of Han-shan Te-ch'ing." See also Chi Wen-fu, *Wan-Ming ssu-hsiang*, pp. 78–97; Richard Shek, "Religion and Society," p. 76; and deBary, "Individualism and Humanitarianism," pp. 176f.

[58] For background on sectarian Buddhism in the Ming, see Daniel L. Overmyer, *Folk Buddhist Religion*, and his "Boatmen and Buddhas," pp. 284–302; and Yü Chün-fang, "Chu-hung and Lay Buddhism." On the relation between Ch'an Buddhism and *hsin-hsüeh*, see Araki Kengo, *Mindai shisō*, pp. 81–99, 265ff., 291, 329–54; and his "Confucianism and Buddhism," pp. 40ff., 54ff.; Tu Wei-ming, "Ultimate Self-transformation," pp. 241ff.; Wing-tsit Chan, *Instructions*, pp. xxxviif.; deBary, Introduction to *Self and Society*, pp. 13ff.; and Julia Ching, *To Acquire Wisdom*, pp. 189f. See also Rodney L. Taylor, "Meditation in Ming Neo-Orthodoxy," pp. 149–82.

[59] On the three-teachings trends in late Ming, see Araki Kengo, "Confucianism and Buddhism," pp. 46ff., 53.; Koyanagi Shikita, "Min-matsu no sankyō kankei," pp. 349–70, esp. 358ff.; and Sawada Mizuho, "Sankyō shisō to engi shōsetsu," pp. 163–67. See also deBary's discussion of "A New Liberalism and Pragmatism in Late Ming," in his Introduction to *Self and Society*, pp. 22ff.; and Kenneth Ch'en, *Buddhism in China*, p. 439.

[60] The more popular side of three-teachings syncretism as the background for one colloquial novel is treated in Judith Berling, "Paths of Convergence," pp. 131ff.; and in her "Curing the Delusions of the Sages in the Streets." See also Liu Ts'un-yan, "Lin Chao-en, the Master of the Three Teachings," pp. 253–78, and his "Yüan Huang and His Four Admonitions," p. 128; and Yü Chün-fang, "Chu-hung and Lay Buddhism," pp. 93–140.

One might say it is the basic premise of all Neo-Confucian thought.[61] But it is in this period that three-teachings syncretism begins to provide the basic language of discourse, horizontally across the entire spectrum of philosophical writing, and vertically from humble exercises in popular wisdom on up to serious philosophical inquiry. This last point needs special emphasis here, since in vernacular fiction we are usually not dealing with the most systematic form of intellectual pursuit, and at times we get from it a quite simplistic view of the human condition. Yet I will argue that the intellectual level reflected in the four masterworks, at the very least, is nothing like the hypothetical shopkeeper's mentality often envisioned in reconstructions of the "popular" audience for these works.[62] We must acknowledge that the authors of colloquial fiction in general, and even the compilers of the crucial sixteenth-century editions of the four masterworks, were not exactly rigorous thinkers in their own right.[63] The most I can claim for them is that they reflect the bedrock conceptions of their intellectual milieu, which were thoroughly grounded in three-teachings formulations, and that they rise at least occasionally to some rather penetrating insights.[64]

Moving on to the broader realm of cultural history, we once again observe in the sixteenth century a period of outstanding achievements following what is largely perceived to be a lull during much of the preceding hundred years.[65] By the second half of the fifteenth century, however, the pace begins to quicken with the appearance of a brilliant new generation marked by such names as Shen Chou 沈周 (1427–1509), and later Wen Cheng-ming 文徵明 (1470–1559), Chu Yün-ming 祝允明 (1460–1526), and T'ang Yin 唐寅 (1470–1523)—members of the same generation that produced Wang Yang-ming.[66]

This burst of creativity around the turn of the sixteenth century covers a wide spectrum of cultural activities, including the major artistic media, as well as various minor arts. Many of these pursuits, such as elaborate garden

[61] See, for example, Liu Ts'un-yan and Judith Berling, "The Three Teachings in the Mongol Yuan Period," pp. 479–509. See also Wing-tsit Chan, "The Ch'eng-Chu School," pp. 44f.

[62] See Shimada Kenji, *Zasetsu*, pp. 130ff., 254, 287, 285f.; and Richard Shek, "Religion and Society," pp. 41ff. This argument will be restated at several points later.

[63] On the other hand, they do show greater depth and breadth of vision than many of their fellow fiction writers in the following century. See my article, "After the Fall," pp. 546ff.

[64] For a recapitulation of some of these moments, see Chapter 6 of this book.

[65] For example, Susan Bush speaks of a "cultural hiatus" with respect to literati painting in the first century of Ming rule in *The Chinese Literati on Painting*, p. 152.

[66] See Bush, *Literati*, pp. 153–58.

design,[67] fine book collecting, and connoisseurship of antiquities and rare objects, were obviously made possible by the new profusion of wealth observed in this period. This is especially true in the lower Yangtze region, particularly in and around Su-chou, whose cultural supremacy was reclaimed precisely at this point.[68]

I should mention here the very significant expansion of book printing and publishing in this same period. A number of recent general descriptions of sixteenth-century social history have paid special attention to this development, and their reports of a publishing boom are corroborated by specialized studies on the history of Ming printing by private studios, government agencies, and commercial publishing houses.[69] We must be cautious, however, in assessing the connection between the spread of printing in this period and the rise of the new genres of prose fiction. It is certainly true that a larger number than ever before of various types of "popular" books were printed at this time. This includes guidebooks to a wide range of subjects, simplified encyclopedias, religious tracts, even digests and simplified editions of the classics and histories, not to mention collections of successful examination essays for the use of upwardly mobile young men.[70] But it is misleading to associate our masterworks of vernacular fiction with this development, as many would have it. At least, this is denied by the fact that many of the earliest known editions of all four works were relatively fine printings, apparently expensive and meant for only limited circulation.[71]

[67] The art of Ming gardens takes in not only the famous actual examples, but also a number of critical treatises on garden design, such as Chi Ch'eng's *Yüan-yeh*. For additional bibliographical references on Ming gardens, see my *Archetype and Allegory in the Dream of the Red Chamber*; Maggie Keswick, *The Chinese Garden*; and Osvald Sirén, *Gardens of China*.

[68] On the cultural revival of Su-chou in the late fifteenth century, see Mote, "Millennium" and "Transformation"; and Murck, "Chu Yün-ming." For a general discussion of Su-chou in Ming-Ch'ing culture, see Robert Hegel, *The Novel in Seventeenth-Century China*, pp. 4ff.

[69] The various general descriptions of Ming printing include Ho Ping-ti, *Ladder*, pp. 212–15; Evelyn Rawski, *Education and Popular Literature*, pp. 115ff.; and her "Economic and Social Foundations," pp. 17–31; Hegel, *Novel*, p. 10; as well as the observations of Matteo Ricci reported in *China in the Sixteenth Century*, pp. 20f. For specialized studies of printing establishments and techniques, see K. T. Wu, "Ming Printing"; Shih Mei-ts'en, *Chung-kuo yin-shua fa-chan shih*, pp. 80–100; Liu Kuo-chün, *Chung-kuo shu-shih chien-pien*, pp. 74–82; Nagasawa Kikuya, *Wakansho no insatsu to sono rekishi*, pp. 73–83; Lo Chin-t'ang, *Li-tai t'u-shu pan-pen chih-yao*, pp. 74–79; Liu Ts'un-yan, *Chinese Popular Fiction in Two London Libraries*, pp. 1–44, and his *Ming-Ch'ing Chung-kuo t'ung-su hsiao-shuo pan-pen yen-chiu*.

[70] For the late Ming printing of certain popularizations of the *Tzu-chih t'ung-chien*, see Andrew Hing-bun Lo, "*San-kuo chih yen-i* and *Shui-hu chuan* in the Context of Historiography."

[71] See Wilt Idema, *Chinese Vernacular Fiction*, pp. xl, lv, n. 81; and Hegel, *The Novel in Seventeenth-Century China*, pp. 10f.

By far the most impressive areas of cultural activity in this period, however, are surely those of painting and calligraphy. The most productive period of late Ming painting neatly conforms to our chronology, with relatively disappointing fifteenth-century output followed by an upswing of both quality and quantity by late in the century,[72] especially thanks to Shen Chou, followed by the masters just mentioned.[73] The standard explanations for this spurt of activity—as a response to general economic development and the leisure afforded by increased personal wealth, or to the need to turn to alternative spheres of cultivation due to blocked channels of official advancement or forced retirement under political pressure —are fairly convincing, especially since the most impressive successes in this period were scored by the Wu School around Su-chou, an area of special economic and political maturity.[74]

The late fifteenth century saw a new impetus in the worlds of both "professional" and "amateur" painting. It is the latter category that is of most interest to us here. The phenomenon of the so-called "literati painter" had already appeared in the Sung, but it now took on new proportions and new ideological bases precisely in this period, when the material circumstances for indulgence in cultivated pursuits happily coincided with refinements in aesthetic theory and technique.[75]

For the purposes of this review of the state of the empire in the sixteenth century, however, the crucial point is not the social basis of this art as much as its ideological commitment to the aesthetic and moral values of literati culture. This is because a number of the literary developments that culminate in the four masterworks display many of the same presumptions observed in the world of painting, based on shared education, common aesthetic expectations, and, most of all, a sense of commitment to self-realization through the practice of the arts of civilization (*wen* 文).[76] With this in mind, I will speak of these fictional masterpieces as "literati novels" (*wen-jen*

---

[72] See Bush, *Literati*, pp. 152ff.; and James Cahill, *Parting at the Shore*, p. 57.

[73] On the painting of Wen Cheng-ming, T'ang Yin, and others, see Cahill, *Parting at the Shore*, pp. 193–218, as well as his *The Compelling Image*, pp. 36–70, and *Distant Mountains*, pp. 87–128.

[74] On the rise of the Wu School, see Bush, *Literati*, pp. 152f., 158f.; and Nelson Wu, "Tung Ch'i-ch'ang," pp. 260–93.

[75] The concept of literati painting is delineated in Nelson Wu, "Tung Ch'i-ch'ang"; Cahill, *Distant Mountains*, pp. 17ff.; Bush, *Literati*, pp. 1–29, 158ff., 169, 180ff.; and Yoshizawa Tadashi, "Nanga to bunjinga," 82:9:257–62 (esp. 259), 82:11:345–50, 82:12:336–81; and 83:1:27ff. See also Joseph Levenson, "The Amateur Ideal in Ming and Early Ch'ing Society," pp. 320–41. Cf. Willard Peterson's argument that the term "literati" should be reserved for the *shih* class 士 of scholar-officials (in *Bitter Gourd*, p. 13).

[76] For this notion of *wen* as an all-inclusive expression of the literati life-style, see Peter Bol, "Culture and the Way in Eleventh-Century China."

hsiao-shuo 文人小說), to the extent that they exhibit many of the same pretensions to high wit and deep seriousness as those found in literati painting—pretensions that set the four works sharply apart from the popular materials out of which they are fashioned.

The notion of literati painting refers at one level to lofty artistic purposes, or at least the affectation of such, but it also takes in a set of specific qualities that comprise the canons of a changing aesthetic of composition. Sixteenth-century painting stands out as somehow different, almost modern, in its outlook, in spite of its basic continuities with the tradition and its normative reliance on models of past masters. This difference can perhaps be summed up in the expression "self-consciousness," with a sense of individualized perspective coming out in a variety of ways in late Ming examples. We see the projection of wit, even whimsy, in such things as choice of subject matter, playful manipulation of the elements of composition, positioning of shapes, use of color, and the like, plus the application of certain innovative techniques: the use of worn-out brushes, for example, or other eccentricities of execution—even experiments that betray the incipient influence of some of the exotic approaches to representation introduced to China by Jesuits at this time.[77]

These features add up to the impression of a strong dose of self-consciousness in relating to the past artistic tradition. This seems to be what Cahill has in mind when he uses the term "irony" to describe certain paintings by Ch'en Hung-shou 陳洪綬 (1598–1652) and others.[78] This aesthetic attitude will form the key to my argument regarding the comparable ironic revision of traditional narrative conventions in the four masterworks of the literati novel.[79]

Many of the same individualistic tendencies that link the world of literati painting to that of prose fiction also run through each of the other genres of the late Ming literary repertoire, to which we now turn. In the rich and varied output of sixteenth-century literature, we find both a qualitative and a quantitative leap beyond the work of the preceding hundred years. Quantitatively, this is immediately evident from a glance at practically any of the later anthologies of Ming poetry or prose, which nearly uniformly give space to a handful of masters from the founding generation—Sung Lien 宋濂, Kao Ch'i 高啟, Wang Wei 王褘, Fang Hsiao-ju 方孝孺 —

[77] See Marilyn Fu and Shen Fu, *Studies in Connoisseurship*; Cahill, *Compelling Image*, pp. 38–60; and Nelson Wu, "Tung Ch'i-ch'ang." See also Richard Barnhardt, "Wild and Heterodox School in Ming Painting," pp. 365–96.

[78] See Cahill, *Compelling Image*, pp. 106–45, esp. 134; *Distant Mountains*, pp. 120ff., 203, 206, 244–66; *Fantastics and Eccentrics in Chinese Painting*; and *The Restless Landscape*.

[79] For the aesthetic concept of irony as a defining feature of the novel genre, see n. 27, and my "Full-length *Hsiao-shuo*," pp. 171ff.

followed by just a sprinkling of fifteenth-century representatives, if any, until we come to the sudden proliferation of major stylists in the Hung-chih and Cheng-te reigns.[80] Granted, this impression is distorted by the selectivity of our collections, but it is by that very reasoning not entirely gratuitous, as this same fact proves that later anthologizers perceived this middle period to offer only a slim harvest of masters.

In any event, a number of the critics of late Ming and Ch'ing saw the turn of the sixteenth century as the start of a new phase in classical prose and poetic literature. For example, the collective biography of the literary world (Wen-yüan 文苑) in the Ming shih specifies the Hung-chih and Cheng-te reigns as a new phase of activity following the "increasingly flaccid style" (ch'i-t'i chien jo 氣體漸弱) of the preceding period.[81] In the more restricted area of ku-wen 古文 classical prose, which I will consider first, a comparable opinion is expressed in prefaces to Huang Tsung-hsi's 黃宗羲 Ming-wen an 明文案 and in the Ming-wen shou-tu 明文授讀, as well as in a preface to the Ch'ung-chen collection Huang-Ming wen-chüan 皇明文雋; and a number of recent scholars have seconded this judgment.[82] Even those Ch'ing critics who regard this entire phase of late Ming culture as essentially decadent also recognize the sharp changes of direction, away from the jejune literary styles of the preceding hundred years that are commonly reduced to the single rubric of the so-called "chancellery style" (t'ai-ko t'i 臺閣體).[83] This rather uninspired aesthetic refers less to a set style of prose composition per se than to the prizing of the measured cadences of documentary style, endowed with a degree of literary respectability by virtue of the high political office of some of its best-known practitioners, notably the "three Yangs" who served as top ministers of state during the fifteenth century.[84]

[80] For example, the Ku-wen kuan-chih 古文觀止 gives a few pieces by Sung Lien, Liu Chi 劉基, and Fang Hsiao-ju; and then skips to Wang Ao 王鏊, Wang Shou-jen (Wang Yang-ming), T'ang Shun-chih 唐順之, Kuei Yu-kuang 歸有光, Mao K'un 茅坤, Wang Shih-chen, and Yüan Hung-tao. Other anthologies include mid-Ming compositions by such figures as Yü Ch'ien 于謙, Wang Chih 王直, Hsüeh Hsüan 薛瑄, Li Shih-mien 李時勉, and Ch'eng Min-cheng 程敏政, etc.

[81] See Ming shih, vol. 24, lieh chuan, no. 174, Wen-yüan 文苑, pt. 2, p. 3348.

[82] For Ming-wen an, Ming-wen shou-tu, Huang-Ming wen-chüan, and Ming-wen ying-hua, see bibliography. Chu Tung-jun also describes the Hung-chih and Cheng-te reigns as a period of unprecedented flourishing (Chung-kuo wen-hsüeh p'i-p'ing shih ta-kang, p. 224). The 1959 Peking University history of Chinese literature, Chung-kuo wen-hsüeh shih, p. 875, speaks of a "crisis" (wei-chi 危機) in literature at this point caused by the influence of the t'ai-ko style.

[83] Cf. the rendering of this term as "censorate—grand secretary style," in the biographies of Li Tung-yang, Yang Shih-ch'i, and others in DMB, pp. 879, 1539, and "cabinet-style," in Daniel Bryant, "Three Varied Centuries of Verse," p. 83.

[84] For background on the t'ai-ko style, see Ch'ien Chi-po, Ming-tai wen-hsüeh, pp. 13–17; Kuo Shao-yü, Chung-kuo wen-hsüeh p'i-p'ing shih, pp. 297, 307–14, 342–48; and Sung P'ei-

When we come to the Hung-chih reign, we observe a marked reaction against this type of writing. It is almost as if the new generation deliberately sets out to overturn the dominance of the *t'ai-ko* style, even though the latter had never been defended as a superior mode in theoretical terms. There is no small measure of irony in the fact that the so-called "restoration" (*fu-ku* 復古) movement in prose, which was later to become a target of attack by more radical literary polemicists, was itself conceived as a reaction against conventionality—and it, too, was associated with men who were often high government ministers. In fact, Li Tung-yang 李東陽, who is regarded as the forerunner and teacher of the "former seven masters" (*ch'ien ch'i-tzu* 前七子), was also known as a master of *t'ai-ko* style. The same inconsistency is true of the succession of polemical "movements" in literary theory that run through much of the century: the "restoration" of ancient style associated with the "former and latter seven masters" (*ch'ien-hou ch'i-tzu* 前後七子); the substitution of models from the more recent past, whose advocates are sometimes referred to as the "T'ang-Sung School" 唐宋派; and later the supposed rejection of the value of imitation in favor of individual expression, ascribed to the Kung-an 公安 and Ching-ling 竟陵 literary cliques.[85]

In reviewing this bewildering array of literary positions, one often gets the impression that each new movement is mostly determined by the need to counter the influence of its predecessors, especially since these so-called "schools" are far indeed from evincing any degree of programmatic purity in their theoretical positions. For one thing, the well-known slogans of the various schools are often taken out of context and interpreted as more extreme pronouncements than they really are. Take, for example, the much-quoted dictum "In prose one must emulate the works of Ch'in and Han, in poetry one must emulate the High T'ang" (*wen pi Ch'in-Han, shih pi sheng-T'ang* 文必秦漢, 詩必盛唐), with which Li Meng-yang himself is

---

wei, *Ming wen-hsüeh shih*, pp. 57–64; etc. See also Juan K'uei-sheng, *Ch'a-yü k'e-hua, chüan* 11, pp. 307f. A large body of such writings is collected in Liao Tao-nan, ed., *Tien-ko tz'u-lin chi*. For the "three Yangs," see n. 118.

[85] For reviews of the literary theories of the "former and latter seven masters" and the T'ang-Sung School, see Kuo Shao-yü, *P'i-p'ing shih*, pp. 333, 343–46; Chu Tung-jun, *P'i-p'ing shih ta-kang*, pp. 224–52; Ch'ien Chi-po, *Ming-tai wen-hsüeh*, pp. 17–51; Sung P'ei-wei, *Ming wen-hsüeh shih*, pp. 89–100, 125–48; and the Peking University *Chung-kuo wen-hsüeh shih*, pp. 877–87; The "former masters" include Li Meng-yang 李夢陽 (1473–1529), Ho Ching-ming 何景明 (1483–1521), Hsü Chen-ch'ing 徐禎卿 (1479–1511), Pien Kung 邊貢 (1476–1532), K'ang Hai 康海 (1475–1541), Wang Chiu-ssu 王九思 (1468–1551), and Wang T'ing-hsiang 王廷相 (1474–1544). The "latter masters" include Wang Shih-chen 王世貞 (1526–90), Li P'an-lung 李攀龍 (1514–70), Hsieh Chen 謝榛 (1495–1575), Tsung Ch'en 宗臣 (1525–60), Liang Yu-yü 梁有譽 (1522–66), Hsü Chung-hsing 徐中行 (1517–78), and Wu Kuo-lun 吳國倫 (1524–93). See also Yoshikawa Kōjirō, "Gen-Min shi gaisetsu," pp. 169ff.; and Hsia Ch'ung-p'u, "Ming-tai fu-ku p'ai yü T'ang-Sung wen-p'ai chih ch'ao-liu," pp. 1219–28.

said to have established his leading role on the Chia-ching literary scene. In actuality, although this line is cited in Li's biography in the *Ming shih*, there is no direct evidence that he ever uttered anything as unequivocal as this; and even if he had, this would not have been unique, as much the same idea was voiced earlier by, among others, Ch'en Hsien-chang.[86]

Moreover, when we take a more careful look at the relevant sources, we find nothing like the consistency of positions implied by simplistic accounts. On the contrary, we see considerable disagreement among the various masters, as in the substantive disputes between Li Meng-yang and Ho Ching-ming, the two most prominent "former masters," over the question of literary models (*fa* 法), or the rather sharp exchanges between Wang Shih-chen 王世貞 and his fellow "latter master" Li P'an-lung 李攀龍. Even individual critics often show a high degree of inconsistency in their theories, especially over the span of their entire careers, and they frequently reverse themselves on key issues, as in the cases of Wang Shih-chen and T'ang Shun-chih, whose later literary theories to some extent contradict their earlier positions. The same is true for the Kung-an critics such as Yüan Hung-tao, whose earlier youthful rejection of T'ang-Sung models later gives way to expressions of basically unqualified praise for Sung masters, especially Su Shih 蘇軾.[87]

In order to understand the vehemence with which the critical battles over these points were joined, we must therefore reconsider the broader context of political, intellectual, even social and economic factors within which they took place. For one thing, the literary alignments of the period were part of a complex network of interlocking relationships based on personal ties, generational affiliations, common places of origin, intertwined official careers, and common degree-years, which so greatly determined the configurations of the Ming intellectual and cultural map. For example, a

---

[86] *Ming shih*, vol. 24, *lieh-chuan* no. 174, *Wen-yüan*, pt. 2, p. 3348. Cf. the line in Ch'en Hsien-chang's poem "Chi Wai-shih Shih-ch'ing Yü-t'ai" 寄外史世卿玉臺, no. 4: "The art of prose declined in Eastern Han, the great masters disappeared; When poetry passed the Mid-T'ang, few writers of stature remained" 文衰東漢無高手, 詩過中唐少作家 in *Pai-sha tzu ch'üan-chi, chüan* 8, p. 12b. This reference was pointed out to me by Chu Hung-lam. Richard Lynn notes in his "Orthodoxy and Enlightenment," p. 232, that Yen Yü's *Ts'ang-lang shih-hua* in the Sung period had already established the exclusive preeminence of High T'ang poetry.

[87] For the disagreement between Li Meng-yang and Ho Ching-ming, see Kuo Shao-yü, *P'i-p'ing shih*, pp. 305ff.; Ch'ien Chi-po, *Ming-tai wen-hsüeh*, pp. 25f.; and Chu Tung-jun, *P'i-p'ing shih ta-kang*, pp. 227f. On the differences of opinion between Wang Shih-chen and Li P'an-lung, see Kuo Shao-yü, *P'i-p'ing shih*, pp. 320ff.; Ch'ien Chi-po, *Ming-tai wen-hsüeh*, p. 33; and Matsushita Tadashi, "Ō Seitei no kobunjisetsu yori no dakka ni tsuite," pp. 72ff. Chu Tung-jun, *P'i-p'ing shih ta-kang*, pp. 237, 252, discusses Wang Shih-chen's change of positions in his later years; and Chou Chih-p'ing points out the later softening of Yüan Hung-tao's literary stands in "The Poetry and Poetic Theory of Yüan Hung-tao (1568–1610)," pp. 133ff.

quick review of biographical data shows that the former seven masters who dominated the literary scene in the 1490s and 1500s were primarily of northern origins, with a disproportionate number of them having roots in Shensi (including Li Meng-yang, Ho Ching-ming, Wang Chiu-ssu, K'ang Hai), whereas all of the latter seven masters, with the exception of Li P'an-lung, came from the south.[88] To give examples of other personal connections, Li Meng-yang was a youthful member of the poetic circle of Li Tung-yang, and Wang Chiu-ssu and K'ang Hai were lifelong friends and political allies.[89] We may also note here that a surprising number of the leading literary figures of this period happen to have been men without impressive pedigrees, often coming from military backgrounds or low officialdom, and their behavior after reaching prominence sometimes displays a bit of the air of the self-made man.[90]

In any event, these various types of relationships were cemented by a wealth of shared experience gained in the same educational path and career ladder, through common interests in intellectual currents such as the teachings of Wang Yang-ming or the later influence of Buddhist savants, as well as by virtue of the binding effect of having gone through political crises together in many cases.[91] For example, Li Meng-yang's rise to prominence is not unrelated to his skillful tightrope walk during the ascendancy of the regime of the eunuch Liu Chin, while Yang Shen 楊慎 and Wang Shih-chen both suffered the bitter consequences of the Chia-ching emperor's misrule. T'ang Shun-chih, on the other hand, primarily benefited from his relationship with the Yen Sung faction.[92] Given these various levels of group

[88] The significance of northern and southern regional affiliations is highlighted in Wang Chiu-ssu's biography in *DMB*, pp. 1366f. The rapid advancement of Li Meng-yang and his Shensi fellows K'ang Hai and Wang Chiu-ssu may be related to the fact that the eunuch politician Liu Chin hailed from the same province (see *DMB*, p. 693). Other examples include Pien Kung, Li P'an-lung, and Li K'ai-hsien, all from Shantung, or the common Yangtze delta origins of Wang Shih-chen, Hsü Chung-hsing, Wu Kuo-lun, Kuei Yu-kuang, T'ang Shun-chih, and Mao K'un.

[89] On the personal connections between Li Meng-yang and Li Tung-yang, see *DMB*, p. 841. For the friendship between K'ang Hai and Wang Chiu-ssu, see n. 88.

[90] For example, Li Meng-yang, Hsü Chen-ch'ing, and Wu Kuo-lun came from military families. Ho Ching-ming, Pien Kung, K'ang Hai, and Wang T'ing-hsiang were sons of minor officials. Li P'an-lung's father was a peasant. Hsü Chung-hsing, T'u Lung, Wang Shih-chen, and T'ang Shun-chih are among the few "masters" of cultivated stock. Li Meng-yang's swift leap to literary prominence is conventionally described with the expression "meteoric rise" (*chüeh-ch'i* 崛起). See, for example, Chu Tung-jun, *P'i-p'ing shih ta-kang*, p. 238.

[91] On the influence of Buddhist ideas on Wang Shih-chen, see Lynn, "Orthodoxy and Enlightenment," pp. 221ff., 253ff.; and Matsushita Tadashi, "Dakka," pp. 81ff. The Kung-an and Ching-ling critics in Wan-li, of course, tend to draw upon Ch'an style and terminology.

[92] See *DMB* biographies of Li Meng-yang, (pp. 841ff.), Yang Shen (pp. 1531ff.), Wang Shih-chen (pp. 1399ff.), and T'ang Shun-chih (pp. 1252ff.). Yang Shen (1488–1559) was a victim of the 1524 purge at the height of the "great rites controversy" (see n. 22). On Wang Shih-chen's struggles with Yen Sung, see Wu Han, "Chin P'ing Mei ti chu-tso" (see below,

interaction, it is not surprising that these literati developed a number of types of formal organizations, from the academies and political associations discussed earlier to the various prose and poetry circles (*wen-she, shih-she* 文社, 詩社) that proliferated in this period.[93]

Against the background of these interlocking relations, the rather perplexing lineup of literary positions frequently emerges as less a question of purely academic debates, and more a matter of newcomers establishing their reputations by staking out polemical territory and maneuvering to form alliances. In many cases, we can observe a direct correlation between extremism of literary advocacy and uncertainty of political and social status.

Another dimension of significance can be perceived in these literary debates when we view them as reflections of the broader philosophical issues of the day. Thus the championing of Ch'in-Han prose may sometimes be taken as a deliberate rejection of Sung Neo-Confucianism (i.e., *li-hsüeh* 理學), rather than as an actual distaste for the prose styles of the T'ang-Sung masters in themselves.[94] By the Wan-li period, the battle lines are already less programmatically drawn, and social mobility seems to have reached the point at which generational and regional origins are less crucial a factor.[95] On the other hand, the various literary qualities advocated by the later Ming critics—notions such as *ch'ü* 趣 and *hsing-ling* 性靈 —are clearly invested with rather pointed implications growing out of post–Wang Yang-ming intellectual currents.[96]

Chapter 2, n. 8); and Barbara Krafft, "Wang Shih-chen," pp. 185ff. T'ang Shun-chih's well-known essay, "Hsin-ling chün chiu Chao lun" 信陵君救趙論, focusing on the danger of factional connections (*p'eng-tang* 朋黨), seems to make a transparent allusion to the anti–Yen Sung forces. See also Ts'ao Chü-jen, "Ming-tai ch'ien-hou ch'i-tzu ti fu-ku yün-tung yu-che tzen-yang ti she-hui pei-ching," pp. 381–85.

[93] For an excellent survey of the various literary groups, see Kuo Shao-yü, "Ming-tai ti wen-jen chi-t'uan," pp. 86–128.

[94] Hence the emphasis on the term *fa* to the exclusion of *li* 理 and *tao*.

[95] We should note, however, that among the major Wan-li literary figures, the majority have origins in the Yangtze delta or adjacent areas. See biographies for T'ang Hsien-tsu (in Arthur Hummell, ed. *Eminent Chinese of the Ch'ing Period*, pp. 708f.), Hsü Wei 徐渭 (*DMB*, pp. 609–12), Yüan Hung-tao (*DMB*, pp. 1635–38), Chung Hsing 鍾惺 (*DMB*, pp. 408f.), Li Chih 李贄 (*DMB*, pp. 807–18), Ch'en Chi-ju 陳繼儒 (Hummell, *Eminent Chinese*, pp. 83–85), Feng Meng-lung 馮夢龍 (*DMB*, pp. 450–53), Tung Ch'i-ch'ang 董其昌 (Hummell, *Eminent Chinese*, pp. 987ff.).

[96] For discussions of these terms, see Kuo Shao-yü, *P'i-p'ing shih*, pp. 316ff., 324ff., 333ff., 337, 340, 353f., 359, 362, 376f., 381ff.; Jonathan Chaves, "The Panoply of Images," pp. 4–15; Richard Lynn, "Orthodoxy and Enlightenment," pp. 237, 239, 247ff.; Chou Chih-p'ing, "Poetry and Poetic Theory," pp. 94ff., and his "P'ing Kung-an p'ai chih shih-lun," pp. 82ff. See, for example, Yüan Hung-tao's famous discourse on *ch'ü* in "Hsü Ch'en Cheng-fu Hui-hsin chi" 敍陳正甫會心集, in *Yüan Hung-tao chi-chien chiao*, pp. 463f.; and Li Chih's well-known essay on *t'ung-hsin* (童心說) in his *Fen shu*, pp. 97–99.

As we have seen, when taken out of the context of their social and political milieu, the debates of sixteenth-century literary theory often present a bewildering array of contradictions and inconsistencies. Several aspects of these debates, however, have a special relevance for the development of the aesthetics of fictional narrative in this period. One of these factors is a heightened interest in the technical side of prose composition. When the literary theorists of this period invoke the term *fa*, for example, they more often than not have in mind a loose conception of the underlying spirit of classical models for imitation. But in certain contexts the point at issue in discussions of *fa* is more one of concrete literary devices.[97] At least, we see increased attention in this period to critical analysis of structural patterns, prose rhythms, and particularly the design of parallel constructions based on the complementarity of paired qualities. The various terms used to discuss these literary patterns (e.g., *chao-ying* 照應, *ch'eng-shang ch'i-hsia* 承上起下, *tun-tso* 頓挫, *shun-ni* 順逆)[98] appear frequently in both theoretical statements and in exercises in practical criticism in interlinear commentary editions of major texts. These terms are by no means new here, but they do gain a wider application at this point to all types of poetry and prose, including *pa-ku* essays and drama. From here, it is just one more step to the incorporation of this vocabulary directly into the emerging aesthetics of prose fiction that began to blossom into full-fledged fiction criticism by the end of the century and into the next.[99]

A second type of influence these developments in prose theory have on the novel form arises out of the greater range of rhetorical strategies and devices now available. For example, nearly all of the sixteenth-century critics, regardless of their positions, opt for language closer to the rhythms of actual speech in the composition of *ku-wen*. In each case, the theoretical justification for this is different. For example, *fu-ku* proponents generally advocate the quality of spare directness associated with pre-T'ang writing,

[97] On the varying uses of the term *fa*, see Kuo Shao-yü, *P'ing-p'ing shih*, pp. 301, 306ff., 312, 340f., 347; and Richard Lynn, "Orthodoxy and Enlightenment," pp. 222, 235, 242.

[98] Most of these terms derive from earlier prose criticism, or are borrowings from poetic or art theory. See, for example, Sung critical works on prose composition such as Lü Tsu-ch'ien's *Ku-wen kuan-chien*; and Chen Te-hsiu's *Wen-chang cheng-tsung*. The most complete compendium of such terms in the sixteenth century is Kuei Yu-kuang's *Wen-chang chih-nan*, especially his introductory analytic schemes under the headings *tsung-lun*, *k'an wen-tzu fa*, and *lun wen-chang t'i-tse* 總論看文字法, 論文章體則, as well as marginal commentaries appended to actual texts presented in the collection. It is perhaps not accidental that Kuei Yu-kuang was known as a master of the technical aspects of prose composition, particularly the crafting of complex parallel constructions.

[99] For background on the development of fiction criticism in China, see David Rolston, ed., *How to Read the Chinese Novel*, Introduction. I will return to this point later in this chapter.

especially that of Ch'in and Han expository style, before the beginnings of
more ornate kinds of patterned prose in the Six Dynasties. The critics of the
T'ang-Sung School also prize Ssu-ma Ch'ien 司馬遷 and Pan Ku 班固, but
they hold that the language of the Sung masters, being closer to contemporary speech, is therefore more smooth and natural (*shun* 順) for them
to imitate.[100] In the Wan-li period, Yüan Tsung-tao 袁宗道 takes the argument one step further to suggest that the changing patterns of spoken
language require a continuous evolution of prose style as well.[101]

Perhaps the most important point of Ming prose theory for our understanding of the great sixteenth-century novels is the strong sense we get
of self-conscious writers trying to forge new relationships to the great
models of the past (this is the other meaning of the term *fa*).[102] Despite the
apparent controversy on this issue, all the leading prose theorists agree on
the crucial role of learning from the old masters. The changing objects of
imitation selected as models through the course of the century would seem
to belie this, but in practice all turn around and insist that the true greatness
of their respective models, that which constitutes the real quality to be
imitated, is actually the attainment of a degree of spontaneous expressivity.
Consequently, nearly all of the prose critics of the time stress the development of a personal voice, whether that be associated with the affecting
conviction of a Ssu-ma Ch'ien, a Han Yü 韓愈, a Su Shih, or an Ou-yang
Hsiu 歐陽修.[103]

---

[100] Cf. Ch'ien Chi-po's characterization of the power and lucidity of Wang Shih-chen's
style, derived from his assimilation of Ch'in-Han prose, in *Ming-tai wen-hsüeh*, pp. 35ff. For a
description of Sung prose style as "smooth," see for example Kuo Shao-yü, *P'i-p'ing shih*,
p. 308. In certain pieces we see not just a loose imitation, but a direct appropriation of Ssu-
ma Ch'ien's language, as for example in Wang Shen-chung's "Hai-shang p'ing-k'ou chi"
海上平寇記.

[101] Yüan Tsung-tao, "Lun wen," pp. 66–70. See translation of this piece by André Lévy in
"Un document sur la querelle des anciens et des modernes *more sinico*," pp. 251–74.

[102] For the understanding of *fa* in this sense of following the inner spirit of the compositions of the great masters, see T'ang Shun-chih, cited in Kuo Shao-yü, *P'i-p'ing shih*,
pp. 310ff.; Ho Ching-ming, among others, draws explicitly on the Buddhist sense of the term
fa, using the perennial play on words by which structured reality ("dharma," *fa*) is likened to
a raft (*fa* 筏), which is discarded as just so much driftwood after it has ferried one to the
"other shore."

[103] For examples of rhetorical variety, even originality, in late Ming *ku-wen* compositions,
see T'ang Shun-chih's adumbration of the word *hsin* 心 in "Hsin-ling chün chiu Chao lun"
(see above, n. 92), Tsung Ch'en's use of a fictionalized dialogue in "Pao Liu I-chang shu"
報劉一丈書, Kuei Yu-kuang's use of emotive detail in "Hsien-pi shih-lüeh" 先妣事略, Kao
P'an-lung's play on the word *k'e* 可 in his "K'e-lou chi" 可樓記, Mao K'un's use of irony in
his "Ch'ing-hsia hsien-sheng wen-chi hsü" 青霞先生文集序, Wang Shih-chen's exercise in
reversal of earlier arguments (*fan-an wen-chang* 翻案文章) in his "Lin Hsiang-ju wan pi kuei
Chao lun" 藺相如完璧歸趙論. See also Iriya Yoshitaka's discussion of Kuei Yu-kuang's
"T'ao chieh-fu chuan" 陶節婦傳, in his *Mindai shibun*, pp. 68–92.

The issue of imitation of prose models takes on a special significance in connection with the *pa-ku* examination essay, which, according to some, is the emblematic literary form of the age. Although the twentieth-century reputation of this form suffers grievously from the descriptions of its worst moments in the writings of early Ch'ing critics such as Ku Yen-wu 顧炎武, as well as from satiric accounts in fictional works such as *Ju-lin wai-shih* and *Hung-lou meng*, through the sixteenth century people still believed by and large that this exercise represented a crucial demonstration of both literary and moral capacity.[104] Li Chih is perhaps being deliberately provocative when he goes as far as to claim that the *pa-ku* essay is the crowning achievement of Ming literature, but he was not the only one to voice such an opinion.[105] The fact that the expression "contemporary prose" (*shih-wen* 時文) came to refer specifically to *pa-ku*-type essays is a bit ironic, as this clashes with the common view of *pa-ku* writing as a kind of slavish imitation of conventional models. But the budding prose stylists of the time, whose essential training and "feel" for prose writing was in most cases formed through the medium of *pa-ku*, do not appear to have been disturbed by this contradiction. In fact, the reputations of many literary figures were made by virtue of proficiency in this medium, and not a few political careers were also launched by young candidates who gained fame as *pa-ku* masters.[106] This cross-fertilization between the art of *ku-wen* composition and the experience of *shih-wen* training is clearly expressed in the well-known critical description of Kuei Yu-kuang as one whose "*shih-wen* partakes of *ku-wen* style" 以古文爲時文.[107]

Aside from the practical value of *pa-ku* composition as a test of a man's ability to think under pressure, to organize his ideas, and to come up with a cogent logical structure in a highly restricted form, the examples of *pa-ku* at its best often amount to a kind of virtuoso performance, with their unprecedentedly long and complex chains of parallel constructions, subtleties of indirect statement, and other features.[108] In addition, the rhetorical

---

[104] Cf. Ku Yen-wu's condemnation of *pa-ku* practice in *Jih-chih lu*. See above, n. 39 for this, as well as other secondary sources on the *pa-ku* essay.

[105] Li Chih, *Fen shu*, p. 98. See also Yüan Hung-tao, "Shih-wen hsü" 時文序, cited in Chou Chih-p'ing, "P'ing Kung-an p'ai," p. 80.

[106] The best example of a career launched by *pa-ku* mastery is that of Wang Ao, who was propelled to national prominence after placing first in the metropolitan examination in 1474. *Pa-ku* composition also figured to some extent in the reputations of Wang Yang-ming, T'ang Hsien-tsu, and others.

[107] For this common judgment, see Ch'ien Chi-po, *Ming-tai wen-hsüeh*, p. 108.

[108] The virtuosity is particularly evident in many examples in which one string of characters is separated from the matching parallel string by considerable distance. The best *pa-ku* stylists also use the insertion of sharp exclamatory statements at certain points, as required by the prescribed form, for maximum aesthetic effect. For additional evaluations of the literary qualities of *pa-ku*, see Ch'ien Chung-shu, *Yeh-shih chi*, pp. 83–88.

requirement of modulation of an implied speaker's voice may have had a
significant impact on the refinement of narrative rhetoric in the novel as
well. At first sight, the stricture that the *pa-ku* writer must "speak in the
voice of the sage" (*tai sheng li yen* 代聖立言) appears to close the door on
individual expression. But, in fact, the best examples of *pa-ku* quickly
go beyond this initial rhetorical requirement to develop more and more
personal modes of expression, punctuated by the mimesis of sagely ardor
through strategically placed exclamatory particles. It has even been suggested that this feature may be directly linked to experiments in dramatic
voice on the late Ming stage, during the heyday of *pa-ku* composition.[109]
Surprisingly, the vital necessity of drawing the attention of examiners by
means of the exposition of a set topic tied to orthodox commentaries called
forth considerable ingenuity on the part of gifted *pa-ku* stylists, who often
come up with unique perspectives, original insights, or at least new nuances
in framing their structured argumentation. This is yet another unexpected
example of the highlighting of personal perspective and literary self-
consciousness, hallmarks of much of the prose writing of this period.[110]

The same sense of heightened personal perspective is also the dominant
feature of a very different kind of "contemporary prose," as opposed to
formal *ku-wen*, which is characteristic of the late Ming. This is the corpus
of so-called "minor pieces" (*hsiao-p'in wen* 小品文).[111] Formally, these pieces
are often indistinguishable from the conventional subgenres of *wen-chang*
that fill the pages of every scholar's *wen-chi* of the traditional period; or
perhaps they may be associated with entries in informal *pi-chi* 筆記 collections.[112] But already during the sixteenth century, this type of writing was
seen to constitute a separate category of literary prose, one distinguished
by the air of informality (*hsien* 閑) accruing to it even when it may observe

[109] See, for example, Ch'ien Chung-shu, *T'an-i lu*, p. 39.

[110] For examples of originality within the restricted *pa-ku* form, see such pieces as T'ang
Hsien-tsu's "Wo wei chien hao-jen che" 我未見好仁者, Tung Ch'i-ch'ang's "So-wei ch'i ch'i
chia" 所謂齊其家, and Yüan Hung-tao's "She-chi ts'ung-jen le ch'ü yü jen i-wei shan"
舍己從人樂取於人以爲善. Many of these pieces can be read in collections such as Kao
T'ang, ed., *Ming-wen ch'ao*.

[111] For a review of criticism on *hsiao-p'in wen* and bibliography, see Ch'en Shao-t'ang,
Wan-Ming hsiao-p'in wen lun-hsi.

[112] See for example pieces in the *yu-chi* 遊記 form, such as Yüan Hung-tao's "Wan yu liu-
ch'iao tai yüeh chi" 晚遊六橋待月記 and "Hu-ch'iu chi" 虎丘記; Chang Tai's 張岱 "Hu-
hsin t'ing hsiao-chi" 湖心亭小記; Ch'en Chi-ju's "Yu t'ao-hua chi" 遊桃花記; and Wang
Ssu-jen's 王思任 "Yu hsiao-yang chi" 遊小洋記. See also fictionalized "biographies" (*chuan*
傳) such as Yüan Hung-tao's "Cho-hsiao chuan" 拙效傳 and "Hui-chün chuan" 回君傳; and
hsü 序 prefaces such as Hua Shu's, "T'i Hsien-ch'ing hsiao-p'in hsü" 題閑情小品序 (see
n. 113), Ch'en Chi-ju's "Wen-yü hsü" 文娛序, and Chang Tai's "T'ao-an meng-i tzu-hsü"
陶庵夢憶自序. See Ch'en Shao-t'ang, *Lun-hsi*, pp. 22–42.

most of the formal requirements of conventional composition.[113] At times we even get the impression of a conscious, perhaps forced, effort on the part of the *hsiao-p'in* writer to convey this sense of casual composition, or to evoke an air of unruffled ease. This is often the true point of a given piece.[114] Otherwise, the *hsiao-p'in* exhibit much the same set of general aesthetic qualities that we have seen to be characteristic of the *ku-wen* and *shih-wen* literature of the period. As an ideal medium for the presentation of personal perspectives, the *hsiao-p'in* go even farther in this direction than more formal types of prose, with their frequent infusion of "painterly" details, special interest in bizarre subjects, delight in plays on words, fresh figures of speech, and wry observations—all of which are very much in line with the rhetorical stance of the vernacular novel.[115] Perhaps the logical conclusion of this increased reliance on private experience and personal perspective is the frequent turn to the self as a subject for *hsiao-p'in* prose treatment. Thus we find a number of pieces in this mode that are framed as self-eulogies, self-portraits, or autobiographies, a thematic shift that at a later stage of development contributes to the rise of autobiographical fiction.[116]

Virtually all of the features that characterize the classical prose literature of the late Ming hold true in the area of poetry as well; and indeed, the critical writings of the period, in keeping with the traditional breadth of the term *wen*, do not normally bother to insist on the separateness of poetry and prose within literary theory. In reviewing the poetic corpus of the sixteenth century, we immediately discover precisely the same hiatus separating the poetic flourish of the fourteenth century from the literary revival toward the end of the fifteenth. This is reflected in most anthol-

[113] The term *hsiao-p'in* appears in book titles, sometimes with slightly different meaning, by late Ming and early Ch'ing. Cf. Ch'en Chi-ju's, *Wan-hsiang t'ang hsiao-p'in* 晚香堂小品; and Hua Shu's *Hsien-ch'ing hsiao-p'in*. At least as early as the eighteenth century, Chi Yün used this term to refer specifically to this body of writing (see Ch'en Shao-t'ang, *Lun-hsi*, p. 141).

[114] See, for example, Hua Shu's discussion of the quality of *hsien* in his preface, referred to in n. 112. Another quality often highlighted is that of "uniqueness" (*ch'i* 奇). Cf. Yüan Hung-tao's discourse on *ch'ü* in "Hsü Ch'en Cheng-fu Hui-hsin chi" (see n. 96).

[115] Examples of painterly details occur in many pieces, especially those by literati who also happen to be proficent in painting, e.g. Li Liu-fang 李流芳 and Wang Ssu-jen. Unexpected subjects include such things as an outcast in Yüan Hung-tao's "Hui-chün chuan," or fighting cocks in his "Shan-chü tou-chi chi" 山居鬭雞記. We get an example of wry observations in Chang Tai's "Hsi-hu ch'i-yüeh-pan" 西湖七月半; bold figures of speech are reused in Huang Ju-t'ing's 黃汝亭 "Yao Yüan-su Huang-shan chi-yin" 姚元素黃山記引 and Yüan Hung-tao's "Man-ching yu-chi" 滿井遊記.

[116] For example, Chang Tai's "Tzu-wei mu-chih ming" 自爲墓誌銘 and Hsü Wei's piece with the same title. See Iriya Yoshitaka's discussion of Chang Tai's piece in *Mindai shibun*, pp. 165–92.

ogies of Ming poetry, as well as in critical discussions.[117] Here, too, the
lackluster performance of the middle period is brightened by only a
handful of talented poets, such as Li Chen 李禎 (Li Ch'ang-ch'i 李昌祺,
1376–1452) and Shen Chou, and sometimes the poetry of the period is
also subsumed under the imprecise label of the "chancellery style" (t'ai-
ko t'i). Only with the emergence of the generation of the Hung-chih
and Cheng-te reigns, sparked by such poets as Li Tung-yang and Shen
Chou later in his career, do we once again get a sense of vital poetic
creativity.[118]

Even after this point, however, the major poets of the late Ming
have not won very high critical acclaim, and they are largely neglected in modern studies of the Chinese poetic tradition. At the same
time, this very period is widely acknowledged to have produced major
achievements in poetic theory.[119] The terms of the sixteenth-century
debates over poetics are slightly different from those in prose theory,
but the basic positions and the alignments among many of the principal
advocates are strikingly similar; thus the same sets of background relationships we have seen to underly the polemics on prose style are also at work
here.[120]

In the debate over the proper models for imitation in poetic composition, however, the concept of fu-ku in its literal sense is not entirely
appropriate. First, to speak of a "return to the past" here raises a possible
confusion between the "poetry of the ancients" (ku-jen chih shih 古人之詩)

[117] The principal seventeenth-century anthologies of Ming poetry include Ch'ien Ch'ien-
i's 錢謙益 Lieh-ch'ao shih-chi 列朝詩集, Shen Te-ch'ien's Ming-shih pieh-ts'ai, Chu I-tsun's
Ming-shih tsung, and Hua Shu's Ming-shih hsüan-tsui. The hundred years from 1381 to 1470
are described as a "poetic desert" by Daniel Bryant ("Three Varied Centuries," p. 83).
Yoshikawa Kōjirō ("Gaisetsu," p. 148ff.) also speaks of a "vacuum" in the first half of the
fifteenth century.

[118] On the t'ai-ko style in poetry, see Liu Ta-chieh, Chung-kuo wen-hsüeh fa-ta shih,
pp. 297f.; Kuo Shao-yü, P'i-p'ing shih, pp. 296, 308; Sung P'ei-wei, Ming wen-hsüeh shih,
pp. 60–80; and Yoshikawa Kōjirō, "Gaisetsu," p. 149. See also Li Yüeh-kang, "Sheng-ming
shih t'ai-ko t'i yü chu pieh-t'i chih liu-pien," pp. 46–93. Other examples of prominent
fifteenth-century poets include such figures as Hsüeh Hsüan (1389–1464), Yü Ch'ien
(1398–1447), as well as the so-called "three Yangs" 三楊: Yang Shih-ch'i 楊士奇 (1365–
1444), Yang P'u 楊溥 (1372–1446), and Yang Jung 楊榮 (1371–1440).

[119] For general reviews of the poetry criticism and poetic theory of the late Ming period,
see Kuo Shao-yü, P'i-p'ing shih, pp. 289–389; Ch'ien Chi-po, Ming-tai wen-hsüeh, pp. 17,
103; Sung P'ei-wei, Ming wen-hsüeh shih, pp. 81–173; Chu Tung-jun, P'i-p'ing shih ta-kang,
pp. 224–72; Yeh Ch'ing-ping, Chung-kuo wen-hsüeh p'i-p'ing tzu-liao hui-pien: Ming-tai and
the Peking University Chung-kuo wen-hsüeh shih, pp. 877–86.

[120] See Kuo Shao-yü, "Ming-tai ti wen-jen chi-t'uan." The network of personal relations
binding many of the major poets of the period together is underscored in the numerous
occasional poems exchanged among them, which occupy a prominent place in the various
anthologies and personal collections.

and the mode of "ancient-style poetry" (ku-shih 古詩).[121] Moreover, since virtually all of the sixteenth-century critics agree on the unparalleled pre-eminence of the High T'ang masters, there is no question of a return to pre-T'ang antiquity for models, and therefore no need for anything corresponding to a T'ang-Sung School. Instead, the question at issue tends to focus more specifically on the exclusiveness of the mantle conferred upon the High T'ang poets, which often boils down to debates over the merits of late T'ang and especially Sung poetry in their own right.[122] Frequently this takes the form of wrangling over the evaluation of particular Sung poets, such as Huang T'ing-chien 黃庭堅 or Su Shih.[123]

With the terms of the argument over "archaism" versus literary evolution thus narrowed, there remains even less room for significant opposition. Certain theorists put more stress on the mastering of the formal aspects of poetry through imitation as a step on the path to self-expression, whereas others pay more attention to the act of directly conveying one's own personal vision. But all seem to accept both of these elements in the poetic process.[124] In addition, despite the forcefulness with which the sixteenth-century critics argue for their views of poetry, in the final analysis they show more continuity with, than divergence from, the ongoing tradition of critical theory. As a matter of fact, the basic positions of both the "classicism" of the "former and latter seven masters" and the Wan-li schools of "expressionism," as they have been imprecisely labeled, draw heavily on some of the same seminal poetic treatises. Chief among these is Yen Yü's 嚴羽 Ts'ang-lang shih-hua 滄浪詩話, which had already embodied this basic contradiction by on the one hand insisting on recognizing the attainment of perfect poetic form in the T'ang, and consequently rejecting much of Sung poetry, while at the same time also advancing the notion of quasi-mystical poetic vision on the analogy of Ch'an enlightenment.[125] By early

[121] Pieces in the ku-shih 古詩 mode, often in direct imitation of well-known Han ballads, such as the Ku-shih shih-chiu shou 古詩十九首 or yüeh-fu pieces, are especially common among the anthologized poems of Li Tung-yang, Li Meng-yang, Ho Ching-ming, Li P'an-lung, and Hsü Chen-ch'ing, etc. See, for example, Ming-shih tsung, chüan 29, pp. 3b–20a; Ming-shih pieh-ts'ai, chüan 4, p. 70; and other places.

[122] For various critiques of Sung poetry, see Kuo Shao-yü, P'i-p'ing shih, pp. 286ff.; Richard Lynn, "Alternate Routes to Self-realization in Ming Theories of Poetry," pp. 9f.; and Jonathan Chaves, "Panoply of Images," pp. 7f.

[123] For this idea, see Ch'ien Chung-shu's T'an-i lu, pp. 166ff.

[124] See discussion of this point by Richard Lynn in "Orthodoxy and Enlightenment." The common use of such terms as "orthodoxy" and "archaism" by Lynn and many others to refer to the fu-ku movement may be misleading in that these often imply a rigid dichotomy between the advocacy of classical models and the aim of individual poetic expression.

[125] On the seminal position of the Ts'ang-lang shih-hua in late Ming poetic theory, see Richard Lynn, "Orthodoxy and Enlightenment," pp. 219ff.; Jonathan Chaves, "Panoply of Images," pp. 9f.; and Yoshikawa Kōjirō, "Gaisetsu," p. 146.

in the Ming, this trend in poetic criticism had already been codified in Kao
Ping's 高棅 *T'ang-shih p'in-hui* 唐詩品彙, which remained very influential
through the late Ming.[126] By the same token, the emphasis on individual
expression in the Kung-an and Ching-ling schools in Wan-li, marked by the
use of such terms as *ch'ü, chen* 真, and *hsing-ling*, also harks back to ideas
put forth in the writings of earlier critics.[127] Thus these latter poetic
"schools" are not nearly as radical as they are pictured by their twentieth-
century supporters and Ch'ing detractors alike.[128]

In any event, the various idealistic pronouncements we get in Ming
literary theory about the process of self-realization through poetry are far
removed from the actual poetic practice of the period. But though the
Chia-ching and Wan-li poets generally fall short of their stated ideals, they
do demonstrate a number of tendencies that, once again, feed into the
development of vernacular fiction in their own day.

First, in apparent violation of the frequent call for the nurturing of formal
proficiency based on the assimilation of the great models of the past, the
poets of the time seem to pay far less attention to the technical aspects of
poetics than they do in their prose compositions. This is true even of those
whose theories stress the imitation of formal modes (*ko-tiao* 格調) derived
from the models of the T'ang giants.[129] Instead, we witness a loosening of
formal restrictions, tonal patterns, and rhyme schemes; or, for example,
such unorthodox devices as the repetition of words within a single poem.
In many cases all this means in practice is the choice of *ku-shih* or *yüeh-fu*
modes, which, to judge by the taste of the anthologizers, seem to dominate
the poetic corpus of the age.[130]

A second relevant feature of sixteenth-century poetry is its apparent
delight in forging plays on words, new figures of speech, and occasionally
elaborate conceits.[131] This stands in contrast to the mimesis of homespun

---

[126] See Lynn, "Orthodoxy and Enlightenment," p. 218; and Yoshikawa, "Gaisetsu,"
pp. 144ff.

[127] On the earlier uses of these terms, see Kuo Shao-yü, *P'i-p'ing shih*, pp. 295ff., 307ff.,
313ff.; Chaves, "Panoply of Images," pp. 12ff.; Lynn, "Alternate Routes," p. 39; and Maeno
Naoaki, "Min shichishi no sensei: Yō I-tei no bungakukan ni tsuite," pp. 41–69. See also
Chou Chih-p'ing, "P'ing Kung-an p'ai," pp. 82ff.

[128] See Chou Chih-p'ing, "Poetry and Poetic Theory," pp. 114f., 139f.

[129] See Kuo Shao-yü's discussion of the term *ko-tiao* in *P'i-p'ing shih*, pp. 301, 320, 323,
327, 330.

[130] See n. 121.

[131] For examples of plays on words, see the following pieces: Hsü Wei, "Yang-fei ch'un-
shui t'u" 楊妃春睡圖, in Hua Shu, *Ming shih hsüan-tsui, chüan* 2, pp. 269ff., and "Po-tzu yün
t'ing yu ch'ien-yeh shih-liu hu tso i fang ju ch'üan" 伯子雲亭有千葉石榴忽作一房如拳, in
Hsü Wen-ch'ang i-kao, 1:3b; T'ang Hsien-tsu, "Chiang su" 江宿, in *T'ang Hsien-tsu shih-wen
chi*, p. 876. Cf. also displays of virtuosity in rhyme, as in Ho Ching-ming's "Wu-p'ing wu-tse
t'i" 五平五仄體, in Chu I-tsun, *Ming-shih tsung*, p. 30:9b, and many others.

diction in the many pieces that directly imitate the "primitive" quality of well-known Han *yüeh-fu* poems. Either way, the impression here is more one of self-conscious manipulation of the poetic medium than of spontaneous self-expression. The other side of the same coin is the observation in much of late Ming poetry of a certain prosy quality, a matter-of-fact tone or discursive ring that is a far cry from the intensity and immediacy of lyric vision sought in the poems of the High T'ang masters. In fact, this is precisely the quality of much late T'ang and Sung poetry that is derided by many Ming critics as the opposite of pure poetic vision.[132] But apparently, by this time the tendencies represented by Sung poetry had become too ingrained in poetic practice to be waved away with a polemic wand, and they continued to condition the poetic language of even the most ardent "intuitionists."

What comes out of these various tendencies in sixteenth-century poetics is, once again, a sense of highly self-conscious cultural activity, one deeply committed to partaking in the achievements of the past, but forever constrained by a feeling of latter-day detachment from pure poetic vision, leaving more a somewhat forced affectation of lightness and spontaneity than the full experience of it.

This point, I believe, must be kept in mind when we read the various types of "informal" verse (i.e., forms other than *shih*) that occupy a considerable portion of the poetic corpus of the Ming period. This type of poetry is of course simply a continuation of the chain of verse forms leading from late T'ang and Sung *tz'u* 詞 through the Yuan *ch'ü* 曲 songs, which had long since become integral parts of literati culture, with their own critical canons and theoretical bases. By the sixteenth century, however, the cumulative bulk of this alternative tradition gives it even more weight within the overall spectrum of Ming poetry.[133]

At the same time, the association of these verse forms with popular culture, especially through the mediation of the pleasure quarters, also

[132] Examples of noticeably discursive poems include Li Chih's "Chang T'ao-t'ing pi-ch'u shang-shan chi huan hsieh chu tseng shih ku i ch'ou-chih" 張陶亭逼除上山旣還寫竹贈詩故以酬之, in his *Hsü Fen shu*, p. 460; "Ju-shan te Chiao Jo-hou shu yu kan" 入山得焦弱侯書有感, in *Hsü Fen shu*, p. 478; T'ang Hsien-tsu's "Hsiang-ju" 相如, in *T'ang Hsien-tsu shih-wen chi*, p. 808; and Yüan Hung-tao's "Ho Ts'ui-fang-kuan chu-jen Lu Yin-shan yün" 和萃芳館主人魯印山韻, in *Yüan Chung-lang ch'üan-chi*, p. 154. We also find a number of explicitly narrative poems, such as Li Meng-yang's "Shih chiang-chün chan-ch'ang ko" 石將君戰場歌, in Shen Te-ch'ien's *Ming-shih pieh-ts'ai*, pp. 4:73f.; and Li Tung-yang's "Feng-yü t'an" 風雨歎, in Chu I-tsun, *Ming-shih tsung*, p. 22:19b. It is indicative of this tendency that the poets of the period so often insert personal pronouns to specify their own individual perspective.

[133] For general descriptions of these types of poetry, see Wang I, *Tz'u-ch'ü shih*; and Yeh Te-chün, *Sung Yuan Ming chiang-ch'ang wen-hsüeh*.

colors our perception of them as genres.[134] In this context, the highly colloquial diction of many *tz'u* and *san-ch'ü* 散曲 pieces and their earthy mimesis of direct speech and intimate, though usually conventional, details give rise to a misleading impression that what we have here is a kind of popular poetry.[135] But this is belied by the frequent displays of virtuosity in rhyme and meter in these verse forms. In this light, some of the major collections of supposedly popular songs attributed to well-known figures on the literary scene, such as Kuo Hsün's 郭勛 *Yung-hsi yüeh-fu* and especially Feng Meng-lung's *Shan-ko* 山歌, should be read as literati exercises in the imitation of popular song, just like Yang Shen's earlier volume of *t'an-tz'u* 彈詞 on historical themes.[136] Thus, where a preface to Feng's collection speaks of the "pure and true" (*ch'ing-chen* 清眞) quality of his "mountain songs," we should understand that this is just one jaded connoisseur's reconstruction of popular expression, and not any simple gathering of pristine material.[137]

This brings us to the fullest development of *ch'ü* poetics, that found in the dramatic literature of the period. The recurring impression that the literary creativity of the Ming begins to take off toward the end of the fifteenth century is even more markedly exemplified in the field of drama. Here we observe in the generation of the Ming founding in the late fourteenth century the undying achievement of the masterpieces *Hsi-hsiang chi* 西廂記 and *P'i-p'a chi* 琵琶記, followed by a period of nearly one hundred years of continued activity not graced by any major works, until the emergence of a series of gifted playwright-poets after the Ch'eng-hua 成化 period.[138]

The revitalization of Ming drama corresponds loosely to the transformation of Chinese dramatic art from the *tsa-chü* 雜劇 form, which reached its zenith in the Yuan period, to the so-called "southern drama" (*nan-hsi* 南戲),

---

[134] Cf. the popular songs incorporated into the text of the *Chin P'ing Mei* (see below, Chapter 3, nn. 5 and 60, for critical studies).

[135] For examples illustrating these qualities, see Ch'ien Nan-yang, ed., *Yuan-Ming-Ch'ing ch'ü-hsüan*: K'ang Hai, "Ch'en-tsui tung-feng" 沉醉東風 (p. 81f.), "Tai yu-jen huan-ti shu huai" 代友人宦邸書懷 (pp. 82ff.), Feng Wei-min 馮惟敏, "Sai-hung ch'iu" 塞鴻秋 (pp. 92f.), "Hung-men tsou k'ai-ko" 鴻門奏凱歌 (p. 92), "Ho-hsi Liu niang-tzu" 河西六娘子 (p. 93f.), "Tsui T'ai-p'ing" 醉太平 (pp. 94f.), Chin Luan 金鑾, "Tsui T'ai-p'ing" (pp. 90f.), Liang Ch'en-yü, "Pai-lien hsü" 白練序 (p. 102).

[136] For Kuo Hsün's *Yung-hsi yüeh-fu*, Feng Meng-lung's *Shan-ko*, and Yang Shen's *Nien-i shih t'an-tz'u chu*, see bibliography. See also Kuan Te-tung, "Feng Meng-lung chi-chi ti kua-chih-erh," pp. 175–81; and his *Chia Fu-hsi mu-p'i tz'u chiao-chu*.

[137] See Feng Meng-lung, *Shan-ko*, "Hsü shan-ko" 敍山歌.

[138] This view of the gap in production of dramatic literature in the fifteenth century is emphasized in Liu Ta-chieh, *Fa-ta shih*, pp. 323, 348. See also Wang I, *Tz'u-ch'ü shih*, pp. 432ff.

which gradually came to be referred to as *ch'uan-ch'i* 傳奇 drama.[139] The designations "northern" and "southern" in this context may be a bit misleading, as they do not indicate a simple division between northern *tsa-chü* of the Yuan and southern *ch'uan-ch'i* of the Ming. In fact, *tsa-chü* continued to be a vital medium through the Ming, even in the southern hands of a playwright such as Hsü Wei 徐渭, whereas *nan-hsi* goes back to earlier periods, before the consolidation of the *ch'uan-ch'i* form.[140] Thus the distinction is more one of technical, musical significance. The gradual dominance of southern musical styles in the Ming theater is crowned by the adaptation of the K'un-shan 崑山 style associated with Wei Liang-fu 魏良輔 as a medium for full-length drama, a development generally credited to Liang Ch'en-yü 梁辰魚 in his play *Huan-sha chi* 浣沙記.[141] *K'un-ch'ü*, with its sensuous delicacy contrasting with the more vigorous rhythms of the other leading musical styles,[142] quickly came to dominate the late Ming dramatic world, only to withdraw into the salon as primarily a chamber art by the mid-Ch'ing.[143]

In any event, *ch'uan-ch'i* drama, particularly in *K'un-ch'ü* style, marks a special contribution of sixteenth-century literati culture and provides a number of major inputs into the development of the aesthetics of prose fiction. First, one of the most obvious features of late Ming *ch'uan-ch'i* drama is the unprecedented size of its texts, generating book-length plays of forty or fifty scenes or more that open up far more complex narrative possibilities for stage art. What is most important about this for the development of the Ming novel is the fact that these longer dramatic works call forth new structural patterns for arranging the lengthy texts. The most characteristic of these patterns involve the juxtaposition of brief scenes embodying contrasting moods, emotions, and imagery in an alternating movement, typically based on a scheme of separation to union, or

[139] On the gradual differentiation of northern and southern dramatic styles, see Wang I, *Tz'u-ch'ü shih*, pp. 424ff.; Ch'ien Chi-po, *Ming-tai wen-hsüeh*, pp. 104ff.; Chang Ching, *Ming-Ch'ing ch'uan-ch'i tao-lun*, pp. 2–7; and Yeh Te-chün, *Hsi-ch'ü hsiao-shuo ts'ung-k'ao*, pp. 3ff. Cf. Hsü Wei's discussion of this subject in his *Nan-tz'u hsü-lu*, pp. 240ff.

[140] For some of the more important examples of Ming *tsa-chü*, see Fu Hsi-hua, *Ming tsa-chü k'ao*; and Wu Mei, *Chung-kuo hsi-ch'ü kai-lun*, pp. 58–65.

[141] For background on the rise of *K'un-ch'ü*, see Wang I, *Tz'u-ch'ü shih*, pp. 423f.; Yao Hsin-nung, "The Rise and Fall of K'un-ch'ü Drama," pp. 63–84; and Josephine Huang Hung, *Ming Drama*, p. 134ff.

[142] Hsü Wei, *Nan-tz'u hsü-lu*, p. 242, describes the new musical style as "sinuous and exotic" (*liu-li yu-yüan* 流麗悠遠). The other principal musical styles are *Wen-chou* 溫州, *Yi-yang* 弋陽, *Yü-yao* 餘姚, and *Hai-yen* 海鹽. See Hsü Wei, *Nan-tz'u hsü-lu*, p. 242; and Yeh Te-chün, "Ming-tai nan-hsi wu ta ch'iang-tiao chi ch'i chih-liu, pp. 1–67.

[143] On the rapid decline of *K'un-ch'ü*, see Yao Hsin-nung, "Rise and Fall"; and Yeh Te-chün, *Hsi-ch'ü hsiao-shuo ts'ung-k'ao*, pp. 47ff.

sorrow to joy (*li-ho pei-huan* 離合悲歡). In charting these fluctuations, the paradigmatic *ch'uan-ch'i* form makes a point of broadening its scope of action to take in a wide sweep of geographical peregrinations, glimpses of high and low society, scenes in court and gentry settings, and forays to the edges of the empire.[144]

All this is tied together within a fairly standard structural frame. As fixed in later critical analyses, this frame is built upon an introductory act (*chia-men* 家門), with exposition of the structure and theme of the play, and an obligatory final "grand reunion" scene (*ta t'uan-yüan* 大團圓, or *ta shou-sha* 大收煞), with its conventional happy ending. Often this is preceded by a minor reunion scene (*hsiao shou-sha* 小收煞), as close as possible to the precise midpoint of the play. Such formal requirements as these were observed with a remarkable degree of uniformity, and are codified in many treatises of dramatic art, notably that of Li Yü in the following century, from where we get many of these technical terms.[145] As I will show in my analyses of the four masterworks, these patterns had a major impact on the formation of the structural parameters of the literati novel genre.[146]

A second aspect of *ch'uan-ch'i* dramatic art that influenced the rise of serious fiction is its complex counterpoint of spoken dialogue, lyric passages, and mimesis of action. Of special importance within this rhetorical mix is the manner in which the virtuosity of *ch'ü* composition is played off against the directness of spoken passages, allowing considerable opportunity for the display of urbane wit and the generation of thick dramatic ironies. The perception of irony in many of the great *ch'uan-ch'i* dramas is a point of special significance, because the tendency to choose sentimental plots (to which the term *ch'uan-ch'i* itself may originally allude) very often gives rise to the wrong impression—if one misses the counterweight of ironic deflation effected by this type of rhetorical manipulation and by the structural juxtaposition of passages of jarring contrast. By far the most brilliant example of this is found in the crowning achievement of the *ch'uan-ch'i* genre, *Mu-tan t'ing* 牡丹亭, where scenes of exquisite lyricism are interleaved with contrasting scenes of bawdy humor, stark military action, or childlike fantasy, thus helping the audience to take this very

[144] The term *li-ho pei-huan* is variously interpreted to apply to geographical distance or personal partings and reunions. See, for example, such plays as *Huan-sha chi*, *Ming-feng chi*, and *Mu-tan t'ing*.

[145] For Li Yü's drama criticism, see *Hsien-ch'ing ou-chi*, sections on *tz'u* aesthetics. For reviews of this formal structure, see Cyril Birch, "Some Concerns and Methods of the Ming Ch'uan-ch'i Drama," pp. 220–58; and Richard Strassberg, "The Peach-blossom Fan," pp. 108–17.

[146] See below, Chapters 2, Part II, and 5, Part II.

appealing pageant of youthful passion with an appropriate grain of salt.[147]

The subtleties of these contrived effects make such plays difficult to read, much less to apprehend in stage performance. It is not surprising, therefore, that sixteenth-century drama is marked by a shift from plays written primarily for performance to plays published as reading matter for gentlemen of means.[148] This fact is corroborated by the fine editions in which these works appeared, frequently graced by elaborate illustrations, critical prefaces, and extensive marginal commentaries.[149]

One final aspect of the literati affiliation of *ch'uan-ch'i* drama of relevance to the rise of the Ming novel is its presumption of a certain degree of intellectual seriousness. Often the reflection of the world of ideas in these plays is a matter of light wit: poking fun at stodgy Neo-Confucian stereo-types or lascivious Buddhist and Taoist figures, even parodying texts of classical learning.[150] But in prefaces and other critical sources, the authors occasionally signal their intentions of taking up serious philosophical ques-tions regarding conflicts between individual desire and the social order, or the reality and unreality of emotional experience (*ch'ing* 情)—the kind of issues that naturally arise in connection with the illusion of lived expe-rience on the stage.[151] I should add here that the *ch'uan-ch'i* plays also regularly bring in rather pointed references to historical and political issues. Indirect allusion to history is, of course, a constant feature of Chinese literary art. But in the vernacular works of this period, the refer-

---

[147] The presence of irony in *Mu-tan t'ing* is pointed out by Wu Mei in a preface in-cluded in an appendix (*fu-lu* 附錄) in Hsü Shuo-fang, ed., *T'ang Hsien-tsu shih-wen chi*, pp. 1569–74.

[148] For the distinction between drama texts for performance and "tabletop" (an-t'ou 案頭) reading, see Tsang Mao-hsün's second preface to his *Yuan-ch'ü hsüan*, pp. 8f. See also Wu Mei colophon to *Tzu-ch'ai chi* 紫釵記, quoted in *Chung-kuo ta pai-k'e ch'üan-shu, Hsi-ch'ü* 中國大百科全書, 戲曲 (Peking: Pai-k'e ch'üan-shu, 1983), p. 567.

[149] On the publishing of Ming drama, see Nagasawa Kikuya, "Mindai gikyoku kankōsha hyō shokō," pp. 2–9. The major texts of Ming drama criticism include Hsü Wei's *Nan-tz'u hsü-lu*; Li K'ai-hsien's *Tz'u-nüeh*; Wang Shih-chen's *Ch'ü-tsao* 曲藻; Ho Liang-chün's 何良俊 (1506–1573) *Ch'ü-lun* 曲論; and Wang Chi-te's 王冀德, *Ch'ü-lü* 曲律. For a convenient collection of these materials, see *Chung-kuo ku-tien hsi-ch'ü lun-chu chi-ch'eng*. Examples of fine commentary editions of dramatic texts include printings of *Ching-ch'ai chi* 荊釵記, *P'i-p'a chi*, and *Huan-sha chi*, all of which are attributed to Li Chih, and later Chin Sheng-t'an's *Hsi-hsiang chi*, Mao Tsung-kang's *P'i-p'a chi*, etc. See Yeh Te-chün, *Hsi-ch'ü hsiao-shuo ts'ung-k'ao*, p. 49f.; *Tz'u-ch'ü shih*, pp. 424f.

[150] An early example of ironic treatment of intellectual issues appears in K'ang Hai's *Chung-shan lang* 中山狼, where Mohist teachings are ridiculed. Cf. the rather didactic treatment of philosophical issues in earlier plays such as *Tung-t'ien hsüan chi* 洞天玄記 and *Wu-lun ch'üan-pei* 五倫全備.

[151] See C. T. Hsia's sensitive discussion of the concept of *ch'ing* in "Time and the Human Condition in the Plays of T'ang Hsien-tsu," pp. 249–90, esp. 250, 262, 276.

ences become more and more explicit, to the point that we get a play like *Ming-feng chi* 鳴鳳記 even before the tears had dried over the traumatic martyrdom of Yang Chi-sheng, and a work such as *T'ao-hua shan* 桃花扇 before the dust of the Manchu conquest had fully settled.[152] As we shall see, the authors of the sixteenth-century literati novel take up some of the same philosophical issues as their counterparts in literati drama, and they also confront some of the same historical and political questions.

Actually, the solidarity between the authors of the novels and dramas of this period goes even farther than this. Many of the individuals who were prominent in the sparkling successes of various fields of literati culture in the sixteenth century, including drama, were directly involved in one way or another in the formation of the vernacular novel genre. For example, the names of such important Chia-ching figures as Wen Cheng-ming, Kuo Hsün, Li K'ai-hsien 李開先, and Wang Tao-k'un 汪道昆 are all connected to a certain extent with the early publication of the full recension of *Shui-hu chuan*.[153] By the same token, a number of the possible candidates for the authorship of *Chin P'ing Mei*—Li K'ai-hsien, T'ang Hsien-tsu 湯顯祖, T'u Lung 屠隆, and Hsü Wei—were leading names in the field of Ming drama, as both playwrights and critics.[154] We may recall, by the way, that Lo Kuan-chung 羅貫中 was also a man of the theater; in fact, what little we know about him derives from this connection alone. Later on the same holds true for such figures as Feng Meng-lung, Ling Meng-ch'u 凌濛初, Li Yü, and Yüan Yü-ling 袁于令, who were intimately involved in the writing and publishing of both *ch'uan-ch'i* drama and vernacular fiction.[155] It was only after the point of the Ming-Ch'ing transition that the enterprise of writing fiction began to pass into the hands of noticeably less cultivated individuals. Thus, in many senses the development of fiction and drama in the sixteenth century is essentially one story. This commonality is partly a matter of the economic and social background of these cultural activities, since the literati stage and novel flourished in the same

---

[152] On the question of the authorship of *Ming-feng chi*, see Hsü Fu-ming, "Ming-feng chi ch'u-t'an," pp. 29–38; and Su Huan-chung, "Ming-feng chi ti tso-che wen-t'i," pp. 82–85. Birch, in "Concerns and Methods," p. 240, notes the possible presence of a contemporary allusion in the character Li Ch'üan 李全 in *Mu-tan t'ing*.

[153] For the connections of Wen Cheng-ming, Wang Tao-k'un, Kuo Hsün, and others to the *fan-pen Shui-hu chuan*, see below, Chapter 4, Part I.

[154] On the possible attribution of *Chin P'ing Mei* to Li K'ai-hsien, Hsü Wei, T'u Lung, T'ang Hsien-tsu, and others, see Chapter 2, Part I.

[155] On the careers of Feng Meng-Lung and Ling Meng-ch'u, see Patrick Hanan, "The Nature of Ling Meng-ch'u's Fiction," pp. 85–144; and *The Chinese Vernacular Story*, pp. 75ff., 140ff. For Yüan Yü-ling, see Robert Hegel, *Novel*, pp. 120ff.

region, especially in the areas around Su-chou and Nanking, and shared many of the same publishing houses and very nearly the same sophisticated reading audience.[156]

This last point regarding the readership of literati fiction and drama must be stressed, since this audience was in fact far less broad than we have been led to believe by misleading descriptions of the "popular" nature of the Ming novel. As we have seen, what little we know about the size, prices, and format of the first editions of our masterworks confirms this, since these books were apparently more the playthings of a select few than the best-sellers of any mass audience of shopkeepers and artisans, as is sometimes imagined.[157] It is true that alongside of this literati fiction and drama—and this is another point that unites the two genres as parallel cultural phenomena—there also continued to exist another more truly popular stratum of storytelling and stage art. But that only serves to set off books such as the four masterworks of fiction and the great ch'uan-ch'i dramas as major cultural achievements.[158] As I shall argue in each of the substantive chapters in this study, the fact that the literati novel continues to adopt the colloquial language, with certain modifications, as its basic medium of narration proves nothing about its social origins. Rather, this must always be understood as a deliberate literary choice directed toward specific aesthetic effects.

Returning now to my century-based periodization, once again we can document a major breakthrough after the Hung-chih and Cheng-te reigns. Here, too, the significant advances in the development of vernacular fiction registered during the late Sung and Yuan periods give way to almost complete silence, until the turn of the sixteenth century ushers in two or three hundred years of remarkable creativity.

This time frame is immediately evident in the development of the colloquial short-story genre through the late Ming. Many modern scholars in the field have demonstrated that the examples of the mature short-story form that we know from the great collections of the early seventeenth century can actually be traced to preexisting sources dating back to the early and mid-Ming, and occasionally even to Sung and Yuan provenance (although the earlier confident identification of certain pieces as "Sung

---

[156] For a useful review of the publishing world of seventeenth-century Su-chou, see Robert Hegel, "Sui-T'ang yen-i and the Seventeenth-Century Literary Elite," pp. 124–59.

[157] See my "After the Fall," pp. 58f.

[158] My use of the term "literati novel" parallels somewhat Wilt Idema's discussion of the "literary novel" in Chinese Vernacular Fiction, pp. xiff., xxii, 118f., 122f. Cf Hanan's discussion of "two literatures" in "The Text of the Chin P'ing Mei," p. 45. See also C. T. Hsia, Classic Novel, pp. 9, 11.

stories" has by now been largely discredited).[159] Yet for the purposes of this discussion, we must be very careful not to confuse antecedent narrative materials with finished literary pieces in the mature generic form. Based on the actual textual evidence in our hands, the earliest extant examples of the Chinese vernacular short story in the so-called *ni-hua-pen* form before the *San-yen* 三言 and *Erh-p'ai* 二拍 collections can only be dated to the mid-sixteenth century, primarily to Hung Pien's six collections known by the collective title *Liu-shih chia hsiao-shuo* 六十家小說 (later designated *Ch'ing-p'ing shan-t'ang hua-pen* 清平山堂話本). The sole exception, a 1498 piece entitled *Ch'ien-t'ang meng* 錢塘夢, was published, significantly, as a supplement to a printing of the drama *Hsi hsiang chi* (and anyway, this minimal story does not really conform to the generic form of the colloquial story that we are talking about here).[160] This means that, for all intents and purposes, the Ming short story as we know it was probably an invention of the Chia-ching period, later refined in Wan-li collections such as Hsiung Lung-feng's 熊龍峯 "Four Stories," and then brought to maturity in the *San-yen* and *Erh-p'ai* anthologies.[161]

The attempts of recent scholars to demonstrate that a significant portion of the extant corpus of late Ming colloquial stories is based on earlier materials represent a major contribution to our understanding of Ming literary history; but in the final analysis these conclusions are still largely speculative. The hypothetical existence of earlier versions of some of the late Ming stories does not change the fact that the colloquial story in the *ni-hua-pen* form cannot be observed before the sixteenth century.[162] This sense of old narrative material in new generic bottles is exactly the same

[159] On the sources of many late Ming short stories, see Hanan, *The Chinese Short Story*, pp. 233ff., passim; Sun. K'ai-ti, "San-yen Erh-p'ai yüan-liu k'ao," pp. 3481–532; Hu Shih-ying, *Hua-pen hsiao-shuo kai-lun*, pp. 357–411; and T'an Cheng-pi, *Hua-pen yü ku-chü*, pp. 2–143. The view of *hua-pen* stories as prompt books for oral storytellers is refuted by Idema, in *Chinese Vernacular Fiction*, pp. 3, 12, 16, 23, 70; by André Lévy in *Le conte en langue vulgaire du XVIIe siècle*, pp. 11–19; and by Charles Wivell, "The Term 'Hua-pen,'" pp. 295–305.

[160] For further background on the Hung Pien collections, see Hanan, *Chinese Short Story*, pp. 103–51, and *Chinese Vernacular Story*, pp. 28ff., 54ff.; Lévy, *Le Conte*, pp. 23–33; and Idema, *Chinese Vernacular Fiction*, pp. xxi, xi, 35, 39, 118–20, 126ff.

[161] For the Hsiung Lung-feng collection, see Hanan, *Chinese Short Story*, pp. 4, 129; Lévy, *Le Conte*, pp. 30ff.; and Y. W. Ma, *Chung-kuo hsiao-shuo shih chi-kao*, pp. 45–76. Another text of similar significance in the development of the colloquial short story is the *Pai-chia kung-an*; see Y. W. Ma, *Chung-kuo hsiao-shuo shih chi-kao*, pp. 147–82, and his "The Textual Tradition of Ming Kung-an Fiction," pp. 190–220, esp. 206ff.; and Hanan, *Chinese Short Story*, pp. 63ff, and *Chinese Vernacular Story*, pp. 72ff.

[162] Hanan divides what he calls the "early" from the "middle" period in the development of the colloquial short story at around 1450, but his argument refers to the dating of source materials incorporated into the stories, not to the appearance of the genre itself.

view I will repeatedly stress in attempting to argue that the earliest extant sixteenth-century editions of the four masterworks represent a completely new phase within their respective narrative traditions.

As I have acknowledged, these sophisticated genres of short and full-length fiction developed alongside a parallel tradition of popular fictional forms. And these two genres were also joined by a third type, the classical-language short story, with its roots as far back as Six Dynasties and T'ang, which continued to be written and published through the Ming and Ch'ing periods. After the publication of Ch'ü Yu's 瞿佑 major collection *Chien-teng hsin-hua* 剪燈新話 soon after the founding of the Ming, later joined by Li Ch'ang-ch'i's 李昌祺 *Chien-teng yü-hua* 剪燈餘話 in the early fifteenth century, no other collection of equal stature appeared among the similar, often imitative, works that continued to be published until we come to *Liao-chai chih-i* 聊齋誌異 in the seventeenth century.[163]

If the maturation of the colloquial short story was a relatively late phenomenon, then the common view of the full-length novel as a linking of short-story units, as implied in the term "linked-chapter novel" (*chang-hui hsiao-shuo* 章回小說), would put the rise of full-length fiction even later. This, however, is not the case. The chronological order is actually the other way around, with the first major examples of the novel actually preceding the short story and establishing many of the rhetorical and structural conventions later adapted in the briefer form.[164] The first of our four sixteenth-century masterworks also had their precursors and antecedents, in three out of four cases going back to hypothetical prototypes in the fourteenth century or earlier, only brought up to their final form in the sixteenth. But still, the mature literati novel stands as a new synthesis of the whole range of literary developments of the Ming period, drawing upon the aesthetic qualities and techniques of late Ming prose style and poetics, compositional principles of the *pa-ku* essay, the informal spirit and rhetorical devices of *hsiao-p'in wen*, and the structural patterns and intellectual attitudes of the literati drama, as well as certain storytelling devices that eventually go into the formation of the colloquial short-story genre.[165]

As I mentioned at the beginning of this introductory essay, the four masterworks of the sixteenth century do not account for the entire output

[163] On the *Chien-teng hsin-hua*, see Herbert Franke, "Eine Novellensammlung der frühen Ming-Zeit," pp. 338–82; William Nienhauser, "Ming Short Fiction, Popular Culture, and the Mass Critique"; Yeh Te-chün, "Tu Ming-tai ch'uan-ch'i wen ch'i-chung," pp. 535–41; and Tai Pu-fan, *Hsiao-shuo chien-wen lu*, pp. 240ff.

[164] On the *chang-hui hsiao-shuo*, see Idema, *Chinese Vernacular Fiction*, p. xxi; and Liu Ts'un-yan, *Two London Libraries*, pp. 20ff.

[165] The *Chin P'ing Mei*, in particular, presents a full synthesis of a broad range of antecedent narrative and dramatic materials. See Hanan, "Sources of the *Chin P'ing Mei*," pp. 23–67; and below, Chapter 2, Part I.

of late Ming full-length fiction. For example, the recent discovery of a series of late fifteenth-century vernacular texts printed under the rubric *shuo-ch'ang tz'u-hua* 說唱詞話 shows that the block carvers of the time were not completely idle.[166] Similarly, certain historical narratives published by Hsiung Ta-mu 熊大木 in the mid-sixteenth century seem to go back to materials of the preceding century.[167] But with few exceptions these are works of a more popular nature, and outside of these, the fine Chia-ching printings of *San-kuo yen-i* and *Shui-hu chuan* were practically alone in the field until well into the Wan-li period, as far as can be determined by extant evidence.

To be more accurate, we do know of a number of other full-length novels that can be dated to the sixteenth century. These include such works as the twenty-chapter *P'ing-yao chuan* 平妖傳 (later revised and expanded by Feng Meng-lung), *Tung-Chou lieh-kuo chih* 東周列國志, *Ts'an-T'ang Wu-tai shih yen-i chuan* 殘唐五代史演義傳, *Ssu-yu chi* 四遊記 (especially the sections entitled *Nan-yu chi* 南遊記 and *Pei-yu chi* 北遊記, *Feng-shen yen-i* 封神演義, and perhaps *San-pao t'ai-chien hsia hsi-yang chi*, 三寶太監下西洋記, *Ying-lieh chuan* 英烈傳, and *Yang-chia chiang* 楊家將 —all of which are extant in Wan-li printings that may derive from somewhat earlier editions.[168] In each of these cases, however, the earliest editions we have actually date only from around the 1590s, which would mean that they should already show the influence of the generic form established by *Shui-hu* and *San-kuo* (and perhaps even that of *Hsi-yu* and *Chin P'ing Mei* if, as some argue, these may also go back to Chia-ching or Lung-ch'ing 隆慶

[166] On the *shuo-ch'ang tz'u-hua*, see David T. Roy, "The Fifteenth-Century *Shuo-ch'ang tz'u-hua* as Examples of Written Formulaic Composition." See also Chao Ching-shen, "T'an Ming Ch'eng-hua k'an-pen shuo-ch'ang tz'u-hua," pp. 19–22; plus additional sources in David Roy, "Written Formulaic Composition," n. 1; and Idema, *Chinese Vernacular Fiction*, pp. xxxvif. Lu Kung's *Ming Ch'ing p'ing-hua hsiao-shuo hsüan*, p. 236, contains one piece, "Ch'ien-t'ang yü-yin Chi Tien-shih yü-lu" 錢塘漁隱濟顛師語錄, with a preface dated 1569.

[167] For the publishing work of Hsiung Ta-mu, see Idema, *Chinese Vernacular Fiction*, pp. xxix, 108; and C. T. Hsia, "The Military Romance," pp. 341, 351ff.

[168] See the following studies on these works: on *P'ing-yao chuan*, Hanan, "The Composition of the *P'ing-yao chuan*," pp. 205, n. 13, 206f. Hanan puts the composition of the original novel before 1560 and probably before 1550. See Idema, *Chinese Vernacular Fiction*, pp. 33f. On *Feng-shen yen-i*, see Liu Ts'un-yan, *Buddhist and Taoist Influences on Chinese Novels*. Liu attributes the novel to Lu Hsi-hsing 陸西星 (1520–1601) and dates it in the Lung-ch'ing or Wan-li reigns. See Hu Shih-ying, *Hua-pen hsiao-shuo*, p. 74; and Liu Hsiu-yeh, *Ku-tien hsiao-shuo*, pp. 89f. On *Ts'an-T'ang Wu-tai shih yen-i chuan*, see Idema, *Chinese Vernacular Fiction*, p. 116. See Chao Ching-shen, "Ch'eng-hua k'an-pen," p. 20. On the four novels reprinted as *Ssu-yu chi*, see Liu Hsiu-yeh, *Ku-tien hsiao-shuo*, pp. 87ff.; as well as Liu Ts'un-yan, *Two London Libraries*, pp. 138ff. On *San-pao t'ai-chien hsia hsi-yang chi*, see J. J. L. Duyvendak, "A Chinese Divina Commedia," pp. 255–316, esp. 262. On *Ying-lieh chuan*, see Hok-lam Chan, "Liu Chi in the *Ying-lieh chuan*," pp. 26–42. On *Yang-chia chiang*, see C. T. Hsia, "The Military Romance," pp. 350f.

composition).[169] Even if further research should prove that some of these other works predate the four masterworks, however, they still would remain primarily examples of the more popular narrative tradition parallel to the literati novel. This, at least, is true of the series of cheaper and cruder printings of *San-kuo*, *Shui-hu*, and *Hsi-yu chi* (often substantially abridged, hence the designation *chien-pen* 簡本), which also appeared during the Wan-li period.[170] In the case of *San-kuo* and *Shui-hu*, as we shall see, some scholars have hypothesized that these *chien-pen* represent a stage of evolution closer to the "original" composition of the novels. For the purposes of this discussion, however, they too may be taken here as examples of the separate tradition of popular printed fiction that paralleled the rise of the literati novel.

This concludes my review of the areas of political, economic, social, intellectual, cultural, and literary history out of which the literati novel emerged in the sixteenth century. In each of the following chapters, I will attempt to demonstrate the remarkable achievements of the four masterworks as cultural monuments of Ming civilization through a close analysis of their structural patterning and rhetorical complexity, followed by an attempt to reinterpret their meaning within the context of the issues of sixteenth-century intellectual life. In each case my argument will turn on the manner in which the rather self-referential structural and rhetorical manipulation in the texts is subordinated to a pervasive ironic focus, as each author engages in a critical reevaluation of the respective traditional materials from which his novel is drawn.

This notion of a fundamentally critical attitude brings me to one final point regarding sixteenth-century culture in China, one which lies at the heart of the art of the literati novel. This is the emergence of what might be called the flowering of an "age of criticism" across the entire spectrum of late Ming cultural life. I have presented above examples of this orientation in the critical and theoretical writings that governed the fields of prose, poetry, and drama, as well as painting and the minor arts, in this period. I might add here the vitality at this time of what may be called "historical criticism," including both the preparation of critical commentaries on certain major historiographical works (*shih-p'ing* 史評) and the frequent practice of engaging in revisionist interpretations of major figures and episodes in the national past (*shih-lun* 史論).[171]

---

[169] For the arguments on the dating of these novels, see below, Chapters 2, 3, 4, and 5, Part I.

[170] On the *Min-pen* printings of *San-kuo* and *Shui-hu*, see below, Chapters 4, Part I, and 5, Part I. In a sense, the slightly briefer alternate recension of *Chin P'ing Mei* may be regarded as an associated phenomenon (see below, Chapter 2, Part I).

[171] Examples of *shih-p'ing* in the sixteenth century include commentary editions of *Shih Chi* and *Han shu* by Mao K'un, Sun K'uang 孫鑛, and others (e.g., *Shih Chi p'ing-lin* 史記

All of these critical pursuits were eventually joined by sophisticated inquiry into the art of fiction, which began to elicit serious critical scrutiny as early as the Wan-li period. This is manifested in a number of prefaces, colophons, and especially marginal commentaries, such as those attributed with at least passing credibility to major literati figures. [172] The adaptation by the early fiction critics of the technical terms of analysis from all these other fields effectively sets much of the groundwork for the blossoming of traditional Chinese fiction criticism in the mid-seventeenth century.[173] In my own analysis of such critical variables as structural patterning and figural recurrence, modulation of narrative voice, innovative uses of verse passages, ironic shifts of meaning, and such extended literati games as allusion and allegory, I will draw constantly upon the penetrating, if somewhat erratic, insights of these early reader-critics.

The reason I am placing such emphasis on this new critical practice as a key factor in the rise of the Ming novel is that this point happens to be central to the justification for borrowing the European term "novel" to describe these works of another cultural sphere.[174] This is not the place to present a full defense of the use of this term in the Chinese context (and in any event it is by now routinely used to stand for the equally imprecise Chinese term *hsiao-shuo* with reference to full-length colloquial fiction). Suffice it to say that, whether or not these sixteenth-century Chinese works should be labeled novels, I believe I can at least show that they *do* what novels are supposed to do, or more to the point, that they lend themselves readily to the types of literary analysis generated by studies of the European and American novel.

In summation, I would like to suggest a few broad propositions regarding sixteenth-century literati culture in general and the novel form in particular. First, we have seen that much of the cultural activity of this period reveals a struggle to define the relationship of the latter-day artist to his ancient heritage. I find W. T. deBary's use of the expression "burden of culture" to be appropriate here in conveying the impression of self-conscious artists of

---

評林 and *Han shu p'ing-lin* 漢書評林, *Shih Chi ch'ao* 史記鈔). Kuo Shao-yü treats these critical editions under the heading of what he calls *p'ing-tien chih hsüeh* 評點之學 in *P'i-p'ing shih*, pp. 389–93. For examples of revisionist interpretations of history, see Li Chih's *Ts'ang shu* 藏書, and Chung Hsing's *Shih huai* 史懷.

[172] For a review of the development of fiction criticism in the Ming, see David Rolston, ed., *How to Read*, Introduction. There has been a surge of interest in traditional fiction criticism in China in recent years, as evidenced by a number of new collections of this material. See, for example, Yeh Lang, *Chung-kuo hsiao-shuo mei-hsüeh*, and Huang Lin and Han T'ung-wen, *Chung-kuo li-tai hsiao-shuo lun-chu hsüan*.

[173] For a review of the terms of fiction criticism, see Rolston, *How to Read*, Introduction.

[174] For a full statement of this argument, see my "Full-Length *Hsiao-shuo*," p. 175.

the period laboring under a strong pressure to restate their own position vis-à-vis a cultural heritage that had already become too massive for any individual to wholly master.[175] It is as if the time-honored conception of the generative interplay of past (*ku* 古) and present (*chin* 今) was by this time beginning to wear thin under the sheer cumulative weight of the centuries, so that we begin to get a feeling of something closer to what T. S. Eliot called the "pastness of the past" than to the perennial Chinese notion of complementary phases within the same ongoing tradition.[176] It is perhaps no accident that in this period and slightly later thinkers start to emphasize the unilinear historical development of art and literature, at the same time that others were beginning to apply similar views to material and historical progress. At least, we now find subtle manifestations of historical relativism as our writers strive to recapture the "original" spirit of traditional forms.[177] As a result, the entire constellation of literati culture often becomes something of an affectation, a rather self-conscious attempt to fulfill a notion of what *wen-jen* should be, instead of simply embodying the ideal spontaneously, as the great Sung masters seemed to have done. Hence, the distortions, inconsistencies, and ironic focus of so much of the outlook of this period.

This groping for identity as *wen-jen* runs through the full range of late Ming cultural life, with the attempt at self-definition more often than not leading only to uneasy compromises. Thus, we see our literati artists playing the game of self-realization from behind a screen of detachment not quite substantial enough to be called alienation, but sufficient to fuel sarcasm and ironic perspective—now coming across as playful bursts of wit, now sinking into rather heavy, even bitter musings.[178]

These remarks on self-consciousness, alienation, and the like may perhaps smack of the intellectual presumptions of contemporary sensibility. But we can anchor them more securely in sixteenth-century Chinese thought by recalling that the central concern of the intellectual life of Ming thinkers

[175] See deBary, *Self and Society*, pp. 8–12. See also James Cahill, *The Compelling Image*, p. 63; and his *Distant Mountains*, pp. 120ff.; and Susan Bush, *Literati*, pp. 180ff., for similar ideas.

[176] T. S. Eliot, "Tradition and the Individual Talent," pp. 47–59. The wide range of varying responses to the past tradition is covered by such terms as *fu-ku* 復古, *ni-ku* 擬古, *shih-ku* 師古, *hsüeh-ku* 學古, etc. For an enlightening discussion of this point, see Frederick W. Mote, "The Arts and the Theorizing Mode of the Civilization," pp. 3–8.

[177] On the notion of progress in literary history, see Kuo Shao-yü, *P'i-p'ing shih*, pp. 295, 333, 361, 357, 401. I am thinking of the theories of figures such as Ku Yen-wu, Wang Fu-chih 王夫之, and Yeh Hsieh 葉燮.

[178] Cf. deBary's discussion of the "experience of the self" in the Ming period, in *Self and Society*, pp. 12ff. See also Irene Bloom's discussion of "personal identity" in her "Concepts of Personal Identity," and Rodney L. Taylor, "The Centered Self."

of all persuasions was the attainment of a degree of cultivation of the social and moral self revolving around a core of individual consciousness. This focus on self-cultivation enables me to bring my readings of these master-works of the Ming "novel" into meaningful comparative perspective with the greatest examples of the European novel, since it, too, from Sterne and Fielding to Joyce and Mann, has been preoccupied with much the same exploration of the boundaries and substance of the self.[179] But at the same time, this central issue marks these literary monuments as crucial expressions of the Neo-Confucian heart of Ming civilization.[180]

[179] See my "Full-Length *Hsiao-shuo*," pp. 173ff.
[180] I will take up these last points in my concluding chapter.

Chapter 69: "The First Dalliance with Madame Lin in the Commissioner's Palace 招宣府初調林太太,
from Ch'ung-chen edition, *Hsin-k'e hsiu-hsiang p'i-p'ing Chin P'ing Mei* (see b.n. I.2), reproduced in 1981
reprint of *Chin P'ing Mei tz'u-hua* (Taipei: Tseng-ni-chih wen-hua shih-yeh), Vol. 2

CHAPTER 2

Chin P'ing Mei:
Inversion of
Self-cultivation

I

Proceeding chronologically backward, I will begin with the *Chin P'ing Mei*, since this work presents the least difficulty for setting up the generic outlines of the "sixteenth-century" Chinese novel. Actually, the first known printed editions of the novel did not appear until early in the following century, but we know from a variety of evidence that at least a portion of the text had begun to be passed around within a small circle of literati by the mid-1590s.[1] This evidence for the early appearance of the novel in manuscript includes a number of letters, diary entries, and colophons, chief among them Yüan Hung-tao's 袁宏道 (1568–1610) letter to Tung Ch'i-ch'ang 董其昌 (1555–1636), interpreted by Patrick Hanan and other scholars as proof that part of the book was in existence by at least 1596, and a later diary entry by Yüan Chung-tao 袁中道 (1570–1624) recalling having seen half the book around the same time.[2] Another reference to an

---

[1] For general information on the editions of the *Chin P'ing Mei*, see Patrick Hanan, "The Text of the *Chin P'ing Mei*"; Cheng Chen-to, "T'an Chin P'ing Mei tz'u-hua," pp. 242–62, esp. 255–62; Sun K'ai-ti, *Chung-kuo t'ung-su hsiao-shuo shu-mu*, pp. 131ff.; Wei Tzu-yün, *Chin P'ing Mei ti wen-shih yü yen-pien*, pp. 51–62; Chu Hsing, *Chin P'ing Mei k'ao-cheng*, pt. 1, "Chin P'ing Mei ti pan-pen wen-t'i," pp. 260–64; James J. Wrenn, "Textual Method in Chinese with Illustrative Examples," pp. 150–99, esp. 154–57; Ono Shinobu, "*Chin P'ing Mei*: A Critical Study," pp. 76–89, esp. 80–85; Torii Hisayasu, "Kinpeibai hanponkō," pp. 335–66; Sawada Mizuho, "Kinpeibai shomokkō" and "Kinpeibai no kenkyū to shiryō," pp. 262–72, esp. 270; and Chang Hung-hsün, "Shih-t'an Chin P'ing Mei ti tso-che, shih-tai, ch'ü-ts'ai," pp. 281–91.

[2] This documentary evidence has been gathered and interpreted in Hanan, "Text," pp. 39–51; Wei Tzu-yün, *Wen-shih yü yen-pien*, pp. 51–62 (follows his earlier articles: "Lun

early manuscript, in a colophon on Yüan Hung-tao's *Shang cheng* 觴政 included in a collection entitled *Shan-lin ching-chi chi* 山林經濟籍 by T'u Pen-chün 屠本畯 (fl. 1596), has recently been used by Liu Hui to tentatively push the circulation of the novel back several years earlier.[3] From this point on, we have a number of miscellaneous reports of partial manuscripts in the hands of individuals who can be shown to have been personally acquainted with one another. The first mention of a complete manuscript, however, does not appear until Shen Te-fu's 沈德符 *Wan-li yeh-huo pien* 萬曆野獲編, in which Shen reports a meeting with Yüan Hung-tao in 1606, at which time he was informed of the existence of a complete manuscript in the possession of the family of Liu Ch'eng-hsi 劉承禧 in the city of Ma-ch'eng 麻城.[4] After this we get conflicting reports of partial and complete copies of the novel, leading some scholars to speculate that we are actually dealing here with more than one type of early manuscript, which may or may not correspond to the two basic recensions of the book that eventually made their way into print.[5]

Despite this uncertainty regarding the precise date of the earliest appearance of the *Chin P'ing Mei*, there is virtual unanimity among scholars that all or part of the book was being read by the middle of the Wan-li period, before the end of the sixteenth century. The question on which there is less agreement, however, is exactly how much earlier the actual composition of this remarkable book may have taken place.[6]

For a long time, the prevailing theory of authorship had it that the novel

---

Ming-tai ti Chin P'ing Mei shih-liao," pp. 18–39, and "Yüan Chung-lang yü Chin P'ing Mei," pp. 255–76); Chu Hsing, "Chin P'ing Mei pei tsuan-wei ti ching-kuo," pp. 263–66 (reprinted in *K'ao-cheng*, pp. 54–63); Y. W. Ma (Ma Yau-woon), "Yen-chiu Chin P'ing Mei ti i-t'iao hsin tzu-liao," pp. 151–56, and "Lun Chin P'ing Mei Hsieh pa shu," pp. 215–19; A Ying (Ch'ien Hsing-ts'un), *Hsiao-shuo hsien-t'an*, pp. 29f.; André Lévy, "Recent Publications on the *Chin P'ing Mei*," pp. 144–49; and Ono Shinobu, "Critical Study," pp. 77ff. See also Hsü Shuo-fang, "T'ang Hsien-tsu ho Chin P'ing Mei," pp. 126f.

[3] See Liu Hui, "Pei-t'u-kuan ts'ang Shan-lin ching-chi chi yü Chin P'ing Mei," pp. 10–26, esp. 20. See also Hanan, "Text," p. 49; and Wei Tzu-yün, "Shih-liao," pp. 34ff.

[4] See Hanan, "Text," pp. 49ff.; Ma Tai-loi, "Ma-ch'eng Liu-chia ho Chin P'ing Mei," pp. 111–20.

[5] The two principal recensions will be described below. For information on the various known manuscripts of the novel, see Hanan, "Text," pp. 39ff.; Hsü Shuo-fang, "T'ang Hsien-tsu," pp. 27f., and "Chin P'ing Mei ch'eng-shu hsin-t'an," p. 37; David T. Roy, "The Case for T'ang Hsien-tsu's Authorship of the Chin P'ing Mei," pp. 2.6, 2.15; André Lévy, "Pour une clarification de quelques aspects de la problématique du *Jin Ping Mei*," pp. 189f.; Ma Tai-loi, "Ma-ch'eng Liu-chia," pp. 111–13; and Chang Yüan-fen, "Hsin fa-hsien ti Chin P'ing Mei yen-chiu tzu-liao ch'u-t'an," pp. 334f. Liu Hui ("Pei-t'u-kuan ts'ang," p. 25) mentions an unidentified manuscript in the hands of a certain Hsüeh Kang 薛岡.

[6] Most scholars have apparently assumed that the partial state of the earliest manuscripts in circulation is not necessarily an indication that the novel was unfinished until a later stage. Hanan suggests this possibility in "Text," p. 45.

had in fact been written much earlier. This view was already fairly common by the end of the Wan-li period, when Shen Te-fu identified the author as "a renowned literary figure of the Chia-ching period" (*Chia-ching chien ta ming-shih* 嘉靖間大名士), an idea put more loosely in one of the prefaces to the first printed edition, which speaks of "a poet of an earlier age" (*ch'ien-tai sao-jen* 前代騷人).[7] By that time, this idea was already beginning to develop into the legendary attribution of the novel to Wang Shih-chen 王世貞 (1526–90), allegedly as an act of revenge against his personal enemy, Yen Shih-fan 嚴世蕃 (1513–65).[8] Other apparently related versions of the story substituted the Chia-ching politician Lu Ping 陸炳 (1510–60) in the role of the villain, or assigned the act of literary revenge to an unnamed retainer of a well-connected officer in the imperial guard (金吾戚里).[9]

By now, the legends of this sort about the authorship of the novel have been nearly fully repudiated by scholars. I say "nearly," because as late as 1979 the attribution to Wang Shih-chen found another champion in the work of Chu Hsing 朱星, although Chu's argument did not succeed in convincing many people.[10] At the same time, other scholars have attempted to see a small kernel of truth in the legendary attributions, based

[7] See Shen Te-fu, *Wan-li yeh-huo pien*, p. 652; and Nung-chu k'e preface in the *Tz'u-hua* and Ch'ung-chen texts (b.n. I). The expression "a former age" has been interpreted by some as referring to a considerably earlier period, perhaps the Ch'eng-hua reign. See Hsü Shuo-fang, "Hsin-t'an," p. 42.

[8] Relevant early documents transmitting this legend include Shen Te-fu's discussion of the novel in his *Yeh-huo pien*, p. 652; the "Nien-kung" 廿公 preface in the earliest editions; the Hsieh I preface in the Chang Chu-p'o edition, as well as Chang's introductory essay, "K'u-hsiao shuo" 苦孝說. See K'ung Ling-ching, *Chung-kuo hsiao-shuo shih-liao*, pp. 81–89. For discussions of the formation of the legend, see Hanan, "Text," pp. 47f.; Wei Tzu-yün, *Wen-shih yü yen-pien*, pp. 19ff.; André Lévy, "Pour une clarification," pp. 191ff.; Ch'ien Ching-fang, *Hsiao-shuo ts'ung-k'ao*, pp. 101f.; Chiang Jui-tsao, *Hsiao-shuo k'ao-cheng*, pp. 57f., 60; Paul V. Martinson, "Pao, Order, and Redemption," pp. 9ff.; and A Ying, *Hsiao-shuo hsien-t'an*, pp. 29–33, 161f. For refutations of the theory, see Wei Tzu-yün, *Wen-shih yü yen-pien*, pp. 25–41; and Wu Han, "Chin P'ing Mei ti chu-tso shih-tai chi ch'i she-hui pei-ching," pp. 15–19. See also Hsü Shuo-fang, "Chin P'ing Mei ti hsieh-ting-che shih Li K'ai-hsien," p. 85.

[9] For the first of these legends, see T'u Pen-chün, "Shang-cheng pa" (discussed by Liu Hui in "Pei-t'u-kuan ts'ang," p. 18); for the second, see Hsieh Chao-che, "Chin P'ing Mei pa" (see discussion below, and n. 48). See Ma Tai-loi, "The Early Textual History of the *Chin P'ing Mei*," pp. 2f. Ma ("Ma-ch'eng Liu-chia," p. 115) suggests that the "officer of the guards" may refer to Mei Kuo-chen, another close acquaintance of the inner circle of early readers of the novel, which, he suggests, would put the composition of the book before 1583. André Lévy has pointed out that T'ang Hsien-tsu, Mei Kuo-chen, Lü T'ien-ch'eng (the probable author of a slightly later novel *Hsiu-t'a yeh-shih* 繡榻野史, which discusses the *Chin P'ing Mei* in its preface), and Lo Yü-jen, along with Liu Shou-yu (守有, Liu Ch'eng-hsi's father), were all *chin-shih* graduates of the same year, 1583.

[10] See Chu Hsing, "Chin P'ing Mei ti tso-che chiu-ching shih shui," pp. 270ff.

on sources indicating the possible possession of an early copy of the novel in the hands of Wang Shih-chen's descendants.[11]

This, however, has not put an end to the theories of Chia-ching authorship. In recent years, considerable effort has been expended by certain leading literary scholars in China, notably Wu Hsiao-ling 吳曉鈴 and Hsü Shuo-fang 徐朔方, to prove that the man responsible for the original compilation of the *Chin P'ing Mei* was none other than the illustrious Chia-ching dramatist Li K'ai-hsien 李開先 (1502–68).[12] The case for attributing the novel to Li K'ai-hsien is based largely on circumstantial evidence regarding Li's geographical origins and literary orientation, but it is also supported by a few more substantive details.[13] One of these is the point that Li K'ai-hsien's play *Pao-chien chi* 寶劍記 (preface 1547) is frequently quoted in the text of the novel. In fact, it seems to be the latest datable piece among the patchwork of source materials that go to make up the text.[14] Hsü Shuo-fang further strengthens the argument by pointing out the curious fact that there is apparently not a single reference to *K'un-ch'ü* 崑曲 dramatic style or the citation of any songs from plays composed' specifically for *K'un-ch'ü* performance in the entire novel, although its pages are otherwise packed with both an extensive mimetic representation of the pleasures of late Ming life (despite the Sung setting of the plot), and many quotations from a broad range of the dramatic literature current in the sixteenth century.[15] On top of this, we find men-

[11] See Ma Tai-loi, "Ma-ch'eng Liu-chia," p. 111; and Liu Hui, "Pei-t'u-kuan ts'ang," p. 18. The validity of Shen Te-fu's report is called into question by Wei Tzu-yün in "Shih-liao," p. 38, and in his "Yüan Chung-lang," pp. 255–76. See also Hsü Shuo-fang, "T'ang Hsien-tsu," p. 127; Chang Yüan-fen, "Ch'u-t'an," p. 332; and A Ying, *Hsiao-shuo hsien-t'an*, pp. 30f.

[12] For this theory, see Hsü Shuo-fang, "Hsieh-ting-che," pp. 78–85. I am grateful to Professor Wu Hsiao-ling for sharing with me an outline of his own argument during a visit to Princeton in June 1982. Li K'ai-hsien was listed as a probable author of the novel in several editions of *Chung-kuo wen-hsüeh shih* put out by the Chinese Academy of Sciences, Institute of Literature. André Lévy reported in a lecture delivered at Princeton in May 1984, "The Question of the *Jin Ping Mei* Authorship: A Reassessment," that Sun K'ai-ti had voiced a similar opinion in a meeting in 1982. Chu Hsing (*K'ao-cheng*, p. 32) ascribes the same theory to Kuan Te-tung.

[13] Li K'ai-hsien was a native of Chang-ch'iu 章丘 in Shantung. I will reconsider below the question of determining the authorship of the novel on the basis of regional origins. Cheng P'ei-k'ai suggests in his article "Chin P'ing Mei tz'u-hua hsü-pa so fan-ying ti she-hui tao-te i-shih," p. 36, that the fact that Li K'ai-hsien lost two sons in his lifetime might support this view.

[14] See Hanan, "Sources of the *Chin P'ing Mei*," pp. 50ff. Hanan notes, however, that the attribution of the entire text of *Pao-chien chi* to Li K'ai-hsien is itself not absolutely certain (p. 50, n. 56).

[15] See his "Hsin-t'an," pp. 50ff. For a general review of the citation of dramatic and popular song materials in the novel, see Hanan, "Sources," pp. 49–63; Feng Yüan-chün, "Chin P'ing Mei tz'u-hua chung ti wen-hsüeh shih-liao," pp. 170–213; and Katherine Carlitz, "The Role of Drama in the Chin P'ing Mei." See below, n. 60.

tion, in scenes of dramatic performance, of every one of the other major musical modes popular around this time. Thus according to Hsü, since we have fairly precise knowledge about the meteoric rise of *K'un-ch'ü* to a position of dominance on the late Ming literati stage after, say, the 1550s, it is possible to conclude that the *Chin P'ing Mei* must have been written at some point between 1547 and approximately 1570, by which time no accurate description of a wealthy household could omit this particular detail.[16]

Ranged against these possible indications of a Chia-ching date of composition for the novel is a formidable array of arguments supporting the view that the work could not have taken on anything like its final form until the Wan-li period. The most influential of these has been Wu Han's 吳晗 seminal study isolating allusions in the novel to datable Ming institutions and scandals associated with the Wan-li reign—notably the misappropriation of funds from the treasury of the Imperial Stud (*T'ai-p'u ssu* 太僕寺) and traffic in contraband lumber from the imperial forests (*huang-mu* 皇木)—as well as reflections of the resurgence of Buddhist influence in the Wan-li period following a time of increased court patronage of Taoism under the Chia-ching emperor.[17] On the basis of these anachronistic details in the novel, Wu set the upper and lower limits for the composition of the *Chin P'ing Mei* at between 1568 and 1606, and suggested that the Ming reality depicted in the novel was most likely a reflection of the period after the death of Chang Chü-cheng 張居正 in 1582, which left the gates open for many of these specific abuses of power. This time frame has been accepted by most scholars over the past generation, but it has not gone completely unchallenged. For example, both Wu Hsiao-ling and Hsü Shuo-fang, among others, have countered that many of the same abuses outlined by Wu Han can be found in other periods of Chinese history, not the least in the equally trouble-wracked reign of the Chia-ching emperor.[18]

On the other side, a number of recent scholars have deepened the connection of the novel to current issues of the Wan-li reign by emphasizing the striking parallel between the destabilizing role of Li P'ing-erh 李瓶兒 in Hsi-men Ch'ing's 西門慶 household and the gross favoritism of the emperor for his consort, Lady Cheng (Cheng Kuei-fei 鄭貴妃), which became a kind of *cause célèbre* throughout this period, producing aftershocks

[16] On the rise of *K'un-ch'ü* style to become the dominant mode on the Wan-li stage, see above Chapter 1, nn. 141 and 143, for further references. The play regarded as the first major work in this mode is Liang Ch'en-yü's *Huan-sha chi* 浣沙記, dated by Hsü Shuo-fang ca. 1540.

[17] See Wu Han, "Chin P'ing Mei ti chu-tso," pp. 19–31. For further discussion of the Buddhist resurgence in this period, see Chapter 1. The scandal over the *T'ai-p'u ssu* funds is discussed in Hanan, "Text," p. 39, n. 45; and David Roy, "The Case for T'ang Hsien-tsu," pp. 1.17f.

[18] See, for example, Hsü Shuo-fang, "Hsin-t'an," pp. 40ff.

that continued to reverberate well into the 1620s.[19] A second bombshell of
Wan-li court politics that some scholars have perceived to underlie the
unflattering portrait of imperial rule given in the pages of *Chin P'ing Mei*
was the submission in 1590 of a scathing memorial by an official named Lo
Yü-jen 雒于仁, castigating the Wan-li emperor for his flagrant violations of
the proverbial "four vices of excess" (*ssu t'an* 四貪), largely in connection
with the Cheng Kuei-fei scandal.[20] According to the argument of David
Roy, this incident may have inspired the writing of this merciless fictional
exposé of abuses of the "four vices" on a smaller scale; and at the same
time it may possibly account for the veil of secrecy surrounding the
authorship and early circulation of the novel, above and beyond any
reluctance of the author to take credit for the pasages of erotic description
responsible for the unsavory reputation of the book.[21]

Another type of evidence that bears on the dating of the novel involves
the source materials quoted within the text, although here, too, the arguments presented to date have been largely inconclusive. Some scholars
have attempted to demonstrate that the novel's extensive borrowing from
the *Shui-hu chuan* was taken directly from the T'ien-tu wai-ch'en edition of
that work, usually dated on the basis of its preface at 1589.[22] As we shall
see in Chapter 4, however, this reading of the date in question is very
tentative; and in any event, this text is generally taken to be a reprint of a
Chia-ching prototype, so we cannot establish a *terminus a quo* for *Chin P'ing
Mei* on this basis.[23] The same is true of the many popular songs quoted
throughout the text. As Feng Yüan-chün, Patrick Hanan, and others have
pointed out, many of these same songs can be found in the various
published song collections of the sixteenth century.[24] Since many of these
collections were published during the Chia-ching period, and many of the
song types most frequently used in the novel are known to have been
popular at that time, one might conclude that the novel should therefore be
a product of Chia-ching authorship—although one can just as easily spe-

[19] For discussion of the Lady Cheng controversy, see above, Chapter 1. For further
background, see Ray Huang, *1587: A Year of No Significance*, pp. 30ff., 83ff.; David Roy,
"The Case for T'ang Hsien-tsu," pp. 1.9f. and n. 23; *Dictionary of Ming Biography*,
pp. 208–11; Wei Tzu-yün, *Wen-shih yü yen-pien*, pp. 63ff.; and Katherine Carlitz, *The
Rhetoric of Chin P'ing Mei*, chap. 2.

[20] For the background of the Lo Yü-jen incident, see David T. Roy, "The Case for T'ang
Hsien-tsu," pp. 2.11f. and n. 134; and Ray Huang, *1587*, pp. 223ff.

[21] For this argument, see Roy, "The Case for T'ang Hsien-tsu," p. 2.5.

[22] See, for example, Huang Lin, "Chung-i shui-hu chuan yü Chin P'ing Mei tz'u-hua,"
pp. 228–32. Huang cites a suggestion by Lu Tan-an 陸澹安 (in *Shuo-pu chih-yen* 說部卮言)
that the borrowing may have gone in the other direction.

[23] See below, Chapter 4, Part I, and n. 26.

[24] See sources cited above, n. 15, and Cheng Chen-to, "T'an Chin P'ing Mei," p. 261; Wei
Tzu-yün, "Chin P'ing Mei tz'u-hua ti tso-che," and *Wen-shih yü yen-pien*, p. 32; and P'an K'ai-
p'ei, "Chin P'ing Mei ti ch'an-sheng ho tso-che," pp. 173–80, esp. 175.

culate that it might have been composed ten or twenty years or more into the following reigns. One small clue supporting the view of later authorship is the citation of a song in chapter 35 that is presented in a later Wan-li collection as the work of Li Jih-hua 李日華 (1565–1635).[25] If correct, this would narrow the time of the novel's formation to the few years between the reasonable start of Li Jih-hua's literary maturity, in the 1580s, and the first circulation of the book in the 1590s.

None of these points provides convincing grounds for the definitive dating of the *Chin P'ing Mei*; but the cumulative weight of these arguments does, I believe, give an edge to the theory of Wan-li composition. Among the scholars who hold this view, a few have gone on to explore the mystery of the authorship of the novel. Until recently, the roster of names brought forward as candidates for this honor included a number of famous sixteenth-century literary figures with a known affinity for vernacular literature, such as Li Chih 李贄 (1527–1602), Hsü Wei 徐渭 (1521–93), Chao Nan-hsing 趙南星 (1550–1628), and even people such as Feng Meng-lung 馮夢龍 (1574–1646), Shen Te-fu, and Yüan Wu-yai 袁無崖 (fl. 1614), not to mention other less prominent individuals.[26] In most of these cases, very little documentary evidence has been cited in support of such speculation.

In the last few years, however, a few intrepid scholars have presented more persuasive documentation regarding various new theories of authorship. One of the candidates put forward is the obscure writer Chia San-chin 賈三近, suggested by Chang Yüan-fen 張遠芬.[27] This theory has

[25] See Wei Tzu-yün, "Shih-liao," pp. 33ff.; and Hsü Shuo-fang, "Hsin-t'an," p. 43.

[26] For earlier speculations on the authorship of the novel, see Cheng Chen-to, "T'an Chin P'ing Mei," pp. 260ff.; Ono Shinobu, "Critical Study," pp. 77f.; Torii Hisayasu, "Kinpeibai shiwa hennenkō oboegaki," pp. 58–80; "Chin P'ing Mei pan-pen ti i-t'ung," in Yao Ling-hsi, ed., *P'ing-wai chih-yen*, pp. 61–67; Chang Hung-hsün, "Tso-che, shih-tai, ch'ü-ts'ai," pp. 282f.; and C. T. Hsia, *The Classic Chinese Novel*, pp. 167f. More recent reviews of these possibilities include Wei Tzu-yün, *T'an-yüan*, pp. 171–80, and *Wen-shih yü yen-pien*, pp. 132ff.; Chu Hsing, *K'ao-cheng*, pp. 31ff.; Huang Lin, "Chin P'ing Mei tso-che T'u Lung k'ao," pp. 31–39; Hsü Shuo-fang, "Hsin-t'an," p. 6; André Lévy, "Pour une clarification," pp. 193f., and "Recent Publications," pp. 145ff.; and Tai Pu-fan, "Chin P'ing Mei ling-cha liu-t'i," in *Hsiao-shuo chien-wen lu*, p. 139 plus Ts'ai Kuo-liang, "Ming-jen, Ch'ing-jen, chin-jen p'ing Chin P'ing Mei," p. 306. Other candidates for the authorship include Hsüeh Ying-ch'i 薛應旂 (1500–73?); Shen Te-fu's father, Shen Tzu-pin 沈自邠 (1554–89); Lu Nan 盧柟 (d. ca. 1560); and Feng Wei-min 馮惟敏 (1511–78?).

[27] See Chang Yüan-fen, "Chin P'ing Mei tso-che hsin-cheng," pp. 7–15. Among the circumstantial evidence presented, one particularly suggestive item is a line in Chia's *Hua-yao chuan hsü* 滑耀傳序: "I have poured out all my pent-up ideas, extending to several thousand words" 罄所蘊語焉，落落數千言. This is strikingly reminiscent of a line in the Hsin-hsin tzu preface to the *Tz'u-hua*: "In doing this, my friend Hsiao-hsiao sheng poured out all that was pent up in him over the years, and wrote this book of one hundred chapters" 吾友笑笑生爲此爰罄平日所蘊者，著斯傳凡一百回⋯.

aroused considerable interest, but the case is based on little more than the conformity of certain features of this writer's biography—his dates, place of origin, political frustration, and literary accomplishments—to preconceived notions regarding the hypothetical author of the novel, in particular the simple fact that he was a native of I-hsien 嶧縣 in Shantung, in the same area as the historical Lan-ling 蘭陵. A second identification of the author, that recently proposed by Huang Lin, singles out the important sixteenth-century poet and dramatist T'u Lung 屠隆 (1542–1605).[28] Here, too, the evidence presented is limited to a patchwork of cirumstantial support. But in this case, the speculation is backed up by a tantalizing identification of the pseudonym Hsiao-hsiao sheng 笑笑生 with T'u Lung in a Wan-li work entitled *Shan-chung i-hsi hua* 山中一夕話. To this we might add the personal and family link between T'u Lung and T'u Pen-chün, one of the early readers of the novel, although obviously this has little bearing on the question of authorship.

Possibly the fullest case yet presented for a tentative identification of the author of *Chin P'ing Mei* is that proposed recently by David Roy, who has marshaled an impressive body of evidence to support his conviction that the novel was written by no less a literary giant than T'ang Hsien-tsu 湯顯祖.[29] Roy's argument consists of two parts. On the one hand, he traces the complex network of personal relations linking T'ang Hsien-tsu to virtually every one of the Wan-li literati connected with the early circulation and printing of the novel, especially to members of the family of Liu Ch'eng-hsi, who, as we have seen, were apparently the first ones fortunate enough to acquire a complete manuscript of the book. He then brings documents to attest to the fact that T'ang Hsien-tsu was working on a major work of a highly controversial nature during the last years of his life, apparently touching upon the heady subject of the "four vices," which was tantamount to sedition in the years following the Lo Yü-jen incident. Unfortunately, this is as far as the evidence goes; and so Roy is forced to make the less convincing assumption of large-scale collusion within T'ang Hsien-tsu's circle of friends to account for that he calls a "smoke screen" of secrecy surrounding this major literary event.[30]

In the other half of his argument, Roy provides extensive analysis of the

[28] See Huang Lin, "T'u Lung k'ao," pp. 31–39. For further discussion of this theory, see Hsü Shuo-fang, "Hsin-t'an," p. 44; Wei Tzu-yün, "Chin P'ing Mei tso-che hsin-t'an"; and Liu Hui, "Pei-t'u-kuan ts'ang," p. 24. Wu Hsiao-ling describes another occurrence of the name Hsiao-hsiao sheng on a poem inscribed in a text entitled *Hua-ying chin-chen* 花營錦陣; see his article "Ta-lu wai ti Chin P'ing Mei je," p. 13. André Lévy, in a note to his masterful French translation *Fleur en Fiole d'Or*, p. 1051, n. 1, reports a copy of this book in the Van Gulik collection, with a date of 1610.

[29] See Roy's article "The Case for T'ang Hsien-tsu."

[30] Ibid., p. 2.5. Roy acknowledges the possibility that the secret work referred to might be the lost sequel to *Chin P'ing Mei* entitled *Yü Chiao Li* 玉嬌麗.

striking parallels in structural and rhetorical devices and in philosophical message linking the *Chin P'ing Mei* to T'ang Hsien-tsu's four dramatic masterpieces known as the "four dreams of Lin-ch'uan" 臨川四夢, especially to the plays *Nan-k'e chi* 南柯記 and *Han-tan chi* 邯鄲記, as well as to other pieces in his extant writings.[31] These examples are quite suggestive but still inconclusive, since they can easily be explained as evidence of T'ang Hsien-tsu's influence on another author, rather than as proof of direct borrowing from his own work. In any event, the leading authority on T'ang Hsien-tsu, Hsü Shuo-fang, while rejecting David Roy's conclusions, still concurs in his perception of a direct textual connection between these plays by T'ang Hsien-tsu and the novel. Hsü, however, sees this as evidence of borrowing in the other direction, arguing that T'ang Hsien-tsu could not have written *Nan-k'e chi*, for example, until after he had had an opportunity to read the entire text of the *Chin P'ing Mei*.[32]

One other aspect of the dispute regarding the composition of the *Chin P'ing Mei* has to do with attempts to identify the regional background of the author on the basis of evidence within the text. Recently, the long-standing assumption that the author had to have been a native of Shantung —which figures in the attribution of the novel to Wang Shih-chen, Li K'ai-hsien, and Chia San-chin, among others—has been countered by scholars who claim to have identified examples of Wu-dialect expressions in the novel.[33] Wei Tzu-yün and other writers have pressed the argument by citing certain details of daily life and customs in the novel, ranging from elegant wine-drinking habits to such mundanities as chamber pots, which they associate with life in central and south China.[34] On the other side, it has been pointed out by Cheng P'ei-k'ai 鄭培凱 and others that most of these examples were by no means exclusive to either the north or the south during the late Ming period.[35] This is especially true in view of the marked degree of mobility we have seen to characterize the life-style of the

[31] Ibid., p. 1.38.

[32] See Hsü Shuo-fang, "Hsin-t'an," pp. 37ff.

[33] Recent attempts to identify Wu-dialect expressions in the novel include Huang Lin, "T'u Lung k'ao," p. 32, and "Shui-hu yü Chin P'ing Mei," pp. 236f.; Tai Pu-fan, "Ling-cha," pp. 137ff.; Hsü Shuo-fang, "Hsin-t'an," pp. 46ff.; and Wei Tzu-yün, *Wen-shih yü yen-pien*, pp. 132ff. Chang Yüan-fen attempts to show Shantung dialect influences in "Hsin-cheng," p. 8.

[34] Wei Tzu-yün's argument that the author must have been a southerner was first presented in "Chin P'ing Mei tz'u-hua ti tso-che," later reprinted in *T'an-yüan* and *Wen-shih yü yen-pien*. For further discussion of the prevalence of Chin-hua wine 金華酒, see David Roy, "The Case for T'ang Hsien-tsu," p. 1.22. Tai Pu-fan argues for a southern authorship on the basis of certain southern *ch'ü* songs in the text. See his "Ming Ch'ing hsiao-shuo chung ti hsi-ch'ü shih-liao" 明清小說中的戲曲史料, in *Chien-wen lu*, pp. 160ff.

[35] See Cheng P'ei-k'ai's refutation in "Chin P'ing Mei tz'u-hua yü Ming-jen yin-chiu feng-shang," pp. 5–44, and in "Chin P'ing Mei chung yin-chiu yü tso ma-t'ung ti wen-t'i." See also André Lévy, "Recent Publications," p. 149; and Hsü Shuo-fang, "Hsin-t'an," pp. 44ff.

sixteenth-century Chinese literati, to the extent that practically any reasonably well-educated and well-traveled individual of the time could easily be familiar with customs, tastes, and even dialect expressions of many places beyond his native region.[36] And nearly all of the Wan-li literati figures whose names are associated with the early history of the novel were demonstrably well-traveled men.

To sum up this rather inconclusive review of the current state of scholarship regarding the authorship and dating of the *Chin P'ing Mei*, we may note for the purposes of this discussion that virtually all scholars working on the background of the novel are in agreement that it was a product of the sixteenth century, with the overwhelming majority favoring theories of Wan-li composition. In fact, the proponents of Chia-ching authorship are not really as far from this position as they may seem, since these theories generally assume that the novel must have come into being after the publication of *Pao-chien chi* around 1547, and perhaps as late as the 1560s. Even the attribution of the novel to Wang Shih-chen, for that matter, would not necessarily put its composition appreciably earlier, since Wang lived well into the Wan-li period. Thus there is substantial agreement that the novel as we have it must be a product of the second half of the sixteenth century. One additional piece of textual evidence supporting this point is the anachronistic mention in chapter 17 of a military hero named Chang Ta 張達, who gained considerable fame for his exploits in the defense of Ta-t'ung in 1550.[37]

The only suggestion of a date of composition, or rewriting, after the sixteenth century was made a few years ago by Wei Tzu-yün, who saw in the printed editions reflections of the later phases of the Wan-li political scandals, especially the infamous "Attack with the Club" (*t'ing-chi an* 梃擊案), the effects of which spilled over into the following reigns.[38] In fact, Wei went as far as to suggest that one particular inconsistency in the internal dating of the story might constitute a hidden allusion to the one-month reign of the T'ai-chang 泰昌 emperor (the erstwhile rival of the son of Lady Cheng), that is, in a later revision of the novel. But more recently Wei seems to have reversed himself to endorse the attribution of the novel to T'u Lung, whose death in 1605 would rule out this possibility

---

[36] For a discussion of the increased social and geographical mobility of the sixteenth-century Chinese literati, see above, Chapter 1.

[37] See David Roy, "The Case for T'ang Hsien-tsu," pp. 1.21f. Hsü Shuo-fang puts the composition of the novel in the later years of Li K'ai-hsien (see "Hsieh-ting-che," pp. 84f.).

[38] See his *Wen-shih yü yen-pien*, pp. 68–78, 93–103. The latter section was published earlier as "Chin P'ing Mei t'ou-shang ti wang-kuan" pp. 221–44. See also his "Chin P'ing Mei tz'u-hua ti ch'eng-shu nien-tai," and "Chin Ping Mei pien-nien shuo," pp. 42–55. Cf. André Lévy, "Pour une clarification," p. 187.

unless we allow for several stages of incremental revision in the process of the novel's composition.[39]

This last possibility, that of a gradual process of development of the text over several phases, is actually quite plausible, and would help to account for the partial state of the earliest reported manuscripts in circulation. For that matter, such a view might easily reconcile the debate over Chia-ching versus Wan-li composition by simply allowing for an earlier prototype of the book in the late Chia-ching period, elaborated into the form of the novel as we know it by mid-Wan-li, not so very long after.[40] For the time being, however, such scenarios remain purely speculative.

This brings us back once again, with a bit more factual support, one hopes, to my initial identification of the *Chin P'ing Mei* as a "sixteenth-century" Chinese novel. This will remain the basic assumption of the following discussion, as I proceed with my critical analysis of the text as an example of the late Ming literati novel genre, and attempt to reinterpret its meaning in line with the specific intellectual currents of this period.

This would seem to dismiss the textual problems regarding the composition of the *Chin P'ing Mei*, but there still remain a number of complexities concerning the dating and filiation of the earliest printed editions of the novel that will require a few comments, as they have a bearing on my own analysis of the text. The various known editions of the novel break down fairly neatly into three main recensions: the *Chin P'ing Mei tz'u-hua* 金瓶梅詞話, the so-called "Ch'ung-chen period" text 崇禎本, and the *Ti-i ch'i-shu* 第一奇書 editions (practically identical to the "Ch'ung-chen" texts except for the addition of the full critical commentary and prefatory pieces by Chang Chu-p'o 張竹坡). These last editions provided the standard text throughout much of the Ch'ing dyansty, until they in turn were replaced by various expurgated versions later in the Ch'ing period and into the twentieth century.[41] Since the rediscovery of the *Tz'u-hua* and Ch'ung-chen editions in the 1930s, the prevailing scholarly opinion has taken the former, with its fuller text and more complete citation of songs and poems, to represent the hypothetical original form of the novel. The idea that the *Tz'u-hua* came first obviously follows from the accepted dating of this edition in 1617, according to the date on the Nung-chu k'e 弄珠客 preface (actually, January 1618), at least a decade before the start of the Ch'ung-

[39] Wei Tzu-yün, "Tso-che hsin-t'an."

[40] This possibility is suggested by Lévy in "Pour une clarification," p. 189; see also his "Recent Publications," pp. 145ff. Wei Tzu-yün ends up saying something like this in *Wen-shih yü yen-pien*, p. 146. See also Chu Hsing's idea that the erotic passages in the novel were a later addition, not present in the original version (*K'ao-cheng*, pp. 57ff.).

[41] For descriptions of the editions used in this study, see b. n. I. 1–3.

chen period.[42] In view of the virtually uncontested critical judgment that the *Tz'u-hua* is the superior text for purposes of study and translation, the Ch'ung-chen text has been dismissed as a commercial abridgment, a kind of footnote to the development of the novel from its original form into the Chang Chu-p'o critical edition.[43]

However, the relationship between the two early recensions of the *Chin P'ing Mei* is somewhat more complex than this. First, the designation of the latter edition as a Ch'ung-chen period printing is based on very flimsy evidence: the signatures of certain engravers on some of its woodcut illustrations, which also happen to reappear in one or two other texts bearing Ch'ung-chen prefaces.[44] Since the same preface used to fix the date of the *Tz'u-hua* text at 1617 is also printed in the Ch'ung-chen text, there remains very little ground for insisting on the chronological priority of the former. This is especially true in view of the fact that the earliest known exemplars of both of these texts bear full titles describing them as "newly reprinted" (*hsin-k'e* 新刻). At the very least, this raises the possibility that neither of these two texts represents an approximation of the *ur*-text of the novel; thus any simple comparison of the examples we have cannot prove the order of filiation.[45]

[42] For discussions of the dating of the *Tz'u-hua* edition, see the following studies. Hanan, following Lu Hsün and Hu Shih, originally put the first printing of the *Tz'u-hua* at 1610, on the basis of the testimony of Shen Te-fu ("Text," p. 54). Recently, André Lévy has argued for a more conservative approach, taking the 1617 printing with the Nung-chu k'e preface to represent the first printed edition. See his "About the Date of the First Printed Edition of the *Chin P'ing Mei*," pp. 43–47. Wei Tzu-yün puts this more loosely as "after 1615" in "Shih-liao," p. 34; and Ono Shinobu ("Critical Study," pp. 79f.) has it sometime after 1617. See also Cheng P'ei-k'ai, "Hsü-pa," p. 32, n. 1. David Roy points out that the lunar month in the date of the Nung-chu k'e preface fell mostly in January 1618 ("The Case for T'ang Hsien-tsu," p. 2.4). On the "rediscovery" of the *Tz'u-hua* edition, see Hanan, "Text," pp. 2f.; Lévy, "Pour une clarification," p. 184, n. 8; and Chu Hsing, *K'ao-cheng*, p. 261. See also Teramura Masao, "Kinpeibai shiwabon yori kaiteibon e no kaihen o megutte," p. 74.

[43] On the dating of the "Ch'ung-chen" edition, see Hanan, "Text," pp. 5f.; Cheng Chen-to, "T'an Chin P'ing Mei," p. 257; Torii Hisayasu, "Hanponkō," pp. 349ff.; Ono Shinobu, "Critical Study," pp. 84ff.; Wrenn, "Textual Method," pp. 151–55; Chu Hsing, *K'ao-cheng*, pp. 260ff.; and André Lévy, "Pour une clarification," p. 187, n. 30. Hanan ("Text," pp. 12f.) characterizes this edition as a commercial abridgment of the *Tz'u-hua* text. See Wei Tzu-yün, *Chin Ping Mei shen-t'an*, pp. 110ff.

[44] See Hanan, "Text," pp. 5f. I have reviewed the problems of assessing the Ch'ung-chen text in "The Ch'ung-chen Commentary on the *Chin P'ing Mei*," pp. 4ff.

[45] See Cheng P'ei-k'ai, "Hsü-pa," pp. 31ff. Liu Hui ("Pei-t'u-kuan ts'ang," p. 25) notes the overlapping of the prefaces, and posits three stages in the development of this text. On the possibility of a common ancestor of both types of editions, see my "Ch'ung-chen Commentary," pp. 6f.; Wrenn, "Textual Method," pp. 184ff.; and Lévy, "Pour une clarification," p. 44. Cf. the speculation of Chu Hsing regarding a lost prototype not marred by erotic description (*K'ao-cheng*, pp. 57ff.). Huang Lin refutes this argument in "Shui-hu yü Chin P'ing Mei," p. 233. See also Hsü Shuo-fang, "Hsin-t'an," p. 78. Cf. references to an "original edition"

One other aspect of these texts deserves mention here. Aside from the most striking differences between the two recensions—the almost completely different contents in chapters 1 and 53–55, the more copious detail of the *Tz'u-hua* narrative, and certain changes in chapter titles and poems quoted in the text—the two also diverge in their division into volumes (*chüan* 卷) and chapters (*hui* 回).[46] Judging from the several examples I have examined, as well as the descriptions of others, the Ch'ung-chen editions are invariably divided into twenty *chüan* of five *hui* each, whereas every known example of the *Tz'u-hua* appears in ten *chüan* of ten *hui* each.[47] This seemingly negligible difference may become a bit more significant in light of the Hsieh Chao-che 謝肇淛 colophon to the *Chin P'ing Mei* recently discovered and published by Ma Tai-loi 馬泰來 and Ma Yau-woon 馬幼垣 (Y. W. Ma), which speaks of an early manuscript in twenty *chüan*.[48] If the text mentioned in this reference is the same one that Hsieh Chao-che borrowed from Yüan Hung-tao—which we know to have been in his hands as early as 1607—then this would connect it directly to the earliest reported manuscripts of the novel. At the very least, this would mean the unchallenged assumption that the earliest manuscripts in circulation must have been something like the *Tz'u-hua* texts now extant would have to be partially qualified.[49]

_____

(*yüan-pen* 原本) in the Ch'ung-chen edition commentary (e.g., *chüan* 4, p. 44a, chapter 47, chapter-commentary), as well as in the Chang Chu-p'o commentary at several points. Later designations of expurgated editions as the "original text" (*ku-pen* 古本) or the "authentic text" (*chen-pen* 眞本), of course, have no bearing on this question. See Cheng Chen-to, "T'an Chin P'ing Mei," pp. 255f.

[46] For a review of differences between the *Tz'u-hua* and Ch'ung-chen editions, see Hanan, "Text," pp. 11–39. On the revisions of chaps. 53 to 57, see Wei Tzu-yün, *Shen-t'an*, pp. 1–29. Hanan notes that the generally fuller citation of source materials in the *Tz'u-hua* is qualified by a number of examples in which it is the Ch'ung-chen version that has fuller citations.

[47] For a review of the division into *chüan* of the various editions of *Chin P'ing Mei*, see the textual descriptions referred to in n. 1. For the literary significance of the five- and ten-*hui* units, see below.

[48] See Y. W. Ma, "Hsin tzu-liao," and "Lun Hsieh pa shu" (see n. 2); and Ma Tai-loi, "Chin P'ing Mei pa." Hanan dates Yüan Hung-tao's letter to Hsieh asking him to return the manuscript in 1607 (in "Text," p. 48). Wei Tzu-yün questions the authenticity of this letter in "Shih-liao," pp. 18ff. See Lévy's discussion of this issue in "Pour une clarification," pp. 190f., and "Recent Publications," p. 147.

[49] One possible refutation of this view might be to argue that the detail of the twenty-*chüan* division mentioned in the colophon applies not to the original portion ("three-tenths" 其十三) borrowed from Yüan Hung-tao, but to the second "half" acquired from Ch'iu Chih-ch'ung 丘志充. But we really have no grounds for associating these two batches of the text with the two respective recensions, any more than we can say that the two types of manuscripts isolated by Hanan and other scholars (the "Tung Ch'i-ch'ang manuscript" and the "Liu Ch'eng-hsi manuscript") themselves reflect separate textual systems.

As far as my critical analysis of the text is concerned, the most significant difference between the two recensions is their totally dissimilar handling of the opening of the novel in the first chapter. A number of theories
have been offered to account for this difference, including Cheng Chen-to's
creative suggestion that the introduction of the principal male character,
Hsi-men Ch'ing, at the start of the Ch'ung-chen version follows the structural requirements of *ch'uan-ch'i* drama, and Wei Tzu-yün's hypothesis that
the opening of the Ch'ung-chen text represents a deliberate softening of
some of the political implications in the first pages of the *Tz'u-hua*.[50] For
the purposes of my argument, however, I would like to understand this
point as an affirmation of the developing aesthetics of the literati novel
form, regardless of whether we follow Hanan's reasoning—that the contrived symmetry the first chapter of the Ch'ung-chen version sheds on the
text reflects the more polished structural conventions of the seventeenth-
century Chinese novel—or, alternatively, we associate this with the formal
features of the genre that go back to the first three of our four masterworks.[51] We should also give the Ch'ung-chen editions more credit than
they have received to date for the critical commentary that is an invariable
feature of this textual system, although this contribution has been largely
eclipsed by Chang Chu-p'o's more impressive achievement in this area. Not
enough attention has been paid to the fact that not only does Chang
Chu-p'o's basic edition simply take over the Ch'ung-chen text, but his
commentary as well is substantially influenced by the work of the earlier
commentator.[52]

Although the textual history of the novel from the time of its original
composition to the later Ch'ing editions is thus a subject of scholarly
debate, the other side of the picture, that leading up to the formation of the

---

[50] See Cheng Chen-to, "T'an Chin P'ing Mei," p. 258. Cf. the identification of characters
in the novel with dramatic role categories in the Nung-chu k'e preface. See also Wei Tzu-
yün, *Wen-shih yü yen-pien*, pp. 81–150; and Lévy, "Pour une clarification," p. 187, and
"Recent Publications," pp. 144f.

[51] See Hanan, "Text," p. 13.

[52] For a discussion of the debt of Chang Chu-p'o to the Ch'ung-chen edition commentary,
see my "Ch'ung-chen Commentary," pp. 8ff. Examples of Chang Chu-p'o comments taken
directly from Ch'ung-chen edition comments include: Chang (hereafter CCP) chapter 39 (1b)
and "Ch'ung-chen" (hereafter CC) 39 (32a), CCP 22 (22b) and CC 22 (15b), CCP 51 (16b)
and CC 51 (13a), CCP 93 (4b) and CC 93 (26a). Additional examples will be cited below. See
also Hanan, "Text," p. 8; and Torii Hisayasu, "Hanponkō," pp. 352ff. For a review of later
Chang Chu-p'o editions, see Cheng Chen-to, "T'an Chin P'ing Mei," pp. 255ff. For further
information on the Chang Chu-p'o editions, see Tai Pu-fan, "Ling-cha," pp. 139ff. Recently,
Liu Hui has discovered in the Peking Library a Kuang-hsü period edition with a hitherto
unknown independent commentary. A transcription of comments, along with critical introduction, has appeared in recent issues of *Wen-hsien* under the title "Pei-t'u ts'ang Chin P'ing
Mei Wen Lung p'i-pen hui-p'ing chi-lu."

text, remains relatively free of controversy. That is, in exploring the genesis of the novel, few scholars have felt any need to speculate on the possible existence of antecedent versions of the same narrative prior to its time of composition. The one notable exception to this is the theory advanced as early as 1954 by P'an K'ai-p'ei, which held that the novel had evolved through the collective efforts of professional oral storytellers (*shuo-shu jen* 說書人). But this theory was immediately refuted by Hsü Meng-hsiang, and then dropped completely out of sight.[53]

Recently, however, a number of scholars in China have gone back to the notion of "collective authorship" (*chi-ti ch'uang-tso* 集體創作) to account for the label *tz'u-hua* on what is probably the earliest text, and, more important, to explain the many glaring inconsistencies of detail in the book, which have led such critics to conclude that the text cannot have come from a single guiding hand.[54] Some of these inconsistencies and errors are so blatant as to practically require a theory of this sort, but the notion of collective authorship entails a number of other problems. First, we have no evidence whatsoever of prior versions of the *Chin P'ing Mei* story—a point that is all the more striking since in the case of all three of the other masterworks we will have to account for the transformation of preexisting versions of the respective narratives as they are recast in the novel form. There do exist a number of examples of popular treatment of episodes from the *Chin P'ing Mei* in various folk genres (especially the *tzu-ti shu* 子弟書), the earliest evidence of which is mentioned in Chang Tai's 張岱 *T'ao-an meng-i* 陶菴夢憶, but these all appear to be materials derived from the novel rather than the other way around.[55]

[53] See P'an K'ai-p'ei, "Ch'an-sheng ho tso-che." Hsü Meng-hsiang's refutation appeared under the title "Kuan-yü Chin P'ing Mei ti tso-che." See Hanan, "Sources," p. 24 n.2; C. T. Hsia, *Classic Novel*, p. 167, nn. 6 and 15; and Sawada Mizuho, "Kenkyū to shiryō," p. 268. André Lévy defends P'an K'ai-p'ei against Hsü Meng-hsiang's attack in "Pour une clarification," p. 195, but he stops short of endorsing the hypothesis.

[54] For discussions of the obvious inconsistencies in the text, see C. T. Hsia, *Classic Novel*, p. 173; André Lévy, Introduction to his French translation *Fleur en Fiole d'Or*, p. LXII; and Wei Tzu-yün, "Wang-kuan," pp. 238ff., where Wei suggests that some of the discrepancies are the result of a process of collective revision. Torii Hisayasu concludes on the basis of a linguistic analysis that the entire text could not have been written by one man ("Kinpeibai no gengo," pp. 259f.). See Hsü Shuo-fang, "Hsieh-ting-che," p. 82, and "Hsin-t'an," pp. 9ff. Hsü notes than Shen Te-fu mentions *Chin P'ing Mei* in *chüan* 25 of *Yeh-huo pien* under the heading of *tz'u-ch'ü* 詞曲, thus emphasizing the performance aspect of the *tz'u-hua* label. Wei Tzu-yün uses the term *chi-t'i ch'uang-tso* again in *Wen-shih yü yen-pien*, p. 146, but in a different sense.

[55] Chang Tai, *T'ao-an meng-i, chüan* 4, p. 1a (867): "... recited a dramatic narrative of the *Chin P'ing Mei* in the northern mode, making the audience double over [with laughter]" 用北調說金瓶梅一劇使人絕倒. Wei Tzu-yün cites this evidence in "Shih-liao," p. 36, to prove that the novel was in circulation by Ch'ung-chen 7 (1628). See also A Ying, *Hsien-t'an*,

It is significant, therefore, that nearly all of the scholars who support the view of collective authorship also grant that the text of the novel as we know it represents the product of considerable revising and shaping to yield the "definitive text" (*hsieh-ting* 寫定), as Hsü Shuo-fang has put it.[56] From my point of view, this is precisely the issue: the transformation of prior narrative materials to conform to the new aesthetic conventions and intellectual concerns of the emerging novel genre in the sixteenth century. However we put this, the *Chin P'ing Mei* is widely regarded as in many senses an astonishingly "original" work of art, conceived, at least to some extent, within the mind of a single author.[57] This impression is based not so much on incontrovertible evidence regarding its process of composition as on the fact that, for all its inconsistencies of style and decorum, the *Chin P'ing Mei* projects a sense of unity of conception virtually unparalleled in the early history of colloquial Chinese fiction.[58] This alone seems to lend credence to the unproven assumption that it was written by one man over one period of time. Chang Chu-p'o, for one, implies as much when he notes in his prefatory essay "How to Read the *Chin P'ing Mei*" ("Chin P'ing Mei tu-fa" 金瓶梅讀法) that " the hundred chapters of this work constitute a single chapter" 一百回是一回.[59] This evaluation of the novel obviously clashes head-on with the views of those critics who emphasize the inconsistencies in the text, but I will attempt to support the position in the remainder of this chapter.

The capacity of the *Chin P'ing Mei* to create within its pages the sense of a single coherent world is all the more remarkable since we know that the text in actuality incorporates a large number of earlier source materials (as opposed to prior versions of the narrative). These sources, as enumerated by Patrick Hanan and others, cut across the entire spectrum of Ming

---

p. 33. For information on examples of the *Chin P'ing Mei* story in the *tzu-ti shu* form, see Fu Hsi-hua, *Tzu-ti shu tsung-mu*, pp. 41, 76, 98, 137, 148. In P'an K'ai-p'ei's rejoinder to Hsü Meng-hsiang ("Ch'an-sheng ho tso-che," p. 180), he refers to a *"shuo-ch'ang Chin P'ing Mei"* and a *"Chin P'ing Mei t'an-tz'u,"* as examples of popular narratives on the same material. See also Hsü Shuo-fang, "Hsin-t'an," p.33.

[56] See Hsü Shuo-fang, "Hsieh-ting-che," pp. 79ff. Hsü credits this later writer (Li K'ai-hsien) with "completely transforming" (*ch'üan-jan kai-kuan* 全然改觀) the text (p. 80). Even P'an K'ai-p'ei, who had originally suggested that the novel was a product of collective authorship by professional storytellers (see n. 53), later admitted that the author must have been a *wen-jen* (see "appended note" in reply to Hsü Meng-hsiang, "Ch'an-sheng ho tso-che," pp. 179f.).

[57] For a good discussion of this idea, see Martinson, "Pao, Order, and Redemption," p. 14. See also Chang Hung-hsün, "Tso-che, shih-tai, ch'ü-ts'ai," p. 93.

[58] Hanan makes this argument in his "Sources," pp. 66f.

[59] Chang Chu-p'o, "Chin P'ing Mei tu-fa," item no. 38, in *Ti-i ch'i-shu*, see b.n. I. 3. See also items 34, 35, 37, 38, 39, 48, and 52 of the *tu-fa*, as well as Chang's *fan-li* 凡例 introduction and his essay "Chu-p'o hsien-hua" 竹坡閒話.

literature, including colloquial materials from drama, the short story, and popular songs, as well as classical-language pieces on erotic subjects, *pao-chüan* 寶卷 religious texts, and even historical writings.[60] But as Hanan himself suggests, the most significant point to be made in this regard is not the simple fact of the novel's debt to a variety of sources, but quite the contrary, the extreme care that has gone into selecting, piecing together, and ultimately transforming these materials to produce a singularly original literary creation.

As I will show in my discussions of the other three Ming novels treated in this study, this process of transforming earlier, often popular, materials is precisely what constitutes the creative mode of the literati novel genre. Moreover, in *Chin P'ing Mei*, as in its three sister novels, the precise manner in which these borrowed materials are shaped into the new narrative genre reveals a highly sophisticated literary sensibility.[61] Of particular importance to the present argument will be the observation, in my analysis of this and the other three texts, of many instances in which there is a very pointed attempt to bring out ironic discrepancies between the original import of the borrowed passages and the uses they are put to in their new contexts.[62]

In the remainder of this chapter I will consider some of the notable features of the *Chin P'ing Mei* that mark it as a self-conscious literary construct. I will begin by devoting considerable space to an elucidation of

[60] See Hanan, "Sources," pp. 23–67. See also the following more specific studies. On the use of drama and popular song materials, see Feng Yüan-chün, "Wen-hsüeh shih-liao," and Carlitz, "Role of Drama." See also Chao Ching-shen, "Chin P'ing Mei tz'u-hua yü ch'ü-tzu," pp. 308–12. For the use of colloquial short-story materials, see John Bishop, "A Colloquial Short Story in the *Chin P'ing Mei*," pp. 226–34; Katherine Carlitz, *Rhetoric*, pp. 71–77; and Hsü Shuo-fang, "Hsin-t'an," pp. 25ff. On the adaptation of the original *Shui-hu chuan* episode, see Hsü Shuo-fang, "Hsin-t'an," pp. 23ff., and his "Chin P'ing Mei ch'eng-shu pu-cheng," pp. 81f.; and Huang Lin, "Shui-hu yü Chin P'ing Mei." For additional information on the use of the *Ju-i chün chuan*, see Hsü Shuo-fang, "Hsin-t'an," pp. 21ff.; and Patrick Hanan, "The Erotic Novel," pp. 2f., 7ff. On the citation of *pao-chüan* texts in the novel, see Sawada Mizuho, "Kinpeibai shiwa shoin no hōkan ni tsuite," pp. 86–98; and Carlitz, *Rhetoric*, pp. 59ff. Martinson provides a good review of these various types of sources in "Pao, Order, and Redemption," pp. 18ff.

[61] Cf. Hanan, "Sources," pp. 24, 46, 63, and 65: "It is not the fact of copying which is important, but its nature and the purpose for which it was undertaken ... the author has relied on literary experience rather than on personal observation...." Hanan makes a similar point in "The Composition of the *P'ing-yao chuan*," pp. 215f.: "The author of *Chin P'ing Mei* delights in turning the original meaning of a passage inside out." See also Lévy, "Pour une clarification," pp. 192f., 196f.; and C. T. Hsia, *Classic Novel*, p. 166. This is the central thesis of Carlitz, *Rhetoric*, passim.

[62] A number of recent studies have set forth the ironic use of allusions to popular songs and drama in the novel. See, especially, the work of Katherine Carlitz and K'ang-i Sun Chang (for bibliographical information see notes 15, 60, and 218).

those aspects of the text that demonstrate its impressive degree of structural manipulation and control of narrative detail, with an eye toward supporting my basic contention that certain apparent patterns of meaning within the novel represent a deliberate projection on the part of the author. Although some of these features may seem self-evident, I will take the time to point them out in this section in order to set up a generic model against which to consider retrospectively comparable aspects of the other three Ming novels under investigation.

The following textual analysis is based on close readings of exemplars of all three of the basic recensions. I will use the *Tz'u-hua* throughout as my primary text for citation of passages, but I will also make reference to the Ch'ung-chen text and the Chang Chu-p'o edition for elucidation of textual variants, and especially for adducing the critical commentaries attached to these latter two editions.[63]

II

Beginning with the overall structural design of the text, I will first draw attention to its invariable hundred-chapter length, with all the potential symmetries and numerological patterns implied by that number. As we shall see, this order of magnitude had become by the time of the composition of the *Chin P'ing Mei*—with some room for variation—a standard generic feature of the literati novel form.[64] The division of the text into *hui*-units, however, should not be taken for granted, since modern scholarship has shown that the *chang-hui* 章回 format was only a later phenomenon in the development of Ming fiction, before which time fictional narratives had been divided into other types of single-episode units (e.g., *tse* 則 and *kuan-mu* 關目).[65] The insistence on creating the patently false impression that such full-length texts are comprised of strings of independent *hui*-units from street-side storytelling is in itself not without significance for the aesthetics of the Chinese novel in general, and this is particularly striking in the case of the *Chin P'ing Mei*, for which we have no evidence of a prior tradition of oral story cycles or other forms of continuous narrative on the same theme.

Of greater importance for our understanding of the underlying structure of the novel, however, is its division into the standard printing units of the *chüan* 卷. As far as I can tell, nearly every known printing of the two earliest

[63] For bibliographical information, see b.n. I.2, 3.

[64] Cf. P'an K'ai-p'ei's discussion of the hundred-chapter length, in "Ch'an-sheng ho tso-che," p. 178.

[65] Cf. Liu Ts'un-yan's discussion in *Chinese Popular Fiction in Two London Libraries*, pp. 20ff.

recensions of the *Chin P'ing Mei* was divided into either ten *chüan* of ten *hui* chapters each, or twenty *chüan* of five *hui* chapters, like many of the earliest editions of *San-kuo yen-i, Shui-hu chuan,* and *Hsi-yu chi,* as we shall see later.[66] This seemingly fortuitous bibliographical detail leads me to my first major point regarding the structural design of the novel, when we note that the narrative continuum of the text also breaks down into a fairly clear rhythm of ten-chapter units—punctuated by events of crucial importance to the structural outlines of the story, or of prophetic significance, in the ninth and tenth chapters of each "decade."

Let us take a moment to set forth in some detail the division of the text into these ten-chapter units.[67] The first of these units is devoted to the expanded retelling of the *Shui-hu* episode of the liaison between Hsi-men Ch'ing and P'an Chin-lien 潘金蓮, the murder of her husband Wu Ta 武大, and Wu Sung's 武松 attempted revenge and banishment, concluding with P'an Chin-lien's acceptance into the Hsi-men household in chapter 9. This is followed immediately by another ten-chapter section covering the parallel story of Hsi-men Ch'ing's adulterous affair with Li P'ing-erh, the unpleasant demise of her two husbands in quick succession, and her own entry into Hsi-men Ch'ing's fold in chapter 19. Chapters 20 to 29 then develop the seeds of internal dissension within the outward prosperity of the Hsi-men household, culminating in the fortunetelling session in chapter 29 and in the double triumph of Kuan-ko's 官哥 birth and Hsi-men's simul-

---

[66] See p. 67 for the division of the *Tz'u-hua* texts into ten *chüan* of ten *hui* each and the Ch'ung-chen editions into twenty *chüan* of five *hui* each. The only exception to this appears to be the text entitled *Hsin-k'e ku-pen pa ts'ai-tzu tz'u-hua* 新刻古本八才子詞話 (Hanan's "B-9"), which seems to be related to the inaccessible *Tz'u-hua* edition held in the Jigendō 慈眼堂 collection in Nikkō (Hanan's "A-3"). See Wrenn, "Textual Method," p. 153. Torii ("Hanponkō," p. 339) describes the latter as consisting of one hundred *hui* divided into sixteen [sic] stitched volumes (*ts'e* 册), which may or may not correspond to *chüan* divisions, although even Torii bewails his inability to examine the Jigendō text himself. (The catalogue of the Jigendō collection, *Nikkō-zan Tenkai zō shuyō kosho kaitai* 日光山天海藏主要古書解題 [1966], p. 113, does not mention this division in its description of the book.) As for the Chang Chu-p'o commentary editions, Hanan's general statement that they are not divided into *chüan* must be qualified by at least one exception: the exemplar in the Gest Oriental Library, which is divided into fifty *chüan* of two *hui* each. See Teramura, "Kaiteibon e no kaihen," pp. 76ff.

[67] Chang Chu-p'o's schematic outline of the contents of the book in a prefatory piece entitled "Ti-i ch'i-shu mu" 第一奇書目 holds to the ten-chapter division for the first three decades, then abandons it and breaks the sequence of chapters at numbers 46, 58, 75, and 96. He does, however, provide an explicit discussion of the textual unit stretching from chapter 20 to 29 in a chapter-commentary at the beginning of chapter 21. See also his discussion of certain larger textual units in his *fan-li* 凡例 introduction. More recently, the ten-chapter rhythm of the novel has been discussed by David T. Roy in "A Confucian Interpretation of the *Chin P'ing Mei*," p. 54. See also Martinson, "Pao, Order, and Redemption," pp. 254ff.; and Katherine Carlitz, "Role of Drama," pp. 15ff.

taneous ascension to official status in chapter 30. The following ten chapters trace the increasingly dangerous behavior of servants and masters
leading up to the discussions of karmic retribution in chapter 39. The ten
chapters starting from chapter 40 develop the deepening enmity between
P'an Chin-lien and Li P'ing-erh and the vulnerability of P'ing-erh's baby, as
Hsi-men Ch'ing's fortunes spiral higher and his sexual powers receive a
boost from the strange foreign monk who appears in chapter 49, followed
by the repetition of images of sickness and intimations of impending
tragedy that lead into the cruel events of chapter 59. From chapter 60 to
69 we witness the rapid waning of P'ing-erh, and her replacement first by
Ju-i 如意 and then by Madame Lin 林太太, after which time the narrative
enters a ten-chapter coda of feverish sexual activity resulting in Hsi-men
Ch'ing's collapse in chapter 79.

Even after the narrative pace slows down and loses its centripetal focus
with the death of the nuclear figure, we can still observe the manner in
which the author maintains a rough ten-chapter rhythm, using chapters 80
to 90 or 91 to empty out the household and send all of the concubines
off to their separate fates, then turning to a final section devoted primarily
to the humbling of Ch'en Ching-chi 陳經濟, bringing us up to the closing
scenes.

Once the reader's attention becomes attuned to the rhythm of these
ten-chapter units of text, certain other related structural patterns also begin
to emerge. On the one hand, within the space of each decade we can
perceive a type of smaller internal patterns of oscillation on the level of
narrative action. Thus, in the same way that I have identified the special
function of the ninth and tenth chapters of each decade within this structural arrangement, we may also note the recurrence of peaks of excitement
—gaiety, anger, or grief—placed in the fifth chapter of many sections,
generally flanked by troughs of relative inactivity in the intervening periods.[68] As many critics have pointed out, it is during these scenes of
apparent inaction that some of the most meaningful developments in the
narrative actually transpire.

On the other hand, these basic ten-chapter units are themselves linked in
various combinations to yield broader structural divisions of the narrative.

---

[68] Cf. the murder of Wu Ta in chapter 5, the intoxicating Lantern Festival festivities in
chapter 15, the combination of springtime abandon and the mounting of violent tensions in
chapter 25, Hsi-men Ch'ing's triumphant visit to the capital in chapter 55, the dangerously
exaggerated funeral for P'ing-erh in chapter 65, the sexual excesses and open conflict
between wives in chapter 75, and P'an Chin-lien's abortion and the disclosure of her ruinous
affair with Ch'en Ching-chi in chapter 85. David Roy argues in "Confucian Interpretation"
(p. 54) that the seventh chapters of each decade comprise a similar sequence. Cf. the string of
scenes of sexual excess and violence in chapters 8, 28, 38, 68, and 78.

For example, we immediately observe the obvious point of articulation that separates the first eighty chapters of the book from the last twenty in terms of a number of literary variables, as well as the apparent symmetry between the opening and closing two decades (1–20 and 80–100), the action of both of which takes place primarily outside the Hsi-men compound. In the same way, the first twenty chapters, in which the household takes shape with the addition of three new wives, clearly balance the concluding twenty chapters, in which the same household breaks up with accelerating rapidity.[69] In all of these schemes the ten-chapter units of the text may be understood as forming the basic building blocks of its overall structure.

The widespread critical observation that the last twenty chapters of the *Chin P'ing Mei* constitute a separate structural division brings us to another generic feature of the Ming-Ch'ing novel form. That is, we see here a good example of the tendency of these narratives to present the downfall and elimination of their central figures at a point only about two-thirds or three-fourths of the way through the text, followed by a lengthy final section in which the remaining actors who had gathered onstage during the early phases are steadily dispersed.[70] In this light, it seems to be less than sheer coincidence that Hsi-men Ch'ing dies in chapter 79 of *Chin P'ing Mei*, almost precisely the same point at which Ts'ao Ts'ao 曹操 falls in *San-kuo yen-i*, ushering in a chain of short-lived successors whose failings quickly bring his dynasty to ruin.[71]

A similar instance of overall structural design in which the *Chin P'ing Mei* exemplifies the generic model of the Ming literati novel is its neat cleavage into two equal textual hemispheres. In a number of senses the celebrations in chapter 49 capped by Hsi-men Ch'ing's acquisition of a magic potency drug mark a great divide between the first half of the book,

---

[69] See C. T. Hsia, *Classic Novel*, p. 178; and David Roy, "Confucian Interpretation," pp. 52f. Most of the central body of the work (from chapter 38 to 78) fits into one year of calendar time. See Torii, "Hennenkō." The structural divisions at chapters 20 and 80 are reinforced by staging important trips to the capital in chapters 30 and 70. K'ang-i Sun Chang has shown that the precise use made of popular songs in the text also changes noticeably in the final twenty-chapter section ("Songs in the *Chin P'ing Mei tz'u-hua*," pp. 26–34). For a comparable pattern of division in *San-kuo chih yen-i*, see below, Chapter 5, Part II.

[70] Cf. also the various critical discussions of the final third of *Hung-lou meng* and *Ju-lin wai-shih*. As far as I know, no one ever suggested that the change of pace and tone in the last twenty chapters of *Chin P'ing Mei* indicates the hand of another author. For a theoretical discussion of this structural pattern, see my "Towards a Critical Theory of Chinese Narrative," pp. 309–52, esp. 338f.

[71] Of course, the analogy is qualified by the 120-chapter length of *San-kuo*, which changes the proportions involved; but at the very least, the parody on chapter 1 of *San-kuo* in the first (or the tenth) chapter of *Chin P'ing Mei* supports the notion of conscious modeling on the *San-kuo* structure.

outlining his steady rise to economic, political, and sexual power, and the second, in which his very triumphs on all these fronts bring upon him an inexorable process of self-destruction. Chang Chu-p'o refers to this fundamental structural division in a number of critical passages as a key to understanding the work, although at some point he uses the terms "first half" and "second half" more loosely to signify the rise and fall of Hsi-men Ching's world.[72] As we shall see, the compositional principle of fashioning two contrasting textual halves is already observable in *San-kuo yen-i* and *Shui-hu chuan*, and in *Hsi-yu chi* this division is charged with a special burden of allegorical significance.

One more aspect of the structure of the *Chin P'ing Mei* that provides a retrospective model of the generic assumptions of the sixteenth-century Chinese novel may be seen in the special functions reserved for its opening and closing sections. For the purpose of my interpretive analysis, the fact that the novel starts with the expanded retelling of an episode from another novel, the *Shui-hu chuan*, is of interest not so much because it is a striking example of the novelist's adaptation of preexisting source materials, as because it demonstrates another major compositional principle: the prefixing of a structurally distinct prologue section to the main body of the work. This common feature of the Ming-Ch'ing novel evidently bears some genetic relation to the prologue section (*ju-hua* 入話) in the colloquial short-story genre, which was being standardized in this same period, although here the common view that this is a direct reflection of the original demands of oral storytelling performance is no longer relevant.[73] Instead, it is more useful to understand this to be a self-conscious literary device, one designed to fulfill the structural function of counterbalancing the formal conclusion, while also setting up a narrative model that alerts the reader to certain issues to be raised more seriously in the main body of the text.

The opening chapters of the *Chin P'ing Mei* are set effectively outside of the central world of the novel, that is, apart from the day-to-day flow of experience within and around the Hsi-men compound. But at the same time, they serve to set in motion the chain of events that leads up to (and later down from) the major events of the narrative, while also contriving to

[72] See Chang Chu-p'o, *tu-fa*, items 1, 6, 82, 83 (in the last instance, he seems to speak of chapters 1 to 80 and 80 to 100 as two "halves" of the book), as well as his interlinear and chapter commentaries in chapters 1 ("chapter-commentary," *tsung-p'ing* 總評, hereafter *tp*), 46 (*tp*), 49 (*tp*), 51 (*tp*), and 67 (12b).

[73] Even in the colloquial short-story form, the structural use of the *ju-hua* section has little to do with actual oral storytelling practice. Wei Tzu-yün discusses the structural function of the opening chapter of the novel in *Wen-shih yü yen-pien*, pp. 81ff. Hanan considers the pattern of seven- or eight-chapter prologue sections in *Hsi-yu chi, Shui-hu chuan*, and *P'ing-yao chuan* in his "Composition of the *P'ing-yao chuan*," p. 218.

bring onstage nearly all of the main characters: Hsi-men Ch'ing and P'an Chin-lien at center stage, Li P'ing-erh and P'ang Ch'un-mei 龐春梅 in the wings by oblique reference, and Meng Yü-lou 孟玉樓 in the interlude of chapter 7.[74] Even more important to this discussion is the fact that the borrowed "prologue" section takes advantage of the fairly straightforward tale it tells of adultery and revenge to implicate—with a greater sense of detachment precisely because it draws on familiar material—some of the more serious issues regarding sexual excess and the larger social order to be taken up in the text, before we are drawn into a more intimate, and hence less objective, view of the main protagonists.

In evaluating the structural significance of the opening of the novel, we must also take into account the prologue to the prologue—the initial disquisition that precedes the start of the narrative proper. Our judgment of this point depends, of course, on which of the two basic recensions we choose to work with. Regardless of whether one feels that the structural integrity of the book is enhanced or distorted by the inclusion of the section on the formation of the boon brotherhood in chapter 1 of the Ch'ung-chen edition (with its obvious parody on the opening scene of *San-kuo yen-i*), it is interesting that the initial verses and discussion of the problem of excessive emotional attachment (*ch'ing* 情) in the *Tz'u-hua* text is matched by the opening verses and discussion of what I have termed the "four vices of excess" (*ssu t'an*) in the other recension, As mentioned earlier, Wei Tzu-yün contends that the pages that, to use his figure of speech, "crown" the opening of the *Tz'u-hua* text represent a pointed reflection of the excesses of the bearer of the imperial crown in the Wan-li period, which had been so scathingly criticized not long before in Lo Yü-jen's shocking memorial. Thus the striking revision in the Ch'ung-ch'en edition, in his view, reveals a politically motivated softening of the blow.[75] For the purposes of the present discussion, however, I will stress instead the fact that the openings of both of these recensions retain the same aesthetic function—that of breaking the narrative ice while explicitly raising some of the fundamental issues to be addressed in the book. Toward the end of this chapter I will have occasion to return to these "issues" regarding the

[74] Chang Chu-p'o notes the oblique presentation of P'ing-erh in the opening chapters, and describes the opening section as a "structural outline" (*tsung-kang* 總綱) for the book as a whole (chapter 1 [13a]). Cf. Cheng Chen-to's interpretation of the revised opening of the Ch'ung-chen edition of the novel in terms of the *ch'uan-ch'i* drama technique considered above, in part I of this chapter.

[75] Wei Tzu-yün, "Wang-kuan," pp. 235ff. (restated in *Wen-shih yü yen-pien*, pp. 81–116). On the Lo Yü-jen case, see n. 20. I will come back to the prefatory disquisition on emotional attachment later in this chapter. Cf. C. T. Hsia's critical remarks (*Classic Novel*, p. 178): "The didactic preamble to chapter 1 is so absurd that even the editor of the Ch'ung-chen edition felt compelled to replace it."

consequences of excessive sensuality and its effect on the larger world order, and I will argue that the seemingly facile observations on human morality thrown out at the beginning eventually come to take on more charged layers of meaning after the reader has made his way through the fictional experience of the narrative.

At the other Aristotelian extremity of the text, the use of the fulfillment of a preordained destiny—the reclaiming of Hsi-men Ch'ing's orphan-heir Hsiao-ko 孝哥 by the monk P'u-ching 普靜—as a device of closure is not ostensibly linked to any specific points in the prologue section. This has left many readers with a sense that the ending, like the beginning, is something tacked on gratuitously, that it leaves us up in the air. Indeed, Chang Chu-p'o seizes precisely on this point to argue that the evocation of a final sense of emptiness is exactly what the author has in mind, and that this, in turn, resonates with the note of vanity of vanities sounded in the opening pages.[76]

Since a comparable sense of final emptiness also arises in all three of the other works to be considered here, I will return to this question in my promised interpretation of the meaning of the novel. In the meantime, however, I will simply add that what the conclusion accomplishes, over and above providing the final dispensation of Hsi-men's estate, is to use the deracination of this "filial son" and the final vision of Hsi-men Ch'ing in chains to close the bracket on the theme of filiality, and thus remind the reader that the issue of filial responsibility in its broadest sense forms a crucial nexus of meaning in the novel.[77] Moreover, the inexorable convergence of the destiny of the household with the fate of the Sung empire in the concluding scenes also sets the final seal on the pattern of cross-reflection between the microcosm of the enclosed compound and the world at large, which accounts for yet another central framework of meaning in the book.

In reviewing some of the more obtrusive structural patterns in *Chin P'ing Mei* that contribute to the generic model of the sixteenth-century Chinese novel, I would also mention certain other spatial and temporal schemes of organization. As for the spatial outlines of the narrative, many readers have been impressed by the degree of detail with which the author constructs his physical setting, to the point at which the novel can serve as a source for the study of Ming urban planning, architecture, and interior design. Chang

[76] Chang Chu-p'o, *tu-fa*, item 26.

[77] Chang Chu-p'o points out in a chapter-commentary in chapter 100 that his edition of the book starts with a parody of brotherhood and ends with a "filial son." See also Chang's prefatory essay entitled "On Filial Martyrdom" ("K'u-hsiao shuo"). The dream procession that settles the novel's karmic accounts may be viewed as the equivalent of the final reunion scene (*ta t'uan-yüan* 大團圓) prescribed in *ch'uan-ch'i* drama.

Chu-p'o, for example, pays particular attention in a number of discussions to the manner in which the positioning of the main characters within the compound sets up more complex relationships in the narrative.[78] Other scholars have drawn attention beyond the household itself to the commercial streets, entertainment quarters, and local temples in Ch'ing-ho 清河 prefecture, or to the geographical routing of Hsi-men Ch'ing's several trips down the Grand Canal and over to Kaifeng.[79] These various aspects of spatial setting take on what I would call structural significance in connection with the periodic contrast between the central mimetic world of the narrative: Hsi-men Ch'ing's compound with the pleasure garden at its heart, and the world beyond its walls. In fact, we can see in *Chin P'ing Mei* the same design later exploited in *Hung-lou meng*: an enclosed garden within a walled compound, leading outward through its immediate neighborhood to the surrounding city, on to the imperial capital, and thus by implication to the entire world scope.[80]

The same degree of attention to significant detail is evident in the author's handling of the temporal coordinates of his narrative. Numerous modern critics have pointed to inconsistencies in this aspect of the text as proof of what they see as the structural weakness of the work.[81] Chang Chu-p'o, on the other hand, defends the book against this charge, claiming that every example of apparent sloppiness in this area in fact indicates

[78] See Chang's prefatory piece "Tsa-lu hsiao-yin" 雜錄小引, in which he speaks of "the points that set up the physical framework" (*li-chia ch'u* 立架處) of the novel. See also his discussions of particular locations in the *tu-fa*, items 12 and 33, as well as his appended list of structures in and around Hsi-men Ch'ing's compound ("Hsi-men Ch'ing fang-wu" 西門慶房屋). Mary Scott has worked out a careful reconstruction of the layout of the house and garden in her study "The Image of the Garden in *Chin P'ing Mei* and *Hung-lou meng*," pp. 2ff. Cf. Martinson, "Pao, Order, and Redemption," p. 21.

[79] Cf. Martinson's guide to the "religious geography" of Ch'ing-ho hsien ("Pao, Order, and Redemption," pp. 235ff.); and Torii's analysis of Hsi-men Ch'ing's trips to the capital in "Hennenkō," pp. 76–80. The symbolic significance of the city walls around the town of Ch'ing-ho comes into play in chapter 100. David Roy emphasizes the author's revision of the *Shui-hu* source to set the novel in Ch'ing-ho hsien, and reads "Ch'ing-ho" as a pointedly ironic expression. See his "Confucian Interpretation," pp. 55f., and "The Case for T'ang Hsien-tsu," pp. 1.13ff. See also Hsü Shuo-fang, "Ch'eng-shu pu-cheng," p. 82. Scenes are staged in the "Temple of the Jade Emperor" (*Yü-huang miao* 玉皇廟) in chapters 1, 39, and 62; in the "Temple of Beneficence Rewarded" (*Pao-en ssu* 報恩寺) in chapters 6, 8, 47, 63, 87, 99, and 100; and in the "Temple of Eternal Prosperity" (*Yung-fu ssu* 永福寺) in chapters 13, 34, 35, 36, 49, 57, 80, 88, 96, 99, and 100. Chang Chu-p'o's allegorical reading of these temple names will be reconsidered later in this chapter.

[80] For a similar kind of spatial patterning in *Shui-hu chuan*, see Chapter 4, Part II, of this book. For an analogous discussion of the relation between the enclosed garden and the outside world in *Hung-lou meng*, see my *Archetype and Allegory in the Dream of the Red Chamber*, pp. 190ff.; and Mary Scott, "Image of the Garden."

[81] See above n. 54.

deliberate manipulation of detail in accordance with the author's grand design.[82] This is also the assumption of Wei Tzu-yün, when he explains one particularly troubling discrepancy in the internal dates of the story as a deliberate allusion to the one-month reign of the T'ai-ch'ang emperor.[83]

Once again, the notion of slipshod design is easy to counter by calling attention to the author's controlling hand in certain other aspects of temporal organization. Chief among these is his masterful manipulation of the details of seasonal change that fill out the three or four years of calendar time spanned by the main body of the novel. The outline of the text is very noticeably constructed on a grid of recurring annual events: festivals and ritual observances, most typically the birthdays of the principal characters. With regard to the latter point, the attention to birthdays is practically unavoidable in a work of "domestic fiction" such as the *Chin P'ing Mei*, but the fact that the author's control in this area goes somewhat beyond mechanical plotting is indicated by the frequency with which these occasions are pointedly pegged to special moments in the seasonal cycle. For example, Wu Yüeh-niang's 吳月娘 birthday falls on the day of the Mid-Autumn Festival 中秋節 (the fifteenth day of the eighth lunar month), that of P'an Chin-lien during the New Year season (the ninth day of the first lunar month), P'ing-erh's on the Yüan-hsiao Festival 元宵節 (the fifteenth day of the first lunar month), Hsi-men Ch'ing's at the passing of summer (the twenty-eighth day of the seventh lunar month). The degree to which

---

[82] Chang Chu-p'o, *tu-fa*, item 37. The Hsin-hsin tzu preface also cites a pattern of significance underlying the round of years and seasons ("故天有春夏秋冬人有悲歡離合…").

[83] Wei Tzu-yün first raised this question in "Ch'eng-shu nien-tai," and he develops it in *Wen-shih yü yen-pien*, pp. 105–16. Wei argues that the proclaiming of a new reign period (*kai-yüan* 改元) in chapter 71, at a point between two consecutive winter solstices—one falling on the twenty-eighth day of the eleventh lunar month and the second falling on the ninth day of the following eleventh month—fits perfectly the situation in the year 1620–21, and thus indicates a late date for the completion of the manuscript. Lévy discusses this point in "Recent Publications," p. 148, citing Torii's earlier indication that this situation applied in the year 1609–10 as well (although, in fact, Torii's calculation is slightly off). See Ch'en Yüan, *Ch'en-shih Chung-hsi-hui shih jih-li*. Recently, Mrs. Lucy Loh has also pointed out to me that the same sequence of solstice dates occurred in Wan-li 10–11 (1583–84), which corresponds even more neatly to prevailing views on the dating of the novel. Chang Chu-p'o also picks up the erratic change of reign period in chapter 71 (*tp*), although he chooses to interpret it in accordance with his own ideas on the structure of the novel. The use of an earlier historical setting to reflect issues current at the time of composition is a standard pattern in the Chinese literati novel, one we shall observe in *Shui-hu chuan* and *San-kuo chih yen-i*, and which is central to the conception of *Ju-lin wai-shih*. Cf. Ono Shinobu, "Critical Study," p. 82. The author of the *Chin P'ing Mei* does, however, as we have seen, insert a glaring—perhaps deliberate—anachronism with the pointed mention of the known Ming historical figure Chang Ta, in a memorial quoted in chapter 17 (5a). See above, n. 37. See Carlitz, *Rhetoric*, pp. 164f., n. 26.

these birthdays coincide with one another further strengthens the impression of deliberate design.[84]

As for the detailed descriptions of the observance of the seasonal festivals themselves, this too is in a sense a requisite of quotidian narrative;
but the author again reveals his guiding hand through his rich interweaving of the traditional imagery of the festivals with the physical
conditions of temperature and precipitation attendant upon the respective
seasons, a dimension of far greater significance than may first appear.[85]
Since, as we shall see, this heightened sensitivity to seasonal plotting (and,
in particular, the rich associations of the Mid-Autumn Festival and the New
Year feasts, culminating in the carnival atmosphere of the Yüan-hsiao
night) marks another common compositional focus of the Chinese novel in
general, I will take some time here to consider this question in greater
detail.

The degree to which the author's control over details of the seasonal
round goes beyond the straightforward description of physical setting or
sheer chronological sequencing of events—and reaches a point at which
we may rightly speak of seasonality as a structural principle—becomes
most evident when we consider the manner in which he constructs his

---

[84] Birthdays are celebrated in chapters 12, 14, 15, 16, 17, 19, 21, 26, 27, 33, 39, 42, 49, 50,
52, 55, 58, 59, 69, 72, 78, 79, 95, 96, 97, and 99, with major attention in chapters 39, 52, 58,
78, and 99. Chang Chu-p'o provides a general discussion of the manipulation of birthdays in
tu-fa, item 37, and comments on the significance of particular birthday celebrations in
chapters 12 (20a), 21 (17a), 30 (24b), 72 (*tp*), 73 (*tp*), 75 (*tp*), 97 (2b), and 98 (*tp*). See also
Ch'ung-chen commentary, chapter 96 (2a). Torii provides a convenient listing of birthdays
among the vital statistics for each main character in his "Hennenkō," pp. 69–76. See also
Martinson, "Pao, Order, and Redemption," pp. 294f.; and Wei Tzu-yün, *Shen-t'an*, pp. 82ff.
In chapter 52 (8b), Yüeh-niang observes that there have been too many birthday celebrations that season, and in chapter 59 the celebration of Yüeh-niang's birthday is canceled on
account of the death of Kuan-ko. Chang Chu-p'o notes that the dates of death of certain
characters are also suggestively placed (65 [*tp*]), as in the case of Li P'ing-erh's expiration
right after the Ch'ung-yang ("Double Yang") Festival.

[85] Annual observances celebrated in the course of the narrative include the Yüan-hsiao
Festival (first lunar month, fifteenth day [1/15]) in chapters 15, 24, 41–46, and 78; the
Ch'ing-ming Festival 清明節 (set by solar calendar, approximately early April) in chapters
25, 48, and 89; the Mang-chung Festival 芒種節 (set by solar calendar, approximately early
June) in chapter 52, the Tuan-wu Festival 端午節 (5/5) in chapter 6; the Chung-ch'iu Autumn
Festival (8/15) in chapters 19, 33, 59, 83, and 95; and the Ch'ung-yang Festival 重陽節
(9/15) in chapter 62; not to mention the extended New Year celebrations in chapters 14, 23,
39, 78, and 96. Chang Chu-p'o comments on the significance of many of these dates. See,
for example, 39 (1b) and 78 (*tp*) on the New Year season, 40 (15b) and 95 (*tp*) on the Mid-
Autumn Festival, and 13 (6a) on the Ch'ung-yang Festival; as well as discussions in 17 (6a)
and 46 (*tp*) on the significance of the sixth lunar month, and 75 (*tp*) on the seventh month. A
convenient aid to following the vagaries of the internal calendar in the novel is provided by
Torii's chronology of events in "Hennenkō," pp. 59–69.

scenes to highlight a sense of incessant alternation between heat and cold. The most notable examples of this include the sultry summer days in chapters 8, 27, and 82; the snowscapes and bitter cold in chapters 20–21, 70–71, and 81; and the brilliant spring garden scenes in chapters 25, 48, and 89.[86] This in itself, again, might be regarded as simply part of the continuity of quotidian description at the heart of the art of the novel. But the artistry of the *Chin P'ing Mei* in this respect demonstrates the particular aesthetics of the Chinese novel in two important ways.

First, the descriptions of shifts in physical temperature in the text are designed in such a way as to bring them into alignment with other more abstract variables, also conceived in terms of "heat" and "cold." The fact that the story as a whole begins in a blithe spring and ends in a desolate autumn immediately alerts us to this sort of correspondence, and throughout the novel we often observe significant correlation between the seasonal moment and the alternation of scenes of heated excitement (*je-nao* 熱鬧) and cold loneliness (*ch'i-liang* 淒涼). Similarly, we can trace a movement analogous to the seasonal cycle in the alternation of hot and cold periods in the vicissitudes of Hsi-men Ch'ing's fortunes.[87] The terms *leng* and *je* and their counterparts virtually stud the text in poems, chapter titles, and narrative details, often going far beyond reference to temperature alone.[88]

[86] Cf. also the winter scenes in chapters 38, 48, 67, and 93; and the hot weather in chapter 6. In the concluding section of the book, the seasonal round is speeded up, so that where one annual cycle went from chapter 38 to 78, we plunge from winter cold into summer heat within the brief span of chapter 81 to 82.

[87] In addition to the overall course of the narrative from its springtime opening to its autumnal close, we may note the assignment of a summer setting to the midpoint in chapter 49, and the pointed correlation between the final ten-chapter phase of Hsi-men Ch'ing's life from chapter 70 to 79 and the approaching end of the long year stretching from chapter 39 to 78, with his death occurring right after the close of the New Year season. Cf. also the contrast between the heat of the first visit to the capital in chapter 30, and the starkly cold backdrop of the second visit in chapters 70–71.

[88] For examples of cold imagery associated with "cold" ideas, see chapters 38 (8b, 9a, 9b), 67 (2a, 5a, 10a), 69 (9b), 71 (3a, 10a, 16a, 17b), 77 (11b), and 93 (2b). See also many songs and poems relating changes in temperature to changes in the narrative mood or pace, in chapters 11 (1a), 12 (6a), 17 (11a), 67 (11b, 17a), 77 (5b), and 80 (1a). Chang Chu-p'o picks up a good many of these usages and frequently uses the metaphors of heat and cold in developing his own interpretation of the work as a whole. See his comments in chapters 30 (*tp*), 32 (*tp*), 39 (3a), 46 (*tp*), 51 (*tp*), 56 (*tp*), 63 (*tp*), 66 (*tp*), 67 (*tp*), 68 (*tp*), 89 (*tp*), and 100 (*tp*), among many others, as well as extended discussions of this principle in the *tu-fa*, items 10, 25, 83, 87, and 88. See also his prefatory essay "Chu-p'o hsien-hua," and especially an additional essay "Leng-je chin-chen" 冷熱金針: "The Chin P'ing Mei opens with a discussion of the two concepts 'cold' and 'hot,' but who could fail to realize that these two words form the key to the entire work?" 金瓶梅以冷熱二字開講抑孰不知此二字爲一部之金鑰乎？ The Ch'ung-chen edition commentator shows a similar interest in this aspect of the meaning of the novel in, for example, chapters 1 (1a), 2 (22a), 12 (21a), 16 (2b), 65 (57a), 68 (30a), 78 (53b), 89 (33a), and 95 (42b). For a good discussion of this point, see Carlitz, "Puns and

And this sort of structural correspondence is rendered more complex and interesting by a second aesthetic sense, whereby, in keeping with traditional Chinese conceptual models, the representation of the ebb and flow of experience is based on patterns of the interpenetration of heat within cold and cold within heat.

With this extension of the meanings of heat and cold in mind, we can see this principle at work in the construction of many major scenes in the book. In the one arc of the seasonal cycle, many of the "hottest" scenes are deliberately set in the coldest months of the year, those same months that happen to contain the season of most intense merrymaking in the Chinese ritual calendar. This principle of composition may partially explain the special fascination for the Yüan-hsiao Festival in the eyes of the Ming-Ch'ing novelists. In the course of the *Chin P'ing Mei*, the annual cycle rolls around and stops on the Yüan-hsiao Festival four times, and each time the general gaiety and abandon, the blazing lights in the crackling air, give rise to events of special significance.[89] Conversely, the author often chooses to

---

Puzzles in the *Chin P'ing Mei*," pp. 221ff., and *Rhetoric*, pp. 79ff.; and Martinson, "Pao, Order, and Redemption," pp. 34f. The heat-cold frame of reference adds unexpected layers of meaning to such innocent terms as the "cold shop" (*leng-p'u* 冷鋪, i.e. "beggars' den"), the uncontrollable shivers (*leng-chan* 冷戰) of Kuan-ko and later Hsi-men Ch'ing, and perhaps even the emblematic fire symbol of the falling Sung dynasty (cf. the terms *yen-Sung* 炎宋, *Yen-ching* 炎京, and *Chien-yen* 建炎).

[89] See above, n. 85. The ambivalence of the Yüan-hsiao holiday is heightened by the fact that its symbols bespeak the warmth of the new spring, while the weather is still very cold. The sense of dangerous abandon in Yüan-hsiao scenes lends deeper meaning to the acceptance of Li P'ing-erh (whose birthday falls on this very holiday) into the circle of wives in chapter 15; the incestuous flirtation of P'an Chin-lien and Ch'en Ching-chi and the fatally rising ambitions of Sung Hui-lien in chapter 24; and the panic over the missing gold in chapter 43. The descriptions of the inevitable fireworks blazing and vanishing in the cold night sky on these occasions (especially in chapters 43 and 79) aptly capture the meaning of this imagery. The author drives at this core meaning by bringing us back to the apartment on "Lion Street" (*Shih-tzu chieh*)—the scene of the initial murder of Wu Ta—for Yüan-hsiao festivities in chapters 15, 24, 42, and 79. Cf. the poem on the Yüan-hsiao Festival at the beginning of chapter 46; the song on the Lantern Festival theme sung at the end of chapter 74 (19a); and the name of the maid Yüan-hsiao-erh 元宵兒, whose death in chapter 93 (2a) marks the last step in the humbling of Ch'en Ching-chi. Chang Chu-p'o provides numerous extended discussions of the meaning of the Yüan-hsiao Festival (e.g., 42 [*tp*], 78 [*tp*], and 31b, 41a, 79 [*tp*]), as does the Ch'ung-chen commentator in chapter 24 (32b). For interesting discussions of the conventional associations of the Yüan-hsiao Festival, see Marcel Granet, *Danses et légendes de la Chine ancienne* (Paris: Alcan, 1926), p. 321 (cited in Kristofer Schipper, *Le corps taoïste*, p. 282); and Victoria Cass, "Celebrations at the Gate of Death," pp. 88ff., 218. Additional examples of the heat-within-cold pattern include the seduction of Wang Liu-erh on a cold day in chapter 37 (reminiscent of the attempted seduction of Wu Sung in chapter 1); the warm camaraderie that replaces the images of cold and rejection in chapter 38; and the lively bustle (*je-nao*) of funeral scenes in chapters 63, 79, and elsewhere (cf. the term "hot mourning," *je-hsiao* 熱孝, used with ironic effect at several points).

dwell on the oppressive heat of the summer months precisely when he wishes to convey a certain chill with respect to the dangerous consequences of sensual excess, as for example in the notorious escapade in the Grape Arbor 葡萄架 in chapter 27, or the ominous fulfillment of incestuous passion in chapter 82.[90]

In such examples, the constant shifting between cold inspiring feverish activity and heat that leaves one cold yields a major overlay of irony that contributes substantially to the rich suggestiveness of the novel. A few more examples may help to demonstrate the extent to which the ironic manipulation of the hot-cold axis governs the use of many specific images and details of the text. One of these may be seen in the intimations of cold that dominate the treatment of the brief existence of Kuan-ko: his incessant shivering (*leng-chan*), the inordinate fear that he may catch a chill, and most pointedly, the furor over his contact with cold metal bangles in chapter 43—all of this set against the hottest phase of Hsi-men Ch'ing's career.[91]

Another example even more explicitly linked to seasonal imagery materializes in the cold backdrop to the ten-chapter section that sees Hsi-men Ch'ing finally burn himself out. After a series of snowy days and frosty nights in chapters 67, 68, and 69, the trip to the capital in chapters 70 and 71 is pointedly set against the bone-chilling cold of the waning year. There, the author masterfully executes a series of scenes combining images of coldness, whiteness, and emptiness, which cut right through the splendor of the court and Hsi-men Ch'ing's own personal glory. Following this point, the cold images continue to pile up as Hsi-men's dizzying spiral of political and sexual advances reaches its climax, just as the festivities of the New Year season move into full swing. In chapter 77 the author once again pulls together imagery of snow, warm inner apartments, and escalating sexual fantasy in Hsi-men's visit to Cheng Ai-yüeh-erh 鄭愛月兒, and this sets the stage for his stark end as he expends the last of his remaining vitality amidst a flurry of fireworks, lanterns, incense, and other images of fragile warmth, all set against the snowy cold whiteness of a late winter scene.[92] Here, in the final flare of Hsi-men Ch'ing's dying embers, the

[90] In many cases, the cold-within-heat pattern takes the form of unsettling violence, e.g., the mistreatment of Ying-erh 迎兒 in chapter 8 and the beating of Sung Hui-lien's father at the start of chapter 27. The link between the first improprieties between P'an Chin-lien and Ch'en Ching-chi in chapter 18 and the ultimate consummation of their affair in chapter 82 is intensified by the repetition of similar heat imagery in the two scenes—particularly the joking allusions to mosquitoes in each case.

[91] Cf. chapter 31 (10b), 33 (8a), 43 (3a), 48 (5a, b), and 53 (1b). The incident of the gold bangles will be reconsidered later in this chapter.

[92] For example, chapters 67 (23b), 71 (9a–b), 72 (4a–b, 11a), 78 (120a), 79 (3b). Chang Chu-p'o frequently comments on the significance of this sort of imagery, e.g.: chapters 42 (*tp*), 43 (13a), 46 (*tp*, 24a), 78 (42a, 44a).

reader is reminded of the ironic linkage of images of heat and cold with scenes of pointless sexuality that had been made repeatedly earlier in the narrative, especially during the first decade of the body of the novel, chapters 20 to 29. The most obvious instance is the heated union in chapter 27, so conspicuously lacking in warmth for all its violent thrashing about, which is set after a cooling shower on a languorous summer day.[93] Lest we miss the connection here between the seasonal setting and the purport of the scene, the author interjects a highly suggestive *tz'u* poem on the heat,[94] and places the action of this white-hot episode in the Grape Arbor near a section of the garden known as the Snow Cave (*Hsüeh-tung* 雪洞)—itself apparently located inside the Grotto of Sequestered Spring (*Ts'ang-ch'un wu* 藏春塢). The reader recalls that this is the same place where in chapter 23 the passionate embraces of Hsi-men Ch'ing and Sung Hui-lien 宋惠蓮 were turned into a night of teeth-chattering cold; and later the same spot is used as the scene of many comparable conjunctions of cold and heat.[95]

These are only a few examples of the complex use of heat and cold imagery in the construction of many major scenes in the novel. Through the exploitation of this device, the cycles of seasonal change that form the temporal warp of the narrative come to merge with the overall patterns of prosperity and decline, gathering and dispersion, that comprise its significant structure. This is the sense in which Chang Chu-p'o speaks of the work as a whole as "a book of heat and cold" (*yen-liang shu* 炎涼書).[96]

III

As for the vast sea of narrative within these structural outlines, what to some may appear to be primarily a straightforward mimetic rendering of the day-to-day realities in the Hsi-men compound reveals, upon closer investigation, innumerable examples of smaller-scale, finer-textured compositional patterning. Although many recent scholars have faulted the novel for weakness in this area, the early critics point very approvingly to what they see as its textural density to account for the greatness of the

[93] For an excellent analysis of the significant manipulation of heat and cold imagery in chapter 27, see Carlitz, "Puns and Puzzles," pp. 221ff. (also in *Rhetoric*, pp. 79ff.).

[94] See Carlitz, "Puns and Puzzles," p. 217.

[95] See, e.g., scenes in chapters 22 (3b), 52 (12a), 53 (5a, b), 56 (2b), 73 (1a)—cf. the use of the phrase "warm as springtime" 暖如春 to describe the artificial warmth of the spot. See Chang Chu-p'o's disparaging remark in chapter 90 (20a). I am reminded in this context of the image of heated sexual transports in the floating "Crystal Palace" of ice devised by the eighteenth-century Russian tsarina Anna for one of her courtiers; see Philip Longworth, *The Three Empresses*, pp. 145ff.

[96] Chang Chu-p'o, 100 (*tp*). See n. 88. On this point he closely follows the wording of the Ch'ung-chen commentator.

work. For example, the writer of the Hsin-hsin tzu 欣欣子 preface attached
to the *Tz'u-hua* text credits the book with a capacity to maintain "a unified
focus in its structural ramifications such that myriad threads face the winds
without becoming entangled 如脈絡貫通如萬絲迎風而不亂; and later the
1695 Hsieh I 謝頤 preface in the Chang Chu-p'o edition uses similar textile
metaphors to praise its "fine needlework and dense texture" 細鍼密線.[97] It
is to Chang Chu-p'o's commentary, however, that we are indebted for
setting forth these various compositional patterns in a thorough textual
analysis. In applying to the *Chin P'ing Mei* a variety of critical concepts and
technical terms borrowed from the vocabulary of earlier prose, poetry, and
painting theory, Chang Chu-p'o was by no means an innovator.[98] His
critical approach is unashamedly modeled on that of his immediate masters,
Chin Sheng-t'an 金聖歎 and Mao Tsung-kang 毛宗崗, and in fact many of
his terms and ideas, as we have seen, can be found in the marginal and
interlinear comments of the earlier Ch'ung-chen period text upon which his
own commentary edition was based.[99] But certainly Chang carries his close
reading of the novel to a point that places it among the greatest examples

[97] Hsin-hsin tzu preface, p. 3; Hsieh I preface, in *Ti-i ch'i-shu* edition, p. 1a. Liu Hui
suggests in "Pei-t'u-kuan ts'ang," p. 23, that Hsieh I may be a nom de plume for Chang
Ch'ao 張潮. Chang Chu-p'o expresses a similar evaluation in his *fan-li*, item 2, in "Chu-p'o
hsien-hua," and in comments in chapters 20 (*tp*) and 87 (*tp*).

[98] For the background of Chang Chu-p'o, see David T. Roy, "Chang Chu-p'o's Commentary on the *Chin P'ing Mei*," pp. 115–23; and Martinson, "Pao, Order, and Redemption,"
pp. 19ff. According to a newly discovered family genealogy, Chang's dates have been fixed
at 1670 to 1698. See Wu Kan, "Chang Chu-p'o sheng-nien shu-lüeh," pp. 74–79. I am
grateful to Wu Kan and to Liu Hui for arranging for me to examine the genealogy (*tsu-p'u*
族譜) in Hsü-chou in November 1984. Ts'ai Kuo-liang provides a review of traditional
criticism on the novel in "Ming-jen, Ch'ing-jen, chin-jen p'ing Chin P'ing Mei," pp. 306–12.
For a general review of the development of traditional Chinese fiction criticism, see the
Introduction of *How to Read the Chinese Novel*, ed. David Rolston. A full translation of Chang
Chu-p'o's *tu-fa* preface by David Roy appears in the same volume.

[99] Chang Chu-p'o explicitly acknowledges his debt to Chin Sheng-t'an in the *fan-li*, item
2, and refers to Mao Tsung-kang's commentary on *P'i-p'a chi* in the *tu-fa*, item 36. See Wu
Kan, "Shu-lüeh," p. 77. His use of such terms as "broken-line trail of a snake in the grass"
(*ts'ao-she hui-hsien* 草蛇灰線) in chapters 20 (*tp*), 67 (4b), 76 (*tp*), and "touching in the clouds
to adumbrate the moon" (*hung-yün t'o-yüeh* 烘雲托月) also derives from conventional usage
(see also *tu-fa*, item 50). His use of terms such as "mortise-and-tenon joint" (*sun* 榫),
"deliberate repetition" (*fan* 犯), in chapter 13 (*tp*), and "Ch'ang [-shan] snake-formation technique" (*Ch'ang-she chen-fa* 長 [sic] 蛇陣法) in chapter 45 (*tp*) seems to reflect Mao Tsung-
kang's critical vocabulary. As for Chang Chu-p'o's reliance on the Ch'ung-chen edition
commentary, several of his comments are quite close to comments in the earlier edition; see
examples cited in n. 52, plus 22 (15b), 39 (*tp*), 43 (20a), 51 (13a), 55 (*tp*), 57 (16b), 70 (62a),
89 (33b), 93 (21a), 96 (2a), and 97 (19a). In this last example, the Ch'ung-chen commentator's declaration: "This proves that the *Chin P'ing Mei* is not a work of pornography"
此則金瓶梅非淫書 seems to provide the inspiration for Chang Chu-p'o's identically titled
essay. In addition, Chang's use of the concepts of heat and cold, his general hostility to Wu

of Chinese fiction criticism, thereby providing us with one of the fullest expositions we have of what David Roy has called the "poetics" of the Ming-Ch'ing novel form.[100] In proceeding to set forth my own reading of the novel, therefore, I will rely heavily on Chang Chu-p'o's assistance.

At this point, those familiar with the various critical discussions of the many loose ends left dangling in the text may be wondering how such inconsistencies can possibly be reconciled with these glowing praises of consummate textual control.[101] Chang Chu-p'o simply waves away the problem by claiming that such instances are deliberately planted to keep the readers on their toes, and Wei Tzu-yün, as we have seen, essentially follows the same line in his attempts to read into the discrepancies in internal dates a key to unlock his own special interpretation.[102] Perhaps it is more reasonable to account for the various inconsistencies as David Roy has done, in terms of what we know of the process of composition—which seems to have taken place over a long period of time, as much as twenty years, and with the manuscript apparently in circulation long before it was completed.[103] In any event, in what follows I will take the position that these inconsistencies of detail in no way detract from the novel's otherwise very high degree of textual control throughout the bulk of the work—a degree of control often astounding not only for its own time and place, but for the artistry of the novel in general. This point will be my justification for proceeding to indulge in a serious interpretation of the meaning of the work, and to relate that interpretation to the contemporary intellectual milieu. In this section, I will try to demonstrate this control over textural density with reference to three aspects of the artistry of the novel: first, its keen attention to significant detail; second, its manifest design in the framing of individual chapters; and, most important, its sophisticated use of the principle of figural recurrence to set up a network of ironic cross-reflection.

Yüeh-niang, his idea of the symbolic merging of Li P'ing-erh and P'an Chin-lien, and his use of other terms such as "putting on the finishing touches" (*tien-chui* 點綴), "a pointedly tangential detail in the midst of action" (*mang-chung hsien-pi* 忙中閒筆), and "lingering ripples of suggestiveness" (*yü-po* 餘波), often coincides with that of the Ch'ung-chen commentary. For discussions of the textual relations between Ch'ung-chen and Chang Chu-p'o editions of the novel, see n. 52, and my "Ch'ung-chen Commentary," pp. 8ff.

[100] See Roy, "Chang Chu-p'o," p. 122.

[101] See n. 54, plus Hsia, *Classic Novel*, p. 180: "structural anarchy"; and Hanan, *"P'ing-yao chuan,"* p. 205. Martinson debates Hsia's evaluation in *"Chin P'ing Mei* as Wisdom Literature,"* pp. 45f.

[102] For example, *tu-fa*, item 37: ". . . that is why he deliberately mixes up his chronology . . ." 故特特錯亂其年譜. See n. 54.

[103] David Roy, "Confucian Interpretation," p. 41. See also Lévy, "Recent Publications," p. 148 (see n. 40).

As for the first of these elements, I have already taken a look at the acute attention to detail in my discussion of the use of seasonal imagery as a compositional framework in the structuring of the text. I argued that the extensive descriptions of fireworks, snow, sleet, and other imagery of heat and cold are more than just decorative touches. As we shall see, this grasp of concrete description extends to details of food, clothing, the physical setting of the house and garden, and of course sexual activity. Nearly all modern critics have taken note of this attention to concrete detail, although they have generally regarded it as simply a measure of the novel's mimetic focus.[104]

In the context of the present discussion, however, I will focus on the manner in which all these mimetic threads are woven into larger patterns of meaning. To take one preliminary example, the melon seeds we see P'an Chin-lien casually cracking as she first comes into view are initially just a vivid touch that helps to convey the sense of careless flirtatiousness in the scene. As the narrative continues, this detail, with its slight hint of erotic significance, develops into something of an emblem for P'an Chin-lien's sexuality, and it is eventually extended to take on broader symbolic implications in scenes involving some of the other women as well. Similar examples include the all-too-penetrable barrier of the rattan blinds (*lien* 簾), discussed by Chang Chu-p'o, and the soaring immodesty of garden swings, the heady abandon of fireworks displays, and many others.[105]

A second aspect of this sort of substructural organization in the *Chin P'ing Mei* is the design of individual *hui*-chapters as independent artistic units within the larger framework. In reviewing the broader structural outlines of the novel, we have seen the special function reserved for the ninth and tenth (and perhaps the fifth) chapters of each decade of the text, and we may also perceive a measure of significance in the precise numbers assigned to certain chapters within the overall sequence. We have seen Hsi-men Ch'ing's trip to the capital in chapter 70 to be deliberately

---

[104] For example, Hanan, "A Landmark of the Chinese Novel," pp. 325–35; Hsia, *Classic Novel*, pp. 174f.; and Cheng Chen-to, "T'an Chin P'ing Mei," p. 244. Chang Chu-p'o pays special attention to details of food and clothing in chapters 7 (8a) and 49 (43b). Cf. the Ch'ung-chen commentator's attention to vivid details in chapters 7 (10b), 20 (45a), and 30 (43a).

[105] The traditional association of melon seeds with fertility (via the pun *to tzu* 多子) may add to the significance of this motif in the novel. Chang Chu-p'o discusses the recurring rattan blinds in chapter 2 (*tp*). See later in this chapter for another use of this motif in chapter 69. The symbolism of such blinds as a social barrier is developed in Cass, "Celebrations," p. 20. Chang Chu-p'o points out the significance of the swing motif in chapter 25 (*tp*). Cf. the association of Ta-chieh's suicide with swing imagery in chapter 92 (12b). Fireworks are set off in chapters 42, 44, 46, 53, 62, 71, 74, 78, and 79. Cf. Chang Chu-p'o comments: 42 (*tp*), 46 (*tp*, 24a), 78 (42a).

pegged at that point (thirty chapters from the end) to match Lai Pao's 來保 earlier visit in chapter 30, just as the author's choice of chapter 82 to bring the long-term dalliance of P'an Chin-lien and Ch'en Ching-chi to its logical conclusion reveals a symmetry with the point of their first meeting in chapter 18 that is too neat to be accidental.[106] Additional examples of this type abound in the *Chin P'ing Mei*, although not to the extent I will trace in my chapter on the *Hsi-yu chi*.

Regarding the internal structure of chapters, we may first take note of the obvious division of each *hui* into two balanced halves, conventionally demarcated by means of the use of parallel couplets as chapter titles. In some cases this feature remains purely formal, but in quite a few it is integrated into the underlying design of the piece. One of the clearest examples of this is chapter 27, where the parallelism of the first line of the title, "Li P'ing-erh Shares a Secret in the Kingfisher Pavilion" 李瓶兒私語翡翠軒, with the second, "P'an Chin-lien Has a Drunken Rampage in the Grape Arbor" 潘金蓮醉鬧葡萄架, marks a very blatant parallelism in the construction of the chapter—one that pointedly juxtaposes a scene of warm, gentle lovemaking with the adjacent scene of wild but passionless sexual aggression.[107] In other cases, the inner structure of the *hui* may not

---

[106] A similar symmetry seems to hold between chapters 25 and 75, linked by the parallel relation to Hsi-men of Hui-lien and Ju-i, by the repeated motif of pregnancy discomfort, and by threats of violence. A little less neat is the return of Meng Yü-lou to center stage in chapter 91, paralleling her first extended treatment in chapter 7. Similarly, Tai-an's autonomous escapade in chapter 50 may be a deliberate counterweight to his assumption of the role of heir of the family in chapter 100. Given this attention to the numbers of chapters, it may be less than accidental that Wang Liu-erh, whose "sixness" appears to be an intended cipher for her *yin* sexuality, comes onstage in chapter 33. See Chang Chu-p'o, 33 (*tp*).

[107] Other examples of pointed parallelism in chapter titles include (in the *Tz'u-hua* recension) chapter 30 (Ts'ai Ching's birthday gifts and the birth of Kuan-ko), 32 (the false intimacy of Li Kuei-chieh and that of Ying Po-chüeh), 34 (the arrogation of favors by Shu-t'ung and then by P'ing-an), 39 (celebrations at a Taoist temple and prophecies by Buddhist nuns), 40 (the contrasting attractions of Li P'ing-erh and P'an Chin-lien), 47 (the venality of Wang Liu-erh and that of Hsi-men Ch'ing), 49 (political and sexual corruption), 52 (immodesty of Ying Po-chüeh and P'an Chin-lien), 69 (petitioners for sexual and judicial favors), 77 (sexual elegance and baseness), 79 (death and birth), 80 (stolen kisses and stolen goods), 91 (conjugal felicity and violent beatings). The Ch'ung-chen edition revises the chapter headings in many cases; but it retains nearly identical wording in chapters 7, 9–17, 19, 21, 26–29, 31, 33, 35, 37, 40, 42, 46, 50, 54, 55, 59, 60, 62, 66, 67, 77, 79, 81, 83, 87, 90, 91, 92, and 99; and presents the same two parallel incidents in chapters 2–6, 8, 18, 22, 24, 30, 36, 38, 41, 43, 48, 49, 52, 58, 71, 80, 82, 86, 89, 94, 98, and 100. It substitutes one new item for half of the title in chapters 20, 23, 25, 32, 34, 47, 56, 57, 61, 63, 64, 68–70, 73, 74, 76, 78, 84, 85, 88, 93, and 96. Only in ten chapters does it change the entire title: 1, 39, 44, 45, 51, 53, 65, 72, 75, and 95. Chang Chu-p'o's revisions of chapter titles are in most cases minor alterations of the wording in the Ch'ung-chen edition (see table of chapter titles provided in Chu Hsing, *K'ao-cheng*, pp. 14–29). Chang Chu-p'o discusses the division of chapters into two halves in chapters 10 (1a) and 35 (*tp*).

necessarily be reflected in a neat couplet, although it may still break down into two parallel halves.

Far more important for our appreciation of the design of individual chapters in the novel, however, is what I might call the internal "image structure," that is, the integration of significant imagery and other details in certain chapters into a unified poetic whole. In order to do justice to this aspect of the novelist's art, I must take the time to run through a brief reading of a few chapters (with the help of Chang Chu-p'o), calling attention to at least some of the many elements that go into their construction.

Let us consider first chapter 15, halfway through the ten-chapter sequence that begins with P'an Chin-lien's entry into the household and ends with the installation of Li P'ing-erh. It is the Yüan-hsiao Festival night (which also happens to be the birthday of both P'ing-erh and Hsi-men Ch'ing's second wife, the former prostitute Li Chiao-erh 李嬌兒), and the air is charged with a sense of excitement in spite of the bitter cold. The title—"A Bevy of Beauties Take Their Mirthful Pleasure in the Lantern-viewing Tower, a Band of Lascivious Patrons Goes A-whoring in the Hall of Springtime Charm" 佳人笑賞翫登 [sic] 樓, 押客幫嫖麗春院 —immediately alerts us to the fact that we will be dealing with two parallel episodes. The chapter opens with a poem on the transcience of beauty and then plunges directly into preparations for a holiday visit to Li P'ing-erh's new house on Lion Street 獅子街 —the original setting of P'an Chin-lien's murderous betrayal of Wu Ta. We are told that of all the wives only Sun Hsüeh-o 孫雪娥 is left behind, and we are treated to descriptions of the gaily decorated house, colorful costumes and hair ornaments, and the unqualified excitement (*shih-fen je-nao* 十分熱鬧) of the lantern-bedecked street scene, viewed from the second-story balcony. There then follows a long *tz'u* poem ostensibly describing the various lanterns on display, but replete with suggestive references to the ladies who are also on display— in keeping with the tradition of this holiday on which throngs of people gather in the streets, on the pretext of viewing holiday lanterns, but mainly in order to watch each other.[108]

At this point, the two older wives, Wu Yüeh-niang and Li Chiao-erh, withdraw from the window to the banquet tables inside, leaving P'an Chin-lien and Meng Yü-lou at the railing.[109] We are curiously not reminded of Li P'ing-erh's presence. In the ensuing scene the two are caught up in the spirit of the occasion and gradually cast aside their reserve.

---

[108] Chang Chu-p'o suggests in the chapter-commentary that each lantern described in the *fu* poem refers to one of the ladies present.

[109] Chang Chu-p'o goes on (p. 5a) to discuss the combined treatment (*ho-hsieh* 合寫) of P'an Chin-lien and Meng Yü-lou in this scene.

Without any hesitation P'an Chin-lien gathered up the sleeves of her white silk outer robe to reveal the sleeves of her gold-twill-lined inner jacket, in the process baring her ten supple "spring-onion" fingers decked with six "golden-stirrup" rings. She leaned half her body out over the railing, cracking melon seeds in her mouth and spitting the cracked shells down to the street. Every time one fell on the people below, both she and Meng Yü-lou went into peals of uncontrollable laughter.

那潘金蓮一徑把白綾襖袖子摟着，顯他遍地金掏袖兒，露出那十指春葱來帶着六個金馬鐙戒指兒。探着半截身子，口中磕瓜子兒，把磕了的瓜子皮兒都吐下來，落在人身上，和玉樓兩個嘻笑不止。

This description strikes a number of notes of déjà vu, as we recall the same pose at the railing in chapter 2, even the melon seeds as both an emblem and an instrument of dangerous flirtation. We nearly forget that we are now in the home of Li P'ing-erh, at a moment midway through her own parallel adultery with Hsi-men Ch'ing that has already caused the death of one husband and is soon to crush yet another. We hear their excited cries of admiration at the strangely shaped lanterns. A sudden gust of wind tears a hole in the bottom half of one of them, shaped in the form of an old woman, sending them into renewed peals of laughter, which in turn attract the attention of a crowd of lantern viewers jostling about in the street below. The focus shifts from a downward view of enchanting lanterns to an upward view of the bewitching attractions at the railing. The implied identity here between the vanity of the Yüan-hsiao lanterns and the fleeting youth of our ladies—which is to become a central metaphor of the book—already begins to add depth to what had seemed to be the shallow message of the opening poem.

A crowd of wanton youths (*fu-lang tzu-ti* 浮浪子弟) begins to discuss the unexpected beauties on display. Who can these lovely creatures be? One reasons, "They must be exquisite concubines of sons of the imperial family who have come here to view the lanterns; otherwise how could they be dressed in forbidden court costume?" 是貴戚皇孫家艷妾來此看燈，不然，如何內家粧束⋯? And we feel a vague suggestion of Li P'ing-erh's shadowy past connections with a well-placed family at the imperial court. We also recall the treasure chests that make up a not insignificant part of her attractiveness, and that are soon to subject her to fateful intrigues within the Hsi-men compound. Another young merrymaker speculates that these beauties may be expensive prostitutes called to keep company with the owner of the house, reminding us of where Hsi-men is at this very moment. Finally, a third voice breaks in and announces that he recognizes the one in the red-lined, gold-twill jacket, warning his fellows not to toy with her, as she is "the wife of the King of Hell" 閻羅大王妻, the same one who had been involved in the scandalous murder of Wu Ta. Yüeh-niang overhears these last remarks, and sensing that the scene may go too far, she calls her sisters in for the remainder of the banquet, before they all return home.

The chapter now shifts to its second locus. Hsi-men Ch'ing has also gone out to enjoy the festive scene in the company of his boon companions, who, despite his protests (he has also appointed a tryst with Li P'ing-erh for later that night), drag him to the brothel where he is a favored patron. After a brief poem decrying the inconstancy of the human heart, we are ushered into the presence of Li Kuei-chieh 李桂姐, and in no time at all another raucous banquet is under way. There is some talk about payment and a weak joke by Ying Po-chüeh 應伯爵 on the same theme, and we learn about the rivalry between Li Kuei-chieh and Wu Yin-erh 吳銀兒, the former favorite of P'ing-erh's late husband Hua Tzu-hsü 花子虛 who is later to enter into an alliance with P'ing-erh parallel to that between Kuei-chieh and Hsi-men Ch'ing's principal wife Yüeh-niang. A few brothel beggars come in selling melon seeds and Hsi-men Ch'ing makes a show of generosity. The banquet begins in earnest, followed by music, singing, and all the ingredients of a festive (*je-nao*) celebration. A few more camp followers of the brothel show up, these too evidently on good terms with Hsi-men and his friends, and Hsi-men invites them to stay for a game of kickball in which Kuei-chieh also takes part, panting with exertion and working up a conventionally appealing sweat.[110] Hsi-men's trusted servant Tai-an 玳安 arrives and whispers that Li P'ing-erh is awaiting his visit, and after a quick seance in Kuei-chieh's room, he begs leave to wash his hands and slips away into the night.

In this chapter, the cross-reflection between the two halves is well planned and pervasive. At first it is the contrast between the elegant gathering of fine ladies and the not-too-elegant denizens of the brothel world that is dominant, but eventually the similarities begin to outweigh the differences, as Chang Chu-p'o insists in his comments on the scene.[111] More important, the full range of imagery and associations of the Yüan-hsiao Festival brought together in the chapter succeeds in producing a rich canvas that captures all of the illusory warmth and empty joys of the season.

My second example is taken from chapter 69, at the last point before the

[110] The conventional narrative *topos* of lovely young girls playing football or engaging in mock combat may be seen in *Sui Yang-ti yen-shih*, chapter 22; *Hsing-shih yin-yüan chuan*, chapter 1; and *Hsi-yu chi*, chapter 72.

[111] See Chang Chu-p'o, chapter-commentary, and the Ch'ung-chen edition commentary, p. 46a.

beginning of the end, right before the ten-chapter sequence that takes
Hsi-men Ch'ing from his highest peak to his low conclusion. This chapter
also breaks down neatly into two parallel halves indicated in its title:
Hsi-men Ch'ing's pursuit of Madame Lin, and his compensatory efforts to
aid her wayward son Wang San-kuan 王三官. The parallelism is even
neater in the Ch'ung-chen version. After an introductory poem with conventional allusions to secret trysts, the curtain rises on the efforts of the
unsavory matchmaker Aunt Wen 文嫂 to sell Hsi-men Ch'ing to an eager
client. In her lengthy enumeration of his desirable qualities—wealth, good
looks, and sexual prowess—she also lists his illegal operations and corrupt
connections, falsely claiming that he is an educated man. In his household,
she boasts, "every night is a Yüan-hsiao Festival" 夜夜元宵. After a narrator's aside on the "watery" (i.e., fickle) nature of women 水性, we are not
surprised by Madame Lin's quick assent to an interview with Hsi-men,
ostensibly to request help for her son, and we now await the meeting
almost as eagerly as the principal participants. The author pauses, however,
to inform us that Hsi-men Ch'ing slept the night before with Li Chiao-erh,
whose favors he rarely seeks in the course of the novel, and whose presence serves mainly as an occasional reminder of venality and vulgarity—
expectations she fulfills immediately after his death, ten chapters hence.

At the appointed hour of the visit, the author appropriately paints his
backdrop with a moonlit winter haze near year's end, as Hsi-men sets out
wearing the same eye covering (*yen-sha* 眼紗) he has donned for many an
earlier midnight ramble. Arriving at Madame Lin's mansion, he is ushered
into a formal sitting room, where he awaits her appearance under the
solemn gaze of a portrait of the founder of the house in full ceremonial
regalia. In the room hangs an inscription designating it as a "Hall of
Integrity and Honor" 節義堂, in commemoration of the qualities of this
noble forebear.[112] All the time that Hsi-men is gazing at the imposing
portrait, he, in turn, is being watched through a bamboo blind (*lien*)[113] by

---

[112] See Chang Chu-p'o, chapter-commentary. David Roy has pointed out to me that the
assignment of the name Wang Ching-ch'ung 王景崇 to this figure is heavily ironic, since
that is the name of a well-known traitor of the Five Dynasties period. When referred to by
his official title, Wang Chao-hsüan 王招宣, this figure is linked to the identically named
character who is suggestively inserted in the author's revision of the original *Shui-hu chuan*
story about the background of P'an Chin-lien. This latter connection is apparently also
based on a figure in the short story "Chih-ch'eng Chang Chu-kuan" 至誠張主管. See
Hanan, "Sources," pp. 34f.; and Hsü Shuo-fang, "Hsin-t'an," p. 33. Professor James T. C. Liu
informs me that the term *chao-hsüan* 招宣 refers to a temporary military position, not to be
confused with *chao-hsüan* 昭宣, a eunuch position in the Sung palace. For this latter, see
Charles O. Hucker, *A Dictionary of Official Titles in Imperial China*, p. 361.

[113] See Chang Chu-p'o comments, pp. 5a, 7a. For information on the *chung-ching kuan*, see
Ch'en Chao, "Chin P'ing Mei hsiao-k'ao;" p. 404.

Madame Lin, who drinks in with her eyes his fine clothes and dashing figure. He is wearing his "loyalty and order cap" (*chung-ching kuan* 忠靖冠) and, we are also reminded, his mourning clothes—literally, "wearing garments of filial piety" (*tai-hsiao* 帶孝)—for the recent death of his favorite wife, P'ing-erh. Madame Lin sees only that he is "a rich and crafty unscrupulous character, oppressor of the good, cheater of the innocent, a man of wine and sex" 就是個富而多詐奸邪輩, 壓善欺良酒色徒, and she is beside herself with delight (*man-hsin huan-hsi* 滿心歡喜).

As she emerges from behind the blinds, we are treated to a head-to-toe description, and she is likewise summed up in a parallel line as "a voluptuous lover of sex in plush apartments, a goddess of fornication in the inner chambers" 就是個綺閣中好色的嬌娘, 深閨內合毯的菩薩, using the conventionally sarcastic but nevertheless suggestive term "bodhisattva" to describe this particular type of compassionate soul. In the ensuing conversation Madame Lin presents her plea to Hsi-men Ch'ing to intercede on behalf of her wayward son in the interest of the reputation of the family, and he accepts with many pious expressions of moral principle and family honor. The business having been concluded, we now turn to the matter uppermost on everyone's mind. Wine is served, Hsi-men learns that Madame Lin's birthday is fast approaching—it is on the fifteenth day of that eleventh month (yet another lover born on the night of the full moon!)—and pledges to pay his respects properly on that occasion. A sumptuous dinner is set before the pair, and then, after quick preliminaries, they shed their ornate clothes and proceed to what is described as a "battle array of love" (*feng-liu chen* 風流陣), recalling the similar use of tongue-in-cheek military metaphors in earlier adulteries, followed by a descriptive poem, more wry than erotic in its catalogue of conventional sexual allusions.[114]

Later, when the new lovers part and Hsi-men Ch'ing sets out for home, the author paints a consummate tableau. At the very moment our exhausted lover steps out into the street he is blanketed by a frosty mist stretching across the sky (the earlier haze has turned to frozen vapor), and all the heat and passion of the previous scene (for the reader as well as for him) is engulfed in cosmic silence 一天霜氣萬籟無聲.

Following this moment of calm emptiness in the middle of the chapter, the author turns his attention to the other half of the bargain. The very next day Hsi-men Ch'ing, in his capacity as local constable, presides over an investigation of trouble in the pleasure quarters. We learn that Wang San-kuan has been seeing Li Kuei-chieh (the same Li Kuei-chieh) and has gotten into a fight over her with other brothel patrons. Hsi-men takes

[114] For other uses of the mock-battle motif, see chapters 16 (5b), 78 (9b), and 80 (2b).

immediate action and strikes the names of his protégés from the official warrants (we recall the striking of his own name from an impeachment writ in chapter 18). After dealing harshly with the other offenders (some of the same ruffians we had met at the brothel in chapter 15), he takes Wang San-kuan under his wing, amidst much self-righteous admonishment, in a relation later formalized in chapter 72 when he takes the unlikely wastrel as his adopted son.

Reading this chapter as a unit, we can see numerous threads running through it, organizing it into a unified whole. Once again, the initial contrasts between a lady and a whore, between elegance and vulgarity, between cold weather and hot doings, eventually give way to an essential identity between the two sides. Of particular interest, we see here a very sarcastic development of the theme of patrimony, as Hsi-men pursues an illicit conquest and uses the pretext of saving a son to commit adultery literally in front of an altar of ancestral honor. When he later adopts Wang San-kuan as his own "son," the entangled ties between the mother, the son, the illicit lover, and the former mistress (who, to top it off, had in the meantime become the adopted daughter of Hsi-men's first wife) become too close to incest for comfort. The stage is set for the final scenes which push him over the brink.

I hope that the above examples may give some idea of the degree of textural density that goes into the making of many chapters of the *Chin P'ing Mei.* I could go on and on, since practically every chapter in the book lends itself to this sort of reading.[115] That, of course, is precisely what Chang Chu-p'o attempts to accomplish in his full textual commentary. Although in his interlinear notes Chang occasionally indulges in idiosyncratic readings and diatribes on pet themes, his lengthy pre-chapter discussions clearly convey the sense that each individual chapter constitutes an artistic whole.

This brings us to the third indicator of self-conscious textual manipulation I proposed earlier: the complex use of the principle of recurrence to build up a rich narrative texture. This intricate use of chains of recurrent narrative elements applies to textual units of various orders of magnitude, from specific motifs to extended patterns of action, as well as to the framing of individual characters. In the following discussion, as well as in the subsequent chapters of this study, I will frequently use the term "figure" to apply to a variety of such units of analysis; thus the instances of recurrence as a principle of composition will be referred to as "figural

---

[115] For similar close readings of chapters in the novel, see Carlitz, "Puns and Puzzles," passim; and David Roy's "Explication de texte" for chapter 1 (unpublished manuscript).

recurrence" and the resulting richness of texture will be termed "figural density."[116]

The reader of the *Chin P'ing Mei*, and for that matter of the Chinese novel in general, soon becomes aware of the fact that this type of text is constructed on the basis of the repeated treatment of similar, and often nearly identical, narrative units. In this case, the endless series of sexual escapades and household quarrels, or the constant round of banquets, with their obligatory songs, jokes, and suggestive conversation, recur with a regularity that may often seem tedious.[117] The sense of repetitiveness in the range of experience depicted in this work is of course not unique to the Chinese novel. In fact, we might say—and many recent theorists of literature would argue—such repetition of scenes is an essential feature of the representation of day-to-day reality in the novel form and, in a broader sense, in narrative art in general.[118]

In singling out this principle as a significant aspect of the art of the Chinese novel, therefore, I will have to ground my discussion more specifically in Chinese literary aesthetics. As I argued in my introductory chapter, it is no accident that the Chinese literati novel emerged as a genre in the sixteenth century, precisely in a period of significant advances in prose theory, inasmuch as this type of theory heavily emphasizes the use of interlocking patterns of recurring elements and parallel constructions. The special form of fictional prose writing we call the Ming novel can be viewed as an outgrowth of this increased interest in complex prose structure from the Chia-ching period on. At the least, the textual commentaries and critical essays that closely accompany the development of the novel genre in the sixteenth century self-consciously transfer to the new form many of the concepts and terms of existing prose (and poetry) criticism, chief among them the principle of recurrence and the manipulation of

[116] In other words, "figure" refers to any identifiable element of textual patterning. This usage of the term is derived from the notion of *figura* frequently applied by medievalists and comparatists in the study of biblical and postbiblical Western narrative. See, for example, Erich Auerbach, *Scenes from the Drama of European Literature*, pp. 11–76, and *Mimesis*, pp. 73ff., 194ff. Although the extension of this term from the field of Western scriptural exegesis to that of non-Western, nonscriptural narrative art may appear a bit specious, I maintain that the concept of the recurring figure as the key element in the projection of meaning in a literary text may be an important critical tool even in works totally unrelated to the phenomenon of "figural typology" per se.

[117] Chang Chu-p'o pays particular attention to the repetition of scenes and details of setting. See, e.g., chapters 72 (17b), 90 (20a), 92 (15b), 93 (10a). Martinson refers to this textual feature as "replication" ("Pao, Order, and Redemption," pp. 270ff.).

[118] For a general discussion of the centrality of patterns of recurrence to the construction of literary texts, see for example Yurij Lotman, *Struktura khudožestvennogo teksta*, pp. 132ff.; and Viktor Šklovskij, *O Teorii prozi*, pp. 33ff.

complex relationships of similarity and difference within parallel construc-tions.[119]

A large number of Chang Chu-p'o's comments serve to focus attention on this particular aspect of the text before him. In his elucidation of these patterns of linkage, he draws on the existing critical terminology used in the Ch'ung-chen commentary and refined by his acknowledged masters, Chin Sheng-t'an and Mao Tsung-kang. For example, Chang points out numerous instances in the *Chin P'ing Mei* of structural patterns involving "forward projection" (*fu-pi* 伏筆, *ying-hou* 映後) or "backward reflection" (*chao-ying* 照應, *fan-she* 反射).[120] He also goes on to observe specific variations on these patterns, such as constructions based on "parallelism at a distance" (*yao-tui* 遙對) separated by large chunks of text (e.g., the periodic restaging of Yüan-hsiao Festival scenes) or those in which he traces an "incremental repetition" (*chia-i-pei hsieh-fa* 加一倍寫法) in chains of figures (e.g., Hsi-men Ch'ing's increasingly impressive and profitable dealings with the imperial court).[121] In analyzing the recurrent use of figurally related material, Chang often takes up the question of textual continuity, since in a certain sense it is the interposition of separate narrative elements that actually gives rise to the rhythm of recurrence. Sometimes he credits the author with the management of smooth transitions, "invisible seams," between narrative units (*wu-hen* 無痕), but he is usually more interested in deliberate breaks in narrative continuity, especially where the author contrives to stretch his threads of continuity across structural joints.[122] To express this idea he is

[119] For a discussion of the relationship between colloquial fiction structure and classical prose criticism, see Rolston, *How to Read*, Introduction; and Plaks, "Full-Length *Hsiao-shuo* and the Western Novel," pp. 163–76. See n. 98.

[120] Examples of the use of these and related terms abound in Chang's commentary, e.g., *fu-pi*: 2 (*tp*), 6(*tp*), 8 (7a), 22 (22a), 27 (10b), 31 (*tp*), 32 (*tp*), 36 (*tp*), 46 (*tp*), 77 (18a), 78 (*tp*), 82 (*tp*), 93 (11a), 98 (16a); *ying-hou*: 1 (19a), 10 (*tp*, 8a), 18 (24b), 20 (*tp*), 37 (12a), 38 (*tp*), 41 (3a), 46 (24a), 57 (*tp*), 59 (4a), 60 (*tp*), 67 (*tp*), 74 (21b), 75 (*tp*), 77 (18a), 78 (*tp*), 86 (23a), 96 (19a–b); *chao-ying*: 7 (7a), 13 (8b), 43 (12b), 48 (*tp*, 21a), 61 (*tp*), 71 (*tp*), 75 (8a), 87 (*tp*, 7b); *fan*: 13 (*tp*), 22 (*tp*), and *tu-fa*, item 45; *yü-po*: 29 (*tp*), 72 (*tp*), 77 (*tp*). The Ch'ung-chen commentator employs similar terms, for example, 1 (6b), 2 (30a), 7 (10b), 10 (17b), 21 (5a), 24 (32b), 30 (44a), 48 (27b), 51 (10b), 68 (29a), 72 (12b), and 91 (7a). For further discussion of these terms, see Rolston, *How to Read*, Introduction.

[121] For examples of Chang Chu-p'o's use of the term *yao-tui*, see 17 (*tp*), 24 (*tp*), 26 (17b), 74 (*tp*), and *tu-fa*, item 9. For *chia-i-pei hsieh-fa*, see 16 (*tp*), *tu-fa*, item 25. See Martinson, "Pao, Order, and Redemption," p. 23, for a discussion of this term.

[122] Examples of the use of such terms include the following: *ch'uan-ch'a* 穿插: 3 (*tp*), 7 (*tp*), 19 (*tp*), 20 (32a), 21 (*tp*), 23 (*tp*), 32 (*tp*), and *tu-fa*, 5, 68; *chia-hsieh* 夾寫: 5 (5b), 11 (*tp*), 40 (*tp*), 89 (*tp*); *mang-chung hsien-pi*: 10 (1a), 20 (25a), 21 (5a), 27 (6a), 30 (24a), 42 (*tp*), 43 (*tp*), 46 (*tp*), 48 (*tp*), 51 (*tp*), 59 (14a), 62 (*tp*), 78 (46a), 86 (13b), 100 (*tp*), and in the Ch'ung-chen edition: 15 (46a), 17 (17b), 72 (12b), 96 (2a); *chien-ko*: 14 (*tp*). Related critical terms include *cheng-wen*, *p'ang-wen* 正文, 旁文: Chang Chu-p'o, 14 (*tp*), 17 (*tp*), 32 (*tp*), 48 (*tp*); *shou-shih*

particularly fond of employing the carpentry metaphor of the mortise-and-tenon joint, generally in the sense of an advance taste of narrative material embedded within a contiguous preceding section, serving as an unobtrusive bridge into a new scene. As examples of this "dovetailed" structure, Chang cites the seemingly offhand mention of Wu Sung's tiger in the course of the conversation of the ten "brothers" in the first chapter of his recension, and the revelation of Li P'ing-erh's pregnancy in chapter 27.[123] Here again, Chang's use of this term is not original, as it appears frequently in the commentaries of Mao Tsung-kang on *San-kuo yen-i*, and it also crops up in the Ch'ung-chen edition on which his edition is based.[124] In actual practice, this term often refers to something not very different from the notion of advance planting of significant details, indicated by the terms *fu-pi* or *fu-hsien* 伏線. For instance, the term is applied to the unexpected recalling of the name Wu Sung in chapter 78, sixty-eight chapters after he had dropped out of the narrative, followed by further mention in chapters 81 and 83, thus gradually preparing the audience for his dramatic return in chapter 87.[125]

The principle of figural recurrence becomes more crucial to our appreciation of the complexity of the novel when we emphasize the implied contrast that emerges from within the initial similarity of repeating figures. The essence of my argument here is that the manifest repetitiveness of the *Chin P'ing Mei* and its sister novels, far from revealing a limitation of resources or imagination on the part of the authors, reflects a deliberate design calculated to bring out patterns of meaning through controlled cross-reflection, the net result of which is the generation of a significant overlay of irony. I will attempt to further elucidate the implications of this ironic focus for the interpretation of the novel in the second half of this chapter. In the meantime, however, let us consider in greater detail how the principle of recurrence functions at the respective levels of the three types of figures enumerated earlier—motifs, narrative events, and characters—to shed a sense of coherence on this sprawling text.[126]

At the level of motifs, we have already seen the principle of recurrence at work in my discussions of the modulation of seasonal imagery, as well

---

收拾 or *shou-sha* 收煞: 10 (*tp*), 21 (*tp*), 26 (*tp*), 28 (*tp*), 73 (*tp*), 76 (*tp*), 89 (*tp*), 94 (*tp*), 95 (*tp*), 99 (*tp*), 100 (*tp*). See also Ch'ung-chen edition: 7 (15b), 57 (16b).

[123] Chang Chu-p'o, 1 (*tp*), 10 (1a), 14 (*tp*), 16 (*tp*), 18 (*tp*), 20 (*tp*, 32a), 27 (10b, 12b), 30 (17a), 38 (*tp*), 72 (23b), and *tu-fa*, items 8, 13, 26. The rendering of the term as "dovetailing" was coined by David Roy in his translation of the Chang Chu-p'o *tu-fa* for *How to Read*.

[124] See below, Chapter 5, Part II.

[125] Cf. the offhand mention of Yang-ku hsien in chapter 65 (1b).

[126] See Martinson's discussion of patterns of cross-reflection in the novel in "Pao, Order, and Redemption," pp. 20ff.

as the manipulation of fine details as an indicator of self-conscious authorial control. A few more examples here may help to further demonstrate the point that the "meaning" of an entire chain of recurrence is often greater than the sum of its individual occurrences.

As the first example, let us take a look at the chain of dogs and cats that rear their heads through much of the work. As the reader of the novel will recall, one of the most dramatic episodes in the narrative (which is otherwise short on drama) involves a snow-white cat with a black patch on its forehead, suggestively named "Charcoal in the Snow" (*Hsüeh-li sung-t'an* 雪裡送炭). In chapter 59 this cat, which had been trained by P'an Chin-lien to pounce on pieces of raw meat wrapped in red cloth, attacks Hsi-men Ch'ing's new heir Kuan-ko (dressed in a red shirt), sending the delicate, high-strung baby into a fit of terror from which he never recovers. This is not an isolated incident, but rather the focal point of an entire procession of menacing cat figures. "Charcoal in the Snow" is not the only cat stalking the garden. Other cats had been mentioned before (in chapters 34 and 52), each time a different-colored animal; and at several points Kuan-ko's inordinate fear of cats is brought out (even though we are told in chapter 59 that the child was basically fond of playing with cats).[127]

Besides the chilling role assigned to P'an Chin-lien's cat in the cold-blooded killing of Kuan-ko, additional occurrences of the cat motif bring out entirely different layers of meaning. In chapter 51, for example, immediately after Hsi-men Ch'ing has embarked upon an increasingly violent spate of sexual activity with the aid of his newly acquired potency drug, the author takes the time to insert a telling detail in the midst of a particularly furious encounter, as Hsi-men and P'an Chin-lien become aware that their transports are being observed by a "snow-lion cat" (*hsüeh shih-tzu* 雪獅子). Whether or not this is supposed to be the cat that executes the gruesome deed at the end of the decade, it is clearly a *fu-pi*, as the Ch'ung-chen commentator duly notes, which brings together several important associations.[128] Not only does the description of the cat as a little "lion" resonate with the name of "Lion Street" (*Shih-tzu chieh*), the scene of P'an Chin-lien's first murder in the name of sexual fulfillment (cf. her own identification with tiger symbolism, to be elaborated later), but the appearance of the snow-white cat in the midst of a white-hot bedroom scene also provides a subtle example of the use of heat-cold imagery outlined

[127] In chapter 34 (10a) it is an amber-colored cat; in chapter 52 (19a), a black cat. Cf. a line in chapter 39 (10a), which tells us that the child was so high-strung that "even a cat or dog would not cross his path" 猫狗都不敢到他根 [sic] 前 without producing a violent reaction.

[128] Ch'ung-chen edition, 51 (10b). See also Chang Chu-p'o's comments in chapters 52 (34a), 58 (24a), 59 (*tp*, 9a), 74 (69a). In the title of chapter 59 of the *Tz'u-hua* edition, "Charcoal in the Snow" is identified as a "snow-lion."

earlier, as well as of the recurrent pattern of rampant sexuality interrupted or watched by intruders, another element I will discuss shortly.[129] Once this connection between the cat motif and sexually inspired violence has been made, the frequent use in dialogue of seemingly innocuous common expressions based on cat imagery takes on a greater significance than may appear at first sight. For example in chapter 57 (12b), shortly before the fatal incident, one of the many instances of somewhat amusing, frustrated attempts by P'an Chin-lien and Ch'en Ching-chi to consummate their flirtation is deflated by the expression "just like a cat who has his eye on a fishy dish" 就是個貓兒見了魚鮮飯; and immediately thereafter, their furtive efforts are described as "just like a rat who has caught sight of the cat" 又像老鼠見了貓來 .... With this potential layer of meaning in mind, one notices on successive readings of the novel numerous other instances of suggestive cat motifs.[130]

In many of these instances cats and dogs are mentioned in the same breath; in other cases, however, the dogs seem to stand out with special associations of their own. The link between dogs and cats in the affair of Kuan-ko is implied at several points, notably in chapter 58, when P'an Chin-lien steps in dog urine, soiling her shoe, and her merciless beating of the offending animal and its howls of pain push the terrified baby to the brink of collapse, ready for the final blow. Once again, this is not an isolated detail, but had also figured in a number of earlier scenes. In chapter 53 (6a), for example, it is a barking dog that interrupts P'an Chin-lien and Ch'en Ching-chi in their first attempt to make love in the garden, and soon thereafter another dog startles a doctor called in to treat P'ing-erh's steadily advancing illness. In addition, the image of a mangy copulating beast also figures in numerous derogatory colloquial expressions voiced in the dialogue, as in chapter 76 (19a), when Yüeh-niang remarks about a case of incest brought before Hsi-men Ch'ing's court: "If the bitch doesn't wag her tail, the male won't mount her" 母狗不掉尾, 公狗不上身.[131] Given the

---

[129] This sexual scene in chapter 51, with its conjunction of cold and heat imagery pointedly emphasized, comes right after "Lion Street" has once again been mentioned. Additional references to Lion Street after the opening section occur in chapters 24 (5a), 29 (4a), 33 (2b), 37 (5b), and most significantly, 79 (4a). In most of these occurrences, the location is tainted with associations of wrongdoing, ranging from Lantern Festival abandon to coldblooded murder. Cf. Chang Chu-p'o's discussions in chapters 24 (*tp*), 39 (1a), 42 (*tp*), and 79 (*tp*).

[130] Other noteworthy uses of cat metaphors occur in chapters 7 (12a), 12 (1b), 39 (10a), 53 (13a), 62 (5a), 68 (14a), 75 (23a), and 86 (11b–12a). Cf. Chang Chu-p'o's discussion in chapter 58 (23a). Martinson ("Pao, Order, and Redemption," p. 20) reminds us that Hsi-men Ch'ing first tests his potency pills on a tomcat.

[131] Other uses of expressions involving dogs appear in chapters 12 (17a), 57 (10a), and 60 (6a). Yüeh-niang's crude expression is repeated in chapter 86 (8a, 9a).

unsavory connotations of the dog imagery used throughout the text, the repeated allusions to the Ming play *The Tale of the Slaughtered Dog* (*Sha-kou chi* 殺狗記) seem to imply even more than its explicit theme of rank unfiliality.[132]

Another chain of recurrent motifs that provides an example of this sort of textual linkage centers around images of shoes and feet. The repeated use of this motif focuses attention on the primary iconographic feature of P'an Chin-lien, the dainty "three-inch golden-lotuses" 三寸金蓮 for which she is named. Given the special importance attached to tiny feet in Ming eroticism, with even earlier historical origins, it is only natural in a novel dealing with the affairs of the bedchamber for attention to be turned so often to this particular part of the female anatomy, especially in view of all the sociological and cultural implications associated with the practice of foot-binding. Since, in a very real sense, the status of P'an Chin-lien and the others in the household depends on the paramount delicacy of their tiny feet, this detail comes to refer both synecdochically and metaphorically to their entire selfhood. The point is amply demonstrated in the initial presentation of Chin-lien; and thereafter, each time a new conquest is introduced into the circle of "sisters," Chin-lien's first gesture is to lift up her skirts to take a peek at the rival pair of feet.[133] The overblown attention paid to dainty feet in this cultural context also gives special importance to shoes, particularly the special bed slippers that often play a part in sexual descriptions. This type of footwear thus also comes to take on symbolic significance as the primary possession of the foot-bound concubine. It is no idle touch, therefore, that P'an Chin-lien is depicted, in addition to her other skills, as being adapt at the art of embroidering slippers.

As the narrative proceeds, these lowly items come to figure more and more in the high mock drama of the plot action. With the arrival in chapter 23 of Sung Hui-lien, whose tiny feet surpass even those of her quasi-namesake (originally her full namesake, as we are told), this immediately becomes a point of competition between them. In chapter 24, shoes again play a role in a scene of flirtation between Chin-lien and Ch'en Ching-chi that takes place, true to form, on the evening of a Yüan-hsiao Festival. This chain of occurrences leads up to chapter 28, when a shoe lost by Chin-lien during the escapade at the end of the previous chapter becomes

---

[132] For a discussion of this play and the allusions to it in the novel, see Carlitz, "Role of Drama," chap. 4 (also in *Rhetoric*, chap. 5). Chang Chu-p'o also discusses this allusion in chapters 80 (*tp*), and 100 (22b), as well as in "Chu-p'o hsien-hua," p. 2a.

[133] For example, chapters 7 (7a), 19 (5b), 23 (7b), and 58 (6b), as well as the glimpses of dainty feet afforded during the swing scene in chapter 25. Chang Chu-p'o notes the emphasis on shoe imagery in chapters 28 (*tp*), 38 (16b), 36 (*tp*), and 43 (12b), and discusses foot sexuality in chapter 73 (*tp*).

a plot node around which converging suggestions of adultery, violence, and incest revolve.[134] Much later, some of these same associations come together again in chapter 58, when P'an Chin-lien's symbolically significant misstep discussed earlier unleashes a series of rabid outbursts. This inelegant combination of dog and shoe imagery not only presents a stark contrast with the dainty feet of Cheng Ai-yüeh-erh described lovingly earlier in the same chapter, but also sets in motion a chain of beatings, recriminations, and tensions that lead right into the cruel demise of Kuan-ko in chapter 59.

These examples may give some idea of the way in which the author singles out special motifs to set up a warp of threads for his rich texture. Additional examples include the description of the garden swing in chapter 25, with its conventional erotic connotations heightened by suggestions of the danger of the excessive liberties taken in the thoughtless presence of Ch'en Ching-chi, the first hints of P'ing-erh's pregnancy, and the approaching violence of the Hui-lien affair. These associations are revived in chapter 48, when Kuan-ko comes under the assault of P'an Chin-lien's poisonous caresses just as Hsi-men Ch'ing is coming under attack for his official misconduct. Finally, the author pulls this thread one more time in chapter 92, when he uses the image of a garden swing to describe Ta-chieh's 大姐 pitiful conclusion at the end of a rope.[135] Here again, we see that it is only in the context of a chain of recurrence that these individual motifs take on their fullest meaning.

A second level of textual figures on which we can observe the workings of the principle of recurrence is that of narrative events. The fact that the same things seem to happen over and over again in the Hsi-men household is to a certain extent due to the limited scope of activity in the day-to-day routine of life in a provincial backwater, especially for the women sequestered in a closed compound. Even the sexual activity depicted in the book is highly repetitive, the reputation of the book notwithstanding. When I come to consider a similar repetitiveness in the other three works treated in this study, I will attribute this partially to their adaptation of conventional narrative *topoi* from their source materials.[136] But since the *Chin P'ing*

[134] Chang Chu-p'o notes the allusion to the play *Liu-hsieh chi* ("The Abandoned Shoe") in chapter 43 (12b). See Carlitz, "Role of Drama," pp. 114f., 168f., for a discussion of this play and its use in the novel. Cf. the scene in which P'an Chin-lien and Li P'ing-erh enjoy a rare moment of harmony as they embroider slippers together in chapter 29 (1a). See Yao Ling-hsi, "Chin P'ing hsiao-cha" 金瓶小扎, in *Ping-wai chih-yen*, pp. 167, 169.

[135] See chapters 48 (6a), 92 (12b). Cf. the use of the swing motif in erotic prints of the Ming period. Other examples of recurrent motifs of this order of magnitude include the bamboo blinds discussed by Chang Chu-p'o, as well as the fireworks and lamp wicks considered earlier.

[136] Cf. Hanan's discussion of the conventional narrative *topoi* worked into a contemporary novel, in "P'ing-yao chuan," pp. 215f.

Mei departs from the other novels in its relative independence from ante-cedent narratives, it will be more useful to accept the recurrence observed at this level, too, as an integral part of the author's literary design.

A few examples will suffice to illustrate this point. First, let us consider the recurring pattern of loss and recovery of objects in the garden. Be-ginning with the incident of the lost shoe in chapter 28, we see a whole series of scenes in which the loss of one object or another—Ch'en Ching-chi's keys in chapter 33, Meng Yü-lou's hairpin in chapter 42, and the metal bangles Kuan-ko plays with in chapter 43[137]—causes a disruption far out of proportion to the value of the objects themselves. In each of these cases, however, the minor losses are tied by a chain of cause and effect to very serious consequences, and each loss chips away at the integrity of Hsi-men Ch'ing's world, until the entire compound is looted and emptied very soon after his death.

Another pattern of recurrence may be seen in the frequent appeals for refuge to Hsi-men Ch'ing, usually by undeserving petitioners. This chain is initiated with the arrival of Ch'en Ching-chi and Ta-chieh in chapter 17, and is later carried on when the prostitute Li Kuei-chieh seeks refuge after chapter 51, as well as in Hsi-men Ch'ing's protection of Miao Ch'ing 苗青 in chapter 47, and finally Wang San-kuan after chapter 69.[138] (This figural link between Li Kuei-chieh and Wang San-kuan is sealed when they be-come carnally linked later in the narrative.) At the same time, the adoption of Wang San-kuan as Hsi-men Ch'ing's "son" in chapter 72—parallel to Li Kuei-chieh's adoption by Yüeh-niang in chapter 32, and the adoption of her rival, Wu Yin-erh by Li P'ing-erh in chapter 42—marks another repeating pattern, which has by then taken in Hsi-men Ch'ing's own adoption by the infamous high minister Ts'ai Ching 蔡京 in chapter 55, reconfirmed in chapter 71 immediately before he, in turn, adopts Wang San-kuan.[139]

One broader scheme of narrative recurrence grows out of the structural division of the novel into a prologue section setting up the basic issues of

[137] The shoe retrieved in chapter 28 and the lost keys in chapter 33 significantly advance the illicit relationship between Ch'en Ching-chi and P'an Chin-lien; the hairpin lost in chapter 42 returns as a focus of the blackmail attempt that results in Ch'en Ching-chi's ruin in chapter 92; the bangle misplaced in chapter 43 takes on a threatening quality in conjunction with the fragility of Kuan-ko; and when trivial objects are discovered missing in chapter 64 (4b) a major incident results. See Chang Chu-p'o's discussions in chapters 43 (*tp*) and 44 (*tp*).

[138] As it turns out, all of these petitioners are linked either contextually or figurally to one another.

[139] I will reconsider the significance of this pattern of linkage later in this chapter. Cf. Ts'ai Ching's "false son," Ts'ai-Yün, in chapter 36, and the final "adoption" of Tai-an as Hsi-men Ch'ing's heir in chapter 100. See also the poem on this theme in chapter 82 (4b). Chang Chu-p'o provides frequent discussions of the pattern of false relations, e.g., in chapters 12 (24b), 30 (*tp*), 31 (*tp*), 32 (*tp*), 44 (*tp*), 51 (*tp*), 55 (*tp*), 69 (*tp*), 72 (27b), 93 (2b), and 97 (*tp*).

the text, the main body developing the central mimetic world, and an extended final section carrying the narrative on beyond the death of the central figure, as discussed earlier.[140] This structural arrangement virtually ensures a large degree of repetition from section to section. In the *Chin P'ing Mei*, we can easily view the yo-yo vicissitudes of Ch'en Ching-chi as a recapitulation, at an accelerated pace, of the self-destructive excesses perpetrated by Hsi-men Ch'ing in the body of the novel. As we shall see, the sense of the inexorable repetition of the failings of the fathers in the generation of the sons applies as a general principle of composition in the traditional Chinese novel, particularly in *San-kuo chih yen-i*.[141]

Moving on to the principle of recurrence in the framing of character, we come to the most complex use of this type of patterning. One of the most noticeable features of the *Chin P'ing Mei* is the apparent redundancy in its cast of characters. This is most obtrusive in the conception of auxiliary roles, where the tendency to present warmed-over versions of stock character types may be partially attributable to preexisting materials. That is, many of the almost indistinguishable members of certain categories—the honey-tongued go-betweens, lustful Buddhist nuns and monks, quack doctors—are apparently taken over ready-made from popular drama and oral storytelling and trotted out onto the stage with little revision on the part of the author.[142] This may be partially explained as a result of the tendency in Chinese fiction to conceive character in terms of composite groupings, with correspondingly less attention paid to the differentiation of individual members. Thus, for example, among Hsi-men Ch'ing's ten sworn brothers only Ying Po-chüeh is singled out for extensive treatment, with the others reduced to caricatures with essentially walk-on parts. And even among Hsi-men's six wives, the second wife, Li Chiao-erh, and the fourth wife, Sun Hsüeh-o, are given nothing like the attention enjoyed by P'an Chin-lien, Li P'ing-erh, Wu Yüeh-niang, and Meng Yü-lou.[143]

In developing these latter figures, it is true, the author is lavish in the application of individualizing detail, and he has been deservedly

---

[140] See above, Part II.

[141] See below, Chapter 5 Part IV, for the use of the generational focus in *San-kuo chih yen-i*.

[142] Particularly noticeable are the midwife Ts'ai in chapter 30 (8a) and the tailor in chapter 40 (9a), whose treatment in the novel appears to be directly borrowed from the stage (see Hanan, "Sources," p. 53). Another example of a stock narrative figure is seen in the chain of mischievous urchins (Yün-ko 鄆哥, Hsiao-t'ieh-kun-erh 小鐵棍兒) who appear in chapters 6, 27, and 41. Cf. Chang Chu-p'o's discussion of the principle of deliberate redundancy in *tu-fa*, item 45, and his reference to the overlapping of go-between figures in chapter 6 (*tp*).

[143] The names of some of the "brothers" vary in the two recensions (see below, n. 205). See Chang Chu-p'o's discussion of the overlapping of the figures of the six wives in *tu-fa*, items 18 and 19, and in chapter 30 (24a).

praised by critics for succeeding in distinguishing each of his main female characters.[144] At the same time, however, the principle of recurrence continues to apply to these figures as well. That is, a large measure of the artistry of the novel is directed toward bringing out a welter of shared attributes, overlapping stories, and interlocking relationships whereby individual characters fall together as linked elements within the dense texture of the narrative as a whole.[145]

In setting up the network of links that binds his characters into joint constructions, the author focuses on several specific kinds of details. With respect to women, these include physical features such as height and build, dark or light complexion, and tiny feet, as well as vital statistics: ages, birthdays, and zodiac signs.[146] In addition, we will observe linking details based on such points as taste in clothing, accomplishment in music and other skills (e.g., embroidery), personal wealth, even habitual practices in lovemaking.[147] The sense of linkage based on shared attributes becomes all but explicit in the frequent use of shared or related names. The ingenuity exercised by the author in the naming of his characters, as we shall see, is all the more striking since the names of all but the initial handful are the

[144] This is particularly true with respect to the characteristic manner of speech of P'an Chin-lien, less so for the other wives.

[145] Chang Chu-p'o uses a number of critical terms to refer to this overlapping of characters, e.g., "prior version" (*chiu-kao* 舊稿) in chapter 57 (8b); "surrogate" (*t'i-shen* 替身) in chapter 78 (46a); "model" (*chang-pen* 張本) in chapter 10 (7b); as well as numerous occurrences of the terms "shadow" (*ying* 影) and "supporting character" (*ch'en* 襯).

[146] For example, P'an Chin-lien is described as "short of stature" (*wu-tuan shen-ts'ai* 五短身材), a trait she shares with Wang Liu-erh, Madame Lin, and Sun Hsüeh-o, but Meng Yü-lou is said to have a "longish figure" (*ch'ang-t'iao shen-ts'ai* 長條身材). The juxtaposition of female characters of contrasting build is a familiar device of traditional Chinese fiction, as, for example, in the story of Chao Fei-yen 趙飛燕 and her sister, Chao-i (see "Chao Fei-yen pieh-chuan 別傳," in *Sung-jen hsiao-shuo* 宋人小說 [Shanghai: Shen-chou kuo-kuang, 1940], pp. 66–72); or that of Yang Kuei-fei 楊貴妃 and Mei Fei 梅妃 (see "Mei Fei chuan" 梅妃傳, in *Sung-jen hsiao-shuo*, pp. 92–97, and in *Sui-T'ang yen-i* 隋唐演義, chapter 79). For a quick review of the vital statistics of the major characters in the novel, see Torii, "Hennenkō," pp. 69–76. See also Martinson, "Pao, Order, and Redemption," pp. 294ff. The birthdays and zodiac signs of individual figures are emphasized in the negotiations of go-betweens in chapters 3, 7, 17, 69, and in the fortunetelling sessions in chapters 29 and 46.

[147] See, e.g., the *p'i-p'a* lute played by P'an Chin-lien (in chapters 6, 18, 27, 38) versus Meng Yü-lou's *yüeh-ch'in* 月琴. Cf. Chang Chu-p'o's interpretation of the significance of Yü-lou's instrument in chapter 7 (*tp*), as well as the discussion by Carlitz in "Puns and Puzzles," p. 232. The clothing in the *Chin P'ing Mei* has been analyzed in Aikawa Kayoko, "Mindai no fukushoku," pp. 429–64. On the one hand, the details of clothing serve to differentiate the female characters according to gradations of status and taste; and on the other, they often serve to link them through shared colors and styles, especially inasmuch as they frequently borrow or otherwise appropriate each other's clothing (e.g., chapters 40, 41, 46, 74, 75, 79). For the sexual predilections of some of the characters as a deliberate element of characterization, see Part IV of this chapter.

product of his own imagination, and this remains an abiding feature of the Chinese novel tradition right up to the twentieth century.[148] Finally, in the course of the narrative, the author's tendency to cast crisscrossing threads of association between characters is reinforced by a shifting ballet of personal relations and alliances, as I will work out in detail in the following analysis.

First let us take a brief look at the figural relation between P'an Chin-lien and Sung Hui-lien, before turning to the core set of figures involving P'an Chin-lien and Li P'ing-erh, and their relations to Hsi-men Ch'ing. The possibility of a significant link between P'an Chin-lien and Sung Hui-lien is immediately suggested by the common *lien* ("lotus") of their names. Of course, the use of the character *lien* is perfectly common in women's names up to the present day, but the author goes on to tell us that Hui-lien's original name was in fact also Chin-lien, referring in her case as well to her exceptionally tiny lotus feet (as we have seen).[149] This connection is driven home in chapter 28, when Hui-lien's shoe is confused with Chin-lien's lost slipper.[150]

At the same time another of the charms boasted by Hui-lien, her dazzlingly white skin, links her figurally not to Chin-lien but to Li P'ing-erh. This apparent contradiction takes on greater significance when we reconsider the story of Hui-lien as the third major adulterous liaison in the course of the novel, occupying the heart of the third "decade" of the text in the same way that the affairs of P'an Chin-lien and then Li P'ing-erh dominated the first two decades. The fact that Hui-lien is by status an underling may seem to distinguish her case, but at the same time it serves to point up the common ground, in that all three of these adulterous affairs with Hsi-men Ch'ing establish a causal chain that directly or indirectly leads to the cruel death of their husbands, and in the course of time each of the women pays with her own life for this indiscretion.[151]

[148] See Chang Chu-p'o, *tu-fa*, item 48; and Martinson, "Pao, Order, and Redemption," pp. 38f., for discussions of this point. I will reconsider this aspect of the text in greater detail later.

[149] In fact, we are told in chapter 1 (10a) that this was Chin-lien's childhood name (*hsiao-ming* 小名). But when she is taken into the household of the wealthy patron Chang as a concubine, along with another similarly described young beauty given the name Pai Yü-lien 白玉蓮, it seems that we are dealing with the common custom of providing linked sets of names for household servants. See Carlitz, *Rhetoric*, p. 39f.; and Cass, "Celebrations," p. 18.

[150] See Carlitz, "Role of Drama," p. 114.

[151] The parallel is deepened by the fact that Lai Wang is actually Hui-lien's second husband (see chapter 22 [1a]), the first (Chiang Ts'ung 蔣聰) having also been a small-time cook cuckolded by Hui-lien and eventually murdered (by fellow gamblers, not by Hui-lien). We may note that the entire episode of Sung Hui-lien is bracketed by mention of Hsi-men Ch'ing's preparation of birthday gifts for his infamous mentor Ts'ai Ching immediately before her introduction in chapter 22 and immediately after the wrap-up of the affair (the beating of her outraged father) in chapter 27.

Still, this complex cross-reflection among the three women leaves room for one more twist, since Hui-lien's final act of compassion for her husband contrasts sharply with the treatment of Wu Ta, Hua Tzu-hsü, and Chiang Chu-shan 蔣竹山. Thus, in this case, an initial impression of marked similarity gives rise in the final analysis to sharp ironic contrast.[152]

Coming now to P'an Chin-lien and Li P'ing-erh, we can also observe various dimensions of difference and similarity that initially divide but ultimately unite the two central female figures in the book. The opening association of Chin-lien and P'ing-erh as two seductive beauties who join the household back to back in the first two movements of the book immediately gives way to a strong sense of opposition between the two figures. This opposition is brought out in a long list of qualities in which the two stand in diametric contrast to one another. Let us review here some of these contrasting qualities.

First, with respect to physical appearance Li P'ing-erh is rather slender and pale, whereas P'an Chin-lien is short, full-figured, and vigorous.[153] P'ing-erh's unusually white skin receives considerable attention and is the point of much envy and imitation on the part of Chin-lien, who is depicted as rather dark in complexion. This black-white distinction between the two is pointedly emphasized in chapter 67 (17b), when Hsi-men Ch'ing's dream of the departed P'ing-erh, dressed in ethereal white, is rudely broken by the intrusion of P'an Chin-lien, dressed in black.[154] It would be an oversimplification to view these details as iconographic markers for pure and impure character traits, especially since black and white faces have a quite different significance on the Chinese stage. On the other hand, however, the author does seem to add some significance to Chin-lien's dark color by setting up an intertextual association with certain other swarthy figures in the sixteenth-century novel, notably the "Black Whirlwind" Li K'uei 李逵 from *Shui-hu chuan*, who may himself be modeled after Chang Fei 張飛 in *San-kuo yen-i*. This association is amply borne out in the characterization of Chin-lien as aggressive, temperamental, given to violent outbursts of in-

[152] Cf. Chang Chu-p'o's discussions of the similarity and contrast between Hui-lien and Chin-lien (chapters 27, 28 [*tp*], and *tu-fa*, item 20). He identifies Hui-lien as a "precursor" (*ch'ien-shen* 前身) of Li P'ing-erh in a note in chapter 71 (17b). See also chapter 26 (*tp*).

[153] See above, n. 146. In chapter 38 (11b), Chin-lien tries to equal P'ing-erh's slimness by claiming to have lost weight. For the correspondences between these two figures, see Mary Scott, "Image of the Garden," pp. 9ff.

[154] Cf. Chin-lien's attempts to whiten her skin with a jasmine-flower cream in chapter 29 (12b). The whiteness of P'ing-erh's skin is emphasized in chapters 27 (5a), 34 (10a), and 67 (14b). See Carlitz, "Puns and Puzzles," p. 22; and Cass, "Celebrations," p. 11. Cf. Hsüeh Pao-ch'ai's association with white clothing and other iconographic markers of whiteness in *Hung-lou meng* (see my *Archetype and Allegory*, pp. 63f.).

vective and even physical assault.[155] This tongue-in-cheek identification with the rough-hewn heroes of the tradition is made quite explicit in her repeated references to herself as "a big strong man who just doesn't wear a turban" 不戴頭巾的男子漢....[156]

P'ing-erh is by way of contrast, at least for the duration of her life in the Hsi-men compound, depicted as a woman of more gentle disposition, weak-willed, prone to suffer in silence. The Ch'ung-chen commentator finds this quality irritating and at a number of points attacks her for being "stupid" (*ch'un* 蠢); but Chang Chu-p'o reads this as the essential nature of the figure, whose very name, "vase" 瓶, points to her tendency to bottle up her feelings.[157] At first sight, this reading seems a bit far-fetched, but in a long series of passages we are told that she "swallowed her rage" (*jen-ch'i* 忍氣), endured Chin-lien's abuse "without a word" (*pu yen* 不言), "could only fume but could not say a word" (*kan nu erh pu kan yen* 敢怒而不敢言).[158] Evidently this yielding disposition is responsible for her description as a woman of "compassion and righteousness" (*jen-i* 仁義). Although her initial presentation as a self-serving adulteress would seem to disqualify her from this honor, still this description does serve to contrast with the spite and venom of her principal rival.[159]

In bringing out this stark contrast between P'an Chin-lien's savage power and Li P'ing-erh's meek helplessness, the author does not miss the

[155] For examples of her juicy cursing, see chapters 2 (2b–3a), 8 (2b), 30 (8a–b), 41 (7b–8a), 43 (5b–6a), 58 (14b), and 75 (23b). Significantly, P'ing-erh is also shown to be capable of dishing out this sort of invective, as e.g. in chapter 19 (6b), although as we shall see shortly, her characterization once she is established in Hsi-men compound goes in the exact opposite direction. See Chang Chu-p'o's discussion of Chin-lien's style of speaking in *tu-fa*, item 51.

[156] In chapter 15 (4a) she is described as "the wife of the King of Hell," and in chapter 7 (7a) and later in chapter 79 (8a) she is identified with a merciless demon known as *Wu-tao chiang-chün*. See Yao Ling-hsi, "Hsiao-cha," p. 112. Cf. also the identification of Chin-lien with the image of a fierce tiger. What I have here translated as "turban" (*chin* 巾), following accepted practice, is the characteristic headband of traditional Chinese rebels.

[157] Ch'ung-chen edition: 17 (18b), 19 (33a, 40a), 51 (2b); Chang Chu-p'o: *tu-fa*, item 51.

[158] See, e.g., chapters 41 (7a) and 58 (15b). The name P'ing-erh, we are told in chapter 10, derives from a gift of a pair of vases presented to her parents upon her birth (see Martinson, "Pao, Order, and Redemption," pp. 40, 285; and Cass, "Celebrations," pp. 28ff.). See Hanan, "Erotic Novel," p. 19, n. 15, for a possible source of this figure. Chang Chu-p'o develops the significance of the vase image in chapter 41 (*tp*). In chapter 19, she is depicted arriving in the Hsi-men household carrying some sort of a "precious vase" (*pao-p'ing* 寶瓶), apparently a marriage ritual object (see *Chung-wen ta-tz'u-tien*, p. 4101). Her final lapse into silence in chapter 62 follows her uncharacteristically voluble farewell speech. These qualities (as well as her attempted suicide in chapter 19) link her figurally to Hsi-men Ch'ing's daughter, Ta-chieh, whom she befriends in chapter 51.

[159] The attribution to her of "compassion and righteousness" comes out in chapters 46 (16a) and 62 (19a). The ambiguous application of these terms here is paralleled in *Shui-hu chuan* and *San-kuo chih yen-i* (see below, Chapters 4, Part V, and 5 Part V).

trick of assigning them, respectively, to the zodiac signs of the tiger and the lamb. Later I will reconsider the use of such zodiac associations as examples of continuous metaphors within the rhetorical complexity of the novel. In the meantime, we may note here that the identification of P'an Chin-lien as a character with tiger symbolism also ties her, by traditional five-elements associations, with the image of gold (i.e., cutting metal) and the killing autumn wind, two further implications of the "gold" and the late-summer "lotus" in her name. All these implications of barren destructiveness are borne out in her murderous and fruitless sexuality in the course of the novel. By neat contrast, for all P'ing-erh's cool reserve and exaggerated whiteness—qualities conveyed in descriptions of her as a "snow maiden" (*hsüeh jen-erh* 雪人兒) and references to her "snow-white body" (*hsüeh-t'i* 雪體)—it is within her womb that the seed of Hsi-men Ch'ing's firstborn son is incubated.[160]

Another point of difference between the two women concerns their prior status and accomplishments. Here the author deliberately alters his received source to have P'an Chin-lien appear on the scene as a well-endowed courtesan before she becomes the wife of the lowly cake seller Wu Ta, after which she enters the Hsi-men household empty-handed. P'ing-erh, by way of contrast, is introduced as the wife of a wealthy neighbor, and before that had been the concubine of a well-placed courtier (Liang Chung-shu 梁中書), so she brings with her coffers of jewels and fine clothes.[161] On the other side of the picture, P'an Chin-lien is redrawn in the novel as a woman of a variety of talents: she is skilled at singing and playing the *p'i-p'a*, proficient in embroidery (especially on the emblematic bed slippers), and she can even read and write.[162] Despite her more elegant past, P'ing-erh boasts of few accomplishments outside of the bedchamber, other than her unique ability to make a certain kind of candy (*p'ao luo-erh* 泡螺兒), which Hsi-men Ch'ing remembers fondly after her death.[163]

This essential contrast between the two principal female figures in the

[160] Cf. the line of verse in the fortuneteller Wu's divination in chapter 61 (26a): "Amidst prosperous union they slaughter the lamb in deference to the tiger's sway" 榮合屠羊看虎威. P'ing-erh's snowy whiteness is emphasized in chapters 13 (1b), 67 (17a, b), and 71 (9b). This set of contrasts between fiery and cool spirits is paralleled in the relationship between Lin Tai-yü and Hsüeh Pao-ch'ai in *Hung-lou meng* (see my *Archetype and Allegory*, chap. 4).

[161] P'ing-erh's wealth is emphasized in chapters 13 (11a, b), 20 (1a, 4a), and 64 (1b), among others. Once again, the more solid social position of P'ing-erh may be reflected in that of Hsüeh Pao-ch'ai in *Hung-lou meng*. On the other hand, however, the fact that she was formerly a concubine of an ill-connected figure lessens the distance between her and Chin-lien, a point suggested by Chang Chu-p'o in chapter 15 (*tp*).

[162] For Chin-lien's musical ability and skill at making slippers, see above, nn. 134 and 147. Her ability to read is brought out in chapters 3 (4b, 5b), 39 (12a), and 78 (22a).

[163] See Chang Chu-p'o's discussions of this point in chapters 58 (20a) and 67 (6b).

novel is carried over into the relationships between each of them and Hsi-men Ch'ing. From the very beginning the bond between Hsi-men Ch'ing and P'an Chin-lien is dominated by the heat of physical desire.[164] As their passion settles down into a more domestic struggle of mutual domination, however, the focus seems to shift in the direction of psychological as much as physical control. For example, in chapter 33 (3a) we are told, "What she really wanted was to ensnare this man's heart" 無非只要牢籠漢 子之心; and again in chapter 72 (11a), "This woman wanted nothing else than to tie down Hsi-men Ch'ing's heart" 無非只是要拴西門慶之心. From this point of view, we may interpret her series of breaches of fidelity, from the early punitive dalliance with the servant Ch'in-t'ung 琴童 to the more consequential forbidden fruit shared with Ch'en Ching-chi, as cases of her own sexual insatiability, complemented by that of her appetitive partner. Even her repeated willingness to wink at Hsi-men Ch'ing's incorrigible infidelity as long as it is carried out with her full knowledge, and hence implied control, may be understood as an example of the same sort of domination—a relationship pressed to the logical conclusion of mutual destruction when she actually does him in during the grotesque final encounter in chapter 79.[165]

On the other side, the affair between Hsi-men Ch'ing and Li P'ing-erh is relatively cool; in fact almost from the moment she moves into the compound the text only occasionally stresses sexuality in their relations. At the same time, the author does present several key scenes in which Hsi-men Ch'ing's feeling for P'ing-erh is presented as something approaching tenderness, and she for her part is a model of fidelity for the rest of her life. For example, Hsi-men Ch'ing's solicitude appears to be genuine in chapter 54 when he rushes home from a party to attend the ailing P'ing-erh, and later in bedside vigils over his expiring lover his repeated refrain "How can I ever let you go" (*she-pu-te ni* 捨不得你) rings with a measure of sincerity. Thus, when P'ing-erh finally dies, we see in his signs of grief—his profuse tears, parting kiss, exaggerated mourning, and continued dream encounters with her after her death—a degree of at least occasional emotional commitment never present in his relations with P'an Chin-lien.[166] This contrast between possessive sexual aggression and ten-

[164] The most memorable examples occur in chapters 6, 8, 27, 29, 39, 73, and 74.

[165] The implications of her infidelity with the servant Ch'in-t'ung and later with Ch'en Ching-chi will be considered below. The tendency toward domination in her relations with Hsi-men Ch'ing comes out in chapters 12 (12a–b), 18 (11a), 43 (5b, 6a), 72 (11a, b), 76 (12a–13b), and, most glaringly, in the final scene to be discussed later. Significantly, Chin-lien refuses to join the other wives in pious vows for Hsi-men Ch'ing's life as he lies in agony (chapter 79 [19b]).

[166] P'ing-erh, for her part, often expresses complete submission to Hsi-men Ch'ing, as in chapter 19 (15b). when she tells him, "You are my Heaven ..." 你是個天…, and calls him

der solicitude in Hsi-men Ch'ing's emotional life is most obvious in chapter 27, where, as we have seen, the basic construction of the chapter is clearly designed to contrapose these two polar alternatives.

In view of the pains taken by the author to frame his portraits of P'an Chin-lien and Li P'ing-erh in terms of diametric contrasts, it is entirely fitting that their inevitable rivalry for the affections of Hsi-men Ch'ing blossoms into deep enmity, leading to the murder of P'ing-erh's baby. From the very beginning, the birth of Kuan-ko becomes the focus of their rivalry, with Chin-lien attempting to detract from P'ing-erh's triumph by claiming—not without some degree of credibility—that the child must have been fathered by Chiang Chu-shan, not Hsi-men Ch'ing.[167] Her hatred for the baby is clearly conveyed through her exaggerated kisses and caresses, and he, for his part, indicates that the feeling is very much mutual by virtually going into shock every time P'an Chin-lien comes near. Chin-lien, meanwhile, rarely misses a change to dig at the baby's dubious paternity, as in her sarcastic query in chapter 41: "I wonder what family this little seed belongs to" 還不知是誰家的種兒哩.[168] For all this, it still comes as something of a shock when we learn that she had methodically trained her cat to carry out the savage attack on Kuan-ko (although we recall the same sort of single-minded forcefulness she exercised in the elimination of Wu Ta).[169] The same sense of seething enmity governs her relationship to P'ing-erh, as her constant stabs at P'ing-erh's wealth and her hold on Hsi-men Ch'ing's affections later develop into open curses. Her venom reaches its peak after P'ing-erh's death, when she finds it within herself to mock Hsi-men Ch'ing's tears of grief—one of the few convincing examples of his humanity in the whole book.[170]

However, in spite of the gulf of opposing qualities, bitter rivalry, and fatal conflict that divides P'an Chin-lien from Li P'ing-erh, the author contrives to counterbalance this view with a number of hints to the effect that the two in fact have much more in common than may at first meet the eye. From the very beginning, as we have seen, the two enter the Hsi-men household one after the other under comparable circumstances: they are

---

"the balm for all my ills" 你是醫奴的藥. Cf. Martinson's discussion of this last metaphor ("Pao, Order, and Redemption," p. 395).

[167] For example, chapters 41 (6b, 7b), 48 (6b, 7a), 58 (15a–16b). The uncertainty about the child's paternity is brought out explicitly in an authorial comment in chapter 31 (9b).

[168] Chapter 41 (7b). See also chapters 30 (8b), 34 (15b), 35 (10b). The Ch'ung-chen commentator emphasizes the ominous implications of Chin-lien's kiss in chapter 48 (26b).

[169] In chapter 75 (27b), Yüeh-niang finally accuses Chin-lien of having deliberately driven P'ing-erh to her death.

[170] See chapters 31 (10a–b), 33 (3b), 41 (10a), 43 (5b, 6a), 51 (21a), 58 (16b), and 64 (1b). Cf. the fortuneteller's prediction in chapter 46 (17b): "Only, she will suffer from disharmony with her peers" 只是吃了比肩不和的虧.

both "turnaround wives" (*hui-t'ou jen* 回頭人) who have directly or indirectly caused the deaths of their previous husbands in order to consummate adulterous relationships with Hsi-men Ch'ing. This point is driven home by the figural similarity between Wu Ta and Chiang Chu-shan (they are both described as small in size and both are cursed by their unsatisfied wives with similar terms of abuse), and is later reemphasized when it is suggested that they finally pay with their lives as retribution for their adulterous excesses (P'an Chin-lien through the agency of Wu Sung, P'ing-erh hounded by guilty apparitions of Hua Tzu-hsü). Immediately after being taken into Hsi-men Ch'ing's fold, both women pass through similar stages of initial neglect on his part: Chin-lien in chapters 8 and 12; P'ing-erh first in chapter 17, then in chapter 19, in the scene of her attempted suicide. This figural similarity is reinforced by the fact that both are referred to as "sixth sister" or "sixth wife" (*liu-chieh* 六姐 or *liu-niang* 六娘) in the course of the narrative: in the case of P'ing-erh because she is in fact Hsi-men Ch'ing's sixth wife, in the case of Chin-lien on the basis of her generational designation in her own original family.[171] In addition, certain other details of presentation, from clothing to sexual practices, further link the two as halves of an overlapping construction.

Although the main outlines of the plot of the novel strongly emphasize the enmity between Chin-lien and P'ing-erh, I should point out here that the author takes care to include certain scenes of amity between the two "sisters," or at least occasional cessation of hostilities between them. Thus Chin-lien welcomes P'ing-erh as a sister in chapter 14, asks that they be allowed to live together in chapter 16, and treats her as a friend in chapters 21, 27, and 29. Even as late as chapter 40 they can still appear together in a scene of warm conviviality as they sit together on the *k'ang* in Hsi-men Ch'ing's study. Perhaps the best example of this occurs at the end of chapter 38. The scene begins with P'an Chin-lien in the role of a neglected lover (for the space of several chapters Hsi-men Ch'ing has virtually abandoned her for the very similar charms of Wang Liu-erh 王六兒), singing her heart out to the mournful strains of her *p'i-p'a*, against the backdrop of a snowy evening—in obvious parody of Yüeh-niang's earlier prayers on a snowy night in chapter 21. By the time Hsi-men finally comes home and proceeds to P'ing-erh's room, she has worked herself up into a pitch of self-pity and continues to sing her refrain louder and louder, refusing their pleas that she come to join them. The scene hovers between humor and

---

[171] Chang Chu-p'o discusses the significance of the designations "fifth" and "sixth" in chapters 9 (2a) and 74 (28b). We have already seen the symbolic significance of the number 6 (the archetypal number of *yin*) in connection with Wang Liu-erh. Cf. the erotic popular song to the tune "Sixth Wife" (*Liu-niang-tzu* 六娘子), which Chin-lien sings in bed with Ch'en Ching-chi in chapter 82 (3a). On the revision of these numerical designations, see Hsü Shuo-fang, "Ch'eng-shu pu-cheng," p. 95.

seriousness for a while, until finally the tension is defused, and she goes to P'ing-erh's room to enjoy a round of games and song, after which, at P'ing-erh's insistence, she wins the pleasure of Hsi-men Ch'ing's company for the night.

This act of sisterly generosity on P'ing-erh's part in one sense represents the traditional ideal of harmonious polygamy, but at the same time it raises the hint of a further degree of conjunction between the two. We recall that at the beginning of Hsi-men Ch'ing's affair with P'ing-erh, P'an Chin-lien had taken on the role of a vicarious participant by demanding to be informed of all the intimate details, as well as appropriating P'ing-erh's sex manuals and other trophies.[172] This relation becomes reciprocal after Kuan-ko is born and P'ing-erh virtually retires from the sexual arena, regularly sending Hsi-men to sleep with Chin-lien.[173] Thus, we see the two con-joined, as it were, as a composite object of Hsi-men Ch'ing's desire, a relation that will take on more and more significance as my discussion proceeds.

It is difficult to say that these various dimensions of mutuality between P'an Chin-lien and Li P'ing-erh ever outweigh the sharp opposition and enmity that divide them. But the traditional critics on the text often do say just that. For example, the Ch'ung-chen commentator frequently calls at-tention to the figural similarity in their parallel entry into Hsi-men Ch'ing's world. And Chang Chu-p'o goes even further to speak of a fundamental identity between the two figures.[174] Perhaps the most we can say here is that this relationship exemplifies the principle of figural recurrence at work in their characterization, resulting in the sort of yoked construct of simi-larity and dissimilarity, balance and opposition, that comes to be a central feature of the literati novel genre.[175]

---

[172] For example, chapters 13 (12a) and 16 (4b, 7a). Chin-lien wears P'ing-erh's clothes in chapters 35 (4b) and 75 (15a), and in chapter 62 (20b) she helps Yüeh-niang do P'ing-erh's hair for lying in state. In chapter 29, they sit side by side embroidering bed slippers (see n. 134).

[173] P'ing-erh sends Hsi-men Ch'ing to Chin-lien's bed in chapter 33 (2b), 38 (12b), and 44 (7a). Chang Chu-p'o points out this last occurrence in chapter 44 (16b).

[174] Ch'ung-chen edition, chapters 9 (16b), 13 (28b); Chang Chu-p'o, chapters 13 (*tp*, 13a), 15 (3a), 77 (*tp*), *tu-fa*, item 23, and prefatory essay, "On the Allegorical Meaning in the *Chin P'ing Mei*" (*Chin P'ing Mei yü-i shuo* 金瓶梅寓意說), p. 1b. Cf. the Nung-chu k'e preface: "Chin-lien dies by adultery, P'ing-erh dies from the burden of sin, Ch'un-mei dies of licentiousness" 金蓮以姦死, 瓶兒以孽死, 春梅以淫死.

[175] Cf. the various links between each of these two and Meng Yü-lou (Chin-lien and Yü-lou's confidential relationship, their musical ability; P'ing-erh and Yü-lou's comparable wealth). Chang Chu-p'o describes Yü-lou and P'ing-erh as virtually identical 二人乃一體之人 in chapter 75 (*tp*), and compares Yü-lou with Chin-lien in *tu-fa*, item 28. Cf. the comparable relationship between Lin Tai-yü and Hsüeh Pao-ch'ai in *Hung-lou meng* (see my *Archetype and Allegory*, pp. 68ff.), or that between Sun Wu-k'ung and Chu Pa-chieh in *Hsi-yu chi* (see below, Chapter 3).

The dense network of textual relations that binds Chin-lien and P'ing-erh also sends out threads that enmesh many other characters in the novel. One of these threads weaves through the repeated figure of the lascivious wives of Hsi-men Ch'ing's managers: Han Tao-kuo's 韓道國 mate, Wang Liu-erh and the figurally similar wife of Pen Ssu 賁四. Chang Chu-p'o points out the obvious redundancy in these two women (both are referred to with number names, both are short in stature), and, I might add, many of their shared points apply to P'an Chin-lien as well. Even P'ing-erh is touched by this reflection, since she, too, is a "sixth sister" formerly married to one of Hsi-men Ch'ing's cronies at the start of their affair.[176] If we extend this connection to include the wives of household servants, then the same network covers Lai Wang's 來旺兒 wife, Sung Hui-lien, whose figural links to P'an Chin-lien and Li P'ing-erh have already been traced; and from there we shuttle forward to the wife of another servant, Lai Chüeh 來爵, whose fleeting encounter with Hsi-men Ch'ing toward the close of the main body of the narrative stretching from chapter 20 to 80 harks back figurally to the affair with the former at the start of this central section.

Even more significant is the chain of figural ties by which Chin-lien and P'ing-erh are linked to Madame Lin and Lady Lan 藍氏 in the final ten chapters of Hsi-men Ch'ing's career. Despite a wide gap in their social status, a certain affinity between P'an Chin-lien and Madame Lin is intimated in their common attributes and their similar sexual relations with Hsi-men Ch'ing; and this is soon reinforced by the warmth with which Chin-lien welcomes this latest partner in Hsi-men's affections in chapter 79. Here, the author's masterful attention to significant detail comes to light, when we recall (or notice in a subsequent rereading) that at the very start of the narrative he had revised his *Shui-hu chuan* source to have Chin-lien begin her career in the service of a certain Commander Wang (Wang Chao-hsüan)—the same name and title given to the illustrious patriarch of Madame Lin's house.[177] At the same time, we see subtle reflections of P'ing-erh in the wealth and status of Madame Lin and, even more, Lady Lan, whose position as the lovely young wife of Hsi-men Ch'ing's crony Commander Ho (Ho Ch'ien-hu 何千戶) parallels that of P'ing-erh at the start of the book.[178] Thus there emerges a certain symmetry between the

[176] See above, n. 171. Chang Chu-p'o notes the figural redundancy of Wang Liu-erh and Pen Ssu's wife in *tu-fa*, items 23 and 45, and points out the overlapping features of Wang Liu-erh and Chin-lien in chapter 52 (*tp*), and "Yü-i shuo," p. 3a. See Martinson, "Pao, Order, and Redemption," p. 191, n. 1.

[177] See above, n. 112.

[178] See Chang Ch·u-p'o, *tu-fa*, item 23. This overlapping figure may also take in Lady Huang 黃氏, the wife of Wang San-kuan. Cf. the description of Lan-shih as a *teng jen-erh* 燈人兒—"[self-consuming] lamp wick," or perhaps "lanternlike [bewitching] beauty"—in chapter 78 (11a).

pair of beauties who initiate Hsi-men Ch'ing's story, and the two who bring it to its logical conclusion.

Another set of parallel relations among the female characters in the novel involves the figural similarity between the ladies of the household and the singing girls in the local brothel. The implied equivalence between the beauties installed within Hsi-men Ch'ing's pleasure garden and those he visits regularly on the outside is a constant source of irony—a point strengthened by the fact that at least two of the wives are in fact former singing girls themselves, and driven home early in the book when admiring viewers of the Yüan-hsiao spectacle in chapter 15 assume that the lovely creatures on the Lion Street balcony must be high-class courtesans.[179]

The key figure who pulls together this area of cross-reflection is Li Kuei-chieh, the courtesan for whom Hsi-men Ch'ing exercises the right of the first night in chapter 12 (thereby pushing Chin-lien, for whom he had just committed adultery, murder, and the corruption of justice, into the arms of a lascivious houseboy). Kuei-chieh's function as a nexus of negative associations is immediately indicated by the fact that she is a blood relative of Li Chiao-erh. As the plot of the narrative progresses, her relations to the Hsi-men household are further complicated when she first swears a bond of allegiance to (i.e., becomes the adopted daughter of) Yüeh-niang, and later takes advantage of this bond to seek refuge in the Hsi-men compound from trouble at the brothel. Later, her position at the center of a convoluted web of intertwined sexual relations is again knotted with the involvement of this "daughter" of Hsi-men Ch'ing in a dangerous affair with Wang San-kuan—the wastrel son of Hsi-men's newest conquest, Madame Lin—himself soon to become an "adopted son" of the Hsi-men house. The web is further entangled by a figural link between Kuei-chieh, the first queen of the night whose charms draw Hsi-men Ch'ing out of his garden, and Cheng Ai-yüeh-erh, the nearly divine creature who draws him into adventures that prove to be beyond his capacity. Chang Chu-p'o calls attention in a number of critical discussions to the similarity between Kuei-chieh and Ai-yüeh-erh, and goes on to tighten the net by pointing out the figural connection between the goddess Hsi-men possesses in the brothel in chapter 68, and the goddess he conquers immediately thereafter in an ancestral hall—even calling Madame Lin a "surrogate" (*t'i-shen*) for the lovely courtesan.[180] The "moon" (*yüeh* 月) in Ai-yüeh-erh's name provides another example of the author's rich texture of associations. Not only does the

---

[179] See discussion of this scene in Part II of this chapter.

[180] On the figural link between Ai-yüeh-erh and Kuei-chieh, see Chang Chu-p'o, chapters 11 (*tp*), 68 (*tp* and 28a), *tu-fa*, item 45, and "Yü-i shuo," p. 3b. On the link between Ai-yüeh-erh and Madame Lin, see Chang Chu-p'o, chapters 67 (*tp*) and 78 (47a). It is during Hsi-men Ch'ing's visit to Ai-yüeh-erh in chapter 68 that he first hears of the charms of Madame Lin.

moon image identify her with the Goddess of the Moon, Ch'ang-o 嫦娥, a conventional symbol of illicit desire in the Chinese tradition, but it also sets up a link with Yüeh-niang, one that means little in terms of any common qualities of the two women, but does serve to tighten even more this tangled skein of relations.[181] At the same time, the "Ai" 愛 ("love") in her name resonates with that of Han Ai-chieh 韓愛姐, the daughter of Han Tao-kuo and Wang Liu-erh sent off early in the narrative as a concubine to repay one of Hsi-men Ch'ing's benefactors at court, only to reappear in a key role toward the end of the book. With the emergence of Han Ai-chieh as the prostitute-lover of Ch'en Ching-chi in chapter 98, the circle is closed, since in a number of senses, as Chang Chu-p'o points out, she presents a final image that reflects all the way back to P'an Chin-lien.[182]

One more obvious level of figural reflection involving female characters is that between the mistresses and the maids of the household. In a loose sense, the overlapping of P'an Chin-lien and Sung Hui-lien may be considered an example of this, and this is even more explicit in the case of Ju-i, who, by virtue of her position as nurse of P'ing-erh's baby, her lovely white skin rivaling that of her hapless mistress, and her eventual relationship with Hsi-men Ch'ing, becomes another surrogate figure, as the commentators do not fail to notice.[183]

The most important relation of this type, however, is clearly the one that binds P'an Chin-lien and her maid Ch'un-mei 春梅. Beyond the equivalence suggested by the inclusion of Ch'un-mei's *mei* among the three characters in the title of the book, this link is cemented by a variety of textual details: physical attributes, behavior, speech, even perhaps their similar-sounding surnames (P'an and P'ang). In the light of my earlier discussion, it is particularly significant that the two figures are often brought into conjunction precisely in the bedchamber. From a certain point on, Chin-lien gives her maid over to Hsi-men Ch'ing's pleasure, and this leads to a recurring chain of scenes in which the three share sexual experiences of an obtrusively cooperative nature. It is therefore nothing more or less than the fulfillment of a symmetrical design when, at the end of the work, Ch'un-mei consummates a pseudo-incestuous affair with Ch'en Ching-chi, causing his violent death, and then rebounds into a symbolically

[181] The link of moon imagery also takes in Kuei-chieh's "cassia tree." Chang Chu-p'o discusses this connection in chapter 59 (*tp*).

[182] Chang Chu-p'o links Han Ai-chieh with Chin-lien in *tu-fa*, item 11, and in chapter 98 (18a). Cf. his discussions of the figural links between Chin-lien and Kuei-chieh, in chapters 8 (5b), 20 (*tp*), and 69 (*tp*).

[183] See Chang Chu-p'o, chapter 72 (17b). Ju-i's white skin is emphasized in chapter 75 (4a). On her name, see n. 205.

incestuous relationship with her new husband's servant, only to die herself through sexual exhaustion in the very same posture in which her erstwhile mistress-model had sapped the last energies of Wu Ta and later Hsi-men Ch'ing. Ch'un-mei, in short, comes from the same place as Chin-lien, and ends up right where she leaves off. This gradually emerging sense of the identity of the two figures is explicitly stated in chapter 83, when she remarks to Chin-lien, "You and I are really one and the same person" 你和我是一個人; and not long afterward it is dramatically represented in her rituals of mourning for her slain soul-mate, and in her rapid rise to succeed her as unlikely mistress of a great house.[184]

Among the male characters in the novel as well, we can observe a parallel design in the rapid recapitulation of Hsi-men Ch'ing's trajectory in the final structural division of the text. That is, Ch'en Ching-chi also quite obviously takes over where Hsi-men Ch'ing leaves off, playing out the remaining implications of his destructive impulses beyond the garden world. I have already pointed out the function of this final section as an example of the tendency of the traditional Chinese novel to repeat its structural patterns through succeeding generations, and here I might add that this general figural linkage between the two leading male characters is shored up by numerous specific details.[185] This is especially clear in Ch'en Ching-chi's sexual misadventures, where his somewhat sympathetic obliviousness to the consequences of his actions reflects back to the initial exuberance of Hsi-men Ch'ing; and even his tireless pursuit of his "mother-in-law" takes up the various hints of incest in the tangled web of the "father's" sexual relations. Although Ch'en Ching-chi is only related to Hsi-men Ch'ing by marriage, he is very much a chip off the old block, so it is not surprising when the depleted Hsi-men Ch'ing refers to him on his deathbed as his true son. I will have a good deal more to say on these last points later in this chapter.

The irony of figural reflection in this uncanonical father-son relationship also informs the contrived link between Hsi-men Ch'ing and the historical villain Ts'ai Ching—a glaring departure from the conventions of realism that nevertheless rings perfectly true in the context of the novel. I will reconsider below the importance of this link for setting up a focus of cross-reflection between Hsi-men Ch'ing's world and the empire at

---

[184] Chapter 83 (6a). Cf. Chang Chu-p'o's discussions of this relationship in chapter 98 (18a). In chapter 11 (*tp*) he suggests a comparable linkage between Ch'un-mei and Sung Hui-lien.

[185] See discussions of this point by Chang Chu-p'o in chapter 4 (*tp*). We may perhaps perceive here a little sardonic reflection from Hsi-men Ch'ing's medicine shop to the "cold shop" (*leng-p'u*) where Ch'en Ching-chi ends up in chapter 93.

large.[186] In the meantime, we may note an interesting play on this linkage in the visits to the Hsi-men compound of Ts'ai Yün 蔡蘊, another patently "false son" (*chia-tzu* 假子) of Ts'ai Ching in chapters 36 and 49. The sense that the one false son reflects on the other is corroborated by Hsi-men Ch'ing's choice of the style name Ssu-ch'üan ("four streams" 四泉) to match Ts'ai Yün's I-ch'üan ("one stream" 一泉), and this little joke is again taken up when Hsi-men Ch'ing's own false son, Wang San-kuan, is given the name San-ch'üan ("three streams" 三泉).[187]

In a less tangible way, one can perceive another sort of reflection of Hsi-men Ch'ing in the presence of certain other shadowy figures in the text. One of these is the totally unprincipled Miao Ch'ing, who comes under Hsi-men Ch'ing's protection in chapter 47. Although certain details in the treatment of this character are affected by textual discrepancies in connection with the "missing" chapters 53 to 57,[188] the main outlines of the portrait—his incestuous affair with the concubine of his adopted father (formerly his master) Miao Yüan-wai 苗員外, followed by the murder of his benefactor, the use of Hsi-men Ch'ing's corrupt influence to release him from punishment, his installation as the neighbor of Wang Liu-erh, his gift of a suggestively named maid Ch'u-yün 楚雲 to Hsi-men in chapter 77, and finally his unhesitating collusion in running off with Hsi-men Ch'ing's money immediately after his death—all mark him as something of a caricature of the basest strokes in Hsi-men Ch'ing's portrait.[189]

---

[186] Although Ts'ai Ching does not really appear onstage in the novel until chapter 55, his name and infamy are mentioned throughout practically the entire book; e.g., chapters 1 (3b), 18 (1a), 22 (1a), 27 (1a), 30 (5a), 36 (3a), 48 (10a ff.), 49 (1b ff.), 55 (1b ff.), 64 (7b), 70 (2b), 71 (15a). Cf. Chang Chu-p'o's discussion of the falsity of the relationship between Ts'ai Ching and Hsi-men Ch'ing in chapter 72 (27b). The fact that a midwife named Ts'ai appears to deliver Hsi-men Ch'ing's son, Kuan-ko, in chapter 30, precisely at the moment that the Grand Minister Ts'ai is providing analogous services in the launching of Hsi-men Ch'ing's official career, is probably not an accident. See David Roy, "Confucian Interpretation," pp. 58f.; and Carlitz, *Rhetoric*, pp. 36ff.

[187] See the interpretation of the term *ch'üan* 泉 in David Roy, "Confucian Interpretation," p. 59; and Martinson, "Pao, Order, and Redemption," p. 181; as well as Sun Shu-yü's reading of Hsi-men Ch'ing's *hao* Ssu-ch'üan in "Hsi-men-ch'ing ti hsing-hsiang yü Chin P'ing Mei ti ch'eng-chiu," pp. 17–23, p. 23, n. 4. Perhaps the *hao* assigned to Commander Ho (Ho Ch'ien-hu, Yung-shou 永壽)—T'ien-ch'üan 天泉—also partakes of this play on words. Cf. Chang Chu-p'o, 51 (16b); and "Allegorical Meaning," pp. 1a, 5a.

[188] See Hanan's discussion of the textual problems involved in the insertion of the Miao Ch'ing episode in "Text," pp. 15ff.

[189] It is not certain whether the Miao Yüan-wai who befriends Hsi-men Ch'ing in chapter 55 is the same Miao Yüan-wai betrayed by Miao Ch'ing in chapter 47 (or to what extent this confusion is the result of the textual problem of chapters 53 to 57). In chapter 55 (*tp*), Chang Chu-p'o suggests that this Miao Yüan-wai is in a sense a double of Hsi-men Ch'ing; see also his comment in chapter 72 (20b). We may note that the description of the Miao Yüan-wai who appears in chapter 47 presents him as forty years old, with one daughter but

A different type of reflection emerges in connection with an even more elusive figure, Ch'iao Hung 喬洪, the wealthy neighbor with remote connections to the imperial family whose presence looms behind many scenes of the novel (although he rarely appears on stage himself), often with indirect links to life-and-death issues within the compound. These links include Yüeh-niang's miscarriage, suffered during a visit to the Ch'iao mansion in chapter 33, and the proposed betrothal of Kuan-ko and the child heiress of the Ch'iao family, beginning in chapter 41. A small hint that something is wrong with this match is suggested in the visit of Madame Ch'iao in chapter 43, right on the heels of the ominous incident of the cold lost bangle, and this becomes more disturbing as arrangements for the marriage are pushed forward precisely in the midst of the corrupt negotiations for the freeing of Miao Ch'ing in chapter 47. Later, Ch'iao Hung himself puts in one of his few personal appearances in chapter 62, where he offers his services to obtain wood for P'ing-erh's coffin. (The reader may recall that it was along the wall of the Ch'iao estate behind P'ing-erh's house that she had seen hallucinations of vengeful fox spirits of the sort that later hound her to death.) Throughout this chain of recurrent hints, we get a sense that Ch'iao somehow represents a shadow image of Hsi-men Ch'ing's rising fortunes, and at the same time a presage of his impending fall.[190]

One final dimension of figural parallelism among characters in the novel may be seen in the constant cross-reflections between masters and servants. Beyond the examples discussed above involving the mistresses of the house and their maids, a large number of scenes are clearly designed to mirror the sexual license, outbursts of violence, and general breakdown of moral order in the compound with the corresponding misbehavior on the

---

no sons, the master of a suggestively named concubine (Tiao-shih 刁氏), formerly a prostitute, who becomes involved in a dangerous affair with his adopted son, Miao Ch'ing. The fact that the plot on Miao Yüan-wai's life is predicted by a monk from the Pao-en-ssu temple, and that the act is carried out right outside Ch'ing-ho hsien, heightens the sense of correspondence between the two.

[190] Cf. Chang Chu-p'o's comments in chapters 30 (*tp*) and 81 (*tp*). In chapter 76 (*tp*), he glosses the name Ch'iao as "tree," evidently based on the compound *ch'iao-mu* 喬木, and perhaps suggesting associations between the Ch'iao family's wealth and power and the sort of illicit enterprises exemplified in Hsi-men Ch'ing's dealings with lumber from imperial preserves (*huang-mu*). See Wu Han, "Chin P'ing Mei ti chu-tso," pp. 27ff., for a discussion of this term. The fact that Ch'iao provides the lumber for P'ing-erh's coffin may add significance to this association. I believe that the author's choice of the name Ch'iao for the family may be influenced by the semantic value of various terms for arrogance, ostentatiousness, and flirtatiousness, which appear frequently in the text; e.g., *ch'iao tso-tso* 喬做作: 53 (18a); *ch'iao-yang* 喬樣: 37 (6a), 68 (13b), 78 (30a); *ch'iao-mo ch'iao-yang* 喬模喬樣: 1 (10a), 8 (12a), 33 (10b), 37 (3a); *ch'iao-ch'iao ti* 趫趫的: 61 (3b), 77 (13b); *ch'iao chang-chih* 喬張致: 2 (3b). Cf. the linguistic connection with *chiao* 驕, *ch'iao* 蹻, etc.

part of the servants who actually manage Hsi-men Ch'ing's home and business. This is most noticeable at those points in the narrative where the absence of the titular head of the household or the principal wives leaves the servants essentially on their own, free to ape their masters' worst traits.[191] The fact that the key figures among them ultimately supersede their former masters—Ch'un-mei rising to high status precisely as the house of Hsi-men Ch'ing crumbles, and Tai-an being named heir of the house by default—is clearly intended to make a sardonic point; and the subsequent self-destruction of Ch'un-mei must lead the reader to take the final restoration of the depopulated family with more than a little skepticism.[192]

In the preceding pages, I have attempted to demonstrate that the various levels of figural parallelism in the *Chin P'ing Mei* constitute a major aspect of the art of the literati novel genre. In what follows I will argue that the aesthetic significance of these patterns may be relevant to an interpretation of the meaning of the *Chin P'ing Mei* in at least three ways. First, the sense that the treatment of individual character in the novel is oriented toward the development of composite figures of overlapping significance may help us to reconcile some of the inconsistencies in textual detail. Second, I will argue that the constant use of cross-reflection between figures is primarily directed toward a fundamentally ironic projection of the meaning in the work.[193] Finally, I will frequently point to this maintenance of a dual perspective among parallel figures on the level of masters and servants, within the household and without, in the local context and the imperial sphere, to support my reading of the text as a serious exploration of certain far-reaching intellectual issues.

IV

A third area of critical analysis in which the *Chin P'ing Mei* may serve as a model of the literati novel genre maturing in the sixteenth century is its sophisticated control of narrative rhetoric. As in the case of the structural and textural arrangement considered in the foregoing sections, the author's

[191] See Carlitz, *Rhetoric*, pp. 39f., for a discussion of this point. I will reconsider the parallelism between masters and servants below.

[192] Cf. Chang Chu-p'o, *tu-fa*, item 17. The survival of Wang Liu-erh at the end of the book, a bit like Liu Lao-lao at the end of *Hung-lou meng*, may also reflect this kind of ironic point.

[193] See Chang Chu-p'o's elucidation of this point in *tu-fa*, item 45, as well as frequent discussions of the way in which the description of one character's behavior is really directed toward the characterization of another.

handling of this aspect of his art also reveals a high degree of pointed manipulation that far outweighs the impression of sloppiness in certain inconsistencies of detail, and virtually rules out the possibility of reading the work as nothing more than an amusing or gripping exploration of daily life and morals in late Ming China. By the term "rhetoric" I refer to the entire range of devices that define and modulate the relationship of the author to his reader and his fictional world.[194] Specifically, this means the controlled use of language, whereby attention is focused on the way the story is being told, as much if not more than on the story itself. In this section, I will outline a number of rhetorical features of the *Chin P'ing Mei* that will enable me to map out the ironic projection of meaning in the novel, while also introducing some of the techniques that will figure in my treatment of the three other masterworks.

The first question we must come to grips with in this context is the problem of how to understand the author's use of the rhetorical conventions of the oral storytelling tradition. As I have already argued in my introductory chapter, the tendency of many modern students of Chinese fiction to assume that the presence of these conventional usages proves a direct connection between street-side narrative and the colloquial novel is both inaccurate and misleading. It is inaccurate because this view of the development of colloquial fiction is simply not supported by what recent literary historians have taught us about the authorship, readership, and publishing of the early Chinese novel; and it is misleading because the implication that the great works of Ming colloquial fiction are essentially products of "popular" culture may result in a failure to appreciate the serious intellectual issues they often address.[195]

If this is true as a general statement about the literati novel, it is even more true for the *Chin P'ing Mei* than for the other three masterworks covered in this study, which do actually stand in a complex relation to earlier popular narratives. Even on this point, however, I will argue that the connection between these novels and their "sources" is not one of direct derivation, but rather a self-conscious transformation of existing materials, so that their imitation of some of the conventional rhetorical features of the popular narrative genres must be understood as a deliberate

[194] For a more general discussion of the rhetoric of Chinese fiction, see my "Towards a Theory of Chinese Narrative," pp. 325–29. See also Katherine Carlitz, *Rhetoric*, chaps. 4, 5.

[195] This is not to deny the importance of the novel as a valuable source of information about daily life in late Ming China. In fact, a number of important studies on food and clothing have relied heavily on the *Chin P'ing Mei* for specific details. See for example Aikawa Koyoko, "Mindai no fukushoku"; Ikemoto Yoshio, *Kinpeibai shiwa no inshoku shishaku kō*; and F. W. Mote, "Yuan and Ming," pp. 248ff. Chang Chu-p'o pays particular attention to details of food and clothing (see above, n. 104) and frequently praises the verisimilitude of the novel (e.g., *tu-fa*, items 54, 62, 63).

element of literary design.[196] I have already discussed the structural function of the use of the prologue section and the *chang-hui* arrangement, along with its chapter titles, and I will return shortly to the specialized use of poems and songs cited in the text. Even the inevitable narrator's tag expressions from the storytelling tradition—expressions such as "listen to the next chapter to find out" (*ch'ing t'ing hsia-hui fen-chieh* 請聽下回分解) and "but now our story divides into two" (*hua fen liang-t'ou* 話分兩頭)— should be seen as not simply decorative, but as playing a significant role in the segmentation and shaping of the narrative continuum. The most significant example of this type of rhetoric is probably the frequent interpolation of authorial asides introduced by the expression "Dear reader, listen to what I have to say" (*k'an-kuan t'ing-shuo* 看官聽說), which carries the charade of the "simulated context" of narrator-audience interaction to the level of dramatization. The fact that these passages occur so often in the course of the novel, and that they often go on at such length, immediately suggests other functions beyond the simple retardation of the flow of the narrative. These functions include providing necessary background information (for example, a number of early instances give details on the past histories of characters not otherwise presented in the text), advance warning of coming eventualities of the plot ("later on . . ."), as well as explanation of possibly puzzling actions or remarks.[197]

Of greater interest are the frequent examples of this type in which the narrator indulges in extended disquisitions on various topics. To be sure, many of these passages maintain the pose of the oral storyteller by dishing up rather uninspired homilies on such themes as the nature of women, the corrupting influence of money, and especially the evil wiles of monks, nuns, and go-betweens.[198] But in certain instances these little asides carry a strong sense of personal conviction and provide meaningful commentary

[196] See above, Part I. Hsü Meng-hsiang speaks of the use of storytellers' phrases as an "imitation" (*mo-ssu* 摹似) of this type of oral rhetoric ("Tso-che," p. 180).

[197] I have counted about forty *k'an-kuan* passages in the course of the novel, in chapters 1 (9a, 12a), 2 (6a–b), 3 (7a–b), 7 (2b), 7 (4b), 9 (2a), 10 (6b), 11 (3a), 12 (18a), 13 (12a–b), 14 (7b), 18 (7a), 18 (11a), 19 (4a–b), 20 (14a), 22 (5a), 24 (2b), 25 (6a), 30 (5a), 31 (4a), 31 (9b), 59 (10b–11a), 62 (14a), 68 (3b), 69 (4a), 70 (15a), 72 (11a), 78 (4b), 79 (9b), 80 (9a), 80 (11b), 82 (10b), 83 (4b), 84 (4a), 84 (5b), 84 (8a), 84 (10a), 87 (5a), 92 (7a), 96 (7a), 98 (3a). Martinson ("Pao, Order, and Redemption," p. 137, n. 1) puts these at forty-eight. See also Carlitz, "Role of Drama," p. 100; and Teramura Masao, "Kinpeibai shiwa ni okeru sakusha kainyūbun," pp. 19–31. Examples of *k'an-kuan* passages providing background information on specific characters include chapters 10 (6b), 11 (3a), 13 (12a), 24 (2b), 84 (5b, 10a). Those giving warnings of coming eventualities include 13 (12a), 19 (4a), 30 (5a), 31 (4a), 59 (10b), 62 (14a), 82 (10b), 84 (8a), 87 (5a). Those that explain puzzling narrative developments include 18 (7a), 31 (9b), 83 (4b), 96 (7a).

[198] See discussions of women: 3 (7a), 9 (2a), 14 (7b), 25 (6a), 69 (4a), 72 (11a), 84 (5a); go-betweens: 7 (2b); nuns: 12 (18a), 20 (14a), 24 (2b), 68 (3b), 84 (4a); money: 7 (4b); good-for-nothing friends: 80 (11b); singing girls: 20 (14a), 80 (9a).

on specific events and characters described in the text, as well as such larger issues as the interrelationship between individual degeneration and the dissolution of the imperial order, or the illusory nature of human experience.[199] Since the specialized use of this particular technique does not really materialize in our three earlier masterworks, but does play a significant role in later literati novels, one might possibly conclude that the author of the *Chin P'ing Mei* deserves the credit for developing this fruitful rhetorical device, at least as far as full-length fiction is concerned.[200]

The net effect of this pointed use of explicit narrative rhetoric is to periodically remind the reader of the presence of the narrator somewhere between himself and the story. The awareness of the shaping hand of the narrator in this and other aspects of the text ultimately serves to drive a wedge between the first and the final impression we form of characters, between the apparent and the underlying meaning of the events related in the book. Here we come to the main point in the discussion of the rhetorical features of the literati novel; that is, its creation and maintenance of a predominantly ironic focus on the figures and events depicted within its pages. In applying the term "irony" here, I wish to use it in the broadest sense, to refer to every possible disjunction between what is said and what is meant, every slippage between the out-of-context and the in-context import of a wide range of figures of speech, literary allusions, lines of dialogue, and even narrative situations.[201]

A number of recent scholars have begun to pay attention to the presence of a thick overlay of irony in the *Chin P'ing Mei*. When Wei Tzu-yün speaks of "ironic allusion" (*feng-yü* 諷喩) in the novel, he has in mind only the veiled criticism of the Wan-li emperor through the figure of Hsi-men Ch'ing. But Sun Shu-yü goes much farther in developing this into a useful critical tool.[202] Although Sun seems to have some hesitation about how best to render the term "irony" (at one point he translates it as *fan-feng* 反諷, elsewhere he falls back on a phonetic transcription of the English word: 艾朗尼), he puts his finger on the essence of the trope when he defines it as "the nonequivalence of surface and underlying meaning" 表裡之別.[203] The critical concept of irony, however, is not new in China,

---

[199] For example, chapters 14 (7b), 24 (2b), 78 (4b), 79 (9b), 98 (3a).

[200] On the use of *k'an-kuan* passages in the Ming short story, see Cyril Birch, "Some Formal Characteristics of the Hua-pen Story," pp. 346–64.

[201] For a general discussion of irony in the traditional Chinese novel, see my "Full-Length Hsiao-shuo," pp. 171ff. My understanding of the use of irony in fiction owes much to Wayne Booth's *The Rhetoric of Irony*, and to Georg Lukacs's *Theory of the Novel*.

[202] Wei Tzu-yün, *Wen-shih yü yen-pien*, pp. 89ff., and "Wang-kuan," p. 233. See also Chu Hsing, *K'ao-cheng*, p. 59; and Tai Pu-fan, "Ling-cha," pp. 111ff.

[203] Sun Shu-yü, *Chin P'ing Mei ti i-shu*, pp. 28–32, 48ff., 112, 120, esp. 55. See André Lévy's review of Sun's discussion in *Chinese Literature: Essays, Articles, Reviews* 3, no. 1, p. 180; and Carlitz, *Rhetoric*, pp. 2f.

and Chang Chu-p'o is frequently talking about the same phenomenon when he describes certain passages as the sort of "pointed" or "hidden" expressions (*ch'ü-pi, yin-pi, shih-pi* 曲筆, 隱筆, 史筆) associated in the Chinese tradition with serious historiography, or as "inversions" (*fan-an* 翻案) of expected patterns.[204]

It remains, however, to set forth as fully as possible the precise workings of irony in a variety of specific constructions. I will begin with a review of some of the more transparent ironic touches visible in puns and other verbal games (perhaps employed as much for amusement or embellishment as for serious reference), and then move on to suggestive uses of extended metaphors and complex literary allusions. In all cases, we will watch for the manner in which these surface features are directed toward the adumbration of certain deeper, only partially hidden, patterns of meaning.

As an example of the lighter side, let us consider first the use of puns in the naming of characters. As a rule, the less important the character, the more transparent the name. For example, among Hsi-men Ch'ing's fellows the names Wu Tien-en 吳典恩 ("without an ounce of generosity") and Ch'ang Shih-chieh 常時節 ("always on the take") are based on stock puns, and the name of the tutor Wen Pi-ku 溫必古 ("warming the rear") only barely masks a reference to his inclination to pederasty.[205]

---

[204] Chang Chu-p'o, chapters 1 (*tp*), 12 (*tp*), 13 (*tp*), 45 (*tp*), 60 (28b), 66 (73a), 96 (25a), 97 (2b). See also Ch'ung-chen edition, 14 (37a) and 23 (26b). The use of the term *fan-an* (e.g., 96 [*tp*]) reminds us of the notion of parody essays (*fan-an wen-chang* 翻案文章) popular in the late Ming. The commentators often put in sarcastic remarks of their own regarding the action of the narrative; e.g., Chang Chu-p'o, 56 (19a), Ch'ung-chen edition, 31 (22b), 72 (18a).

[205] Some of the names of Hsi-men Ch'ing's sworn brothers are written differently, and the puns are slightly more camouflaged, in the Ch'ung-chen recension (see above, n. 143). Chang Chu-p'o frequently suggests glosses on the names of characters, e.g., chapters 7 (*tp*), Meng Yü-lou; 19 (6a), Chin-lien; 24 (20b), Han Tao-kuo and Pen Ssu; 41 (*tp*), P'ing-erh; 51 (5b), P'ing-erh; 56 (*tp*), Wen Pi-ku; 59 (*tp*), Cheng Ai-yüeh-erh; 65 (*tp*), Ju-i; 67 (12a), Ying Po-chüeh; 68 (*tp*), Kuei-chieh; 70 (*tp*), Pen Ssu's wife; 76 (*tp*), Wen Pi-ku; 77 (*tp*), Pen Ssu's wife; 78 (*tp*), P'ing-erh, Hsi-men Ch'ing; 79 (*tp*), Chou Shou-pei; 80 (*tp*), Li Ming; 82 (*tp*), Ch'en Ching-chi; 88 (*tp*), the Taoist Wu; 91 (3b), the matchmaker T'ao; 92 (*tp*), Yang Ta-lang; 94 (16a), Yü-t'ang, Chin-kuei; 99 (8a), Ch'en Ching-chi; and 100 (*tp*), Chou Shou-pei. He repeats many of these points in "Allegorical Meaning" (see Martinson, "Pao, Order, and Redemption," p. 38; Wei Tzu-yün, *Shen-t'an*, pp. 86ff.; and Sun Shu-yü, "Chin P'ing Mei ti ming-ming," pp. 9–16). In a number of places, the author inserts additional tongue-in-cheek allusions to the names of his characters in certain lines of verse. For example, chapter 46 contains several references to "golden lotus" lanterns (p. 1a, 3b); chapter 52 (19b) follows up a tryst with Kuei-chieh in the garden with a poem to the title "plucking the cassia" (*che-kuei ling* 折桂令), an association repeated in chapter 74 (8b) after Hsi-men Ch'ing literally "breaks off" with Kuei-chieh. The name of the obliging wet-nurse Ju-i is neatly glossed in a line of verse in chapter 78 (16a): "Sir, you may do as you will" 任君隨意. Perhaps we also have here an offhand allusion to the erotic story *Ju-i chün chuan* used as a source for the novel (see Hanan, "Sources," pp. 43ff.). For the significance of the change of the name of the town in which the story takes place to Ch'ing-ho hsien, see David Roy, "Confucian

When we come to the main characters, it becomes more difficult to come up with neat interpretations of their names, although many still appear to have a measure of suggestiveness. Chang Chu-p'o, for one, exercises considerable ingenuity in deciphering the names of all the central figures. For example, he glosses the "Ch'ing" in Hsi-men Ch'ing's name with the homophone *ch'ing* 罄 ("depletion"), a reading that resonates well with the essence of the figure, but seems to lose sight of the fact that this name is taken over ready-made from *Shui-hu chuan*.[206] Chang's imaginative readings become a bit more convincing when he attempts to link the names of a number of female characters into a web of associated plant and flower imagery. Beginning with the title of the novel, he first suggests that the three characters *Chin, P'ing,* and *Mei* may be read not simply as abbreviations for the three heroines, but also as a single phrase "plum blossom in a golden vase."[207] At first sight this seems a bit forced, but at the same time, we have seen that the association of Li P'ing-erh with the vase image does have certain significant connotations in terms of her character. This "vase" association takes on an additional layer of meaning in connection with the bond between P'ing-erh and Wu Yin-erh, whereby the golden vase now becomes a silver vase, an image that recurs at a number of points in the novel.[208] A similar poetic word game may be seen in the parallel relationship between Yüeh-niang ("Moon Lady") and Kuei-chieh, whose *kuei* 桂 ("cassia") is traditionally associated with moon imagery.

In his essay "On the Allegorical Meaning of *Chin P'ing Mei*", which I have cited in the above discussion, Chang clearly goes too far with his horticultural metaphors, stretching his interpretation to cover Madame Lin (*Lin* 林, "forest") and Pen Ssu's wife (whose surname, *Yeh* 葉, means "leaf"), and identifying P'ing-erh—with little textual support—as a fragrant hibiscus (*fu-jung* 芙蓉). Although Chang clearly misses the mark in many of these far-fetched readings, his instincts are not completely groundless within the context of the stereotyped traditional associations of flower

---

Interpretation," p. 55. (See above, n. 79.) This idea is expressed in a line of verse in chapter 76 (18a). See also Hanan, "Sources," p. 26. Significant scenes in the Grotto of Sequestered Spring occur in chapters 22, 23, 27, 36, 52, 55, 56, 67, 73, 84.

[206] Chang Chu-p'o, "Allegorical Meaning," p. 1a, and chapter 78 (*tp*).

[207] Chang Chu-p'o, *tu-fa*, items 1, 48, and 106; "Allegorical Meaning"; and chapter 7 (*tp*). See Carlitz, "Puns and Puzzles," pp. 237ff. This reading is followed in several recent translations of the novel, including André Lévy's *Fleur en Fiole d'Or*; and V. Manukhin's *Cveti slivy v zolotoj vaze*.

[208] The expression "silver vase" seems to have had erotic reference in the Ming period, as did the term *che-kuei* (see *Mu-tan t'ing*, Scenes 10, 26). See Cass, "Celebrations," p. 37. Carlitz ("Puns and Puzzles," p. 233, n. 20) glosses "Yin-erh" with "debauchery" (*yin* 淫) and notes that Wu Yin-erh had been the mistress of P'ing-erh's erstwhile husband, Hua Tzu-hsü. Cf. Chang Chu-p'o, chapter 100 (*tp*). The image of a silver vase appears in chapter 54 (6b), and that of a golden vase appears in chapters 10 (5b), 31 (12b), 71 (1b).

imagery with the themes of delicate beauty, inevitable decay, illusory splendor, and all the rest—and precisely these associations are stressed countless times in the poetry cited in the text.[209]

Still more important, the plant and flower images take on a richer layer of meaning within the setting of the pleasure garden at the heart of Hsi-men Ch'ing's world.[210] The fact that the garden in the *Chin P'ing Mei*, like many a garden of delights in European literature, is intended to serve as a global metaphor for Hsi-men Ch'ing's fleeting life of the senses is suggested by the way in which his own rise and fall are tied to the history of the garden. This is already evident in the coordination of the construction of the garden (from chapter 16 to 19) with the gathering of his complete bouquet of wives over the first two decades of the text, and the ceremonies of its completion simultaneous with the arrival of Li P'ing-erh. Thereafter, we see the expanding glory of Hsi-men Ch'ing's sexual and political powers celebrated in a series of scenes of garden delights and visits by influential court officials.[211] In the second "half" of the book, however, we witness the gradual decline of the garden. The demise of Hsi-men Ch'ing in chapter 79, in effect, spells the end of the garden; thus, after the last fleeting escapades of P'an Chin-lien and Ch'en Ching-chi, it is quickly reduced to ruin in the final section, as most poignantly emphasized in the return of Ch'un-mei in chapter 96.[212] In much of the framing of this garden construct, we can detect the blueprint for the monumental literary garden later realized in the *Hung-lou meng*.[213]

There are many other examples of extended metaphor used as a means

[209] For example, Chang Chu-p'o, chapters 7 (*tp*) and 82 (*tp*). In chapter 32 (1aff.), Ying Po-chüeh jokes about the link between Kuei-chieh's cassia and P'ing-erh's vase. Cf. related flower imagery in chapters 17, 19 (1b–2a), 49 (9a–b, 10a), 51 (17b), 52 (13b), 56 (2b), 60 (4a), 61 (11b, 12a), 73 (4b), 77 (9b, 10a), 91 (7a–b), 92 (11a), 97 (6a–b). See Carlitz, "Puns and Puzzles," pp. 232ff. The choice of the rare surname Hua ("flower") for P'ing-erh's evanescent husband seems quite pointed.

[210] For a general discussion of the significance of garden imagery in Chinese literature, see my *Archetype and Allegory*, chap. 7; and Mary Scott, "Image of the Garden." Chang Chu-p'o comments on the significance of the garden in chapters 5 (*tp*), 9 (*tp* and 1b), 15 (*tp*), 17 (13a), 34 (16a), 54 (*tp*), 71 (*tp*), 82 (*tp*, 19a), and 96 (18b).

[211] The plans for the garden are first mentioned in chapter 14, and the construction is carried out in chapters 16, 17, 18, and 19. See Carlitz, "Puns and Puzzles," pp. 225f. Major garden scenes include the swing scene in chapter 25; the grotto escapade in chapter 27; the official visit in chapter 36; butterfly chasing in chapter 52; continuing improprieties in chapters 56, 57, and 58; autumn festivities in chapter 61; and snowscapes in chapters 71 and 77. Hsi-men Ch'ing visits other people's gardens in chapters 30, 54, 71.

[212] Cf. Chang Chu-p'o, chapter 96 (*tp* and 18b).

[213] For example, the Ta-kuan garden is also built from chapters 16 to 18, also gives rise to swinging, butterfly chasing, and snowscape pleasures, and also passes into a phase of decay and destruction (see my *Archetype and Allegory*, chap. 8).

of directing the reader's vision beyond the surface of the text. We have already seen the imagery of lantern wicks and candles burning themselves out, as well as the symbolism of blanketing snow melting away into nothingness. I might add here the matching of the tiger symbolism used in the treatment of P'an Chin-lien with references to Hsi-men Ch'ing as a "dragon," a metaphoric attribution that supports his role as a miniature "emperor" in his enclosed world. Not only does the identification of Chin-lien with a ferocious cat resonate with the ominous cat imagery traced earlier in this chapter, but it also taps traditional symbolism to evoke the powerful attraction that locks her with Hsi-men Ch'ing's dragon in an embrace of mutual destruction.[214]

In reviewing these examples of extended metaphor in the *Chin P'ing Mei*, I must acknowledge that the "other" meaning to which these figures point never falls together into a unified allegorical scheme, Chang Chu-p'o's essay on "Allegorical Meaning" notwithstanding. This does not rule out the possibility of a network of *roman à clef* references, as in the reading suggested by Wei Tzu-yün. At the very least, we should still credit the *Chin P'ing Mei* with moving toward the sort of multiple correspondences among linked figures that is later developed into a more articulated allegorical structure in the *Hung-lou meng.*[215]

Turning now to other means of setting up an ironic disjunction between first and final impressions, we may note briefly a few more general techniques employed in the novel. One of these is the manipulation of point of view, whereby the author gives us, through the eyes of one or another character, impressions that turn out to be at variance with the true picture. Perhaps the best example of this is the presentation of Cheng Ai-yüeh-erh, who appears to us first in the infatuated gaze of Hsi-men Ch'ing as a veritable goddess, but later turns out to be far from divine.[216] An even more important technique consists in the citation of literary source ma-

---

[214] For such imagery, see chapters 1 (5a), 3 (11a), 4 (5a), 26 (17a), 39 (4a), 71 (16b), and 85 (5a). The fact that Hsi-men Ch'ing deliberately falsifies his zodiac sign in chapter 29 actually adds to the symbolic significance of the attribution. See Martinson, "Pao, Order, and Redemption," pp. 346ff., and Carlitz, *Rhetoric*, pp. 54ff., on the "garbled horoscopes" in the novel.

[215] For a discussion of allegorical schemes in Chinese fiction, see my *Archetype and Allegory*, chap. 5, and "Allegory in *Hsi-yu chi* and *Hung-lou meng*," pp. 163–202. The author of the *Chin P'ing Mei* begins to play with five-elements correspondences, but only in a very loose way. Chang Chu-p'o, of course, reads the whole text as a carefully contrived structure of significant imagery. See his "Allegorical Meaning," and comments in chapters 20 (*tp*), 70 (*tp*), 72 (*tp*), 75 (10b), 82 (*tp*), 93 (*tp*), 94 (*tp*), 99 (8a), and 100 (*tp*).

[216] Cf. also the treatment of Hsi-men Ch'ing's first visit to Madame Lin's mansion in chapter 69 (see above, Part II). Chang Chu-p'o frequently notes the presentation of certain scenes "through [a certain character's] eyes"; e.g., chapters 9 (3b), 13 (8b), 55 (7b), and 82 (*tp*).

terials that ill suit the new context in which they are set. This applies immediately to the various uses of material borrowed from *Shui-hu chuan*, where the many deliberate changes introduced by the author in both plot outlines and specific details must certainly have encouraged his more attentive readers to ponder his intentions.[217]

The most brilliant successes scored by the author in the revalorization of such borrowed material are in his characteristic citation of popular songs and dramatic pieces from the contemporary repertoire, as several recent scholars have demonstrated.[218] The extensive use made of this literature in the *Chin P'ing Mei* should not be surprising, in view of the symbiotic relationship described earlier between the emerging novel form and the literati stage in the late Ming period; and indeed, many of the patterns of structure and rhetoric analyzed here are derived from or influenced by formal features of *ch'uan-ch'i* drama.[219]

The case of *Chin P'ing Mei*, however, is somewhat unique, not only in its use of contemporary popular songs in addition to excerpts from dramatic works, but also in the degree and kind of use it makes of these materials. That is, if this meant simply the insertion of suggestive verse at various points in the narrative in order to interrupt the action, recapitulate scenes, heighten emotional intensity, or set the mood, then we would be dealing with a phenomenon familiar in all Chinese colloquial fiction of the period. But in a number of ways the author reveals a self-conscious expansion of this technique to serve his own ironic purposes.

The precise manner in which this material is inserted into the text in many cases alerts us to the possibility of hidden intentions. The majority of scenes of singing performance, it is true, may be taken as mimetic representations of this particular aspect of life in the merchant salons and urban entertainment quarters of the time, as well as in the round of banquets and formal celebrations in official life. But as we shall see, the number of instances in which the background songs provide a kind of choric commentary on the actions taking place at center stage is just too great to dismiss in this way. In some cases, the author advertises the unusual function of these songs by presenting them with certain contrived special effects, as for example in the swan-song duet sung by Hsi-men Ch'ing and Wu Yüeh-niang in chapter 79 (apparently the only instance in which

[217] Many critics have pointed out the differences between the P'an Chin-lien episode in *Shui-hu chuan* and the opening section of *Chin P'ing Mei*, for example Chang Chu-p'o chapters 1 (*tp*), 3 (*tp*), 10 (*tp*). See Hanan, "Sources," pp. 25ff.

[218] See Hanan, Feng Yüan-chün, K'ang-i Sun Chang, and Katherine Carlitz, works cited in nn. 15 and 60. See also Wei Tzu-yün, *Shen-t'an*, pp. 70ff.

[219] For a discussion of the application of the terminology of drama criticism to colloquial fiction, see Rolston, *How to Read*, Introduction.

Hsi-men Ch'ing himself sings), or the repeated interruption of a song sequence in chapter 52 with irreverent comments by Ying Po-chüeh, set off by the device of double-column reduced-size printing (normally reserved for commentaries of a more serious sort).[220]

However, it is the way the songs themselves reflect ironically on the scenes in which they are placed that is most crucial here. Sometimes this irony arises out of the choice of a particular dramatic piece to be performed on a given occasion. We have already noted the ironic associations between the singing of pieces from the plays *Sha-kou chi* (*Sha kou ch'üan fu* 殺狗勸夫) and *Liu-hsieh chi* 留鞋記 and the significant use of dog and shoe imagery in certain scenes. This sort of irony is thickened when we take into account the implied comparison between the context of a given song in its original play and the use to which it is put in the novel. Thus, when songs from *Sha-kou chi* are introduced in chapter 80, the sixteenth-century reader could not have failed to recall the theme of a faithless brother in the original play, right at the point when Hsi-men Ch'ing's "brothers" are robbing his widow blind, as Chang Chu-p'o duly notes.[221] Similarly, the theme of worldly renunciation sounded in the play *Han Hsiang-tzu* 韓湘子 is brought in with unsettling effect at the celebrations of the birth of Kuan-ko held in chapter 32; and lest the reader miss the point, the author alerts us by having guests comment on the inappropriateness of certain songs earlier at the same banquet (at the end of the preceding chapter), and later on bringing back songs from the same play, *Han Hsiang-tzu*, immediately before the baby's cruel death in chapter 58.[222] There are numerous other examples of this type, many of which have been collected and analyzed in the very valuable study by Katherine Carlitz.[223]

Even among the independent popular songs (*hsiao-ch'ü* 小曲) that stud the text, we can observe a similar tendency to choose tune titles (*ch'ü-p'ai* 曲牌) that provide ironic reflection on the situation of the narrative. This practice is particularly striking since, as a rule, a given tune title is not supposed to affect the contents of a song. Yet enough examples exist to convince me that this is indeed one of the devices employed in the *Chin*

[220] In the Ch'ung-chen edition I have used, the double columns have been pasted over and reprinted as separate columns. See also the special uses of verse in chapters 93 (2b–4b) and 100 (11b). In chapter 31 (13aff.) a substantial portion of a *yüan-pen* dramatic script is copied directly into the text. See Carlitz, "Role of Drama," pp. 258ff.

[221] See Chang Chu-p'o, *tu-fa*, item 107, and comment in chapter 100 (22b).

[222] See Chang Chu-p'o, *tu-fa*, item 6. The inappropriate play in chapter 31 (see n. 220) is a performance about the T'ang figure Wang Po 王勃.

[223] Carlitz, "Role of Drama," chaps. 4, 5, 6, ad 7. See also Carlitz, "Puns and Puzzles," pp. 228ff., on the use of allusions to *P'i-p'a chi* in chapter 27. Cf. references to *Hsi-hsiang chi* in chapters 42 (2b) and 68 (2b).

P'ing Mei, as Chang Chu-p'o insists in a number of comments.[224] One such example may be seen in the choice of a song to the tune "Eternal Union" (*Yung t'uan-yüan* 永團圓), sung at the party given to welcome P'ing-erh into the circle of wives in chapter 20. Here the superficial amity of the occasion only papers over the shock of P'ing-erh's attempted suicide immediately before, and the chapter goes on to reveal seething rivalries within the household, followed by Hsi-men Ch'ing's abandonment of his new wives for the charms of Li Kuei-chieh, leaving the unlikely guardian Ch'en Ching-chi in charge of the garden. Significantly, it is P'an Chin-lien who objects at this point to the choice of this song. Similar implications seem to be suggested in chapter 41, when a song to the tune "Fighting Quails" (*tou an-ch'un* 鬭鵪鶉) wryly undercuts the surface felicity of Kuan-ko's betrothal. (There may be a hint of this little joke in the expression *tou-ch'i* 鬭氣 in the title of this chapter.)

Perhaps the most convincing example of this type is the recurrent use of the tune "Lamb on a Precipice" (*Shan-p'o yang* 山坡羊). The favored status of this particular tune may be partially explained by the fact that it seems to have been very popular precisely at the time of the novel's composition; but the sheer frequency with which it is heard makes it something of a theme song for the work as a whole, one that provides frequent ironic digs at the little lost sheep among the women in the compound.[225] This is especially true with respect to P'ing-erh, whose identification with lamb symbolism was noted earlier, and whom we can easily find ourselves pitying as an innocent little lamb. It is precisely by lulling us into sentimental sympathy, however, that the author ensures that we never forget the fact that this little lamb has committed adultery and worse.

In the majority of cases, these tune titles are less significant than the specific lyrics included in the text. It is perhaps possible to take certain instances as positive expressions of the singer's inner feelings, as Hanan has suggested.[226] For example, Chin-lien's *Shan-p'o yang* song of rejection in chapter 8 may be taken as a lyrical outpouring of her sincere attachment to Hsi-men Ch'ing (as long as one is prepared to overlook her cruel treatment

---

[224] Chang Chu-p'o, *tu-fa*, item 49, and chapters 6 (18a), 27 (*tp*), 61 (15b), 73 (*tp*). See, for example, the tune "Long-lived as the Southern Hills" (*Shou pi nan-shan* 壽比南山), sung after a major exposure of the baby Kuan-ko's fragility. One *k'an-kuan* passage in chapter 96 (7a) pointedly asks why a certain song has been sung. Cf. the sardonic use of a poem to the tune "In Praise of the New Groom" (*Ho hsin-lang* 賀新郎) at the beginning of chapter 100 in the novel *Hsing-shih yin-yüan chuan* 醒世姻緣傳. See my "After the Fall," p. 563.

[225] Examples occur in chapters 1 (11b), 8 (2a), 33 (6a f.), 44 (2b–3b), 50 (7b), 59 (15b, 19b), 61 (4a–b), 75 (13a), 89 (4b, 8b, 11b), and 91 (13b). I am grateful to Chang Ch'ung-ho (Mrs. Hans Frankel) for her reconstruction of the *Shan-p'o yang* song form presented in a demonstration-recital held in the Ming Garden Court of the Metropolitan Museum of Art in New York on April 13, 1981.

[226] Hanan, "Sources," p. 67.

of her step daughter, Ying-erh, in the same chapter, or her quick resort to the substitute caresses of Ch'in-t'ung on the next occurrence). Similarly, Hsi-men Ch'ing's grief over the loss of P'ing-erh is often accepted as proof of deep affection (once again, setting aside his substantial responsibility for her death and his quick rebound into other beds). Perhaps most convincing is Ch'en Ching-chi's long plaint in chapter 93, which, coming in the midst of his manifold sufferings, carries a strong note of appealing conviction.

Usually, however, the planting of such lyrics goes in the direction of undermining their literal meaning, as both singers and listeners fail to understand the import of the words they mouth. A fine example of this appears in the song Chin-lien croons to the strains of her *p'i-p'a* on that snowy night in chapter 38. At first sight, this sounds like a sincere, even moving, expression of her feelings of rejection. But as the scene progresses and her repeated refrain "You've ruined my springtime, turned my youth upside down; you've left me up in a tree and I can't get down" 悮了我 青春年少, 你撇的人有上稍來沒下稍 grows louder and more impatient, the song is emptied of its emotional content and turned into something of a farce, until Hsi-men Ch'ing and P'ing-erh are finally brought around by the ludicrousness of the situation. The author, meanwhile, does not forget this refrain; he sounds it one final time in chapter 86 (13b), immediately before the return of Wu Sung brings a swift end to P'an Chin-lien's trials. A similar example occurs in chapter 33 (6a–b), where Ch'en Ching-chi, just at the point when his involvement with Chin-lien is proceeding beyond harmless flirtation, sings a long *Shan-p'o yang* song loaded with hints of the inevitable consequences that are to overtake and finally destroy his own thoughtless garden of delights.[227]

These sorts of hints of the inevitable cooling of illusory passions also run through the background songs sung on appropriate occasions in nearly every chapter. Since these popular songs, like love songs everywhere, generally dwell on loneliness, parting, and grief, it is not surprising that sentiments of this nature crop up repeatedly in these pieces. But as the cycle of the narrative rolls into its downward arc, these hints become more and more insistent, yielding long chains of conventional images (snuffed candles, moonlight on snow, and the like) expressing cold loneliness (*ch'i-liang*) and emptiness (*k'ung* 空), and directing the reader's vision away from immediate warmth and gaiety toward impending desolation.[228]

[227] These hints include the expressions "cruel lover" (*yüan-chia* 冤家) and "steaming blood" (*je-hsüeh* 熱血).

[228] For example, 44 (2b–4b), 46 (2b–3a, 6a–6b, 7b–8a), 49 (5b–10a), 52 (9b–11b), 61 (4a–5a, 11b–12b, 17a–b), 65 (15b), 73 (3b), 75 (13a–b). Many of these associated images are brought together with particular density in poems in chapters 43 (9a–10a) and 71 (3a–5b).

V

Having catalogued some of the specific devices used by the author to impose an ironic perspective on his story, we are now ready to move on to the other side of the coin of irony: its implicit challenge to the reader to pursue the meaning it keeps beneath an unreliable surface. From here on, the plane of discussion will shift from analysis to interpretation, as I attempt to set forth some of the patterns of meaning left behind after our initial expectations are stripped away.

One might justifiably raise at this point the question of whether or not this sort of elusive layer of meaning must necessarily lurk beneath a textual surface sufficiently engrossing in its own right. Granted, there is no reason to assume that such exists, since in narrative literature in general, and Chinese fiction in particular, this is probably the exception rather than the rule. On the other hand, the probability that there is some serious intention here beyond the simple pleasure of storytelling becomes greater as we begin to appreciate the high degree of control the author of *Chin P'ing Mei* exercises over his text—control that extends from structural patterning to rhetorical complexity. Eventually, the impression one gains after successive readings of the text is that practically nothing has been left to chance, that every thread is carefully plotted in advance—in spite of the well documented gaps and inconsistencies that remain in the earliest extant editions. This is apparently what Chang Chu-p'o has in mind when he warns his reader not to be "fooled" (*man-kuo* 瞞過) by the surface of the text, or what the Ch'ung-chen commentator means when he advises us not to take certain passages as "idle words" (*mo tso hsien-hua* 莫作閒話).[229] It is also a point made by many (admittedly, not all) of the other early critics of the novel. For example, when the author of the Nung-chu k'e preface to the earliest editions says that "the author definitely has his own intentions" 作者亦自有意, or when the colophon writer who signs himself Nien-kung 廿公 says that "there is an object to its ironic stabs" 蓋有所刺也, they seem to accept the notion that the structural manipulation of the text is not purely aesthetic in intent, but that the sum total of its figural patterning adds up to a significant framework of meaning.[230] In their enthusiasm, Chang

[229] For example, Chang Chu-p'o, chapter 10 (*tp*); Ch'ung-chen edition, chapter 2 (29a). Chang Chu-p'o enjoins the reader to scrutinize the text with high seriousness in the *tu-fa*, items 36, 37, 39, 40, 42, 94, 95, 96, 97, 98, 99. See also his use of the term "deep indignation" (*fen-man* 憤懣) in item 77, with its clear allusion to *Shih Chi*.

[230] Yüan Hung-tao, for one, seems to be talking about the entertainment value of the novel in the famous passage in his *Shang-cheng*, although none of the other early documents that claim this is an exceptionally important book pay much attention to its amusing side. For reviews of the late Ming response to the novel, see Ono Shinobu, "Critical Study," pp. 85ff.; A Ying, *Hsien-t'an*, pp. 29ff.; Hanan, "Text," pp. 45ff.; Ts'ai Kuo-liang, "Ming-jen,

Chu-p'o and even Nung-chu k'e go so far as to claim that the work as a whole should be read as a kind of allegory.[231] While I acknowledge that this possibility does not really materialize, still at a number of points the author does set out clear signposts of linked figure and meaning of the sort that we find in true allegorical composition, to the extent that they challenge the reader to engage in active interpretation.

Examples of these pointed nodes of correlation are found in chapter 26, where the miscarriage suffered by Yüeh-niang is juxtaposed with a case of rank miscarriage of justice in Hsi-men Ch'ing's courtroom, or chapters 29 and 30, where the festivities surrounding the birth of Kuan-ko (the star-crossed "little official") are set against the rapid advancement of Hsi-men Ch'ing's own career as a *kuan* official. This parallel coordination of the short life of Kuan-ko with the rising fortunes of Hsi-men Ch'ing is pulled together in a series of subsequent scenes. For example, in chapter 39 the Taoist rituals for the sickly child overlap the gay celebration of P'an Chin-lien's birthday (also the occasion for prophetic homilies by visiting Buddhist nuns); in chapter 48 the baby's advancing debilitation is set against increasingly uninhibited garden frolics with Ch'en Ching-chi (in the family graveyard on the Ch'ing-ming Festival), reaching a crisis on the same day that Hsi-men Ch'ing is threatened with impeachment by the censor Tseng Hsiao-hsü 曾御史, 孝序; and in chapter 49 the frail child's rapid deterioration is mirrored in Hsi-men Ch'ing's rapid ascendance at court, crowned by his meeting with the strange monk who boosts his vigor to the point of no return.[232]

In the same vein, the author does not miss the chance to link the chilling demise of the baby in chapters 58 and 59 with a warm family celebration of Hsi-men Ch'ing's birthday (coming at a time of rising fortunes in business). As a final sardonic touch, he insists on setting the death of the child precisely on a day designated *jen-tzu* 壬子 in the cyclical reckoning, a day that already had been invested with a special significance as a day for

---

Ch'ing-jen, chin-jen"; C. T. Hsia, *Classic Novel*, p. 168; Carlitz, "Role of Drama," pp. 76ff., 366ff.; and Wei Tzu-yün, "Yüan Chung-lang," pp. 268f. (See below, Chapter 4, Part V, for a discussion of the late Ming response to *Shui-hu chuan*.)

[231] Chang Chu-p'o, "Allegorical, Meaning," p. 1a: "For the most part it may be taken as allegorical writing" 大半皆屬寓言.

[232] The connection between the birth of Hsi-men Ch'ing's baby and the launching of his career is sealed in the prophecy in chapter 29 (5b): "After the official is wounded, wounded beyond return, his fortune will be restored." The fact that Yüeh-niang suffers a miscarriage while she is viewing the new contruction on the Ch'iao family estate adds further meaning to the incident. Other examples of significant correlation of narrative events include the arrival of Ch'en Ching-chi in the middle of the affair with P'ing-erh (and in the middle of the construction of the pleasure garden to house her), and the coinciding of Hsi-men Ch'ing's final spiral of sexual excess with events at Court.

conception (based on the homophone *jen-tzu* 妊子, "to conceive a child"), in connection with the repeated attempts of Yüeh-niang and later Chin-lien to become pregnant.[233]

Perhaps the principal reason readers of the *Chin P'ing Mei* have been so reluctant to pursue the serious level of meaning to which these textual nodes and correlations ostensibly point is, paradoxically, the very fact that the book does offer within its pages an explicit didactic framework. From the opening disquisition on the wages of sin to the final "redemption" of Hsi-men Ch'ing's progeny Hsiao-ko, the reader is presented with a succession of pointed passages stressing the conception of karmic retribution that, in a simplistic sense, governs the entire plot of the novel. This message is periodically reemphasized in the various scenes of prophecy or Buddhist parables (literally, "tales of karmic consequence" 說因果) occurring at the close of certain textual decades, as well as through the frequent mention of metaphors of such things as the day of reckoning or the payment of one's dues, which were of considerable currency in popular religious thinking at the time of the novel's composition.[234] Therefore, if one were to follow the argument of Wu Han and others that the time of composition falls in a period of resurgence of Buddhist thought (and even

---

[233] The plans of Yüeh-niang, and later Chin-lien, for the productive use of *jen-tzu* nights are described in chapters 52, 53, 59, 62, 68, 73, and 75. Not accidentally, Yüeh-niang first learns this conception witchcraft in chapter 50, at the very moment that Hsi-men Ch'ing is trying out his own new secret of potency with Li P'ing-erh (an act to have tragic consequences). The fact that he receives the magic pills on Wang Liu-erh's birthday adds to the symbolic significance. See Martinson, "Pao, Order, and Redemption," p. 191, n. 1; and Carlitz, *Rhetoric*, pp. 66ff.

[234] Expressions of Buddhist concepts of the payment of debts or obligations for one's actions occur in chapters 10 (1a): "If you plant melons you get melons, if you plant beans you get beans" 種瓜得瓜, 種豆得豆; 29 (3b): "Every injustice has its responsible party, every debt has one to whom it is due" 冤有頭, 債有主; and 59 (18a). This is especially sarcastic in chapter 80 (11b): "Everything has its ultimate master" 物各有主. Chang Chu-p'o emphasizes these ideas in chapters 59 (*tp*), 60 (*tp*), 81 (*tp*); in his *tu-fa*, items 20, 78, and 92; in the prefatory essay "The Chin P'ing Mei is Not a Work of Pornography" (*Ti-i ch'i-shu fei yin-shu* 第一奇書非淫書); as well as in frequent comments on the name of the temple Pao-en ssu (literally, the "Temple of Beneficence Rewarded"). See also Chang's comments in chapters 14 (15b), 47 (2a), 49 (*tp*), 57 (*tp*), 67 (*tp*), 71 (*tp*), 88 (*tp*), and 100 (*tp*). In addition to instances of prophetic Buddhist narrations or fortunetelling in chapters 29, 39, 40, 46, 58, 62, 73, 74, 75, 82, 83, 88, and 95, this dimension of meaning is emphasized in suggestive dreams and visions at several points, especially chapters 71 and 100. The problematic digression of the Miao Ch'ing story in chapter 47 may be regarded as an exemplum of this sort embedded in the narrative. Many of the *k'an-kuan* passages also emphasize the later consequences of ongoing patterns of behavior, e.g., chapters 19 (4a–b), 30 (5a), 31 (4a), 62 (14a), 82 (4a), 87 (5a). For discussions of the various aspects of the concept of retribution in the novel, see Martinson, "Pao, Order, and Redemption," esp. chap. 5, pp. 328–408; Carlitz, *Rhetoric*, pp. 141ff.; Cheng P'ei-k'ai, "Hsü-pa," p. 32.

court patronage, at the expense of Taoism), then it should be easy to conclude that this is as far as the author has to go in providing a "message" for his book.[235]

Unfortunately, this obtrusive didactic framework of Buddhist retribution has left the majority of readers largely unconvinced. For one thing, the focus of the story is too intricately enmeshed in the sphere of human relations to admit any simple denial of the existential validity of the entire narrative world so painstakingly assembled in the novel.[236] More important, the author rarely foregoes a chance to call into question the credibility of the representatives of Buddhist wisdom who appear in the narrative in the guise of monks, nuns, and various old women mouthing pious platitudes. Among the *k'an-kuan* passages of authorial commentary, a number specifically decry the hypocrisy, venality, stupidity, and above all lust of these stereotyped figures.[237] And this conventional image is played up in many scenes in which these dubious celibates are caricatured, in accordance with the proverbial expression, as "hungry devils of lust" (*se-chung o-kuei* 色中餓鬼).[238]

This constant debunking begins as early as the uproarious scene in chapter 8, when a troop of monks rhythmically chanting sutras over the bier of Wu Ta gets caught up in a very different sort of rhythm that reaches their ears from the adjacent bedroom, and is carried through in the unholy concourse depicted among nuns, go-betweens, and other outcast social types.[239] This savage stripping away of monastic pretense to reveal a pudendous core culminates in the brilliant depiction of the "foreign monk" (*hu-seng* 胡僧), who bestows on Hsi-men Ch'ing the secret potency pills that eventually do him in. As David Roy has unflinchingly pointed out in a recent article, and as both the Ch'ung-chen commentator and Chang Chu-p'o clearly indicate in their marginal notes on the passage in question, the stylized description of this monk is couched in striking terms ("one-eyed dragon," "flesh-red cloak," and "sunken-eye in panther head" 獨眼龍,

---

[235] Wu Han, "Chin P'ing Mei ti chu-tso," pp. 24ff. For a review of the development of Buddhism in the late Ming period, see above, Chapter 1.

[236] Chang Chu-p'o (*tu-fa*, item 105) claims that the focus of the book is primarily "this-worldly" (*ju-shih* 入世), but at the same time "otherworldly" (*ch'u-shih* 出世). See Wei Tzu-yün's use of these terms in "Wang-kuan," p. 224.

[237] Chapters 12 (18a), 24 (2b), 68 (3b), 84 (4a). See above, nn. 197, 198.

[238] This proverbial expression occurs frequently in late Ming colloquial fiction. See, for example, *P'ai-an ching-ch'i*, no. 6, opening verse. The Ch'ung-chen commentator uses this expression in a biting remark in chapter 73 (28b–29a). Cf. the dark caricature of this type of celibate in the Taoist temple where Ch'en Ching-chi finds unwelcome solace in chapter 93.

[239] Cf. Hanan, "Sources," p. 31. Chang Chu-p'o rails at Yüeh-niang's susceptibility to pseudo-Buddhist preaching in many comments, for example, chapters 72 (16a), 75 (1a), and 100 (23a).

肉紅直裰, 豹頭凹眼, which undeniably identify him as a personification of the male organ.[240] The intrusion of this startling image precisely at the midpoint of the book ushers in the second half, in which the self-destruction of Hsi-men Ch'ing (followed by that of his tailing shadow, Ch'en Ching-chi) is causally linked to the overuse of this gift, leading to the conflation of his entire being down to this organ alone. In symbolic terms, what we witness in the final scenes of Hsi-men Ch'ing's demise is his gradual metamorphosis into the image of the strange monk—into a Priapus-like grotesque constituted of virtually nothing more than eyes and a phallus.

Toward the end of the book, this image of dubious salvation once again comes into play when another lone monk mysteriously appears, first in chapter 84 to rescue Yüeh-niang from dishonor (at the price of forfeiting Hsi-men Ch'ing's posterity), and then again in chapter 100 to collect his pledge.[241] At this point, the earlier identification of Kuan-ko as a "little monk" (*hsiao ho-shang* 小和尚) rings in its special irony.

The procession of these linked figures leads to a point at which the Buddhist monks, with all their pronouncements on the eternal "Void" (*k'ung* 空), come to symbolize its conceptual opposite: *se* 色, signifying worldly illusion in general and sexuality in particular. Even without the consistent undercutting of these Buddhist spokesmen, however, the lip-service paid thorugh repeated admonitions to awaken from the illusion of sensual reality to the truth of emptiness still rings somewhat hollow within the context of what is arguably the most convincing mimetic presentation of worldly experience in all of Chinese literature (with the possible exception of the *Hung-lou meng*, which is greatly indebted to the *Chin P'ing Mei*, precisely on this point).[242] Ultimately, even Chang Chu-p'o himself must throw up his hands and admit that the author's bodhisattva-like intimations

[240] See Ch'ung-chen commentary, 49 (43a): "Just look at this monk; what does he look like?" 看此僧, 却像何物…; and further on: "The deportment of this monk is actually not very different from that of a male organ" 和尚擧止與陽物原差不遠; and Chang Chu-p'o, 49 (12b–13b): "Of all the myriad characters in the book, only this monk is written unambiguously" 一部萬言人物, 此僧獨顯然寫出… "What does he look like" 像甚麼… "It's what the people in *Shui-hu chuan* would call 'one of those damned things'" 水滸中人所云一片鳥東西也. See David Roy, "Confucian Interpretation," pp. 52f.; and Martinson, "Pao, Order and Redemption," pp. 205ff. See also the early poems in which Hsi-men Ch'ing and P'an Chin-lien are humorously identified with their sexual organs (4: 4a–b, 5b–6a). Chang Chu-p'o describes Hsi-men Ch'ing's final transformation into a phallus figure in comments in chapter 80 (*tp* and 30b).

[241] This figural chain is reinforced with the appearance of another "Indian monk" in chapter 57. See Chang Chu-p'o, 57 (8b).

[242] For discussions of the debt of *Hung-lou meng* to *Chin P'ing Mei*, see K'an To, "Hung-lou meng chüeh-wei" and "Chin-Hung ts'o-yü," in *P'ing-wai chih-yen*, pp. 78–99; Hsü Shuo-fang, "Hung-lou meng ho Chin P'ing Mei," pp. 143–62; and Chu Hsing, *K'ao-cheng*, pp. 96–100. See Mary E. Scott, "Image of the Garden," for discussion and additional references.

of transcendent emptiness in the final resolution leave him somewhat cold. He complains, in one of the most revealing discussions in his *tu-fa* introduction, that if the author had gone one step beyond the presentation of emptiness into the realm of "nonemptiness" (*pu-k'ung* 不空), he would have written a better book.[243]

Because of the unconvincing nature of this Buddhist message, many of the readers of the novel have concluded that its entire didactic framework is nothing more than a pretentious sham or, at best, an elaborate excuse on the part of the author for writing what is essentially a work of pornography—perhaps hoping to deceive the more moral-minded among his readers (or his censors) with a few choice protestations of pious intent, or perhaps deluding himself into believing that his own interests in exploring sexual experience were something other than prurient. More to the point, I might add that by the time of the composition of the *Chin P'ing Mei* the use of Buddhist didactics had been incorporated into the generic outlines of the novel as a conventional narrative framework to provide fixed structural outlines even where the doctrinal message does not really apply.[244] Before my interpretation of the novel reaches its conclusion, however, I will attempt to show that the idea of Buddhist retribution and the concepts of sensual illusion and emptiness do, in fact, play a very significant role in the projection of meaning in the book, as long as we do not take them at face value.

In order to refute the view of *Chin P'ing Mei* as no more than a positive or negative exploration of sexual behavior in general, or at least that of one jolly fellow in particular, it will be necessary at this point to take a careful look at the passages of erotic description that loom so large in the impression of the book for most readers over the past four centuries. Perhaps Chang Chu-p'o is being too facetious when he claims that "anyone who says that the *Chin P'ing Mei* is an obscene book has probably only taken the trouble to read the obscene passages" 凡人謂金瓶梅是淫書者想必伊止知看其淫處也, but his impassioned argument in the essay entitled *"Chin P'ing Mei* Is Not a Work of Pornography" ("Ti-i ch'i-shu fei yin-shu") in actuality follows a line already set out in the Nung-chu k'e and Nien-kung prefaces, and closer to Chang, in the Ch'ung-chen commentary.[245] In this light, Chu Hsing and other recent scholars seem to miss the point when

---

[243] Chang Chu-p'o, *tu-fa*, item 75. Chang describes the work as a vehicle of enlightenment in items 57, 72, 75, 79, 91, 100, and 101. See also his comments in chapters 1 (*tp*), 25 (*tp*), 39 (*tp*), 57 (7a), 79 (*tp*), and 100 (*tp*).

[244] For discussions of the use of the notion of karmic retribution as a structural rather than a doctrinal framework, see my *"After the Fall"*; and Martinson, "Pao, Order, and Redemption," pp. 59ff., 126ff.

[245] Chang Chu-p'o, *tu-fa*, item 53. Similar ideas appear in items 52, 56, and 82, and also in "Not Pornography," p. la: "That is why they view it as a pornographic book, not realizing that in fact it is the licentious who are thus perceiving their own licentiousness" 所以目為

they attempt to prove that the "obscene parts" were only added in the seventeenth-century editions and do not represent the original intention of the author.[246]

In attempting to come to terms with the function of these erotic passages, we must recognize, first, that in terms of sheer quantity they do not occupy as large a space as many readers—perhaps guilty of the type of reading insinuated by Chang Chu-p'o—have felt. This has long since been pointed out by Cheng Chen-to and others.[247] In fact, the total number of passages of true extended erotic description is fairly limited, to the extent that a thorough student can easily recall nearly all of the major examples. For this reason, as Cheng Chen-to remarks, the later expurgated editions do not significantly alter the shape of the novel—as they would, say, in a book like *Jou p'u-t'uan* 肉蒲團.[248] This point is especially noticeable since, as we know, the sixteenth century in China was a time of considerable publication of erotic fiction—some of which figures among the sources of *Chin P'ing Mei*. Thus, any restraint the author shows in this regard—the reputation of the novel notwithstanding—must be viewed as a deliberate artistic choice.[249]

The real question we have to consider, therefore, is the quality rather than the quantity of the sexual description in the novel. Granted, this is a matter of personal sensibility, but I would hazard to say that in the entire vast narrative of *Chin P'ing Mei* the number of scenes depicting erotic experience in sympathetic terms are no more than a handful, and those that could by any stretch of the imagination be taken as a glorification of the sex act, of the sort modern apologists of pornography might seek here, are practically nonexistent.[250] One does find a few scenes in which we can see

---

淫書, 不知淫者自見其爲淫耳. Cf. the comment in the Ch'ung-chen edition (97 [19a]) referred to above, n. 99. See also Wei Tzu-yün, *Shen-t'an*, pp. 94ff., 155ff.

[246] For example, Chu Hsing, *K'ao-cheng*, pp. 260ff. See Carlitz, *Rhetoric*, pp. 44ff., and "Puns and Puzzles," pp. 216ff.; and Hou Chien 侯健, "Chin P'ing Mei lun," introduction to reprint of *Chin P'ing Mei tzu-hua* (Taipei: Tseng-ni-chih wen-hua shih-yeh, 1980).

[247] Cheng Chen-to, "T'an Chin P'ing Mei," pp. 253ff. This idea is echoed in Wei Tzu-yün, *Wen-shih yü yen-pien*, pp. 63f.; André Lévy, review of Sun Shu-yü, *I-shu*; and Chu Hsing, *K'ao-cheng*, pp. 59f. Even in Robert H. van Gulik's *Sexual Life in Ancient China*, the *Chin P'ing Mei* is described as a relatively mild reflection of Ming erotica (pp. 287ff.).

[248] If anything, the most damaging result of expurgation is that the practice of inserting empty squares in the place of excised words may encourage the reader to fantasize, weaving scenes in his imagination that may outdo the original.

[249] For a review of Ming erotic literature, see van Gulik, *Sexual Life*, passim. See also Hanan, "Sources," pp. 43–47, and his "Erotic Novel"; and Lévy, "Une texte burlesque du 16ᵉ siècle dans le style de la chantefable," pp. 119–24; R. K. McMahon, "The Gap in the Wall," chapter 3; and Cheng P'ei-k'ai, "Hsü-pa."

[250] A sensitive, nonscholarly reading of this aspect of the novel is provided by Liu Shih-ku (pseudonym, Tung-kuo hsien-sheng), in *Hsien-hua Chin P'ing Mei*.

something resembling warm affection, mutual pleasure, or at least honest desire. Among these I would list the first half of chapter 27, Hsi-men Ch'ing's night with Yüeh-niang after a long absence in chapter 55, or Ch'en Ching-chi's sexual respite with Feng Chin-pao 馮金寶 in chapter 93 after experiencing much frustration and abuse.[251] But in virtually every other instance it can be demonstrated that, in one way or another, the author deliberately withholds the potential pleasure he has led the reader to eagerly await, so as to ultimately deny or deflate the sort of vicarious release that some pornography pretends to offer. In the following pages, I will attempt to support the above generalization by analyzing in detail various devices by means of which the author achieves this end.

One of the most obvious ways in which the author manages to put a measure of distance between the reader and his vicarious delight is through the use of humor in the treatment of sexual acts.[252] In addition to such examples as the burlesque in chapter 8 and the grotesque tour de force in chapter 49, already discussed, there are the early pair of poems on the respective sexual parts of Hsi-men Ch'ing and P'an Chin-lien in chapter 4, the "mosquito double-entendre" (*wen-tzu shuang-kuan* 蚊子雙關) in chapter 18, the bawdy poem on plucking "the flower in the rear courtyard" (*hou-t'ing hua* 後庭花) in chapter 38 (5a–b), and especially the mock-heroic treatment of sexual combat with P'an Chin-lien in chapter 16, and with Madame Lin in chapter 69 (*feng-liu chen*)—all of which effectively deflate our tendency to become emotionally involved in the acts portrayed.[253] Elements of these various jokes come together in chapter 80, when the eulogy for Hsi-men Ch'ing penned by his erstwhile scholar-brothers turns out to be a mock-serious parody, nearly every line of which refers quite transparently to his principal part.[254]

This same tongue-in-cheek irreverence also governs the continuing series of scenes involving the gradually advancing relations between P'an Chin-lien and Ch'en Ching-chi, whose fumbling attempts to commit incest are foiled time after time. Throughout the body of the novel this chain of incidents reads like a sexual farce of the first order, becoming more serious only after the death of Hsi-men Ch'ing leaves them free to indulge their

[251] For an appreciation of the affectionate half of chapter 27, see Frederick W. Mote, "Yuan and Ming," pp. 248ff.

[252] See Carlitz, "Role of Drama," pp. 69, 74ff., and "Puns and Puzzles," pp. 236f.

[253] The mosquito image is brought back in a comparably sweaty sexual scene in chapter 82 (6a–b). The mock-heroic description of the first encounter with Madame Lin is introduced again in a subsequent tryst in chapter 78 (9b). See also 29 (13a).

[254] See David Roy, "Confucian Interpretation," p. 57. Both Chang Chu-p'o (80 [*tp*, 30b]) and the Ch'ung-chen commentator (80 [78b]) point out the presence of this joke. A similar example of double-entendre in chapter 78 (9b–10a) identifies Hsi-men Ch'ing as "an adamantine demon of sex and wine" 一員酒金剛色魔王.

fancies. One might also include as an example of this comic treatment the deflation of erotic solemnity through the frequent use of hyperbolic expressions, especially stereotyped metaphors about mating phoenixes and frolicking fish, although it seems to be laughter of another sort when the author turns increasingly to animal imagery to mock his heroes' sexual indiscretions.[255]

This last point brings us to an important general statement about narrative technique, one that applies in the discussion of our other three novels as well. In setting up chains of recurrent figures, the classic Chinese novelist tends to begin with a lighter treatment of his basic themes, before moving gradually toward more serious implications. Whether we conclude that the author of *Chin P'ing Mei* carefully plotted this sort of unfolding of significance, or that it is simply a case of slowly coming to grips with the underlying meaning of the human experience he re-creates, we may observe here a more or less steady movement from lighthearted, even boisterous treatment of the sexual escapades of Hsi-men Ch'ing, P'an Chin-lien, Ch'en Ching-chi, and others—not without its own prurient interest—to a point at which the erotic scenes are no longer funny, or for that matter sexy, and ultimately become deadly serious.

This is particularly clear in the treatment of the relationship between Hsi-men Ch'ing and P'an Chin-lien. In the opening ten-chapter section adapted from *Shui-hu chuan*, the author maintains a light touch and exercises considerable ingenuity to ensure that the tale of corruption, infidelity, and even brutal murder does not evoke a reaction of shock or horror. Instead, it reads like an exuberant tale on the age-old theme of cuckoldry, which, like so many examples in Boccaccio and elsewhere in European literature, cannot help but amuse the reader in spite of any general reservations he may have regarding adultery and murder. The fact that practically every reader of the novel, I suppose, must be pleased to see Hsi-men Ch'ing jump from an upper-story window and escape his just deserts (which are visited upon him by Wu Sung at that point in the *Shui-hu* original) is probably a direct function of the rhetorical tone employed in this section. It is also a function of the obvious attempt on the part of the author to make P'an Chin-lien, at this stage at least, genuinely attractive—both physically alluring and admirably self-possessed. Several comments by the Ch'ung-chen editor demonstrate that it is not just the modern reader's predisposition to sympathize with brash self-reliance that makes her an attractive figure at this point.[256] But as soon as the author goes beyond his

---

[255] For example, chapters 19 (3a), 57 (12b), 75 (23a), and 85 (5a).

[256] Ch'ung-chen edition, chapters 4 (42b), 12 (17b), and especially 79 (58b): "Even though I am fully aware that she is the instrument of his destruction, I can't help feeling an irresistible attraction to her" 雖明知其爲送死之具, 使我當之亦不得不愛. Cf. the attrac-

ready-made source materials and moves deeper into his own development of characters and themes, the mood of playful spontaneity and infectious exuberance of his initial treatment turns increasingly sour. The sexual encounters between the two become less and less pleasurable, more and more exercises in mutual domination, until by the final bout in chapter 79 the ground has been prepared for a scene of sexual horror scarcely matched in all literature.

A second device by which the author of the *Chin P'ing Mei* contrives to dampen the enthusiastic response of the reader to his sexual scenes is through his manipulation of the placement of these scenes within the flow of the narrative. That is, a good many of the passages of sexual description appear immediately contiguous to instances of violence or corruption, so as to produce negative associations that cannot but detract from the pleasurable effect. For example, the rampant sexual excesses in chapter 27 are sandwiched between the wrap-up of the Hui-lien affair, concluding with the cruel treatment of Hui-lien's father and the beating of servants that occupies much of chapter 28. Similarly, the amusing bedroom scene in chapter 38 follows immediately upon an instance of corruption and torture in the case of Wang Liu-erh's brother-in-law, Han Erh 韓二 (Han Tao-kuei 韓搗鬼).

A particularly favored variation on this pattern is the device of interrupting passionate embraces with the intrusion of a third figure, who provides a reminder of the context in which the scenes are played out. For example in chapter 11, just as P'an Chin-lien is struggling to consolidate her position in Hsi-men Ch'ing's household, their lovemaking is interrupted by her mother's visit to the compound, and this pattern is repeated in chapter 20, when Hsi-men Ch'ing's consummation of P'ing-erh's installation within the circle of wives is broken up by the sudden intrusion of Chin-lien and Meng Yü-lou—the same pair who appear on the scene to dispel another tender love scene between these two in the beginning of chapter 27.[257] As the narrative proceeds, Chin-lien's frequent intrusions into the intimacy of Hsi-men Ch'ing and P'ing-erh appear more and more deliberate—as in the example just mentioned in chapter 38, again in chapter 41 when she wakes up the sleeping baby whose crying then pulls P'ing-erh

---

tive descriptions of Chin-lien in the first few chapters, e.g., chapters 2 (4b–5a) and 3 (8a). As late as chapter 12, we still do not really hold her vindictive affair with Ch'in-t'ung against her. Chang Chu-p'o provides among his prefatory pieces a tongue-in-cheek listing of all the individuals with whom Chin-lien, and Hsi-men Ch'ing carry on their sexual excesses ("P'an Chin-lien yin-kuo jen mu" 潘金蓮淫過人目).

[257] Additional examples include the arrival of Ch'un-mei during a tête-à-tête between Hsi-men Ch'ing and P'ing-erh in chapter 34, the intrusion of Ying Po-chüeh on Hsi-men Ch'ing's seclusion with Ai-yüeh-erh in chapter 68, and Ch'un-mei's discovery of Chin-lien and Ch'en Ching-chi at the moment of their long-awaited union in chapter 82.

from Hsi-men Ch'ing's embrace, and in chapter 78, when she sends Ta-chieh to interrupt a visit by Hsi-men to Sun Hsüeh-o's room. In another recurrent variation on the pattern, the author several times reserves the role of the intruder for a waggish child or other prankish figure (e.g., Tai-an in chapters 16 and 78 and Hsiao T'ieh-kun-erh in chapter 27, an obvious figural replay of the appearance of Yün-ko in chapter 4). Sometimes, as we have seen, this function degenerates into the uncomprehending stares of dogs or cats.[258]

The device of interrupting sexual scenes is used with most pointed effect in the repeated unsuccessful attempts of P'an Chin-lien and Ch'en Ching-chi to fulfill their incestuous infatuation. As already mentioned, this long chain of last-minute interruptions produces a farcical effect that teases the reader by keeping him waiting through the entire main body of the book, from their first advances in chapter 20, until their final union in chapter 82. But a number of cutting hints indicate that more is involved here than long-term titillation. Thus, one near embrace in the garden in chapter 52 is interrupted by the arrival of P'ing-erh, out for a stroll with her baby, and in the next chapter it is the barking of a dog, signaling the return of Hsi-men Ch'ing, that cuts short an incipient scene of passion. This latter occurrence is one of the most sardonic, since Hsi-men Ch'ing not only intrudes into their incomplete embrace, but goes on to take over where Ch'en Ching-chi abruptly leaves off, carrying it to its physical conclusion—with only perfunctory measures of hygiene on the part of Chin-lien.[259]

Aside from such examples of the rhetorical debunking or structural overshadowing of the allure of sexual scenes, the key question for us here is, again, the *quality* of the sexual behavior that is shown. On this score we find the strongest evidence against the view of *Chin P'ing Mei* as a work of pleasurable pornography. In order to establish this point beyond doubt, it will be necessary to dwell in considerable detail on some of the more unsavory aspects of the sexual behavior presented in the book, for which I beg the reader's indulgence.

First, we should note that the vast majority of the sexual connections in the novel are the expression of illegitimate unions. These relations range from lightly treated instances of infidelity (such as Chin-lien's dalliance with Ch'in-t'ung in chapter 12), to liaisons that are flagrantly adulterous (such as Hsi-men Ch'ing's afternoons with Pen Ssu's wife and Wang Liu-erh, in which the ready collusion of the husband in each case stains the match still further), and finally to relations that are patently or symbolically

---

[258] See above, Part III.

[259] Similar examples occur in chapter 73, when Chin-lien takes over for Ch'un-mei, and 78, when Tai-an and P'ing-an replace Hsi-men Ch'ing in the arms of Pen Ssu's wife.

incestuous. For that matter, even Hsi-men Ch'ing's circle of lawful conjugal partners includes P'an Chin-lien and Li P'ing-erh, whose relations with him are conceived in blood; Li Chiao-erh, a former prostitute who runs off with his money and his friends before his body is cold; and Sun Hsüeh-o, who despite her nominal status remains a caricature of lowliness throughout the book.[260] The figural parallels that are set up between Hsi-men Ch'ing's legitimate wives and the prostitutes he frequents, as considered in my analysis of vertical parallelism, also constantly remind us of this side of the picture. In several places the author manages to manipulate brilliantly the narrative point of view to have us see these courtesans (especially Li Kuei-chieh and Cheng Ai-yüeh-erh) through the eyes of Hsi-men Ch'ing as visions of surpassing loveliness. But we are shown in other scenes that what seem at first to be elegant beauties of the type catalogued in classics such as *Pan-ch'iao tsa-chi* 板橋雜記 are, in fact, little more than yamen call girls, who, as we learn, are easily bought for the night by gross merchants and wanton youths. This deliberate cheapening is underscored in the frequent depiction of vulgar patrons, rapacious madames, and ugly brawls in the "pleasure quarters."[261]

The roster of unsavory sexual relations depicted in the novel must also include the several examples of homosexuality presented: Hsi-men Ch'ing's dalliance with Shu-t'ung 書童 in his study in chapter 34, his unconcealed infatuation for the singing boys given by Miao Yüan-wai in chapter 55, his recourse to the bed of Wang Ching 王經 in chapter 71, and his jealous rage at the old tutor Wen Pi-ku for practicing pederasty with one of his favorites in chapter 76. It may perhaps be objected that these aberrations are intended more as evidence of heterosexual insatiability spilling beyond normal boundaries, and are not necessarily intended as affronts to the reader's sensibility. But within the context of the novel itself, these escapades are invariably hushed up by the participants as something shameful and, when discovered, are the subject of intense ridicule. The author himself rarely misses an opportunity to take a poke at these proclivities by assigning punning names to figures such as Wen Pi-ku (discussed earlier)—and I suspect also Wang Ching—and taking repeated potshots at "southern-style" love (*nan-feng* 南風), in which *nan* (南 "southern") puns on

---

[260] I will consider the treatment of Yüeh-niang and Meng Yü-lou below. The only bedroom scenes I can find between Hsi-men Ch'ing and Sun Hsüeh-o, in chapters 58 (1b) and 78 (12b–13a), are strikingly unerotic and seem designed mainly to prepare the reader for the distasteful scenes about to occur.

[261] Such brawls occur in chapters 12 and 20. Cf. the brawl that takes place in the Yung-fu-ssu temple in chapter 57. On the reflection between wives and prostitutes, see Carlitz, *Rhetoric*, pp. 47f. Hanan notes in "Erotic Novel" (p. 15) that prostitutes do not figure in any major scenes in Ming erotic fiction.

nan (男 "male").[262] In any case, this sarcasm reaches its peak toward the end, when Ch'en Ching-chi is more than once raped by gangs of hoodlum priests, and is himself made into the "wife" of the leader of a beggar band.

Moving on to the actual detailed description of heterosexual practices, we may note the special care taken by the author to inform the reader of the particular predilections of Hsi-men Ch'ing's principal partners. Of course, anyone familiar with the literature and engravings of the period is aware that the use of metaphorical terms such as "flower in the rear courtyard" would have been received more with amusement than shock.[263] But in practically every instance of close-up description, the author manages to take us beyond initial titillation to leave us with profoundly negative impressions. Here the use of the principle of figural recurrence: first setting up a pattern then plumbing it for significance, comes into full play. The clearest instance of this is the repeated description of P'an Chin-lien's predilection for mounting her sexual partner. Early in the book this is nothing more than one possible variation of sexual posture, one that, incidentally, provides an additional figural link between Chin-lien and Li P'ing-erh.[264] But by the time we arrive at chapter 79, the image of Chin-lien astride Hsi-men Ch'ing's limp body emerges with full horror as nothing more or less than that of a vampire, relentlessly draining away his life essence (a striking parallel to the pose of Acrasia in Book II of Spenser's almost exactly contemporary epic). At this point it becomes clear that the author has carefully laid out a path of figural recurrence leading up to this final fulfillment of the image of domination. The reader now recalls that it was precisely in this straddling posture that she had snuffed out the life of Wu Ta, and is thus well prepared for the brilliantly conceived symmetry in the final chapter, when Ch'un-mei also dies of sexual exhaustion "astride the body of Chou I" 死在周義身上.

The same development can be seen in the treatment of a number of other sexual practices, ranging from the mildly kinky to the out-and-out perverse—where the author moves from an initially playful mood to later force the reader to confront the implications of what he is viewing. To take one more example of this, the author sets up another chain of recurrence in the book involving the tying up of one partner in sexual play. The reader with a tolerance for this sort of thing may perhaps laugh off the notorious

---

[262] On Hsi-men Ch'ing's fascination for the singing boys offered him by Miao Yüan-wai in chapter 55, the Ch'ung-chen edition's version of the title of the chapter is a little bit more explicit. Instances of "southern-style" love appear in chapters 34 (18a), 35 (3b, 9a), 36 (6a), and 49 (6b). See Yao Ling-hsi, "Hsiao-cha," p. 191; and van Gulik, *Sexual Life*, p. 289.

[263] Chang Chu-p'o tries, quite unconvincingly, to apply an allegorical reading to the term *hou-t'ing hua* in his "Allegorical Meaning," p. 3b. See van Gulik, *Sexual Life*, p. 289.

[264] For example, chapter 16 (3b).

scene under the grape trellis in chapter 27, but by chapter 73, when it is Chin-lien who devises a certain kind of strap to boost the nearly spent Hsi-men Ch'ing, the full implications of mechanical manipulation of the sexual partner as an object become unmistakable.[265] A similar case of role reversal links an incident in chapter 29, in which Hsi-men Ch'ing possesses his exhausted partner in her sleep, with its final inversion in chapter 79. Likewise, the multipartner frolic in chapter 27 is echoed with more serious implications in instances of shared sex in chapters 53, 73, and elsewhere.

This tendency to color the treatment of sex as mutual dominance and destruction is intensified after the turning point in chapter 49, when Hsi-men Ch'ing receives his transforming drug from the phallic monk. It completely takes over during the course of the final ten-chapter phase of his life, in which he is sucked into a whirlpool of frenzied pursuits, with each chapter introducing a new example of unsalutary sexuality. In all of these instances, the author carefully manipulates his details to emphasize the constant theme of sexual domination. This conclusion is inescapable in chapter 72, when an especially distasteful act is depicted as a deliberate attempt by Chin-lien to break down Hsi-men's self-control in order to extract favors from him (in particular, the gift of P'ing-erh's cloak, at once a symbol of her wealth and of Hsi-men Ch'ing's affection for her). And lest the reader miss the point, he repeats the same detail in a scene soon afterward with Ju-i, once again to obtain a special favor—this time a promise to elevate her to fill the conjugal position (*pu-wo* 補窩) vacated by P'ing-erh.[266] Another example of the recurrent theme of sexual activity directed toward physical and psychological domination appears in the encounters with Madame Lin and with Ju-i in chapter 78, in which one of the most bizarre practices in the book—burning moxa on the female pudenda (this act is repeated for emphasis in two separate scenes)—sets the stage for Hsi-men Ch'ing's demand for absolute submission with the words "Whose woman are you?" 你是誰的老婆?, before he finally grants his sexual bounty.

Scenes of sexual aggression such as this need not necessarily be viewed as sadomasochistic, but no matter what they clearly resonate with the textual linkage observed earlier between sexual and nonsexual violence to establish yet another core of meaning for the novel. We have just seen the very strong implication of sexual murder in the final image of P'an Chin-lien as succubus, and this is only the final realization of a long chain

[265] The numbers 27 and 73 make this even more interesting. See also chapters 28 (1b), 61 (6a), 82 (6a), and 83 (9a, b) for additional examples. Cf. Yao Ling-hsi, "Hsiao-cha," pp. 137, 194; and R. K. McMahon, "Eroticism in Late Ming Fiction" (unpublished paper), pp. 21ff.

[266] See, especially, chapters 72, 73, 77, 78, and 79. the Ch'ung-chen commentator protests the first incident in chapter 72 (18a).

of hints in the text (even before the cruel murder of Wu Ta, Chin-lien had already drained the vitality of Chang Ta-hu 張大戶), which eventually leads to the fulfillment of Hsi-men Ch'ing's own pledge in chapter 5: "If I ever betray your love, may I end up just like Wu Ta" 我若負了心, 就是武大一般.[267]

Of key importance here is the mirror-opposite relationship of sexual destruction that holds between Hsi-men Ch'ing and Li P'ing-erh. As the narrative proceeds, numerous hints are dropped to the effect that Hsi-men is himself somehow responsible for the death of his beloved P'ing-erh—in a more direct sense than simply his general failure to keep the unsettling rivalries in the household in check. These hints are not missed by either of our seventeenth-century commentators, but they are easy to overlook and must be pulled together here.[268]

This chain of significance begins in chapter 50, immediately after the crucial midpoint of the book, when Hsi-men Ch'ing insists on trying out his newly intensified sexual power on P'ing-erh during her menstrual period, despite her pleas for forbearance. This point sends a flash of recollection back to chapter 27, to a figurally similar scene in which P'ing-erh had complained of pain in intercourse during her early pregnancy, and casts light ahead to her progressive decline marked by frequent references to profuse vaginal bleeding as the central symptom of her debilitation.[269] This is explicitly stated in the doctors' diagnoses in chapters 54 and 55, and in chapter 61 her problem is unflinchingly attributed to "an infusion of semen in her blood" 精冲了血....[270]

Aside from these examples of the pointed connection drawn between sex and suffering, we observe many instances in which the desired pleasure

[267] Chapter 5 (9a–b). Cf. Hanan's discussion of the connection made between sex and power in the novel, in "Landmark." See also Carlitz, *Rhetoric*, pp. 48ff.; Hanan, "Erotic Novel," pp. 21ff.; and McMahon, "Eroticism in Fiction," pp. 18ff. Another example may be seen in Hsi-men Ch'ing's cruel humiliation of Li P'ing-erh upon her entry into the family in chapter 19. Cf. the *k'an-kuan* passage in chapter 13 (12a). Hanan identifies the source of the description of moxa burning in "Sources," p. 45.

[268] Cf. Ch'ung-chen edition comment in chapter 73 (38a): "If he is willing to go to such lengths in the 'cultivation of the self' and the 'pursuit of learning,' can there be any fear that he will not reach the utmost in his endeavors?" 修身爲學肯如此何患不造其極？ See Martinson, "Pao, Order, and Redemption," p. 394; and Sun Shu-yü, "Ming-ming," p. 12.

[269] See Chang Chu-p'o, chapter 51 (4b), and Ch'ung-chen commentary, chapter 50 (54a), which isolates this incident as the "root of the problem" (*ping-ken* 病根).

[270] See chapters 50 (10a), 54 (10b, 12b, 13a), 55 (1a, b), 60 (1b), 61 (21b). David Roy discusses this in "Confucian Interpretation," p. 53. In Chapter 53 (6b) Yüeh-niang puts Hsi-men Ch'ing off (it is not a *jen-tzu* day) by claiming that her period has come unexpectedly 月經左來日子, and in chapter 75 (18a) we see Hsi-men Ch'ing make love to Meng Yü-lou in her sickbed. See Carlitz, "Role of Drama," pp. 127f., and *Rhetoric*, pp. 49f.; and Cass, "Celebrations," p. 35.

is reduced to a minimum, if it is not totally absent. In a more comic sense, this applies to the recurrent scenes of the frustrated desire of P'an Chin-lien and Ch'en Ching-chi, described in metaphors of furtive animals in chapter 57; and even when they finally begin to achieve their long-sought aim, their transports are hurried and are usually immediately interrupted. This same sense seems to govern the final phases of Hsi-men Ch'ing's sexual trajectory, as even his most frenetic experiences are progressively emptied of emotional fulfillment. This trend reaches rock bottom in chapter 78, when the spent hero, literally on the run, pauses to lie in an alleyway with a maid whose name he hardly knows—an encounter almost totally devoid of any human feeling other than momentary release.

This is just one of a whole chain of scenes built around the inconsequentiality, or emptiness, of Hsi-men Ch'ing's spiral of sexual incontinence. By the time of the chilling end in chapter 79, it becomes clear that what we have witnessed is the progressive draining or drying up of Hsi-men Ch'ing's vital essence, a final state of profound symbolic significance within the context of the larger philosophical issue of emptiness and sensory illusion (*se-k'ung*) seriously raised in the novel. As David Roy has convincingly argued, this pattern of meaning seems to be behind the author's frequent use of images expressing the leaking away, or exhausting, of both his monetary and his sexual potency, as he careers uncontrollably toward his end.[271] Chang Chu-p'o also takes due note of this as a key to his interpretation of the novel. He seems to be indulging in a fanciful reading when he argues, in his essay "Allegorical Meaning in the *Chin P'ing Mei*," that the name of the "Temple of Eternal Prosperity" (*Yung-fu ssu* 永福寺) ought to be glossed as *yung yü fu-hsia* 湧于腹下 ("leaking out below the belly"), but in a number of other discussions he backs up this reading with more convincing textual support.[272] At any rate, many lines in the text emphasize precisely this point at the time of Hsi-men Ch'ing's death, for example in the poem on his last bout with Madame Lin in chapter 78 (10a–b): "... she seized his vital essence and sucked his marrow" (*to-ching hsi-sui* 奪精吸髓); or in the author's pseudo-medical explanation in a *k'an-kuan* passage in chapter 79 (9b–10a): "... he didn't realize that his oil was running dry, his lamp about to be extinguished, that his marrow would be exhausted and his life would be lost" ⋯不知油枯燈盡, 髓竭人亡. And as we have seen, the author does not fail to conclude his vast narrative, true to form, with a final restatement of this theory in very

[271] Roy, "Confucian Interpretation," pp. 58. See also Carlitz, *Rhetoric*, pp. 46ff.; and Sun Shu-yü, "Chin P'ing Mei ti ch'eng-chiu," p. 18.

[272] Chang Chu-p'o, "Allegorical Meaning," p. 5a, and chapters 72 (20a), 79 (12a), and 99 (11a). The compound *yung-ch'üan* appears in the text itself in a crucial line in chapter 78 (16a).

similar language in his description of Ch'un-mei's fatal exhaustion in the last chapter.[273]

These various expressions of the draining or emptying of sexual vitality are not isolated metaphors; in fact, the author carefully sets up this axis of meaning for his book. One most telling example occurs in a passage in chapter 71, where in the midst of his triumphal visit to the imperial court, capping the very height of his dreams of grandeur, Hsi-men Ch'ing sleeps alone (we had been told of his loneliness and discomfort in sleeping alone at the time of his first visit to the capital in chapter 55), and his restless dreams of the lost P'ing-erh end in involuntary ejaculation. The author brilliantly captures the cold emptiness of this experience through his manipulation of imagery: the cold room, the brittle moonlight (*yüeh-se* 月色), P'ing-erh's snowy body. The Ch'ung-chen commentator captures all the vacuousness of the moment in the following comment:

> This depiction of the world of dream can be called a consummate evocation of the sense of cold desolation, and when he adds the touch of the involuntary ejaculation, I can only respond with a laugh. In the free play of the author's literary sensibility he is not the slightest bit confined by the limitations of his prose.
> 寫夢境可謂幽冷有致又帶夢遺發一笑文心戲處決不爲筆墨縛來.

The implications of this empty dream are again driven home the next day, when he seeks solace in the homosexual embrace of Wang Ching, and the following night he finds himself cold and alone in an ancient temple on the way home.[274]

The same imagery of cold emptiness is woven in and out of the final phase of Hsi-men Ch'ing's destruction. This is crystallized in chapter 79 (7b) when, leaving the bed of Wang Liu-erh after a wild and exhausting bout, he steps out again into the bright emptiness of the moonlight (*yüeh-se*). As he passes over a stone bridge, a dark shadow crosses his path and his horse rears, sending him into a fit of shivers (*leng-chan*)—a term that refers back figurally to the ominous chills of Kuan-ko, while also preparing him for the final assault at the hands of P'an Chin-lien.[275]

---

[273] Cf. Hsi-men's complaints of "flagging vital energy" 沒精神 in the last phase of his life (e.g., chapter 79 [3b]). The description of Ch'un-mei's self-destruction in chapter 100 (6b) includes the following expressions: "She had depleted her vital energy, her body was as thin as a stick of wood, yet her insatiable lust continued unabated ..." 消了精神, 體瘦如柴, 而貪淫不已…

[274] See the Ch'ung-chen commentary (71 [6a]) and Chang Chu-p'o (71 [*tp*]). Given the layers of meaning in this episode, I am convinced that the name Wang Ching 王經 is intended to pun on 亡精. Cf. Chang Chu-p'o's gloss in "Allegorical Meaning," p. 3a–b.

[275] The author may be indulging in an additional play on the word *chan* 戰, as it also figures in the final destruction of Hsi-men (cf. the expressions *liang-chan* 兩戰 and *chiu-chan* 久戰). See Carlitz, "Role of Drama," pp. 126ff.

One final theme through which the author explores the vacuity of inconsequential sexuality is seen in recurrent instances of voyeurism. In a number of scenes this is simply a matter of the playful peeking of a variety of pranksters (T'ieh-kun-erh in chapter 27, Ch'in-t'ung in chapter 50, the maids Ying-ch'un 迎春 in chapter 13 and Yü-hsiao 玉蕭 in chapter 23, even Ying Po-chüeh, who spies on Hsi-men Ch'ing and Li Kuei-chieh in chapter 52, not to mention the curious cat in the same chapter)—all of which seems designed largely to fulfill the function of narrative interruption mentioned earlier as a device of deflation.[276] In other cases, however, the act of spying introduces a threatening element of conflict. For example, when Sung Hui-lien catches a glimpse of the early flirtation of P'an Chin-lien and Ch'en Ching-chi in chapter 24, or when the maid Ch'iu-chü 秋菊 discovers the same couple in flagrante delicto and rushes to tell Yüeh-niang in chapter 83, this propels the plot forward toward its fatal consequences, a sense reasserted at the end with the violent death of Ch'en Ching-chi, after he is caught one more time, by Chang Sheng 張勝 in chapter 99, in the consummation of a forbidden match.

This pattern applies most consistently to P'an Chin-lien, whom we watch in the act of spying (or at least eavesdropping) no less than eight times in the course of the narrative, each time exacerbating rivalries and extorting greater favors, leading to more dangerous consequences.[277] In particular, the very frequent repetition of scenes of P'an Chin-lien spying on her rivals in bed with Hsi-men Ch'ing seems to suggest something beyond the requirements of plot alone.

This interest in voyeurism reaches its ultimate conclusion as we follow Hsi-men Ch'ing through the later phases of his Quixotic pursuit of the vain image of his own desire. From the very beginning, we observe that Hsi-men Ch'ing is possessed of a roving eye. That is, after all, what gets him and P'an Chin-lien into the story in the first place. It is only after the midpoint of the book, as we trace his gradual transformation into the Priapus figure, that our attention is drawn more and more to his ogling and less to the active fulfillment of his desire. We see him smitten at the sight of the troupe of boy actors sent as a gift by Miao Yüan-wai in chapter 55; in chapter 59 we view through his eyes the not-quite-unattainable loveliness of Cheng Ai-yüeh-erh; and, with him, we feast our eyes from head to

---

[276] Other examples include Hua-t'ung's spying on Hsi-men Ch'ing and Shu-t'ung in chapter 34, and the cat in chapter 51. Cf. Chang Chu-p'o, *tu-fa*, item 14. Chang wryly includes in his list of Chin-lien's sexual partners (see n. 256): "Yün-ko by word of mouth," "the monks [in chapter 8] by hearsay," "the cat by its eyes," "T'ieh-kun-erh by the tip of his tongue," and "Ch'iu-chü by means of her dream" (all of these under the obscure heading "Hibiscus Mirror of the Sequestered Spring" 藏春芙蓉鏡).

[277] Examples of Chin-lien's spying and eavesdropping occur in chapters 20, 22, 23, 27, 41, 50, 64, 67.

toe on the willing Madame Lin in chapter 69, while she in turn drinks him in with hers.[278]

This development reaches its peak in the final New Year's festivities, as he spins back and forth, goggle-eyed, from one vain object of desire to the next, until finally he catches a fleeting glimpse—through window blinds—of Lady Lan, about whose breathtaking beauty he had already heard so much. This incident, coming at the height of his dizzying spiral, pushes him over the edge. We are told, "If he had never seen her the matter would have rested at that; but once he had caught sight of her his soul took wing to beyond the heavens ... his heart was rocked and his eye bedazzled" 不見則已, 一見魂飛天外…心搖目蕩—language reflecting back to his first full view of Wang Liu-erh in chapter 37, and brought back later to describe Ch'en Ching-chi's instantaneous infatuation with Wang Liu-erh's daughter, Han Ai-chieh, in chapter 98.[279] The party goes on. Hsi-men, carried away by flights of fantasy, falls asleep, while the players joined by Madame Lin sing a dramatic piece with unheard words of fading glory. He awakens to the sound of exploding fireworks (the display prepared by Pen Ssu's wife) in time to have a final look at the departing vision of Lady Lan. "By this point Hsi-men Ch'ing was reduced to a state of hungry eyes about to pop, his mouth emptily swallowing saliva; he would gladly have coupled with her right on the spot" 這西門慶正是餓眼將穿, 饞涎空嚥, 恨不能就要成雙, we are told, as he steps out through the garden, into the arms of the first nameless female that crosses his path.

Following this strong image of what might be called in the European tradition "fornication of the soul," it is easy to accept Chang Chu-p'o's comment that "it is Lady Lan who sends Hsi-men Ch'ing to his death" ... 送西門慶之死.[280] It is scarcely an idle touch, therefore, when we are told that all through the final throes of his penultimate bout with Wang Liu-erh "his thoughts were all on Lady Lan" 心中只想着何千戶娘子藍氏…, driving him beyond his overextended capacities, out into the cold moonlight, back to the vampire embrace of P'an Chin-lien.

The manner in which the author of *Chin P'ing Mei* brings a long series of unfulfilling sexual acts to their logical conclusion in empty voyeurism is a stroke of genius. As our attention is drawn more and more to the mental images of the objects of Hsi-men Ch'ing's desire, we gradually become aware that we, too, are in effect watching through a keyhole over the

[278] See above, n. 262.

[279] See chapters 78 (28a) and 37 (3b). Cf. Madame Lin's ogling of Hsi-men Ch'ing through the blinds of her sitting room in chapter 69, as discussed earlier.

[280] Chang Chu-p'o, "Allegorical Meaning," p. 2a. Cf. Spenser, with his description of "readie spoyle/of hungry eies" (e.g., Book II, 12:78f.), who provides one of the best contemporary analogues in European literature.

shoulders of P'an Chin-lien and the other voyeurs.[281] This is a crucial element in the design of the novel: by luring the reader into a vicarious affirmation of the reality of his illusory fictional world, the author succeeds in concretizing the very abstract relationship of mutual implication between reality and illusion, or form and emptiness, and takes a step toward the realization of the state of nonemptiness alluded to by Chang Chu-p'o. I will return once more to this point in my concluding section.

In the meantime, lest I become irretrievably immersed in the idea of the evocation of sensual illusion and lose sight of the point of the discussion, I will return to the original line of the argument. I have devoted considerable space to an analysis of the passages of sexual description in the novel in order to demonstrate the consistent use of ironic undercutting in its presentation of sex, and thus to refute the view of the work as any kind of affirmative treatment of this area of human experience. As I have argued, however, the point of true irony is always predicated on at least the hypothetical existence of a positive dimension of meaningfulness to which the various denials and negations obliquely point. Since I have rejected the simplistic framework of karmic retribution as insufficient to account for this perception of meaning in the novel, I will have to continue now my own pursuit of the proper interpretation of the book.

Clearly, something is wrong in Hsi-men's world. One might say that the profoundly negative view of sex and other aspects of life in the household is simply a mimetic reflection of the sordid side of Wan-li mores, but the problem appears to go deeper than that. This feeling that something is wrong is not just the sensibility of a modern reader, but finds expression in many of the more serious comments of Chang Chu-p'o, the Ch'ung-chen commentator, and the early preface writers.[282] Even the characters within the fictional text, I might add, are depicted as not quite comfortable with their own behavior, often exhibiting what appears to be shame for such things as sodomy and incest.

Neither the gathering of six wives in a garden of delights nor the seeking of extramural liaisons presents absolute transgression of moral law for the sixteenth-century Chinese reader. But the central thread running through all the sexual abuses in the novel is the flagrant violation of another law that is of equivalent sanctity in the context of traditional Chinese civilization: that is, the horror of excess.

This "message" is already sufficiently clear in the consistent depiction of sex gone beyond simple pleasure into the realm of violent self-destruction.

---

[281] Carlitz makes the same point in her "Puns and Puzzles," p. 239, and *Rhetoric*, p. 51f.

[282] See Chang Chu-p'o, *tu-fa*, item 36; Ch'ung-chen commentary, 14 (39a), 23 (26b). Similar ideas are expressed in both the Hsin-hsin tzu and the Nung-chu k'e prefaces, as well as in the recently uncovered Wen Lung commentary (see above, n. 52).

This is patently what is at issue in the dizzying merry-go-round of sexual encounters that fills Hsi-men Ch'ing's last days. But lest the reader miss the point, the author hammers away at the idea of desire gone wild. At every point where the narrator's voice is heard—in chapter verses, descriptive metaphors, and *k'an-kuan* asides—we are bombarded with expressions of "desire flaring out of control" (*yü-ch'ing ju huo* 慾情如火), "unbounded sexual appetite" (*se-tan ju t'ien* 色胆如天), or behavior gone "beyond limits" (*wu-tu* 無度), etc.[283]

In a number of passages this idea is also pointedly broached in dialogue, as for example in chapter 57 (9b), when Yüeh-niang urges Hsi-men Ch'ing to curb his philandering, and he replies that with his money and power he could rape goddesses like Ch'ang-o and Chih-nü 織女 and get away with it.[284] Hsi-men Ch'ing's pride in his sexual prowess takes on a special taint after he boasts of being one who "loves sensuality" (*hao-se* 好色) in chapter 18. Outside of the particular meanings assigned to this expression as a term of Chinese philosophical discourse, it also has special associations in the colloquial fiction tradition, as a mark of the effeminate opposite of the manly *hao-han* 好漢, with his loudly professed scorn for temptations of the flesh.[285] The author provides a fairly explicit hint in this direction when he has the *Shui-hu* chieftain Sung Chiang 宋江 profess his aversion to female sensuality (*pu chin nü-se* 不近女色) in chapter 84 (9b), and he packs more seriousness into the idea in the portrait of Commandant Chou 周守備, whose resistance to feminine wiles, we are told, leaves him free to fight valiantly against the Tartar onslaught—at the very moment that his new wife, our Ch'un-mei, is destroying herself through sexual indulgence.

What finally does Hsi-men Ch'ing in is thus the scourge of his own insatiability, coupled with that of P'an Chin-lien. The author provides a

[283] See examples in chapters 8 (9a), 9 (1a), 12 (6a), 37 (9b), 73 (19b), 79 (6b), 80 (4b), 100 (6b). A *k'an-kuan* passage in chapter 79 (9b) discusses this issue at length. See also Chang Chu-p'o discussions in chapters 51 (*tp*), 73 (*tp* and 6a), and 97 (*tp*), and Ch'ung-chen commentary, chapters 67 (16b), and 99 (38b). I will reconsider the "four vices of excess" later.

[284] Cf. the line in chapter 79 (1a): "He was quite aware how to lust after other men's wives, but he was unaware that death was soon to catch up with him" 自知淫人妻子而不知死之將至. A similar point is made in Hsi-men Ch'ing's prophecy in chapter 29, and in a crucial passage in 61 (9b): "If you could give free rein to your desires, you would take your pleasure with every woman in the world" 若是信着你意兒把天下老婆都耍遍了罷.

[285] This reading of the term *hao-se* is a radical distortion of the positive concept in the Four Books (*Lun Yü*, 9:18, 15:13; *Meng-tzu*, 1B:5, 5A:1). In chapter 70 (11b), the infamous minister Chu Mien is praised for his love of sensuality (*hao-se*). See also the description of the emperor in chapter 71 (14b). In chapter 99 (10a), Chou Shou-pei warns his family to "reduce their desires" (*kua-yü* 寡欲) before he sets out for a hero's death. The Ch'ung-chen commentator brings up these terms in comments in chapters 21 (2a) and 37 (8a). Cf. the manifestation of this same issue in *Shui-hu chuan* (see below, Chapter 4, Part IV). See Sun Shu-yü's discussion in "Chin P'ing Mei ti ch'eng-chiu," pp. 17f.

quasi-allegorical key to this point in chapter 49 (16a), when the foreign monk (whom we have identified as a personification of Hsi-men Ch'ing's sexuality) warns him that the aphrodisiac pills he has bestowed upon him must not be used to excess—advice Hsi-men Ch'ing, as expected, proceeds to utterly disregard. P'an Chin-lien's part of the bargain is well documented in the chain of incidents leading up to the graphic pose in Hsi-men Ch'ing's final scene, in which insatiability is turned inside out to yield incontinence and depletion.[286]

The theme ultimately takes on a wider scope of meaning in terms of the rise and fall of Hsi-men Ch'ing's world in general. As Hsi-men's bloated sexuality distends from chapter 50 to 79, it parallels a period of fullness in other phases of his life as well. In chapter 57 (7b), for example, he tells another foreign monk that all his wishes have been fulfilled 萬事已是足了, and in the next ten chapters we see the convergence of his financial, political, and sexual gratification. Within the traditional Chinese world view, unfortunately, such expressions of the attainment of maximum fulfillment are the surest possible sign of impending doom, and so Hsi-men Ch'ing's peaking fortunes are accompanied by frequent soundings of the traditional refrain that "When joy reaches its zenith it gives rise to sadness" (*le-chi sheng-pei* 樂極生悲).[287] Oblivious to these clear signals, Hsi-men goes on trying to hold on to his cake while consuming it. He continues to enclose himself in places like the Grotto of Sequestered Spring and the Temple of Eternal Prosperity, trying to hold fast to his self-contained world of eternal springtime as the seasons roll by around him.[288]

We may recall at this point that at the very start of the book, in both of its variant recensions, the author subjects us to a lengthy homily precisely on the problem of the fatal consequences of sexual overindulgence. In the *Tz'u-hua* edition this is followed up with a line by the Six Dynasties literary figure Wang Yen 王衍: "It is people like ourselves who are most affected by passion" 情之所鍾正在我輩. In its original context, this line is used to describe obsessive grief, but as used in the *Chin P'ing Mei* it comes to refer more to a kind of self-indulgent wallowing in sensuality. This, at least, is

---

[286] Chapter 49 (16a). See also chapter 72 (18a): "Her lustful desire was unsatiated" 淫情未足. The theme of insatiability is also brought out in Ch'en Ching-chi's chronic inability to learn his lesson, as for example expressed with the term *chiu-hsin pu-kai* (see below) or *chiu-ch'ing pu-kai* 舊情不改; see, e.g., chapters 87 (6b) and 93 (12a).

[287] For example, chapters 57 (7a), 63 (12b), 78 (29a), and 92 (1a, 15b). The peak of this transient joy is apparently reached in chapter 78 (16a), where once again the same refrain is sounded. Sun Shu-yü discusses this idea in "Ming-ming," pp. 10ff. See also Hsin-hsin tzu preface, p. 8.

[288] Cf. Wang Liu-erh's line in chapter 79 (7a): "As long as your pine tree is forever green, winter and summer, then everything will be all right" 只要你松柏兒冬夏長青便好; as well as frequent descriptions of the garden as a world with "flowers unfading through all the seasons" 四時有不卸之花; e.g., chapters 19 (2a) and 56 (2b).

the sense the same line conveys in the short story "The Blissful Union of Lovers with Their Throats Cut" 刎頸鴛鴦會, another piece of sixteenth-century colloquial fiction (which appeared in print not long before the probable time of composition of *Chin P'ing Mei*), in which the connection between sex and violence is also a central issue.[289] In any event, in both recensions of the *Chin P'ing Mei* the prologue discussion brings in yet another traditional formulation of the problem of excess: the proverbial sins of drunkenness (or gluttony), lust, avarice, and wrath, which I have rendered earlier as the "four vices of excess" in order to emphasize the parallel with the four cardinal sins in the European tradition. In the Ch'ung-chen edition this discussion follows directly; in the *Tz'u-hua* it is implicit in the discussion of "passion and sensuality" (*ch'ing-se* 情色), made explicit in the introductory verses on the subject.

As we shall see in the remainder of this study, the notion of the "four vices" recurs as a major framework of meaning in the three other sixteenth-century novels under investigation here. In *Chin P'ing Mei*, this formula helps to account for the wide range of excessive behavior we witness in all four of these areas: drunkenness and gluttony (in such scenes as the rowdy banquets in chapters 12 and 52); venality (in Hsi-men Ch'ing's business dealings and political corruption); and wrath (in various instances of violence and murder)—all of which are pointedly linked to excessive sexuality.[290] The connection between sex and money in particular dominates much of the narrative—especially with respect to the exchange of sexual favors for clothes, as has been discussed by Hanan, C. T. Hsia, and others.[291] This is also one of Chang Chu-p'o's favorite topics of discussion.

In all these cases, the consistent emphasis on the harmful consequences of excessive self-indulgence infuses new meaning into the didactic framework of karmic retribution. That is, although I have rejected the simplistic Buddhist interpretation of the novel as unable to do justice to its

[289] David Roy has pointed out that the original context of this line, as cited in the *Shih-shuo hsin-yü*, is different from that to which it is applied here (see "The Case for T'ang Hsien-tzu," pp. 1.4ff.). The story "The Blissful Union ..." appears in Hung Pien's *Ch'ing-p'ing-shan t'ang hua-pen*, pp. 154–67. See Hanan, "Sources," pp. 33f. and n. 23; and André Lévy, *Études sur le conte et le roman chinois*, pp. 187–210. I suspect that the name Tsung-mei 宗美 given to Ch'en Ching-chi during his unpleasant monastic experience in chapter 93 may reflect a similar idea.

[290] Additional scenes of excess in food and drink include chapters 22, 24, 27, 75, and 79. The connection between food and sex is emphasized in chapter 27, and is again highlighted in chapter 49. See Mote, "Yuan and Ming," pp. 248–52, for a discussion of this aspect of the novel. Scenes of violence either directly or indirectly related to sexual tensions appear in nearly every chapter, and these lead to unnatural death in chapters 5, 14, 26, 35, 79, 92, and 100.

[291] See Hanan, "Landmark," pp. 329ff.; C. T. Hsia, *Classic Novel*, pp. 200f.; and David Roy, "Confucian Interpretation," pp. 59.

complex unfolding of the consequences of human action, it is still not surprising to find here expressions of the popular Buddhist ideas of the repayment of one's worldly debts, of the clearing of accounts, or "retribution in this world" (*hsien-shih pao* 現世報), ideas Chang Chu-p'o often uses to describe the structural as well as the doctrinal design of the novel.[292] The very fact that so many warnings are delivered, however, results in shifting the emphasis from the grand scheme of universal justice to individual responsibility for excessive behavior.[293] This is most forcefully expressed in the repeated line of proverbial wisdom: "It is not sensual desire that leads men astray, but men themselves who fall into error" (*se pu mi-jen, jen tzu-mi* 色不迷人人自迷).[294] This gives a special function to the structure of recurrence traced above, which itself becomes a kind of metaphor for the flagrant recidivism of those who continually fail to learn their lessons or heed their warnings. As another frequently cited cliché has it, "The old heart just couldn't change its ways" (*chiu-hsin pu-kai* 舊心不改).

Such ideas of guilt and retribution clearly smack of the popular Buddhism that was current in the later Ming, with its "personal registers" of good and bad deeds (*kung-kuo ko* 功過格) and its institutionalized confessions—the sort of religious phenomena reflected in the Buddhist recitations (*shuo yin-kuo* and *pao-chüan*) included in the text. But at the same time, this reinterpretation of the Buddhist framework in terms of essentially moral rather than metaphysical meaning raises the possibility that the same ideas could just as well be explained in Confucian terms. At any rate, the entire scheme of karmic justice comes to be quite indistinguishable from the concept of "universal principle" (*t'ien-li* 天理) invoked repeatedly by the commentators.[295]

---

[292] Chang Chu-p'o, chapters 1 (*tp*), 4 (20b), 7 (*tp*), 21 (*tp*), 33 (*tp*), 38 (14b), 43 (*tp*), 45 (*tp*), 46 (*tp*), 56 (*tp*), 75 (*tp*), 79 (*tp*), 80 (*tp*), 91 (*tp*), 97 (*tp*); *tu-fa*, items 19, 23; and "Hsien-hua," p. 2a–b. Chang discusses the general idea of all four "vices of excess" in comments in chapters 34 (21a) and 100 (30b). See Wei Tzu-yün, "Wang-kuan," p. 239. For examples in which articles of clothing are at stake, see chapters 22, 35, 40, and 41.

[293] See Chang Chu-p'o's discussions of this point in chapters 3 (*tp*), 24 (*tp*), 33 (9b), 58 (23a), 69 (*tp*), 79 (*tp*), 93 (*tp*), and 100 (*tp*).

[294] See, e.g., chapter 3 (1a). For a good discussion of this idea, see Carlitz, "Role of Drama," p. 90, and "Puns and Puzzles," p. 238. Cf. the related notion of "calling forth one's own troubles" (e.g., 74 [6a]), as well as repeated refusals to heed warnings, prophecies, and dreams. This is especially true in the case of Ch'en Ching-chi, whose roller-coaster vicissitudes in the final chapters remind me of the narrative pattern established in the T'ang story "Tu Tzu-ch'un" 杜子春. See also Sun Shu-yü, "Ming-ming," p. 9.

[295] Chang Chu-p'o, chapter 1 (*tp*); Ch'ung-chen commentary, chapters 98 (21b) and 100 (42b). On the notion of accountability for individual actions that was so widespread in the popular Buddhism of the late Ming period, especially in connection with the practice of maintaining "personal registers," see references cited above in Chapter 1, n. 52. See Martinson, "*Chin P'ing Mei* as Wisdom Literature," pp. 44–56.

VI

With this in mind, I can now proceed to develop in full detail my interpretation based on what a number of readers have perceived to be an essentially Confucian vision in the *Chin P'ing Mei*. The idea that, for all its Buddhist preaching, the novel may be more Confucian in its basic spirit is not new. Chang Chu-p'o openly states as much in quite a few of his critical discussions, and recently this idea has been further developed by David Roy and other scholars. In Professor Roy's view, the presentation of human failings in the novel makes most sense as a specific reflection of the philosophy of Hsün Tzu 荀子—which would help to explain the author's choice of the pseudonym Lan-ling Hsiao-hsiao sheng ("the Scoffing Scholar of Lan-ling" 蘭陵笑笑生).[296] I believe that this is a cogent argument worthy of the most serious consideration, particularly as the author himself raises the question of good and evil in human nature at several points.[297]

The reading I would like to pursue here, however, will rely primarily on the core teachings of the Four Books as the repository of Neo-Confucian wisdom reflected most directly in the novel.[298] As discussed in my introductory chapter on late Ming cultural history, and as I shall again mention in my final review of the intellectual groundwork of the four novels, the sixteenth century saw a significant deepening of the Neo-Confucian synthesis based on the notion of the "unity of the three teachings" (*san-chiao ho-i* 三教合一) and a general shift of emphasis from external patterns of order to the internal dimension, that is, the mind (*hsin* 心) as the locus of self-cultivation.[299] The resulting redefinition of basic Confucian values in a more relativistic manner was accompanied by a new focus on individual consciousness that opened the door to various extreme tendencies, for example those associated with the T'ai-chou School. By the time of the

---

[296] David Roy, "Confucian Interpretation," passim. See also Martinson, "Pao, Order, and Redemption," p. 160; and Carlitz, "Role of Drama," pp. 40, 375ff. Chang Chu-p'o describes the vision of the novel in terms of Confucian concepts in *tu-fa*, items 56, 63, 103. In a sense, the legend attributing the novel to Wang Shih-chen rests on related assumptions regarding the Confucian motivation of the work. Cf. the opening poem in chapter 99, which brings Buddhist and Confucian ideas into conjunction.

[297] For example, chapters 47 (3b, 10b), 57 (1a, 6a, 8a), 75 (1a), 79 (1a), and 100 (11b, 16b).

[298] This in no way excludes the possibility of significant reference to the ideas of Hsün Tzu, since in many ways the Neo-Confucian interpretation of Mencius allows for the incorporation of Hsüntzian positions. For that matter, I would argue that the apparently irreconcilable gap between these two positions on the problem of the inherent good or evil of human nature is not unbridgeable.

[299] For general discussions of the Neo-Confucian background of the sixteenth-century novel, see Chapters 1 and 6 of this book.

composition of the *Chin P'ing Mei* late in the century, however, the pendulum was already swinging back in reaction against the more extreme of these positions.

In suggesting that these broad movements in intellectual background may be relevant to the interpretation of the novel, I must hasten to acknowledge that our author, whoever he may have been, was obviously not a professional philosopher (if such ever existed in China), nor was he necessarily a partisan of any particular school. The argument here is simply that as a participant in contemporary literati culture he was demonstrably attuned to the intellectual issues of the day, chief among them the redefinition of the concept of self-cultivation. The complexity and controversiality of this question arises from differences of opinion on the nature of the individual self, the possibility of its integrality, and the extent of its autonomy. On the one side, certain post–Wang Yang-ming thinkers tend to emphasize the cultivation of the self in isolation, the pursuit of inner enlightenment largely in disregard of the surrounding world, leading at best to "cultivating one's own garden," and at worst to self-indulgence and ego-gratification.[300] Ranged against this tendency, the more orthodox schools take the view of self-cultivation outlined in the Four Books and expanded in the Neo-Confucian philosophical writings as a matter of nearly metaphysical significance, in the sense of the hierarchical ordering of the proper relations between self and world. Given the centrality of this issue for the generations that saw the composition of the novel, I believe we can interpret the entire vast text as a kind of negative reflection—in fact, a parody—of the ideal of self-cultivation. In this sense, what is "wrong" in Hsi-men Ch'ing's world can be explained as the failure to understand and practice the central teachings of the Four Books on this all-important question. It is quite possible that the author himself was not fully conscious of this pattern of meaning when he first set his brush to paper to expand one suggestive episode from *Shui-hu chuan*. But as he plunges deeper into the creation of his fictional world, and as his ironic vision begins to take over, what emerges is a deeply searching exploration of the meaning of Confucian ideals in an age of dissolution.

In the remaining pages I will attempt to set forth in detail the parody of Confucian self-cultivation realized in the novel. In doing so, I find it most convenient to frame my analysis in terms of one particular core passage in the text of the "Great Learning" (*Ta-hsüeh* 大學), although these ideas, of course, are by no means confined to this passage or this text alone. In the opening section of the *Ta-hsüeh*, it will be recalled, the behavioral model for

---

[300] In this sense, the initial term of the *Ta-hsüeh* text ("to make bright one's illustrious virtue," *ming ming-te* 明明德) may, paradoxically, take on the meaning of polishing one's own inner mirror.

the ordering of self and world is schematized in terms of a set of concentric circles of ever-broadening significance, centering on the individual self with its own inner constitution, and radiating outward to encompass the entire universe:

> Through the investigation of things, one's knowledge is extended; once one's knowledge is extended, his will can be stabilized; once one's will has been stabilized, his mind can be rectified; once one's mind has been rectified, one's self can be cultivated; once one's self has been cultivated, one's family can be ordered; once one's family has been ordered, the state can be properly ruled; once the state is properly ruled, the entire world can be kept in harmony.
> 物格而後知至，知至而後意誠，意誠而後心正，心正而後身修，身修而後家齊，家齊而後國治，國治而後天下平．[301]

In the following discussion I will attempt to relate Hsi-men Ch'ing's glaring violation of the canonic injunction to keep his own house in order (*ch'i ch'i chia* 齊其家) to a corresponding disequilibrium (*luan* 亂) at each of the other levels of the system. My analysis will begin with the microcosm of Hsi-men Ch'ing's individual self, both mind and body, and proceed through his widening circles of relations to the household, the sphere of his external affairs, and ultimately to the macrocosm of the imperial world order.

Let us begin at the "heart" of the system, in the individual consciousness (*hsin*, literally "heart") that is the locus of the first three levels of cultivation, even though it appears rhetorically in the middle of the chain sequence. As every reader of the *Chin P'ing Mei* is aware, the focus of this narrative is more attuned to the life of the body—its drives for food (酒), sex (色), money (財), and power (氣)—than to the life of the mind. At many points it almost seems as if the central figures Hsi-men Ch'ing, P'an Chin-lien, and even Li P'ing-erh are in a sense devoid of mind—that is, empty inside, except for momentary appetites or at best emotional affinities, but without self-consciousness. But in line with the late Ming focus on mind as the essential ground of self-cultivation, certain recurring expressions in the novel still appear to reflect an interest in this side of the self. For example, after the author reminds us in a *k'an-kuan* passage in the first chapter that

---

[301] *Ssu-shu chi-chu*, p. 2. For alternate translations see Wing-tsit Chan, "The Great Learning," in *A Source Book in Chinese Philosophy*, pp. 84–94; James Legge, *The Four Books*, pp. 317–46; E. R. Hughes, *The Great Learning and the Mean in Action*, pp. 145–66. The link between this ancient text and the later novel is cemented by the broad currency during these few centuries of the Sung work (*Ta-hsüeh yen-i* 大學衍義) by Chen Te-hsiu, and its Ming expansion, *Ta-hsüeh yen-i pu* 大學衍義補, by Ch'iu Chün 邱濬 (1420–95). See Carlitz, *Rhetoric*, pp. 30ff.

"it is the human heart, more than anything else in the world, that is most prone to evil" 世上惟有人心最歹, numerous expressions identify the mind as the locus of destructive impulses, marking it as "malicious" (*hsin-hsieh* 心邪), "venomous" (*hsin-tu* 心毒), "weak" (*hsin-juan* 心軟), or subject to violent "flare-ups of desire" (*hsin-shang yü-huo* 心上慾火).[302] These innate tendencies are singled out as the heart of the matter, so that sexual domination is explained as the attempt to "ensnare a man's heart" (*lao-lung han-tzu hsin* 牢籠漢子心) or, as spelled out in chapter 72, "This woman wanted nothing more or less than to bind Hsi-men Ch'ing's heart" 這婦人…無非只是要拴西門慶之心 (see above, p. 110).[303]

Such expressions may easily be brushed aside as common figures of speech that do not necessarily bear special meaning here. The same may probably be said of certain traces of the vocabulary of *Hsin-hsüeh* that appear at various points. In chapter 62, for example, the term "let the mind go" (*fang-hsin* 放心) appears a few times in connection with P'ing-erh's apparitions of guilt, and later in the same chapter we find a reference to the "Prajnaparamita Heart Sutra" (*Hsin ching* 心經), which is cited so pointedly in *Hsi-yu chi*.[304] The most convincing evidence of this potential dimension of meaning, however, comes in with the repeated description of Hsi-men Ch'ing's gradual self-destruction in terms of the notion of "disorder of the mind" (*hsin-luan* 心亂).[305] I cannot really prove that the author makes much of these hints, but I believe that the endemic disorder at this level, owing to Hsi-men Ch'ing's failure to "rectify his mind" (*cheng ch'i hsin* 正其心), is intended to bear out the disorder that reigns on the other rungs of the *Ta-hsüeh* ladder.

Continuing along the chain, we may now consider the corresponding disorder in the context of Hsi-men Ch'ing's "cultivation of the self" (*hsiu-shen* 修身) in the more narrow sense of the development of personal

[302] For example, chapters 35 (9a), 59 (12a), 68 (13b), 75 (17b, 23a, 25a), 76 (12a, 13a). The line "It is the human heart ..." in chapter 1 (9a) is repeated in chapters 19 (1a), 84 (10a), and 94 (1a). Cf. the *k'an-kuan* passage elucidating this point in chapter 62 (14a). In chapters 74 (3a), 76 (2b), and 78 (23a) we are told that Chin-lien "had no heart."

[303] Chapter 72 (11a). See also chapters 33 (3a), 67 (17b, 18a), and 78 (11a).

[304] Chapter 62 (7b, 8b). Cf. the proverbial expression "monkey of the mind, horse of the will" (*hsin-yüan i-ma* 心猿意馬) in chapters 8 (11a), 41 (5a), and 80 (9a). In chapter 57 (8a) there is a discussion of the equation of Buddha and mind; in chapter 29 (6a–b) we are given a parody lecture on the interrelation of mind and external signs (*hsin-hsiang* 心相); and in chapter 93 (9b) we find a sardonic inversion of the phrase "purge the mind return to the proper path" (*hsi-hsin kai-cheng* 洗心改正). Cf. the use of the term *hsi-hsin* in the Hsin-hsin tzu preface (p. 6).

[305] For example, chapters 55 (8a), 60 (8a), 68 (13b–14a). The expression "his heart was rocked and his eye bedazzled" (*hsin-yao mu-tang*) appears in a number of scenes (see n. 279). Cf. the inversion here of the Mencian concept of "the (un)moved heart" (*pu tung hsin* 不動心), in chapter 57 (6b) for example.

virtues. The novel presents abundant evidence of Hsi-men Ch'ing's failure
in this area. Chief among these is the fact that he is not only lacking in the
learning of Confucian moral education, but he is also barely able to read
and write.[306] This deficiency is revealed in several scenes (for example, in
chapter 48 he is unable to read an official bulletin absolving him of the
accusation of corruption), although it does not stop the go-between in
chapter 69 from describing him to Madame Lin as a master of all the
schools of learning (*chu-tzu pai-chia* 諸子百家). Chang Chu-p'o puts his
finger on this disqualification as the "root of his ills" 病根 in chapter 1, and
in a number of other comments both he and the Ch'ung-chen editor decry
his "vulgar" (*shih-ching* 市井) mentality.[307]

Skipping for a moment past the level of family harmony, we see these
same personal defects of Hsi-men Ch'ing's character directly reflected in his
performance as a bogus official, a supposed participant in the grand enterprise of maintaining order in the state (*chih ch'i kuo* 治其國). Here the
picture of Hsi-men Ch'ing in action is uniformly dismal. For the most part
he simply neglects his duties, leaving them in the hands of dubious assistants. But even when he does take an active role in several cases, he is
depicted as corrupt, venal, and cruel, one whose efforts primarily "serve the
interests of his superiors at the expense of his inferiors" (*sun-hsia i-shang*
損下益上), an expression used repeatedly in the text and cited by Chang
Chu-p'o.[308] In his capacity as judge, we see him resort readily to intimidation and torture, with particular alacrity in cases of adultery and incest.[309]
This is especially obvious in the Miao Ch'ing affair, for the mishandling of
which he is nearly impeached in chapter 48, only to be let off by virtue of
liberal bribery and the intercession of Chai Ch'ien 翟謙.

Given this flagrant abuse of the imperial trust, it is no accident that his
baby son, Kuan-ko, whose very name marks him as a symbol of Hsi-men
Ch'ing's official career, is born, takes sick, and dies in coordination with his
father's fortunes in office—in fulfillment of the prophecy in chapter 29
(5b): "When the *kuan* is wounded, wounded beyond recovery, he will then
recover wealth ..." 傷官傷盡復生財 .... Similarly, we have seen the striking
parallelism between Hsi-men Ch'ing's rising official career and his sexual

---

[306] Cf. descriptions of Hsi-men Ch'ing as a "broken-down scholar" (*p'o sha-mao* 破紗帽)
in chapter 43 (6a) and elsewhere.

[307] See Chang Chu-p'o, chapter 1 (13a), and Ch'ung-chen commentary, chapters 16 (3a),
51 (13a), and 73 (38a). Perhaps a little joke about Hsi-men Ch'ing's version of self-cultivation
is intended in chapter 67 (3a), when he is reminded that he has been growing quite fat.

[308] For example, chapter 49 (1b). See Chang Chu-p'o, chapter 12 (*tp*). In P'ing-erh's
deathbed exhortation in chapter 62 (17b), she urges him not to spend so much time in the
bedchamber to the detriment of his official duties.

[309] See the adultery case in chapter 34 and the incest case in chapter 38. For a review of
Hsi-men Ch'ing's judicial cases, see Martinson, "Pao, Order, and Redemption," pp. 228ff.

advances, such that his highest promotion comes simultaneously with the onset of his final sexual whirl beginning in chapter 70. I might add that his rather unlikely network of protection and influence at court is largely the fruit of his services in procuring a concubine (Han Ai-chieh, the daughter of his own sexual partner Wang Liu-erh) for Chai Ch'ien, the majordomo of Ts'ai Ching, in chapter 36, The fact that Hsi-men Ch'ing's rank defilement of the ideal of state service is seen here as more than the fault of the corrupt system is indicated by the author's inclusion of a number of examples of honorable officials in the narrative, notably the censor Tseng in chapter 48, and Magistrate Li 李通判(李昌期, 李達天), the father of Li "Ya-nei" 李衙內, 李拱璧, in chapter 92, not to mention Chou Shou-pei at the end.[310] I should also mention as a further dimension of the disorder of Hsi-men Ch'ing's worldly affairs the considerable attention paid to his questionable business dealings. Here, too, we see him abdicating responsibility into the unreliable hands of Ch'en Ching-chi, Han Tao-kuo, and Pen Ssu, and cultivating connections in the proverbially illicit lines of salt smuggling, trading in contraband lumber from imperial forests (*huang-mu*), and other such activities.[311] Once again, the author takes care to ironically link the progress of Hsi-men Ch'ing's business affairs with the regression of his infant son, especially in chapters 48 to 60, where the baby's cruel end takes place against a background of great profits and expansion in his financial life.[312]

The transition from the level of lower official service to the level of imperial order (*p'ing t'ien-hsia* 平天下) brings us to one of the central axes of meaning in the entire work. In the early stages of the narrative, the doings in the provincial backwater of Ch'ing-ho hsien may appear to have little to do with the fate of the Sung empire at large. But throughout the text, the author takes pains to direct the reader's gaze outward from the microcosm of the enclosed garden to the macrocosm of the world beyond.

[310] Other examples of proper official vigilance appear in chapters 10, 14, and 72. Cf. the references to the Confucian heroics of Chou Shou-pei in chapters 98 (1a) and 100 (4b). See Chang Chu-p'o's discussions in chapter 48 (*tp*), and in *tu-fa*, item 89.

[311] For references to dealings in salt (e.g., 51 [5a]), appropriation of imperial lumber (e.g., 34 [5b], 49 [5b]), and "granary bills" (*ts'ang-ch'ao* 倉鈔), see Wu Han, "Chin P'ing Mei ti chu-tso," pp. 27ff. It is strongly suggested that Li P'ing-erh's wealth, both that appropriated through Hua Tzu-hsü—whose position as nephew of a powerful court eunuch already suggests illegitimacy—and that which she seems to have retained after her disastrous connection with Liang Chung-shu, derives from illicit sources. See chapters 10 (6b) and 64 (1b–2a). Passages that describe Hsi-men Ch'ing's business dealings are found in chapters 16, 25, 31, 38, 42, 48, 55, 56, 58, 59, 60, 66, 71, 75, 77, and 81, not to mention instances of moneylending in chapters 42, 45, 55, and 56.

[312] In this context, the panic over the baby's contact with the cold bangles in chapter 43 takes on fuller meaning. Cf. P'an Chin-lien's assumption of responsibility for some of the family finances in chapter 77 (3a).

One way in which he does this is by weaving into his plot numerous threads that tie the local story directly or indirectly to the affairs of the imperial court. These threads are at first quite unconvincing, as when we are casually informed of P'ing-erh's past status as a concubine of Ts'ai Ching's son-in-law, Liang Chung-shu, or when Ch'en Ching-chi arrives on the Hsi-men doorstep from the capital and we are told in a somewhat offhand manner that Hsi-men Ching's daughter had married into a well-placed family at court.

As the narrative proceeds, Hsi-men Ch'ing's connections with court politics come into play more and more, securing his release from responsibility in the Wu Sung case in chapter 10, and the removal of his name from an impeachment bill in chapter 18. Later, these unseen connections are fleshed out in the depiction of several trips between Ch'ing-ho hsien and the capital, first by the servant Lai Pao in chapter 30 (followed by the reception of Ts'ai Ching's dubious "son" in chapter 36, and the dispatch of bribes to Ts'ai in chapter 48), and later with two visits by Hsi-men Ch'ing himself in chapters 55 and 70–71.[313] By the midpoint of the book it becomes increasingly clear that the political advancement of this small-time figure is being blown far out of realistic proportion—to a degree that parallels his soaring sexual adventures. As his sexual conquests spiral higher and higher, his contacts at court become more and more impressive. Thus the initial connection with Chai Ch'ien and the agreement to provide him with a hometown beauty pave the way for a meeting with Ts'ai Ching himself, capped by his adoption as Ts'ai's "son." Hsi-men Ch'ing's soaring ambitions bring him to the presence of the very pinnacle of imperial power in chapter 70. In this scene, the author exercises masterful control of structure and point of view, first heightening expectations through several frustrated attempts to meet the haughty minister Chu Mien 朱勔, then having us see through Hsi-men Ch'ing's bedazzled eyes the pomp and spectacle of an imperial procession, climaxed by a glimpse of the emperor himself. All of this, we recall, is juxtaposed against the presentation of some of the starkest imagery of cold emptiness and futility in the whole book.[314] Following this point, Hsi-men Ch'ing becomes tangentially involved in the historically infamous project known as "the flower and stone mission"

---

[313] For a review of the visits to the capital and the intercourse with Ts'ai Ching, see Martinson, "Pao, Order, and Redemption," p. 227; and Torii, "Hennenkō," pp. 76–80. Cf. the linkage between the preparation of birthday gifts for Ts'ai and the sexual excesses of chapter 27, mentioned earlier. Cf. also the link between Hsi-men Ch'ing and another member of the notorious clique of evil ministers, Yang Chien 楊戩, in chapter 17. See Carlitz, *Rhetoric*, pp. 37f.

[314] I will consider some further implications of this cold imagery in the following discussion.

(*hua-shih kang* 花石綱), by which the resources of the entire tottering empire were marshaled for the gathering of rare plants and stones for the Ken-yüeh pleasure garden of the emperor.[315] This detail is of special significance, not only because it intensifies the forewarning of Hsi-men Ch'ing's downfall, but also because it is the crowning touch to the symbolic structure of flower and garden imagery at the heart of the novel's conception.

In the final section of the book, after Hsi-men Ching's death, the author again throws open the gates of the compound and takes us out, on the trail of Ch'en Ching-chi's adventures, into the wide world. As we near the end of his trials, the long intimated convergence between the breakdown of Hsi-men Ch'ing's family and the collapse of the Sung empire is brought to a thunderous conclusion as the invading Chin forces overrun Ch'ing-ho hsien in their drive south, and Yüeh-niang, along with throngs of refugees, is swept out through the city gates.

The fact that this novel of domestic manners ends up in a head-on confrontation with historical events of great magnitude cannot be dismissed lightly. As we shall see, this intersection of fiction and history is a salient feature of Chinese narrative in general and the novel in particular, and it will figure in my interpretation of our other three works as well. In the *Chin P'ing Mei*, the connections between the fictional tale and historical fact are numerous and insistent. Besides repeated discussions of the responsibility of the "four evil ministers" (*ssu chien-ch'en* 四奸臣) for the eventual loss of half of the Sung empire, we may note many other specific allusions to such historical figures as Wang An-shih 王安石, Hou Meng 侯蒙, Chang Shu-yeh 張叔夜, and others.[316] In the light of this apparent interest in the causes of dynastic collapse, the opening discussion of the tragic downfall of Liu Pei 劉備 and Hsiang Yü 項羽 takes on greater meaning than is initially evident.

The ultimate point of the deliberate interweaving of the fate of Hsi-men Ch'ing and the fate of the dynasty is driven home in a number of passages in which the figure of Hsi-men as master in his own self-contained world is compared with the figure of the ruler of the world at large; that is, as a parody of the role of the emperor in the *t'ien-hsia* realm. Hsi-men Ch'ing's performance in this role is, to say the least, unexemplary. His failure to provide a moral example, susceptibility to the influence of unprincipled

---

[315] The *hua-shih kang* is mentioned in chapters 65 (2b), 68 (5a), and elsewhere; and the Ken-yüeh garden is mentioned in chapters 65 (2b) and 78 (26a).

[316] Reference to Wang An-shih in chapter 78 (7b), to Chang Shu-yeh in chapter 97 (7b). Cf. general discussions on the fall of the Sung dynasty in chapters 1, 49, 64, 68, 73, 99, and 100. See Hanan, "Sources," pp. 47ff.; and Martinson, "Pao, Order, and Redemption," chap. 6 for discussions of the historical references in the novel.

advisers, and general abdication of responsibility in the pursuit of sensual pleasure all conform precisely to the qualities associated with the traditional stereotype of the "bad last ruler" in falling dynasties, as recent critics have pointed out.[317] Indeed, this analogy is made fully explicit at a number of points in the text, where Hsi-men Ch'ing is actually described as a "benighted ruler" (*hun-chün* 昏君).[318]

But what is the purpose of the analogy? Obviously we cannot really say that the misbehavior of Hsi-men Ch'ing in his own little world is responsible for the collapse of the world at large, causing untold suffering for countless others. But what I do believe the author is trying to work out through the medium of his fictional narrative is the Confucian understanding of the interrelation of the individual self and the world order, an idea stated programmatically in the same *Ta-hsüeh* passage, and repeated tirelessly in Neo-Confucian thought. According to this view, the emperor acts as the keystone of the entire hierarchical structure. When he fails to exercise his functions, then the edifice as a whole collapses, or, as in the common expression repeated many times in the novel, "when the roofbeams are not straight, the rafters will be crooked" 上梁不正下梁歪.[319] When there is no longer a ruler at the top, as we are told in chapter 100 (7a): "there was no one to rule in the Central Plain" 中原無主, the entire empire degenerates into a state of disorder (*luan*), in this case barbarian conquest. At the same time, the obverse of the same theory insists that the small man does have the capacity to at least contribute concretely to this disorder, an idea expressed with considerable passion in several *k'an-kuan* passages.[320]

The identification of Hsi-men Ch'ing with the perennial image of the bad last ruler lends considerable weight to the reading of the novel as a specific commentary on the world of the author's own time. Chang Chu-p'o, at

[317] Carlitz, *Rhetoric*, pp. 29ff., and "Role of Drama," pp. 57, 366ff. See also Martinson, "Pao, Order, and Redemption," pp. 59ff.; and Roy, "Confucian Interpretation," p. 49. The conception of the "bad last ruler" is developed by Arthur Wright in "Sui Yang-ti: Personality and Stereotype," pp. 69ff.

[318] Hsi-men Ch'ing is called a *hun-chün* in chapters 26 (5a) and especially 29 (3a): "These days chaos is the rule in the house ... causing catastrophic disorder for the helpless ruler" (如今這一家子亂世爲主 ⋯ 把昏君禍亂的). Cf. Hsi-men's association with dragon symbolism discussed earlier. In this context, Hsi-men Ch'ing's frequent dealings with court eunuchs—usually in matters of illegitimate business or official corruption—add to the analogy. At the least, the analogy between Hsi-men Ch'ing surrounded by his six wives, and the Sung emperor surrounded by his eunuch advisers, is suggested by Chang Chu-p'o and others. See Carlitz's discussion of Hsi-men Ch'ing's arrogation of titles, and his building of a mausoleum, as reflections of this level of meaning (*Rhetoric*, pp. 37ff.).

[319] For examples of this expression, see chapters 26 (8b) and 78 (5a), and a similar idea in chapter 76 (19a): "When the great ones are not in order, then the small ones have no respect" 大不正則小不敬.

[320] For example, chapter 70 (15a). See Carlitz, *Rhetoric*, pp. 37ff.; Wei Tzu-yün, *Wen-shih yü yen-pien*, pp. 117ff.; David Roy, "The Case for T'ang Hsien-tsu," pp. 1.28.

least, seems to suggest such an interpretation at several points.[321] Such a reading makes most sense in the context of the excesses of the Wan-li emperor, as a number of critics have recently argued, particularly with reference to that willful monarch's scandalous infatuation for the imperial consort Cheng Kuei-fei.[322] But since a similar case could also be made regarding the Chia-ching emperor, perhaps it is more useful to understand this as a more general indictment of bad rulership.

Returning now to the ideal of maintaining order within the sphere of the family (*ch'i ch'i chia*), we find an analogous situation of lapsed authority. In fact, it often seems as if the entire novel can be read as a gloss on this brief phrase from the *Ta-hsüeh* text. From the presentation of the initial completion of the household by chapter 19 or 20, at which time, on the surface at least, an uneasy peace seems to prevail, the narrative reads as an accelerating breakdown of family order. This is most obvious among the wives, whose relations proceed from protestations of sisterly affection to mutual antipathy and fatal clashes; but it also applies in the relations between the rulers and the ruled within this miniature empire, that is, between the mistresses and the maids, or the masters and the servants. The relation of mutual contempt is most flagrant in the cruel treatment meted out by Hsi-men Ch'ing and P'an Chin-lien to their underlings, punctuated by beatings and forced suicides, often connected to sexual intrigues.[323] At the same time, the servants pay them back in kind, first engaging in petty theft, and eventually trespassing on their masters' sexual territory. It is especially ironic, therefore, that it is the maid Ch'iu-chü who discloses to Yüeh-niang the incestuous affair already known to everyone else, sending P'an Chin-lien to her doom in chapter 85.

We also observe the same disorder among the servants and maids themselves, with many humorous scenes in which they mirror the behavior of their masters.[324] This is particularly highlighted in those chapters in which misdeeds at the two levels of the household are brought into

---

[321] Chang Chu-p'o, chapters 33 (7b) and 70 (*tp*). See also Ch'ung-chen commentary, 71 (9a).

[322] See Wei Tzu-yün, *Wen-shih yü yen-pien*, p. 110, and "Wang-kuan," p. 21b; Roy, "Confucian Interpretation," p. 50; and Carlitz, "Role of Drama," pp. 366ff. See discussion of this reference in Part I of this chapter.

[323] For example, chapters 11, 12, 26, 31, 43, 44, 50, 53, 58, 72, 75, 78, and 91.

[324] For example, chapters 30, 31, 34, 43, 44, 46, 47, 50, 78, and 91. This chaotic situation is explicitly condemned, for example, in a poem in chapter 22 (5a): "Hsi-men Ch'ing's excessive lust eliminated the distinction between high and low" 西門貪色失尊卑; and in Yüeh-niang's tirade in chapter 75 (21a): "I can't tell anymore who is the master and who is the servant" 不知那個是主子，那個是奴才. Particularly ironic instances of servants arrogating the role of masters occur in chapter 48, when the impious servant Shu-t'ung is called in to read the official bulletin announcing Hsi-men Ch'ing's promotion, and in chapter 78, when Tai-an and P'ing-an treat themselves to Hsi-men Ch'ing's sexual spoils.

structural juxtaposition, as for example in chapter 50, where Tai-an visits the "Lane of Butterflies" (*Hu-tieh hsiang* 蝴蝶巷) at the same time that Hsi-men Ch'ing is trying out his magic medicine with Wang Liu-erh,[325] or in chapter 75, when squabbles between the maids set up the serious clash between Yüeh-niang and P'an Chin-lien that gives the first concrete suggestion of the breakup of the family.[326]

The understanding that these various levels of disorder are a direct result of the failure to provide guidance at the top is spelled out unequivocally at frequent intervals. In addition to numerous examples of proverbial expressions of this idea, the author devotes more than one extended *k'an-kuan* passage to unambiguous statements of this principle.[327] Chang Chu-p'o is especially preoccupied by this theme, and he returns to it for impassioned discussions at many points, often explicitly drawing upon the language of the *Ta-hsüeh* to blame Hsi-men Ch'ing for his manifest failure to keep his house in order (*ch'i ch'i chia*), to pursue his individual cultivation (*hsiu-shen*), or to model the ordering of his household on the harmonious rule of the empire (*p'ing t'ien-hsia*).[328]

Once again, the key term in all of these discussions is "disorder" (*luan*). This term occurs through the text in a manner too profuse to be gratuitous. Sometimes the "disorder" in question is simply a matter of disturbing the normal routine—even in the sense of holiday excitement. But more often it is linked to negative associations—the confusion of illnesses and funerals, the flare-up of domestic squabbles into serious violence, and especially scenes of unleashed sexual excess.[329] In this context, the repeated use of the term "chaos" (*nao* 鬧) has a similar range of meaning, from simple excitement (*je-nao*) to more ominous challenges to orderly authority.[330] It is possible to argue, I suppose, that we are dealing only with

---

[325] One of the primary symptoms of the breakdown of order here is the sexual concourse of masters and servants, as in Hsi-men Ch'ing's relations with Shu-t'ung, Ch'un-mei, and for that matter, Sung Hui-lien. Cf. a *k'an-kuan* passage on this issue in chapter 22 (5a).

[326] Cf. the repeated incidents of beating servants which help to prepare the oversensitive Kuan-ko for his final trauma.

[327] For example, chapters 20 (14a) and 78 (4b).

[328] Chang Chu-p'o, chapters 24 (*tp*), 26 (27b), 34 (*tp*), 46 (14b), 69 (*tp*), 75 (*tp*), 83 (3b), and 84 (*tp*).

[329] For example, the term *luan* appears in the sense of family excitement in chapters 15, 18, 20, 30, 38, 46, 49, 54, and 68; in the sense of discord in chapters 11, 12, 31, 34, 35, 43, 58, 72, 75, 80, 92, and 100; in the context of sickness and death in chapters 48, 59, 63, and 90; in sexual descriptions in chapters 73 and 78; and in descriptions of pomp at the court in chapters 55 and 71.

[330] The term is used in chapter titles in chapters 26, 73, 84, and 92, and is emphasized in the text in chapters 78, 80, 95, and 99. Cf. the conventional *ta-nao* scenes in colloquial storytelling and on the popular stage (see below, Chapters 4, Part V, and 5, Part I).

common words in the language, but given their exaggerated usage I am convinced that more is at stake here. If there is any validity to my citation of the key *Ta-hsüeh* passage in this interpretation, then we may see another provocative allusion in the warning immediately following: "If the roots are in disorder, it is impossible for the branches to be ordered" 其本亂而末 治者否矣.

Thus, we see that the symptoms of disorder explored within the context of the family have far-ranging implications for the entire world structure. This lends much greater significance to the author's choice of the largely insignificant events in the private camp of a petty tyrant for the focus of his narrative. That is because the world of the household is the crucial heart of the entire system, at once the fullest extension of the world of the individual self and a microcosmic model for the world at large.

Having said this, one is reminded of another canonic formula of Confucian values related to this conceptual framework for interpreting the novel. This is the notion of the "five cardinal relations" (*wu-lun* 五倫): those between ruler and minister, father and son, husband and wife, elder and younger brother, friend and friend.[331] Here again, we observe the blatant, almost systematic, subversion of these ideals by Hsi-men Ch'ing and the others in every phase of the paradigm.

With regard to the relationship between ruler and ruled, I have already discussed the novel's projection of debased standards of rulership from the imperial level down to Hsi-men Ch'ing's own private empire; just as we see the prostitution of ideals of government service in the other direction, from Hsi-men Ch'ing's miserable performance as a local official on up to the "four evil ministers" in the capital. In the latter direction (i.e., minister to ruler), the paradigmatic relation is that of loyalty (*chung* 忠). Given the consistent subversion of this ideal into cynically opportunistic manipulations at both the macrocosmic and microcosmic levels—with disastrous results on both—it is important to recall that the book still presents certain positive examples of loyal service, with the corollary ideal of "personal honor" (*i* 義) that in the context of official conduct becomes nearly synonymous with loyalty. These include Magistrate Li, whose upright ordering of his own house provides Meng Yü-lou with an honorable exit from the world of the narrative, and Commandant Chou, whose personal loyalty and honor, despite the hopelessness of his cause, outweigh even the

---

[331] This paradigm forms the core of the discussion in the Hsin-hsin tzu preface. These ideas are treated in various classical sources with changes in terminology, notably in the *Chung-yung*, section 20, and in Meng Tzu's discussion of the "four cardinal relations" (*ssu-tuan* 四端) in his "Kung-sun Ch'ou" chapter (2A:6). See Martinson, "Pao, Order, and Redemption," pp. 138ff.; and Carlitz, "Role of Drama," pp. 44, 194f.

degradation of his ill-chosen wife, Ch'un-mei. This sheds an especially ironic light on the name of Chou I 義, the son of the old servant Chou Chung 忠, who figures in Ch'un-mei's final self-destruction.[332]

Moving ahead to the relationship between brothers, we see this blasted in the novel from the opening parody of brotherhood (at the start of the body of the novel proper in the *Tz'u-hua*, moved up to the head of the text in the Ch'ung-chen edition), and through a succession of unbrotherly brothers (e.g., Han Tao-kuo and Han "Erh tao-kuei") and out-and-out false brothers (e.g., Ch'en Ching-chi's masquerades in chapters 92 and 94). In discussing this point, Chang Chu-p'o notes the significance of the fact that the leader of the brotherhood, Hsi-men Ch'ing (and Ch'en Ching-chi, for that matter), are in the position of having no natural siblings.[333] This also accounts for the conspicuous lack here of the mutual faith ideally ascribed to the relationship between friends (*p'eng-yu yu hsin* 朋友有信). This is most pointedly satirized in the unstinting exploitation, on the part of the "brothers," of Hsi-men Ch'ing's dubious generosity as leader of their little society. This is the object of another ironic dig when Hsi-men's very reluctant loans to his sponging friends win him conventional praise as one who "holds fast to honor, and slights worldly goods" (*chang-i shu-ts'ai* 仗義疏財). Later he is suitably rewarded for his reluctant largesse when his friends lose not a moment in robbing his widow as soon as he breathes his last.[334] In a broader sense, if we define the relationship between "friends" more loosely to cover all forms of good faith between man and man, then we may speak here of the entire range of subverted values that, as Martinson has pointed out, is taken in by the recurrent

---

[332] The conjunction of *chung* and *i* is implicit in Meng Tzu's formula "in relations between ruler and minister there is [the ideal of] honorable behavior" 君臣有義. Cf. the use of the combined term *chung-i* in *Shui-hu chuan* and *San-kuo chih yen-i* (below, Chapters 4, Part V, and 5, Part V). Hsi-men Ch'ing's unsuitability for the true exercise of *chung* is perhaps satirized in his frequent donning of a "cap of loyalty and steadfastness" (*chung-ching kuan*), with its vague reminder of the rallying cry of Yüeh Fei; see, e.g., chapters 46 (3b), 56 (2b), and 67 (7a). See Yao Ling-hsi, "Hsiao-cha," p. 195; and Martinson, "Pao, Order, and Redemption," p. 183, n. 1. In this context, the scene in the Hall of Integrity and Honor (*Chieh-i t'ang*) in chapter 69 is particularly cutting. Cf. ironic distortions of the principle of *i* in chapters 72 (1a, 13b), 80 (11b, 12a), 84 (1a), and 85 (9b, 10b).

[333] Chang Chu-p'o, *tu-fa*, item 107; chapters 76 (53a) and 100 (22b); and "Hsien-hua," pp. 1b–2a.

[334] See chapter 56 (1a). Hsi-men is again described with the expression *chang-i shu-ts'ai* in the go-between's pitch in chapter 69 (4b). See also a *k'an-kuan* passage in chapter 80 (11b). Here, the requital of Hsi-men's erstwhile open-handedness is bewailed by Ying Po-chüeh (1b): "In those days what we ate was his, what we used was his, what we took advantage of was his, what we borrowed was his, what we gobbled up was his ..." 當時也曾吃過他的, 也曾用過他的, 也曾使過他的, 也曾借過他的, 也曾嚼過他的.

ironic use of the term "human feeling" (*jen-ch'ing* 人情) throughout the novel.[335]

This brings us back to the bond between husband and wife, biologically at the core of all human relations. The fact that this prototypical "novel of human relations" (*jen-ch'ing hsiao-shuo* 人情小說) focuses on the subversion of the proper relationship between man and wife on practically every page needs little further comment here. As mentioned above, the somewhat unwieldy assemblage of six wives in Hsi-men Ch'ing's house is not in itself a violation of this canonical relation; in fact, it initially purports to present a conventionally ideal state of family harmony. But the author immediately proceeds to puncture this myth with an endless procession of ironic scenes of bitter rivalry, insatiability, adultery, cuckoldry, sexual domination, and, finally, mutual destruction. From this point of view, the cause of all this disorder may be understood to be the inversion of the proper hierarchy of marriage—the kind of "upsidoun" situation known to students of English literature in the figure of Chaucer's Wife of Bath, a comparison particularly meaningful in light of the straddling posture in the violent deaths that begin and end Hsi-men Ch'ing's story.[336]

It is important to note, therefore, that these topsy-turvy relations are due as much to the overemphasis as to the neglect of conjugal affection. Thus, one reading of the novel would have it that the major factor in the dissolution of the family is the disequilibrium of Hsi-men Ch'ing's attachment to P'ing-erh, as manifest in favoritism during her life and the over-elaborate funeral after her death.[337] At any rate, this is the key to the view of the novel as a *roman à clef* reflection of the Wan-li emperor's infatuation for Cheng Kuei-fei and his subsequent attempts to undo the mechanism of legitimate succession. Another, more puzzling, side of the distorted marital relations pictured in the novel is seen in the warm mutual understanding

[335] Martinson, "Pao, Order, and Redemption," pp. 300ff. See also Carlitz, "Role of Drama," p. 56. Cf. the line in a poem in chapter 49 (12a): "Universal principles and personal relations, both are subject to value judgments" 公道人情兩是非.

[336] Cf. the warning in Hsi-men Ch'ing's fortune, which is told in chapter 29: "Only when the house of the wives is brought into submission can you [escape a disastrous fate]" 妻宮剋過方可. The failure of Hsi-men Ch'ing's wives to maintain the traditionally prescribed chastity (*chieh* 節) of widowhood after his death contrasts ironically with the solemn vows taken by Han Ai-chieh after Ch'en Ching-chi's death in chapter 100 (9a). Cf. P'an Chin-lien's refusal to pray for Hsi-men Ch'ing's recovery in chapter 79. Chang Chu-p'o discusses the subversion of marital relations in full in chapter 93 (*tp*), and drives home his point by appending to his prefaces charts outlining all the illicit relations of Hsi-men Ch'ing and P'an Chin-lien respectively (see above, n. 256).

[337] Chang Chu-p'o emphasizes this point in chapter 65 (*tp*, 3b, 9b). See discussions in Martinson, "Pao, Order, and Redemption," pp. 280ff.; and Cass, "Celebrations," p. 186.

between Han Tao-kuo and Wang Liu-erh as they cooperate in her lucrative seduction of Hsi-men Ch'ing—an ambiguity that lingers at the end of the book when she marries her brother-in-law and outlives the other, less brutally honest, women in Hsi-men Ch'ing's life.

Another riddle remains in connection with the role of Yüeh-niang as Hsi-men Ch'ing's principal wife. From one point of view, that of Chang Chu-p'o, the image of Yüeh-niang presented in the novel is profoundly negative. In her early acquiescence in Hsi-men Ch'ing's expansionist liaisons, her tendency to look the other way from household disputes, and especially her naive vulnerability to the false preaching of Buddhist para-sites, Yüeh-niang may be viewed as an inversion of the proper Confucian role of a wife in maintaining order within the household. This is particularly true with reference to her failure to admonish her wayward husband.[338]

The most glaring example of this lapse is seen in her thoughtless intro-duction of Ch'en Ching-chi into the circle of wives, likened by the Ch'ung-chen commentator to "inviting a wolf into the house" 引狼入室; and the author hints that she is not completely oblivious to the implications of his presence when she hurriedly sends him away upon hearing that Hsi-men Ch'ing has returned.[339] By the same token, her acceptance of her husband's whore, Kuei-chieh, as an adopted daughter is naive at best and calculating at worst. Chang Chu-p'o is especially outraged by the behavior of Yüeh-niang—even more than by that of Chin-lien—and frequently rails against her for her own failure to "keep her house in order".[340] In many comments the Ch'ung-chen editor expresses a similar view, but interestingly, he reverses himself at certain points and defends Yüeh-niang as basically well intentioned.[341] Even Chang Chu-p'o, I should add, finds it within himself to allow that the presence of Ch'en Ching-chi in the garden is not entirely her fault.[342] With this in mind, we should note that in a few scenes in the novel she does actually exercise her proper authority. In chapter 72, for example,

---

[338] Yüeh-niang's leniency is brought out in chapters 11 and 13; her obtuse naiveté is emphasized in chapters 32, 35, 81, and 83. Her susceptibility to Buddhist preaching is ridiculed in chapters 39, 40, 51, 84, 88, and 100. All these qualities are discussed in a *k'an-kuan* passage devoted to the wives in chapter 11 (3a). Chang Chu-p'o attacks Yüeh-niang in comments in chapters 14 (*tp*), 16 (18b), 18 (*tp*), 19 (2a), 31 (*tp*), 32 (*tp*), 33 (*tp*), 43 (7b), 58 (*tp*), 68 (28a), 75 (*tp*), 80 (*tp*), 82 (14a), 84 (*tp*), 87 (*tp*), 89 (*tp*), 90 (*tp*), 94 (21a), 96 (16a), and 97 (*tp*); as well as in the *tu-fa*, items 24, 26, and 27. The vitriolity of Chang's attack seems almost a sign of some personal grudge.

[339] See Ch'ung-chen commentary, 18 (25a), 85 (31b); and Chang Chu-p'o, 25 (*tp*), 44 (*tp*), 58 (*tp*).

[340] For Chang Chu-p'o's condemnation of her "failure to keep her house in order," see chapters 75 (*tp*) and 84 (*tp*).

[341] Ch'ung-chen commentary, chapters 12 (14a), 29 (34a), 43 (21b), 48 (25b), 75 (63b), 81 (7b), and 88 (31a).

[342] Chang Chu-p'o, 24 (*tp*).

she runs a tight ship during Hsi-men Ch'ing's absence, and in chapter 75 she summons the courage to confront P'an Chin-lien head-on.[343] Later on, after slipping back into her weak posture for a while to allow the incest of Chin-lien and Ch'en Ching-chi to run its course, she asserts herself quite forcefully in the successive expulsion of the two in chapters 85 and 92.

A similar ambiguity applies to the treatment of Hsi-men Ch'ing's third wife, Meng Yü-lou. Yü-lou's position as a confidante of P'an Chin-lien, on top of certain figural links to Chin-lien and others, add a hint of guilt by association to her otherwise sympathetic portrait. On the other hand, she is first presented in chapter 7 as a remarkably level-headed and self-reliant woman, whose well-considered marriage to Hsi-men Ch'ing stands in stark contrast to the circumstances of his acquisition of P'an Chin-lien and Li P'ing-erh in the same part of the book. Moreover, she ends up at the close of the story with a modest, salutary fate, which strongly suggests that she is intended to be a positive model of some sort. Chang Chu-p'o frequently praises Yü-lou with the same enthusiasm with which he heaps scorn on Yüeh-niang, and he even goes as far as to identify her as a kind of "self-allusion" (*tzu-yü* 自喻) on the part of the author. Regrettably, he does not provide sufficient evidence to support this assumption. Perhaps the most we can say is that the portraits of Yüeh-niang and Yü-lou help to fill out a spectrum of possibilities through which the author explores the positive and negative aspects of his two principal female characters.[344]

The issue of proper conjugal hierarchy is closely linked to the fifth paradigmatic relation explored in the novel, that between parents and children, or fathers and sons. The key term here is *hsiao* 孝. The common translation of this term, "filial piety," fails to do justice to its significance as the central axis running through all the other cardinal relations, often conceived as a quasi-metaphysical model of vertical continuity at the heart of the cosmic order.[345] Curiously, whereas the depiction of Hsi-men Ch'ing is apparently conceived in terms of pointed violations of all the other paradigmatic relations, the question of his filiality is completely obviated, since he appears in the novel as an orphan. On the other hand, there

---

[343] See chapters 72 (1a) and 75 (22aff.).

[344] For Chang Chu-p'o's comments on Meng Yü-lou, see chapters 41 (*tp* and 6b), 72 (32a), 85 (*tp*), and 100 (*tp*); and "Hsien-hua," p. 1a. See also Ch'ung-chen commentary, chapter 90 (4a).

[345] The canonic statement of this view of filiality is found, of course, in the "Classic of Filial Piety" (*Hsiao Ching* 孝經), which is mentioned in chapter 62 (26a). Cf. the songs from the play *Yü-huan chi* sung during the visit of the "false son" (*chia-tzu*, i.e., Ts'ai Yün) of Hsi-men Ch'ing's "fake father" (Ts'ai Ching) in chapter 36 (5bff.). Later Hsi-men Ch'ing renders "filial homage" (*hsiao-shun* 孝順) to Ts'ai Ching in chapter 55. Chang Chu-p'o provides frequent comments on this aspect of the text; see *tu-fa*, items 28, 29, 30, 31, and 32. See also "Not Pornography," p. 1b; and "Filial Martyrdom."

is no lack of affronts to the ideal of filial respect on the part of other characters. P'an Chin-lien, for example, shockingly mistreats her mother in a number of scenes, often in the course of her sexual misbehavior. Similarly, Ch'en Ching-chi shamelessly neglects the required funeral sacrifice for his father and then goes on to cheat his mother, driving her to her death, in his hot haste to fulfill his incestuous liaison with P'an Chin-lien in chapter 92. Soon thereafter he again defiles his father's memory by wasting the kind assistance of a family friend, Wang Hsing-an 王杏菴.[346] But these are all limited examples of explicitly unfilial behavior. The concept of filiality and its inversion is taken up with much greater seriousness in the development throughout the narrative of two other associated themes: childlessness and incest.

In view of the intense focus on the ordering of the family as a model of both individual and universal harmony, it is certainly significant that, for all the seed Hsi-men Ch'ing scatters in the course of the novel, he remains ultimately childless, proverbially the greatest violation of filial duty (不孝有三無後為大). Although of course he does father three children, all of these natural offspring are creatures of dubious origins and tragic ends. His daughter Ta-chieh, born before the narrative opens, remains a pitiful peripheral character whose eternal suffering in silence links her figurally to Ying-erh (the daughter of Wu Ta, later cruelly mistreated by P'an Chin-lien), as well as to the bottled-up Li P'ing-erh.[347]

Kuan-ko, as we have seen, comes into the world with unclear paternity,

---

[346] P'an Chin-lien's mother arrives unbidden in chapters 6, 11, 33, 58, and 78. In chapter 58 (17b) Yü-lou takes Chin-lien to task for her grossly unfilial behavior, and in chapter 78 (21a), Chin-lien's mother complains that her daughter falls far short of P'ing-erh in human decency. Fittingly, Chin-lien ends up with "no kin in sight" (*chü-yen wu-ch'in* 舉眼無親) to bury her in chapter 88 (5b). Cf. Hsi-men Ch'ing's hypocritical admonition on Wang San-kuan's unfiliality in chapter 69. The rank unfiliality in the book is underscored by the various sexual adventures that take place while the participants are in the midst of mourning for first-degree relatives (literally, "wearing the robes of intense filial obligations": *ch'uan-hsiao* 穿孝 or *tai je-hsiao* 帶熱孝); see chapters 14, 16, 67, and 68. The other side of this coin is the failure of parents to provide proper moral instruction to their children (*shih-chiao* 失教), a problem raised in chapters 31, 34, 35, and 79. Additional examples of shocking unfiliality occur in the case of Miao Ch'ing in chapter 47, and the plaint of the mirror polisher in chapter 58. For comments of Chang Chu-p'o on the above scenes, see chapters 1 (*tp*), 6 (16a), 57 (1a), 58 (*tp* and 17a), 78 (*tp* and 35b), 92 (16b); and *tu-fa*, items 85 and 89. *See* Katherine Carlitz, *Rhetoric*, pp. 29ff.

[347] The figural link between P'ing-erh and Ta-chieh is underlined by their friendship, brought out in chapter 51, as well as in the image of attempted suicide by hanging, unsuccessful in P'ing-erh's case in chapter 19, successful in Ta-chieh's case in chapter 92. In chapter 4 (5a), Hsi-men Ch'ing eagerly points out that he has no children (*wa-erh* 娃兒), other than his married daughter, to inhibit his relationship with Chin-lien.

and passes quickly through this sea of suffering under a constant threat of extinction—burning out amidst repeated images of fireworks, candlewicks, and the like, just as Hsi-men Ch'ing's official career starts to blaze. Likewise, Yüeh-niang's child bearing the allegorical name Hsiao-ko (literally, "filial son") is born—like so many figures in traditional Chinese narrative—at the precise moment of Hsi-men Ch'ing's death, making him something of a reincarnation of his own father (the later clarification of Hsi-men Ch'ing's rebirth notwithstanding). Not long thereafter he is pointedly extracted from family ties in the final scene of the novel. The spectacle of this incarnation of "filiality" taken into the ranks of celibacy is but the last affront to the ideal of family continuity, and the mockery is topped off as the crafty slave Tai-an becomes Hsi-men Ch'ing's heir by default. At the same time, however, the principle of figural reflection obviously links Hsiao-ko to his short-lived elder brother, who, we now recall, had also been described as a "little monk" in certain earlier scenes.[348]

The sense of the fragility, in effect the nonentity, of all of Hsi-men Ch'ing's offspring helps to explain why his wives and concubines invest so much time and effort in their attempts to become pregnant—the key to their status and even survival, as we see in the fatal rivalry between P'an Chin-lien and Li P'ing-erh that ultimately destroys Kuan-ko. In this context, Yüeh-niang's painstaking efforts to bear a son emerge as a pattern of recurrence covering the entire central body of the novel. This chain stretches from the moonlight prayers on a snowy night in chapter 21, through her miscarriage in the Ch'iao family's treasure house in chapter 33, and her acquisition of a fertility drug in chapter 50. The implied parallel here to Hsi-men Ch'ing's potency pills is made explicit in chapter 53 (10a), when Yüeh-niang boasts, "He has that foreign monk's magical art and I have the nun's divine potion" 他有胡僧的法術, 我有姑子的仙丹. Finally, the chain of occurrences achieves its logical end in chapter 79, when Yüeh-niang gives birth to a new heir precisely as Hsi-men Ch'ing expires.

It is quite interesting that a number of links in this chain unexpectedly bind P'an Chin-lien to Yüeh-niang. We may recall the figural similarity between Yüeh-niang's snowy-night prayers and P'an Chin-lien's plaint in chapter 38, and in chapter 52 it is Chin-lien whom Yüeh-niang asks for assistance in deciphering her calendar (here the detail of Chin-lien's ability to read comes into play) in order to plan the timing of her conception.

---

[348] For example, chapters 39 and 54. Chang Chu-p'o notes the figural connection between the two short-lived sons in chapter 58 (19a). It should be noted that Hsi-men Ch'ing shows strong affection for Kuan-ko. Cf. Ch'ung-chen commentary, 48 (25a). In chapter 78, Hsi-men Ch'ing sucks Ju-i's milk originally intended for Kuan-ko. The fact that Tai-an replaces Hsi-men Ch'ing at the end suggests an easy gloss on his name (for 玳 read 代).

Later, after P'an Chin-lien also acquires a similar pill in chapter 73, the question of who will sleep with Hsi-men Ch'ing on the fateful day becomes a matter of intense rivalry between them, as in chapter 74, thus setting up their bitter confrontation in chapter 75.[349]

Coming after Chin-lien's long history of abortive efforts, it is one of the most sharply ironic touches that, when she finally becomes free to fully exercise her desire with Ch'en Ching-chi, she becomes pregnant almost immediately. And when her illicit fetus is tossed into the privy six months later in chapter 85, it turns out, of course, to be a boy.[350] By the same token, Ch'un-mei also proves quite fertile in the house of Commandant Chou.[351] Even more ironic, the author has Ying Po-chüeh appear in chapter 67 to interrupt a session of garden sex between Hsi-men Ch'ing and P'an Chin-lien bearing the unwelcome news that his wife has given birth to an unwanted child.[352]

The theme of childlessness also helps to account for the recurrent motif of adopted parents and children that runs through the entire text. Here, as we have seen, true natural bonds of filiality are replaced by false and unnatural ones: between wife and whore, local tyrant and imperial villain, wastrel son and mother's lover.[353]

All these implications are drawn together in the key issue of incest, the most damaging inversion of the proper hierarchical order in cardinal human relations. Given the repeated emphasis we have seen on the concept of disorder (*luan*) at all the levels of the *Ta-hsüeh* paradigm, we can see that

---

[349] In chapter 53 Yüeh-niang refuses to sleep with Hsi-men Ch'ing because it is not the *jen-tzu* day (she lies that her period has come unexpectedly), and sends him to the bed of P'an Chin-lien—whom he interrupts on the verge of consummating the incestuous affair with Ch'en Ching-chi. In chapter 75 Chin-lien waits for Hsi-men Ch'ing on a *jen-tzu* day, but he goes instead to spend the night with Meng Yü-lou, in spite of her illness. Cf. Chin-lien's demand to the servants Shu-t'ung and Yü-hsiao in chapter 64 to reveal Yüeh-niang's secret method for conception. Since Hsiao-ko is born on the twenty-first day of the first month of the following year, we must assume that he was conceived on the *jen-tzu* day in chapter 53 (late in the fourth month of that year). Yüeh-niang's complaints in chapter 75 (27b) about discomfort in pregnancy may perhaps indicate that she is nearly due. In any case, her competition for Hsi-men Ch'ing's favors in chapter 74 is no longer a question of conception. See Hanan, "Text," pp. 35f. Chang Chu-p'o considers this point in chapters 17 (*tp*), 19 (6a), 30 (*tp*), 48 (21a), and 53 (*tp*).

[350] Chapter 85 (3a). In the same chapter (p. 1a), early in the tenth month, we are told that Chin-lien is putting on girth, and that her last period had been in the third month. The first explicit consummation of the union between Ch'en Ching-chi and Chin-lien appears to occur in the fourth month in chapter 82 (3a–b).

[351] For Ch'un-mei's fertility, see chapter 94 (4a).

[352] Chapter 67 (19b). Chang Chu-p'o inserts a cutting remark on Ying Po-chüeh's blessed event in chapter 67 (*tp*).

[353] See discussions by Chang Chu-p'o in *tu-fa*, item 86, and "Hsien-hua," pp. 1b–2a; and Martinson, "Pao. Order, and Redemption," p. 215.

the term for incest, *luan-lun* 亂倫 (literally, "disorder in human relations") sums up all of the dimensions of disorder presented in the novel.[354]

The most glaring example of such "overrating of personal relations" is set before us in the developing relationship between P'an Chin-lien and Hsi-men Ch'ing's son-in-law, Ch'en Ching-chi, which gradually deepens from casual flirtation through farcical frustration to illicit union and mutual destruction.[355] This chain of development is marked by such memorable scenes as Ch'en Ching-chi's first admission to the garden (through Yüeh-niang's good offices) in chapter 18, his barter of Chin-lien's shoe lost in the Grape Arbor encounter for a love token in chapter 28, and their repeated near consummation—interrupted by barking dogs in chapter 53, by the return of Hsi-men Ch'ing from the capital in chapter 55, and by the arrival of guests in chapter 57. Many of the implications of this forbidden love are brought together in chapter 33, where their advancing intimacy is presented almost simultaneously with the introduction of the author's icon of female sexuality, Wang Liu-erh, and is followed by the miscarriage of a son and rumors of another incestuous affair, between Wang Liu-erh and her own brother-in-law, Han Erh.[356]

Technically, of course, Ch'en Ching-chi is not Hsi-men Ch'ing's son; but Hsi-men Ch'ing does call him his "son" in his deathbed farewells, and P'an Chin-lien is labeled his mother-in-law in chapters 82 and 83, so the liaison is clearly identified as incestuous in the eyes of all.[357] The full revulsion we feel at this son-in-law "mounting his father's couch" is driven home in chapter 53, when Hsi-men Ch'ing returns unexpectedly to finish the job started by Chen Ching-chi, or when P'an Chin-lien delivers to Ch'en Ching-chi his late father-in-law's bequest of sexual paraphernalia in chapter 82. The irony is further underlined by a number of cases of incest that come before Hsi-men Ch'ing's local court, to which he invariably responds with outrage and merciless punishment.[358]

[354] The problem of incest is brought up in chapter 22 (5a), and especially in the most disorderly chapter: 33. See Sun Shu-yü, *I-shu*, p. 98; and Martinson, "Pao, Order, and Redemption," pp. 172ff.

[355] In addition to those examples noted, this chain of development is marked out by instances in chapters 19, 20, 24, 25, 29, 52, 54, 55, 72, 80, 82, 83, and 85. See Chang Chu-p'o, chapter 57 (10a).

[356] In the same chapter P'ing-erh refuses to sleep with Hsi-men Ch'ing, fearing that her baby will be disturbed, and sends him to Chin-lien's bed. Soon afterward, Chin-lien's mother arrives for a visit. See Chang Chu-p'o's assertion (*tp*) that all the threes and sixes in the chapter have a deeper meaning.

[357] See chapter 82 (4b): "On the false presumption of the close affection of a son-in-law, he had repeatedly engaged in topsy-turvy acts of abduction with his mother-in-law" 假認做女婿親厚, 往來和丈母歪偷. See also Chapter 83 (3a).

[358] For example, in chapters 33 and 76.

By the time the budding relationship between Chin-lien and Ch'en Ching-chi bears its forbidden fruit, the seeds planted long before are well rooted. We recall the key role of Yüeh-niang in first bringing these lovers together when it is she herself who fatally separates them from their scandalous embrace. This sets the stage for the delivery of Chin-lien over to the avenging sword of Wu Sung, and we suddenly remember that it was her unsuccessful seduction of Wu Sung himself, her own brother-in-law, that got our story started in the first place.

Beyond this most explicit instance of incest in the novel, the author goes to extraordinary lengths to entangle Hsi-men Ch'ing in a web of more subtle quasi-incestuous relationships. Thus, the initial whiff of illicit desire in Chin-lien's attempted seduction of Wu Sung is repeated when Hsi-men Ch'ing takes P'ing-erh, the wife of his own sworn "brother" Hua Tzu-hsü (turning simple adultery into incest). For that matter, P'ing-erh's earlier status as a concubine of Liang Chung-shu (the son-in-law of Ts'ai Ching) adds a further layer of entanglement when Hsi-men Ch'ing is later adopted as Ts'ai's "son." All this prepares the soil well for the affair of P'an Chin-lien and Ch'en Ching-chi.

Thereafter, a number of other connections provide hints of less blatant, but symbolically at least, equally taboo relations. For example, when Li Kuei-chieh ingratiates herself as the adopted daughter of Yüeh-niang, her past history with Hsi-men Ch'ing in the brothel is retroactively turned into a kind of second-degree incest. This tenuous connection is made more substantial later on, when Hsi-men Ch'ing takes as his adopted son Wang San-kuan, whose mother Madame Lin had become his lover shortly before; and the circle is closed with the ongoing sexual relations between Wang San-kuan and Kuei-chieh.[359] In the concluding section of the work, the author continues to hammer away at this pattern of significance, so that Ch'en Ching-chi's unsuccessful attempt to pose as Meng Yü-lou's brother in chapter 92 is followed by his successful ruse of passing himself off as Ch'un-mei's brother in chapter 97, in this case leading immediately to the consummation of a pseudo-incestuous match. Even after Ch'en Ching-chi's efforts win him a violent death, Ch'un-mei provides a final echo of the theme when she sleeps with the son of her husband's servant, dying suitably in bed. Thus, every one of the three main female figures whose names form the title of the book, plus the two successive central male

[359] Chang Chu-p'o discusses many of these convoluted relationships in chapter 69 (*tp*). Other liaisons involving a slight hint of pseudo-incestuous entanglement include the sexual favors enjoyed by Tai-an (Hsi-men Ch'ing's ultimate heir) with Pen Ssu's wife (Hsi-men's lover) in chapter 78. Cf. the false rumors accusing Yüeh-niang of carrying on an affair with Tai-an in chapter 94. Ch'en Ching-chi's final romance with Han Ai-chieh (the daughter of his father's lover) may also be viewed in this light. See Sun Shu-yü, *I-shu*, p. 98; Martinson, "Pao, Order, and Redemption," pp. 172ff., 281; and Carlitz, *Rhetoric*, pp. 50ff.

characters, eventually stray into actually or symbolically incestuous ties, which lead them by an inexorable chain of cause and effect to pay for their sins with their lives.

The relentlessness with which the author drives these sinners toward their final punishment brings us back to the structure of karmic retribution that frames his tale. As argued above, the precise manner in which the novel works out these consequences, first as a function of personal responsibility ("it is not sexual desire that leads men astray..."), and second, in the wider context of the interlinking of successive levels of relations, smacks more of the Confucian concept of *pao* than the Buddhist notion of *pao-ying* 報應, a point developed in depth by Martinson.[360] In effect, what the author succeeds in doing is to turn an unconvincing mechanical framework into a credible exposition of the dynamics of a moral universe in the flesh. That he is more interested in working out "retribution in this life" (*hsien-shih pao*) in terms of human ends than in witnessing the awesome power of divine judgment is borne out by the weakness of the reincarnation scheme he concocts for his main characters in the final vision in chapter 100, where they all go to markedly nondescript destinations that can only be explained as the deliberate planting of an outline for a sequel volume.[361]

There still remains, however, one additional framework of meaning that cannot be easily divorced from its original context in Buddhist thought. This is the frequent citation of the two correlative terms *se* ("color,"

---

[360] Martinson, "Pao, Order, and Redemption," pp. 59ff., 126f.

[361] The karmic rebirths specified in chapter 100 are as follows: Chou Shou-pei reborn as Shen Shou-shan 沈守善, second son of Shen Ching 沈鏡, in the capital; Hsi-men Ch'ing reborn as Shen Yüeh 沈鉞, second son of a rich man, Shen T'ung 沈通, in the capital; Ch'en Ching-chi reborn as son of Wang family in the capital; P'an Chin-lien reborn as daughter of Li 黎 family in the capital. Wu Ta reborn as son of Fan 范 family in peasant village near Hsü-chou 徐州; Li P'ing-erh reborn as daughter of Captain Yüan 袁指揮 in the capital. Hua Tzu-hsü reborn as son of Commander Cheng 鄭千戶 in the capital; Sung Hui-lien reborn as daughter of Chu 朱 family in the capital; P'ang Ch'un-mei reborn as daughter of K'ung 孔 family in the capital; Chang Sheng reborn as son of Kao 高 family of street beggars in the capital; Sun Hsüeh-o reborn as daughter of poor peasant family Yao 姚 outside the capital; Hsi-men Ta-chieh reborn as daughter of government clerk P'an Chung-kuei 潘鐘貴 outside the capital; Chou I reborn as son of Kao 高 family outside the capital, with name Kao Liu-chu-erh 留住兒.

The deaths of Hsi-men Ch'ing, P'an Chin-lien, and Li P'ing-erh are, of course, explicitly framed as fitting retributions for the crimes with which the narrative begins. The bitter end of Sun Hsüeh-o in chapter 94 is a bit more problematic, since she is generally depicted more as sinned against than sinning in the course of the narrative (although the lowness of her fate does match the meanness of her life). Yü-lou, on the other hand, appears to basically deserve her happy ending with Li Ya-nei, and even after their indiscretion results in a scandal, they end up in a state of peace and harmony in more modest circumstances. Cf. the actual sequel volumes *Hsü Chin P'ing Mei* 續金瓶梅 and the condensed version *Ko-lien hua-ying* 隔簾花影. See Martinson, "Pao, Order, and Redemption," pp. 43–47.

"appearance," "sensuality," "sexuality," "illusion") and *k'ung* ("emptiness," "vanity," "the Void") at various points in the text. In a simplistic reading of the novel it is possible to understand the invocation of various combinations of these terms as describing the transition from the illusion of excessive sensuality to a kind of redemptive awakening after the bubble has burst.[362] But too many of these occurrences push us toward a more complex apprehension of these two faces of existence to allow for such an easy solution.

In order to grasp the depth of this pattern of meaning, we must review here, in conclusion, the logical relation between illusory reality and emptiness in the novel. As Chang Chu-p'o astutely observes in more than one critical passage, the book as a whole begins and ends on a note of emptiness (although even he admits that it does not carry it through to its ultimate conclusion).[363] But the ocean of narrative between these two shores is, if anything, *full*—and it is the experience of plenitude that leaves the most lasting impression on the reader. When we take a closer look, however, we can see that intimations of emptiness hover over the text at every level of analysis.

I suggested earlier that the overall structure of the novel may be viewed as a gradual filling in of the narrative world in the first "half" of the book, followed by its steady depletion. Thus the process of inclusion by which P'an Chin-lien, Meng Yü-lou, and Li P'ing-erh are brought into the garden compound (and the subsequent addition of other flowers to Hsi-men Ch'ing's bouquet) is reversed after Hsi-men's death, until the household is rendered empty and desolate by chapter 91. This trajectory of physical fullness and emptiness also mirrors the rising and falling fortunes of Hsi-men Ch'ing's house. Thus, on the very eve of the first blow of adverse fortune, Hsi-men Ch'ing's complacent boast that all his desires have been fulfilled immediately brings to mind the inviolable law of the alternation of joy and sorrow (樂極生悲), discussed earlier, which is associated with broader patterns of alternating fullness and emptiness frequently evoked in chapter-opening and closing poems throughout the text.[364]

We have also seen at the level of thematic development a recurrent

---

[362] This sense seems to come out in the Hsin-hsin tzu preface. See Carlitz, "Role of Drama," p. 90f.; and Sun Shu-yü, *I-shu*, pp. 103–17.

[363] See Chang Chu-p'o, *tu-fa*, items 75, 76, 102, 103. A similar claim is made for *San-kuo chih yen-i* by Mao Tsung-kang (see below, Chapter 5, n. 476).

[364] See Chapter 91 (10a). Hsi-men Ch'ing's irreverent boast is in chapter 57, right after the Indian monk's discussion of the inexorable cycles of fortune. The idea that "when joy reaches its zenith it gives rise to sorrow" is brought out in chapters 8 (9a), 54 (1a), 56 (1a), and 92 (1a, 15b), among other places. Cf. the related discussions of "waxing and waning" (盛衰消長) in the Hsin-hsin tzu preface, "prosperity and decline" 得失榮枯, 興亡, 否極 泰來 in chapters 30 (1a), 71 (1a), 78 (1a, 29a), etc. See discussions by Chang Chu-p'o in chapters 95 (*tp*) and 96 (*tp* and 24a).

emphasis on the emptiness of excessive sexuality as manifested in various kinds of inconsequential sexual activity (voyeurism, homosexuality), and the corollary emphasis on childlessness and loss of posterity.[365] This, in turn, leads to the symbolic drying up or exhaustion of Hsi-men Ch'ing's resources, both financial and sexual, in the last ten-chapter phase of his life.

Perhaps the most pervasive treatment of the concept of emptiness, however, takes place at the level of specific imagery. This includes concrete images woven into the fabric of the narrative and the presentation of allusive images in lines of verse and in songs and plays cited in the text. I have traced the recurrence of specific symbols of evanescence such as fireworks, snuffed candles, and particularly snow—whether we are talking about its effect of obliterating outlines, or its tendency to melt away into dissipated slush.[366] In a number of scenes all of these images come together in complex concatenations of heat and cold, light and darkness, perception and nothingness, often linked directly to the term "emptiness." Perhaps the most striking example of this kind is found in chapter 61, where singers at the celebration of one late-autumn festival (*Ch'ung-yang chieh*, literally, "double-*yang* day") sing an incantational refrain of "empty...empty... empty" 空…空…空 even as P'ing-erh exudes a colorless discharge and fades into nothingness.[367]

All these suggestions of emptiness take on their fullest meaning at the dramatic close of the narrative, when the entire edifice of the novel melts away just as the foundations of imperial world order evaporate before the advancing Chin armies. The author captures all this in an unforgettable scene, as Yüeh-niang, having abandoned the now-empty compound, falls in with waves of other refugees and is swept out past the protective walls of her enclosed compound. The moment she passes through the city gates, the entire outside world simply falls away, leaving her in starkly open fields (*k'ung-yeh* 空野) ready to receive the final vision.[368]

It would be tempting to simply understand this final vision of emptiness

---

[365] Chang Chu-p'o emphasizes this dimension of meaning in chapters 61 (*tp*), 78 (21b), 79 (22a), 93 (4a). In chapter 79 (10a), Hsi-men Ch'ing's state of fatal sexual exhaustion is described with the term "empty at the core" (*k'ung-hsin* 空心). Cf. the undercurrent of sickness and weakness that is brought out at many points (e.g., chapters 12, 13, 14, 17, 51, 54, 62, and 80.

[366] See examples in chapters 68 (1a), 69 (9a), 71 (3a–b, 9a–10a), 74 (12b), 78 (12b). Cf. Chang Chu-p'o's reading of certain "empty" imagery in chapters 68 (*tp*) and 77 (*tp* and 17a), and in "Allegorical Meaning," pp. 3b–4a.

[367] Chapter 61 (17a–b). Similar imagery occurs in songs in chapters 2 (4a), 38 (8b), 51 (17b), 57 (1a, 13b), 65 (1a, 7a), 66 (11a), and 73 (3b, 4b, 16b). See Chang Chu-p'o, chapter 61 (15b).

[368] Cf. Chang Chu-p'o's discussion in *tu-fa*, item 26. The appearance of the Buddhist term "gate of right and wrong" (*shih-fei men* 是非門) in the final chapter (1a) strongly suggests an allegorical reading of the image of the city gates.

as a kind of resolution of the problem of worldly illusion through the redemption of Yüeh-niang and Hsiao-ko. Or conversely, one might wish to read into the modest survival of Meng Yü-lou—and perhaps even the survival of figures as unlikely as Wang Liu-erh and Han Erh to work the land—a message of redemption of another sort.[369] But I believe that it is closer to the intended meaning of the author for us to turn back to an understanding of the dual relation of illusory reality and emptiness (*se-k'ung*) worked out in the novel as two sides of the same coin. This, at least, is the sort of "message" of the identity of *se* and *k'ung* that would have made the most sense to the sixteenth-century reader, and this is invoked in many comments by Chang Chu-p'o.[370]

These abstract dialectics of reality and emptiness may sound like a bit of sophistry, but they have a special significance here for the art of the novel, which in a sense consists in turning the empty illusion of fiction into an affecting, and to that extent "real," human experience. The author of the *Chin P'ing Mei* is a consummate master at this. Admittedly, the philosophical pretensions of this book may be limited, but the dialectic of *se* and *k'ung* will serve us well as we turn now to the interpretation of another Wan-li masterwork, *Hsi-yu chi*.

---

[369] This reading would find its parallel in the common interpretation of the survival of Liu Lao-lao after the collapse of the world of *Hung-lou meng*.

[370] Chang Chu-p'o, chapters 78 (32b), 97 (*tp*), 100 (*tp*). See also the Ch'ung-chen commentary, chapter 79 (64a). The notion of the identity of *se* and *k'ung* is raised in chapters 1 (1a–2b), 65 (7a), 88 (9a), and elsewhere. Cf. the monastic name assigned to Hsiao-ko upon his withdrawal from the world of illusion: Ming-wu 明悟 (literally, "unclouded enlightenment"), as well as the question the monk P'u-ching asks of Yüeh-niang at the final moment: "Have you finally attained enlightenment now?" 你如今可省悟得了麼? This inspires the following comment on the part of Chang Chu-p'o (100 [28b]): "These words are intended to awaken all mankind. That is, the author is posing the question to the infinite multitudes of humanity in later ages; it is not just the Master P'u-ching asking Yüeh-niang alone. I would like to ask the reader who has finished reading the *Chin P'ing Mei* how he would answer this question" … 一語喚醒天下人, 是作者問天下後世萬萬人, 非普淨問月娘一人也。試問看過金瓶梅者何以答此一句?

Chapter 37: "A Ghostly Prince Visits San-tsang at Night" 鬼王夜謁唐三藏 , from "Li Chih" commentary edition, *Li Cho-wu hsien-sheng p'i-p'ing Hsi-yu chi* (see b.n. II.4)

CHAPTER 3

Hsi-yu chi:
Transcendence of
Emptiness

I

The second work to be considered here as an example of the literati novel form coming of age in sixteenth-century China is *Hsi-yu chi*. At first sight, the transition from *Chin P'ing Mei* to *Hsi-yu chi* might seem to invalidate the notion of a unified literary genre, since these two books could not be further removed from one another in subject matter and style. But I hope to show that these two disparate works share a very wide and firm common ground of both form and meaning. It is on this common ground that I will stake out the generic boundaries of the Ming literati novel, which will then enable me to treat *San-kuo chih yen-i* and *Shui-hu chuan* as sixteenth-century novels despite the more problematical assignment of their composition to this period.

The connection between *Hsi-yu chi* and *Chin P'ing Mei* is immediately borne out in the prevailing theories regarding their composition. The common attribution of *Hsi-yu* to Wu Ch'eng-en 吳承恩 (ca.1506–ca.82)—which we will see below to be less than unassailable—would probably put its creation sometime around mid-century, from the late Chia-ching period to the beginning of Wan-li.[1] This, together with the date 1592 on the

---

[1] The attribution of the novel to Wu Ch'eng-en is based on a bibliographical entry in a T'ien-ch'i period gazetteer of Huai-an prefecture (*Huai-an fu-chih* 淮安府志), printed in 1648, *chüan* 19, *I-wen chih* 藝文志, p. 3b. See citations in K'ung Ling-ching, *Chung-kuo hsiao-shuo shih-liao*, pp. 64–81; Chiang Jui-tsao, *Hsiao-shuo k'ao-cheng*, pp. 42–47; and Lu Hsün, *Hsiao-shuo chiu-wen ch'ao*, pp. 62–75. One of the first persons to connect the book mentioned in this entry with our novel appears to have been Wu Yü-chin 吳玉搢 (1698–

earliest extant full edition (the Shih-te t'ang 世德堂 text), would parallel fairly nicely the assumed late Chia-ching or more likely Wan-li composition of the latter, with a nearly full manuscript appearing in circulation by 1595 or 1596.[2]

This would appear to provide sufficient grounds for proceeding with an interpretive analysis of *Hsi-yu chi* as an exemplar of the sixteenth-century Chinese novel form. However, a number of unresolved problems in connection with the origins of *Hsi-yu chi* will require reopening the file before I turn to the primary focus of my discussion.

One aspect of the genesis of *Hsi-yu chi* that throws off the neat parallel to *Chin P'ing Mei*, and even casts doubt on their contemporaneity, is the fact that the former work is unquestionably the culmination of a long tradition of antecedent versions dealing with the same narrative outlines. This immediately distinguishes its process of composition from that of *Chin P'ing Mei*, although at the same time it sets up striking parallels to those of *Shui-hu chuan* and *San-kuo chih yen-i*. The materials in question include the accounts of the actual journey of the historical Hsüan-tsang 玄奘 (596–664), gradually embellished in the popular imagination into a full story cycle, as well as certain other types of popular religious narratives, and more sophisticated prose and dramatic works covering various parts of the story.[3] Among these, the most important are the *Ta-T'ang San-*

1773), a fellow native of Shan-yang hsien 山陽縣 (for his dates see Ogawa Tamaki, "Saiyūki genpon to sono kaisaku," p. 90), in his *Shan-yang chih-i* 山陽志遺, *chüan* 4 (cited in K'ung, *Shih-liao*, pp. 65–67). For problems regarding the absence of this entry in later editions, see n. 11. Other early references include Ting Yen (1794–1875, see Ogawa, "Saiyūki genpon"), *Shih-t'ing chi-shih hsü-pien*; Ch'ien Ta-hsin, *Ch'ien-yen t'ang wen-chi*, *chüan* 29, p. 461; and a discussion in Juan K'uei-sheng's *Ch'a-yü k'e-hua*, pp. 674f. A slightly different quotation is given in Yeh Te-chün, "Hsi-yu chi yen chiu ti ts'ai-liao," pp. 556–560, and in Chiao Hsün, *Chü-shuo*, *chüan* 5 (in K'ung, ibid.). See Liu Hsiu-yeh, "Wu-ch'eng-en chu-shu k'ao," and "Wu ch'eng-en lun-chu tsa-shih k'ao," pp. 232–46, esp. 234f.; Chao Ching-shen, "Hsi-yu chi tso-che Wu Ch'eng-en nien-p'u," pp. 251–63, esp. 253f.; and Liu Ts'un-yan, "Wu Ch'eng-en: His Life and Career," pp. 1–97, esp. 65ff., and his entry on Wu Ch'eng-en in *Dictionary of Ming Biography*, pp. 1479–83. See also the following general studies: Lu Hsün, *Chung-kuo hsiao-shuo shih-lüeh*, pp. 167ff.; Glen Dudbridge, "The Hundred-chapter *Hsi-yu chi* and Its Early Versions," pp. 187ff.; Anthony Yu, *The Journey to the West*, vol. 1, Introduction, pp. 16f.; Ogawa Tamaki, "Saiyūki genpon," pp. 88f.; Hu Shih, "Hsi-yu chi k'ao-cheng," pp. 354–99, esp. 376ff.; Kuo Chen-i, *Chung-kuo hsiao-shuo shih*, pp. 302ff.; and Yeh Te-chün, "Ts'ai-liao," pp. 556ff. I will reconsider the shakiness of this attribution in further discussions and in nn. 11, 22, and 23.

[2] For the dating of the hundred-chapter edition, see the following discussion. For the dating of the *Chin P'ing Mei*, see above, Chapter 2, Part I.

[3] For general reviews of the various sources of the novel, see Hu Shih, "K'ao-cheng," pp. 358–76; Liu Ts'un-yan, "Wu Ch'eng-en," pp. 70ff.; Glen Dudbridge, *The Hsi-yu chi*; Cheng Ming-li, *Hsi-yu chi t'an-yüan*; Chu I-hsüan and Liu Yü-ch'en, *Hsi-yu chi tzu-liao hui-pien*; Anthony C. Yu, *Journey*, pp. 1–13; Kuo Chen-i, *Hsiao-shuo shih*, pp. 276–92; Chao Ts'ung, *Chung-kuo ssu ta hsiao-shuo chih yen-chiu*, pp. 143–53; Ota Tatsuo, "Kaisetsu,"

tsang ch'ü-ching shih-hua 大唐三藏取經詩話 and the *Hsi-yu chi tsa-chü* 西遊記雜劇, which attest to the earlier treatment of the basic narrative in more or less continuous form, plus the fragments contained in the *Yung-lo ta-tien* 永樂大典 and the Korean text *Pak t'ongsa ŏnhae* 朴通事諺解, which enable us to postulate the existence of prior versions of the entire narrative.[4] Since these materials have been amply treated in recent scholarship, notably in the work of Hu Shih, Liu Ts'un-yan, Glen Dudbridge, Anthony C. Yu, and others, there is no need to rehearse here the particulars, except where they affect my interpretation of the hundred-chapter novel.

The possible existence of one or more full-length narratives covering the outlines of the entire story cycle prior to the Ming period, and perhaps as early as the late Sung or Yuan, is of no small importance to this study.[5] This is especially true since the notion of a nonextant *p'ing-hua* 平話 version as the missing link between the Sung-Yuan *shih-hua* 詩話 and the later Ming novel roughly parallels the theory of a hypothetical *tz'u-hua* 詞話 posited between *Hsüan-ho i-shih* 宣和遺事 and *Shui-hu chuan*, or the key position of the *San-kuo p'ing-hua* in the development of *San-kuo chih yen-i*.[6] As in these latter cases, there is not enough verbal correspondence between the later Ming novel *Hsi-yu chi* and any antecedent narratives to prove a direct textual relationship, but a careful comparison of the text with the

---

pp. 431ff., and his *Saiyūki no kenkyū*; Saitō Akio and Itō Keiichi, "Saiyūki no kenkyū to shiryō," pp. 210f.; and Hu Kuang-chou, *Wu Ch'eng-en ho Hsi-yu chi*, pp. 45–62.

[4] For a review of the specialized studies on the use of the respective source materials in the novel, see b.n. I.

[5] The extrapolation from the *Yung-lo ta-tien* and the *Pak t'ongsa ŏnhae* fragments to a hypothetical full-length narrative is largely speculation. The former, which covers only a peripheral anecdote from the prologue section, could easily derive from some common source material, as is often the case in prologues in Ming colloquial fiction. The latter, with its brief outline of the entire story line and its full presentation of one episode from the body of the narrative, provides a more convincing case; but here, too, the argument is just as plausible that what we have are two independent traditions drawing upon common sources. For that matter, the fact that the editions of this work available to us date only from the late fifteenth through the seventeenth centuries make possible any amount of revision or even interpolation by that time (for bibliographical information, see Dudbridge, *Hsi-yu chi*, pp. 60ff.; and Isobe Akira, "Genpon Saiyūki ni okeru Son Gyōja no keisei," pp. 103–27, esp. 103ff.). See also Liu Ts'un-yan ("Wu Ch'eng-en," pp. 76f.), who downplays the significance of these fragments; and Yen Tun-i, "Hsi-yu chi ho ku-tien hsi-ch'ü ti kuan-hsi," pp. 149f. For optimistic assessments of the possibility of a fourteenth-century *p'ing-hua* antecedent, see Dudbridge, *Hsi-yu chi*, pp. 63, 82f.; Kuo Chen-i, *Hsiao-shuo shih*, pp. 289f., 297; Cheng Chen-to, "Hsi-yu chi ti yen-hua," pp. 270, 273; Ogawa Tamaki, "Saiyūki genpon," p. 85; Anthony Yu, *Journey*, pp. 11f.; and especially Lo Chin-t'ang, "Clues Leading to the Discovery of the *Hsi-yu chi P'ing-hua*," pp. 176–94; and Hu Shih-ying, *Hua-pen hsiao-shuo kai-lun*, pp. 198, 293. For further information on the *Pak t'ongsa ŏnhae* texts, see Ōta Tatsuo, "Boku tsūji genkai shoin Saiyūki kō," pp. 1–22.

[6] For theories regarding *p'ing-hua* or similar antecedents of the novels *San-kuo chih yen-i* and *Shui-hu chuan*, see below, Chapters 4, Part I, and 5, Part I.

two narrative fragments, especially that in the *Pak t'ongsa ŏnhae*, does reveal a few such echoes.[7] Thus, it is quite reasonable to hypothesize about a direct chain of development linking the main known antecedent materials.

But though the novel *Hsi-yu chi* is undeniably the end-product of a long chain of development, to read it as simply the final stage in an expanding story cycle is to miss the quantum leap that transpired between the middle and the end of the process. As I have argued in my discussion of *Chin P'ing Mei* and will again insist in treating *San-kuo yen-i* and *Shui-hu chuan*, the relation of the novel to various antecedents is of far less consequence than is the radical structural transformation and revalorization of meaning effected on these materials when they are recast in the new generic mold.

Nearly all of the modern scholars working on this subject have taken due note of the fact that the hundred-chapter novel goes far beyond anything before it.[8] Beyond the simple fact that this text brings the narrative and dialogue to its fullest development, it has been pointed out that the restruc-

[7] See, for example, a passage in chapter 46 of the novel in which Sun Wu-k'ung transforms himself into a centipede and then clamps onto the nose of a villain ⋯ 道士鼻凹裏叮了一下. See *Hsi-yu chi*, 1972 Jen-min wen-hsüeh edition (hereafter *HYC*), vol. 2, p. 638 (citations by volume and page number, e.g., 2:638). This line may echo the corresponding line in the *Pak t'ongsa ŏnhae* version: 大仙鼻凹裏放了 (see Dudbridge, *Hsi-yu chi*, p. 187, l. 301). Cf. also the expression "one hundred percent accuracy" (*pai-hsia pai-cho* 百卜百著) in the *Yung-lo ta-tien* fragment (facsimile edition, *chüan* 13139, p. 8b), which is echoed in the novel version (1:124, l.5). Another term that figures in the scene (1:128), the "dragon- slicing platform" (*kua-lung t'ai* 剮龍臺), appears in the *Yung-lo* fragment (p. 9a), but not in the Yang Chih-ho version of the incident (*Ssu-yu chi*, p. 116, to be discussed below). The only weak verbal reflections I can discern in the *shih-hua* version are such expressions as "wait while I go on ahead" (*tai wo ch'ien-ch'ü* 待我前去), "it is obviously a demon" (*ting shih yao-kuai* 定是妖怪), and "to destroy the weeds you must remove the roots" (*chan-ts'ao ch'u-ken* 斬草除根).

[8] For example, Lu Hsün (*Chung-kuo hsiao-shuo shih-lüeh*, p. 169) describes the changes effected in the hundred-chapter edition as a complete "transformation" (*kai-kuan* 改觀), the same expression he uses to describe the *fan-pen Shui-hu chuan* (see Chapter 4, n. 76, of this book). Hu Shih ("K'ao-cheng," pp. 59ff.) describes this development as one of "elaboration and definitive revision" (*chia-kung hsieh-ting* 加工寫定). See also Cheng Chen-to, "Yen-hua," p. 264; Chao Ts'ung, *Ssu ta hsiao-shuo*, p. 152f.; Yen Tun-i, "Hsi-yu ho hsi-ch'ü," p. 150f.; and Anthony Yu, *Journey*, p. 37; etc. The opposite view is voiced by Ch'en Tun-fu in the Introduction to his *Hsi-yu chi shih-i*, p. 6 (see b.n. II.10 for information). Dudbridge treats the "hundred-chapter novel" as the basic text of his study, but he is slightly ambiguous on this point (see *Hsi-yu chi*, 103f.). Cf. Chang P'ei-heng's assertion that the text was modified by adding some Wu-dialect expressions at a later stage. See his "Pai-hui-pen Hsi-yu chi shih-fou Wu Ch'eng-en so-tso," p. 303. Earlier, in Wu Yü-chin's discussion of the Shan-yang gazetteer entry (see above, n. 1), the contribution of Wu Ch'eng-en was described as the transformation of an earlier text into a "popular elaboration" (*t'ung-su yen-i* 通俗演義), and a similar view is suggested in Juan K'uei-sheng's *Ch'a-yü k'e-hua*, p. 675. Hu Shih's remark ("K'ao-cheng," p. 377) that this passage was absent in his edition of *Ch'a-yü k'e-hua* indicates that it may be an interpolation. See below, n. 11 for further discussion of this question. A similar comparison of Wu Ch'eng-en's role to that of Lo Kuan-chung is suggested by Kuo Chen-i (*Hsiao-shuo shih*, p. 297) and by some of the traditional commentators.

turing of the work with the story of the Monkey King as an extended
prologue to the narrative proper, the interjection of suggestive philosophical terminology, and the extensive addition of incidental verse, mark major
changes that put the novel into a new literary class.[9] In addition, a number
of episodes in the novel, some of which are of key significance for the
allegorical framework, do not appear in any of the known antecedent
materials.[10]

The question that remains unanswered, however, is precisely when this
leap took place, that is, when were the story-cycles in the popular storytelling and dramatic traditions, and perhaps even a lost *p'ing-hua*, recast as
the hundred-chapter novel? Did this occur only around or shortly before
the time of the appearance of the Shih-te t'ang edition in 1592? Was it the
handiwork of Wu Ch'eng-en roughly a generation earlier? Or does the
credit go back still farther, to the unnamed author of a *p'ing-hua* version in
the Yuan or early Ming period?

[9] The shift of the Monkey King story to the head of the text is noted by Liu I-Ming in
his *tu-fa* introduction to the edition entitled *Hsi-yu yüan-chih* (see b.n. II.8 for information).
In the *Hsi-yu chi tsa-chü* version, Sun Wu-k'ung first appears only in Scene 9. There is no
narrative presentation of this material in the *Shih-hua*, although one speech in section 11
does fill in some of the details (see 1954 reprint, pp. 24f.). On the sources of the Monkey
King legend, see Dudbridge (*Hsi-yu chi*, pp. 114–54); Li Shih-jen and Ts'ai Ching-hao
("Ta-T'ang San-ts'ang," pp. 24f.); Isobe Akira ("Son Gyōja," pp. 103–27); Chu T'ung, "Lun
Sun Wu-k'ung," pp. 68–79; Chang Ching-erh, "The Monkey-hero in the *Hsi-yu chi* Cycle,"
pp. 191–217, 537–91, and his "Lun Hsi-yu ku-shih chung ti Wu-k'ung," pp. 14–59; Na
Tsung-hsün, "Hsi-yu chi chung ti Sun Wu-k'ung," pp. 66–78. For other unique materials in
the hundred-chapter novel, see Nicholas Koss, "The Xiyouji in Its Formative Stages,"
chaps. 1, 3, and 4. (I have read this dissertation only in incomplete draft sent to me by the
author, so my references are by chapter number only.)

[10] Among those elements in the allegorical framework of the book that do not seem to
show up in any of the antecedent materials, I would include the renaming of Dual Border
Mountain (*Liang-chieh shan* 兩界山) in chapter 14 (1:182); the episode of the *jen-shen* (人參)
fruit at the Temple of the Five Estates (*Wu-chuang kuan* 五莊觀) in chapters 24–26; the two
exiles of the mind-monkey in chapters 27–31 and 56–58 (although the Black Pine Forest
[*Hei-sung lin* 黑松林] in which the first of these incidents takes place is a stock setting of the
vernacular tradition, as for example in *Mu-lien chiu-mu ch'üan-shan hsi-wen*, Act 62 [see Ōta,
"A New Study on the Formation of the Hsi-yu chi," pp. 101f.]; in the *Hsiao-shih chen-k'ung
pao-chüan* [see Dudbridge, *Hsi-yu chi*, p. 94]; and in certain episodes in *Shui-hu chuan* [see
below, Chapter 4, Part I]); the moonlight meditation scene in chapter 36; the episode in the
Black Cock Kingdom (*Wu-chi kuo* 烏雞國) in chapters 37–39; as well as the episodes
involving the One-horned Rhinoceros Demon (*Tu-chiao ssu ta-wang* 獨角兕大王) in chapters 50–52; the temptation by the centipede spirits (*wu-kung ching* 蜈蚣精) in chapters
72–73; the parody on medical lore in chapters 68–71; the episode in the Land of Dharma
Destruction (*Mieh-fa kuo* 滅法國) in chapters 84–86 (this place-name is mentioned in the
Hsiao-shih chen-k'ung pao-chüan, but it apparently is a different story); and the near submission of the Master to the temptations of the Jade Hare in chapters 93–94. The poetry-
composing scene in chapter 64 also appears to be unprecedented, although we may perceive
here a trace of the tree spirits who appear in section 8 of the *Shih-hua*.

In attempting to solve this riddle, we must note at the outset that the accepted attribution of the novel to Wu Ch'eng-en is itself far from certain. In fact, it is based on evidence of the sort commonly dismissed by literary historians. As a number of recent scholars have acknowledged, this evidence consists primarily of a few laconic entries in local gazetteers assigning the authorship of a book called *Hsi-yu chi* to Wu Ch'eng-en. The identification of this title with our novel is supported only by a set of circumstantial arguments: the occurrence of certain regional dialect expressions in the text, Wu Ch'eng-en's reputation for wit, and certain passages in his collected writings that exhibit an interest in supernatural phenomena.[11] In short, the attribution of the book to Wu Ch'eng-en is of the same order as that of *Shui-hu chuan* and *San-kuo yen-i* to Lo Kuan-chung 羅貫中 or Shih Nai-an 施耐庵, which I will call into serious question in the following two chapters.[12]

[11] For the gazetteer references in question, see n. 1. See also Lu Hsün, *Chiu-wen ch'ao*, pp. 62ff.; Liu Ts'un-yan, "Wu Ch'eng-en," p. 65; and Anthony Yu, *Journey*, pp. 16f. A Ying (Ch'ien Hsing-ts'un) points out in *Hsiao-shuo hsien-t'an*, pp. 176ff., that the title *Hsi-yu chi* is deleted in most later printings of the Shan-yang gazetteer. Tanaka Iwao argues in "Saiyūki no sakusha," p. 37, that the description of Wu's book as a "miscellany" (*tsa-chi* 雜記) in Wu Yü-chin's reference would not fit a work of colloquial fiction such as this. Isobe Akira ("Saiyūki ni okeru Cho Hakkei zō no keisei," p. 185) suggests that this entry may in fact refer to an edition of the drama *Hsi-yu chi tsa-chü*. Cf. an additional reference to a book entitled *Hsi-yu chi* in the late seventeenth-century catalogue *Ch'ien-ch'ing t'ang shu-mu* 千頃堂書目 of Huang Yü-chi 黃虞稷. Chang P'ei-heng argues ("Pai-hui-pen," p. 296) that the listing of this book under the category of historical and geographical works in this catalogue shows that it is a different sort of book, perhaps a travelogue recording Wu's journey to take up his official post at the court of the Prince of Ching (see n. 20). Su Hsing rejects this (in "Yeh t'an pai-hui-pen Hsi-yu chi shih-fou Wu Ch'eng-en so-tso," pp. 250 ff.) on the basis of evidence that Wu never actually went to take up this position. See also Liu Ts'un-yan, "Ch'üan-chen chiao ho hsiao-shuo Hsi-yu chi," pt. 1, p. 55. The passages in Wu Ch'eng-en's *wen-chi* resonating with the language of the novel include those on pp. 15, 19, 28, 75, 77, 95. (See Liu Hsiu-yeh edition, cited in n. 1.) See especially Wu's poem "Erh-lang-shen sou shan t'u ko" 二郎神搜山圖歌 and his preface to a work entitled *Yü-ting chih* 禹鼎志, included in *She-yang hsien-sheng ts'un-kao*, chüan 2, p. 7b (see Ogawa Tamaki, "Saiyūki genpon," p. 88f.; and Chang P'ei-heng, "Pai-hui-pen," pp. 303ff.). The attribution to Wu of the *tz'u* collection *Hua-ts'ao ts'ui-pien* containing material drawn from colloquial fiction would, if true, also link Wu to the latter medium. See Hanan, *The Chinese Short Story*, p. 166. The presence of Huai-an dialect expressions is discussed in Ogawa Tamaki, "Saiyūki genpon," p. 90; Liu Ts'un-yan, "Wu Ch'eng-en," p. 67; and Huang Su-ch'iu, "Hsi-yu chi ti chiao-ting ho chu-shih kung-tso," pp. 180f. See also Chang P'ei-heng, "Pai-hui-pen," pp. 298ff. Another link between Wu Ch'eng-en and the field of colloquial fiction may be seen in a reference in Juan K'uei-sheng's *Ch'a-yü k'e-hua*, p. 641, indicating that Wu wrote a laudatory piece (*tsan* 贊) on certain illustrations of the thirty-six *Shui-hu* heroes. See also Wu's friendship with Li Ch'un-fang, to be discussed in n. 22.

[12] For general discussions of the weakness of the attribution of the novel to Wu Ch'eng-en, see Glen Dudbridge (Tu Te-ch'iao), "Hsi-yu chi tsu-pen k'ao ti tsai-shang-ch'üeh," pp. 497–519; Tanaka Iwao, "Saiyūki no sakusha"; Arai Ken, "Saiyūki no naka no Saiyūki,"

Even if one chooses to adopt a less critical approach and accept the indications that Wu Ch'eng-en did write a book entitled *Hsi-yu chi*, a number of problems still remain. Chief among these is the question of whether the hundred-chapter novel, as represented by the 1592 Shih-te t'ang edition, actually constitutes a close approximation of Wu Ch'eng-en's putative work.

This issue has been beclouded by scholarly debate over the precise relationship between the Shih-te t'ang text and two other early texts: the *T'ang San-tsang hsi-yu shih-o chuan* 唐三藏西遊釋厄傳, compiled by Chu Ting-ch'en 朱鼎臣, and *San-tsang ch'u-shen ch'üan-chuan* 三藏出身全傳, compiled by Yang Chih-ho 楊致和 (陽至和) appearing in roughly the same period.[13] Since these two texts cover more or less the same outlines of the

---

p. 600; Anthony Yü, *Journey*, pp. 17f.; Yen Tun-i, "Hsi-yu ho hsi-ch'ü," p. 556; Liu Ts'un-yan, "Wu Ch'eng-en," pp. 65f.; Chang Ching-erh, *Hsi-yu chi jen-wu yen-chiu*, pp. 11–17. The latest and most thorough refutation of the "evidence" linking the novel to Wu is that by Chang P'ei-heng in "Pai-hui pen," pp. 295–305. See also Ch'en Yü-p'i, "Wu Ch'eng-en Hsi-yu chi ch'eng yü wan-nien shuo hsin-cheng," pp. 3f.; and Huang Su-ch'iu, "Chiao-ting ho chu-shih," pp. 180ff. Ch'en Tun-fu, for his own reasons, gives the most absolute rejection of this theory (see *Shih-i*, pp. 4ff., 10ff., 18). The fact that the writer of the preface in the Shih-te t'ang edition, Ch'en Yüan-chih, claims to have no idea who the author might be has also been taken as a weak point in the theory of Wu Ch'eng-en's authorship, since he was a fairly well-known literati figure associated with some of the "latter seven masters" (*hou ch'i-tzu* 後七子), discussed above in Chapter 1. Additional acknowledgments of the tentative nature of the attribution to Wu Ch'eng-en can be found in Ōta Tatsuo, "Saiyū shōdōsho kō," and in his "Kaisetsu," p. 439; Isobe Akira, "Hsi-yu chi ti chieh-na yü liu-ch'uan," p. 151; C. T. Hsia, *The Classic Chinese Novel*, pp. 116, 124.

[13] For bibliographical information regarding the Chu and Yang editions, see b.n. II. 2–3. Liu Ts'un-yan treats this issue in "Ssu-yu chi ti Ming k'e-pen," pp. 344ff., 355, 363. The same argument also appears in his *Chinese Popular Fiction in Two London Libraries*, pp. 138–44, 204ff., and in his *Ho-feng t'ang tu-shu chi*, pp. 379–432, as well as in his "The Prototypes of Monkey," pp. 55–71, and his "Wu Ch'eng-en," pp. 75, 81. See also Dudbridge, "Early Versions," pp. 159ff.; Chao Ts'ung, *Ssu ta hsiao-shuo*, pp. 163ff., 172ff.; Cheng Chen-to, "Yen-hua," pp. 266ff., 275ff., 286; Chang P'ei-heng, "Pai-hui-pen," p. 300; Chang Ching-erh, *Jen-wu yen-chiu*, pp. 27ff.; Chao Ching-shen, "Tu Ssu-yu chi" and "Ssu-yu chi tsa-chih," pp. 221–28; Ōta Tatsuo, "New Study," pp. 106–12, and his "Saiyūki zakkō," pp. 1–18. For a comprehensive treatment of this question, see Nicholas Koss, "Formative Stages," chap. 1. See also Kuo Chen-i, *Hsiao-shuo shih*, pp. 299ff.; C. T. Hsia, *Classic Novel*, pp. 122ff.; Hu Shih, "K'ao-cheng," pp. 332ff., and "Pa Ssu-yu chi pen ti Hsi-yu chi-chuan," pp. 408–11; Sun K'ai-ti, *Jih-pen Tung-ching so chien Chung-kuo hsiao-shuo shu-mu*, pp. 79ff., 83, 95, and his *Chung-kuo t'ung-su hsiao-shuo shu-mu*, p. 190; Dudbridge (Tu Te-ch'iao), "Tsai-shang-ch'üeh," pp. 497–519; Anthony Yu, *Journey*, pp. 13f.; and Ogawa Tamaki, "Saiyūki genpon," pp. 86f. Within these studies, the priority of the Chu version was first suggested by Lu Hsün in *Chung-kuo hsiao-shuo shih-lüeh*, and is upheld by Liu Ts'un-yan and Nicholas Koss. Hu Shih tried to show that the Shih-te t'ang edition preceded the Chu text. This line of reasoning is followed by others, including Dudbridge and Sun K'ai-ti. Ōta ("Kaisetsu," p. 438) puts the Chu text even after the Yang edition. Cheng Ming-li, in "Lun Hsi-yu chi san pan-pen chien chih kuan-hsi," pp. 173–234, argues for an earlier prototype (*tsu-pen* 祖本).

story, but are briefer (sixty-seven and forty-one chapters, respectively), discussion has centered on the question of whether what we have here is an expansion of a shorter text or an abridgment of a longer one. This issue parallels the debate over the priority of the *fan-pen* 繁本 or the *chien-pen* 簡本 recensions of *Shui-hu chuan*, that of the *San-kuo chih t'ung-su yen-i* or the *San-kuo chih-chuan* 志傳, and perhaps that of the *Chin P'ing Mei tz'u-hua* or what is commonly known as the Ch'ung-chen 崇禎 edition of that work.[14] This analogy is thrown off somewhat by the fact that the printing of the Shih-te t'ang edition is not appreciably better than that of the Chu edition. But on the other hand, the name of the Fukien publisher Yü Hsiang-tou 余象斗, known for his work on various *chien-pen* editions of *Shui-hu*, also appears on an earlier printing of a companion volume to the Yang edition of *Hsi-yu chi*, which suggests that we are dealing with an associated chapter of literary history.[15]

The debate over the chronological priority of the Shih-te t'ang, the Chu, or the Yang text has seesawed back and forth for half a century without leading to any definitive conclusions in the matter.[16] To my mind, all of these efforts suffer from a tendency to lose sight of the possibility (which all generally admit but then disregard) that both the longer and shorter versions may derive from earlier prototypes, so that any comparison of the

[14] For the somewhat similar debate over the priority of the different recensions of our other three masterworks, see below, Chapters 2, Part I, 4, Part I, and 5, Part I. The early editions of *Hsi-yu chi* are also discussed in terms of the distinction between "fuller" and "simpler" recensions (*fan-pen, chien-pen*) by various scholars, including Sun K'ai-ti (*Jih-pen*, p. 84), Cheng Chen-to ("Yen-hua," p. 285), Ogawa Tamaki ("Saiyūki genpon," p. 116, n. 18), Ota Tatsuo ("New Study," p. 107), and Saitō Akio and Itō Keiichi ("Saiyūki no kenkyū to shiryō, p. 211). See also Ch'en Hsin, "Ch'ung-p'ing Chu Ting-ch'en T'ang San-tsang Hsi-yu shih-o chuan ti ti-wei ho chia-chih," pp. 61–67.

[15] Both the Chu edition and certain Wan-li reprints of the Shih-te t'ang text appear in the split-page format, with woodcut illustrations positioned above the text, which is characteristic of the Fukien editions known by the abbreviated designation *Min-pen* 閩本. Cf. certain later Wan-li editions in *Min-pen* format described by Sun K'ai-ti (*Jih-pen*, p. 73); Chao Ts'ung, *Ssu ta hsiao-shuo*, pp. 163ff.; and Liu Ts'un-yan, *Buddhist and Taoist Influences on Chinese Novels*, p. 152. See also Nicholas Koss "Formative Stages," chap. 3; and Ōta Tatsuo, *Saiyūki no kenkyū*, pp. 261f. Cheng Chen-to uses this detail to date the Chu edition earlier than the Shih-te t'ang text ("Yen-hua," p. 281). Cf. also the use of the term *chi-chuan* 記傳 in certain editions, which recalls similar usage in various *chien-pen* editions of *San-kuo chih yen-i* and *Shui-hu chuan* (see Chapters 4 and 5 of this book). For the connection between Yü Hsiang-tou and the printing of colloquial fiction in the Wan-li period, see Chapter 4, n. 63, of this book.

[16] See, for example, Dudbridge, "Early Versions," pp. 167ff.; and Nicholas Koss, "Formative Stages," chaps. 3, 4, 6, 7. Koss's conclusions regarding the probable priority of the Chu edition are based on close comparisons of chapter titles and concluding verses, certain narrative details, general style, linguistic style-markers, and the use of poetry in the two texts. Cf. Huang Su-ch'iu's identification of the Shih-te t'ang edition as Wu Ch'eng-en's original text ("Chiao-ting ho chu-shih, p. 180). See also Cheng Ming-li, "Lun Hsi-yu chi san pan-pen," pp. 173–234.

secondary editions that have by chance come down to us cannot prove much about the original filiation of the three versions.[17]

The idea that there must have been an edition of *Hsi-yu chi* earlier than the extant Wan-li texts is unavoidable, since Wu Ch'eng-en died around 1582. This is supported by a number of other pieces of evidence. The most obtrusive of these appears at the head of the Shih-te t'ang and the Chu texts themselves, where we get the explicit mention of a prior text entitled *Hsi-yu shih-o chuan* (not to be confused with the identically titled Chu edition).[18] More tantalizing evidence occurs in the early Ch'ing *Hsi-yu cheng-tao shu* 西遊証道書, edited by Wang Hsiang-hsü 汪象旭 and Huang T'ai-hung 黃太鴻. The commentary in this edition speaks in several places about an "original edition" (*ku-pen* 古本), different from the later text on a number of points, which it identifies as a "Ta-lüeh t'ang" 大略堂 edition.[19] Even more suggestive is a preface signed by Ch'en Yüan-chih 陳元之 in the 1592 edition claiming that this text is based on an earlier manuscript

---

[17] The possibility that neither of these editions represents the "original text" is implied by Koss in discussions in chap. 6; and also by Chao Ts'ung, *Ssu ta hsiao-shuo*, pp. 174f.; Yen Tun-i, "Hsi-yu ho hsi-ch'ü," pp. 149f.; Anthony Yu, "Narrative Structure and the Problem of Chapter Nine in the *Hsi-yu chi*," p. 5; Cheng Chen-to, "Yen-hua," pp. 275–86; and C. T. Hsia, *Classic Novel*, p. 124.

[18] In the Yang edition, this title is given as *San-tsang shih-ni chuan* 三藏釋尼傳 (the character *ni* here obviously a misprint for *o* 厄). See *Ssu-yu chi*, p. 100. See also Ōta Tatsuo, "New Study," pp. 111f.; and Dudbridge (Tu Te-ch'iao), "Tsai-shang-ch'üeh," pp. 500ff. The fact that the Chu version also begins with the same reference, notwithstanding its own identical title, seems to prove that it is a yet earlier text that is at issue.

[19] For bibliographical information on the Wang Hsiang-hsü edition, see b.n. II.5. In a note in chapter 9 (p. 1b) he refers to the earlier "Ta-lüeh t'ang" edition as *Shih-o chuan* (*Shih-o chuan ku-pen* 釋厄傳古本). In another place (chapter 100 [14a]), the co-editor Huang T'ai-hung enumerates the differences between this edition and the "original edition" (*ku-pen*), including the well-known point about the interpolated story of Hsüan-tsang's birth and early adventures, plus certain differences in the use of popular verse and dialect expressions. Another note in chapter 22 (p. 1b) raises the possibility that this "ku-pen" may perhaps refer to a Wan-li edition such as the *Li Cho-wu hsien-sheng p'i-p'ing Hsi-yu chi* (see b.n. II.4). For additional discussions of the Ta-lüeh t'ang reference, see Chao Ts'ung, *Ssu ta hsiao-shuo*, pp. 169, 182f.; Dudbridge, "Tsai-shang-ch'üeh," pp. 509f.; Ōta Tatsuo, "Kaisetsu," p. 438, "Shōdōsho," pp. 10f., and "New Study," pp. 111f.; C. T. Hsia, *Classic Novel*, p. 124; Isobe Akira, "Genpon Saiyūki o meguru mondai," pp. 10f. The identity of the Ta-lüeh t'ang text remains a mystery. Liu Ts'un-yan speculates that this may refer to a prototype of the Chu Ting-ch'en edition in his "Ch'üan-chen chiao," pt. 1, p. 57; and in pt. 5, p. 72, he tentatively identifies this as an original "Ch'üan-chen" Taoist version. I have found no mention of this publishing house in any of the general studies on Yuan and Ming printing mentioned in Chapter 1, n. 69, of this book, including K. T. Wu, "Ming Printers and Printing;" Liu Ts'un-yan, *Ming-Ch'ing Chung-kuo t'ung-su hsiao-shuo pan-pen yen-chiu*; Lo Chin-t'ang, *Li-tai t'u-shu pan-pen chih-yao*; Liu Kuo-chün, *Chung-kuo shu-shih chien-pien*; Rawski, *Education and Popular Literacy in Ch'ing China*; and Nagasawa Kikuya, *Wakansho no insatsu to sono rekishi*. Nor has it turned up in the detailed lists of printing houses given in Shih Mei-ts'en, *Chung-kuo yin-shua fa-chan shih*; P'an Ch'eng-pi and Ku T'ing-lung, *Ming-tai pan-pen t'u-lu*

associated with an unspecified "princely house" (*Wang-fu pen* 王府本). Since Wu Ch'eng-en at one point in his career may have served as a tutor in the household of a Prince of Ching 荆王, this has led scholars to speculate that this notice may refer to none other than the lost book by Wu Ch'eng-en himself.[20]

One frequently overlooked document indicating an even earlier text akin to the hundred-chapter novel is the preface by Yang T'i 楊悌 to Yang Shen's 楊慎 *tsa-chü* play *Tung-t'ien hsüan-chi* 洞天玄記, in which the allegorical scheme of this play is explained with reference to a prose work called *Hsi-yu chi* that seems quite close to the novel we know from the Shih-te t'ang edition. If that is so, then the early date on another preface to this play, 1542, would suggest the existence of such a text somewhat

---

ch'u-pien; Nagasawa Kikuya, "*Genson Mindai shōsetsu-sho kankōsha hyō shohen*," pp. 41–48; or Nancy Lee Swann, "Seven Intimate Library Owners," pp. 363–90. I have also found no trace of it in my browsing through the bibliographical descriptions in Ming *pi-chi* writings, such as Hu Ying-lin's *Shao-shih shan-fang pi-ts'ung* and Liu Jo-yü's *Cho-chung chih*.

[20] This theory is based on the reading of an ambiguous passage in the Ch'en Yüan-chih preface, where three unclear phrases—"produced in the domain of a certain nobleman of the imperial family" 出天潢何侯王之國, "produced by a follower of the eight masters" 出八公之徒, and "produced under the private sponsorship of the prince" 出王自製 —have led scholars to the conclusion that the novel was sponsored by a certain Prince of Ching, or at least written during the tenure of Wu Ch'eng-en as "tutor" (*chi-shan* 紀善) in his household. (For bibliographical information regarding this edition, see b.n. II.1. A convenient reprint of the preface is provided by Sun K'ai-ti in *Jih-pen*, p. 75. The first scholar to suggest this reading appears to have been Cheng Chen-to ("Yen-hua," p. 269). For later discussions of the theory, see Ōta Tatsuo, "New Study," pp. 106ff., 111f., and "Kaisetsu," pp. 439f.; Liu Ts'un-yan, "Ssu-yu chi," p. 375; and Hu Kuang-chou, *Wu Ch'eng-en ho Hsi-yu chi*, p. 18. In "Wu Ch'eng-en," p. 72, Liu Ts'un-yan brings evidence of patronage of dramatic literature by this same Prince of Ching. In addition, Ōta Tatsuo ("Kaisetsu," p. 439) cites a late Ming *pi-chi* work (*Hsiu-an ying-yü* 休菴影語 by Sheng Yü-ssu 盛于斯) that speaks of *Hsi-yu chi* as the product of another princely house, this time a *Chou-wang fu* 周王府 (*Chou-ti* 周邸). Cf. also another reference to a *Lu-fu pen Hsi-yu chi* 魯府本西遊記, based on an entry in Chou Hung-tsu's *Ku-chin shu-k'e*, p. 377, discussed by Ōta Tatsuo in "Saiyūki seiritsu shiryaku," p. 29, and in his *Saiyūki no kenkyū*, pp. 239ff. 244–59. See also Isobe Akira ("Cho Hakkei no keisei," pp. 185f.), who suggests that this may refer to a dramatic work. The possibility of identifying the Ching-wang in question depends on whether one follows Liu Hsiu-yeh's dating (see "Wu Ch'eng-en nien-p'u" 吳承恩年譜, in *Ts'ung-k'ao*, p. 224), which would place Wu in this position in the year 1562 or 1563, or Liu Ts'un-yan's counter-argument that he may have held this post as early as 1553. For further information, see Ch'en Kan, "Wu Ch'eng-en ti Ching-fu chi-shan chih pu ho Hsi-yu chi ti hsieh-tso k'an-k'e," pp. 206–14. According to the genealogical charts (*piao* 表), no. 4, in the *Ming shih* (*chüan* 103, p. 2876), the holder of the hereditary title of Ching-wang from 1554 to 1570 was Chu I-chü 朱翊鉅 (the position seems to have been briefly vacant in 1553). See also Ōta Tatsuo, "Zakkō," pp. 13ff. Ch'en Yü-p'i reviews this piece of evidence in "Wu Ch'eng-en Hsi-yu chi ch'eng yü wan-nien shuo hsin-cheng," and cites a paper presented by Liu Ts'un-yan in China in 1981, which tries to link Chu I-chü's three sons with the three princes in Yü-hua-chou 玉華州 in chapter 89 of the novel.

sooner than is normally assumed.[21] If it is a book by Wu Ch'eng-en that this writer is talking about, then at the very least this would contradict the theory that the novel was a product of Wu's later years.[22]

Given the wide acceptance of the prevailing theory of authorship, there is no reason for me to deny that Wu Ch'eng-en had some role in the development of the novel. But once again, there are no grounds for assuming that any one of the extant early editions provides a close replica of the text hypothetically assigned to Wu. On the other hand, the remote possibility that the novel as we know it was already in existence by the Chia-ching period leads us to reconsider the theories of a yet earlier *ur*-text of the novel, one that Wu—if he indeed had any hand in the history of the novel at all—may have revised, edited, or perhaps only composed a preface for, as one inventive commentator has recently suggested.[23] It bears repeating here that the two fourteenth- or fifteenth-century fragments that have been taken, a bit optimistically, as evidence of a full-length text of *Hsi-yu chi* by the beginning of the Ming period do not really prove the point.[24]

[21] *Tung-t'ien hsüan-chi*, in *Ku-pen Yuan-Ming tsa-chü*, vol. 2, *ch'ien-hsü* 前序. Dudbridge (*Hsi-yu chi*, p. 172, n. 3) mentions this work, but he does not consider the relevance to the problem of dating.

[22] On the life and career of Wu Ch'eng-en, see sources cited in n. 1, and Chao Ching-shen, "Hsi-yu chi tso-che Wu Ch'eng-en nien-p'u," pp. 251–63; Hu Kuang-chou, *Wu Ch'eng-en ho Hsi-yu chi*, pp. 3–44; and Chao Ts'ung, *Ssu ta hsiao-shuo*, pp. 154–60. The idea that *Hsi-yu chi* was written late in Wu's life is expressed in Ogawa Tamaki, "Saiyūki genpon," p. 91; Liu Ts'un-yan, "Wu Ch'eng-en," p. 84; and Hu Kuang-chou, *Wu Ch'eng-en ho Hsi-yu chi*, p. 20. See also Ch'en Kan, "Hsieh-tso k'an-k'e," p. 213. Cf. Liu Ts'un-yan's suggestion that the author of *Hsi-yu chi* may have seen and borrowed from a manuscript of the *Chin P'ing Mei* ("Wu Ch'eng-en," p. 80). Hu Shih "K'ao-cheng," pp. 376ff.) puts the composition of the novel in the period from 1540 to 1550. See also *Hsi-yu chi*, "Tsai-pan shuo-ming" 再版說明, in the 1972 Jen-min wen-hsüeh edition, p. 1. The argument that the book was written in the first half of Wu's life is voiced in Su Hsing, "Kuan-yü Hsi-yu chi ti chi-ko wen-t'i," pp. 134–48, esp. 134ff., 145. Another biographical connection between Wu Ch'eng-en and the novel may be derived from his documented friendship with Li Ch'un-fang 李春芳 (1511–85), whose name has been suggested as a possible identification of the Hua-yang tung-t'ien chu-jen 華陽洞天主人 mentioned as compiler of the Shih-te t'ang edition (see b.n. II.1). For discussion of this evidence, see Liu Yin-po, "Hsi-yu chi Ming-Ch'ing liang-tai ch'u-pan shih k'ao," pp. 76–79. See also Su Hsing, "Yeh t'an," p. 249.

[23] This last theory, suggested by Ch'en Tun-fu (*Shih-i*, p. 18), is based on a rather imaginative repunctuation of the list of Wu's writings in the *Huai-an fu-chih*. Wu's preface to *Ch'un-ch'iu lieh-chuan* 春秋列傳序 appears in *She-yang hsien-sheng ts'un-kao* (*chüan* 2, p. 1a). See Liu Hsiu-yeh, *Shih-wen chi*, p. 50.

[24] See nn. 5 and 7. Examples of this sort of hasty conclusion are found in Dudbridge, *Hsi-yu chi*, p. 103: "...within clear sight of the story told in the hundred-chapter work of the sixteenth-century." Similarly, Cheng Chen-to speaks of the *Yung-lo ta-tien* fragment as a kind of *ur*-text of the novel ("Yen-hua," p. 273), while Ogawa Tamaki speaks confidently of the "Yuan edition" of the novel ("Saiyūki genpon," pp. 85, 103). Cf. Lo Chin-t'ang's "Clues Leading to the Discovery of the *Hsi-yu chi P'ing-hua*," pp. 176–94.

With this in mind, it becomes less far-fetched to reexamine the earlier attribution of the novel to "Ch'ang-ch'un chen-jen" 長春眞人, the late Sung Taoist master Ch'iu Ch'u-chi 丘處機. This attribution was quite widespread during much of the Ch'ing period and finds expression in a number of relevant documents, the most important of these being the preface bearing the name Yü Chi 虞集 attached to the influential Wang Hsiang-hsü *Hsi-yu cheng-tao shu* edition.[25] By the eighteenth century, scholars had pointed out the apparent confusion, at the basis of this attribution, between the Ming novel *Hsi-yu chi* and the Yuan text *Ch'ang-ch'un chen-jen hsi-yu chi* 長春眞人 西遊記, a well-known account of Ch'iu Ch'u-chi's travels through Central Asia of much interest and importance in its own right, but totally unconnected to our novel.[26] This theory persisted to the end of the Ch'ing, and thus twentieth-century scholars have still felt the need to refute it by pointing out the source of the confusion between these two unrelated books.

For the past few generations, practically no one has seriously entertained the possibility that the *Hsi-yu chi* was written by a thirteenth-century

[25] For the "Yü Chi" preface, see *Hsi-yu cheng-tao shu*, "Original preface" (*yüan-hsü* 原序). See b.n. III for bibliographical information and for further discussion. The piece bears the date T'ien-li *chi-ssu* 天曆己巳 (1329). Additional examples of the attribution to Ch'ang-ch'un chen-jen are found in Wu Yü-chin's *Shan-yang chih-i* (cited in n. 1); in Liu T'ing-chi's *Tsai-yüan tsa-chih*; T'ao Tsung-i's *Ch'o-keng lu*, pp. 429–31. See n. 34 for other Ch'ing period references. Liu Ts'un-yan reviews this evidence in "Ch'üan-chen chiao," pt. 1, pp. 55f.

[26] Early examples include Ch'ien Ta-hsin's "Pa Ch'ang-ch'un chen-jen hsi-yu chi," in *Ch'ien-yen t'ang wen-chi*; Yü Yüeh's 俞樾, *Hsiao fu-mei hsien-hua* 小浮梅閑話 (cited in K'ung Ling-ching, *Shih-liao*, p. 75); and Lu I-t'ien 陸以湉, *Leng-lu tsa-chih* 冷廬雜識 (cited in K'ung Ling-ching *Shih-liao*, p. 70). See also Juan K'uei-sheng, *Ch'a-yü k'e-hua*, chüan 21 (also cited in Yeh Te-chün, "Hsi-yu chi yen-chiu ti ts'ai-liao," p. 559), and a preface by Wang T'ao 王韜 printed in a nineteenth-century lithograph edition of *Hsin-shuo Hsi-yu chi* (cited in Chao Ts'ung, *Ssu-ta hsiao-shuo*, pp. 170ff.). Among twentieth-century scholars, this point was first restated by Hu Shih "K'ao-cheng," p. 354), and in an appendix to Wang Kuo-wei's annotated edition of *Ch'ang-ch'un chen-jen Hsi-yu chi chu* (*fu-lu*, p. 123), in Yen I-p'ing, ed., *Tao-chiao yen-chiu tzu-liao*, no. 2 (Taipei: I-wen, 1974), as well as by Lu Hsün (*Hsiao-shuo chiu-wen ch'ao*). For a good review of this issue, see Isobe Akira, "Genpon Saiyūki o meguru mondai," pp. 60–75; and Ōta Tatsuo, "Shōdōsho," p. 93. Ōta points out the faulty basis of Lu Hsün's citation. See also Ch'ien Ching-fang, *Hsiao-shuo ts'ung-k'ao*, p. 50. Ch'en Tun-fu, predictably, defends the attribution to Ch'iu Ch'u-chi in *Shih-i*, pp. 15ff., citing additional sources that repeat the claim. There exist a number of modern editions of the *Ch'ang-ch'un chen-jen hsi-yu chi*, the best being the Wang Kuo-wei annotated edition mentioned in this note. Cf. Arthur Waley's translations in *Travels of an Alchemist*. In his preface to this volume (p. x), Waley also points out the apparent confusion. For additional studies in connection with Ch'iu Ch'u-chi, see b. n. III. Some passages in the Ch'iu Ch'u-chi *Travels* do seem to vaguely resonate with the novel: certain settings (e.g., the Long Pine Ridge 長松嶺, p. 36), descriptions of cities, gardens, etc. (e.g., p. 71), monsters and demons (e.g., pp. 43, 91), mountain and water barriers (e.g., pp. 28, 41, 47, 67, 81), and even certain philosophical terms (e.g., *ling-hsing* 靈性, p. 92, *hsin* 心, pp. 87, 103, 106).

Taoist master. It simply makes more sense to dismiss this as an example of the all-too-common phenomenon in Chinese literature in general, and colloquial fiction in particular, of attributing the composition and editing of books to celebrated literati figures. But in exploring this question I have come across a number of points that, though insufficient to salvage the long-dead theory, do, I believe, warrant at least leaving the case open.

To begin with, it is curious that of all the modern scholars who mention the "Yü Chi" preface, only to dismiss it as referring to a different book, surprisingly few go on to label the preface itself spurious.[27] In fact, a number of discussions speak of this as an actual, verifiable piece by the great Yuan scholar Yü Chi, one that forms part of his extant writings. Lu Hsün, for example, states flat out that the preface is taken from Yü's *Tao-yüan chi* (an abbreviation for the *Tao-yüan hsüeh-ku lu* 道園學古錄).[28] In my unsuccessful attempts to track down this preface, I have encountered a bibliographical tangle due to the incomplete state of most of the extant copies of this collection; thus the possible existence of the piece remains unverified.[29]

What is most important about this preface is not simply its impressive endorsement of the novel by a major intellectual figure, or its assignment of the authorship of the novel to a famous religious personality like Ch'iu Ch'u-chi. All of this is to be expected in fiction prefaces. What is significant for us is its interpretation of the allegorical framework of the novel in terms

[27] Recent scholars who note the misplacement of the Yü Chi preface but do not deny its authenticity include Hu Shih ("K'ao-cheng," p. 378), Sun K'ai-ti (*Jih-pen*, p. 78, and *Shu-mu*, p. 191), Chao Ts'ung (*Ssu ta hsiao-shuo*, pp. 141, 168), Kuo Chen-i (*Hsiao-shuo shih*, p. 274), Ōta Tatsuo ("Kaisetsu," p. 433, and *Saiyūki no kenkyū*, p. 285), and Saitō and Itō ("Kenkyū to shiryō," pp. 214f.). Ota Tatsuo ("Shōdōsho," p. 4) goes the farthest in affirming the existence of the piece, arguing that it does not read like a forgery. Dudbridge does brand it a "forgery" in "Early Versions," p. 151, but he is less unequivocal in "Tsai-shang-ch'üeh," p. 509. Liu Ts'un-yan dismissed the piece as a forgery by Wang Hsiang-hsü in "Ssu-yu chi," p. 372, but more recently he has given the evidence serious reconsideration. See his "Ch'üan- chen chiao," pt. 1, pp. 58ff., and pt. 5, pp. 71ff., and especially his discussion of Yü's association with certain Taoist figures mentioned in the preface whose writings are actually quoted in the novel. The most comprehensive treatment of the problem is found in Isobe Akira, "Genpon Saiyūki o meguru mondai," pp. 60–75. Isobe also accepts the authenticity of the preface (p. 72), suggesting that perhaps Yü Chi himself had not seen the Ch'ang-ch'un chen-jen *Travels*, thus leading to the confusion. He also calls attention to a similar preface attributed to Yü Chi in a printing of another Yuan work of colloquial fiction, *Chiao-hung chi* 嬌紅記, mentioned in Itō Sōhei, "Kaisetsu," pp. 465f., appended to the Japanese translation of that work included in the *Chūgoku koten bungaku taikei* series edition of *Chin-ku ch'i-kuan* (Tokyo: Heibonsha, 1973).

[28] Lu Hsün, *Hsiao-shuo chiu-wen ch'ao*, p. 69. A volume of selected pieces by Yü Chi under the abbreviated title *Yü Tao-yüan chi* (copy in Gest Oriental Library, Princeton) also does not contain the preface.

[29] For bibliographical information, see b.n. III.

of Taoist terminology, plus its description of the text as "several hundred thousand words" in length 數十萬言 —two points that accurately describe our hundred-chapter novel, but none of the other known earlier versions of the narrative.[30] In the unlikely event that the piece was actually written by Yü Chi, then, even if the attribution to Ch'iu is groundless, this would still mean that a text fulfilling some of the defining features of the novel already existed by Yü Chi's time.

Having already come this far in deference to a dubious theory, we may now go one step further to reconsider the unlikely attribution to Chi'iu Ch'u-chi. A few tantalizing scraps of evidence make this a little less fanciful than it might appear. For example, in one preface to Ch'iu Ch'u-chi's collected works we are told that among his various writings he left several volumes: two poetry collections, *P'an-hsi chi* 磻溪集 and *Ming-tao chi* 鳴道集, and another book called *Hsi-yu chi*.[31] Recalling now that the famous *Ch'ang-ch'un chen-jen Hsi-yu chi* was not actually written by Ch'iu himself but by his disciple Li Chih-ch'ang 李志常 (who in fact narrates the

---

[30] Of particular interest is the discussion of the term *fang-hsin* 放心 to be considered later in this chapter. As for the estimation of the length of the book, my own rough calculation comes to around 500,000 characters. Isobe Akira ("Son Gyōja," p. 105) suggests the figure 300,000 and says that the Yü Chi estimation is exaggerated. Ch'en Tun-fu (*Shih-i*, p. 18) puts it at 700,000. Cf. the description in the Ch'en Yüan-chih preface, which substitutes *ch'ien* 千 for *shih* 十, thus yielding an astronomical figure. The Yuan Yü-ling preface (see b.n. II.4) reduces this by a factor of ten 數百萬言 but still gives an unreasonable length. Ota Tatsuo ("Shōdōsho," p. 4) agrees that the contents of the preface can only refer to our novel. Additional details of interest in the preface include the mention of a certain Tzu-ch'iung tao-jen 紫瓊道人, identified as the Yuan Taoist figure Chang Mo 張模 (see his biography in *Shang-yang tzu Chin-tan ta-yao, lieh-hsien chih* 上陽子金丹大要列仙誌 by Ch'en Chih-hsü). See Liu Ts'un-yan, "Ch'üan-chen chiao," pt. 1, pp. 59ff; Ōta Tatsuo, "New Study," pp. 99ff., and "Kaisetsu," pp. 433, 432; and Isobe Akira, "Son Gyōja," p. 105. In earlier articles ("Shōdōsho," p. 6, and "Saiyūki seiritsu shiryaku," pp. 21f.), Ōta suggests that this Chang Mo himself may have been the author or redactor of a prototype of the novel. The mention of both Chang Mo and Hsi-yüeh tao-jen 西月道人 (Wang Shou-yen 王壽衍) tallies with the experience of Yü Chi, although these figures seem to have been sufficiently well known that they might easily be cited by a later Ch'ing forger. The same is true with respect to Yü Chi's familiarity with the life and works of Ch'ang-ch'un chen-jen. Ōta Tatsuo ("Shōdōsho," p. 4) also identifies the Wei Ching-fu mentioned in the preface with Wei Su, with whom Yü Chi was known to have had connections.

[31] The passage in question reads: 有磻溪鳴道集西遊記行于世. See *Ch'iu-tsu pen-chuan* 邱祖本傳, included in Ch'iu Ch'u-chi, *Ch'iu-tsu ch'üan-shu chieh-chi*, p. 5a. Cf. a similar title mentioned among Ch'iu Ch'u-chi's writings in a biographical sketch given in T'ao Tsung-i's *Ch'o-keng lu*, p. 431. See Liu Ts'un-yan, "Ch'üan-chen chiao," pt. 1, p. 56; Ōta Tatsuo, "New Study," pp. 99ff.; and Isobe Akira, "Genpon Saiyūki," pp. 66f., for other sources of this citation. Ōta's reference curiously adds the number "two" before the name of the book, thus leading to speculation that more than one text of this title is at issue here. Liu Ts'un-yan gives a similar citation in "Ch'üan-chen chiao," pt. 3, pp. 72f., but he rejects Ōta's punctuation.

death of his master in the course of the book), we have to assume that this entry, if authentic, must refer to yet another work by the same title.

As a matter of fact, there is no scarcity of journeys to the West or books entitled "Journey to the West" in Chinese literature, particularly in the period of Mongol rule. But a few other passages in Ch'iu's extant writings seem to point to a text closer to our own *Hsi-yu chi*. In one place, for example, the reader is reminded of the use in his book *Hsi-yu chi* of the term "seven apertures" (*ch'i-ch'iao* 七竅).[32] This expression does not occur in the Ch'ang-ch'un chen-jen *Travels*, but a slight variation ("nine apertures") does figure in some memorable lines in the novel. Still more suggestive is another line that speaks of the *Hsi-yu chi* of Master Ch'iu as "a guide to the True Scriptures in the western region" 指示眞經在西天 —a description that cannot apply to the Ch'iu Ch'u-chi *Travels* but sounds suspiciously like our *Journey to the West*.[33] Obviously, these small indications are not enough to substantiate this improbable theory; but at least they should force us to consider the possibility a bit more seriously. I might add that a number of Ch'ing scholars, including respected figures such as Mao Ch'i-ling 毛奇齡 —who should have known the difference between the novel *Hsi-yu chi* and the *Ch'ang-ch'un chen-jen Hsi-yu chi*—still granted credence to the Yuan attribution.[34] A cogent objection raised as early as the seventeenth

[32] See *Ch'iu-tsu yü-lu*, in *Ch'iu-tsu ch'üan-shu*, p. 8a, preface by P'an Ching-kuan 潘靜觀, dated Yung-lo 13 (1415). For further information on this text, see Liu Ts'un-yan, "Ch'üan-chen chiao," pt. 1, p. 56. Isobe discusses the dating of this text in "Genpon Saiyūki," pp. 69f., 74, n. 33. Of course it is entirely possible that this work was compiled, if not fabricated, by someone else. Other works of the Yuan period with similar titles include a *Hsi-yu lu* 西遊錄 by Yeh-lü Ch'u-ts'ai 耶律楚材, described by Paul Pelliot in "L'édition collective des oeuvres de Wang Kuou-wei," p. 172; and a work entitled *Hsi-yu chi* 西遊集 mentioned by Yü Yüeh in an entry in his *Chiu-chiu hsiao-hsia lu* 九九消夏錄, cited in K'ung Ling-ching, *Shih-liao*, p. 75. Lu Hsün cites a reference to another *Hsi-yu chi* by Hsü Ch'ien 許謙 in *Hsiao-shuo chiu-wen ch'ao*, p. 64. The passages in the novel dealing with the idea of "nine apertures" occur in chapter 2 (1:21) and 3 (1:42). Liu Ts'un-yan ("Ch'üan-chen chiao," *Ibid.*) notes similar terminology in chapters 6, 17, and especially 41 of the novel.

[33] The passage in question reads: 紫陽翁，悟眞篇，盡把參同奧旨宣；西遊記，邱祖傳，指示眞經在西天 (in *Ch'iu-tsu ch'üan-shu*, p. 256). The line seems to be written in third person. Cf. the name Li Kung-ch'en 李拱辰, credited with "presenting" (*ching* 敬) this set of poems in the *Ch'iu-tsu ch'üan-shu* (p. 18a). See n. 36. The *Wu-chen p'ien* referred to in the first half of the quotation is by the eleventh-century master Chang Po-tuan (Tzu-yang; see n. 145). Ōta Tatsuo ("Kaisetsu," p. 442) identifies a poem from this collection in chapter 36 of the novel (2:503).

[34] See above, n. 25. Mao Ch'i-ling's acceptance of the attribution (apparently based on the *Ch'o-keng lu* entry noted earlier) is mentioned by Ting Yen in his *Shih-t'ing chi-shih hsü-pien* (cited in K'ung Ling-ching, *Shih-liao*, p. 71). Juan K'uei-sheng raises a doubt about the reliability of some of Mao Ch'i-ling's citations in *Ch'a-yü k'e-hua*, pp. 260f. See also Ch'en Tun-fu, *Shih-i*, p. 20. Ōta, "Shōdōsho," p. 3, reports the absence of this point in Mao's *Hsi-ho ho-chi* 西河合集.

century, to the effect that the presence of Ming place-names in the novel seems to rule out the possibility of Yuan composition, is an important point; but it is by no means conclusive, especially considering the long and complicated history of the novel's redaction.[35] More to the point, given the above assertion that one of the key distinguishing features of the hundred-chapter novel is its overlay of Taoist terminology, we should also note that virtually all of these terms are very much the language of discourse of Sung-Yuan Taoism in general, and the writings of Ch'iu Ch'u-chi and his disciples in particular.[36] At the very least, this helps to explain why the

[35] See Ting Yen, *Shih-t'ing chi-shih*; and Ch'ien Ta-hsin, "Pa Ch'ang-ch'un chen-jen Hsi-yu chi" (see above, n. 1). Discussions by Ting Yen are found in sections entitled "Huai-yin ts'o-lu" 淮陰脞錄, pp. 4b–5a, and "Shu Hsi-yu chi hou" 書西遊記後, p. 22a (in *I-chih chai ts'ung-shu*). A similar idea is brought out by an anecdote recorded by Chi Yün 紀昀 in his *Ju-shih wo wen* 如是我聞, *chüan* 3, in *Yüeh-wei ts'ao-t'ang pi-chi* 閱微草堂筆記 (cited in K'ung Ling-ching, *Shih-liao*, p. 69, and Lu Hsün, *Chiu-wen ch'ao*, p. 65). See Liu Ts'un-yan's discussion of this point in "Wu Ch'eng-en," p. 66. Ch'en Tun-fu argues against denying the attribution to Ch'iu Ch'u-chi on the basis of Ming terminology in *Shih-i*, pp. 17f. For a comparable discussion of the significance of Yuan place-names in the 1522 edition of *San-kuo yen-i*, see below, Chapter 5, Part I.

[36] Of course Ch'iu Ch'u-chi has no monopoly on the use of these common Taoist terms, but by the same token the traditional association of many of these concepts with Ch'iu and his school remains quite strong. For example, the poems in Ch'iu Ch'u-chi's *P'an-hsi tz'u* include such lines as the following: *sheng-t'ien ju-ti chü tsai hsin-wei* 昇天入地俱在心爲, p. 5a; *wu k'ung-hua pi-an kao teng* 悟空華彼岸高登, p. 10a; *lien-ch'u ts'un-hsin ju t'ieh* 鍊出寸心如鐵, p. 15a; *chien-chien fang-k'ai hsin-yüeh, wei-wei she-t'ou ling-t'ai* 漸漸放開心月, 微微射透靈台, p. 24b; and *hsi-yu ... ta-tao wu hsing fang-ts'un ho p'ing* 西游⋯大道無形方寸何憑, p. 28b. Cf. also the occurrences of such expressions as *fa-shen* 法身, p. 1a; *shen wai shen i* 身外身易, p. 3b; *wu-tsei* 五賊, p. 4a; *chih-chi ts'ung* 枳棘叢, p. 4b; *p'ang-men* 旁門, p. 7b; *san-chiao* 三教, p. 9b; and *huan-tan* 還丹, p. 29b. Other terms used in the novel appear in the poems included in the *Ch'iu-tsu ch'üan-shu*; e.g.; *chin-kung* 金公, *fu-hu* 伏虎, *se-k'ung* 色空, p. 21b; *ch'iao-nei ch'iao-chung* 竅內竅中, p. 24a; *chin-tan ts'ung wai lai ku fei tzu-chi wu* 金丹從外來, 固非自己物, p. 25a; *ying-erh* 嬰兒, *ch'a-nü* 姹女, p. 25a; *tu-yang ch'i neng ch'üan* 獨陽豈能全, p. 25b; *kung ch'eng sui tso fo sheng-hsien* 功成隨作佛聖仙, *ku-yin tu-yang ch'i neng ch'üan* 孤陰獨陽豈能全, *ch'un-yang chen chung-tzu neng t'ung t'ien-ti shou ch'i nien* 純陽眞種子, 能同天地壽齊年, p. 25b; *huo-kung* 火功, *hsin-huo* 心火, *k'an-li chiao-kou* 坎離交姤, p. 26a; *liu-tsei chieh lai jao-luan hsin-shen* 六賊皆來, 擾亂心神, p. 27a; and *yüan-shen huo-hou* 元神, 火候, p. 27b. Similar language is found in another text attributed to Ch'iu Ch'u-chi, the *Lung-men mi-chih*, pp. 45–60, esp. 49f.: "Hsiao chou-t'ien huo-hou k'ou-chüeh ko" 小周天火候口訣歌, which provides a presentation of the cycle of hours reminiscent of the opening segment of the novel, as well as such terms as *hsün-feng* 巽風, *huo-hou* 火候, *hua-kuo* 花果, and *ying-erh* 嬰兒 (p. 57). For general discussions of the Taoist terminology current in the Yuan and Ming periods, see Sun K'e-k'uan, *Yuan-tai Han wen-hua chih huo-tung*, plus his *Sung-Yuan tao-chiao yüan-liu*, and articles cited in b.n. III; and Ch'en Ming-kuei, *Ch'ang-ch'un tao-chiao yüan-liu*. See also Nakano Miyoko, *Saiyūki no himitsu*, pp. 250–59; Liu Ts'un-yan, "Taoist Self-cultivation," pp. 291–330; and several articles in his *Ho-feng t'ang tu-shu chi* (see above, n. 13). Ch'en Tun-fu (*Shih-i*, pp. 5f.) sees in the novel specific reflections of the text entitled *Chung-Lü ch'uan-tao chi*, attributed to the legendary

seventeenth-century editor of the *Hsi-yu cheng-tao shu*, in promoting his own interpretation of the novel as a Taoist allegory, might have created a false preface by Yü Chi. And this would also account for the most recent commentary edition, which presents the novel as a tract in Ch'üan-chen Taoist verities.[37]

The upshot of all this speculation is, unfortunately, a state of uncertainty. Having expended considerable effort to undermine the accepted theory of composition, I can now only do an about-face and reaffirm my reading of the novel as essentially a product of the sixteenth-century intellectual milieu.[38] The remote possibility I have entertained that the novel, or at least a prototype, may in fact be a Yuan (or even a late Sung) composition would contradict this; but at the same time, it would strengthen the parallel to *Shui-hu chuan* and *San-kuo chih yen-i*. These, as we shall see, present roughly the same situation: with verifiable full texts not appearing much before the sixteenth century, despite accepted theories of fourteenth-century authorship.[39] This, at the very least, will ultimately reinforce the idea of the generic commonality of three of our four masterworks.

---

figures Chung-li Ch'üan and Lü Yen (Lü Tung-pin). (See *Tao-tsang ching-hua* ed.) Anthony Yu has uncovered certain other Taoist poems apparently alluded to in the novel (see his *Journey*, 1:41, 49, and 2:430, n. 22). See also Ōta Tatsuo, "Kaisetsu," p. 442, and "Shōdō-sho," pp. 6–8, for additional examples, especially a poem in chapter 2 of the novel (1:20), which according to Ōta is attributed to Ch'iu Ch'u-chi in *Ch'uan-ch'i hui-k'ao* 傳奇彙考. See below for a reconsideration of the use of Taoist terminology in the allegorical framework of the narrative.

[37] See above, nn. 26 and 36. For Ch'en Tun-fu's reading of the novel as a Ch'üan-chen tract, see *Hsi-yu chi shih-i* (see b.n. II.10). On the development of Ch'üan-chen Taoism, see Sun K'e-k'uan works cited, especially "Yü Chi and Southern Taoism," pp. 214, 228, 253; Ch'en Ming-kuei, "Ch'üan-chen chiao tsung-lun," in *Ch'ang-ch'un tao-chiao yüan-liu*, pp. 4–10; and Yoshioka Yoshitoyo, *Dōkyō no kenkyū*, "Zen-shin-kyō no seiritsu" 全真教の成立, pp. 175–95. See also Liu Ts'un-yan, *Buddhist and Taoist Influences*, pp. 128ff; and Ōta Tatsuo, "Shōdōsho," pp. 8f. Liu Ts'un-yan reviews the key Ch'üan-chen terminology in the novel in "Ch'üan-chen chiao," pt. 2, pp. 59ff.

[38] This will lead me to revise my interpretation later in this chapter of the significance of the Taoist and Buddhist terminology in the text. On the fluctuating popularity of Buddhist and Taoist ideas in the sixteenth century, see Wu Han's discussion of the intellectual background of the Wan-li period, in his "Chin P'ing Mei ti chu-tso shih-tai chi ch'i she-hui pei-ching" (see above, Chapter 1, n. 55, and Chapter 3, n. 8,). The Chia-ching emperor's flirtation with Taoism is the subject of an entire chapter in the *Ming-shih chi-shih pen-mo* 明史紀事本末 (*chüan* 52, pp. 547–58). See also Liu Ts'un-yan, "The Penetration of Taoism into the Ming Neo-Confucian Elite," pp. 31–102 (also in Chinese in *Ho-feng t'ang tu-shu chi*, 1:233–72; originally published in *Hsin-ya hsüeh-pao* 8, no. 1 [1967]); Miyakawa Hisayuki, "Min no Kasei jidai no dōkyō," pp. 631–43.

[39] See below, Chapters 4, Part I, and 5, Part I, for discussions of this point in relation to the analogous gap between fourteenth-century and sixteenth-century drama. See previous references comparing the role of the author of *Hsi-yu chi* to that of Lo Kuan-chung (n. 8).

The parallel with *San-kuo yen-i* and *Shui-hu chuan* gains an additional measure of credence when we consider the links of intertextual allusion that bind these works together. This is an aspect of the text that was noticed by the traditional commentators and has also been pointed out by a number of modern scholars.[40] For example, Sun Wu-k'ung's 孫悟空 impersonation of a bride in a nuptial chamber in order to lure Chu Pa-chieh 豬八戒 into his clutches in chapter 18 obviously parallels Lu Ta's 魯達 similar trick in chapter 5 of *Shui-hu chuan*. To take a more subtle example, the cluster of associations between sexual vulnerability and wrath brought out in a temple haunted by "centipede spirits" (*wu-kung ching* 蜈蚣精) in chapter 93—where the ambiguous incident of the girl in the back room of a monastery seems to somehow lead into the temptations of the Jade Hare 玉兔 immediately following—is reminiscent of the strange episode of the lascivious Taoist and his ambiguous female partner, who call forth the wrath of Wu Sung 武松 at the Centipede Ridge (Wu-kung ling 蜈蚣嶺) in chapter 31 of *Shui-hu*.[41] In addition, there are several passages in which the intertextual linkage goes beyond the level of similar scenes to the point of actual verbal correspondences. Examples of this include the proverbial expression used in chapter 39, "There are several types of crying ..." 哭有 幾樣, the very same words that appear in the scene of P'an Chin-lien's

---

[40] For further comments on the intertextual relations among the four masterworks, see Chapter 6. References in the commentaries to intertextual allusion to other novels include the following examples. Relating *Hsi-yu chi* to *Shui-hu chuan*, Wang Hsiang-hsü, in chapter 5 (5b), points out the similarity of Sun Wu-k'ung's behavior to the entry of the bandits, with flowers in their hair, into the gardens of the Forbidden Palace in chapter 72 of *Shui-hu*, and in another place, 48 (1b), he calls attention to the obvious parallel between Sun Wu-k'ung's boudoir lure of Chu Pa-chieh and that by Lu Ta in chapter 5 of *Shui-hu*. With regard to *San-kuo yen-i*, Chang Shu-shen, in chapter 54 (14a), compares Hsüan-tsang's imperfect fortitude with Kuan Yü's resistance to Ts'ao Ts'ao's blandishments; Wang Hsiang-hsü, 59 (1b), and Ch'en Shih-pin, 61 (618f.), relate the trebling pattern in the episode at Huo-yen shan to the "three visits to the thatched cottage" episode (see n. 58); "Li Cho-wu" sees in the repeated temptation of Hsüan-tsang a reflection of Chu-ko Liang's sevenfold manipulation of Meng Huo, 72 (3b). See additional examples in Chang Shu-shen, 12(1b), 47(1a–2a), 48 (13b, 14a), 49 (1b, 16a–b); Wang Hsiang-hsü, 8 (1a), 29 (1a), 59, 81 (1b, 2a); "Li Cho-wu" preface. Chang Shu-shen, chapter 30 (17a), notes an interesting connection to *Chin P'ing Mei*—Cf. Liu Ts'un-yan's discussion of source material shared by *Hsi-yu chi* and *Chin P'ing Mei* (in n. 22)—and sees reflections of *Feng-shen yen-i* in comments in chapters 12 (1b), 33 (1b), 67 (15a), and 95 (13b). See also Ts'ai Yüan-fang, *tu-fa*, item 4. Also of interest are Chang Shu-shen's frequent references to similarities between the novel and certain dramatic works, especially *Hsi-hsiang chi*, e.g., chapters 12 (1b), 37 (2a), 81 (1b), 83 (11a); and *P'i-p'a chi*, e.g., chapters 52 (16a–18a), 81(15a); as well as *Ming-feng chi*, chapter 51 (12b).

[41] For discussion of the relevant passages in *Shui-hu chuan*, see below, Chapter 4, Part IV. The centipede spirits (*wu-kung ching*) had already appeared earlier in chapter 73. A similar example of intertextual resonance with *Shui-hu chuan* is seen in Chu Pa-chieh's descent into a well in chapter 38 (cf. *Shui-hu*, chapter 54.)

crocodile tears in *Shui-hu chuan* (chapter 25—and thus taken over into *Chin P'ing Mei* as well); or perhaps the following line in chapter 82: "... if it were any other common man subject to the temptations of wine and sex ..." 若是⋯第二個酒色凡夫⋯, which seems to me to echo a very similar line applied ironically to Sung Chiang in chapter 72 of *Shui-hu*.[42]

What do such instances tell us about the relationships between these separate works? The most reasonable explanation is that the author of *Hsi-yu chi* borrowed these passages from *Shui-hu chuan*, which might place its composition sometime after the appearance of the *fan-pen* text of *Shui-hu* in the Chia-ching period. However, the comparable uncertainty of the dating of the full text of *Shui-hu* makes it impossible to say this with absolute confidence. In fact, the borrowing could conceivably go in the other direction, especially if we are willing to entertain the possibility of an earlier text of the *Hsi-yu chi*. By the same token, the verbal reflection of certain other passages from *Hsi-yu chi* in the *Chin P'ing Mei*, as pointed out by Liu Ts'un-yan, seems to indicate that *Hsi-yu chi* came first; although the theory of late Chia-ching or early Wan-li composition for the latter work makes the possibility of reverse borrowing just as plausible, not to mention the even more likely explanation that the passages in question were adapted in both from other common sources. At the very least, the presence of intertextual allusion is of major significance for my argument, since it reinforces the sense of commensurability binding these four very different narrative works together within a single literary genre.

The main thrust of my argument, however, is not the textual history of these works, but the definition of their common ground of form and meaning. With this in mind, I will now turn to an interpretive analysis of the text itself. I will begin by observing the points on which *Hsi-yu chi* conforms to the structural features outlined in the chapter on *Chin P'ing Mei*, with the intention of expanding this common ground in the chapters on *Shui-hu chuan* and *San-kuo chih yen-i*. In doing so, my analysis will follow primarily the hundred-chapter text based on the Shih-te t'ang edition, though I will refer wherever relevant to discrepancies between the novel and its antecedents or later versions. In attempting to unravel the meaning of the allegory, I will rely heavily on several later commentary editions. These editions include the *Li Cho-wu hsien-sheng p'i-p'ing Hsi-yu chi* 李卓吾先生批評西遊記, Wang Hsiang-hsü's 汪象旭 *Hsi-yu cheng-tao shu*, *Hsin-shuo Hsi-yi chi* 新說西遊記 by Chang Shu-shen 張書紳, and *Hsi-yu chen-ch'üan* 西遊眞銓 by Ch'en Shih-pin 陳士斌, as well as the prefatory essays in a revised edition of *Hsi-yu cheng-tao shu* by Ts'ai Yüan-fang 蔡元放, a late

---

[42] The first example is found in *Shui-hu chuan*, chapter 25 (1:399); see also *Chin P'ing Mei*, chapter 5 (9a). For the second passage, see chapter 82 (3:1135), and *Shui-hu*, chapter 72 (4:1338). For discussion of these passages, see below, Chapter 4, Part IV.

eighteenth or early nineteenth-century edition entitled *Hsi-yu yüan-chih*
西遊原旨 by Liu I-ming 劉一明, additional comments in a late Ch'ing
reprint of a Ch'en Shih-pin text, another Ch'ing commentary suggestively
entitled *T'ung-i Hsi-yu cheng-chih* 通易西遊正旨, and a recent edition prepared in Taiwan by Ch'en Tun-fu under the title *Hsi-yu chi shih-i*.[43] Admittedly, these commentaries, like that of Chang Chu-p'o, are quite uneven in
the quality of their insights. But even where this is so, it is easy to justify
using them, because they provide a firmer basis for interpreting the novel
as a reflection of the immediate intellectual milieu of the Ming-Ch'ing era.

II

Starting again with the overall shape of the work, we immediately note that
the hundred-chapter length, by which I have identified the basic form of the
genre, is an invariable feature of all the full editions. This is itself does not
say much, since all of the later editions are based on the Shih-te t'ang text.
This also arbitrarily excludes from consideration the shorter Chu and Yang
recensions for the sin of not comprising one hundred chapters.[44] But there
is more to the hundred-chapter length of the novel than meets the eye. Not
only does this length conform neatly to the generic dimensions of the *Chin
P'ing Mei*, but, more important, this precise number of chapters provides a
numerological grid for several significant structural patterns to be explored
in the following pages.

The aesthetic commitment to the hundred-chapter length is indirectly
demonstrated by the juggling of material occasioned by the variations in
chapter 9 in the different editions.[45] The implications of the absence in the
1592 edition of the section on Hsüan-tsang's childhood tribulations (which
is presented in the ninth chapter in most other editions) have occupied a
number of scholars, most recently Anthony Yu, who has convincingly
shown that practically all the important details of this story are conveyed
elsewhere in the Shih-te t'ang text.[46] Viewed from the perspective of this

---

[43] For detailed descriptions of the editions used in this study, see b.n. II.1–10.

[44] For the position of the Shih-te t'ang edition as the basic text, see *Hsi-yu chi*, "Tsai-pan
shuo-ming," pp. 1–2; and Huang Su-ch'iu, "Chiao-ting ho chu-shih," p. 180. See also Sun
K'ai-ti, *Jih-pen*, pp. 74ff.; Cheng Chen-to, "Yen-hua," pp. 267ff.

[45] Cf. Wang Hsiang-hsü's explicit indication of this point in his comments in chapters 9
(1b) and 100 (14a); and Ts'ai Yüan-fang's discussion of certain implausible aspects of chapter
9 in his own received text (*tu-fa*, item 51). See also *T'ung-i Hsi-yu cheng-chih*, chapter 9 (94a).

[46] See Anthony C. Yu, "Narrative Structure and the Problem of Chapter Nine in the
Hsi-yu chi," pp. 295–311; plus the following studies: Huang Su-ch'iu, "Lun Hsi-yu chi ti
ti-chiu-hui wen-t'i," pp. 172–77; Su Hsing, "Wu Ch'eng-en Hsi-yu chi ti-chiu-hui wen-t'i,"
pp. 31–36; Dudbridge, "Tsai-shang-ch'üeh," pp. 501f., and "Early Versions," pp. 170ff.;

discussion, however, what is most significant about this debate is the fact
that at least one of the early editors (who that was depends on whether one
says that the editor of the Shih-te t'ang edition removed this material or
that Wang Hsiang-hsü inserted it) thereby reaffirms the inviolability of the
hundred-chapter length.[47]

In the preceding chapter I observed that the unalterable hundred-
chapter length of the *Chin P'ing Mei* is rationalized by the implicit division
of that text into ten ten-chapter units, and that this demarcation is arguably
borne out in the essential rhythms of the narrative structure itself. In the
case of *Hsi-yu chi*, I have been unable to come up with convincing evidence
that the author intended sets of ten chapters to bear the same sort of
structural significance I have outlined in the *Chin P'ing Mei*, and will repeat
in *San-kuo yen-i* and *Shui-hu chuan*. For this very reason it is quite noteworthy with respect to my argument about a generic model, that several
editions of the novel maintain the formal feature of dividing the text into
five- or ten-chapter *chüan*-units.[48] For that matter, one might even perceive
a less precise sense of these aesthetic proportions in both the Chu text,
which is divided into ten *chüan* of unequal length, and the Yang text,
whose forty-one chapters are broken up into four *chüan*. The insistence on
equal *chüan*-units is given special emphasis in the Shih-te t'ang edition,
where the twenty *chüan* of five chapters each are enumerated according to
the sequence of words in a twenty-word poem by Shao Yung 邵雍, one
word standing at the head of each *chüan*.[49]

Cheng Chen-to, "Yen-hua," pp. 287–80; Liu Ts'un-yan, "Wu Ch'eng-en," pp. 73f., and
"Ssu-yu chi," pp. 362f., 369ff.; Ōta Tatsuo, "Shōdōsho," pp. 12ff., and "New Study,"
pp. 97f., 109f.; Li Shih-jen, "Lüeh-lun Wu Ch'eng-en Hsi-yu chi chung ti T'ang-seng ch'u-
shih ku-shih"; and Ogawa Tamaki, "Saiyūki genpon," p. 87. The problem of chapter 9 is
complicated by the fact that certain editions omit the material on Hsüan-tsang's birth but
retain the same chapter titles as those that include it.

[47] Cf. Chang Shu-shen's comment on the inviolability of the overall structure, cited
below. For the somewhat comparable problem of the interpolation of material in chapters
53–57 of *Chin P'ing Mei*, see above, Chapter 2, Part II.

[48] See b.n. II.1–10 for the *chüan* divisions of the various major editions. At least one printing of the Ch'en Shih-pin *Hsi-yu chen-ch'üan* is divided into ten *chüan* of ten *hui* each, as is the
T'ung-i Hsi-yu cheng-chih. The structural configurations of the Chu, Yang, and Shih-te t'ang
editions can be conveniently compared in a table provided by Ōta Tatsuo in "Kaisetsu,"
pp. 436f; and a similar table in Chang Ching-erh, *Jen-wu yen-chiu*, pp. 261–66.

[49] The poem by Shao Yung is entitled "Song of the Clear Night" (*Ch'ing-yeh yin* 清夜吟).
It reads as follows: "The point where the moon reaches the heart of heaven,/The moment
when the breeze touches the surface of the waters./The sense of the universal purity of
mind./Few, it seems, can ever fully understand." (月到天心處 / 風來水面時 / 一般清
意味 / 料得少人知.) See Ch'ien Mu, ed., *Li-hsüeh liu-chia shih-ch'ao*, p. 25. Cf. the pointed
mention of Shao Yung's thought in the opening disquisition in chapter 1, to be discussed
shortly in this section. On the citation of Shao Yung's name in some of our other novels,
see above, Chapters 2, Part II, and 4, Part II.

Although the author of *Hsi-yu chi* does not punctuate his ten-chapter units with clear narrative subclimaxes, as in the *Chin P'ing Mei*, the fact that this is more than a simple formality or a publishing convenience is revealed in certain other ways. One of these ways emerges in the correlation, in terms of content, of certain chapters that appear at corresponding numerical positions of the different "decades." To take one very noticeable example, the problem of sexuality in one form or another seems to be taken up around the third and fourth chapters of each cycle (23, 53–55, 72–73, 82–83, 93–95).[50] A similar example of parallel slots may be seen around the seventh chapters, where we note for example the link between chapters 27–31 and 56–58 (the two exiles of the "mind-monkey"). Once the reader becomes attuned to the possibility of such patterns, a number of more subtle examples begin to emerge. To give a few of these, chapters 64 and 94 both portray the writing of poetry; chapter 98 realizes the gift of scriptures promised at a similar assembly in chapter 8; in chapters 19–20 and 79–80 we have allusions to the Heart Sutra; and chapters 9, 49, and 99 all present perilous water crossings. Granted, none of the above examples alone is sufficiently compelling to prove that this is a matter of conscious design; but taken together they do seem to indicate at least the loose aesthetic sense of a structural rhythm built on a framework of ten-chapter units.

Perhaps the principal reason the author does not articulate these ten-chapter units as clearly as in *Chin P'ing Mei* is that his eye is on other numerological patterns—chiefly the use of nines. In view of the special significance of the number nine in the allegorical scheme of attainment defined as a sequence of nine times nine trials, it seems to be no accident that the author plans his text so that the fulfillment of the quest, "the attainment of the nine nines" 九九功完, comes to pass precisely in chapter 99. The fact that this sort of number game was dear to the author is underscored by the reaffirmation of the formula $9 \times 9 = 81$ at the close of the journey, with the pointed addition of one more trial to fill out this required number. In fact, just as we get to chapter 90 we get a rash of demons and places with the number nine in their names.[51]

We will reconsider soon some possible interpretations of the numerol-

[50] Chang Shu-shen calls attention to one such resonance between chapters 23 and 73; see chapter 73 (14a). Cf. the repeated appearance of the centipede spirits in chapters 73 and 93, as well as the reflection in chapter 93 of the female domination presented in the Land of Women in chapter 53. The figural reflection between chapters 27 and 56–57 may perhaps be picked up in Sun Wu-k'ung's more merciful treatment of bandits in chapter 97.

[51] Cf. the "Primal Sage of the Nine Spirits" (*Chiu-ling yüan-sheng* 九靈原聖) in chapters 89–90, dwelling in the "Cave of Ninefold Twists and Turns" (*Chiu-ch'ü p'an-yüan tung* 九曲盤桓洞), a demon who turns out to be a nine-headed lion (*chiu-t'ou shih-tzu* 九頭獅子). Cf. also the Nine-headed Son-in-law (*Chiu-t'ou fu-ma* 九頭駙馬) in chapters 62–63. Some of the numerological implications of the nines are suggested in a poem in chapter 90

ogy of nines within the context of Buddhist, Taoist, and *I Ching* concepts, or perhaps as a general cipher for the concept of multiplicity. In the meantime, we may note in passing the parallel between the allegory of nines within a structure of tens in *Hsi-yu chi*—whereby the nine times nine trials are completed in 99 + 1 chapters—and the 3 times 33 + 1 structure of Dante's *Divina Commedia*, as a vehicle for the attainment of a "nine" of another sort.[52] This might also, incidentally, add a further layer of significance to the problem of chapter 9. Unfortunately, however, not all of the ninth chapters fall into this pattern, but at least chapters 9, 19, 39, 49, and 99 seem to betray a consciousness of numerology that cannot be entirely gratuitous.

Once the idea of the author's attention to numerological patterns in arranging his chapter numbers is accepted, then we may consider some other, even more tenuous, patterns that can add to our appreciation of the structural intricacy of the text and also support certain points of interpretation. One such pattern grows out of the sense of a contrived symmetry linking the two ends of the hundred-chapter text. For example, the lecture by the Master Subodhi that caps the opening mini-quest of the Monkey King 美猴王 in chapter 2 is restaged at the feet of the Buddha on the Holy Mountain in chapter 98. This might be explained away in terms of the general tendency of narrative works to provide some recapitulation of their beginnings close to their ends. But once one begins to look at the text in this way, a number of additional examples suggest themselves. For instance, it seems less than pure coincidence that the motif of tossing an embroidered ball in chapter 9 is repeated, not without pointed meaning as we shall see, in chapter 93. Similarly, the crossing of the pale of T'ang jurisdiction in chapter 13 neatly counterbalances the reentry of the band into settled civilization in chapter 88 (3:1205), at which point we are told that the orderly rule in Yü-hua hsien 玉華縣 reached by the pilgrims here is "no different from that in China" 與中華無異. Other possible examples of this principle of organization may be at work in the recasting of the hunter

---

(3:1239). See discussion by Ch'en Tun-fu in *Shih-i*, p. 1062. The link between the water crossings in chapters 9, 49, and 99 is emphasized by Wang Hsiang-hsü in chapter 49 (1a). Cf. the highlighting of the "resuscitation pill compounded nine times" (*chiu-chuan huan-hun tan* 九轉還魂丹) in chapter 39.

[52] On the symbolism of the number 9 in Dante see discussions of his *Vita Nuova*, where *nova* (*nove*, nine) suggests the new (Latin, *nova*) life of redemption. See, for example, Robert Hollander, "*Vita Nuova*: Dante's Perceptions of Beatrice," *Dante Studies*, pp. 1–18. Cf. the Tantric iconographic emblem of nine skulls worn around the neck of the Sand Monk (this detail appears already in the *tsa-chü* version, appropriately enough in Scene 9). Ch'en Shih-pin provides an interesting discussion of the numerological implications of chapters 19 (201) and 99 (1003), and compares this with the use of 3's in chapter 33 (341f.). See also comments in chapters 69 (703f.) and 82 (835). The numerological significance of the nine-times-nine trials is taken up in Hsü Chen-chi, "Hsi-yu chi pa-shih-i nan yen-chiu."

figure Liu Po-ch'in 劉伯欽 met at the start of the journey as the woodcutter whose rustic retreat is visited in chapter 86.[53]

A still more whimsical example of numerical plotting seems to emerge in a number of special chapters that are singled out for treatment of allegorical issues in self-contained episodes. Often these happen to coincide with the numbers of perfect squares: chapters 9, 36, 49, and 64. To be sure, this pattern is not complete. Most disappointing, I can detect no comparable highlighting of chapter 81 (although, as we have seen, the author is saving his fulfillment of 9 × 9 for another point). On the other hand, chapters 16 and 25 do seem to bear a special degree of emphasis. Thus, in view of the author's general sensitivity to the numbers of his chapters, I am convinced that he was not unconscious of this sort of positioning. At least, this is a possible avenue of interpretation not overlooked by the more zealous of the commentators.[54]

A second aspect of the overall structural design of *Hsi-yu chi* that bears out the generic expectations observed in the *Chin P'ing Mei* is the manner in which the hundred-chapter text divides into two distinct halves. Perhaps even more than in *Chin P'ing Mei*, the line between chapters 49 and 50 in *Hsi-yu chi* is clearly a great divide, as is symbolized by the midway water-crossing that takes place at this point. Here, several textual details reinforce the sense that we have arrived at the midpoint of the book. Most obvious is the fact that the crossing in chapter 49, which marks the end of the first half of the novel, is restaged at the end of the second half in chapter 99—down to the detail of the *yüan* 黿 tortoise that ferries the pilgrims across on both occasions. This point is duly noted by the commentators.[55] Immediately thereafter, the author again contrives to sustain the sense of a second beginning by inserting a number of details that hark back to the first beginning. For example, in chapter 51 the two divinities No-ch'a 哪吒 and Li T'ien-wang 李天王, who had figured prominently in the opening section and then retreated into the wings, are now trotted back onto the stage. The motif of Lao Tzu's "diamond snare" (*chin-kang cho* 金剛琢), mentioned in chapter 6, is similarly repeated in chapter 52.[56]

[53] The symmetry between the beginning and the end of the novel is discussed by Chang Shu-shen in a comment in chapter 100 (14b).

[54] For examples of commentators' discussions of the numerological significance of particular chapters, see Chang Shu-shen, chapter 19 (16a); Ch'en Shih-pin, chapter 33 (341f.); and Wang Hsiang-hsü, chapter 47 (1a, 1b). It is perhaps not accidental that the issue of the "five elements" is treated most explicitly in chapter 25.

[55] See, for example, Chang Shu-shen, chapters 47 (15b) and 98 (17a); and Wang Hsiang-hsü, chapter 47 (1a). See also Ts'ai Yüan-fang, *tu-fa*, item 49.

[56] Another example of this sort may be seen in Sun Wu-k'ung's recollection of his earlier theft of the "peaches of longevity" (*p'an-t'ao* 蟠桃) in chapter 55. Perhaps the plaint that the mission is on the verge of being "abandoned midway" (半途而廢, 中道而止) in chapter 57 (2:795) reflects more than a simple cry of despair in this context.

Although the use of hemispheric divisions as a formal feature closely parallels that in *Chin P'ing Mei*, the associated sense of a gathering of actors onstage in the first half of that book, followed by their inexorable dispersal in the second, is only partially fulfilled here. Perhaps this is because the unilinearity of the quest journey does not lend itself to the cyclical pattern of rise and fall that governs each of our other three texts.[57]

At the other end of the scale of textual divisions, the relentless continuity of the narrative of *Hsi-yu chi* is broken up into smaller episode units, varying from two or three to four or even five chapters in length.[58] In addition, we have seen that there are a certain number of episodes confined to the space of a single chapter that often seem to bear a special signifi-

[57] For the significance of this pattern in the other three novels, see above, Chapters 2, Part II, 4, Part II, and 5, Part II. Chang Ching-erh sees a certain sense of climax at the point of chapters 74–77 ("The Structure and Theme of the *Hsi-yu chi*," pp. 169–88, 179, 186). Wang Hsiang-hsü describes the gathering of the pilgrims in chapter 22 (1a) as a "minor reunion scene" (*hsiao t'uan-yüan* 小團圓), later followed by a "major reunion scene" (*ta t'uan-yüan* 大團圓) in chapter 100 (1a). Cf. Wang's use of the term "minor rest" (*hsiao-hsieh* 小歇) to describe a structural break in chapter 7 (1a). Many modern critics pay attention to the broad structural divisions of the text, for example, Cheng Chen-to, "Yen-hua," pp. 290, 294ff.; Hsü Chen-chi, "Pa-shih-i nan," pp. 73ff.; Arai Ken, "Saiyūki no naka no Saiyūki," pp. 591–96. Chang Shu-shen posits a division after chapter 26 in his "General Commentary" (*Tsung-p'i* 總批), item 26, which seems to demonstrate his sense that the preparatory phases of the narrative come to an end at this point, a pattern he goes on to relate to contemporary prose structure.

[58] For example, two-chapter episodes include chapters 16–17, 18–19, 20–21, 65–66, 72–73, 78–79, 91–92, and 96–97. Three-chapter units include 24–26, 37–39, 40–42, 44–46, 50–52, 53–55, 56–58, 59–61, 84–86, 88–90, and 93–95. The episodes in chapters 32–35, 68–71, 74–77, and 80–83 cover four chapters, and the long episode in chapters 27–31 stretches over a full five chapters (actually four plus an introductory section, a special pattern I will reconsider shortly). Cf. the spread of episodes over three or four scenes in the *Hsi-yu chi tsa-chü* (e.g., Scenes 1–4 on Hsüan-tsang, 9–10 on Sun Hsing-che, 13–16 on Chu Pa-chieh, and 19–20 on the Huo-yen shan episode). In the *Shih-hua*, on the other hand, every section comprises a separate episode. The commentators use a variety of terms to refer to these episode units. Liu I-ming, for example (*tu-fa*, item 9), speaks of "cases" (*kung-an* 公案) made up of two or three *hui* each, whereas Chang Shu-shen uses the terms "segment" (*chieh* 節) in *Tsung-p'i*, item 28 (7a, 7b), and "compositional unit" (*chang* 章) in item 29 (7b). In other places (e.g., *Tsung-p'i*, items 25, 26, 28, 29, 62) Chang speaks of the linking together of "chapters" (*p'ien* 篇) made up of related episodes, and elsewhere (e.g., *Tsung-p'i*, items 26 and 62), he speaks of separate narrative "topics" (*t'i-mu* 題目). This last usage is reminiscent of the "items" (*kuan-mu* 關目) that form the basic building blocks of *San-kuo yen-i* and, to a lesser extent, *Shui-hu chuan* (see below, Chapter 5, Part II). Liu I-ming (*tu-fa*, item 19) distinguishes between the narration of continuous and discontinuous episodes (*fen-shuo, ho-shuo* 分說, 合說). Cf. Wang Hsiang-hsü's discussion of the uneven matching of *nan* 難 to episode units in a note in chapter 99 (1b). The "trebling" pattern observable in the narrative sequence in many episode units is pointed out by Ch'en Shih-pin, 61 (618f.), and by Wang Hsiang-hsü, 59 (1b). On the generic significance of the *hui* organization in the hundred-chapter novel, see above, Chapter 2, Part II. See Liu Ts'un-yan, "Ssu-yu chi," pp. 370f.; and Koss, "Formative Stages," chap. 3. See also Ogawa Tamaki, "Saiyūki genpon," pp. 81ff.

cance. Within the overall framework of the quest journey, with its hemispheric and decade divisions, these episode units give the text its primary
structural coherence. Here *Hsi-yu chi* departs from *Chin P'ing Mei*, although
the episode structure brings it more into line with *San-kuo yen-i* and *Shui-hu
chuan*.[59]

One particularly interesting pattern unique to *Hsi-yu chi* is that seen in
episodes constructed of two or three chapters prefaced by one additional
chapter that is thematically linked to, but technically separate from, the
main body of the episode unit. The clearest examples of this type include
the sequence from chapters 53 to 55, in which the two-chapter episode in
the Land of Women at Hsi-liang 西梁女國 (chapters 54 and 55) is introduced by the incident of the pilgrims' "pregnancy" immediately before
(chapter 53)—which raises the issue of inverted sexual hierarchies even
before we get to the topsy-turvy kingdom. Thematically, these two parts
of the section are of a piece, although in terms of narrative flow the events
of chapter 53 constitute a separate incident concluded within the space of
the chapter. A similar example occurs in the encounter with the Lady of the
White Bones (Pai-ku fu-jen 白骨夫人) in chapter 27, which sets the allegorical stage for the exile of the mind-monkey, but is actually independent
from the main part of the episode stretching from chapter 28 to 31.[60]
This function of what one might call "pivotal" or "lead-in" chapters seems
to be a deliberate part of the author's organizational scheme, and the
commentators call attention to it.[61]

The structural design of *Hsi-yu chi* comes even closer to that outlined in
Chin P'ing Mei with respect to the shape and significance of its opening and
closing sections. There is room for debate over whether the main body of
the narrative begins in chapter 9, 12, or 13, or perhaps only with the
completion of the pilgrim group in chapter 22; but it is obvious that we
have here in the story of the Monkey King another extended prologue.
This is all the more striking since, as I have noted, the moving up of this
traditional material to the head of the narrative appears to be the unique
design of the novel, as opposed to any of the known antecedents.[62] As in
the case of *Chin P'ing Mei*, the use of the prologue section goes beyond the
simple formal feature of the delayed beginning (what has been related to

[59] See below, Chapters 4, Part II, and 5, Part II.

[60] A similar pattern of organization can be seen in chapter 37–39, preceded by 36, and
chapters 48–49, preceded by 47. Other, albeit less clear, examples include the prefacing of
chapter 62 to 63–64, 80 to 81–83, and 88 to 89–90.

[61] See, for example, Ch'en Shih-pin, chapters 10 (114f.) and 47 (477f.).

[62] See above, n. 9. That is not to say, of course, that the story of the Monkey King does
not appear in the antecedents, only that its shift to the beginning of the text suggests a
revised interpretation. On the other hand, we can observe that the extended treatment
of Hsüan-tsang's birth and early trials in Scenes 1–4 of the *Tsa-chü* fulfills a comparable
prologue function in the play.

the *ju-hua* 入話 in oral storytelling and the *hsieh-tzu* 楔子 in *tsa-chü* drama)
to fulfill the specific function of setting up some of the central issues to be
taken up in the body of the novel.[63]

It has been pointed out by many critics that what we have in the first eight
chapters of *Hsi-yu chi* is in effect a structural model for the rest of the book:
a mini-quest for salvation complete with many of the motifs later developed, in a kind of parody of the enlightenment process.[64] The manner in
which the novel ostensibly begins with light treatment of popular material
conforms to a pattern we have seen in *Chin P'ing Mei* and will trace in
subsequent chapters. But at the same time it also lays much of the termin-
ological groundwork for the allegory, and ultimately begins to outline such
weighty problems as the constraints of mortality, the impossibility of self-
contained perfection, even questions of social order and chaos, which cast a
shadow over the otherwise amusing career of the "Great Sage Equal to
Heaven" 齊天大聖 and the story of his ultimate submission to the all-
encompassing power of the Buddha nature. As we shall see, all of these
issues are brought to bear on the interpretation of the main body of the
narrative as well. I should also note here that some of the central motifs
of the opening sequence—the birth of the hero, perilous water crossings,
an attempt to cheat the forces of destiny—are repeated in the additional
section that falls between the eight-chapter prologue and the body of the
narrative. In this light, we can view this section as a second prologue,
regardless of how we choose to deal with the problem of the function of
chapter 9. The sense of a line demarcating these preparatory sections from
the rest of the world of the novel is made quite explicit with the renaming
of Five Elements Mountain as Dual Border Mountain (*Liang-chieh shan*),
clearly signposting the entry into a new narrative realm.[65]

[63] Wang Hsiang-hsü uses the term *hsieh-tzu* 楔子 in chapters 10 (1a) and 11 (1a). See also
Wu Pi-yung, "Hsi-yu chi yen-chiu," pp. 12f.

[64] The function of the first few chapters as a model of the quest pattern in the novel as a
whole is discussed in Liu I-ming, *tu-fa*, items 27 and 29. A number of recent critics have
suggested the same idea; for example, James Fu, *Mythic and Comic Aspects of the Quest*,
pp. 90ff.; Karl S. Y. Kao, "An Archetypal Approach to *Hsi-yu chi*," pp. 63–98; and Chang
Ching-erh, "Structure and Theme," p. 184. A more contrived reading of the same structural
pattern is give in Okuno Shintarō's "Mizu to honō no denshō," pp. 225ff, where he attempts
to relate the Monkey King's mini-quest to a term for the quest journey of particular
currency in Japanese narrative theory: "the tale of the wandering nobleman" (*kishū ryūri tan*
貴種流離譚).

[65] Other examples of recurring motifs that link the two introductory sections include the
"grand assemblies" (*ta-hui* 大會) and the frustration of the powers of the dragon king in
chapters 3 and 10. The melons delivered by Liu Ch'üan 劉全 to the underworld in chapter
11 to effect a rebirth may also give a faint symbolic echo of the stone egg in chapter 1. In
addition, the stone marker at Dual Border Mountain (*shih-chieh* 石碣) also suggests an
intertextual allusion to the similar monument in chapter 1 of *Shui-hu chuan*, where the
release of potentially destructive forces is also at issue.

On the other side of the prologue, we observe yet another instance of striking conformity to the structural model of *Chin P'ing Mei*. Here, too, we find an initial disquisition that presents something of a prologue to the prologue. Whereas in *Chin P'ing Mei* this took the form of a homily on the deleterious effects of passion, here we get a quick review of the cyclical movements of cosmic and earthly time, leading up to the spontaneous emergence of the Monkey King out of his timeless rock.

It would be possible to take these added sections on the birth and origins of the main characters of the book as examples of a common device in Chinese fiction: the tendency to begin by running through the historical origins of the story down to the time of the narrative itself. But the topic of discussion in the opening disquisition, for all its pseudo-philosophical jargon, takes up a theme that is of central importance to the conception of the novel.[66] This is the concept of "nonbeginning," as expressed in the terminology of the *I Ching* in the formula *chen-hsia ch'i-yüan* 貞下起元, here worked out in several frames of reckoning and supported by an appeal to one of the most deeply metaphysical of all Chinese philosophers, Shao Yung. This, too, can easily be brushed aside as a reflection of the more popular image of Shao Yung as a soothsayer, rather than as a serious philosophical "message."[67] But I believe the opening exercise in cosmology goes right to the heart of the crucial question of how to relate the unilinear trajectory of the end-oriented quest to other, nonlinear, concepts of attainment. At the very least, it provides a basis for understanding the various sets of philo-sophical terms—notably the five elements and hexagram designations worked into the text—in terms of cycles with neither beginning nor end.[68]

This gives a special meaning to the other primary point of structural articulation; i.e. the conclusion of this long work. If the story so pointedly begins at a moment of cyclical renewal, then should we take the literal end of the quest, with its songs of praise and apotheosis, at face value as a final

[66] Ōta Tatsuo ("Kaisetsu," p. 440) speculates that the earlier *Shih-o chuan* began with the recounting of the myth of creation associated with P'an-ku, and argues that the entire section preceding this is a later interpolation by the Shih-te t'ang editor, one he regards as superfluous.

[67] For example, Ōta Tatsuo, "Kaisetsu." See above, n. 49. Cf. the poem attributed to Shao Yung at the start of chapter 79 in *Chin P'ing Mei*, and the reference to Shao Yung as a master of the occult precisely in chapter 79 of *Hsing-shih yin-yüan chuan* 醒世姻緣傳.

[68] The commentators take the *chen-hsia ch'i-yüan* formula quite seriously. See, for ex-ample, Wang Hsiang-hsü, chapter 99 (1a, 6b); Ch'en Shih-pin, chapters 10 (115), and 50 (509); and Liu I-ming, *tu-fa*, item 13 and preface. Liu I-ming also brings into his discussion the *I Ching* terms *i-fa* 已發 and *wei-fa* 未發. The significance of this preoccupation with beginnings and endings within the context of the allegorical structure will be explored below. For further discussion of the concept of *hai-mo tzu-ch'u* 亥末子初, see Liu Ts'un-yan, "Taoist Self-cultivation," pp. 297f.

fulfillment? I will have a good deal to say about this in the following interpretation of the allegorical level of the text. In the meantime, I will consider the structural implications of the ending with respect to the aesthetic shape of the novel. We have already seen in *Chin P'ing Mei* the manner in which that sprawling narrative draws to a close with an apocalyptic flourish of national cataclysm and personal salvation, which, however, fails to flesh out its parting note of emptiness. The *Hsi-yu chi* can be read as a variation on the same theme, and here, too, the inexorable unilinearity of the quest pattern sheds upon the moment of the consummation of the meandering journey only a superficial sense of finality.

In terms of simple narrative aesthetics, this makes perfect sense. Every story, like every banquet, must have an end. This sense of closure is recognized by the commentators, such as Wang Hsiang-hsü for example, who sees in the final chapter the function of the sort of "grand reunion scene" (*ta t'uan-yüan*) mandatory in Ming literati drama.[69] But although the aesthetics of the quest narrative demand a grand finale, the author is at evident pains to bring out at several points the idea that the literal-minded pursuit of the end is basically misguided. In effect, then, the wearying trek to the ends of the earth really goes nowhere and ends up where it began. Or, in other words, it ends with a reinterpretation of the meaning of final attainment, such that the metaphoric expression "creating the fruit" (*ch'eng-kuo* 成果) comes to mean the same thing as "returning to the point of origin" (*huan-pen* 還本).[70] I will have more to say about this issue toward the end of this chapter.

Finally, let us consider the author's use of certain other spatial and temporal schemes of structural arrangement that also link *Hsi-yu chi* to the artistry of our other sixteenth-century literati novels. The possibility of some sort of spatial design, such as the juxtaposition of the microcosm and macrocosm in *Chin P'ing Mei*, or the geographical sweep and countermovements in *Shui-hu chuan* and *San-kuo chih yen-i*, are more or less eclipsed in *Hsi-yu chi* by the unilinear path of the quest journey. The most we can say on this point is that the author develops a certain alternating movement

[69] See Wang Hsiang-hsü, chapter 100 (1a), where he compares the ending of *Hsi-yu* to that of other novels. The same term (*ta t'uan-yüan*) is used by Arai Ken in "Saiyūki no naka no Saiyūki," p. 604ff. See note 57.

[70] The rather pointed joke about the "wordless scriptures" (*wu-tzu ching* 無字經) may follow a hint of nonfulfillment in section 15 in the *Shih-hua*, where the glorious bestowal of scriptures is marred by the conspicuous omission of the Heart Sutra. On the allegorical significance of the attainment of the perfect "fruit" of cultivation (*ch'eng-kuo*), and the "return to the source" (*fan-pen* or *huan-pen*), see section V of this chapter, below. Some interesting parallels to the idea of ending at the beginning may be observed in Dante's *Commedia*, in Proust's *A la recherche*, and other works. See Wu Ta-yün, "T'ien-ti pu ch'üan," pp. 80–109.

between settled civilization and trackless wastes, or between land and water perils, as at least one commentator has noted.[71]

With respect to the temporal arrangement of the narrative, on the other hand, we can find more evidence of a conscious design, although this too is obscured by the plodding progression through the eight-one trials. One aspect of the temporal design of the novel that may be more significant than it appears is the intimation of a dual focus between the real time frame of the early T'ang and the mythical time referred to in the story of the Monkey King's prehistory, and in the additional passages relating the prior existence of the other pilgrims and demons. In the course of the novel, the discrepancy in time between these two ages is more than once described as a gap of "five hundred years."[72] Generally this number can be understood as a loose reference to the misty past *in illo tempore*, such as we find in Buddhist and Confucian scripture.[73] But another possible explanation is suggested by the fact that five hundred years before the time of the narrative in the early T'ang happens to fall (by very rough arithmetic) in the mid-Han era. Thus the occasional references to Wang Mang 王莽 in descriptions of unbridled demons help to set up a historical and philosophical resonance of some significance, as I will discuss later.[74]

Coming back closer to our generic model, it is interesting that despite the apparent timelessness of many of the fantastic episodes, the author of *Hsi-yu chi* still seems to pay attention to seasonality as an organizing

[71] See Wang Hsiang-hsü, chapter 50 (1a), on the "cycle" of mountain and water scenes. This idea is discussed by Hsü Chen-chi in "Pa-shih-i nan," pp. 82ff.; and Arai Ken, "Saiyūki no naka no Saiyūki," pp. 597f.

[72] For examples, see chapters 2 (1:21), 24 (1:328f.), 28 (2:377), and 56 (2:777). The commentators frequently call attention to the reckoning of years within the temporal frame of the narrative; e.g., Chang Shu-shen in *Tsung-p'i*, item 43 (11b); Liu I-ming, *tu-fa*, items 13, 15, 17, 41; Ts'ai Yüan-fang, *tu-fa*, item 48. Cf. the chronological discrepancy regarding the number of years of the journey's duration. See Koss, "Formative Stages," chap. 4; and Arai Ken, "Saiyūki no naka no Saiyūki," pp. 594ff., 605f.

[73] See, for example, Mencius's idea of the appearance of a true king every 500 years (2.B.13 and 7.B.38); plus certain well-known passages in the *Chin-kang ching*, e.g., *Chin-kang ching chien-chu*, pp. 9b, 22a. The sense of timelessness comes out in the expression "time has no sequence in the mountains" (*shan chung wu chia-tzu* 山中無甲子), cited in chapter 1 (1:3). The associated proverbial idea that "one day in heaven equals one year on earth" had been expressed earlier in the *Shih-hua*, section 3, and in the *Tsa-chü*, Scenes 9 and 10. See Wang Hsiang-hsü, chapters 60 (1a), 63 (1b), and 76 (1b); Liu I-ming, *tu-fa*, item 41; and Ch'en Shih-pin, chapters 1 (8), 5 (54), 7 (77), 23 (241), 37 (377).

[74] I will reconsider the implications of Wang Mang in part V of this chapter. Sun Wu-k'ung is associated with Wang Mang at the start of chapter 14 (1:182). This is, of course, the literary image of Wang Mang, deliberately fostered in certain writings for political and ideological reasons, which differs sharply from the actual career of the man. Cf. the expression "500-year nemesis" (*wu-pai-nien yüan-chia* 五百年冤家), which appears frequently in *Chin P'ing Mei*.

principle in ordering his text.[75] In a simple sense, the use of seasonal tags and motifs in the iconography of demons and their abodes is to be expected within the context of the fabric of colors, directions, and other details that go to make up the allegorical groundwork. But we do seem to have a more self-conscious development of a seasonal rhythm when the author contrives, for example, to stage the introduction and incorporation into the band of Chu Pa-chieh—his icon of material life force and animal vigor—precisely amidst the imagery of spring, or when he pegs the dead center of the novel, the crossing of the frozen river in chapter 49, in the dead of winter (*yen-tung* 嚴冬).[76] In these and other examples, he demonstrates a sensitivity to the cyclical alternation and interpenetration of cold and heat such as I have posited as a key to the temporal structure of *Chin P'ing Mei*.[77] Here, cold and heat imagery take on a heightened degree of significance in connection with the water and fire symbolism that contributes to the allegorical structure. Given the special sensitivity to seasonal symbolism as a central structuring principle in the literati novel, it is not surprising that we find in *Hsi-yu chi*, as in all three of our other masterworks, a highlighting of the Yüan-hsiao Festival, here used as a setting in chapter 91 for one of the most perilous trials faced by the pilgrims.[78]

A second area of analysis in which the *Hsi-yu chi* conforms to the generic criteria of the literati novel outlined in the previous chapter is in its capacity

[75] The commentators also draw attention to this aspect of the work. See, for example, Wang Hsiang-hsü, chapter 22 (1b): "The advent of each of the members of the group is in accordance with the proper season" 四衆之來各以其時 .... See a similar comment by Chang Shu-shen in chapter 94 (1a). For another discussion of this point, see Arai Ken, "Saiyūki no naka no Saiyūki," pp. 591ff.

[76] Other examples include the early winter setting (*ch'u-tung* 初冬) at the start of the narrative proper and the late summer backdrop for the wind and fire imagery in chapters 20–21. The pegging of the pseudo-enlightenment scene in chapter 36 to the Mid-Autumn Festival (*Chung-ch'iu chieh* 中秋節) is all but obligatory. A similar sense is at work in the playing of scenes of sexual implications in chapters 53, 73, and 93 in the springtime.

[77] See above, Chapter 2, Part II, and below, chapters 4, Part II, and 5, Part II. This principle is enunciated by Wang Hsiang-hsü in chapters 26 (1a) and 61 (1a). In the latter note, Wang relies heavily on an earlier "Li Cho-wu" comment, chapter 61 (16a). See also "Li Cho-wu," chapter 48 (9b); and Chang Shu-shen, chapters 15 (1a), 38 (1a), and 40 (1a). The alternations of heat and cold are explained by Wang Hsiang-hsü in terms of *yin-yang* cycles. See, e.g., chapters 13 (1a), 26 (1a), 43 (2a), 55 (1b), 59 (1b), 63 (1a), and 80 (1a). See also Ch'en Shih-pin, preface and comments in chapters 5 (55), 7 (78), 17 (185), 19 (201), 22 (229), 26 (272), 38 (387), 54 (549), 59 (598), 69 (702), 72 (739), 73 (746), 82 (839), 92 (929), 94 (949), 95 (960), 99 (1003), 100 (1014); and Chang Shu-sheng, chapters 34 (9a), 43 (11b), and 44 (11b), as well as in the *T'ung-i Hsi-yu cheng-chih*, chapters 15 (57b), 20 (94b).

[78] Ch'en Shih-pin discusses the significance of the Yüan-hsiao setting at length in a comment in chapter 91 (921). Cf. the poem on the Yüan-hsiao Festival interjected in that chapter.

to develop what I have termed textural, or "figural," density.[79] Here, too, as in the *Chin P'ing Mei*, we have an intricate composition whose intricacy lies not only in the sort of global structural patterns discussed above, but also in its weaving of finely textured local linkages. The very special nature of the contents of *Hsi-yu chi* has diverted the attention of most modern critics away from this aspect of its artistry, to questions of sources on the one hand, and allegorical interpretation on the other. But we do find among the remarks of the Ming-Ch'ing commentators on the novel considerable interest in this aspect of the work.

In this case, we do not have one preeminent guide to lead us through the labyrinthine passages of the text, such as we had in Chang Chu-p'o, and we will see again in Chin Sheng-t'an and Mao Tsung-kang.[80] However, this is more than compensated for by the cumulative contributions of several full-length commentaries still extant.[81] The commentator who is by far the most interested in this critical area is Chang Shu-shen, whose quite slanted interpretation of the novel is nevertheless packed with textual analyses couched in the terms of fiction criticism inherited from Chin and Mao. Chang, for example, uses language reminiscent of descriptions of *Chin P'ing Mei* cited earlier to evaluate the overall intricacy of the text of *Hsi-yu chi*:

> Not a single episode could be added, nor could a single part be taken away, since the vital spirit of the composition, from start to finish and all the way through, is intricately interwoven.
> 欲添一章，欲去一節，亦不得，蓋以上下前後之文氣脈絡，遞相聯貫也.[82]

[79] For additional explanations of the concept of "figural density," see above, Chapter 2, Part III, and below, Chapter 5, Part II. See also my article "Conceptual Models in Chinese Narrative Theory," pp. 25–47, esp. 32ff.

[80] On Chang Chu-p'o, see above, Chapter 2, Part II. For Chin Sheng-t'an and Mao Tsung-kang see below, Chapters 4, Part II, and 5, Part II.

[81] For bibliographical information on these commentaries, see b.n. II. The work of these individual critics does not represent entirely independent efforts, but rather a dense network of acknowledged and unacknowledged borrowings. For example, Ch'en Shih-pin reproduces comments by Wang Hsiang-hsü in chapters 45 (456), 54 (549), 59 (599), 68 (693), 78 (796), 81 (824), 84 (855), 85 (866), 88 (894), and 92 (930); and perhaps by Chang Shu-shen in chapters 62, 63 (639), 69 (704), 82 (834), and 84 (855). Ch'en also mentions Li Chih in a comment in chapter 90 (911). Liu I-ming discusses the Wang Hsiang-hsü commentary, as well as that of Ch'en Shih-pin in his *tu-fa*, item 44. In fact, Liu I-ming makes it clear that he sees his own work as essentially an expansion of the Ch'en Shih-pin commentary. Chang Shu-shen mentions Chin Sheng-t'an in comments in chapter 12 (22b) and especially *Tsung-p'i*, items 37 (9b) and 40 (10b), where he nearly reproduces a line from Chin's *Shui-hu chuan tu-fa*. The *T'ung-i Hsi-yu cheng-chih* commentator complains of the inadequacy of some of Ch'en Shih-pin's comments in chapters 94 (39b) and 95 (49b).

[82] Chang Shu-shen, chapter 18 (1b). See above, n. 47. Chang expresses similar ideas in his *Tsung-p'i*, 18 (5b), 19 (5b), 28 (7b, 8a), 40 (10b), 49 (13b), 67 (18a), and in chapters 8 (1a),

Writing during the Ch'ien-lung period, Chang had the full benefit of the contributions of the giants Chin Sheng-t'an and Mao Tsung-kang to traditional fiction criticism, but even in the earlier "Li Cho-wu" commentary we already find considerable interest in this aspect of the novel.[83]

In any event, the terminology and critical concepts applied by the commentators to the novel are very much the language of discourse of sixteenth- and seventeenth-century criticism. In attempting to analyze the perceived density of the text into its structural patterns, for example, the commentators on *Hsi-yu chi* also distinguish between examples of forward projection (*fu-pi* 伏筆, *mai-fu* 埋伏, *ko-nien hsia-chung* 隔年下種)[84] and retroactive reflection (*chao-ying* 照應, *hui-chao* 回照).[85] At the same time, they pay special attention to problems of narrative continuity, discussing transitions between textual units (*kuo-chieh* 過節, *p'o-chan* 破綻), as well as matters of narrative pace and sequencing of episodes. This last topic will be reconsidered later, in my interpretation of the direction and pace of the quest.[86]

---

54 (1a), 59 (2a–b), 65 (1b), and 68 (15a). Chang's application of the terms of classical prose analysis is quite in keeping with his Confucian reading of the novel, but nearly all of the other commentators also draw upon similar critical terminology; for example, "Li Cho-wu," chapter 11 (13a, *tp*); Ch'en Shih-pin, chapter 20 (212); *T'ung-i Hsi-yu cheng-chih*, chapter 73 (34b); Ts'ai Yüan-fang, *tu-fa*, item 5.

[83] Regardless of whether or not the attribution to Li Chih is dismissed, all scholars agree that the "Li Cho-wu" edition dates roughly from his lifetime, which makes it the earliest of the extant commentaries on the novel. See Liao Nan, "Kuo-nei fa-hsien Ming-k'an Li Cho-wu p'ing Hsi-yu chi." Cf. Wang Hsiang-hsü's extensive reliance on this commentary, as observed above (see b.n. II.5). On the complexities of the problem of the attribution to Li, see the Appendix of this book. See also my paper "The Ch'ung-chen Commentary on the *Chin P'ing Mei*," pp. 2ff.

[84] For examples of the term *mai-fu*, see Chang Shu-shen, chapters 1 (18b), 39 (1b), and 53 (1b), and *Tsung-p'i*, items 40 (10b) and 45 (12b); Ch'en Shih-pin, chapter 20 (212); Wang Hsiang-hsü, chapter 39 (1b); for *ko-nien hsia-chung*, see Chang Shu-shen, chapter 57 (14a). Similar terms include *ts'ao-she hui-hsien* 草蛇灰線; see, e.g., Ch'en Shih-pin, 20 (212), 47 (477), and *Chia-p'i Hsi-yu chi*, *chüan* 3 (27b). "Li Cho-wu" occasionally uses such terms as *yin-tzu* 引子 and *chang-pen* 張本 to describe this function, as does Wang Hsiang-hsü, 13 (2a). See also *Chia-p'i Hsi-yu chi*, *chüan*, 1 (10b, 11b), 2 (1a, 4b, 5a, 5b, 9b, 20a), 3 (18a, 22a, 22b), 4 (1b, 6b, 15b), 5 (15a, 17b), 6 (12a), 7 (1a, 3a, 18b), 9 (20a, 25a).

[85] Variations on the term *chao* 照 appear in Chang Shu-shen, chapters 8 (1a), 35 (15a), 43 (1a), 45 (15a), 51 (1b), and *Tsung-p'i*, items 29 (7b), 76 (19b); Ch'en Shih-pin, chapters 18 (192), 20 (212), 21 (219), 43 (437); "Li Cho-wu," chapter 60 (1a); Wang Hsiang-hsü, chapters 44 (1a), 61 (8b); *Chia-p'i Hsi-yu chi*, *chüan* 6 (2b), 7 (6b, 17b, 19b), 8 (15a, 16a), 9 (6b), 12 (1a, 18a); *T'ung-i Hsi-yu cheng-chih*, chapters 88 (82b), 94 (34b), 97 (91b). In addition, the terms *tou-ch'u* 逗出 or *tien-tou* 點逗 are sometimes used in the special sense of the retroactive evocation of an earlier motif; e.g., Chang Shu-shen, chapter 39 (3b).

[86] For example, the term *kuo-chieh* occurs in Chang Shu-shen, chapters 8 (1a), 43 (1a), 65 (1b); Ch'en Shih-pin, chapters 84 (856), 87 (884), 91 (922), 98 (992); Wang Hsiang-hsü, chapter 10 (1a). *P'o-chan* is used in Liu I-ming, *tu-fa*, item 15. Other terms that treat the

In all of these critical discussions, the aesthetic sense of prose density in the novel again rests on the principle I have called "figural recurrence." As in *Chin P'ing Mei*, the simple fact that textual elements tend to be repeated over and over again can easily be taken as evidence of haphazard composition, quite the opposite of the consummate control claimed by the commentators.[87] Or it can be ascribed to the influence of popular storytelling, with its use of predictably recurrent narrative materials.[88] Therefore, in order to demonstrate that what we have here are instances of *significant* recurrence, I will quickly review several types of recurrent figures in the following pages, before returning in the second half of this chapter to try to specify where this significance lies.

For a text that otherwise displays such inventiveness, it is a bit surprising that the same figures seem to reappear again and again in the novel. Sometimes we see precisely the same characters introduced at several points. For example, Li T'ien-wang and No-ch'a, as I have noted, are first brought in to combat the errant Monkey King, and later provide the means to subdue other figurally similar creatures in chapters 42, 51, 61, and 83.[89] The same is true for Erh-lang shen 二郎神, whose early prowess is restaged in chapter 63.[90] Similarly, the wayward Green Lion under the command of the bodhisattva Manjusri (Wen-shu 文殊), first introduced in chapter 39, puts in more than one appearance, as do the Bull Demon King (Niu mo-wang 牛魔王) and others.[91] In some cases, this is just a question of the early mention and later recall of a name, as, for example, in the reappearance of the Red Child (Hung-hai-erh 紅孩兒) in chapter 59, leading into the related episode of the Mountain of Flames (Huo-yen shan), or the

problems of narrative pacing and sequencing include *ch'i-po* 起波: e.g., Chang Shu-shen, chapters 54 (1a), 99 (11b); Wang Hsiang-hsü, chapter 76 (1a); Ch'en Shih-pin, chapter 83 (844); *shou-sha* 收煞: Chang Shu-shen, 77 (1a), 95 (13b); and Ch'en Shih-pin, chapter 100 (1013), etc.

[87] Certain instances of loose threads or other discrepancies in the text are pointed out by Liu Ts'un-yan, "Wu Ch'eng-en," 84, n. 172; Cheng Chen-to, "Yen-hua," pp. 265f.; and Su Hsing, "Hsi-yu chi so-t'an," pp. 62f.; among others. A more positive assessment of the author's repetitions is given by James Fu, *Quest*, p. 16. Cf. discussions of this point by the commentators, e.g., Wang Hsiang-hsü, chapter 80 (1b); Chang Shu-shen, chapter 49 (1a); Ch'en Shih-pin, chapter 97 (981).

[88] Such examples as the "trebling" pattern (see below, Chapter 5, Part II) or the repeated use of stock settings (e.g., the Black Pine Forest) reflect such storytelling conventions.

[89] See chapters 33 (2:461), 42 (2:587), 51 (2:710), 58 (2:805), 61 (2:853), 80 (3:1101), and 83 (3:1142, 1146).

[90] Chapters 6 (1:74ff.), 63 (2:876ff.).

[91] Wang Hsiang-hsü takes note of this repeated appearance in chapters 51 (1a), 74 (1b), 83 (1a); and Ch'en Shih-pin calls this a case of "transformation" (*hua-shen* 化身). See also Ts'ai Yüan-fang, *tu-fa*, item 32. Cf. Su Hsing, "Hsi-yu so-t'an," p. 62.

introduction of the term "Jade Hare" in a poem in chapter 81 (3:1113), long before a figure with this name actually appears in chapters 93–95. At the very least, I would suggest that these instances fulfill the literary function of tightening up the "figural density" of the text.[92]

In other cases, the sense of redundancy is based on recurring types of characters rather than the same specific figures. For example, the woodcutter who provides a refuge for the band in chapter 86 seems somehow linked to the hunter who rescues the fledgling pilgrim in chapter 13, as I have mentioned.[93] By the same token, we can see a number of chains of demon figures who share either a false form (e.g., the temptresses Pai-ku fu-jen and Ti-yung fu-jen 地湧夫人) or a camouflaged "true form" 本相 (e.g., the various animal or insect spirits who bar the pilgrims' way).[94]

A similar redundancy may be seen at the level of smaller textual details. For one thing, though the journey ostensibly makes its way through vast stretches of territory, the landscape through which the pilgrims pass is remarkably repetitive, with its recurrent round of mountains, caves, and deep pools. Even the cities have a certain sameness about them, with the resulting sense of circularity in the path of the pilgrimage.[95] This principle

[92] In other words, these can be viewed as instances of forward (*fu*) or backward (*chao*) reflection. Other examples include the repeated mention of such figures as the bodhisattva Ling-chi 靈吉菩薩 in chapters 21 (1:288f.) and 59 (2:823); and Shan-ts'ai t'ung-tzu 善財童子 in chapters 42 (2:591), 49 (2:687), 57 (2:791), and 84 (3:1152). See also the recall of Wu-ch'ao ch'an-shih 烏巢禪師, first glimpsed in chapter 19 (1:263ff.), in chapter 93 (1266).

[93] See chapter 13 (1:175ff.) and 86 (3:1187ff.). Also cf. the woodcutter who directs Sun Wu-k'ung to the Master Subodhi in chapter 1 (1:10f.), and the woodcutter who appears in chapter 32 (1:434). This repetition is noted by the commentator in *T'ung-i Hsi-yu cheng-chih*, chapter 86 (64b).

[94] Pai-ku fu-jen appears in chapter 27, Ti-yung fu-jen in chapters 82–83. For the appearance of these figures in the antecedent sources, see Part I of this chapter. The taxonomy of animal spirits includes foxes (chapters 34, 70); deer (*pai-lu* 白鹿), chapters 45, 70, 79; tigers (chapters 13, 29, 45, and 90); lions (chapters 52 and 89–90), a hare (chapter 95); apes (chapters 58, 83); a rhinoceroslike creature (*ssu* 兕), chapter 50; a panther (chapter 86); a python (*mang* 蟒), chapter 67; spiders (*chih-chu ching* 蜘蛛精), chapter 73; and centipedes (*wu-kung ching* 蜈蚣精), chapter 93. For an analysis of the various categories of demons see Kao Ming-ko, "Hsi-yu chi li ti shen-mo wen-t'i," pp. 118–27; and Hsü Chen-chi, "Pa-shih-i nan," pp. 51–72. Cf. comment by Wang Hsiang-hsü in chapter 71 (10a), enumerating various types of demons.

[95] We see mountain caves in, among others, chapters 1, 8, 15, 17, 18, 20, 28, 29, 32, 33, 50, 59, 63, 72, 74, 81, 88, 90, and 91; we cross water barriers in chapters 1, 3, 5, 9, 11–12, 14, 15, 22, 26, 30, 37–38, 44, 47–49, 53, and 87; we visit cities in chapters 29, 37, 44–46, 54–55, 62, 68, 76, 78, 84, 87, 91, 93, and 96. Ch'en Shih-pin, in chapter 97 (981), notes the similar urban landscape that links Mieh-fa kuo 滅法國 to Chu-tzu kuo 朱紫國. Cf. the advance mention of Hsi-liang nü-kuo in chapter 48 (2:674).

also applies, as we have seen, at the level of specific motifs, such as the recurring "diamond snare" and the embroidered ball.[96] But we will find more fertile ground for this interpretive analysis at the level of recurrent patterns of narrative action. Here, again, many of the repeated figures are associated with basic *topoi* of the storytelling tradition (e.g., the boatman's trick given in several chapters).[97] Yet, a number of these recurring scenes set up patterns that demand more rigorous interpretation. This is true of the three quests for salvation, the multiple water crossings, the predictable self-enclosure of demons—all of which function within the allegorical framework.[98] It is also quite evident in the restaging of the "exile" of the mind-monkey,[99] or in the several episodes in which the pilgrims are stymied by replicas of their own selves.[100] All of these instances will be treated in greater detail in my full allegorical reading of the novel. Here the point is simply to stress the extent to which the text is constructed on the principle of significant recurrence, in line with the general aesthetics of the literati novel form.

One final aspect of the figural density of the text that deserves mention is the manner in which the main figures are woven into a composite scheme

[96] The "diamond snare" (*chin-kang cho*) is introduced in chapters 6 (2:80) and 52 (2:732). Wang Hsiang-hsü, in chapter 50 (1a), notes the reappearance of this motif, as does Ts'ai Yüan-fang (*tu-fa*, item 49). See n. 56. Besides the embroidered ball, cf. the "banana fan" (*pa-chiao shan* 芭蕉扇), which is mentioned in chapters 34 (2:465), 39 (2:535), and 52 (2:732) before becoming a focus of attention in chapters 59–61. Cf. the various transformations into small creatures (fly, bee, gnat, crab, bat, fish, moth, rat, butterfly) in order to gain entry into a closed lair (see n. 224). In other cases, such recurrent motifs indicate the persistence of certain allegorical issues, as in the "false" weapons that confuse the pilgrims in chapters 34–35, 71, 73, and 87, or the "encompassing" objects that dominate a number of scenes. I will discuss this last category in Part V of this chapter.

[97] The boatman's trick is staged in chapters 9, 15, 43, 48, and 53. For the corresponding motif in *Shui-hu chuan*, see below, Chapter 4, Part II. It is also mentioned in the *Tsa-chü*, Scene 12. Set pieces derived from popular storytelling can also be identified in other conventional scenes, such as the resuscitation of expired heros in chapters 9 and 38–39; the staging of formal or burlesqued "assemblies" (*hui* 會) in chapters 5, 7, 8, 12, 17, and 89; the scenes of "wreaking havoc" (*nao* 鬧) presented in chapters 7, 25, 52, 58, 70, 79, 81, and 95. For this latter pattern in *Shui-hu chuan*, see below, Chapter 4, Part II.

[98] This point is brought out by Chang Shu-shen, in chapter 49 (1a), and Liu I-ming (*tu-fa*, item 27). I have already considered the structural implications of the parallel quests. Other recurrent themes of special significance for the allegory include the theft of spiritual weapons, instances of sexual temptation, the danger of false compassion—all of which will be taken up later in my interpretation of the allegory. Cf. the pattern of recurrence that links the "six thieves" with the "seven passions."

[99] See Part V of this chapter.

[100] For example, the false Master in chapter 39, the two "mind-monkeys" in chapter 58, the false Chu Pa-chieh in chapter 61. Wang Hsiang-hsü, chapter 39 (1b), suggests that the two Masters in that chapter prefigure the two mind-monkeys in chapter 58.

based on five-elements correspondences.[101] This scheme is not entirely consistent (Sun Wu-K'ung, for one, seems to straddle the area between fire and metal); nor is it fully worked out (Chu Pa-chieh is exclusively linked to the element wood, but both Hsüan-tsang 玄奘 and the Sand Monk 沙和尚 share certain affiliations with earth, while the dragon-horse only has an identification with water by implication). In like manner, the emblematic colors and directions woven into the presentation of various demons frequently draw upon five-elements associations, but nowhere are these articulated into a uniform scheme. Later I will consider the ramifications of this arrangement for the allegorical structure of the novel.[102] In the meantime, let me simply call attention here to the use of the five-elements scheme as an aspect of the aesthetic patterning of the text, one we have seen in a very loose sense in the *Chin P'ing Mei*, and that later forms a crucial framework of meaning in the *Hung-lou meng*.[103]

III

The third category of analysis I used to account for the textual richness of the *Chin P'ing Mei* included a range of special rhetorical effects. I argued that its deliberate adaptation of the characteristic rhetorical devices of the colloquial fiction tradition, far from indicating a direct link to popular storytelling, identifies that work instead as an exemplar of the literati novel genre.[104] In the case of *Hsi-yu chi*, this argument goes in a somewhat different direction, since the hundred-chapter novel is undeniably linked to an actual oral tradition. But here, too, the final impression the reader gets in assessing this aspect of the novel is one of selective adaptation for specific literary functions, rather then the simple preservation of fossils of

[101] I will consider the allegorical implications of this pattern in greater detail later. For additional discussions, see Fu Shu-hsien, "Hsi-yu chi chung wu-sheng ti kuan-hsi," pp. 10–17; Chang Ching-erh, "Structure and Theme," pp. 170ff.; Anthony Yu, *Journey*, pp. 49ff., and my "Allegory in *Hsi-yu chi* and *Hung-lou meng*," pp. 176ff. The commentators do not neglect these references. See, e.g., Wang Hsiang-hsü, chapters 43 (1a, 1b), 49 (4a); "Li Cho-wu", chapter 46 (15b, *tp*), Liu I-ming, *tu-fa*, items 33 and 37. This aspect of the text is also emphasized in most of the prefaces, as it is in Liu T'ing-chi's critical review of the novel in *Tsai-yüan tsa-chih*.

[102] For the allegorical significance of the five-elements labels, see discussion in Part V of this chapter.

[103] See above, Chapter 2, Part III. I have attempted to set forth the implications of the five-elements scheme in *Hung-lou meng* in my *Archetype and Allegory in the Dream of the Red Chamber*, chap. 4.

[104] See discussion of this point above, Chapter 1. I have made a more extensive argument on this issue in "Full-Length *Hsiao-shuo* and the Western Novel," pp. 163–76.

oral performance. Thus on this point as well, *Hsi-yu chi* falls squarely within the generic criteria of the sixteenth-century novel.

The fact that the basic medium of narration in *Hsi-yu chi* shows less variation than in our three other works probably says more about the artistic control of the author than the lack of it.[105] We find, for example, liberal use in *Hsi-yu chi* of the conventional tag expressions of the colloquial narrator, especially the chapter-ending formula, uniformly given as "just listen to the next chapter for the explanation" (*ch'ieh t'ing hsia-hui fen-chieh* 且聽下回分解).[106] Interestingly, *Hsi-yu chi* fails to exploit the device of *k'an-kuan t'ing-shuo* 看官聽說 passages of authorial commentary, which we saw to play a key role in *Chin P'ing Mei*—probably because the voice of an omniscient narrator would clash with the deliberate opacity of the allegory.

Another clear indication of the purposeful adaptation of the rhetorical devices of the colloquial fiction tradition traced in the last chapter was seen in the innovative use of quoted songs and dramatic arias, plus other special effects in the citation of incidental verse. The author of *Hsi-yu chi* also demonstrates a high degree of creativity in this area, although here the use of poetry within the narrative takes somewhat different directions. One of these is the use of highlighted opening and closing verses in each chapter, as well in the interpolated poems, to carry much of the burden of the allegory.[107] Often this is just a matter of injecting suggestive philosophical terminology into otherwise uninspired poems, but in some cases the author's wit turns these expressions into quite clever conceits.[108] In addition, in terms of sheer versification the *Hsi-yu chi* stands out among the four masterworks for the exuberance of its poetic style, particularly in its modification of existing poetic conventions to convey a certain mock-epic quality consonant with the nature of the quest.[109]

[105] For other discussions of this issue, see Ōta Tatsuo, "New Study," p. 113; Ogawa Tamaki, "Saiyūki genpon," p. 113; Koss, "Formative Stages," chaps. 6 and 7.

[106] Wang Hsiang-hsü discusses the use of the chapter-ending formula in a comment in chapter 100 (14a). See also Liu I-ming, *tu-fa*, items 10 and 12, on the special function of chapter titles.

[107] On the use of opening and closing verses, see Ts'ai Yüan-fang, *tu-fa*, item 10.

[108] The special poetic effects achieved in the verse passages are analyzed by Anthony Yu in "Heroic Verse and Heroic Mission," pp. 879, 897, and in his *Journey*, pp. 24ff. See also Francis So, "Some Rhetorical Conventions of the Verse Sections of *Hsi-yu chi*," pp. 177–94; Chao Ts'ung, *Ssu ta hsiao-shuo,* pp. 185f.; and Dudbridge, "Tsai-shang-ch'üeh," pp. 515f. On the particular device of delayed amplification, see Koss, "Formative Stages," chaps. 3 and 7. Some poems in a similar pattern can be found in the *Tsa-chü*; e.g., Scenes 12, p. 665, and 16, p. 676. The enthusiasm with which the best of these pieces were received by the sixteenth-century readers may be gauged by "Li Cho-wu's" liberal application of "critical dots" (*p'ing-tien* 評點) to mark particularly fine examples.

[109] Cf. the possibly tongue-in-cheek comment by "Li Cho-wu," chapter 1 (2b): "All the poems and other verse in *Hsi-yu chi* are just meant to be fine-sounding, ... anyone who tries

Once again, however, the key element of fictional rhetoric—the point on which I am identifying the four disparate Ming novels as members of the same generic class, and that which, in fact, justifies the use of the imported term "novel" in the first place—is the reliance on irony to undercut the conventional significance of traditional figures.[110] Here, however, I will have to modify my earlier working definition of irony as any discrepancy between surface meaning and underlying intent in a text to allow it to take in the more fully articulated disjunction of meaning that materializes in allegory. As in the *Chin P'ing Mei*, here too the author's ironic wit ranges from very light to quite heavy, from occasional jokes and parodies to the serious allegorical framework of meaning that will occupy the bulk of the remainder of this chapter. Let us begin with the lighter side. The text of *Hsi-yu chi* is liberally sprinkled with innumerable little jokes and puns. These are most transparent in the names of many of the characters and places in the narrative, from witty stabs at false pretenses, as in the Jade-faced Princess (Yü-mien kung-chu 玉面公主), to hints of a more doctrinal nature (e.g., the *yüan* tortoise).[111] The traditional commentators devote considerable ingenuity to deciphering names of this sort. I should point out that these include quite a few instances of sexual innuendo, both in names—for example, the Bodhisattva Below the Belt (Pan-chieh Kuan-yin 半截觀音) in chapter 83, and in other details.[112]

---

to interpret them according to literary principles is a foolish pedant" 凡西遊詩賦只要好聽 … 若以文理求之則腐.

[110] See review of the use of ironic rhetoric in the four masterworks below, Chapter 6.

[111] Yü-mien kung-chu makes her appearance in chapter 60 (2:829). We may note the common iconography that links her with Pai-ku fu-jen in chapter 27, and the Jade Hare (Yü-t'u 玉兔) in chapters 93–95. The commentators frequently gloss the suggestive names of characters and places in the text. For example, "Li Cho-wu" glosses the name of the Sand Monk in chapter 22 (15a); Pai-ku fu-jen in chapter 26 (14a); Yü-mien kung-chu in chapter 60 (1b); and he expresses delight at suggestive names in a number of places (e.g., 67 [1b]). See also Wang Hsiang-hsü, on the Chia widow and daughters in chapter 23 (5a), on Chin-tou Mountain 金峴洞 in chapter 50 (1b), and on the Cave of Coiling Threads 盤絲洞 in chapter 72 (1a). See also Ch'en Shih-pin on Pai-ku fu-jen in chapter 30 (339) and on the centipede spirits in 73 (746); and Chang Shu-shen on the Pao-hsiang kuo 寶象國 in chapter 28 (2b, 3b), on Wen-shu in chapter 37 (16b), on the Buddha Ju-lai in chapter 58 (14a), and on the lions in chapter 90 (14b). In *Tsung-p'i*, item 11 (4a), Chang explicitly states the principle of significant naming. See also Wang Hsiang-hsü, comments in chapters 44 (1b), 49 (1b), and 99 (1a).

[112] Chapter 83 (3:1146). Chang Shu-shen notes the suggestiveness of this name in chapter 80 (5a), and "Li Cho-wu" all but spells out the joke in chapter 83 (14a, *tp*): "I wonder whether this 'half Kuan-yin' is the top half or the bottom half? I wish people would tell me whether it is the top half they prefer or the bottom half. Ha!" 半截觀音不知是上半截不知 是下半截。請問世人還是上半截好還是下半截好，一笑一笑! Other examples of more or less subtle sexual hints seem to be present in the white jade scepter (*pai-yü kuei* 白玉珪), in chapter 37 (2:511), *yü-t'u* in the same chapter (2:514); and the warning not to "leak heavenly

In addition, the author apparently enjoys concocting elaborate word games to jolt his reader into considering the discrepancy between text and meaning. For example, in the very first chapter he indulges in a little joke on the name of Sun Wu-k'ung, playing the old game of "character splitting" (*ch'ai-tzu* 拆字) to get "small child" out of the name Sun. When he goes on to relate this to the Taoist term "newborn babe" (*ying-erh* 嬰兒), the joke turns in a more suggestive direction, and this is further developed when Sun proceeds to claim that he has no surname (*wu-hsing* 無姓), punning on the expression "no nature" (*wu-hsing* 無性) to stress the idea of his spontaneous birth.[113] Later, this is taken up again in chapters 34 and 35, where the confusion between the true monkey-pilgrim (Sun Hsing-che 孫行者) and the false Che Hsing-sun 者行孫 and Hsing-che Sun 行者孫 leaves Sun Wu-k'ung's identity literally turned inside out. The tendency to begin with a pun and then plumb it for additional layers of meaning also applies to the "monkey of the mind" metaphor (*hsin-yüan i-ma* 心猿意馬), which begins as not much more than a conventional joke, but is eventually plugged into the larger allegorical scheme. One of the most intriguing instances of wordplay in the book is found in a puzzling line of verse that appears in chapter 20 and is then repeated, with variations, in chapter 40:

> A cave to collapse faces a cave to collapse,
> When the cave becomes about to collapse, the cave becomes a
>   mountain.
> 當倒洞當當倒洞, 洞當當倒洞當山 .[114]

---

secrets" (*hsieh-lou t'ien-chi* 洩漏天機) in chapter 44 (2:620), in a scene dealing with a leak of another sort. I think we can also detect a lascivious pun in the catfish spirit (*nien-yü ching* 鮎魚精) into which Chu Pa-chieh transforms himself in order to join the bathing goddesses in chapter 72 (3:999); most particularly in chapter 95, where references to a "short staff" (*tuan-kun* 短棍) and to a "Downy Hill" (*Mao-ying shan* 毛穎山) make unmistakable reference to the sort of salvation proffered by the Jade Hare (3:1291, 1295). The Jade Hare herself, of course, bears strong erotic connotations, which may hark back to the pursuit of a white hare in the episode at Wu-chi kuo. In response to such innuendo, the commentators are occasionally willing to indulge in little jokes of their own, as in "Li Cho-wu's" rather crude derision of the Master as a catamite in chapters 54 (9a) and 29 (3b); and Chang Shu-shen's quip in chapter 29 (3b): 和尚走後門, 其惡絕妙. The most puzzling example of this type is seen in repeated mention of the "lute bone" (*p'i-p'a ku* 琵琶骨), which is pierced to subdue a number of demons, including the Monkey King himself; see, e.g., chapters 6 (1:80), 43 (2:606), and 63 (2:880). This term has generally been taken in its modern sense to refer to the clavicle, but a small piece of evidence (see below, n. 193) indicates the possibility of sexual associations in the expression. Cf. the P'i-p'a Cave in a scene of sexual affront in chapter 55.

[113] Chapter 1 (1:14).

[114] Chapters 20 (1:272), and 40 (2:551). In the second occurrence the word *tang* 當 is changed to *t'ang* 堂, and the final *shan* 山 becomes *hsien* 仙, perhaps suggesting that this is nothing but a nonsense rhyme. But at least one commentator, Ch'en Shih-pin (32:331f.), picks up on this combination of sounds and images.

Although I do not claim to fully understand this line (and in fact it may be nothing more than nonsense syllables), I suspect that what the joke is talking about has to do with the complementary concepts of mass and void, which not only inform the landscape of mountains and caves collapsing into one another—as in the opening sequence of the enclosed vault of heaven within a waterfall cave—but also resonate with more abstract qualities of solidity and emptiness of special significance to the author's vision. At the very least, witticisms like these force the reader to look beyond the amusing surface of the story to consider the possibility of hidden patterns of meaning.[115]

One additional area in which the author applies his ironic brush may be seen in his presentation of individual figures. Sometimes this is a matter of hyperbole in the delineation of character traits: Chu Pa-chieh's sloth, Sun Wu-k'ung's temper, the Sand Monk's exaggerated moroseness. This is of course one of the basic elements in the humor of the book. More significant for my argument is the tendency to expose the weak underside of the heroes of the popular *Hsi-yu* tradition. In the case of Hsüan-tsang's helplessness and nervousness, or the self-destructive rivalry between Sun Wu-k'ung and Chu Pa-chieh, this is quite transparent. But also in those significant instances in which Hsüan-tsang reveals his inner weakness precisely where he should be strongest (i.e., in certain cases of sexual temptation), the irony begins to cut a bit deeper.[116] The same is true in certain scenes in which Sun Wu-k'ung is shown to be all too vulnerable, or else to reach the limits of his extraordinary powers. This type of ironic undercutting is of special significance, since I will appeal to the same idea to explain the reduction in the stature of the popular heroes of *San-kuo yen-i* and *Shui-hu chuan* when their stories are reworked in the novel form.

Before turning now to the serious dimension of the author's bifocal ironic vision, I must pause a moment to acknowledge the humorous side of the novel. For the remainder of this chapter I will focus exclusive attention on a serious reading of the allegory, but it would be a grave error to deny that the humorous side of the novel also exists. Hu Shih was not the first critic to dismiss the forced interpretations of the Ch'ing commentators and praise instead the sheer good fun of the book; but his has been the most influential argument. It finds its way into the writings of many twentieth-

---

[115] Additional examples of extended plays on words include the attribute "overmindfulness" (*to-hsin*) applied to Hsüan-tsang (cf. the propensity to tears ascribed to Sung Chiang and Liu Pei, to be discussed below, Chapters 4, Part IV, and 5, Part IV).

[116] Hsüan-tsang's obtuseness in the face of self-evident peril is emphasized in chapters 27, 33, 40, and 80, among other places. His exaggerated innocence and sexual vulnerability are the central issues in a number of chapters. The commentators are predictably sensitive to this issue; e.g., Chang Shu-shen, chapters 47 (15b), 73 (1b). See Anthony Yu, *Journey*, pp. 43f.; James Fu, *Quest*, pp. 45f.

century critics of Chinese fiction, and also dominates the reputation of the book in the West, thanks to Waley's brilliant *Monkey*.[117] Although I personally feel that the serious side of the novel is far more interesting, given the intellectual context of Hu Shih's evaluation in the midst of the literary revolution in the early part of this century, his reading is fully understandable as a reflection of the spirit of the times. And, for that matter, nothing is wrong with it as far as it goes. *Hsi-yu chi* is after all a very funny book. But it is also quite a serious book, not dead serious perhaps, but it does raise serious intellectual issues. Having made this apology, I can move on to my own attempt to make something of the serious side of the text.

IV

To pursue the argument that there is more to the *Hsi-yu chi* than its amusing surface narrative, we must move from the notion of irony into the adjacent territory of allegory. Irony and allegory are, after all, sister tropes: they both describe ways in which texts can say one thing and mean another.[118] But where the emphasis in irony is on the undermining of the authority of what is "said," in allegorical compositions we get a more fully articulated projection of what is ultimately "meant."

This essential function of allegory to shift the reader's vision from patterns of narrative shape to corresponding patterns of meaning sets *Hsi-yu chi* apart from our other three novels, which, for all their varying

[117] Hu Shih, "K'ao-cheng," p. 390; Lu Hsün, *Chung-kuo hsiao-shuo shih-lüeh*, p. 173; Chao Ts'ung, *Ssu ta hsiao-shuo*, pp. 184ff. See also Ou-yang Chien, "Hsi-yu chi ti wan-shih chu-i ho hsien-shih ching-shen," pp. 54–71. The commentators discuss the mix of humor and seriousness at many points; e.g., "Li Cho-wu," chapters 19 (14a, *tp*) and 25 (15a, *tp*); Wang Hsiang-hsü, 3 (8b), 17 (1b); Chang Shu-shen, 4 (16a, b), 18 (7a), 25 (3a); Ch'en Shih-pin, 26 (273), 45 (458), 55 (560); *T'ung-i Hsi-yu cheng-chih*, 67 (70b). For general discussions of the reception of the novel by Ming readers, see Su Hsing, "Hsi-yu so-t'an," pp. 54–63, esp. 57ff.; Isobe Akira, "Hsi-yu chi ti chieh-na yü liu-ch'uan," pp. 147ff.; and Lo Lung-chih, "Hsi-yu chi ti yü-yen ho hsi-nüeh t'e-chih," pp. 11–19.

[118] This minimal definition of allegory is reflected in the term *alienoloquium* attributed to Isidore of Seville. For a review of the sources and various definitions of allegory in Western literature, see my *Archetype and Allegory*, pp. 87ff., and "Allegory in *Hsi-yu chi*," pp. 163ff. A crucial aspect of the theoretical basis of Western allegory lies in the distinction between "allegorical composition" and "allegorical reading" (roughly equivalent to Dante's "allegory of the poets" and "allegory of the theologians," that is, texts that are composed in accordance with an allegorical scheme versus those that are simply susceptible to allegorical interpretation). In what follows, my analysis is based on the conviction that the *Hsi-yu chi* qualifies as a self-consciously programmed allegorical composition, which demands a rigorous allegorical reading. Chang Ching-erh discusses this issue in *Jen-wu yen-chiu*, pp. 17ff.

degrees of ironic deflation and suggestive use of language, cannot really be said to deliver this sort of message. In *Chin P'ing Mei*, it is true, we do find a strong hint of the allegorical impulse—strong enough to have inspired Chang Chu-p'o's essay "On the Allegorical Meaning in the *Chin P'ing Mei*" ("Chin P'ing Mei yü-i shuo" 金瓶梅寓意說).[119] But clearly neither this nor either of the other sixteenth-century masterworks comes close to working out a consistent allegorical scheme.

The idea that *Hsi-yu chi* ought to be read allegorically is seconded by virtually all of the traditional commentators whose readings are still extant. In the prefaces and marginal comments of these critics, we find numerous passages that explicitly proclaim the allegorical foundations of the book. For example, the preface attributed to Yü Chi warns us that

> What is said refers to Hsüan-tsang, but what is meant is actually not about Hsüan-tsang. What is recorded refers to the fetching of scriptures, but what is intended is not about the fetching of scriptures. It just deliberately borrows this to allegorize the great Tao.
> 所言者在玄奘而意實不在玄奘。所紀者在取經，而志實不在取經，特假此以喻大道耳.[120]

Similarly, the nineteenth-century critic Liu I-ming insists that "the intended meaning of the work lies completely beyond the given words" 其用意處盡在言外, and nearly all the traditional critics refer at one point or another to the "hidden meaning" (*shen-i* 深意, *yin-i* 隱意, *yin-yü* 隱寓) underlying its surface texture.[121] This does not mean, of course, that such readers fail to appreciate the humor for which the novel is justly praised. But that does not keep them from insisting on the presence of a serious level

---

[119] For discussions of Chang Chu-p'o's "Chin P'ing Mei yü-i shuo," see above, Chapter 2, pp. 125, 127. As in the case of Western allegory, fully realized examples of this mode are less common than shorter sequences within longer narrative works. Other examples of what I could call allegorical composition in the Chinese fiction tradition include *Hsi-yu pu* 西遊補, and portions of *Lü-yeh hsien-tsung* 綠野仙踪, *Ching-hua yüan* 鏡花緣, and *Lao-ts'an yu-chi* 老殘遊記, etc.

[120] On the attribution of this preface to Yü Chi, see Part I of this chapter and b.n. II.5, and III.

[121] Liu I-ming, *tu-fa*, item 2. See b.n. II.8. Examples of occurrences of the other terms are as follows; *shen-i* 深意: Chang Shu-shen, 9 (1b), Wang Hsiang-hsü, 24 (2a), "Li Cho-wu," 4 (14a), *T'ung-i cheng-chih*, 14 (47b); *yin-i* 隱意: Chang Shu-shen, *Tsung-p'i*, 23 (11a), Ch'en Shih-pin, 11 (124), Liu I-Ming, *tu-fa*, item 17; *yin-yü* 隱喻: Ch'en Shih-pin, 43 (438), 55 (559), 77 (784), 91 (921), Chang Shu-shen, *Tsung-p'i*, 8 (3b), 13 (4b), 70 (18b); "Li Cho-wu," 14 (12a), 16 (16a), and 63 (14b); *yü-i* 寓意: Chang Shu-shen, 28 (1a), 29 (1a), 32 (17b), 59 (17b), 72 (17a), and *Tsung-p'i*, 1 (1b), 3 (2a), 6 (2b), 33 (8b), 52 (14b). Other examples include Wang Hsiang-hsü, 24 (1b), 69 (1a), 78 (1b); Ch'en Shih-pin, 9 (104), 30 (309), 37 (378), 50 (509), 54 (550), 59 (599), 69 (703), 72 (734), 94 (949); Chang Shu-shen, 6 (2b), 13 (5a), and *Tsung-p'i*, 72 (19b); and *T'ung-i Cheng-chih*, 14 (47a).

of meaning beneath the amusing surface, as they explicitly argue in many comments.[122]

Now, when these critics use such terms as "allegorical figure" (*yü* 寓) or "metaphoric expression" (*yü* 喻) to refer to this unarticulated dimension of meaning, what they often seem to have in mind is simply the presence of some kind of a didactic "message," short of true allegorical reference.[123] For this reason, in order to push ahead with my reading of the novel as an allegorical text, it will be necessary to lay out in full the articulated structure of meaning I contend to be present.[124] In doing so, I will first set forth some of the key terms in which the allegory is couched, and then will consider the manner in which these are worked together into interlocking schemes—especially those whereby they are integrated into the dynamic movement of the narrative itself. With that done, I will be able to turn to my own interpretation of the "intended" meaning of the book.

As observed earlier, one of the things that distinguishes the hundred-chapter *Hsi-yu chi* from all other extant antecedents and parallel versions of the Hsüan-tsang story cycle is the imposition onto the text of an extensive

---

[122] This is the general assumption underlying the notion of a "hidden" layer of meaning. See, e.g., "Li Cho-wu," 2 (14b, *tp*), Wang Hsiang-hsü, "Yü Chi" preface; Ts'ai Yüan-fang, *tu-fa*, item 4 and passim, Liu I-ming, *tu-fa* and prefaces passim, and *Hsi-yu chi shih-i*, preface. Cf. the *Tung-t'ien hsüan chi*, Yang T'i preface (see n. 21), where the *Hsi-yu chi* is characterized in similar terms.

[123] For example, Ts'ai Yüan-fang, *tu-fa*, item 55: "Within its bantering tone there is always a profound meaning" 科諢中皆有妙理. Similar ideas are expressed in the Ch'en Yüan-chih preface, the Man-t'ing kuo-k'e preface, and in "Li Cho-wu" comments 2 (19b), 6 (13b), 16 (16a), 19 (14a), 25 (15a), and 46 (16a); Chang Shu-shen, *Tsung-p'i*, items 1 (1a), 3 (2a–b), 8 (4a), 11 (4b), 13 (15a), 17 (5b–6a), 19 (6a), 21 (6b), 31 (8b–9a), 33 (9a–9b), 36 (10a–10b), 45 (13b), 52 (15a), 65 (18a), 66 (18a–18b), 69 (19a), 70 (19a), 72 (19b), 75 (20a); the Yu T'ung preface and 50 (509), 53 (539), 59 (594), 69 (703), 72 (734). Hu Shih's rejection of allegorical readings is found in his "K'ao-cheng," p. 390. An earlier critic, Juan K'uei-sheng (*Ch'a-yü k'e-hua*, p. 675), also brushed aside any forced attempt to find deeper meaning in the novel. Chang Hsüeh-ch'eng, on the other hand (see K'ung Ling-ching, *Shih-liao*, p. 69), provides an oblique affirmation of the more serious readings when he states, "Although it is basically a sort of didactic fable, it still contains a measure of ultimate truth" 雖屬寓言, 却有至理. A very similar view is expressed in Hsieh Chao-che, *Wu tsa-tsu*, 15:36a; as well as in Liu T'ing-chi's *Tsai-yüan tsa-chih* (2:24b), and in the *Tung-t'ien hsüan-chi* preface. Liu Ts'un-yan defends the Ch'en preface as "original" (*hsin-hsien* 新鮮) in "Ssu-yu chi," p. 374. See also my "Allegory in *Hsi-yu chi*," pp. 173ff.

[124] "Li Cho-wu," in chapter 14 (12a–b, *tp*), emphasizes the painstaking efforts required for this allegorical composition. This notion of strict allegorical design contrasts with the sort of loose didactic parable or fable that Wu Ch'eng-en seems to have in mind when he uses the term *yü* 寓 in a passage often cited as evidence of his allegorical intentions (see above, n. 11). I am aware of the controversial implication of intentionality in this view of allegory, but I would argue that if speculation about an author's intentions is anywhere valid, it is here in allegorical narrative, where what we have is essentially an intellectual exercise, a challenge to the reader to decode the author's intended meaning.

overlay of suggestive philosophical terminology. If the speculations on the role of Ch'iu Ch'u-chi in the history of the novel ever prove to have some basis in fact, then the isolation in the "Yü Chi" preface of some of the key terms of the allegory would shift the first introduction of these terms into the story back to the thirteenth or fourteenth century. But for the time being, all other available evidence indicates that this allegorical framework is the contribution of a sixteenth-century author.

In either case, the primary distinguishing feature of the novel text is precisely this injection of allegorical terms. These tag words do not simply crop up at random points; they are strategically inserted in a certain number of predictable locations. One of these places is in the names applied to the fictional characters within the story: both the principal pilgrims with their various appellations, and the demons bearing such suggestive names as the Lady of the White Bones (Pai-ku fu-jen), the Red Child (Hung-hai-erh), the Iron Fan Princess (T'ieh-shan kung-chu 鐵扇公主), the Jade Hare (Yü-t'u), and the Many-eyed Demon (To-mu kuai 多目怪). Of course, in those cases in which these names are taken over from preexisting sources we obviously cannot say that the author has deliberately created them for roles in his allegory, only that he has perceived the potential significance of these names and gone on to develop them within his own allegorical framework.[125] On the other hand, a good many of the interesting names given to these figures do, in fact, seem to be original with the author of the hundred-chapter novel.[126] The same is true for many of the iconographic details attached to specific characters. The metal band that encloses the head of the mind-monkey as well as those that enclose the tip of his magic cudgel, the nine-toothed rake used by Chu Pa-chieh both as a weapon and as a tool to clear allegorical brambles and muck from the true path, the necklace of nine skulls worn by the Sand Monk as trophies of his unredeemed past, not to mention the emblematic colors, elements, and weapons that define each of the major demons who bar the pilgrims' way to

---

[125] Some very suggestive examples are in fact found in antecedent versions of the narrative. For example, Pai-ku fu-jen appears in the *Shih-hua*, section 4. See T'an Chia-chien, "Sun Wu-k'ung san ta pai-ku ching ku-shih t'an-yüan," p. 66; and Chang Ching-erh, "The Monkey-hero in the *Hsi-yu chi* Cycle," pp. 208f. Ti-yung fu-jen is mentioned in the *Pak t'ongsa ŏnhae*, transcribed in Dudbridge, *Hsi-yu chi*, p. 183, and in the *Hsiao-shih chen-k'ung pao-chüan*, l. 38 (see Dudbridge, *Hsi-yu chi*, p. 94; and Hu Shih, "Pa Hsiao-shih chen-k'ung pao-chüan," p. 3612). The monastic name of Sun Wu-k'ung is a case in point. Although this designation is not unprecedented, we can readily perceive the manner in which the author gets allegorical mileage out of its different levels of meaning (see n. 288). For studies on the sources regarding Sun Wu-k'ung and Chu Pa-chieh, see b.n. I. The same is also true of the development of the significance of certain place-names, such as Huo-yen shan (see *Tsa-chü*, Scene 18, and *Pak t'ongsa ŏnhae*).

[126] See above, nn. 9 and 10.

salvation—all of these derive from prior sources, so their use here is more a question of exploiting allegorical potential than of inventing entirely new imagery.[127]

These allegorical clues become more obtrusive when they appear in certain special positions in the text, primarily in chapter-title couplets and in the other forms of incidental verse described earlier. For example, such chapter headings as "Tripitaka Does Not Forget His Original Source; the Four Sages Put to Trial the Mind of Meditation" 三藏不忘本, 四聖試禪心 in chapter 23; "Perverse Teachings Lead the True Nature Astray, the Primal Spirit Aids the Essential Mind" 外道迷真性, 元神助本心 in chapter 33; and "Where the Mind-monkey Is Rectified the Various Affinities Are Quelled, Slashing through the Devious Gate, the Brightness of the Moon Comes into View" 心猿正處諸緣伏, 劈破傍門見月明 in chapter 36 quite explicitly label the allegorical significance of the narrative figures and events in question.[128] The same is true for a large number of other lines of incidental verse in the text, many of which I will cite in the following discussion.[129]

What are these terms used to transform the received story cycles into an allegorical novel?[130] To begin with, we may quickly pass beyond the various terms associated with Mahayana Buddhism. In view of the fact that the narrative is framed as a quest for scriptures for the purpose of saving the lost souls of an entire empire, it is hardly surprising that there is so much mention of the Buddha and principal bodhisattvas. Among these, Kuan-yin is singled out for particular attention, not only by virtue of her dominant place in Mahayana soteriology, but also because the specific iconographic details associated with this figure, especially her "vase of purification" (*ching-p'ing* 淨瓶), resonate with some of the crucial imagery in the novel.[131]

[127] On the iconographical details associated with the *Hsi-yu* figures, see Dudbridge, *Hsi-yu chi*, pp. 18ff., 47ff.; Su Hsing, "Hsi-yu so-t'an," pp. 54–63; Kao Ming-ko, "Hsi-yu chi li ti shen-mo wen-t'i," pp. 118–27.

[128] Another good example is found in chapter 14: "The Mind-monkey Returns to the True Way; the Six Thieves Vanish without a Trace" 心猿歸正, 六賊無踪.

[129] Cf. Liu I-ming's discussion of the allegorical function of the chapter titles and concluding verses in his *tu-fa*, items 10 and 12.

[130] For a thorough review of the allegorical terminology programmed into the novel, see Anthony Yu, *Journey*, pp. 36–62; and my "Allegory in *Hsi-yu chi*," pp. 175–81. Nicholas Koss has some of these in mind when he notes the insertion of "literati terms" to heighten the didactic flavor of the Shih-te t'ang edition ("Formative Stages," chap. 4).

[131] Kuan-yin appears in chapters 6, 8–12, 14, 15, 17, 22, 26, 41, 83, 84. On the *ching-p'ing*, see Ts'ao Shih-pang, "Hsi-yu chi jo-kan ch'ing-chieh ti pen-yüan tsai-t'an," pp. 35f. For additional background on the Buddhist terminology in the novel, see Anthony Yu, *Journey*, pp. 53f.; Dudbridge, *Hsi-yu chi*, p. 14; and my "Allegory in *Hsi-yu chi*," pp. 179ff. Liu Ts'un-yan considers the significance of some Buddhist terms in "Ch'üan-chen chiao," pt. 3, p. 87.

The use of some of the principal icons of Mahayana salvationism, insofar as it is dictated by the prior tradition, should not be unique to the hundred-chapter novel—and indeed these figures are well represented in the extant antecedent versions of the story.[132] By the same token, the recurrent evocation of the concept of "crossing over" to the "other shore" of salvation (*tu* 渡, *teng pi-an* 登彼岸) may be viewed as a necessary part of the tale of the quest journey. These also appear frequently in the sources, although, as we shall see, the diminished weight of the end point within the structure of the novel significantly alters the new meaning of the arrival on that other shore.[133]

As for explicit references to Buddhist scriptures, there is no lack of these in the antecedent materials. Especially prominent are the Lotus Sutra (*Fa-hua ching* 法華經) and the Diamond Sutra (*Chin-kang ching* 金剛經). In the novel, however, allusions to these texts are minimal, while the corresponding highlighting of the Prajnaparamita Heart Sutra (*Hsin ching* 般若波羅蜜多心經) sets up one of the central frames of meaning in the book.[134]

Within the general area of Buddhist thought, the author does not unequivocally favor the teachings of any particular sect. For example, he stages a fairly weak conventional debate on Mahayana and Hinayana doctrine in chapter 12, and as we shall see he does not appear to present a clear choice in the theological controversy over self-attained versus externally bestowed enlightenment (*tzu-li* 自力, *t'a-li* 他力), or between sudden and gradual attainment.[135] On the other hand, however,

---

[132] For example, Manjusri appears in the *Shih-hua*, section 4. See Ts'ao Shih-pang, "Pen-yüan tsai-t'an," pp. 34ff.

[133] The image of crossing over a water barrier (*tu*) figures prominently in a number of chapters, including 1, 15, 22, 49, 50, and 98. Of course, this motif is an integral part of the prior narrative cycle; e.g., in the *Shih-hua*, section 17. The commentators frequently pick up on this motif and its traditional associations. Cf. the metaphor of the raft (*fa* 筏) with its conventional gloss as *dharma* (*fa* 法), on which one is absolutely dependent to stay afloat throughout one's "passage," but which is then rejected as utterly useless once one has reached the "other shore." See *Chin-kang ching*, p. 11a.

[134] The *Hsin ching* is introduced with much fanfare in chapters 19–20 and is recalled several times thereafter at key points. It is also mentioned in some of the antecedent materials, including the *Shih-hua*, section 17, where it is singled out for special attention, although the significance of its message is not developed. See Anthony Yu, "Two Literary Examples of Religious Pilgrimage," p. 222. The *Chin-kang ching* is brought up for more substantive, though essentially humorous, treatment in the *Tsa-chü*, Scene 21 (it is mentioned again in Scene 22). Ch'en Shih-pin makes pointed reference to the *Hua-yen ching* 華嚴經 in chapter 38 (387), as does the Yu T'ung preface. See also *T'ung-i cheng-chih*, 44 (31b), 56 (61b), 82 (13b), and 98 (88b).

[135] See more detailed discussion of the implications of this issue in interpreting the novel in Part V of this chapter. The debate on Mahayana versus Hinayana doctrines is staged in chapter 12. See comments by Wang Hsiang-hsü, chapters 13 (1a), and 42 (1b).

he does provide for a special focus on Ch'an thought and imagery.[136] This is notable, since the historical Hsüan-tsang of course had no connection with the Ch'an School (unless we exaggerate the common ground between Ch'an and "Mere Ideation" philosophy). In any event, the allegorical level of the novel draws heavily upon Ch'an elements, both for ideas regarding the "true nature" (*pen-hsing* 本性) of reality, and for favored imagery such as the autumn moon in the enlightenment scene that forms the nucleus of chapter 36.[137] This emphasis on Ch'an places the primary focus of interest on the enlightenment of the mind, and this will contribute one of the central axes of my own interpretation.

It is in the introduction of specifically Taoist terminology, however, that we find the clearest evidence of recasting of the source narratives into our allegorical novel. Although one can perceive traces of certain such terms in the antecedent materials, there is no question about the fact that this overlay represents a crucial element in the conception of the hundred-chapter novel.[138]

The most prominent terms within the province of Taoist lore are those derived from cinnabar alchemy (*lien-tan* 鍊丹).[139] Aside from the actual cinnabar itself, we also find references in the novel to certain implements involved in this occult art: crucibles, firing furnaces (*lu* 爐), cauldrons (*ting*

---

[136] The most prominent images with strong Ch'an associations are the refulgent moon and the subdual of dragons or tigers of consciousness (*fu-hu, fu-lung* 伏虎, 伏龍). These concepts are often emphasized by the commentators; e.g., Wang Hsiang-hsü, 13 (1a); Ch'en Shih-pin, 19 (202), 23 (241f.), 36 (368), 40 (405), 46 (467), 47 (478), 58 (588f.), 85 (867), 86 (875), 90 (911f.); Ts'ai Yüan-fang, *tu-fa*, item 23. Hsüan-tsang's inaccurate identification as a Ch'an master also appears in the *Tsa-chü*, Scenes 4 and 5. On the relationship between Ch'an and the historical Hsüan-tsang's "Mere Ideation School" of Buddhist philosophy, see Fung Yu-lan, *History of Chinese Philosophy*, 2:299ff., 388ff.; Kenneth Ch'en, *Buddhism in China*, pp. 235ff., 297–364, and esp. 323ff.

[137] See especially chapters 64 and 93. The moon symbolism is also emphasized in the *Tsa-chü*, Scene 23.

[138] For a review of the Taoist terminology in the novel, see Anthony Yu, *Journey*, pp. 36–52, and his "Pilgrimage," pp. 223ff.; Liu Ts'un-yan, "Wu Ch'eng-en," pp. 82f.; Chang Ching-erh, "Structure and Theme," pp. 170ff.; and my "Allegory in *Hsi-yu chi*," pp. 176–82. For additional background on this terminology, see for example Liu Ts'un-yan, "Taoist Self-cultivation," pp. 291–330, and his "Ch'üan-chen chiao," plus studies cited in n. 36.

[139] The terms of cinnabar alchemy are emphasized in all of the commentaries; for example, Wang Hsiang-hsü, chapters 39 (1a), 52 (1a), 53 (1a); Ts'ai Yüan-fang, *tu-fa*, item 8. Predictably, they also figure prominently in the interpretations of Ch'en Tun-fu. See, for example, pp. 29ff., and his *Tsung-lun*, pp. 29–32. Cf. the emphasis on this frame of meaning in the early descriptions of the novel; e.g., Ting Yen (see n. 35), cited in K'ung Ling-ching, *Shih-liao*, p. 72. For further analysis and background on this alchemical lore, see Anthony Yu, "Pilgrimage"; Judith Berling, "Paths of Convergence," pp. 123–47; Kristofer Schipper, *Le corps taoïste*, pp. 144ff., 226–36; and works cited in n. 138.

鼎), a kind of measuring spoon called *tao-kuei* (刀圭), etc.[140] Most significant are the various uses of alchemical terms based on *yin-yang* and five-elements designations to refer to some of the central figures in the narrative: Mother of Wood (*Mu-mu* 木母) for Chu Pa-chieh, Lord of Metal (*Chin-kung* 金公) for Sun Wu-k'ung, Yellow Hag (*Huang-p'o* 黃婆) for the Sand Monk.[141] A second set of Taoist terminology of relevance to the novel is that associated with various forms of physical cultivation: quiet-sitting, breath control, and, most important, sexual exercises.[142] As we shall see, these oblique references to late Ming sexual cults occupy a special place in the novel, where they play upon the *yin-yang* symbolism worked into many scenes.

These separate sets of Taoist terms begin to merge when we note that many of the expressions for sexual union and its issue—"the conjugal joining of *yin* and *yang*" (*yin-yang chiao-kou* 陰陽交媾), "the lovely maiden" (*ch'a-nü* 姹女), and especially "the newborn babe" (*ying-erh* 嬰兒)—are applied with equal currency to the union of alchemical substances and the corresponding gestation of a "child" of the elements.[143] The connection between these two sets of terms is strengthened by the use of the term "firing time" (*huo-hou*), not only because it refers literally to the crucial question of the timing of the process of cultivation, but also because it lends itself to a nice pun on the name of the fire-monkey (also *huo-hou* 火猴) who is the principal guardian of the pilgrim band.[144] As in the case of the Buddhist lore considered earlier, the loose insertion of these terms

[140] Ch'en Shih-pin glosses the term *tao-kuei* in chapter 38 (388). See Anthony Yu, *Journey*, p. 51.

[141] Examples of the use of the terms *Chin-kung* and *Mu-mu* occur in poems and chapter titles throughout the text. On the term *Huang-p'o*, see Wang Hsiang-hsü, 47 (1a), and 53 (1b). Cf. the use of practically all of these terms in *Tung-t'ien hsüan-chi* (e.g., pp. 12b, 13a). For a thorough analysis of the five-elements terms in the novel, see Alice Nai-yin Lung, "An Interpretation of the *Hsi-yu chi* Pilgrims in terms of the Five Elements." See also Nakano Miyoko, *Saiyūki no himitsu*, pp. 72–145.

[142] On sexual practices and other physical cultivation in Ming Taoism, see Liu Ts'un-yan, "Taoist Self-cultivation," pp. 301ff.; and Kristofer Schipper, *Le corps taoïste*, pp. 144ff., 171ff., and passim.

[143] These overlapping terms occur throughout the text, and are especially prominent in chapters 19, 24, 40, 53, 78, and 94. The commentators frequently link their interpretations to these terms; e.g., Wang Hsiang-hsü, 38 (1a), 44 (1b), 47 (1a), 53 (1b), 80 (1a–1b); Ch'en Shih-pin, 17 (185), 22 (229), 54 (548), 69 (702), 72 (734), 82 (834), 92 (929), 94 (949). Once again, a proximate literary source for much of this terminology is found in *Tung-t'ien hsüan-chi*, especially pp. 12b, 13a, 14a–b, 15a–b.

[144] For examples of the use of the term *huo-hou* in the novel, see chapters 73 (3:1008) and 88 (3:1214). The term is emphasized in comments by Wang Hsiang-hsü, 4 (3b), 92 (1b); Ch'en Shih-pin, 4 (44), 32 (333), 91 (921), 99 (1003); *T'ung-i cheng-chih*, 84 (41b); and Ts'ai Yüan-fang, *tu-fa*, item 8. An earlier occurrence of the term can be found in the *Tsa-chü*, Scene 9.

makes it difficult to identify with any precision the sectarian origins of particular expressions. But it is worth repeating that though the bulk of these terms belong to the common vocabulary of Ming Taoism found in abundance in practically any of the texts in the *Tao Tsang* 道藏, nearly all of them can be traced back at least to the teachings of southern Taoism in the late Sung and Yuan period—particularly to the writings of Ch'iu Ch'u-chi and other Ch'üan-chen luminaries.[145] One other Taoist idea read by certain commentators between the lines of the novel is the notion of the "dual cultivation of the physical and essential self" (*hsing-ming shuang-hsiu* 性命 雙修), which by the Ming period had come to refer fairly specifically to cults of sexual union, while still retaining more abstract philosophical significance beyond the exclusive bounds of Taoism.[146]

Another set of terms that figures prominently in the allegorical framework of the novel involves expressions derived from the *I Ching* and associated texts. In a loose sense, we might relate some of the numerological patterns in the book, particularly the repeated formula of nine nines, to the *yang* number, nine, in which case the expression "the execution of the three threes" (*san san hsing* 三三行) used to describe the fulfillment of the mission, would yield a similar reading.[147] Some more strictly scriptural

[145] For background on Sung and Yuan Taoism, see above, n. 36. Some examples of Taoist texts I have read that seem to have particular relevance to the terminology imposed on the narrative include *Wu chen p'ien chi-chu*, attributed to Chang Po-tuan (Tzu-yang chen-jen) (see n. 33). Cf. references to Tzu-yang chen-jen in Wang Hsiang-hsü, 62 (1a); Ch'en Shih-pin, 22 (229), 29 (294), 39 (396), 68 (692), 69 (703), 91 (920); *T'ung-i cheng-chih*, 18 (82b), 57 (72a), 61 (10b), 71 (8a), 95 (49b); and the *Chin-tan ta-yao* by Ch'en Chih-hsü, which makes liberal use of such terms as *huo-hou, huan-tan, t'ai*, and *kuei*. The author of this text is linked by Ōta Tatsuo ("Shōdōsho" p. 4) through a chain of associations to Yü Chi. Cf. Ch'en Tun-fu's assertion that the allegory follows the *Chung-Lü ch'uan-tao chi* (see n. 36). For a review of this terminology, see Liu Ts'un-yan, "Ch'üan-chen chiao," Pt. 1, pp. 58ff. Although the novel evinces little interest in classical Taoist sources, Chang Shu-shen occasionally draws analogies to the thought of Chuang Tzu; e.g., *Tsung-p'i*, 13 and 78. See also *T'ung-i cheng-chih*, 18 (80b), 19 (92b), 97 (72a); and Ch'en Shih-pin, 15 (168), 18 (192), 45 (456), 48 (486), 57 (576), 64 (651), 75 (763), 77 (784), 78 (795), and 98 (993).

[146] For further explication of the Ming Taoist interpretation of this particular term, see Liu Ts'un-yan, "Taoist Self-cultivation," pp. 307f., 318f. A more extensive treatise dealing with this concept is *Hsing-ming kuei-chih* 性命圭旨 (see biblio.). The term appeared in Sung and Yuan Taoist writings, but it may not have taken on this specific range of meaning until the Ming period (cf. the different application of the terms *hsing* and *ming* in Neo-Confucian thought). See *T'ung-i cheng chih*, 14 (47a), 80 (99b).

[147] The formula *san-san hsing chiu-chiu kung* 三三行九九功 is invoked in chapters 1 (1:13), 36 (2:503), and 43 (2:595), etc. The "three threes" may perhaps refer to the six stacked horizontal lines in the *Ch'ien* hexagram ☰; see my "Allegory in *Hsi-yu chi*," p. 179. The idea comes up for discussion by Chang Shu-shen in chapter 99 (1a–b); as well as by Wang Hsiang-hsü, chapters 3 (10a), 19 (7b); Ch'en Shih-pin, preface and chapters 19 (201), 32 (331), 33 (341f.), 37 (378), 69 (704), 70 (713), 82 (835), 99 (1003), 100 (1015); and Ts'ai Yüan-fang, *tu-fa*, item 8.

usages occur in the references to particular hexagrams in lines of verse and other allegorically charged positions. These terms go beyond their common use as pseudo-philosophical ornamentation to take on greater meaning when the author draws upon specific implications, such as the pure *yin* and pure *yang* of *ch'ien* and *k'un* (乾坤), or the fire and water trigram components (*k'an* 坎, *li* 離) that go to make up the hexagrams *chi-chi* and *wei-chi* 既濟, 未濟 —these latter endowed with special significance due to their literal reference to water crossings.[148] The *chi-chi* and *wei-chi* hexagrams are also given heightened attention since the inverted order that puts *chi-chi* ("fully completed") before *wei-chi* ("not yet completed") in the "Later Heaven" sequence of hexagrams provides a key for dealing with the problem of the paradoxical fulfillment of the quest at the close of the narrative.

It would shed a certain balance on this review if these various allusions to *I Ching* lore could be pigeonholed as "Confucian" terms, as opposed to the Buddhist and Taoist expressions outlined earlier. But, of course, the language of the *I Ching*, like that of *yin* and *yang* and the five elements, really belongs to none of the three "schools" exclusively. But this very fact may be more help than hindrance to us, since it is precisely in the syncretic breadth of Ming Neo-Confucianism that I will seek the principal focus of my interpretation.[149]

I hope this cursory review of the terms of discourse of the novel will give some idea of the universe of words within which the allegorical pilgrimage takes place. At this point, I must go on to pursue what are the more crucial functions of allegorical composition: first, the linking of these isolated symbolic terms into complex interlocking schemes; and second, the interaction of these symbolic figures in the context of the narrative itself. Although the text is studded with allegorical labels of the type I have discussed above, the simple identification of textual figures with suggestive philosophical designations does not in itself constitute true allegory, especially since many of these tags appear in the prior sources.[150] This is only the raw material of allegorical composition, which must

[148] The hexagram terms *chi-chi* and *wei-chi* figure in a number of chapters, notably 61 (2:847, 856). The commentators frequently discourse on the symbolism of the fire (*li*) and water (*k'an*) components of these hexagrams. See, for example, Wang Hsiang-hsü, 2 (2a), 4 (1b), 15 (1a), 16 (1a), 18 (1a), 20 (2a), 43 (1a). The *T'ung-i Hsi-yu cheng-chih*, despite its promising title, only rarely bases its interpretations on *I Ching* concepts; e.g., 77 (82a), 79 (95b). In fact, it seems to come out strongly on the side of three-teachings syncretism in a final colophon (*hou-pa* 後跋). Similar terms are used in the *Tsa-chü*, Scenes 19, 20, and in *Tung-t'ien hsüan-chi*, pp. 5a, 13a, and passim.

[149] I will reconsider, however, certain more explicitly Neo-Confucian ideas in the text later.

[150] See n. 127.

be drawn into a fabric of dynamic interaction for the allegory to really function.

This principle is most obvious with respect to the *yin-yang* and five-elements terms liberally applied to specific characters. The simple labeling of characters with one element or another does not really tell us much. True, the tagging of Sun Wu-k'ung and Chu Pa-chieh as Lord of Metal and Mother of Wood, respectively, does convey something of their essential qualities—Sun Wu-k'ung's mercurial energy, Chu Pa-chieh's vegetative life-force. But these terms only take on their full allegorical significance within the context of the overall framework of interaction worked out in the narrative itself.

The same holds true for the use of hexagram terms, in keeping with the fundamental understanding of the *I Ching* whereby the essential meaning of each separate hexagram phase of reality resides only within the framework of the complete cycle of phenomenal change—an understanding with direct bearing on my interpretation of the apparent circularity of the quest journey in the body of the text.[151] In this light, the various schemes become much more interesting when we note the extent to which they reinforce one another. Just as the terms of cinnabar alchemy and sexual cultivation come together in their common use of *yin-yang* and five-elements jargon to evoke the shared concept of generative harmony, so do the fire and water components in the two hexagrams of most relevance to the narrative (*chi-chi* and *wei-chi*) set up a mutual resonance with associated imagery in Buddhist, Taoist, and even Confucian texts. This is particularly true with respect to the common focus on the cultivation of the mind in sixteenth-century Chinese thought, which, as promised, will provide the key to my interpretation of the novel as an allegory of self-cultivation.

Even this complex interrelation of symbols, however, becomes what can be accurately termed "allegorical" only when the individual symbols enter into the dynamic flow of the narrative; i.e., when we press the button and set the entire scheme in motion.[152] The fact that the author expects his readers to work at decoding the surface texture of his narrative is signaled in a number of fairly explicit allegorical figures. In the very first obstacle

[151] For additional discussions of the nonfinality of the ending of the narrative, see Parts II and V of this chapter.

[152] I have stressed this dynamic definition of allegory in my "Allegory in *Hsi-yu chi*," p. 165. A similar idea is expressed in the 1801 preface to Liu I-ming's *Hsi-yu yüan-chih*: "Each term and each idea is brought out in the actual course of concrete experience" 一辭一意 俱在履實踐中發出. See also the 1778 preface: "It uses concrete events to elucidate principles" 以事明理. Cf. the "Yü Chi" preface: "It is a text in which the principles of transformation take on concrete images" 夫大易皆取象之文.

faced by the Master after crossing the frontier of civilization and taking on his principal disciple in chapter 14, the doctrinal label "the six thieves" (*liu-tsei* 六賊) is attached to the problem of misguided reliance on the senses; and later on, in chapter 72, a similar cartouche is applied in a scene of temptation by seven beauties who are unambiguously labeled "the seven passions" (*ch'i-ch'ing* 七情).[153] There are many other passages in which these labels become less obtrusive, but still outline narrative situations that are often just too scriptural to be read as anything but doctrinal exempla—as in the treacherous crossing of the River of Communion with Heaven on thin ice (*lü-ping* 履冰) in chapter 48, the descent into a well (*ju-ching* 入井) in chapter 38, the subdual of ferocious tigers (*fu-hu* 伏虎) in chapters 13, etc.[154] The traditional commentators regularly take the trouble to gloss such examples, not because their significance is opaque, but simply to emphasize the type of allegorical reading demanded by the text.[155]

Slightly less obvious, but still fairly transparent, are certain narrative relationships that draw upon the symbolic designations of the principal figures in five-elements terms. For example, once Sun Wu-k'ung and Chu Pa-chieh have been identified with the elements metal and wood, respectively, the overcoming of the wayward pig in chapter 19 emerges as a simple enactment of the principle that metal conquers wood (*chin k'e mu* 金剋木). This, in turn, provides an easy gloss on the necessary role of Chu Pa-chieh in bringing the unruly Sand Monk into line in chapter 22 (*mu k'e t'u* 木剋土, or *mu k'e shui* 木剋水). The same elemental symbolism further explains why Sun Wu-k'ung is for the most part invulnerable to fire but

---

[153] Despite the proverbial familiarity of the designation *liu-tsei*, the commentators still feel the need to point out its significance. See, for example, Wang Hsiang-hsü, 56 (1a), 72 (1a–b), 96 (1a). The term also figured in the earlier *Tsa-chü*, Scene 21, as well as in *Tung-t'ien hsüan-chi*, where the "six thieves" occupy a key role in the dramatic plot.

[154] The image of treading on thin ice (*lü-ping*) brings to mind the *I Ching*, *k'un* hexagram, line 1 (*Chou-i che-chung*, pp. 140, 758). See Wang Hsiu-hsü, 48 (1a). The descent into a well (*ju-ching*) may hark back to *Lun-yü*, 6:26 or to Mencius (2A:6, 3A:5). Cf. the scene involving a descent into a well in *Shui-hu chuan* (see below, Chapter 4, Part IV). Examples of the subduing of tigers (*fu-hu*) occur in chapters 13 and 21. For the cluster of traditional associations linking images of tigers, damaging winds, poison, cutting metal, and autumn in *Chin P'ing Mei*, see above, Chapter 2, Part III. See comments by Wang Hsiang-hsü, 13 (1a), 68 (1a).

[155] For example, Wang Hsiang-hsü discusses the Nine-headed Son-in-law (Chiu-t'ou fu-ma) in chapter 63 (1a), as does Chang Shu-shen in chapters 62 (1a) and 63 (14a). Chang glosses the binding of Chu Pa-chieh to a tree in chapter 24 (2a, 2b) as "setting the fruit" (*chieh-kuo* 結果), the Many-eyed Demon (To-mu kuai) in chapter 72 (1b, 2a) as an incarnation of sensuality (*se* 色); the hollow bamboo in chapter 14 (17b) as "without a heart" 無心; the spider demons (*chih-chu*) in chapter 73 (9b) as obsession (*ch'ih* 痴). See also Ch'en Shih-pin, chapters 47 (478), 49 (501), and 64 (651).

nearly helpless in water, and is forced to call upon the services of Chu Pa-chieh, who is quite at home in water, every time a denizen of the depths needs to be overcome.

This sort of prescribed reading of allegorical figures also applies to the central metaphor of the text: the identification of the irrepressible monkey with the human mind, by way of the expression "monkey of the mind, horse of the will" (*hsin-yüan i-ma*).[156] Although this is after all a quite common locution—in fact, it appears in some of the antecedents of the novel—here it is very obviously raised to the level of a key to the entire allegory, as our commentators do not fail to note.[157]

With all this allegorical apparatus at our fingertips, it might appear that it would be a simple task to decode the meaning of this text. As in the case of *Chin P'ing Mei*, there is no lack here of seemingly straightforward didactic preaching. After all, this is the story of a group of "pilgrims" engaged in an ecclesiastical mission crowned with success, and the book closes with hymns of praise and thanksgiving. Given the insistence of the allegorical signposts, the critical commentators on the novel have felt no hesitation in assuming that a didactic message is present in the book.[158] Significantly, however, not a single one of them accepts at face value the Mahayana pieties with which the journey begins and ends as exhausting the intended meaning of the work.[159] Instead, they all seem to recognize

[156] Among the innumerable uses of this expression in the text, we may cite as examples occurrences in the titles of chapters 7, 14, 15, 30, 36, 41, 46, 51, 54, 75, 81, 83, 85, and 88. For a review of the sources of this metaphor, see Dudbridge, *Hsi-yu chi*, pp. 167–76; Anthony Yu, *Journey*, pp. 59f.; Hsü Chen-chi, "Pa-shih-i nan," pp. 11f; and Liu Ts'un-yan, "Ch'üan-chen chiao," pt. 2, p. 63. As these discussions show, the originally Buddhist associations of the term were diffused by the time of the novel's composition, and it was reduced to a nondoctrinal expression for libidinous energy. Hsieh Chao-che singles this out as the main idea in his description of the novel in his *Wu tsa-tsu*, pp. 1286f.

[157] For example, the term occurs in the *Tsa-chü*, Scene 10, and in the *Tung-t'ien hsüan-chi* preface (see Dudbridge, *Hsi-yu chi*, p. 172). Our earliest commentator, "Li Cho-wu," takes due note of the term in chapter 14 (12a–b, *tp*), as does Wang Hsiang-hsü, 15 (1a). Liu I-ming (1778 preface) criticizes Wang Hsiang-hsü for overemphasizing this idea. Ts'ai Yüan-fang (*tu-fa*, items 15, 16, 17, 18) lists various examples of this usage. See also Ch'en Shih-pin, 7 (78), 14 (158), 36 (369). Chang Shu-shen goes one step further, in chapter 4 (14b), to link the term *i* in the "horse of will" with the Neo-Confucian concept of *ch'eng-i* 誠意. He expands on this idea in chapters 15 (1a), 22 (1a), and *Tsung-p'i*, 11 (4a), 16 (5a).

[158] For a general review of the traditional interpretations of the allegory, see Cheng Chen-to, "Yen-hua," pp. 263, 274; Huang Su-ch'iu, "Chiao-ting ho Chu-shih," pp. 180ff.; and Chang Ching-erh, Jen-wu yen-chiu, pp. 17ff. For a list of commentary editions available today, see b.n. II. Ch'en Tun-fu (*Shih-i*, p. 20) adds to this list a *Hsi-yu chi chu* 西遊記註, compiled by a certain Ts'ai Chin 蔡金, which I have been unable to identify. Sun K'ai-ti (*Shu-mu*, p. 191) listed this edition, but he also had not seen it.

[159] The sole exception is discussed in P'eng Hai, "Hsi-yu chi chung tui fo-chiao ti p'i-p'an t'ai-tu," pp. 160ff.

that the overlay of Taoist terms and other symbols must radically modify the meaning of the Buddhist story.

With the exception of one recent commentator, none of the critics have gone to the other extreme of concluding that the insertion of Taoist terms into the text requires a thoroughly Taoist interpretation of the allegory as a whole.[160] Instead, they have taken due note of the fact that these two sets of terms are not at all incompatible, and have chosen to emphasize the confluence of Buddhist and Taoist ideas (*hsien-fo t'ung-yüan* 仙佛同源) as the ground of meaning of the book. The clearest and most consistent exposition of this position is that in Wang Hsiang-hsü's *Hsi-yu cheng-tao shu*, seconded and restated in Ts'ai Yüan-fang's reissue, and a similar interpretation eventually emerges in Ch'en Shih-pin's far more sophisticated and difficult critical commentary.[161] This syncretic ground again underlies the nineteenth-century commentary of Liu I-ming, even though his somewhat disappointing introductory essay, "How to Read The Original Meaning of *Hsi-yu chi*" ("Hsi-yu yüan-chih tu-fa" 西遊記讀法), has been reprinted in a collection of Taoist treatises.[162]

[160] This is, of course, Ch'en Tun-fu, whose *Hsi-yu chi shih-i*, bearing the subtitle "Record of the Mind According to Lung-men Teachings" (*Lung-men hsin-chuan* 龍門心傳), was issued under the auspices of the Ch'üan-chen society in Taiwan (see b.n.II.10). Ch'en outlines the principles of his Taoist interpretation in a series of prefaces, esp. pp. 15, 16, 18, and goes on to provide a "General Discussion" (*Tsung-lun* 總論), complete with a glossary of Taoist terminology (see also his commentary on p. 1151). Wang Hsiang-hsü's renaming of the novel as *Cheng-tao shu* ("a book to validate the Tao") is misleading, since his reading is actually a syncretic amalgam. To the extent that the overlay of Taoist terminology may represent at least one level of the novel's meaning, this may have a bearing on the question of its date of composition, since the mid-sixteenth century was marked by a pendulum swing from infatuation with Taoism under the Chia-ching emperor to a minor renaissance of Buddhist thought fostered by the patronage of the Wan-li emperor, and boosted by the intellectual authority of influential monks such as Chu-hung and Chih-hsü (see above, Chapter 1). Attempts to pin down the authorship of the novel on this basis have not been altogether convincing, but at least this line of inquiry parallels attempts to date the composition of the *Chin P'ing Mei* on similar grounds, notably that by Wu Han (see above, Chapter 2, Part I).

[161] See, for example, Wang Hsiang-hsü's comments in chapters 1 (1a), 44 (11b), 78 (1b), and 98 (1a, 1b). A good example of the sort of blend of Buddhism and Taoism followed by Wang can be seen in the Wan-li text *Wu-Liu hsien-tsung ch'üan-chi* by Wu Ch'ung-hsü, especially the section entitled "Hsien-fo ho-tsung" 仙佛合宗, which is liberally sprinkled with many of the allegorical terms of our novel (e.g., *huo-hou*). See also Ts'ai Yüan-fang, *tu-fa*, items 1, 3, 5, 7, 9, 10, 11; "Li Cho-wu," chapter 98 (3a); and *Hsi-yu yüan-chih*, 1778, 1798, 1801 prefaces. Liu T'ing-chi (in his *Tsai-yüan tsa-chih*) acknowledges that Wang Hsiang-hsü's reading is essentially valid, but he criticizes him for unconvincing interpretations of specific points. See also Isobe Akira, "Genpon Saiyūki o meguru mondai," pp. 72f.

[162] See Liu I-ming, *tu-fa*, item 4, and passim (see b.n. II.8). The three-teachings reading is discussed by Liu Ts'un-yan, in "Wu Ch'eng-en," p. 83; Anthony Yu, *Journey*, p. 38; Cheng Chen-to, "Yen-hua," p. 274; James Fu, *Quest*, p. 58; and the explanatory introduction

At the other end of the spectrum, Chang Shu-shen reads the work as an allegorical exposition not of Buddhist or Taoist occultism, but of exclusively Confucian learning. Chang's stubborn insistence on reading the entire novel as a sort of gloss on the basic teachings of the Four Books must strike most modern readers as idiosyncratic, to say the least.[163] But I will try to show here that a less dogmatic application of Chang's instincts may be quite compatible with the intellectual underpinnings of the novel; and in any case, Ch'en Shih-pin frequently invokes some of the same Confucian concepts in working out his own far-reaching interpretations.[164]

With the possible exception of the Ch'en Shih-pin commentary, most of these readings suffer from a tendency to force the novel's allegory of salvation into an exclusive dogmatic mold. The chief problem with any simplistic reading of the text, however, is the fact that the ever-present sting of irony sooner or later undercuts even the didactic pronouncements that the author himself provides. For one thing, we immediately note that representatives of all three of the teachings come in for rather consistent debunking in the course of the narrative. Regarding the bearers of Mahayana salvation, the author appears to present the saving grace of Bud-

---

("Ch'u-pan shuo-ming") to the 1956 reprint of *Ssu-yu chi*, p. 1. The earlier commentators had already suggested the same approach. See "Li Cho-wu," Yüan Yü-ling preface; Wang Hsiang-hsü, chapter 88 (10b); Chang Shu-shen, *Tsung-p'i*, 1 (1a), 3 (1b), 5 (2b); Ch'en Shih-pin ed., Yu T'ung preface, and 47 (477), 64 (653), 100 (1014ff.); plus *T'ung-i cheng-chih*, 86 (59b), 97 (72a–b). Cf. the reflection of this range of meaning in the *Tsa-chü*, Scenes 5, 12, 17; as well as in *Tung-t'ien hsüan-chi*.

[163] See especially Chang's general discussion (*Tsung-p'i*), items 1 (1a), 3 (1b), and numerous textual comments, with the fullest exposition occurring in comments in chapters 25 (1a, 14b), 49 (1b), 52 (1a). Chang links his reading to the *Ta-hsüeh* in comments in chapters 1 (19a), 22 (1a, 1b), 30 (1a), 47 (1a), 48 (1a, 1b), 50 (1a, 1b), 57 (1a), 61 (1a), 62 (14b), 71 (19a), 79 (20a, b) (cf. a reference to the *Ta-hsüeh yen-i* in *Tsung-p'i*, 71:19a); he refers to the *Chung-yung* in chapter 50 (1a), to Mencius in *Tsung-p'i*, item 8 (14a); to Ch'eng-Chu teachings in chapters 10 (1b), 19 (16a), 70 (1b), and 96 (14a), and in the *Tsung-p'i*, 35 (9a, b), 59 (15b, 16a), 70 (20a, b). See also Ts'ai Yüan-fang, *tu-fa*, item 20.

[164] See Ch'en Shih-pin comments in chapters 2 (21), 3 (35f.), 5 (54), 6 (65), 18 (192), 24 (251f.), 26 (272), 28 (289), 35 (361), 37 (378), 40 (406f.), 41 (418f.), 42 (426f.), 50 (509), 52 (528), 56 (568f.), 58 (588), 64 (652ff.), 65 (664), 66 (672), 85 (868), 86 (874f.), 98 (993f.). In chapter 100 (1014), he concludes with a position close to the slogan of *san-chiao kuei-ju* 三教歸儒 ("the three teachings converge in Confucianism"), espoused by a number of his contemporaries. The other major commentators also fall back on Confucian ideas at certain points; e.g., Wang Hsiang-hsü, 4 (5b), 15 (1a), 62 (1b), 68 (1a–b), 88 (10b); *Chia-p'i Hsi-yu chi*, 1 (2b, 3a, 3b, 4b, 6b, 7a, 10a, 15a), 2 (2a, 4a, 11b, 14a, 18a, 22a), 6 (8a), 9 (18a), 12 (20a, 20b, 21a, 21b); and *T'ung-i cheng-chih*, 12 (16b), 61 (10b), 65 (50b), 66 (59a), 86 (62b), 97 (72a), 98 (87b). Nicholas Koss notes the conspicuous interjection of Confucian terms in the Shih-te t'ang edition of the novel ("Formative Stages," chaps. 4, 5, 6). Cf. the appearance of *hsin-hsüeh* terms in the *Tsa-chü*, Scenes 2, 3, 4, 12, 13.

dhas and bodhisattvas in many episodes, but this is qualified by an abundance of other scenes in which it is their failure or limitations that are stressed.[165]

The undercutting of literal-minded Buddhist dogma is even more to the point, however, in the parody of individual enlightenment through calm meditation presented in the caricature of the master Hsüan-tsang, whose incessant nervousness, susceptibility to hunger and cold, and fear for his personal safety in the novel contrast with the aura of imperturbable saintliness that radiates from his visage in traditional iconography.[166] This is clearest in those incidents—especially in chapters 36 and 64—in which he ostensibly undergoes classic enlightenment experiences, replete with images of the refulgent moon. In each case this turns out to be a pseudo-enlightenment—one that gives rise to new entanglements with pointedly sexual overtones.

This would seem to clear the way for a serious interpretation of the novel as an exposition of Taoist concepts, except for the fact that the actual Taoist figures portrayed in the book are also subjected to ridicule, appearing primarily in the guise of various heretical wizards (*p'ang-men wai-tao* 旁門外道), charlatans, medicine men, and rainmakers (*hu-feng huan-yü* 呼風喚雨), not to mention all the demons decked out with their own Taoist trappings.[167] Here, too, a telling connection is drawn between pseudo-enlightenment and sexual sublimation, a point of particular significance in light of the emphasis on certain sexual practices within sixteenth-century Taoist "cultivation." Nor can we say that the Confucian types fare much better in the author's hands, since in the few cases where such figures appear, they come off as benighted rulers and helpless advisers rather than as paragons of moral courage. More to the point, those in-

---

[165] For example, chapter 52, 98–99. Among the commentators, "Li Cho-wu," in particular, is quick to point out the more ludicrous aspects of the Buddhist saviors, as for example in chapters 8 (4a) and 42 (7b). See also Ch'en Shih-pin, chapter 65 (662). Cf. P'eng Hai, "Hsi-yu chi chung tui fo-chiao," pp. 158–71.

[166] See above, n. 116.

[167] The most derogatory treatment of Taoist masters is presented in chapters 37–40, 44–45, 78–79, 87. In this context, the turning of the Buddhist figure Subodhi (Hsü-p'u-t'i 須菩提) into a Taoist Master in chapter 2 is quite suggestive. Cf. the highlighted role of Hsü-p'u-t'i in the Heart Sutra and the *Chin-kang ching* as one who truly "understands the meaning of emptiness" (*wu-k'ung* 悟空). At this point in the novel, his disciple, Sun "Wu-k'ung," pointedly fails to grasp this message. See the sarcastic comments by "Li Cho-wu" in chapters 4 (5a), 21 (14b, *tp*), and passim; Wang Hsiang-hsü, chapters 44 (11b), 78 (1b); and Chang Shu-shen, chapter 20 (1b). See James Fu, *Quest*, p. 79; Ōta Tatsuo, "Kaisetsu," p. 442; Kao Hsi-tseng, "Hsi-yu chi li ti tao-chiao ho tao-shih," pp. 153–59; Chao Ts'ung, *Ssu ta hsiao-shuo*, 190f. Cf. the use of the term *wai-tao* in the *Tsa-chü*, Scene 21. I will consider below the special treatment of the problem of sexual disequilibrium in the allegory.

stances in which Confucian values are explicitly expressed often call forth denunciations as "false moralism" (*tao-hsüeh ch'i* 道學氣) from the commentators.[168]

If the author denies us an easy interpretation of his text in terms of the didactic values of Buddhism, Taoism, or Confucianism, what are we to make of the allegorical journey with its apparent message of attainment through perseverance, or transcendence of worldly temptation, in the pursuit of a higher aim? What, then, is the purpose of all the excess baggage of philosophical terminology added here to the traditional narrative? The majority of twentieth-century critics would simply reply that these have no particular significance at all, that this is just literary embellishment, at most a kind of literati joke designed to mock the naive reader. To my mind, however, the sheer amount of allegorical terms, as well as the manner in which they are integrated into the narrative structure, rule out such a blanket dismissal. At the very least, the Ming-Ch'ing commentators, presumably closer to the intellectual and literary presuppositions of the time of composition, refuse to allow such a conclusion.

Unfortunately, the task remaining before us—that of working out this allegorical interpretation in detail—is by no means an easy one. The allegorical framework is not necessarily fully articulated or even consistent. In fact, even our intrepid guides among the traditional commentators on occasion admit their own frustration in attempting to crack the author's allegorical code. For example, Ts'ai Yüan-fang and Liu I-ming acknowledge a number of undecipherable passages, and even the ingenious Ch'en Shih-pin throws up his hands at one point and complains:

> I have read this chapter over and over a number of times from start to finish, then closed the book and pondered deeply; but in the end I am unable to grasp its meaning.
> 此篇從頭至尾，翻覆數過，掩卷沈思，而終莫得其解. [169]

But since I cannot claim to have reached the level of Ch'en Shih-pin's insight, I also need not give up without a struggle. As is undoubtedly clear by now, my own understanding of the allegorical meaning of the novel rests on locating the allegory within sixteenth-century Chinese thought, especially its central focus on what is commonly called the "philosophy of

---

[168] See for example "Li Cho-wu," chapters 17 (2b), 41 (3b), 57 (*tp*); Wang Hsiang-hsü, 29 (1a); Ch'en Shih-pin, 30 (309), 78 (796). This theme gives added significance to the highlighting of T'ang T'ai-tsung's somewhat tainted role as a spiritual leader in the narrative.

[169] Ch'en Shih-pin passage is found in chapter 93 (938). For similar admissions of difficulty, see Ts'ai Yüan-fang, *tu-fa*, item 56; Liu I-ming, *tu-fa*, item 26; Chang Shu-shen, 43 (17a), 93 (13b); and *T'ung-i cheng-chih*, 56 (61b).

mind" (*hsin-hsüeh*).[170] I will for convenience refer below to this body of intellectual groundwork as primarily Neo-Confucian, although this does not mean that Buddhist and Taoist ideas are completely effaced within the amalgam. The point is that it is precisely within the sphere of "philosophy of mind" that the various sets of terms used by the three schools show the greatest degree of compatibility; thus, we can speak of the "convergence of the three teachings" as something more integral than any particular movement of contrived syncretism. If the idea of a Neo-Confucian synthesis in this looser sense is a valid description of the intellectual foundations of the literati milieu to which this allegorical novel belongs, this has a special importance for my argument, since it reinforces what I have claimed to be the Neo-Confucian dimension of meaning in the *Chin P'ing Mei*, and what I will stress in my subsequent chapters on *San-kuo yen-i* and *Shui-hu chuan*.

This convergence of meaning within the post-Sung philosophy of mind is borne out in the novel with the appearance of certain terms of special relevance to each of the respective schools of Ming thought. Among Buddhist ideas, we find an emphasis on the "mind of (Ch'an) meditation" (*Ch'an-hsin* 禪心) and the "illumination of the mind" (*ming-hsin* 明心), in addition to references to the Prajnaparamita Heart Sutra highlighted at several key points in the text—not to mention the identity of Buddha-nature and mind invoked at the start of the journey in chapter 14 (佛即心 兮心即佛).[171] Within the province of Taoist thought, the crucial indicator pointing in this same direction is the reinterpretation, standard by this time, of all references to cinnabar alchemy in terms of the notion of the "internal

---

[170] For general discussions of the philosophy of mind in the Ming period, see Fung Yu-lan, *History*, pp. 572–629; Wing-tsit Chan, "The Ch'eng-Chu School of Early Ming," pp. 29–52; Shimada Kenji, *Chūgoku ni okeru kindai shii no zasetsu*; Araki Kengo, *Mindai shisō kenkyū*; Hou Wai-lu, *Chung-kuo ssu-hsiang t'ung-shih*, vol. 4; and other works. See above, Chapter 1, for further discussion. If there should prove to be any substance to the possibility of the fourteenth-century authorship of an allegorical work similar to our novel, this would obviously weaken my case; but at the same time, I could easily cite earlier phases of this same intellectual movement (e.g., Lu Chiu-yüan 陸九淵 (Hsiang-shan 象山), Yang Chien 楊簡, Wu Ch'eng 吳澄 to account for this dimension of meaning. The commentators occasionally refer to the thought of Wang Yang-ming in elucidating certain passages; e.g., Wang Hsiang-hsü, 4 (9a), and Chang Shu-shen, 18 (1a). Cf. the late Ming attempts to reconcile Neo-Confucian and Buddhist ideas through the medium of *hsin-hsüeh* concepts (see Yü Chün-fang, "Some Ming Buddhists' Responses to Neo-Confucianism," esp. pp. 2, 10f. 18f.). See Anthony Yu, "Pilgrimage," pp. 222ff.; and Wen Chi, "Hsi-yu chi cha-chi," pp. 55ff.

[171] The idea of the identity of Buddha and mind is expressed in chapter 14 (1:182). See comments by Wang Hsiang-hsü, 74 (1b); Chang Shu-shen, 1 (17b), 19 (1a, 16a), and *Tsung-p'i*, 37 (9b), and additional citations in n. 284. On the highlighted invocation of the *Heart Sutra*, see C. T. Hsia, *Classic Novel*, pp. 127f. The use of the *Hsin ching* in the novel parallels the pointed citation of the *Chin-kang ching* in the *Tsa-chü*, Scene 21.

cinnabar" (*nei-tan* 內丹), nearly always a cipher for the inner core of the self.[172] These ideas, however, are fully compatible with the Ming redefinition of Confucian self-cultivation as primarily a cultivation of the mind (*hsiu-hsin* 修心), a term that in fact takes in all of the other ideas cited above.[173] Our commentators are fully aware of this confluence of terms and ideas within their intellectual heritage. Chang Shu-shen's attempt to read all the examples of *hsin-hsüeh* terminology in the novel as placeholders for Four Books concepts is more than a little forced,[174] but the Yu T'ung preface goes to the heart of the matter in its opening discussion of the equivalence running through the Buddhist notion "illumination of the mind to perceive the true nature" (*ming-hsin chien-hsing* 明心見性), the Taoist idea of "cultivating the mind to refine the true nature" *hsiu-hsin lien-hsing* 修心練性), and the Confucian concept of "preserving the mind to nourish the true nature" (*ts'un-hsin yang-hsing* 存心養性).[175] Yu's choice of the yoked terms "mind" (*hsin*) and "nature" (*hsing*) in each of these three parallel expressions serves to deepen this convergence, since these two levels of being are often taken as virtually interchangeable with respect to Buddhist attainment (e.g., *Ch'an-hsing*) or Taoist immortality, and they also appear in this sense in many Neo-Confucian contexts.[176]

[172] On the concept of the "internal cinnabar," see Judith Berling, "Paths of Convergence," pp. 123–47; Anthony Yu, *Journey*, pp. 51f.; Liu Ts'ung-yan, "Taoist Self-cultivation," pp. 292f., and his "Ch'üan chen chiao," pt. 2, pp. 61ff. See comments by Ch'en Shih-pin, 24 (251), 36 (369ff.), 68 (692f.), and other discussions in chapters 27 (281), 33 (342), 39 (397), 40 (405), 43 (438), 49 (498), 50 (509), 70 (713), 71 (724), 73 (744), 74 (753), 98 (996), 99 (1003).

[173] On the Neo-Confucian shift of the understanding of "self-cultivation" from the *Ta-hsüeh* stress on the balance of inner and outer selfhood (*hsiu-shen*) to focus more on the interior dimension (*hsiu-hsin*), see works cited in n. 170, and W. T. de Bary, "Individualism and Humanitarianism in Late Ming Thought," pp. 145–248, passim. See Anthony Yu, "Pilgrimage," p. 222; and Tu Wei-ming, review of *Journey* (see n. 180).

[174] Chang provides the fullest expositions of this reading in chapters 16 (3a) and 39 (1a). See n. 163. A similar transfer of ideas is suggested at certain points by Ch'en Shih-pin in chapter 66 (672), "Li Cho-wu" in chapter 44 (16b, *tp*), and Ts'ai Yüan-fang, *tu-fa*, items 19, 20.

[175] See Ch'en Shih-pin edition, Yu T'ung preface, and 2 (22), 7 (78), 8 (89, 93), 13 (145f.), 14 (158f.), 21 (219), 27 (281f.), 39 (397), 40 (405ff.), 42 (428), 43 (438), 86 (874), and 93 (939). Cf. the use of the expression *ming-hsin chien-hsing* in *Tung-t'ien hsüan-chi*, p. 7a; it also occurs in a couplet at the end of chapter 98 (3 : 1343). See also Chang Shu-shen, chapters 19 (1a, 16a), 39 (1a), 58 (14a); Ts'ai Yüan-fang, *tu-fa*, item 8; *T'ung-i cheng-chih*, 12 (16b).

[176] See, for example, chapters 67 (2 : 682f.) and 85 (2 : 866f.); and comments by "Li Cho-wu," 12 (13a, *tp*), 37, (16a, *tp*), 91 (19a, *tp*); Wang Hsiang-hsü, 80 (1b); and Liu I-ming, *tu-fa*, item 20. Cf. the use of the expression *ts'un-hsing* in the *Tsa-chü*, Scene 14. For further discussion of certain related concepts—e.g., *pen-hsing* and *shuang-hsiu hsing-ming*—see my remarks later in this chapter.

V

With this frame of reference in mind, I can now move on with my allegorical reading of *Hsi-yu chi*. At the very outset, I must take due note of the author's considerable efforts to undermine the notion of a simple pattern of quest and attainment. Despite the constant crossing of trackless wastes and impassable barriers by our not-so-intrepid pilgrims, we still get the sense of a certain circularity in the progress of the band.[177] At the least, they seem continually to be passing through the same landscapes, vulnerable to the same external and internal trials; and when they finally reach their promised land it is suspiciously reminiscent of the T'ang capital from which they set out.

Even more troubling are the doubts cast over the necessity of the entire journey. More than once the question is raised as to why the cloud-soaring monkey cannot simply somersault over the Himalayas and fetch the long-sought scriptures without further trials on the part of his earthbound master.[178] The final irony of the "wordless scriptures" (*wu tzu chen-ching* 無字眞經) is a rather transparent joke, unless we choose to emphasize the proverbial desirability of "empty" scriptures in Chinese philosophical discourse, in which case the final restoration of the "real" scriptures itself further diminishes the ultimate attainment of the quest.[179] Since the parting touch of withholding the scriptures appears only in the novel, in contrast to the triumphal endings in the *Shih-hua* and *Tsa-chü* versions, we can only take this as a final undermining of the fulfillment of the mission.

The solution to this problem lies in reading the quest narrative not as a kind of literal "Pilgrim's Progress," as has been suggested by certain recent critics, but rather as an internal pilgrimage of the mind.[180] This is already strongly suggested by the inclusion of so much *hsin-hsüeh* terminology,

---

[177] This circularity is emphasized in comments by "Li Cho-wu," 29 (1a); Wang Hsiang-hsü, 15 (1a); and Ch'en Shih-pin, 19 (202f.). In a sense, the pilgrimage only ends when it returns to the midpoint and re-crosses the River of Communion with Heaven.

[178] "Li Cho-wu" asks the same question in chapter 12 (13a, *tp*), as does Liu I-ming in his preface, and *tu-fa*, item 26.

[179] Cf. comparable deficiencies in the scriptures bestowed in the *Shih-hua*, sections 15, 16, and *Tsa-chü*, Scene 22. The insistence on a precise total number of scriptures also figures in *Tung-t'ien hsüan-chi*, p. 13a. See "Li Cho-wu," 57 (14a), and 99 (11a).

[180] The parallel with *Pilgrims Progress* has been suggested by C. T. Hsia, *Classic Novel*, pp. 126ff.; Chang Ching-erh, "Structure and Theme," p. 22; and Wu Pi-yung, "Hsi-yu chi yen-chiu," pp. 102ff. Anthony Yu ("Pilgrimage") elucidates the notion of the pilgrimage of the mind, as does Tu Wei-ming, in his review of *Journey to the West* in *History of Religions* 19, no. 2 (November 1979); 177–84. The internal nature of the quest is stressed by Ch'en Shih-pin, in 76 (774) and 85 (866).

and it is stated almost outright at a number of points in the text. Thus, for example, the Holy Mountain to which the pilgrims later direct their steps is obliquely identified in the very first chapter with the mind, in the little anagram of the Cave of the Crescent Moon with Three Stars (*Hsieh-yüeh san-hsing tung* 斜月三星洞). Much later, as they come nearly within sight of the journey's end in chapter 85, they are told that "the Holy Mountain is nowhere but in your mind" (*Ling-shan chih tsai ju hsin-t'ou* 靈山只在汝心頭).[181]

But to simply state that the allegorical journey is a pilgrimage of mind raises as many questions as it answers. In order to put some flesh on this skeleton interpretation, we must work out the allegorical significance of such things as the precise course and pace of the spiritual progress, the sequence of episodes, and the nature of the obstacles barring the path. I will also have to reinterpret the meaning of the goal of final attainment, as well as the reason the hundred-chapter novel reorganizes the traditional material to give us not one, but in effect three quest stories.

Let us begin by analyzing the obstacles to the spiritual progress of the pilgrim group. At first sight, what we have is a series of external hurdles to surmount, from the physical barriers: the ever-present mountains and rivers, to the more imaginative blockages: the expanse of brambles in chapter 64, the stretch of rotten persimmons in chapter 67—all of which refer to spiritual rather than physical hindrances.

As for the various demons (*yao-mo* 妖魔) who bar the way, here too the initial sense of simple maliciousness soon gives way to more complex kinds of symbolism. For one thing, the iconographic details of secluded mountain lairs and caves, with their characteristic stone furnishings, strongly suggest the abodes of Taoist immortals—even before we learn, in the majority of cases, that these "demons" are in fact denizens of the world of the immortals only temporarily banished to this world for the sin of earthly desire. And this same sort of origin is shared by all of the disciples in the pilgrim band: Chu Pa-chieh, the Sand Monk, the dragon horse, and most pointedly, Sun Wu-k'ung, whose prior existence is lavishly staged for us in the prologue section lest we miss the point. In later scenes, Sun Wu-k'ung goes on to disclose his earlier links to some of the demon figures now imperiling the journey, most noticeably the Bull Demon King (Niu mo-

---

[181] Chapters 1 (1:12) and 85 (3:1166). See comments by "Li Cho-wu," 8 (14a) and 39 (16a): "[The goal of the quest] is not outside yourself" 不在身外也; Wang Hsiang-hsü, 13 (2a): "One need not search for it afar" 何必遠求; chapters 24 (2a), 25 (1b), and 74 (1b), where he points out that Sun Wu-k'ung is "none other than one's own mind" 行者即此心. See also Ch'en Shih-pin edition, Yu T'ung preface and chapter 76 (775); Chang Shu-shen, 18 (6a), 32 (15b), 33 (5b), 96 (14a); and Ts'ai Yüan-fang, *tu-fa*, item 31. In my discussion below, I will draw additional distinctions between the external and internal obstacles to the quest.

wang).[182] But by this time we have already been informed that "the bodhisattvas and the demons are all manifestations of a single concept" (*p'u-sa yao-ching tsung shih i-nien* 菩薩妖精總是一念). Indeed, at the very start of the mission, this understanding of the internal locus of the demons was stated quite explicitly: "With the emergence of consciousness, all types of demons come forth; with the extinction of consciousness, all the demons are extinguished" 心生, 種種魔生, 心滅, 種種魔滅. In other words, all the demons who threaten the life and limb of the travelers are essentially manifestations of the unenlightened state of the mind in its process of cultivation.[183]

At this point, I will go on to consider in greater detail the specific pitfalls in the cultivation of mind that are allegorized in the separate episodes.[184] One of the least problematical types of obstacles arises in those cases in which it is primarily carelessness, or lack of vigilance, that gives rise to a serious setback to the progress of the group. This includes the predictable complacency of the pilgrims at the start of each episode, where we see them freshly delivered from the preceding peril, whistling down their road to the West, only to fall heedlessly into the clutches of the next waiting demon. In some cases this negligence entails the violation of specific instructions, as for example in the inability of the group to remain within the protective circle (*ch'üan-tzu* 圈子) drawn on the ground by Sun Wu-k'ung in chapter 50, or their failure to guard properly certain divinely bestowed tokens of salvation: for example, the Master's cassock whisked away in chapter 16, or the weapons snatched in chapter 88, just as they reach a stage of self-satisfaction with the degree of attainment under their belts.[185]

The most pointed instance of this problem is found at the pivotal point

---

[182] The linked prehistory of Sun Wu-K'ung and the various demons is emphasized in comments by Wang Hsiang-hsü, chapters 28 (1a), 32 (1a), 41 (1b), 61 (1a); Chang Shu-shen, chapter 61 (7a); Ts'ai Yüan-fang, *tu-fa*, item 44; and "Li Cho-wu," chapter 17 (15a). See Tu Wei-ming review of *Journey*; and Cheng Ming-li, "Huo-yen shan ku-shih ti hsing-ch'eng," p. 8f. This same sense is brought out in the *Tsa-chü*, Scenes 9 and 10.

[183] Chapter 13 (1:169). See comments by "Li Cho-wu," 17 (16b); Liu I-ming, *tu-fa*, item 23; Wang Hsiang-hsü, 49 (1a), 57 (1a), 59 (1b), 60 (1a), 70 (1a); Chang Shu-shen, chapter 92 (1b) and *Tsung-p'i*, 37 (9b), 38 (9b), 42 (11a–b), 46 (13b–14a); and *T'ung-i cheng-chih*, 51 (55b).

[184] This question is emphasized in Ts'ai Yüan-fang, *tu-fa*, items 1, 2, and especially 35. See discussions by Chang Ching-erh, "Structure and Theme," p. 185; Hsü Chen-chi, "Pa-shih-i nan," pp. 51ff.; and Wu Pi-yung, "Hsi-yu chi yen-chiu," pp. 47ff.

[185] The incident of negligence in chapters 88–90 is followed immediately in chapter 91 by a peril brought on by the Master's "relaxation of his meditative nature" 寬了禪性 (see 3:1247). The commentators frequently raise this point; e.g., Wang Hsiang-hsü, 24 (1b), 47 (1a), 53 (1a), 83 (1a), 89 (1a); Ch'en Shih-pin, 62 (629); Ts'ai Yüan-fang, *tu-fa*, 29; and Chang Shu-shen, 23 (4a, 11a).

in chapter 36, where the Master's premature bid for enlightenment in a classic scene replete with symbols of all-pervading illumination, terminates not in the final attainment that is sought but in the issue, out of his own dream consciousness, of a new trial—one not without sexual overtones. The allegorical labels attached to this scene are quite explicit on this point. We are first told, "When one's merit has reached the proper degree, the [attainment] will be fulfilled spontaneously" (*kung tao tzu-jan ch'eng* 功到自然成); and then we are informed that "his merit was not yet complete" (*kung wei-wan* 功未完).[186]

Not all of the spiritual obstacles presented in the allegory are simply manifestations of insufficient attainment or a premature relaxing of vigilance, however. Instead, certain episodes bring into focus a small number of separate but interrelated philosophical issues current in sixteenth-century thought.

Among the principal pitfalls of this type is the problem of disunity, which threatens the progress of the group at several key points. This is most graphically presented in the episodes that literally recount the breakup of the pilgrim body: namely, the two instances of the "exile" of the mind-monkey (*fang-hsin* 放心, see below), both of which lead to a perilous state of dis-integration. As Wang Hsiang-hsü rather succinctly puts it, "The mind and body were split asunder" (*hsin-shen hsiang-li* 心身相離).[187] These two episodes are transparent enough, and may seem to convey nothing more than the humorous playing out of the petty rivalries and clash of wills within the band—one of the common arenas of the humor of the novel. But when we proceed to a detailed exegesis of the *fang-hsin* concept later in this chapter, we will see that a number of more specific philosophical implications are raised here.

One of the primary conceptual axes of the book is the drawing of a contrast between primal unity and discordant division. This is the idea with which the book begins, with its opening discourse on cycles of cosmic harmony, before moving immediately into a world of undifferentiated innocence and its loss. This is mythically expressed in the Monkey King's leap through the water curtain into a world of pristine perfection, only to succumb to the anguish of mortality lurking within his enclosed paradise. A similar idea is stressed at the opening of the main body of the quest

---

[186] Chapter 36 (2:492) and (2:503). See also chapter 57 (2:795): "to desist mid-journey, to stop halfway" 半途而廢, 中道而止. See comments by Wang Hsiang-hsü, 23 (1b): "They have not yet penetrated deeply into the Way" (*ju-tao wei-shen* 入道未深); Chang Shu-shen, 36 (15b), 64 (1a); Ch'en Shih-pin, 24 (253), 36 (369), 40 (406), 50 (510), 53 (558); and *T'ung-i cheng-chih*, 47 (83a), 61 (12a), etc.

[187] Wang Hsiang-hsü, chapter 28 (1b). Cf. the frequent use of the expression "disperse like wildfire" (*san-huo* 散火) in, for example, chapters 30 (1:412), 32 (1:438), 57 (2:795).

narrative itself, where the transition from a state of heavenly grace to the pitfall-strewn path of uneven progress toward enlightenment is marked by the crossing of a conceptual demarcation at the Dual Border Mountain (*Liang-chieh shan*)—a sense reinforced soon after when we arrive at the Ridge of the Double Fork (*Shuang-ch'a ling* 雙叉嶺).[188]

Right after this, the author's concern with the issue of division is dramatized in the episode of the "six thieves." Here, our attention is directed to a particular side of this issue: the problem of multiplicity as an impediment to the singularity of consciousness demanded for spiritual cultivation. This theme is continuously allegorized by means of the various number-named demons who threaten to tear asunder the unity and integrality of the group, as in the cases of the Six-eared Ape (Liu-erh mi-hou 六耳彌猴) in chapter 58 and the Nine-headed Son-in-law (Chiu-t'ou fu-ma) in chapters 62 and 63.[189] The "Li Cho-wu" commentator, for one, explicitly glosses this latter creature as a symbol of the "multiplicity of man's consciousness" ... 喻人之頭緒多也.[190] The incident of the Six-eared Ape in chapter 58 is a particularly telling example of this idea, since here the disunity caused by the second "exile" leads directly into the appearance of this many-eared monster, who immediately confronts the pilgrims with the bogey of multiplicity in the form of a false doubling of the mind-monkey himself.[191] The connection drawn between the "cloning" of the monkey and the dangerous refraction of the mind into discordant impulses reminds us of yet another side to this issue: that of excessive centrifugality as allegorized, among other places, in the episode of the Many-eyed Monster (To-mu kuai), also known as the Hundred-eyed Prince of Demons (Pai-yen mo-chün).[192]

This brings us to the problem of excessive emotional attachment, and in particular the destabilizing power of sexual desire. For a narrative dealing almost exclusively with a group of monks on a quest for scriptures, it is striking—although often overlooked—that a good many of the episodes specifically treat the problem of sexual temptation. This theme is already quite pointed in the depiction of the entanglement of Chu Pa-chieh, literally in a web of desire, in chapter 23; and in the second half of the book this

[188] See discussion of the structural significance of this dividing line in Part II of this chapter. This is treated by James Fu in *Quest*, pp. 50ff., 57ff., 69ff.

[189] Other examples of demons of multiplicity appear in chapter 73 (the Hundred-eyed Prince of Demons 百眼魔君) and chapter 90 (the Primal Sage of the Nine Spirits). See n. 51 and comments by Wang Hsiang-hsü, 63 (1a), 90 (1b).

[190] "Li Cho-wu," chapter 63 (14b, *tp*).

[191] See comments by "Li Cho-wu," 58 (13b, *tp*), and Chang Shu-shen, 59 (1a). The figure of false duplication here is reminiscent of the duplicitous Duessa in the first few books of Spenser's *Faerie Queene*.

[192] See above, n. 189. Cf. also the centipede spirits who inhabit Hundred-leg Mountain 百脚山 in chapter 93 (3:1269).

subject begins to dominate the stage, constituting the central focus of the episodes in chapters 53—55, 72—73, 80—83, and 93—95. In some of these cases, it is entirely possible to read the sexual motifs as simple instances of assault on the purity of the Master, or humorous slaps at the sexual incontinence of Chu Pa-chieh. In fact, I have noted that in a number of passages the author himself indulges in sexual innuendo, as for example in the pun on the Gate of Ch'an (*Ch'an-men* 禪門) in chapter 53, or the little joke on what I have rendered as Bodhisattva Below the Belt (Pan-chieh Kuan-yin) in chapter 83.[193]

But there seems to be more at stake in these instances than the simple matter of fortitude in the face of temptation. For one thing, the author lavishes considerable effort on making some of the temptations in question as sensually appealing as possible. This is true in chapter 23 (as several commentators admit); and in chapter 72, in the scene of Chu Pa-chieh transformed into a slippery fish frolicking in a bathing pool with naked temptresses, we get imagery that rivals Spenser's Bower of Bliss in its evocative sensuality.[194] By the time we come to the episode of the Jade Hare in chapters 93—95, the ground has been prepared for the convincing portrayal of Hsüan-tsang's apparent submission to demonic designs on his pure essence, right at the point where the goal of the quest comes within sight.[195]

---

[193] See chapters 53 (2:738) and 83 (3:1146). See above, n. 112. Another, less transparent, example of sexual overtones can be seen in the repeated mention of the *p'i-p'a ku* (see also, n. 112). This has been rendered by translators in its modern usage (e.g., Waley, *Monkey*, p. 71: "lute-bone"; Yu, *Journey*, 1:169: "breastbone"), but according to an entry in *Ch'a-yü k'e-hua* (p. 154), the expression seems to have referred to either the pelvis or perhaps the thighs. Could this simply be a pun for *p'i-ku*? In any case, the expression seems to have carried certain unmistakable sexual connotations, as we see in comments by Chang Shu-shen, 4 (6b), 27 (16a), 30 (17a), 31 (1a), 56 (1b, 15b), 60 (3a), 73 (1a), 78 (1b, 14a), 80 (1a, 5a); and Ch'en Shih-pin, 17 (185), 55 (559f.). The commentator who is most interested in this area of meaning is "Li Cho-wu"; see chapter 5 (1b), 23 (15a—b), 27 (196), 54 (9a), 70 (12a), 71 (2b), 72 (14b), 74 (16a), 79 (13a), 82 (13b), 83 (14a), 95 (13b).

[194] Cf. "Li Cho-wu's" comment in chapter 23 (15a)—"Who today wouldn't be brought to ruin by [these girls]; we shouldn't just laugh at our friend the pig" 今人那一個不被… 弄壞了, 不要獨笑老豬也 —reproduced with different wording by Wang Hsiang-hsü, 23 (9a). See also Wang's comments in chapter 24 (2a), 27 (1a), 54 (1a), 55 (1b), 56 (1a), 59 (1b), 60 (1a), 72 (1a, 1b), 82 (1a), and 95 (1b).

[195] This entire episode is heavily laden with sexual suggestiveness. Aside from the connotations of the name of the seductive Jade Hare, such details as the "Downy Hill" (*Mao-ying shan*) and the "short staff" (*tuan-kun*) corroborate the impression of sexual innuendo (see above, n. 112). Ch'en Shih-pin, in chapter 94 (949), sees in this episode hints of "southern-style" (*nan-feng* 南風) love—that is, homosexuality—as does "Li Cho-wu," 95 (13b). Other comments by Ch'en Shih-pin bring in a variety of other concepts of Ming sexual lore; e.g., 18 (191) 23 (241): "seizing the Yin to replenish the Yang" (*ts'ai-yin pu-yang* 採陰補陽); 54 (548f.), 60 (609): "the external wife and the internal wife" 身外之妻,

Once again, we could read these sections as straightforward parables of resistance to the temptations of the flesh, or perhaps as sarcastic digs at the proverbial lust burning beneath the robes of Buddhist monks. But within the context of the allegorical framework set up in the book, it may be more useful to relate this theme to several other philosophical issues.

One of these is the problem of emotional attachment, in a broader sense than sexual desire alone.[196] There are a number of episodes in which it is the compassionate nature of the Master, more than anything else, that leads him into extreme peril. The notion of emotional attachment as a block to enlightenment, even when this attachment is essentially chaste, is emphasized by many of the commentators as one of the principal obstacles on the path to salvation. Chang Shu-shen, for example, frequently brings in the Confucian concept of "material desire" (*wu-yü* 物慾) as a gloss on these passages.[197] The "Li Cho-wu" commentator, on the other hand, draws upon the more specifically Buddhist idea of the "net of desire" (*yü-wang* 慾網) to explain this entanglement of consciousness.[198] In this context, the author's insistent use of the image of greedy eyes to bring out the illusory nature of sexual experience marks another point of common understanding that links *Hsi-yu chi* to *Chin P'ing Mei*.[199]

A somewhat different side of this theme comes out in those scenes in which it is not sexuality per se but rather its tendency to throw off the equilibrium of the self that is at issue. This idea refers primarily to the disorientation of individual consciousness—the crucial problem of "losing oneself in sensuality" (*mi-se* 迷色), which I have discussed in the chapter on *Chin P'ing Mei*—that is conveyed in the text with such terms as the "disorder of the mind" (*luan-hsin* 亂心), the "disturbing of the mind" (*tung-hsin* 動心), and "forgetting one's basic nature" (*wang-pen* 忘本), all of which

---

身內之妻; 78 (796), 80 (815), 92 (929), 93 (939), 95 (960). Wang Hsiang-hsü notes the preponderance of female demons in a comment in chapter 23 (2a), repeated in chapter 82 (1a); and a similar idea is found in "Li Cho-wu," chapter 82 (13b, 15b). See also *T'ung-i cheng-chih*, 37 (67b), 55 (51b); Ts'ai Yüan-fang, *tu-fa*, item 28.

[196] The most obvious examples of such emotional vulnerability appear in the recurrent scenes of demons masquerading as damsels (or babes) in distress; e.g., chapters 27, 33, 40, 64, 80. Cf. *Tsa-chü*, Scenes 10 and 12. See Ch'en Shih-pin comments in chapters 27 (281) and 62 (629).

[197] See examples in chapters 16 (10a), 18 (13b, 14a), 27 (1b), 31 (17b), 32 (1b), 33 (3b, 5b, 8a), 37 (1a, 4b, 16a), 40 (2a), 44 (1a, 16b), 71 (1a), 73 (14b), 79 (14b), 91 (1a), 95 (1a), 98 (1a); and *Tsung-p'i*, 10 (4a), 21 (6a), 23 (6b), 26 (7a), 42 (11a, b), 56 (15b), 58 (15b), 59 (15b, 16a), 60 (16b), 65 (18a). See also Wang Hsiang-hsü, 72 (1a–b); Ch'en Shih-pin, 71 (725), 72 (734f.); and *T'ung-i cheng-chih*, 21 (9b).

[198] "Li Cho-wu," chapter 74 (16a).

[199] See above, Chapter 2, Part V. Chang Shu-shen discusses this issue in chapters 72 (1a) and 80 (1a). Once again, we find a striking analogue in Spenser's allegorical epic (e.g., Book II, Canto XII, 69, 73, 78).

I will reconsider later.[200] Both chapters 23 and 72, for example, are unmistakably captioned with labels of similar import, and expressions of the same idea are abundant in the episode of the Lady of the Earthly Wellsprings (Ti-yung fu-jen) in chapters 81–83.[201] Here, by the way, we have another example of a narrative figure that had already appeared within the sources of the novel, now being singled out by the author for special treatment within his own allegorical framework.[202]

The same can be said for the inverted sexuality in the Country of Women at Hsi-liang in chapters 54 and 55, which also appears in one form or another in most of the narratives of the Hsüan-tsang cycle, even in the records of the historical monk's journey to the West. But here it is invested with a heightened allegorical function in exploring the problem of sexual disequilibrium.[203] Of particular interest in this regard is the application to certain figures in the novel of the term "lovely maiden" (*ch'a-nü*). In view of the association of this metaphor with late Ming Taoist alchemical and sexual cults, it is hard to avoid the conclusion that the insertion of such terms as these reflects a kind of backlash reaction to sixteenth-century literalist excesses in this area. Ch'en Shih-pin makes a strong statement of this view in a comment in chapter 54:

> ... granted, the process of becoming an immortal or a Buddha is inextricably linked to the Way of sexual generation, but this is not talking about union of the flesh giving free run to one's desire, only a spiritual union. ...
>
> …成仙作佛雖不能離男女化生之道, 第非形交而順其所欲, 乃神交…
>
> ....[204]

[200] See, e.g., chapters 23 (1:311), 27 (1:373), 64 (2:888), 94 (3:1270). See comments by "Li Cho-wu," 72 (14a); Wang Hsiang-hsü, 23 (1b), 27 (1a), 54 (1b), 56 (1a), 59 (1b), 70 (1a), 72 (1a, 1b), 80 (1b); Ch'en Shih-pin, 81 (823ff.), and *Chia-p'i Hsi-yu chi*, 1 (12a), 3 (11a, 22a, 22b), 4 (6b, 7b, 8a, 9b, 14a, 14b, 15a, 15b, 16a), 8 (13b), 10 (7b, 8a, 10a, 13a). This aspect of the allegory is discussed by C. T. Hsia (*Classic Novel*, 155ff.); James Fu (*Quest*, 24ff., 37, 41ff.); Liu Ts'un-yan ("Wu Ch'eng-en," pp. 82ff.); Wu Pi-yung, "Hsi-yu chi yen-chiu," pp. 51ff., Hsü Chen-chi, "Pa-shih-i nan," pp. 23f., 32f.

[201] See Ts'ai Yüan-fang, *tu-fa*, items 26, 27, 28, 35.

[202] See above, n. 111, and Chang Ching-erh, "Monkey-hero," pp. 215ff.

[203] Earlier versions of the Land of Women can be seen in the Nü-erh kuo of the *Shih-hua*, section 10; in the *Tsa-chü*, Scenes 13, 14, 15, 17, 18, 19; and in the *Pak t'ongsa ŏnhae* (see Dudbridge, *Hsi-yu chi*, p. 74). For an example in the quasi-historical accounts of Hsüan-tsang's journey, see Dudbridge, *Hsi-yu chi*, pp. 13f. I might add to this the later reworking of the Land of Women *topos* in *Ching-hua yüan*, chapters 32–34. A similar example is the Iron Fan Princess (T'ieh-shan kung-chu), who appears in the *Tsa-chü*, Scenes 17 and 18, and in the *Nan-yu chi* section of *Ssu-yu chi*, among other places. See Ch'en Yü-p'i, "Kuo Huo-yen shan." Here it is clearly the problem of "flames of desire" (*yü-huo* 慾火) that is at issue in this figure.

[204] On Ming sexual practices, see Liu Ts'un-yan, "Taoist Self-cultivation," pp. 292ff.; R. H. Van Gulik, *Sexual Life in Ancient China*, esp. pp. 263–336, 339–59; and R. K.

Perhaps the reason the issue of sexuality occupies so much of the allegory is that it covers virtually all of the aspects of the unenlightened consciousness treated in the text: loss of inner calm, disproportionate emphasis on individual fulfillment, and disruption of concentration. In many of the allegorical obstacles outlined above, we can see that the various problems of consciousness reduce themselves to a failure or block-age of vision. Sometimes this is dramatized in the blindness of the pilgrims to the presence of real dangers, or their refusal to heed warnings and injunctions. It is certainly significant that Sun Wu-k'ung is depicted as a bearer of superior visual perception, an attribute included in the initial description of the Monkey King in chapter 1. But in his case as well, the author insists on including examples in which his eyes are also subject to malfunction—especially due to the effects of the smoke from "demonic fire." [205]

At other times, this failure of perception is presented as the result of deliberate subterfuge on the part of hostile creatures. Thus, we have epi-sodes constructed around the idea of the false masquerading as the true, or alternatively, a confusion between true and false versions of various things: weapons, pilgrims, temples. [206] If we take this in a looser sense, then the majority of episodes involve some form of impersonation or mis-representation. In the majority of cases, the state of blocked vision culmi-nates in the concealment of the demon within a locked enclosure, from which it is made to emerge only when it is forced to "reveal its true form" (*hsien pen-hsiang* 現本相). [207]

This brings us to a final category of philosophical problems confronting our seekers of scriptural truth in the form of implacable demons along their path. Just as in practically every episode the demons eventually shut them-selves up in a mountain cave, underwater lair, or some such, in a majority of these cases these same demons attempt to subdue the pilgrims by encompassing them within one or another kind of enclosing object. These "weapons" range from actual metal rings or snares to a variety of rather whimsical variations on the theme: gourds, vases, girdles, even bronze bells

---

McMahon, "The Gap in the Wall," for fuller discussion of the literary significance of these associations. See comments by Ch'en Shih-pin, especially 34 (353), 47 (478), 54 (548f), 78 (796), 92 (929). I will reconsider the significance of the term *ch'a-nü* later.

[205] Instances of smoke damage to the eyes of Sun Wu-k'ung occur in chapters 5, 20, 41, 75.

[206] For examples in which the pilgrims are temporarily confounded by false weapons, or by false demons masquerading as true souls, see Part II of this chapter. See comments by "Li Cho-wu" in chapters 57 (14a) and 65 (14a); Wang Hsiang-hsü, 21 (1a), 23 (5a), 39 (1b), 51 (1a), 53 (1a), 57 (1b), 66 (1a), 80 (1a), 93 (8b), 97 (1b); Chang Shu-shen, 27 (1a), 39 (16a), 42 (4a), 58 (13a–b), 85 (1b), 91 (1a); Liu I-ming, *tu-fa*, item 25; Ts'ai Yüan-fang, *tu-fa*, items 25, 26; and Ch'en Shih-pin, 13 (146), 34 (352), 65 (662f), 66 (672), 92 (929) 95 (959f.).

[207] For discussion of this pattern, see remainder of this chapter.

or the hemisphere of a brass cymbal.[208] In view of the ingenuity exercised in developing this pattern, it is evident that the author has more in mind here than simply an original arsenal of outlandish kinds of weapons. At several points it is strongly suggested that the image of entrapment carries a special burden of meaning, as the commentators often point out.[209] For example, one of the clearest uses of this type of image is found in chapter 33, where it is another "vase of purification" (*ching-p'ing*)—this time not Kuan-yin's vase containing healing waters, but one capable of "swallowing up the entire world" (*chuang-t'ien* 裝天)—that threatens to engulf and annihilate the pilgrims by reducing them to a few drops of pus. Only by being able to counter the symbolic import of these encompassing devices can the pilgrims escape the prospect of extinction. The question of how this impossible task is to be accomplished will occupy us shortly.

Having reviewed some of the obstacles barring the path to salvation through the cultivation of the mind, let us now move on to the manner in which our pilgrims confront and surmount these barriers in the course of their allegorical quest. First, we must reconsider the overall direction and pace of the journey taking shape in the narrative. As already outlined, the majority of the extended episodes that make up the text fall into a recurrent pattern of development: we begin with our happy pilgrims on the road, buoyant and satisfied with themselves for having overcome their preceding ordeal, only to find their equanimity disturbed by cold, hunger, or discomforts of some other sort. Out of this ruffling of consciousness emerges

[208] See the following examples: a red gourd in chapters 22 (1:303) and 33 (2:460); various sorts of sacks: *ta-lien* 褡褳 in chapter 25 (1:343), *ju-i p'i-tai* 如意皮袋 in chapter 41 (2:574), *jen-chung tai* 人種袋 in chapters 65 and 66 (2:917); a bell (*chin-ling* 金鈴) in chapter 70 (3:973); a metal cymbal (*chin-nao* 金鐃) in chapter 65; variously shaped bottles (especially the *ching-p'ing*) in chapters 12 (1:165), 26 (1:360), 33 (2:455), 42 (2:584), 74 (3:1030) (see following note); a snare in chapters 6 (1:74), 34 (2:469), 50 (2:696), 52 (2:721), 59 (2:826); a box in chapter 84 (3:1153). We may also consider the web spun out by spider demons to ensnare the pilgrims in chapters 72 and 74; and attempts to spin them (*chüan* 捲) into their mouths or snort them into their noses in chapters 41 (2:579), 74 (3:1029), 77 (3:1063) as variations on the same concept.

[209] Ch'en Shih-pin puts his finger on this range of meaning in chapter 35 (362): "... Is not [enlightenment] a matter of man's mind being able to encompass what is beyond heaven and earth? But people always [fall into] the 'gourd that engulfs heaven and earth'" 非心包天地 之外乎, 人固有裝天地之葫蘆也; and chapter 51 (519): "... but his vision could not yet penetrate to the entire ground of being, and so he ultimately failed to extricate himself from the snare" 未能洞見全體, 而終難脫彼圈套也. See also comments by "Li Cho-wu" 5 (6b), 6 (13b), 33 (15b); Ch'en Shih-pin, 6 (69), 26 (273), 33 (341ff.), 41 (417), 42 (426f.), 49 (498), 53 (538). 65 (663), 75 (763); Chang Shu-shen, 34 (16b); Ts'ai Yüan-fang, *tu-fa*, item 32; and Wang Hsiang-hsü, 42 (1a), 50 (1a), 53 (1a), 71 (1a), 75 (1a). In chapter 75 (1a), Wang Hsiang-hsü compares the various weapons of this sort. See additional comments by Wang, 35 (1a), 52 (1a), 65 (1a); *Chia-p'i Hsi-yu chi*, 1 (19a), 5 (4a), 7 (5a), 10 (6a), 11 (1a); and *T'ung-i cheng-chih*, 74 (42a).

a demon, who after one or repeated attempts manages by stealth or sheer force to snatch the Master and perhaps other pilgrims away from their protective circle and entrap them in a secluded lair. Sun Wu-k'ung, who is usually not among those initially captured, employs his powers of vision (or the help of others) to locate the prisoners, but fails in his initial attempts to break through the spell. In most cases it is only after he seeks external aid—the bestowal of either a secret formula or a magic weapon, or the direct intervention of powers of salvation—that the demon is finally subdued: its true form revealed, and the thralldom dispelled, leaving the pilgrims free to continue on their way until the quick emergence of the next peril.

Within the predictability of this general pattern over the course of the narrative as a whole, a number of significant variations arise along the way.[210] First, in view of the pains taken by the author to undercut the basic concept and the necessity of the unilinear quest journey as a whole, it is difficult to grasp what is intended by the precise sequence of episodes within the overall framework of the allegorical circuit. It would be helpful if we could discern some sort of logical progression, a step-by-step ladder of ascents to be serially mounted on the path to enlightenment. This is precisely what the commentators attempt to do in numerous discussions. For example, Wang Hsiang-hsü explains the fording of the River of Communion with Heaven (*T'ung-t'ien ho*) crossed with help in chapter 49, on the heels of the figurally similar river crossing at the River of Black Waters (*Hei-shui ho*) in chapter 43, as follows:

> Having eliminated the heterodox Taoists and passed through the Double Pass (*shuang-kuan* 雙關), the true waters of the individual self can now merge unassisted with those of the universe.
> 外道已除, 雙關已過, 則吾身眞水自可通天.[211]

This type of reading, however, is rarely more than locally convincing. I may put the argument on slightly firmer ground by trying to show that certain types of spiritual progress are emphasized at different points as the journey inches toward its destination. I have observed the fact that the author seems to take up the problem of sexuality in greater earnest in the

---

[210] This generalized pattern describes most accurately the following episodes: 27–31, 32–35, 40–43, 50–52, 56–58, 59–61, 65–66, 72–73, 74–77, and 80–83. Of course, every one of the other episodes presents at least one or more of these elements. Cf. Wang Hsiang-hsü's discussion of the transition from one trial to another in chapter 83 (1a): "No sooner do they extricate themselves than they become ensnared once again" 脫而復陷.

[211] Wang Hsiang-hsü, chapter 47 (1a). See also chapters 43 (1a, b), 44 (1b), 59 (1a), and 80 (1b). See also Ch'en Shih-pin, chapters 16 (177), 24 (251), 53 (538), 62 (629), 68 (692), 80 (814), 91 (920), 94 (949), 96 (968); Chang Shu-shen, chapter 47 (15b); and *T'ung-i cheng-chih*, 26 (60b), 55 (51b), 77 (77b), 88 (83b, 84a), 95 (49a, b).

second half of the book, and I will argue that there is a noticeable rise in the degree of integration of the pilgrim group as they move into the final phases of their mission.[212] But for all this, we cannot really say that the pilgrimage progresses steadily toward the goal of perfect attainment. Quite the contrary, we are given abundant evidence of backsliding late in the novel: the old rivalry between Sun Wu-k'ung and Chu Pa-chieh surfaces as late as chapter 85, and despite all his accumulated experience in the paths of salvation, Hsüan-tsang is just as nervous and hesitant as ever even as he is forcibly ferried to the other shore. Perhaps more serious, we witness the most troubling undermining of Hsüan-tsang's impenetrable resistance to temptation on the very edges of enlightenment, in the incidents of Ti-yung fu-jen and the Jade Hare.

The question of whether the fulfillment of the quest is to be viewed as a cumulative process of attainment or an instantaneous flash of deliverance conforms precisely to the perennial issue of sudden versus gradual enlightenment in Chinese Buddhist philosophy. From the point of view of this issue, the fact that the apparent progress of the pilgrimage is subverted by the persistence of the same obstacles at the very end as at the beginning gives rise to the idea that the illusion of progress may itself be the greatest impediment to ultimate attainment. At least this idea would help us to understand the not overly hidden point, made fairly explicit in the novel, that the goal of the quest lies in the path itself, not in the prize of dubious scriptures waiting at the end of the road. The most recent commentator on the novel, Ch'en Tun-fu, aptly expresses this point within his otherwise idiosyncratic reading, when he glosses the term "scriptures" (*ching* 經) as "the path" (*ching* 徑).[213]

In any event, the author's allegorical reflection of this question does not seem to be unequivocal; or, at least, the traditional commentators find much room for disagreement on the point. The "Li Cho-wu" commentator, for one, denies the value of sequential stages and insists that ultimate enlightenment must be instantaneous:

> [Enlightenment] certainly does not reside in [progress] from beginning
> to end; it is a matter of a single instant. 豈居前後, 悟即刹那.[214]

[212] See below in this chapter for further discussion. The sense of gradual spiritual progress through the course of the journey is discussed by Chang Ching-erh, "Structure and Theme," p. 177; and James Fu, *Quest*, p. 29. For example, the chain of figurally linked occurrences staked out by chapters 16, 27, 57, and 97 shows a clear "improvement" of sorts from wrathful destruction to more merciful subdual of the allegorical "thieves" of the senses. Cf. Chang Shu-shen's invocation, in chapter 99 (1b), of the Confucian metaphor of "the last basketful of earth" needed to raise a mound (*wei shan wei ch'eng i-k'uei* 爲山未成一簣). See *Lun Yü*, IX:19.

[213] Ch'en Tun-fu, *Shih-i*, p. 2. Some of the early commentators give the same gloss.

[214] "Li Cho-wu," chapter 29 (1a). He expresses a similar idea in chapter 90 (14a).

Those commentators who advocate a more strictly Taoist reading of the allegorical quest tend to favor the idea of gradual attainment. As Ts'ai Yüan-fang astutely observes, instantaneous enlightenment makes enough sense in Buddhist thought, but within Taoist learning the idea of final attainment is predicated on a slow process of cultivation.[215] Ch'en Shih-pin, with his characteristic breadth of vision, allows that both aspects may be necessary: the steady advance of cultivation on the one hand, and the quantum leaps of illumination on the other.[216]

Another side of the same question comes out in the apparent contradiction between the promise of attainment through one's own efforts, and salvation bestowed by the grace of external forces, what in Buddhist thought is often expressed in terms of salvation "through one's own powers" (*tzu-li*) and that brought about "by virtue of the power of others" (*t'a-li*). Within the province of Neo-Confucian thought, and perhaps within Taoism as well, we find a similar debate on the extent to which the Mencian dictum of "every man a sage" may be interpreted literally.[217] On the face of it, the novel provides a very significant role for the principle of externally bestowed salvation. After reciting parables of salvation in both prologue sections, the narrative presents a chain of episodes in which deliverance from allegorical perils is effected only through the intervention of divine beings, especially the bodhisattva Kuan-yin, leading up to the final granting of the long-sought scriptures by the Buddha himself in chapter 98.[218]

[215] Ts'ai Yüan-fang, *tu-fa*, item 7: "In Buddhism there are both types, sudden and gradual, but in Taoist attainment there is only the gradual kind, not the sudden" 佛教有頓漸兩樣, 道教工夫只有漸而無頓.

[216] See chapter 98 (996): "That is to say, the wordless [scriptures] represent sudden attainment and those with words represent the gradual way. The sudden way is without deliberate effort and the gradual way takes deliberate effort. To proceed from the gradual to the sudden, from the deliberate to the nondeliberate, is the path of the true scriptures" 蓋無字爲頓法, 有字爲漸法, 頓爲無爲, 漸爲有爲, 由漸而頓, 由有爲而無爲, 皆眞經也. See also chapter 100 (1015): "Although there is a distinction between gradual and sudden, between ease and effort, respectively, in attainment they are united" 雖各有漸頓安勉之殊, 而成功則一.

[217] Chang Shu-shen addresses the issue of "every man a sage" with a bit of sarcasm in chapter 18 (1a), and more seriously in chapter 100 (16a–b). "Li Cho-wu," with his characteristic wit, mocks the mass-produced sages in a comment in chapter 41 (3b): "What a lot of sages! It's just like those people who expound on 'innate knowledge'; no sooner do they get to the lecture hall than they start calling themselves 'great sage'" 何聖人之多也極衆, 講致良知者, 一入講堂便稱大聖人矣.

[218] For example, soteriological intervention is required in chapters 7, 14, 17, 21, 22, 26, 31, 35, 39, 42, 43, 49, 52, 55, 58, 61, 66, 69, 71, 73, 77, 83, 87, 90, 92, and 95. The deus ex machina is Kuan-yin in chapters 14, 17, 21, 26, 42, 49, 55, 58, and 71. We may recall, of course, that it is Kuan-yin who initiates the quest journey in the first place. Wang Hsiang-hsü, in chapter 49 (1a), compares the various instances of divine intervention, distinguishing between instances in which Kuan-yin comes herself and those in which she sends an agent,

The other side of this coin is the inability of Sun Wu-k'ung to work his own salvation, as Wang Hsiang-hsü observes in chapter 52.[219] This point is of importance here not only because the frustration of the self-generated attainment of the Monkey King is the obvious message of the expanded prologue, but also because this reduction in his heroic stature from that which he enjoys in the popular tradition reminds us of the focus on the limitations of individual potential in all the literati novels, a pattern I will appeal to again in my discussions of *San-kuo chih yen-i* and *Shui-hu chuan*.[220]

In any event, we may note here several additional variables of major importance in the process of effecting the mode of salvation allegorized in the *Hsi-yu chi*. First I would distinguish between those episodes that culminate in a titanic clash—related with all the narrative flourish the author can bring to bear, and leading to the physical destruction of the demons, or at least their defeat in formal debate or some other contest,[221] and those in which the pilgrims simply escape by sneaking away in the dead of night. This distinction is conceptually related to the contrast between those scenes in which the final submission of a demon leads to the recall of the wayward creature by a divine master, and by contrast those that require the uncompromising destruction of the demons, their abodes, and all the creatures in their train.[222] The significance of this latter alternative is suggested in the frequent use of the expression "to remove the weeds one must eliminate the roots" (*chan-ts'ao ch'u-ken*). This extreme solution is called for most consistently in the episodes involving threats of a sexual

---

and between those in which her assistance is sought and those in which she appears unbidden. See also comments by Ts'ai Yüan-fang, *tu-fa*, items 28, 45. Ironically, the very first assault on the full pilgrim band occurs at a "Temple of Kuan-yin." The role of the various savior figures is discussed by Hu Shih ("K'ao-cheng," p. 367); Anthony Yu ("Pilgrimage," p. 221); and Hsü Chen-chi ("Pa-shih-i nan," pp. 141ff.).

[219] Wang Hsiang-hsü, chapter 52 (1a): "Sun Wu-k'ung's ... wits and powers were both exhausted, he had no choice but to seek a savior" 行者…智力俱竭, 勢不得不尋主人公矣.

[220] On the recurrent theme of the limitations of heroic capacity, see below, Chapters 4, Part IV, and 5, Part IV. See also Chang Ching-erh, "Monkey-hero," pp. 561ff., 572ff.

[221] Full-scale pitched battles (aside from the titanic struggles of the prologue section) are staged in chapters 17, 19, 20, 22, 25, 29, 31, 34, 35, 37, 39, 41, 42, 43, 48, 50, 51, 52, 53, 55, 57, 58, 59, 60, 61, 63, 65, 66, 67, 70, 71, 72, 73, 76, 81, 83, 85, 86, 89, 91, 92, 95. The struggle takes the form of a debate in chapters 64 and 78, and a contest of magical arts in chapters 35, 45, 46, 66, 69, 75, 84, 87, 97. In chapters 92 and 95 the pilgrims sneak away after subduing their foes, a pattern repeated at the last stop on their journey in chapter 99.

[222] The wayward demons are recalled to their prior estate in chapters 31, 35, 39, 42, 43, 46, 49, 52, 61, 64, 66, 71, 77, 79, 83, and 90. They are mercilessly destroyed in chapters 55, 58, 72, 73, 74, 79, 89, and 92. See comments by Wang Hsiang-hsü, 63 (1b); Ch'en Tun-fu, *Shih-i*, p. 983; and in *T'ung-i cheng-chih*, 92 (18b).

nature, which we have seen to stand out particularly in the second half of the book.[223]

Perhaps the most bizarre means of overcoming the demons—yet apparently one very dear to the author—is found in those numerous episodes in which the monster must be subdued not by a frontal assault but, in one way or another, *from the inside*. This is in a sense the other side of the coin of encompassment and self-enclosure considered earlier. This pattern is worked out in many different forms, often showing considerable imagination. In chapter 17, for example, it is in the guise of a cinnabar pill that Sun Wu-k'ung manages to penetrate one demon's defenses; and in chapter 82 he first tries, unsuccessfully, to enter his enemy in the froth of a cup of wine, and later gains access in the form of a luscious peach.[224] One of the most fully articulated examples of this type is presented in the episode at the Little Thunderclap Temple (*Hsiao Lei-yin ssu* 小雷音寺) in chapters 65 and 66. In this episode Sun Wu-k'ung is first entrapped under the edge of a brass cymbal (*chin-nao*), from which he escapes by borrowing out with the aid of a dragon's horn, only to be "bagged" once again in the girdle (*ta-pao-erh*) of the demon. Eventually the spell of encompassment is broken, not by enclosing the demon with another bag, but rather by getting inside him, this time in the form of a juicy melon.[225] This game of outwitting the engulfing power of demonic forces seems also to be behind another conceptually related pattern, in those cases in which the secret of subduing the hostile creature lies in tricking him into identifying himself, as if, by defi-

[223] For example, the following episodes conclude with the total annihilation of the offending demons: Ch'e-ch'ih kuo (chapter 46), Hsi-liang nü-kuo (chapter 55), Six-eared Ape (chapter 58), python demon (chapter 67), spider demons (chapter 73), Mieh-fa kuo (chapter 86). See also chapters 64, 79, and 92. Notable exceptions include chapters 83 and 95, both instances of sexual assault ending with the recall of a wayward temptress to her prior state. The expression *chan-ts'ao ch'u-ken* may be susceptible to more than one interpretation: "to mow down the weeds and then dig up the roots" or "in order to get rid of the weeds, you must first remove the roots." This common term is also used in various antecedents, e.g., the *Shih-hua*, section 6; the *Tsa-chü*, Scene 2; and at a number of points in *Tung-t'ien hsüan-chi*.

[224] The commentators find this imagery interesting. See Ch'en Shih-pin, 4 (44), 22 (230), 39 (396), 59 (599), 82 (835), 83 (844), and *Chia-p'i Hsi-yu chi*, 8 (6b); Wang Hsiang-hsü, 75 (1b); Ts'ai Yüan-fang, *tu-fa*, items 30, 33, 34; and *T'ung-i cheng-chih*, 17 (75a), 39 (85b), 64 (38b), 83 (21b). See also Ch'en Tun-fu, *Shih-i*, p. 917. Sun Wu-k'ung transforms himself into the following tiny creatures to penetrate his enemies' defenses: bee, 16, 55, 78, 94; gnat, 32, 59; flea, 49; louse, 71; fly, 34, 41, 51, 70, 72, 75, 82; firefly, 92; ant, 86; butterfly, 89.

[225] Chapter 66 (2:917f.). The same pattern is again driven home in the later episode in which the python demon is also subdued by means of a *bellum intestinum*. Cf. the traditional symbolic significance attached to the melon image, similar to that of the *hulu* gourd (e.g., chapters 32–35) endowed with power to encompass the universe (*chuang-t'ien*). See N. J. Girardot, *Myth and Meaning in Early Taoism*, for further discussion of gourd symbolism in China.

ning its own being, the force is reduced to the vulnerable proportions of a finite self.[226]

All of these examples provide important counterweights to the simple saving grace bestowed upon the pilgrims in some of the episodes, since here the question of confronting and overcoming the demonic power is clearly more conceptual than physical. In the last few examples cited, what we witness is an abstract form of solution to the problem of self-enclosure, whereby the encompassing force is neutralized not by the expansion, but by the contraction of the bounds of selfhood.

This brings us back to the original focus of the reading of the allegory of *Hsi-yu chi* as essentially a *psychomachia* of the process of the cultivation of the mind as construed by sixteenth-century thinkers. Having reviewed some of the principal obstacles to this process and the means of overcoming them, as presented through the medium of allegorical narrative, we can now reconsider these same issues in terms of the problems and their solutions at the level of individual consciousness. A careful reading of the novel now establishes that there is much more to it than a set of Taoist terms imposed on a Buddhist fable; that it is heavily charged with the language of syncretic *hsin-hsüeh*, which substantially conditions the meaning of its allegorical figures. This philosophical language both redefines the problems raised in the allegorical journey and suggests possible solutions in terms of various conceptualizations of the cultivation of the mind.

The most immediately obvious of these formulations is seen in the use of the notion of the "lost mind" (*fang-hsin*), which is very pointedly programmed into two key episodes, in chapters 27–31 and again in chapters 56–58. In each of these cases, the mind-monkey is "let go" (literally, "exiled," in the harsher meaning of the same word, *fang*). And in both incidents, the crisis resulting from the ensuing state of "mindlessness" raises the same theoretical problem of consciousness: the loss of unitary focus due to conflicting claims of compassion—in this case misguided—and pride. The contrived design of the two scenes leaves little room for doubt that what is intended is an allegorical exemplum of the Neo-Confucian concept of mind cultivation, based on Mencius's definition of true "learning" (*hsüeh-wen* 學問) as "seeking the lost mind" (*ch'iu ch'i fang hsin* 求其放心).[227]

---

[226] This divulging of identity is a more pointed manifestation of the revealing of one's true form (*hsien pen-hsiang*). The most explicit example occurs in chapter 58, where a "demon-reflecting mirror" (*chao-yao ching* 照妖鏡) brings to light the slippery identity of the Six-eared Ape. Of course, this may also be recognized as a common folktale motif. See comments by Wang Hsiang-hsü, 42 (1b), 58 (1b), 73 (1a), 77 (1a).

[227] Mencius, VI:A:10a (*Ssu-shu chi-chu*, pp. 168f.). The pun based on the two levels of meaning of *fang-hsin* is used for humorous effect in chapters 27 (1:375) and 56 (2:776), and perhaps also in chapter 23 (2:314). Other pointed occurrences of the expression are found in chapters 14 (1:190), 28 (1:381), 32 (2:437), 48 (2:671), 49 (2:681), 54 (2:754), 55 (2:769), 56–58 (2:776–88), 67 (3:921), 74 (3:1019–24), 83 (3:1145), 85 (3:1166), 86

This is abundantly clear from the way in which the episodes in question are developed. In the first instance, the dismissal of Sun Wu-k'ung immediately causes the band to drift apart, leaving them easy prey for the Yellow-robed Demon 黃袍怪, until they are finally forced to beg the exiled mind-monkey to return, a situation obviously conceived in terms of the original Mencian passage. When the scene is restaged in the second half of the novel, the author deepens the significance of the lost-mind state through his allegorical treatment of the problem of false identity that arises with the appearance of the false "double mind-monkey" (二心猿). In the latter case, the spectacle of the two mind-monkeys battling for supremacy further defines the problem as one of refraction of consciousness, a point driven home when we learn that it is an aptly named Six-eared Ape who is responsible for the entire disorder. Since the problem in these episodes is so canonically defined in terms of "letting the mind go," the prescribed solution consequently lies in "keeping" it (*ts'un-hsin* 存心) or else "recovering" it (*ch'iu-hsin* 求心, *shou-hsin* 收心), as the text itself specifies at a number of points.[228]

A slightly different conception of more or less the same issue surfaces in the many scenes in which the problem is the disequilibrium of the mind, the opposite of what Mencius would call the "unmoved mind" (*pu tung hsin* 不動心).[229] We can see reflections of this idea in practically every episode in which an initial state of harmony is subverted by restlessness and discomfort, giving rise to perils according to the formula cited earlier: "with the emergence of consciousness ..."[230] Typically, the "moving" of the

(3:1186), 88 (3:1206f.), 89 (3:1224), 94 (3:1287). See comments by "Li Cho-wu," 13 (6a); Chang Shu-shen, chapters 14 (17a), 19 (15a), 56 (1a–1b), 57 (8b, 14a), 58 (12b), and *Tsung-p'i*, 24 (6b); Wang Hsiang-hsü, 3 (8b), 27 (1a–2a), 30 (1a), 56 (1a, 6b); Ch'en Shih-pin, 36 (369), 56 (569); and *T'ung-i cheng-chih*, 29 (86b), 30 (99a), 31 (11b), 56 (61b). See Hsü Chen-chi, "Pa-shih-i nan," pp. 5ff., 127ff.

[228] For example, *ts'un-hsin* occurs in 74 (3:1032), 81 (3:1118), 85 (3:1166). See comments by Ch'en Shih-pin, 2 (21), 3 (35), 36 (368f.), 43 (437), 56 (568); Wang Hsiang-hsü, 3 (1b), 4 (5b), 14 (2a), 19 (1a), 31 (1a), 32 (1b), 57 (1a); Chang Shu-shen, 3 (1a), 14 (17a), 19 (15a), 56 (1a, 1b), 57 (8b, 14a), 58 (12b), 59 (12a), 60 (18a), 79 (14a), and *Tsung-p'i*, 24 (6b), 68 (18a); Ts'ai Yüan-fang, *tu-fa*, items 1, 15, 17; and *T'ung-i cheng-chih*, 87 (70a). These terms also occur in the *Tsa-chü*, Scenes 16 and 21.

[229] Mencius, II:A:2 (*chüan* 2, p. 36f.). The expression *tung-hsin* occurs in chapters 16 (1:215, 221), 23 (1:311), 50 (2:694), 78 (3:1084), and 82 (3:1130). See comments by Chang Shu-shen, 34 (1b), 72 (17a); Wang Hsiang-hsü, 77 (1a); and *T'ung-i cheng-chih*, 48 (90b).

[230] Chapters 13 (1:169) and 20 (1:266). "Li Cho-wu" seizes on this idea as the "basic meaning" (*tsung-chih* 宗旨) of the book; see chapter 13 (13a). See also Ch'en Shih-pin, 20 (210f.), 23 (242), 43 (437), 50 (570f.); Chang Shu-shen, 34 (1b), 51 (14b), 56 (1b), 60 (16b), 62 (1b), 92 (1b). In chapter 72 (2a, 17a) Chang applies the variation *tung-ch'ing* specifically to the problem of sexual disequilibrium. In chapter 16 (1:216–21) the expressions *fang-hsin*, *tung-hsin*, *tu-hsin* 毒心, and *pu hsiao-hsin* 不小心 are introduced in rapid succession. See also *Tsa-chü*, Scene 21.

heart takes the form of wrath, from the peevish outbursts that prompt Hsüan-tsang to "lose his mind" in the "exile" scenes, to the unbridled fury personified in the Red Child (Hung-hai-erh), with his blazing carts and other iconographic emblems of rage.[231] The traditional association between the heart as a bodily organ and the element fire, as allegorized in the figure of the monkey-pilgrim with his alternate connections to fire and metal symbolism, helps to account for a good deal of this sort of imagery in the novel. This covers both his general mastery of fire of the natural sort, and his vulnerability to "demonic" fire (*hsieh-huo* 邪火) blazing out of control, allegorically presented in the two linked episodes of the Red Child and the Iron Fan Princess, as well as in several other incidents in the narrative.[232]

At the same time, similar associations are evoked through various uses of the wind motif, taking in both the relatively benign gusts (*hsün-feng* 巽風) harnessed by the Monkey King and the blustery squalls summoned up by various demons, many of whose names refer specifically to demonic winds.[233] In a word, what I believe is suggested by all this huffing and puffing is the notion of "disorder of the mind" (*luan-hsin*), already familiar to us from the chaos at the heart of the *Chin P'ing Mei*.[234] The obvious antidote to the poison of unbridled consciousness is a cooling of psychic energy. This is precisely the idea behind the central metaphor of the novel's conception: the "stilling" of the mind-monkey (*ting hsin-yüan*

[231] The figure of Hung-hai-erh reminds me of Spenser's icon of Wrath in Book I, Canto IV: 33, and also his Pyrochles (Book II, Cantos IV–VI) whose famous line "I burne, I burne, I burne" (VI: 44) could well have been uttered by Hung-hai-erh.

[232] The allegorical significance that underlies the figure of Hung-hai-erh is brought out again in the episode of his parents at Huo-yen shan, where it is also supported by the identification of the element fire with the heart; see chapter 61 (855). See Wang Hsiang-hsü, 4 (1b), 25 (1a); "Li Cho-wu," 41 (1a), 42 (3a, 7b), 56 (15b), 59 (15a). On the discrepancy of the five-elements assignment of Sun Wu-k'ung to both metal and fire, see "Li Cho-wu," 41 (16a); Wang Hsiang-hsü, 59 (1b), 62 (1a), 70 (1a); Ch'en Shih-pin, 17 (184f.), 41 (415ff.); Chang Shu-shen, 60 (16b, 17a); *T'ung-i cheng-chih*, 42 (20b). In a comment in chapter 40 (1a), Wang Hsiang-hsü explains that Hung-hai-erh represents "fire in its ascendancy as a single element" 一行偏至之火, whereas Sun Wu-k'ung represents "fire as the complete amalgam of all the five elements" 五行全備之火.

[233] The traditional five-elements symbolism brings into association images of autumn winds, tigers, cutting metal, and poison. Cf. the iconographic color of this quarter, white, which figures in such names as Pai-hu shan-ling and Pai-ku fu-jen. Unusual winds blow in chapters 16, 18, 20, 28, 38, 40, 43, 44, 47, 49, 54, 58, 59, 61, 63, 64, 67, 68, 69, 75, 78, 81, 85, 91, 98; tigers appear in chapters 13, 14, 20, 27, 29, 34, 36. See comments by Wang Hsiang-hsü, 13 (1a), 68 (1a), 73 (1a); and Ch'en Shih-pin, 13 (146), 14 (158), 15 (166), 21 (219), 56 (569).

[234] See above, Chapter 2, Part VI. The idea of *luan-hsin* is emphasized in comments by Wang Hsiang-hsü, 23 (1b), 24 (1b); *T'ung-i cheng-chih*, 62 (21b), 63 (29b), 80 (1b); Ch'en Shih-pin, 28 (289), 40 (407), 50 (511); and Ts'ai Yüan-fang, *tu-fa*, item 36.

定心猿).[235] Not only does this conception represent a pointedly stressed reversal of the adapted metaphor of the mind-monkey, with its own long history in various literary sources, but it also informs the structural design of the novel whereby the unprecedentedly extended prologue treatment of the insurrection of the mind-monkey precedes his subdual and harnessing, without which the quest journey could not even get under way.

Aside from the prominently signposted instance of stilling the mind-monkey in chapter 7, the term *ting-hsin* does not occur often in the novel. But other expressions containing the character *ting* recur throughout the text, the most important among them being "stilling one's nature" (*ting-hsing* 定性), substituting for *hsin* (心) the term *hsing* (性), which we have seen above to be so closely linked as to become nearly interchangeable in many contexts. And once this nexus of meaning has been established, then such details as Sun Wu-k'ung's iron cudgel made from the staff used by the Great Yü to "fix the depths" of the seas (*ting-ti* 定底), which he acquires in chapter 3 and puts to significant use in the conquest of Chu Pa-chieh in chapter 22; the "spirit-calming post" (*ting-hun chuang* 定魂桩) to which Hsüan-tsang is tied in chapter 28; and several instances of "quelling the winds" (*ting-feng* 定風)—all of these take on a more specific range of meaning.[236]

At the same time, a whole range of other terms of nearly synonymous import are used in the text and in the commentaries to convey similar ideas. These include "calming the mind" (*ning-hsin* 寧心) and "quieting the mind" (*ching-hsin* 靜心), as well as "pacifying the mind" (*an-hsin* 安心), "ordering the mind" (*chih-hsin* 治心), "subduing the mind" (*hsiang-hsin* 降心)—not to mention the terms *shou-hsin* and *ts'un-hsin* mentioned earlier.[237] This per-

---

[235] Chapter 7 (2:82). This expression, however, is not original to the hundred-chapter novel. It occurs in Scene 21 of the *Tsa-chü*, and in fact is also the title of a separate dramatic piece (see Hu Shih, "K'ao-cheng," p. 368). See Ch'en Shih-pin, 36 (368), and Wang Hsiang-hsü, 46 (1b). Wang states this even more strongly in a comment in chapter 57 (6b), when he insists that "the return of the mind-monkey back to within the passes" 心猿復進關 "completely wraps up all the hidden subtleties of the *Tao Tsang*" 括盡道藏之精蘊.

[236] Examples of the use of *ting-hsing* occur in chapters 10 (1:122f.), 16 (1:212), 31 (1:432), 36 (2:491), 45 (2:632), 50 (2:699), 59 (2:823), 60 (2:832), and 64 (2:885–87). Associated expressions include *ju-ting* 入定: 12 (1:158), 21 (1:201); *tso-ting* 坐定: 41 (2:573); *ting-feng* 定風: 21 (1:280), 59 (2:824), etc. For the epithet *ting-ti* applied to the magic staff, see chapters 3 (1:34) and 22 (1:293). For the philosophical implications of the term *ting-hsing*, see Yü Chün-fang, "Buddhists' Responses," pp. 8f., reference to Chang Tsai's "Ting-hsing shu" 定性書. See Chang Shu-shen, 21 (13a, 15a); and Ch'en Shih-pin, 3 (35), 7 (78), 36 (368), 77 (784f.).

[237] Examples include *ning-hsin*: 21 (1:285); and *ching-hsin*: 93 (3:1270). See comments by "Li Cho-wu," 4 (14a); Wang Hsiang-hsü, 4 (5b), 50 (32); Ch'en Shih-pin, 42 (426); and Chang Shu-shen, 15 (16a), 20 (14b).

sistent emphasis on the stilling of conscious energy, by the way, has special relevance in connection with the practice of "quiet-sitting" (*ching-tso* 靜坐), shared by adherents of all three of the major schools of thought in this period.

By the late Ming, however, quiet-sitting had in itself become a point of considerable controversy.[238] We may perhaps see a minor reflection of this issue in the provocative use of certain other terms in the novel. The "unmoved mind," for example, may describe an ideal state of unperturbed equilibrium of consciousness, but if by virtue of remaining stationary the mind begins to gather moss, then this state becomes something less than desirable. This is the danger of taking on a film of dust, as it were, what is expressed in Neo-Confucian language by the concept of the "beclouding of the mind" (*hsin-pi* 心蔽), understood to refer to selfish desires that block one's vision of the ultimate nature of things. I cannot cite any instances of the explicit expression of this idea in the text—although we do find plenty of associated ideas, and the commentators occasionally bring this into their discussions.[239] On the other hand, certain accepted correctives to this condition find frequent mention in the course of the narrative. One of these is the notion of "cleansing the mind" (*hsi-hsin* 洗心).[240] This is originally a Buddhist concept, but it is fully assimilated within Neo-Confucian terminology and occurs in several passages in the novel, where it often merges with the idea of the "illumination" of the mind (*ming-hsin* 明心). In chapters 36 and 64, for example, the ironic treatment of the immediate outcome of Hsüan-tsang's "illumination" in the dazzling white moonlight forces the reader to look beyond the superficial Buddhist sense of the term.[241]

Two other specific obstacles to the cultivation of the mind treated in the allegory deserve a closer look here. The first of these is the problem of duplicity and multiplicity treated earlier. We have already seen the use of the term "double-mind" (*erh-hsin* 二心) in the allegorization of this idea in

---

[238] For background discussion on the practice of "quiet-sitting," see Jen Yu-wen, "Ch'en Hsien-chang's Philosophy of the Natural," pp. 78ff.; and Rodney Taylor, "Meditation in Ming Neo-Orthodoxy," pp. 149–82. The concept is reflected in comments by Wang Hsiang-hsü, 46 (1b); Chang Shu-shen, 63 (14b); Ch'en Shih-pin, 50 (511) and 74 (754), where he refers specifically to Ch'en Hsien-chang's ideas on this subject.

[239] For example, Chang Shu-shen, 37 (1a), 78 (14b), and *Tsung-p'i*, 21 (6b), 23 (6b); "Li Cho-wu," 32 (1b); Wang Hsiang-hsü, 14 (2a). See the idea of "cleansing from dust" (*ti-kou* 滌垢) in chapter 62 (2:857).

[240] For *hsi-hsin*, see chapter 8 (1:100), 53 (2:735), 62 (2:857), 64 (2:887), 87 (3:1202). See comments by Ch'en Shih-pin, 67 (702), 72 (733f.); and Chang Shu-shen, *Tsung-p'i*, 65 (18a).

[241] These ideas are brought out in comments by Ch'en Shih-pin, chapters 19 (193), 36 (369f.). Cf. the initial discussion of *ming-hsin chien-hsing* in the Yu T'ung preface to the Ch'en Shih-pin edition. This expression also appears in Ch'en's comments in chapters 80 (814) and 94 (949). See also Chang Shu-shen, 36 (15b), and *Tsung-p'i*, 14 (5a); Wang Hsiang-hsü, 92 (1b); and Ts'ai Yüan-fang, *tu-fa*, item 8.

chapters 57 and 58.[242] And now we can add the frequent citation of the expression "multiple-minded" (*to-hsin*), taken for the most part in its humorous sense in colloquial usage to mock the excessive mindfulness of Hsüan-tsang.[243] In addition, we may perhaps catch a bit of a joke in the repeated references to the Prajnaparamita Heart Sutra by the elliptic title *To-hsin ching* (obtained by adding the final syllable of the transcription from Sanskrit to the descriptive Chinese title).[244] In at least one episode, however, the issue of multiplicity of mind is clearly worked up into an allegorical tableau. This is the scene in chapter 79 in which Sun Wu-k'ung dissects himself to reveal a large number of hearts pumping within his breast.[245] This in itself may be taken lightly, as a witty parody of Taoist side-show antics, but since this scene comes in the middle of an episode dealing with the striking imagery of the gathering of human hearts for a king's medicine prescribed by a Taoist wizard, the spectacle of Sun Wu-k'ung's multiple hearts is not entirely gratuitous.

A final set of related concepts involves spiritual disorder caused by the straying of the mind from the proper path, as expressed in such terms as "the straying of the mind" (*mi-hsin*), "stubborn attachment of the mind" (*chih-hsin* 執心), and "one-sidedness of the mind" (*p'ien-hsin* 偏心).[246] As used by both the author and the commentators, these terms refer within the context of the novel primarily to the venom of sectarian heterodoxy, the antidote for which is a return of the mind to its proper course (*cheng-hsin* 正心).[247]

[242] For discussions by the commentators, see, e.g., Wang Hsiang-hsü, 57 (1a–b), 58 (1b); "Li Cho-wu," 58 (13b); Ch'en Shih-pin, 57 (579), 58 (588f.), 59 (598); and *T'ung-i cheng-chih*, 57 (71b).

[243] For example, chapters 40 (2:550), 76 (3:1060), 79 (3:1088). See comments by Wang Hsiang-hsü, 19 (7b); and Chang Shu-shen, 20 (2a), 79 (14a). The exact opposite of *to-hsin* is the quality of *i-hsin* 一心, the "single-minded" devotion often ascribed to Sun Wu-k'ung (e.g., chapters 32 (1:437) and 58 (2:811).

[244] This version of the title of the Heart Sutra is not altogether uncommon. For example, it appears in the *Shih-hua*, sections 15, 16. This discrepancy is pointed out by Liu Ts'un-yan in "Wu Ch'eng-en," p. 84, n. 172, who cites additional examples. See also his "Ch'üan-chen chiao," pt. 3, p. 90, n. 41. The sutra is given as *Mi-to hsin-ching* in chapter 45 (2:632).

[245] This issue is taken up by Ch'en Shih-pin, 21 (221), 48 (487), 85 (867f.), 93 (939f.); Wang Hsiang-hsü, 79 (1a); and Chang Shu-shen, 74 (4b), 79 (14a), and 93 (1b), as opposed to a "reduction of mindfulness" (*kua-hsin* 寡心).

[246] These and similar terms are used in comments by "Li Cho-wu," 62 (14b), 73 (15a); Wang Hsiang-hsü, 71 (1a); Ch'en Shih-pin, 29 (299), 47 (477); Ts'ai Yüan-fang in *tu-fa*, item 29.

[247] See Wang Hsiang-hsü, 3 (1a), 15 (1a); Chang Shu-shen, 28 (14a), 36 (1a), 63 (1a), and *Tsung-p'i*, 3 (2a–b); "Li Cho-wu," 7 (12a, *tp*); Ch'en Shih-pin, *Chia-p'i Hsi-yu chi*, 1 (2a, 2b, 3b), 2 (24a, 31b), 3 (14a, 15b, 16b, 18a), 4 (24b), 8 (13a), 10 (9b, 10a, 11b, 12a), 12 (6b, 15a); Ts'ai Yüan-fang, *tu-fa*, item 36. Cf. the opposition between "the constancy of mind" (*hsin chih ch'ang* 心之常), represented by the Buddha, and the mercurial mutability of mind (*hsin chih p'ien* 心之變), symbolized by Sun Wu-k'ung's monkey nature.

In the last few pages, the focus of my discussion has turned exclusively on the idea of cultivation of the mind as the ground of the allegorical meaning of *Hsi-yu chi*. I have argued earlier, however, that the key to understanding this book has to do with the concept of an integration of the separate elements of the self within an organic whole. This apparent contradiction can be resolved easily in accordance with the Neo-Confucian concept of self-cultivation, embracing as it does both mind and body within the comprehensive boundaries of the "self." In this sense the separate terms "cultivation of the mind" (*hsiu-hsin*) and "cultivation of the physical self" (*hsiu-shen* 修身) become virtually interchangeable with reference to the conjoining of the external and internal facets of existence. Based on this understanding, we can now proceed to explore in greater detail the concept of the integration of the self presented in the allegory.

To begin, let us pay a bit more attention to the external aspect of this two-sided coin of cultivation: the harmonizing of the self within a network of human relations in society and the world at large. Although the allegory of *Hsi-yu chi* is clearly oriented toward the problems of the inner self, it is important to recognize that the other side of the picture is not entirely absent. The most obvious area in which the question of social integration arises is with respect to the pilgrimage group itself. I have observed earlier that, despite all the rivalry and contrariness that disturbs the harmonious functioning of the band right up to the end of their journey, we can still see a certain gradual improvement on this point as they proceed through the stations of their pilgrimage. Moreover, in the course of the narrative the author takes rather evident pains to manipulate his material to allow for significant contributions to the quest by each of the members of the group. Aside from Sun Wu-k'ung's central role, Chu Pa-chieh raises his rake to remove sticky obstacles or plunges into deep water to defend his comrades in chapters 22, 64, and 67; the Sand Monk brings healing water to his pregnant fellows in chapter 53; and even the dragon-horse manages to transform himself into a dancing girl and wield an unlikely weapon to save the master on one occasion in chapter 30.[248]

The fact that the author intends to make the on-again off-again spirit of cooperation among the members of the little band something more than a subject for humorous exploitation is made quite clear in his consistent application of abstract allegorical terms describing their fluctuating degree of integration. I have already discussed some of the allegorical labels used for certain instances of flagrant disunity, and in those short-lived moments when the pilgrims are reunited, their state is described with such expres-

---

[248] The dragon-horse also performs an indispensable function in the final rescue in chapter 99. See comments by Chang Shu-shen, 32 (17b), 64 (4a); Wang Hsiang-hsü, 67 (1a); and *T'ung-i cheng-chih*, 58 (76a).

sions as "the four comrades in harmonious concord" (*ssu-chung ho-ho* 四衆 和合), "with a common will and a single mind" (*ho-i t'ung-hsin* 合意同心), and "with a single mind and intense efforts" (*t'ung-hsin lu-li* 同心戮力).[249] These expressions often draw quite pointed discussions from the traditional commentators.[250]

Although these references to integral relationships apply primarily to the nuclear group adrift in the wilderness, we should also take note of certain intimations of a broader social context in the book. For one thing, the fact that the author's tale is focused exclusively on a group of monastic pilgrims does not keep him from displaying considerable interest in the realm of family ties. In fact, quite a few episodes involve specific issues of filial relationships, both in the positive ideal set up in the parable of Hsüan-tsang's rescue of his parents in chapter 9—which in a sense qualifies him for this noble mission in the first place, and in the negative examples of violations of sacred bonds, calling forth the valiant efforts of the pilgrim heroes to restore proper hierarchical order.[251]

The disordering of family relations receives its most sarcastic treatment, of course, in the episode of the Land of Women at Hsi-liang. Against this background the question of filial piety, taken in its broadest sense, seems to resonate with some of the various metaphors for attainment that I will treat later. Thus, the violation of this principle is tantamount to a denial of the subordination of the individual self to the chain of existence, as we see in the vaunt of self-procreation by the unredeemed Monkey King in chapter 1.[252] This brings the author's vision into line with one of the key problematic areas traced in my interpretation of *Chin P'ing Mei*. Chang Shu-shen may be exaggerating a bit when he puts the concept of *hsiao* (孝) at the core of his interpretation, but his argument may not be as far out of line as it first appears when he goes on to insist on the reflection of other Confucian virtues in the novel. At the least, as quite a few critics have

---

[249] See, for example, *ho-ho ssu-hsiang*, 100 (3:1362); and *t'ung-hsin lu-li*, 81 (3:1122).

[250] See, for example, Wang Hsiang-hsü, 16 (1a), 22 (1b), 27 (1b), 32 (1a); Ch'en Shih-pin, 27 (282), 59 (598), 72 (734f.); "Li Cho-wu," 50 (1b); and Chang Shu-shen, 98 (1a–b). A good discussion of this point is found in Wu Ta-yün, "T'ien-ti pu ch'üan," pp. 80–109.

[251] Cf. the issue of filiality suggested in the question of the "parentage" of various demons; e.g., Hung-hai-erh in chapters 40–42, Ti-yung fu-jen in chapter 83, or in the episode involving usurped patrimony in Ch'e-ch'ih kuo. See also the figure of the filial woodcutter in chapter 86. Cf. Chang Shu-shen's discussion in a comment in chapter 50 (1a–b). This idea is discussed by James Fu in *Quest*, pp. 26ff.

[252] See Chapter 1 (1:14). See discussion by "Li Cho-wu," 1 (14a); and *T'ung-i cheng-chih*, 12 (25b, 26a). We can perhaps detect in the presentation of the Monkey King's spontaneous generation a parody of the ideas in Chang Tsai's *Hsi-ming* 西銘. This parallels the sense of the unparented state of Hsi-men Ch'ing in *Chin P'ing Mei*, discussed above, Chapter 2, Part V.

pointed out, the number of scenes in which the pilgrims provide valuable service to other humans in need seems to be more than gratuitious, despite the problematic nature of the issue of compassion within the terms of the allegory.[253]

Having come this far in considering the human context of our allegorical fantasy, we may also take a bit more seriously certain reflections of the concrete historical frame of reference in the novel. I have observed above that the author makes somewhat more of the historical setting than he would have had to in arranging his temporal structure. For example, he introduces the tangential subject of the T'ang founder Li Shih-min not only in chapter 11, but also in chapter 39; and at various points he hints at a certain conceptual connection between the unruly arrogance of the Monkey King and other demons and the proverbial image of Wang Mang "five hundred years" earlier. The commentators do not necessarily have this in mind when they bring into their discussions analogies to a wide range of controversial historical figures from ancient times down to the Ming to make their points; but I am convinced that the author of *Hsi-yu chi* is vitally concerned with this aspect of his text.[254] If that is so, then this provides another unexpected link between this allegorical novel and our other three more mimetically grounded texts, all of which, in their different ways, are deeply enmeshed in the exploration of historical issues. Of course, I cannot really claim that the author makes very much of this dimension of meaning. Perhaps the most that can be said is that he, too, like our other authors, has learned his Four Books catechism well, and that he is therefore fully aware of the social, historical, and other interpersonal contexts that form the matrix of individual human consciousness.[255]

---

[253] The commentators treat these implications quite seriously. For example, Chang Shu-shen identifies the protective circle (*ch'üan-tzu* 圈子) in chapter 50 (1a) as symbolizing the network of ritual propriety (*li* 禮). Ch'en Shih-pin, 24 (253), associates the five elements with the five cardinal relations (*wu-lun* 五倫). See also Anthony Yu, *Journey*, pp. 56f.; James Fu, *Quest*, p. 73; and Chang Ching-erh, "Monkey-hero," pp. 582f., who reviews the instances of service to others rendered by our pilgrims in the course of their journey.

[254] See above, nn. 73 and 74. Various historical parallels are suggested by the commentators. For example, Wang Hsiang-hsü draws parallels to such figures as Shen-sheng 申生, Wang Mang, Chu-ko Liang, and Wen T'ien-hsiang 文天祥. Chang Shu-shen repeats many of these, e.g., 47 (2a, 4a), 91 (1b), and adds Yüeh Fei, 57 (1a). Ch'en Shih-pin, 46 (468), strikes closer to home with a reference to Fang Hsiao-ju 方孝儒. More recently, Chang Ching-erh has suggested that the muddle-headed Master of our pilgrimage may reflect a veiled portrait of the Wan-li emperor ("Monkey-hero," pp. 202f.). Cf. Su Hsing's argument that the novel was intended as an attack on the Chia-ching emperor, in his "Hsi-yu chi tui Ming Shih-tsung ti yin-yü p'i-p'an ho ch'ao-feng," pp. 33–53. See Part II of this chapter for the possible significance of references to Wang Mang in the temporal scheme of the text.

[255] I might point out that Wu Ch'eng-en, if he is the author of our text, was not entirely uninvolved in political life, despite the image he presents of a recluse. Cf. his

But for all this, the novel ultimately focuses more on *hsiu-hsin* than on *hsiu-shen*; in other words, it is the internal integrality of the individual self that concerns the author more than the integration of the self into a wider set of relations—even though these are, in the final analysis, two sides of the same coin. The theoretical issue of the wholeness of the self is fleshed out in the allegory in a number of ways. First, many of the allegorical tags convey to us a sense that the Master and his four disciples together constitute a single composite entity. The fact that each of the disciples and even the Master himself are usually singled out as separate elements does not contradict this; it only emphasizes the point that his is the aggregate identity of which they all individually partake. The text is fairly explicit on this point, referring to the pilgrim band as a "single body" (*i-t'i* 一體) in a number of passages.[256] Once we recognize this principle, the entire narrative process of disintegration and reintegration yields a fairly easy allegorical interpretation. In fact, from this perspective all of the obstacles outlined above—the tendency to disunity, various forms of the disorienting push of desire, the blockages of vision, and especially the problem of self-replication—can be taken as aspects of the loss and recovery of the integrality of the self.

Beyond this, the author further relates this ground of meaning to other schemes of analyzing the components of self that were current in his intellectual milieu. Thus, in certain scenes he speaks of the unity of "mind" and "will" (*hsin-i* 心意), drawing at one and the same time on the key terms of the "monkey of the mind" metaphor, on the common Ming Taoist division of the self into "mind," "spirit," and "will" (*hsin, shen, i*), and on the two crucial internal foci of Neo-Confucian self-cultivation: "the rectification of the mind" and "the stabilization of the will" (*cheng-hsin, ch'eng-i* 正心誠意), as I would like to render these terms.[257] In other places, he frames this conceptual division in terms of distinctions between "mind" and "nature"

---

relations with Hsü Chung-hsing 徐中行, a committed partisan of Yang Chi-sheng, and other figures, discussed in Liu Ts'un-yan, "Wu Ch'eng-en," pp. 18ff.

[256] The expression *i-t'i* occurs in chapters 32 (1:433), 58 (2:802), 77 (3:1062), 84 (3:1151, 1162), 90 (3:1239), 99 (3:1347, 1349), 100 (3:1362). The commentators frequently discourse on this subject, insisting that the separate pilgrims must be understood as comprising a single self. See, for example, "Li Cho-wu," 49 (7b); Wang Hsiang-hsü, 16 (1a), 20 (2a), 22 (1a), 27 (1b), 28 (1a, 1b), 32 (1a), 34 (1a), 44 (11b), 56 (1b), 67 (1a), 94 (1a); Chang Shu-shen, 22 (14b), 23 (1a), 94 (8a), 99 (1a), and *Tsung-p'i*, 7 (3b); Ch'en Shih-pin, 8 (92f.), 29 (299), 57 (579), 58 (587), 85 (866), 87 (884); Liu I-ming, *tu-fa*, item 30. Cf. the allegorical theme of disunity discussed earlier. See Okuno Shintarō, "Mizu to honō," p. 228.

[257] Various combinations of the terms *hsin* and *i* occur in many chapters; e.g., 19 (1:262), 50 (2:694), 54 (755, 761), 58 (2:814), 77 (3:1075). See comments by Chang Shu-shen, 33 (1a), 49 (1b); "Li Cho-wu," 49 (14b); and Wang Hsiang-hsü, 15 (1a), who criticizes narrow-minded Confucianism for taking the rectification of mind 心 and will 意 as two separate levels.

(*hsin-hsing* 心性),²⁵⁸ or between "ultimate nature" and "physical existence" (*hsing-ming* 性命), whose "dual cultivation" (*shuang-hsiu*) we have seen to have had a special interpretation within Ming Taoist thought.²⁵⁹

One additional allegorical scheme of particular relevance to the idea of integration is provided by the use of five-elements symbolism in the text. Aside from the generative and destructive relations among the pilgrims themselves, frequently labeled with five-elements tags (e.g., chapter 31, "Metal follows, wood conforms to reach the true fruition" 金順木馴成 正果; or chapter 57, "When earth and wood have no attainment, then metal and water are split asunder" 土木無功金水絕),²⁶⁰ a number of entire episodes are patently mapped out on a grid of five-elements interaction.²⁶¹ The key to the interpretation of these references lies in the realization that the five elements can be both components of harmonious integration and forces of mutual destruction. This seems to be behind the frequent association of the unleashed fury of the most savage demons with one or another of the five elements in their unchained separate phases, as for example in the noxious image of the Red Child, the Iron Fan Princess, and various other color-labeled creatures.²⁶²

Significantly, the threat to the harmonious integrality of the mission through the disordering of the five elements forms the allegorical core of

²⁵⁸ See the following uses of the term *pen-hsing*: 13 (1:173), 77 (3:1062), 83 (3:1138), 98 (3:1330). Cf. the use of the terms *ting-hsing* and *ming-hsing*, discussed earlier. See comments by Ch'en Shih-pin, 1 (11), 3 (34), 8 (89), 18 (193), 19 (201), 26 (272), 27 (283), 33 (341), 34 (351), 35 (359), 40 (406), 41 (415), 43 (437), 47 (477), 50 (509), 53 (538), 55 (559), 77 (784), 83 (844), 98 (993); Liu I-ming, *tu-fa*, items 33, 38; Ts'ai Yüan-fang, *tu-fa*, items 12, 19, 46; and *T'ung-i cheng-chih*, 13 (33b). In the *Tung-t'ien hsüan-chi* preface Hsüan-tsang is identified with the term "true nature" (*chen-hsing* 眞性).

²⁵⁹ Liu I-ming in particular emphasizes this concept at a number of points. See also Ch'en Shih-pin, 27 (282), 36 (370), 40 (406), 50 (509), 55 (559), 100 (1015); and *T'ung-i cheng-chih*, 14 (47a).

²⁶⁰ Chapters 31 (2:417) and 57 (2:793).

²⁶¹ In addition to the episode at Wu-chuang kuan in chapters 24−26, to be discussed below, we can also see the same allegorical focus in the following episodes: the conflict with Hung-hai-erh in chapters 40−42; crossing the River of Communion in chapter 49; the incident at Huo-yen shan in chapters 61−62; the clash with Sai-t'ai-sui 賽太歲 in chapters 70−71. See comments by "Li Cho-wu," 46 (15b), 92 (14b); Wang Hsiang-hsü, 1 (1b), 7 (1a), 14 (1b), 23 (2a), 24 (1a), 40 (1a), 43 (1a−b); Chang Shu-shen, 40 (1a, 16b, 17a), 60 (18a); Ch'en Shih-pin, 1 (8), 4 (44), 7 (77), 22 (229), 24 (251ff.), 34 (351), 35 (359f.), 41 (415f.), 58 (587), 61 (620), 68 (693), 91 (921), 99 (1003); and Liu I-ming, *tu-fa*, items 33 and 37. This is discussed in James Fu, *Quest*, p. 69, and his "Wu-sheng ti kuan-hsi," pp. 10−17 (under Fu Shu-hsien). See also Wen Chi, "Hsi-yu chi cha-chi," p. 52.

²⁶² See comments by Wang Hsiang-hsü, 1 (1b), 7 (1a), 18 (1a), 19 (5b), 32 (1b), 34 (7b), 40 (1a), 43 (1a, b), 49 (4a), 50 (2a), 51 (1a), 59 (1a, 1b), 62 (1a), 70 (1a), 92 (1a, b); and Chang Shu-shen, 22 (14b), 44 (2a), 64 (2a, 16b). For additional comments on the assignment of respective pilgrims and demons to the five elements, see Wang Hsiang-hsü, 32 (1b); Ch'en Shih-pin, 34 (351f.); "Li Cho-wu," 46 (16a, *tp*); Liu I-ming, *tu-fa*, item 30.

one of the first fully realized trials faced by the pilgrims after reaching their full complement (of five). Here, in the episode that unfolds within the precincts of the Temple of the Five Estates (*Wu-chuang kuan*)—placed, true to form, in the chapter numbered 25—there grows a fruit of perfect completeness on a "ginseng" tree (*jen-shen kuo* 人參果), whose very name suggests the triple harmony of heaven, earth, and man (人參天地). The greed and impatience of the pilgrims, however, give rise to the force of "five-elements repulsion" (*wu-hsing hsiang wei* 五行相畏), which in turn leads to discord and peril that can be finally salved only through the healing power of Kuan-yin's "sweet-dew elixir" (*kan-lu shui* 甘露水), another symbol of all-inclusive, integral harmony in chapter 26.[263] We cannot but recall at this point the message proclaimed to be the secret of immortality long before this at the start of the Monkey King's pseudo-quest in chapter 2:

> Fully integrate the five elements and apply them backward and forward; when this is accomplished you can become a Buddha or immortal at will.
>
> 攢簇五行顛倒用, 功完隨作佛和仙.[264]

Within the context of the allegorical treatment of the five elements in the novel, I would like to interpret this ambiguous formula as saying that the proper understanding of five-elements harmony lies in moving *both* backward *and* forward, thus combining both directions—that is, the generative and destructive functions (*sheng k'e* 生剋) of elemental process—within a larger totality. This principle is well formulated in the following discussion by Ts'ai Yüan-fang:

> Only when the five elements have been successfully integrated does one have the necessary foundation, so that his subsequent attainment will remain in the proper path without deviation . . . he must not relax his vigilance for a moment, lest they lapse back into disorder, each seeking one-term dominance, and thus becoming destructive forces.
>
> 五行既合方有其基，後面工夫正自不易…不可一刻懈弛。稍一不謹則合者仍復散亂偏勝而爲賊矣.[265]

[263] See Wang Hsiang-hsü, 24 (1a, 1b); Ts'ai Yüan-fang, *tu-fa*, item 29.

[264] Chapter 2 (1:20). This idea is discussed by Wang Hsiang-hsü in chapters 14 (1b), 34 (7b); and Ch'en Shih-pin, chapters 12 (139), 22 (229), 23 (241), 35 (360), 58 (587), 82 (835), 88 (893), 92 (929f.).

[265] Ts'ai Yüan-fang, *tu-fa*, item 29. See also items 13, 21, 51; and Wang Hsiang-hsü, 6 (1a), 14 (1b), 19 (5b), 59 (1a); Chang Shu-shen, 23 (1a), 36 (15b), 38 (1a), 40 (1a); "Li Cho-wu," 12 (13a, *tp*), 14 (12a, *tp*); and *T'ung-i cheng-chih*, 81 (1a). See also Chang Ching-erh, "Structure and Theme," p. 180. A similar pattern of meaning emerges in various references in the text to the concept of *yin* and *yang*, as in the *yin-yang erh-ch'i p'ing* 陰陽二氣瓶 in chapters 74–77, and the sexual imbalances in chapters 82–83 and 93–95. See comments by Wang Hsiang-hsü, 43 (2a), 48 (1a), 59 (1b); and Ch'en Shih-pin, 5 (55), 12 (139), 14 (158), 22 (229), 23 (241), 32 (331f.), 36 (368f.), 59 (508f.), 69 (702f.), 70 (713), 82 (834ff.), 83 (844), 88 (893),

The desirability of attaining a degree of completeness within the self is certainly an attractive enough idea. But this very notion of self-containment presents a certain conceptual problem that appears to trouble our author. As Yuan Yü-ling, the writer of the Man-t'ing kuo-k'e 幔亭過客 preface to the "Li Cho-wu" edition, puts it, "The demons are none other than the individual self" (*mo fei t'a chi wo* 魔非他即我).²⁶⁶ This little rhyming epigram may be a bit too precious to take at face value, but it does zero in on what is perhaps the central issue of the allegorical text: the danger that the completeness of individual consciousness *within* the self may give rise to the illusion that the self is complete *unto* itself.²⁶⁷

The degree to which the author recoils from such a possibility explains many of the allegorical figures in his text. At the very start of the book, in the expanded version of the Monkey King parable put at the head of his composition, he confronts head-on the inner contradiction of self-containment and self-sufficiency. The image of the unparented generation of the Monkey King, followed by his spontaneous establishment of a harmonious community after the leap through the divisive barrier of the Water Curtain Cave (*Shui-lien tung* 水簾洞) into the enclosed paradise of the Mountain of Flowers and Fruit (*Hua-kuo shan* 花果山), immediately sets up the outlines of the issue.²⁶⁸ It does not take long for there to develop trouble in paradise—in the form of despair over the limitations of mortal existence. The Monkey King's attempted solution to this problem is to seek immortality in a parody journey of self-cultivation, the pursuit of which leads him to the point of arrogating the title Great Sage Equal to Heaven (Ch'i-t'ien ta-sheng 齊天大聖).²⁶⁹ Although this title does appear in some of the sources of the novel, it obviously struck our author as particularly mean-

---

92 (929), 95 (959f.). For a good discussion of this understanding, see Wu Ta-yün, "T'ien-ti pu ch'üan."

²⁶⁶ Yüan Yü-ling preface. I suspect that the character *t'a* 他 should be given its alternate reading *t'o* here to add to the little rhyming game. Ch'en Shih-pin indulges in a similar play on these words in chapter 74 (754): "When my self occupies the demon and the demon is reduced to my self, then the demon submits of its own accord" 我主魔而魔亦歸我, 魔自伏. James Fu discusses similar ideas in *Quest*, pp. 20, 35.

²⁶⁷ See discussions by Ch'en Shih-pin, 20 (212), 47 (477), 53 (539), 62 (630f.), 63 (639), 69 (702), 72 (734). See also Wu Ta-yün, "T'ien-ti pu ch'üan."

²⁶⁸ This is perhaps the point of the joke about the mythical Monkey King's "lack of a nature" (*wu-hsing*), referred to earlier (n. 113). See pointed discussions of this issue by Ch'en Shih-pin, 54 (549); "Li Cho-wu," 42 (4b); and Chang Shu-shen, 51 (14b), 88 (1a), 89 (1a), 90 (1a). See also James Fu, *Quest*, p. 34.

²⁶⁹ For the title Ch'i-t'ien ta-sheng in the antecedents see e.g., *Pak t'ongsa ŏnhae*, the *Hsiao-shih chen-k'ung pao-chüan*, and *Tsa-chü*, Scene 9. It also occurs in various versions of the story of the white ape described by Dudbridge (*Hsi-yu chi*, pp. 119–23, 127, 129), and other popular sources (cf. the play *Erh-lang shen so Ch'i-t'ien ta-sheng* 二郎神鎖齊天大聖 (see Dudbridge, *Hsi-yu chi*, 158f.). But our allegorist must still be credited with bringing out its full implications.

ingful, since he repeats the same idea in the name of another demon, the King Who Merges with the World (Hun-shih mo-wang 混世魔王), whom he has occupying the Mountain of Flowers and Fruit in the Monkey King's absence (an early instance of the pattern of destructive self-replication), and again in the name of the master of the ginseng tree: the Prince Coeval with the World (Yü-shih t'ung chün 與世同君) in chapter 24.[270] This hubristic challenge to the authority of heaven proves quite unstoppable to all who try to combat the monster of ego on its own terms. It is only after demonstrating the actual smallness of the monkey's bloated self in the shadow of the Buddha's fingers in chapter 7, that the overblown mind-monkey is reduced to finite proportions, and his rehabilitative imprisonment under Five Elements Mountain (the inverted image of the five fingers of the Buddha) can begin.[271]

After the unruly monkey of the mind is "stilled" and the journey gets under way, the author continues to press this same issue in numerous other allegorical figures. We have already noted the pattern by which the inability of the pilgrims to stay within their protective circle leads directly into allegorical perils, and conversely, we have seen Sun Wu-k'ung's success in subduing demons by first getting inside them. More important, from this perspective the encompassing weapons that so dominate the author's *psychomachia* may be understood as allegorical symbols for the tendency of the self to fall into the trap of taking its own scope of vision as a total frame of reference. This idea is brought out in the imagery presented in chapter 33, where the illusory attempt to "engulf the heavens" (*chuang-t'ien*) within a false version of Kuan-yin's "purification vase" nearly leads to the literal "dissolving" of the band. Here the falsity of this premature attempt to grasp the meaning of totality contrasts sharply with the symbolism of the River of Communion with Heaven (T'ung-t'ien ho), whose crossing marks the midpoint of the book.[272] And the same illusion of the totality of the self seems to underlie the demon of self-gratification in many of the episodes devoted to sexual temptation.

The traditional commentators do not fail to recognize this pattern of meaning. For example, "Li Cho-wu" glosses the cage formed by the Buddha's hand that finally entraps the mind-monkey in chapter 7 as "the

[270] Cf. the similarly chaotic state on Hua-kuo shan discovered by Sun Wu-k'ung at the time of his "exile" in chapter 28. A similarly named figure, T'ung-t'ien ta-sheng 通天大聖, appears as a brother of Ch'i-t'ien ta-sheng in some of the sources (Dudbridge, *Hsi-yu chi*, pp. 120, 129). Cf. the use of this latter name (T'ung-t'ien ta-sheng) for Sun Wu k'ung himself in the *Tsa-chü* (see Scene 10).

[271] Cf. the inverse relationship between Five Elements Mountain and the "Eight-trigrams furnace" (*pa-kua lu* 八卦爐), which fails to temper the Monkey King's elemental imbalance in chapter 7.

[272] The expression "T'ung-t'ien" in this context now means the exact opposite of the same words in the name T'ung-t'ien ta-sheng (see above, n. 270).

circle of self-containment out of which he ultimately cannot leap 究竟跳
不出自在圈子, and Ch'en Shih-pin and Chang Shu-shen express similar
ideas in a number of discussions.[273] In all of these examples, it is the
distortion of self-containment into self-indulgence or selfishness that gives
rise to allegorical peril—what is expressed in Neo-Confucian terms as the
beclouding focus on individual desires (*ssu* 私).[274] Thus it is Sun Wu-k'ung's
discontent (*pu chih tsu* 不知足) that leads to the inevitable destruction of
the initial paradise at the Mountain of Flowers and Fruit, just as it is the
impatience and greed of the pilgrims that turn the five-elements fruit
into a hostile force in chapter 25. The enunciation of this principle is what
originally wins the chastened Monkey King a promise of deliverance in
chapter 8:

> When the human mind gives rise to any single thought
> Heaven the Earth must always be aware.
> For if good and evil were without their proper recompense,
> Then the universe would be subject to selfish one-sidedness.
> 人心生一念，天地盡皆知，善惡若無報，乾坤必有私。

And this very formula is repeated for final emphasis as the pilgrims near
their destination in chapter 87.[275]

The same sort of paradox between the attractive ideal and the inherent
danger of self-containment also hangs over the allegorical presentation of
the goal of the quest. I have already discussed in several different contexts
the provocatively unfinished nature of the end of the novel.[276]

[273] See "Li Cho-wu," 6 (13b, *tp*); Chang Shu-shen, 24 (16a), 49 (15b), 90 (1a); Wang
Hsiang-hsü, 14 (2a); Ch'en Shih-pin, 4 (43), 33 (341), 35 (362), 49 (498), 53 (538), 55 (560),
65 (664), 75 (764), 76 (774); *T'ung-i cheng-chih*, 25 (46a), 52 (12b, 17b), 53 (29b), 75 (48b,
54a). The problem of entrapment within the self may also be behind the crushing of
Wu-k'ung under the proverbial burden of T'ai-shan 泰山, as allegorized in chapter 33; and
perhaps we can see a little joking reference to this idea in the frequent resort to the trick of
"getting outside oneself" (*shen-wai-shen fa* 身外身法) in many of the battle scenes. A similar
idea is singled out for special attention in the seventeenth-century novel *Hsi-yu pu*, where
the solution to the problem of illusory self-containment is conveyed in the following line
from the *I Ching*: "In it are contained the forms and scope of all the transformations of the
universe, so that nothing goes beyond it" 範圍天地之化而不過 (See *Chou-i che-chung*,
p. 980, and Hellmut Wilhelm, *The I Ching, or Book of Changes*, p. 296).
[274] The author cannot have missed the ironic implications of the name of the Monkey
King's original paradise in *Ao-lai kuo*, which I would render as the "Land of Burgeoning
Pride." Liu Ts'un-yan suggests a source for this name in "Ch'üan-chen chiao," pt. 5, pp. 71f.
This overweening pride characterizes the essential nature of the unchained mind-monkey in
the prologue chapters, as well as his unredeemed side throughout the journey.
[275] Chapters 8 (1:104) and 87 (3:1200). See Chang Shu-shen, 49 (15b).
[276] See Part II of this chapter, and comments by Chang Shu-shen, 36 (15b), 90 (13b), 98
(14a), 99 (1b); and "Li Cho-wu," 99 (11a).

This undermining of the surface finality of the successful fulfillment of the quest is underscored in the two principal metaphors applied to the attainment of the long-sought end. One of these is the notion that the goal of self-cultivation is in some sense a return to the "source" or "root" of existence (*fan-pen*). This idea is explicitly stated at a number of points, and underlies those many scenes in which selfish deviation from this sacred mission is labeled "forgetting the root" (*wang-pen*) or "straying from the source" (*mi-pen*), especially in instances of sexual confrontation.[277] In particular, the notion of straying from, or returning to, the root is inserted at the point of the most severe trials: in the two instances of "exile" and in the ultimate temptation by the Jade Hare. Within this context, we can perhaps say that this "source" (*pen*) refers to the "original nature" (*pen-hsing*)—a term of currency in all three of the three teachings.[278]

At the same time, we have in the text another set of metaphors that refer not to the starting point of the original "root," but to a newly created "fruit" of attainment.[279] The symbolism of fruit can be seen to inform some of the underlying conceptions spanning the entire narrative: from the original world of harmonious self-containment on Hua-kuo shan, and the episode of the ginseng fruit in chapter 25, to the final "attainment of the fruit" of enlightenment (*ch'eng-kuo* 成果). Significantly, in several cases the premature grasp of self-containment is abused or, to put it another way, gives rise to the natural desire to have one's perfect fruit and eat it too. In this light, it seems less than an accidental touch that the original paradise on Hua-kuo shan must be destroyed, like Dante's purgatorial Eden, before the true "attainment of the fruit" can be realized.[280]

[277] See the following occurrences of these terms: *fan-pen*, 35 (2:485); *wu-pen*, 49 (2:691); *wang pen*, 23 (1:306), 64 (2:888); *mi-pen*, 72 (3:989). Cf. the notion of *mi-se* considered in *Chin P'ing Mei* earlier. The term *kuei-yüan* 歸元 reminds me of the opening formula *chen-hsia ch'i-yüan*, and this idea is driven home when the *yüan* tortoise becomes the instrument of bringing our pilgrims back to their starting point. See comments by Ch'en Shih-pin, 5 (53), 23 (241), 24 (251, 253), 25 (263), 31 (321), 62 (629), 72 (733f.), 80 (814), 98 (993); "Li Cho-wu," 72 (12b, *tp*); Chang Shu-shen, 23 (1a, 17a); and *Tsung-p'i*, 75 (20a); Liu I-ming, preface and *tu-fa*, item 20; and Wang Hsiang-hsü, 72 (1b).

[278] For examples of the expression *kuei pen-hsing*, see 31 (2:417) and 95 (3:1301). I should add that the return to one's original form (*hsien pen-hsiang*), which marks the submission of many demons, also provides the means of their salvation. See comments by "Li Cho-wu," 7 (12a), 12 (13a); Wang Hsiang-hsü, 4 (1a); Ch'en Shih-pin, 29 (299), 33 (343); and Chang Shu-shen, 26 (1a), 49 (1a), and *Tsung-p'i*, 74 (19b).

[279] Probably the fullest development of this metaphor is found in chapters 24–26. For sources of this episode, see Ts'ao Shih-pang, "Hsi-yu chi jo-kan ch'ing-chieh ti pen-yüan wu-t'an," pp. 34f. Cf. the counterpart of this idea in Buddhist terms discussed by Anthony Yu in *Journey*, p. 61.

[280] This is especially clear in the opening sequence on Hua-kuo shan, where it is the problem of insatiety that leads to the loss of the primal world of self-containment. For the

The symbolism of creating fruit also resonates meaningfully with the metaphors of birth that occupy a prominent place in the allegorical apparatus of the novel—from the opening pseudo-myth of self-generation of the cosmos, and the birth of the Monkey King from a stone egg, through the birth of the foundling Hsüan-tsang, to various allegorical tours de force, not the least of which is the inversion of pregnancy in the Land of Women.[281] As we have seen, the notion of organic procreation links up with the language of alchemical gestation, so that the terms "internal cinnabar" and "newborn babe" become nearly interchangeable with reference to the tangible results of the process of cultivation.

When we arrive at this point, it is not so hard to reconcile the apparent paradox between the metaphors proclaiming a return to primal unity and those that bespeak the attainment of a new state, since in all three of the philosophical contexts of Ming thought the notion of attainment is inseparable from the idea of a solid core of selfhood—regardless of whether we are talking about trees and fruit, parents and babes, or elemental gold and cinnabar.

The idea that the fruit of attainment is organically linked to the root of the self brings us back to the meaning of the problem of self-containment we have found underlying many of the allegorical figures of the novel. The resolution of this paradox seems to lie in the understanding that neither of the two principal metaphors for the goal of the quest are really talking about any kind of ultimate transcendence of the self, but rather a return to the basic bedrock of selfhood.[282] In other words, the figurative pursuit of Taoist immortality or Mahayana salvation points to a kind of self-cultivation that remains within the sphere of conscious existence; thus the manifest nonfinality of the quest may be explained more as a lesson in nonattainment than in terms of steady progress toward a final goal. This is precisely the sort of revisionist position that marks Chinese thought in general, but especially that of the late Ming and Ch'ing reaction to the excesses of T'ai-chou intuitionism; and it finds frequent expression in the commentaries on the novel.[283]

---

parallel to Dante's fallen Eden, see *Purgatorio*, 28–32, esp. 32. Cf. Wang Hsiang-hsü's remark in chapter 24 (1b): "When Sun Wu-k'ung steals the forbidden fruit, it is used as a metaphor for the mind's impatient desire [for immortality]" 行者之竊人參果, 亦借以喻此心之急.

[281] Given the prominence of certain Mencian ideas in the allegory, we may perhaps detect in these instances another hint of an oblique reference to Mencius's concept of the newborn babe (*ch'ih-tzu* 赤子). Chapters involving births, babies, or children include 1, 9, 12, 24–26, 37, 47–49, 53, 66, 77, 78, and 94. See Ts'ai Yüan-fang, *tu-fa*, items 20, 23, 25, 26; and Ch'en Shih-pin, 40 (406), 74 (754).

[282] See n. 173 on the concept of self-cultivation within the late Ming intellectual context.

[283] The *T'ung-i cheng-chih* commentator, for example, insists on the cultivation of *shen* alongside *hsin*, 13 (34a), 27 (70b), 59 (92a).

Perhaps I can most conveniently sum up this issue by returning to the Heart Sutra, which is bestowed as a key to enlightenment in chapter 19 (by a Ch'an monk) and which remains an occasional point of reference later on in the journey.[284] The best-known line from this brief classic, the one most often cited in works of colloquial fiction, is the formula that tells us "Perceived reality is no different from emptiness, emptiness is no different from perceived reality, reality is emptiness, emptiness is reality" 色不異空, 空不異色, 色即是空, 空即是色.[285] It is possible to understand this line as a simple declaration of the illusory nature of reality 色即是空. But I would like to give the author and the commentators credit for recognizing that the message is actually a two-way street. That is, I believe that the allegory of *Hsi-yu chi* is designed to demonstrate the principle that, though the sensory perception of reality (*se*) is ultimately an empty illusion, at the same time the converse is also true—meditation upon emptiness itself tends to turn into an illusory experience. From this perspective, the chief obstacle to be overcome on the path to enlightenment is the conscious pursuit of enlightenment itself, an idea most clearly allegorized in the abortive illumination of the Master in chapter 36.

The author comes close to stating something like this at several points in the text, and the commentators frequently take up his challenge.[286] In chapter 94, for example, Wang Hsiang-hsü points to this kind of nominalist approach to enlightenment (*i wu wei ming* 以悟爲命) as the principal remaining obstacle, and in chapter 25 Ch'en Shih-pin explains that "the attempt to intuitively grasp the empty-ness of emptiness means a failure to grasp the fruit of emptiness" 悟空中之空而不識空中之果.[287]

This last comment can perhaps help us to redefine the author's understanding of the name of the principal figure in his book: the "heart" of the pilgrimage, Sun Wu-k'ung. To the extent that he is not simply using the name ironically, as a dig at the incomplete state of the monkey's attain-

---

[284] Chapters 19–20 (1:264ff.). Later references to the Heart Sutra occur in chapters 32 (1:433), 58 (2:811), 80 (3:1102), 85 (3:1166), 93 (3:1266), 100 (3:1364). See n. 244. Among the writings of recent critics, the use of the *Hsin ching* is discussed by C. T. Hsia, *Classic Novel*, pp. 127ff.; James Fu, *Quest*, pp. 76ff., 90; Anthony Yu, *Journey*, p. 48; Dudbridge, *Hsi-yu chi*, pp. 14f.; and Hsü Chen-chi, "Pa-shih-i nan," pp. 8f.

[285] "Reality," in this rendering, of course means only the illusion of reality based on sensory perception. The well-known formula is also cited in *Chin P'ing Mei*, chapter 62 (21a), for the soul of Li P'ing-erh. See above, chapter 2, Part VI.

[286] See discussions by Wang Hsiang-hsü, 4 (1a): "Emptiness is inadequate by virtue of being empty" 空失其空···, 14 (2a–b); Ch'en Shih-pin, 19 (201), 56 (568), 72 (734), 82 (834), 84 (855), 85 (866); Chang Shu-shen, 98 (6b); Ts'ai Yüan-fang, *tu-fa*, item 50; "Li Cho-wu," 99 (11a, *tp*); and *T'ung-i cheng-chih*, 57 (71b), 65 (50b).

[287] Wang Hsiang-hsü, 94 (1a), and Ch'en Shih-pin, 25 (264). Similar ideas are expressed by Ch'en in 20 (211), 52 (527), 75 (764), 96 (968).

ment, perhaps it would be better to take this as signifying not an awakening from illusion *into* "vacuity," as translators have tended to render it in
English, but rather as an awakening *about* the meaning of emptiness, as just
one side of the coin of existence; or, at least, an awakening to the vanity of
distinguishing betweeen reality and emptiness.[288] This, then, would mean
that the path to enlightenment involves a coming to terms with the self,
rather than the obliteration of the self through some kind of loincloth
nirvana. Recalling the central place of the dialectics of *se* and *k'ung* in the
Chin P'ing Mei, we have now arrived at a final link between our two
sixteenth-century masterworks. And we shall see that even in *San-kuo chih
yen-i* and *Shui-hu chuan*, despite the primary concern with their respective
spheres of concrete historical experience, sooner or later meditations on
emptiness begin to occupy their authors' minds.[289] Such questions were,
after all, very much in the air in sixteenth-century China. In each of our
other three works it is possible to dismiss this dimension as not really
central to the authors' concerns. But here in *Hsi-yu chi* it can help us to
recognize that this most penetrating exploration of the realm of emptiness
is intended to be much less empty than it at first appears.

[288] See Arthur Waley, *Monkey*, p. 31; and Anthony Yu, *Journey*, p. 82. On the sources and
prior uses of the name Sun Wu-k'ung, see b.n. I.5. Isobe Akira ("Son Gyōja," p. 115) points
out the existence of an actual monk named Wu-k'ung at the time of T'ang Hsüan-tsung. For
the adoption of this name by various later religious figures, see Richard Shek, "Religion and
Society in Late Ming," p. 205. The commentators are aware of the more pointed use of the
name in the hundred-chapter novel. See "Li Cho-wu," chapter 8 (13b); Ch'en Shih-pin, 4 (44),
19 (201), 73 (746); Chang Shu-shen, 98 (6b); Wang Hsiang-hsü, 14 (2a–b). Cf. the formula
tzu-se wu-k'ung 自色悟空 invoked in chapter 1 of *Hung-lou meng*.

[289] See above, Chapter 2, Part VI, and below, Chapters 4, Part V, and 5, Part V. Other
expressions of the idea of emptiness occur in chapters 32 (1:433), 39 (2:540), 62 (2:859),
73 (3:1016), 78 (3:1084), 96 (3:1302), 100 (3:1355, 1358, 1362). On the late Ming
polemics over the concept of emptiness, see Yu Chün-fang, "Buddhists' Responses," pp. 1,
3, 4.

Chapter 69: "Sung Chiang Honorably Releases the Double-lance General" 宋公明義釋雙鎗將, from T'ien-tu wai-ch'en preface edition, *Chung-i shui-hu chuan* (see b.n. II.1)

CHAPTER 4

Shui-hu chuan:
Deflation of Heroism

In the preceding two chapters, in which I used *Chin Ping Mei* and *Hsi-yu chi* to set forth the generic outlines and intellectual substance of the Ming literati novel, I had few qualms about claiming that both of these works were products of the sixteenth century. True, we saw that the *Chin P'ing Mei* was not actually put to blocks until early in the following century, whereas in the case of *Hsi-yu chi* I explored certain tantalizing hints that the allegorical novel as we know it may have derived from a much earlier prototype. But for both the hundred-chapter *Hsi-yu chi* and the *Chin P'ing Mei tz'u-hua*, the overwhelming bulk of current testimony supports the conclusion that the two books reached their most mature forms during the second half of the sixteenth century.[1]

In this and the following chapter, my discussions of the remaining two masterworks of the Ming novel, *Shui-hu chuan* and *San-kuo chih yen-i*, will have to go in a somewhat different direction. Like *Hsi-yu chi* (and to a minimal extent *Chin P'ing Mei*), these two works represent the culmination of long histories of textual evolution—from a variety of historical sources and a wide range of treatments of similar narrative material in such forms as oral storytelling, popular song narratives (*tz'u-hua* 詞話), and drama, down to antecedent prose works that cover more or less the entire narrative outlines in rudimentary form.[2] And here, too, these antecedent versions lead the way

---

[1] See above, Chapters 2, Part I, and 3, Part I.

[2] For general reviews of the sources of the *Shui-hu* narrative material, see Cheng Chen-to, "Shui-hu chuan ti yen-hua," pp. 101–10; Hu Shih, "Shui-hu chuan k'ao-cheng," pp. 9–31;

to full-length works of prose fiction that, according to considerable bibliographical evidence, began to appear in print during the sixteenth century.
But the difference here is that in the case of *San-kuo* and *Shui-hu* much of
this same evidence speaks fairly convincingly of fourteenth-century authorship, thus giving rise to the prevailing scholarly assumption that the novels
had already taken on their recognizable shape long before the appearance
of the sixteenth-century editions.[3] As a result, the burden of proof in these
cases now shifts to the attempt to demonstrate that the composition of
these novels as we know them in their mature generic form did not occur
until close to the time the first known printed editions came to light in the
Chia-ching and Wan-li periods. This also makes more problematical the
task of interpreting the works as specific reflections of the cultural and
intellectual concerns of the late Ming literati milieu.

This situation is essentially the same as what we encountered in the
consideration of *Hsi-yu chi*, only here the strength and insistence of the
claims of fourteenth-century authorship require a more thorough reassessment. In the following review of the available evidence regarding the
authorship and early publication of *Shui-hu chuan*, I make no claim to
uncovering any new theories or sources; the material is simply presented in
order to support my contention that the sixteenth-century incarnations of
the ongoing *Shui-hu* textual tradition ought to be read and interpreted in
their own right as examples of an independent literary phenomenon of
great significance.

Before I proceed, it may help to make it clear at the outset that my
reading of the *Shui-hu chuan* as a "sixteenth-century novel" focuses on only
one of the two basic recensions that came into currency during that period.
This is the so-called "full recension" (*fan-pen* 繁本) represented by several
known editions.[4] The question of whether it is these or the editions of the

---

Richard Irwin, *The Evolution of a Chinese Novel*, pp. 33–43; Yen Tun-i, *Shui-hu chuan ti
yen-pien*, pp. 41–121; and Ho Hsin (Lu Tan-an), *Shui-hu yen-chiu*, pp. 3–19. For more specific
studies, see b.n. I.

[3] See the following reassessment of the attempts to identify Lo Kuan-chung or Shih
Nai-an as the original authors.

[4] The term *fan-pen* seems to have been coined in this context by Lu Hsün in *Chung-kuo
hsiao-shuo shih-lüeh* (p. 153 in *Lu Hsün san-shih-nien chi* and p. 145 in *Lu Hsün ch'üan-chi*). See
also Cheng Chen-to, "Lun wen-tzu ti fan, chien," pp. 1174–77. For a review of the extant
editions in the *fan-pen* system, see Sun K'ai-ti, *Chung-kuo t'ung-su hsiao-shuo shu-mu*,
pp. 209–16. See also Cheng Chen-to, *Shui-hu ch'üan-chuan*, preface, pp. 4f; Hu Shih, "K'ao-
cheng," pp. 101ff; Yen Tun-i, *Yen-pien*, pp. 140–205; Ho Hsin, *Yen-chiu*, pp. 32ff; Irwin,
Evolution, pp. 61–97; Andrew Lo, "*San-kuo chih yen-i* and *Shui-hu chuan* in the Context
of Historiography," pp. 265–68; Y. W. Ma (Ma Yau-woon), "Liang-shan chü-pao chi,"
pp. 23ff., and "Hu-yü yen-chiu chien-pen Shui-hu i-chien shu," p. 186. A convenient table
of *Shui-hu* editions is provided by Cheng Kung-tun in *Shui-hu chuan lun-wen chi*, 1:87–94.
For detailed information on the editions used in this study, see b.n. II.

"simpler recension" (*chien-pen* 簡本) that represent a closer approximation of the "original" form of the novel will occupy us briefly, but it will not substantially affect the object of this study, since it is the *fan-pen* texts alone that conform to the structural and rhetorical conventions outlined in my analysis of *Hsi-yu chi* and *Chin P'ing Mei*, and it is this recension that sets the stamp on the basic text of the novel through all of its subsequent transmutations, right down to the twentieth century.

As already mentioned, a wealth of bibliographical and other evidence puts the first appearance of the *fan-pen* early in the sixteenth century. By the Chia-ching period, we already begin to get reports of the circulation of a text bearing certain similarities to the *fan-pen* we know from later editions. The earliest of such sources include the Pao-wen t'ang 寶文堂 library catalogue of Ch'ao Li 晁瑮 (*chin-shih*, 1541), which contains two different entries for the novel, one under the same title: *Chung-i shui-hu chuan* 忠義水滸傳 with which most later *fan-pen* are headed; plus the *Pai-ch'uan shu-chih* 百川書志 catalogue of Kao Ju 高儒 (preface, 1540), which lists a hundred-chapter book apparently covering the story cycles of the full complement of 108 heroes.[5] Other Chia-ching sources include Lang Ying's 郎瑛 (1487–1566) *Ch'i-hsiu lei-kao* 七修類稿 and T'ien Ju-ch'eng's 田汝成 (1500–63) *Hsi-hu yu-lan chih-yü* 西湖遊覽志餘, both of which also seem to indicate the existence of full narratives of the *Shui-hu* cycles, as well as a roughly contemporary bibliographical compilation, the *Ku-chin shu-k'e* 古今書刻 of Chou Hung-tsu 周弘祖 (fl. 1559), which informs us of the existence of an edition printed under the auspices of the imperial censorate bureau called the Tu-ch'a yüan 都察院. One may well imagine that this latter book would have been something more serious than a cheap commercial printing.[6] To this we may add other sources of information

[5] Ch'ao Li, *Pao-wen t'ang shu-mu*, pp. 100, 108. Irwin (*Evolution*, p. 98, n. 12) cites evidence to date this catalogue in the 1540s or 1550s. Regarding the question of the two separate editions listed in this reference, see Huang Lin, "I-chung chih-te chu-mu ti Shui-hu ku-pen," p. 89. Tai Pu-fan (*Hsiao-shuo chien-wen lu*, p. 100) speculates that the second title may not refer to the same edition. See also George Hayden, "A Skeptical Note on the Early History of *Shui-hu chuan*," p. 375. If the second title is indeed a *fan-pen* text, this would be the only early example not entitled *Chung-i shui-hu chuan*, except for the Shanghai Library fragment, to be discussed shortly. The *Pai-ch'uan shu-chih* reference is found in a modern reprint (Shanghai, 1957), p. 82 (also available in Ma T'i-chi, *Shui-hu tzu-liao hui-pien*, p. 351; Chu I-hsüan and Liu Yü-ch'en, *Shui-hu chuan tzu-liao hui-pien*, p. 131; and K'ung Ling-ching, *Chung-kuo hsiao-shuo shih-liao*, p. 12).

[6] See Lang Ying, *Ch'i-hsiu lei-kao*, pp. 352f. The mention here of a "basic text" (*ti-pen* 的本 [*sic*]) by Shih Nai-an evidently follows the information used by Kao Ju. The second reference is found in T'ien Ju-ch'eng, *Hsi-hu yu-lan chih-yü*, p. 468, and is repeated by Wang Ch'i (1564–1614) in his *Hsü wen-hsien t'ung-k'ao, chüan* 177, pp. 10687f., and his *Pai-shih hui-pien*, pp. 1558f. The *Ku-chin shu-k'e* has been reprinted together with the *Pai-ch'uan shu-chih* (see n. 5), p. 325. Citations also in Ma T'i-chi, *Tzu-liao*, pp. 471, 503f.; Chu I-hsüan, *Tzu-liao*,

indicating the circulation of one or more fine editions of the novel within Chia-ching literary circles. For example, Li K'ai-hsien 李開先 (1502–68) speaks in his *I-hsiao san* 一笑散 about the high regard for the novel in the eyes of some of his illustrious literati contemporaries, including T'ang Shun-chih 唐順之 (1507–60) and Wang Shen-chung 王愼中 (1509–59); and he specifies that this book comprised twenty volumes (*ts'e* 冊) in length, a figure that conforms to later configurations of the known *fan-pen* texts.[7] This is corroborated by a description in a late Ming catalogue of a fine manuscript reportedly copied personally by the great Chia-ching painter and calligrapher Wen Cheng-ming 文徵明 (1470–1559), which according to one reference was also a text measuring some twenty volumes (*chüan* 卷) in length.[8]

These skeletal references to the approximage length and quality of certain

---

pp. 85f., 130ff.; and K'ung Ling-ching, *Shih-liao*, pp. 12f. For further discussion of these sources, see Ch'en Chung-fan, "Shih-lun Shui-hu chuan ti chu-che chi ch'i ch'uang-tso shih-tai," p. 112. Charles Hucker, *A Dictionary of Official Titles in Imperial China*, p. 536, renders the official term *Tu-ch'a yüan* as the "chief surveillance bureau." See also Yen Tun-i, *Yen-pien*, p. 160; and Chin Tai-t'ung (Yü Sung-ch'ing), "Li Chih yü Shui-hu," p. 80.

[7] See Li K'ai-hsien, *I-hsiao san*, p. 106. The same passage also appears in Li's *Tz'u-nüeh*, p. 286. The source is apparently derived from a Ch'ing edition of this work. See Wang Li-ch'i, "Kuan-yü Shui-hu ch'üan-chuan ti pan-pen chi chiao-ting," p. 399. It is also available in Ma T'i-chi, *Tzu-liao*, p. 351; and Chu I-hsüan, *Tzu-liao*, p. 187. Tai Pu-fan (*Chien-wen lu*, p. 109) argues that this passage shows a complete *fan-pen* was already in existence by the 1530s. Li K'ai-hsien's remark on the novel raises the question of whether or not his drama *Pao-chien chi* was directly based on an early edition of the novel, and if so, which edition. The Chia-ching prefaces to the play do not mention the novel explicitly (see Yen Tun-i, *Yen-pien*, p. 179; and Ma T'i-chi, *Tzu-liao*, p. 78f.). Another piece of evidence that has been cited as an indication of a Chia-ching edition is a line quoted in Yang Shen's *Tz'u-p'in* 詞品 from a late Sung work entitled *Weng-t'ien ts'o-yü* 甕天脞語, which matches a verse in chapter 72 of the *fan-pen* novel. This was already pointed out by Hu Ying-lin (1555–1602) in his *Shao-shih shan-fang pi-ts'ung*, *chüan* 41, pp. 571f. (also available in Chu I-hsüan, *Tzu-liao*, pp. 86f.). Of course, the presence of this line in a *fan-pen* text does not prove it dates from Yang Shen's time, since it could easily have been borrowed at any later stage. We have a similar case in the line from a poem included in the *Hua-ts'ao ts'ui-pien* 花草粹編 (preface, 1583, comp. Ch'en Hui-wen 陳耀文) sometimes attributed to Wu Ch'eng-en 吳承恩, which also appears in the novel in a chapter-opening verse in chapter 11 of the T'ien-tu wai-ch'en edition. See Wang Li-ch'i, "Pan-pen chi chiao-ting," p. 398; and Wen Ying, "Shui-hu chuan liu-pien ssu-chang," pp. 206f.

[8] See Chang Ch'ou, *Chen-chi jih-lu*, *chüan* 5, p. 8a. The passage reads: "an original edition of *Shui-hu chuan* copied in elegant formal characters by Wen Cheng-ming" 文徵明精楷古 本水滸傳. This reference is noted by Li Tzu in "Shui-hu ti pan-pen ho Shui-hu ti cheng-chih ch'ing-hsiang," p. 41, n. 2, where he adds the words "in twenty volumes" 二十卷 in his quotation, perhaps based on an alternate version. For a description of Chang Ch'ou's catalogue, see H. C. Lovell, *Annotated Bibliography of Chinese Painting Catalogues and Related Texts*, p. 26, in which she dates the work to the 1620s. Wen Ying ("Liu-pien," p. 213) argues that *chüan* and *ts'e* may not be equivalent terms in this context. Tai Pu-fan presents an opposite opinion in *Chien-wen lu*, pp. 100f. See Yüan Liang, "Wen Cheng-ming hsieh-pen Shui-hu."

Chia-ching versions do not really enable us to identify these books with any certainty with the later *fan-pen* editions. But we do get a more substantive clue in the *Pao-wen t'ang shu-mu* entry designating one of the two editions it cites as a "Wu-ting edition" 武定本.[9] This label has been accepted by all scholars as a reference to the well-known political and cultural personality of the early Chia-ching period Kuo Hsün 郭勛 (or 勳) (1475–1542), who in 1507 assumed the title of Marquis of Wu-ting 武定侯, originally granted to his illustrious forebear Kuo Ying 郭英.[10] Ch'ao Li's reference is picked up and repeated by a number of later sources, thus strengthening the claim that such a Chia-ching edition did in fact exist.[11]

Since certain details of the descriptions of this text that we get in other places conform to the outlines of the hundred-chapter *fan-pen* we know from extant editions, and, moreover, the association with Kuo Hsün fits with the descriptions of the work as a "fine edition" 善本, this theory has been given widespread credence—although there is of course no guarantee that this is the same book as that reported in other Chia-ching references.[12]

[9] *Pao-wen t'ang shu-mu*, pp. 100, 108. The citation reads *Wu-ting pan* 武定板, though it is most often quoted as *Wu-ting pen*.

[10] For biographical information on Kuo Hsün, see *Dictionary of Ming Biography*, pp. 770–73; and *Ming shih, chüan* 130, pp. 3823f. Tai Pu-fan (*Chien-wen lu*, pp. 113ff.) reviews the career of Kuo Hsün, and notes Kuo's unhappy entanglement with the Tu-ch'a yüan (p. 115), putting his death at 1542. Wen Ying ("Liu-pien," pp. 217ff.) attempts to refute the argument regarding the priority of the Kuo edition.

[11] See T'ien-tu wai-ch'en preface; Yüan Wu-yai edition, *fa-fan* preface; Shen Te-fu, *Wan-li yeh-huo pien*, p. 139; Ch'ien Hsi-yen, *Hsi-hsia*, 1:11a–b, 3:22b–24a; Chou Liang-kung, *Yin-shu-wu shu-ying*, p. 378. Citations also available in Ma T'i-chi, *Tzu-liao*, pp. 1, 13, 356, 360, 377; Chu I-hsüan, *Tzu-liao*, pp. 147, 248 150f., 152, 187; and K'ung Ling-ching, *Shih-liao*, pp. 14, 15, 17, as well as in Ch'en Hsi-chung, ed., *Shui-hu chuan hui-p'ing pen*, 1:25ff. See also Nieh Kan-nu, "Shui-hu wu-lun," pp. 29, 149. Shiroki Naoya, "Kaku Butei hon shikō," p. 157, expresses skepticism regarding the *Yeh-huo pien* passage. (The Library of Congress catalogue reads this scholar's name as Shiraki; I follow Nihon Gakujutsu Shinkōkai 日本学術振興会, *Daigaku kenkyūsha kenkyū daimoku sōran* 大学研究者研究題目総覧 [Tokyo, 1971], p. 397.)

[12] The text is described as a "fine edition" in the T'ien-tu wai-ch'en preface, and in the *Yeh-huo pien* and *Hsi-hsia* passages. A similar statement also appears in another preface attributed to the late Ming poet and dramatist Chang Feng-i, dated by Hsü Shuo-fang slightly earlier than the T'ien-tu wai-ch'en preface (see below, n.27). For the relevant citation, see Ma T'i-chi, *Tzu-liao*, p. 8; or Chu I-hsüan, *Tzu-liao*, p. 190. See Cheng Chen-to, "Yen-hua," pp. 117f. The idea of a "fine edition" may remind us of Wen Cheng-ming's hand-copied text, although there is no reason to assume any connection. Anyway, Wen Cheng-ming outlived Kuo Hsün by some seventeen years. Other features ascribed to the Kuo edition include the appending of introductory narrative sections to each chapter, as well as a larger quantity of incidental verse, the omission of the two campaigns against T'ien Hu and Wang Ch'ing and the addition of the Liao expedition, and the shift of narrative material in the Yen P'o-hsi episode (see analysis of T'ien-tu wai-ch'en preface, in following pages). For further discussion, see Ho Hsin, *Yen-chiu*, pp. 83ff., and Y. W. Ma, "Chü-pao chi," p. 23.

Recently, however, scholars have begun to raise serious doubts about this speculation. Some have wondered whether Kuo Hsün's putative role may have been limited to that of financial patron of this edition, or whether he may have simply been the owner of the text, if he had any connection whatsover to the book.[13] To further complicate the issue, one scholar recently uncovered another Ming reference specifically crediting Kuo Hsün with producing an "imitation" of *Shui-hu*, along with similar texts of *San-kuo* and *Ying-lieh chuan* 英烈傳.[14] This, by the way, would obviously imply that the "Kuo Hsün edition" was based on a yet earlier prototype, a possibility I will return to shortly.[15]

The primary reason for all this uncertainty lies in the fact that no authoritative exemplar of the Kuo edition believed to have existed during the sixteenth century is now extant. This is not to say that no pretenders have come forward to claim the honor. The last report of a complete copy of a Kuo text was by Miao Ch'üan-sun 繆荃孫 in the early Kuang-hsü period.

[13] For the idea that Kuo Hsün's role was that of the sponsor of this edition, see Tai Pu-fan, *Chien-wen lu*, pp. 117ff. Chang Kuo-kuang, "Shui-hu tsu-pen t'an-k'ao," p. 39, concurs with this opinion, and puts the date of the edition around 1533–34. The idea that Kuo may have simply been the owner of the text derives from the expression "[this text] was the one handed down in his family" 即其家所傳 in *Yeh-huo pien* (see above, n. 11). See also Tai Pu-fan, *Chien-wen lu*, p. 110.

[14] See Tai Pu-fan, *Chien-wen lu*, p. 117. The text in question is a quasi-historical compilation entitled *Huang-Ming ts'ung-hsin lu*, by Ch'en Chien, *chüan* 30, p. 1a. The passage reads: "At that point Kuo Hsün, Marquis of Wu-ting, wishing to elevate his ancestor Kuo Ying for his contribution to the founding of the dynasty to a position in the Imperial Ancestral Temple (*T'ai-miao* 太廟), made imitations of the colloquial *San-kuo chih* and the *Shui-hu chuan*, and made the *Record of the Illustrious Heroes of Our Dynasty [Ying-lieh chuan]* ..." 至是武定侯郭勛欲進其立功之祖英于太廟乃倣三國志俗說及水滸傳, 爲國朝英烈記 . Tai also notes on the preceding page the fact that the *Pao-wen t'ang shu-mu* omits mention of any copy of the *Ying-lieh chuan*. Tai notes four missing characters in his citation, but the Gest Oriental Library copy is apparently complete.

[15] This is precisely what the T'ien-tu wai-ch'en preface unequivocally states: "Kuo Wu-ting reprinted the book" 郭武定重刻其書. For discussions of this point, see Nieh Kan-nu, "Wu-lun," p. 147; Shiroki Naoya, "Sōzō to iu koto," pp. 99ff., 117, and "Haiin Suiko zenden e no hihan to teigen," pp. 57–73. See also Wen Ying, "Liu-pien," pp. 202ff.; and Huang Lin, "Ku-pen," p. 89. On the specific changes allegedly made by Kuo Hsün to revise an earlier text, see below, n. 35. For further discussions of the specific points of difference between the Kuo text and its hypothetical precursor, see Cheng Chen-to, "Yen-hua," p. 155; and Shiroki Naoya "Sōzō to iu koto," p. 122. Huang Lin ("Ku-pen," p. 87) cites evidence from the Ming work *Hsiao-ch'uang tzu-chi* of a lost early edition in which the two campaigns were interpolated before the surrender of the Liang-shan band to the imperial forces (see n. 22). On the shift of material in the Yen P'o-hsi episode, see Nieh Kan-nu, "Wu-lun," p. 68. For the removal of some incidental verses and the "appended narratives" (*chih-yü*), see later discussion in this chapter. For explanation of the latter term, see Cheng Chen-to, "Yen-hua," pp. 111f.; Hu Shih, "K'ao-cheng," pp. 75ff., and appendix, pp. 96–100; and Nieh Kan-nu, "Wu-lun," p. 194. Some of these points are repeated in the *fa-fan* preface to the Yüan Wu-yai edition (to be discussed shortly) and in Ch'ien Hsi-yen's *Hsi-hsia* (see n. 11).

This purchase was recorded by Teng Chih-ch'eng 鄧之誠 in his *Ku-tung so-chi* 骨董瑣記, after which time the book dropped completely out of sight.[16] But when Cheng Chen-to managed to obtain a five-chapter section of a *fan-pen* text in 1931, he unhesitatingly identified it on the basis of this description as a copy of the lost Kuo edition. This fragment was later joined by an additional three-chapter section obtained by the Peking Library in 1958, plus a single folio fragment belonging to the great book collector Ma Lien 馬廉, to make up a sizable chunk of the book.[17] Since these pieces gave sufficient evidence to establish that they were the remains of a hundred-chapter text in twenty *chüan*, they at one time seemed to provide the missing link to the lost Chia-ching editions. At least, the respected bibliographer Chao Wan-li 趙萬里, while expressing reservations as to whether or not this was a Kuo text, concurred that these were indeed authentic examples of Chia-ching printing.[18] In the past several years, however, Cheng Chen-to's hasty conclusion has largely given way to skepticism.[19]

In the meantime, a fragment of another early edition was discovered in the bowels of the Shanghai Municipal Library in 1975.[20] Although this piece is also evidently part of a twenty-*chüan fan-pen* edition, it differs

[16] Teng Chih-ch'eng, *Ku-tung so-chi ch'üan-pien*, p. 103; also available in Chu I-hsüan, *Tzu-liao*, pp. 185f.; K'ung Ling-ching, *Shih-liao*, pp. 25f. See Nieh Kan-nu, "Wu-lun," pp. 144f.; and Irwin, *Evolution*, p. 65. Miao Ch'üan-sun's role in the spurious printing of the *Ching-pen t'ung-su hsiao-shuo* 京本通俗小說 collection probably compromises his credibility in this context as well.

[17] For the story of Cheng Chen-to's discovery of this text, see his *Chieh-chung te-shu chi*, pp. 114f., cited in Chu I-hsüan, *Tzu-liao*, p. 511. He claims that this is a Kuo text remnant in his preface to *Shui-hu ch'üan-chuan*, p. 4. See Irwin, "Water Margin Revisited," pp. 395f. Regarding the three-chapter fragment in the Peking Library, see Y. W. Ma's description in "Chü-pao chi," p. 24. Ma (same article) also mentions an additional one-page fragment at one time belonging to Wu Hsiao-ling. The single folio fragment belonging to Ma Lien was reproduced in KLPPTSKKK 8:2 (March–April, 1934), p. 5939. See Chao Ching-shen, "Shui-hu chuan chien-lun," p. 139. I am grateful to the Rare Book Division of the Peking Library, and especially to the curator, Li Chih-chung 李致忠, for allowing me to examine the Chia-ching fragments as well as the T'ien-tu wai-ch'en text during the winter of 1984–85. Microfilm copies of the latter are available in the Far Eastern Library of the University of Chicago and in Gest Oriental Library, Princeton.

[18] Y. W. Ma affirms the judgment of Chao Wan-li in "Hu-yü yen-chiu," pp. 194.

[19] See Y. W. Ma's refutation in "P'ai tso-tz'u i-hou Shui-hu chuan ti ch'ing-chieh ho jen-wu," p. 85, and in his "Chü-pao chi," p. 24. Liu Ts'un-yan ("Sur l'authenticité des romans historiques de Lo Guanzhong," p. 261) also rejects Cheng Chen-to's claim that this is a remnant of the Kuo text, but he still accepts the fragment as a Chia-ching printing (p. 284). See also Nieh Kan-nu, "Wu-lun," p. 195. In order to avoid misunderstanding, Nieh calls this text the "large-character edition" (*ta-tzu pen* 大字本).

[20] On the discovery of the Shanghai fragment, see Ku T'ing-lung and Shen Chin, "Kuan-yü hsin fa-hsien ti Ching-pen chung-i chuan ts'an-yeh," pp. 34–35. Ku and Shen conclude on the basis of printing features that this text must have been published earlier than the hypothetical Kuo Hsün edition. I am grateful to Mr. Shen for allowing me to see a copy of this fragment in the Shanghai Library in December 1984.

from the Cheng Chen-to text on a number of points, including its linguistic style, and most noticeably its title, *Ching-pen chung-i chuan* 京本忠義傳, which provides a unique exemplar of what was apparently a separate line of textual development.[21] Yet the consensus of scholarly opinion accepts this as an authentic Chia-ching text of the novel, possibly the earliest in existence. In addition to this, a trace of one more early edition, representing yet another textual strain, has recently been uncovered by Huang Lin in a *pi-chi* collection entitled *Hsiao-ch'uang tzu-chi* 小窗自紀 by Wu Ts'ung-hsien 吳從先, dating from the early seventeenth century.[22] Over the years, there have occasionally been other reports of rediscovered Ming editions of the *Shui-hu chuan*, but none of these have provided any concrete evidence regarding the early history of the novel.[23]

It is only in the Wan-li period that we begin to get convincing material evidence of the nature of the *fan-pen* editions of *Shui-hu* in circulation by that time. By far the most significant of these is the edition entitled *Chung-i shui-hu chuan* bearing a preface signed by T'ien-tu wai-ch'en 天都外臣 with the date 1589.[24] According to a slightly later description in Shen Te-fu's 沈德符 (1578–1642) *Wan-li yeh-huo pien* 萬曆野獲編, this preface marks the text in question as a reprint of an original Kuo Hsün edition; and Shen goes on to identify "T'ien-tu wai-ch'en" as a sobriquet of the well-known sixteenth-century literati figure Wang Tao-k'un 汪道昆 (1525–

---

[21] Y. W. Ma ("Chü-pao chi," p. 24) agrees with Ku and Shen's assessment that this text belongs to the *fan-pen* system, since it appears to have been a twenty-*chüan*, hundred-chapter text. Ou-yang Chien, "Shui-hu chien-pen fan-pen ti-shan kuo-ch'eng hsin-cheng," pp. 215f., argues on the basis of occurrences of nonstandard orthography (*su-tzu* 俗字) similar to examples found in the early prototype of *Hsi-yu chi*, *Ta-t'ang San-tsang ch'ü-ching shih-hua* and in *San-kuo chih p'ing-hua* (see Chapters 3, Part I, and 5, Part I) that this should not be considered a *fan-pen*. Recently the assessment of this text has been debated by Liu Tung and Ou-yang Chien ("Ching-pen chung-i chuan p'ing-chia shang-tui") versus Chang Kuo-kuang ("P'ing Chung-i chuan ts'an-yeh fa-hsien i-i fei-ch'ang chung-ta lun"). See also Shiroki Naoya, "Ko-shi Shin-shi kyōcho kanyo shinhakken teki Kyōbon chūgiden zanya hihan."

[22] See Huang Lin, "Ku-pen," pp. 86–89. The passage cited in *Hsiao-ch'uang tzu-chi* is in a section entitled "Tu Shui-hu chuan" 讀水滸傳. This source speaks of something it calls a "historical fiction" (*pai-shih* 稗史) version of *Shui-hu chuan*, whose contents are apparently not identical to any extant *fan-pen* or *chien-pen* text. The citation is also available in Chu I-hsüan, *Tzu-liao*, pp. 218ff.

[23] For example, Yeh Te-chün (*Sung-Yuan-Ming chiang-ch'ang wen-hsüeh*, p. 49) speaks of the discovery "three years earlier" of a Chia-ching text, with no further information provided (despite the publication date of 1959, the author dates his conclusion of the book 1952). Ogawa Tamaki provides a similar note in a review of this book in *Chūgoku bungaku hō* 1 (October 1954): 136.

[24] The sole known exemplar now extant is held in the Peking Library. For the story of the acquisition of this copy, see Wu Hsiao-ling, "Man-t'an T'ien-tu wai-ch'en hsü-pen Chung-i shui-hu chuan."

93).[25] If this information is accurate, then the date 1589 on the preface would provide a very convenient point of reference, as it would put the reprinting of this text right around the time of the Shih-te t'ang printing of *Hsi-yu chi*, during the same years in which the manuscript of *Chin P'ing Mei* was probably taking shape.

Unfortunately, a number of problems detract from the usefulness of this piece of the puzzle. First, the widely cited date 1589 is actually based on a very shaky reconstruction of a few virtually illegible marks remaining on the edge of a page that has been cut away.[26] In addition, Hsü Shuo-fang has recently shown that the T'ien-tu wai-ch'en preface itself was apparently an expansion of a slightly earlier preface written by the poet and dramatist Chang Feng-i 張鳳翼 (1527–1613). The edition for which this latter preface was written is no longer extant, but the piece is preserved in Chang's collected prose, and has been dated by Hsü at 1588 or 1589.[27] For that matter, the identification of T'ien-tu wai-ch'en as Wang Tao-k'un is itself subject to some doubt.[28] And even if this could be confirmed, the only extant exemplar of this edition is in fact a much later printing done in Hsin-an in the following century, by which time, it has been demonstrated, a number of blocks had already been recut.[29] For all these reasons, this

[25] Shen Te-Fu, *Yeh-huo pien*, p. 139. See Yen Tun-i, *Yen-pien*, pp. 180ff.; and Irwin, *Evolution*, pp. 65f.

[26] All that remains of the data is a few truncated ink strokes, looking like a line of dots. The nearly universal decipherment of these marks takes them to be the cyclical date *chi-ch'ou* 己丑 (1589), although this reading is hard to see, even if one assumes a partial imprint from faulty blocks. Other possible pairs of calendrical terms whose edges might yield the requisite marks include *i-wei* 乙未 (1595) and *chi-hai* 己亥 (1599), but as far as I know the accepted reading has never been questioned. Wu Hsiao-ling describes the process of decipherment in "Man-t'an" (see n. 24), and admits that the conclusion was far from certain.

[27] Hsü Shuo-fang, "Kuan-yü Chang Feng-i ho T'ien-tu wai-ch'en ti Shui-hu chuan hsü." For further discussion of the relationship between the two prefaces, see Wu Hsiao-ling, "Man-t'an," and Wang Hsiao-i, "Kuan-yü T'ien-tu wai-ch'en Wang Tao-k'un." Cf. Ho Hsin's assumption that this preface was attached to the original Chia-ching book (*Yen-chiu*, p. 100). In any case, the text cannot be a copy of the "fine edition" known from Chia-ching sources. See Nieh Kan-nu, "Wu-lun," p. 147. A similar conclusion is voiced by Y. W. Ma, "Chü-pao chi," p. 23; Wen Ying, "Liu-pien," pp. 214ff.; and Fan Ning, "Shui-hu chuan pan-pen yüan-liu k'ao," p. 67.

[28] For the doubts about the identification of T'ien-tu wai-ch'en as Wang Tao-k'un see, e.g., discussion by Nieh Kan-nu ("Wu-lun," p. 146f.). Cheng Chen-to went as far as to speculate that Wang Tao-k'un himself may have been the compiler of this edition ("Yen-hua," p. 138). See Wang Hsiao-i, "T'ien-tu wai-ch'en." Wang Tao-k'un is known to have lived for some time in retirement near the famous T'ien-tu peak of the Huang-shan range.

[29] Hsin-an 新安 (formerly Hui-chou 徽州, area of modern She-hsien 歙縣) was a major publishing center during the Ming known for finer printings than those produced in a similar center in Chien-yang 建陽, Fukien. See K. T. Wu, "Ming Printers and Printing," pp. 204f. See also Yen Tun-i, *Yen-pien*, pp. 185f.; and Y. W. Ma, "Chü-pao chi," p. 23. For the

particular text cannot really serve as an accurate model of the Kuo Hsün edition or other hypothetical Chia-ching forms of the *fan-pen Shui-hu chuan*.

One other possible example of the lost early editions is the hundred-chapter text discovered by Li Tsung-t'ung 李宗侗 (Hsüan-po 玄伯) in 1924, and subsequently reprinted by Li under the title *Chung-i shui-hu chuan*. Whether or not Li's judgment that he had found a Kuo text was accurate, Sun K'ai-ti, for one, saw it and accepted it as being a product of the 1570s, which might put it at least earlier than the T'ien-tu wai-ch'en edition. However, this question is now entirely academic, since the Li Hsüan-po edition is today virtually inaccessible, and is known only by secondhand description.[30]

This leaves us with no reliable exemplar of the early *fan-pen Shui-hu* until the 1610 printing by the Jung-yü t'ang 容與堂 of the text entitled *Li Cho-wu hsien-sheng p'i-p'ing Chung-i shui-hu chuan* 李卓吾先生批評忠義水滸傳. This date of publication falls inconveniently outside of the framework of our century. But it does, again, nicely parallel the date of the earliest printed edition of the *Chin P'ing Mei*, a coincidence less random than it may immediately seem, in light of the connection of both of these books with the Yüan brothers 三袁, Feng Meng-lung 馮夢龍, and other Wan-li literary figures involved in fiction publishing. Anyway, we do have several well-preserved exemplars of this text, so it can provide a reasonable specimen of the sixteenth-century *fan-pen* system.[31] Aside from the heated controversy

---

identification of blocks cut by Shih-ch'ü ko 石渠閣, see Cheng Chen-to, *Shui-hu ch'üan-chuan*, preface, p. 6; Wang Li-ch'i, "Pan-pen chi chiao-ting," pp. 399ff.; and Fan Ning, "Yüan-liu k'ao," pp. 67f. A text entitled *Shih-ch'ü ko ching-ting Huang-Ming ying-lieh chuan* 石渠閣精訂皇明英烈傳 is held in the Tōyō bunka kenkyūjo at Tokyo University.

[30] The Li Hsüan-po edition, reprinted in 1925, is discussed by Hu Shih in "K'ao-cheng," pp. 103f.; Irwin, *Evolution*, pp. 66; and Ho Hsin, *Yen-chiu*, pp. 33f. Shiroki Naoya ("Kaku Butei hon," p. 145f.) states that certain other printings of this text held in Japanese collections had marginal commentaries. Sun K'ai-ti ("Shui-hu chuan chiu-pen k'ao," p. 193) describes this as a "fine printing" on the basis of his examination of the book in 1931, but he goes on to bemoan its subsequent disappearance. Fan Ning ("Yüan-liu k'ao," p. 67) suggests that certain details of the Chieh-tzu yüan Ta-ti yü-jen preface edition held in the Peking Library, which conform to descriptions of the Li Hsüan-po text, may indicate a direct textual derivation. The fact that this text is no longer accessible is affirmed by Y. W. Ma ("Chü-pao chi," p. 25) and Irwin ("Water Margin," pp. 406f.). Cheng Chen-to ("Yen-hua," p. 150) also admits that he had been unable to see the original Li Hsüan-po text firsthand. On the other hand, the illustrations from this edition were apparently reprinted by Cheng Chen-to in a separate publication in 1958. See Ma Tai-loi, "Ming-pan Shui-hu chuan ch'a-t'u erh-chung shu hou," p. 123, n. 7. Y. W. Ma believes that the original copy of the text may still be in the possession of Li's family.

[31] For bibliographical information on the Jung-yü t'ang edition, see sources cited in n. 4. See Sun K'ai-ti, *Jih-pen Tung-ching so chien Chung-kuo hsiao-shuo shu-mu*, pp. 106ff. A complete set of photographic reproductions of an early eighteenth-century Japanese copy prepared by Wang Ku-lu 王古魯 is in the library of the Institute of Literature of the Chinese

over the authenticity of the attached critical commentary attributed to Li Chih,[32] the general scholarly consensus tells us that, as far as its basic text is concerned, the Jung-yü t'ang edition can be taken as representative of the chain of filiation leading down from the hypothetical Chia-ching, Kuo Hsün, and T'ien-tu wai-ch'en editions.[33]

From there, the same chain of development splits off through various lines of filiation to yield all of the later variants of the *fan-pen* system. The most influential of these is the 120-chapter *Li Cho-wu p'ing Chung-i shui-hu ch'üan-chuan* 李卓吾評忠義水滸全傳 (*Chung-i shui-hu ch'üan-shu* 全書) printed by Yüan Wu-yai 袁無涯 in 1614.[34] The relation of this edition to the *fan-pen* system is obscured by certain textual problems. First, the *fa-fan* 發凡 preface included in this volume, containing as it does a number of knowing or unknowing misstatements, has raised doubts about the facts of its publication.[35] This skepticism is then carried over to the appended

Academy of Social Sciences in Peking. I am grateful to Professor Liu Shih-te for allowing me to examine these in February 1985. I have seen similar but not identical copies of this edition in the Jinbun kagaku kenkyūjo of Kyoto University and the Tōyō bunka kenkyūjo of Tokyo University. The idea that the Jung-yü t'ang edition represents the earliest *fan-pen* text now extant is voiced by Ou-yang Chien ("Ti-shan kuo-ch'eng," p. 223) and Nieh Kan-nu ("Wu-lun," p. 103). A number of scholars assume that the Li text was not substantially different from the Kuo edition; see Fan Ning, "Yüan-liu k'ao," p. 68; and Y. W. Ma, "Chü-pao chi," p. 23. Fan Ning notes certain discrepancies between the Peking Library copy and certain Japanese exemplars. Nieh Kan-nu ("Wu-lun," p. 104, 144ff.) also speaks of two types of Jung-yü t'ang editions, one with a preface by Sun P'u 孫樸 and one without.

[32] For the various bibliographical and critical issues regarding the "Li Cho-wu" commentaries on *Shui-hu chuan* and the other novels, see the Appendix of this book.

[33] Nieh Kan-nu ("Wu-lun," pp. 103ff.) enumerates some minor differences between the Jung-yü t'ang and earlier *fan-pen* texts. Y. W. Ma ("Ch'ing-chieh ho jen-wu," p. 85) hypothesizes that a prototype of the Jung-yü t'ang edition may have preceded the T'ien-tu wai-ch'en edition. For charts of the filiation of known *fan-pen* editions, see Irwin, "Water Margin," p. 415; Yen Tun-i, *Yen-pien*, p. 201; and Hu Shih, "K'ao-cheng," p. 149. Cheng Chen-to, assisted by Wang Li-ch'i and Wu Hsiao-ling, chose the T'ien-tu wai-ch'en edition as the basic text for the variorum edition of *Shui-hu ch'üan-chuan* (except of course for chapters 90–110).

[34] For bibliographical information, see b.n. II.3. See Yeh Lang's appendix "Yeh Chou p'i-tien Shui-hu chuan k'ao-cheng," in *Chung-kuo hsiao-shuo mei-hsüeh*, p. 290, n. 1, where he asserts that this edition may have been printed as early as 1612, after the publication of the *Hei hsüan-feng chi* mentioned in the afterword to the "Huai-lin" prefatory essay in the Jung-yü t'ang text (see my Appendix). A reprint of this edition printed by the Yü-yü t'ang 郁郁堂 is held in the Nanking Library and in the Naikaku Bunko and Seikadō libraries in Tokyo (see Sun K'ai-ti, *Shu-mu*, p. 216). For further information on Yüan Wu-yai, see Wang Li-ch'i, "Shui-hu Li Cho-wu p'ing-pen ti chen-wei wen-t'i," pp. 377f.

[35] For further discussion of these points in the *fa-fan* preface, see Cheng Chen-to, "Yen-hua," pp. 151f.; Hu Shih, "K'ao-cheng," pp. 75ff., 109ff.; Shiroki Naoya, "Ippyaku nijūkai Suikozenden no kenkyū: hatsubon o tsūjite kokoromita," pp. 125ff., 134f.; and Irwin, "Water Margin," pp. 402ff. The most glaring misstatement in the *fa-fan* piece, other than the report

critical commentary, also attributed to Li Chih, though substantially different from that in the Jung-yü t'ang edition. Although most scholars have
tended to give credence to the sources that deny the attribution advertised
in the title, instead ascribing this commentary to Yeh Chou 葉晝, some
have been willing to at least partially accept the testimony of Yang Ting-
chien 楊定見 and grant a measure of authenticity to the commentary.[36]
This, however, still leaves open the question of whether the text itself bears
a relation to the one Li Chih had written a commentary upon, or derives
from some other independent source. In any event, aside from the interpolated twenty chapters covering the campaigns against the bandits T'ien
Hu 田虎 and Wang Ch'ing 王慶, which have no corresponding material in
the hundred-chapter texts, the remainder of this edition differs only in
superficial details from the other extant *fan-pen* versions.[37]

---

that the Kuo edition was responsible for adding the section on the Liao campaign and
removing the T'ien and Wang campaigns, is the claim that Li Chih was responsible for
restoring the words *Chung-i* to the title of the book. See Nieh Kan-nu, "Wu-lun," p. 119.
Since certain portions of the *fa-fan* are apparently based on the T'ien-tu wai-ch'en preface,
or on its sources, the writer should have been aware that the title of that text also includes
the words *Chung-i*. See also Ou-yang Chien, "Ti-shan kuo-ch'eng," p. 267, and Wang Li-ch'i,
"Chen-wei wen-t'i," pp. 373ff. For the text of the *fa-fan* preface, see Ma T'i-chi, *Tzu-liao*,
pp. 12ff.

[36] See Appendix of this book for discussion and references.

[37] The fact that the Yüan Wu-yai edition does not represent an untouched original text
is stated in its full title, which begins with the term "newly reprinted" (*hsin-chüan* 新鐫). See
Nieh Kan-nu ("Wu-lun," p. 151), who specifies the object of this revision to be the original
Li Chih text, as opposed to the Jung-yü t'ang edition. The same conclusion can be drawn
from Yüan Chung-lang's remark to the effect that this edition contained "minor additions"
稍有增加耳. There is a difference of opinion as to whether this expression refers to the
addition of the critical commentary itself, or perhaps only to minor changes in the commentary or the text. See Yeh Lang, "Yeh Chou p'ing-tien," pp. 291f.; Ou-yang Chien,
"Ti-shan kuo-ch'eng," p. 261; and Huang Lin, "Shui-hu ch'üan-chuan Li Chih p'ing yeh shu
wei-t'o," p. 96. Another interpretation (e.g., Chin Tai-t'ung, "Li Chih," p. 75) takes this as a
reference to the addition of the two campaigns, a textural modification that occurs in no
other *fan-pen* examples, although this does appear in many of the early *chien-pen* texts. Fan
Ning ("Yüan-liu k'ao," p. 71) cites an example of the modification of a poem in chapter 42
to foreshadow the interpolated campaigns. We can recall the complaint in the T'ien-tu
wai-ch'en preface that the addition of these sections was a superfluous encumbrance on the
text (*t'ien-tsu* 添足). Cheng Chen-to (*Shui-hu ch'üan-chuan*, preface, p. 1) notes that only the
Fang La campaign is covered in the narrative in *Hsüan-ho i-shih*, although some have
interpreted a line that speaks of "three expeditions" (*san-lu* 三路) as a reference to the other
campaigns. Cf. Wang Yung-chien's note in his "Ts'ung Ming-ch'u ti Shui-hu hsi k'an Shui-hu
chuan tsu-pen ti ch'eng-shu nien-tai," p. 241, that the Liao and Fang La campaigns are
already mentioned in Yuan and Ming dramas on *Shui-hu* themes, but the other two
campaigns are never suggested. Ou-yang Chien ("Ti-shan kuo-ch'eng," p. 213) argues that
this interpolation reveals a deliberate attempt to add to the glory of the Liang-shan heroes,
and points out that the text of the *fan-pen* treatment of the Liao and Fang La campaigns, as
represented by the Jung-yü t'ang and Yüan Wu-yai editions, is fairly consistent with that in

As for additional examples of hundred-chapter *fan-pen* texts, I should mention yet another *Li Cho-wu p'i-tien Chung-i shui-hu chuan*, published by the Chieh-tzu yüan 芥子園 printing house and bearing a preface by Ta-ti yü-jen 大滌餘人.[38] According to certain scholars, this text was actually produced by abridgment of the Yüan Wu-yai 120-chapter edition, rather than through direct filiation from the 100-chapter line; others, however, see this fine printing as closer to the original Chia-ching editions.[39] This latter position is supported by the fact that the Ta-ti yü-jen preface, perhaps borrowed here from the Li Hsüan-po edition, shows signs of being directly or indirectly based on the T'ien-tu wai-ch'en preface.[40] Ma Tai-loi, in a recently published article, has attempted to demonstrate on the basis of the woodcut illustrations that this line of filiation should predate the Yüan Wu-yai version.[41] Another edition of the *Chung-i shui-hu chuan* in one hundred chapters, bearing a preface and commentary attributed to the late Ming literary maverick Chung Hsing 鍾惺 (1574–1624), has been accepted by many scholars as a direct descendant of the Jung-yü t'ang edition.[42] Not only is the preface in this text closely modeled on the Li Chih preface, and

---

the *chien-pen*, but diverges in the narration of the T'ien Hu and Wang Ch'ing campaigns. He also states that the T'ien Hu and Wang Ch'ing sections are better integrated in the 120-chapter edition than in the *chien-pen* examples where they also appear. A number of scholars, including Cheng Chen-to ("Yen-hua," p. 114), Y. W. Ma ("Ch'ing-chieh ho jen-wu," pp. 87ff.), Shiroki Naoya ("Sōzō," p. 123), and Ch'en Chin-chao ("Li Cho-wu p'i-tien Shui-hu chuan chih yen-chiu," p. 48), note the discrepancy in the fact that the first three campaigns are conducted with practically no casualties, after which the band is virtually wiped out in the fourth, as proof that these sections were not by the same author. Li Tsung-t'ung ("Tu Shui-hu chi," pp. 12ff.) speaks of these sections as a separate work, which he refers to as *Shui-hu ssu-cheng* 水滸四征.

[38] For bibliographical information, see b.n. II.5, and Sun K'ai-ti, *Shu-mu*, p. 212. A number of shoddy later editions of *Shui-hu chuan*, *Hsi-yu chi*, and *San-kuo* advertise themselves as Chieh-tzu yüan editions (e.g., one copy in Metropolitan Library, Peking), but they can have little to do with the elegant printing of the true Chieh-tzu yüan texts.

[39] A number of scholars follow Sun K'ai-ti (*Shu-mu*, p. 212) in proclaiming this to be an abridgment of the 120-chapter edition. See Yeh Lang ("Yeh Chou p'ing-tien," p. 294), Ch'en Chin-chao ("Li Cho-wu p'i-tien," p. 45), Irwin ("Water Margin," p. 409). Others speculate that this text may derive directly from the T'ien-tu wai-ch'en edition, and thus may be a close descendant of the Kuo Hsün text. See Shiroki Naoya, "Ippyaku nijūkai Suikozenden no kenkyū: hatsubon o tsūjite kokoromita," pp. 131f.; Fan Ning, "Yüan-liu k'ao," pp. 67, 70, 72.

[40] See Sun K'ai-ti, *Shu-mu*, p. 212.

[41] See Ma Tai-loi, "Ch'a-t'u," pp. 121–26.

[42] For information on the "Chung Hsing" commentary edition, see Sun K'ai-ti, *Jih-pen*, p. 109; Shiroki Naoya, "Ippyaku nijūkai: hatsubon," pp. 131f.; and his "Shō Hakkei hihyō Shichikan kanpon no kenkyū," pt. 1, pp. 103f., pt. 2, p. 171, and pt. 3, pp. 116–48. See also Ch'en Hsi-chung, "Kuan-yü Chung Po-ching hsien-sheng p'i-p'ing Chung-i shui-hu chuan," pp. 42–52; Liu Hsiu-yeh, *Ku-tien hsiao-shuo hsi-ch'ü ts'ung-k'ao*, pp. 84f. and Shiroki Naoya, "Zanya hihan," p. 79.

its commentary largely derivative, but it also reprints prefatory material based on certain pieces signed by the monk Huai-lin 懷林, which are also attached to the Jung-yü t'ang text.[43] Thus, although the attribution to a notorious figure like Chung Hsing is naturally suspect, it still retains a small measure of plausibility. Among the extant hundred-chapter editions, I might also mention here a number of other texts primarily preserved in Japan, including the Mukyūkai 無窮會 and Kuraishi 倉石 texts described by Irwin and others.[44]

All of these editions, however, were completely eclipsed by Chin Sheng-t'an's 金聖歎 seventy-one-chapter abridgment first published in 1644, which became the standard text for three centuries of Chinese readers as well as that used for virtually all translations into other languages, until very recently.[45] Chin's treatment of the novel has become the focus of intense critical controversy, especially with respect to the ideological impli-cations of his truncation of the text and substitution of a new ending, and on account of his hostile attitude toward Sung Chiang expressed in the commentary. Chin's claim to be restoring the status of an earlier prototype (*ku-pen* 古本) was never really taken seriously, except in connection with his naming of Shih Nai-an 施耐庵 as the original author of the work.[46] But as for the rest of his text itself, beyond a certain amount of minor textual emendations used to bring out points of his own interpretation, Chin's

[43] See especially "A critique of characters in *Shui-hu chuan*" (*Shui-hu chuan jen-p'in p'ing* 水滸傳人品評), which duplicates much of "A Comparative Ranking" (see below, n. 130). Nieh Kan-nu compares the two prefaces in "Wu-lun," p. 106. On the "Huai-lin" prefatory pieces, see Appendix.

[44] See Irwin, "Water Margin," pp. 395, 399; and Nieh Kan-nu, "Wu-lun," pp. 150f.

[45] For further background regarding the genesis of the Chin Sheng-t'an edition, see Cheng Chen-to, "Yen-hua," pp. 122ff.; Sun K'ai-ti, *Jih-pen*, p. 112; Yen Tun-i, *Yen-pien*, pp. 239ff.; Irwin, *Evolution*, pp. 87ff. Irwin (*Evolution*, pp. 89, 108, n. 1) notes the date 1641 on the third Chin Sheng-t'an preface, although the actual date of publication was apparently 1644. Ch'en Chin-chao claims that Chin's text was based on the Yüan Wu-yai edition (see *Wen-lun*, pp. 114ff., and his "T'an Kuan-hua t'ang Chin Sheng-t'an p'i-pen Shui-hu chuan," pp. 59f. Irwin (*Evolution*, p. 91) says it was based on both editions.

[46] Chin Sheng-tan's claim to have obtained a *ku-pen* text is rejected by practically all scholars. One exception is Hu Shih ("K'ao-cheng," pp. 40, 45), who accepted this claim; and more recently Ou-yang Chien ("Ti-shan kuo-ch'eng, p. 212) has been willing to at least entertain the possibility. Y. W. Ma ("Ch'ing-chieh ho jen-wu," p. 91) concludes after a detailed study of the latter part of the text that the five major sections of the 120-chapter version following the ceremony of inauguration in chapter 71 all derive from different hands, thus implying that the first seventy chapters may represent a preexisting integral work. Nieh Kan-nu ("Wu-lun," p. 114) also notes this, but he denies Chin's claim of having acquired an earlier Kuan-hua t'ang edition, explaining the name "Kuan-hua" as an allusion to the *hao* of one of Chin Sheng-t'an's close friends. At least one aspect of Chin's revised text may have a prior source. That is the final dream of doom, an element that, according to Wang Ch'i's *Pai-shih hui-pien*, pp. 1558f. (see above, n. 6), was a part of an early version of the narrative.

edition does not depart radically from the basic *fan-pen* text—that is, of course, through the first seventy chapters.[47] With this, the final form of the *fan-pen* was established, to be reissued periodically during the Ch'ing dynasty, occasionally with new commentaries such as that by Wang Wang-ju 王望如, but with no substantive changes until the rediscovery of the 100- and 120-chapter *fan-pen* texts in the early twentieth century.[48]

On the basis of all these pieces of evidence, we can put together a fairly complete picture of the process of textual development of the *fan-pen* *Shui-hu chuan* during the late Ming period: from the first appearance of a hundred-chapter text in the Chia-ching period, its subsequent printing with some sort of connection to the house of Kuo Hsün, its reprinting in the Wan-li period after 1589 and again toward the end of the Wan-li period in 1610 and 1614, and finally its truncation and reediting at the very end of the dynasty.

But this oversimplified scenario is complicated by at least two major areas of uncertainty. Most immediately, we can recall that the very same bibliographical evidence used to document the circulation of the *fan-pen* recension by the Chia-ching period nearly unanimously asserts that the novel had been composed much earlier, naming as its principal compiler either Lo Kuan-chung 羅貫中 or Shih Nai-an. To this is added the fact that virtually every edition from the sixteenth century down to the present day clearly states on its title page that one or both of these men were responsible for its original compilation.[49]

---

[47] This is obviously a matter of subjective judgment. Cheng Chen-to speaks in his preface to *Shui-hu ch'üan-chuan* (p. 4) of "large-scale revisions" 大加修改, and Nieh Kan-nu ("Wu-lun," pp. 121–27) emphasizes the extent of Chin's editorial changes. For examples of hostile criticism of Chin Sheng-t'an, see Ho Man-tzu, *Lun Chin Sheng-t'an p'ing-kai Shui-hu chuan*. In the past few years some attempts have been made to rehabilitate Chin's reputation. See, for example, Chang Kuo-kuang, *Shui-hu yü Chin Sheng-t'an yen-chiu*, pp. 91–111. Cheng Kung-tun, in *Shui-hu chuan lun-wen chi*, pp. 415, 464, 598, appeals for an objective evaluation of Chin Sheng-t'an's contributions as a fiction critic. Lu Hsin, "Chin-p'i Shui-hu ti ch'ü-pi yü Sung Chiang," p. 52, distinguishes between the prefaces, with their anti-Sung Chiang bias, and the actual comments in the text, which occasionally show sympathy for the aims of the band.

[48] For bibliographical information on the Wang Wang-ju edition, see b.n. II.7.

[49] See, for example, *Pai-ch'uan shu-chih*, *Ch'i-hsiu lei-kao*, and *Hsi-hu yu-lan chih-yü* (cited in nn. 5 and 6), as well as *Yeh-shih-yüan shu-mu* and *Yin-shu-wu shu-ying*. See citations in Ma T'i-chi, *Tzu-liao* pp. 351, 377; Chu I-hsüan, *Tzu-liao*, pp. 130ff., 152; and K'ung Ling-ching, *Shih-liao*, pp. 12f. The T'ien-tu wai-ch'en preface also credits Lo Kuan-chung with the authorship, although the title page of the K'ang-hsi reprint does cite Shih Nai-an as the principal author (see Nieh Kan-nu, "Wu-lun," p. 147). On the personal names of Lo Kuan-chung, see Nieh, "Wu-lun," p. 155; and Wang Li-ch'i, "Lo Kuan-chung yü San-kuo chih t'ung-su yen-i," pp. 68ff. Ch'en Chung-fan reviews the transmission of this information from source to source in his "Shih-lun," p. 112. See also Cheng Chen-to, "Yen-hua," pp. 111–17, esp. footnote on page 115.

These attributions, rather than solving the question of authorship of the
novel, in fact only pose further puzzles. First, Lo Kuan-chung has been
readily identified as a fourteenth-century dramatist, at least one of whose
plays is still extant. A certain amount of background information about him
is available, including a biographical notice in the *Hsü Lu-kuei pu* 續錄鬼簿
of Chia Chung-ming 賈仲明 and other sources. But nowhere in this material
do we find any documentary evidence of his alleged activity as a novelist,
such as we get later in the Chia-ching bibliographical sources.[50] Liu Ts'un-
yan's suggestion that the appearance of an oracular figure with the name
Hsü Kuan-chung 許貫中 in a *chien-pen* text of the novel may constitute
a signature on Lo's part is intriguing but inconclusive.[51] More recently,
Wang Li-ch'i has uncovered what he believes to be complete proof of Lo's
authorship in the giving of the name Ch'en Wen-chao 陳文昭, the same as
that of a highly respected friend and colleague of Lo Kuan-chung, to a
noble-minded official who provides a unique example of judicial integrity
in chapter 27.[52] But aside from these tantalizing hints, we have no solid
evidence linking Lo to the novel. As a result, the debate has revolved
around the question of whether or not the ideological leanings expressed in
the book, or the style in which these are presented, conform to those in
San-kuo yen-i—also attributed to Lo Kuan-chung, but on equally insubstan-
tial grounds.[53]

The same situation holds true for Shih Nai-an, since with the exception
of one reference (which does, however, happen to be the earliest in hand:
Kao Ju's *Pai-ch'uan shu-chih*), Shih was as a rule mentioned only in a subsid-
iary capacity, until Chin Sheng-t'an's inclusion in his edition of a pretended
preface by Shih established the claim of Shih's authorship for succeeding
centuries.[54] If Lo Kuan-chung is a somewhat shadowy figure despite the

[50] See Chia Chung-ming, *Hsü Lu-kuei pu*, p. 148 (cited in Ma T'i-chi, *Tzu-liao*, p. 502; Chu
I-hsüan, *Tzu-liao*, p. 130; and K'ung Ling-ching, *Shih-liao*, p. 12). Tai Pu-fan notes certain
problems with this source in *Chien-wen lu*, pp. 103ff.

[51] Lin Ts'un-yan, "Sur l'authenticité," pp. 281f.

[52] Wang Li-ch'i, "Shui-hu chuan shih tsen-yang tsuan-hsiu ti," pp. 86–101.

[53] The idea that the authors of the two books cannot be the same person was suggested
as early as the late Ming period, by Hu Ying-lin (*Pi-ts'ung*, p. 572). Recently, Wang
Hsiao-chia has raised this question in "Shui-hu chuan tso-che hsi Lo Kuan-chung k'ao-pien,"
pp. 148ff., adopting the opposite position. Nieh Kan-nu explains the term *pien* 編 as proof of
what he calls "collective authorship" (*chi-t'i ch'uang-tso* 集體創作) in "Wu-lun," pp. 27ff.,
repeated on p. 46.

[54] See *Pai-ch'uan shu-chih*, *Ch'i-hsiu lei-kao* (citations in nn. 5–6). Hu Ying-lin (*Pi-ts'ung*,
pp. 571, 573) also chooses Shih over Lo. See also Chou Liang-kung, *Yin-shu-wu shu-ying*,
chüan 1, p. 75 (cited in K'ung Ling-ching, *Shih-liao*, p. 22). Tai Pu-fan (*Chien-wen lu*, p. 129)
adds a reference to another Chia-ching work entitled *Hsin-k'an wan-i hsüan hsin-chih lu*
新刊玩易軒新知錄, by Liu Shih-i 劉仕義, which also attributes the novel to Shih Nai-an.
See also Wen Ying, "Liu-pien," pp. 210f; and Li Ling-nien, "Shih Nai-an tsa-k'ao," pp.

proof of his historicity, Shih Nai-an's identity is even more obscure. Over
the past few decades, considerable effort has been expended, primarily by
descendants of the Shih family in Chiang-su 江蘇 province, to produce
documentary evidence sufficient to confirm the credit for their forebear
established by Chin Sheng-t'an; but recently a number of scholars have
systematically refuted the authenticity of most of these documents.[55] Nor
has the attempt by the eminent drama expert Wu Mei 吳梅 and others to
identify Shih Nai-an as Shih Mei-chün 施美君 (Shih Hui 施惠) gained much
of a following.[56] Tai Pu-fan even went so far as to deny that Shih Nai-an ever
existed, explaining that his persistently cited name may be a pseudonym
for an anonymous compiler working under the patronage of Kuo Hsün.[57]

Despite this lack of positive evidence to settle the question, the cumulative weight of testimony makes the nearly universal attribution of the
novel to these names difficult to dismiss. Actually, the value of the voluminous evidence regarding Lo-Shih authorship is even less than it appears,
since all of the sources in question copy each other, and thus depend on the
correctness of the earliest attribution. On the other hand, we do have
ample grounds for assuming that the Chia-ching or Kuo Hsün editions
would not have been original compositions, but rather revisions of a prior
text or texts. The T'ien-tu wai-ch'en preface says as much when it enumerates certain editorial changes allegedly effected by the Kuo edition: namely,
the cutting of the two narrative sections dealing with the campaigns
against T'ien Hu and Wang Ch'ing, the addition of the expedition against
the Liao forces, and the removal of certain introductory material known as
"appended narratives" (*chih-yü* 致語), which were allegedly attached to the

---

61–66. Chin Sheng-tan's attribution of the novel to Shih Nai-an is discussed by Tai Pu-fan
in *Chien-wen lu*, p. 105.

[55] This evidence is collected in *Shih Nai-an yen-chiu chuan-chi*, put out under the sponsorship of the local government of Ta-feng hsien in 1983. This view is supported by Pan 'In
(P'ang Ying), in "K voprosu ob avtorstvje i vremeni sozdanija romana Recnije zavodi,"
pp. 200–208. Recently, it has been refuted by Chang Kuo-kuang, in "Lu Hsün ti Shih Nai-an
wei fan-pen Shui-hu tso-che chih t'o-ming shuo wu k'e chih-i," pp. 52ff.; Tai Pu-fan,
Chien-wen lu, pp. 106ff.; and Liu Shih-te, "An Analysis of the Historical Relics and Materials
Concerning Shi Naian," pp. 186f. See also Chang P'ei-heng, "Shih Nai-an mu-chih pien-wei
chi ch'i-t'a," pp. 11–30. Chang Hsiao-hu ("Shih Nai-an wei chiang-hu i-jen shuo," pp. 89–
100) suggests that Shih Nai-an was a "wandering entertainer" by profession.

[56] For Wu Mei's identification of Shih Nai-an as Shih Hui, see Tai Pu-fan, *Chien-wen lu*,
p. 105; Ho Man-tzu, "Ts'ung Sung Yuan shuo-hua chia-shu t'an-so Shui-hu fan-chien-pen
yüan-yüan chi ch'i tso-che wen-t'i," p. 43; Fan Ning, "Yüan-liu k'ao," p. 69. This theory is
based on an entry in Hsü Fu-tso's 徐復祚 *San-chia ts'un-lao wei-t'an* 三家村老委談, reprinted
in Chu I-hsüan, *Tzu-liao*, pp. 221f. This was later copied over in a Ch'ien-lung work entitled
Pao-tun lou ch'uan-ch'i hui-k'ao mu 寶敦樓傳奇滙考目 (see Fan Ning, "Yüan-liu K'ao,"
p. 69). The identification was accepted by Sun K'ai-ti in *Shu-mu*, p. 209.

[57] For discussions of this issue, see Irwin, *Evolution*, pp. 64f.; and Wen Ying, "Liu-pien,"
pp. 210ff.

head of each chapter.[58] Lately, a number of scholars have attempted to prove that the text as we know it could not have been a fourteenth-century composition by citing such points as the occurrence of Ming dynasty place-names and official terminology, or the fact that the expansion of the story cycles to cover 108 heroes was apparently unknown in the dramatic treatments of the same subjects as late as the early fifteenth century.[59] But, of course, these points do not exclude the possibility of later superficial revisions of a text that was already substantially complete by that time.[60] To add to the confusion, we should note that even the attribution to Lo Kuan-chung or Shih Nai-an seems to indicate not an original composition, but instead a form of contribution labeled with such terms as "editing," or "compiling" (*pien-tz'u* 編次, *chi-chuan* 集撰, *tsuan-hsiu* 纂修). Only Kao Ju's early reference credits Shih Nai-an with authorship of a basic text (*ti-pen*) of the novel.[61] As a result the question at issue becomes not whether a Lo-Shih text ever existed, but rather what sort of book the lost prototype attributed to them might have been, and in what relation this book would have stood to the sixteenth-century *fan-pen* texts under study here.

One way to make some sense out of this tangle may emerge when we move to a second area of speculation complicating the early history of the novel. This has to do with the existence of another body of *Shui-hu* texts known as the "simpler recension" (*chien-pen*), which roughly parallels the "full recension" in terms of basic characters and events covered by the narrative, but differs on various points such as generally shorter overall length, different division into narrative units and chapters, relative economy of narrative detail, more classical linguistic medium, and variant handling of certain key episodes—not to mention the inclusion of the two additional

[58] For the restatement of these points in the *fa-fan* preface, see above, n. 35. See also Tai Pu-fan, *Chien-wen lu*, pp. 90–135 (see n. 15). A similar argument is given in Chang Kuo-kuang, "Tsu-pen t'an-k'ao," pp. 43f. This is refuted by Wang Ken-lin in "Shui-hu tsu-pen t'an-k'ao chih-i," pp. 79–88. Irwin (*Evolution*, p. 47) renders *chih-yü* as "fillers."

[59] On the occurrence of Ming place-names in the novel, see Chang Kuo-kuang, "Tsu-pen t'an-k'ao," p. 39; and counterargument in Wang Ken-lin, "Chih-i," p. 80. Tai Pu-fan (*Chien-wen lu*, p. 122) similarly notes the occurrence in chapter 78 of the expression "imperial court" (*huang-ch'ao* 皇朝), which was only current during the Ming period. Liu Ts'un-yan ("Sur l'authenticité," p. 89) notes other details of Ming history and culture which would indicate late composition. See the argument presented by George Hayden in "A Skeptical Note," esp. p. 375. Since then, similar arguments have been provided in Sun Shu-yü, *Shui-hu chuan ti lai-li, hsin-t'ai, yü i-shu*, p. 204; Tai Pu-fan, *Chien-wen lu*, p. 119; and Wang Yung-chien, "Ch'eng-shu nien-tai," p. 241. See also Wilt Idema, "Zhu Youdun's Dramatic Prefaces and Traditional Fiction." We know from Chia-ching sources that narratives covering the full complement of *Shui-hu* heroes were current by the sixteenth century.

[60] For the same sort of argument regarding the appearance of Yuan and Ming place-names in the earliest editions of *San-kuo*, see below, Chapter 5, Part I.

[61] See above, nn. 5–6. See also Nieh Kan-nu, "Wu-lun," pp. 27ff. Ho Hsin provides a convenient list of the various attributions in *Yen-chiu*, pp. 20f.

campaigns in many of these editions.[62] These points, taken together with
the generally less elegant printing of most of the extant Ming *chien-pen*
editions in comparison with the contemporary *fan-pen*, typically by a
certain group of Fukien printing houses, have given rise to a simple impression that they represent a more primitive stage of development, and perhaps even the missing link between the hypothetical earlier prototype and
the mature sixteenth-century versions.[63]

The situation regarding the "simpler recension," however, is not so
simple. The relation between the *fan-pen* and *chien-pen* texts, their literal
labels notwithstanding, is one of complex interrelation. This was understood by Sun K'ai-ti, Cheng Chen-to, and other scholars, who saw that the
degree of fullness in prose style on the one hand, and the fullness of
narrative coverage on the other, were two separate variables, so that some
editions could be characterized as "simple in style but full in detail" (*wen
chien shih fan* 文簡事繁), and others as "full in style but simple in detail"
(*wen fan shih chien* 文繁事簡).[64] This distinction applies most directly to the

[62] The most comprehensive review of *chien-pen* materials is provided by Y. W. Ma in his
article "Hu-yü yen-chiu," pp. 186–204. See also his more recent "Hsien-ts'un tsui-tsao ti
chien-pen Shui-hu chuan." For general discussions of the differences in these texts, see Yen
Tun-i, *Yen-pien*, pp. 152ff.; Sun K'ai-t'i, *Jih-pen*, pp. 97–105, 109ff.; Ho Hsin, *Yen-chiu*,
pp. 76ff.; Cheng Chen-to "Yen-hua," pp. 139; and Nieh Kan-nu, "Wu-lun," pp. 153–58,
171–77. See also C. T. Hsia, *The Classic Chinese Novel*, pp. 80f.; Liu Hsiu-yeh, *Ku-tien
hsiao-shuo*, pp. 84f. Comparisons of the prose in the two recensions are provided in Cheng
Chen-to, "Yen-hua," pp. 123ff.; and Kao Ming-ko, "Lun Shui-hu ti chien-pen hsi-t'ung,"
pp. 223ff. For more detailed information on the *chien-pen* editions used in this study, see b.n.
III.

[63] Besides the *P'ing-lin pen*, in which the Fukien publisher is clearly advertised, the *Ch'a-
tseng pen*, Oxford text, and other fragments share the split-page format characteristic of this
type of Fukien edition (*Min-pen*). Cf. the similar printing of *Hsi-yu chi* and *San-kuo yen-i*
discussed in Chapters 3 and 5 of this book. For further information on Yü Hsiang-tou and
his work, see K. T. Wu, "Ming Printing," pp. 229–38; Cheng Chen-to, "Yen-hua," p. 144;
Liu Ts'un-yan, "Sur l'authenticité," p. 264f., and his *Chinese Popular Fiction in Two London
Libraries*, pp. 68ff.; Yen Tun-i, *Yen-pien*, pp. 190f.; C. T. Hsia, *Classic Novel*, p. 78f.; Nieh
Kan-nu, "Wu-lun," p. 196; and especially Y. W. Ma, "Niu-chin ta-hsüeh so ts'ang Ming-tai
chien-pen Shui-hu ts'an-yeh shu hou," p. 63, and his "Ying-yin liang-chung Ming-tai hsiao-
shuo chen-pen hsü," pp. 133f. Shiroki Naoya ("Haiin," pp. 242ff.) reports on other Yü
Hsiang-tou products held in Japanese collections. Nieh Kan-nu ("Wu-lun," p. 155) expresses
some doubt about the attributions to Yü Hsiang-tou. Cheng Chen-to ("Yen-hua," p. 143)
notes the inferior printing of the Yü edition, but praises it for fine illustrations. Yeh Lang
("Yeh Chou p'i-t'ien," p. 298) gives Yü credit for composing the first marginal commentary
on the novel.

[64] As far as I can determine, the distinction between fullness of prose and fullness of the
narrative was first drawn by Sun K'ai-ti in *Shu-mu* (pp. 215ff.) and in *Jih-pen* (p. 97), and it is
followed by Cheng Chen-to in his preface to *Shui-hu ch'üan-chuan*. Nieh Kan-nu ("Wu-lun,"
pp. 170f.) distinguishes between the results of prose writing efforts and those of publishing
efforts 文字工作, 出版工作, that is, comparing the prose of the different texts on the one
hand, and their contents (prefaces, commentaries, etc.) on the other.

addition of certain episodes in some of the *chien-pen* texts, especially the
T'ien Hu and Wang Ch'ing sections. These, we are told by the problematic
T'ien-tu wai-ch'en preface, were part of the "original" structure of the
novel, before being excised by Kuo Hsün. But since the earliest example
we have of their treatment seems to be in the *chien-pen* fragment entitled
*Hsin-k'an ching-pen ch'üan-hsiang ch'a-tseng T'ien Hu Wang Ch'ing Chung-i
shui-hu ch'üan-chüan* 新刊京本全像插增田虎王慶忠義水滸全傳, some
scholars have given the credit to the "simpler" texts for inventing these
added plot complications. Other examples of cross-fertilization between
the two recensions include sharing of such terms as *ching-pen* 京本, *ch'üan-
chuan* 全傳, and *chung-i* 忠義 in overall titles, interchangeable chapter
headings and chapter-ending formulas, and mutual borrowing of incidental
verses cited within the narrative.[65] In at least one set of editions, the Wen-
hsing t'ang 文杏堂 or Ying-hsüeh ts'ao-t'ang 映雪草堂 printings, the mixing
of *fan-pen* structure with *chien-pen* style makes it difficult to decide to which
of the two recensions the texts actually belong.[66]

To further complicate matters, the convoluted textual relations among
the *chien-pen* editions themselves are equally uncertain, showing no clear
lines of filiation or consistent points of comparison. For example, the
fragmentary *Ch'a-tseng* text, which has been appraised as one of the earliest
chien-pen editions, not only adds the campaigns advertised in its title, but
also boasts more extensive narrative prose than certain other *chien-pen*

---

[65] Cf. the term *chung-i* in the titles of the *P'ing-lin, Ch'a-tseng,* and *Han-Sung ch'i-shu*
editions. I should also mention the common attribution of most of these texts to Lo
Kuan-chung or Shih Nai-an. (See Nieh Kan-nu, "Wu-lun," pp. 153ff.) On the sharing of
poetic lines, see Liu Ts'un-yan, "Sur l'authenticité," pp. 260f., 271; and Ho Hsin, *Yen-chiu,*
pp. 78ff., 357ff. Cf. Hu Ying-lin's complaint (*Pi-ts'ung,* p. 572) about the cutting of the poems
from the cheap popular editions on the market in his day. An example of the interchange-
ability of chapter-ending formulas can be seen in the use of the expression *yu-fen chiao*
... 有分教 in the *Ying-hsiung p'u.* This latter *chien-pen* text includes an opening *tz'u* verse as in
the *fan-pen* editions, and also separates the opening passages of the text along the lines of
the Jung-yü t'ang treatment. See Ōuchida Saburō, "Suikoden hanponkō: hyaku nijūyon kai
bon ni tsuite," no. 4, p. 2. Liu Ts'un-yan ("Sur l'authenticité," p. 284) also notes certain
common features between the Cheng Chen-to fragment and the 115-chapter *chien-pen*
version. The question of the two interpolated sections further demonstrates the complex
interrelationship of the two recensions. See Nieh Kan-nu, "Wu-lun," pp. 190ff.

[66] See b.n. III.5 for further background information on the Wen-hsing t'ang edition. See
also Liu Shih-te, "T'an Shui-hu chuan Ying-hsüeh ts'ao-t'ang k'an-pen ti kai-k'uang, hsü-wen,
ho piao-mu," pp. 134–62; Y. W. Ma, "Hu-yü yen-chiu," p. 186, n. 3; and especially Nieh
Kan-nu, "Wu-lun," pp. 158ff. Nieh notes that this text follows the *fan-pen* in its narrative
outlines, but has particularly simplified prose. There are two known variants of this edition,
represented by the Pao-han lou text in Paris and the Ying-hsüeh ts'ao-t'ang text in Tokyo.
The latter should be distinguished from the similarly designated Ku-su ying-hsüeh t'ang
姑蘇映雪堂 124-chapter text, which in turn differs from the 124-chapter edition described
by Sun K'ai-ti (*Shu-mu,* p. 215). On this edition, see Ōuchida Saburō "Suikoden hanponkō:
hyaku nijūyon kai bon ni tsuite," no. 3, pp. 1–10.

examples. Moreover, it has been suggested that the *Chung-i shui-hu chuan p'ing-lin* 忠義水滸傳評林 in twenty-five *chüan*, with the earliest known (albeit minimal) marginal commentary, may actually derive from a twenty-*chüan* prototype, in which case it may have some closer textual relation with the *fan-pen* system.[67]

In spite of these formidable textual difficulties, the *chien-pen* editions are still of crucial importance for pursuing the origins of the *fan-pen* novel. Since the two recensions, for all their mutual influence, still clearly reflect separable lines of development, the scholarly debate about them has centered on the obvious question of which came first: whether the *chien-pen* texts represent an earlier stage of development later elaborated into the more polished *fan-pen*, or are perhaps the end product of abridgment or cheaper reprinting.

The former possibility, that the *chien-pen* preceded the *fan-pen*, was suggested by Lu Hsün, and more recently Liu Ts'un-yan, Ho Hsin, and others, who see in these texts fossils of the "original" novel by Lo Kuan-chung.[68] This theory makes good sense in terms of the logic of literary evolution, especially in light of the clearly traceable process of develop-

---

[67] For the latter suggestion, see Fan Ning, "Yüan-liu k'ao," pp. 71, 74. For detailed comparison of the various texts of the *chien-pen* system, see the following studies. Nieh Kan-nu ("Wu-lun," pp. 153–58) describes the complex relations between the different editions but emphasizes the commonality between them. Y. W. Ma, in "Ch'ing-chieh ho jen-wu," p. 89, "Hu-yü yen chiu," pp. 198f., and "Chü-pao chi," p. 24, distinguishes at least two separate strains to demonstrate the differences within the *chien-pen* system. Kao Ming-ko ("Chien-pen hsi-t'ung," pp. 222ff.) provides specific textual comparison of the prose in the different *chien-pen* editions, as does Nieh Kan-nu in "Wu-lun," pp. 163–67. Y. W. Ma in his "Niu-chin," p. 51, also gives a comparison of the narrative prose of the *Ch'a tseng* and *P'ing-lin* editions, and in "Chü-pao chi" (p. 22) he concludes that the *Ch'a-tseng pen* is directly related to the Oxford fragment. See also Yen Tun-i (*Yen-pien*, pp. 183f.), Ou-yang Chien ("Ti-shan kuo-ch'eng," p. 224), and Irwin, "Water Margin," pp. 411ff. Ōuchida Saburō ("Hanponkō," no. 2, p. 6, and no. 4, p. 15) attempts to show the filiation of the *Ying-hsiung p'u* and *P'ing-lin* texts along different routes from an earlier 115-chapter edition, one which is more *fan* in its prose style.

[68] For reviews of this debate, see Nieh Kan-nu, "Wu-lun," pp. 198ff.; Chang Kuo-kuang, *Shui-hu yü Chin Sheng-t'an*, pp. 21–43; Y. W. Ma, "Hu-yü yen chiu," pp. 189ff.; Liu Ts'un-yan, "Sur l'authenticité," pp. 259, 268ff.; and Ōuchida Saburō, "Suikoden hanponkō: hanpon to kanpon no kankei o chūshin ni," no. 1, pp. 51ff. Lu Hsün's view that the direction of development proceeded from simpler to fuller is repeated by Liu Ts'un-yan ("Sur l'authenticité," pp. 259ff.), Ho Hsin (*Yen-chiu*, pp. 76f.), and Cheng Chen-to ("Yen-hua," pp. 139ff.), although Cheng later reversed himself (in his preface to *Shui-hu ch'üan-chuan*, p. 2). Nieh Kan-nu ("Wu-lun," pp. 142ff., 189f.) makes this case on the basis of the laws of cultural development from simpler to more complex forms, pointing out (p. 171) that the prefaces of the *fan-pen* editions, for example, are almost uniformly more sophisticated than those in the *chien-pen* editions, with the exception of the Hsiung Fei preface to the *Ying-hsiung p'u*. Ōuchida Saburō ("Suikoden hanponkō: Suiko shiden hyōrin-pon no seiritsu katei o chūshin ni," no. 2, p. 10) gives a similar argument on the basis of the gradual development of sophisticated literary vernacular style away from simple classical diction.

ment of the *Shui-hu* story cycles from popular storytelling to the *Hsüan-ho i-shih* 宣和遺事, and from numerous dramatic pieces in the Yuan and early Ming periods through the emergence of the full-length novel version in the late Ming. Liu Ts'un-yan actually refines this scheme to allow for not one but two early prototypes: one by Lo Kuan-chung, the progenitor of the *chien-pen* system, and another by Shih Nai-an, ancestor of the latter-day *fan-pen*, with the two parallel strains borrowing from one another until they finally contribute to the formation of the "complete" edition of 1614.[69]

On the other side of the picture, this logic has not prevented other scholars from drawing the exact opposite conclusion. These critics argue that the less polished *Min-pen* 閩本 printings executed by Yü Hsiang-tou 余象斗 and other Fukien publishers represent cheap commercially inspired popularizations of the fine Chia-ching and Wan-li volumes. This theory fits the data in hand in that the earliest extant datable *chien-pen* text is only from 1594, and is borne out in the complaints of several writers of the next generations that the cheap imitations by Fukien booksellers had eclipsed the fine editions of years gone by.[70] Some textual support for this conclusion also has been found by means of the comparison of parallel passages in the two recensions to uncover traces of the assumed process of abridgment. For example, Ou-yang Chien has enumerated a series of errors of omission and interpolation that in his view give away the process by which the shorter text was allegedly derived.[71]

[69] See Liu Ts'un-yan, "Sur l'authenticité," pp. 288f. Ho Man-tzu ("Shui-hu fan-chien-pen yüan-yüan," p. 38) makes a less convincing attempt to account for two separate strains by positing the development of the *chien-pen* from the *chiang-shih* 講史 branch of the oral storytelling tradition, and the *fan-pen* from that designated *hsiao-shuo*. We may recall here the two different titles for the Chia-ching *Shui-hu* cited in the *Pao-wen t'ang shu-mu* entries (see above, n. 5). Liu Ts'un-yan ("Sur l'authenticité," pp. 284f.) suggests that these may be separate ancestors of the two recensions, as does Ho Man-tzu ("Shui-hu fan-chien-pen yüan-yüan," p. 21). Tai Pu-fan (*Chien-wen lu*, p. 100) argues that the two references may have been to one book. See also Nieh Kan-nu, "Wu-lun," p. 145.

[70] The view of the *chien-pen* as later popularized abridgments of the *fan-pen* versions was first espoused by Hu Shih, "Pai-erh-shih hui pen Chung-i shui-hu chuan hsü," pp. 126ff.; and Sun K'ai-ti, *Jih-pen*, pp. 97ff.; and is followed by Cheng Chen-to in his later years (see n. 68), Irwin (*Evolution*, pp. 66–75), and Fan Ning ("Yüan-liu k'ao," pp. 71, 74). This idea is apparently supported by the testimony of the T'ien-tu wai-ch'en preface and of Hu Ying-lin, Chou Liang-kung, Ch'ien Hsi-yen, and other late Ming writers decrying the cheap popularizations flooding the market (for references, see n. 11). Nieh Kan-nu reviews these statements in "Wu-lun," pp. 145, 193ff. Although the late date of 1594 on the earliest *chien-pen* text, the *P'ing-lin pen*, seems to support this view, there is considerable evidence to indicate that the Ch'a-tseng and Oxford fragments may be considerably earlier (see above, nn. 62, 67).

[71] See Ou-yang Chien, "Ti-shan kuo-ch'eng," pp. 219f. Cf. Ho Hsin's interpretation of the occurrences of the term *yüeh* 曰 in place of *tao* 道 in the 120-chapter edition, refuted by

As I have said in my review of the comparable controversy over the priority of the Shih-te t'ang 世德堂 *Hsi-yu chi* versus the shorter Chu Ting-ch'en text 朱鼎臣,[72] this seesaw debate is necessarily inconclusive, since it relies on comparing those extant texts that have by chance come down to us to determine historical priority, when we have every reason to suspect that none of these are in fact original exemplars of their respective systems, and may not even be particularly representative.[73] If, on the other hand, we find that we are dealing with two parallel strains, which only after a certain point enter into a relationship of mutual influence, then there is no contradiction in viewing the *chien-pen* line in general as evidence of an earlier stage of development, while still recognizing that the particular *chien-pen* examples we have in hand may be the result of a later process of abridgment of the sixteenth-century *fan-pen* texts.[74] Or, to look at it from another direction, we can accept that the *fan-pen* must have had earlier prototypes, without falling into the trap of assuming that any of the *chien-pen* as we have them must provide models of this "original" form.

My own speculation would in fact run along something like these lines: I would bow to the persistent attribution to Lo Kuan-chung or Shih Nai-an of a simpler prototype, which may have eventually fed into the *chien-pen* system; yet I would also insist on the notion of a separate development of the *fan-pen* recension, with this later exercising a conditioning influence on the *chien-pen* exemplars now extant.

Ōuchida Saburō in "Hanponkō," no. 1, pp. 59f. Additional examples are given by Kao Ming-ko in "Chien-pen hsi-t'ung," pp. 223ff.

[72] See Chapter 3, Part I of this book.

[73] Y. W. Ma, in "Hu-yü yen-chiu," pp. 191ff., provides some helpful diagrams of filiation based on the assumption that the extant exemplars are not "original" versions of each type. A similar assessment is given by Nieh Kan-nu, in "Wu-lun," p. 192. See also Ho Hsin, *Yen-chiu*, pp. 76ff.; and C. T. Hsia, *Classic Novel*, pp. 80f., 338f., n. 10.

[74] This is the implication of Liu Ts'un-yan's argument (see above, n. 69). This scenario of mutual influence has particular relevance for the textual problems of the four campaigns. Ou-yang Chien ("Ti-shan kuo-ch'eng," pp. 211ff.) posits three stages of development: first, a *fan-pen* model produced by removing the T'ien Hu and Wang Ch'ing campaigns from and adding the Liao expedition to a preexisting prototype that had the former two sections and lacked the latter; a second stage, in which the first *chien-pen* was produced by abridgment of this; and a third, in which the two campaigns were reinserted into the later *fan-pen* (sometime after the appearance of the *Ch'a-tseng pen*). This is essentially an argument for development from *fan-pen* to *chien-pen*, but it allows for more than one type of operation on the text going on at the same time. Y. W. Ma, in "Ch'ing-chieh ho jen-wu", p. 88, sees the four campaigns as independent textual units, and points out (p. 90) the fact that the Fang La section in the *fan-pen* texts is relatively simple in style, whereas the Wang Ch'ing section is written in fuller prose even in the *chien-pen* editions where it appears. I should note that we have no basis for concluding that the early Chia-ching citations must refer to *fan-pen*, except for the indication of one or more "fine editions" in twenty *chüan* (presumably one hundred chapters).

Regardless of how we formulate this, the possibility that the *chien-pen* texts may ultimately derive from an early prototype only points up the signal contribution—as in the case of *Hsi-yu chi*, a quantum leap—taken by the sixteenth-century *fan-pen* in recasting the *Shui-hu* narratives into a new generic mold marked by the aesthetic sophistication and intellectual seriousness characteristic of the late Ming literati milieu.[75] This has been acknowledged by most modern critics, who allow that the book was radically transformed in the Chia-ching editions, even when they continue to grant the basic credit for authorship to Lo Kuan-chung or Shih Nai-an.[76] My argument here puts the primary emphasis on the end point of this process of transformation, the point at which the *Shui-hu* story cycles become the novel *Shui-hu chuan*. By this reasoning, I begin with the observation that many of the most significant aspects of structure and interpretation in which the *fan-pen* *Shui-hu* departs from its antecedent source materials happen to coincide strikingly with certain features of the mature sixteenth-century novel form I have outlined in *Hsi-yu chi* and *Chin P'ing Mei*. On the basis of this sense of common generic form—an impression supported by the instances of explicit borrowing and implicit cross-reference that further link the *Shui-hu chuan* to these other works in a network of intertextual relations—I will now proceed to a close-reading and analysis of the *fan-pen* text within the context of sixteenth-century aesthetic and philosophical concerns.

This is not to deny the view of the novel as a gradual evolution of narrative materials out of a variety of prior sources. Certainly the link between the novel and the earlier *Shui-hu* story cycles has been clearly demonstrated. But it is still difficult to show any direct textual connections

[75] This idea that the novel could not have taken on anything like the generic form of the *fan-pen* until the sixteenth century is also expressed by Tai Pu-fan, *Chien-wen lu*, pp. 120f.; Nieh Kan-nu, "Wu-lun," pp. 27, 43ff.; Ch'en Chung-fan, "Shih-lun," p. 115; Lo Te-jung, "Ying-hsiung ch'uan-ch'i ti k'ai-shan chih tso Shui-hu chuan," pp. 127–33.

[76] For acknowledgments of the far-reaching changes in the sixteenth-century editions, see Lu Hsün (*Shih-lüeh*, p. 146): "nearly completely transformed its appearance" 幾乎改觀; C. T. Hsia (*Classic Novel*, p. 78): "Whoever he was, this redactor must be honored as the second most important author of *Shui-hu Chuan*," and p. 82: "He not only recast the original novel in a more colloquial language and enlarged its narrative; he has also accentuated the notes of savagery and sadism in scenes of vengeful killing ..."; and Hanan (*Chinese Short Story*, pp. 31f.), where he cautiously suggests that it can be demonstrated on the basis of linguistic criteria that the text was substantially revised in the Wan-li period. Irwin is somewhat self-contradictory on this point. On pp. 43f. of *Evolution* he presents evidence for the original contributions of the "novel" (based on the sixteenth-century editions), but later on (p. 58, n. 3) he pushes all this back to the fourteenth century: "Even at the risk of erring, I prefer to credit the compiler of the original novel with whatever material is not of demonstrably earlier origin."

to these materials, even to the *Hsüan-ho i-shih* segments that are sometimes taken as a kind of blueprint for the novel.[77]

Once again, the point at issue in this study is not the definitive dating of
the major Ming novels, but instead the problem of their more meaningful
interpretation. Thus, even if future discoveries should prove that the form
of the *fan-pen* novel was, as I suspect, a product of Chia-ching authorship,
or if the hypothetical role of Lo Kuan-chung or Shih Nai-an may eventually
be documented, one might still argue that the *Shui-hu chuan* ought to be
interpreted according to the generic model observable in the Wan-li classics *Hsi-yu chi* and *Chin P'ing Mei*. This would leave a rather long, unexplained time gap between the inception of the genre and the appearance of
the major editions of the four masterworks in the sixteenth century, but it
would conform fairly neatly to my observation of a fifteenth-century "slack
period" across the entire spectrum of Ming literature. It would also parallel
the early appearance of the drama masterpieces *Hsi-hsiang chi* 西廂記 and
P'i-p'a chi 琵琶記, which by the fourteenth century had laid most of the
groundwork for the *ch'uan-ch'i* dramatic form, even though that form did
not reach its full flowering until the sixteenth century.[78]

In the remainder of this chapter I will attempt to substantiate this
approach to *Shui-hu chuan* by considering a number of structural and
rhetorical features of the *fan-pen* texts that to my mind reflect the same
generic underpinnings analyzed earlier in connection with *Hsi-yu chi* and
Chin P'ing Mei. Wherever possible, I will draw comparisons between the
fan-pen and the *chien-pen* treatment of the novel's source materials, as well
as between the novelistic handling of the central figures and that in the
ongoing popular tradition. Specifically, I will attempt to show that the *fan-
pen Shui-hu chuan* should be read as a deeply ironic revision of its inherited
source materials, such that all discussions of the heroic stature of the
leading figures in the Liang-shan 梁山 band, though to some extent valid
with respect to the earlier and subsequent popular imagination, cannot accurately describe the situation in the novel version under consideration here.[79]

---

[77] For studies on the known sources of the novel, see b.n. I. Cf. the citation of storytellers'
titles for specific parts of the narrative, as in chapters 16 (*Shui-hu ch'üan-chuan*, Vol. 1:236,
hereafter cited *SHCC*, 1:236) and 40 (2:649), or the quotation of a long *tz'u* poem in
chapter 48 (2:796), which bears marks of direct derivation from oral performance. See Irwin,
Evolution, pp. 40f., 46. See also Hsü Shuo-fang, "Ts'ung Sung Chiang ch'i-i tao Shui-hu chuan
ch'eng-shu."

[78] This impression of a "slack period" in Ming cultural life during the fifteenth century is
discussed above, in Chapter 1. Yen Tun-i (*Yen-pien*, p. 140) attempts to account for this in
terms of the cultural retrenchment that followed after the Yung-lo usurpation.

[79] Even within the so-called "popular" sources , the evaluation of the activities of the
Liang-shan band is far from unequivocal. This is especially true with respect to the treatment

II

In my initial area of analysis, that of structure, *Shui-hu chuan* would seem at first sight to differ radically from the two novels already considered. That is, the impression here of a meandering, loosely linked plot structure (which has often been described as episodic and has even been associated, quite inaccurately, with the picaresque form in certain examples of Western narrative) seems to present a clear contrast to the sense of unity imparted by the well-anchored spatial setting in *Chin P'ing Mei* and by the frame of the quest journey in *Hsi-yu chi*. The fact that the outline of the novel has gone through so many different editions, and that even its "dismemberment at the waist" (*yao-chan* 腰斬) has been generally accepted on aesthetic grounds by three centuries of readers within the Chinese tradition, would also appear to argue against any notion of inviolable structural integrity intrinsic to the *Shui-hu* narrative.[80] When Chin Sheng-t'an characterizes the entire text as something like a single well-wrought prose essay in its tight structural organization (evidently the source of Chang Chu-p'o's similar comments on *Chin P'ing Mei*), and praises the degree of conscious effort manifested in the author's structural manipulation, the reader might well question the basis for such a description, particularly in view of the extreme liberties Chin himself has taken with the outer shape of the work.[81] This is particularly true since Chin is in a sense patting himself on the back for his own editorial improvements worked into the text. But Chin Sheng-t'an was not the first traditional critic to appreciate the structural intricacy of the

---

of the principal heroes in *tsa-chü* drama. See, for example, Yen-Tun-i, *Yen-pien*, pp. 142f.; Irwin, *Evolution*, p. 38. I will refer to these divergent images at various points in the following discussion. For a convenient presentation of the popular view, see James J. Y. Liu, *The Chinese Knight-Errant*, pp. 108–15, 172–82.

[80] A number of recent critics have undertaken an open-minded reassessment of the aesthetics of the Chin Sheng-t'an text. See, for example, discussions by Y. W. Ma, "Ch'ing-chieh ho jen-wu," p. 86; Chang Han-liang, "Shih hsi Shui-hu chuan ti chieh-kou," pp. 45–47; and Ko Ch'u-ying and Chin Chia-hsing, "Chin Sheng-t'an yao-chan Shui-hu ti i-shu kou-ssu," pp. 50–53.

[81] See *Ti-wu ts'ai-tzu shu*, "Tu Ti-wu ts'ai-tzu shu fa" 讀第五才子書法 (hereafter *tu-fa*), *chüan* 3, p. 3a: "... its over two thousand pages of writing is all of a piece, and many of the events contained within it are examples of the prose techniques known as 'exposition,' 'development,' 'transfer,' and 'conclusion' ..." …其二千餘紙只是一編文字, 中間許多事體便是文字起承轉合之法; and p. 3b: "*Shui-hu* gives rise to events on the basis of prose patterns ... paring down excess and filling in gaps in accordance with the tone of the argument; it always follows the author's own intent" 水滸是因文生事…順着筆性去削高補低都緣我. Interestingly, Chin Sheng-t'an faults *Hsi-yu chi* for the same charge of being "episodic" that is so often leveled at *Shui-hu chuan* (see *tu-fa*, p. 2b): "It is patched together section by section ... with no central thread at all" 只是逐段捏捏撮撮…中間全沒貫串.

fan-pen Shui-hu chuan. We may note the critical assessment of this text as "subtly complex in its fine detail, with its underlying structural outlines informing the entire composition" 委曲詳盡, 血脈貫通 in Li K'ai-hsien's early report; or the praise it receives in the T'ien-tu wai-ch'en preface for being "varied in its texture and depth, a masterful example of subtle adumbration, like a long expanse of brocade with interwoven colors and not a thread out of place" … 濃淡遠近點染盡工, 又如百尺之錦, 玄黃經緯, 一絲不紕.[82]

When one takes a look at the text to analyze its internal principles of organization, some of this solid sense of structural control begins to come into view. As soon as we have set aside the varying outlines of the *chien-pen* editions as a separate problem, a quick glance at all of the remaining extant early *fan-pen* texts immediately establishes a basic length of one hundred chapters, up until the appearance of the expanded 1614 edition, followed by Chin Sheng-t'an's seventy-chapter truncation. This basic number of chapters, which the *fan-pen Shui-hu* shares with *Chin P'ing Mei* and *Hsi-yu chi*, is corroborated in nearly all of the bibliographical references cited earlier, whether the number one hundred itself is given or the division into twenty *chüan* of five chapters each, as in the various Chia-ching fragments.[83] Yüan Wu-yai's expansion of the text to 120 chapters by means of the "interpolation" of the campaigns against T'ien Hu and Wang Ch'ing does not really contradict this. This editorial revision can be explained on different grounds, either as a practical response to pressure from the bookselling competition of *chien-pen* editions that included these additional sections, or perhaps for more technical storytelling purposes, such as accounting for the "four bandits" named on the screen in the

[82] For sources of these citations, see nn. 7 and 24. Similar appreciations of the intricacy of the text can be found in Hu Ying-lin, *Pi-ts'ung*, *chüan* 41, p. 572 (cited in Ma T'i-chi, *Tzu-liao*, p. 353); Liu T'ing-chi, *Tsai-yüan tsa-chih*, *chüan* 2:24a (cited in Ma T'i-chi, *Tzu-liao*, pp. 382). For additional examples of this type, see Andrew Lo, "Historiography," pp. 121ff. In a prefatory essay attributed to Huai-lin entitled "A Comparative Evaluation of the Hundred Chapters of *Shui-hu chuan*" 水滸傳一百回文字優劣 (cited in Ma T'i-chi, *Tzu-liao*, pp. 6f., and Huang Lin and Han T'ung-wen, *Chung-kuo li-tai hsiao-shuo lun-chu hsüan*, pp. 183ff.), the text is described in similar terms, but this is judged to be a critical fault that at times may even become tedious (*k'e-yen* 可厭). Also cited in Ch'en Hsi-chung, *Shui-hu chuan hui-p'ing pen*, p. 26.

[83] For the *chüan* divisions of the earliest editions, see b.n. II. Irwin (*Evolution*, pp. 46, 114) speculates that the "original" novel covered only the equivalent of ninety chapters of the hundred-chapter *fan-pen* (minus the Liao campaign), distributed differently to make up one hundred *hui* of varying lengths. In the earliest Chin Sheng-t'an edition, four *chüan* of prefatory pieces are added to his seventy-one substantive *chüan* (seventy chapters plus prologue), to give a total of seventy-five *chüan*. This arrangement of one *hui* per *chüan* follows a similar practice in some of the earlier hundred-chapter editions (e.g., T'ien-tu wai-ch'en, Jung-yü t'ang, and "Chung Hsing" editions).

imperial palace in chapter 72.[84] But this arrangement can still be viewed as a kind of oblique affirmation of the hundred-chapter form, one that retains much of the obvious numerical balance and symmetry of the former length, simply raised to a higher power. Chin Sheng-t'an's truncated text, again, would seem to deny the structural significance of the 100- or 120-chapter length from which it was derived, but the move also betrays, alongside of Chin's unconcealed ideological motivations, certain aesthetic considerations that by their very denial serve to reaffirm the lengthier blueprint. This is to say, although the effect of bringing the development of the Liang-shan band to a sudden halt at the apogee of its power seems to dispense quite readily with the final sections of the book, in fact it still carries the implication, within the general aesthetics of the Ming novel, of the existence of additional narrative sequences outlining the inevitable dispersal of the brotherhood. Curiously, however, Chin's own artificially obtained seventy-chapter length seems at some points to carry a certain structural logic of its own. For example, we can observe the structural division that falls around the middle of Chin's text, punctuated by the miniature ceremony of dedication in chapter 35, and then the major escalation in chapter 40, which brings to a close the localized banditry of his first "half" and marks the emergence of the band as a serious threat to centralized power in the second.[85]

A similar situation may be observed with regard to the larger structural divisions within the overall shape of the text. Once again, the initial impression here of a random linking of narrative materials derived from popular sources ultimately gives way to a strong sense of the careful ordering of constituent segments. To my knowledge no extant *fan-pen* editions of *Shui-hu chuan* are divided into *chüan* of ten chapters each, but the various editions in twenty *chüan* of five chapters each obviously yield the same type of numerical proportions.[86] Moreover, in a loose sense, this text also breaks down into basic ten-chapter rhythms such as we have seen to varying degrees in *Chin P'ing Mei* and *Hsi-yu chi*. This is most discernible in the textual decades numbering from chapter 2–11 (the chain of figures comprised by Shih Chin 史進, Lu Ta 魯達, and Lin Ch'ung 林沖, leading up

---

[84] Irwin (*Evolution*, pp. 66ff.) attributes this interpolation to commercial purposes. The *fa-fan* preface pretends that it is simply restoring the original length of the book, and criticizes the editor of the Kuo edition for "removing the campaigns against the bandits T'ien Hu and Wang Ch'ing, and adding the Liao campaign" as an example of "a petty artist's technique of cross-reflection" 小家照應之法. See citation in Ma T'i-chi, *Tzu-liao*, p. 13. The addition of the extra two campaigns also has the function of retarding the dispersal of the band.

[85] This structural division is described as a "watershed" in Yüeh Heng-chün, "Liang-shan po ti ti-tsao ho huan-mieh," pp. 77f.

[86] The Li Hsüan-po edition was reportedly not divided into *chüan* at all; nor is the Chieh-tzu yüan edition (see nn. 4, 30–38).

to the initial presentation of the Liang-shan lair), 22–31 (the exploits of Wu
Sung 武松), 61–70 (the recruitment of Lu Chün-i 盧俊義, his capture of
Shih Wen-kung 史文恭, and the contest for hegemony of the band), and
72–81 (encounters with imperial authority paving the way for the imple-
mentation of the *chao-an* 招安 policy). This pattern continues to apply
fairly neatly in the final sections of the "complete edition," relating the four
campaigns against the Liao 遼 forces (chapters 83–89), T'ien Hu (chapters
91–100), Wang Ch'ing (chapters 101–110), and Fang La 方臘 (chapters
111–119).

In the rest of the ten-chapter units this impression is admittedly more
subjective, since the narrative contents in question are more miscellaneous
in nature, but the pattern still seems to hold true. For example, we may say
that chapters 12–21 cover the early history of Liang-shan po 梁山濼 prior
to the first coming of Sung Chiang 宋江, that chapters 32–41 or 42
describe the fluctuating fortunes through which Sung is propelled into the
position of the de facto leader of the band, and that chapters 51–60 depict
the development of the group into a serious challenge to imperial authority. Thus, it is quite common for scholars to refer loosely to some of these
ten-chapter units as quasi-independent sections, such as the "ten Wu Sung
chapters" 武松十回 or the "ten Sung Chiang chapters" 宋江十回.[87] Significantly, Chin Sheng-t'an's radical alteration of the text does nothing to
upset this underlying structural rhythm. In fact, it may be even more
evident in his version, since his renumbering of the chapters following his
separate prologue chapter (*hsieh-tzu* 楔子) puts more of the turning points
at the beginning of numerical decades (e.g., 1, 11, 21, 31).

Within these larger textual divisions we can sometimes perceive the
outlines of smaller structural units corresponding to individual hero cycles.
For example, the narrative focus is dominated by Lu Ta in chapters 3–7, by
Lin Ch'ung in chapters 7–12, Yang Chih 楊志 in chapters 12–17, and Yang
Hsiung 楊雄 in chapters 44–46. Similarly, the attack on the Chu family
village 祝家莊 occupies chapters 46–50, and the ensnarement of Lu Chün-
i, chapters 61–63.[88] This pattern roughly parallels the use of three- or four-
chapter episodes in *Hsi-yu chi*; and the compiler of *Shui-hu chuan* also
occasionally employs another structural technique observed in *Hsi-yu chi*,
that of inserting single-chapter interludes between or within these other
episode-length units, as for example in chapters 53 and 65.

Looking at the structural significance of the opening of the novel, one

[87] See, e.g., Liu Ts'ao-nan, "Lun Wu shih-hui," pp. 484–96; as well as Y. W. Ma's
"Shui-hu chuan chan-cheng ch'ang-mien ti lei-pieh ho nei-han," pp. 20ff.

[88] For the notion of story cycles embedded in the novel, see Hu Shih-ying, *Hua-pen
hsiao-shuo kai-lun*, p. 54; Nieh Kan-nu, "Wu-lun," pp. 32f.; and Chang Han-liang, "Chieh-
kou," p. 46. The modern novelist Mao Tun emphasizes this point in an essay on *Shui-hu*
entitled "T'an Shui-hu ti jen-wu ho chieh-kou," pp. 1–5.

immediately notices once again the presence of an initial narrative section (the release of the star-spirits) that is set clearly apart from the spatial-temporal frame of the main body of the work. This justifies setting off the separate "prologue" chapter in the Chin text, itself based on the separation of a small portion of this material as an "introduction" (*yin-shou* 引首) in the earlier *fan-pen* editions. The fact that this opening chapter presents the outline of a minimal supernatural framework of sorts for the novel, what was eventually to become a common feature of later examples of colloquial Chinese fiction, might seem to provide further evidence linking the novel to the popular tradition. But here this section seems to be in fact a new addition appearing only in the novel, with no corresponding material in antecedent versions; so it can best be explained as a deliberate device, a structural frame rather than a reflection of the popular imagination. This is especially true if one realizes that the notion of the baneful star-spirits presented in chapter 1 is somewhat at odds with the remainder of the narrative. Not only does the section avoid giving any clear rationalization of the function of the star-spirits or the meaning of their order of presentation, but also the actual narration of the opening scene is replete with ambiguities regarding the role of Commander Hung 洪太尉 himself, as well as the imperial court he serves. If anything, what the prologue chapter does add to the novel is what can only be called an ironic reflection on what is to come: an advance warning that the treatment of the heroes of the popular tradition in this novel will not necessarily conform to simplistic expectations.[89]

As in the first two works considered in this study, we can also perceive in *Shui-hu chuan* several overlapping layers of introductory material, such that even after the initial episode of the release of the star-spirits, there still remains an extended narrative section in which we only gradually approach the initial presentation of the central mimetic world of the novel. In this case this is the outlaw community on Liang-shan, which comes into view only at the moment of Lin Ch'ung's arrival in chapter 11.[90] As in *Chin P'ing Mei* and *Hsi-yu chi*, this lead-in section serves to introduce a number of major figures whose early portrayal begins to bring out certain character models

[89] The commentator of the Yüan Wu-yai edition describes the addition of this incident as a point of "profound meaning" (*shen-i* 深意) in his chapter-commentary to the first section (see *Hui-p'ing pen*, 1:53). See Chin Tai-t'ung, "Li Chih," p. 77. Yüeh Heng-chün ("Ti-tsao ho huan-mieh," p. 76) sees in the scene a kind of "allegory" (*yü-yen* 寓言). Of course, the terms *T'ien-kang* 天罡 and *Ti-sha* 地煞 derive from the popular tradition; see, for example, E.T.C. Werner, *Dictionary of Chinese Mythology* (Shanghai: Kelly and Walsh, 1932), pp. 496, 506.

[90] Chin Sheng-t'an suggests in a chapter-commentary on chapter 11 (his chapter 10, p. 1b) that the story only begins with Lin Ch'ung's arrival at the lair. Nieh Kan-nu ("Wu-lun," p. 58) discusses the possibility that the first thirteen chapters represent a later addition. This would closely parallel the situation in the first twelve or thirteen chapters of *Hsi-yu chi*.

and central thematic issues to be treated in the main body of the work. Here the primary focus seems to be on the themes of recognition of individual capacity (*chih-jen* 知人) and identifying a leader worthy of serving (*ch'iu-chu* 求主). At the least, these themes provide a strong linking thread that ties together the various adventures of Wang Chin 王進, Shih Chin, Lu Ta, and Lin Ch'ung and prepares the way for developing the extensive parallels between Lin Ch'ung and Yang Chih.[91] Reconsidered from this point of view, the opening chapters of *Shui-hu chuan*, seemingly among the most peripatetic in the book (and thus largely responsible for the criticism of its "episodic" structure), can be seen to establish the favored structural pattern of the "billiard ball" shift in narrative focus, according to which we follow the course of one figure until he runs into another, whereupon the narrative then follows the new trajectory of the latter's adventures, leaving the former in his tracks, perhaps to be reintroduced at a later juncture.[92] This discontinuous movement may appear disturbingly erratic at times, but in fact it conceals a very significant narrative function, as it lays the groundwork for the pattern of figural recurrence that governs the meaning of the text to such a great extent.

One more interesting point in chapter 1 that seems to link *Shui-hu chuan* with the formal conventions of the later sixteenth-century novels may be

[91] The case of Wang Chin is particularly intriguing and deserves some additional comment here. Yüan Wu-yai notes in his *fa-fan* preface that the figure of Wang Chin appears to have been "completely dropped after opening up [the text proper]" 王進開而不復收繳, but he goes on to suggest that this may represent a deliberate device, "one that distinguishes this from other novels, and makes it superior" 此所以異於諸小說, 而爲小說之聖也歟. Chin Sheng-t'an, in his chapter-commentary before chapter 50 (49:3a–b), similarly calls attention to the fact that Wang Chin had been left hanging in limbo; and he too goes on to suggest that this is a point with a hidden message (寓言). Yen Tun-i (*Yen-pien*, pp. 166f.) picks up on this point and informs us that although the name of Wang Chin does not appear in *Hsüan-ho i-shih* as one of the thirty-six original bandits, one might guess, since the name Chin was reportedly quite common among military men of the time, that the characters Wang Chin and Shih Chin are derived from Wang Wen 王溫 and Shih Pin 史斌 in that text. Although it would be virtually impossible to prove the point, I am convinced that the revision that gives both of these figures the name Chin 進, and their positioning as the first two figures who begin the chain of events leading into the world of the novel, involves a very pointed hint that the author is fully aware of the "lead-in" function for which they are employed in the text. If there is any validity to this supposition, then the fact that the later novel *Ju-lin wai-shih* also begins with two figures named Chin linked by the same functional role—in contrast to a prologue figure named, neatly enough, Wang Mien (for 晃 read 免)—might possibly betray a conscious imitation of this little novelistic joke. See Nieh Kan-nu ("Wu-lun," pp. 55f.) for additional sources on some of these names.

[92] The traditional commentators sometimes use the term "wavelike motion" (*i-po* 一波) to describe narrative rhythms of this sort. One recent critic has modified this idea as a point of analysis; see Lin Wen-shan, "Shui-hu ti ch'ing-chieh an-p'ai," pp. 187ff. See also Mao Tun, "T'an Shui-hu," p. 3, for a similar discussion.

seen in the opening verse, which functions much like the introductory piece later inserted on the first page of the Mao Tsung-kang edition of *San-kuo*. In *Shui-hu*, this poem is attributed to none other than Shao Yung, whose corresponding citation on page one of *Hsi-yu chi* clearly betrays a self-conscious linkage on the part of at least one of the two authors.[93]

In evaluating the ending of the 100- and 120-chapter *fan-pen* texts, we must not forget that the final scenes of collective suicide and dream vision cited by many critics as a high point of the novel are missing or modified in the truncated Chin edition by which the work has been judged for centuries. Regarding the structural significance of this section, we may note that it serves to lend a sense of aesthetic symmetry by closing the bracket on the destiny of the stars released in chapter 1, while at the same time tying up the loose ends of the fates of the remaining characters.[94] Even more important for the purposes of this discussion, the final scenes invite the reader to undertake a sober reconsideration of all he has witnessed in the course of the novel. To be more specific, by bringing to its logical conclusion the relationship of mutual destruction between Li K'uei 李逵 and Sung Chiang, the author casts a final ironic reflection not only on the heroic stature of these two individual figures, but also on the purposes and achievements of the entire brotherhood.

In this light, it is quite significant that Chin Sheng-t'an's truncated version also maintains essentially the same function in his own invented ending. His seventy-first chapter, stopping at the grand ceremony of inauguration, also provides a symmetrical counterweight to the opening chapter, and hence a strong aesthetic sense of closure. At the same time, Chin does not fail to insert a note of impending doom and futility at the end in the final twist of Lu Chün-i's dream vision.[95] Given Chin Sheng-t'an's loud declarations of hostility to the aims and methods of Sung Chiang and his men, the addition of this prophecy of doom is all but obligatory, as his text would otherwise close with the band at their greatest point of triumph. It is

[93] For Mao Tsung-kang's addition of the opening poem in *San-kuo*, see below, Chapter 5, Part II. Pointed citations of poems by Shao Yung also occur in chapter 79 of *Chin P'ing Mei*, as well as in the same exact position in *Hsing-shih yin-yüan chuan* (see above, Chapter 2, Part II). The opening *tz'u* poem at the head of the Wen-hsing t'ang edition starts with the same words (試看…). The *Ying-hsiung p'u* text I have used starts with a different *tz'u* poem, but follows with the same *shih* verse as the *fan-pen* texts (紛紛五代…).

[94] I will discuss the "emptiness" of the concluding scenes below. For an interesting critical discussion of the ending of the book, see Chang Shu-hsiang, "Ts'ung ching-t'ien tung-ti tao chi-t'ien mo-ti: Shui-hu ch'üan-chuan chieh-chü chih ch'üan-shih," pp. 138–57. See also Chang Han-liang, "Chieh-kou," p. 4.

[95] Wang Ch'i notes in the *Pai-shih hui-pien* passage cited above (n. 6) that the final dream balances the opening supernatural scene. See Chang Shu-hsiang, "Ch'üan-shih," pp. 138, 150; and Weng Po-nien, "Ching-o meng hsin-hsi," pp. 402–10.

true that by eliminating the later episodes he also deprives the bandits of their chance to perform honorable service to the nation, but at the same time his truncation leaves them unscathed, and unpunished, at the height of their powers. This sense of ambiguity in Chin Sheng-t'an's ending, however, is not unparalleled in the earlier *fan-pen* versions, where the final touch of the emperor's dream also serves to defuse somewhat the drama of the band's self-destruction acted out in the concluding scenes. I will attempt to unravel some of these ambiguities below in my interpretive discussions.

In reviewing here some of the most noticeable structural patterns that link the *fan-pen Shui-hu* to *Chin P'ing Mei* and *Hsi-yu chi* as examples of the literati novel genre, I would like to restate the fact that this text follows the broad pattern of building up its central mimetic world gradually through the first half or two-thirds of the body of the text, followed by a lengthy final section devoted primarily to its accelerating dissolution. In the Chin Sheng-t'an edition, of course, the latter phase is pointedly discarded. But in the other *fan-pen* texts this aesthetic principle is embodied in the methodical elimination of the members of the band in the course of the final campaigns, as emphasized in the body-count appended to the final chapters and in repeated images of disillusion and extinction throughout the concluding sections, as the inevitable end draws near.[96]

Under the heading of structural devices, I might also mention the manner in which the author arranges his narrative in accordance with certain other complex schemes of temporal and spatial progression. Examples of the former are most noticeable in the use of the seasonal cycle for key points of reference in the plotting of the novel. As in *Chin P'ing Mei*, the choice and treatment of the seasonal setting for a given scene often result in the element of seasonality (or the yearly cycle of ritual occasions) becoming of central importance in itself. As we have seen in earlier discussions of *Chin P'ing Ming* and *Hsi-yu chi*, one of the favored points of the annual ritual cycle in the consciousness of the Ming novelists seems to have been the Yüan-hsiao 元宵 Festival, with its carnival atmosphere of phantom lights and shapes, and its relaxed inhibitions on mingling of the sexes.[97] In *Shui-hu*, it seems less than accidental that a number of crucial scenes are set precisely on this day. These include the capture and binding

---

[96] Cf. Y. W. Ma's interesting discussion of the obtrusive counting of casualties in the additional campaigns (see above, n. 37).

[97] For a discussion of the Yüan-hsiao scenes in the novel, see Andrew Lo, "Historiography" pp. 191f. Cf. interpretations of this theme in *Chin P'ing Mei*, *Hsi-yu chi*, and *San-kuo yen-i*, in Chapters 2, 3, and 5 of this book. Chao Ching-shen provides additional background on the practice of "lantern fairs" (*teng-shih* 燈市) in *Hsiao-shuo hsi-ch'ü hsin-k'ao*, p. 543. The Yü-lan p'en Festival, I might add, the setting for a shocking scene in chapter 51, is also observed by lighting lanterns.

of Sung Chiang at Ch'ing-feng chai 清風寨 in chapter 33, the rescue of Lu Chün-i and Shih Hsiu 石秀 from execution in Ta-ming fu 大名府 in chapter 66, Li K'uei's riot in the capital in chapter 72, and his similarly conceived return to the capital with Yen Ch'ing 燕青 in chapter 110. Many of the implications of these scenes are brought together in Li K'uei's troubling dream in chapter 93, which also takes place in a post–New Year season. Other clear examples of the author's linking of seasonal moment and narrative content may be seen in his use of the seventh-month Festival of the Dead (*Yü-lan p'en* 盂蘭盆) in chapter 51 as a backdrop for Li K'uei's hideous murder of a small child, or the choice of the Mid-Autumn Festival (*Chung-ch'iu* 中秋節), with its conventional symbolism of the cold fullness of the harvest moon, as the proper season for Lu Ta's death in chapter 119— an extinction described with the Buddhist term "merging into the void" (*yüan-chi* 圓寂), an expression often associated with autumnal moon imagery.

In light of the attention to images of heat and cold seen as a self-conscious structuring device in my discussion of *Chin P'ing Mei*, one can cite numerous other narrative details in *Shui-hu* as examples of a similar sensibility to patterns of heat-within-cold or cold-within-heat.[98] These include the combining of images of fire and snow in the depiction of Lin Ch'ung's helpless rage at the burning fodder depot in chapter 10, the staging of Wu Sung's heated encounter with a tiger amidst a snow scene in chapter 23, or the use of hot summer backdrops to set off both Yang Chih's chilling fall in chapter 15 and Sung Ch'ang's final demise in chapter 120.

In his use of patterns of spatial arrangement, the author also shows considerable ingenuity in handling the geographical limitations dictated by his antecedent story cycles. Early in the narrative, the alternating movement between the Liang-shan region and other centers of power seems to underscore the remoteness of the mountain lair. But as the military potential of the band grows, the sphere of control of the Liang-shan complex gradually swells, until it becomes a major center of power in its own right. These expanding circles of influence also seem to be reflected in the spatial structure of Liang-shan po itself, in that its own physical situation—a fortress within a valley ringed by mountain peaks within a lake within a marsh—comprises a formidable set of concentric rings whose impenetrability is emphasized in many scenes. In addition, the locations of scenes set away from the stronghold reveal a certain geographical orientation radiating outward in all directions from the core area in Hopei and western

[98] For commentators' discussions of the heat-cold axis in the novel, see Yüan Wu-yai edition, chapter-commentaries on chapters 10(12b) and 110(12a), and Chin Sheng-t'an's chapter-commentary on chapter 24(23:3a).

Shantung, taking us to, among other places, Ch'ing-chou 青州 in the east, Ts'ang-chou 滄州 and Ta-ming-fu in the north, the capital region and Meng-chou 孟州 to the west, and Chiang-chou 江州 in the south. This pattern is then taken up once again in the framing of the concluding portions of the complete editions, so that the four campaigns can be viewed in terms of a counterclockwise sweep: against the Liao in the north, T'ien Hu to the northwest, Wang Ch'ing to the southwest, and Fang La in the south, culminating in the monumental sieges of the great cities of the Chiang-nan region.[99] In the end, however, the author drops these attempts at geographical verisimilitude and stages his final scenes of emptiness and desolation in a kind of limbo, in a place called Liao-erh wa 蓼兒洼 that is not quite the same as the part of the Liang-shan fastness we had known by that name earlier.[100]

The sort of large-scale patterns of arrangement I have been considering here are of major importance for appreciation of the aesthetic model of the *fan-pen Shui-hu chuan*; but they are less crucial for my interpretation of the work than the fine weaving of details that goes to make up its narrative texture. This was central to my critical analysis of the first two sixteenth-century novels investigated in this book. In evaluating this dimension of the artistry of *Shui-hu chuan*, I will again place primary emphasis on the principle of figural recurrence, observing how this goes to set up the patterns of ironic reflection at the heart of my reading of the novel.

In the critical appreciation of the narrative texture of *Shui-hu chuan*, we are greatly aided by the easy availability of Chin Sheng-t'an's relatively thoroughgoing analysis of the narrative devices at work in the novel, as set

---

[99] Most of the action following the victory at Chiang-chou takes place within the core area around Liang-shan in Shantung and Hopei, up to the movement to Ta-ming-fu during much of chapters 61–70. The pattern in the last four campaigns is somewhat obscured by the fact that some of the place-names there appear to be fictitious. But if we follow the statement of the T'ien-tu wai-ch'en preface that the T'ien Hu and Wang Ch'ing campaigns take place, respectively, in "Ho-pei" (actually western Hopei and eastern Shanshi, around the T'ai-hang range) and "Huai-hsi" 淮西 (actually a variety of locations ranging from the capital area to Hopei, Hunan, and eastern Szechwan), then the progression through the four campaigns does trace a fairly neat counterclockwise movement. Cf. the theories about separate regional strains in the *Shui-hu* story cycles, one relating to the T'ai-hang area and one to the Liang-shan area. See discussions in Y. W. Ma, "Chan-cheng ch'ang-mien," p. 21; Sun Shu-yü, *Lai-li, hsin-t'ai, i-shu*, pp. 171ff, 194ff.; and Irwin, *Evolution*, pp. 31f. Nieh Kan-nu points out some of the discrepancies of geographical detail in the novel in "Wu-lun," pp. 28f. Yüeh Heng-chün considers the symbolic significance of some of the mountains in the book in "Ti-tsao ho huan-mieh," p. 77.

[100] Liao-erh wa is mentioned in the concluding poem in chapter 1 (*SHCC*, 1:10), and again in chapters 11 (1:163) and 19 (1:273) as a part of the Liang-shan complex; but in chapter 120 (4:1810) it appears to be a separate place, one that "looks just like Liang-shan po" 和梁山濼無異.

forth programmatically in his well-known *tu-fa* 讀法 essay, and applied
throughout in his interlinear and prechapter commentary. To be sure, Chin
Sheng-t'an does not deserve the credit for originating the terminology and
critical concepts he applies to the artistry of *Shui-hu chuan*. Most of these
he simply took over from the criticism of classical poetry, painting, and
especially the *ku-wen* 古文 essay, which we have seen to have acquired
greater technical sophistication precisely at the time that the literati novel
form was taking shape during the last century of the Ming. Closer to home,
even within the field of fiction criticism per se, Chin takes up where earlier
commentators on the novel leave off.[101] Regardless of whether one accepts
the attribution of these earlier commentaries to well-known literati figures
such as Li Chih and Chung Hsing, or assigns them to relatively obscure
individuals such as Huai-lin or Yeh Chou, or to editors such as Yü Hsiang-
tou and Yüan Wu-yai, it is easy to show the debt of Chin Sheng-t'an to
what went before him. In fact, it has been demonstrated that a large portion
of Chin's interlinear comments were borrowed directly from the 120-
chapter "Li Cho-wu" commentary. But certainly that does not diminish the
fact that Chin carries this serious critical approach to the fictional text
through to an unprecedented degree of thoroughness, thus setting a model
for fiction criticism followed very closely by Mao Tsung-kang 毛宗崗 and
Chang Chu-p'o 張竹坡, and setting the standards for the appreciation of
the art of the novel during the Ch'ing period.[102]

Putting aside the heated political and ideological controversies regarding
Chin Sheng-t'an's interpretation of the book, I believe his primary contribution lies in his close reading and literary analysis of the specific narrative
techniques that comprise the dense texture of the work. In the context of
my discussions in this book, it is most significant that Chin Sheng-t'an's
wide-ranging critical vocabulary can be reduced to a central focus on the
ways in which the principle of figural recurrence operates in this text. In his
tu-fa introduction, Chin enumerates fifteen "compositional devices" (*wen-fa*
文法), to which he attributes the superiority of *Shui-hu* over *Shih Chi* 史記

---

[101] For a review of the development of the vocabulary of traditional Chinese fiction
criticism, see David Rolston, ed., *How to Read the Chinese Novel*, General Introduction. A full
translation of Chin's *tu-fa* by John C. Y. Wang is included in this volume. For a detailed
consideration of the attribution of the "Li Cho-wu" commentaries, see the Appendix of this
book.

[102] For the indebtedness of Mao Tsung-kang, Chang Chu-p'o, Wang Hsiang-hsü and
others to Chin Sheng-t'an's commentaries, see discussions in Chapters 2, 3, and 5 of this
book. On the extent of Chin Sheng-t'an's influence on the other critics, see Rolston, ed.,
How to Read, Introduction. For evidence of Chang Chu-p'o's debt to Chin Sheng-t'an, see
David T. Roy, "Chang Chu-p'o's Commentary on the *Chin P'ing Mei*," pp. 115–23. On the
importance of Chin's critical approach for the early commentaries on the *Hung-lou Meng*,
see John C. Y. Wang, "The Chih-yen chai Commentary and the *Dream of the Red Chamber*,"
pp. 189–220.

and *Hsi-yu chi*. From my point of view, these terms overlap considerably, and in fact they are reducible to a much smaller number of critical concepts. Many of these revolve around the author's practice of framing his narrative on the basis of repetition of textual units of various orders of magnitude, from individual motifs to larger patterns of action. Although this method of composition is partly responsible for the impression of a haphazard stitching together of preexisting source materials, a closer examination reveals that, beneath the very noticeable similarity in repeating narrative patterns that make up much of the text, there lies a level of careful differentiation and cross-reflection within the various manifestations of recurrent figures much like what we have seen in analyzing *Chin P'ing Mei* and *Hsi-yu chi*.[103]

Let us take a closer look at some of this overlapping terminology and the specific manner in which it is applied in Chin's analysis of the text. On the one hand, Chin's critical sights often zero in on the repetition of specific motifs or narrative details. For example, he makes a point of noting the repeated mention of Wu Sung's club in the tiger-slaying episode, or of the curtain blinds (*lien* 簾), which take on an important symbolic function in the P'an Chin-lien 潘金蓮 segment. To describe these instances, he adapts the prose term "broken-line trail of a snake in the grass" (*ts'ao-she hui-hsien* 草蛇灰線) in a sense that departs somewhat from the more common use of this metaphor in critical writings. In fact, Chin demonstrates his special interest in this aspect of the text by actually counting up the occurrences of repeated images in certain passages.

At the same time, Chin also pays considerable critical attention to patterns of repetition at the level of more complex narrative units: settings, events, even entire scenes. Of particular interest is his attempt to define the precise degree of similarity or dissimilarity present in certain recurrent figures, distinguishing for example between what he calls "full redundancy" (*cheng-fan* 正犯) and "partial redundancy" (*lüeh-fan* 略犯). As examples of the former pattern he lists such things as the several tiger-slaying scenes, the very similar cases of adultery involving P'an Chin-lien, Yen P'o-hsi 閻婆惜, and P'an Ch'iao-yün 潘巧雲, and the predictable last-minute rescues on the execution ground. In applying the latter concept he emphasizes the subtle differentiation of figurally linked scenes such as Lin Ch'ung's buying versus Yang Chih's selling of a precious sword, or Lu Ta's handling of Cheng the Butcher 鄭屠 versus Wu Sung's encounter with Chiang the Gate God 蔣門神.[104]

---

[103] See Andrew Lo's discussion of "linkage patterns" in "Historiography," pp. 135ff.

[104] Other examples not mentioned by Chin Sheng-tan include such *topoi* as the portentous shooting of wild geese (chapters 35, 62, 110), the trick of rolling down a hill wrapped in felt (chapters 5, 49, 57, 86, 116), contests of physical strength and skill (chapters 13, 74,

Chin Sheng-t'an's interest in interlocking textual figures also applies at the level of specific characters in the text. Only one of his *wen-fa* terms relates explicitly to the juxtaposition of individual characters in the narrative. This is his "technique of applying powder on the reverse side" (*pei-mien p'u-fen fa* 背面鋪粉法), describing the use of one character as a foil for another, such as we see in the treatment of Sung Chiang and Li K'uei, or Yang Hsiung and Shih Hsiu. But on the other hand, he frequently uses examples of recurring character types to illustrate other categories of structural analysis.[105] Beyond the examples of this type that Chin provides, we may also note here that the principle of paired characters clearly applies to Lu Ta and Wu Sung, Lu Chün-i and Yen Ch'ing, and the various pairs of brothers (Hsieh 解, Ts'ao 曹, Sun 孫, K'ung 孔) that fill the text. In some of these cases it may be said that there is no real differentiation between the two figures yoked together; but in other pairs, for example Yang Hsiung and Shih Hsiu, Lu Ta and Wu Sung, Lei Heng 雷橫 and Chu T'ung 朱仝, and others, the author very quickly moves beyond a simplistic joining of similar types (or complementary opposites) to a deeper exploration of the serious differences brought out in the respective comparisons. This is most obvious in the case of Sung Chiang and Li K'uei, whose complex relationship of similarity and difference sets up a central axis of meaning for the novel. The same can be said for the expansion of this principle of composition to cover groups of three or more recurring figures, as for example in the chain of heroes comprised by Lu Ta, Wu Sung, and Li K'uei, or the progression of leaders that takes us through Wang Lun 王倫, Ch'ao Kai 晁蓋, and Sung Chiang. I will attempt to show below that in each of these chains of recurrent types the author's chief aim is to manipulate the conflicting aspects of similarity and difference involved in the juxtapositions of roles and types in order to cast an ironic reflection on the final interpretation of all the figures involved.

In developing his analysis of the figural density of the novel, Chin Sheng-t'an also goes on to consider a second category of narrative devices, those dealing with the manner in which the author contrives to join discrete narrative units by various techniques of transition, or conversely,

---

102), drawing lots to match military prowess (chapters 69, 94, 108, 116), the Trojan-horse grain barge trick (chapters 70, 83, 106), meddling by two court-appointed supervisors (chapters 16, 75), thwarting of naval attacks on Liang-shan po (chapters 19, 78), the demand of three conditions from Li K'uei (chapters 43, 53, 74), old men showing the route of escape (chapters 47, 117), the burning of besieged cities by spies (chapters 50, 66, 84, 92), and many more.

[105] One example of the long-range repetition of character types involves the remote link between Wang Chin and Wang Ch'ing, suggested by Li Tsung-t'ung (Hsüan-po), in "Tu Shui-hu chi" p. 13; and Hu Shih, in "K'ao-cheng," pp. 77ff.

introduces deliberate breaks or retardation of narrative continuity. For example, in his discussion of "the technique of lead-in elements" (*nung-yin fa* 弄引法) he describes the device of introducing unessential narrative material in order to prepare the way for a subsequent topic, as in the enumeration of the "five prerequisites for a lover" followed by the "ten stages of seduction" in his treatment of the first tryst of Hsi-men Ch'ing 西門慶 and P'an Chin-lien in chapter 24. On the other hand, his term "technique of the otter's tail" (*t'a-wei fa* 獺尾法) deals with the gradual tapering or winding down of major scenes by adding descriptive passages that keep the scene in focus after the main action has been concluded, as for example in Wu Sung's encounter with a party of hunters immediately after he has slain the tiger. Other devices of retardation of narrative continuity described by Chin include the technique of "deliberately letting matters go in different directions with the intention of pulling it all together" (*yü-ho ku-tsung* 欲合故縱), as in the seemingly disconnected series of meetings and adventures that set the stage for the dramatic reunion at Pai-lung miao 白龍廟 in chapter 40, or the use of quiet interludes within action-filled episodes, what he refers to by a term from painting criticism, "horizontal clouds cutting across mountain peaks" (*heng-yün tuan shan* 橫雲斷山).[106]

Certain other compositional patterns delineated by Chin Sheng-t'an have less to do with instances of figural recurrence than with other points of analysis of relevance to this discussion. One of these is the element of narrative causality. In view of the common impression that the *Shui-hu chuan* is nothing more than a series of adventures loosely strung together on the thread of the Liang-shan brotherhood, it is extremely interesting to note that Chin Sheng-t'an insists the author of the novel must have been highly conscious of the network of causal relations that forms the linkage between separate scenes. Thus, he distinguishes between chains of events in which the elaboration of logical causality is minimized, what he terms the "technique of maximum narrative economy" (*chi-sheng fa* 極省法)—for example the transition from Wu Sung's tiger-slaying to the P'an Chin-lien episode by means of the chance meeting of Wu and his brother, as opposed to scenes in which no detail is spared to evoke a sense of inexorable determinism in the unfolding of events, what he terms the "technique of minimum narrative economy" (*chi-pu-sheng fa* 極不省法), such as the chain of events leading up to Sung Chiang's killing of Yen P'o-hsi. Along similar lines, Chin also draws attention to scenes that are fully delineated, to which he applies the expression "technique of total depiction" (*ta-lo-mo fa* 大落墨法). Examples of this include Wu Yung's recruitment of the Juan

---

[106] Here Chin has in mind the interruption of long narrative units such as the attacks on the Chu family village or Ta-ming fu with seemingly extraneous incidents.

阮 brothers, the episode of Wu Sung and the tiger, and the three attacks on the Chu family village. To these he counters passages of subtle innuendo, to which he applies the metaphorical expression "the prick of a needle in cotton wadding" (mien-chen ni tz'u 綿針泥刺)—for example, the undercurrents of tension between Sung Chiang and Ch'ao Kai that precede each foray from the mountain lair. Chin Sheng-t'an's attention to this latter aspect of the text is of particular interest to us here, since by this he points directly at what I will attempt to establish as the crucial element in the proper interpretation of the fan-pen novel: the dimension of ironic reflection on the heroics of the Shui-hu band.

III

With this, we begin to shift our attention to the third area of analysis considered in Chapters 2 and 3 of this study, that of narrative rhetoric. Once again, my discussion of this aspect of the text will focus on the key element of irony in the fan-pen revision of its narrative material. Before proceeding to elucidate the workings of irony in this text, however, I will pause to note certain other rhetorical features that govern the projection of meaning in this deceptively simple book. First, we should acknowledge the significant contribution of the Shui-hu chuan to the expansion and enrichment of the literary colloquial language as a medium for sophisticated prose fiction. Despite the common misconception of this book as an example of pure colloquial expression, the text is in fact composed of a complex mix of various levels of diction.[107] The consistent exploitation of the expressivity of colloquial speech applies not only in the mimesis of dialogue per se, which remains a central element in the texture of Shui-hu despite the action-oriented nature of its subject matter, but also in passages of scenic and character description reserved in lesser works of the colloquial tradition for conventional formulas in semiclassical verse or parallel prose. Two of the most memorable examples of this sort are the treatment of the clatter of flying hooves in Yang Chih's joust with Chou Chin 周謹 in chapter 13 and the intrusion of Lu Ta's staff into our field of vision as he comes to Lin Ch'ung's rescue in Chapter 9, both of which approach the cinematographic in their attention to the expressivity of detail.[108] A second

[107] The subtlety of the language used in the novel is emphasized by Lu Hsin in "Ch'ü-pi," pp. 49–53.

[108] Other noteworthy passages of concrete description include chapters 41(SHCC, 2:658), 59(3:986), 61(3:1033), 73(3:1237), 90(4:1471f.), 111(4:1665ff.), 113–14(4:1696, 1716), and 120(4:1810). Cf. C. T. Hsia's description of the vivid detail in certain scenes (e.g., Classic Novel, pp. 99f.).

aspect of the rhetorical complexity of the novel that deserves greater critical attention is the use of the incidental verse occupying a conspicuous place in most of the Ming editions. Although our own experience of this part of the work is sharply curtailed by later excision, the remarks of the Ming and Ch'ing commentators sometimes show a more hospitable appreciation of these poems than we may imagine today.[109]

This brings me to the crucial element in my analysis of the great sixteenth-century novels, the central role of irony. This is ultimately what distinguishes the *fan-pen* versions of *Shui-hu* from the antecedent source materials and to a lesser degree from the contemporary *chien-pen* and other popular treatments of the same materials. It is also, as I have argued, the primary justification for speaking of these works as "novels" in the first place.[110] The idea of an ironic reading of the *Shui-hu chuan* obviously goes against the impression of the book as an essentially positive treatment of the deeds of the Liang-shan band, a sense that may be true of the alternate versions of the story cycles, which are often understood as celebrations of an anti-authoritarian bandit spirit of the Robin Hood sort. In fact, I suspect that in many cases the reader's impression of the events depicted in the novel is largely colored by prior conceptions of the story based on images from the popular tradition. But in the case of the *fan-pen* texts, I am convinced that the transfer of these popular images into an interpretation of the novel leads to a serious misreading of its literary significance.[111]

[109] The *fa-fan* preface deplores the cutting of poems in certain prior editions and explains the special functions of the verse in the novel to "describe the appearance of characters" 形容人態 and "bring the mood of a passage to an abrupt conclusion" 頓挫文情. Hu Ying-lin, *Pi-ts'ung* (cited in Ma T'i-chi, *Tzu-liao*, p. 353) also criticizes the cutting of poems in the popular editions. C. T. Hsia points to the cutting of the poems as an improvement in the text (*Classic Novel*, p. 100). See additional discussions by Ch'en Chou-ch'ang, "Lun Shui-hu yün-wen ti i-shu tso-yung," pp. 278–90; Ōuchida Saburō, "Hanponkō," no. 2, p. 62; and Shiroki Naoya, "Ippyaku nijūkai," pp. 136ff.

[110] For the centrality of irony in the rhetoric of the novel genre, see above, Chapter 1. A number of recent critics have paid attention to the ironic dimensions of the novel. See, for example, Chang Han-liang, "Chieh-kou," p. 47; and Chang Shu-hsiang, "Ch'üan-shih," p. 141. Nieh Kan-nu ("Wu-lun," p. 125), credits Chin Sheng-t'an with adding many of the ironic touches.

[111] At the very least, a reading of the novel as some sort of indirect statement is suggested by the Yüan Wu-yai *fa-fan* preface, which speaks of the "lingering meaning in the spirit of the Ch'un-ch'iu classic" 有春秋之遺意焉. I also take this as the implication of the last line in the opening verse of chapter 71 in the T'ien-tu wai-ch'en edition (moved to the end of the inauguration scene in the Yüan Wu-yai and Chieh-tzu yüan editions, omitted in most others): "This I present to my readers for their careful perusal" 付與諸公仔細看. For that matter, one may say that the repeated advice of the Jung-yü t'ang and Yüan Wu-yai commentaries to "pay attention" (*cho-yen* 着眼) to a given passage often implies that there is a hidden meaning involved. Chin Sheng-t'an provides a fairly explicit discussion of the ironic dimension of the text in his chapter-commentary to chapter 19 (18:2a, b).

Here we are indebted to the eye-opening discussions of C. T. Hsia, Sun Shu-yü, and other recent critics on the tendency of the *Shui-hu chuan* to dwell on the darker side of the traditional Chinese mentality.[112] In the light of the definition of irony developed in this study, I might restate this thesis to say that what we have in the novel is neither a blind approval of the Liang-shan mentality in disregard of its more troubling implications, nor a bitterly cynical denunciation of all that the band stands for, but rather a manifestation of a basic uncertainty. This is the other side of ironic narrative: a questioning of some of the most deep-seated beliefs about the nature of the individual hero and the significance of human action. On this other side of the coin, I will emphasize the fact that the novel also takes pains to present a certain number of positive figures and ideals, alongside its more somber portraits, in order to keep before the reader's eyes the possibility of a more balanced understanding of the meaning of the events portrayed.

In my earlier discussions of the ironic dimensions of *Chin P'ing Mei* and *Hsi-yu chi*, it was helpful to proceed from the lighter to the heavier side of the ironic reflection perceived in those two books. In *Shui-hu chuan* as well, we see similar gradations of seriousness. Sometimes the ironic touch in passages in the novel seems to amount to nothing more than light mockery, as in the grotesque exaggeration we see in the depiction of Wang Ying 王英 (Wang Ai-hu 王矮虎), or in the use of ribald double-entendre in chapter 45 to describe one Buddhist monk's devotional fervor.[113] In other cases, the playful tone comes out in the timeworn practice of using punning personal names, a conventional feature of Chinese narrative that enjoys increased possibilities in *Shui-hu* due to the unusual abundance of nick-names, star-names, and the like for its various key figures. For example, the frequent labeling of warriors as a "junior" (*hsiao* 小) or "sick", i.e. deficient (*ping* 病) copy of an earlier hero seems to poke fun at the small-time status of some of the *Shui-hu* warriors.[114] Although of course most of these names were simply inherited by the author as part of his source materials, there is

[112] See C. T. Hsia, *Classic Novel*, pp. 75–114; and Sun Shu-yü, *Lai-li, hsin-t'ai, i-shu*, pp. 25–46, and passim.

[113] *SHCC*, 2:738. Chin Sheng-t'an (chapter 44:20b) adds to the fun by changing "sharing a pillow, they took their pleasure" 共枕歡娛 to "they fulfilled their heartfelt vows" 了其心願.

[114] These characters include Hua Jung (Little Li Kuang 小李廣), Yang Hsiung (Sick Kuan So 病關索), Sun Li 孫立 (Sick Yü-ch'ih 病尉遲), Lü Fang (Little Marquis Wen 小溫侯), Chou T'ung 周通 (Little Hegemon 小霸王), Hsüeh Shui 薛水 (Sick Man-eater 病大蟲), Sun Hsin 孫新 (Little Yü-ch'ih 小尉遲), and possibly Kuo Sheng 郭盛 (Rival Jen-kuei 賽仁貴). On the identification of the elusive figure Kuan So, see below, Chapter 5, n. 410. Wang Li-ch'i argues that the epithet "sick" (*ping*) is simply a descriptive tag for a sallow complexion (see "Shui-hu ying-hsiung ti ch'o-hao," p. 282).

also considerable evidence of tampering on his own part, as for example in the transfer of the nickname I-chang-ch'ing 一丈青 from a male bandit in earlier sources to the female warrior Hu San-niang 扈三娘 in the novel.[115] The name given in the novel to Sung Chiang's principal adviser is particularly noteworthy in this context. As far as I can tell, the use of the name Wu Yung, with its very obvious stock pun (for 吳用 read 無用, "good-for-nothing"), is not to be found in the earlier sources, where this figure is known by the designations Wu Chia-liang 吳加亮 or Wu Hsüeh-chiu 吳學究 (both of which, by the way, also provide possibilities for ironic interpretation), and only becomes attached to the tradition at about the time of the appearance of the *fan-pen* novel in the Chia-ching period.[116]

However, this sort of light ironic touch is far less significant for my purposes than the manner in which the author generates ironies regarding some of the central figures in the text by means of the manipulation of specific details in their presentation, and by setting up a network of cross-reflections between figurally linked characters and actions. In the following pages, I will take up in considerable detail some of the principal examples of this sort.

IV

As our first case, let us consider Wu Sung, the indomitable hero of the popular sagas. The treatment of the Wu Sung figure in the episodes of the tiger-slaying and his methodical revenge on P'an Chin-lien and Hsi-men Ch'ing in the *fan-pen* novel is not drastically different from popular versions of these legends (and, conversely, much of the popular image of Wu Sung may ultimately reflect these particular scenes in the novel itself). The

---

[115] For this name, see Wang Li-ch'i, "Shui-hu ying-hsiung ti ch'o-hao," p. 284; Sun Shu-yü, *Lai-li, hsin-t'ai, i-shu*, pp. 261–66. In the Kung Sheng-yü "encomium" (see b.n. I), this name is used to describe Yen Ch'ing, in the puzzling line: "He was a great master of sensual delight, he had I-chang ch'ing" 大行春色, 有一丈青. Perhaps the expression *ta-hsing* here should be read *T'ai-hang*, as the underlining in the citation of this passage in K'ung Ling-ching, *Shih-liao*, p. 10, suggests. As we will see below, "master of sensual delight" is an apt epithet for Yen Ch'ing. In the *Hsüan-ho i-shih* this same epithet is applied to a male figure named Li Heng 李衡.

[116] The name Wu Chia-liang appears in *Hsüan-ho i-shih*, and the figure appears most often in Yuan drama under the name Wu Hsüeh-chiu. See Ho Hsin, *Yen-chiu*, pp. 356f. One early example of the use of the name Wu Yung may be found in Lang Ying's *Ch'i-hsiu lei-kao*, p. 386. The one exception to this is the play entitled *Nao t'ung-t'ai* 鬧銅臺. See Nieh Kan-nu, "Wu-lun," p. 33; and Hayden, "A Skeptical Note," p. 394. Nieh notes that this play may be a Ming rather than a Yuan work. For some imaginative readings of several of the names in the novel, see the late Ch'ing essay "Shui-hu chuan ming-ming shih-i" 水滸傳命名釋義, cited in Chu I-hsüan, *Tzu-liao*, pp. 399ff.

encounter with the tiger in chapter 23 is basically good fun, and the extracting of P'an Chin-lien's debt of blood not long after is not without a certain degree of dramatic intensity.[117] But by the time we come to the replay of Wu Sung's vengeful wrath in subsequent chapters, the author begins to approach the fine line between heroics and havoc that comprises one of the central thematic dimensions of his work.

The darker side of Wu Sung's portrait come out most powerfully in the chilling massacre at the Yüan-yang lou 鴛鴦樓 in chapter 31. On the face of it, Wu Sung's murderous rage is perfectly justified—his victims had, after all, conspired to arrange his own coldblooded murder immediately before. So it is only the author's fine brushwork details—the hopeless pleas of the innocent servants, the theft of the gold and silver dishes, and, in retrospect, Wu Sung's subtly disclosed vulnerability to the attractions of the girl Yü-lan 玉蘭 —that, taken together, add up to the final impression of excessive, even wanton bloodletting.[118] In other words, what our author does is take the theme of merciless revenge and present it first in one set of circumstances, then in another, in order to force the reader to consider some of the deeper implications involved.

From this point on, the treatment of the fortunes of Wu Sung turns perceptibly sour. Most telling, I believe, is the incident at Wu-kung ling 蜈蚣嶺 immediately following. Here the motivation for Wu's fury is shrouded in the thickest of ambiguities. The cause of his explosive indignation at the Taoist priest's dalliance with an apparently willing partner is not made very clear; and his own attitude toward the girl he has saved remains suggestively ambivalent, in sharp contrast with the unequivocal sense of a damsel in distress in the treatment of the scene in the more recent oral cycles.[119]

Finally, the section of the novel devoted to the Wu Sung hero-cycle closes with this invincible slayer of beasts and avenging angel rendered nearly powerless. By the end, we have seen him beaten to the point of making a false confession in chapter 30, bound for slaughter in chapter 31,

[117] This special intensity in the killing of P'an Chin-lien is noticeably subdued in the *Ying-hsiung p'u* treatment of the same incident (p. 4:19a; the arrangement of material in this section shows some sloppy cut-and-paste work).

[118] *SHCC*, 1:461ff., 475ff. The excuse that Wu Sung was feeling the effects of his wine at the time of the killings is canceled out by his prodigious capacity for wine exhibited in chapter 23. See Yüeh Heng-chün, "Ti-tsao ho huan-mieh," p. 85. The theft of the dishes is strongly reminiscent of Lu Ta's identical act at T'ao-hua shan in chapter 5. Y. W. Ma also takes note of the excessive quality of this scene in "Liang-shan po fu-ch'ou kuan-nien pien," p. 106. See C. T. Hsia's extremely vivid translation of this scene in *Classic Novel*, pp. 97ff.

[119] For popular storytelling treatment of this scene, see Wang Shao-t'ang, *Yang-chou p'ing-hua Shui-hu: Wu Sung*, pp. 927ff.

and, most graphically, floundering helplessly in a river in chapter 32. At this point, one recalls the introduction of the figure as a sullen beggar wracked with sickness in chapter 22, and we look ahead to his ultimate fate when he is described as a one-armed cripple, a "wreck of his former self" (*fei-jen* 廢人), by the close of the work.[120]

A similar process of narrative development may be seen in the parallel treatment of Li K'uei, who is figurally linked to Wu Sung by a number of shared attributes. In this case, however, the negative implications in the character surface sooner, and they are subsequently carried to more deeply troubling conclusions.

In a number of early scenes, the reader is introduced to examples of Li K'uei's disruptive behavior, but in a manner that is governed by a generally light tone of presentation, which ensures that the incidents will be taken in good humor. This more or less positive image of the "Black Whirlwind" 黑旋風 as an uninhibited free spirit with basically good intentions is predominant in the disturbance among the fishermen at Chiang-chou in chapter 38, in his antics in official robes in chapter 74, and even in the abortive ax murder of the Taoist master Lo Chen-jen 羅眞人 and Li's subsequent penance in chapter 53. In these examples, we get the sort of sympathetic view of Li K'uei that we find in a number of Yuan and Ming dramatic treatments, and that was apparently the basis for the separate narrative devoted to Li that is advertised in one of the "Huai-lin" prefaces to the Jung-yü t'ang edition.[121]

In the text of the *fan-pen* novel, however, some of the darker implications of Li K'uei's anarchistic tendencies soon become too insistent to be ignored. For example, Li's forced abduction of his own mother in chapter 43 begins with a light enough tone at the outset, when his grotesquely distorted feelings of filial piety present a parody of similar sentiments expressed by Kung-sun Sheng 公孫勝 and Sung Chiang himself immediately before. The encounter with his own double, Li Kuei 李鬼, whose name and attributes mark him as a reflection of the savage side of Li's character, begins to become more suggestive, although this is still essentially a humorous touch. But when this little escapade is shown to result in the

---

[120] *SHCC*, 4:1791.

[121] See Liu Ching-chih, "Yuan-tai chih hou ti Shui-hu hsi," pp. 274f., for a discussion of the generally positive treatment of Li K'uei in Yuan drama. Nieh Kan-nu ("Wu-lun," p. 66) notes certain inconsistencies in this treatment. For a full discussion of the Li K'uei image in the novel, see Ch'ang Ch'ung-i, "Shui-hu chung ti Li K'uei hsing-hsiang chih-i," pp. 351–59. Some of the historical sources for the Li K'uei figure are presented by Wang Li-ch'i in "Ch'o-hao," p. 299. See also Nieh Kan-nu, "Wu-lun," p. 36; Hsiung Wen-ch'in and Shih Lin, "Ts'ung Shui-hu hsi tao Shui-hu chuan, k'an Li K'uei hsing-hsiang ti fa-chan," pp. 141–48. For the obvious parallel to Chang Fei's role in *San-kuo*, see Wang Hsiao-chia, "Shui-hu chuan tso-che hsi Lo Kuan-chung k'ao-pien," p. 150. I will reconsider this parallel in the following chapter of this book.

mauling of his mother by a tiger, the humor begins to take a different turn. This is another excellent example of the complexity of figural recurrence at work in the novel. Not only is Li K'uei's escape with his mother on his back modeled on Wang Chin's Aeneas-like flight from the capital at the start of the narrative, but the encounter with the four tigers also forces a comparison with the tiger-slaying episode of Wu Sung. Only in this case, Li K'uei's recklessness is shown to have fatal consequences. Here the author's acid wit comes out in the fine details. Where Wu Sung conquers his beastly foe in face-to-face combat, the author has one of Li K'uei's thrusts find its mark, to put it nicely, under the tail of the animal.[122]

A similar case may be seen in the incident at Ssu-liu ts'un 四柳村 in chapter 73, where Li K'uei's offer to enter a maiden's chamber to exorcise a demon assumed to be tormenting her, figurally reminiscent of Lu Ta's comparable position in chapter 5 (itself similar to the first encounter of Sun Wu-K'ung 孫悟空 and Chu Pa-chieh 猪八戒 in chapter 22 of *Hsi-yu chi*), leads to one of the most coldblooded killings in the book.[123] Once again, we have a good example of a scene that begins lightly enough, with the reenactment of a stereotyped popular story. But the author's treatment soon becomes more serious as he injects a strong measure of pathos for the desperate young couple and the helpless parents of the girl, and we are left with a sense that there is more at stake here than a simple case of frontier justice.

In fact, there are a number of scenes in the novel in which it is specifically a female figure who unwittingly provokes Li K'uei's rage, as for example at the end of chapter 38, when the singer Sung Yü-lien's 宋玉蓮 unwise interruption of Li's manly boasting triggers a disproportionately violent reaction. The ironic tone of these scenes is unmistakable, given the fact that among the members of the brotherhood it is most often Li K'uei who voices the *hao-han* 好漢 code of sexual pride.[124] This is perhaps most noticeable in chapter 72, when it is Li's nervous impatience outside the apartment of Li Shih-shih 李師師 that undermines the chance for an early amnesty for the band. Many of these associations are brought together in Li K'uei's very suggestive dream in chapter 93, in which he first rescues a damsel in distress and refuses to take her as his wife, later wipes out all the

---

[122] *SHCC*, 2:699. The ironic import of this scene is later reemphasized in Li K'uei's dream vision in chapter 93. Chin Sheng-t'an mockingly compares Li K'uei's pursuit of a white rabbit 白兔 through the underbrush at the start of the chapter to Sung Chiang's relationship to the mysterious "dark goddess" 玄女 in the preceding chapter, in his chapter-commentary on chapter 43 (42:7b).

[123] See Wang Yung-chien, "Ch'eng-shu nien-tai," p. 236.

[124] For C. T. Hsia's discussion of this point, see *Classic Novel*, pp. 105f. See also Sun Shu-yü, *Lai-li, hsin-t'ai, i-shu*, pp. 32–38.

evil ministers at the imperial court, and finally sees his own mother back in the woods, threatened by another tiger.

The most unforgivable example of the problematic side of the portrait of Li K'uei, however, is surely the brutal killing of the small child in Chu T'ung's protection in chapter 51. I suppose that it would not be entirely impossible to interpret this act as a necessary evil in the cause of fulfilling the preordained numerical strength of the Liang-shan band. But the author invalidates this interpretation by carefully portraying Chu T'ung's relationship with his superior as one based on mutual respect, and by pressing the point of sincere affection between Chu and the child. But it is the sheer glee with which Li K'uei reveals his handiwork, leading Chu T'ung on a hopeless chase through the woods with the taunt "Come and get me!" (*Lai, lai, lai!* 來來來), that seals the case that there must be more to the author's construction of the Li K'uei figure in such scenes than simple delight in the exploits of a totally uninhibited fellow.[125]

This understanding comes out most strongly in connection with the development of Li K'uei's role within the Liang-shan band. From very soon after his introduction in the novel, at which point he already voices whole-hearted support for the sentiments expressed in Sung Chiang's poem of rebellion, all the way to his final parting cry of defiance, "So let's rebel!" (*Fan le pa* 反了罷) in chapter 120, Li serves as the main focus for the ominous implications of the growing strength and numbers of the band. As couched in Li's own characteristically crude language, these frequent exhortations to insurrection are as a rule humorous. But it becomes increasingly clear that his impulses toward the overthrow of authority are directed not only against the imperial regime, but also against the authority within the band itself. This surfaces in his bitter opposition to Sung Chiang's proposals to yield the leadership to Lu Chün-i in chapter 67, and in his repudiation of the *chao-an* policy at several points.[126] Eventually his rallying cry (*fan*) takes on overtones that go beyond the literal conception of rebellion to constitute an attack on all order and control. Given the insistent association of the Li K'uei figure with this impulse to destroy, I cannot help thinking that the depiction of his role in the burning and looting of the great cities of Su-chou and Hang-chou in the course of the Fang La campaign must have been particularly difficult for the sixteenth-century literati

---

[125] *SHCC*, 2:847. The telling detail of Chu T'ung's hair standing on end is absent in the *Ying-hsiung p'u* treatment of the scene. The problem of how to deal with the generally positive assessments of the Li K'uei figure in many early critical commentaries will be reconsidered below.

[126] For examples of this aspect of Li's role, see chapters 41 (*SHCC*, 2:666), 67(3:1136), 68(3:1163), 71(3:1206). Cf. his cutting of the *t'i-t'ien hsing-tao* banner in chapter 73, and his destruction of the first *chao-an* proclamation in chapter 76.

audience, centered as they were in the urban areas of the Yangtze delta region, to swallow uncritically. At any rate, the portrayal of this warrior revolves around descriptions of indiscriminate killing. We are told repeatedly that "he killed everything he saw" 見一個殺一個見兩個殺一雙 or that he was itching for a chance to kill again. Among other things, the force of this association is captured in the author's repetition of one particular detail in several scenes describing Li's ax-play: his habitual practice of chopping off the hooves of the horses of his foes. It is also clearly identified in the epithet "killing and burning" applied to Li K'uei in a number of sources, as well as in the star-name Star of Celestial Murder (T'ien-sha 天殺星), assigned to him in the ceremony of inauguration in chapter 71.[127]

In view of this association between the Li K'uei figure and the unbridled forces of destruction implicit within the emergence of the Liang-shan band, it is quite significant that, as we have seen in the case of Wu Sung, the author of the *fan-pen* novel takes pains to give us a number of scenes in which Li's physical powers are sharply undermined. Part of this treatment is amusing, as in the graphic illustration of his strange vulnerability to control by Tai Tsung 戴宗 and Yen Ch'ing at several points. More important, even in the area of military prowess, we observe that in numerous battle scenes Li K'uei's skills as a warrior are limited to his mindless charge with broad-axes flying, a tactic that rarely proves to be of military value, and is often downright detrimental.[128]

In light of the above discussion, it is of particular interest that the author seems to inject at a number of points vague hints that there may be a connection between Li K'uei's overstated misogyny and his frequent failure in physical confrontations. The treatment of this side of Li K'uei's portrait goes even further than the comparable exploration of the limitations of strength we have seen in the case of Wu Sung. At least, in the course of the novel we see him bound by the wife of the impostor Li Kuei in chapter 43, pointedly helpless against the martial arts of I-chang-ch'ing in chapter 48 and Ch'iung-ying 瓊英 in chapter 98, and wounded (of all places in the thigh) in the crucial battles of chapter 68. Toward the end he appears to wane irretrievably, so that by chapters 94 and 115, after additional staging of the recurrent scene in which he begs Sung Chiang to permit him to join the fray, his flailing attack fails utterly, and in the last case he returns to

---

[127] For example, *SHCC* 2:660f. See also chapter 40: "He did not care if they were soldiers and officials or common people" 不問軍官百姓 (2:647); and chapter 50: "killing with delight" 殺得快活 (2:829). For examples of his "itching" to kill, see chapters 47 (2:785) and 63 (3:1072). In chapter 88 his bloody rampage results in his own capture, and in chapter 91 Lu Chün-i forcibly restrains him in order to save innocent lives.

[128] On the limitations of Li K'uei's value as a fighter, see Ch'ang Ch'ung-i, "Li K'uei hsing-hsiang," p. 358.

camp in tears of humiliation. Two chapters later he is allowed a compensatory show of rescuing Sung Chiang at T'ung-lu 桐廬, but this, too, leads directly to another serious defeat.

As soon as we note some of these broad similarities in the treatment of the popular heroes Wu Sung and Li K'uei in the *fan-pen Shui-hu*, we are reminded of one more figure, Lu Ta, who is not only physically similar to Wu Sung and Li K'uei, but also shares certain other details of characterization with them. Eventually, the common features of proverbial strength, prodigious appetite, and unbridled violence are pushed one step further, when Lu Ta is explicitly paired with Wu Sung as comrades on Two Dragon Mountain 二龍山, and later as the "two pilgrims" 二行者 whose fates are ultimately linked in chapter 119 in the fulfillment of the prophecy of the Ch'ien-t'ang bore.

In a certain sense, we can see in the narrative progression through these three figures the same principle of rising intensity or seriousness that governs the gradual deepening of ironic implications in the portrayal of each of the individual heroes. In the early recounting of the adventures of Lu Ta in chapters 3–7, the author maintains a relatively light touch. In the episodes of the killing of Cheng the Butcher, Lu's naked riot in the monastery at Wu-t'ai shan 五臺山, and his stint as a gardener in the capital that positions him to rescue Lin Ch'ung, the author does little to qualify the reader's delight in the adventures of an irrepressible hero. He does, in fact, begin to introduce the theme of weakness within strength in the strange incident at the Wa-kuan ssu 瓦罐寺 in chapter 6, but this suggestion is not pressed to its logical conclusions in this case, so that Lu Ta's final attainment of enlightenment in chapter 119 reads as a well-motivated fulfillment of the image of the naked monk (赤條條) projected early in the work.[129] When this character type is recast in the person of Wu Sung in chapters 22–31, delight gives way to awe and troubling ambiguity in certain scenes, but the portrait still generally continues to command the reader's sympathies. In the figure of Li K'uei, however, the implications that are present in the earlier two instances of the chain reach their ultimate conclusions, so, at least from the point of the gratuitous killing of the child in chapter 51, the violent actions portrayed are no longer very funny or awe-inspiring. They are at best grotesque, and at worst profoundly negative.

This range of treatment, from light humor to bitter irony, must be kept in mind when we come to consider the complex image of Sung Chiang as developed in the *fan-pen* novel, since in a number of senses Li K'uei and

---

[129] For a discussion of this side of the Lu Ta figure, see Sun Shu-yü, *Lai-li, hsin-t'ai, i-shu,* pp. 246ff. Lu Ta's final dispensation is set up in his parting speech to Sung Chiang in chapter 119 (*SHCC*, 4:1787), at which time he tells him, "My heart has long since turned to ash" 酒家心已成灰. Nieh Kan-nu discusses the image of Lu Ta on the stage in "Wu-lun," p. 33.

Sung Chiang comprise the most crucial pair of linked opposites in the book.[130] In evaluating the role of Sung Chiang within the *Shui-hu* narrative, both traditional and modern critics have tended to dwell on the political implications of the rising power of the Liang-shan band, either indulging in wholesale condemnation of the lawlessness and banditry they represent, or else flatly rejecting the "defeatist" mentality that leads them to give up their anti-authoritarian ideals and throw in with the government forces. I will consider these issues later in this chapter, but my assessment of the portrait of the Sung Chiang must first take into account the fine brush-work details with which he is delineated in the *fan-pen* text.

Beginning at the level of physical attributes, the first thing we notice is that Sung Chiang does not cut a very imposing figure. He is described from the very outset as small and swarthy, and at certain points we are told that he is a bit on the heavy side. His diminutive stature is played up for ironic effect in chapter 33, when he is forced to stand on his tiptoes and peer through a crowd to get a look at Yüan-hsiao Festival lanterns. His dark complexion, as indicated by his nicknames Black Third Son (Hei san-lang 黑三郎) and Black Sung Chiang (Hei Sung Chiang 黑宋江), is not simply an idle detail, as it sets him apart from the ideal physiognomic qualities of a noble ruler, and more to the point, also gives the first suggestion of a figural link to several other problematic individuals in the novel. These include the lustful dwarf Wang Ying—the "dwarf tiger" (Ai-hu)—the gnarled cuckold Wu Ta, and a series of swarthy outlaws beginning with Liu T'ang and culminating in Li K'uei, who himself calls attention to Sung's dark color at their first meeting in chapter 38.[131]

Sung Chiang is endowed with more nicknames and descriptive tags than any other character in the book.[132] In addition to the references to his

---

[130] Chin Sheng-t'an discourses at length on the significance of the Sung Chiang–Li K'uei pair in a chapter-commentary to chapter 43(42:7a–8b). See also the "Huai-lin" prefatory essay "A Comparative Ranking of the 108 Liang-shan Heroes 梁山濼一百單八人優劣," which puts this pair on an equal level with the more positive comradeship of Shih Hsiu and Yang Hsiung.

[131] *SHCC*, 1:259f., and 2:570. Cf. Sung Chiang's later curse of Li K'uei as a "black beast" in chapter 110 (see n. 164). Another nickname that provides associative links with some of Sung's rougher fellows is Tiger of Yün-ch'eng 鄆城虎, mentioned in chapter 33, which brings to mind the figural connection to Wang Ai-hu, as well as his bond to the "tiger monk" 虎行者, Wu Sung.

[132] For reviews of the sources of Sung Chiang's various appellations, see studies on historical sources mentioned in b.n. I, plus Wang Li-ch'i, "Ch'o-hao," pp. 272ff.; Chang Cheng-lang, "Sung Chiang k'ao," pp. 207–33; etc. The image of Sung Chiang presented in Yuan drama is fairly consistent, as outlined in his own introductory speech repeated with little variation in most of the plays where he appears. See, for example, passages from the plays *Cheng pao-en san-hu hsia-shan* 爭報恩三虎下山 and *Lu Chih-shen hsi-shang Huang-hua yü* 魯智深喜賞黃花峪 (cited in Ma T'i-chi, *Tzu-liao*, pp. 468f.). See also Ch'ü Chia-yüan,

swarthiness, he is also known variously as Guardian of Valor (Hu pao-i 呼保義), Timely Rain (Chi-shih yü 及時雨), and the Filial and Noble (Hsiao-i hei san-lang 孝義黑三郎).[133] At one level, this multiplicity of names simply reflects the various kinds of historical sources and popular legends regarding Sung. But in the medium of the literati novel, this provides very fertile ground for the author to plant some of his ironic wit.

For example, the issue of Sung Chiang's filiality comes up for quite a bit of questioning in the text.[134] At first we are led to believe that this is indeed one of Sung's finest attributes. This is strongly affirmed precisely by its pretended negation in the ruse by which his father denounces him for unfilial behavior in chapter 22. But as the novel progresses, repeated points in the dialogues draw a clear link between the lawlessness of the band and the concept of dishonor to parents and family. This idea is particularly emphasized in the pivotal debates in chapter 36. Significantly, it was the suggestion of an archetypal act of unfiliality, failure to minister to his father during his dying hours, that had cut short Sung's first tentative alignment with the outlaw community in chapter 35, and it is clearly restated in chapter 42 that the events set in motion at Chiang-chou have placed his family in grave danger.[135] Much later, in chapter 102, the centrality of this issue is emphasized once again in the lengthy debates between Wang Ch'ing and his own parents over the significance of his irresponsible and antisocial behavior.

The same sort of ironic undercurrents may easily be perceived in Sung's nickname Timely Rain, an expression usually glossed in the sense of beneficent generosity, as an indication of his reputation as an unstinting patron of *hao-han* fellows.[136] In this metaphor of bounteous rain we may perhaps note a hint of ironic reference to Sung Chiang's very noticeable propensity to tears, a reading that may appear less far-fetched if one

---

"Shui-hu i-pai tan pa chiang ch'o-hao k'ao-shih," p. 63. This image is essentially the same as that given in the *Hsüan-ho i-shih*.

[133] A number of recent scholars have attempted to decipher the obscure name Hu pao-i. Most agree that the last two characters, *pao-i*, represent an official title in the Sung bureaucracy. In at least one occurrence (in the parallel prose passage celebrating the triumph in chapter 71), it is understood literally in the sense of a "guardian of righteousness." The addition of the word *hu* has been interpreted as indicating that, in this case, Sung Chiang is only *claiming* such honorable intentions, by "calling himself a guardian of the people." See, for example, Wang Li-ch'i "Ch'o-hao," pp. 272ff.; Tai Wang-shu, *Hsiao-shuo hsi-ch'ü lun-chi*, p. 54; Ch'ü Chia-yüan, "Ch'o-hao k'ao-shih," pp. 64f.; Ho Hsin, *Yen-chiu*, p. 239; and Li T'o-chih, "Hu pao-i k'ao," pp. 248–54.

[134] For a discussion of this issue, see Ch'en Chou-ch'ang, "Sung Chiang hsing-ko chieh-kou shih-t'an," pp. 151f.

[135] See, for example, chapter 36 (*SHCC*, 2:565).

[136] For this meaning of the name, see Lü Hsing-ch'ang, "Shui-hu chuan ch'u-t'an: ts'ung hsing yü ch'üan-li ti kuan-tien lun Sung Chiang," p.32.

considers the parallel to Liu Pei in *San-kuo* on this same point.[137] At any rate, in many scenes in the novel Sung's actions are depicted as anything but timely, and this is especially true with regard to his planning and execution of military strategy.

One other designation for Sung Chiang that is technically not one of his nicknames but is applied to him so often in the course of the book that it takes on the force of an epithet, is the expression "holding fast to honor, slighting wordly goods" (*chang-i shu-ts'ai* 仗義疏財). This is cited at the very first introduction of Sung in the novel, where we are told of his great renown for liberally dispensing favors to "good fellows."[138] The long-range value of this reputation is made clear in recurrent scenes in which, for want of other physical prowess, it is his good name alone on which he must rely to save his own skin. Early in the book, however, we are also shown another implication of this particular quality, as it is precisely Sung Chiang's indiscriminate generosity ("He took in one and all, regardless of status" 若高若低無有不納) that puts him in league with various unsavory characters and soon involves him, at the crucial point in chapter 18, in an act of defiance for which he has in principle no ideological sympathy. This immediately sets in motion a chain of events that threatens the welfare of his family and, in the course of time, the empire.[139]

One particularly telling episode that develops out of this side of Sung Chiang's character is the killing of Yen P'o-hsi. Let us consider this scene in greater detail. At the start of this episode, we are informed that it is Sung's weakness for requests of all sorts—in this case to provide a coffin for the head of a very unlikely family—that originally involves him in the fateful match. As the section develops, the author brings out deeper ironies in the relationship between Sung Chiang and Yen P'o-hsi through a variety of figural juxtapositions and pointed details; thus, what was presented in *Hsüan-ho i-shih* as a simple act of revenge for adultery becomes in the novel a far more complex exploration of human motivations.

At first sight, the positioning of this episode nearly contiguous to Wu

[137] On the parallel between Sung Chiang and Liu Pei, see, for example, Sun Shu-yü, *Lai-li, hsin-t'ai, i-shu,* pp. 225ff. I will reconsider this point in the following chapter.

[138] Cf. Sun Shu-yü's discussion of this point in *Lai-li, hsin-t'ai, i-shu,* pp. 333ff. See also Y. W. Ma's treatment in "Fu-ch'ou kuan-nien," p. 106. We have seen a similar undercutting of this term in *Chin P'ing Mei,* where the expression *chang-i shu-ts'ai* is invested with particular irony in scenes depicting Hsi-men Ch'ing's pointedly reluctant largesse to manifestly unworthy recipients.

[139] He appears to be genuinely shocked by news of the birthday-gift robbery in chapter 18, and is visibly discomfited by Liu T'ang's approaches in chapter 20. We know, of course, that the Yen P'o-hsi section was conspicuously revised in the sixteenth-century versions of the novel, as attested by Yüan Wu-yai in his *fa-fan* preface. See also Ho Hsin, *Yen-chiu,* pp. 63ff.; and Huang Lin, "Ku-pen," p. 88.

Sung's figurally similar vengeance wrought on P'an Chin-lien (down to the detail of the nearly identical street-urchins T'ang Niu-erh 唐牛兒 and Yün-ko 鄆哥), to which it is also structurally linked through the chance meeting of Sung and Wu both immediately before and after the "Wu Sung section," would seem to invest Sung Chiang's act with some of the aura of righteous rage that characterizes his "brother's" chilling revenge.[140] But in the unusually protracted presentation of the scene, stretching over several pages, this view is eroded by numerous narrative details emphasizing the weakness and uncertainty, and even the ambiguity of motivation, that characterize this particular hero.[141] One indication of this may be seen in the repeated refrain describing Sung's submissive posture: "just hanging his head" 只低着頭. This, together with strong intimations that the final blow is actually triggered at the suggestion of Yen P'o-hsi's own words, gives a picture not of wrathful indignation, but of indecisiveness and helplessness, especially as contrasted with the consummate deliberateness with which Wu Sung (the "stalwart hero with his head held high and his feet on the ground" 頂天立地的好漢) dispatches P'an Chin-lien. It is probably not accidental that in the treatment of this scene in the novel the explanation that Sung killed the girl under the influence of wine (*tai-chiu* 帶酒), which we get in a number of the prior sources, is conspicuously omitted. At best we can say that Sung Chiang is caught up in an inexorable chain of cause and effect beyond his control. This is what Chin Sheng-t'an seems to be suggesting in his discussion of this passage as an example of the "technique of minimum narrative economy," mentioned earlier. But this is clearly a far cry from the bold act of defiance seen in the Wu Sung cycle.

When the Yen P'o-hsi scene is read in this way, numerous additional details seem to chip away at the foundations of the heroic image of Sung Chiang, as for example in the clever touch of having Sung mistaken for Yen P'o-hsi's real lover, Chang San-lang 張三郎, when he is announced as "your darling San-lang" 你親愛的三郎. Interestingly, the author avoids turning Chang into the stereotype of the adulterer that he used for Hsi-men Ch'ing in the Wu Sung sequence. In the painfully slow-paced description of the long night at opposite ends of the bed, we get more than one hint that Sung is quite ready to swallow insult and be reconciled with the tramp at the slightest hint of reciprocal feeling.[142] Thus, if anything, Sung

[140] Sung Chiang's heroism is further linked to that of Wu Sung by the fact that his signing of his own name on the *fan-shih* in chapter 39 parallels Wu Sung's signature in blood in chapter 26. Significantly, it is in connection with the Yen P'o-hsi killing that Sung makes his claim to fame in *Hsüan-ho i-shih* and various Yuan drama appearances.

[141] *SHCC*, 1:312ff.

[142] This scene is much quicker and less suggestive in the *Ying-hsiung p'u* treatment. We may perhaps perceive an additional cut in Sung's reference to himself by the typical false

Chiang's role in the Yen P'o-hsi affair is curiously reminiscent not of Wu Sung, but more of his brother, the short dark cuckold Wu Ta.

In line with the suggestion that the portraits of both Wu Sung and Li K'uei carry certain hints of sexual vulnerability despite their loud protestations to the contrary, I wish to take a closer look now at the problematic issue of heroism and sexuality implied by some of these last points. After the initial descriptions of Sung Chiang as a patron of warriors and thus by association a member of the *hao-han* class, supposedly beyond sexual temptation, we move directly into the ambiguous episode of Yen P'o-hsi. From this point on, a great many other details in Sung's characterization seem to further emphasize his vulnerability in this area. For example, immediately after the focus of the narrative shifts back from Wu Sung to Sung Chiang following chapter 32, we witness his intercession to rescue the wife of stockade commandant Liu 劉知寨 from the grotesque clutches of Wang Ying, only to have his solicitude repaid when he is betrayed and bound up by the woman in the following chapter. Later, his insistence on inflicting a bloody penalty on his tormentress once again amounts to denying Wang Ying his much-sought prize, a loss to be compensated later when Sung plays matchmaker for Wang and I-chang-ch'ing.

The treatment of Sung's attitude toward this last female figure is even more pregnant with ironic undertones. Through his subtle control of fine details, the author of the *fan-pen* version informs us of Sung Chiang's "secret sighs of admiration" 暗暗的喝采 for the female knight's prowess in chapter 48. When she is finally captured (by the mighty arms of Lin Ch'ung) and Sung has her sent back to the custody of his father on Liang-shan-po to be disposed of later, all those present naturally assume that he intends to take the girl for himself. At this point, the author of the *fan-pen* text takes the time to add a telling touch: Sung spends that entire night sleepless.[143] Thereafter, when he delivers her into the unsavory hands of Wang Ying, one might take this as further evidence of Sung's generosity of spirit, but in view of the ludicrous mismatch of valiant maid-in-arms to dwarf, on top of the figural linkage we have noted between Sung and Wang, it is hard to avoid seeing in this resolution a rather sardonic note.[144]

name Chang San 張三 in chapter 33, where he is again shown to be vulnerable to feminine wiles. Cf. Y. W. Ma's interesting suggestion that Sung Chiang himself is responsible for "letting the wolf into the bedroom" (*yin lang ju shih* 引狼入室), in his "Fu-ch'ou kuan-nien," p. 118. Nieh Kan-nu also sees the sexual vulnerability of Sung Chiang in this scene, even in some of the prior sources ("Wu-lun," pp. 51f.).

[143] *SHCC*, 2:798, 800. Some of these details are omitted in the *Ying-hsiung p'u* treatment (pp. 7:38a, 40a). Of course, "sighs of admiration" is a formulaic expression also used, e.g., in the depiction of Ch'ao Kai's admiration for Yang Chih's prowess in chapter 14.

[144] The author gets in one last laugh at this relationship by depicting Wang Ai-hu's lustful glances at Ch'iung-ying, described with the term *i-ma hsin-yüan* 意馬心猿, in chapter 98 (3:1542).

In the light of recent critical discussions of the taint of misogyny as one key element within a larger complex of problematic themes in the novel, one may view these ironic sexual connotations in many of Sung Chiang's actions as manifestations of an issue that goes deeper than sexuality alone. Many modern readers have sensed that what is ultimately behind the link between bravado and vulnerability in the character of Sung Chiang and others is an understanding of the implicit connection between the ostensible denial of one form of gratification and the simultaneous grasping for another, in this case the mutual implication of sex and power.[145] That is, I believe, alongside the political and historical issues involved in the re-evaluation of the Liang-shan legends, what is really being addressed in the figure of Sung Chiang involves questions of human ambition and the will to power in the broadest sense.

This understanding of the connection between physical desire and ambition in the novel puts the author's repeated exploration of the fine line between weakness and strength close to the heart of the matter. Within this context, it is probably not accidental that the author chooses to precede the fateful incident in which Sung Chiang writes a poem of rebellion on the wall of the Hsün-yang lou 潯陽樓 in chapter 39 with a section depicting the man who is about to commit an act of arrogant defiance put out of action by an attack of dysentery brought on by overeating. The fact that it was Li K'uei's meddling that led Chang Shun 張順 to provide the feast of fish on which Sung had gorged himself obviously adds to the irony here. In any event, the possibility of viewing this poem as an intrepid call to arms is undercut by the fact that the next morning Sung has no recollection of the incident, and is so horrified when he hears of his own deed that he is willing to endure base humiliation, to the point of feigning madness and eating human waste, to avoid prosecution. Nor does the suggestive reference to the calligraphy of Su Tung-p'o on display in the pavilion lend much dignity to Sung Chiang's rather shallow and pretentious poem. Throughout this scene, a number of suggestive details in the *fan-pen* treatment point up ironies that are not nearly as pronounced in the *chien-pen* versions.[146] And once again, the principle of figural reflection forces us to recall the very similar poem penned on the wall of a tavern by Lin Ch'ung in chapter 11. In that case, however, Lin Ch'ung's expres-

---

[145] For an interesting discussion of this issue in psychological terms, see Lü Hsing-ch'ang, "Hsing yü ch'üan-li," cited in n. 136. See also Y. W. Ma's treatment in "Shui-hu chuan li ti hao-se jen-wu," pp. 225–31.

[146] For examples of the different treatment of this key scene in the *chien-pen* texts I have used, see the *Ying-hsiung p'u* (p. 6:86–9a), where the details of the sickness and the morning-after reaction are not given, and the *P'ing-lin* (8:156) where it is given in full. See Nieh Kan-nu, "Wu-lun," pp. 3f. Cf. Chin Sheng-t'an's citation of this sequence of details as an example of the technique of "maximum narrative economy."

sion of thwarted ambition seemed to carry a greater sense of conviction, and it was backed up soon thereafter by an impressive demonstration of physical fortitude.

Much later in the work, in the meeting between Sung Chiang and Li Shih-shih in chapter 72, we are witness to another situation in which wine and sensual stimulation induce Sung Chiang to reveal his ambitions in verse. Here, in Sung's second exercise in lyric expression, we once again get a clear expression of his burgeoning self-importance, this time adding the pretension of a dashing patron of the pleasure quarters.[147] Just as in the first case some very serious consequences—the massacre at Chiang-chou and the first major challenge to imperial authority—followed directly afterward, this time too the scene pointedly concludes with the sudden appearance of the emperor himself, to cut Sung short at the moment he is about to disclose his true identity and ambitions. Once again, the *chien-pen* handling of this scene is noticeably less provocative.

For all of this subtle deflation of Sung Chiang's ballooning ambition, however, we must also recognize that the author of the *fan-pen* novel does not seem to undercut Sung's sincerity with regard to his stated aim of ultimately fighting for the imperial cause. Instead, he allows for fairly consistent expressions of his desire to accept honorable surrender (*chao-an*). But that does not in any way curtail his exploration of the gradual expansion of Sung Chiang's self-image. In the course of the novel, Sung's conception of himself and his noble-sounding appeals to others to join his "cause" become increasingly pompous and arrogant. In chapter 48, for example, he refers to himself as a "valiant knight" (*i-shih* 義士), and by chapter 61 he is known in the surrounding area as an outlaw "prince" (*ta-wang* 大王), a designation that in this case seems to carry more ominous implications than it does in its common use for any small-time bandit chieftain.[148] As these delusions of grandeur come closer and closer to attainment, the ultimatums issued to resisting forces become more and more convincing. One extremely graphic presentation of this supreme haughtiness takes place in chapter 59, when Sung professes his honorable intentions with exaggerated courtesy to the imperial envoy Commander Su 宿太尉, while directly behind his back loom the glowering figures of Sung's strong-arm men, weapons at the ready, conveying the true import of his words. This attitude is summed up accurately by Huang Wen-ping 黃文炳 in chapter 39, when he comments

---

[147] *SHCC*, 3:1222. See especially the lines "As present master of the Shantung fortress of misty waters, I come to shop for springtime beauty in the city of Phoenixes" 借得山東煙水寨, 來買鳳城春色. Y. W. Ma gives special emphasis to this implication in "Fu-ch'ou kuan-nien," p. 107. The *Ying-hsiung p'u* treatment of this scene lacks the detail of Sung's readiness to spill the beans about the band's ambitions.

[148] *SHCC*, 2:794, and 3:1029.

that the writer of the *fan-shih* must be "a man of no mean self-image" 這人自負不淺.[149]

Within the context of the rising swell of Sung Chiang's ambition, it is of crucial significance that the author once again carefully modulates his narrative details to bring out the underlying weakness and vulnerability of the figure within the apparent heroics of the popular tradition with which he begins. Sung Chiang is obviously powerless when left to his own devices. This is demonstrated in the recurrent scenes in which he is captured and bound, only to be spared by grace of his prior reputation. At times the presentations of this side of the Sung Chiang figure reach the point of ludicrousness, as for example when he is put in a cage in chapter 33, wrapped and bound like a dumpling in chapter 37, carried out of Chiang-chou in a daze in chapter 40, and left hiding in a cupboard in chapter 42.[150]

Even when backed by an entire army, however, Sung's role as military commander leaves much to be desired—although that does not stop him from rolling up his sleeves and bragging about his martial skills to Li Shih-shih in chapter 72.[151] Specifically, Sung Chiang's generalship is repeatedly marred by the rash or reckless use of his forces. For example, his tendency to lose patience and commit his troops to ill-conceived offensives leads to serious setbacks in numerous battle scenes, and in chapter 115 he himself acknowledges this particular fault. Even after he gains possession of a supposedly divine manual of warfare (*t'ien-shu* 天書), time after time he is described as "at a loss for strategy" (*wu-chi* 無計), and at certain points the schemes suggested by his "heavenly book" are either ridiculously obvious or result in failure. (Interestingly, we are told in chapter 100 that Fang La also has a similar book.)[152]

Since Sung is after all a civil official by profession, his deficiency in military prowess is entirely forgivable. But if he did possess the Con-

[149] *SHCC*, 2:620.

[150] In the pages leading up to the scene of the *fan-shih*, the expression "all alone" (*tu-tzu i-ko* 獨自一個) is repeated many times to emphasize the existential insecurity that is really behind this act.

[151] *SHCC*, 3:1221. See Y. W. Ma's treatment in "Ch'ing-chieh ho jen-wu," p. 87, and "Fu-ch'ou kuan-nien," p. 107.

[152] *SHCC*, 4:1660. Cf. the ridicule of the divine manual in the "Chung Hsing" commentary on chapter 88 (cited in Ch'en Hsi-chung, "Kuan-yü Chung Po-ching," p. 50). Scenes involving the failure of the manual's divine strategy may be found in chapters 52 and 64. Variations on the expression *wu-chi* appear in chapters 52, 55, 59, 64, 116, and 118 (in this last case it is the fail-safe grain barge trick that fails). Sung also seems to have a propensity to take sick during major campaigns, as in chapters 65 and 108. Exceptions to this military ineptitude include chapter 57 (where victory is in any case assured by the special training in grappling-hook warfare provided by the newly recruited Hsü Ning), and in chapter 76 (the Nine Palaces Eight Trigrams Maze).

fucian learning he claims in chapter 120, he should have gained a measure of the perspicacity and judgment he so often lacks in the leadership of the band.[153] Instead, each setback pushes him to the brink of despair, and he must be constantly reminded by Wu Yung and others of the obvious principle that a military commander must be ready to accept reverses (兵敗爲常事).

The most serious flaw of Sung Chiang's performance as a leader is one he shares with many other figures of narrative literature in China and elsewhere: his tendency to allow his own personal desire for revenge to govern his actions as a military commander. In particular, the parallel to his counterpart in the *San-kuo* hero cycles, Liu Pei, is quite striking in this regard and probably indicates a conscious attempt at intertextual reference. In any event, one of the first acts Sung undertakes after being recognized as de facto leader of the bandits is to turn around his men, who had only shortly before fought their way out of a very difficult position, and send them back into Wu-wei chün 無爲軍 in order to consummate his grudge against Huang Wen-ping—with particularly bloody consequences for the townspeople in his path, as well as for Huang himself. Curiously, in this case certain *fan-pen* texts spare the most grisly details of Huang's subsequent execution.[154] By the same token, the two miniature "campaigns" against the Chu family village and Tseng-t'ou shih 曾頭市 in chapters 46–50 and 60 and 68, which comprise the structural focus of the middle section of the book, are both instigated in order to redress petty grievances, and in both cases the adversaries are depicted as basically honorable men who suffer losses entirely out of proportion to their errors.[155] Near the end, the death of Chang Shun in chapter 114 triggers in Sung Chiang a reckless desire for revenge that leads to an immediate blunder, despite Wu Yung's desperate warnings, and very nearly thwarts the entire undertaking against Fang La.[156]

This implication of the relation between rising external forces and simul-

---

[153] *SHCC*, 4:1810. Cf. Sung's speech: "From my tender years I have been a scholar of Confucian classics. By the time I grew up I was fully conversant with the skills of office" 我自幼學儒, 長而通吏. The Jung-yü t'ang commentator ridicules Sung at this point (see Chin Tai-t'ung, "Li Chih," p. 76).

[154] *SHCC*, 2:661. See Y. W. Ma's discussion in "Fu-ch'ou kuan-nien," pp. 107ff., for further elucidation of this point. See, for example, the treatment of the scene in the *Ping-lin* text (p. 9:4a).

[155] The first case results from Shih Ch'ien's theft of a chicken in chapter 46, the second is precipitated by the appropriation of a horse meant for Sung Chiang in chapter 60; but we are given to believe that there was already a history of bad blood between these two groups (*SHCC*, 3:1006).

[156] For Wu Yung's warning to Sung on the danger of overreaction to Chang Shun's death, see *SHCC*, 4:1718.

taneous erosion of inner strength, which forms one of the key concepts in the *fan-pen Shui-hu*, is played out most conspicuously in the precarious balance that governs the relationship between Sung Chiang and Li K'uei. In the convoluted interaction between the two, we can see one of the best examples of the author's technique of using contrastive character pairs to explore certain deeper problems of human motivation at a higher level of abstraction.

The relationship of mutual implication that holds between Sung Chiang and Li K'uei begins to surface from the time of their very first meeting at the P'i-p'a t'ing 琵琶亭 in Chiang-chou in chapter 38. This scene is so rich with suggestive details that it warrants a much closer analysis. From the moment of their first encounter, we are given a variation on the recurring theme of mutual recognition. At the outset, Sung is visibly amused by Li K'uei's disruptive behavior in the black-and-white struggle with Chang Shun, which begins to highlight the color labels that contribute a significant layer to the symbolic treatment of these two figures. Immediately following this scene, we witness a display of Li's gluttony that provokes Sung Chiang's enthusiastic remark, "Brilliant! A true man of mettle!" 壯哉！眞好漢也！To which Li replies, "This guy Sung know exactly what's on my blasted mind" 這宋大哥便知我的鳥意.[157] The fact that these are not idle touches soon becomes clear when Sung Chiang follows Li's example of overindulgence, with the giddy consequences that lead directly into the incident of the poem of rebellion.

After this point, Li K'uei comes increasingly to occupy a central position as the real source of power behind Sung Chiang's manipulative exercise of authority. Perhaps the most telling example of this occurs in chapter 41, when Sung asks who of his followers will carry out his revenge on Huang Wen-ping, and not surprisingly it is Li who steps eagerly forward, knife in hand. Immediately thereafter, it is Li's only half-joking threats to cut down any objectors—"Come on! Let's get going! If anybody doesn't go, he'll get a taste of my blasted axe!" 都去，都去，但有不去的，吃我一鳥斧！—that in effect bring to realization the first full-scale escalation of their resistance, with the result that the reins of authority are irrevocably placed in Sung's hands.[158]

Ultimately, one may say that in the recurrent scenes in which Sung Chiang expresses an initial reluctance to unleash Li K'uei, but later turns to his broadax charge as the final weapon in his military arsenal, the figure of the Black Whirlwind serves as a surrogate for Sung's own impulses in his rise to power. It may be more than an idle joke, therefore, when Sung calls

[157] *SHCC*, 2:604.
[158] *SHCC*, 2:662.

Li "a child born of my own household" 家生的孩兒 in chapter 72. Li, at any rate, is manifestly serious when he claims the status of "a petty demon in his brother's command" 哥哥部下一個小鬼 at the close of the work.[159]

In the course of the novel, however, we witness a continued series of clashes between the two figures—some basically humorous, others pointedly personal and bitter. In chapters 52 and 54, for example, Li K'uei first tells Sung he is not afraid of him: 我不是怕你 ..., then accuses him of malicious intentions: 你們也不是好人.[160] By chapters 66 and 67, he raises very serious objections to Sung's stated policy of yielding his position to Lu Chün-i, even threatening to kill him for such a move. Of course, the more cynical reader may take these latter examples as evidence of Sung's deliberate manipulation of Li, rather than of genuine opposition on Li's part.

In view of the issue of latent sexuality lurking within the manly heroics of the band, it is particularly striking that it is Li K'uei, Sung Chiang's chief co-spokesman for the misogyny of the *hao-han* code, who alone raises doubts as to Sung's true intentions regarding I-chang-ch'ing in chapter 50, and Li Shih-shih in chapter 72. Immediately thereafter, in the *fan-pen* reworking of the episode widely known from the Yuan *tsa-chü* drama "Li K'uei Shoulders Thorns" (*Li K'uei fu-ching* 李逵負荊), Li not only shows a very quick readiness to believe Sung's alleged vulnerability to sexual temptation, but he goes as far as to suggest a link between the sexual stimulation intimated in the Li Shih-shih affair and Sung's supposed abduction of the girl soon after. Li's speech at this point reveals an insight into Sung Chiang's personality that is clearly out of character, but at the same time it provides a major hint on the part of the *fan-pen* author:

> At first I respected you for being a *hao-han* beyond the pull of lustful desire, but now I see that you are a pursuer of wine and sex after all. Killing Yen P'o-hsi was just a small example of this; going to the capital to patronize Li Shih-shih was the major example.
> 我當初敬你是個不貪色慾的好漢，你原正是酒色之徒。殺了閻婆惜便是小樣，去東京養李師師便是大樣.[161]

Even more damaging is the fact that Li uses the occasion of this accusation to go on to cast some very cutting aspersions on Sung's entire leadership role, charging him with duplicity (*k'ou shih hsin fei* 口是心非), and suggesting his deliberate manipulation of the men under him to support his own case.[162]

---

[159] *SHCC*, 3:1221, 4:1811. See the discussion of this relationship in Wang Yüan-p'ing, "Shui-hu ti hsing-ko k'e-hua yü ch'ing-chieh an-p'ai," pp. 69–73.

[160] *SHCC*, 2:861, 2:908. The scene in chapter 54 is noticeably less intense in the *Ying-hsiung p'u* version (p. 8:37a, chapter 46), and omits the line 你們也不是好人.

[161] *SHCC*, 3:1232.

[162] Ibid.

Through all of this, Sung Chiang's attitude toward Li K'uei remains somewhat ambiguous. As we have seen, the recurrent scenes of Sung's reluctance to unleash his unpredictable friend (chapters 43, 47, 48, 75, 115) can probably be read either way—as examples of sincere restraint and caution on Sung's part, or as evidence of tactical delay in committing his most powerful weapon. Given the centrality of the theme of the proper "use" of talent (*yung-jen* 用人) in this novel, as in the Chinese narrative tradition as a whole, it has special significance here that his initial refusals are often expressed in the words "I have no use for you" 用不着你. Gradually, however, Sung becomes more and more aware of the potential danger Li K'uei's behavior poses for his cause, so that his apologies for having "forgotten" Li K'uei at the bottom of a well in chapter 54 are not quite convincing, least of all to Li himself.[163] And in chapter 67 he seems to be genuinely shocked by the news of Li's unauthorized foray (although in this case it produces positive results). By chapter 78, Sung is dead serious when he denies Li permission to participate in a key mission to the capital and replies to his entreaties with only mocking laughter. And when, in a fit of anger in chapter 110, he calls his loyal comrade a "black beast" (*hei ch'in-shou* 黑禽獸), Li is the only one who does not laugh off the remark.[164] At any rate, the author seems to add a bit of conceptual underpinning to this relationship in chapter 72, when he has Sung very pointedly characterize Li as "evil by nature," using the pregnant Confucian term *hsing pu-shan* 性不善, to which Li unabashedly replies—with his characteristic mixture of innocence and cynicism—"Why? Did I ever scare anyone to death?"[165]

Against this background of the love-hate relationship between Sung Chiang and Li K'uei, I find it hard to read the final scene of joint suicide as a paean to the shining *in ultima* loyalty of Li to his chief. He had, after all, already challenged Sung's authority on numerous occasions, threatened his life, and in general forced him into a position of confronting the embarrassing implications of his actions. Instead, I believe that the concluding scene is deliberately staged in order to set the final seal on the relationship of mutual self-destruction that pertains to the two figures in particular and the band as a whole. In any event, Sung Chiang's discussion of his motivations for taking Li with him to the grave center more on the defense of his own reputation than on the fact of their sworn brotherhood.[166]

The view I have been presenting of Sung Chiang's hypocrisy is perhaps somewhat colored by Chin Sheng-t'an's one-sided reading of the text.

[163] In connection with the well episode, I suspect that the author may have had the passage in the *Analects* (VI:24) in the back of his mind. See Chapter 6, below.

[164] *SHCC*, 4:1654.

[165] *SHCC*, 3:1220.

[166] For the idea of a "love-hate" relationship between the two, see Lü Hsing-ch'ang, "Hsing yü ch'üan-li," pp. 38f.

Obviously, one does not want to fall into the trap of judging the fictional representation of Sung Chiang on the basis of traditional or contemporary reevaluations of the figure in the context of nonliterary, i.e., political issues, as opposed to a close reading of the text itself.[167] For that matter, I must acknowledge that there does materialize a certain rise in Sung Chiang's stature in the concluding sections of the book, although this impression materializes, if at all, only in the sections dealing with the first three of the four campaigns, and the figure presented in the final ten chapters seems to revert back to the earlier, less than towering image of the man. As I have already indicated, the author does not seem to cast any doubts on the consistent sincerity of Sung's espoused aim of ultimately joining up with the imperial forces. But in any case, I feel that a careful examination of the narrative details in the *fan-pen* text turns up so much ironic under-cutting of Sung Chiang's words and actions that by the time the band swells to proportions sufficient to seriously challenge the established order, it is too late to avoid judging the ultimate significance of the movement in a darker light.

These intimations of hypocrisy are most sardonic in the treatment of the process by which Sung Chiang rises to the top position in the outlaw hierarchy. Since Sung's move comes as the third instance in a repeated series of takeovers, one cannot help but evaluate this with reference to the careers of his two predecessors. Here we have another prime example of the compositional principle of cross-reflection through figural similarity. The model of Wang Lun early in the book is clear enough in its implica-tions, even without the overworn pun in this particular name (for Wang Lun read *wang-lun* 亡倫, "without human decency"), a sense immediately backed up in the depiction of Wang's crass, if perhaps honest, defense of his own narrow self-interest.[168] The case of Ch'ao Kai is somewhat more complicated, in view of the generally positive image of Ch'ao in the early sections of the novel. But the fact that the treatment of Ch'ao Kai's role in the novel departs significantly from many of the prior narrative sources forces us to pay greater attention to the manner in which his portrait is drawn here.[169] In spite of Ch'ao's protestations of brotherly devotion, the

---

[167] For discussions of the perceived hypocrisy on the part of Sung Chiang, see Yüeh Heng-chün, "Ti-tsao ho huan-mieh," p. 89; and Nieh Kan-nu, "Wu-lun," p. 3. A good example of the sort of denunciations of Sung Chiang that were prevalent during the "Cultural Revolution" can be seen in Chang P'ei-heng and Huang Lin, *Sung Chiang hsi.*

[168] For a curious attempt to defend Wang Lun, see Lo Tung-pien, "Man-shuo Shui-hu li ti Wang Lun," pp. 372–78. An allusion to a certain Sung traitor with the same name is suggested by Sheng Yü-ssu 盛于斯 in a late Ming commentary entitled "Tsung-p'i Shui-hu chuan" 總批水滸傳 (cited in Ma T'i-chi, *Tzu-liao*, p. 357).

[169] For a discussion of the changing image of Ch'ao Kai in the various *Shui-hu* materials, see Sun K'ai-ti, "Chiu-pen k'ao," pp. 2487ff. In the *Hsüan-ho i-shih*, Ch'ao is dead before Sung Chiang's arrival at the lair, so there is no issue of their rivalry.

author makes it quite clear that he too, like Wang Lun before him, is jealous of his own position and wary of his chief contender for supremacy, not without justification. Thus, after first suggesting that the top spot rightfully belongs to Sung, Ch'ao Kai registers only token objection to Sung's repeated insistence on joining the vanguard in a series of dangerous missions. As it becomes increasingly obvious that these external forays are working to consolidate Sung Chiang's growing following within the band, however, Ch'ao's offers to take personal command become more and more insistent (as, for example, in chapters 52 and 58), though in each case he is forced to defer to his rival's powers of persuasion. This ironic tug-of-war becomes all but explicit in chapter 60, when in finally winning his point Ch'ao protests, "It is not that I want to steal your glory" 不是我要奪你的功勞, thus dispelling any remaining pretense of innocence on his part. As a result, the copious tears that Sung Chiang sheds in chapter 60 upon hearing the news of the untimely death of Ch'ao Kai, whom he mourns as a lost father, cannot but recall his earlier tears of (unfounded) bereavement.[170] In this light, Chin Sheng-t'an seems to hit the mark when he goes as far as to denounce Sung's passive complicity in Ch'ao's death with the starkest Confucian term of opprobrium: *shih* 弒, normally reserved for instances of patricide or regicide.[171]

From this point on, the ironies in Sung Chiang's takeover of the band become more and more bitter. Thus when Sung, with a Caesarian show of reluctance, consents to "provisionally" take on the leadership spot (*ch'üan tang tz'u wei* 權當此位), and when he adopts the seemingly open-ended vow to yield command to the avenger of Ch'ao Kai's death, but then allows himself to be convinced—by a groundswell of mass support—to forego his earlier promise in favor of the contest with Lu Chün-i, a number of narrative details seem to suggest in these moves something less than nobility of purpose. Lu, for his part, clearly sees that this is all a charade, and protests: "Why must you make a mockery of me?" 何故相戲?[172] In the ensuing parallel attacks on Tung-p'ing fu 東平府 and Tung-ch'ang fu 東昌府, Sung makes a display of assigning both of his top strategists to Lu's detachment, but they immediately find themselves pinned down by

---

[170] *SHCC*, 3:1010f.

[171] See chapter-commentary on chapter 67 (68:1a). The author's obvious linking of all of the palace-coup episodes is emphasized when he has Ch'ao Kai recall Wang Lun's name in chapter 58. A final staging of the recurrent scene takes place in Wang Ch'ing's takeover at Fang-shan chai in chapter 104.

[172] *SHCC*, 3:1044. The implications of the "contest" are brought out several times in the latter sections of the book, when the scene of drawing lots for military objectives is repeated in chapters 94, 108, and 116. Significantly, in all of these later cases Lu Chün-i performs much better, further suggesting a stacked deck in the first draw. In any event, some of the lines suggesting collusion in the first contest do not appear in the *Ying-hsiung p'u* version (e.g., p. 11:5a).

the seemingly invincible barrage of Chang Ch'ing's 張清 rock missiles. Curiously, then, after Sung's troops make short work of their own objective and come to Lu's assistance, it is both Wu Yung and Kung-sun Sheng who soon provide the keys (tactical and magical, respectively) to a quick victory. And if this is not enough to raise suspicions of collusion, the author has Sung claim, most transparently, that he had deliberately assigned his two most trusted advisers to Lu's camp in order to let him win the contest. This reading is bolstered by a number of additional touches: the fact that Sung shows visible discomfiture at reports of Lu's successes in chapter 68, that he takes no chances and leaves Li K'uei behind in chapter 69, and that at the very height of the contest with Lu Chün-i he actually presents his litany of yielding the command to another adversary, Tung P'ing 董平 —all of which make it impossible to take Sung Chiang's words at face value.

We should not, however, place all the blame for this cynical manipulation of Lu Chün-i on Sung Chiang's shoulders, since very much the same sort of ironic undercutting is also at work in the depiction of Sung's closest cohort. After all, it was Wu Yung (the implications of whose name have already been noted) who pulled the strings in Lin Ch'ung's overthrow of Wang Lun; it was he who planned and supervised the recruitment of Lu Chün-i from start to finish; and it is he whom we can perceive behind the scenes in chapters 67 and 68, giving secret signals and orchestrating the rumblings of opposition to Sung Chiang's proposal of stepping down in favor of Lu Chün-i. In this light, it may be more a matter of cynical manipulation than simply wily cleverness that is expressed in Wu Yung's famous trademark, the two-fingered salute.

In keeping with the pattern of the gradual revelation of weakness within strength, it is worth noting that Wu's strategical brilliance, at its best in the "conquests by guile" (*chih-ch'ü* 智取) in chapters 16, 41, and 50, is shown to fail in chapter 39, due to his ludicrous blunder in the forged letter to the capital. At other points, he is clearly shown to be at a loss without the magical arts of Kung-sun Sheng (chapters 53, 68, and 70). Thus, even the iconographic details that identify him, as his own nickname suggests, as a "super Chu-ko Liang" (Chia-liang 加亮) are undercut by the more telling resemblance of his colleague Kung-sun Sheng to the earlier master of wind and fire. (And as we shall see below, the image of Chu-ko Liang is in any event not free from irony in itself.) In fact, Chang Hsüeh-ch'eng 章學誠 seizes upon precisely this comparison to argue for the superiority of *San-kuo*, in his view, over *Shui-hu chuan*.[173] As a result, even the final scene of

---

[173] For examples of the two-fingered salute, see chapters 14 (*SHCC*, 1:208), 48 (2:801), and 60 (3:1013). Cf. Chang Hsüeh-ch'eng's remark, in Ma T'i-chi, *Tzu-liao*, p. 385. For additional discussions of Wu Yung, see Hu Chen-wu, "T'an Wu Yung," pp. 360–71; Wang Yüan-p'ing, "Hsing-ko k'e-hua," p. 70; Sun Yung-tu, "Lun Liang-shan i-chün chung ti Chih-to hsing Wu Yung," pp. 376–86; and Sun Shu-yü, *Lai-li, hsin-t'ai, i-shu*, pp. 330ff.

his double suicide with Hua Jung 花榮, pointedly parallel to the end of Sung Chiang and Li K'uei, may also serve to leave a concluding suggestion of the bond of equivalence linking Wu Yung's ultimate purposes to those of his less inscrutable chief.

Suspicions regarding the duplicity of Sung Chiang and his principal adviser are nowhere more troubling than in the recurrent pattern of the forced recruitment of warriors. This is not only an important structural element linking many of the separate narrative units within the larger framework of the gathering of forces, but it also provides a central illustration of the ironic revision of the image of the Liang-shan bandits in popular materials. Some of the major examples include such key scenes as the liquidation of Ch'in Ming's 秦明 family in chapter 34, Li K'uei's murder of Chu T'ung's small ward in chapter 51, the burning of Li Ying's 李應 proud estate in chapter 50, the framing of Hsü Ning 徐寧 as a thief in chapter 56, the actions taken "to foreclose any thought of return" (*chüeh … nien-t'ou* 絕…念頭) on the part of Hu-yen Cho 呼延灼 in chapter 58,[174] and of course the calculated plot to bring Lu Chün-i into the fold in chapters 60–62. Particularly ironic is the presentation in chapter 42 of a similar pattern of abducting unwilling family members and putting a noble manor to the torch, only this time it is Sung Chiang's father who is the object of the move, once again raising the question of Sung's proverbial filiality. Sung Chiang's own hand in the plot concerning Ch'in Ming is freely admitted immediately upon Ch'in's surrender, and the shock is even greater in chapter 52, when we are told that it was Sung who personally ordered the murder of the child in order to ensure Chu's answer to the call. In this light, the fact that in both of these latter cases Sung's admission of premeditation is explicitly coupled with entreaties to his victims to "join in the great cause" (*kung hsing ta-i* 共興大義) seriously undermines both the method of recruitment itself and the broader claims regarding the noble purposes of the band.

The care with which the author has framed these particular scenes is evident, from the overall pattern of merciless coercion down to the level of specific language with which this is presented. For example, Ch'in Ming's cry of anguish upon hearing of the murderous scheme perpetrated against him: "But you have treated me just too cruelly!" 只是害得我忒毒些個!— is closely echoed by Chu T'ung after he undergoes a similar ordeal.[175]

In the preceding discussion, I have considered at some length the ironic undercutting that characterizes the *fan-pen Shui-hu chuan*. In defining irony as a principle of narrative rhetoric, however, I have also insisted on the notion of some kind of projection of a positive ground of meaning. It is

---

[174] *SHCC*, 3:975.

[175] *SHCC*, 2:539, 2:848. An Tao-ch'üan 安道全 expresses similar sentiments with the word *t'e* 忒 in chapter 65 (3:1111).

extremely important, therefore, to point out that the author of the novel also provides a counterweight to the darker aspects of his treatment of these figures, through a string of characters who present a more upright embodiment of the traditional Chinese conception of the hero.

The first fully developed example of this type of figure materializes early in the book, in the case of Lin Ch'ung. In fact, the model for this character type was already set up in the very first chapter of the book in the treatment of Wang Chin, who is clearly linked to Lin Ch'ung by profession, character traits, and even parallel clashes with the power of Kao Ch'iu 高俅. Lin Ch'ung is not without his problematic side, but he clearly continues this model, and passes it on to a long list of individuals, including Yang Chih, Ch'in Ming, Yang Hsiung, Chu T'ung, Kuan Sheng 關勝, Hu-yen Cho, and Lu Chün-i, most of whom are also professional military men of the sort later labeled "crack generals" (*hsiao-chiang* 驍將).[176] The contrived link between Lin Ch'ung and Yang Chih is especially obvious, since these two warriors not only share a variety of attributes and similar fates, but their separate stories are also set into a kind of parallel construction through the common motif of the treasure sword (*pao-tao* 寶刀).

Although the stories of each of these men are differentiated by varying circumstances, they all share a fairly compact set of physical and psychological qualities. Most important among these is a very strong sense of personal honor (*i-ch'i* 義氣), an element that provides a pointed contrast to the sort of compromising behavior I have traced above in the cases of the principal Liang-shan heroes. When first confronted with the choice of throwing in with the bandit group, each of these men expresses initial revulsion at the thought of betraying the dynasty, typically formulated in one particular refrain: "I'm a man of the Sung for as long as I live, and I'll be a ghost of the Sung when I die" 生是大宋人死爲大宋鬼. Given the insistent repetition of this formulaic line throughout the narrative, we may perhaps perceive a note of parody in Li K'uei's parting speech in chapter 120—with the added irony of substituting the name of Sung Chiang for the Sung empire, a joke Li himself makes in chapter 75.[177] In any event, the sincere commitment of this sort of hero to the fate of the dynasty is shored up by blood links to some of the most heroic figures of Chinese history and

---

[176] I might also include other figures such as Tai Tsung, Chang Ch'ing 清, and perhaps Ch'ai Chin 柴進. Chin Sheng-t'an notes that Lin Ch'ung and Lu Chün-i comprise the first and last links in this chain; see chapter-commentary on chapter 2 (61:5b). Cf. Sung Chiang's own enumeration of the personal and professional qualities in which he falls short of Lu Chün-i: physical presence, inborn capacity to rule, and command of civil and martial arts (3:1162). See also C. T. Hsia's evaluation of the character of Lin Ch'ung (*Classic Novel*, pp. 340f., n. 14). All of these hero figures are gathered together on stage in chapters 55 and 69–70, and again in chapter 76, where we get the label *hsiao-chiang*.

[177] *SHCC*, 3:1258.

legend. For example, Yang Chih traces his descent from the great Yang family generals and Hu-yen Cho comes from the line of the glorious general Hu-yen Tsan 呼延贊, all of which gives added meaning to the frequent mention of the defenders of the frontier under the Ch'ung family military commissioners 种經略 in Yen-an. Similar conclusions can be drawn from the association of Lü Fang 呂方 with Lü Pu 呂布, or the family and iconographic links that tie Chu T'ung and Kuan Sheng to Kuan Yü 關羽. Even at the end, the author leaves us with indications of later military contributions beyond the close of the novel proper by Chu T'ung (like those of Hu Ch'eng 扈成 foretold in chapter 50 [2:828]), and more pointedly, we are told at the end that the son of Sung Chiang's brother later grew up to a distinguished official career. In this light, the fact that these true warriors of noble stock are so often "forced to climb Liang-shan" 逼上梁山 in a manner that distorts this popular notion from valiant desperation into the area of kidnapping and murder cannot but intensify the ironic light in this particular aspect of the novel.

On the other hand, the development of this alternative image of the hero in the *fan-pen* novel does not exempt these figures from the pattern of weakness within strength that we have seen to be so central to the novel's conception. The weaker side of these mighty warriors is most movingly manifested in their common tendency to exhibit a kind of loner mentality, so often expressed in the nearly formulaic epithet "sunk in hopeless depression" (*men-men pu-i* 悶悶不已). The portraits of these potentially epic figures are also clouded by a common flaw of excessive pride. This is obviously true of the treatment of Lu Chün-i's overblown self-assurance, which leads to his first capture by the Liang-shan men in chapter 61. And we can see a similar sense in the treatment of Yang Chih's arrogant behavior in chapter 16, although here his uncompromising harshness to his men is probably justified under the circumstances.

In each case, it is this unbending attachment to proud self-image that places such men in a position of total isolation, "with neither home nor country to turn to for refuge" 有家難奔有國難投.[178] This is the obverse of another issue raised in this book, and in so much of Chinese narrative in general: that of seeking a lord worthy of serving (*ch'iu-chu*) or a comrade who can appreciate one's own individual capacity (*chih-chi*). We have already seen the manner in which the fates of Lin Ch'ung and Yang Chih are intertwined through the recurring *topos* of the treasure sword, to be bought or sold by one who appreciates its true value (*mai yü shih-huo*

---

[178] See *SHCC*, 2:533, and 2:712, etc., in addition to the use of the term in the sections on Lin Ch'ung and Yang Chih. A good example of the ultimate limitations of such warriors is seen in the case of the human fish Chang Shun, who finds himself strangely in need of a boat in chapter 111, and then is cut down, literally like a fish out of water, in chapter 114.

賣於識貨).[179] All of these instances of symbolic treatment of the honorable "use" of other men surely place Sung Chiang's primary methods of recruitment in the darkest light, as both a blow to these heroes' physical pride and an affront to their sense of honor.

There is one character presented in the *Shui-hu chuan* who, while loosely falling into the category of these positive heroes, still manages to escape from the inexorable process of ironic undercutting. This is not one of the professional military men considered just now but rather the less pretentious figure of Lu Chün-i's retainer, Yen Ch'ing. In his initial appearance, Yen is not particularly impressive—he appears to be yet another member of the class of idlers (*lang-tzu* 浪子) we saw burlesqued earlier. Throughout the second half of the book, however, we gradually come to know and appreciate some of the exceptional attributes of the man (in this case it is the reputation that is petty and the man who is substantial).[180] In addition to a few outstanding physical attributes that are gradually revealed—his unexpectedly fine physique highlighted by a most glorious tattoo and a whiteness of skin rivaling that of Chang Shun—the author also grants Yen Ch'ing a remarkable number of special skills. He is an accomplished wrestler, a fine singer, an unfailing archer, and even proficient in a variety of local dialects, a skill that has an important use in a number of scenes.[181] In addition, he is a man of intrepid fighting spirit, as we see in the psychological manipulation that crushes his opponent even before the start of the wrestling match in chapter 74. He also possesses an admirable sense of personal loyalty, as he demonstrates in his intense emotional commitment to his lord Lu Chün-i in chapter 62.

The most significant example of Yen Ch'ing's heroism, however, surfaces not in feats of strength or skill, but rather in his emotional self-mastery. This is fully developed in chapter 81, where it is Yen's self-control in resisting the careless flirtations of Li Shih-shih that finally enables Sung Chiang to legitimize his ambitions. Yen's behavior here reflects back to the weak-kneed figure of Sung Chiang in a similar situation in chapter 72 where, significantly, it was the dash and skill of Yen that brought about that meeting in the first place. In this scene, Yen's graceful solution of

[179] See Yüeh Heng-chün, "Ti-tsao ho huan-mieh," for discussion.

[180] For sources of the Yen Ch'ing figure, see Wang Li-ch'i, "Ch'o-hao," pp. 286ff.; and Ch'ü Chia-yüan, "Ch'o-hao k'ao-shih," pp. 66f. For discussions of the treatment of Yen in the novel see, for example, Y. W. Ma, "Ch'ing-chieh ho jen-wu," p. 87; Chang Shu-hsiang, "Ch'üan-shih," pp. 145f.; Sun Shu-yü, *Lai-li, hsin-t'ai, i-shu,* pp. 231ff.; and Wang Ch'i-chou, "Li Shih-shih hsing-hsiang ti su-tsao yü Shui-hu chuan ti ch'uang-tso ssu-hsiang," pp. 77f.

[181] This is how I read the expression *ta hsiang-t'an* 打鄉談, which appears in chapters 61 (3:1026), 74 (3:1242), 81 (3:1335), and most explicitly 111 (4:1669), where the dialect in question is specified. Yen's skill at wrestling is foregrounded again in the bout with Kao Ch'iu in chapter 80.

sidestepping the lovely courtesan's advances by leading her into an oath of brotherhood is expressed in one of the finest examples in the book of the suppleness of literary colloquial language: "[With these bows], he bowed away the woman's lascivious impulse" 拜住那婦人一點邪心. When the author goes on to pointedly state, "If this had been another man subject to the attractions of wine and sex, the grand undertaking would have been undermined" 若是第二個在酒色之中的, 也壞了大事, the object of his barb is fairly obvious.[182]

Given the efforts the author has expended on drawing a nearly unblemished portrait of Yen Ch'ing, it is not surprising that in the final dispensation of the fortunes of the survivors Yen Ch'ing figures among the small number granted the right to finish out their natural lives in peace and comfort. In the end, Yen's timely withdrawal from the faded dream of glory is credited to a kind of insight or experiential wisdom, whereby he "understood the secret hinge of commitment and withdrawal, life and death" 知進退存亡之機.[183]

This wide range of physical and spiritual qualities in the very appealing image of Yen Ch'ing may be summed up in the ambivalent term *feng-liu* 風流, applied to him at several points in the text. In Yen's case, the sense conveyed by this term falls more on the positive side of its semantic range, so that it means something like "affectionate and dashing." [184] This leads us to reconsider one more time the intimations of hostile vulnerability we have seen in the relations between the nominal "heroes" Wu Sung, Li K'uei, and Sung Chiang and members of the opposite sex. The treatment of these figures in the novel, as opposed to that in certain prior drama versions of their respective stories, emphasizes the underlying sexual hostility in several famous scenes. This stands in sharp opposition to the other, more manly heroes, who are as a rule married, and what is more often display sincere emotional attachment to their wives and families.[185] This is brought out dramatically early in the book, in the poignant interchanges between Lin Ch'ung and his wife (who happens to be one of the few more extensively drawn female portraits in the book not associated with either the female-

---

[182] *SHCC*, 3:1338.

[183] *SHCC*, 4:1792. Cf. Liu Ts'un-yan's theory (n. 51) that the relationship between Yen Ch'ing and Hsü Kuan-chung reveals a signature of Lo Kuan-chung. One of the lucky few granted a happy end that is not cut short by early death is Juan Hsiao-ch'i 阮小七. See *SHCC*, 4:1806f., for the final status of the surviving bandits.

[184] Cf. the association of Yen Ch'ing with "sensual delight" in the Kung Sheng-yü encomium (see above, n. 115).

[185] See Cheng Chen-to, "Lu Chih-shen ti chia-t'ing" and "Wu Sung yü ch'i ch'i Chia-shih," pp. 759–62. Huang Lin ("Ku-pen," p. 88) mentions certain sources that ascribe a wife and children to Sung Chiang. See also Hayden, "A Skeptical Note," p. 377; Sun Shu-yü, *Lai-li, hsin-t'ai, i-shu*, pp. 314ff.; and Wang Yung-chien, "Ch'eng-shu nien-tai," p. 237.

warrior stereotype or the chain of adulteresses represented by Yen P'o-hsi, P'an Chin-lien, and P'an Ch'iao-yün). These relationships are not fully developed in our novel, and are limited to a few scenes, but I find in these scenes a crucial counterweight to the emblematic misogyny of the *hao-han* stereotype.[186] In the cases of Yang Hsiung and Lu Chün-i, to be sure, this attachment is betrayed, although in the treatment of the latter case the author does exercise particular care to avoid casting Lu's wife in the simple adulteress mold, allowing her to voice arguments of justification for her course of action which are not altogether unconvincing.[187]

The same depth of feeling we can observe in the marital relations of the more positive martial heroes also carries over into certain other related areas of human attachment. For example, Lei Heng's filial devotion to his mother in chapter 51 provides a primary focus for his own display of heroism, and sheds further ironic light on some of the parodic distortions of filiality presented in the novel, notably that of Li K'uei.[188] By the same token, the presentation of the deep bond of friendship that links Yang Hsiung and Shih Hsiu, or Lu Chün-i and Yen Ch'ing, can only reflect badly on the sort of tainted brotherhood embodied in the relationship between Sung Chiang and Li K'uei.

V

Having reviewed the range of variation bracketed by these negative and positive models of human character in the novel, we may now be in a position to consider a few possible interpretations of overall patterns of meaning in the text. As I have stressed in earlier discussions, I believe a proper reading of the ironic figures worked out in the *fan-pen Shui-hu* demands that we abandon any simplistic association of the Liang-shan band as a whole, and Wu Sung, Li K'uei, and Sung Chiang as individuals, with the familiar heroic images known from popular stage and storytelling. At the same time, we should also beware the common error of being drawn into an attitude of "real-life" condemnation of these literary constructs. Unfortunately, this sort of reading has colored the criticism of the *Shui-hu*

---

[186] For a discussion of the types of women portrayed in the novel, see Sun Shu-yü, *Lai-li, hsin-t'ai, i-shu*, pp. 293ff.; and Sun Shou-wei, "Man-t'an Shui-hu li ti fu-nü hsing-hsiang," pp. 417–25.

[187] This judgment hinges, of course, on one's interpretation of the suggestion that Chia-shih and Li Ku had already had relations before this.

[188] The Yüan Wu-yai chapter-commentary on this scene (*Hui-p'ing pen*, 2:947) calls it the "main guiding principle of the book" 傳中第一綱領. The striking juxtaposition of Lei Heng's archetypal act of filiality with Li K'uei's gross violation of paternal compassion in the second half of the chapter makes this a very pointed treatment of the theme.

chuan over the centuries, from the understandably bitter denunciation of the code of banditry by Chin Sheng-t'an and others at the fall of the Ming, down to the "reverse educational materials" (*fan-mien chiao-ts'ai* 反面教材) campaign of the mid-1970s.[189]

Instead, what seems to be at stake in the sixteenth-century novelistic revision of the Liang-shan hero cycles is a rather far-ranging exploration, partly of the glories but more of the inner limitations and contradictions, of heroic action. This helps to explain the thematic undercurrent of weakness and failure that we have seen to govern both the internal organization of the separate hero cycles and, in a certain sense, the overall structure of the entire novel. This is dramatized in the choreographic pageant of frustration that takes place before the gates of Tung-ch'ang fu (immediately before the panegyrics of chapter 71), and it again eats away at the nominal victories in the final sections of the book, most obviously in the Pyrrhic triumphs of the Fang La campaign. In the final analysis, this exploration of ambiguities of motivation and limitations of capacity goes beyond the narrow scope of banditry and rebellion. With this in mind, I can now attempt to restate my earlier interpretations of the *fan-pen Shui-hu* within the context of the sixteenth-century Chinese intellectual milieu.

To begin, let us recall at this point the manner in which the novel is structured on a spatial scheme that gradually radiates outward from the isolated backwater of the Liang-shan marshes to reach a sphere of action of empire-wide scope. As in the case of the *Chin P'ing Mei*, *Shui-hu chuan* also builds upon its spatial setting in such a way as to intensify the parallel between the microcosm of the bandit lair and the macrocosm of the Confucian world order. In terms of the sphere of operations of the outlaw confederacy itself, the novel begins at a level that is essentially humorous, with the scruffy bandidos from T'ao-hua shan 桃花山 in chapter 5 (and 57), or the small-time gamblers such as Juan Hsiao-wu 阮小五 and later Wang Ch'ing. Nor is the original nucleus of the Liang-shan band, before the advent of Ch'ao Kai, a very impressive lot. Of course, one might say that this simply serves to point up the more attractive qualities of the growing Liang-shan fellowship under Ch'ao Kai and Sung Chiang. But the irony probably cuts both ways. At least, for all their noble-sounding rhetoric, the leaders of the reconstituted band never quite get away from their petty origins, as the author continues to remind us by bringing in a variety of

---

[189] Other examples of "real-life" denunciation of the Liang-shan heroes, after Chin Sheng-t'an and before the anti-Sung Chiang campaign, include discussions by Wang Kuo-wei in *Jen-chien tz'u-hua*, p. 49 (cited in Ma T'i-chi, *Tzu-liao*, p. 439); Lu Hsün, "Liu-mang yü pien-ch'ien," pp. 160ff., etc. Cf. the sequel *Tang-k'ou chih* 蕩寇志, written with the express purpose of bringing the fictional bandits to their proper punishment. See Nieh Kan-nu, "Wu-lun," p. 81.

low figures such as ragged poachers (the Hsieh brothers) and a chicken thief (Shih Ch'ien 時遷).[190] At the same time, however, he gradually orchestrates a rise in seriousness from small-scale larceny and confrontations with the local gendarmerie to successful stands against punitive forces of the central government, and then increasingly audacious raids on prefectural towns, larger cities, and eventually (symbolically, at least) the capital itself.

In view of this progressive escalation we are forced to consider, as in *Chin P'ing Mei*, the obvious analogy between the enclosed world of Liang-shan and the broader context of the imperial state. In his role as lord of the lair (*chai-chu* 寨主), Sung Chiang is frequently described as a kind of miniature emperor within his own realm. This is made all but explicit in chapter 60, where the imperative of unbroken dynastic succession (國不可一日無主) is invoked to "convince" Sung Chiang to assume full control after Ch'ao Kai's death. For that matter, the high-sounding motto "carry out the way on behalf of heaven" (*ti-t'ien hsing-tao* 替天行道) obviously carries an unambiguous arrogation of imperial prerogatives.[191]

In drawing this parallel between Sung Chiang's leadership of the Liang-shan brotherhood and the conduct of the affairs of the empire, the author presses a number of implications of the analogy. First, at the level of both the imperial court and Sung Chiang's surrogate empire, we observe a dependence on advisers of questionable morality, with the constant threat and actual experience of palace intrigues. Here, moreover, the contrast between the low estate of those who join the outlaw band willingly and the thwarted nobility of those who are brought into the fold under the cruelest duress takes on its fullest significance, as a bitter manifestation of Sung Chiang's distortion of the classical function of legitimate government: to attract and "use" worthy public servants (expressed by the terms *te-shih* 得士 and *yung-jen* in historical prose). By the same token, the frequent protestations by the Liang-shan leaders of deep concern for the welfare of "the people" are sharply undercut by the behavior of the band. This is not simply a question of the unnecessary sacrificing of innocent lives in many battles, but is brought to dramatic issue in the basically unprovoked destruction of the Chu family village and Tseng-t'ou shih (and later Tung-p'ing fu and Tung-ch'ang fu), which are narrated in great detail in the *fan-pen* texts. In each of these cases, one of the principal justifications for the attack lies in the stated desire to plunder for provisions, and the adver-

---

[190] Cf. the touch of having these low types stick flowers in their hair at their first appearance. This is repeated in a similar decoration for the Liang-shan bandits at the time of their presentation at court in chapter 82.

[191] See *SHCC*, 3:1011. Sung Chiang's rage at Juan Hsiao-ch'i for dressing up in Fang La's captured regalia in chapter 119 (4:1785) also seems to betray a sensitivity to these implications.

saries are by no means "enemies of the people." If anything, these people are more representative of the populace than the Liang-shan fighters themselves, whose presence, we are told, is a heavy burden on the surrounding countryside.[192] It may be significant, in this context, that in chapter 82 we are told that over two-thirds of Sung's loyal men choose not to join him in the final campaigns for the government side.

Within this context of flawed rulership, the initial model of Kao Ch'iu's rise to favor and his subsequent persecution of Lin Ch'ung, which comprises the very start of the novel proper with only tangential connections to the subsequent plot structure, takes on greater significance as an example of both unwise recruitment and the improper use of power. It seems significant, therefore, that after the initial section and up to the start of the later campaigns the "four evil ministers" are only barely developed in the narrative. Our only contact with them is through the relatives who represent them in a number of scenes (notably Liang Chung-shu 梁中書 in chapters 12, 17, and 62–67; Kao Lien 高廉 in chapters 52–54), where they are portrayed in terms that are far from the expected stereotypes of treachery. And the Emperor Hui-tsung 徽宗 himself, for all his vacillation and weakness, is spared in the novel the demeaning stamp of the "benighted ruler" (*hun-chün* 昏君).[193]

The fact that the author of the *fan-pen* novel has gone so far to break free of the simplistic stereotyping of both his heroes and his villains, relying instead on the subtle cross-reflection of figural parallels, adds to the complexity of interpreting the meaning of some of the central moral concepts evidently at issue in the work. The most obvious of these ideas are represented by the two Confucian terms *chung* 忠 and *i* 義 that cap the titles of virtually all the sixteenth-century *fan-pen* editions of the novel. As far as the latter term is concerned, I have translated it in various contexts above as "valor," "honor," "generosity," or "nobility." [194] But we have seen the

---

[192] In chapter 15 the Juan brothers explain that all the people in the Liang-shan area live in fear of the original band, and in chapter 84 Sung himself acknowledges the hardships his band has caused for the local populace, which he attempts to repay with the proceeds of the auction held before quitting the lair. Cf. Li K'uei's indiscriminate killing noted earlier.

[193] Even Ts'ai Ching, we are told, had originally sincerely wanted to recruit the bandits to the imperial side, until the savage attack on his son-in-law at Ta-ming fu pushed him to the opposite position. In chapter 72 (3:1220) the state of the empire is described in the following stereotyped terms: "the land was prosperous, the people at peace" 國富民安. The opening of the *fan-pen* version also provides us with a view of one of the evil ministers, Kao Ch'iu, that is strikingly similar to certain aspects of the careers of Sung Chiang, Wang Ch'ing, and other bandit leaders.

[194] For additional discussions of the various meanings of the term *i* in the novel, see Andrew Lo, "Historiography," pp. 144–60; Sun Shu-yü, *Lai-li, hsin-t'ai, i-shu*, pp. 42ff., 275–92, 333ff.; Yüeh Heng-chün, "Ti-tsao ho huan-mieh," p. 95.

author's unflinching exposure of the manner in which this high-sounding ideal is distorted or cheapened to a point at which the compound *chang-i* 仗義 comes to mean little more than loose pursestrings, where *chieh-i* 結義 can be assumed by any confederation of thugs, and where *chü-i* 聚義 takes on the menacing message "join us or else." We have discussed the bitingly sardonic use of such expressions in connection with the "recruitment" of Ch'in Ming and Chu T'ung, as well as the undercutting of the notion of righteous popular uprising also associated with the concept of *i*.

But this is only half of the picture. At the same time, the pages of the novel also contain examples of precisely the sort of noble selflessness implicit in the term. One important instance of this is seen in Chu T'ung's "unselfish release" 義釋 of Sung Chiang in chapter 22. Here we have yet another fine example of the density of figural reflection at work in the novel. This scene is not only figurally linked to Sung Chiang's comparable release of Ch'ao Kai in chapter 18, but the label *i-shih* also sets up an intertextual parallel to the famous scene of Kuan Yü's release of Ts'ao Ts'ao 曹操 in chapter 50 of *San-kuo chih yen-i*. It is, of course, no coincidence that Chu T'ung is iconographically linked to Kuan Yü, both by his impressive beard and by his nickname based on this feature. Here, however, the effect of the parallel is to put Sung Chiang on a par with Ts'ao Ts'ao, an idea that is not entirely without foundation within the overall significance of his rise to power as depicted in the novel. At the same time, the parallel brings out a bit of ambiguity regarding Sung Chiang's own release of Ch'ao Kai. This possibility is subtly suggested in the label of the scene—"secret (or selfish) release" (*ssu-fang* 私放)—in contrast to the expression "unselfish release" in the former case. But this only begins to take on its full implications as the uneasy relations between Sung and Ch'ao Kai continue to develop. Later, after the death of Ch'ao Kai, the author adds a third ironic instance of "unselfish release" on the part of Sung Chiang, this time directed toward Tung P'ing, a man he has never met before, in circumstances that raise serious doubts about his true motivations.

This leads us to a consideration of the other Confucian concept set off in the titles of the *Chung-i* editions: that of loyalty to the state. In the course of the novel numerous debates are staged that weigh rather carefully the causes and consequences of taking to the "green woods" 綠林. In many of these instances it is emphasized that what is at stake in this concept is not so much the simple fact of personal or professional loyalty to the imperial government as a deeper commitment to the basic structure of the Confucian world order. That is why a reading of the *Shui-hu chuan* as a kind of partisan attack on either brigandry or "defeatism" can be just as misleading as taking it to be a wholehearted celebration of anti-authoritarian elan. This is particularly evident in those discussions in which filial duty to one's parents and loyal service to the empire are drawn into a vertical equation, such that the violation of one necessarily implies the violation of the other. It is against the background of this sort of understanding that the author frames his text in such a way as to place the rising ambitions of Sung Chiang and the Liang-shan band, even with their dubious protestations of loyalty to the dynasty, into situations of conflict in which the demands of family welfare and personal commitments are sacrificed to a "greater cause." [195] This issue becomes most pressing in the extensive debates between Sung Chiang and his father in chapter 36, but the question is never settled and crops up again in parallel debates between Wang Ch'ing and his parents in the latter part of the book. As a result, the very obvious discrepancy between noble ideals and petty motivations that make a mockery out of the repeated swearing-in ceremonies in the Hall of Honorable Union (Chü-i t'ang 聚義堂) continues to undercut the more impressive claims to noble purpose after that hall is renamed Chung-i t'ang 忠義堂 and the missions issuing from it begin to affect the fate of the dynasty.

By the time the scope of action of the Liang-shan brotherhood reaches empirewide proportions, the sixteenth-century author begins to press the issues of loyalty and honor beyond simple ethical or political considerations into a more abstract contemplation of order and disorder 治亂 within the framework of Confucian political theory. Something like this is implicit in the recurrent series of episodes that explicitly take up the theme of chaos or havoc (nao 鬧).[196] A few of these scenes, Lu Ta's "riot" in the Wu-t'ai shan monastery for example, can be understood as simply stock narrative *topoi* taken over from popular drama and storytelling. But gradually these incidents become more and more costly and involve more and more innocent lives, until they finally reach the precincts of the imperial capital and challenge the central foundations of world order.

It is tempting to interpret the reflections of this perennial issue in our novel in the light of the particular political situation during the last few generations of the Ming, at the time the novel as we know it was being finalized. Even those critics who assume that the book was written in something like its present form in the fourteenth century have tried to see in its pages reflections of the chaos of the Yuan-Ming transition, citing

[195] For discussions of this issue, see Sun Shu-yü, *Lai-li, hsin-t'ai, i-shu*, pp. 289f.; Yüeh Heng-chün, "Ti-tsao ho huan-mieh," pp. 70ff.; Chin Tai-t'ung, "Li Chih," p. 77; Chang Kuo-kuang, "Tui Lo Erh-kang hsien-sheng Shui-hu chen-i k'ao i-wen chih shang-ch'üeh," pp. 43f.; and Ko Ch'u-ying, "T'an Shui-hu ti chung-i," pp. 129–40.

[196] See chapters 2, 4, 5, 8, 22, 24, 30, 33, 34, 37, 46, 67, and 93. Ho Hsin gathers some of these examples in *Yen-chiu*, p. 339.

hidden references to the rebel Fang Kuo-chen 方國珍, or to the swarthy victor Chu Yüan-chang 朱元璋.[197] Others, placing greater weight on the transformation of the book in the sixteenth century, have looked for parallels to the catastrophic insurrection of Li Tzu-ch'eng 李自成 or the forces of destruction unleashed by Nurhaci from over the northeastern frontier; while yet others have turned their gaze inward, looking for parallels in the disequilibrium associated with the Tung-lin 東林 purges of the early seventeenth century.[198] In the light of my guiding hypothesis that the *fan-pen Shui-hu chuan* under study here was essentially a product of the Chia-ching period, it is difficult to come up with a reading that can pin its depiction of rampant disorder on any specific upheavals during that relatively tranquil age.[199] But, if anything, the issues of order and chaos raised in this novel are perennial ones within the traditional Confucian vision, so that by 1644 Chin Sheng-t'an could, with considerable conviction and pathos, take it as a nearly allegorical exploration of what was causing the world to crumble all around him.

There is one more dimension of meaning in this novel, however, against which I believe we must also weigh the entire texture of experience presented in the novel. This is the backdrop of cosmic futility or emptiness (*k'ung* 空) out of which the monumental plot emerges with its opening poem, and into which it dissolves with the final dispensation of the band. The repeated foregrounding of this perspective includes a good deal of conventional imagery drawing upon Buddhist and Taoist symbolism (e.g., Lu Ta's nakedness in chapter 5 and his later enlightenment, or the pronouncements of the Taoist Lo in chapters 53 and 85). A number of recent critics have in fact suggested a more serious reading of some of these Taoist associations, citing the well-known resurgence in Taoist patronage

[197] See, for example, Chang Kuo-kuang, "Shang-ch'üeh," p. 44; Wang Li-ch'i, "Lo Kuan-chung yü yen-i," p. 70; and Tai Pu-fan, *Chien-wen lu*, p. 98.

[198] The parallel to the Manchu menace under Nurhaci is suggested in the "Chung Hsing" preface (see Ma T'i-chi, *Tzu-liao*, p. 8; Chu I-hsüan, *Tzu-liao*, p. 226). See Yen Tun-i, *Yen-pien*, p. 166; Ch'en Hsi-chung, "Kuan-yü Chung Po-ching," p. 4; and Shiroki Naoya, "Shō Hakkei," pt. 1, p. 100, pt. 2, p. 178. Other more general discussions of the reflection of the late Ming political and military situation in the novel include Chin Tai-t'ung, "Li Chih," p. 81; Shiroki Naoya, "Sōzō," p. 123; Hsü Shuo-fang, "Ts'ung Sung Chiang ch'i-i tao Shui-hu chuan ch'eng-shu." One interesting connection between these fictional upheavals and the political problems of the day is seen in the use of the Liang-shan nicknames to disparage the leading members of the Tung-lin group, for example in the text entitled *Tung-lin tien-chiang lu* 東林點將錄 (partial citation in Chu I-hsüan, *Tzu-liao*, pp. 502f.). See Chu T'an, "Tung-lin tien-chiang lu k'ao-i," pp. 569–601; and Andrew Lo, "Historiography," pp. 225f., 375, n. 44. See also Nieh Kan-nu, "Wu-lun," pp. 85f.

[199] Cheng Chen-to suggests a reference to the Chia-ching situation in "Yen-hua," pp. 120f.

and scholarship that began during the Chia-ching period.[200] But there is no denying that the textual basis in the novel for such an interpretation is extremely thin. At best, we can say that there are floating around here a few loose ideas about enlightenment of the nondescript three-teachings sort, as is pointed out in an early preface attributed to the Wan-li reader Huai-lin.[201]

This, at least, is the overpowering sense we are left with at the close of the work. The idea that all the sound and fury has come to naught reverberates in a number of poems toward the close, and is finally captured in the inconclusive dream of the final page, an element that, as we have seen, even Chin Sheng-t'an felt compelled to retain in his radically different ending. The Jung-yü t'ang commentator seems to put his finger on this when he says in a final comment:

> ... using a dream to tie up the plot as it approaches the end is full of deeper meaning; it is evident that all the various things that went before were like the recounting of a dream ... to read it at face value would be like a madman telling his own dream.
> 臨了以夢結局極有深意，見得從前種種都說夢⋯讀去認眞便是痴人說夢.[202]

In any event, as the cycle of action turns toward the phase of dissolution, the interjection of images of emptiness becomes more and more insistent. Examples such as the bare mountain visited by Tai Tsung and Shih Hsiu in chapter 90, the empty clack of the castanet-like *hu-ch'iao* 胡敲 in chapter 110, and the disturbing shooting of wild geese in the same chapter mount as the author brings the final chaos to a close.[203] In view of the frequent use of such images in traditional Chinese fiction in a rather shallow sense, the reader may perhaps be justified in dismissing them from consideration here as well. But in the context of the particular structural pattern of gathering and dispersal that we have observed in the novels of the sixteenth century, this ever-present suggestion of futility may add something to the interpretation of the problematical figures in this text as well.

In the preceding pages, I have attempted to demonstrate that the *fan-pen*

---

[200] See Sun Shu-yü, *Lai li, hsin-t'ai, i-shu*, pp. 176ff., 246ff.; Tai Pu-fan, *Chien-wen lu*, p. 123; Chang Kuo-kuang, "Tsu-pen t'an-k'ao," pp. 42ff.; and Hsiao Tso-ming, "T'an Shui-hu tso-che ti tao-chia ssu-hsiang," pp. 175–81.

[201] See "Yu lun Shui-hu chuan wen-tzu" 又論水滸傳文字 (cited in Ma T'i-chi, *Tzu-liao*, p. 7). See also Shiroki Naoya, "Shō Hakkei," p. 176.

[202] Jung-yü t'ang edition, chapter-commentary, chapter 100 (cited in Ma T'i-chi, *Tzu-liao*, p. 109).

[203] Chapter 110 (4:1649f., 1658). For a good discussion of these associations, see Chang Shu-hsiang, "Ch'üan-shih," pp. 138ff. See also Chang Kuo-kuang, "Shang-ch'üeh," p. 44.

Shui-hu was composed, or at least reframed, with an eye toward ironic reflection on the parameters of individual human action, and that it was directed toward a sophisticated audience that could be expected to look beyond the surface of its popular source materials. If there is any validity to this argument, then there still remains the very difficult problem of how to account for some of the remarks of late Ming and Ch'ing critics who seem to express general approval for some of the more disturbing actions of the Liang-shan band. This is true not only of "radical" literary critics such as the pseudo Li Chih and Chung Hsing, whose reputation for anti-establishment sentiments—though not entirely deserved—would make such an attitude quite understandable, but also for a wide range of late Ming readers including, according to one report, no less than the Wan-li emperor himself.[204]

Particularly troubling is the widespread praise on the part of sixteenth- and seventeenth-century commentators for Li K'uei as a totally honest individual, an unbridled free spirit, a veritable "living Buddha." Such commendation is easy to see if we are talking about Lu Ta, or perhaps Wu Sung, where their earlier position in the book and general tone of presentation ensure a more sympathetic treatment. (Curiously, Wu Sung does not seem to draw much enthusiasm on the part of the late Ming critics.) But some of the ecstatic appreciations of Li K'uei expressed in the commentaries seem to present a blind eye to the darker sides of his characterization. Interestingly, even Chin Sheng-t'an basically concurs in this view, and at numerous points in his commentary he departs from his unconcealed disgust for the aims and purposes of the band as a whole to express a preference for Li's forthrightness and daring over the qualities of his less transparent brother.[205]

Given the occasional acuteness of these commentators' critical insights— including the Jung-yü t'ang commentator despite his generally shallow marginal notes—we cannot simply dismiss such remarks as based on an uncritical reading of the text. It may be possible to explain these comments as referring more to the familiar image of Li K'uei and the others known from the popular stage than to the specific character constructs developed in the novel. But from the perspective of my reinterpretation of the *fan-pen*

---

[204] See Liu Luan 劉巒, *Wu-tan hu* 五石瓠, *chüan* 6, cited by Chin Tai-t'ung, "Li Chih," p. 80, n. 2. Cf. Nieh Kan-nu's discussion of three types of readings of the novel, in "Wu-lun," pp. 83f.

[205] For a review of the Yüan Wu-yai and Jung-yü t'ang comments on Li K'uei, see Ch'en Chin-chao, "Li Cho-wu p'i-tien," pp. 52f. Cf. chapter-commentary in chapter 71 of the Yüan Wu-yai edition (in *Hui-p'ing pen*, 2:1273), praising Li as a man of "unfeigned loyalty and personal devotion" 眞性忠義. A similar judgment is given in the Jung-yü t'ang commentary at this point (71:15b).

Shui-hu as a reflection of its sixteenth-century intellectual background, it may be more useful to relate such views directly to the variously conceived ideals of spontaneity—Li Chih's concept of the "childlike mind" (*t'ung-hsin* 童心), Yüan Hung-tao's 袁宏道 idea of "spontaneous delight" (*ch'ü* 趣), or the notion of "nonrational insight" (*hsing-ling* 性靈)—which were so current at precisely the time that the printed editions of the novel were gaining wider circulation. In fact, Li Chih makes the connection all but explicit in his discussion of the *t'ung-hsin* concept in his *Fen shu* 焚書, where he cites *Shui-hu chuan* as a prime example of his notion of the free expression of the childlike mind.[206]

On the other hand, some of the late Ming commentators whose works are still extant take care to balance their enthusiasm for the Li K'uei types with a more sober evaluation of the remaining figures in the novel. For example, in the prefatory piece attributed to Huai-lin entitled "A Comparative Ranking of the 108 Liang-shan Heroes", printed in certain Jung-yü t'ang and Chung Hsing editions, the critic qualifies his initial appreciation of Li K'uei, Sung Chiang, and Wu Yung by adding that Li K'uei is surpassed by Lu Ta in the latter's "cleverness within crudeness" (*ts'u chung hsi* 粗中細); that despite Sung Chiang's ability to "take in men's minds" (*shou-shih jen-hsin* 收拾人心), he is still essentially a bandit; that Wu Yung represents "treachery incarnate" (*ch'üan-shen chien-cha* 全身奸詐); and that by and large the remainder of the band are hoodlums pure and simple, in sharp contrast to the genuinely heroic figures such as the "three heroes" of the Chu family and the five "tiger generals" at Tseng-t'ou shih.[207] This last point is repeated twice for special emphasis. In view of the fact that within the late Ming intellectual context the sort of natural openness associated with Li K'uei was pointedly contrasted to the narrow moralizing of the Confucian pedant (*tao-hsüeh ch'i* 道學氣), the evaluation of Sung Chiang as "a false moralizer, a true bandit" 假道學眞强盜 is particularly damning.[208]

Regardless of the specific readings these commentators apply to characters and events in the text, the very fact that they indulge in the time-consuming labor of textual commentary in itself provides a significant corrective to the common view of the *Shui-hu chuan* as a naive celebration of the popular imagination. Well before Chin Sheng-t'an, a number of late Ming critics had already given expression to a uniform view of the novel as a very serious piece of writing, rather than as nothing more than a delightful collection of heroic adventures. The T'ien-tu wai-ch'en preface, for example, argues that the models in the novel may be as instructive as those

---

[206] Li Chih, *Fen shu*, p. 98.
[207] "Huai-lin" preface cited in Ma T'i-chi, *Tzu-liao*, p. 6; and Chu I-hsüan, *Tzu-liao*, p. 209.
[208] Ibid. Similar ideas are expressed in the Wu-hu lao-jen preface (cited in Ma T'i-chi, *Tzu-liao*, p. 10; Chu I-hsüan, *Tzu-liao*, p. 213). See Shiroki Naoya, "Shō Hakkei," p. 183.

in serious historical writing, in spite of the fact that the men of Liang-shan do not measure up to true historical heroes. The Li Chih preface centers on the notion that the novel, like Ssu-ma Ch'ien's immortal work, was written "to give vent to deep indignation" (*fa-fen* 發憤) at the historical tragedy that befell the northern Sung—one with obvious analogues in Li's own age.[209] Another prefatory piece attributed to Huai-lin gives a more balanced assessment of the vision of the novel:

> ... passages designed to amuse the world comprise seven parts in ten; passages designed to take the world in hand, the remaining three. But even the parts for amusement all contain a visceral intention of putting the world in order.
> 玩世之詞十七，持世之語十三。然玩世處亦俱持世心腸也．[210]

On the basis of the discussions in this chapter, I believe it is possible to argue that a close reading of the text of the *fan-pen Shui-hu* may support a revised interpretation of its significance as a sixteenth-century literati novel. We have seen a number of examples in which the *fan-pen* texts depart from the *chien-pen* recensions at precisely those points where suggestive details come to the fore. Moreover, a comparison of the various editions of the novel with other more popular versions of the Liang-shan cycles reveals an even wider discrepancy in the treatment of figures such as Li K'uei, Wu Sung, and Sung Chiang. This is particularly evident when we review the episodes that were apparently embroidered onto the earlier cycles to form the basic outlines of the *fan-pen* text, and see that, in practically every case, what these sections add is a pronounced ironic cast.[211] Once again, this is not to deny the parallel existence of the traditional popular images of the "watermargin" heroes. It is only to insist that the *fan-pen* novel is simply no longer working along these lines; that it is doing with its own source materials the same sort of things that the *Chin P'ing Mei* and *Hsi-yu chi* were to do with theirs.

[209] See Appendix for references. See also Lu Hsin, "Ch'ü-pi," p. 49.

[210] "P'i-p'ing Shui-hu chuan shu-yü" 批評水滸傳述語, cited in Ma T'i-chi, *Tzu-liao*, p. 5; and Chu I-hsüan, *Tzu-liao*, p. 208.

[211] Episodes we may tentatively call "original" in the *fan-pen* novel include the release of the star-spirits, the Lin Ch'ung section, the Yang Chih story, the overthrow of Wang Lun, Li K'uei's parody of filiality in chapters 42 and 43, the recruiting of Hsü Ning and An Tao-ch'üan, the expansion of the Tseng-t'ou shih battles, the contest with Lu Chün-i, the ceremony in chapter 71, the riot in the capital in chapter 72, the killings in chapter 73, and the finale in chapter 120. See Irwin, *Evolution*, pp. 44f.; and Hu Shih, "K'ao-cheng," pp. 125f., for other speculation on the "original" material in the *fan-pen* novel.

Chapter 38: "[Chu-ko Liang] First Emerges from the Thatched Hut and Determines the Tripartite Divison" 定三分初出茅廬, from "Li-Yü" commentary edition, *Li Li-weng p'i-yüeh San-kuo chih*" (see b.n. I.4)

CHAPTER 5

San-kuo chih yen-i:
Limitations of Valor

I

I have left for last the work that is most likely the earliest of our four masterworks of Ming fiction, because it presents in a number of senses a different case of my argument regarding the rise of the Chinese literati novel in the sixteenth century. Not only does the date on the earliest extant edition of *San-kuo chih yen-i* precede by as much as a generation the probable date of the first appearance of the *fan-pen* recension of *Shui-hu chuan* (itself a half century or more before the publication of *Hsi-yu chi* and *Chin P'ing Mei* in the Wan-li period), but also with respect to certain key aspects of form this text departs noticeably from the model I have tried to set up in the preceding chapters. Yet, on balance, it may be possible to demonstrate that *San-kuo* still shares with these other three works a sufficient number of common points of structure and meaning to enable me to speak of it as a member (most likely the initiator) of the same literary class. As in each of the preceding chapters, my discussion will ultimately come to focus on the thesis that *San-kuo* ought to be read as an essentially ironic revision of the various source materials on which it is based, a contention I will attempt to support as far as possible through comparison with alternate versions of the *San-kuo* narrative in popular fiction, drama, and historical writings.

I will take a few pages to review here the question of the dating of the novel as it bears upon my argument. The earliest text now extant is the *San-kuo chih t'ung-su yen-i* bearing two prefaces: one signed with the pseudonym Yung-yü tzu 庸愚子 (identified as Chiang Ta-ch'i 蔣大器) and dated Hung-chih 7 (1494), and another signed by Hsiu-jan tzu 修髯子 (identified as Chang Shang-te 張尚德) and dated Chia-ching 1 (1522).[1] If, as caution would dictate, we take only the second of these two prefaces to fix the date of this edition, then the appearance of the novel falls safely within the designated span of the sixteenth century. But, of course, one could just as well accept the preface dated 1494 as proving the existence of the text by that year, following the same reasoning that puts the date of the T'ien-tu wai-ch'en edition of *Shui-hu chuan* at 1589 according to a preface that we actually have only in a much later reprint.[2] In fact, judging by the testimony of the 1522 preface itself, it is possible that the text for which the 1494 preface had been composed was a hand-copied manuscript, which was subsequently put to blocks only in or around 1522.[3] If this is so, then for want of any specific evidence of radical revision of the text at the time of printing, we might conclude that the seal had been set on the text by the year 1494.[4] Even this, however, would leave us only a few years short of our imported time frame; and more to the point, this would still put the assembling of the earliest extant text of *San-kuo* in the Hung-chih reign, precisely the period I described in my opening chapter as a time of marked new directions across the entire spectrum of Ming culture.[5]

To accept the composition of *San-kuo chih yen-i* as falling within—or on the verge of—the sixteenth century, however, immediately flies in the face of the prevailing scholarly opinion, which attributes the primary role in the authorship of the novel to Lo Kuan-chung 羅貫中, sometime in the fourteenth century.[6] To begin with, Lo Kuan-chung's name actually appears at

---

[1] See *San-kuo chih t'ung-su yen-i*, "Ch'u-pan shuo-ming" 出版說明, p. 1a. All later editions derive from this recension, including the seventeenth-century Mao Tsung-kang edition read almost exclusively today. See b.n. I.1 for bibliographical information.

[2] See above, Chapter 4, Part I.

[3] This is the conclusion drawn by the editors of the Jen-min wen-hsüeh reprint. See "Ch'u-pan shuo-ming," p. 1b.

[4] Hence the common designation "Hung-chih text" (*Hung-chih pen* 弘治本). Cheng Chen-to explains that this designation derives from an edition in which only the earlier preface appeared. See his "San-kuo chih yen-i ti yen-hua," p. 208. For information on the rediscovery of this edition, see ibid., pp. 240f.

[5] See above, Chapter 1.

[6] For information on the background of Lo Kuan-chung, see above, Chapter 4, Part I. On Lo's relation to *San-kuo-yen-i*, see Cheng Chen-to, "Yen-hua," pp. 191ff.; Tung Mei-k'an, *San-kuo yen-i shih-lun*, pp. 23ff.; Liu Ts'un-yan, "Sur l'authenticité des romans historiques de Lo Guanzhong," pp. 231ff.; and Winston L. Y. Yang, "Lo Kuan-chung." The most convincing case for establishing Lo Kuan-chung's identity and connection to colloquial fiction has been made by Wang Li-ch'i, in "Lo Kuan-chung yü San-kuo chih t'ung-su yen-i." The scene known as "Visiting a Recluse Sage" (*Fang-hsien* 訪賢) in the play *Lung-hu feng-yün hui* 龍虎風雲會, usually accepted as Lo Kuan-chung's work, has also been taken by many scholars as proof of Lo's authorship of the *Yen-i*.

the head of the 1522 text.[7] One might point out that Lo is credited there with the "editorial arranging" (*pien-tz'u* 編次) of the book, but that, of course, would put its original composition even earlier. Numerous other bibliographical references, including many from the sixteenth century, attest to this same attribution.[8] The theory of fourteenth-century composition also gains a measure of support from the fact that some of the interlinear notes in the 1522 printing identify certain obscure Three Kingdoms place-names for the reader in terms of their Yuan period equivalents, thus suggesting to some scholars the idea that the entire text as we have it must have been assembled in or shortly after the Yuan period.[9]

Given the number and persistence of the bibliographical references attributing to Lo Kuan-chung a fictional narrative dealing with the history of the Three Kingdoms period, it is difficult to deny the assumption that such a work existed. The question remains, however, whether the book described by the Ming bibliographers was identical to the book we are dealing with here. It has been quite natural for modern scholars to assume that the 1522 text is for all intents and purposes a reprint of Lo Kuan-chung's original work, but the grounds for this conclusion are not appreciably sounder than those underlying the attribution of *Shui-hu chuan* to Lo Kuan-chung or Shih Nai-an 施耐庵.[10] As in the case of *Shui-hu*, it is entirely possible that this lack of evidence simply reflects the incompleteness of our knowledge. But for the purposes of the present discussion, I will once again leave the burden of proof on those who wish to establish Lo Kuan-chung's authorship, and proceed to analyze and interpret the *San-kuo chih yen-i*, as

[7] See Wang Li-ch'i, "Lo Kuan-chung yü yen-i," p. 68.

[8] These early references include citations in the *Pai-ch'uan shu-chih* of Kao Ju, *Ku-chin shu-k'e* of Chou Hung-tsu, and the *Yeh-shih-yüan shu-mu* of Ch'ien Tseng (1629—99). For information on these works and authors, see above Chapter 4, Part I. See citations in K'ung Ling-ching, *Chung-kuo hsiao-shuo shih-liao*, pp. 39ff.; and Cheng Chen-to, "Yen-hua," p. 209. Andrew Hing-bun Lo, "*San-kuo chih yen-i* and *Shui-hu chuan* in the Context of Historiography," pp. 207f., 370, n. 1, adds to these references a description by the eunuch Liu Jo-yü of an early text in a palace library in the Wan-li period (see Liu Jo-yü, *Cho chung chih, chüan* 18, pp. 1a—9b.

[9] The editors of the 1975 reprint of the 1522 edition state this case in "Ch'u-pan shuo-ming," pp. 1b—2a. The 1522 edition notes also make references to Sung terminology as equivalents for Three Kingdoms terms (e.g., *chüan* 1, p. 23b), a fact that may weaken the conclusions drawn from the references to Yuan terminology. See Wang Li-ch'i, "Lo Kuan-chung yü yen-i," pp. 66f.; Chang Kuo-kuang, "San-kuo chih t'ung-su yen-i ch'eng-shu yü Ming chung-yeh pien," pp. 269f.; and Ou-yang Chien, "Shih lun San-kuo chih t'ung-su yen-i ti ch'eng-shu nien-tai," pp. 280ff.

[10] See above, Chapter 4, Part I. The assumption that the 1522 edition is a close replica of the hypothetical Lo text is implicit in the discussions of Cheng Chen-to and Sun K'ai-ti, and is reflected in the arguments of Wilt Idema, "Some Remarks and Speculations Concerning P'ing-hua," p. 156; and C. T. Hsia, "The Military Romance," p. 347.

we know it from the 1522 text and later editions, as an example of the sixteenth-century literati novel, one that was either newly created during the second Ming century or was substantially altered by that time.[11]

One small piece of evidence that indicates the 1522 edition cannot be considered an exact reproduction of a fourteenth-century text is the inclusion of a eulogy for Chu-ko Liang 諸葛亮 in chapter 104 that is identified as a piece by the fifteenth-century writer Yin Chih 尹直 (1427–1511), as noted by the editors of the 1975 facsimile reprint of the 1522 edition.[12] This addition may be considered nothing more than an insignificant editorial alteration, but at the very least it calls into question the significance of the appearance of the Yuan place-names in the notes of the 1522 edition— since these can be taken as good evidence of fourteenth-century composition only if one insists that the text was absolutely untouched between then and 1522.[13]

Among those modern scholars who believe that the standard texts of *San-kuo chih yen-i* are not necessarily exact reproductions of the work of Lo Kuan-chung, some have paid special attention to a group of less familiar late Ming editions of the narrative, including the *San-kuo chih-chuan* 三國志傳, *San-kuo ch'üan-chuan* 三國全傳, *San-kuo chih-chuan p'ing-lin* 三國志傳評林, and others.[14] Many of these are printings of the so-called

---

[11] In a recent article, Wilt Idema concludes that the great dramatist Chu Yu-tun 朱有燉, in the early fifteenth century, probably did not know the *San-kuo chih yen-i* text as we have it in the 1522 edition. This would be strange, although of course not impossible, if the known dramatist Lo Kuan-chung had indeed written the novel only shortly before. See Idema, "Zhu Youdun's Dramatic Prefaces and Traditional Fiction," p. 20f. This point harks back to my statement in the preceding chapter: that in the event new evidence proves Lo Kuan-chung's authorship of an equivalent of the 1522 version of the novel, the long time gap between this achievement and the later novel masterpieces of the sixteenth century would parallel the appearance of the full-length dramas *Hsi-hsiang chi* and *P'i-p'a chi* in the fourteenth century, more than a century before the consolidation of the *ch'uan-ch'i* dramatic form. Cf. the occasional attribution of the authorship of *San-kuo chih yen-i* to Wang Shih-fu 王實甫 (see, for example, K'ung Ling-ching, *Shih-liao*, p. 56).

[12] See reprint of 1522 edition, "Ch'u-pan shuo-ming," p. 2a–b. For information on Yin Chih's historical compilations, see Andrew Lo, "Historiography," p. 19f. Wang Li-ch'i ("Lo Kuan-chung yü yen-i," p. 66) concludes on this basis that the 1522 edition cannot be the "original form" 本來面目 of the novel.

[13] In fact, these notes could just as well have been incorporated into the 1522 edition from an altogether different source work on Three Kingdoms history. See Chang Kuo-kuang, "Ch'eng-shu pien," pp. 273ff.

[14] See especially Sun K'ai-ti, "San-kuo chih p'ing-hua yü San-kuo chih-chuan t'ung-su yen-i"; and Liu Ts'un-yan, "Sur l'authenticité," pp. 239–43. For descriptions of these editions, see Sun K'ai-ti, *Chung-kuo t'ung-su hsiao-shuo shu-mu*, pp. 35–44; Cheng Chen-to, "Yen-hua," pp. 210ff.; Ma Lien, "Chiu-pen San-kuo yen-i pan-pen ti tiao-ch'a"; and Ogawa Tamaki, "Kan Saku no densetsu sono hoka," pp. 165ff. An additional rare edition of the *Chih-chuan* housed in the Escorial Library in Madrid is described by Andrew Lo in "Historiography," p. 260.

"Fukien type" (*Min-pen* 閩本), which we have encountered in the publishing history of *Hsi-yu chi* and *Shui-hu chuan*, and some are associated with the printing establishment of Yü Hsiang-tou, whom we also met in those cases.[15] Specifically, the physical printing format of these texts, with running woodcut illustrations above the text proper on each page, is strikingly similar to that in some of the *chien-pen* 簡本 editions of *Shui-hu chuan*.[16] Proceeding from this similarity, Liu Ts'un-yan and others have gone on to consider the question of which system of texts came first: these relatively crude editions or the technically superior editions represented by the 1522 text and the later commentary editions attributed to Li Chih 李贄, Li Yü 李漁, and Mao Tsung-kang 毛宗崗. They arrive at the conclusion that the *Chih-chuan* texts represent a closer approximation of the hypothetical "original" Lo Kuan-chung edition, either directly or by way of intermediate stages.[17] This conclusion would obviously help to sort out some of the confusion over the date of the composition of the novel. But it, too, remains little more than speculation, since outside of their format and generally inferior workmanship, these editions do not present very major differences from the 1522 edition as far as their basic narrative text is concerned, and so, unlike the *chien-pen* editions of *Shui-hu chuan*, they cannot be said to comprise a separate textual system.[18] Moreover, since none of the extant examples of these texts can be reliably dated before the Wan-li period, it appears that as far as we can tell the chain of known editions of *San-kuo* proceeded not from crude beginnings to later refinement, as implied by such theories, but rather from the highly polished 1522 edition to more popular versions.[19] Mao Tsung-kang, for one, argues that his seventeenth-century revisions are aimed simply at restoring the original character of the text, which had been watered down in crude popular versions by his time.[20]

[15] See Sun K'ai-ti, *Shu-mu*, pp. 37ff.; and Cheng Chen-to, "Yen-hua," pp. 213ff. For further information on Yü Hsiang-tou, see Chapter 4, n. 63.

[16] For the distinction between *fan-pen* and *chien-pen* editions, see above, Chapter 4, Part I. I have also noted certain editions of *Hsi-yu chi* in the same format; see above, Chapter 3, Part I.

[17] See b.n. I for bibliographical information on these editions.

[18] I will refer to some of the minor discrepancies between the 1522 edition and these other editions in the course of the discussion in this chapter.

[19] Tung Mei-k'an (*Shih-lun*, p. 2) speaks of the popular "Wan-li editions," as opposed to the elegant "early Ming edition." An example of one of these more popular Wan-li editions is the *Ching-pen ta-tzu San-kuo chih yen-i* 京本大字三國志演義 (see Sun K'ai-ti, *Shu-mu*, p. 37).

[20] For Mao Tsung-kang's references to the "popular editions" (*su-pen*) current in his time, see below, n. 52. See also his *fan-li*, p. 1. A similar view seems to underlie a note by the commentator of the "Li Cho-wu" edition decrying the "grave injustice" done to Lo Kuan-chung's original intentions in the more recent popular versions. See *Li Cho-wu hsien-sheng p'i-p'ing San-kuo chih yen-i*, chapter 102 (p. 14b). See b.n. I.3 for description of this edition.

Since the primary aim of this study is close-reading and interpretation rather than background scholarship, I need not get too deeply entangled in the problem of dating—which, in any case, cannot be solved conclusively on the basis of the existing evidence. There are, however, a few ramifications of this question that are worth mentioning at this point, as they may shed light on my reading of the novel. First, there is a general tendency among modern readers of *San-kuo* to understand the book as a specific reflection of the fourteenth-century historical situation, with pointed reference to such perennial issues as dynastic legitimacy or the conflict of northern and southern interests within the context of Mongol rule. According to this view, Lo Kuan-chung is seen as a stereotyped loyalist (*i-min* 遺民) in conformance with the common image, now outdated, of the frustrated Han literati who supposedly turned to fiction and drama in desperation after all other avenues of individual expression had been closed off by their alien rulers.[21] Some scholars have gone on to note Lo Kuan-chung's alleged association with the abortive cause of Chang Shih-ch'eng 張士誠, and have concluded that the pessimistic tone of the novel is directed more against the self-made autocrat Chu Yüan-chang 朱元璋 than against the excesses of the Mongols.[22] Such theories are reasonable enough as long as one accepts the hypothesis that the book reportedly written by Lo Kuan-chung and the book we are investigating are one and the same. But as soon as we deny the absolute certainty of this claim, we must immediately shift our interest in the novel's reflection of its historical context to the political and intellectual developments of later Ming reigns— when we know for certain that the book as we have it was published and read.

A second important implication of the bibliographical sources mentioned above arises from the observation that in a large number of these references *San-kuo chih yen-i* and *Shui-hu chuan* seem to go hand in hand. For example, the *Ch'i-hsiu lei-kao* 七修類稿, *Pai-ch'uan shu-chih* 百川書志, *Ku-chin shu-k'e* 古今書刻, and *Shao-shih shan-fang pi-ts'ung* 少室山房筆叢 all mention both of these works in parallel citations.[23] Of particular interest among these is the reference that indicates the existence of government-sponsored editions of the two novels, put out by the same censorate

---

[21] For a recent refutation of this stereotyped view, see Stephen H. West, "Mongol Influence on the Development of Northern Drama," pp. 434–65.

[22] This is based on a reference in a colophon by the Ch'ing writer Hsü Wei-jen 徐渭仁 to Hsü Ping's 徐鈵 "Illustrations of the 108 Warriors of the Water Margin" 水滸一百單八將 圖題跋. See Chao Ts'ung, *Chung-kuo ssu ta hsiao-shuo chih yen-chiu*, p. 116. See also a similar reference in Wang Li-ch'i, "Lo Kuan-chung yü yen-i," p. 71.

[23] Citations available in K'ung Ling-ching, *Shih-liao*, pp. 15ff., 39ff. See above, Chapter 4, Part I, note 6.

bureau, the Tu-ch'a yüan 都察院, plus a later laconic entry in the *Pao-wen t'ang shu-mu* 寶文堂書目 that speaks of a *Wu-ting* 武定本 edition of *San-kuo*.[24] If this latter designation means the same thing here as it means in the references to the similarly labeled Kuo Hsün 郭勛 edition of *Shui-hu chuan*, then perhaps we have in our fine extant Chia-ching printing of *San-kuo* an example of what the format of the missing *Shui-hu* text might have been like. Later on, we find the publication of what seem to be almost paired sets of the two works by the Fukien printers (i.e., Yü Hsiang-tou's crude commentary editions of the *San-kuo chih-chuan p'ing-lin* and *Chung-i shui-hu chih-chuan p'ing-lin*), culminating in the publication of a split-page combined printing of both works in the *Ying-hsiung p'u* 英雄譜 and other seventeenth-century editions. All this bespeaks a strong sense in the late Ming publishing world that these two novels belonged to the same literary class—an understanding also implicit in the publication of parallel commentary editions attributed to Li Chih, Chung Hsing 鍾惺, and Li Yü.[25] Now, it is possible to say that the chief significance of linking *San-kuo* and *Shui-hu* in these parallel editions lies in the fact that they both deal with heroic chapters in history, and both seem to bring into relief the issues of loyalty and personal honor (*chung-i* 忠義)—this seems to be all that the editors of the *Ying-hsiung p'u* had in mind in their tandem printing.[26] But for the purposes of the present discussion I would like to propose that we also have here evidence that the sophisticated vernacular novel was emerging as an identifiable literary genre by the early sixteenth century—even before the various texts came to be grouped by critics among the "four masterworks" or the "six works of genius". In view of this perceived generic linkage between *San-kuo* and *Shui-hu*, I will repeat here my earlier assertion that, in the event that future discoveries should succeed in proving the fourteenth-century authorship of these two works, the chronological neatness of my theory of the sixteenth-century novel would have to be sacrificed, but the sense of a well-defined narrative genre taking in our two earlier and two later masterworks would remain intact.

One more aspect of the composition of *San-kuo chih yen-i* that might appear to go against my view of it as an early example of the literati novel, but which ultimately locates it squarely within that generic tradition, is the

[24] Ch'ao Li, *Pao-wen t'ang shu-mu*, p. 109. See Chapter 4, Part I, note 5.

[25] For descriptions of the "Chung Hsing" commentary edition, see Sun K'ai-ti, *Shu-mu*, p. 40; and Andrew Lo, "Historiography," p. 260. For this and the "Li Cho-wu" and "Li Yü" editions, see b.n. I.3, I.4, and II.

[26] See above Chapter 4, Part I. I will refer in the following discussion to numerous points of apparent intertextual reference between the two works, especially to the figural similarity between Liu Pei and Sung Chiang, Kuan Yü and Wu Sung, and Chang Fei and Li K'uei. See Andrew Lo, "Historiography," pp. 207ff., for a "convergent reading" of the two works.

fact that it, too, is to a large extent derived from preexisting popular and semipopular sources dealing with the same narrative subjects. These sources, broadly defined to include any evidence of treatment of the figures and events of the history of the Three Kingdoms period in fiction and drama, have been collected and discussed in the writings of numerous modern scholars.[27] We know from certain references, for example, that stories of these heroes were the subject of various forms of popular entertainments, perhaps as early as Sui and T'ang times. One of the earliest examples is a possible reference to a Sui period pageant known as "Liu Pei Crosses the T'an River on his Mount" 劉備乘馬渡檀溪. By Sung times several contemporary accounts inform us that there existed professional oral storytellers who specialized in the Three Kingdoms hero cycles.[28] Some of the evidence regarding this type of material may be misleading, however. For example, Y. W. Ma (Ma Yau-woon) has recently called into question the relevance of the line in a poem by Li Shang-yin 李商隱 that is often cited as proof of well-developed T'ang storytelling on the San-kuo theme. And I might add that Su Shih's 蘇軾 well-known description of a young audience's response to the performance of the story, upon closer investigation, turns out to be secondhand information.[29] But we can still be fairly certain, from various kinds of evidence, that from an early period on the hero cycles that grew up around the exploits of the San-kuo figures became a major subject of oral storytelling, and this tradition has continued right down into the twentieth century.[30] On the other hand, the fact that recent oral storytelling examples can be shown to be largely based on the written *Yen-i* text reminds us that the line of development from oral storytelling to the full-length novel is by no means simple or one-directional.[31] The real point here, as I have argued in each of the preceding

[27] See Sun K'ai-ti, "P'ing-hua yü yen-i"; and Cheng Chen-to, "Yen-hua"; Tung Mei-k'an, *Shih-lun*; Andrew Lo, "Historiography"; Wang Li-ch'i, "Lo Kuan-chung yü yen-i," pp. 72f.; etc.

[28] The reference to the Sui example is found in *Ta-yeh shih-i chi*, available in the *T'ai-p'ing kuang-chi, chüan* 226, pp. 1735–37. See Andrew Lo, "Historiography," pp. 15, 335, n. 5. For further evidence of T'ang and possibly earlier treatments of *San-kuo* materials, see Chou Shao-liang, "T'an T'ang-tai ti San-kuo ku-shih." See also Cheng Chen-to, "Yen-hua," pp. 169ff.; Tung Mei-k'an, *Shih-lun*, pp. 17ff.; Idema, "Some Remarks," pp. 76ff.; and Chang Cheng-lang, "Chiang-shih yü yung-shih shih."

[29] See Y. W. Ma, "The Beginnings of Professional Storytelling in China," p. 233. The citation from Su Shih may be found in *Tung-p'o chih-lin, chüan* 1 (*Huai-ku* 懷古), p. 5. Also available in Wang Sung-ling edition, p. 7.

[30] For a thorough description of recent oral storytelling on the San-kuo cycles, see Boris Riftin, *Istoricheskaya epopeia i fol'klornaya traditsia v Kitae*, pp. 251–432.

[31] Riftin, *Istoricheskaya epopeia*, pp. 260ff. A popular contemporary San-kuo storyteller, Yüan K'uo-ch'eng 袁闊成, has acknowledged in a private interview in Peking in February 1985 that he bases his work largely on the printed *Yen-i* text.

three chapters, is not the simple fact of prior narrative treatment, but rather the manner in which the literati novel pointedly transforms the earlier material as it casts it into a new generic mold.

This is particularly true with respect to the *San-kuo chih p'ing-hua* 三國志平話. Given the various bibliographical references ostensibly pointing to a date of composition for the *San-kuo chih yen-i* sometime in the latter half of the fourteenth century, the rediscovery of the printed *P'ing-hua* text bearing a date in the Chih-chih 至治 reign (1321–23) of the Yuan period appeared to provide the missing link in the development of the novel, an assumption supported by the somewhat analogous relation of *Shui-hu chuan* to the late Sung or Yuan text *Hsüan-ho i-shih* 宣和遺事. In fact, the 1494 preface attached to the *T'ung-su yen-i* itself speaks of an earlier, less satisfactory *p'ing-hua* version.[32] On the basis of this hypothesis, Sun K'ai-ti and other scholars have undertaken detailed comparisons of corresponding passages of the *P'ing-hua* and the *Yen-i*, working from the assumption that the text of the novel they were using (either the 1522 edition, a Mao Tsung-kang edition, or a *Chih-chuan* edition, as the case may be) derives from the pen of Lo Kuan-chung, only slightly later than the printing of the extant *P'ing-hua*.[33]

The aim of such comparisons is invariably the isolation of verbal or narrative parallels which may prove that the author of the *Yen-i* used the

[32] See facsimile reprint of the *San-kuo chih p'ing-hua* included in *Li-shih t'ung-su yen-i*, to which my page numbers refer. The text is also available in *Ch'üan-hsiang p'ing-hua wu-chung*, and in a 1955 typeset edition. The text was rediscovered and published in Japan in 1926, and acquired by Chang Yüan-chi 張元濟 and reprinted in China in 1929. James Crump describes the first modern reprints of the *P'ing-hua* in "*P'ing-hua* and the Early History of the *San-kuo chih*," p. 250. Of course the assumption that the *p'ing-hua* referred to in the 1494 preface is the same text is pure speculation. An additional text entitled *San-fen shih-lüeh* 三分事略 is nearly identical to the *P'ing-hua*. This text is usually dated as a Chih-yüan period printing. Liu Shih-te, however, puts this back to 1294, which would make it a possible prototype of the *P'ing-hua*. See his "T'an San-fen shih-lüeh," pp. 99–111. The *San-fen shih-lüeh* text is available on microfilm in Gest Oriental Library, Princeton, courtesy of Tenri University Library. In comparing the *San-fen* and *P'ing-hua* texts, I have found a few trivial but curious differences. In addition to a larger number of simplified and incorrect characters, this text is missing a few pages in each separate *chüan* (*chüan* 1, pp. 20–22; *chüan* 2, pp. 21–22; and *chüan* 3, pp. 19–21). The illustrations also show some strange discrepancies. For example, the dog in the illustration on p. 1a of the *P'ing-hua* here has his head pointing out from behind the figure rather than inward, and on p. 4a the dog is omitted altogether. Similarly, on p. 7b, the entire background of the engraving is omitted. These details, as well as the cruder workmanship throughout the illustrations, would support the view of this text as a copy of the *P'ing-hua*. See Nagasawa Kikuya, *Shoshigaku ronkō*, pp. 190f.

[33] For such comparisons of the *P'ing-hua* and the *Yen-i* texts, see Sun K'ai-ti, "P'ing-hua yü yen-i," pp. 109–20 (using the *Chih-chuan* text); Cheng Chen-to, "Yen-hua," pp. 176–90; and Boris Riftin, *Istoricheskaya epopeia*, passim (using the Mao Tsung-kang edition).

P'ing-hua as a blueprint for his more elaborate text. But this goal has remained elusive. In fact, Sun K'ai-ti ultimately comes around to emphasizing the novel's "large-scale transformation" 大改舊觀 of the *P'ing-hua*, and even finds himself obliged to posit the existence of an intermediate stage, a hypothetical *San-kuo tz'u-hua* 三國詞話, to account for the gap between the two texts—along the lines of his hypothesis regarding a missing *tz'u-hua* version of *Shui-hu chuan*.[34] From the point of view of my discussion, the difficulty of demonstrating direct textual links between the *P'ing-hua* and the novel is not a problem; on the contrary, it confirms the assertion that it is precisely the transformation of prior narrative materials that distinguishes the four great Ming novels under study here. In the following analysis, therefore, I will have frequent occasion to contrast the treatment of specific figures and events in these two different narrative forms, in order to cast light on the divergent patterns of meaning that emerge when the same heroes come to be treated in the novel.

The assessment of the debt of the novel to preexisting dramatic treatments of the *San-kuo* materials presents a similar case. On the one hand, we have a copious amount of extant dramatic texts that correspond in varying degrees to episodes in the novel, and these are supplemented by a large number of nonextant works described in various bibliographical sources.[35] Since these plays are primarily Yuan pieces in the *tsa-chü* 雜劇 *form*, they

[34] Sun K'ai-ti, "P'ing-hua yü yen-i," pp. 113f., 119. See also Cheng Chen-to, "Yen-hua," p. 186. For the theories regarding a *Shui-hu chuan tz'u-hua*, see above, Chapter 4, Part I, and Chapter 4, b.n. I. Wang Li-ch'i ("Lo Kuan-chung yü yen-i," p. 65) uses the expression "blueprint" to describe this textual relationship.

[35] For lists of the extant and nonextant Yuan and Ming dramas, see Fu Hsi-hua, *Yuan-tai tsa-chü ch'üan-mu*, *Ming-tai ch'uan-ch'i ch'üan-mu*, and *Ming-tai tsa-chü k'ao*, etc. See also Wang P'ei-lun, *Hsi-ch'ü tz'u-tien*. The texts of most of the extant *tsa-chü* on San-kuo themes are conveniently found in the *Ku-pen Yuan-Ming tsa-chü*. These include "The Lone Swordsman Attends a Banquet" (*Tan-tao fu-hui* 單刀赴會), vol. 1, no. 2; "The Banquet at Hsiang-yang" (*Hsiang-yang hui* 襄陽會), vol. 1, no. 4; "Three Duels with Lü Pu" (*San-chan Lü Pu* 三戰呂布), vol. 1, no. 6; "The Yellow Crane Tower" (*Huang-ho lou* 黃鶴樓), vol. 1, no. 7; "A Lone Journey for a Thousand Leagues" (*Ch'ien-li tu-hsing* 千里獨行), vol. 1, no. 8; "Burning the Camp at Po-wang" (*Po-wang shao-t'un* 博望燒屯), vol. 1, no. 8; "The Oath of Brotherhood in the Peach Garden" (*T'ao-yüan chieh-i* 桃園結義), vol. 1, no. 15; "The Lone Swordsman Slashes the Four Bandits" (*Tan-tao p'i ssu-k'ou* 單刀劈四寇), vol. 1, no. 16; "At Hsing-lin Village" (*Hsing-lin chuang* 杏林莊), vol. 1, no. 16; "Single Combat with Lü Pu" (*Tan-chan Lü Pu* 單戰呂布), vol. 1, no. 16; "Three Sorties from Hsiao-p'ei" (*San-ch'u Hsiao-p'ei* 三出小沛), vol. 1, no. 16; "In the Garden of Pomegranates" (*Shih-liu yüan* 石榴園), vol. 1, no. 17; "P'ang T'ung Seizes the Four Commanderies" (*P'ang lüeh ssu-chün* 龐掠四郡), vol. 1, no. 17; "On the Road to Ch'en-ts'ang" (*Ch'en-ts'ang lu* 陳倉路), vol. 1, no. 17; "The Five Horsemen Crush Ts'ao Ts'ao" (*Wu-ma p'o Ts'ao* 五馬破曹), vol. 1, no. 17; "Kuan P'ing Put to Death in Anger" (*Nu-chan Kuan P'ing* 怒斬關平), vol. 1, no. 18; and "Seeking the Hand of Hsiao-Ch'iao" (*Ch'ü Hsiao-Ch'iao* 娶小喬), vol. 1, no. 18. Other *tsa-chü* not included in the *Ku-pen* collection include "The Double Dream Visit" (*Shuang-fu meng* 雙赴夢), full title: "Kuan and Chang March Together to the Dream of Western Shu" 關張雙赴西蜀夢, in

seem again to strengthen the case for fourteenth-century composition closer to the Yuan period.[36] But when one reviews the extant plays, one finds very little in the way of textual overlap that might indicate direct reliance on any of these dramatic works as sources, and even the basic story elements often depart very radically from the narratives of the *Yen-i*.[37]

Once again, my guiding principle here is that it is one thing to discover prior or parallel treatment of the same figures, and quite another to say that such materials represent a direct input into the process of composition. Thus, in my analysis of *San kuo chih yen-i*, the points of comparison I will draw between the novel version and its dramatic precursors will generally aim at bringing out the divergence rather than the conformance of the later text and these "source materials." As I have said, the list of known dramas on *San-kuo* themes contains practically no examples in the full-length *ch'uan-ch'i* form, with the exception of *Lien-huan chi* 連環計 and the Ch'ing work *Ting-chih Ch'un-ch'iu* 鼎峙春秋. This is a bit curious, since we know from the large number of *San-kuo yen-i* editions published from 1522 through the end of the Ming, many in popular format, that there was no flagging of interest in the San-kuo cycles during the heyday of southern drama in the sixteenth century. Perhaps this may be explained by the simple fact that *ch'uan-ch'i* dramatists tend to specialize in romantic themes, especially of the *ts'ai-tzu chia-jen* 才子佳人 type, to the exclusion of heroic historical subjects (just as the colloquial short-story form developing in this period also tends to neglect materials from the storytelling tradition of historical narrative [*chiang-shih* 講史], as something essentially outside of its scope). This does not mean, however, that the connection between the novel *San-kuo chih yen-i* and Ming drama is simply a matter of the common cultural milieu out of which they both emerged. In fact, there are a number

---

Ch'üan Yuan tsa-chü ch'u-pien, pp. 55–67; "A Battle of Wits Across the River" (*Ko-chiang tou-chih* 隔江鬥智), in *Yuan-ch'ü hsüan*, pp. 651–57; "The Linked-ring Plot" (*Lien-huan chi* 連環計)—not the *ch'uan-ch'i* drama of the same name—in *Yuan-ch'ü hsüan*, pp. 771–78; "Honor and Valor Refuse a Reward" (*I-yung tz'u-chin* 義勇辭金), in *Ming-jen tsa-chü hsüan*, pp. 141–68. Sun K'ai-ti provides a partial list of *San-kuo* dramas in "P'ing-hua yü yen-i", pp. 111f., and recently a more complete list of the known dramas on *San-kuo* themes has been compiled by Fang Tsu-shen, "Lo Kuan-chung yü San-kuo chih yen-i," pp. 54–57. The existence of most of the nonextant plays is known from the *Pao-wen t'ang shu-mu*, the *Yeh-shih-yüan shu-mu*, and the *Lu-kuei pu*. For an analytic study of *Tan-tao fu-hui* and *Shuang-fu meng*, see Liu Ching-chih, *Kuan Han-ch'ing San-kuo ku-shih tsa-chü yen-chiu*.

[36] The earliest example of such materials may be a Chin period *yüan-pen* play entitled *Hsiang-yang hui* 襄陽會, cited by Hu Shih in "San-kuo chih yen-i hsü," p. 468.

[37] Mao Tsung-kang points out certain examples of episodes in the *ch'uan-ch'i* dramas known to him that do not correspond to the contents of the novel (e.g., "Kuan Yü Kills Tiao-ch'an" 關公斬貂蟬 and "Chang Fei Captures Chou Yü" 張飛捉周瑜). See his *fan-li* 凡例 introduction, item 10. The former play is listed in Fu Hsi-hua (*Yuan-tai*, p. 362) and is mentioned in the seventeenth-century novel *Hsing-shih yin-yüan chuan* 醒世姻緣傳 (chapter 69).

of points of structural design and patterns of meaning on which *San-kuo* draws upon the conventions of dramatic literature, and the traditional commentators frequently turn to the terminology of drama criticism in their analyses of the novel text.[38]

The main reason so much emphasis has been placed by scholars on the sources of the novel in the *P'ing-hua* and Yuan *tsa-chü* seems to grow out of the common view of *San-kuo chih yen-i* as basically a product of the popular tradition—an idea I tried to refute in the opening chapter of this book. One extremely important counterweight to this view may be found in the far more significant relationship between the *Yen-i* and the extensive body of historiographical materials on the Three Kingdoms period. The title of the 1522 edition proclaims it to be an "elaboration of the meaning" (*yen-i* 演義) of the official dynastic history of the Three Kingdoms: the *San-kuo chih* 三國志, and nearly every preface attached to the various Ming and Ch'ing editions proceeds from the assumption that this is the primary aim of the book.[39] Some recent scholars have gone on to elucidate the relationship between the *San-kuo chih* and the *Yen-i* by comparing specific passages of the two texts.[40] In spite of the key role of the *San-kuo chih* in the conception of the novel, however, examples of actual verbal borrowing, in which it can be demonstrated that the novel bases itself directly on the historical text, are limited to a small number of passages. These include famous lines of dialogue, such as Hsü Shao's prophecy on Ts'ao Ts'ao's career (治世之能臣, 亂世之奸雄), or Liu Pei's deathbed injunction to Chu-ko Liang (若嗣子可輔則輔之, 如其不才, 君可自取), plus capsule biographies, historians' evaluations, and similar passages.[41] In assessing the

---

[38] For example, Mao Tsung-kang uses the term *shou-k'e* 收科 ("concluding speech") in chapters 37 (*chüan* 6, p. 33, hereafter cited as 6:33) and 81 (13:33), refers to Shan Fu 單福 as a *fu-mo* 副末 role in chapter 36 (6:22), and describes the novel's conclusion with the term *sha-wei* 煞尾 ("finale") in chapter 120 (19:50). He also discusses the novel's structure in terms of the dramatic alternation of "union and separation" (*li-ho* 離合) in chapters 51 (8:36) and 58 (10:1). All references to the Mao Tsung-kang text and commentary are taken from the Hong Kong (Shang-wu, 1978) edition, since this is most widely available (see b.n. I. 2).

[39] This is most explicit in the opening section of the Hsiu-jan tzu preface to the 1522 edition. For discussions on the significance of the term *yen-i*, see Wang Li-ch'i, "Lo Kuan-chung yü yen-i," p. 64; C. T. Hsia, *The Classic Chinese Novel*, pp. 38f.; Andrew Lo, "Historiography," pp. 113ff.; and Y. W. Ma, "The Chinese Historical Novel."

[40] See C. T. Hsia, *Classic Novel*, pp. 39f.; Winston L. Y. Yang, "The Literary Transformation of Historical Figures in the *San-kuo chih yen-i*"; and Boris Riftin, *Istoricheskaya epopeia*, pp. 21ff. The "Li Cho-wu" commentator draws comparisons between the "popular *yen-i*" and the "official history" at several points, as for example in a discussion in chapter 21 (12a), where he deplores the novel's change for the worse.

[41] The first line appears in a note in the biography of Ts'ao Ts'ao (Wei Wu-ti 魏武帝) in the *Wei shu* 魏書 section of *San-kuo chih* (1959; reprint ed., Peking: Chung-hua, 1982), 1:3, and in chapter 1 of the *Yen-i* (1:6). The second appears in the biography of Chu-ko Liang in the *Shu shu* section, 4:918, and in the *Yen-i*, in chapter 85 (14:13). For a discussion

debt of the novel to the official history, therefore, we must again bear in mind that it is the former's manipulation—its "fictionalization"—of the historical materials, in conformance with the structural demands of its continuous narrative form, that is the primary area of concern here.[42]

It should be pointed out that besides the tomes of officially sanctioned historiography that serve as sources for the novel, the text also draws on a wide sampling of semiofficial, unofficial, and even popular historical materials. These range from the P'ei Sung-chih 裴松之 commentary on the *San-kuo chih* (which itself draws frequently on such largely pseudo-historical sources as *Ying-hsiung chi* 英雄記 and *Ts'ao Man chuan* 曹瞞傳) to popularized historical verse such as the *yung-shih* 詠史 poems of Hu Tseng 胡曾 and Chou Ching-hsüan 周靜軒 (Chou Li 周禮), as well as echoes of Yang Shen's 楊愼 collection of historical poems in the *t'an-tz'u* 彈詞 form.[43]

An even more direct link than these between the novel and the historiographical tradition, however, can be found in the continuous narratives of the *pien-nien* 編年 chronicle type, namely Ssu-ma Kuang's *Tzu-chih t'ung-chien* 資治通鑑 and Chu Hsi's *Tzu-chih t'ung-chien kang-mu* 資治通鑑綱目 and, to a lesser extent, the topically arranged *T'ung-chien chi-shih pen-mo* 通鑑記事本末 of Yüan Shu. This connection was in fact advertised in the full titles of a number of early editions of the novel, which described them as "collated according to the *Tzu-chih t'ung-chien*" (*an-chien* 按鑑), as well as in discussions in certain prefaces.[44] It seems to be no accident that the

---

of the capsule biographies (what Mao Tsung-kang terms *hsiao-chuan* 小傳), see Riftin, *Istoricheskaya epopeia*, p. 226. I will discuss and translate these historical quotations later in this chapter.

[42] See C. T. Hsia's appreciation of the *Yen-i*'s contribution of fictionalization of its materials, in *Classic Novel*, pp. 35ff.

[43] For a good review of the quasi-historical sources of the *San-kuo chih*, see Rafe de Crespigny, *The Records of the Three Kingdoms*; and Winston L. Y. Yang, "The Use of the San-kuo chih as a Source of the San-kuo chih yen-i." Yang Shen's collection *Li-tai shih-lüeh shih-tuan chin tz'u-hua* 歷代史略十段錦詞話 is available in a modern reprint under the alternate title *Nien-i shih t'an-tz'u chu*. On the adaptation of popularized historical verse in the development of the novel, see Chang Cheng-lang "Chiang-shih yü yung-shih shih"; James Crump, "Ping-hua and San-kuo chih"; and Cheng Chen-to, "Yen-hua," pp. 221f. For an excellent review of these and other materials demonstrating the linkage of the novel to historiography and semipopular versification, see Andrew Lo, "Historiography," pp. 17–20, 231–36. Information about the identification and career of Chou Li may be found in Liu Hsiu-yeh, *Ku-tien hsiao-shuo hsi-ch'ü ts'ung-k'ao*, pp. 66f. Cf. Mao Tsung-kang's explicit reference to the addition of the poems attributed to Chou Li, in his *fan-li* introduction, item 8.

[44] For example, certain Fukien *Chih-chuan* editions and the Lien-hui t'ang *San-kuo chih* (see Sun K'ai-ti, *Shu-mu*, p. 37f.). Cf. 1494 preface and Lien-hui t'ang preface. Andrew Lo ("Historiography," p. 19) discusses a reference to Lü Tsu-ch'ien's 呂祖謙 *Hou Han shu hsiang-chieh* 後漢書詳解 in an interlinear note of the 1522 edition. For further discussion of the term *an-chien*, see Wang Li-ch'i, "Lo Kuan-chung yü yen-i," p. 66.

publication of the earliest extant edition of the novel followed on the heels of a period that saw a number of relatively popular printings of *Tzu-chih t'ung-ch'ien* and the *T'ung-chien kang-mu,* including editions and commentaries by Chou Li, the same Chou Ching-hsüan whose *yung-shih* poems also appear in many later editions of the novel, and by Yin Chih, whose writing is also quoted in the 1522 edition of *San-kuo t'ung-su yen-i.*[45] The role of these materials in the evolution of the novel has recently been explored in detail by Andrew Hing-bun Lo, who has established convincingly that it is the *Kang-mu* in particular that leaves its imprint on the *Yen-i,* both in its segmentation of the historical continuity of the raw material into units of episode length, a matter I will return to shortly, and in its adoption of the unsentimental evaluative standards associated with the *Ch'un-ch'iu* classic.[46]

Much of the critical discussion of the *Yen-i,* from Ming times to the present day, has centered on the extent to which the novel is judged to be faithful or unfaithful to the historical facts, as reconstructed from the *cheng-shih* 正史 and *pien-nien* historiographical sources. For example, Chang Hsüeh-ch'eng 章學誠, writing in the eighteenth century, credits the novel with fidelity to historical truth in the major portion of the work (七分 實事, 三分虛構), although he faults it in another place for its mixing of fact and fancy. More recently, Sun K'ai-ti has argued that even the "factual" parts of the text are loaded with fiction, while C. T. Hsia, as noted, points precisely to this "fictionalization" as the primary achievement of the work.[47] Within the context of the present study, however, the departure of the *Yen-i* from its sources, both historical and ahistorical, is taken as a consequence of the degree of structural manipulation demanded by the emerging novel genre. I will attempt to show in this chapter that these formal transformations are also linked to a changing historical consciousness, one I would like to interpret against the background of the intellectual developments of the later Ming period. Although the explicit connection between *San-kuo chih yen-i* and historiography per se make it a uniquely "historical" novel, we will see that the specific historical issues that emerge in the text in fact link it all the more closely with *Shui-hu chuan, Chin P'ing Mei,* and even *Hsi-yu chi,* as members of the same literary class.[48]

In the remainder of this chapter I will attempt to support my contention

[45] See Liu Hsiu-yeh, *Ku-tien hsiao-shuo,* pp. 66–67; and Andrew Lo, "Historiography," pp. 17–20, 231–36, esp. 20.

[46] See Andrew Lo, "Historiography," pp. 42–48. Mao Tsung-kang refers explicitly to the *T'ung-chien kang-mu* in comments in chapters 69 (11:40) and 73 (12:22).

[47] For Chang Hsüeh-ch'eng's remarks, see *Ping-ch'en cha-chi,* p. 63b (citation in K'ung Ling-ching, *Shih-liao,* p. 44). See also Sun K'ai-ti, "P'ing-hua yü yen-i," p. 117; and C. T. Hsia, *Classic Novel,* pp. 35ff.

[48] See Chapter 6 of this book for a discussion of the treatment of historical issues in the four novels.

that *San-kuo chih yen-i* should be read not as a popular narrative but as a serious, often ironic revision of its various sources, through a detailed structural and interpretive analysis of the text as compared with corresponding *p'ing-hua, tsa-chü,* and historiographical versions of the same narrative material. In doing so, I will base my analysis primarily on the 1522 text and the mid-seventeenth-century Mao Tsung-kang edition, but I will also draw upon the following late Ming and early Ch'ing editions: the "Li Cho-wu" commentary edition, the "Li Yü" commentary edition, and the less familiar *San-kuo chih-chuan, San-kuo ch'üan-chuan, San-kuo chih-chuan p'ing-lin,* and *Lien-hui t'ang ch'ih-ti yü-pien,* plus a Ch'ung-chen period text printed in one edition of the *Ying-hsiung p'u.*[49] I have already mentioned the fact that the basic text of the *San-kuo chih-chuan,* which Liu Ts'un-yan has attempted to link to the hypothetical Lo Kuan-chung text, does not actually differ from the 1522 edition on other than minor points; and it can also be shown that all of the other editions listed here derive directly from the 1522 edition (or else some common prototype).[50]

The only text that does present significant differences from the basic text is the Mao Tsung-kang commentary edition. The changes introduced by Mao, as enumerated in his introductory remarks (*fan-li* 凡例), amount mostly to minor alterations of detail, although they also include the re-organization of certain larger textual units: cutting and substitution of poems, changing of many chapter titles, correction of factual errors, and cutting, insertion, or deletion of certain episodes.[51] Mao, as I have pointed out, describes his work as a deliberate reaction against the "popular edition(s)" (*su-pen* 俗本)—from his description, this appears to mean something like the text put out by the Fukien publisher Cheng I-chen—and a return to what he calls the "original edition" (*ku-pen* 古本)—perhaps the 1522 text?[52] I will make mention of the changes made by Mao wherever

---

[49] For detailed information on the texts used for this study, see b.n. I.

[50] See Cheng Chen-to, "Yen-hua," pp. 213–23, for a full exposition of this point. See above, n. 14.

[51] *San-kuo chih yen-i,* Mao Tsung-kang edition (hereafter MTK), *fan-li,* pp. 1–2. For a translation and discussion of Mao's introduction, see Andrew Lo, "Historiography," pp. 27–38.

[52] According to the description in items 5, 6, 7, and 8 of the *fan-li,* Mao's *su-pen* was marred by such things as uneven chapter divisions without parallel chapter-title couplets, by a commentary spuriously attributed to Li Chih—including disparaging remarks against Liu Pei and Chu-ko Liang—and the insertion of unpolished verses by Chou Ching-hsüan. This description seems to correspond most closely with the late Ming *Hsin-chüan chiao-cheng ching-pen ta-tzu yin-shih ch'üan-tien San-kuo chih yen-i* 新鐫校正京本大字音釋圈點三國志演義, edited by Cheng I-chen 鄭以楨 (last character written 禎 in Cheng Chen-to, "Yen-hua," p. 212), which bears a commentary attributed to Li Chih and numerous Chou Ching-hsüan poems, but is not divided into 120 *hui* as are the other "Li Cho-wu" editions. (See Sun K'ai-ti, *Shu-mu,* p. 37; and Cheng Chen-to, "Yen-hua," pp. 209, 212, 223.) Of course, Mao

relevant to my discussion, but in spite of such differences it is still true that, as far as literary analysis is concerned, the 1522 edition, the Mao edition, and even the other more popular editions all represent the same basic text.

Before moving on, at last, to my promised analysis of the ways in which the novel conforms to the structural model established for *Chin P'ing Mei*, *Hsi-yu chi*, and *Shui-hu chuan*, I must make one final interruption to acknowledge the fact that our ability to appreciate both the larger-scale structural design and the smaller compositional patterns in *San-kuo* is once again largely indebted to one particular traditional critic: in this case, Mao Tsung-kang.[53] Mao, like Chin Sheng-t'an and Chang Chu-p'o, is in fact only building upon an existing body of commentary editions, such as those attributed to the flamboyant literary figures Li Chih and Chung Hsing, and later to Li Yü.[54] Moreover, even the 1522 edition, it should be noted,

---

may be referring to some other *Min-pen* edition no longer extant. Mao also mentions the *su-pen* in a number of textual comments, e.g., in chapters 21 (4:1) and 26 (4:38). Cheng Chen-to ("Yen-hua," pp. 224f.) also agrees that the changes introduced by Mao are of minor significance, and he goes on (p. 236) to deny Mao's claim of having based himself on an earlier *ku-pen*. See also Sun K'ai-ti, "P'ing-hua yü yen-i," p. 119; Fang Tsu-shen, "Lo Kuan-chung yü yen-i," p. 50; and Tung Mei-k'an, *Shih-lun*, p. 3, for comparisons of the 1522 and Mao Tsung-kang texts. One particular, albeit minor, point of substance on which the various early editions of *San-kuo* differ is the introduction of Kuan Yü's son Kuan So 關索. See n. 410, for a discussion of this point.

[53] In granting Mao Tsung-kang the credit for this contribution we must acknowledge that the project of composing the *San-kuo* commentary was apparently begun by his father, Mao Lun 毛綸. The prevailing scholarly opinion does, however, conclude that the lion's share of the work was completed by the son. See Andrew Lo, "Historiography," p. 339, n. 25; C. T. Hsia, *Classic Novel*, pp. 37, 332, n. 7; and Huang Lin, "Yu-kuan Mao-pen San-kuo yen-i ti jo-kan wen-t'i." See also David Rolston, ed., *How to Read the Chinese Novel*, Introduction. A full translation of Mao's *tu-fa* by David Roy is included in this volume.

[54] As in the case of the "Li Cho-wu" commentary editions of *Hsi-yu chi* and *Shui-hu chuan* considered earlier (see Chapter 3, n. 83, and the Appendix), most modern scholars dismiss this attribution out of hand, most often accepting the theory that the *Li Cho-wu hsien-sheng p'i-p'ing San-kuo chih yen-i* commentary is also a forgery by Yeh Chou 葉晝, or some similar contemporary of Li Chih (see, for example, Lu Lien-hsing, "Li Chih p'i-p'ing San-kuo yen-i pien-wei"; and Huang Lin, "Mao-pen," p. 335, both of whom note the appearance of Yeh Chou's name in comments in chapters 96, 105, and 117). I have noted in my discussion of the question of the authorship of the Jung-yü t'ang 容與堂 commentary on *Shui-hu*, however, that the revised attribution to Yeh Chou is itself based on shaky evidence. (See Appendix). On the other side of the picture, certain points in this commentary, such as a reference to Matteo Ricci in chapter 59 (10b), an expression of indignation at Liu Pei's execution of Liu Feng in chapter 79 (10b) that seems to reflect some of Li's personal frustration, and a variety of irreverent expressions (e.g., chapter 86[12a–b] and chapter 90[14a]) lead me to entertain the possibility that this might conceivably be the work of Li Chih himself. In that case, the fact that the form and terms of these critical comments closely parallel those in the other "Li Cho-wu" novel texts, as well as the critical style in the *Shih-kang p'ing-yao* (another

contains mixed among its generally factual interlinear notes a certain number of comments of a critical nature, some of which I will refer to below.[55]

Although these earlier commentaries already use some of the critical terminology later applied by Mao, and they contain, as we will see below, quite a few gems of insight (amidst much dross), Mao Tsung-kang still deserves the credit for going far beyond his predecessors, perhaps even farther than Chin Sheng-t'an and Chang Chu-p'o, in his exploration of the structural complexities of the literary novel form. Recently, students of *San-kuo* have begun to take more seriously Mao's programmatic introductory essay "How to Read the *San-kuo chih*" ("Tu San-kuo chih fa" 讀三國志法), in which he develops the categories of structural analysis introduced by Chin Sheng-t'an in his earlier *tu-fa* essay (and later taken up again by Chang Chu-p'o) in fuller detail and with more cogent examples.[56] But the most impressive contribution of Mao Tsung-kang lies in his chapter discussions and line-by-line commentary, and these have unfortunately remained underexploited by most modern readers.[57] As we proceed with our analysis of *San-kuo* with Mao at our elbow, many of his comments will

---

doubtful attribution, but one which is more often accepted as the work of Li Chih), may further support this possibility. For an argument against accepting the *Shih-kang p'ing-yao* commentary as genuine, see Ts'ui Wen-yin, "Problems Concerning the Authenticity of the *Shih-kang p'ing-yao*," pp. 125–51, 169f. Or, perhaps the existing editions purporting to present the commentary of Li Chih in fact represent the work of more than one writer in successive accretions. For example, in chapter 85 the "Li Cho-wu" commentary expresses first strong praise (p. 5b), then immediately afterward sharp condemnation (p. 14a), of Liu Pei's deathbed injunction to Chu-ko Liang. As for the seventeenth-century edition attributed to Li Yü, Ogawa Tamaki has argued that this commentary is spurious and is based on the Mao Tsung-kang commentary. See his "Sankoku engi no Mō Seizan hihyōbon to Ri Ryūōbon." To be fair, we should note that the editor of this text freely acknowledges his debt to Mao Tsung-kang in the preface. The fact that Li Yü and Mao Tsung-kang were associated with the same literary circles makes it not inconceivable for Li Yü to have composed this commentary, although there is no factual basis for this assumption. In any event, the commentary includes a significant number of points of interest not borrowed from Mao Tsung-kang that are worth considering in their own right. See Cheng Chen-to, "Yen-hua," p. 236.

[55] For examples of comments of a critical nature among the 1522 edition interlinear notes, see *chüan* 3, p. 12b (hereafter cited as 3:12b), 5:19b–20a, and others below. The next earliest commentary edition of the novel now extant appears to be the 1592 *San-kuo chih-chuan p'ing-lin*. See Sun K'ai-ti, *Shu-mu*, p. 37f.; and Cheng Chen-to, "Yen-hua," p. 215.

[56] For translation and discussion of the *tu-fa*, see David T. Roy, "How to Read the Romance of the Three Kingdoms," in Rolston, *How to Read*; Winston Yang and Robert Ruhlmann have also translated portions of this essay into English. See Boris Riftin's analysis in *Istoricheskaya epopeia*, pp. 231ff.; and Yeh Lang, *Chung-kuo hsiao-shuo mei-hsüeh*, pp. 143ff.

[57] For example, Cheng Chen-to dismisses the importance of Mao's interlinear commentary in "Yen-hua," p. 235. A similar evaluation is given by Wu Chien-li, "San-kuo yen-i k'ao-shu," p. 22. For the influence of Chin Sheng-t'an on Mao, see Huang Lin, "Mao-pen," p. 341.

help to deepen our understanding of the sophisticated degree of textual manipulation that marks the *San-kuo chih yen-i* as an early example of the self-conscious artistry of the sixteenth-century novel form.

II

To begin this review of the structural design of *San-kuo*, we may note with regard to the overall dimensions of the book that it is in all cases divided into 240 discrete narrative units.[58] This common denominator, however, still leaves considerable room for variation between editions. The 1522 edition, for example, is arranged into twenty-four *chüan* 卷 volumes of ten items each, combined in certain later Wan-li editions into twelve *chüan* of twenty items each; in the *Chih-chuan*, the *Chih-chuan p'ing-lin*, the *Ch'üan-chuan*, the *Ying-hsiung p'u*, and other texts this total number of units is reshuffled into twenty *chüan* of twelve items each.[59] It is not until the Wan-li period, in certain "Li Cho-wu" commentary editions, that these 240 basic units are organized into 120 double-item *hui* chapters, the format later taken over in the Mao Tsung-kang and "Li Yü" editions to yield the familiar shape of all modern editions.[60] This 120-chapter length obviously diverges from the 100-chapter basic length of *Chin P'ing Mei*, *Hsi-yu chi*, and the *fan-pen* 繁本 *Shui-hu chuan*. But for the purposes of the present argument, I will still maintain that the 120-chapter outline embodies the same aesthetic sense of symmetry and comprehensiveness as the 100-chapter length of the other examples.[61]

The basic commensurability of the structural outlines of *San-kuo* with those of the other three novels under study here comes into clearer focus when we turn our attention to the manner in which the text breaks down into smaller units. Here, too, the earliest extant editions of the novel

[58] The sole possible exception is the edition described in the *Pai-ch'uan shu-chih* (p. 82) as containing "two hundred and four *chüan*" 二百四卷, although this is surely an error for "two hundred and forty." (See also K'ung Ling-ching, *Shih-liao*, p. 40.)

[59] See Sun K'ai-ti, *Shu-mu*, pp. 35–44. One rare edition described by Sun (*Shu-mu*, p. 41) divides its 240 *tse* sections into only six *chüan*-units. The reference in Liu Jo-yü's *Cho chung chih* (see above, n. 8) speaks of "twenty volumes" (*erh-shih pen* 二十本). Cf. Ogawa Tamaki's discussion of three basic recensions of the novel: twenty-*chüan*, twelve-*chüan*, and 120-*hui* (in "Kan Saku no densetsu," pp. 165ff.). See Liu Ts'un-yan, *Chinese Popular Fiction in Two London Libraries*, pp. 20f., for a general discussion of the textual divisions of early editions of Chinese fiction.

[60] Mao Tsung-kang's *chüan* divisions will be considered later in this chapter.

[61] Sun K'ai-ti ("P'ing-hua yü yen-i," p. 118) suggests that there may have been only 100 or so basic units at an earlier stage of development. Apparently, the 120-chapter *Shui-hu chuan* published by Yüan Wu-yai in 1614 comes around the same time as the consolidation of the 120-*hui* format for *San-kuo* toward the end of the Ming.

are divided into the same sort of ten-item (or twenty-item) units (that is, the equivalent of five- or ten-chapter *chüan*) that we have noted in the early editions of *Shui-hu chuan*, *Hsi-yu chi*, and *Chin P'ing Mei*.

Once again, we find that these technical divisions are borne out in the internal rhythms of the narrative itself.[62] For example, using for convenience of reference the chapter numbers of the later 120-*hui* editions (as I will continue to do throughout the remainder of this discussion), we observe in chapter 9 the neat conclusion of the rise and fall of Tung Cho 董卓, which occupies the center of attention throughout the first ten-chapter decade; and the same pattern repeats with the second decade revolving around the story of Lü Pu 呂布, culminating in his dramatic end in chapter 19. Later on, the climactic events of chapter 49 bring to a head the first brilliant phase of Chu-ko Liang's official service launched at Po-wang p'o 博望坡 in chapter 39, in the same way that the demise of Ts'ao Ts'ao 曹操 and the ensuing confusion of chapters 78 and 79 clearly mark a major structural division in the narrative. As further markers of this sort of periodic movement, one might cite the formal recognition of Liu Pei's 劉備 rise to prominence in chapter 20, his final takeover of I-chou 益州 in chapter 60, and his assumption of the Han throne, on the heels of the crowning of the first Wei emperor, in chapter 80. Granted, the ten-chapter rhythms in *San-kuo* are far less pronounced or consistently articulated than in *Chin P'ing Mei* (but perhaps even more so than in *Shui-hu chuan*). Still, enough evidence does exist to convince me that the text is, in fact, designed around such a structural framework.[63]

Curiously, Mao Tsung-kang seems to disregard the ten- or twelve-chapter *chüan* arrangement of the earlier editions, dividing his text into sixty *chüan* of two chapters each. Moreover, a number of extant "Mao Tsung-kang" editions completely abandon the compositional symmetry of such arrangements, organizing the 120 *hui* into nineteen *chüan* containing from five to seven chapters each, which only coincide with the divisions of the 1522 text at occasional points.[64] Unless perhaps this uneven division

[62] Mao Tsung-kang occasionally uses the term "summation" (*tsung-chieh* 總結) to describe the function of wrapping up this short of periodic division in the novel.

[63] The visible articulation of this ten-chapter rhythm in the text also seems to shed a special significance on the midpoint of each such division, that is, around the fourth and fifth chapters of each decade. Thus, we see Liu Pei isolated and on the threshold of ruin precisely at the close of chapters 14, 24, and 34, and we witness the downfall of a succession of great heroes in chapters 75–77, 85, and 104.

[64] For examples of this type of text, see the following editions: *Ssu ta ch'i-shu ti-i-chung* 四大奇書第一種 (Shan-ch'eng t'ang edition 善成堂), in Peking Metropolitan Library; Tsao-ssu t'ang edition 藻思堂, held in Sinologisch Instituut Library, Leiden (see Andrew Lo, "Historiography," p. 263); and two Korean printings listed in the *Ming-Ch'ing shan-pen hsiao-shuo ts'ung-k'an* 明清善本小說叢刊 catalogue, p. 25. The Hong Kong reprint used for textual references in this study also follows a 19-*chüan* format. In this arrangement, *chüan* 3

is adopted simply to equalize the length of the *chüan*-units for printing purposes, the reasoning involved is not at all clear. Mao himself, in his introductory analysis of the structure of the novel, discusses what he sees as "six beginnings and six conclusions" (*liu-ch'i liu-chieh* 六起六結) forming the structural skeleton of the novel, but these divisions have no real correspondence to this *chüan* arrangement.[65] We should also note here that the twelve-chapter *chüan*-units in most of the *Min-pen* editions also show less concern for the ten-chapter structural rhythms described here (although at least this arrangement does yield a ten-*chüan* book). Recalling the fact that some of the physically similar and genetically related *chien-pen* editions of *Shui-hu chuan* also stray from the structural clarity of the hundred-chapter basic length of the *fan-pen* recension, I would suggest that these divergences represent a later phase of the development of the novel, in which some of the formal features of the genre were either submerged in more popular printings, or were subjected to the strong-minded editorial whims of critics such as Chin Sheng-t'an and Mao Tsung-kang.

Besides the division of the novel into periodic movements corresponding to the *chüan* divisions of the text, we can also perceive several other broad structural configurations reminiscent of the overall shape of the other three works. We have seen the manner in which the authors of *Chin P'ing Mei* and *Hsi-yu chi* divide their texts into two distinct halves, pivoting around a midpoint in chapters 49 and 50 that presents a significant culmination of the plot development of the first half, while also giving way to a sense of the recapitulation of the opening phases of the work.[66] When

---

ends at chapter 20, *chüan* 11 ends at chapter 69, *chüan* 14 ends at chapter 89, right at the peak of the Meng Huo campaign, *chüan* 16 ends at chapter 100, and, of course, the final *chüan* ends at chapter 120.

[65] In the nineteen-*chüan* arrangement, *chüan* 6 does mark out quite neatly the structural unit depicting Liu Pei's relations with Hsü Shu and the subsequent employment of Chu-ko Liang, but several other *chüan* break off abruptly in the middle of extended episodes. For example, *chüan* 4 ends with chapter 26, halfway through the episode of Kuan Yü's sojourn with Ts'ao Ts'ao; *chüan* 8 continues past the climactic point of chapter 50 to end after chapter 51, well into the first of the "enraged three times" sequence; *chüan* 12 ends abruptly at chapter 76, in the midst of Kuan Yü's gripping downfall; and *chüan* 13 leaves off at chapter 83, at the height of the revenge campaign (see also n. 64). But this pattern of ending *chüan* divisions at points of suspense in the action is also not consistently observed. Mao's *tu-fa* discussion of beginnings and conclusions is found in item 6 (MTK, *tu-fa*, p. 4f.). One possible explanation of the 19-*chüan* arrangement might be that these nineteen "volumes" plus an additional *chüan* of prefatory pieces would yield a proper 20-*chüan* fictional text. This is apparently what was done in the Korean printings mentioned in the previous note. This would also parallel Chin Sheng-t'an's combining of seventy-one one-*hui chüan* plus four prefatory *chüan* to produce his seventy-five-*chüan* Kuan-hua t'ang edition.

[66] This pattern parallels the use of the so-called "minor finale" (*hsiao shou-sha* 小收煞) in *ch'uan-ch'i* drama—a miniature reunion scene falling precisely at the midpoint of the dramatic text. See above, Chapters 2, Part II, and 3, Part II.

the reader of *San-kuo* reaches chapter 60, he again finds himself at a comparable point in the narrative. Ts'ao Ts'ao has reached the peak of his power over the first half of the book and is beginning to show signs of weariness, and Liu Pei has also finally attained, with the conquest of I-chou, the safe power base that had eluded him ever since the start of the novel. At this point, the author reveals his awareness that he has reached the point of a second beginning by adding a number of specific details that hark back to the opening of the story. For example, the uprising of Chang Lu 張魯 precisely in chapters 59 and 60, so reminiscent of the revolt of the Yellow Turbans that launched the narrative action in chapter 1, and the recalling of the Peach Garden oath shortly thereafter, seem to deliberately turn the reader's thoughts back to the beginning of the first half of the book.[67]

Since the greater length of *San-kuo* obviously leaves its midpoint ten chapters later than that of *Chin P'ing Mei* and *Hsi-yu chi*, it is interesting that the climactic watershed of the plot of *San-kuo*, the Battle at the Red Cliffs, falls precisely in chapters 49 and 50. One might say that the positioning of this event in the narrative is to a certain extent conditioned by the fixed chronology of the historical records. But at the very least, I would like to suggest that the highlighting of the fifty-chapter mark in *Chin P'ing Mei* and *Hsi-yu chi*, for their part, is modeled on this structural division in *San-kuo*.

Another instance of such modeling is seen in the fact that in *Chin P'ing Mei* the gruesome death of Hsi-men Ch'ing—hounded by visions of guilt after a life of gross self-indulgence—is narrated almost precisely at the point reserved for Ts'ao Ts'ao's death scene in *San-kuo*.[68] This instance of imitation is especially noteworthy as it brings to light a common pattern of structure in the Chinese novel, already apparent in *San-kuo*, whereby the phases of the gradual gathering of forces and the unfolding of the mimetic world of the novel pass a watershed around the midpoint, and reach the point of greatest fullness around two-thirds or three-fourths of the way through the text, after which the process is reversed and attention is shifted to the gradual dismantling of the stage and the dispersal of the principal players.[69] Thus, in terms of structure, the death of Ts'ao Ts'ao in chapter 78

---

[67] Mao Tsung-kang dryly notes the parallel between Chang Chiao 張角 and Chang Lu 張魯 in a comment in chapter 59 (MTK, 10:9). Similarly, the opening line of chapter 51 (8:37) recalls the Peach Garden oath back in chapter 1.

[68] This model is already evident in the opening parody of the Peach Garden brotherhood staged in chapter 1 of the Ch'ung-chen recension of the *Chin P'ing Mei*, and chapter 10 of the *Tz'u-hua* version.

[69] For a fuller discussion of this point, see my "Towards a Critical Theory of Chinese Narrative," in *Chinese Narrative*, pp. 338f. Mao Tsung-kang frequently discusses this pattern in terms of the conventional expressions "gathering and dispersal" (*chü-san* 聚散) and "separation and reunion" (*li-ho*), commonly applied to dramatic structure. Cf. n. 38. Within

of *San-kuo* marks the anchor of a phase in which a number of the central figures pass away in rapid succession: Kuan Yü first in chapter 77, Chang Fei 張飛 in chapter 81, and Liu Pei in chapter 85. Although Chu-ko Liang continues to dominate the stage for another twenty chapters, his death in chapter 104 also leaves a lengthy final section of fifteen chapters in which noticeably lesser men play out the conclusion of the drama.

With regard to the use of structural units on a smaller order of magnitude, one particular characteristic of *San-kuo chih yen-i* is its frequent framing of numbered sequences of events. In sequences such as "Chou Yü is enraged three times" (*san-ch'i Chou Yü* 三氣周瑜), "Meng Huo is captured seven times" (*ch'i-ch'in Meng Huo* 七擒孟獲), "[Chu-ko Liang] marches forth from Ch'i-shan six times" (*liu-ch'u Ch'i-shan* 六出祁山), and "[Chiang Wei] launches nine campaigns against the Central Plain" (*chiu-fa chung-yüan* 九伐中原), the author is clearly interested in the aesthetic effect of suspenseful retardation in working out the individual episodes, since he could just as easily have dismissed each of these series with one or two vivid examples. Mao Tsung-kang notes the structural significance of such sequences and distinguishes between continuous treatment (*lien* 連), as in the Meng Huo series, and discontinuous treatment (*tuan* 斷), as in the Chou Yü series.[70] In addition, we also find in *San-kuo* the use of the three- or four-chapter episodes we observed in *Shui-hu chuan*, even clearer in *Hsi-yu chi*. For example, the section in chapters 25–27 dealing with Kuan Yü's captivity and escape clearly comprises an independent structural unit— reminiscent of the independent cycle devoted exclusively to Wu Sung 武松 in chapters 23–32 of *Shui-hu*; and the text later shifts its focus back to Kuan Yü for the similarly self-contained episode of his final heroics and downfall in chapters 73–76.[71]

This brings us to the single narrative units that form the basic building blocks out of which every edition of the work is constructed. As we have seen, the combination of these separate headings (*mu* 目) into double-item *hui* chapters was a late development in the evolution of *San-kuo*, as it was in the history of the Chinese novel in general.[72] This later conception of two-

---

the outlines of the *San-kuo* narrative, the former term is a more accurate description than the latter. Cf. Mao Tsung-kang's addition of the line "What has long been united must be divided ...." (*fen chiu pi ho* 分久必合) at the head of the text, to be considered later in this chapter.

[70] The "Li Cho-wu" commentator expands on the principle of numbered sequences in a chapter-commentary (*tsung-p'i*, hereafter *tp*) in chapter 115 (p. 10a). For Mao's distinction between continuous and discontinuous sequences, see *tu-fa*, item 12, p. 9.

[71] Mao refers to the former sequence as a separate "biography" (*chuan* 傳) of Kuan Yü (MTK, 5:1). See Riftin, *Istoricheskaya epopeia*, p. 226.

[72] This fact is reflected in item 5 of Mao Tsung-kang's *fan-li* preface. See n. 59. Cheng Chen-to uses the term "section" (*chieh* 節) to refer to these single narrative units ("Yen-hua,"

part chapters labeled with chapter titles in the form of parallel couplets, emphasizing the underlying parallelism of the narrative elements conjoined therein, is in itself of major importance for the subsequent development of the aesthetics of the Chinese novel. But for my analysis of structure here it will be more useful to focus attention on the single narrative units, the *mu*, which have special significance for a number of reasons.

First, an investigation of these *mu*-units in the early editions of *San-kuo chih yen-i* gives us further insight into the relationship between the novel and its "popular" sources. The use of a seven-character line, normally naming the central figure and action of the section, apparently follows the practice in Yuan *tsa-chü* of taking a seven-character line from the concluding couplet (sometimes known as *hsia-ch'ang shih* 下場詩) for use as the title of the piece (although later this is generally abbreviated to a three-, four-, or five-character title). When we compare the *mu* titles of the 1522 edition with the titles of extant and known dramas based on the Three Kingdoms cycles, we find a total of 15 out of 240 that show an exact correspondence.[73] This intersection between narrative fiction and drama is even more striking in the *P'ing-hua*, where ten out of the forty *mu* headings inserted into the extant fourteenth-century printing reproduce known Yuan *tsa-chü* titles.[74] Here, moreover, nearly all of the titles appear in their more popular, abbreviated forms.

It is worth noting, by the way, that many of the *mu*-units shared in this way represent a common pool of stock episodes that occur in many other works of fiction and drama. For example, the many *San-kuo* plays and fictional episodes based on the triple occurrence of a pattern of events— "Three duels with Lü Pu" (*San-chan Lü Pu* 三戰呂布), "Three retreats from Hsü-chou" (*San-jang Hsü-chou* 三讓徐州), "Chi-p'ing is interrogated three times" (*San-k'an Chi P'ing* 三勘吉平), "Chang Fei is enraged three times" (*San-ch'i Chang Fei* 三氣張飛), "Chou Yü is enraged three times" (*San-ch'i*

---

p. 209). More recently, Boris Riftin (*Istoricheskaya epopeia*, p. 205ff.) has applied to these units the Russian formalist term "plot move" (*sjužetnij khod*).

[73] These are chapters 1a, 桃園結義; 5b, 三戰呂布; 12a, 三讓徐州; 19b, 白門曹操斬呂布; 23b, 三勘吉平; 25b, 刺顏良; 27a, 千里獨行; 28b, 五關斬將; 34a, 襄陽赴會; 37a, 三顧草廬; 39b, 博望燒屯; 63b, 義釋嚴顏; 66a, 單刀赴會; 79a, 七步成章; 84a, 夜走白帝城; and 104a, 五丈原. See Andrew Lo, "Historiography," Appendix II-C, pp. 318–23.

[74] *San-kuo chih p'ing-hua*, p. 378, 三戰呂布; 379, 獨戰呂布; 386, 三出小沛; 391, 白門斬呂布; 395, 曹操勘吉平; 400, 刺顏良; 404, 千里獨行; 406, 斬蔡陽; 407, 古城聚義; and 427, 赤壁鏖兵. See Andrew Lo, "Historiography," Appendix II-B, pp. 307–17; and Sun K'ai-ti, "P'ing-hua yü yen-i," pp. 111ff. Of course, this sort of comparison overlooks the more numerous instances in which the narrative content overlaps without identical titles (what Sun calls *yu shih wu mu* 有事無目). The 1610 *Chih-chuan* adds captions to its illustrations (as do many other *Min-pen* texts, such as the 1596 *Ch'üan-chuan*) that frequently correspond to the abbreviated episode titles of *tsa-chü* drama and the *P'ing-hua*.

Chou Yü 三氣周瑜), "Three sorties from Hsiao-P'ei" (*San-ch'u Hsiao-P'ei* 三出小沛), "Three visits to the thatched hut" (*San-ku ts'ao-lu* 三顧草廬)—obviously rely upon the common "trebling effect" observed by scholars of folklore and popular literature.[75] In the Chinese tradition, the framing of certain episodes in terms of such stock *topoi* as the hero who "wreaks great havoc" (*ta-nao* 大鬧) is a pattern we have already noted for its frequent occurrence in *Shui-hu* and *Hsi-yu* materials.[76] From this perspective we may see here evidence of the 1522 edition backing away, so to speak, from its popular sources in its comparatively limited use of such formulaic patterns.

At the same time, we can also see in the framing of the single narrative units of the *San-kuo chih yen-i* the clear influence of the *Tzu-chih t'ung-chien kang-mu*, referred to earlier. Comparing the *Kang-mu* entries for the Three Kingdoms period with the *mu* headings in the 1522 edition, we find a number of instances in which the wording in the novel comes fairly close to that of the historical text, as for example in chapters 12 (second half), 25 (second half), 56 (first half), 65 (second half) 66 (second half), 62 (both halves), and 73 (first half).[77] In the second line of his *hui* title for chapter 65, Mao Tsung-kang conspicuously revises one term of the 1522 title in order to reproduce more exactly the *Kang-mu*'s original wording.[78] Although it must be admitted that such clear examples of borrowing account for only a small number of cases, still it can be seen that the novel, in a looser sense, does follow the outline of events in the *T'ung-chien kang-mu* for a large portion of its narrative skeleton.

In reviewing the sixteenth-century texts *Chin P'ing Mei* and *Hsi-yu chi*, as well as the *fan-pen Shui-hu chuan*, I assigned special structural significance to

[75] See above, n. 35 for extant texts of these plays. For discussion of the "trebling" effect, see Vladimir Propp, *The Morphology of the Folktale*, pp. 74f.

[76] See above, Chapters 3 and 4, Part II. Mao Tsung-kang's revision of the title of chapter 42 inserts the term *ta-nao*. The expression also appears in the full title of the Yuan drama: *Mang Chang Fei ta-nao Shih-liu yüan* 莽張飛大鬧石榴園. Other examples of stock *topoi* shared by the fiction and drama traditions include "attending a banquet" (*fu-hui* 赴會), as in the plays *Tan-tao fu-hui* and *Hsiang-yang hui*, and "single-handed combat" or "lone journey" (*tu-chan* 獨戰, *tu-hsing* 獨行), as in the episodes *Ch'ien-li tu-hsing* and *Chang Fei tu-chan Lü Pu*.

[77] For example, chapter 12b, 曹操定陶破呂布, follows the *Tzu-chih t'ung-chien kang-mu* (hereafter TCTCKM) entry: 二年春正月曹操敗呂布於定陶 (cited from Chu Hsi, *Yü-p'i tzu-chih t'ung-chien kang-mu*, 13:9a); chapter 66b, 曹操杖殺伏皇后, follows TCTCKM 14:28a: 十一月, 魏公操殺皇后伏氏及皇子二人; chapter 72a, 劉玄德智取漢中, follows TCTCKM 14:42b: 夏五月, 操引還, 備遂取漢中; chapter 72b, 曹孟德忌殺楊修, follows TCTCKM 14:45a: 魏王操殺丞相主簿; and chapter 73a, 劉備進位漢中王, follows TCTCKM 14:43b: 秋七月, 劉備自立爲漢中王. For a fuller comparison of 1522-edition chapter titles and TCTCKM entries, see Andrew Lo, "Historiography," pp. 44–49, 52ff., and Appendix II-A, pp. 271–306.

[78] In this case 劉玄德平定益州 is changed to 劉備自領益州牧.

the opening and closing sections of the texts. In *San-kuo chih yen-i* this function is more attenuated due to the framework of historical chronology that demarcates the beginning and end of the San-kuo period. But we can still see in the opening pages of the 1522 text—with its general description of the state of the Han empire in its final reigns—something of the prologue function that was defined in the context of the other three novels; that is, setting up a generalized pattern of significance for the interpretation of the work as a whole, while also setting in motion the chain of causality that leads into the body of the narrative. From this point of view, we see that the section right before the event signalling the start of the narrative proper (the uprising of the Yellow Turbans) not only evokes a clear sense of the cyclical theories of dynastic decline, but even more important, relates this breakdown of order to certain specific issues of Han history—the improper exercise of imperial authority, the destabilizing influence of special-interest groups (eunuchs, imperial clansmen), the problem of factional and individual idealism carried to the point of civil strife—all of which eventually surface in the body of the narrative.[79]

Moreover, we can also see in the initial ten-chapter unit of the novel the same extension of the prologue function observed in *Chin P'ing Mei*, *Hsi-yu chi*, and *Shui-hu chuan* over much of the first decade of the respective texts. Thus, the narration of the meteoric rise and fall of Tung Cho, clearly viewed by the author not as an isolated accident of history but as a striking model for the career of Ts'ao Ts'ao and the later hegemons who displace his dynasty, falls precisely within the span of the first ten chapters of the text.

Admittedly, the structural function of the opening passages and sections of *San-kuo* is not as fully articulated as in the other three works. But this very fact may have a special significance here, since on this point the *Yen-i* again diverges very sharply from its alleged popular source, the *San-kuo chih p'ing-hua*, with its drawn out, barely integrated prologue section.[80] Later editors, perhaps under the influence of the consolidation of the formal features of the genre by the time of *Chin P'ing Mei* and *Hsi-yu chi*, seemingly attempt to improve upon the basic text of *San-kuo* by expanding its lead-in section. For example, one edition attempts to soften what Cheng Chen-to once termed the "stabbing abruptness" (*tan-tao chih-ju* 單刀直入) of

---

[79] Cf. Mao Tsung-kang's discussion of the cause-and-effect chain of events underlying the plot of the novel, in item 7 of the *tu-fa* (p. 5), under the heading "the marvelous device of tracing matters to their root causes and pursuing them back to their original sources" (*chui-pen ch'iung-yüan chih miao* 追本窮源之妙).

[80] For a discussion of the prologue section of the *P'ing-hua*, see Cheng Chen-to, "Yen-hua," pp. 172ff.

the opening words of the 1522 text ("With the passing of Emperor Huan of the Latter Han ..." 後漢桓帝崩) by appending a list of all the preceding reigns of the Han dynasty.[81] The *Min-pen* edition entitled *San-kuo ch'üan-chuan* expands this to a breathless race through the cycles of Chinese history from the origin of the universe down to the Han, which it incorporates as the start of the text itself.[82]

It remained only for Mao Tsung-kang to complete the text universally read today by adding the prefatory *tz'u* poem on the vanity of human glory, and the now proverbial introductory generalization "In the grand scheme of the affairs of this world, what has been long divided is sure to be reunited, and what has been long united is sure to be divided" (*T'ien-hsia ta-shih fen chiu pi ho, ho chiu pi fen* 天下大勢分久必合，合久必分), known to every reader of Chinese novels. Even here, however, Mao's contribution is not entirely original, as this *tz'u* appears to be taken verbatim from an introductory verse to the section on Ch'in-Han history in Yang Shen's collection *Nien-i-shih t'an-tz'u* 廿一史彈詞.[83] I have been unable to locate an exact source for the maxim on the cycles of unity and division 合分, but I have come across a strikingly similar formulation in the *tu-fa* introductory remarks to the popular historical text *Yüan-Wang kang-chien ho-pien* 袁王綱鑑合編, which was most likely familiar to Mao Tsung-kang.[84] What is most important about this for my discussion is the fact that Mao's handling of the beginning of the text seems to reflect his strong awareness of the aesthetic requirements of the prologue section within the generic canons of the mature literati novel.[85]

As for the ending of the text, it is again dictated by the close of the historical period with the establishment of the Chin dynasty. Still, we can perceive an awareness of the structural significance of the concluding phases of the work in the manner in which a sense of closure is evoked as the end draws near. One particular device employed to signal the closing of the bracket of the novel's structure is the frequent mention toward the end of textual details that had marked the opening of the narrative so

[81] "Yen-hua," pp. 193, 217. Cheng is referring to the Cheng I-chen edition, which I have tentatively identified as Mao's *su-pen* text (see above, n. 52).

[82] For bibliographical information, see b.n. I. 6.

[83] Yang Shen, *T'an-tz'u*, *chüan* 3, pt. I, section 3, p. 69 (for more bibliographical information see above, note 43). Lines with similar expressions occur before the introductory section (*Tsung-shuo* 總說), *chüan* 1, section 1, p. 1, and *chüan* 2, section 2, p. 25, plus at the conclusion of section 3, part 2, p. 143. The source of this poem was pointed out to me by Andrew Lo (see "Historiography," p. 233).

[84] Yüan Huang (Liao-fan) 袁黃（了凡） and Wang Shih-chen 王世貞, *Yüan Wang kang-chien ho-pien* (attrib.), *tu-fa*, p. 3.

[85] C. T. Hsia (*Classic Novel*, p. 37) describes this addition as "in conformity with the style of popular historical novels ... to lessen *San-kuo*'s dissimilarity to that genre of fiction."

many chapters earlier. For example, the long-forgotten names of Li Chüeh 李傕 and Kuo Ssu 郭汜 are recalled in chapter 112,[86] in chapter 115 we are reminded of the "ten constant attendants" (*shih ch'ang-shih* 十常侍), and in chapter 118 we witness one more example of sworn brotherhood, followed in the next chapter by a renewed appearance of the Yellow Turbans, as the historical process comes full circle.[87] Similarly, in chapter 114 Ts'ao Mao's 曹髦 defiant cry: "I am the emperor!" 吾乃天子也 may echo Liu Pei's use of similar words as a child in chapter 1; and in chapter 120 we are given a replay of the chain-boat strategy that we witnessed much earlier at the time of the climax of the action of the narrative.[88]

Mao Tsung-kang draws our attention to the device of recapitulation at several points; he posits this as a basic structural principle in a note in chapter 115, and provides further extended discussions of this principle in his *tu-fa* introduction.[89] Mao's sharply refined "sense of an ending" leads him to revise the title of chapter 120 to wrap up the completion of the historical cycle ("With the Surrender of Sun Hao the Tripartite Division Returns to Unity" 降孫皓三分歸一統),[90] although he retains virtually unchanged the concluding *ku-feng* 古風 poem summing up the outline of the entire narrative, as does every other edition of the novel I have examined.

As we have seen in each of our other examples above, the various devices of closure employed in the literati novel form are not simply mechanical features, but are in each case integrated through the articulation of structure into the patterns of meaning that take shape in the course of the works. Likewise, in *San-kuo* there is a certain sense of didactic fulfillment attached to the conclusion of the work: a sense that the moral complexities of the main body of the text have become noticeably simpler toward the end, as case after case of disproportionately evil or stupid behavior is shown to lead directly to self-destruction. Thus, Mao Tsung-kang argues that in the interest of poetic justice the end of the narrative must be delayed up to the final destruction of Wei to repay Ts'ao Ts'ao for his

[86] MTK, 18:37. The fact that chapter 112 is exactly nine chapters from the end (Li and Kuo were last mentioned in chapter 9) suggests the possibility of deliberate symmetry, of the sort we have seen in the composition of *Hsi-yu chi*. If one wishes to credit the author of *San-kuo* with this degree of textual manipulation, then the mention of Lü Pu in chapter 103 may also be more than pure accident.

[87] MTK, 19:11, 19:30, 19:38.

[88] MTK, 19:3.

[89] MTK, 19:7: "One reads up to the final chapters, and it again resonates with the opening lines at the very start of the book" 又有讀至終篇, 而復與最先開卷之數行相應. See also 19:13 for a similar point. Mao develops the idea of resonance between beginning and end in items 4, 7, and 8 of the *tu-fa*.

[90] The final section of the 1522 edition is entitled "Wang Chün Takes Shih-t'ou ch'eng by a Clever Plan" 王濬計取石頭城.

strangulation of the Han.[91] On the other hand, the ending of *San-kuo* also shares with those of the other three novels a sense that the initial impression of the simplistic workings of retribution is ultimately submerged within a larger conception of futility—a futility underscored by the harsh ironies of Chu-ko Liang's end and scarcely offset by the beginning of a new short-lived cycle that can in no way be viewed as a final salvation.

The last area of global structural patterning that we have observed in the other three novels is the use of certain schemes of spatial and temporal organization. In *San-kuo*, the central fact of tripartite division governs the spatial layout of the narrative from early on in the book, even before the actual establishment of three rival states. Within this fixed framework, however, we can perceive certain examples of apparent manipulation on the part of the author. For example, there may be observed a certain circularity of movement through the course of the novel, with the central theater of action in the capital region of northern China during the first thirty chapters, shifting to the Yangtze valley for most of the next thirty, then moving around to Shu in the west for a comparable number of chapters, before turning back eastward for the final clashes between Shu and Wei, fought mostly in the mountainous areas lying between these two states.[92]

At other times the broad tripod configuration is conflated in such a way that the focus shifts around all three of the key areas one by one within the space of a single chapter, further indicating the author's control over the geographical setting.[93] Evidence of this sort of spatial design may be seen in the detailed treatment of Ts'ao Ts'ao's mopping-up drive into the northeastern steppes to consolidate his rear after wiping out the remnants of the rebellious forces under Yüan Shao's 袁紹 contentious sons—which later turns out to be a mirror image of Chu-ko Liang's thrust against Meng Huo deep into the jungles of the southwest, ostensibly launched for the same purpose of securing his own rear lines.[94]

[91] See Mao's comments on chapter 120 (19:42). Similar ideas are expressed in sections 1 and 8 of the *tu-fa*. Mao's revision of the title of chapter 119 seems a further reflection of this sense of the ending of the work.

[92] See Andrew Lo, "Historiography," p. 180ff., and his "The *San-kuo chih yen-i*: A Study of Its Overall Structure and Narrative Patterns," pp. 4–5.

[93] Mao discusses this pattern in a comment on chapter 28 (MTK, 5:10). In chapter 65, he uses the expression "the device of parallel narration in two separate places" (*liang-pien shuang-hsü fa* 兩邊雙敘法) to describe the problems of simultaneous narration (11:10), and at other points he pays particular attention to the shift of the narrative focus from the north to the south (e.g., chapter 34, 6:10).

[94] The fact that the northeastern campaign in chapter 32 is symmetrically mirrored in the southwestern campaign just about thirty-two chapters from the end provides another tantalizing instance of structural overdetermination (see n. 86).

The evidence of the author's deliberate control over structure is even stronger with respect to the temporal organization of the text, contrary to the expectation that the pegging of the narrative to dates drawn from the historical sources might preclude any possibility of manipulation in this area. Andrew Lo has pointed out one broad scheme of temporal structure, according to which the first decade and the last two decades of the text run quickly through twenty or more years of historical time, but this drops sharply to several years per decade, then only one or two years per decade for the central portion of the novel, before speeding up again as we move into the final sections.[95] This pattern is of special interest to us here, because it parallels the 20-60-20 structural division of the chapters of *Chin P'ing Mei*, with a comparable slowdown in the central section, as described in Chapter 2.

Another important dimension of temporal structure that is repeated in each of the other three novels is the linking of key scenes in the text to significant moments in the seasonal cycle. As might be expected, this practice applies chiefly to the most patently fictional episodes in the narrative. For example, the snowy setting of Liu Pei's second visit to Chu-ko Liang's retreat, as well as the springtime splendor of his third, and successful, excursion, are not based on details in the historical record of the incident. Similarly, the evocation of a bleak autumn scene adds to the starkness of the fall of Kuan Yü from chapter 74 on, and is strongly emphasized in the scene depicting the death of Chu-ko Liang at Wu-chang yüan 五丈原, where the conventional motifs of the Mid-Autumn Festival—with its central symbol of the full yet cold harvest moon—are worked into the text in a manner highly reminiscent of the circumstances of Lu Ta's 魯達 passage to oblivion in *Shui-hu chuan*.[96]

The most striking example of controlled seasonality, however, is the pointed use of the special day of the Yüan-hsiao Festival, which we have seen to have unique associations for the art of the sixteenth-century novel. The frenetic unreality of this holiday is specified three times in the course of the *San-kuo* text, each time forming a backdrop to appropriately sensational episodes. In chapter 23 the account of Chi P'ing's 吉平 conspiracy with Tung Ch'eng 董承 to poison Ts'ao Ts'ao is set on this day, as is another

---

[95] See Andrew Lo, "Historiography," pp. 56ff. The "Li Yü" commentator notes the possibility of obtaining heightened emotional effects through the device of ticking off chronological markers (chapter 3, pp. 5b–6a). See Riftin, *Istoricheskaya epopeia*, pp. 225f.

[96] Another example of special emphasis on the seasonal setting for dramatic events is seen in the winter setting for Lü Pu's fall in chapter 19 (3:36). Mao Tsung-kang takes note of the special significance of these occasions in comments on chapter 114 (19:6). However, his use of the terms "heat" and "cold" in item 15 of the *tu-fa* refers to an entirely different literary variable from that in Chang Chu-p'o's usage (see above, Chapter 4, Part II). See Andrew Lo, "Historiography," pp. 190ff.

abortive assassination attempt (involving Chi P'ing's sons) in chapter 69. On this latter occasion, Mao Tsung-kang signals his awareness of the special associations of relaxed vigilance connected with this day by adding the following line to the basic text: "Indeed, the *chin-wu* guards failed to enforce the prohibitions, nor was anyone hastened by the jade water-clock" 眞箇金吾不禁玉漏無催 .⁹⁷ Later, in the chaotic final phases of the novel, the author again chooses the Yüan-hsiao Festival as a time frame for the abortive palace coup of Chung Hui 鍾會 and Chiang Wei 姜維 in chapter 119, giving way to the total breakdown of order that ushers in the start of a new cycle.

Several additional aspects of the temporal arrangement of the text that we may point to as examples of the structural manipulation characteristic of the genre involve questions of modulation of narrative pace and sequencing. As already noted, the ratio between narrative time and historical time varies within the larger structural divisions of the book according to a discernible pattern, and we can detect a similar control of narrative speed in smaller units of the text as well.⁹⁸ The most obvious example of this is of course the treatment of the episode of Liu Pei's three visits to the thatched hut of Chu-ko Liang, since, as many scholars have observed, the development of this scene in the novel far exceeds that in the *P'ing-hua* and dramatic sources in volume and detail.⁹⁹ Mao Tsung-kang discusses at length in chapters 36 and 37 the manner in which the author draws out the narration of the first two visits, and he goes on in chapter 38 to add the astute observation that in many cases the primary factor responsible for narrative suspense is the deliberate retardation of the pace of movement by the interjection of nonessential material.¹⁰⁰ This aspect of narrative sequencing is a concern Mao and the other traditional Chinese fiction critics often have in mind when they point out the manner in which an author may turn aside at a moment of furious narrative pace (*pai-mang-chung* 百忙中) to introduce seemingly irrelevant material (*mang-chung hsien-pi*

⁹⁷ MTK, 11:45. Mao discusses the significance of the Yüan-hsiao setting in a chapter commentary in the same chapter (11:41) and in an interlinear note in chapter 119 (19:35).

⁹⁸ Mao Tsung-kang frequently uses the critical terms "fast-paced" (*chi* 急) and "slow-paced" (*huan* 緩) to describe this variable of narrative speed.

⁹⁹ For comparisons of the pacing of the "three-visits" sequence in the *Yen-i* and other materials, see Cheng Chen-to, "Yen-hua," pp. 194–204; Winston L. Y. Yang, "Literary Transformation," p. 55; Tung Mei-k'an, *Shih-lun*, p. 127ff.; C. T. Hsia, *Classic Novel*, p. 52.

¹⁰⁰ MTK, 6:22, 6:29f., 6:36, and esp. 6:37. Mao's frequent discussions of the technique of "interposed passages" (*chia-hsieh* 夾寫, *ch'a-hsieh* 插寫) often amount to the same thing (see examples in chapters 1, 3, 7, 8, 16, 18, 28, 40, 49, 104). Boris Riftin (*Istoricheskaya epopeia*, pp. 232f.) draws explicitly on the narrative theory of V. Šklovskij to elucidate this principle in *San-kuo*.

忙中閒筆).[101] Further examples of deliberate breaks in narrative continuity include the insertion of supplementary material (*pu* 補), or the occasional use of flashbacks in the text.[102]

Moving on now to a consideration of the network of more finely calibrated compositional patterns—those described in my analyses of *Chin P'ing Mei*, *Hsi-yu chi*, and *Shui-hu chuan* as features of "narrative texture"—we find in *San-kuo chih yen-i* a sense of common design and execution that once again places it within the generic outlines of the sixteenth-century literati novel. Here, too, the dominant principle of organization at this level of analysis may be identified as what I have called "figural recurrence": the deliberate repetition of textual units of different orders of magnitude to build up a sense of solid coherence within the overall structural skeleton of the text.[103] Every reader of *San-kuo* must become aware sooner or later of the fact that this vast text is composed of a limited number of recurring units, and he may even at times become impatient with the incessant repetition of familiar patterns. Hu Shih, for one, condemns this feature as evidence of a lack of imagination on the part of the author, especially in the patently fictional episodes of the text.[104] Similarly, the critic of the "Li Cho-wu" commentary edition seems to lose patience by the final chapters of the work, and complains that "reading *San-kuo* up to this point is like chewing wax, bland and flavorless, ... it has all been told and told again" 讀三國志演義至此等處眞如嚼蠟, 淡然無味… 都是說了又說…; and in another place: "When I read through the *Yen-i* up to this point I start to doze off, because all of this has been said before in the earlier chapters, and is being replayed with only the names changed" 讀演義至此惟有打頓而已，何也，只因前面都已說過，不過改換姓名重疊敷演云耳.[105] In arguing here, therefore, that the manifest repetitiveness of *San-kuo chih yen-i*

[101] See, e.g., MTK, chapter 114 (19:6), and numerous other instances (e.g., in chapters 1, 3, 5, 12, 18, 20, 22, 59). Sometimes (e.g., 1:19) Mao applies the metaphorical distinction between narrative "heat" and "cold" to this device (see n. 96); at others he may discuss it in terms of "direct" versus "indirect" narration (*cheng-hsieh*, *p'ang-hsieh* 正寫, 旁寫) (examples in chapters 48, 62). See also items 12 and 16 of the *tu-fa* (pp. 9f.).

[102] Examples of the term "supplementary passages" occur in chapters 18, 21, 57, 72, and 98. The use of flashbacks is a standard device of Chinese historical narrative, typically introduced by the word *earlier* (*ch'u* 初). For examples of flashbacks in the novel, see chapters 22 (4:10), 108 (18:14), and 112 (18:38). For other critical discussions of the temporal sequencing of the narrative, see the "Li Yü" commentary (10:7a and 37:4a), and MTK chapter 40 (7:8).

[103] Riftin discusses the principle of textual repetition in *Istoricheskaya epopeia*, pp. 236, 250.

[104] Hu Shih, "Yen-i hsü," pp. 472f.

[105] "Li Cho-wu" edition, chapters 110 (p. 11a) and 112 (p. 10a). See also chapter 113 (p. 10b). Mao Tsung-kang notes the repetition of "the same situation" 同一局面 in chapters 34 (6:11) and 40 (7:13).

(as in its sister novels) does not represent a failure of narrative resources, but on the contrary points to one of the key aspects of its greatness as a sophisticated literary vehicle, it will be necessary to distinguish among several different types of patterns of recurrence.

First, I must allow that a large portion of the recurring figures in the text may be accounted for in terms of the realia of the subject matter of the novel. Given the sheer repeatability of historical situations and events, it is practically inevitable that the same kinds of scenes appear over and over in the text. Within the setting of the imperial and provincial courts, we witness a succession of state banquets, royal hunts and entertainments, policy debates, and presentation of memorials. The predictable round of court business and amusements is frequently quickened by chilling omens, and these are regularly fulfilled in the form of assassinations, palace coups, forced removal or sack of the capitals, and in some cases outright usurpation of the throne, the latter following a familiar sequence of stages.[106] Particularly memorable are the recurrent scenes in which loyal ministers pay with their lives for their intrepid counsel in the face of adversity (*chien-ssu* 諫死), or those in which a passably honorable but weak-willed ruler vacillates (*yu-yü pu-chüeh* 猶豫不決) when decisive action is imperative, until the situation is past the point of saving.[107]

Out on the battlefield, we witness a comparable predictability of the military moves and countermoves included within the repertoire of contemporary warfare, most frequently following the pattern of a preliminary skirmish, confrontation of armies in full battle array, a challenge to individual combat of picked champions, followed by full-scale clash of troops. Besides such formal engagements with limited room for maneuvering, a whole range of more crafty acts of war—ambushes, surprise raids on enemy camps, defections, holing up in walled fortresses and subsequent laying of sieges, the burning of supply depots; and even more devious types of stratagems: fake surrender, counterfeit messages of support or information, and such tricks as luring the enemy with beautiful women (*mei-jen chi* 美人計), driving a wedge of suspicion between allies (*fan-chien chi* 反間計), or voluntary submission to corporal punishment to gain the confidence of an enemy (*k'u-jou chi* 苦肉計)—all are employed with a frequency that would appear to eliminate any power of deception.[108] Sometimes, partic-

---

[106] For example, royal hunts: chapters 20, 56; omens (especially broken flags): chapters 1, 11, 24, 31, 53, 62, 63, 80, 91, 112, 116; moves of the capital 遷都: chapters 6, 13, 61, 75, 80; usurpations: chapters 17, 61, 107, 111.

[107] For example, executions of loyal advisors: chapters 2, 4, 30, 60, 68, 80; vacillation: 27, 30, 31, 39, 43, 61, 107.

[108] For example, sieges: chapters 94, 95, 108, 111, 112, 115; ambushes: chapters 12, 98; fake surrender 詐降: chapters 97, 114; defections: chapters 31, 79, 82, 107; lure by beautiful

ular stratagems or modes of combat are presented as the personal trademark of individual heroes (for example, Chu-ko Liang's use of brocade bags
for secret messages, his practice of sitting conspicuously on top of a mound
of earth to infuriate his enemy, or his appearance in the thick of battle in the
unlikely cart and garb of a Taoist immortal), which also results in a redundancy of detail in the battle scenes.[109]

This same element of thematic recurrence may also help to account for
the repetitiveness of the novel in its framing of characters. Of the hundreds
of individuals who play a role in the narrative, all except a handful of
central figures can easily be reduced to a set of repeating images, not so
much fixed character types as recurring patterns of human behavior: the old
warrior still more than a match for his foes despite his years, the noble
adviser faithful to his lord unto death, the arrogant commander, the dull-
witted strong man, among others.[110] Mao Tsung-kang seems to put his
finger on this recurrence when he illustrates the most successful types of
characterization in the novel by means of a long list of secondary figures
grouped according to the qualities and capacities they represent (those
with an ability to predict human behavior: Kuo Chia 郭嘉, Ch'eng Yü 程昱,
Hsün Yü 荀彧, Chia Hsü 賈詡, Pu Chih 步騭, Yü Fan 虞翻, Ku Yung 顧雍,
Chang Chao 張昭; those who can charge enemy lines and break a battle
formation: Ma Ch'ao 馬超, Ma Tai 馬岱, Kuan Hsing 關興, Chang Pao
張苞, Hsü Ch'u 許褚, Tien Wei 典韋, Chang Ho 張郃, Hsia-hou Tun
夏候惇, Huang Kai 黃蓋, Chou T'ai 周泰, Kan Ning 甘寧, T'ai-shih Tz'u
太史慈, Ting Feng 丁奉; those who are quick-witted: Ts'ao Chih 曹植,
Yang Hsiu 楊修; recluses: Ts'ui Chou-p'ing 崔州平, Shih Kuang-yüan
石廣元, Meng Kung-wei 孟公威).[111]

This sort of recurrence of textual elements, sometimes governed more
by the nature of the materials than by authorial control, is also observed
at the level of particular words and formulaic expressions used to carry
forward the narrative. For example, nearly every scene of policy debate at
court is introduced by the words "one man rose to his feet" (*i-jen t'ing shen*
一人挺身) leading into the presentation of a dramatic confrontation, while
out in the field it appears obligatory for every extended battle scene to be

---

women: chapters 5, 8–9, 53, 55, 85, 105 (see *tu-fa*, item 10, pp. 6–7); wedge driven between
allies: chapters 59, 65, 87, 91, 114.

[109] Brocade bag: chapters 50, 99, 105; sitting on hill above battle: chapters 25, 30, 32, 65,
98; the special headgear (*kuan-chin* 綸巾) worn by Chu-ko Liang: chapters 64, 65, 83, 89, 90,
92, 93, 97, 98, 99, 100, 101, 104, 105.

[110] For example, old warriors: chapters 53, 63, 70, 83, 87, 91, 92, 93. This list of character
types might also include the chain of noble suicides; see Robert Ruhlmann, "Motives and
Meanings of Suicide in the *San-kuo chih yen-i*."

[111] See *tu-fa*, item 3, p. 3.

broken up by the sudden arrival of new forces announced with the formula "suddenly there appeared a troop of horses and riders" (*hu-chien i-piao jen-ma* 忽見一彪人馬). It would be going too far to take this use of recurrent fixed formulas as evidence of oral composition buried in the source materials, or to view them as indicators of some kind of "epic" quality of the text. Instead, we should recognize that the use of these formulas is not completely gratuitous, and very often they seem to be inserted to fulfill specific structural functions in demarcating the significant units of the narrative.[112]

A second category of recurrent units that we may distinguish in *San-kuo* includes those representing not repeated thematic aspects of the subject matter, but set patterns of the literary tradition out of which the novel emerged. I have already discussed the fact that many of the basic narrative units (*mu*) of the novel parallel stock episodes in the popular fiction and drama traditions.[113] Particularly noticeable among such examples are those in which the recurrent scenes in *San-kuo* also recur in other novels, especially in *Shui-hu chuan*. For example, the oath of brotherhood that sets the plot in motion (and is then repeated at several later points in the course of the book) is quite familiar as a staple of Chinese heroic narrative, as are scenes framed according to the pattern of "honorable release" of a captive (*i-shih* 義釋), or "the capture by guile" (*chih-ch'ü* 智取) of an enemy stronghold.[114] By the same token, the successive instances of superhuman feats of strength—such as Liu Pei's cleaving a boulder with his sword in chapter 54 or the miraculous leap across the T'an River in chapter 34—often seem to be isolated units better understood as motifs of folklore than in terms of the development of the immediate narrative context. The same can be said for the obligatory mention of such motifs as the "wild wind" (*k'uang-feng* 狂風) blowing up as a prelude to a disproportionately large number of dramatic scenes.[115]

However, these examples of repeating patterns dictated by traditional associations are less important for my discussion than those in which the

---

[112] Other examples of quasi-formulaic usage include such expressions as "depressed and disgruntled" (*men-men pu-le* 悶悶不樂), "those who follow me will live ..." (*shun wo che* 順我者), and "hesitating, unable to make up his mind" (*yu-yü wei-chüeh* 猶豫未決). See n. 107.

[113] See Part I of this chapter for discussion of the sources of the novel.

[114] "Honorable release" scenes appear in chapters 50, 53, and 63. See also above, Chapter 4, Part V, and the discussion of "great havoc" (*ta-nao*) and "attending a banquet" (*fu-hui*) scenes above, n. 76. An additional example of this type is the setting of "three conditions" in several episodes (e.g., chapters 25, 52).

[115] Examples of the wild wind occur in chapters 1, 7, 9, 10, 24, 36, 41, 68, 83, 84, 86, 89, 90, 91, 97, 103, 104, 105, 106, 108, 111, 113, and 116.

principle of figural recurrence works to build up the structural coherence of the narrative itself. For example, the restaging in chapter 111 of the dramatic scene of the emperor's forced march from the capital (which we first witnessed back in chapter 6) serves to emphasize the structural linkage between the opening and the closing phases of the story. At closer range, an unmistakable echo of the hounding of Sun Ts'e 孫策 to death by the ghost of Yü Chi in chapter 29 recurs again in the supernatural attack on Ts'ao Ts'ao by the magician Tso Tz'u 左慈 in chapter 68, also producing a structural resonance that lends coherence to the body of the text.[116]

In pursuing this aspect of the artistry of the novel, I will continue to rely heavily on Mao Tsung-kang's critical analysis. In his *tu-fa* introduction, Mao praises what he terms the "structure" (*chieh-kou* 結構) of *San-kuo* for the manner in which it achieves a dynamic integration of textual elements, such that "the earlier sections leave room for later reflection, and the later sections reflect back on the earlier sections" 前能留步以應後, 後能回照以應前.[117] In a number of subsequent passages in chapter and interlinear commentary he develops this idea by using the military metaphor of the "Ch'ang-shan snake formation" (*Ch'ang-shan she* 常山蛇), and he goes on to point out the interlocking of narrative threads throughout the entire text (although the examples are more noticeable in the beginning and the end).[118] Thus, Mao's concept of "structure" turns out to be closer to what I have termed "texture," in the sense of the fine interweaving of smaller-scale units of recurrence to lend internal cohesion and meaning to the narrative text.

A number of the seemingly hit-and-miss categories of analysis drawn in Mao's *tu-fa* introduction seem to come into a more meaningful focus when we observe that they are often based on the fundamental concept of significant recurrence, considered from different points of view. One of these perspectives focuses on the planting of narrative figures earlier in the

---

[116] As further examples, the gruesome details of Ssu-ma Shih's excruciating eye disease in chapter 110 (18:23) may resonate with Hsia-hou Tun's wounded eye in chapter 18; and Mao Tsung-kang's introduction of Tu Yü's penchant for study of the *Tso chuan* in chapter 120 (cf. *fan-li*, item 3) clearly balances his earlier specification of Kuan Yü's interest in the *Ch'un-ch'iu* text.

[117] See *tu-fa*, item 21, p. 12f., and chapter 113 (18:39) for the term *chieh-kou*. See also item 18, p. 11, for the integration of earlier and later sections such that "the entire composition reads like a single sentence" (*i-p'ien ju i-chü* 一篇如一句), and item 23, p. 13, for the resonance of start and finish. Cf. Chang Chu-p'o's similar description of *Chin P'ing Mei* (see chapter 3, n. 59). Similar discussions appear in chapters 53 (9:9), 57 (9:38), 94 (15:34), 115 (19:7), 116 (19:13), and 120 (19:50). The same point is also emphasized in the preface to the "Li Yü" edition.

[118] See discussions in chapters 94 (15:34) and 115 (19:11).

text in order to anticipate, or lead up to, the later development of major elements of similar or linked significance. Mao's most explicit treatment of this function appears in the section of his *tu-fa* headed "the marvelous device of planting seeds a year in advance, laying down patterns before-hand" (*ko nien hsia chung hsien shih fu-cho chih miao* 隔年下種, 先時伏着 之妙), a critical concept he identifies in the course of the discussion with the common term "foreshadowing" (*fu-pi* 伏筆).[119] Similarly, the composi-tional element described in the *tu-fa* with the metaphoric expression "the marvelous device whereby when it is about to snow, sleet appears; when it is about to rain, thunder is heard" (*chiang hsüeh chien hsien, chiang yü wen lei chih miao* 將雪見霰將雨聞雷之妙) turns out to be equivalent to the lead-in function (*yin* 引): the early introduction of a specific detail or even a fully developed prior model of a narrative figure or situation, such as Mao describes at various points in his interlinear commentary with terms like *chang-pen* 張本 and *hsiao yang-tzu* 小樣子.[120] A related term used by Mao of particular interest here, since we have observed its frequent use by Chang Chu-p'o, is the carpenter's metaphor of the interlocking "mortise and tenon" joint (*sun* 榫), which may be understood as a combination of the foreshadowing and lead-in functions.[121]

Looking at these patterns from the opposite direction, we can see that a number of items emphasized in Mao's discussion of narrative texture in the *tu-fa* focus attention on the placing of later elements to reflect back on earlier instances of the same or comparable figures. The most common terms employed by the traditional fiction critics for this function include *hui-chao* 回照, *ying-tai* 影帶, and *chao-ying* 照應; Mao's *tu-fa* heading enti-tled "the marvelous device whereby rippling patterns follow after waves, and a light drizzle follows after the rain" (*lang hou po-wen, yü hou mai-mu chih miao* 浪後波紋, 雨後霢霂之妙) also turns upon such patterns. The other critical commentaries on *San-kuo* frequently use the same metaphor of "after-waves" or "ripples" (*yü-po* 餘波) to emphasize the later follow-up effect.[122] We have already seen how this particular function takes on an even more significant role toward the close of the text, at which time the

[119] *Tu-fa*, item 17, p. 10. See also discussion in chapter 27 (5:1) and frequent use of the term *fu-pi*.

[120] *Tu-fa*, item 13, p. 9. See also Mao's use of the term *yin* in e.g., chapters 1 (1:2) and 53 (9:10); *chang-pen*, in chapter 13 (2:34); and *hsiao yang-tzu*, in chapter 2 (1:9). This idea is also reflected in the discussion of the use of auxiliary figures in item 4 of the *tu-fa*, p. 3.

[121] This term appears in discussions in chapters 32, 33, 52, 57, 64, 65, 78, 80, 86, 94, 98, 99, 102, 105, 113, 114, and 115. See above, Chapter 2, Part II, for Chang Chu-p'o's use of the term.

[122] See *tu-fa*, item 14, p. 9, and numerous examples in the interlinear comments, chapter 116 (19:14) for one. The term *yü-po* appears in Mao's comments in chapters 2, 8, 13, 34, 39, 41, 68, 78.

frequent recalling of details from the beginning of the story contributes to the aesthetics of closure.[123]

In applying the principle of figural recurrence, Mao Tsung-kang adds a number of further refinements. One of these, which I touched upon earlier, is the distinction between continuous and discontinuous sequences of linked episodes, what Mao calls *lien* 連 and *tuan* 斷. This concept is developed at length in the item of the *tu-fa* entitled "the marvelous device of horizontal clouds cutting across mountain peaks, horizontal bridges locking in streams" (*heng-yün tuan ling, heng-ch'iao so hsi chih miao* 橫雲斷嶺, 橫橋鎖溪之妙), as well as in numerous interlinear comments.[124] In effect, the notion of "planting seeds a year in advance" is another example of discontinuous recurrence, the sort of thing commonly referred to as "parallelism at a distance" (*yao-yao hsiang tui* 遙遙相對).[125] Mao also notes the fact that some cases of figural recurrence stand apart in that they mark out a gradual rise in intensity through a series of occurrences, a pattern to which he applies the term "incremental repetition" (*chia-i pei* 加一倍), which we have already seen in Chang Chu-p'o's analysis of the structural complexities of *Chin P'ing Mei*.[126]

It can be seen in all of the above cases that the function of textual linkage producing a sense of aesthetic cohesion depends primarily on the similitude between analogous narrative figures. In what follows I will explore a fourth type of recurrent figures in *San-kuo*, in which the emphasis is shifted to the discrepancy, rather than the similarity, between comparable elements. Of course, to the extent that all instances of analogy imply both similarity and difference, it is always a matter of subjective judgment which of these two principles may be dominant in a given equation. But we can still isolate in the structure of recurrence in *San-kuo* certain examples in which difference rather than similarity seems to be the point at issue. Thus, for example, in the sequence that includes Kuan Yü's escape with Lady Mi 糜夫人 and Lady Kan 甘夫人 in chapter 28, Chao Yün's 趙雲 rescue of the two wives in chapter 41, and the escape of Lady Sun 孫夫人 in chapter 55, the common element of rescued wives of Liu Pei seems to be the dominant factor pulling the separate instances together into a pattern of similarity. But when we consider such examples as the parallel rise of Ts'ao Ts'ao,

[123] Cf. comparable use of this device in *Hsi-yu chi* (see above, Chapter 3, Part II).

[124] See, e.g., *tu-fa*, item 12, p. 9; and discussion in interlinear comment in chapter 64 (11:6).

[125] See comments in chapters 7, 27, 34, 64, 112 (e.g., chapter 21 [4:2]). Mao's use of the term "the broken line trail of a snake in the grass" (*ts'ao-she hui-hsien* 草蛇灰線) also refers to the delayed repetition of figural details (e.g., chapter 21, 4:5); cf. Chin Sheng-t'an's somewhat different use of the same term, above, Chapter 4, Part II.

[126] See Mao's discussions in chapters 20, 21, 49, 51, 109 (e.g., chapter 21 [4:1]). For Chang Chu-p'o's use of the term, see above, Chapter 2, Part II.

Liu Pei, and Sun Ch'üan 孫權, or the recurrent scene of the humbling of the mightiest warriors in the cases of Lü Pu, Kuan Yü, and Chang Fei, we may say that the possibility of significant contrast is more important than the concurrent function of structural linking.[127]

Some of Mao Tsung-kang's most interesting discussions deal with this particular aspect of *San-kuo*. Two lengthy sections of the *tu-fa*—"the marvelous device of different branches on the same tree, different leaves on the same branch, different flowers on the same leaf, and different fruits from the same flower" (*t'ung-shu i-chih, t'ung-chih i-yeh, t'ung-yeh i-hua, t'ung-hua i-kuo chih miao* 同樹異枝, 同枝異葉, 同葉異花, 同花異果之妙) and "the marvelous device of singular peaks placed face to face, brocade screens looming opposite one another" (*ch'i-feng tui-ch'a, chin-p'ing tui-chih chih miao* 奇峯對插, 錦屏對峙之妙)—are devoted to pointing out the varying emphases on similarity and difference in recurring figures in the text.[128] In the former case, Mao comes to focus on a contrastive pair of terms, "deliberate commission [of redundancy]" (*fan* 犯) and "avoidance [of redundancy]" (*pi* 避), and in the latter he develops the distinction between "direct parallelism" (*cheng-tui* 正對) and "reverse parallelism" (*fan-tui* 反對)—all terms he employs frequently throughout his interlinear commentary.[129] With reference to the structural significance of parallelism between specific human figures, Mao again emphasizes the use of this sort of contrastive pair in another *tu-fa* section headed "the marvelous device of using the guest to set off the host" (*i pin ch'en chu chih miao* 以賓襯主之妙), as well as in a number of interlinear comments.[130]

I should also mention within this category a final group of instances in which it is not initial similarity giving way to difference, but rather an ultimate sense of convergence that serves to undercut an earlier impression of clear contrast between related figures. Many of the popular images of characters and actions formed by readers of *San-kuo chih yen-i* are based on a sense of the uniqueness or unparalleled greatness of the major heroes. It is extremely important, therefore, to point out that in example after example the most memorable heroic deeds are set in a narrative context that explicitly or implicitly diminishes this uniqueness by including parallel instances of figurally similar actions. Thus, for example, we find Chang Fei's

[127] Mao Tsung-kang discusses in detail the parallel careers of Liu Pei, Ts'ao Ts'ao, and Sun Ch'üan in *tu-fa*, item 5, p. 4. Another example of this may be seen in the similarity between the scenes depicting the downfall of Lü Pu (chapter 19) and Chang Fei (chapter 81).

[128] See *tu-fa*, item 10, p. 6, and item 20, p. 11. Mao describes this pattern more explicitly as "the same narrative material with different treatment" at a number of points. See Wang Hsiao-chia, "Shih-t'an San-kuo yen-i ti tui-pi shou-fa," pp. 119–28.

[129] See comments in chapters 32, 40, 52, 53, 69, 84, 86, 108, and esp. 113 (18:39).

[130] See *tu-fa*, item 9, p. 5, and comments in chapters 7, 21, 41, 42, 44, 45, 47, 64, 76, 94, 98, and esp. 37 (6:30).

exploits at Ch'ang-pan 長坂 Bridge in chapter 42 repeated in another
bridge defense in chapter 64, and Liu Pei's magical leap over the T'an River
is restaged by Sun Ch'üan in chapter 67. Similarly, even some of the most
popular exploits of Chu-ko Liang appear to be reduced in magnitude when
we see others employing magical arts of warfare, or engaging in contemplation of the heavens in planning strategy.[131] The same principle of
similarity within difference appears to be at work in other cases in which an
act of questionable wisdom or morality, justified on the grounds of unique
circumstances, is set into a sequence of similar acts that seriously weaken
this justification. For example, when Sun Ch'üan "surreptitiously occupies"
(*an-ch'ü* 暗取) Ching-chou 荊州 in chapter 75, the ironic reflection back on
Liu Pei's earlier seizure of the same city is unmistakable. In the same way,
when Ts'ao P'i 曹丕, Liu Pei, and Sun Ch'üan all assume the imperial throne
in parallel scenes in rapid succession in chapter 80, the distinctions between
the motivations and justifications of the three individuals are outweighed
by the repetitive sameness of their coronations.[132]

III

In the remainder of this chapter I will pay particular attention to the way in
which the author plays off similarity and difference in his repeated use of
recurrent figures in order to bring out the dimension of ironic reflection I
have proposed as the key to my interpretation of this masterwork. First,
however, I will briefly consider some of the other elements of rhetoric that
govern the generation of meaning in the novel.

At the beginning of this chapter, I acknowledged that my attempt to link
San-kuo chih yen-i to the genre of the sixteenth-century literati novel represented by *Chin P'ing Mei*, *Hsi-yu chi* and *Shui-hu chuan* is encumbered by
the fact that its basic medium of narration diverges noticeably from that
of the other three. In spite of the expression "popular" (*t'ung-su* 通俗) in
the title of the 1522 edition, the *Yen-i* is basically composed in a simple
classical idiom with only the occasional use of colloquial diction.[133] The
1494 preface notes this linguistic compromise: "While its prose is not
profound, neither is its language vulgar" (*wen pu shen shen, yen pu shen su*
文不甚深, 言不甚俗). And the Ming bibliographer Kao Ju appears to be

---

[131] For example, chapters 101, 104. Other examples include Chiang Wei's "self-demotion"
(*tzu-pien* 自貶) in chapter 111, reflecting on Chu-ko Liang's similar act, or Ssu-ma I's formal
visit to the advisor Yang Hu in chapter 120, reminiscent of Liu Pei's "three visits."

[132] See *tu-fa*, item 5, p. 4.

[133] The use of colloquial diction is mainly limited to such nonsubstantives as *che* 着, *i-ko*
一個. See, e.g., MTK, 1:3 (1522, 1:6a).

describing the same text when he reports: "It is not in the archaic prose of historiography, yet it avoids the comical air of the blind storytellers" 非史氏蒼古之文, 去瞽傳詼諧之氣.¹³⁴ Interestingly, the hints of colloquial diction that do appear in the 1522 text are generally found in the "straight narrative" passages rather than in the representation of direct speech, which is for the most part in pure *wen-yen*.

At the same time, we should note that the 1522 *Yen-i* does make use of certain colloquial storytellers' expressions, including conventional chapter endings such as "[to find out] what became of his life, just listen to the following *hui* and it will become clear" (*hsing-ming ju-ho, ch'ieh t'ing hsia-hui fen-chieh* 性命如何, 且聽下回分解), as well as introductory phrases such as "but let us tell how" (*ch'ieh shuo* 且說) at the start of new narrative units.¹³⁵ Significantly, the *San-kuo chih p'ing-hua*, with its supposedly direct connection to oral storytelling performance, shows limited use of these conventional tags, although, as Boris Riftin points out, they do appear in some of the other extant *p'ing-hua* texts.¹³⁶

Mao Tsung-kang, for his part, brings the text more into line with the later refinements of the novel form by regularizing these chapter ending and opening tags, as well as adding such structural markers as "now our story splits into two directions" (*hua fen liang-t'ou* 話分兩頭) or "but lest our tale become too entangled" (*hua hsiu fan-hsü* 話休繁絮). On this particular point, at least, we have another clear example to demonstrate that the use of colloquial stylistic markers, which is often taken as evidence of connections to popular performance, was only gradually and deliberately incorporated into the emerging novel genre.

A second rhetorical feature of the sixteenth-century novel form I have considered in the preceding chapters is the specialized use of verse passages within the narrative. We have seen in *Chin P'ing Mei* and *Hsi-yu chi* some very creative uses of originally popular verse forms, and I have suggested that the poems included in the complete editions of *Shui-hu chuan* deserve more serious critical attention. In the case of *San-kuo*, the evolution of the prose narrative has also been linked to certain forms of popular versification, notably in Chang Cheng-lang's 張政烺 theory, expounded in the West by James Crump, of the development of the *San-kuo*

¹³⁴ Kao Ju, *Pai-ch'uan shu-chih* (cited in K'ung Ling-ching, *Shih-liao*, p. 40). For additional assessments of the level of the *San-kuo* prose, see Cheng Chen-to, "Yen-hua," p. 204; the "Li Yü" commentary edition, preface (pp. 4b–5a); C. T. Hsia, *Classic Novel*, p. 80; and Riftin, *Istoricheskaya epopeia*, p. 240.

¹³⁵ See, for example, chapter 17 (1522, 4:22a–b). Cf. Cheng Chen-to's ("Yen-hua," p. 213) discussion of the interpolation of such chapter endings in the Cheng I-chen edition.

¹³⁶ Riftin, *Istoricheskaya epopeia*, pp. 227ff. The *P'ing-hua* does use such expressions as *hua fen liang-shuo* 話分兩說 [sic] (e.g., p. 352) and *ch'üeh-shuo* 却說.

narrative out of prose commentary combined with the *yung-shih* poems of the T'ang poet Hu Tseng.[137] Although the importance of this factor has been overstated, the connection between popular verse on historical themes and the development of historical fiction in the *Yen-i* is clear enough, especially in the incorporation of numerous poems by Hu Tseng and similar poets into the 1522 edition (and later editions), as well as in the links of the *yung-shih* poems of Chou Li and the *t'an-tz'u* verses of Yang Shen to the history of the novel.[138] Although the simple diction and predictable rhythms of this type of verse usually mark it as a product associated with popular culture (even when produced by literati such as Yang Shen), the net effect of inserting these poems, with their attributions to "historians" (*shih-kuan* 史官) or to named or unnamed Sung scholars— aside from the structural functions of retardation and segmentation— seems to be an appeal to classical authority, in contrast with the explicit tapping of folk wisdom and imagination in *Shui-hu* and *Hsi-yu chi*.[139] The *P'ing-hua*, it should be noted, also contains twenty-six verses of comparable style, and some of these are similarly labeled as the work of "historians." A number of these are repeated in the 1522 edition, most interestingly a eulogistic piece attributed to Su Shih, placed curiously before Ma Su's 馬謖 defeat in the *P'ing-hua*, which is identical to one of the pieces included after the death of Chu-ko Liang in the *Yen-i*.[140]

Mao Tsung-kang cuts the number of poems in his edition to half of the four hundred odd pieces in the 1522 edition, and half of these, in turn, are taken over completely unaltered. Decrying the predominance of the "ludi-crously vulgar" 俚鄙可笑 historical verse of Chou Li in what he calls the "popular edition" (*su-pen*), Mao promises to restrict inclusion of poems in his own edition to works of the greatest T'ang and Sung masters. In doing so, he gives particular prominence to the works of Tu Fu, adding pieces by him at key points and, moreover, taking the unusual editorial liberty of

[137] For the Chang Cheng-lang article, see above, nn. 28 and 43. For Crump's study, see above, n. 32.

[138] For a thorough discussion of this aspect of the development of the *San-kuo* materials, see Andrew Lo, "Historiography," pp. 232ff.

[139] The list of poets of high classical prestige cited in this way in the 1522 text includes, in addition to Tu Fu (see n. 142), Tu Mu 杜牧 (10:29b), Fan Ch'eng-ta 范成大 (12:18b), Ssu-ma Kuang (18:55a–b), Po Chü-i 白居易 (21:60a), Ch'eng I 程頤 (21:60a), Tseng Kung 曾鞏 (8:37b), and Su Shih (21:84a–b). Of particular interest to us here is a citation of a verse attributed to Shao Yung (2:50b), since we have already noted citations of Shao's poems in each of the other three novels considered above. See Cheng Chen-to, "Yen-hua," pp. 194, 218ff.

[140] See *San-kuo chih p'ing-hua*, p. 475, and 1522 edition, 21:84a–b. One curiosity about the citation of poems in the 1522 edition is the fact that one particular poem is repeated twice (with very minor alterations): on pp. 21:59b and 21:84b. See also Riftin, *Istoricheskaya epopeia*, pp. 246ff.

incorporating his own critical reading of these poems into the text itself in two cases.[141] This emphasis may, as has been suggested, reflect changes in poetic taste after the Chia-ching period, but it also indicates that Mao, too, wishes to maintain a sense of authoritative monumentality in his handling of this aspect of the rhetorical structure of the novel.[142]

In considering this rhetorical effect of the inserted poems on the novel, one must acknowledge at the same time that the point of view expressed in them leans very heavily toward the popular appreciation of the central heroes of the narrative, and generally follows images known from the stage and oral storytelling. This is already clear in the first two poems in the text—significantly devoted to Chang Fei and Kuan Yü rather than to Liu Pei or Ts'ao Ts'ao, who had already been introduced earlier with no poetic flourishes—which stick closely to the popular images of the two martial heroes. Seldom do the poems reflect either the critical attitude of the historiographical tradition or the ironies brought out by figural reflection within the narrative itself.

On the other hand, however, the basically one-sided perspective in the use of verse is counterbalanced to a large extent by the full citation of written documents within the body of the narrative—primarily memorials, imperial decrees, and personal letters, as well as formal speeches. *San-kuo* is not unique in its use of this device, but in terms of both frequency and length of quotations it once again diverges from colloquial fiction in general and the other three "classic" novels in particular.[143] Apart from the structural function exercised by such material in breaking up and retarding the narrative movement, as well as providing a pretense of historical veracity, we may note in the context of the present discussion that the voluminous citation of all this material serves to provide a more balanced perspective on the events in the narrative by representing in full conflicting points of view on many issues.

This brings us back to what I have identified as the primary rhetorical

---

[141] See Mao's *fan-li* preface, items 8 and 9, and 14:13f, 17:30, and 17:37f.

[142] The 1522 edition contains the same Tu Fu poem that appears in Mao's chapter 84. On the other hand, the 1522 edition contains two additional Tu Fu poems—one after Chu-ko Liang's assent to Liu Pei's plea in chapter 38 (8:37b) and one after his death (21:83a)— which do not appear in the Mao text. The former poem differs slightly from the standard version (see Tu Fu, *Tu-shih yin-te*, p. 487). Interestingly, all the poems that appear at this point in Mao's chapter 104 are by T'ang poets. In one comment in chapter 6 (1:39), Mao praises a particularly moving passage as "equivalent to a few *huai-ku* poems by the T'ang masters" 可當唐人懷古詩數首. For the elevation of the T'ang poets during the late Ming period, see above, Chapter 1.

[143] The *P'ing-hua* text also quotes a few such documents (e.g., pp. 394, 419ff.), but this is nothing like the use made of these materials in the *Yen-i*.

principle generating the meaning of the literati novel: the pervasive use of irony. In the preceding discussions I have defined the term "irony" in the art of narrative fiction as the entire range of structural and rhetorical devices by which the author signals a radical disjunction between appearance and reality with respect to the meaning of his text. Often this takes the form of discrepancies between illusions or expectations in the consciousness of characters on the one hand, and later eventualities on the other. In each of the three novels considered above, this ironic perspective has emerged in a somewhat different form: sardonic undercutting in *Chin P'ing Mei*, allegorical projection in *Hsi-yu chi*, and deflating of popular myths and stereotypes in *Shui-hu chuan*.

In the case of *San-kuo*, the rhetoric of irony again takes on its own particular form in the context of the historical dimension of the work. A large measure of the sense of undercutting in *San-kuo*, no doubt, derives from the inherent contradictions of political life—the sharp discrepancy between rhetoric and motive, or between ambition and fulfillment—which is the stuff of history. This is particularly true of the Three Kingdoms period, with its special circumstances of overlapping claims to legitimacy and multiple spheres of power, thus making it a favorite subject for essays in historical criticism (*shih-lun* 史論), a number of which are actually quoted in the 1522 text.[144]

We must be careful, however, to avoid confusing the ironies inherent in the historical situation with the deliberate use of ironic language as a generic feature of the literati novel. Given the many-sided connections between the *Yen-i* and the historiographical tradition, it is not surprising that Mao Tsung-kang and other early commentators find in the novel many examples of the sort of ironic expressions common in historical narrative per se—which they regularly label, using the technical terms of historiographical criticism, as "pointed rhetoric" (*ch'ü-pi* 曲筆), "the rhetoric

---

[144] For an excellent review of essays in historical criticism on *San-kuo* figures and events, especially those weighing the deeds at the fall of the Han against those of the founding generation, see Andrew Lo, "Historiography," pp. 68–88, 324f. Among such materials actually quoted in the 1522 edition, I might mention citations from the P'ei Sung-chih commentary (6:17a, 9:29a–b, 24:52a–b); Hsi Tso-ch'ih's 習鑿齒 *Han Chin Ch'un-ch'iu* 漢晉春秋 (9:6a–b, 21:63b–64a); Sun Sheng 孫盛, *Chin yang-ch'iu* 晉陽秋 (7:3a–b, 19:7a, 22:13a); to Chu Hsi (21:83b–84a); not to mention Ch'en Shou's evaluative comments taken directly from *San-kuo chih* (16:44b, 17:8a, 17:69a–b, 19:7a, 21:58b–59a, 22:12b), as well as numerous evaluative comments (*lun* 論, *tsan* 贊) by unnamed "historians" 史官 (e.g., 1:54a, 2:51b–52a, 5:8a–b, 8:68b–69a, 70b–71a, 13:12b–13a, 16:27b–28a, 43b–44a, 44b, 22:49b–50a, 24:38a, 59b–60a). Mao Tsung-kang consistently cuts all these materials. The *Han Chin Ch'un-ch'iu* and *Chin yang-ch'iu* may be found in *Huang-shih i-shu k'ao*, ed. Huang Shih (reprint ed., Taipei: I-wen, 1971), vol. 31.

of the historian" (*shih-pi* 史筆), or in a more restricted sense, "the rhetoric of the Spring and Autumn Annals" (*Ch'un-ch'iu pi-fa* 春秋筆法).[145] In my close reading of the novel in the following pages, I will have frequent occasion to mention places in which the novelist, very much in the tradition of the *ch'ü-pi* of the historian, uses pointed turns of phrase to subtly turn the reader's attention to the discrepancy between the simplistic surface of noble aims and heroic deeds, and the underlying complexities of historical judgment. Although the specific nature of the historical sources of *San-kuo* leaves less room here than in the other three novels for manipulating such details as proper names and chronology, the author still manages to employ a wide range of devices to reinforce his ironic perspective—from the placement of single loaded words to the insertion of larger units such as quoted speeches and documents.[146] For the purpose of my discussion of the *San-kuo yen-i* together with the other Ming masterworks, however, I will again focus on the manner in which many of these ironies are generated by figural reflection and plot reverses within the text itself—principally through the creation of ironic resonances among recurrent figures in the narrative.[147]

[145] For examples of Mao's use of the term *ch'ü-pi*, see chapters 9 (2:11) and 22 (4:12); for his frequent use of the expression "pointed treatment" (*wen-ch'ü* 文曲), see chapter 26 (4:43). The term *shih-pi* occurs in Mao's comments on chapter 97 (16:18), as well as in the "Li Cho-wu" commentary edition, chapter 111 (p. 1b). Mao uses the expression *Ch'un-ch'iu chih i* 春秋之義 in chapter 117 (19:31), and "Li Cho-wu" uses it in chapter 114 (p. 10a). One might also read into the "Li Yü" commentator's frequent references to "deeper meaning" (*shen-i* 深義) or "profound stabs" (*tz'u te shen* 刺得深) an interest in this sort of further level of meaning (e.g., chapter 26, p. 6b; 40, p. 2b). The 1494 preface also seems to have the *Ch'un-ch'iu* type of pointed use of terms in mind when it discusses "the moral judgment evident within every single word" (⋯一字之中以見當時君臣父子之道). For a related discussion on the rhetorical touches of the *San-kuo chih* treatment of this material, see Winston L. Y. Yang, "Literary Transformation," pp. 51ff.

[146] The author's use of personal names in the narrative is of course predetermined by his historical sources. But he must have noticed the parallel in the style-names of Liu Pei (Hsüan-te 玄德) and Ts'ao Ts'ao (Meng-te 孟德), the fact that the downfall of both Shu and Wu revolves around a figure named "Hao" (Huang Hao and Sun Hao), or the neat opposition in the names of the two figures Wang Chün 王濬 and Wang Hun 王渾, who engage in a debate over the final strategy of the Chin conquerors in chapter 120. The "Li Cho-wu" commentator, at any rate, takes the time to point out some of the punning implications of certain personal names in a note in chapter 105 (p. 16b). In the same vein, we may imagine that the author perceived the irony in the name of Liu Pei's first official post in chapter 2 (An-hsi hsien 安喜縣), with which he is noticeably less than "delighted," as well as the title awarded to his son Liu Shan (An-le kung 安樂公) after his humiliating surrender in chapter 119. The author may also have been familiar with an association in the popular tradition between the locale Pai-ti ch'eng 白帝城 and the story of usurpation of imperial prerogatives by the renegade Shu leader Kung-sun Shu 公孫述 (see Hu Tseng, *Hsin tiao-chu yung-shih-shih, chüan* 3, p. 9b).

[147] See Mao Tsung-kang's discussion of the ironic reverses in the narrative, in his *tu-fa*, item 11, pp. 7f., and in chapter 38 (6:37).

Insofar as the identification of irony in a narrative text necessarily rests on the reconstruction of authorial intention, we must come to terms here with the problem of the basic sympathies and prejudices of the author vis-à-vis the central figures of Three Kingdoms history. Much ink has been spilled—from both Ming-Ch'ing brushes and modern pens—over the apparent fact that the author of the *Yen-i* basically sides with Shu-Han rather than with Wei in the debate over the legitimate succession to the Han, and consequently seeks to "exalt Liu Pei and denigrate Ts'ao Ts'ao" (*ch'ung Liu ch'u Ts'ao* 崇劉黜曹).[148] This attitude is entirely in keeping with my earlier observation regarding the novel's major debt to popular sources—the *P'ing-hua* and drama—on the one hand, and specifically to the *T'ung-chien kang-mu* among historiographical works on the other, since all these sources agree on this point.

However, this tendency has left many modern scholars at a loss for how to interpret those aspects of the text that appear to place Liu Pei in particular and the Shu-Han cause in general in an ironic light. Hu Shih, among others, concludes that such passages simply indicate the failure of the author to fully realize the picture he really wishes to convey, a view shared by Lu Hsün, Sun K'ai-ti, and Cheng Chen-to, and repeated more recently by Tung Mei-k'an and Winston Yang.[149] In another place, however, Hu Shih explains a bit apologetically that the author was simply following the prevailing opinion on the issue of legitimate succession, but that that did not prevent him from improving the image of Ts'ao Ts'ao at the expense of Liu Pei.[150] C. T. Hsia effectively refutes the simplistic reading of the novel as an unsuccessful attempt to champion the Shu cause, and explains the darker aspects of the text in terms of the more profound insight into the historical process and human character on the part of Lo Kuan-chung.[151]

For the purposes of my own discussion, I will say that the perceived

---

[148] See for example Mao Tsung-kang's extended discussion of the question of the legitimate succession (*cheng-t'ung* 正統) in his *tu-fa*, item 1, p. 1. More recently, the question has been taken up in C. T. Hsia, *Classic Novel*, pp. 40ff.; Tung Mei-k'an, *Shih-lun*, pp. 18ff.; and Andrew Lo, "Historiography," pp. 89ff.

[149] Hu Shih, "Yen-i hsü," pp. 473f. See Lu Hsün, *Chung-kuo hsiao-shuo shih-lüeh*, pp. 135f.; Sun K'ai-ti, "P'ing-hua yü yen-i," pp. 115f.; Cheng Chen-to, "Yen-hua," pp. 208ff.; Tung Mei-k'an, *Shih-lun*, pp. 1ff.; and Winston L. Y. Yang, "Literary Transformation," p. 56. The "reverse" treatment of Ts'ao Ts'ao is described with the term *fan-mien jen-wu* 反面人物 by Liu Chih-chien, "Lo Kuan-chung wei shen-mo yao fan-tui Ts'ao Ts'ao," pp. 335f. Cf. the similar approach to *Shui-hu chuan* (see Chapter 4, Part V).

[150] Hu Shih, "Ta Ch'ien Hsüan-t'ung shu," p. 41.

[151] C. T. Hsia, *Classic Novel*, pp. 40ff., 48. See esp. p. 41, where he points out that Hu Shih's critical reading of the novel is restricted by the fact that it is based primarily on the Mao Tsung-kang edition.

ambiguity on this question in fact locates *San-kuo* precisely within the generic bounds of the literati novel. On the one hand, when we compare the *Yen-i* with the historian's view presented in the *San-kuo chih*, the *Tzu-chih t'ung-chien*, and especially with *shih-lun* essays on the Three Kingdoms history, we find here in the novel an explicitly more sympathetic treatment of the vicissitudes of Liu Pei's career.[152] Even in the *T'ung-chien kang-mu*, after all, there is little in the way of propagandistic flourishes to support its stated position in Liu Pei's favor on the legitimacy question. On the other hand, a careful comparison shows a marked divergence of the novel from the simplistic hero images of popular fiction and drama, particularly in the fine details of presentation. The contribution of the 1522 edition is even more evident on this point, in view of the changes later introduced by Mao Tsung-kang to shore up his own view of the legitimate succession, stated polemically in the first section of his *tu-fa* introduction.[153] The net effect of this ambivalent position of the novel, halfway between the enthusiastic sympathy of the popular hero cycles and the assumed objectivity of official historiography, is a pervasive projection of irony throughout the work. As in our other three novels, we have in *San-kuo* an ironic juxtaposition of popular images with a serious consideration of intellectual issues character-istic of the classical literary tradition—one that dictates neither simple-minded lionization nor cynical deflating, but seeks to explore the parameters of historical achievement through positive and negative examples. With this perspective in mind, I will proceed to consider the ironic treatment of the central figures in the novel—first one by one, and then as they reflect on one another in structural groupings—with an eye out for the diver-gence of the images in the novel from both historical and popular sources.

IV

I will begin my review as the narrative does with the three sworn brothers, taking first among them Kuan Yü, since his case presents the clearest contrast between the popular image of the figure and that devel-

---

[152] The "Li Cho-wu" commentator notes in several places the discrepancy between the novel and the view of the official histories: e.g., chapters 76 (p. 12a) and 113 (p. 5b).

[153] Beyond the obvious fact of the inclusion of a number of more objective essays of historical criticism within the 1522 text, some of the interlinear notes added by the compiler (or later editor) of this edition also emphasize a more critical view. In addition to numerous textual comments touching on the *cheng-t'ung* question, Mao Tsung-kang's hand is visible in such things as his revision of chapter titles (e.g., chapter 80, from "The King of Han-chung Proclaims Himself Emperor in Ch'eng-tu" 漢中王成都稱帝 to "The King of Han Assumes the Throne to Continue the Grand Succession" 漢王正位續大統).

oped in the literati novel.[154] To anyone whose judgment of Kuan Yü in the *Yen-i* is based on a careful reading of the text and not on preconceptions brought from the stage and oral storytelling, it is clear that what we view in the pages of the novel is something less than the awesome figure of a god, such as he had become in the popular tradition by the time of the novel's publication.[155] The later canonization of Kuan Yü in the pantheon of Chinese popular religion is, in fact, only barely reflected in the pages of the novel, and that only after the end of a career of strictly human proportions.[156] Modern critics have attempted to rationalize this discrepancy with various arguments, but within the context of this study I would simply observe that we have here a prime example of the critical revision of source materials, what I have posited as the key to the development of the Ming literati novel.[157]

The portrayal of Kuan Yü in the novel does not make as much out of his physical qualities and military prowess as we would expect. We are given a perfunctory description of his imposing stature and exceptional physiognomy in the passage drawn from the *San-kuo chih* with which he is introduced in chapter 1, and the first poem in the text is a patently popular verse identifying him with his weapon: the Green Dragon Scimitar 青龍刀.[158] But a bit surprisingly, these features are rarely stressed in the ensuing episodes. Instead, the novel focuses attention on less tangible qualities of spirit: his supreme self-confidence in dispatching Hua Hsiung 華雄 in chapter 5, his single-minded loyalty to Liu Pei in the sojourn with

---

[154] See Cheng Chen-to, "Yen-hua," pp. 189f.

[155] For the early canonization of Kuan Yü, see Chao Ts'ung, *Ssu ta hsiao-shuo*, p. 103; Hu Shih, "Yen-i hsü," p. 470; Cheng Chen-to, "Yen-hua," pp. 167f.; Tung Mei-k'an, *Shih-lun*, p. 76; and Fang Tsu-shen, "Lo Kuan-chung yü yen-i," p. 57. This tendency in the popular tradition seems to have been accentuated in the Ch'ing period, with direct influence on the twentieth-century apprehension of the figure in the novel.

[156] That is, in the "theophany" (*hsien-sheng* 顯聖) episode in chapter 77 and the supernatural intervention in chapter 83. This aspect of the Kuan Yü cult is reported in a long citation from the Ch'an text *Ch'uan-teng lu* 傳燈錄, which is quoted in chapter 77 of the 1522 edition (16:22b–23b). The "Li Cho-wu" commentator's frequent application to Kuan Yü of the epithets "A true Buddha! A Sage!" 佛, 聖 refers to human rather than divine attributes.

[157] See Hu Shih and C. T. Hsia remarks, nn. 149 and 151.

[158] For a full treatment of the iconography of Kuan Yü in the *Yen-i* and other materials, see Riftin, *Istoricheskaya epopeia*, pp. 238f., and *Ot mifa k romanu*, pp. 220ff., 271–76. He appears at one point identified solely with the iconographic emblems of his sword and his book in a passage in the 1522 edition (3:6b). Curiously, the various editions of the novel differ on Kuan Yü's height: it is given as nine *ch'ih* 尺 and three *ts'un* 寸 in the 1522 edition; but this becomes nine-five in the "Li Cho-wu" and "Li Yü" commentary editions and the *Ying-hsiung p'u*, and a flat nine *ch'ih* in the Mao text. (The Yuan *tsa-chü* play *T'ao-yüan chieh-i* gives the figure as nine-two.) The initial descriptive poem appears in the 1522 edition on page 1:11a (it is cut by Mao Tsung-kang). For all citations to *tsa-chü* texts in the following discussion, see n. 35.

Ts'ao Ts'ao in chapters 25–28. Mao Tsung-kang concentrates on these qualities in his *tu-fa* discussion of Kuan Yü as one of the "three paragons" (*san-chüeh* 三絕) and significantly, he caps his list of praises with the term "exceptional integrity" (*ta-chieh* 大節).[159] Mao's mention of this last quality is of particular interest, since this expression often refers to the sort of sexual abstemiousness we have observed in the hero figures in *Shui-hu chuan* (and it will come up again at several points in the following pages), although in fact the 1522 text provides very little narrative evidence for this attribute.[160] Mao, however, obviously felt this added point to be obligatory, since he insists on interpolating into his text the episode of "holding a candle until dawn" (*ping-chu ta-tan* 秉燭達旦) to bring out this aspect of Kuan Yü's portrait.[161] Among the leading examples of heroic exploits assigned to Kuan Yü in the course of the narrative, the majority— such as "the killing of Yen Liang" (*tz'u Yen Liang* 刺顏良), "a lone journey for a thousand leagues" (*ch'ien-li tu-hsing* 千里獨行), "cutting down the generals at the five passes" (*wu-kuan chan-chiang* 五關斬將), and "the lone swordsman attends a banquet" (*tan-tao fu-hui* 單刀赴會)—correspond to fixed episode units of drama and popular storytelling.[162] It is all the more significant, therefore, that in practically every one of these cases we can observe an ironic note, or a suggestion of moral ambiguity, which reveals the mind of the author probing beneath the heroic surface toward the underlying issues.

The most obvious "problem" in the character of Kuan Yü is his arrogance, as explicitly identified in the words of the final evaluation in his *San-kuo chih* biography, which the novelist puts into the mouth of Chu-ko

---

[159] See *tu-fa*, item 2, p. 2.

[160] This point about Kuan Yü's resistance to temptation is underscored in chapter 25 (1522, 5:58a; MTK, 4:35), when Ts'ao Ts'ao sends his "guest" a harem of ten lovely maidens, whom he promptly turns over to the service of Lady Mi and Lady Kan. This detail is included in the *P'ing-hua* (p. 402), and the play *I-yung tz'u-chin* (Act 1), p. 141, but is cut out in the *P'ing-lin* and *Ying-hsiung p'u* versions. A further example of this side of the Kuan Yü image in the popular tradition is seen in the nonextant play entitled *Kuan Yü Kills Tiao-ch'an on a Moonlit Night*, mentioned in Chai Hao *T'ung-su pien*, *chüan* 20, p. 227; cited in Fu Hsi-hua, *Yuan-tai*, p. 352 (see Mao's *fan-li*, item 10, and above, n. 37). Cf. Kuan Yü's demonstrative refusal of a marriage for his daughter in chapter 73.

[161] Mao insists in his *fan-li* preface, item 3, that he is following the "original text" 古本 as opposed to the "popular edition" 俗本 in this revision. I have been unable to find any trace of the *ping-chu ta-tan* episode in the extant *tsa-chü* dramas, but the *P'ing-hua* (pp. 398, 402) does record Kuan Yü's insistence on separate quarters, as does the 1522 edition (5:57b). The *Lu-kuei pu* records the title of one play entitled "Holding a Candle at Dawn" (*Ping-chu tan* 秉燭旦), but from the description it seems to be an entirely different story (see Fu Hsi-hua, *Yuan-tai*, p. 197). See also Chai Hao, *T'ung-su pien*, *chüan* 20, p. 227.

[162] See the *P'ing-hua*, pp. 400, 404, 406, and above, n. 35.

Liang in chapter 78.[163] Of course, staunch pride cannot be considered a fault in a military hero, and this, no doubt, is the sense in which Kuan Yü's towering haughtiness is taken in the popular tradition. In the novel, however, the admirable side of this image is sharply undercut as the author focuses attention on a series of scenes in which Kuan Yü's pride out only fails to bear out its promise, but ultimately leads to his own destruction.

Hints of weak points in the armor of his invincibility begin to appear early in the text. For example, soon after the famous incident in chapter 5 in which Kuan Yü makes quick work of an opposing champion before his wine has time to cool, his image as a supreme warrior is diminished when he is shown to be powerless against Lü Pu, even with the help of his two "brothers"; and in chapter 31 he is soundly defeated by Ts'ao Ts'ao's forces. Even in the celebrated episode known in the popular tradition as "the lone swordsman attends a banquet" (*tan-tao fu-hui*), the image of Kuan Yü's courage is here compromised by his carefully laid plans for back-up forces to extricate himself from possible danger, an aspect of the scene in the novel not found in the *P'ing-hua*.[164]

The implications of Kuan Yü's image as a lone warrior are deepened in the novel by developing the accompanying dimension of his frequent hostility toward his own peers. This is most evident in his violent reaction to the inclusion of his name alongside those of his comrades-in-arms in the ranking of the "five tiger generals" upon Liu Pei's ascension as King of Han-chung; but it also applies to his tense relations with Chang Fei, whom he opposes at several points, and to his uneasy partnership with Chu-ko Liang.[165] The various texts differ on whether Kuan Yü is displeased from

[163] Cf. Ch'eng Yü's 程昱 remark in MTK, chapter 50 (8 : 34): "I have known for some time that Kuan Yü is arrogant toward his superiors but displays sentimental weakness toward those in an inferior position to him" 某素知雲長傲上而不忍下. The "Li Cho-wu" commentator points to Kuan Yü's "unmitigated arrogance" (*i-wei chiao-ao* 一味驕傲) in chapter 75 (11b). See also Hu Shih's complaint ("Yen-i hsü," p. 473) that the noble hero "has become an arrogant warrior with no sense of strategy" 關羽竟成了一個驕傲無謀的武夫.

[164] The ironic treatment of the *tan-tao fu-hui* scene in the *Yen-i* is pointed up by Kuan Yü's boasting, and by the fact that he admits that his principal motivation for the gesture is the preservation of his own reputation (MTK, 11 : 20). The scene appears in the *P'ing-hua*, but there it comes after the incident of Kuan Yü's wounded arm (p. 457).

[165] Mao Tsung-kang (12 : 27) cuts Kuan Yü's tears of remorse after Pi Shih's 費詩 speech to soothe his initial rage at the "five generals" list (cf. 1522, 15 : 44a). The precise order of the five generals also varies from edition to edition. In the 1522 text (15 : 43b) and the *P'ing-lin* it is reported as Kuan, Chang, Ma, Chao, Huang, although in Liu Pei's earlier announcement (15 : 36a) it is Kuan, Chang, Ma, Huang, Chao, as it also appears in the *Ying-hsiung p'u*; in the *Chih-chuan* and *Ch'üan-chuan* it becomes Kuan, Ma, Chang, Huang, Chao; in the "Li Cho-wu" and "Li Yü" and Mao Tsung-kang editions it is given as Kuan, Chang, Chao, Ma, Huang. Kuan Yü's early opposition to Chang Fei appears in MTK,

the outset with Liu Pei's courting of Chu-ko Liang, but tension between the two is clearly felt in a number of scenes.[166]

Of particular importance are Kuan Yü's frequent expressions of contempt for the older warriors, whose presumption in fighting against, or even alongside, of him presents a grave affront to his sense of dignity. This attitude is emphasized in chapter 53, for example, in his disdain for Huang Chung 黃忠. As Kuan Yü himself grows older in the course of the narrative (he is fifty-eight when he is killed), the irony of this arrogance towards older warriors becomes increasingly pointed.

From the time of Liu Pei's ascendance to the status of royalty in chapter 73, the trajectory of Kuan Yü's fall becomes more and more precipitous. In that chapter, his burst of wounded pride at the five-generals ranking and his arrogant rejection of Sun Ch'üan's offer of a marriage to his daughter are followed by the highly suggestive dream in which he is wounded in the thigh by a wild boar, the pain from which continues even after he wakes up.[167] Thereafter, the stark contrast between boundless self-confidence and flagging powers becomes more and more apparent. Although the author withholds direct description of Kuan Yü's advancing age, the reader is reminded of this in chapter 74 when Kuan P'ing 關平 begs to be allowed to replace his father in the fight against P'ang Te 龐德.[168] This reaches its culmination in chapter 75, in the famous scene known to all readers from the popular tradition of Kuan Yü laughing and playing chess while a surgeon lays his arm open to the bone.[169] This scene certainly presents one of the most impressive positive examples of Kuan Yü's force of will, but at the same time it marks the beginning of the end. Soon after the operation

---

chapter 14 (2:49) and 16 (3:12), and this sense of rivalry reaches its peak when he challenges Ma Ch'ao to a tournament in chapter 65 (11:16).

[166] For example, MTK, 6:32ff. The repeated expression "displeased" (*pu-yüeh* 不悅) appears in the historical sources (cf. *T'ung-chien kang-mu*, 13:76b, *San-kuo chih*, 4:193, as well as the *T'ung-chien chi-shih pen-mo* version of the scene), but in the *P'ing-hua* only Chang Fei expresses this attitude and Kuan Yü rebukes him for it (p. 411). This detail is trimmed in the *P'ing-lin* edition. In a comment in chapter 84 (14:1), Mao Tsung-kang attributes Kuan Yü's downfall to his failure to heed Chu-ko Liang's advice (see also Tung Mei-k'an, *Shih-lun*, p. 76ff.).

[167] MTK, 12:28. Cf. the K'ang-hsi essay on Kuan Yü entitled "Han ch'ien chiang-chün Chuang-mou Kuan-hou tz'u-pi" 漢前將軍壯繆關侯祠壁, by Tai I 戴易, pp. 1b–2a, attached as a preface to some "Li Cho-wu" commentary editions: "One might say that this refusal of a marriage proposal was a gross overstatement" 或以拒婚爲太甚.

[168] In editing this scene, Mao Tsung-kang cuts Kuan P'ing's plea (1522, 15:54b): "Father, you have maintained your heroic dignity for thirty years; I hope you won't throw away the towering importance of your person over a single word of insult...." 父親守三十年之英風, 不可因一言之辱, 而棄泰山之重....

[169] Cf. Kuan Yü's boast in this scene (MTK, 12:38): "How can you compare me with the common run of mankind?" 吾豈比世間俗子.

we learn that the wound has seriously weakened the aging warrior, and his continued boasts and refusal to admit defeat are belied when he falls from his horse, suffers a series of crushing setbacks, and causes the symbolically crucial loss of Ching-chou. By the end in chapter 77, he reaches a point at which his undaunted spirit also begins to flag. Plagued, like Chou Yü earlier, by the reopening of his wound, he loses his will to continue the battle and is finally caught in a net and easily beheaded by his enemies.[170]

The manner in which the *Yen-i* insists on presenting the fall of Kuan Yü as a gradual process of debilitation, rather than a simple case of a hero tragically cut down at the peak of his glory, brings to mind certain aspects of the treatment of Wu Sung in the *fan-pen Shui-hu chuan*, as considered in the preceding chapter. In addition to the comparable strength and person-alities of the two heroes, we may recall that Kuan Yü, like Wu Sung, first appears in chapter 1 as a fugitive from justice, having slain a man in righteous indignation, and his encounter with the monk P'u-ching 普淨 (and his later posthumous enlightenment at Yü-ch'üan shan 玉泉山) raise an aspect of his character that seems a bit out of place in the portrait in *San-kuo*, but resonates noticeably with the concluding scenes of Wu Sung's depiction in *Shui-hu*.[171]

In reviewing the critical treatment of the Kuan Yü figure in *San-kuo chih yen-i*, I wish to suggest that the central problem raised by the author in this context is not a deficiency, but a surfeit, of valor. In each of the major scenes focusing on Kuan Yü as an individual, we witness what might be called an overplaying of the role of the noble hero. This is brought out at several points in the narrative where his insistence on cleaving to his own self-image as an honorable man leads to serious moral quandaries or else to costly defeats.

In the treatment of the series of episodes involving his sojourn in Ts'ao Ts'ao's camp, for example, the author at no time hints that Kuan Yü's behavior is guided by anything other than selfless loyalty to Liu Pei. (His initial conditions of surrender to Ts'ao Ts'ao in chapter 25 cover him from any suspicion of collusion, and he steadfastly resists being swayed by all of Ts'ao Ts'ao's blandishments.) But at the same time, certain details in the narrative cast a shadow of ambiguity over his heroic stance. First, the killing of Yen Liang 顏良 as a demonstration to Ts'ao Ts'ao of his own good faith need not, I suppose, be read sentimentally—although Yen Liang

---

[170] See MTK, 13:2, and 1522, 16:18b.

[171] The fact that a monk of the same name (written 普靜 in Mao edition) also figures prominently in *Chin P'ing Mei* indicates that this role constitutes a *topos* of the Chinese fiction tradition. The initial description of Kuan Yü as a fugitive is developed in the play *T'ao-yüan chieh-i* (p. 2b). I will consider in Part V of this chapter a passage in the novel in which Kuan Yü gives voice to Taoist sentiments.

is fighting on the same side as Liu Pei at the time. The 1522 edition, however, inserts a telling note at this point, informing us that Yen Liang was actually bringing Liu Pei's personal message to Kuan Yü and was therefore completely unsuspecting when Kuan Yü cut him down.[172] The sense that this is more than an isolated accident of war seems to emerge in the following pages when, after a number of well-intentioned men have fallen victim to Kuan Yü's sense of honor in his dash through the five passes to fulfill his personal bond to Liu Pei, he cuts down Ts'ai Yang 蔡陽 in cold blood, again with the exclusive aim of vindicating his own personal reputation.[173]

The most damaging example of Kuan Yü's overrating of personal honor is surely his "honorable release" (*i-shih* 義釋) of Ts'ao Ts'ao after the Battle of the Red Cliffs in chapter 50—with its fateful consequences for the course of the Three Kingdoms history. Significantly, Kuan Yü had already refrained from killing Ts'ao Ts'ao once before, ostensibly in deference to Liu Pei's will in chapter 20, and in chapter 42 he expresses regret for this omission.[174]

The fact that the author of the *Yen-i* makes this a point of ironic focus, rather than simply a dramatic confrontation between heroes, becomes clear when we compare this treatment of the scene with other versions of the narrative: the historical sources, which only mention Ts'ao Ts'ao's escape in passing, or the *P'ing-hua*, which tells of Ts'ao Ts'ao slipping away in a fog.[175] The novel further presses the issue in the fine details of its presentation. When faced with Ts'ao Ts'ao's last-ditch plea for release on the grounds of his earlier largesse toward Kuan Yü, we are told in the 1522 edition that Kuan Yü "hung his head for a long while in silence" (*ti-shou liang-chiu pu-yü* 低頭良久不語), and several later editions add the sugges-

---

[172] 1522, 5:66a. In many versions of the narrative the killing of Yen Liang is coupled with a similar victory over Wen Ch'ou 文醜. See, for example, the play *Ch'ien-li tu-hsing*, pp. 8a–b. In the historical sources it is Ts'ao Ts'ao who actually disposes of Wen Ch'ou (*San-kuo chih*, 1:19).

[173] MTK, chapter 28 (5:14). Mao Tsung-kang attempts to put this act in a positive light by changing the chapter title from "As the Drums Roll, Kuan Yü Puts Ts'ai Yang to Death" 雲長搷鼓斬蔡陽 to "Ts'ai Yang Is Put to Death and All Suspicion between the Brothers is Dispelled" 斬蔡陽兄弟釋疑. In the historical sources (e.g., *San-kuo chih*, 4:876) it is Liu Pei himself who dispatches Ts'ai Yang. The former title follows that of a nonexistent Yuan *tsa-chü* (see Fu Hsi-hua, *Yuan-tai*, p. 352).

[174] MTK, 7:28. Liu Pei, in reply, repeats his claim that at the time of the earlier confrontation he was "reluctant to take aim at the rat for fear of harming the dish" 投鼠忌器. This expression is derived from the "Biography of Chia I" 賈宜, in *Hou Han shu*, 5:2255. The "Li Cho-wu" commentator heaps praise on Kuan Yü in this scene (chapter 20, pp. 4a, 10b), although it is not clear whether his remarks are directed toward Kuan Yü's righteous indignation or his dutiful restraint.

[175] See *P'ing-hua*, p. 429; *San-kuo chih*, 1:31, 4:915; and *Tzu-chih t'ung-chien*, pp. 2093f.

tive words "his sentiments were moved" (*tung ch'i hsin* 動其心).[176] When
called to account by Chu-ko Liang in the ensuing scene, Kuan Yü admits
that he has committed a grave error (he does not do so in the *P'ing-hua*),
but only three chapters later the author uses the restaging of an *i-shih* scene
(this time with Huang Chung) to reopen the issue.[177]

Kuan Yü's overblown sense of personal honor raises one of the most
agonized issues of the entire work: the conflict between private and public
standards of morality, or that between self-image and responsibility to
others. Presumably Tung Mei-k'an's statement that Kuan Yü is "the incarnation of a sense of valor" (*i chih hua-shen* 義之化身) is meant to be a
positive evaluation, but in this remark he also puts his finger on one of the
central questions raised in the novel.[178] The association between the Kuan
Yü figure and the concept of personal honor (*i*) is, to be sure, an integral
part of the popular tradition, and is especially common in drama. We need
only think of examples such as the play "Honor and Valor Refuse a Reward"
(*I-yung tz'u-chin*). But the *Yen-i* raises this problem to the level of a serious
intellectual issue, one I will now consider in several other instances.[179]

In the case of Chang Fei, the difference in emphasis between the literati
novel and the popular image in storytelling and drama is even more
striking. Although Chang Fei is basically a less towering figure than Kuan
Yü—both in physical size and in heroic stature—and as such lends himself
more readily to critical deflation, still it will be fairly easy to demonstrate
that the generally positive image in the *P'ing-hua* and several extant *tsa-chü*
plays is severely undercut in the pages of the *Yen-i*.[180]

[176] The expression "hung his head" appears in 1522, 10:62a. Significantly, it is Ts'ao
Ts'ao's reminder of Kuan Yü's unjustified killing of the generals at the five passes that seems
to sway him. The expression "his sentiments were moved" appears in the *Chih-chuan*,
Ch'üan-chuan, *P'ing-lin*, and other versions. In the play *Huang-ho lou* (Act 4, pp. 14a ff.) Kuan
Yü twice acknowledges his error in releasing Ts'ao Ts'ao, and in another *tsa-chü* drama,
P'ang lüeh ssu-chün (p. 6a), it is even suggested that Kuan Yü's action may have been
motivated by gratitude for gifts. See also Tung Mei-k'an, *Shih-lun*, pp. 73f.

[177] Mao Tsung-kang emphasizes this restaging by changing the chapter title from
"Huang Chung and Wei Yen Deliver Ch'ang-sha" 黃忠魏延獻長沙 to "Kuan Yü Honorably Releases Huang Chung" 關雲長義釋黃漢升. See also *tu-fa*, item 20, p. 12.

[178] Tung Mei-k'an, *Shih-lun*, p. 76.

[179] In some editions of the *San-kuo chih*, Kuan Yü is given a posthumous title of Chung-i
hou 忠義侯 (e.g., *Erh-shih-liu shih* 二十六史 [Taipei: Ch'i-ming, 1961], *Shu chih* 蜀志, *chüan*
6, p. 201), but this is corrected in other editions to Chuang-mou hou 壯繆侯 (*San-kuo chih*,
4:942). This aspect of the popular image of Kuan Yü is emphasized in many dramas, such
as *Nu-chan Kuan P'ing* (in which Kuan Yü resolves to execute his own son in punishment
for a mistaken killing) and *I-yung tz'u-chin*. The association of Kuan Yü with the *Ch'un-ch'iu*
classic seems to emphasize this same point (this detail also appears in the *P'ing-hua*, p. 357).

[180] See, for example, Chang Fei's heroic posture in the *tsa-chü* plays *San-ch'u Hsiao-p'ei*,
Tan-chan Lü Pu, *San-chan Lü Pu*, and *Hsing-lin chuang*. The first three of these titles are taken

In various phases of the popular tradition, Chang Fei is consistently portrayed in terms of his image as an incorrigible ruffian. Evidence of the formation of this stereotype exists as early as T'ang storytelling, as seen in the well-known line in a poem by Li Shang-yin—"Sometimes they would make fun of Chang Fei's coarseness" (*huo nüeh Chang Fei hu* 或謔張飛胡)— and appears in the virtually inseparable epithet "rude" (*mang* 莽) applied in a number of Yuan *tsa-chü* plays dealing with him.[181] The irrepressible energy implied by these epithets in their more positive sense is tapped in Chang Fei's most heroic deeds, notably in the famous shout at Ch'ang-pan Bridge in chapter 42, a scene reminiscent of last-ditch stands on bridges in the hero cycles of other literatures.[182] Mao Tsung-kang apparently senses this when he adds to the title of this chapter the stock term "wreaks great havoc" (*ta-nao* 大鬧).

The image of Chang Fei running wild, of course, parallels that of Li K'uei 李逵 in *Shui-hu chuan* (and this was later to become a staple figure in the "military romance" genre). In fact, this association is confirmed early in the novel when he reverts to banditry at several points.[183] It is not surprising, therefore, that many traditional and modern readers have expressed enthusiastic praise for Chang Fei's appealing freedom from inhibition. For example, the "Li Cho-wu" commentator frequently interjects the remark "A refreshing character!" (*k'uai-jen* 快人) or even "A Sage!" (*sheng-jen* 聖人) in

---

over as episode titles in the *P'ing-hua* (pp. 378, 379, 386), a fact that points up the corresponding amplification of the Chang Fei figure in that text. In the play *Shuang-fu meng*, much of Act 3 is devoted to an enumeration of Chang Fei's heroic deeds. See Tung Mei-k'an, *Shih-lun*, pp. 83f. Cf. the term "heroic" (*hsiung-chuang* 雄壯) applied to Chang Fei in the *San-kuo chih*, 4:942.

[181] See the poem "Chiao-erh shih" 驕兒詩, in *Li I-shan shih-chi* 李義山詩集, *Ssu-pu ts'ung-k'an* edition, *ch*. 1, p. 1. See also the above *tsa-chü*, plus *Shih-liu yüan* (full title: "*Mang Chang Fei ta-nao Shih-liu yüan*"—referred to in n. 76). For a discussion of the interpretation of the term "rudeness," see C. T. Hsia, *Classic Novel*, n. 26 to Introduction (pp. 327–28). See also Riftin, *Ot mifa*, pp. 220ff., 276ff. The final evaluation of Chang Fei in *San-kuo chih* (4:951) applies to him the term "violent" (*pao* 暴).

[182] The Ch'ang-pan Bridge episode is recorded in the *San-kuo chih* (4:939), as well as in the *Tzu-chih t'ung-chien* (p. 2084) and the *Kang-mu* (13:83b). It is also described in the play *Shuang-fu meng*, p. 64. In the novel, the impressiveness of Chang Fei's feat is offset somewhat by the more significant contribution of Chao Yün's rescue of Liu Pei's wives in the adjacent narrative. The motif of Chang Fei's crushing shout is again brought out in chapter 53 (9:10). Cf. the comparable motif in the Japanese historical narratives on Yoshitsune.

[183] Cf. the figure Ch'eng Yao-chin 程咬金 in *Sui-T'ang yen-i* or Niu Kao 牛皋 in *Shuo-Yüeh ch'üan-chuan*. The "Li Yü" commentator seems to have the Wu Sung figure in mind when he remarks in chapter 70 (3a) that "the drunk Chang Fei is actually the sober Chang Fei" 醉張飛却是醒張飛. The description of Chang Fei's reversion to banditry in chapter 23 (1522, 6:40b) is cut by Mao Tsung-kang. Cf. an earlier scene in chapter 16 (1522, 4:10b), in which Chang Fei poses as a horse thief to steal some of Lü Pu's mounts.

response to Chang Fei's antics, much as the commentators applaud Li K'uei in *Shui-hu chuan* with similar exclamations.[184] On the other hand, the early critics sometimes attempt to justify this praise for Chang Fei's roughness by explaining that this may be just a deceptive exterior masking what is actually sharp cunning within. Thus "Li Cho-wu" refers at several points to Chang Fei's "cleverness within roughness," and even the editor of the 1522 edition adds an interlinear note pointing out an instance in which "the rough man can accomplish fine deeds" (*ts'u-jen tso hsi-shih* 粗人做細事).[185]

In assessing the revision of this popular image in the literati novel form we observe, once again, that these particular aspects of character are pointedly linked to serious problems in the course of the narrative. It is immediately clear that, for all his rough-hewn charm, Chang Fei's relations with the other heroes in the novel are marked more by bitter hostility than by brotherly camaraderie. First, Kuan Yü's less than wholehearted respect for his sworn brother, already noted, is clearly mutual. Chang Fei's harsh accusation of Kuan Yü for treason in chapter 28, dispelled only after Kuan Yü cuts down Ts'ai Yang, is probably justified in the light of the circumstantial evidence. But this distrust erupts into head-on rivalry in the campaigns of chapters 65 and 66, as Liu Pei comes into his own in Shu and his two sworn brothers jockey for position in the new military hierarchy.[186]

The same situation holds in his relations with Chu-ko Liang. Chang Fei's hostile opposition to Liu Pei's three visits to the "reclining dragon," punctuated by the repeated formula "he was displeased" (*pu-yüeh* 不悅), may perhaps be read as a sort of comic relief to the mock seriousness of the scene, although his curses and threats to burn down Chu-ko Liang's house cut a bit deeper.[187] In any event, starting from Chu-ko Liang's first battle at Po-wang p'o, where he immediately objects to his new colleague's tactics, through a whole series of operations in which he is allowed to participate only on condition of a humiliating pledge, Chang's deep resentment toward his brother's chief adviser is never dispelled.

These feelings of hostility are also directed toward a number of other

---

[184] See especially the Jung-yü t'ang commentary edition of *Shui-hu chuan* (for a discussion of the attribution of this commentary to Li Chih, see Chapter 4, p. 289, and the Appendix of this book). Tung Mei-k'an (*Shih-lun*, p. 81) also sees fit to describe Chang Fei's antics as "appealing" (*k'e-ai* 可愛).

[185] "Li Cho-wu" edition, chapters 13 (1b), 39 (12a), and 70 (11b); 1522 edition, 9:13a. See also "Li Yü" edition, chapter 73 (2a). One example of the rare exercise of clever strategy on the part of Chang Fei occurs in chapter 63 (10:47), in the capture of Yen Yen.

[186] Later, this rivalry is to govern the relationship between the two sons of the original "brothers," Chang Pao and Kuan Hsing.

[187] MTK, 6:39. See n. 166. This peeved opposition indicated by the term *pu-yüeh* expands on the accounts in the *Tzu-chih t'ung-chien* (p. 2075f.) and the *T'ung-chien chi-shih pen-mo*, 3:787. See also Wang Fu-chih, *Tu T'ung-chien lun*, pp. 293f.

comrades in the Shu camp, notably Chao Yün,[188] but it is in Chang Fei's
relations with Liu Pei that this tendency is pushed to its logical conclusion.
The fact that the spiritual bond between the two men is less than absolute
surfaces almost immediately after the ritual of brotherhood in the Peach
Garden, when Chang Fei—who had initiated and hosted the ceremony in
his own house—threatens to quit the trio after clashing with Liu Pei over
his wish to kill Tung Cho. This tension continues into the following
chapter, in the well-known scene of Chang Fei's whipping of an arrogant
local inspector (*tu-yu* 督郵), an incident that delights Liu Pei far less than it
does the popular audience.[189] As early as this scene, the author makes the
connection between Chang Fei's violence and his excessive drinking that
is to figure prominently throughout the novel; and here he significantly
specifies that this is not the fun-loving intoxication of a Lu Ta, but rather
unpleasant "drunkenness on account of depression" (*men-chiu* 悶酒).

From this point on, the fact that Chang Fei is more often a liability than
an asset to Liu Pei is emphasized in a series of scenes in which the
commander is forced to check his brother/subordinate, and cites his excessive violence, his drinking, and even his lack of military skill as the reasons
why the rough captain is "of no use" to him.[190] Chang Fei, for his part,
grows more and more surly as the novel proceeds, first complaining about
Liu Pei's lack of understanding, and later condemning him for failure to
appreciate his true worth.[191]

By now it must be clear that the relationship between Liu Pei and Chang
Fei is roughly parallel to that between Sung Chiang 宋江 and Li K'uei in
Shui-hu chuan. This is particularly noticeable in several scenes in which
Chang Fei takes on the role of the principal voice pushing for Liu Pei's
accelerating rise to power, pressing him to accept Liu Piao's 劉表 offer to
yield Hsü-chou in chapter 12, and urging him in chapter 73 to dispense
with the step of assuming the rank of King of Han-chung and instead
proclaim himself emperor directly. In this latter occurrence, his words
"Even if you proclaim yourself emperor, what would be wrong with that?"

---

[188] The rivalry with Chao Yün surfaces in chapters 41 (7:21) and 52 (9:5, 9:8). Cf. Chang
Fei's opposition to P'ang T'ung in chapter 57 (9:42). This enmity is reflected in certain
tsa-chü plays (e.g., *P'ang lüeh ssu-chün*, especially Act 3), as well as in the *P'ing-hua*, where
Chang Fei attempts to kill P'ang T'ung but ends up killing his dog instead (p. 441).

[189] Liu Pei's "shock" (*ching* 驚) at Chang Fei's rash act (MTK, chapter 20, 1:11; 1522,
1:25a) is lessened in the *Chih-chuan* and *Ch'üan-chuan* editions. In the *San-kuo chih*, it is
Liu Pei himself who beats the official (4:872). Early in this chapter, at the point where Liu
Pei restrains Chang Fei from killing Tung Cho, Mao Tsung-kang cuts the term "rebuke"
(*ch'ih* 叱) appearing in the 1522 edition (1:17b). See *P'ing-hua*, pp. 367ff., esp. 369, where
Chang Fei's wrath is turned upon the wife and concubine of the offending official.

[190] Examples of this occur in chapters 13, 14, 16, 21, and 22. See esp. chapters 40 (7:13),
42 (7:28), and 52 (9:5–8).

[191] For example, chapters 22 (4:16) and 70 (12:2).

(... *chiu ch'eng huang-ti yu ho pu k'e* 就成皇帝有何不可) are strikingly similar to sentiments expressed by Li K'uei at several points in *Shui-hu chuan*.[192]

This parallel between Chang Fei and Li K'uei with respect to their relationships with their leaders brings us to a number of additional details linking the two figures as workings of the same basic literary mold. Outside of the external similarity shared by the two figures with their dark complexions and rude temperaments, as pointed out by Chang Hsüeh-ch'eng and later critics, a number of specific scenes—for example, Chang Fei's parody of a government official during his stay in Ku-ch'eng 古城 in chapter 28—recall comparable adventures of Li K'uei in *Shui-hu chuan*.[193] Even the precise words used to describe his lusty bellicosity at one point— "His blood was up with killing" (*sha-te hsing-ch'i* 殺得性起)—seem to recall similar details in the treatment of Li K'uei in the other work. (Although the text of *San-kuo yen-i* does not explicitly attribute to Chang Fei the misogynistic attitude so central to the character of Li K'uei, this does seem to surface in one passage in the *P'ing-hua*.)[194]

For the purposes of this discussion, the most important point to derive from the intertextual comparison of these two figures is the fact that in the treatment of Chang Fei, just as in that of Li K'uei (and this is also true regarding the shared characteristics of Kuan Yü and Wu Sung), the novel appears to be less interested in tracing the positive aspects of heroic character than in exploring the inherent limitations, and ultimately the breakdown, of these towers of strength. The treatment of Chang Fei also takes in a continuous chain of defeats, broken only rarely by examples of heroic successes. In the seesaw battles in and around Hsü-chou in the second decade of the novel, for example, Chang Fei's military might is dwarfed by that of Lü Pu—in stark contrast to the well-known scenes in *tsa-chü* drama and the *P'ing-hua* in which Chang Fei fares much better against this adversary.[195] In subsequent battles, we see Chang Fei's attempts at strategy fail miserably in chapters 23 and 24; he is rendered

---

[192] MTK, 12:24. See above, Chapter 4, Part IV.

[193] Chang Hsüeh-ch'eng, *Ping-ch'en cha-chi*, p. 16:63a (cited in K'ung Ling-ching, *Shih-liao*, p. 30). See also Tung Mei-k'an, *Shih-lun*, p. 85.

[194] MTK, chapter 28 (5:13), cf. *Shui-hu chuan*, chapter 74; and chapter 65 (11:12), cf. *Shui-hu chuan*, chapter 50. I will consider in Part V of this chapter a note in the 1522 edition (23:51a) in which Chang Fei's immunity to sexual temptation is compromised. See the *P'ing-hua* passage cited in n. 189, in which Chang Fei unleashes his violence on several women (p. 369).

[195] See the plays *San-chan Lü Pu*, *San-ch'u Hsiao-p'ei*, and *Tan-chan Lü Pu*, and the *P'ing-hua*, pp. 378–90. Mao Tsung-kang revises the title of chapter 5 from the preexisting drama and *P'ing-hua* heading "At Hu-lao Pass [Chang Fei] Battles Lü Pu Three Times" 虎牢關張飛三戰呂布 to "Crushing the Troops at the Pass, the Three Braves Battle Lü Pu" 破關兵三英戰呂布, thus lessening the focus on Chang Fei's individual exploits.

helpless in chapter 31; and in chapter 39 he and Kuan Yü are completely eclipsed by Chu-ko Liang.[196] In a number of these engagements the author takes care to demonstrate the connection between Chang Fei's drinking and his failures on the battlefield, as in the loss of Hsü-chou to Lü Pu in chapter 14 and again in chapter 70 (although here Chu-ko Liang turns his drunkenness around to the Shu advantage).

This connection is particularly striking in the scenes depicting Chang Fei's final downfall. Here his harsh treatment of his own men and the resulting mutiny and murder by Chang Ta 張達 and Fan Chiang 范疆 are matters of historical record, but the novel's insistence on linking the assassination scene to Chang Fei's drunken rage is a deliberate touch, which brings to its logical conclusion a suggestion developed throughout the work.[197] Significantly, Chang Fei, too, has aged considerably by the end (he is fifty-five when he is killed), and in the final scenes we see him as a raging bull powerless to ward off the death he has brought upon himself.[198]

These intimations of self-destruction remind us of the circumstances of Kuan Yü's death, in spite of the many differences in the characterization of the two men.[199] In comparing the two figures, it may be helpful to recall the relative distinction drawn in the preceding chapter on *Shui-hu chuan* between varying degrees of gravity used in the exploration of the limits of heroic action. Due to the very nature of the character, Chang Fei is evidently not to be taken as seriously as Kuan Yü. To take one example, his reenactment of Kuan Yü's *i-shih* scene with Yen Yen 嚴顏 in chapter 63 is more a parody of the former than a profound consideration of the issues raised in connection with that incident, and it serves primarily to cast an additional ironic reflection on the release of Ts'ao Ts'ao in chapter 50.[200] Nevertheless as the novel progresses, and certainly by the time of his downfall, Chang Fei's story is no longer amusing; his loss of Hsü-chou

---

[196] Chapters 24 (4:29), 31 (5:40), 39 (7:5–6).

[197] See *San-kuo chih*, 4:941; and *Tzu-chih t'ung chien*, p. 2189.

[198] See chapter 81 (13:31), and the *P'ing-hua*, p. 467.

[199] For example, the depiction of Kuan Yü's downfall avoids any suggestion of drinking. See the explicit comparison of the respective faults of Kuan Yü and Chang Fei in the *San-kuo chih* (4:944), also cited in the *Tzu-chih t'ung-chien*, p. 2189. Mao Tsung-kang discusses the contrast between Kuan and Chang as an example of "reverse parallelism" (*fan-tui* 反對) in his *tu-fa*, item 20, p. 11.

[200] In the *San-kuo chih* evaluation of the two historical figures (see n. 199), Chang Fei's act is treated with greater seriousness. In the novel version his release of Yen Yen is presented as a simple case of admiration for the latter's courage, rather than as a question of personal honor. In the *P'ing-hua* version (p. 453), the expression "honorable release" (*i-shih*) is written *i-she* 議攝 ("discusses taking into his service"), indicating that the novelist revised the words to specifically emphasize the figural parallelism of the two scenes. This episode is based on the historical sources: see the *Tzu-chih t'ung-chien*, p. 2127; and the *Chi-shih pen-mo*, p. 794.

in chapter 14 nearly cuts short Liu Pei's fledgling career; he undermines the crucial alliance with Wu in chapters 80 and 81; and the subsequent revenge campaign on Chang's behalf signals the end of the brothers' noble cause.[201]

This brings us to Liu Pei. Critical evaluations of Liu Pei as a figure in the *Yen-i* have largely been sidetracked by the question of the novel's sympathy for his claim to be the legitimate successor to the Han.[202] We have seen how, rather than siding fully with Liu Pei, the novel takes a position midway between the wholehearted adulation of the popular tradition and the relatively critical view that emerges in the writings of traditional historians—even those who assign dynastic legitimacy to Shu-Han rather than Wei.[203] The uncertainty on this point is entirely appropriate for the ironic rhetorical stance of the sixteenth-century novel, where the primary emphasis is not on the hypothetical question of whether or not Liu Pei's cause deserved to fail—that ineluctable fact is firmly implanted in the reader's consciousness by his prior knowledge of the story—but rather on the *process* by which he failed, and the significance of that failure for our understanding of human limitations.

Something of this basic contradiction is already evident in the initial portrait of Liu Pei at the start of the novel, which is essentially a patchwork of historical sources and popular myths. The capsule introduction in chapter 1 is taken largely from the official biography in the *San-kuo chih*, which itself betrays considerable folk influence in its depiction of the iconographic features conventionally assigned to the sage ruler.[204] The description of Liu Pei as one who "all his life was never particularly fond of book learning ... but enjoyed fraternizing with the swashbucklers of the realm" (*p'ing-sheng pu shen le tu-shu ... hao chiao-yu t'ien-hsia hao-chieh* 平生不甚樂讀書…好交游天下豪傑) appears to set him in the mold of a martial hero of the *Shui-hu chuan* type: a man of action with disdain for Confucian learning and the pleasures of the court. This image is reflected later in the text, in chapter 34, when he bemoans the discovery that he is out of shape (*chien chi-shen pi-jou fu-sheng* 見已身髀肉復生), as well as in his own self-description—"I am not an educated man, I have only a rough understanding of the broader outlines of things" (*chen pu tu-shu ts'u chih ta-*

---

[201] See Tung Mei-k'an, *Shih-lun*, p. 85.

[202] See, for example, Tung Mei-k'an, *Shih-lun*, pp. 16f., 30, 58ff.

[203] See Andrew Lo, "Historiography," pp. 58ff., for a discussion of the limitations on Chu Hsi's approval of Liu Pei; and pp. 84–100, esp. citations from Wang Fu-chih, Su Shih, Su Ch'e, and Chang P'u. The *Shu-fa* commentary on the *T'ung-chien kang-mu* (by Liu Yu-i 劉友益) frequently points out the negative aspects of Liu Pei's actions. Even Mao Tsung-kang, as we shall see later, does not shrink from serious criticism of Liu Pei at certain points.

[204] See Riftin, *Ot mifa*, pp. 216ff., 276ff.

lüeh 朕不讀書, 粗知大略)—in his deathbed speech in chapter 85.[205] In fact, in the *P'ing-hua* he is depicted as falling into the bandit pattern (*lo-ts'ao* 落草) in the early stages of his career.[206]

Throughout his presentation in the body of the narrative, however, we see very little in the way of martial prowess, and quite a bit of courtly pretensions. By the same token, the initial description of Liu Pei as a man of stone-faced self-control—"neither joy nor anger were revealed in his countenance" (*hsi-nu pu hsing yü se* 喜怒不形於色)—is also frequently belied in the narrative by examples of emotional weakness, as we will see.[207] His reputation as a man of compassion, an ideal ruler guided by deep concern for his people,[208] does find expression at various points—not only in fawning speeches by underlings, but also in actions depicted in the narrative itself—especially in his relatively benevolent rule in Szechwan after his assumption of the title of King of Han-chung.[209] Occasionally he is shown to be an astute judge of individual character (*chih-jen* 知人) as well, as we see in such examples as his relationship with Chao Yün and in his correct evaluation of Ma Su in his parting speech in chapter 85. But as I will try to show below, the main thrust of the figural reflection applied to Liu Pei in the text goes toward deflating precisely these aspects of his popular image.

The degree to which the *Yen-i*'s treatment of Liu Pei is indebted to popular sources, especially drama, is evident in its retention of several familiar episodes, such as the "three visits to the thatched hut" (*san-ku ts'ao-lu* 三顧草廬), which clearly smack of the popular imagination—although even these scenes are not entirely free of ironic elements in the novel. In a few instances, the novelist even appears to appropriate from the popular tradition the view of Liu as a figure of mythical proportions, as we have

[205] Chapters 1 (1:3), 34 (6:12), 85 (14:12–13). The *pi-jou* incident is recorded in the P'ei Sung-chih commentary on *San-kuo chih* (4:876), as well as in a text entitled *Chiu-chou Ch'un-ch'iu* 九州春秋, attributed to Ssu-ma Piao 司馬彪, in *Huang-shih i-shu k'ao* (33:19a), and is repeated in the *Tzu-chih t'ung-chien* (p. 2042) and the *T'ung-chien chi-shih pen-mo* (p. 786). In the play *T'ao-yüan chieh-i* (p. 7b), Liu Pei is described as "adept in both civilian and military capacities" (*wen-wu shuang-ch'üan* 文武雙全). Cf. his association with the eminent Confucian scholar Cheng Hsüan 鄭玄; see *MTK*, chapter 1 (1:3).

[206] See *P'ing-hua*, p. 370.

[207] Chapter 1 (1:3). This quality of self-control attributed to Liu Pei seems to be behind the scene in chapter 21 (4:3), in which he patiently tends his own vegetable garden while the events around him move toward a crisis. (This detail is also drawn from the P'ei Sung-chih commentary, *San-kuo chih*, 4:875f.).

[208] Cf. the *San-kuo chih* description of Liu Pei (4:892) as "eminently fair" 至公. See Riftin, *Istoricheskaya epopeia*, pp. 197f. The novel's indication of his intimacy with Cheng Hsüan and Kung-sun Tsan seems to derive from this aspect of his image.

[209] See chapter 77 (13:6).

noted in his miraculous mounted leap over the T'an River in chapter 34, and his hewing of a huge rock with his sword in chapter 54.[210] But in a thorough reading of the novel as a whole, we find that such examples of heroic feats fade in comparison to the consistent picture of failure that dominates the portrait of Liu Pei.

Leaving aside for the moment the ultimate collapse of the larger enterprise of restoring the Han dynasty under his own sway, we can observe how the narrative traces a long chain of setbacks and defeats. With a limited number of exceptions, Liu Pei's military campaigns are marked by a pattern of failure each time he himself takes command, including major battles in chapters 24, 31, 43, 63, 83, and 84.[211] In a number of these instances, Liu Pei's failure is noticeably tied to his own overconfidence. For example, in the revenge campaign in chapter 83 he is supremely arrogant, marching out in full battle regalia, refusing to accept surrender, and bragging of his own ability to vanquish the foe without assistance from Chu-ko Liang— only to commit a needless blunder and quickly lose the field. In the following chapter he continues to deploy his troops recklessly, and he is finally routed in the battle, effectively dooming both himself and the entire cause.[212]

To be fair, not all of the blame for Liu Pei's military setbacks can be laid to his own shortcomings as a commander. But it seems significant that the author consistently emphasizes Liu's personal weakness in dealing with these defeats, particularly in view of the interest he shows in the limitations of the heroes Kuan Yü and Chang Fei. As the novel progresses, we perceive a clear pattern of recurrence, according to which an impressive array of forces always seems to melt away, leaving Liu Pei alone and

---

[210] Chapters 34 (6:15) and 54 (9:21). The leap over the T'an river is recorded in the P'ei Sung-chih commentary on *San-kuo chih* (4:876), and is depicted in the play *Hsiang-yang hui* (p. 6a–b). It may be recalled that this incident was reportedly attached to the popular tradition as early as the Sui period (see above, n. 28). The description of Liu Pei's state of mind after the leap—"as if drunk or dazed" 似醉如癡—qualifies the idea of a feat of epic boldness.

[211] Chapters 24 (4:30), 31 (5:40), 41 (7:17ff.), 63 (10:45), 83–84 (13:49–14:6). Mao Tsung-kang softens the impact of Liu Pei's defeat in chapter 31 by changing the title from "Liu Pei Goes in Defeat to Ching-chou" 劉玄德敗走荊州 to "Liu Pei Throws in with Liu Piao in Ching-chou" 玄德荊州依劉表. Similarly, in chapter 41 he changes "Liu Pei Goes in Defeat to Chiang-ling" 劉玄德敗走江陵 to "Liu Pei Leads the People Across the River" 劉玄德攜民渡江. In chapter 42, however, he retains the expression "goes in defeat" 敗走 in the title. An exception to this pattern is seen in chapter 36 (6:24f.), where Liu Pei exercises considerable ingenuity to win a strategic victory at Fan-ch'eng (with considerable assistance as well).

[212] Chapter 83 (13:49). Cf. the phrase "had a good sense of the art of warfare" 頗知兵法 in this passage. In chapter 84 Mao Tsung-kang completely eliminates the 1522 heading: "The Former Emperor (Liu Pei) Retreats by Night to Pai-ti ch'eng" 先主夜走白帝城.

helpless.[213] He is forced to seek assistance (*ch'iu-chiu* 求救) from anyone, even individuals for whom he has no sympathy or affinity, men such as Lü Pu in chapter 15, Ts'ao Ts'ao in chapter 19, and Yüan Shao in chapter 24 (the latter shortly after he has killed Liu Pei's close friend Kung-sun Tsan 公孫瓚).[214] Liu's reaction to these setbacks is typically despair rather than heroic determination. He is prone to fits of tearful depression and tends to blame Heaven for his plight.[215]

The same weakness of will that characterizes Liu Pei's performance on the battlefield also surfaces in a variety of other narrative situations. In numerous scenes Liu falls into the recurrent state of paralysis of the will (*yu-yü*) we have seen to afflict a whole range of other figures in the novel, notable among them Yüan Shao. This treatment takes on particular irony in those scenes in which the popular imagination actually credits him with heroic force of will, despite his own indecision. This is most noticeable at the time of his sojourn in the capital under Ts'ao Ts'ao's protection in chapters 19–21. The first major example occurs in chapter 20, when he signals Kuan Yü not to cut down Ts'ao Ts'ao at the imperial hunt, a move he justifies as an act of deference to the emperor, but then admits was a grave error.[216] By the same token, his association with the ill-fated plot of the "imperial sash decree" (*i-tai chao* 衣帶詔) is essentially forced upon him, and his participation is far less decisive than his co-conspirators originally hope.[217]

---

[213] Liu Pei is seen in serious trouble in scenes in chapters 19, 41, 42, 58, 72, 79, 80, and 84, and is specifically described as "all alone" at a number of points, e.g., chapter 64 (11:3). We see him sick in chapters 79 (13:20), 80 (13:26), and 85 (14:12). He is sixty-three years old at the time of his death and he himself points out that he is past his prime 吾年已半百 in chapter 54 (9:19).

[214] Other examples of this recurrent seeking of refuge occur in chapters 1, 14, 21, 25, 26, and 45.

[215] Cf. chapters 31 (5:40), "Why is heaven making me suffer such hardship?" 天何使我 受此窘極耶; and 64 (11:3), "Heaven is destroying me!" 天亡我也. The *Chih-chuan* adds to the passage in chapter 31 (6:6a) the line "his way of thinking was basically wrong" 心才不正. His propensity to fits of depression (*men* 悶) is seen as early as chapter 2 (1:10ff.) and at many other points. The "Li Cho-wu" commentator takes frequent potshots at this manifestation of weakness. In chapter 21 (p. 4a) he berates his childishness, and in chapter 38 (p. 5a) he ridicules him for crying "like one of our singsong girls today" 極似今日之妓女.

[216] Chapters 20 (3:44) and 42 (7:28). See n. 174.

[217] Chapter 21 (4:3). In chapter 72, however, he claims to be acting under a similar imperial order to take I-chou (12:18). Ts'ao Ts'ao also bases his assassination attempt on Tung Cho in chapter 4 on such a document. In the *San-kuo chih* treatment of this incident (4:875) there is a more explicit indication of Liu Pei's connection with the plot. See also the *Tzu-chih t'ung-chien*, p. 2023, where the term *ch'eng* 稱 ("claimed") adds a further element of doubt as to Liu Pei's connection with the plot. Wang Fu-chih (*Tu T'ung-chien lun*, p. 287) describes both Tung Ch'eng's plot and Liu Pei's acquiescence as precipitous, ill-considered moves.

The familiar scene shortly before this, during which Liu Pei drops his chopsticks when subjected to psychological pressure from Ts'ao Ts'ao, is another case in point. In the differing versions of this incident in the historical sources, the *P'ing-hua*, and drama, Liu Pei's act is sometimes depicted as a calmly executed ruse calculated to distract Ts'ao Ts'ao. But more often (even in the Mao edition) he appears to lose his self-control and is only saved by a fortuitous clap of thunder which allows him to cover up his mistake.[218] The discrepancy between his behavior in this scene and his earlier description as a man whose "inner feelings were never revealed on his face" is instructive, especially in contrast to the numerous dramas in which he is shown to be a man of intrepid spirit.[219] The loss of self-control displayed in the scene of the dropped chopsticks is repeated again in certain other episodes; for instance chapter 34, where Liu Pei commits a "slip of the lip" (*shih-yen* 失言) at Ching-chou, thereby placing himself in mortal danger from which he is extricated only through the supernatural aid of his horse. And this scene is replayed again in chapter 62, when he reveals under the influence of wine his true motivations regarding I-chou, only to regret his loose tongue after his head clears.[220]

The connection drawn in these last scenes between indulgence in wine and loss of presence of mind leads us to another aspect of Liu Pei's weakness of particular relevance to this study. That is, in several passages the author sees fit to emphasize in his portrayal of Liu Pei a certain weakness to sexual temptation, something we have seen to be a sensitive issue within the conceptual framework of the sixteenth-century novel. The treatment of Liu Pei's marriage to Lady Sun, to be sure, is rooted in the popular tradition, where it is viewed as an example of heroic behavior, a fact underlined by the inclusion of the interlude in which he hews a rock

---

[218] The 1522 edition presents the incident more as a deliberate ruse than does the Mao Tsung-kang text. In the *San-kuo chih* version of the incident (4:875) no thunderclap is mentioned (it is added in a later note); whereas in the *T'ung-chien kang-mu* (13:50b) Liu Pei first drops his chopsticks in fear, then seizes the opportune thunderclap to cover his error. The late Ming critic Chung Hsing assumes in his *Shih-huai* (16/1a–b) that Liu Pei's gesture was due to genuine fright, and was not a cover-up trick. See the *P'ing-hua*, p. 395, which recounts the banquet and the dropped chopsticks, also with no thunderclap. The *Ying-hsiung p'u* shifts this scene to a later point in the narrative (4:19a), perhaps deliberately to make it appear alongside Wu Sung's execution of P'an Chin-lien in the parallel *Shui-hu* text. In the play *Shih-liu yüan* (pp. 9b–10a), Liu Pei is shown to cover up his ears upon hearing the thunder.

[219] In a comparable situation (*Hsiang-yang hui*, p. 10a) Liu Pei is depicted as helplessly gullible, whereas in a similar case in *Huang-ho lou* (p. 3a–b) he appears fearless to the point of arrogance.

[220] Chapters 34 (6:12) and 62 (10:37). Mao Tsung-kang's comment on the latter scene relates it explicitly to the earlier occurrence. This scene does not appear in the *P'ing-hua* (see p. 408). See Tung Mei-k'an, *Shih-lun*, p. 68.

with his sword.[221] The development of this episode in the novel, however, places special emphasis on certain telling details: for example, his psychological need for a new wife (玄德自沒甘夫人, 晝夜煩惱) and his trepidation at entering the bridal chamber of this warlike maiden (to the point of wearing armor under his robes as he goes to his marriage bed). More important, it goes on to describe Liu Pei as "losing himself in sensual pleasure" (*mi-se* 迷色) for a long period of time, apparently oblivious to the original mission that led him to accept the marriage offer in the first place—a detail conspicuously absent in the *P'ing-hua* version of the incident.[222]

Despite his basic sympathy for Liu Pei, Mao Tsung-Kang finds this whole incident ludicrous. In a sarcastic note in chapter 54 he mockingly suggests that Liu ought to preen himself with a black pomade to make himself more attractive to his intimidating bride, and in chapter 55 after the wedding, he mocks him for being tied to the apronstrings of his new wife (*chü-nei* 懼內).[223] Another, less striking example occurs in chapter 77, when Liu Pei agrees to enter into one more marriage. Now, for a contender for the imperial throne to take steps to ensure added progeny is certainly beyond reproach. But the fact that this discussion occurs immediately on the heels of the death of Kuan Yü (news as yet unknown to Liu Pei but set glaringly before the reader's eyes), and immediately before the arrival of reports of Kuan Yü's rejection of a marriage for his own daughter, seems to suggest a certain inappropriateness in this match—a shadow not appreciably brightened by Liu Pei's initial reluctance due to his shared surname with the intended bride.[224]

It might be conceivable to interpret these various manifestations of weakness in the character of Liu Pei as traits that are in keeping with his reputed compassionate, yielding nature. But the ground is pulled from under such a view by the numerous passages in the novel that raise serious

[221] See Part I of this chapter for discussion of this point.

[222] Chapters 54 (9:18) and 55 (9:24–25). See the *P'ing-hua*, p. 436. Liu Pei's timidity in the marriage chamber is recorded in the *T'ung-chien kang-mu* (14:2b). Mao Tsung-kang's revision of the chapter titles of chapters 54 and 55 emphasizes the romantic side of this episode. Liu Pei cuts a similarly dashing figure in the play *Huang-ho lou* (full title: "Liu Pei, in his cups, goes to the Huang-ho lou" 劉玄德醉走黃鶴樓).

[223] MTK, 9:21, 23.

[224] MTK, 13:6. In the Mao edition it is the adviser Fa-cheng 法正 who suggests this match, but in the 1522 edition (16:30a), as well as the *Chih-chuan* (13:19a), *Ch'üan-chuan* (13:11b), *Lien-hui t'ang* (13:30a), *P'ing-lin* (13:37a), and *Ying-hsiung p'u* (13:29a) texts, it is Chu-ko Liang who presents the proposal. The figural reflection between this instance and Chao Yün's rejection of another match involving a vaguely incestuous tie in chapter 52 is brought out in a comment by Mao Tsung-kang (9:2), which declares Chao Yün's superiority to Liu Pei in this regard.

doubts about his honorable intentions. Of course, much of the reader's response to such passages depends on the strength of the conviction that Liu Pei's cause is just, and granted, the *Yen-i* often appears to adopt this position. But at the same time, neither does the novel shy away from portraying some of the less noble moments of Liu Pei's career. The same attitude governs the readings of the traditional commentators, whose substantial labors are usually motivated by a strong commitment to the Shu-Han side, but who nevertheless frequently level harsh criticism at Liu Pei, even to the point of equating him with Ts'ao Ts'ao at certain points as an "unscrupulous hero" (*chien-hsiung* 奸雄, or *hsiao-hsiung* 梟雄).[225]

The author of the *Yen-i* never calls into question the legitimacy of Liu Pei's claim to special status as an "imperial uncle" (*huang-shu* 皇叔), nor does he seem to notice that Liu Pei's connection to the imperial line is remote at best—a fact pointed out explicitly by P'ei Sung-chih in a comment in the *San-kuo chih*.[226] In the novel's treatment of Liu Pei, however, the question is implicitly raised as to whether his chief aim is the restoration of the Han house, or his own elevation to power.[227] From the opening passages relating his childhood ambition to become an emperor and then his impatience with low status in chapter 2, through a long series of radical side-switching over the first thirty chapters as he jockeys for position, it becomes increasingly clear that Liu Pei is aiming for imperial authority long before the Ts'ao family finally removes the existing Han line.[228]

Unless the reader is prepared to condone any actions whatsoever as necessary expedients in assuring Liu Pei's rise to the top, he may be disturbed to discover in the novel a series of major actions on Liu's part that are presented in a less than favorable light. At the very least, the manner in which the author develops the chain of recurrence marked by Liu's successive seizures of power—first in Hsü-chou, then in Ching-chou, and finally in I-chou, before he installs himself as King of Han-chung and

[225] For example, "Li Cho-wu" commentary, chapters 11 (p. 14b), 60 (p. 12b), and 85 (p. 14a). Liu Pei's enemies often revile him with the term *hsiao-hsiung*; e.g., MTK, chapter 62 (10:35). Cf. a similar statement ascribed to Chou Yü in Yang Shen's *T'an-tz'u*, p. 149.

[226] *San-kuo chih* (4:890). In several Yuan plays, Liu Pei presents his pedigree a bit defensively, introduced by the line "If anyone should come and ask about my ancestry" 有人來問宗和祖. For example, *Huang-ho lou* (p. 2a), *Hsiang-yang hui* (p. 1a), *Po-wang shao-t'un* (p. 1a), *Hsing-lin chuang* (p. 3a).

[227] That is, the question is whether Liu Pei's career is modeled after that of Kao-tsu's founding or the Kuang-wu emperor's restoration. The *T'ung-chien kang-mu* grapples with this question at several points (e.g., 14:58a–b, as does the *Shu-fa* note on p. 57b). See n. 422.

[228] See chapters 1 (1:3) and 2 (1:11). Liu Pei's childhood game of playing emperor is recorded in the *San-kuo chih* (4:87). Mao Tsung-kang takes note of the pattern of side-switching in the novel in extended comments in chapters 28 and 29 (5:10, 19).

ultimately Emperor of Han in Shu—demands serious reflection on the reader's part.[229]

As is usual in cases of figural recurrence, the first instance in the chain is not particularly troubling. T'ao Ch'ien's 陶謙 desire to yield his authority over Hsü-chou is apparently sincere, especially since Ts'ao Ts'ao is breathing down his neck at the time. Several details planted in this first rehearsal of what eventually becomes a set pattern only take on their full significance with later occurrences. The repetition of the stereotyped formula of "three refusals," for one thing, is not only an example of narrative "trebling," but also an obvious foreshadowing (*fu-pi* 伏筆) for Liu Pei's "three refusals" of the imperial crown almost seventy chapters later. Similarly, the specific expression used by Liu Pei in declining the first two offers: "You are forcing me into a dishonorable position" (*hsien wo pu-i* 陷我不義), as well as his histrionic gesture of drawing his sword and threatening to cut his own throat rather than accept, are elements that will eventually become part of a fixed litany.[230] Mao, for some reason, finds this last point objectionable and cuts the detail, although at the same time he adds speeches by Kuan Yü and Chang Fei urging Liu Pei to accept the offer. And where Liu finally relents, he inserts the key term "assume temporary control" (*ch'üan-ling* 權領), which figures prominently in later stages of Liu Pei's advancement. In any event, all of this posturing is further undercut when, shortly after finally accepting the authority over Hsü-chou, Liu Pei turns around and yields it to the dubious stewardship of Lü Pu.

A nearly identical situation pertains in the case of Ching-chou, although by this time Liu Pei's actions are guided by Chu-ko Liang, who has singled out this area as the first stepping stone in his master plan to gain the empire. Once again an essentially honorable local ruler, partly due to knowledge of his own weak position in the shifting power structure and his personal weariness, and partly due to sincere admiration for Liu Pei and a desire to ensure peace for his own people, urges Liu to take command and assume control of the area. Even the basic geographical situation, with the focus shifting between Ching-chou and its satellite town Hsin-yeh 新野, duplicates the setting at Hsü-chou and Hsiao-p'ei 小沛 in the earlier instance. Liu Pei's reluctance to accept Liu Piao's plea that he take his heir under his protection (*t'o-ku* 託孤) in chapter 40, in spite of Chu-ko Liang's

[229] The term *wang* is rendered here as "king" rather than "prince," in the sense that it is in this case clearly seen as a stepping stone *toward* the imperial throne, not as an appointment *from* the throne.

[230] See MTK, 2:22f., 29f.; and 1522, 3:14b, 26a–b. The *P'ing-hua* reports Liu Pei's acceptance of the offer with no show of reluctance (p. 382). Wang Fu-chih points out that Liu Pei's early moves were not completely honorable, thus leading to his ultimate failure (*Tu T'ung-chien lun*, p. 280).

urging that he do so, appears sincere and closes the door on this move for the time being.

But ten chapters later, when the chance to occupy Ching-chou again presents itself after the Battle of the Red Cliffs, Liu Pei's motives are presented in a less favorable light. In the struggle with Chou Yü for control over the strategic objective of Ching-chou, Liu Pei continues to voice the argument that "the empire belongs to no one individual" 天下者, 非一人之天下, and claims to be interested only in supporting Liu Piao's son Liu Ch'i 劉琦.[231] The deal worked out, whereby Liu Pei's troops occupy the town as long as Liu Ch'i remains alive, seems fair enough; but when Liu Ch'i unexpectedly takes sick and dies a few months later, it becomes immediately obvious that Liu Pei has not the slightest intention of fulfilling his end of the bargain. At this point Liu Pei's claim that he only wishes to "borrow" the city to protect the legacy of his clansman Liu Piao rings exceedingly hollow, especially when he adds a threat to take even more land if pressed.[232] Even Mao Tsung-kang finds it hard to swallow this line, and though probably aware that the expression "borrow Ching-chou" (*chieh Ching-chou* 借荊州) appears in the historical sources, he interjects: "Who ever heard of 'borrowing' a city!" 豈有城池而可以契借者乎 ![233] The ensuing narrative proves the hypocrisy of Liu Pei's noble-sounding arguments, as he holds onto the city for the rest of his life, frequently reiterating his claim to be only "borrowing" it; and later on, after he has entrusted it to Kuan Yü, he cynically apologizes that he is powerless to return it.[234]

By the time we get to the takeover of I-chou less than ten chapters later, the pattern is too well established to admit any other than an ironic reading of Liu Pei's arguments that he only needs a temporary resting place.[235] It

---

[231] For example, 1522, 11:3b, 42b. Mao Tsung-kang's version of these scenes: chapter 51 (8:38), chapter 54 (9:16f.) cuts this line. Earlier occurrences of the *t'o-ku* scene are found in chapter 40 (7:11, 13).

[232] MTK, chapter 54, (9:17–18). In the *P'ing-hua* (p. 412), Chu-ko Liang's scenario of Liu Pei's rise to power presented at the time of the "three visits" specifically calls for "borrowing" Ching-chou.

[233] See Mao's chapter-comment on this point, chapter 54 (9:16) and interlinear comment (9:17). The term "borrow Ching-chou" appears in a note in the *San-kuo chih* (4:879ff.).

[234] MTK, chapter 66 (11:19). Mao Tsung-kang comments here on Liu Pei's shifting of the blame to Kuan Yü, and follows this up by inserting an additional line in which Kuan Yü notes that "a general in the field need not follow all orders from his sovereign" 將在外, 君命有所不受, a rationalization delivered frequently in the course of the novel.

[235] MTK, chapter 60 (10:20). Chu-ko Liang repeats here the claim that they are only "borrowing" Ching-chou. Mao Tsung-kang's comment at the beginning of the chapter (10:16) assumes the fact that Liu Pei is also playing along with this charade. Chung Hsing emphasizes Liu Pei's hypocrisy in his discussion of this incident in *Shih huai* (16:2a): "If he was so moved by the suffering of Liu Ts'ung, why was he unsentimental in the case of Liu Chang?" 何其不忍于琮而獨忍于璋也?

seems instead to be, quite literally, a case of "taking Lung, then looking toward Shu" (*te-Lung wang-Shu* 得隴望蜀). At best, we can say that Liu Pei may have sincere reservations about displacing his kinsman—in chapter 60 he does angrily reject P'ang T'ung's 龐統 plan to assassinate Liu Chang 劉璋, and in some editions he expresses fear for the probable damage to his good reputation and credibility.[236] But in any event, he soon allows himself to be persuaded to go along with this serious violation of honor, as his enemies are quick to point out.

Liu Pei's interview with Chang Sung 張松 provides a good example of this sort of gradual capitulation of the will, a process we see repeated in later occurrences in the chain. At first Liu Pei sticks firmly to his loud refusal to participate in the overthrow of Liu Chang, but later he lets on that the main reason he cannot consider the plan is the logistical nightmare of a campaign across virtually impassable mountain barriers, and so he quickly consents as soon as Chang Sung presents him with a map to guide his men through the passes.[237]

In short, one can view the seizure of I-chou as a well planned and executed political takeover, as Liu Pei and Chu-ko Liang squeeze Liu Chang out step by step, first forcing him to vacate the capital and camp in an outlying district, then seizing the pretext of insult (when Liu Chang sends them a contingent of worn-out soldiers in response to their demand for a levy of troops) to make a complete break with him and consolidate their own hold without further political impediments.[238] As late as chapter 65, Liu Pei still claims allegiance to family feeling for Liu Chang, goes through the ritualistic motions of refusal, and continues to plead that, due to events beyond his control, he could not help taking I-chou from him.[239] But the evidence

---

[236] MTK, chapter 60 (10:25–28), 1522, 12:88a–b, 13:1a–2b. See also *P'ing-hua*, p. 450. Liu Pei is not outraged in the various other editions (e.g., *Chih-chuan*, 10:34a; *Ch'üan-chuan*, 10:19a; *Lien-hui t'ang*, 10:35a). In an earlier passage (p. 10:21), Liu Pei points out to Chang Sung that the justification of taking Szechwan as a springboard for a righteous restoration of the dynasty is negated by the fact that Liu Chang, too, has the same claim to be the restorer of the Han house. The irony here is compounded by Liu Chang's staunch defense (chapter 60, 10:25) of his kinsman's motives (calling him a "true man of honor and compassion" 真仁義之人), against objections by most of his advisers, including Wang Lei's 王累 unforgetable plea for attention by hanging upside down from the city gate.

[237] MTK, 10:21. This turnabout is made even more explicit in the *Ying-hsiung p'u* edition (10:44b), where Liu Pei remarks to Chang Sung, "Even if I did want to occupy [I-chou], what plan could I use to do this?" 雖欲取之，用何良策？

[238] MTK, chapter 62 (10:35). In the *P'ing-hua* (p. 456), Liu Pei reassures Liu Chang that he will grant his request for a fief to provide sustenance for his old age, but one line later we are told that Chu-ko Liang "secretly imprisoned him" (*an-ch'iu* 暗囚).

[239] See esp. MTK, 11:15. Mao Tsung-kang's comment on this line insists that Liu Pei's protestations are sincere 實話, although he allows that the expression "couldn't help it" (*pu te-i* 不得意) is most often used as an excuse for unrighteous behavior (the "Li Yü"

adds up to a quite different picture. In this case, we can conclude that the *Yen-i* is farther from the popular view and much closer to the position of the historians, who almost unanimously criticize Liu Pei's treatment of Liu Chang as a serious breach of moral principle.[240] The *Shu-fa* 書法 commentary on the *T'ung-chien kang-mu*, for example, remarks bitterly that such a flagrant case of dishonor (*pu-i* 不義) should not be glossed over. Even Mao Tsung-kang puts aside his strong sympathy for Liu Pei and follows the *San-kuo chih* here, changing the title of chapter 65 to "Liu Pei Takes Unauthorized Control of I-chou" (*tzu-ling* 自領).[241]

The same message of an essentially just cause exceeding the bounds of principle rings out in the last two stages of Liu Pei's rise to the level of imperial stature. Although in these final cases Liu Pei's advancement does not actually entail the displacement of anyone else, the author deftly orchestrates the elements of figural recurrence in his narrative details to set the assumption of the title of King of Han-chung in chapter 73 and finally his self-coronation in chapter 80 on a par with the earlier stages of accession to power.

A comparison of the treatment of the historical fact of Liu Pei's ascension as King of Han-chung in the *Yen-i* and in historiography is quite instructive. First, the basic sources in the *San-kuo chih* and *Tzu-chih t'ung-chien* record the move as a predictable stage in the power struggles of the imperial system, with no indication of any particular hesitation or doubts on the part of Liu Pei.[242] At the same time, a number of historical critics have zeroed in on this act as a prime example of the unauthorized assumption of power. In fact, readers with an eye for *Ch'un-ch'iu*-style rhetoric easily see in the seemingly neutral expression "assumed the position on his own

---

commentator [p. 9b] expands on this note to make the point even more explicit). The ambiguity of Liu Pei's position in I-chou is emphasized in the *Tzu-chih t'ung-chien* account (pp. 2135f.).

[240] See the *Tzu-chih t'ung-chien*'s description of Liu Pei's "seizure" (*hsi* 襲) of I-chou (based on a note in the *San-kuo chih* treatment of the incident (4:881ff.). Su Shih, in his famous essay "Chu-ko Liang lun," cites this act as the principal cause of Liu Pei's "loss of the confidence of the honorable men of the empire" 失天下義士之望. Cf. the section of the *Chi-shih pen-mo* (pp. 782–802) entitled "Liu Pei Occupies Szechwan" 劉備據蜀. Wang Fu-chih (*Tu T'ung-chien lun*, p. 290) departs in one passage from his generally critical view of Liu Pei to justify this move, although elsewhere (e.g., *Tu T'ung-chien lun*, p. 305), he states flatly that Liu Pei had no right to the mandate. For additional examples of this sort, see Andrew Lo, "Historiography," pp. 86f.

[241] See *San-kuo chih* (4:881f.), and *T'ung-chien kang-mu* (pp. 14:23aff.). The 1522 edition describes the takeover more directly: "Liu Pei Pacifies I-chou" 劉玄德平定益州. Cf. the title of a nonextant *tsa-chü* play: "A Plot to Seize Han-chung" 智取漢中.

[242] See *San-kuo chih*, (4:884): 群下上先主爲漢中王; *Tzu-chih t'ung-chien*, p. 2159: 自稱漢中王; and *T'ung-chien kang-mu*, p. 14:30a: 自立爲漢中王. The *T'ung-chien* wording follows that in *Hou Han shu* (1:389).

initiative" (*tzu-li* 自立) something more than a simple descriptive phrase—
a point emphasized caustically in the *Shu-fa* comment cited above.[243]

In the *Yen-i* the treatment of this move appears to follow the pattern
established in the earlier cases, by focusing on the psychological process of
Liu Pei's gradual assent to a morally ambiguous act. The novel depicts Liu
as fully aware of all the political and moral difficulties of taking upon
himself his elevation to a position within striking distance of the imperial
throne, while simultaneously avowing allegiance to the Han house that
is still in existence, if under the adverse conditions of domination by the
Ts'ao family. The justification of the move as a "temporary expedient"
(*ch'üan-pien* 權變), however, is counterbalanced in the debates preceding
the official declaration by discussions of precedents of self-appointment
among sage emperors of antiquity.[244] As a result, the reasoning by which
Liu Pei is swayed hinges not so much on the political circumstances in Shu
as on his final acknowledgment of his own imperial pretensions, as Chang
Fei, with his characteristic lack of dissimulation, tactlessly asserts when he
complains that if Liu Pei refuses to take the final logical step, "a lifetime of
heroic deeds will turn into a lost dream" 半世英雄成一夢矣.[245] Chu-ko
Liang more disingenuously reminds Liu Pei that his best years are already
behind him, and finally sways him with a "now or never" argument, with
an only slightly veiled threat that failure to act now would lead to the
evaporation of the support of his men and to large-scale desertions. Mao
Tsung-kang apparently finds the implication of conscious empire-building
in this scene too damaging to the image of Liu Pei and softens Chu-ko
Liang's plea, and later in his commentary he attempts to justify Liu Pei's
self-appointment with the argument that Ts'ao Ts'ao's domination of the
imperial court left him with no alternative.[246]

The final link in the chain of recurrence traced here from Hsü-chou
through Ching-chou and I-chou up to Liu Pei's assumption of the imperial

---

[243] The *Shu-fa* commentary (14:30b) insists that the *Kang-mu's* application of the term
tzu-li ("self-coronation") to Liu Pei is set out glaringly in the heading of the section to
emphasize the awesome gravity of the relationship between the sovereign and his ministers,
which Liu Pei's presumptuous act violates. For additional historians' discussions of this
incident, see Andrew Lo, "Historiography," pp. 90f.

[244] MTK, chapter 73 (12:24); 1522, 15:33a–b. Chu-ko Liang's explicit recommendation
that Liu Pei follow in the footsteps of the sage emperors Yao and Shun 法堯禪舜 (1522,
15:32b) is cut by Mao Tsung-kang (as it is in various other editions).

[245] 1522, 15:33b. Mao Tsung-kang's version of Chang Fei's speech (12:24) resembles
more Li K'uei's urgings to Sung Chiang (see Chapter 4, Part IV, of this book), and he cuts
the point about the "lost dream." This appears in the *Chih-chuan* (13:1b), "Li Cho-wu"
(p. 2b), "Li Yü" (p. 2a), and *Ying-hsiung pu* (13:2a) texts, but not in the *Ch'üan-chuan*.

[246] 1522, 15:32b–33b. See Mao's comment (12:22), as well as his revision of the title of
chapter 72 from "Liu Pei Seizes ... " to "Chu-ko Liang Seizes. ... "

title in chapter 80 represents the culmination of repeated patterns of presentation: initial hesitation, the three Caesarean refusals, followed by debates, and then the final persuasion. At this point, the arguments we have
heard voiced at various stages of Liu Pei's rise take on their full significance.
For example, at each earlier stage Liu Pei had resisted acceding to acts
that could be construed as disloyal or dishonorable. In this final instance,
Chu-ko Liang turns the tables and argues that a refusal, in fact, would be
"disloyal and unfilial." [247] In addition, the argument that "the empire does
not belong to any individual" also rings with special irony at this moment
when Liu Pei is in fact assuming the very singular authority of the imperial
throne.[248]

Of particular interest here is the manner in which the *Yen-i* text once
again focuses on the process of persuasion and capitulation that the historical sources take for granted and the *P'ing-hua* glosses over.[249] The author's
handling of this subject is nothing short of brilliant as he takes us through
Liu Pei's "three refusals," each of which brings him a little closer to the final
assent. At first Liu sticks to the by now familiar position that the move
would be contrary to his sense of honor, but later he changes this to
emphasize instead the potential damage to his popular image (恐天下人議
論耳).[250] On the second try, he takes one more step and grants to Chu-ko
Liang that he does have a legitimate claim to the throne, but declines on
the grounds of his own insufficient charisma (並未有德澤以布於民).[251]
Finally, in his third "refusal" he allows himself to be swayed by the fervent
sickbed plea of Chu-ko Liang. I suppose it is possible to take this scene as a
shining example of the deep bond between lord and minister ascribed to
the pair by both the popular and the historical tradition. But certain touches
added to the scene in the *Yen-i*—the fact that no less than sixteen high
officials in full state robes pop out from behind a screen immediately upon
Liu Pei's acceptance; Chu-ko Liang's instantaneous recovery ("he leapt to
his feet with a bound," *yüeh-jan erh ch'i* 躍然而起)—inject a note of parody
that suggests to me that Liu Pei is hypocritically playing along with the

---

[247] 1522, 16:77a. Mao's version, chapter 80 (13:26), is slightly milder. Cf. Liu Pei's rebuke
to the reluctant Chu-ko Liang in chapter 38, admonishing him that to refuse to join his cause
would also be "disloyal and unfilial" (1522, 8:33a–b). Mao (6:40) cuts this line.

[248] In the 1522 edition, the convenient "discovery" of an imperial seal (*hsi* 璽) is narrated
in full before the final debates (16:74b–75b). This detail is also included in the "Li Cho-wu"
(p. 8a–b), *Lien-hui t'ang* (14:11a), *Chih-chuan* (14:10a), *Ch'üan-chuan* (14:7a), *Ying-hsiung p'u*
(14:12b), and *P'ing-lin* (14:12b) texts (in the latter, the discovery of the seal is singled out
for a caption on one of the illustrations in the chapter), but the Mao Tsung-kang text does
not account for the provenance of the seal used in Liu Pei's coronation (13:27).

[249] See *T'ung-chien kang-mu* (14:56aff.), and *P'ing-hua* (p. 466).

[250] 1522, 16:78a; MTK, 13:26ff.

[251] Ibid.

charade.[252] This impression of hypocrisy is heightened in the words with which Liu Pei signals his assent: "There will be plenty of time to take care of this after you have recovered" 軍師病可行之未遲, which sounds neutral enough but is immediately taken by all those present as a declaration of full and final acceptance.[253]

The conclusion that the novel version of San-kuo history is designed in such a way as to bring out the hypocritical aspects of some of the major acts of Liu Pei may suggest a parallel to the role of Sung Chiang in *Shui-hu chuan*—along the lines of the parallels traced above between Kuan Yü and Wu Sung, or Chang Fei and Li K'uei. The impression that there is more to the similarity between Liu Pei and Sung Chiang than the simple fact that they share a common role as the central figures in confederations of heroes is based on numerous specific details of presentation. These range from their initial description as minor officials with a penchant for supporting local stalwarts,[254] to such major scenes as the near betrayal of their own intentions through their loose tongues (*shih-yen*); or the recurring scenes in which, as military commanders, they find themselves alone and helpless (*tu-tzu i-ko* 獨自一個). Certain other fine touches, such as the fact that Liu Pei, like Sung Chiang, is put out of action by sickness at climactic moments in his career, also support the sense that the two heroes are figurally related.[255] Moreover, we have already observed that the uneasy relationship between Liu Pei and his two sworn brothers provides a striking parallel to the relations between Sung Chiang and his own captains.[256]

In making this comparison between Liu Pei and Sung Chiang, however, we must take more seriously Liu Pei's reputation as a man of compassion and honor (*jen-i chih shih* 仁義之士), which is attached to him from the

---

[252] The 1522 edition lacks Chu-ko Liang's "leap" to his feet, and the "Li Yü" text (14:10b) revises the adverbial expression "with a bound" (*yüeh-jan* 躍然) to "with alacrity" (*fen-jan* 奮然), as do the *Ying-hsiung p'u* (14:14a) and *Lien-hui t'ang* (14:12a) texts.

[253] In the *Chih-chuan* version (14:12a), as well as the *Lien-hui t'ang* (14:12a) and *Ying-hsiung p'u* (14:14a), Liu Pei is allowed to voice one final grumble after the court officials have made their appearance: "You gentlemen are the ones who are forcing me into an act of infamy" 陷孤於不義, 皆卿等也. Mao Tsung-kang has Liu Pei go through the motions of a ritual triple refusal 再三推讓 on the coronation platform (13:27), whereas the 1522 version and the *Chih-chuan*, *Lien-hui t'ang*, and *Ying-hsiung p'u* editions only have him bow in humility to the four directions 四面讓之. The *Ch'üan-chuan* text cuts this detail altogether.

[254] MTK, chapter 1 (1:3); and above, Chapter 4, Part IV.

[255] Cf. the "poem of rebellion" (*fan-shih* 反詩) forged in Liu Pei's name by Ts'ai Mao in chapter 34, here too leading to a figurally similar river escape.

[256] See Part V of this chapter for further discussion. On a number of occasions Liu Pei is shown, like Sung Chiang, to bolster his power of intimidation by stationing his captains directly behind his back while he engages in verbal combat. See, e.g., chapter 45 (7:50), as noted by Mao Tsung-kang (7:46).

beginning of his career and is largely responsible for his rise to power.[257] In the course of the novel, a number of scenes seem to be designed to depict Liu Pei as a man of mercy. Although in certain other scenes we witness treatment of captives in which he is anything but merciful (e.g., his grisly *Shui-hu*-style execution of Mi Fang 糜芳 and Fu shih-jen 傅士仁 with his own hands in chapter 83), there are no real grounds for concluding that the author wishes to deny this aspect of Liu Pei's character.[258]

Even more important for our understanding of the *Yen-i* is the fact that a number of passages in the text support the impression that Liu Pei is sincerely bound by the self-image of a man of compassion and honor. Giving Liu Pei the benefit of the doubt, we can say that this self-image lies behind his repeated protestations of reluctance to take actions that might appear to be dishonorable. In chapter 60, for example, the *Yen-i* cites a speech from the official histories in which Liu Pei proclaims that "where Ts'ao Ts'ao rules by force I rule by compassion ..." 操以暴, 吾以仁. And in chapter 62 he argues, "As long as I treat people with compassion and honor, they will not betray my trust" 吾以仁義待人, 人不負我.[259] In other places, he compares himself to the sage emperors, the Han founder, and even King Wen of Chou.[260]

We have seen that the novel does not lack examples in which this righteous self-image is belied by unrighteous behavior. But in the light of my earlier discussion of the destructive self-image of Kuan Yü, it seems that the central issue brought out in the novel's treatment of Liu Pei is again not a lack but an excess of moral fiber: an overemphasis on simplistic matters of principle to the point of blindness to more complex moral realities.

[257] For example, chapters 2 (1:11), 13 (2:34), 22 (4:15f.), 53 (9:12), and 64 (11:5).

[258] 1522, 17:37b. In the Mao Tsung-kang text (13:46), Liu Pei has Kuan Hsing carry out the execution. In the *Ch'üan-chuan* (14:18a), Kuan Hsing does the killing, but the grisly details are omitted. See also *Chih-chuan* (14:15b), *Lien-hui t'ang* (14:16a), and *P'ing-lin*. Other examples of less than merciful behavior are found in chapter 22 (4:14–16), where Liu Pei's display of mercy toward Wang Chung 王忠 and Liu Tai 劉岱 turns out to be a case of "killing with a borrowed sword" 借刀殺人; and chapter 52 (9:5), in the treatment of Hsing Tao-jung 邢道榮. Mao Tsung-kang revises the title of chapter 62 from "Liu Pei Executes Yang Huai and Kao P'ei" 玄德斬楊懷高沛 to "In the Seizure of Fu Pass, Yang and Kao Submit Their Heads" 取涪關楊高授首, although, curiously, he also changes the 1522 text's indication (13:33a) of Liu Pei's compassion in this incident: 玄德終有慈心, 不忍殺之 to a more simple case of vacillation: 玄德還猶未決. See MTK, chapter 62 (10:37).

[259] Chapters 60 (MTK, 10:23) and 62 (10:40). Liu Pei's first line appears in the following sources: see *Tzu-chih t'ung-chien* (p. 2110), *Chi-shih pen-mo* (p. 791), and *T'ung-chien kang-mu* (14:10b). Of course, anyone can claim credit for compassion, as Ssu-ma Chao does in chapter 115 (19:12).

[260] For example, MTK, chapter 38 (6:39). In the 1522 edition (8:30a), it is Kuan Yü who makes this comparison.

One manifestation of this sort of excess may be seen in Liu Pei's tendency to sentimentality, his characteristic moods and tears.[261] The traditional commentators do not fail to note the exaggeration in this trait. Mao Tsung-kang, in a note in chapter 41, remarks that Liu Pei is "going too far in his compassion" 過於仁, and "Li Cho-wu" mocks him in chapter 38 for crying "like a singsong girl."[262] Even among his closest comrades, Chu-ko Liang faults Liu Pei in chapter 65 for his tendency to lapse into "womanish sentimentality" 婦人之仁; and in chapter 13 Chang Fei bemoans Liu Pei's excessive good-heartedness 心腸忒好, only to be rebuked by Liu.[263]

Far more serious are the many instances in the novel in which Liu Pei's stubbornness in matters of perceived honor results in distortion of the ideals in question and harm to other people and the entire cause. For example, his ideological commitment to protect the people under his rule seems to be presented in the novel as essentially sincere, although the more cynical reader may judge this in the light of frequent expressions of the political need to "capture the hearts of the people" 收民心. But this is shown to cause more harm than good in the forced evacuation in chapter 41, as Liu himself admits.[264]

From this perspective we may now reconsider the brotherhood, which in a sense forms the overall framework of the plot of the novel, from the ritual oath of chapter 1 through the fulfillment of the pledge in chapter 85, with the unfolding of its consequences for the remainder of the book. Although the sworn brotherhood between Liu Pei, Kuan Yü, and Chang Fei is not really a matter of historical record,[265] it is of course a staple of the popular tradition, and provides the basic situation incorporated into virtually every extant drama on San-kuo themes as well as the *P'ing-hua*. What is most important here for the purposes of this discussion is the manner in which the *Yen-i* injects irony into the relationship between Liu Pei and his blood brothers. I have already mentioned some of the tensions and hostilities lying beneath the surface of brotherly devotion joining Kuan Yü and Chang Fei and in the relationship of each of them to Liu Pei. Now we may

[261] See above discussion of this point, and the implied connection to Sung Chiang.

[262] MTK, chapter 41 (7:15); "Li Cho-wu" edition, chapter 38 (p. 5a). It is not entirely clear whether this simile refers to insincerity or weakness. See above, n. 215.

[263] Chapters 65 (11:15) and 13 (2:34).

[264] Chapter 41 (7:18). In chapter 65 (11:10, 14), we are told that Liu Chang shows more concern for the welfare of his people than Liu Pei. The terms *te min-hsin* 得民心 and *te chung-hsin* 得衆心 appear in the *San-kuo chih* (1:14, 4:875). In chapter 62 (10:35) the term *shou min-hsin* 收民心 is used in a patently pejorative sense.

[265] Cf. *San-kuo chih* (4:939), which goes only as far as stating that "they were as close as brothers" 恩若兄弟. See Part V of this chapter for a discussion of the brothers' reunion scenes (*chü* 聚).

go on to observe that Liu Pei's feelings toward the other two are undercut in equal measure in the novel by hints of mistrust and even hostility.

First, Liu Pei's relations with Chang Fei are marked by a long series of discordant notes: he is visibly shocked by his dangerous outbursts as early as chapters 1 and 2; he resents his behavior in chapter 13; and clashes openly with him over strategy in chapters 15 and 21. Growing more and more hostile, by chapter 40 he warns Chang to hold his tongue; and he declares that he has no trust in him in chapters 65 and 70.[266] Liu Pei's relationship with Kuan Yü is generally characterized by greater mutual respect. But this still does not prevent the leader from declaring his lack of faith in his captain precisely at the time of the latter's greatest demonstration of loyalty to him in chapter 26.[267] For that matter, it is a bit curious that the novel is silent on the question of why, after Kuan Yü's fall in chapter 77, Liu Pei fails to activate the pledge of their brotherhood to die on the same day, and does not put his own life on the line in a campaign of revenge until after Chang Fei too has been eliminated.

In Liu Pei's relationship to Chu-ko Liang we again see hints of ironic discrepancy between the sort of total commitment lauded in both the historical sources and the popular tradition, and the actual personal situation presented in the novel.[268] In the popular imagination, the bond between Liu Pei and Chu-ko Liang is conceived as complementary to the brotherhood of three, simply expanded (like that of the Three Musketeers) to take in a fourth. But we have already seen that the recruitment of Chu-ko Liang, known to all from the popular story of the three visits, is tarnished in the novel by repeated suggestions of hostility to Chu-ko Liang on the part of Chang Fei and even Kuan Yü, a hostility that continues to dominate their relations throughout the remainder of the narrative.

In the present context, one may say that much of the blame for this slippage lies in Liu Pei's exaggerated assertion of his own image of himself as a stereotype of the noble ruler seeking out sage advisers. This self-importance is parodied in the "three visits" episode in his own pomposity—especially his overblown presentation with full name and titles, delivered at more than one point to the wrong person, and appropriately deflated by Chu-ko Liang's young attendant, who replies, "I can't possibly remember so many names" 我記不得許多名字.[269] Immediately after Chu-

---

[266] Chapters 1 (1:7−8), 2 (1:11), 13 (2:34), 15 (3:2), 21 (4:8), 40 (7:13), 65 (11:11), 70 (12:2).

[267] Chapter 26 (4:43).

[268] This is particularly noticeable in chapters 81−85, where Liu Pei repeatedly disregards Chu-ko Liang's advice; e.g., chapter 83 (13:49).

[269] MTK, chapter 37 (6:33), and 38 (6:39). Liu Pei's announcement of his own titles is slightly longer in the 1522 edition (8:19a). As Cheng Chen-to demonstrates ("Yen-hua",

ko Liang is attached to Liu Pei's camp, the novel emphasizes Liu Pei's excessive intimacy with his new-found confidant: "they ate at the same table and slept in the same bed" 食則同桌，寢則同榻, which serves to undermine some of the earlier bonds of loyalty between him and his men.[270]

This question of the immoderate personal bond in Liu Pei's relationship to Chu-ko Liang is raised by a number of traditional commentators in connection with the familiar scene of Liu Pei's deathbed charge to his sage adviser to undertake the regency for his unpromising son Liu Shan 劉禪, and, if necessary, to assume the imperial authority himself. This scene, by the way, represents yet another "set piece" of the narrative tradition, as is evident from the fact that such *t'o-ku* scenes recur several times in the novel, including those instances in which it is Liu Pei himself who is offered the regency by leaders with sincere concern for the fate of their people. With our hindsight on Liu Pei's use of the opportunities presented at Hsü-chou to consolidate his own position, it is not difficult to understand why Mao Tsung-kang finds it necessary to defend this as a perfectly "true" case, as opposed to other "false" instances, and "Li Cho-wu" condemns it in no uncertain terms as "the words of an unscrupulous hero" 奸雄之言.[271]

In addition to the ironic disequilibrium introduced into the three-party brotherhood with the inclusion of Chu-ko Liang in the inner circle, the novel also uses the technique of figural reflection to chip away at the unique honor seemingly attached to another fixed *topos*: the solemn vows of the Peach Garden ritual in the opening chapter. It turns out that Kuan and Chang are not the only ones to whom Liu Pei swears eternal brother-hood in the course of the novel.[272] His early bond to Kung-sun Tsan, for example, is deeply undercut when he throws his lot in with Yüan Shao in

---

p. 196ff.), the treatment of this scene in the novel is roughly five times longer than that in the *P'ing-hua*. The treatment in the 1522 edition and that in the Mao edition are about equal except for certain details, such as Ts'ui Chou-p'ing's speech on the historical cycles of order and disorder (*chih-luan* 治亂) in chapter 37 (6:33), which is more fully developed in the 1522 edition. The "Li Cho-wu" commentator (chapter 38, pp. 2b, 3b) finds the pomposity and false modesty of Liu Pei and Chu-ko Liang in this scene unforgivable, and curses them both as "vulgar creatures" (*su-wu* 俗物). Cf. the treatment of the "three visits" episode in the *Tzu-chih t'ung-chien*, p. 2075.

[270] MTK, 6:42.

[271] MTK, chapter 85 (14:9), "Li Cho-wu," chapter 85, p. 14a. Liu Pei's *t'o-ku* speech to Chu-ko Liang is recorded in the *San-kuo chih* (4:918); see also *Tzu-chih t'ung-chien*, p. 2213, and *T'ung-chien kang-mu*, p. 14:75b. Wang Fu-chih (*Tu T'ung-chien lun*, p. 321) is particularly critical of this act. Other instances of the *t'o-ku topos* occur in chapter 41 (7:11, 13), 91 (15:14), and 106 (17:46). See n. 231.

[272] Other examples of sworn brotherhood in the novel include those between Chao Yün and Chao Fan in chapter 52 (9:6), and between Chung Hui and Chiang Wei in chapter 118 (19:30). See Part V of this chapter for further discussion.

chapter 22, only shortly after Yüan has done in his unfortunate friend—a point cited by Mao Tsung-kang as an example of the unpredictability of the narrative.[273]

The most incisive counterexample of sworn brotherhood, however, is developed in Liu Pei's relationship to Lü Pu, which occupies the center of attention for much of the second decade of the text. Liu Pei's declaration of faith in this man is naively undiscriminating at best, and crassly opportunistic at worst. But the author goes far beyond this in utilizing the relationship with Lü Pu to cast ironic light on Liu Pei's motivations. Although Lü Pu is branded early in the novel as a paragon of ingratitude because of his betrayal of his adopted father (*i-fu* 義父), Ting Yüan 丁原, for the gift of a horse, a balance of respect holds between the two: each has occasion to seek refuge with the other and later they displace each other in turn from Hsü-chou to Hsiao-p'ei, leaving them on very much the same level. For all his ruthlessness, Lü Pu does show a certain measure of human decency in taking Liu Pei's family under his personal protection each time he retakes Hsü-chou, and Liu does explicitly acknowledge this service in chapter 15.[274] But after Lü Pu is finally brought to his knees by Ts'ao Ts'ao, Liu Pei's role in the final scene—when Ts'ao Ts'ao, for his own reasons, places Lü Pu's fate in Liu Pei's hands, and the latter not only refuses to intervene on his behalf, but even convinces Ts'ao Ts'ao to execute him—seems to be accurately summed up in Lü Pu's curse: "This boy is utterly faithless!" (*shih erh tsui wu-hsin-che* 是兒最無信者).[275] The seriousness with which the novel treats this scene can be appreciated by comparing the different versions of the incident. Where the historical sources record Liu Pei's role, but explain it as basically passive acquiescence in a distasteful act, the popular tradition glosses over Liu Pei's involvement (the *P'ing-hua* omits his own role in the execution entirely).[276] Interestingly, Mao Tsung-kang attempts to skirt the issue altogether by changing the chapter title from

---

[273] MTK, 4:8. Wang Fu-chih comes down hard on Liu Pei on this point in his *Tu T'ung-chien lun*, p. 294.

[274] MTK, 3:2.

[275] MTK, chapter 19 (3:40).

[276] The *T'ung-chien kang-mu* entry (p. 13:38b) credits Ts'ao Ts'ao with the killing of Lü Pu (although in the full narrative below it is Liu Pei who stops Ts'ao Ts'ao from releasing him). See also *Ying-hsiung chi*, p. 16b. In the *Hou Han shu* treatment of the incident Ts'ao alone puts Lü Pu to death in one recounting (1:381), while in another place (5:2451f.) the role of Liu Pei is related as in the *Yen-i*. See also *Tzu-chih t'ung-chien*, pp. 2006f. "Li Chih" first notes in the *Shih-kang p'ing-yao*, p. 329, that Liu Pei did not recommend killing Lü Pu, and then adds the comment "Wonderful! Kill him!" 好, 殺了罷. Wang Fu-chih emphasizes Liu's role in his *Tu T'ung-chien lun*, pp. 260, 284. See also the *P'ing-hua*, p. 391, and the drama *Shih-liu yüan*, p. 3a (where the act is attributed to both Ts'ao Ts'ao and Liu Pei together).

"Ts'ao Ts'ao Executes Lü Pu at Pai-men" 白門曹操斬呂布 to "Lü Pu Forfeits his Life at Pai-men Tower" 白門樓呂布殞命.

A second set of relationships developed in the novel reflecting ironically on the manner in which Liu Pei's excessive fixation on his own righteous self-importance forces him into morally ambiguous situations are those concerning his family. As the reader makes his way through the book, he is struck by the frequency with which scenes where Liu Pei loses touch with his wives and children recur.[277] Now, of course, fighting the battles of the empire is a dangerous business, in which it is to be expected that a hero's family must be ready to accept being placed in jeopardy. Nevertheless, the sheer number of instances in which Liu Pei is separated from his family, or more specifically opts to leave them behind (*ch'i-ch'i* 棄妻) in pursuing his cause—including examples in chapter 24, when his wives are left in the protection of Kuan Yü in Ts'ao Ts'ao's camp, and the famous gesture of throwing his infant son to the ground in chapter 42—calls forth a variety of remarks from the traditional commentators.[278] Mao Tsung-kang, for example, draws attention to the pointed parallel in the novel between Liu Pei's almost casual abandonment of his wives and children and Liu An's 劉安 grotesque sacrifice of his own wife to the cause of his kinsman. And "Li Cho-wu" comes right to the point in chapter 82, when he faults Liu Pei for "giving up a true-hearted wife [Lady Sun] for a false brother" 是爲假兄弟而失眞夫人也.[279]

One of the most troubling instances in the novel of the sacrifice of family ties to an overweening sense of a higher calling is seen in Liu Pei's execution of his adopted son Liu Feng 劉封 in chapter 79. One might easily read this scene as an essentially positive example of the archetypal Confucian dilemma of conflict between personal bonds and a sense of duty. But, once again, the fine details inserted into the treatment in the novel seem to demand a darker interpretation. Liu Feng is, in any case, a shadowy

---

[277] For example, chapters 19 (3:32), 24 (4:30), 42 (7:27f.). Li Chih, in his review of Liu Pei's career in his *Ts'ang shu*, mockingly inserts the comments: "first time," "second time," "third time" after each instance in which Liu Pei's wives and child are captured (pp. 66f.). In a comment in chapter 24 (4:26), Mao Tsung-kang justifies this behavior on the part of Liu Pei.

[278] Cf. the proverbial expression "Liu Pei flings his child" 劉備甩孩, which conveys the sense of an unnecessarily exaggerated gesture. In chapter 21 (4:5), Kung-sun Tsan sacrifices his wife and children before taking his own life, and in chapter 64 (11:7) we witness Ma Ch'ao's loss of his wife and children.

[279] MTK, 3:33; "Li Cho-wu," chapter 82 (p. 1b). See also a "Li Cho-wu" comment in chapter 19 (p. 14b) taking Lü Pu to task for sacrificing himself for a woman, as well as Mao Tsung-kang's discussion of several examples of defending women's honor in chapter 14 (2:41).

figure in the *Yen-i*. His adoption by Liu Pei in chapter 37 (against the advice of Kuan Yü) is presented in an ambiguous light, and though he does figure in certain episodes, he is not as important a character here as he is in *tsa-chü* drama, where he contributes significantly to the cause in several incidents.[280]

The same ambiguity hovers over Liu Feng's acquiescence in the downfall of Kuan Yü, where it is not entirely clear whether his behavior is motivated by circumspection, simple cowardice, or some deeper resentment toward the adopted brother of his adopted father. When he is captured and brought before Liu Pei, however, the latter does not entertain the slightest possibility of innocence or mitigating circumstances, and dispatches him directly to the block with no further investigation. In view of the heinousness of his crime in Liu Pei's eyes this might perhaps seem justified, but the author of the novel insists on carefully manipulating the irony—by placing the scene immediately contiguous to the best-known example of fraternal hostility in the novel (Ts'ao P'i's mistreatment of Ts'ao Chih), by providing the reader with knowledge of Liu Feng's innocence not available to Liu Pei, and by going on to narrate the arrival of a letter clearing Liu Feng, too late of course to save his head. In the presentation of the scene there are several telling details in the 1522 edition (but cut or toned down by Mao Tsung-kang)—Liu Pei's initial, but short-lived, hesitation (*yu-yü*), followed by his bitter tears of regret upon realizing his "momentary lapse" (*i-shih tsao-tz'u* 一時造次), after which he becomes suddenly ill—all of which add up to the impression of a serious blemish on his self-image as a wise and compassionate ruler. This impression is later reinforced by "retroactive reflection" when Sun Ch'üan acts to spare his own brother's adopted son in comparable circumstances in chapter 86.[281] Mao Tsung-kang cuts or softens most of these details and drastically revises the chapter title from "The King of Han-chung, Enraged, Puts Liu Feng to Death" to "A Nephew Betrays his Uncle: Liu Feng is Subjected to the Law." But in his chapter commentary he admits that "although Liu Feng was not without guilt, for

---

[280] Liu Feng's best-known act of "delivering warm clothing" 送暖衣, as a ruse to smuggle a weapon to Liu Pei, figures in the plays *Huang-ho lou*, pp. 3a, 14b (where he is pointedly reluctant to undertake the mission), *Po-wang shao-t'un*, and *Ko-chiang tou-chih*. In the play *Shuang-fu meng* (Acts 3 and 4, p. 21), Kuan Yü and Chang Fei express their rage toward Liu Feng. David Hawkes cites Chang Fei's trussing up of Liu Feng in *Huang-ho lou* as one of the few known examples of literal representation of physical action on the Yuan stage ("Reflections on Some *Yuan Tsa-chü*," p. 81). Cf. the play *Nu-chan Kuan P'ing*, in which Kuan Yü similarly resolves to execute his own son for wrongdoing, but is finally persuaded by his fellows to spare him.

[281] See 1522 edition, 16:62b; and MTK 13:20. The incident involving Sun Ch'üan occurs in chapter 86 (14:24).

the Former Emperor to put him to death was also off the mark" 劉封雖有罪, 而先主殺之, 亦未得其當也.[282] The "Li Cho-wu" commentator, as might be expected, roundly curses both Liu Pei and Chu-ko Liang for this act, and the editor of the "Li Yü" commentary edition even takes the liberty of concretizing this suggestion of collusion by adding a whispered exchange between the two right before Liu Pei sends his son to his death.[283]

The culmination of the novel's treatment of the issue of Liu Pei's destructive overemphasis on personal honor is the revenge campaign launched after the death of Chang Fei. Here again, we observe a sharp contrast between the popular tradition, in which this is viewed as an act of noble heroism, and the historical sources, which record the strategic fiasco involved in what amounts to the first and only major act of Liu Pei's reign as emperor in Shu.[284] Liu Pei's renewed commitment at this point to avenging his brother's death also contrasts with his earlier circumspection. In the *P'ing-hua*, for example, he had restrained Chang Fei when he clamored for blood; and in the 1522 edition, for all his histrionics, he allows himself to be dissuaded by Chu-ko Liang's counsel of patience.[285]

In the *Yen-i*, to be sure, we share some of the vicarious sympathy of the popular view (although this is nothing like the sense of blood obsession conveyed in, for example, the play *Shuang-fu meng*). But the main thrust of the treatment here is to subject the issue to intense, and inconclusive, debate on the rightness of the revenge policy. In these debates, the discussion turns very pointedly on Liu Pei's excessive fixation on his own sense of honor (*i* 義), which leads to a stereotyped conflict between personal honor and public trust (*ssu-i, kung-i* 私義, 公義), or between the greater and the lesser good (*hsiao-i, ta-i* 小義, 大義). Significantly, this is not the first example in the novel (nor is it the last) in which the concept of *i* is linked ironically to the specific issue of revenge.[286] In the light of the serious

---

[282] MTK, chapter 79 (13 : 15). Mao's revision of the incident omits the expression "hesitated" (*yu-yü*), as well as Liu Pei's confession of his "momentary loss of control," and he changes his "seeing the light" (*hui-hsin* 回心) to a milder "he felt somewhat regretful" (*hsin-chung p'o hui* 心中頗悔), afterwards directing his subsequent grief to Kuan Yü alone.

[283] "Li Cho-wu" edition, chapter 79, pp. 10b, 12a; "Li Yü" edition, chapter 79, p. 10a.

[284] See *San-kuo chih* (4 : 890) and *Tzu-chih t'ung-chien* (pp. 2189ff.).

[285] 1522, 16 : 32b–34a; compare MTK, chapter 78 (13 : 9–10). Later (chapter 81, 13 : 30f.) he does present another plea to at least postpone the revenge campaign. See also the *P'ing-hua*, p. 467, and the 1522 edition, 17 : 3bff. Mao Tsung-kang changes the title of chapter 81 from "Liu Pei Raises Troops to Attack Wu" 劉先主興兵伐吳 to "Liu Pei Raises Troops to Expunge the Wrong to his Brother" 雪弟恨先主興兵.

[286] See esp. chapters 80 (13 : 26f.), 81 (13 : 29f.), and 82 (13 : 36). Other cases in the novel in which a sense of personal honor takes the form of revenge occur in chapters 10 (2 : 19), 29 (5 : 20), 53 (9 : 14), 102 (17 : 10). See further discussion below, Part V.

exploration of the meaning of this term that is a central concern of both *Shui-hu chuan* and *San-kuo chih yen-i*, the fact that Liu Pei destroys both himself and his cause in this single-minded pursuit of honor is but the final irony in his presentation in the novel.

Moving on to Chu-ko Liang, we again find an uneasy conjoining of the veneration accorded him in the popular imagination with the more sober judgment of historiography. Here the ambiguity is compounded by the fact that even within the area of historical writings the evaluations of this figure vary widely, from praise in *San-kuo chih* for the impartiality of his administration as prime minister in Shu, to later historical critics who more often emphasize his crafty exercise of power. In the well-known essay "On Chu-ko Liang" ("Chu-ko Liang lun"), for example, Su Shih speaks of Chu-ko Liang's "mixed application of compassion and justice with deceitful force" (*jen-i cha-li chih tsa-yung* 仁義詐力之雜用).[287]

The reflection of this moral ambivalence in the *Yen-i* has left many modern critics at a loss to account for the divergence of Chu-ko Liang's portrait from the familiar popular image on the stage and in oral storytelling. Hu Shih repeats his theory here that the author was simply unsuccessful in his attempt to depict a sage adviser, instead turning his portrait into that of a "villainous, treacherous scoundrel" (*chien-tiao hsien-cha ti hsiao-jen* 奸刁險詐的小人). Cheng Chen-to argues that although the author basically intended to write the novel as a biography of Chu-ko Liang, that still does not mean his portrayal must be uniformly positive, and so he is presented in many instances in the mold of a *Shui-hu*-type military adviser.[288] This impression of contradictory assessments is only barely alleviated by certain editorial touches inserted on Chu-ko Liang's behalf by Mao Tsung-kang; and although he devotes an extended discussion to Chu-ko Liang as one of the "three paragons" in his *tu-fa*, in which he lauds him as a "sage minister" (*hsien-hsiang* 賢相), even Mao finds frequent cause for serious criticism of

---

[287] Su Shih, "Chu-ko-liang lun," p. 71. On the other hand, another essay entitled "Record of a Visit to the Temple of Chu-ko Liang" 武侯廟記, quoted and attributed to Su in the 1522 edition (21:84a), gives a more positive evaluation of the figure. This essay does not appear in the extant collections of Su's writings and is probably spurious. See also, for example, an essay entitled "On the Relative Merits of the Rulers of Wei, Wu, and Shu" ("Wei, Wu, Shu san-chu yu-lieh lun" 魏吳蜀三主優劣論) by the T'ang scholar Yü Shih-nan, which gives a similarly glowing view of Chu-ko Liang's contribution to Liu Pei's cause; this essay is cited in a note in Hu Tseng's *Yung-shih-shih* (1:13). I have been unable to locate this piece as an independent essay, but Yu's piece entitled "Lun-lüeh," included in *T'ang-wen shih-i* (13:3–4), contains an extended discussion that would fit this title. See also Lü Wen (fl. 798), "Chu-ko Liang Wu-hou miao chi," pp. 9a–10b.

[288] Hu Shih, "Yen-i hsü," p. 474; Cheng Chen-to, "Yen-hua," p. 204. C. T. Hsia (*Classic Novel*, p. 41) points out the narrowness of Hu Shih's evaluation, although he himself emphasizes the popular view of Chu-ko Liang's selfless devotion in his subsequent discussion (pp. 52–62). See also Tung Mei-k'an, *Shih-lun*, p. 9.

him in the course of his interlinear commentary.[289] In the following discussion of Chu-ko Liang as an example of the principle of ironic reflection
governing the sixteenth-century literati novel, I will pay less attention to
the positive aspects of the Chu-ko Liang figure, and focus more on the
problematic elements in his characterization in the text, many of which
conform to the same problems we have already met in the preceding pages.

The most immediately obvious feature compromising Chu-ko Liang's
image in the novel is his extreme arrogance. Even before he actually
appears on stage himself, his image is already inflated by the exaggerated
recommendation of Hsü Shu 徐庶, including among other things the point
that Chu-ko Liang "considered himself the equal of Kuan Chung and Yüeh
I" 自比管仲樂毅, a vaunt that elicits from the reluctant suppliant Kuan Yü
the remark, "He really shouldn't go so far" (*wu nai t'ai kuo* 毋乃太過).[290] In
the ensuing narration of the "three visits" episode—which is developed in
the novel far beyond not only the simple record of the historical sources,
but even that in *tsa-chü* drama and the *P'ing-hua*—it is possible to read the
repeated pattern of anticipation and disappointment as a simple exercise in
narrative suspense. But the repeated suspicions of Chang Fei and Kuan Yü
that Chu-ko Liang is arrogantly toying with them gains a measure of
confirmation when Liu Pei finally catches him at home in chapter 38, only
to be kept standing in attendance for hours, to the point of exhaustion.
Chu-ko Liang, meanwhile, blissfully finishes his afternoon nap, first stirring
then rolling over and going back to sleep.[291] When in the following
encounter Liu Pei and Chu-ko Liang go through their pompous ritual of
courtship, the "Li Cho-wu" commentator cannot resist mocking them as
"boorish creatures" (*su-wu* 俗物); nor can he pass up the chance to suggest
that Chu-ko Liang had been waiting for the visit all along, as he plunges
from fervent disavowals directly into a lengthy discourse on the present
and future state of the empire.[292]

[289] *Tu-fa*, p. 2, item 2. For interlinear commentary, see following notes.

[290] MTK, chapter 36 (6:28) and 37 (6:32). Mao seems to reveal a bit of sarcasm
when he comments further on (6:34): "If K'ung-ming can compare himself to Kuan Chung
and Yüeh I, then Liu Pei can read Mencius" 孔明能比管樂, 玄德能讀孟子. The point
about Chu-ko Liang's self-image is based on the historical sources (e.g., *Chi-shih pen-mo*,
pp. 786ff.). See Riftin, *Istoricheskaya epopeia*, p. 246.

[291] The *San-kuo chih* (4:912) laconically mentions Liu Pei's "three trips" 三往, and the
following note specifies this as a reference to the "three visits to the thatched cottage"
episode. Cf. also *Tzu-chih t'ung-chien* (p. 2075). A number of Yuan *tsa-chü* plays treat this
theme: "Three Visits to the Thatched Cottage," "The Story of the Thatched Cottage"
草廬記, and "Wo-lung kang" 臥龍崗, etc. See Fu Hsi-hua, *Yüan-tai*, p. 272. The "three visits"
episode is also portrayed in Act 1 of the play *Po-wang shao-t'un*. In Mao Tsung-kang's treatment of Liu Pei's bedside vigil, he omits the mention of Liu's physical exhaustion (6:39).

[292] "Li Cho-wu," chapter 38 (p. 2b, 3b); MTK, chapter 38 (6:40); "Li Yü," chapter 37
(pp. 4a–5b). Cf. Mao's label "empty formalities" (*t'ao-hua* 套話) applied to the initial
protestations in the encounter (6:40).

After he is firmly established as the principal adviser in Liu Pei's service, Chu-ko Liang continues to display the same arrogance. This is characteristically expressed in his haughty laughter—both in civilian debate, where he frequently boasts of his ability to "rely on his three-inch tongue" to advance his empire-building plans, and on the battlefield, where his habitual pose of blithe indifference, whether in his Taoist cart and headgear or sitting at his ease on a nearby hill, conveys a message of supreme self-confidence to his own men and enemy troops alike.[293] Of course, these last examples may be viewed as nothing more than clever ploys of psychological warfare, and in the early stages of Chu-ko Liang's career they are certainly part of what C. T. Hsia has termed a "gladsome comic mode" that characterizes his actions up to the Battle of the Red Cliffs.[294] From that point on, however, the recurring image of self-assurance begins to raise more and more serious questions, and in the course of the narrative it ultimately becomes a major factor in his downfall.

One area in which Chu-ko Liang's attitude quickly crosses the line from exuberant self-confidence to destructive egotism is in his relations with his comrades in the Shu-Han camp. For example, his attitude toward his fellow adviser P'ang T'ung (who is linked together with him in Hsü Shu's original recommendation) is clearly dominated by jealous rivalry, and in his treatment of Wei Yen 魏延 this is carried to the point of open conflict.[295]

We have already seen the tense hostility of Chang Fei toward Chu-ko Liang, and he himself clearly reciprocates by holding Chang down in a dependent position, alternately checking him or goading him into action at his own convenience.[296] Chu-ko Liang's relationship with Kuan Yü is

[293] Examples of Chu-ko Liang sitting at ease on a hill or mound occur in chapters 39, 65, 98, etc.; his appearances in the *kuan-chin* headgear (see n. 109), or the "Chu-ko Liang turban" occur in chapters 52, 64 (111:4), 65, 83, 87, 89, 90 (15:9), 92 (15:24), 93 (15:30), 97 (16:23), 98 (16:33), 99 (16:44), and 100 (17:3). His "three-inch tongue" and mocking laughter are emphasized in chapters 42, 43, 44, 45, 46, 47, 87, 88, 92, 99, etc. These aspects of his character are brought out—with full admiration—in the *tsa-chü* plays *Po-wang shao-t'un* and *Wu-ma p'o Ts'ao.*

[294] C. T. Hsia, *Classic Novel*, p. 70.

[295] See, for example, chapter 63 (10:43–44), where he sabotages P'ang T'ung's campaign in Szechwan, leading to his death. Chu-ko Liang's hostility to Wei Yen is brought out in chapters 90 (15:7, 9), 92 (15:20), 100 (16:41), and esp. 103 (17:20, 26), 104 (17:28, 31), and 105 (17:33–36). In this last case, Mao Tsung-kang defends Chu-ko Liang's actions to nip Wei Yen's rebelliousness in the bud (17:33), and he changes the title of chapter 105 from "Chu-ko Liang Leaves Behind a Plan to Execute Wei Yen" 武侯遺計斬魏延 to "Chu-ko Liang Lays Down in Advance the Brocade Bag Scheme" 武侯預伏錦囊計. On the other side, a note in chapter 53 of the 1522 edition (11:35a) warns us in advance that Chu-ko Liang will deliberately induce Wei Yen to rebel after his death; and the "Li Cho-wu" commentator repeats this charge explicitly and bitterly in chapter 104 (p. 14b).

[296] Cf. chapter 70 (12:2–3), where he uses Chang Fei's legendary drunkenness to entrap Chang Ho 張郃. Chu-ko Liang's manipulation of Chang Fei appears to be the subject of a

marked by less explicit clashes, but it is also characterized by the same underlying tension. The clearest example of his deliberate manipulation of Kuan Yü is seen in the "honorable release" of Ts'ao Ts'ao on the Hua-jung Road, which is presented in the novel as a calculated risk on the part of the prescient adviser; thus, the ultimate responsibility for this fateful error is also shifted onto Chu-ko Liang's shoulders. In the treatment of this scene in the novel, the impression of cynical premeditation is heightened when he casually announces that he only wants to "do a favor" to Kuan Yü by giving him this assignment, and this is even more striking in the following chapter, when he harshly rebukes Kuan Yü for a blunder he himself, in effect, has brought to pass.[297] The "Li Cho-wu" commentator comes down predictably hard on Chu-ko Liang at this point, calling him a "bandit" (*tsei* 賊); and Mao Tsung-kang revises the chapter title from "Ts'ao Ts'ao, in Defeat, Flees by the Hua-jung Road" 曹操敗走華容道 to "Chu-ko Liang Cleverly Calculates the Hua-jung Affair" 諸葛亮智算華容道 to show his perception of the incident.[298] In view of the special tension in the collision of these two extraordinary egos, it is more than a little ironic that the author of the novel later puts into Chu-ko Liang's mouth the historian's evaluation of Kuan Yü as "unyielding and self-important" (*kang erh tzu-chin* 剛而自矜).[299]

The sort of crafty manipulation seen in Chu-ko Liang's handling of Chang Fei and Kuan Yü is also presented in the repeated scenes in which he induces other proud warriors to carry out his own will. The device most typically used to do this is the recurrent motif of the "brocade bag" (*chin-nang*) containing written instructions to be opened only at specified intervals.[300] The way Chu-ko Liang "uses his men" (i.e. *yung-jen*) by relying on insults and other tricks to goad (*chi* 激) them into action crosses the line from a simple practice of sound generalship to something more problematic when he applies such pressure specifically to the older warriors, such as Huang Chung, by insulting their advanced years.[301] The shock of these blatant affronts to the hallowed respect for age in China may lead us to

---

nonextant *tsa-chü* play entitled *San-ch'i Chang Fei* or *Chu-ko Liang kua-yin ch'i Chang Fei* 諸葛亮掛印氣張飛, cited in Fu Hsi-hua, *Yuan-tai*, p. 362.

[297] MTK, chapter 50 (8:28), and 51 (8:36–37).

[298] "Li Cho-wu," chapter 50 (p. 10a); cf. also chapter 51 (p. 9b). Mao Tsung-kang adds an interesting comment (8:35) to account for Chu-ko Liang's troubling behavior in literary terms: "It is true that Chu-ko Liang was not necessarily this deceitful, but the author could not dispense with this degree of narrative deviousness" 雖孔明未必如此之詐, 而作文者不可無如此之曲.

[299] MTK, chapter 78 (13:9).

[300] For example, chapters 54 (9:19), 99 (16:35), 105 (17:28). Cf. the nonextant *tsa-chü* drama entitled *Chin-nang chi* 錦囊計.

[301] For example, chapters 70 (12:5–7), 87 (14:31), 91 (15:18).

recall that Chu-ko Liang, for all his image as a venerable and sage adviser, is actually a young man throughout the course of the novel—only twenty-seven years old at the time of his emergence from Wo-lung kang 臥龍岡 and fifty-four at the time of his death—a factor that no doubt increases the bad feelings about his quick elevation to effective control of Liu Pei's forces.[302]

In addition to the use of goads and taunts, Chu-ko Liang's psychological manipulation of his men is also furthered by the frequent encouragement of open rivalry between them, often in the form of set contests, such as that between Chao Yün and Huang Chung in chapter 71 or that between Kuan Yü and Ma Ch'ao in chapter 65. One is reminded here of the similar contests in *Shui-hu chuan*.[303] An even more ruthless device, again employed by Chu-ko Liang in a pattern of repetition that demands serious consideration on the part of the reader, is the extraction of a formal statement (*chuang* 狀) by the warrior pledging to forfeit his life in the event of failure in a given mission. While basically a legitimate technique of warfare, this repeated motif also brings out the psychological tug-of-war between Chu-ko Liang and his own men—as in the case of Chang Fei in a number of occurrences, Kuan Yü in chapter 50, and especially Ma Su in chapter 95.[304]

Even in his relationship to his lord Liu Pei, the Chu-ko Liang of the *Yen-i* falls short of the ideal of "perfect selflessness between lord and minister" (*chün-ch'en chih chih kung* 君臣之至公) established in the *San-kuo chih* and epitomized in the tearful farewell in chapter 85.[305] It may be going too far to look here for additional examples of the sort of flagrant manipulation considered above, but we have already seen the manner in which Liu Pei's major decisions are largely conditioned by the effective persuasions of Chu-ko Liang: from his veiled threats in chapters 54 and 73 to his feigned illness in chapter 80. As early as his first military engagement in chapter 39, the novel records an example in which Liu Pei's expressions of reluctance to undertake the battle are silenced by a stern glance from the new comrade, leading him to reconsider the idea.[306] In the light of this sort of

---

[302] The *P'ing-hua* (p. 412) gives his age at the outset as twenty-nine years old. In MTK, chapter 39 (7:5), the hostility of Kuan Yü and Chang Fei is specifically linked to Chu-ko Liang's youth.

[303] Chapters 71 (12:13) and 65 (11:16). Cf. the contest of borrowing arrows in chapter 46, the contest between Chou Yü and Liu Pei for territory after the Red Cliffs battle (chapters 51–52), the tournament staged in chapter 56, the contest between Huang Ch'ao and Wei Yen in chapter 62, the contest of battle formations in chapter 113.

[304] Chapters 50 (8:27) and 95 (16:3). See also chapter 99 (16:35).

[305] *San-kuo chih* (4:892), quoted in 1522 edition (17:69a). The "Chung Hsing" commentator cites this quality as the sole basis for the Shu claim to legitimacy in a chapter-commentary in chapter 113.

[306] MTK, chapter 39 (7:4) and chapter 54 (9:17). See n. 285.

patronizing control over his master, Chu-ko Liang's position regarding the disastrous revenge campaign is puzzling. At first he opposes the plan as counterproductive, but at a certain point he changes his ground and gives what amounts to full acquiescence in the project. Since it is arguably within his power to reverse Liu Pei's impulsive decision, the implication made is that Chu-ko Liang himself is in large measure responsible for this major failure, and with it the accompanying death of his sovereign.

The sort of cynical manipulation that Chu-ko Liang displays toward his own men is naturally employed in handling his adversaries as well. Throughout the course of the novel, we witness a series of examples of this type, ranging from amusing tricks to the more ruthless exercise of power. The case of the protracted psychological defeat of Chou Yü, for example, as stylized in the novel in the discontinuous sequence known as "Chou Yü is enraged three times" (*san-ch'i Chou Yü*), is presented more as a celebration of his indomitable wit in the early stages of his career (in the spirit of a number of dramas in which similar provocations are used against Ts'ao Ts'ao)[307] than as a serious consideration of the clash between two heroic personalities. At the same time, however, much of the amusement begins to be dampened by the way that Chu-ko Liang hits below the belt with his sly insinuation that Ts'ao Ts'ao has designs on Chou Yü's young wife, Hsiao-Ch'iao 小喬, or by the exaggerated suffering of Chou Yü when his wounds burst open from rage. In any event, his revealing response when Chou Yü finally dies of mortification: a delighted laugh followed immediately by mock-serious mourning as if for a deeply respected adversary, seems designed to bring out the hypocrisy in Chu-ko Liang's attitude—a sense confirmed when P'ang T'ung's disparaging remarks about the display of feigned mourning elicit a sly smile from his friend. Later, this is reechoed when Chu-ko Liang sheds crocodile tears after the untimely death of P'ang T'ung himself.[308]

In other cases, however, Chu-ko Liang's calculated moves appear less and less amusing, as for example in the deliberate frame-up of Chiang Wei in chapter 93, a trick disturbingly reminiscent of the forced recruitments in *Shui-hu chuan*. This reaches the point of ruthlessness when he puts Chang Jen 張任 to death in chapter 64 in order, as we are told, "to preserve his own reputation" (*i ch'üan ch'i ming* 以全其名), and when he threatens to wipe out the entire population of Ling-ling in pressing for surrender in

[307] Cf. the plays *Ko-chiang tou-chih, Ch'en-ts'ang lu*, Act 2, and *Wu-ma p'o-Ts'ao*, Act 2.

[308] MTK, chapters 57 (9:39–40) and 63 (10:46). Mao Tsung-kang changes the title of chapter 63 from "At Fallen Phoenix Slope P'ang T'ung Is Felled by an Arrow" 落鳳坡箭殺龐統 to "Chu-ko Liang Weeps Bitterly for P'ang T'ung" 諸葛亮痛哭龐統. In chapter 66, his tearful plea on his colleague's behalf is patently false, as Mao Tsung-kang admits (11:19).

chapter 52.[309] Even Mao suggests that his actions are too cruel when he puts an entire army of men, who are bound in vine armor as protection against arrows, to the torch.[310]

Interestingly, the author of the novel does not seem to question Chu-ko Liang's iron rule over Shu, and in fact he describes his legalist measures at length in ideal terms, following in this the judgment of the historians, who credit him with absolute impartiality in the strict enforcement of law and order.[311] In other words, the issue in the *Yen-i* is not simply Chu-ko Liang's pragmatic toughness—in diametrical contrast to Liu Pei's weak-willed sentimentality—but the fact that he goes too far in pursuit of his basically justifiable ends. This is the same sense of excess that we have seen to be responsible for the deflation of the popular images of the other Three Kingdoms heroes, as they are cut down to size in the novelistic treatment of their stories.[312]

This becomes clear when we review Chu-ko Liang's role in the successive stages of Liu Pei's rise to power. The first case I will consider is that of the seizure of Ching-chou, the incident that Su Shih has in mind when he says that Chu-ko Liang is only barely distinguishable from Ts'ao Ts'ao.[313] Even before leaving his thatched cottage, he had specifically targeted Ching-chou as an objective that would have to be "borrowed" if there was to be any hope of achieving Liu Pei's long-term aims.[314] And when the opportunity to take the prize presents itself after Ts'ao Ts'ao's forces are temporarily put out of the picture at the Battle of the Red Cliffs, the author of the novel takes care to indicate Chu-ko Liang's hand in the operation, in

[309] Chapters 93 (15:29–30), 64 (11:5), and 52 (9:5).

[310] MTK, chapter 90 (15:1).

[311] MTK, chapters 65 (11:16), and 96 (16:12). This description is fuller in the 1522 edition (14:79a). Cf. the *P'ing-hua*, p. 482. For the historical sources of this passage, see *San-kuo chih* (4:919ff.) and *Tzu-chih t'ung-chien* (pp. 2131f.). The latter text's indication that the population subject to Chu-ko Liang's draconian rule was not completely sanguine about his theories of social order contrasts with Ch'en Shou's evaluation (p. 934) to the effect that "there were none who considered it unjust" 無怨者. See Mao Tsung-kang's discussion of this point, chapter 96 (16:10). Two examples of Chu-ko Liang's enforcement of his legalist policies occur in chapter 100 (16:45), when he is quick to order the execution of Kou An 苟安 for negligence (the fact that this figure's name describes his essence probably indicates its fictionality); and chapter 101 (17:8), when he again loses his temper 大怒 and orders the execution of a subordinate (Li Yen 李嚴), only to relax the application of the law in deference to personal connections.

[312] Cf. Tung Mei-k'an, *Shih-lun*, pp. 124f.

[313] Su Shih, "Chu-ko Liang lun," 18:72: "The difference between him and Ts'ao was negligible" 此其與曹操異者幾希矣. Cf. several remarks to the same effect by the "Li Cho-wu" commentator in chapters 51 (p. 10a), 80 (p. 13a), and 96 (p. 3b–4a).

[314] MTK, chapter 38 (6:41).

his whispered command to Liu Pei "to do such and such" (*ju-tz'u ju-tz'u* 如此如此), the import of which we soon learn when the latter seizes Ching-chou in violation of a prior arrangement with Chou Yü. Mao Tsung-kang omits the damaging evidence of Chu-ko Liang's whispered instructions and changes the chapter title from "Chu-ko Liang Occupies the Four Commanderies by Indirect Attack" 諸葛亮傍略四郡 to "Chu-ku Liang Cleverly Dismisses Lu Su" 諸葛亮智辭魯肅.[315] We witness here an example of extreme arrogance in Chu-ko Liang's argument of justification to Lu Su: "Everything must eventually revert to its rightful owner" (*wu pi kuei chu* 物必歸主). The hypocrisy is intensified in chapter 54, when he delivers a high-sounding speech on Liu Pei's noble motives, only to renege on his agreement not long after.[316] Mao Tsung-kang indulges in understatement when he labels this maneuvering as "mischievous" (*wan-p'i* 頑皮) in a comment in chapter 56, but elsewhere he does not hesitate to describe Chu-ko Liang (not without some appreciation) as "deceitful" (*cha* 詐).[317] We have already seen the guiding hand of the master in a number of other problematic episodes: his engineering of the coup in I-chou (where he still maintains that the move is only a temporary expedient); his persuasion of Liu Pei to abandon the dictates of narrow ritual propriety and take upon himself the assumption of the title of King of Han Chung in chapter 73; and his histrionic sickbed plea to Liu Pei to assume the throne in chapter 80, followed by his sudden recovery and leap to his feet. In addition, I have noted the manner in which the editor of the "Li Yü" commentary edition accentuates Chu-ko Liang's role in the execution of Liu Feng by inserting a whispered exchange between him and Liu Pei. Even without this added touch, "Li Cho-wu" condemns him as even more culpable in this than Liu Pei, since his action stems from full knowledge rather than impulsive ignorance.[318]

It must be allowed, at this point, that all of the problematic aspects of Chu-ko Liang's behavior I have reviewed here may be taken as tolerable, even admirable, to the extent that a preconceived sympathy for the cause of Liu Pei dominates the judgment of his character as portrayed in the novel. In other words, one can hardly take a sworn Machiavellian to task for acting as if the end justified the means. The key to my interpretation of the treatment of the Chu-ko Liang figure in the *Yen-i*, therefore, hinges on the further observation that, in his presentation in the novel, he also falls

[315] The whispered instructions appear in the 1522 edition (11:4a), and in MTK, chapter 51 (8:38).

[316] Chapters 52 (9:3) and 54 (9:17).

[317] Chapters 56 (9:36) and 50 (8:35).

[318] "Liu Cho-wu" commentary, chapter 79, p. 10b.

markedly short of the *ends* that these questionable means are supposed to attain.

Leaving aside for the moment the ultimate collapse of the entire cause for which Chu-ko Liang is fighting, let us consider a number of aspects in which the popular image of his invincibility is undermined in the novel. There is no denying that a large measure of the *Yen-i*'s interest in this figure focuses on his image as a master strategist (this in contrast to the *San-kuo chih*, which surprisingly points to military strategy as his principal weak point).[319] In fact, in the narration of his early successes at Po-wang p'o and especially at the Red Cliffs, the novel even outstrips the popular sources in ascribing to Chu-ko Liang full credit for the brilliant victories, as opposed to the *P'ing-hua* and drama, which stick closer to the historical sources in granting more credit to Chou Yü for the ruse of "borrowing arrows" and other contributions to the allied cause.[320]

But it is precisely in the excessive treatment of Chu-ko Liang's brilliance in the novel that the irony begins to emerge. One good example of this undercutting through over-presentation is seen in connection with his proverbial wizardry. His ability to call down the wind and rain or to harness fire, and in general his clairvoyant grasp of heavenly phenomena, are the main focus of the early victories. As the novel proceeds, however, sheer repetition begins to lessen the impact of these powers. Not only does the author detract from his impressiveness by providing counterexamples in which the same magical powers are cultivated by others, but he also takes care to insert scenes in which Cho-ku Liang either fails to heed heavenly signs, or the signs themselves prove wrong.[321] The same is true

[319] *San-kuo chih* (4:930). This point is taken up by Wang Fu-chih in his *Tu T'ung-chien lun*, pp. 292, 313f. Some early examples of Chu-ko Liang's imperfect generalship occur in the strategic defeats in chapters 41 and 42, immediately following the initial victory at Po-wang p'o.

[320] See the *P'ing-hua*, p. 424. In chapter 52 (9:4), the general Hsing Tao-jung disputes Chu-ko Liang's claim of credit for the Red Cliffs victory. See also Tung Mei-k'an, *Shih-lun*, pp. 120ff. The *San-kuo chih* (1:31, 2:878) is noncommittal on this point, but the *Hou Han shu* (1:385) gives full credit for Ts'ao Ts'ao's defeat at the Red Cliffs to Chou Yü. Even Hu Tseng's verse on the Red Cliffs battle (*Yung-shih shih*, 1:46), quoted in the 1522 edition (10:54b), speaks only of Chou Yü's role in the victory. The *Fa-ming* commentary by Yin Ch'i-hsin 尹起莘 on the *T'ung-chien kang-mu* (13:91b), however, insists on the contribution of Liu Pei and Chu-ko Liang. Cf. Hu Ying-lin's argument that the silence of the historical sources on this issue actually implies Liu Pei's contribution to the victory (cited in K'ung Ling-ching, *Shih-liao*, p. 40). See n. 397.

[321] Cf. the magical arts practiced by the Yellow Turbans in chapter 1, and by Meng Huo in chapter 90. The popular scene of Chu-ko Liang summoning the east wind in chapter 49 stands out in clear contrast to the chance appearance of an opportune breeze recorded in the *Tzu-chih t'ung-chien* (p. 2093). The popular view is reflected in Chu-ko Liang's

regarding his seemingly inexhaustible supply of ingenious stratagems, most notably the use of fire—which becomes his trademark after Po-wang p'o but is shown to lose its effect in later battles, and even to fail miserably in chapter 97 and elsewhere—and the "empty-city ruse" (*k'ung-ch'eng chi* 空城計), which is repeated in chapters 95, 98, 101, and 115 to the point of becoming perfunctory.[322] Even the famous Eight Trigrams Maze in chapter 84, I might add, is in effect thwarted by Huang Ch'eng-yen's 黃承彥 assistance (as Tu Fu laments), making it less a celebration of Chu-ko Liang's powers than a demonstration of Lu Hsün's 陸遜 own self-possession.

One of the best examples of this sort of ironic undercutting through overpresentation is the campaign against Meng Huo, which dominates the first phase of Chu-ko Liang's operations in Shu after Liu Pei's death. Most historical commentators tend to accept his argument, voiced in chapter 89 in the novel, that the drive was necessary to consolidate his rear in the south before launching a full-scale invasion of Wei in the north (and Mao Tsung-kang also endorses this position in the *tu-fa* and several other discussions). But we observe the bankruptcy of this strategy when desperate appeals for assistance from the Man tribes in the final days of the Shu state in chapter 118 go unanswered.[323] Thus, in the development of the episode in the *Yen-i*, a number of details raise serious questions about the wisdom of the move.

First, there is a logical contradiction between the treatment of the Man

---

opening speeches in the plays *Huang-ho lou* and *Ko-chiang tou-chih*. Chu-ko Liang's use of the proverbial expression "There are many unexpected winds blowing in the skies" 天有不測之風雲 immediately beforehand betrays the tongue-in-cheek tone of the novel version of the incident. Cf. the repeated use of opportune winds to burn the enemy's forces in chapter 98 (16:26). The "Li Cho-wu" commentator expresses his contempt for this hocus pocus in a note in chapter 102 (p. 14b). In chapter 91 (15:17), Chu-ko Liang refuses to heed the heavenly signs that foretell the failure of the first campaign against Wei, and in chapter 102 (17:10) he contemptuously disregards the portents against his second campaign.

[322] The fire strategy fails in chapters 97 (16:21) and 103 (17:26). In chapter 98 (16:26), Chu-ko Liang himself claims the fire strategy as his personal trademark. The "empty-city ruse" appears in chapters 95 (16:7–8), 98 (16:29), 101 (17:7), in which case Ssu-ma I sees through the trick, and 115 (19:9). See Tung Mei-k'an, *Shih-lun*, pp. 137f.

[323] For Chu-ko Liang's justification of the campaign, see chapter 89 (14:45); for the refusal of the Man tribes to come to Shu's aid, see chapter 118 (19:27f.) A similar justification of the campaign is presented in Hsi Tso-ch'ih, *Han Chin Ch'un-ch'iu*, p. 5a: See Mao Tsung-kang's discussions in the *tu-fa*, item 9, p. 6, and chapter 87 (14:25f.). In the popular tradition, these strategic arguments are disregarded. In the relevant verse by Hu Tseng, for example (*Yung-shih shih*, 3:4b), the southern campaign is described as a kind of prize offered to repay Liu Pei's earlier beneficence to Chu-ko Liang; while a line in the *t'an-tz'u* of Yang Shen (*T'an-tz'u*, p. 154) treats the campaign as a "slack season" activity 乘閒暇. See also Tung Mei-k'an, *Shih-lun*, p. 135.

people as savages in need of the civilizing influence of Han culture, and Chu-ko Liang's insistence on attaining total psychological capitulation before accepting surrender (*kung-hsin* 攻心)—a policy that would probably make more sense in the case of a respected adversary of a comparable level of civilization.[324] This is particularly ironic in the case of Meng Huo, who is portrayed in the novel as a reasonable, even a noble leader. In this regard, "Li Cho-wu" sarcastically questions Chu-ko Liang's view of Meng Huo as a barbarian and quips that the "barbarian" is really his equal. Meng Huo's own words are even more on target when he says, "I may be a man from beyond the pale of civilization, but at least I don't share your honor's treachery" 吾雖是化外之人, 不似丞相專施詭計.[325] Through the protracted narrative of the "sevenfold capture of Meng Huo" (*ch'i-ch'in Meng Huo* 七擒孟獲), Chu-ko Liang's grinning arrogance continues to dominate the picture, seemingly pushing from view the stated strategic and moral aims of the campaign. After the reader has made his way through seven repetitions of Meng Huo's capture and release, therefore, it is difficult to accept without question Chu-ko Liang's tears of regret for the lives lost in the campaign after his final objective has been won, particularly when he solemnly proclaims at the sacrifice at the Lu River before departing for home in chapter 91: "How could I ever cause the unnecessary death of even a single individual?" (*an-k'e wang-sha i-jen* 安可妄殺一人?).[326]

In view of the popular image of Chu-ko Liang as an infallible adviser, it is quite significant that the novel also takes care to include instances of egregious and costly failures of judgment on his part. After the release of Ts'ao Ts'ao in chapter 50 (which, as the presentation in the novel implies, is largely his own responsibility), the most glaring error in judgment committed by Chu-ko Liang is in the case of Ma Su.[327] In light of the key importance placed in the novel on the perception of individual worth (*chih-jen*), this overestimation of Ma Su's ability emerges as a serious failing, as he himself eventually admits, and as the commentators are quick to point out. This is all the more ironic since in this case Liu Pei's otherwise all-too-

---

[324] In the *Tzu-chih t'ung-chien* (p. 2222), the policy of insisting on psychological capitulation is advocated by Ma Su rather than Chu-ko Liang. The "Chung Hsing" commentator (chapter 90, *tp*) takes this aspect of the campaign seriously, and suggests that such an approach might be useful in controlling the Manchus threatening his own world. For a similar point in the "Chung Hsing" commentary on *Shui-hu chuan*, see chapter 4, n. 198.

[325] Meng Huo's speech occurs in chapter 89 (14:43). He expresses similar sentiments in chapter 90 (15:10). See "Li Cho-wu" commentary, chapters 87 (p. 8b), 88 (pp. 11a, 11b), and 89 (p. 4a, 12a), where he reads the entire incident as an allegory directed toward later periods.

[326] Chapters 90 (15:10) and 91 (15:13f.).

[327] Cf. the *tsa-chü* play *P'ang lüeh ssu-chün* (p. 6a), in which Chu-ko Liang is taken to task for "using Kuan Yü in the wrong way."

fallible judgment of men proves to be correct.[328] In the scene of dramatic confrontation when, as the chapter title puts it, Chu-ko Liang "brushes away his tears and puts Ma Su to death" (*hui-lei chan Ma Su* 揮淚斬 馬謖)—killing a man with whom he claims a bond of brotherhood (吾與汝 義同兄弟), and then punishing himself with the symbolic act of ritual demotion—all the problematic elements (hypocrisy, jealous rivalry, and fallibility) in Chu-ko Liang's characterization seem to converge and take on deeper meaning.[329]

My earlier discussions of the special interest of the sixteenth-century novel in probing the limitations of the heroes of the popular tradition may help here to interpret the depiction of Chu-ko Liang's final downfall. Although the dramatic death scene in chapter 104 may be read as the tragic, untimely loss of a great hero in his prime, in fact the novel carefully prepares for this moment with intimations of gradual weakening and decline at many points in the twenty-chapter span between the death of Liu Pei and that of his principal adviser. By the time of the full-scale engagements against Ssu-ma I 司馬懿, it has become clear to many that Chu-ko Liang's former powers are already beginning to fade. Yet in spite of more and more setbacks, he continues to show his habitual arrogance, like Kuan Yü at a comparable phase of his own life.[330] For example, in a battle in chapter 97 he confidently predicts an easy victory, only to find that his favored strategy, attack with fire, fails to gain the field. His unique powers again prove to be not so unique in chapter 99, when Ssu-ma I also contemplates the heavens and predicts the rain that denies Chu-ko Liang a victory that is nearly within his grasp after initial successes. And even his attempts at psychological warfare—insulting Ssu-ma I with the gift of a woman's headgear and other attempts to cast aspersions on his manliness in chapter 103—also fail to provoke Ssu-ma I to play into his hands.[331] In

---

[328] See Mao Tsung-kang's discussion in chapter 95 (16:7). Cf. the treatment of this incident in the *San-kuo chih* (4:922ff.), and in the *Tzu-chih t'ung-chien* (pp. 2241f.), as well as Wang Fu-chih's discussion in *Tu T'ung-chien lun*, p. 314.

[329] Later, Chiang Wei goes through the same motions of ritual demotion (*tzu-pien* 自貶) in chapter 111 (18:31). See n. 131.

[330] In chapter 100 (16:41), Ch'en Shih 陳式 and Wei Yen discuss Chu-ko Liang's failing powers, and later (chapter 107, 18:3) Ssu-Ma Chao mocks Chu-ko Liang's helplessness in the final days. In chapter 102 (17:10), Ssu-ma I estimates that his arrogant assurance of his own cleverness 自負才智 will now lead him to ultimate defeat; in chapter 107 (18:3) Ts'ao Hsi 曹羲 states confidently that Chu-ko Liang was no match for Ssu-ma I. See also the *P'ing-hua* (p. 476), in which Ssu-ma I notes that Chu-ko Liang has grown old. Cf. his physical collapse upon hearing of the death of Liu Pei (14:16) and later that of Chang Pao (chapter 99, 16:36).

[331] Chapters 99 (16:38) and 103 (17:24). The sending of the woman's headpiece, as Mao Tsung-kang points out, picks up on Ssu-ma I's earlier pledge to Ts'ao Chen 曹眞 (100, 16:40) that he will don a woman's clothing 女衣 and makeup if he should fail. It may also

the meantime, Ssu-ma I outguesses Chu-ko Liang in chapter 101 and again in chapter 102, and the Wei general continues to plan his moves on the basis of careful observation of the heavenly signs (天象)—at a time when his opponent, with obvious irony, acts in contravention of these signs and suffers a crushing defeat (chapter 102).[332] By this time his will is nearly broken: he acknowledges that he has met his match (*pi shen chih wo* 彼深知我), and in a last-ditch effort even offers to divide the empire with Wu if they will join him in pushing back Ssu-ma I's onslaught.[333] Toward the end he is depicted as sick and weak, and although he is granted a final compensation in the episode where "the dead Chu-ko Liang drives away the live Ssu-ma I" (*ssu Chu-ko tsou sheng Chung-ta* 死諸葛走生仲達), the end in chapter 104 comes as no shock.[334]

The special treatment of the death of Chu-ko Liang in the novel, underscored by an unparalleled number of eulogistic poems and essays in the 1522 edition, and by the interpolated exegesis of Tu Fu's poem in the Mao edition, brings us back to the question of the larger irony inherent in Chu-ko Liang's wholehearted participation in a losing cause. The story of his emergence from reclusion is fraught with paradoxes. On the one hand, the portrayal of the Reclining Dragon at Nan-yang is drawn with all the iconographic trappings of a perfectly enlightened Taoist sage, and even Liu Pei recognizes and pays homage to this image in a discussion with Kuan Yü on the way to his third visit.[335] On the other hand, however, for all the show of reluctance with which he allows himself to be courted, he makes a notice-

---

[332] The "Li Cho-wu" commentator in one place curses both Chu-ko Liang and Ssu-ma I as "idiots" 最愚最蠢之人 indulging their own egos (chapter 98, p. 12a–b). Cf. Mao Tsung-kang's reduction of Ssu-ma I's credit by revising the title of chapter 95 from "Ssu-ma I Uses Clever Strategy to Seize Chieh-t'ing" 司馬懿智取街亭 to "Ma Su Rejects Advice and Loses Chieh-t'ing" 馬謖拒諫失街亭.

reflect the frequent mutual challenges by Chu-ko Liang and Ssu-ma I to "determine who is a man and who a woman" 決雌雄; e.g., chapter 100, 16:45 (see Mao's comment, 16:39). This incident is recorded in the historical sources, both official (e.g., *Chin shu*, 1:8) and pseudo-popular (e.g., *T'an-tz'u*, p. 156). See also the *P'ing-hua*, p. 477.

[333] Chapters 102 (17:12) and 103 (17:24). Cf. his willingness to congratulate Sun Ch'üan on his usurpation of the imperial title in chapter 98 (16:28).

[334] The episode of "the dead Chu-ko Liang drives away the live Ssu-ma I" appears in the biography of Ssu-ma I in the *Chin shu* (1:9), and in a note in the *San-kuo chih* (4:927) based on the *Han Chin Ch'un-ch'iu*. The Mao Tsung-kang edition, as well as all the other later editions I have used, record Chu-ko Liang's death with the term *hung* 薨, normally reserved for royalty, but in the 1522 edition this is given with the more neutral term *shih* 逝. In the historical sources (*San-kuo chih*, 4:925; *Tzu-chih t'ung-chien*, p. 2299) the term used is even lower on the scale of honor: *tsu* 卒.

[335] Cf. the motif of the irreverent novice (*tao-t'ung* 道僮), as well as Chu-ko Liang's affinity for the song "Liang-fu yin" 梁父吟, with its Taoist as well as Confucian associations. Cf. the nonextant *tsa-chü* play entitled *Nan-yang lo* 南陽樂, cited in Wang P'ei-lun, *Hsi-ch'ü tz'u-tien*, p. 260. For the conversation between Liu Pei and Kuan Yü, see Part V of this chapter.

ably sudden commitment to Liu Pei, based on Liu's impressive persistence and the briefest of acquaintances, and immediately throws himself into plans for the conquest of the empire, this after he had earlier complained bitterly to Hsü Shu that he had made him into a kind of "sacrificial offering" by recommending him to Liu Pei in the first place.[336]

Within the traditional Chinese world view, of course, the impulse toward passionate commitment to the human order, associated with Confucianism, and that toward withdrawal from worldly entanglements, as expressed in Taoist symbolism, are by no means mutually contradictory. The usual bridge between these seemingly antagonistic positions lies in the understanding that if and when a true sage meets up with a leader worthy of his service, and if the times are favorable, then he not only may but must abandon his life of self-containment and dedicate all energies to his cause. This is the easiest explanation of Chu-ko Liang's commitment to Liu Pei and it is offered in various discussions, including those of Mao Tsung-kang.[337] But in the context of the above analysis of the ironic undercutting of Liu Pei's image in the *Yen-i*, it is difficult to accept such an interpretation. Not only does Liu Pei fall far short of the qualities of a perfect leader in many ways, but also the popular notion of untainted mutual understanding between Chu-ko Liang and Liu Pei (the *San-kuo chih* notwithstanding) is seriously questioned in the novel.

Once Chu-ko Liang has thrown in his lot with the cause, several other contradictions emerge. One of these is the gap between the infallibility ascribed to Chu-ko Liang in the popular tradition and the successive instances of defeat and ultimate collapse we witness in the novel. Why, we may ask, after predicting the tripartite division of the empire while still in reclusion, is Chu-ko Liang later driven to pursue the ill-fated six campaigns for reunification, which result in his own death and the collapse of his lord's enterprise? This is a question the "Li Cho-wu" commentator does not fail

---

[336] Mao Tsung-kang argues, chapter 38 (6:37), that the abruptness of Chu-ko Liang's commitment ("he assented when he first laid eyes on him" 一見便允) is compensated by the retardation of the three visits. Cf. C. T. Hsia (*Classic Novel*, p. 56), who explains that Chu-ko Liang was "touched by Liu Pei's sincerity." In the passage treating his earlier protests to Hsü Shu against being made into a "sacrificial offering" (*hsi-sheng* 犧牲), the editor of the 1522 edition, curiously, feels that this term needs to be glossed for his readers (8:13b).

[337] Cf. the lament of Ssu-ma Hui 司馬徽 in chapter 37 (6:32): "He has found a lord [fit to serve], but, alas, he has not yet found the [proper] hour" 臥龍雖得其主, 不得其時. In the *tu-fa* (item 2, p. 2), Mao Tsung-kang uses the conventional distinction between phases of "seclusion" (*ch'u* 處) and "emergence" (*ch'u* 出) to explain Chu-ko Liang's greatness, claiming that he was indeed "in full mastery of the heaven-ordained hour" 達乎天時. On a more popular level, a note on a piece of historical verse by Hu Tseng (1:9a) optimistically describes Chu-ko Liang's emergence as "in accord with the times" (*yü-shih* 遇時).

to point out?[338] In a chapter-commentary before chapter 97, even Mao Tsung-kang describes Chu-ko Liang as "inimitably stupid" for proceeding along a course that he knew full well was certain to fail, although in a discussion in the same chapter he reads into the line "and only cease upon my death" (*ssu ehr hou i* 死而後已), in the famous "Second Memorial for Launching the Imperial Troops" (*Hou ch'u-shih piao* 後出師表), a hint that the implied threat of extinction at the hands of Wei left Chu-ko Liang little real choice in the matter.[339]

Chu-ko Liang's attempt to fight to the end against clearly insurmountable odds, as in the line cited above, smacks of both the timeworn spirit of Confucianism and the romantic revolutionary, and this is also the spirit of combined resignation and defiance in which the famous line: "The planning of great deeds is the province of man, the fulfillment of great deeds is the province of heaven" 謀事在人, 成事在天 is probably taken by most readers. That is, this line can be understood as emphasizing the value of human struggle just as much as the inexorability of universal determinism.[340] For all the aura of sagelike wisdom attributed to Chu-ko Liang in the popular tradition, however, within the context of the arrogance and hypocrisy that color his portrait in the novel it is probably not inaccurate to read even lines such as these in an ironic light.

Having considered the leading figures in the Shu-Han camp, let us turn now to Ts'ao Ts'ao. Virtually all critics of the Chinese novel have pointed out that the Ts'ao Ts'ao of *San-kuo chih yen-i* is a far cry from the Ts'ao Ts'ao whose defeat on the popular stage delighted children in Su Shih's time and gratified countless generations of later audiences. For that matter, weighing the entire tradition, it is probably fair to say that the stereotyped image of Ts'ao Ts'ao as an arch-villain is the exception rather than the rule. The treatment of Ts'ao Ts'ao in the hands of official historiography is generally a more balanced view of a great, but flawed, statesman—regardless of the ideological position of a given writer on the issue of legitimate succession (*cheng-t'ung*). Even in the popular tradition the negative image does not seem to have become firmly established until at least the Sung period.[341]

---

[338] "Li Cho-wu" edition, chapter 91 (p. 12a).

[339] MTK, chapter 97 (16:16, 18). See also 16:25. Cf. Chiang Wei's rhetorical question in the *P'ing-hua* (p. 481): "The master is proficient in all the medical arts; why can't he cure his own illness?" 師父善能通醫, 豈不能治己病?

[340] Cf. the line in Ch'en Shou's discussion of Chu-ko Liang in the *San-kuo chih* (4:931): "When the course of the mandate of Heaven is fixed, no man's wits or force can oppose it" 蓋天命有歸, 不可以智力爭也. See also Tung Mei-k'an, *Shih-lun*, p. 140.

[341] See passages in *San-kuo chih* (1:55), *Tzu-chih t'ung-chien* (2173–76), and *T'ung-chien kang-mu* (14:51b). For the argument that Ts'ao Ts'ao's negative image had taken shape by

Despite its open sympathy for the Shu-Han cause, the *Yen-i* generally treats Ts'ao Ts'ao with a balanced view closer to historiography than to popular literature, and the same is true of the traditional commentators, who liberally acknowledge Ts'ao Ts'ao's admirable qualities whenever appropriate.[342] This includes even Mao Tsung-kang who, to be sure, pays respect to popular sentiments by changing certain chapter titles at Ts'ao Ts'ao's expense, but still expresses grudging admiration in his discussion of the Wei leader as one of the "three paragons" in the *tu-fa*, as well as granting frequent approval of specific actions in his interlinear notes.[343]

This is not to say that the author of the novel makes any effort to cover up Ts'ao Ts'ao most glaring faults. Certainly, the *Yen-i* does not flinch from presenting many serious violations of human decency on Ts'ao Ts'ao's part, notably the coldblooded killing of his own kinsman Lü Po-she 呂伯奢 in chapter 4, "borrowing a sword" to kill Ni Heng 禰衡 in chapter 23, the execution of Yang Hsiu in chapter 72, and the most difficult to swallow, the brutal murder of Empress Fu 伏后 and her entire family in chapter 66.[344] Nor does the evidence of Ts'ao Ts'ao's redeeming poetic sensitivity,

---

the Sung period, see Hu Shih, "Yen-i hsü," p. 470; and Tung Mei-k'an, *Shih-lun*, p. 19. Thus, for example, Su Shih already cites Ts'ao Ts'ao as a model of political ruthlessness in his "Chu-ko Liang lun" and "K'ung Pei-hai tsan" 孔北海贊, although he still opts for the legitimacy of Wei in his "Cheng-t'ung lun" 正統論. For that matter, we might contrast Li Shang-yin's reference to oral performance of the San-kuo cycles, which makes no mention of Ts'ao Ts'ao, with Su Shih's reference to his emergence as a stock villain figure by his own time (see above, nn. 29, 181). Cheng Chen-to ("Yen-hua," p. 221) argues that the negative popular image of Ts'ao Ts'ao was largely due to the influence of Yüan Liao-fan's *Kang-chien* from the Chia-ching period on. See also Chao Ts'ung, *Ssu ta hsiao-shuo*, pp. 129f. For a review of the historical treatment of Ts'ao Ts'ao, see Liu Chih-chien, *Ts'ao Ts'ao lun-chi* (above n. 149). For a more recent historian's defense of Ts'ao Ts'ao, see Lü Ssu-mien, *San-kuo shih-hua*, pp. 90–98.

[342] For example, "Li Cho-wu" commentary edition, chapter 19 (12b).

[343] See *tu-fa*, item 2, p. 2, and comments in chapters 6 (1:36), 7 (1:42), 12 (2:31), 16 (3:11), 24 (4:27), 30 (5:26), and 50 (8:31). In the titles of chapters 23, 24, 69, and 78, Mao substitutes a curse for the name of Ts'ao Ts'ao.

[344] Chapters 4 (1:28), 23 (4:21), 24 (4:28), 66 (11:24), 72 (12:21). Cf. Mao Tsung-kang's addition of the expression "commits an atrocity" (*hsing-hsiung* 行凶) in the title of chapter 24. The "Li Cho-wu" commentator, in chapter 24 (8a), calls this a "crime crying out to the heavens" 通天之罪. In his revision of the title of chapter 66, on the other hand, from "Ts'ao Ts'ao Beats to Death Empress Fu" 曹操杖殺伏皇后 to "Empress Fu Sacrifices Her Life for Her Land" 伏皇后為國損生, as well as in his substitution of a completely new title in chapter 72, he takes the focus off Ts'ao Ts'ao's heinous acts. The *Fa-ming* commentary on the *T'ung-chien kang-mu* treatment of the killing of Empress Fu (14:29a) points to the text's use of the term "regicide" (*shih* 弒) as an instance of "rectification of terms to assign the guilt" 正名定罪; and a note in the 1522 edition (14:15a) follows this view in proclaiming this to be "the greatest wrongdoing in Ts'ao Ts'ao's life" 此是曹操平生最不是處. The execution of Yang Hsiu is treated in the *tsa-chü* plays *Ch'en-ts'ang lu* (Act 4) and *Wu-ma p'o Ts'ao* (Act 3). As other examples of Ts'ao Ts'ao's misdeeds, I might mention the

which is displayed in the scene of the "Brief Ballad" (*tuan ko-hsing* 短歌行)
sung in chapter 48, really compensate for the atrocities he commits in the
course of the narrative as some modern critics have suggested.[345] This is
particularly true as this poem functions less as a lyric piece here than to
bring out the ironic discrepancy between Ts'ao Ts'ao's expansive spirit on
this occasion and the fateful blunders he is on the point of committing
(as driven home in the ominous conclusion of the famous scene). In short,
the issue here is not just a question of determining whether Ts'ao Ts'ao is
portrayed as a positive hero or an evil one, but as before, the manner in
which the novel endeavors to bring out the internal contradictions and
ironic ambiguities that abound in the sphere of human motivations.

What is most significant for my purposes about the treatment of Ts'ao
Ts'ao in the *Yen-i* is the degree to which this text develops a striking
parallelism between the careers of Ts'ao Ts'ao and Liu Pei—from the early
phases when they are linked by ties of mutual support and promise,
through their simultaneous rise through ranks and titles, culminating in
their dramatic deaths seven chapters apart, followed by the swift disintegration of their respective dreams. In the following discussion, I will
attempt to demonstrate that this rough parallelism between the two main
figures is not simply a function of their dramatic opposition in terms of plot
(and, in any case, the novel rarely if ever emphasizes personal hatred
between the two), but more important, provides an example of ironic
cross-reflection giving way to mutual definition of character.[346] In line with
the view of the *Yen-i* as a self-conscious revision of black-and-white

---

evacuation of the capital in chapter 14 (2:45), the psychological abuse of Tung Ch'eng and
the affront to the emperor at the imperial hunt in chapter 20 (3:45), the assassination of
Liu Ts'ung 劉琮 and his mother in chapter 41 (7:20), the killing of Ts'ai Mao 蔡瑁 and
Chang Yün 張允 in chapter 45 (7:54), and the mistreatment of Chang Sung in chapter 60
(10:19).

[345] See, e.g., Winston L. Y. Yang, "Literary Transformation," p. 62.

[346] Cf. Mao Tsung-kang's *tu-fa*, item 5, p. 4, in which he compares the founders of the
Three Kingdoms on a number of points, as well as his comparative discussion of Liu Pei and
Ts'ao P'i in chapters 79 (13:14) and 80 (13:22). The open conflict between Liu Pei and
Ts'ao Ts'ao does not surface until chapter 20, with the imperial hunt and the "discussion of
heroes," and passes the point of no return only with the killing of Ch'e Chou by Kuan Yü
in chapter 21 (4:8). Before that time, Ts'ao Ts'ao appears in the position of Liu Pei's
protector. See Tung Mei-k'an, *Shih-lun*, p. 68, on Ts'ao Ts'ao's early appreciation of Liu Pei.
Cf. Ts'ao Ts'ao's welcome of Liu Pei to his camp in chapter 16 after the loss of Hsü-chou
(3:16): "Liu Pei and I are brothers" 玄德與吾兄弟也. In the *tsa-chü* play *San-chan Lü Pu*,
Ts'ao Ts'ao actively recruits Liu Pei's assistance in the fight against Lü Pu, and in the
Ying-hsiung chi (p. 1a) it is related that Ts'ao Ts'ao entrusted secrets to Liu Pei only to have
him pass the information on to Yüan Shao. Later on, Liu Pei and Ts'ao Ts'ao occasionally
exchange insults (e.g., chapters 31, 5:39, and 72, 12:18f.), but the novel does not develop
their hostility into a dramatic clash of wills.

popular notions, I will pay special attention to points on which either Ts'ao Ts'ao is demonstrably superior to Liu Pei, or else Ts'ao Ts'ao's undesirably negative features may be shown to cast an ironic reflection on the parallel figure of Liu Pei as well.

The manner in which the *Yen-i* deliberately frames the two heroes in parallel fashion is evident at the very beginning of the book, where the first appearance of both is marked by the same expression: "There came forth a hero" (*ch'u i-ko ying-hsiung* 出一個英雄), followed by similar capsule biographies relating matters of birth and childhood. In the *P'ing-hua* no such symmetry exists, as Ts'ao Ts'ao simply appears on the scene with no introduction among a troop of soldiers, including Yüan Shao and Yüan Shu 袁術.[347] The initial descriptions of the two, moreover, are strikingly parallel: both display remarkable precocity and ambition as children, to the displeasure of their families, and both grow into youths who prefer amusements and the company of martial types to formal education.[348] Although Liu Pei's descent from a branch of the imperial line clearly contrasts with the adoption of Ts'ao Ts'ao's father into the Ts'ao clan by a eunuch, the 1522 edition pays protracted attention to the not unimpressive patrimony of the Ts'ao family, especially to the integrity of Ts'ao Chieh 曹節 to emphasize the sense that Ts'ao, too, stems from a noble line. (This information is entirely omitted by Mao Tsung-kang, although he does note in his *tu-fa* the similarity between the two heroes as "self-made men" (*tzu wo-shen erh ch'uang-yeh* 自我身而創業).[349]

---

[347] Chapter 1 (1522, 1:6a–b, 13a–15a; MTK, 1:3, 1:6); *P'ing-hua*, pp. 357, 374. Cf. the capsule biography of Cheng Hsüan in chapter 22 (4:10f.). See Riftin, *Istoricheskaya epopeia*, pp. 226f.

[348] E.g. Ts'ao Ts'ao "was fond of falconry and dog racing, loved singing, dancing, and music making ..." 好飛鷹走犬喜歌舞吹彈… (1522, 1:14a); and Liu Pei "was not particularly fond of book learning, but delighted in dogs and horses, loved music, prized clothing ..." 不甚樂讀書喜犬馬愛音樂美衣服… (1522, 1:6a). Both of these descriptions follow closely their *San-kuo chih* biographies (1:2, 4:871f.). In Ts'ao Ts'ao's case this information (as well as the anecdote of Ts'ao's trick played on his uncle) is given in a note drawn from the *Ts'ao Man chuan* (see n. 43). Ts'ao Ts'ao's early winning of official distinction as "filial and incorrupt" (*hsiao-lien* 孝廉) calls forth the scorn of the "Li Cho-wu" commentator (p. 10b): "If Ts'ao Ts'ao could have gained this distinction, anybody today could claim it!" 曹操也曾舉孝廉, 孝廉之名無人不可爲也. But in fact his filiality is demonstrated in chapter 10, and resonates with Liu Pei's filial labors for his mother as a sandal weaver in his early years.

[349] *Tu-fa*, item 5, p. 4. The fact that Ts'ao Ts'ao's father, Ts'ao Sung 曹嵩, was only adopted into the Ts'ao clan by the eunuch Ts'ao T'eng 曹騰 does not seem to have affected this point. The 1522 edition follows a note in the *San-kuo chih* (1:1f.) that identifies Ts'ao Sung's parentage with the Hsia-hou clan, although Ch'en Shou's basic text at this point states that "no one could determine the details of his parentage" 莫能審其生出本末.

The connection drawn between the Ts'ao family and eunuch power would immediately appear to be not only a blight on Ts'ao Ts'ao's personal honor, but also a specific political black mark in the context of the role of eunuchs in the disintegration of the Han empire. And in the first few chapters Ts'ao does seem to be taking the side of the eunuchs when he moves to block Ho Chin's 何進 attempt to exterminate the "ten constant attendants" (*shih ch'ang-shih*). As it later turns out, significantly, Ts'ao Ts'ao's hegemony is not noticeably marred by eunuch power, while on the other hand Liu Pei's short-lived dynasty is pointedly brought down under the influence of the eunuch Huang Hao 黃皓 over his heir Liu Shan.[350]

After the two men move into their respective positions, the key area of comparison between them lies in their qualities of leadership. Here we can observe a number of points on which Ts'ao Ts'ao as depicted in the novel is clearly superior to Liu Pei, especially with respect to the cardinal virtues of the leader in the historical tradition: the ability to attract worthy followers (*te-shih* 得士), the capacity to judge human potential (*chih-jen*), and the wisdom to make fullest use of varying capacities (*yung-jen*).

From the earliest stages of his career, Ts'ao Ts'ao displays an extraordinary ability to attract worthy followers to his camp. This is already evident in his initial maneuvering in the first decade of the text, and blooms into full flower in the large scale recruitment in chapter 10, after his father and other family members have been murdered, and again in the mass recruitment in chapters 14 and 15. One might even say that the arrival of Liu Pei himself into Ts'ao Ts'ao's fold in chapters 19 and 20 represents the most startling success of this capacity, before subsequent developments force Liu Pei's hand and push him into the opposing camp. Mao Tsung-kang, in fact, singles out this quality of *te-shih* as one of the most outstanding traits of Ts'ao Ts'ao in the *tu-fa* discussion, and "Li Cho-wu" similarly points to Ts'ao's ability to "gather around him human talent" (*shou-shih jen-ts'ai* 收拾人才).[351]

If we attempt to identify the precise basis for this ability of Ts'ao Ts'ao, however, it is difficult to pin it down to either the oratorical skill he

---

[350] Cf. Wang Fu-chih's discussion of the Wei regime's restraint of eunuch power, in his *Tu T'ung-chien lun*, p. 312.

[351] MTK, *tu-fa*, item 2, p. 2; "Li Cho-wu" commentator, chapter 15 (4a). See also Mao, chapter 12 (2:31). The same ability is attributed to Sun Ts'e at the start of chapter 8 (2:2). In the *San-kuo chih* (1:28, 32), Ts'ao Ts'ao is shown as one who seeks out sage advisers; and we observe the same quality in the *Tzu-chih t'ung-chien* (pp. 1991f.). Cf. a note in chapter 30 of the 1522 edition (6:85a): "This describes Ts'ao's ability to draw in all the men in the empire. It is due to this that he won the empire itself" 此言曹公能撈攏天下之人，因此而得天下也.

displays in court debates in the opening scenes, or to any great martial prowess or personal charisma.[352] Instead, the answer lies on the other side of the coin of this pulling power, namely, his proven success in making proper use of those who do throw their lot in with him. This quality of *yung-jen* is specifically cited by all the traditional commentators, including Mao Tsung-kang and "Li Cho-wu," in explanation of Ts'ao Ts'ao's consistent advantage over Liu Pei in the first third of the book.[353] With certain exceptions, Ts'ao Ts'ao's "use" of his followers is marked by openness to criticism and willingness to accept advice from a wide range of sources, including defectors.[354] The contrast to Liu Pei's tendency to draw in upon a small circle of personal intimates is striking, in spite of the image of one who "seeks sage advice" attached to him by virtue of the "three visits to the thatched hut." This is rendered all the more ironic in view of the underlying tensions we have seen between Liu Pei and P'ang T'ung, even Kuan Yü, Chang Fei, and occasionally Chu-ko Liang himself.[355]

In this context it is worth noting that the image of Ts'ao Ts'ao as an oppressive tyrant is not strongly reflected in the *Yen-i*. Outside of the atrocities perpetrated on a few individuals, there is little evidence in the novel of depredations visited on the populace at large, other than those presumably caused by the removal of the capital to Hsü-tu.[356] On the other

---

[352] In the first half of the novel we witness a few examples of clever strategy on Ts'ao Ts'ao's part: e.g., his dissimulation of his lack of supplies in the face-off with Yüan Shao in chapter 30; his exploitation of the rivalry between Yüan Shao's sons in chapter 32; his provision of a contingency plan (*i-chi* 遺計) for Ts'ao Jen 曹仁 to follow after the Red Cliffs defeat in chapter 51 (8:40). Cf. Kuo Chia's self-serving enumeration of Ts'ao Ts'ao's "ten points of superiority" (*shih sheng* 十勝) over Yüan Shao in chapter 18 (3:28f.), the tenth of which is "superiority in warfare" (*wu sheng* 武勝). On the other hand, we witness a number of grave military blunders on Ts'ao Ts'ao's part, not the least of which is the Red Cliffs debacle (see *San-kuo chih*, 1:28). Cf. Ts'ao Ts'ao's spurious "classic" of military strategy (*Meng-te hsin shu* 孟德新書), debunked by Chang Sung in chapter 60 (10:18f.). In chapter 71 (12:9) he takes personal command of his troops and marches off in full regalia, only to suffer a resounding defeat.

[353] MTK, chapters 16 (3:11) and 24 (4:27). Cf. the fourth "point of superiority" enumerated in chapter 18. "Li Chih" also attributes Ts'ao Ts'ao's successes to this point in his *Shih-kang p'ing-yao*, p. 328.

[354] This openness to advice is emphasized in the "ten points of superiority," nos. 1, 2, 5, and 6. For example, chapter 41 (7:19). Wang Fu-chih emphasizes this point in his *Tu T'ung-chien lun*, p. 312. Costly exceptions to this occur in chapter 48 (8:18), when he disregards the threatening omens interpreted in Liu Fu's 劉馥 words of warning, and chapter 40 (7:10), when he rejects the admonitions of K'ung Jung and puts him to death, etc.

[355] Cf. Wang Fu-chih's discussion of Liu Pei's failure to "use" Kuan Yü (*Tu T'ung-chien lun*, pp. 300f.), cited in Andrew Lo, "Historiography," p. 85.

[356] MTK, chapter 14 (2:45). The description of the move to Hsü-ch'ang gives no indication of hardships, although coming after the disastrous forced evacuation in chapter 6

hand, we are told that Ts'ao Ts'ao has won the respect of peasants in chapter 31, that he establishes schools in chapter 66, and that he avoids confiscating the people's property after each victory.[357] If anything, Ts'ao Ts'ao's administration is represented more along the lines of the strict but fairly executed legalist rule associated with Chu-ko Liang—and this is the basis of some of the comments cited above equating both of the two rival leaders.[358] It is possible to object that demonstrative acts of fairness, such as cutting his own hair in an extravagant gesture of equal application of his new ordinances in chapter 17, are nothing more than tricks to win public confidence. But in that case, the same stricture might be applied just as well to Liu Pei's frequent expressions of concern for the people's welfare, which we have seen to be explicitly designated in many places as attempts to "win the people's hearts."[359]

Ts'ao Ts'ao's superior ability to "use people," in the best sense of the term, is predicated on his ability to judge them, and to appreciate their varying capacities. In the first chapter of the novel we are told that "he had a reputation for appreciating individual worth" (*yu chih-jen chih ming* 有知人之名), such as is dramatized in the "discussion of heroes" (*ying-hsiung lun* 英雄論) in chapter 21, and in his far-sighted acquiescence in the "escape" of Kuan Yü in chapter 27. A further example of this quality is seen in his extravagant mourning for Tien Wei in chapter 18, and later for Kuo Chia in chapter 50, which the novel seems to present as sincere expressions of appreciation, in contrast to some of Liu Pei's less convincing displays of grief.[360]

---

it might be assumed that this move, too, caused suffering among the populace. In chapter 75 (12:39), Ts'ao Ts'ao again wishes to move the capital, but is dissuaded by the arguments of Ssu-ma I and others. One counterexample occurs in chapter 12 (2:32), when he confiscates grain from the people at Chi Commandery.

[357] Chapters 31 (5:37) and 66 (11:22).

[358] See n. 313. Cf. the discussion of Ts'ao Ts'ao's legalist tendencies in the *San-kuo chih* evaluation (1:55); and the evaluation of his career at the point of his death in the *Tzu-chih t'ung-chien* (pp. 2175f.): "He applied the law with vigor. Any violator met certain punishment; some might confront him with tearful pleas, but in the end they would never be pardoned ..." 用法峻急, 有犯必戮, 或對之流涕, 然終無所赦. Cf. chapters 31 (5:37) and 41 (7:17). Wang Fu-chih (*Tu T'ung-chien lun*, p. 302) states that the people were fortunate under the Wei regime. The "ten points of superiority" in chapter 18 include three (3, 6, and 9) that refer to fairness in administration. Cf. Tung Mei-k'an's discussion of Ts'ao Ts'ao's "progressiveness" (*chin-pu hsing* 進步性), in *Shih-lun*, p. 40.

[359] Chapter 17 (3:25). A note on this passage in the 1522 edition (4:38b) calls this an example of Ts'ao Ts'ao's ability to use his wits in difficult situations. Cf. the "Li Cho-wu" commentator's remark in chapter 31 (p. 12b): "Even if it was a false display of benevolence and generosity, still he had to take the people into serious consideration in order to carry out his enterprise at all" 即假仁仗義, 亦須以民爲念, 方幹得些少事業.

[360] Chapters 18 (3:27) and 50 (8:35). Cf. Ts'ao Ts'ao's more cynical use of this point in chapter 41 (7:19)—"Who says I don't see through these men?" 吾豈不識人？—to justify

From the point of view of my discussion of the art of the novel, however, the portrayal of Ts'ao Ts'ao's superior qualities is less interesting than the signs of weakness and instances of failure developed in the text. That is, this is not a question of the popular audience "delighting in Ts'ao Ts'ao's defeat," but rather the same fascination with exploring the existential limitations of heroic greatness that I have already traced in the treatment of Kuan Yü, Chang Fei, Liu Pei, and Chu-ko Liang.

Although Ts'ao Ts'ao is extolled at one point (to be sure, by his own adviser) as a "godlike military commander," and we are allowed to witness several brilliant moves on his part in the course of the narrative, the path of Ts'ao Ts'ao's seemingly invincible juggernaut is marked more by strategic defeats than by smashing victories.[361] Most memorable, of course, is the Battle of the Red Cliffs, where the total collapse of his offensive is fully commensurate with his boundless self-confidence in the banquet scene on the eve of the conflict.

Of particular relevance to my consideration of the parallel between Ts'ao Ts'ao and Liu Pei in the novel are the recurring scenes in which, in the thick of battle, Ts'ao finds himself alone—separated from his troops and himself physically trapped by enemy forces, only to be delivered by the timely arrival of his men.[362] In a number of such scenes too frequent to be gratuitous, the author sees Ts'ao Ts'ao through to deliverance only at the cost of physical injury, so that as the novel progresses, he has been wounded in the shoulder in chapter 6, had his beard singed in chapter 12, been wounded in the right arm in chapter 16, taken an arrow in his helmet in chapter 32, been knocked from his mount by Chang Fei's deafening roar

---

his protection of the turncoats, Ts'ai Mao and Chang Yün. This quality is emphasized in the *T'ung-chien kang-mu* (14:51b) in its evaluation of Ts'ao Ts'ao at the time of his death: "Ts'ao Ts'ao had knowledge of men and exceptional insight, so that it was hard to delude him with falsity. He recognized and promoted unusual talent without regard for [the candidate's] lowly position, and so he was able to make full use of people, always gaining their best services" 操知人善察難眩以偽, 識拔奇才不拘微賤, 隨能任使皆獲其用. Cf. Mao Tsung-kang, *tu-fa*, item 2, p. 2, where Ts'ao Ts'ao's ability to "know men" is acknowledged. See Tung Mei-k'an, *Shih-lun*, p. 73, for a discussion of Ts'ao Ts'ao's relationship of mutual appreciation with Kuan Yü. Ts'ao's fatal misjudgment of Ni Heng is an obvious exception.

[361] For example, chapter 71 (12:9), where he rides out in full regalia at the head of his troops, only to lead his men into a series of costly defeats (see above, n. 352).

[362] For example, Ts'ao is delivered from dire straits in chapters 11 (2:26), 12 (2:28), 49 (8:29), 50 (8:31–35), and 72 (12:18–20). Cf. his escape after the unsuccessful assassination attempt on Tung Cho in chapter 4 (1:26). Liu Pei finds himself in such straits more often than not in the first half of the novel (see above, n. 213) and is shown escaping from near capture in a number of scenes. Ts'ao P'i is surrounded and saved, like his father, at the last moment in chapter 86 (14:25).

at the bridge in chapter 42, been seriously injured in chapter 58, and had his teeth knocked out in chapter 72.[363] One might understand this strongly emphasized point as simply suggesting Ts'ao Ts'ao's intrepid participation in the vanguard of his struggles; but to my mind this is more meaningful in the context of the fine line between power and helplessness that so intrigues our author. In any event, the figural similarity to Liu Pei is underlined in a number of scenes, as when he throws off his battle robe to avoid capture in chapter 58 (Liu Pei does the same in chapter 84), and in the unwholesome outcome when he takes refuge with his kinsman in chapter 4, a scene noticeably parallel to Liu Pei's experience of refuge in similar circumstances with Liu An.[364]

A strong sense of contrast emerges from within this degree of figural similarity, however, when we consider the manner in which the two principal "heroes" respond to the series of setbacks and defeats they face in the novel. Here we immediately observe the diametric opposition between Liu Pei's propensity to tears of despair and Ts'ao Ts'ao's characteristic laugh, which resounds as a kind of leitmotif throughout the text.[365] The Wei ruler's emblematic laughter might well be taken as a sign of blind arrogance, as it certainly is in the banquet scene in chapter 48. But the novel's repeated depiction of Ts'ao Ts'ao laughing in the face of defeat soon forms a pattern, one that culminates, in chapter 50, in his echoing peals of laughter as he stumbles into one ambush after another while fleeing from the debacle at the Red Cliffs—a spirit even Mao Tsung-kang credits as "commanding sympathy" (*k'e-ai* 可愛).[366]

It is true that Ts'ao Ts'ao does occasionally lapse into the sort of brooding we have seen to characterize Liu Pei, but in general he is depicted as a commander with the strength of mind to absorb setbacks, and we never see him on the verge of giving up the fight, as we see Liu Pei

---

[363] Chapters 6 (1:39), 12 (2:29), 16 (3:18), 32 (5:48), 42 (7:27), 58 (10:5-6), 72 (12:22). Cf. the *San-kuo chih* mention of Ts'ao Ts'ao's wounds (1:7).

[364] Chapter 84 (14:6). In the *P'ing-hua* (p. 476), Ssu-ma I also escapes from a trap by shedding his battle robe. Mao Tsung-kang emphasizes Ts'ao Ts'ao's act by revising the title of chapter 58 from "Ma Ch'ao Fights Six Battles at the Wei River" 馬孟起渭河六戰 to "Ts'ao Ts'ao Cuts His Hair and Sheds His Robe" 曹阿瞞割髮棄袍. The incident is mentioned in the *tsa-chü* plays *Ch'en-ts'ang lu* (p. 12a) and *Wu-ma p'o Ts'ao* (p. 13b).

[365] For example, chapters 2 (1:15) and 41 (1:25). We see Ts'ao Ts'ao shed tears in chapters 16 (3:18), 18 (3:27), 19 (3:33), and 33 (6:2). See Mao Tsung-kang's long comment on Liu Pei's tears before chapter 119 (19:32): "The fact the Former Emperor's dynastic enterprise had some success was half due to his weeping ..." 先主基業半以哭而得成.

[366] MTK, 8:31. In this case, Ts'ao Ts'ao actually forbids his men to weep, so as not to succumb to despair. The "Li Yü" commentator (p. 4a) remarks in regard to this scene: "He keeps on laughing, but, who knows, he may be laughing his way into disaster" 笑出禍來.

despairing on the bank of the T'an River in chapter 31 or ready to take his own life in chapter 41.[367] This tenacious will to survive is already demonstrated early in the book in his regrouping after the abortive attempt to assassinate Tung Cho in chapter 4, and especially in chapter 10, when the cruel murder of his family prompts him to redouble his efforts to organize his forces (in contrast to Liu Pei's precipitous revenge campaign)—a spirit that draws an approving comment from "Li Cho-wu." [368]

What seems to be at issue in these instances is not so much sheer courage as presence of mind—the sort of force of will with which he stares down Liu Pei in the near confrontation during the imperial hunt in chapter 20, or the quick thinking he uses to extricate himself from a variety of perilous situations. One memorable example of this occurs in chapter 12, when Lü Pu (who does not recognize him) demands to be shown to Ts'ao Ts'ao, and he unflinchingly replies, "He's right over there in front of you!" [369]

It is true that the novel does present a few important lapses in this strength of will. For example, in one of Ts'ao Ts'ao's darkest hours, in chapter 72, his loss of self-control (*hsin-luan* 心亂) leads directly to the morally and tactically unforgivable killing of Yang Hsiu and a subsequent military debacle. Similarly, the scene in chapter 56 in which he is startled into dropping his writing brush by the news of Liu Pei's marriage alliance to the Sun family reflects back on the episode of the dropped chopsticks in chapter 21.[370] The most serious weakness the novel brings out in its treatment of Ts'ao Ts'ao is seen in the recurrent emphasis on his inordinate vulnerability to supernatural forces, as in the encounters with the Taoist

---

[367] Ts'ao Ts'ao broods in chapters 6 (1:41), 46 (8:6), and 59 (10:10). Cf. Liu Pei's attitude in chapters 31 (5:40) and 41 (7:18). See n. 215.

[368] "Li Cho-wu" edition, chapter 58 (p. 12a): "After every time Ts'ao Ts'ao suffers a defeat his fighting spirit is redoubled. What a true "unscrupulous hero" 老瞞每到敗後, 愈有精神, 眞奸雄也. "Li Chih" inserts a similar comment in his *Shih-kang p'ing-yao* (p. 322) after the abortive assassination attempt on Tung Cho: "The hero hastens to rise" 英雄促起. The novelist appears to draw on the Ching K'e 荆軻 episode in the *Shih Chi* in his treatment of this scene in chapter 4.

[369] Chapters 20 (3:44) and 12 (2:28). The same might be said of his gesture of cutting his own hair in chapter 17 (cf. the 1522 edition comment cited in n. 359).

[370] Chapters 72 (12:20) and 56 (9:34). Ts'ao Ts'ao's interpretation of the "chicken rib" 雞肋 sign to retreat would seem to be an example of his flexibility, but his implacable resentment toward Yang Hsiu for second-guessing him turns this around into an example of his failing self-control. The incident is mentioned in the *tsa-chü* plays *Ch'en-ts'ang lu* and *Wu-ma p'o Ts'ao* (see above, n. 344). The killing of Yang Hsiu is cited in the *Shih-shuo hsin-yü* chapter on "Deceit and Treachery" (*Chia-chüeh*, 假譎), *chüan* 6, p. 211, as an example of Ts'ao's ruthlessless (cf. MTK, 12:21). See also chapter 71 (12:10), where Yang Hsiu also outdoes Ts'ao Ts'ao in the decipherment of the riddle at the retreat of Ts'ai Yen 蔡琰.

wizard Tso Tz'u in chapter 68, and in his final days, when he is hounded to death by specters.[371]

In this context, I should point out that the crucial theme of vulnerability to sexual temptation, which we have seen to be a major concern in the treatment of Liu Pei and other figures, also surfaces in the portrayal of Ts'ao Ts'ao. The *Yen-i* touches upon this aspect in a number of scenes: in chapter 16 we see him drunk, asking for the possession of another man's wife; in chapter 44 he is accused by Chu-ko Liang of being a "lecher" (*hao-se chih t'u* 好色之徒); and toward the end of his life he is sometimes reported to have withdrawn from public affairs into a life of self-indulgence.[372] But significantly, the author of the novel seems to skirt this issue, only ambiguously suggesting this side of the story of the Bronze Sparrow Pavilion (*T'ung-ch'üeh t'ai* 銅雀台) and avoiding the image of a lustful tyrant that is associated with this episode in the popular tradition.[373] A similar ambiguity also hangs over Ts'ao Ts'ao's last act: his order to distribute incense to his favorite palace ladies and to make provision for

[371] Chapters 68 (11:38–40) and 78 (13:10–14). Here the author reflects back to Sun Ts'e's figurally similar encounter with Yü Chi in chapter 29 (5:20–24). Cf. Mao Tsung-kang's comments on p. 24. Cf. also the dream of the three suns in chapter 61 (10:32) and the killing of Yang Hsiu "in a dream" in chapter 72 (12:21). Mao Tsung-kang adds a new title for chapter 77 ("In Loyang, Ts'ao Ts'ao Is Moved by a Spirit" 洛陽城曹操感神) to emphasize the effect on Ts'ao of seeing Kuan Yü's disembodied head.

[372] Chapters 16 (3:16–17), 44 (7:42), 60 (10:17). See also chapter 56 (9:32). The "Li Yü" commentator, following Mao Tsung-kang (3:17), describes Ts'ao Ts'ao's behavior in chapter 16 (pp. 10a, 12b) as "his true lustful nature" 因酒及色, 殊露本相, although in the presentation of the scene the woman seems to acquiesce to Ts'ao Ts'ao's blandishments quite readily. Cf. his support of Ts'ao P'i's "recruitment" (*na* 納) of Yüan Hsi's captured wife in chapter 33 (6:2), as emphasized in Mao Tsung-kang's new chapter title.

[373] The depiction of Ts'ao Ts'ao's pleasures in the pavilion in chapter 56 (9:32) is confined to more elegant displays, as opposed to Chu-ko Liang's wily suggestion of more lustful designs in chapter 44 (7:42), and even his own intentions stated in chapter 48 (8:18). A note at this point in the 1522 edition (10:29a) suggests that "earlier Chu-ko Liang only presumed this idea to persuade Chou Yü; at this point Ts'ao Ts'ao himself got the same idea" 先是孔明借意說周瑜, 到此曹操亦有此意. The 1522 edition, following Chou Yü's biography in the official history, uses the character 橋 instead of 喬 for the name of the two sisters. (Could the confusion be a result of textual corruption at some point, based on the two bridges [*erh-ch'iao* 二橋] connecting the two towers? Cf. MTK, 9:32.) See explanation of this point in Chai Hao, *T'ung-su pien* (cited in K'ung Ling-ching, *Shih-liao*, p. 43). Cf. the more noble motives ascribed to the building of the *T'ung-ch'üeh t'ai* pavilion in the *San-kuo chih* (1:32) in a note drawn from *Wei Wu ku-shih* 魏武故事. See the final evaluation of the *Tzu-chih t'ung-chien* (p. 2176): "He was of a refined nature, quite sparing, and not particularly fond of luxury" 雅性節儉, 不好華麗. In the popular tradition, on the other hand, the view of the pavilions as a shameless pleasure palace dominates. See, for example, Hu Tseng's verse on the subject (*Yung-shih shih*, 1:13), and the *tsa-chü* play *T'ung-ch'üeh ch'un shen* 銅雀春深, cited in Wang P'ei-lun, *Hsi-ch'ü tz'u-tien*, p. 509.

their future livelihood, a seemingly innocuous wish interpreted by the commentators as a shocking display of self-indulgent and irresponsible sentimentality.[374]

In general, however, we may say that the character of Ts'ao Ts'ao as presented in the novel is clearly contrasted with that of Liu Pei on the crucial point of self-knowledge. For all the morally reprehensible acts committed by him in the narrative, the Ts'ao Ts'ao of the *Yen-i* text is remarkably willing to admit his own mistakes, and only rarely indulges in extravagant self-praise.[375] This aspect of Ts'ao Ts'ao's portrait is expressed most clearly in his relationship with Ch'en Kung 陳宮 in the early part of the book, when he replies to Ch'en Kung's rebuke: "My motivations may have been unrighteous, but why did you have to serve Lü Pu of all people?" 吾心不正, 公又奈何獨事呂布.[376] Even earlier, Ts'ao Ts'ao had boldly expressed similar sentiments in chapter 4, accounting to Ch'en Kung for his killing of Lü Po-she with a singular lack of self-justification: "I would rather have myself betray the trust of the entire world, than have anyone else in the world betray me" 寧教我負天下人, 休教天下人負我.[377] The 1522 edition adds here, in a note incorporated directly into the text itself in later editions, that these words of unabashed egocentrism have "called forth the curses of countless generations."[378] But in the context of my discussion of the parallel treatment of Ts'ao Ts'ao and Liu Pei, I would go on to note the strong echo set up in the *Yen-i* between this unforgettable statement and a later speech by Liu Pei: "As long as I treat people with compassion and justice, they will not betray my trust 吾以仁義待人, 人不負我.[379] If the

---

[374] See Su Shih, "K'ung Pei-hai tsan," in *Su Tung-p'o chi, chüan* 4:120, for a sharp denunciation of these acts as an example of "showing one's true nature at death" 死見眞性.

[375] He indulges in self-praise in chapter 56 (9:33), a passage that is fuller in the 1522 edition (12:7a–b). Cf. his speech recorded in the *San-kuo chih* (1:26): "If I muster all the wisdom and power in the world and guide them with the Way, there is nothing I cannot do" 吾任天下之智力, 以道御之, 無所不可.

[376] MTK, chapter 19 (3:40).

[377] MTK, 1:28. This entire episode is not treated in the *P'ing-hua*, although it is presented, along with this famous line, in a note in the *San-kuo chih* (1:3).

[378] In the 1522 edition (1:65a) the line is preceded by the following note: "Later, Huan Wen in the Chin period uttered these two sentences, which have led countless generations to curse him: 'He may not have "released a fragrant reputation for a hundred generations, but he has in fact left behind an odor for ten thousand years'" 後晉桓溫說兩句言語, 教萬代人罵道:「是雖不流芳百世, 亦可以遺臭萬年」. Cf. Huan Wen's own similar reputation as one "not worthy of the term minister" (*pu-ch'en* 不臣). In the *Ch'üan-chuan* edition (1:20a), the *Ying-hsiung p'u* (1:28b), the *Lien-hui t'ang* (1:24b), and the *P'ing-lin* (1:10a), this note is incorporated into the text itself. Cf. Chung Hsing's discussion in his *Shih-huai* (17:16): "Although this statement carries a certain pathos, Ts'ao Ts'ao's entire career was covered by these eight words, and so they have become the rationalization of evil men for countless ages" 雖帶感愴, 然老瞞一生受用在此八字, 遂爲千古惡人口實.

[379] MTK, chapter 62 (10:40). See above, n. 259.

depiction of Liu Pei's deeds in the novel did indeed bear out this profession, then this speech would provide a sharp distinction in Liu's favor between moral scruples and sheer self-interest. But given the heavy filter of irony through which the novel bids us judge Liu Pei's actions, we can only conclude that we have here two sides of a troubling moral dilemma.[380] Significantly, even Mao Tsung-kang, whose passion for moral rectitude is unequivocal, admits at this point that the sentiments expressed in Ts'ao Ts'ao's remark are universal and that his very enunciation of them demands a certain respect.[381]

Although Liu Pei's self-righteous contrast between his own "benevolence" (*jen* 仁) and Ts'ao Ts'ao's "violence" (*pao* 暴) conforms to the popular imagination, it is not an accurate description of the picture we get in the novel.[382] As mentioned earlier, in revising the simplistic popular stereotypes the author does not flinch from presenting a number of examples of ruthlessness on Ts'ao Ts'ao's part. But significantly, we find in the traditional commentaries a tendency to give Ts'ao Ts'ao the benefit of the doubt in many cases. For example, an interlinear note in the 1522 edition all but justifies Ts'ao Ts'ao's cynical "borrowing" of Wang Hou's 王垕 head in chapter 17 to appease his troops; and even in the most unforgivable act—the killing of Lü Po-she—Mao Tsung-kang sees fit to excuse as an unfortunate misunderstanding the killing of Lü's wife and children, and only condemns him for the subsequent murder of Lü Po-she himself.[383] The 1522 edition, in fact, goes one step further and credits Ts'ao Ts'ao with "a spirit of broad-minded compassion and great virtue" (*k'uan-jen ta-te chih hsin* 寬仁大德之心) when he refuses to pursue Kuan Yü in chapter 27, an evaluation to which Mao Tsung-kang also gives a halfhearted

---

[380] The two statements put forth, respectively, the most cynical and the most idealistic interpretations of the golden rule. The line does not seem to be taken from the historical sources. In the presentation of Liu Pei's pretentious line in chapter 62, P'ang T'ung serves as an ironic foil to Liu Pei's noble declarations. Cf. his mocking laughter, and Liu Pei's quick change of heart in a slightly earlier passage (10:37).

[381] MTK, chapter 4 (1:19): "When readers reach this point they invariably heap scorn and curses on him, and would be quite ready to kill him. But they don't realize that this is in fact a point on which Ts'ao Ts'ao surpasses normal men. I would just like to ask my fellow men: who does not possess this attitude? ... As for all the gentlemen who expound on moral philosophy, they would reverse this statement ... by all means a fine-sounding declaration, but when we examine their actual practice, then at every step they are secretly following the words of Ts'ao Ts'ao...." 讀書者至此無不詬之詈之, 爭欲殺之矣。不知此猶孟德之過人處也。試問天下人, 誰不有此心。至於講道學諸公, 且反其語非不說得好聽。然察其行事, 却是步步私學孟德二語者… Cf. the popular expression "one whose indignation is limited cannot be a *chün-tzu*; without wrath one cannot be a real man" 恨小非君子, 無毒不丈夫, cited occasionally by the commentators.

[382] See p. 433.

[383] See 1522 edition (4:35b); MTK, chapter 4 (1:28).

nod.[384] This characterization seems grossly exaggerated in terms of the popular view of Ts'ao Ts'ao, but it is not entirely out of line with the novel's depiction of such acts as his care for Ch'en Kung's family, a number of instances of generous treatment of defectors and captives, and his refusal to allow a hidden archer to cut down Chao Yün with a "shot in cold blood" (*leng-chien* 冷箭).[385] To be sure, one may well argue that such instances are examples of favors calculated to win popular support—as Ts'ao Ts'ao himself explicitly states at several points—but that again only reinforces the similarity to Liu Pei's overemphasis on cultivating his self-image as a compassionate ruler. Rarely does Ts'ao Ts'ao lapse into the sort of hypocritical self-righteousness I have pointed out in the case of Liu Pei.[386]

This brings us to the most common epithet applied to Ts'ao Ts'ao in various phases of the tradition: that of an "unscrupulous hero" (*chien-hsiung* 奸雄).[387] I should point out that the meaning of this term is not uni-

[384] See 1522 edition (6:17b). This note follows the P'ei Sung-chih evaluation of Ts'ao Ts'ao's act cited on the preceding page of the 1522 text (see *San-kuo chih*, 4:940). A similar view is taken in the *Tzu-chih t'ung-chien* (p. 2027). Cf. Chung Hsing's attribution of "sensitivity" 有情 to Ts'ao Ts'ao in *Shih-huai* (18:1a), cited in Andrew Lo, "Historiography," p. 94. "Li Chih," on the other hand, chooses to view the historical incident (in *Shih-kang p'ing-yao*, p. 330) with his characteristic cynicism, noting that "he realized he couldn't overtake him; that is why he made this great display of compassion" 亦知追不得, 故發大慈悲心. In chapter 27 (5:1) Mao Tsung-kang admits his admiration for Ts'ao Ts'ao's "nobility" (*i* 義) in spite of his treachery (*chien* 奸), although in chapter 36 (6:23), comparing Ts'ao Ts'ao's release of Kuan Yü to Liu Pei's release of Hsü Shu, he insists that Ts'ao's act was one of "overtly releasing him while covertly blocking him" 陽縱之而陰阻之. See also chapter 28 (5:8). In the *P'ing-hua* (p. 403) we are told of a plot by Ts'ao Ts'ao to ambush Kuan Yü in his flight.

[385] Chapters 19 (3:40), 31 (5:37), 33 (6:4, 6–7), 41 (7:24). The "Li Yü" commentator remarks on his treatment of Ch'en Kung's family in chapter 19 (1b): "No one should say that he was ultimately a dishonorable man...." 莫說竟是無義之徒…. See *Tzu-chih t'ung-chien*, p. 2007. Cf. the seventh "point of superiority" in chapter 18. See also Riftin (*Istoricheskaya epopeia*, p. 192), for a discussion of this side of Ts'ao Ts'ao's character.

[386] Cf. Mao Tsung-kang's discussion of Ts'ao Ts'ao's "apparent" loyalty and honor, etc. 似乎忠, 似乎順, 似乎寬, 似乎義 in the *tu-fa*, item 2, p. 2. Ts'ao Ts'ao's refusal to have Liu Pei assassinated in chapter 16 (3:16) is characteristically justified by him in terms of political realities rather than ethical abstractions: "We are presently right at the point of taking men of heroic stature into service ... we cannot afford to lose the faith of the entire empire by killing a single man" 方今正用英雄之時, 不可殺一人而失天下之心. This speech is drawn from the *San-kuo chih* (1:14). The *San-kuo chih* evaluation of Ts'ao Ts'ao (1:55) describes him as a man of "pretentiousness and unstinting calculation" 矯情任算. Examples of hypocrisy on Ts'ao Ts'ao's part include his display of grief for Yüan Shao in chapter 33 (6:2), immediately after he has helped appropriate Yüan Shao's daughter-in-law for his son Ts'ao P'i; and his vaunt of "promoting the Way on behalf of heaven" (*t'i-t'ien hsing-tao* 替天行道) in chapter 47 (8:14). Cf. the ironic ring of this expression in *Shui-hu chuan* (see Chapter 4, Part IV).

[387] The 1522 edition seems to be more sparing in its use of this term than the later editions, particularly that of Mao Tsung-kang. Cheng Chen-to ("Yen-hua," p. 220) attributes

formly pejorative, or at least does not exclude the possibility of sincere admiration of extraordinary talent (*hsiung* 雄) alongside the attribution of an "unscrupulous" (*chien* 奸) nature, as we see in the use of the term in numerous traditional comments.[388] Thus, Ts'ao Ts'ao is in no way offended when, while still a youth, he is given the prophecy by Hsü Shao 許劭 that he is destined to be "a capable minister in times of peace, an unscrupulous hero in times of disorder" (*chih-shih chih neng-ch'en, luan-shih chih chien-hsiung*), and he smiles when Hsü Yu 許攸 calls him a *chien-hsiung* in chapter 30.[389]

Granted, the expression *chien-hsiung* is most often applied in the popular tradition to separate the evil heroics of Ts'ao Ts'ao from what are seen to be the true, legitimate heroics of Liu Pei. In comparing the justice of the claims of the two rivals, it is important to bear in mind that both Ts'ao Ts'ao and Liu Pei have legitimate claims to power: the one on the basis of his name, the other by virtue of his achievements. At the same time, both are engaged throughout the course of the novel in the gradual, but unmistakable usurpation of imperial authority.[390] If there is any distinction to be made between the two main contenders on this point, it is the difference pointed out by Mao Tsung-kang: that Liu Pei, for all his professed reluctance, personally assumes the imperial mantle, whereas Ts'ao Ts'ao abides by his decision to refrain from seeking the throne, contenting himself with seeing it passed to his descendants (an act explained in the *Tzu-chih t'ung-*

---

the increased use of the term to the insertion of Chou Ching-hsüan's poems in the later editions. Cf. Tung Mei-k'an (*Shih-lun*, p. 48). Mao Tsung-kang adds the term to the title of chapter 78. See n. 343.

[388] For example, the "Li Cho-wu" commentator, chapter 5 (p. 14b): "People nowadays all curse Ts'ao Ts'ao as a *chien-hsiung*, but in my opinion the *chien-hsiung* should not be cursed by ordinary men ... instead it is Ts'ao Ts'ao who should curse people for *not* being *chien-hsiung*"今人都罵孟德奸雄, 吾恐奸雄非尋常人所可罵也⋯, 還應孟德罵人不奸雄耳; chapter 78 (4a): "In the final analysis the old *chien-hsiung* is really a true hero" 畢竟老奸是個英雄. In chapter 11 (p. 14b), he calls Liu Pei's refusal of Hsü-chou "the handiwork of a great *chien-hsiung*" 劉玄德不受徐州, 是大奸雄手段. Cf. Mao Tsung-kang's application of the term to Ssu-ma I in chapter 107 (18:4).

[389] Chapters 1 (1:6) and 30 (5:31). For Hsü Shao's prophecy see n. 43, and the *Shih-shuo hsin-yü*, chapter entitled "Recognizing Models" (*Shih-chien* 識鑒), *chüan* 3, p. 95 (where *chien-hsiung* is given as *chien-tsei* 奸賊). "Li Chih" comments at one point in his *Shih-kang p'ing-yao* (p. 320) that "it is regrettable he did not meet with times of peace" 可恨曹操不逢治世. Cf. a remark by the "Li Yü" commentator in chapter 14 (p. 3a): "At this time Ts'ao Ts'ao was a 'capable minister,' not an 'unscrupulous hero'" 此時操是能臣, 非奸雄也. Kuan Lu brings back these lines in his reading of Ts'ao Ts'ao's physiognomy in chapter 69 (11:43).

[390] Of particular significance is the term "by his own authority" (*tzu-li* 自立) used in the *Hou Han shu* (1:387) to describe Ts'ao Ts'ao's assumption, first of the rank of Duke of Wei 魏公, then that of King of Wei 魏王, strikingly parallel to the term applied to Liu Pei at various stages of his assumption of power. See above n. 243.

chien as the effect of the lingering moral influence of the Han empire).[391] In view of the gripping narration of Ts'ao Ts'ao's incessant, and at times ruthless, struggle to climb to the top of the imperial hierarchy through most of his life, it is possible to discount this as just one final hypocritical claim of an "unscrupulous hero"—although a number of historical critics grant him a large measure of credibility on this point.[392] But in any event, in interpreting the *Yen-i* text one should be aware that a certain weariness seems to dominate Ts'ao Ts'ao thinking as old age and years of struggle take their toll, so that by the end it is entirely credible for him to prefer withdrawal from the affairs of state.[393] From the point of view of my discussions here, this means that the focus on the limitations of heroism in the sixteenth-century novel applies not only to the ideal *ying-hsiung*, but also to the supposedly diabolical designs of the *chien-hsiung*.

Among the remaining figures in the novel, few are singled out for the sort of withering critical scrutiny focused on the major characters reviewed so far in this chapter. But we can still perceive in the treatment of a number of secondary characters the same principle of self-conscious revision of images drawn from the popular tradition. Lü Pu, for example, while undeniably cast in the mold of a simple-minded strong man on the popular stage, comes off as far more complex in the novel. We have seen that, despite the initial presentation of Lü Pu as a totally unprincipled wretch, the depiction of his flip-flop relations with Liu Pei is not completely devoid of honorable moments (occasionally showing Liu Pei himself in a comparatively bad light).[394] Of particular interest is the treatment of the affair of Tiao-ch'an 貂蟬, which begins as a predictable trap for the base impulses of a mindless fool, but by the end is described with motifs that suggest an association with the parting scene of Hsiang Yü 項羽 and Yü-mei-jen 虞美人, thus

---

[391] *Tu-fa*, item 2, p. 2, and esp. item 5, p. 4. See the *Tzu-chih t'ung-chien* (p. 2174).

[392] "Li Chih" praises Ts'ao Ts'ao's decision in *Shih-kang p'ing-yao* (p. 336) as "the words of a great hero" 大英雄語, although he later curses him for likening himself to King Wen of the Chou in this regard (p. 345). See MTK, chapter 56 (9:33). This same issue comes up for discussion again in chapter 119 (19:39), when Ssu-ma Chao is accorded the title of Wen-wang.

[393] See chapter 56 (9:33): "I have already reached the pinnacle of exaltation for a public servant, what else can I hope for?" 人臣之貴已極，又復何望哉？ And chapter 68 (11:38): "I myself have been thinking for some time about a 'bold withdrawal from the rushing stream' …" 我亦久思急流勇退… . Mao Tsung-kang argues in chapter 67 (11:25) that Ts'ao Ts'ao is in fact insatiable, and only slackens his drive for total supremacy out of fear of his adversaries.

[394] See discussion of Lü Pu's honorable dealings with Liu Pei in section on Liu Pei, above. The stereotyped image of Lü Pu as a faithless wretch is epitomized in chapter 3 (1:21) in his betrayal of Ting Yüan, his own adopted father, for the prize of a horse (an act labeled as "forgetting one's honor at the first sight of profit" 見利忘義), Cf. Wang Fu-chih's evaluation (*Tu T'ung-chien lun*, p. 285): "Lü Pu's evil lay solely in his inconstancy" 布之惡無他，無恆而已.

considerably raising his moral standing in preparation for the final confrontation with Liu Pei.[395] The "Li Cho-wu" commentator, for one, finds Liu Pei's dishonorable treatment of Lü Pu particularly regrettable, and goes as far as to imply that Liu Pei's overall failure is in large measure due to his inability to "use" Lü Pu properly.[396]

In the case of Chou Yü, a comparison between the treatment in the novel and in the source materials shows a sharp reduction of his heroic stature. This applies not only to the historical sources, where he is a leading figure of the day, but even in Yuan drama and the *P'ing-hua*, where he comes off as a far more capable commander—most conspicuously in the Battle of the Red Cliffs, where he is given credit for the "borrowing arrows" scheme that is transferred to Chu-ko Liang in the *Yen-i*.[397] Mao Tsung-kang gives a nod to the popular image in the *tu-fa* when he lists him, along with Lu Hsün and Ssu-ma I, as an example of exceptional generalship, but he does little to alter the picture of Chou Yü in the text itself.[398] The same is true in the highlighting of his self-destructive jealousy and implied sexual overindulgence with Hsiao-Ch'iao, in contrast to the treatment in the drama *Ch'ü Hsiao-Ch'iao* 娶小喬, where this relationship is portrayed as one of exemplary propriety.[399]

The novel's recasting of Chou Yü as a gullible, overly jealous, egotistical fool is noteworthy for several reasons. First, the downfall of Chou Yü helps to establish the pattern of linkage between egotism in general, and sensual indulgence in particular, as factors in the limitations of heroic stature. In setting Chou Yü up as something like a comic foil to Chu-ko Liang, the novel highlights the invincible cleverness and determination of Chu-ko Liang; but at the same time it provides an early example of Chu-ko Liang, at the height of his powers, going too far. Outside of the purely aesthetic pattern of trebling in the "enraged three times" (*san-ch'i*) sequence, we observe in the three-part episode another example of the manner in which the author moves from light, essentially comic treatment of Chou Yü's slapstick attempts to do his rival in, to a point at which Chu-ko Liang's

[395] In the *P'ing-hua* (pp. 379f.), Tiao-ch'an is described as originally the wife of Lü Pu, separated from him at the time of the downfall of Ting Yüan. See also the *Ying-hsiung chi*, p. 17a, where Lü Pu is accused of speeding his own downfall by pursuing the wives of his fellow generals.

[396] "Li Cho-wu" edition, preface, p. 2b.

[397] For comparisons of the historical and fictional images of Chou Yü, see Tung Mei-k'an, *Shih-lun*, pp. 110–24, esp. 120ff., and Winston Yang, "Literary Transformation," pp. 68ff. The *P'ing-hua* treatment of Chou Yü's credit for "borrowing the arrows" for the Red Cliffs battle can be found on p. 424 (see above, n. 320).

[398] *Tu-fa*, item 3, p. 3. Cf. his comments in chapter 44 (7:45), where he says that Chou Yü shows true appreciation of Chu-ko Liang; and chapter 49 (8:21), where he argues that the two generals both needed the other for the Red Cliffs victory.

[399] *Ch'ü Hsiao-Ch'iao*, see above, n. 35.

excessive arrogance turns quite sour, and his very triumph begins to turn our attention to some of the more troubling issues involved.

Even in the treatment of Chao Yün, we can again perceive the injection of a certain measure of irony into an otherwise positive portrait. To be sure, in a superficial reading of the text Chao Yün comes off as a composite of the classic attributes of the hero: he is a paragon of loyalty, a warrior of great strength and fortitude (*i-shen tou shih tan* 一身都是膽), and from the very first he enjoys a relationship of mutual appreciation with his lord Liu Pei.[400] But in several episodes the author seems to introduce certain shadows of doubt into this shining popular image.

First, with respect to the moral issue discussed in connection with the seizure of Ching-chou in chapter 52, Chao Yün plays the key role in taking the city—in violation of the prior agreement with Chou Yü. Of course, it is reasonable to defend him in this instance as simply following the secret instructions of Liu Pei and Chu-ko Liang, but the glee with which he announces the capture of the city is a bit troubling, and in fact Mao Tsung-kang cuts this line from his edition.[401] Almost immediately there-after, Chao Yün's image as a stereotyped hero is deepened when, in true *hao-han* fashion, he violently rejects Chao Fan's 趙範 offer of the hand of his widowed sister-in-law. His refusal is technically based on the argument that his oath of brotherhood with Chao Fan shortly before would make the marriage incestuous (not to mention the problem of their common sur-name), but the vehemence with which he expresses his opposition to the match smacks of the misogynistic mentality of the *Shui-hu*-type heroes, and when he reports the affair upon his return, Chu-ko Liang questions his exaggerated principles.[402] In addition to this, we may also note that Chao Yün, too, for all his devotion to Liu Pei, is not free of the flaw of jealous

[400] Cf. their first meeting and instantaneous mutual recognition in chapter 7 (1:45), their reunion at the same time as the reassembly of the three brothers in chapter 28 (5:17), his rescue of Liu Pei in chapter 31 (5:40), his deliverance of Liu Pei's wife and child in chapter 41 (7:23), and Liu Pei's praise of him as "a real man" (眞丈夫) in chapter 52 (9:8). Tung Mei-k'an (*Shih-lun*, p. 91) discusses the enlargement of the Chao Yün figure in the *Yen-i* over that in the *P'ing-hua*. See also C. T. Hsia, *Classic Novel*, p. 45. The famous line "He was a man of fortitude in all his being" appears in the historical sources; see *Tzu-chih t'ung-chien* (p. 2158) and *Chi-shih pen-mo* (p. 800).

[401] See 1522 edition, p. 11:22b (Mao's version is found on p. 9:5).

[402] MTK, chapter 52 (9:7f.). Chu-ko Liang's response is much more explicit in the 1522 version (11:27a). Mao Tsung-kang, in his chapter discussion, cites this as an example of Chao Yün's superiority to Liu Pei (9:2); but later in an interlinear comment (9:7) he ridicules Chao Yün's overstated indignation as "an extreme case of moralizing" 道學之極. Liu Pei's later offer to find Chao Yün a wife to compensate for the one he gave up is reminiscent of Sung Chiang's similar offer to Wang Ying in chapters 32 and 48 of *Shui-hu chuan*; and Chao Yün's initial vulnerability to temptation followed by exaggerated rejection parallels the behavior of Wu Sung in chapter 30 of *Shui-hu*. His defense of Liu Pei's wives in chapter 41 also reflects figurally on Kuan Yü's actions in chapters 25 and 26.

rivalry toward his comrades-in-arms—most clearly in the clashes with Chang Fei in chapter 52, and with Huang Chung in chapter 70. Significantly, the depiction of his heroic career in the novel winds down with graphic descriptions of him as an old warrior, still valorous in spirit but increasingly burdened by age and weakness.[403]

Finally, we may take Ssu-ma I as one more example of the self-conscious revision of popular materials in the *Yen-i*. As the moving force, first of the conquest of Shu and then of the overthrow of Wei, he is conceived as very much the spiritual successor to Ts'ao Ts'ao—and this sense is supported by certain examples of cruelty and self-indulgence on his part.[404] But at the same time, his similarity to Ts'ao Ts'ao also includes much of the ambivalence we have seen to characterize the novel's handling of the latter hero figure. This refers not simply to the fact that the novel clearly depicts him as very much a match for Chu-ko Liang, as we have seen, but more specifically to his outstanding qualities of self-control (in the face of Chu-ko Liang's personal provocations) and, more important, his ability to outguess Chu-ko Liang—that is, in a very real sense, to "know" him.[405]

In the foregoing analysis of the ironic revision of the images of some of the main characters in *San-kuo*, I have relied heavily on the notion that the meaning projected through the treatment of character materializes primarily on the basis of figural reflection among pairs and other groupings of figures. This sort of overlapping treatment of individual figures often results in the sense that what we have in the novel are essentially composite portraits, as the traditional commentators have pointed out.[406] But at the

---

[403] See chapters 91 (15 : 18), where he is described as too old to take part in the campaign against Wei, and 92 (15 : 22), where he finds himself trapped and helpless.

[404] For example, chapters 106 (17 : 44f.), where he kills his own generals, then wipes out Kung-sun Yüan's 公孫淵 entire family, and 107 (18 : 5), where he slaughters Ts'ao Shuang 曹爽 and his entire family. His coup in chapter 107 (18 : 2), carried out during an imperial hunt, clearly reflects back to Ts'ao Ts'ao's consolidation of his grip in chapter 20. Cf. Mao Tsung-kang's description of Ssu-ma I as a *chien-hsiung* in chapter 107 (18 : 4), and his comparison of Ts'ao Ts'ao and Ssu-ma I in chapter 108 (18 : 8). See also Chung Hsing's contrast of Ts'ao Ts'ao's "sensitivity" with Ssu-ma I's "lack of human feeling" (see above, n. 384).

[405] His self-control is demonstrated in chapter 103 (17 : 24), in the incident of the woman's headgear. He outguesses Chu-ko Liang in chapter 102 (17 : 11). He expresses admiration for Chu-ko Liang in chapters 95 (16 : 3, 9) and 99 (16 : 34). See aove, n. 331.

[406] For example, MTK, chapter 75 (12 : 36): "Chi P'ing and Hua T'o 華陀 are a single person, not two people" 吉平華陀是一人不是兩人; "Li Cho-wu" commentator, chapter 69 (p. 12a): "I would like to ask my fellow men whether in the final analysis Tso Tz'u and Kuan Lu are one person or two people" 還問世上人, 左慈管輅畢竟是一個人, 是兩個人. The technique of pairing characters in the novel has a parallel in dramatic practice. For example, the two wives of Liu Pei (e.g., in the play *Ch'ien-li tu-hsing*) frequently speak in unison as one voice on the stage. Cf. the frequent use in the dramatic texts of the formula "if one survives, all three survive; if one dies, all three die" 一在三在, 一亡三亡 to refer to the pledge of the three brothers, as for example, in *San-chan Lü Pu* (p. 8a), *T'ao-yüan chieh-i*

same time, we have also seen that within groupings such as the three brothers of the Peach Garden oath and the "five tiger generals" the surface commonality actually masks deeply divisive contrasts and tensions between the individual members. The subsurface divisiveness that undercuts the fabled devotion of the Peach Garden "brothers" is also carried over into the treatment of a long list of pairs of natural brothers in the text—Yuan T'an 袁譚 and Yuan Shang 袁尚, Chu-ko Liang and Chu-ko Chin 諸葛瑾, Liu Ch'i and Liu Ts'ung, Ts'ao P'i and Ts'ao Chih, Ssu-ma Chao 司馬昭 and Ssu-ma Shih 司馬師 —where the recurrent pattern of fraternal disharmony (pu-mu 不睦) gives rise to significant irony in many episodes.[407]

An even more crucial area of ironic reflection in the novel is generated through the special attention paid to the contrast between successive generations of heroes. To be sure, in a narrative work that covers more than eighty years of historical time, it is practically inevitable that the children of some of the central figures in the first half will appear in the second half of the book. But the sheer number of occurrences, and the emphasis given to them, especially in the concluding sections, seem to indicate here a self-conscious pattern of composition.[408] This pattern, which applies not only to the sons of main characters (Kuan Hsing, Chang Pao, Chu-ko Chan 諸葛瞻, Liu Shan), but even to minor figures such as Hsü Ch'u and Yüeh Chin 樂進, takes on even greater significance against the background of the consistent references to the age gap between older and younger warriors. We have seen how this last factor adds particular irony to Chu-ko Liang's sudden rise, as well as to the fall of Kuan Yü, Chang Fei, and other heroes of the first generation.[409]

(pp. 10b, 11a), Huang-ho lou (p. 2a), Ch'ien-li tu-hsing (pp. 2a, 5b). In the play Nu-chan Kuan P'ing (p. 12a–b), the formula is expanded to "five" to include the "five tiger generals". I might also mention in this context the occurrence in San-kuo of the fictional topos of a character confronting his own double, such as we have seen in Hsi-yu chi and Shui-hu chuan. See, for example, Chang Fei in chapter 63 (10:48), Chiang Wei in chapter 93 (15:29).

[407] Examples of fraternal disharmony occur in chapters 31–32 (Yüan T'an and Yüan Shang), 34 (Liu Ch'i and Liu Ts'ung), 62 (Chang Sung and Chang Su 張肅), 78–80 (Ts'ao P'i and Ts'ao Chih), 89 (Meng Huo and Meng Chieh 孟節), 108 (Sun Teng 孫登 and Sun Ho 孫和). Cf. Mao Tsung-kang's discussion of this pattern in the tu-fa, items 9, 11, and 20.

[408] For example, the appearance of Chi P'ing's sons in chapter 69, Han Te's 韓德 sons and Ch'eng Yü's son in chapter 92, Chao Yün's two sons in chapter 97, the sons of Chang Liao 張遼 and Yüeh Chin in chapter 98, Sun Chien's grandnephew Sun Chün 孫峻 in chapter 109, Chia K'uei's 賈逵 son in chapter 111, Teng Ai's 鄧艾 son in chapter 112, Hsü Ch'u's son in chapter 116, Lu Hsün's son in chapter 119. The "Chung Hsing" commentator (chapter 82, tp) takes Kuan Hsing and Chang Pao as fully adequate replacements for their fathers.

[409] The age gap is also given particular emphasis in chapter 65 (10:39): the contest between Huang Chung and Wei Yen; chapter 70 (12:5): Chu-ko Liang's use of rivalry between his younger and older captains; chapter 83 (13:42): Huang Chung's heroics and later demise; and (13:48): Liu Pei's disdain for his younger opponent Lu Hsün; chapter 87 (14:31): Chu-ko Liang's reference to the age of Chao Yün and Wei Yen; chapter 91 (15:18):

As I have argued earlier, the ironic slippage between generations implied by these examples may be seen to cut two ways. On the one hand, the fact that something of the imposing stature of the heroes of the central body of the work is revived and brought back onstage in the context of the sons' generation (Chang Pao has a thunderous voice like his father, Chang Fei; Kuan Hsing inherits his father's martial prowess; and Chu-ko Chan uses the same tricks as Chu-ko Liang) gives rise to the impression that nothing has changed with the passing of the original heroes—that they were not unique and irreplaceable. As "Li Cho-wu" remarks in a comment in chapter 82, "Once again the cast of characters has been replaced—Kuan and Chang have not died!"[410] A similar sense is expressed at the point when Chiang Wei appears to be filling Chu-ko Liang's shoes with remarkable success (in a series of clashes with Ssu-ma Chao reminiscent of Chu-ko Liang's duel with Ssu-ma I), although of course this is not actually a case of natural heredity.[411]

On the other hand, the sense that dominates the exploits of the second generation is more often one of qualitative decline from the greatness of an irretrievable past. This sense is intensified by the constant comparisons voiced throughout the text between the hopeless heroics of this age of decay and the true glory of the age of the founding of the Han.[412] As mentioned earlier, the concluding section of the book is punctuated by lines

---

Chao Yün's advancing years. See above, p. 444. Cf. Liu Chang's dispatch of "old and feeble" troops to Liu Pei in chapter 62 (10:35).

[410] "Li Cho-wu" edition, chapter 82 (7b). For Chang Pao's shout, see chapter 83 (13:43); for Chu-ko Chan's resemblance to his father, see chapter 117 (19:24ff.). The treatment of Kuan Yü's sons in the novel presents certain problems. The *Yen-i* pays most attention to Kuan Hsing, very little to Kuan P'ing (although he figures more prominently in *tsa-chü* drama; e.g., *Nu-chan Kuan P'ing, Huang-ho lou*), and completely disregards Kuan Ting 關定 after his adoption by Kuan Yü in chapter 28 (5:16). A fourth son assigned to Kuan Yü by the popular tradition, Kuan So 關索, is completely absent in the 1522 edition and is only mentioned in the Mao edition in chapters 87, 88, and 89. This is puzzling, since, although his name is not recorded in the historical sources (see K'ung Ling-ching, *Shih-liao*, pp. 41 and 52), he does appear in the *P'ing-hua* (p. 470), his name is parodied in the *Shui-hu chuan* (see Chapter 4, n. 114), and he is the central figure in a recently discovered *tz'u-hua* narrative (for details, see Andrew Lo, "Historiography," p. 379, n. 26). In addition, Kuan So does appear in several other editions of the novel. The *Chih-chuan* edition introduces him in chapter 70 (12:17b), and his role is also highlighted in the caption of an illustration in chapter 71 (12:20b). The *Lien-hui t'ang* edition assigns him an even larger role, adding his name to the "tiger generals" in chapter 73 (13:2b). See Ogawa Tamaki, "Kan Saku no densetsu," pp. 163–72; A. McLaren, "Chantefable and Textual Evolution"; Chou Shao-liang, "Kuan So k'ao"; and Riftin, *Istoricheskaya epopeia*, p. 245.

[411] Chapters 114 (19:2) and 115 (19:8, 11).

[412] For example, in the self-conscious restaging of the famous "Meeting at Hung-men" 鴻門會 in chapters 21 (4:15) and 61 (10:28). See also chapters 17 (3:20), 20 (3:45), 29 (5:25), and 43 (7:34). See Andrew Lo ("Historiography," pp. 68–88) for a thorough review of the references to the founding of the Han in *San-kuo chih yen-i*.

of dialogue recalling earlier phases of the narrative, and frequently these remarks specifically mourn the absence of Kuan Yü, Chu-ko Liang, or other heroes.[413] The "Li Cho-wu" commentator sums up this impression in the following sarcastic remark: "[Chu-ko Liang] used up all his cleverness ... he was unwilling to leave any to his descendants" 把聰明都使盡了⋯不肯留些與子孫也.[414]

This sense of loss is most keenly felt in the failure of the sons to fulfill the promise of the fathers. We may see this in the recurrent pattern of the eruption of internecine strife immediately upon the death of ruler after ruler. Perhaps the best example, however, appears in the performance of the heir of Liu Pei himself. It is not entirely clear whether the author intends the self-debasement of Liu Shan—as he is reduced from the last scion of a noble line to a groveling puppet in the final chapter—to inspire revulsion or simply pity for his abject helplessness as the inheritor of a lost cause (and some traditional readers have even seen in his behavior hints of well-camouflaged defiance).[415] But from the perspective of the larger pattern of progressive decline, the humbling of Liu Shan functions to bring the diffused irony of the final fifteen chapters to its logical conclusion.

V

I have attempted to demonstrate in the foregoing pages that what distinguishes the *San-kuo chih yen-i* from other treatments of the Three Kingdoms cycles, and at the same time associates it with the sixteenth-century literati novel form, is the ironic revision it effects on its narrative sources. At this point, I must take the next step to consider whether or not there also materializes in *San-kuo* the other side of this approach to the novel: the assumption that the ironic undercutting of popular images is directed toward a positive rethinking of serious issues and values. In other words, I must attempt to refute Hu Shih's evaluation of the author and later editors as "mediocre Confucians, not talented men of literature or lofty thinkers" 平凡的陋儒, 不是有天才的文學家, 也不是高超的思想家.[416]

[413] For example, 113 (18:43).

[414] "Li Cho-wu" edition, chapter 117, p. 11b.

[415] For an essay defending Liu Shan's behavior, see a passage by the Ming writer Hsü I-sun 徐益孫, quoted in Andrew Lo ("Historiography," pp. 98ff.). The "Li Cho-wu" commentator (chapter 119, p. 12b) also suggests that Liu Shan's actions may have been a clever trick, like Liu Pei's planting vegetables and dropping his chopsticks in chapter 21. Liu Shan's final title in chapter 119 (安樂公) resonates with the name of his father's first official post in chapter 2 (安喜縣尉). The final image of the humbled monarch—"He tried to cry but had no tears" 欲哭無淚—remains ambiguous. See above, n. 146.

[416] Hu Shih, "Yen-i hsü," p. 473.

As might be expected, the prefaces to nearly every Ming and Ch'ing edition loudly proclaim the didactic intent of the work. For example, the 1522 preface declares, "this work is not merely intended to provide material for the mouth and ear, but rather aims to restore the patterns of order of highest antiquity" 此編非直口耳資,萬古綱常期復振.[417]

Unfortunately, when we attempt to pin down the substance of such noble purposes, we find a singular scarcity of explicit didactic pronouncements on the part of the narrator.[418] To be sure, the text is liberally spinkled with judgmental statements in the form of speeches, historical documents, poems, and especially the historian's evaluations (*shih-p'ing* 史評) quoted directly from a variety of sources—including Ch'en Shou's judgments from the *San-kuo chih*, as well as those of P'ei Sung-chih, Sun Sheng, Hsi Tso-ch'ih, and later historians. But as I have argued throughout, the unambiguous judgments expressed in such materials are often counterbalanced by the use of ironic reflection in the narrative itself, and even the various evaluative pieces cited at given points in the text are not always consistent with one another. How, then, can the preface of the 1522 edition claim that in the text "all questions of right and wrong are perfectly clear to the mind's eye" 是是非非,了然於心目之下?[419]

One useful solution to this problem, that suggested by Andrew Lo, is to insist on a distinction between explicit statement and implicit presentation of meaning; that is, between the stated judgment (*lun-tsan* 論贊) inherited as a formal element of the historiographical tradition, and the evocation of patterns of meaning in the fictional text, which may be implicitly obvious but are rarely if ever spelled out.[420] Perhaps the clearest example of this deemphasis of explicit didactic statement is seen in connection with the concept of retribution. The generalized notion of an inexorable chain of actions and consequences is very much present in the novel, and elicits considerable attention from the traditional commentators. For example, in a note in chapter 77 "Li Cho-wu" explains Kuan Yü's repayment of his debt to Yen Liang with the analogy of a loan for which "both principle and interest have simultaneously come due" 本利一時俱到. And Mao Tsung-kang discusses the concept of Buddhist causality (*yin-kuo* 因果) at length in chapters 109, 110, 113, and 119, among other places, and changes the title of chapter 109 to "Ts'ao Fang Is Deposed, as the House of

---

[417] See 1522 edition, Hsiu-jan tzu preface, p. 5a.

[418] One exception to this is the author's condemnation of Ts'ao Ts'ao following his renunciation of conventional morality in chapter 4 (see n. 378). Cf. the irony of the "peaceful death" (*shan-chung* 善終) of the last rulers of the Three Kingdoms, as reported in chapter 120 (19:50).

[419] Hsiu-jan tzu preface, p. 1b.

[420] See Andrew Lo, "Historiography," pp. 58–65.

Wei Reaches Its Final Retribution" 廢曹芳魏家果報.[421] But with the exception of occasional references in dialogue to this sort of Buddhist conceptions of karmic causality (especially in chapters 77, 78, and 79), the text
itself does little to impose this conceptual framework on the story—a fact
that sharply distinguishes the novel from the *P'ing-hua*, with its obtrusive
structural frame of retribution through reincarnation.

In the remainder of this chapter, I will consider some alternate patterns
of meaning that emerge in the novel on the basis of figural reflection within
the text—with or without explicit authorial commentary directing the
reader's attention to them. The first area of significance to be explored is
the overall conception of the historical process. Obviously, some degree of
serious interest is shown in the novel in the concept of the dynastic cycle;
this is built into the very choice of this interregnum as the focus of the
narrative, as well as in frequent references to the contrast between the
founding of the Han and its fall. It is also reaffirmed by Mao Tsung-kang
and other editors in their modifications of the opening section of the text, as
discussed in part I of this chapter.

Despite the simplistically symmetrical slogan about unity and disunity,
however, what we witness in the novel is far more complex than a single
turn of the wheel. True, the initial situation of the narrative conforms
precisely to popular dynastic-cycle theories, with all the conventional symptoms of the end of an era: effete rulers, natural disasters, bad omens,
mass uprisings; but this is qualified by a conflict of fundamental perspectives on the Three Kingdoms period: as constituting a brief dynastic
cycle in itself, or simply as a chaotic interregnum that sets in with the last
throes of the Han and does not really usher in a lasting new dynastic order
until the Sui-T'ang empire. Thus, within the context of dynastic-cycle
thinking, Liu Pei's objective is initially that of a (second) glorious restoration of the Han empire; but as the narrative progresses it becomes increasingly clear that what is at stake is not a restoration at all, but the initiation
of a new era.[422] At the same time, as soon as the scope of the novel is
narrowed down from the empire at large to the three separate "kingdoms,"
then we can trace in each case miniature cycles that run predictably through
the conventional course of two- or three-generation dynasties.[423]

[421] See "Li Cho-wu" edition, chapters 77 (p. 12b) and 10 (p. 9b); MTK, chapters 109
(18:15), 110 (18:21), 113 (18:39). The "Chung Hsing" commentator (chapter 109, *tp*)
emphasizes the poetic justice of Ssu-ma Shih's repetition of Ts'ao Ts'ao's misdeeds.

[422] MTK, chapter 85 (14:14), suggests that Liu Pei's posthumous title, "the Chao-lieh
Emperor" 昭烈帝, is intended to parallel the emblematic terms of the Han restoration under
Emperor Kuang-wu 光武帝. Cf. also the name of his reign period, Chang-wu 章武. See
above, n. 227.

[423] Cf. Ts'ui Chou-p'ing's extended discussion of the cycles of order and disorder in
chapter 37 (6:33).

Within the broader outlines of historical development embodied in the dynastic-cycle theories, we can perceive more serious attention paid to certain specific historical issues in the novel. The restricted question of the legitimate succession to the Han, for example, is not simply a matter of which of the two principal contenders has the rightful claim to the emperor's throne, but also involves certain more basic assumptions about the nature of authority in the traditional imperial system.[424] In spite of its basic sympathy for the Shu-Han side, the *Yen-i*'s treatment of Liu Pei and Ts'ao Ts'ao, as we have seen, is a far cry from the clear dichotomy between legitimacy and illegitimacy ascribed to their opposition in the popular tradition. On the one hand, Liu Pei's emphasis on blood lineage carries a certain amount of conviction, although his claims to moral superiority are severely undercut in the novel. Ts'ao Ts'ao, on the other hand, is portrayed in the text as the possessor of a more impressive ability to rule; and even his position of "governing the feudal lords with the emperor under his wing" (*hsieh t'ien-tzu erh ling chu-hou* 挾天子而令諸侯) commands a considerable degree of respect and acceptance.[425] But still, it cannot be denied that Ts'ao Ts'ao's image in the novel is conceived more in line with the notion of the "hegemon" (*pa* 霸) than that of a legitimate king.

In view of the sharp limitations placed on the claims of both Liu Pei and Ts'ao Ts'ao, it is interesting that the third major camp contending for the empire, that of Sun Ts'e and later Sun Ch'üan in Wu, appears to base its claim to power less on extravagant arguments of legitimacy than on unabashed power politics.[426] This gives added significance to the idea voiced repeatedly in the novel that "the empire does not belong to any

[424] Cf. Mao Tsung-kang's lengthy polemic on the *cheng-t'ung* issue, which heads his *tu-fa*, and his use of the dynastic cycle theory in chapter 120 (19:40). See also full discussions of the implications of Liu Pei's assumption of the throne in the *Tzu-chih t'ung-chien* (pp. 2185ff.), and the *T'ung-chien kang-mu* (14:57b–61a). In such examples of *pien-nien* historiography, the question of whose reign periods to follow is as much a practical as a theoretical problem. The *cheng-t'ung* issue comes up for explicit discussion in the novel in chapters 56 (9:33) and 60 (10:20).

[425] For a discussion of Ts'ao Ts'ao's claims to legitimacy in *cheng-t'ung* terms, see Liu Chih-chien, "Lo Kuan-chung fan-tui Ts'ao Ts'ao," pp. 322–26, esp. citations from essays by Ou-yang Hsiu and Su Shih. See also Tung Mei-k'an, *Shih-lun*, p. 26. The Ts'ao house, it should be remembered, is also eventually linked by marriage to the royal line through Ts'ao Ts'ao's daughter, Ts'ao Chieh 曹節, a fact that makes her bitter denunciation of Ts'ao P'i in chapter 80 (13:23) all the more ironic. The incident is based on the *Hou Han shu* (1:455). Cf. Mao Tsung-kang's insistence on correcting this detail in his own redaction (see *fan-li*, item 2). The phrase "with the emperor under his wing" derives from the *San-kuo chih* (4:912). See also *Tzu-chih t'ung-chien* (p. 2075). Cf. chapters 38 (6:40), 43 (7:35), 61 (10:33), 119 (19:39).

[426] See chapter 82 (13:37). Cf. the earlier attempts at usurpation by Yüan Shu and Yüan Shao.

single individual"—an argument we have seen to be invested with particular irony at a number of points.[427] This ironic subversion of the Confucian conception of the right to rule comes out in full force and clarity toward the end, when, in chapter 119, Ssu-ma Yen 司馬炎 justifies his seizure of power by pointing out to Ts'ao Huan 曹奐 that his forebear had also stolen the throne from the Han.[428]

The larger question of the right to rule also involves certain other aspects of political theory that are raised more or less explicitly in the novel. One of the most pointed of these is the perennial issue that has plagued every period of division in Chinese history: that of total commitment to the struggle for unification versus willingness to settle for peaceful rule over less than the entire empire (*p'ien-an* 偏安). Although as the narrative progresses lip service continues to be paid to the moral imperative of reunification (and no small amount of blood is shed in its name), by the latter part of the book it becomes clear that the ponderous balance of the tripod division will not be overturned in favor any of the three "kingdoms," and this inertia elicits serious discussion in chapter 97.[429] In fact, in a comment on a poem inserted in chapter 105, Mao Tsung-kang singles out the evil of *p'ien-an* defeatism as the chief obstacle to the realization of the Shu-Han dream.[430] The question of *p'ien-an* separatism is most often tied up with north-south regionalism in later periods of division in Chinese history, and with this in mind it is interesting to note that considerable attention is paid to this point in the novel, quite anachronistically, with the Wei forces consistently identified as "northerners" invading the south, even though the regional alignments of the period obviously do not conform to a simple north-south division.[431]

[427] See n. 231. The "Li Cho-wu" commentator seems to endorse the use of this line in chapter 54 (1b)—"What a grand argument!" 好大議論 —an attitude that would accord well with our image of the actual Li Chih. (I am not sure how sarcastically this comment is meant to be taken.) Significantly, this argument is used by both sides, and its real effect is to undercut the basic authority of the imperial institution. See also 1522 edition (12:75a). In chapter 119 (19:38), Ssu-ma Chao revises this to "The empire is the possession of my brother" 天下者乃吾兄之天下也.

[428] MTK, 19:39.

[429] Chapter 97 (16:18). The imperative of reunification is stated in chapters 91 (15:17), 101 (17:9), 110 (18:25), and 115 (19:11). Wang Fu-chih points out the limited options for reunification in *Tu T'ung-chien lun*, p. 313.

[430] MTK, chapter 105 (17:37).

[431] It has been suggested that north-south loyalties are partially responsible for the differences between Ch'en Shou and Hsi Tso-ch'ih, or later between Ssu-ma Kuang and Chu Hsi, on the question of the legitimate succession in the Three Kingdoms period. The same is true in discussions of Lo Kuan-chung's apparent preference for the Shu-Han side, in which case the Yuan rulers presumably become identified, as "northerners," with the Wei "usurpation." Cf. the "Li Yü" commentator's disparagement of southerners in comments in chapters 68 (3b) and 81 (9b).

In addition to such geopolitical considerations, a number of other crucial issues of a social or political nature are also reflected in the novel. I have already touched upon the subject of eunuch power, which brackets the text from the "ten constant attendants" in the opening chapters to the evil influence of Huang Hao toward the end; and at several points Mao Tsung-kang singles this problem out for discussion.[432] Similarly, the political involvement of "outer clans" (*wai-ch'i* 外戚), which play such a crucial role in Han history, also comes up for treatment in the novel.[433] One more type of rival power group of particular importance in the history of the Han is that associated with factionalism (*tang* 黨), and the *Yen-i* does not pass over this topic in silence. On the very first page of the text the chaos accompanying the breakdown of the imperial order is linked to the names Ch'en Fan 陳蕃 and Tou Wu 竇武, whose role in the formation of power groups is best known from the "Great Proscription" (*Tang-ku* 黨錮) chapter of the *Hou Han shu*. Perhaps it would not be going too far to suggest that a certain layer of the irony in the depiction of the sworn brotherhood immediately following derives from this early hint of the controversial issue of horizontal loyalties within the imperial system.[434] Finally, I have noted that the novel also takes up quite explicitly the historical issue of strict legalist administration versus more "compassionate" modes of governing. This question is brought into relief in the treatment of the administrative policies of Chu-ko Liang and Ts'ao Ts'ao, and is subjected to extensive discussion in chapters 65 and 96.[435]

What is most significant about the reference to such historical problems in the novel is the fact that practically all of the issues of Han geopolitics that spill over into the *San-kuo* period have a direct relevance to later periods as well. The traditional commentators are quick to point to historical analogies to events in other dynasties. For example, Mao Tsung-kang draws attention to the similarity between Liu Pei's journey through snow to engage the services of Chu-ko Liang and the legendary visit of Sung

[432] MTK, chapter 91 (15:12). The eunuch problem is referred to in chapters 1–3 (esp. 1:2), 101 (17:2), 106 (17:47), 113 (18:40), 115 (19:10f.), 120 (19:42). A note in the 1522 edition (23:28a) points out that the term *huang-men* 黃門 in this case indicates a particular palace position rather than eunuch status. See Andrew Lo, "Historiography," pp. 243f. The *Chi-shih pen-mo* marks this problem as a chapter heading on the fall of the Han (p. 607: 宦官亡漢). See also Wang Fu-chih, *Tu T'ung-chien lun*, p. 266.

[433] Mao Tsung-kang discusses this issue at length in chapter 2 (1:8). Cf. Ts'ao Ts'ao's link to the Han house through his daughter, as well as the elevation of Chang Fei's daughter as consort of Liu Shan. Wang Fu-chih discusses this point in his *Tu T'ung-chien lun*, pp. 264, 303.

[434] The *tang-ku* group is mentioned in chapters 1 (1:2), 2 (1:14), 6 (1:41). Mao discusses this issue in the *tu-fa*, item 9, p. 5. For a full treatment of the *tang-ku* episode in Han history, see Rafe de Crespigny, "Political Protest in Imperial China."

[435] Chapters 65 (11:16) and 96 (16:12).

T'ai-tsu 宋太祖 to Chao P'u 趙普, also through snow; and in another place he brings up the name of Yüeh Fei 岳飛 as an analogy between Three Kingdoms and Sung events. (In fact, the analogy of Yüeh Fei's fate is mentioned within the text itself, in the concluding poem in chapter 113.)[436]

Aside from occasional references to north-south regionalism, there do not seem to be any specific allusions here to the Chin or Yuan historical experience. However, analogies to the Ming political situation are many and far-reaching. From the treatment of the Yellow Turban uprising in the opening chapters (which "Li Cho-wu" immediately relates to the White Lotus rebellion of his own day—and the more cynical reader might even see here a comment on the origins of the Ming state itself), and the mention of tang-ku factionalism (which finds its parallel in the late Ming political societies), to the special emphasis given in the novel to eunuch influence and legalist administration, there are many points on which it is easy to read San-kuo as a commentary on the Ming political scene.[437] Even more crucial is the central issue of legitimate succession in the novel, which can be assumed to have had a particular resonance in the post–Yung-lo era, when the text as we know it was most likely taking shape. Certainly no sensitive reader of the Chia-ching and Wan-li eras can have failed to notice the implications of such questions for the bitter succession controversies of their own day.

But as I argued earlier, the author of the Yen-i seems to be less interested than other writers in the questions of imperial politics per se—taking them, I suppose, as the basic outlines of his material—and more concerned with exploring the motivations and significance of individual human action against the backdrop of the broad historical context. In reviewing the treatment of certain key individual figures in the novel, we have seen a consistent emphasis on the discrepancy between simplistic popular images and complex realities. One area in which this is most striking is in the contrast between the ideals of the noble hero stated and restated interminably, and the actual picture of "heroes" whose stature is sharply constricted by existential limitations. In some instances, these limitations are explored in the recurring theme of failure due to weakness, sickness, and old age; in others they are traceable to specific failings of human character.[438]

---

[436] MTK, chapters 37 (6:36), 23 (4:18), 77 (13:1), 113 (18:45). In the Chih-chuan (19:25a) this poem is attributed to Chou Li, which, if correct, would mean that Mao Tsung-kang overlooked this one. Cf. Mao's comparison of Liu Pei with Sung Kao-tsung in the tu-fa (item 1, pp. 1f.), the "Liu Yü" commentator's discussion of T'ang T'ai-tsung (chapter 90, p. 14a–b), etc.

[437] "Li Cho-wu" edition, chapter 1, p. 3b. Cf. the "Chung Hsing" commentator's reference to the Manchu threat (see above, n. 324).

[438] In addition to the examples of weakness and sickness seen above in the cases of Kuan Yü, Chang Fei, Liu Pei, Ts'ao Ts'ao, and Chu-ko Liang (see above, Part IV of this chapter),

To bring this discussion into the focus of the preceding chapters, I would like to point out that here, too, the treatment of human failings may be subsumed under the headings of what I have called the "four vices of excess" (*ssu t'an* 四貪): wine, sex, wealth, and wrath (*chiu, se, ts'ai, ch'i* 酒色財氣). The theme of drunkenness, for one, is by no means unexpected in a narrative about red-blooded heroes, but the novel makes a point of linking excessive drinking with military and political failure in a series of dramatic scenes: Chang Fei's loss of Hsü-chou, Lü Pu's capture, and many others.[439] This pointed connection is even more striking in the case of sexuality—most often going hand in hand with drunkenness—which might easily be omitted in a tale of martial deeds, but in fact occupies a very noticeable place in the *Yen-i*. In addition to the examples concerning Liu Pei, Ts'ao Ts'ao, and Lü Pu considered earlier, we also have the case of the self-destruction of Liu Ch'i, linked fairly explicitly to his life of dissipation.[440] Even Chang Fei, we are informed in an interlinear note in the 1522 edition, is not exempted by his rough-and-tumble heroics from infatuation for a maiden captured in battle.[441] Toward the end of the novel, the connection between wanton indulgence and the loss of the empire is revealed in the cases of both Liu Shan in Shu, and Sun Hao in Wu.[442]

As for wealth, there are no major examples in the novel of anyone selling out his cause for money, but if one defines "wealth" more loosely to indicate the vice of greed in general, then there is no shortage of examples of those who, like Lü Pu, "forget their ties of honor at first sight of personal gain" (*chien-li wang-i* 見利忘義). Going one step further, we may say that the problem of excessive gain is not unrelated to the crucial issue of greed with respect to territory, as expressed in the popular expression of special relevance to the plot of the novel: "gaining Lung while looking toward Shu" (*te-Lung wang-Shu*).[443] Finally, the fourth vice of excess, that of un-

---

I might also mention the depiction of Sun Ch'üan's vulnerability in chapter 29, as well as similar examples in chapters 110 (18:22f.), 119 (19:36, 38), and 120 (19:44). Cf. Ch'en Shou's remark in his evaluation of the failures of Kuan Yü and Chang Fei in the *San-kuo chih* (4:951): "For a man to end in failure due to his shortcomings is a constant principle of the workings of human destiny" 以短取敗, 數理之常也.

[439] Cf. the loosening of Liu Pei's tongue in chapters 34 and 62, the temptation of Chao Yün in chapter 52, Chang Fei's dangerous drunkenness in chapter 70 (12:2) and that of Hsü Ch'u in chapter 72 (12:19), Chang Fei's drunken self-destruction in chapter 81, and later the destructive effects of drink on Meng Huo (chapters 88, 14:35, and 89, 14:47), Kou An (chapter 100, 16:45), Liu Shan (chapter 115, 19:12), and Sun Hao (chapter 120, 19:42).

[440] MTK, chapter 52 (9:3). For the sexual vulnerability of Liu Pei, Ts'ao Ts'ao, Lü Pu, and Chou Yü, see discussions in Part IV of this chapter.

[441] See 1522 edition, 23:51a. We are told that the maiden, a sister of Hsia-hou Pa 夏侯霸, later gave birth to the daughter who was to become the consort of Liu Shan. See n. 194.

[442] Chapters 115 (19:12) and 120 (19:42). See the *P'ing-hua*, p. 475.

[443] See Mao Tsung-kang's discussion of this issue in chapter 67 (11:25).

bridled wrath, is developed in many scenes dealing with arrogant fury, most graphically in the recurrent theme of self-destructive revenge.

In the chapter on *Shui-hu chuan*, I argued that the long list of deficient or deflated heroes in that text is offset by the presentation of a number of figures depicted in a much more consistently positive light. In the case of *San-kuo*, I dwelt primarily on the ironic revision of the popular images of the major figures in the novel. Even when this revision goes in the direction of lightening negative images, as in the cases of Lü Pu, Ssu-ma I, or even Ts'ao Ts'ao, one cannot say that they are therefore to be interpreted as models of ideal qualities.

There do appear, however, several characters whose treatment focuses on heroic mettle with virtually no dimension of ironic undercutting. Among these I would include Lu Hsün, Lü Meng 呂蒙, and Yang Hu 羊祜 (to a lesser extent Chiang Wei), who have much in common with figures such as Yen Ch'ing 燕青 and Lu Chün-i 盧俊義 in *Shui-hu chuan*.[444] It is worth mentioning in this context that nearly every female character in the novel (e.g., Tiao-ch'an, Lady Kan and Lady Mi, Lady Sun, Hsü Shu's mother) is depicted in a positive light.[445] The traditional commentators pay special attention to the women in the novel. Mao Tsung-kang comments in a number of places that the women in the narrative are superior to the

[444] Both Lü Meng and Lu Hsün, like Chu-ko Liang, are conspicuously young when they emerge upon the scene. See also Tung Mei-k'an's discussion of Lu Su and Sun Ch'üan (*Shih-lun*, pp. 99, 104ff.). In his treatment of Yang Hu, Mao Tsung-kang not only inserts a different poem in chapter 120 (19:45), but he also removes Yang Hu's name from the title of the chapter. On the other hand, he accords particular praise to Yang Hu in several comments (chapter 120, 19:41, 43–44). See Andrew Lo, "Historiography," for additional discussion of Yang Hu.

[445] Additional examples of feminine fortitude include Chiang Hsü's 姜叙 mother in chapter 64 (11:8); Ts'ao Chih's mother, Pien-shih 卞氏, in chapter 79 (13:17); Ts'ao Ts'ao's daughter, the consort of the last Han emperor in chapter 80 (13:23); the female warrior Lady Chu-jung 祝融夫人, who comes to Meng Huo's aid in chapter 90 (15:3f.); Ts'ao Shuang's niece, who disfigures herself to avoid dishonor in chapter 107 (18:5)—cf. the appended poem in the Mao Tsung-kang edition: " ... no stalwart man could match the integrity of the maid in skirts and hairpins" 丈夫不及裙釵節; Wang Ching's 王經 mother in chapter 114 (19:4); and Ma Miao's 馬邈 wife in chapter 117 (19:23). In addition to the description of Lady Sun's martial spirit and boldness in chapters 54 and 55, we again witness her intrepid determination in chapter 61 (10:30), and learn obliquely of her dramatic end in chapter 84 (14:7). Mao Tsung-kang reports in his *fan-li* (item 2) that the incident of Lady Sun's suicide that he inserts in his edition derives from a text entitled "Biographies of Ruthless Maidens" 梟姬傳, possibly in the *Hou Han shu*. I have been unable to identify this text. One counterexample of *Shui-hu-* type female treachery occurs in chapter 57 (9:44), where Huang K'uei's 黃奎 concubine, Li Ch'un-hsiang 李春香, betrays his plot against Ts'ao Ts'ao. Cf. the "Li Cho-wu" commentator's remark in chapter 8 (p. 11a): "This is really a case of an extreme treachery that is camouflaged within extreme submissiveness" 眞個是至險伏於至順 ···. See also Chien-feng, "Chin-wei pu jang hsü-mei: lun San-kuo yen-i chung ti fu-nü ti i-shu hsing-hsiang."

men, and he interpolates the passage in which Chu-ko Liang's saintly wife
is described in chapter 117.[446]

But, of course, all of these examples are only minor figures in the novel.
The fact that a fully realized model of ideal heroism never materializes in
the text does not mean, however, that the predominantly ironic perspective
is not offset by a positive dimension of meaning. In fact, a number of key
passages seem specifically designed to provide illustrations of noble behavior. One such ideal may be seen in the perennial theme of the perception
of individual worth (*chih-jen*). This theme marks both the start of the novel
proper, in the narrative of the instantaneous bond of the spirit that brings
the three "brothers" together and leads immediately into the oath of the
Peach Garden, and the conclusion, with Ssu-ma Yen's uncommon appreciation of Yang Hu and the latter's recommendation of another worthy man:
Tu Yü 杜預.[447] As we have seen, the picture of the brotherhood in the
novel turns out to be something less than a perfect embodiment of fraternal
devotion (or it may perhaps be read as a deliberate parody of this ideal), but
in the course of the narrative we do witness certain more or less positive
versions of the sort of mutual appreciation at issue. Among these I would
mention the extreme case of Ts'ai Yung 蔡邕 given in chapter 9. Here, a
personal commitment and reciprocal obligations are cherished in disregard
of the utter baseness of the man to whom they are directed (and this in
spite of the fact that the bond between Ts'ai Yung and Tung Cho was
sealed under duress, thus presumably releasing Ts'ai from formal obliga-
tion).[448] The "Li Cho-wu" commentator, with his characteristic defiance of
social norms, lauds this ultimate statement: "The reason I approve of the
death of Ts'ai Yung for Tung Cho is that he did not betray the faith put
in him by one who appreciated him" 余取蔡之死董卓, 取其不負知己.[449]
Other early examples of the mutual appreciation *topos* include Liu Pei's
immediate bond of friendship with Kung-sun Tsan (which is later undercut),
and that with Chao Yün, which remains constant throughout his life. This
topos is singled out as a particular quality of the hero in many discussions
by the traditional commentators, especially the frequent remark "it takes a
hero to recognize a hero" 英雄識英雄.[450]

---

[446] See MTK, chapters 55 (9:23) and 118 (19:27), and *tu-fa*, item 16, p. 10. The interpolated passage about Chu-ko Liang's wife appears on pages 19:23–24.

[447] Cf. the following line in the poem on Yang Hu's death in the 1522 edition, 24:64b:
"He was a man who appreciated real men" 是箇男兒識丈夫.

[448] Cf. Tung Cho's threat, "If you do not come, I will wipe out your entire clan"
如不來, 當滅汝族, in chapter 4 (1:23). See Wang Fu-chih, *Tu T'ung-chien lun*, pp. 265, 270,
271.

[449] "Li Cho-wu" edition, chapter 9, p. 14a.

[450] For example, MTK, chapter 43 (7:31, 32); "Li Cho-wu" edition, chapters 18 (p. 8b) and
115 (2a). See Mao's discussions of the theme of recognition of human worth in the cases of

In my earlier discussions, I identified the capacity of mutual appreciation of worth as the conceptual core of a larger set of recurrent ideals—namely, seeking a master to serve (*ch'iu-chu*), gathering worthy followers (*te-shih*), and making proper use of human potential (*yung-jen*)—a set of relationships that one might say underlies nearly every significant episode in the novel.[451] One might argue that in the context of fictionalized history treating an age of shifting alliances and newly rising power bases, the preoccupation with the evaluation of human ability is simply an integral part of the realpolitik of the time. But for the purposes of this discussion, it may be more useful to recognize these linked themes as basic *topoi* of the Chinese literary tradition—elements that provide structural coherence and intertextual linkage with other narrative works, while also entailing a serious consideration of the ideals in question.[452]

In the pages of the novel, we also find attention paid to certain other more specifically Confucian ideals. For example, considerable interest is shown in moral conflicts associated with filiality (*hsiao* 孝) in a few key scenes, notably in Hsü Shu's abandonment of Liu Pei's cause for the protection of his mother, and later in Chiang Wei's commitment to his mother's welfare (the latter not without considerable irony).[453] But it is one other, more intangible Confucian concept—"honor" (*i*)—that constitutes the central focus of the novel, and at the same time links its interpretation to

---

Chang Fei and Lü Pu (chapter 15, 3 : 1), Chou Yü and Chu-ko Liang (chapter 44, 7 : 45), Kuan Yü and Huang Chung (chapter 53, 9 : 8–9), and Chu-ko Liang and Ssu-ma I. Cf. also the "discussion of heroes" in chapter 20, Ts'ao Ts'ao's failure to appreciate Ni Heng in chapter 23, Liu Pei's judgment of Ma Su in chapter 85, and Yang Hu's assessment of Tu Yü in chapter 120.

[451] Cf. the "Li Cho-wu" commentator's remark in chapter 15 (p. 15b): "The *San-kuo* heroes consistently make the gathering of heroic individuals their basic priority" 三國英雄一味以收拾英雄爲本.

[452] Cf. the *loci classici* for the *topos* of mutual recognition (*chih-chi*) found in the *Shih Chi* (e.g., Biographies of the Assassin Retainers, Biography of Ssu-ma Hsiang-ju, etc.). For a discussion of this *topos*, see my "Towards a Theory of Chinese Narrative," p. 346.

[453] See chapter 36 (6 : 26–27) for Hsü Shu's conflict between loyalty and filiality; chapter 43 (7 : 35) for Chu-ko Liang's use of these concepts to score points in the debates at the court of Wu; chapter 54 (9 : 20f.) for Sun Ch'üan's exceptional filiality and its dangerous consequences; chapter 58 (10 : 2–3) for Ma Ch'ao's dedication to his father's cause (see Mao's discussion, p. 11 : 1) and Chao Ang's wife's charge to him to choose loyalty to his father's ideals over his son's life in chapter 64 (11 : 7), 93 (15 : 28ff.) for Chiang Wei's filial protection of his mother (cf. Mao Tsung-kang's discussion on p. 15 : 27); and chapter 114 (19 : 4) for the common resolve of mother and son (Wang Ching). Chapter 79, in particular, revolves around the issue of parent-child relations, in its parallel narration of Ts'ao P'i's treatment of his brothers and mother, and Liu Pei's execution of his adopted son. Cf. Liu Pei's dubious invocation of filial obligations to justify his flight from Wu in chapter 55 (9 : 25).

that of *Shui-hu chuan* and *Chin P'ing Mei*.[454] The term *i*, of course, covers an extremely broad range of concepts, from justice and righteousness to generosity and personal loyalty, but in the context of *San-kuo* it seems to revolve around the honorable relations between individual men. There is no lack of depiction of honorable deeds in the novel, and very frequently these are specifically labeled as instances of *i*. As examples I could cite the refusal of the Wu general Yü Ch'üan 于詮 to surrender to Wang Chi 王基 in chapter 112, which is said to be dictated by a sense of honor that rules out that course of behavior (*i so pu wei* 義所不爲); the decision of Ts'ao Shuang's daughter to disfigure herself rather than endure disgrace, which is labeled "honor steadfast as the hills" (*i ju shan* 義如山);[455] and innumerable other instances. But we have seen that the author's intense scrutiny of questions of honor relating to the main figures of the novel more often than not goes in the other direction to yield a less than perfect picture, in quite a few cases involving flagrantly "dishonorable" (*pu-i* 不義) be-havior, or at least a disregard of the dictates of honor (*wang-i* 忘義).[456]

In the most significant cases, however, the chief problem on which the novel focuses is not that of holding honor too lightly, but rather the overemphasis of a perceived sense of honor often leading to unwanted consequences.[457] The swearing of a "bond of honor" 結義 is a case in point. Ideally, this conventional notion describes an act of individual men forging an undying commitment on the basis of a shared conception of honor, so that it also presupposes a high degree of mutual understanding 知己. But in *San-kuo*, as much as in *Shui-hu*, the net effect of the excessive emphasis on the brotherhood is to displace the perception of shared vision on which it is hypothetically based, leaving a sheer personal loyalty that can easily give rise to gang morality. Chang Hsüeh-ch'eng puts his finger on the anal-

---

[454] In his penetrating discussion of the ramifications of the concept of *i* in the novel, Andrew Lo ("Historiography," pp. 101–16) sees a double significance of the character *i* in the title of the work. The 1522 preface, by the way, also seems to imply a similar two-level understanding of the term (see esp. p. 1b). See also the 1494 preface (pp. 1a, 3a) for similar implications.

[455] Chapters 112 (18:35) and 107 (18:5). The term *i ju shan* is applied to Kuan Yü in chapter 50 (8:34).

[456] For example, Lü Pu's flagrant "disregard of honor at the first sight of profit" (*chien-li wang-i*) in chapter 3 (1:20), perhaps even more ironic in view of the fact that it is his adopted father (*i-fu* 義父, literally "honorary father") whom he betrays here; Liu Pei's protestations that he is being "forced into a dishonorable position" (*hsien wo pu-i*) in the takeovers at Ching-chou and I-chou; Lu Su's charge that Liu Pei's displacement of Liu Chang reveals "greed, in violation of the dictates of honor" 貪而背義 in chapter 66 (11:21), and many others.

[457] See my earlier discussions of this character flaw in Kuan Yü and Liu Pei. P'ang T'ung mocks Liu Pei in chapter 60 (10:23) for his "rigid adherence to conventional principle" (*chü-chih ch'ang-li* 拘執常理). Cf. "Li Cho-wu" commentary, chapter 52 (p. 9b).

ogy between the two works when he relates this "exclusive emphasis on brotherhood to the extent of forgetting the duty of servant to lord" 忘其君臣, 而直稱兄弟, in *San-kuo*, to the comparable situation among the *Shui-hu* figures.[458]

To be sure, Liu Pei's circle of followers is a far cry from the Liang-shan po bandits. But at a number of points in the novel a similarity seems to emerge. Thus, in certain details of description in the early stages of the narrative Liu Pei and his men operate very much in the manner of an autonomous band, and at several points later on the expansion and regrouping of the company is labeled a "gathering for a noble cause" (*chü-i* 聚義), especially in chapter 65, where the ceremony of inauguration following the takeover of I-chou shares with *Shui-hu* a significant undercurrent of irony.[459] The intensely personal bond that dwarfs all other considerations in the *chü-i* scene at Ku-ch'eng in chapter 28 is dramatically emphasized in the hostilities and needless slayings leading to the reunion. And the posthumous reunion of Liu Pei and Kuan Yü in a dream in chapter 77 (evidently based on the Yuan drama *Shuang-fu meng*) calls to mind the ambivalent events in chapter 120 of *Shui-hu chuan*.

We have seen similar implications in the overplaying of personal honor in the case of Kuan Yü's "honorable release" of Ts'ao Ts'ao, another set piece that also finds its parallels in *Shui-hu*. The most glaring example of this, however, is the transfer of the emotional intensity of the bond of brotherhood to the enterprise of collective revenge. The connection between the concept of *i* and the issue of revenge is made early in the novel, when banners of *i* are raised in Ts'ao Ts'ao's camp to avenge his father's murder.[460] In Liu Pei's case, the fact that the debt of blood to the personal bond (*i*) of the brotherhood irretrievably destroys the noble cause (*i*) of the

---

[458] Chang Hsüeh-ch'eng, *Ping-ch'en cha-chi* p. 16:63a–b (see n. 193), cited in K'ung Ling-ching, *Shih-liao*, p. 44. Even in the *Shih Chi* and *Han shu* treatments of the sort of noble brotherhood associated with the *yu-hsia* 遊俠 image, there remains a sense of the dangerous disequilibrium of horizontal loyalties (see contrasting views in *Shih Chi* and *Han shu* versions of the "Biographies of the Knights-Errant"). See Andrew Lo, "Historiography," pp. 194ff., for discussion.

[459] Cf. Chang Fei's association with *Shui-hu*-type outlaws in chapters 16 (3:15) and 28 (5:13). In the *P'ing-hua* (p. 370), we are told that the three brothers "took to the fields" (*lo-ts'ao* 落草) after Chang Fei's beating of the local official. Cf. the parallelism between the three sworn brothers and the three rebels in chapter 1, as pointed out by Mao Tsung-kang (*tu-fa*, item 9, p. 5). See the full-scale *chü-i* scenes in chapter 65 (11:15f.), and also chapters 19 (3:35) and 28 (5:13f., 17). Mao Tsung-kang brings out this point in discussions in chapters 28 (5:9f.) and 81 (13:28, 33). Cf. Andrew Lo, "Historiography," pp. 194ff.

[460] Chapter 10 (2:19). Wang Fu-chih discusses Ts'ao Ts'ao's actions in *Tu T'ung-chien lun*, p. 277. The issue of revenge as an expression of personal honor also surfaces in chapters 29 (5:20), 39 (7:3), 53 (9:14), 102 (17:10).

empire clearly exemplifies the sense that what we have here is excessive justice giving way to injustice.

These last examples raise a more acute problem explored in the novel: the moral dilemma brought about by conflicting claims on the hero's sense of honor. The stereotyped depiction of heroes torn between loyalty to the empire and personal obligations is of course a staple of the Chinese narrative tradition.[461] As his own story proceeds, the author frequently refines this by framing scenes in such a way as to emphasize the specific conflict between "greater" and "lesser" claims of honor (*ta-i, hsiao-i*), and the commentators discuss these issues at length in various places.[462] The implied moral imperative of choosing the greater over the lesser good in such cases is also expressed when the same problem is viewed as a conflict between "public" and "private" obligations (*ssu-i, kung-i* 私義, 公義). In most cases this is more or less the same thing, although the special significance of the terms *kung* and *ssu* in Neo-Confucian thought may lead us to look for deeper implications in the scenes constructed explicitly around this issue (especially Kuan Yü's "honorable release" of Ts'ao Ts'ao and Liu Pei's final revenge campaign).[463] In any event, the traditional commentators are particularly sensitive to this point as well, and often devote extended discussions to it.[464]

In addition to the framing of symbolic conflicts between the advantage of a special group and the good of the empire at large, the author of the novel appears to take great interest in pursuing specific clashes between duty to the empire and obligations to one's family. I mentioned earlier the recurrent pattern whereby Liu Pei's struggles to find a place in the sun necessarily entail the abandonment of his wives and child; a similar dilemma is faced by a number of other figures.[465] Mao Tsung-kang defends Liu Pei for favoring his commitment to his sworn brothers over his love for

[461] For a useful discussion of conflicting Confucian values in the *Yen-i*, see Riftin, *Istoricheskaya epopeia*, pp. 190ff., esp. 192–93. Mao Tsung-kang develops the issue of loyalty versus personal honor in a discussion in chapter 50 (8:29f.).

[462] See especially examples in chapters 81 (13:29f.) and 82 (13:36). Cf. Mao Tsung-kang's discussion of this issue in chapter 28 (5:9f.).

[463] See examples in chapters 50 (8:34); 76 (12:45), in which case Hsü Huang pointedly refuses to allow his debt for Kuan Yü's earlier honorable release to outweigh his immediate duty to capture him; 81 (13:29), in which case it is Chao Yün who tries to make Liu Pei see reason; 101 (17:8); 115 (19:8), etc.

[464] See discussions by Mao Tsung-kang in chapters 58 (10:1) and 81 (13:28), and the "Li Cho-wu" commentator in chapter 67 (p. 12a).

[465] For example, Kung-sun Tsan takes his family with him in death in chapter 21 (4:5), Ma Ch'ao's wife and three young sons are sacrificed in chapter 64 (11:7), and even Kuan Yü is forced to abandon his family at Ching-chou to the mercy of Lü Meng in chapter 75 (12:41). See above, nn. 277, 278.

his wife in a discussion in chapter 83, just as he mocks Liu Piao in chapter 34 for excessive deference to his wife.[466] By the same token, Liu Pei's demonstrative ejection of his infant son in chapter 42 is contrasted with Yüan Shao's excessive affection for his son, which contributes directly to his defeat and the delivery of the empire into the hands of Ts'ao Ts'ao by default. Such cases underscore the moral complexity of conflicting claims of honor, since here the "lesser" or "private" duty is by no means unequivocally to be sacrificed to a greater good. The idealized image of Liu Pei supposedly brings into harmony various honorable commitments at several levels: loyalty to his comrades 義, faithfulness to his family 孝, devotion to his sovereign 忠, and compassionate commitment to the welfare of the people 仁. But in working out the numerous ramifications of these commitments in the novel, the author constantly emphasizes the practical impossibility of harmonizing all of these conflicting claims.[467]

The fact that Liu Pei doggedly cleaves in his own mind to this impossible vision brings us to a final root cause of the failure to realize the demands of honor. This is the problem of self-image discussed earlier in the separate cases of Kuan Yü, Liu Pei, and Chu-ko Liang. We cannot really blame these heroes for their presumptuous illusion of modeling themselves on the ideal figures of their past (King Wen of Chou in the case of Ts'ao Ts'ao, Kuan Chung and Yüeh I in the case of Chu-ko Liang, and the Han founder in the case of Liu Pei). But a considerable portion of the impact of the novel is based precisely on the ironic discrepancy between lofty reputation and flawed reality, whether that is due to stubborn clinging to an overblown self-image or to cynical fostering of an image for the eyes of others.[468] In this context, failure to keep a realistic grip on one's own self-image may be interpreted as the ultimate conclusion of failure to "know" and appreciate other people.[469]

The persistent emphasis on failure and progressive decline in the novel—even as the dynastic cycle moves back into an arc of approaching reunification—raises more difficult questions regarding ultimate responsibility for this state of affairs. The views voiced in the novel and picked up by the commentators seem to stress two ways of understanding this problem. In the first view the historical process, as schematized in the

---

[466] MTK, chapters 83 (13:41) and 34 (6:9f.).

[467] Cf. Yang Yung's 楊顒 speech to Ssu-ma I in chapter 103 (17:24) outlining the view of "the proper way of ruling the family" 治家之道 as an explanation of Chu-ko Liang's slipping control over the Shu state.

[468] Particularly cutting is the fact that Liu Pei and Ts'ao Ts'ao both claim to be modeling themselves after King Wen.

[469] Cf. the expression "to know others and to know oneself" 知彼知己, cited frequently in the text and commentaries (e.g., chapter 107, 18:7, where it is attributed to Sun Tzu).

dynastic cycle, is conceived in terms of a strictly deterministic system. This may be understood as an abstract force, as in frequent references to the "mandate of Heaven" (*t'ien-ming* 天命), or it may be seen as the embodiment of the dynamics of the historical process itself, governed by the limitations of human nature.[470] This distinction seems to be behind an interesting passage in chapter 93, in which Chu-ko Liang and Wang Lang 王朗 engage in a formal debate involving the question of whether it is the "will of Heaven" (*t'ien-i* 天意) or the "natural course of events" (*tzu-jan chih li* 自然之理) that governs the development of human actions.[471] Mao Tsung-kang seems to take the conception of external volition the farthest, and borrows a term from Chuang Tzu to speak of a "creator of corporeal forms" (*tsao-wu-che* 造物者) whose whimsical manipulation of events and outcomes may often clash with the natural desires of the reader.[472]

Most often, however, the concept of Heaven is invoked not to contemplate the first cause of earthly events, but rather to remove from the shoulders of men the responsibility for their actions. Time after time, heroes faced with defeat lift their eyes skyward (*yang-t'ien* 仰天) and voice the plaint: "It is Heaven that is destroying me" (*t'ien sang wo* 天喪我).[473] Only rarely is heaven awarded the converse credit for aiding the heroes of the novel, a fact supported by the relative scarcity of instances of supernatural intervention in the narrative.[474]

The implication of such renunciation of responsibility for human actions, when sincere, reflects the second understanding of the meaning of heaven-ordained determinism: the evocation of a sense that the variously conceived cycles of change—dynastic or otherwise—express not meaningful determinacy, but rather cosmic futility.[475] It is important to point out in this

[470] See, for example, references to the "will of Heaven" in chapters 16 (3:13), 34 (6:15), 41 (7:19), 97 (16:21), 116 (19:18), 119 (19:36, 40), and 120 (19:45), etc. For discussions of the problem of *t'ien-ming* in the novel see Riftin, *Istoricheskaya epopeia*, pp. 188f.; and Wang T'o, "San-kuo yen-i chung ti ting-ming kuan-nien."

[471] Chapter 93 (15:32).

[472] MTK, *tu-fa*, item 8, p. 5. In the *Chuang Tzu* passage that Mao most likely has in mind (see the "*Ta-tsung-shih*" chapter 大宗師), the term *tsao-wu-che* is restricted to a primeval molder of physical forms, as opposed to a creator of the universe. Mao also uses the term in chapters 41 (7:16), 102 (17:9), and 109 (18:15).

[473] For example, chapters 31 (5:39, 40), 64 (11:3), 116 (19:19). See Mao's discussions in chapter 65 (10:42): "Although he claimed that it was the work of Heaven, it was obviously in the hands of man" 雖曰天也, 豈非人哉; and in chapter 100 (16:39).

[474] For example, Chu-ko Liang's cynical claim of Heaven's favor in chapter 89 (14:47). In chapter 103 (17:18), Mao asserts that Heaven is on the side of the Chin forces. Cf. the instances of supernatural intervention in the form of "theophanies" (*hsien-sheng* 顯聖): Kuan Yü in chapter 77, Chu-ko Liang in chapter 116.

[475] The concept of such cycles finds expression in Ts'ui Chou-p'ing's speech on order and disorder (*chih-luan*) in chapter 37 (6:33), as well as in the arguments for Ts'ao P'i's usurpa-

context that in spite of subject matter more firmly grounded in historical reality than its three sister texts of the Ming literati novel, *San-kuo* also shares with them considerable interest in the concept of emptiness (*k'ung* 空). From the opening pages of the novel right down to the completion of the epicycle 120 chapters later, we experience a relentless stream of dashed hopes, lost causes, and failed models of heroism. Mao Tsung-kang intensifies this sense by adding the opening *tz'u* with the line "Right and wrong, triumph and defeat, in a turn of the head all comes to naught" (*shih-fei ch'eng-pai chuan-t'ou k'ung* 是非成敗轉頭空) to balance the line in the final *ku-feng* poem: "And the laments of later generations are but plaints of emptiness" (*hou-jen p'ing-tiao k'ung lao-sao* 後人憑弔空勞騷)—an editorial touch for which he later congratulates himself, observing that the novel (in his edition, at least) now begins and ends on a note of emptiness.[476] In the body of the novel, the reader experiences a number of passages patently designed to bring out Buddhist notions of the vanity of existence, notably Kuan Yü's encounter with the monk P'u-ching in chapter 27, his enlightenment after death in battle in chapter 77, and the tapestry of conventional images of emptiness (the harvest moon, a snuffed candle) worked into the death scene of Chu-ko Liang in chapters 103 and 104.[477] Quite significantly, each of these instances involves intertextual linkage to the other sixteenth-century novels: the monk P'u-ching reappears in the final stages of *Chin P'ing Mei,* and the enlightenment of Kuan Yü and the extinction of Chu-ko Liang's light parallel scenes involving Wu Sung and Lu Ta in *Shui-hu chuan.*[478]

It must be acknowledged that the sense of world-weariness that hangs over the final phases of the narrative is as much an inherent feature of the monumental literary form as it is evidence of interest in Buddhist doctrine on the part of the author. But at any rate, *San-kuo* again parallels the other

---

tion in chapter 80 (13 : 23). Cf. Mao Tsung-kang's discussion of cycles of joy and sorrow in chapter 46 (8 : 15, 18); and the "Li Cho-wu" commentator's discussion of "the fixed principle of waxing and waning" 盈虧之定理 in chapter 118 (p. 12b). See also the poem in chapter 119 (19 : 40) with the line "the heavens revolve in cycles that no man can escape" 天運循環不可逃.

[476] MTK, chapter 1 (1 : 1) and 120 (19 : 50). Cf. Mao's statement in chapter 77 (13 : 1) that the line "What has become of Kuan Yü?" is equal to the teachings of the entire Diamond Sutra 雲長安在, 抵得一部金剛經妙義, as well as his discussion of the intimations of enlightenment in chapter 69 (11 : 40). See also the "Li Yü" commentator's reference to Ch'an Buddhist insights in chapter 48 (p. 1a).

[477] MTK, 5 : 5f., 13 : 4, 17 : 26. See also the instances of prophetic dreams and omens, for example, in chapters 58 (10 : 3), 61 (10 : 32), 72 (12 : 21), 77 (13 : 12), 105 (17 : 34), 113 (18 : 42), 114 (19 : 2), 116 (19 : 15), 119 (19 : 36).

[478] See above Chapters 2, Part VI, and 4, Part V.

three texts in its presentation, as a serious alternative, of the conventional desire for withdrawal from the web of worldly ambitions. The most celebrated example, no doubt, is the image of the "reclining dragon" in reclusion, an image carefully emphasized by the narrative retardation that fences Chu-ko Liang around with a chain of other recluse figures, such that the reader's own impatience to see him is embodied in Liu Pei's frustrating unfulfilled visits.[479] We have seen, however, that the presentation of this episode in the *Yen-i* is not without its own ironic touches. Curiously, in a passage in the 1522 edition cut by Mao Tsung-kang, it is Liu Pei—on his way to coax Chu-ko Liang out of reclusion into what turns out to be a tragic commitment to human affairs—who gives voice to the ideal of withdrawal and the sacrifice of those who are forced to take up the cause of history. This sentiment is seconded by Kuan Yü, much to Liu Pei's approval: "You truly understand my heart" 雲長知我心也.[480] Toward the end, Chiang Wei is given a role vaguely reminiscent of that of Yen Ch'ing in *Shui-hu chuan* as a spokesman for the path of detachment, suggesting to Chung Hui in chapter 119: "Why not just drift off in a boat and lose yourself, climb to the top of Mount O-mei and roam with the Red Pine Master?" 何不泛舟絕跡, 登峨嵋之巓而從赤松子遊乎?[481]

It is virtually impossible to pin down with certainty whether the author is referring to these conceptions in full earnest, or merely working with an inherited pose of his literary tradition in general, and narrative fiction in particular.[482] But whatever his intentions in this regard, the bulk of the novel is really about decisive, at times heroic, human actions and con-

---

[479] For an example of the popular image of Chu-ko Liang as a Taoist adept, see the *tsa-chü* play *Po-wang shao-t'un* (p. 3a), where he is described as a master of Taoist cultivation (*hsiu-shen yang-hsing* 修身養性).

[480] See 1522 edition, 8:22a. This passage also appears in the *Lien-hui t'ang* edition (p. 7:4a).

[481] MTK, 19:34. This drift is deepened with the withdrawal, albeit involuntary, of Yang Hu in the final chapter.

[482] Some of the terminology associated with the late Ming Confucian "philosophy of mind" does appear occasionally in the novel—for example, the expression "his mind was stirred" (*tung-hsin* 動心), used to describe Kuan Yü's fateful act in chapter 50 (8:34); the expression "his mind was out of joint" (*hsin pu-cheng* 心不正), used to describe Ts'ao Ts'ao's vulnerability to Tso Tz'u in a poem in chapter 69 (1522 edition, 14:50a); the expression "his mind was in disequilibrium" (*hsin-luan* 心亂), used to describe Ts'ao Ts'ao's lapse of control in the killing of Yang Hsiu in chapter 72 (12:20); and perhaps even in the emphasis on the "subdual of the mind" (*kung-hsin* 攻心) in the Meng Huo campaign (see Mao Tsung-kang's discussion in chapter 106, 17:42). Unfortunately, the early composition of *San-kuo yen-i* (even if we move it up to the early sixteenth century) may place it a bit too early to reflect the post-Wang Yang-ming intellectual trends that I have considered in discussions of the *Chin P'ing Mei* and *Hsi-yu chi*. See below, Chapter 6, for a reconsideration of this question.

sequences, in a context in which human striving does really matter and frequent protestations of the inability to do anything about impinging forces (*pu te i*) ring out as no more than an excuses for personal failings.[483] Despite his tendency to fall back on despairing recriminations of heaven, Liu Pei admits this principle in chapter 37, when he exclaims, "How could I presume to leave it up to fate or predestination?" 何敢委之數與命?[484] And for that matter, even Chu-ko Liang's most famous statement of resignation in chapter 103—謀事在人, 成事在天—in fact cuts two ways: the fulfillment of ambition (*ch'eng-shih*) may be beyond human control, but man's striving (*mou-shih*) remains very much in the hands of the *ying-hsiung*.[485]

Thus, for all the protestations of emptiness that we get, it is only on the basis of the narration of significant human striving in the novel that we can account for the sense of loss approaching the tragic that materializes by the end.[486] This sense accruing to both Liu Pei's doomed cause and Chu-ko Liang's wasted commitment is expressed with greatest grandeur in the poems of Tu Fu inserted after the deaths of these two figures, as underscored in Mao Tsung-kang's added critical readings.[487] Such familiar lines as "a legacy of regret for the failure to swallow up Wu" 遺恨失吞吳, "From this day on, never again will be heard the sound of his noble song" 於今無復雅歌聲, and "But in the end, the Han line has passed on, never to

---

[483] For example, chapters 27 (5:4), 65 (11:15), 66 (11:19), 88 (14:36), 90 (15:9), 95 (16:8). Mao Tsung-kang's comment on the example in chapter 65 proclaims Liu Pei's sincerity, but admits that the expression is most often used as an excuse, citing several historical examples of internecine strife (including T'ang T'ai-tsung's murder of his brothers in order to secure the throne) to make his point.

[484] MTK, 6:33.

[485] MTK, 17:23. See translation above. "Li Cho-wu" (103, p. 146), predictably, bristles at this line: "The line 'the fulfillment of human ambition ... ' is nothing more than an expression of Chu-ko Liang's humiliation and fecklessness. How could anyone say this is a true maxim?" 若夫「謀事在人, 成事在天」八個字, 乃孔明羞慚無聊之語, 豈眞格言哉? This is somewhat in contradiction to his earlier comment in chapter 94 (p. 12a): "If Kuan Yü's spirit could save his son from the dire danger of the iron carts, but could not pacify Wu and wipe out Wei on behalf of the Second Emperor, this proves that the will of Heaven is fixed, so that even an immortal spirit of loyalty and honor such as Kuan Yü could do nothing about it" 雲長之靈能救其子鐵車之危, 不能爲後主平吳削魏, 乃知天命有定, 即忠義神聖如雲長, 亦不可爲也.

[486] This, at any rate, is the attitude of the historians. For example, the *Fa-ming* commentary on the *T'ung-chien kang-mu* (15:35b) comments on the downfall of Chu-ko Liang: "How can men of substance be evaluated in simple terms of success or failure?" 豈可以成敗論人物哉? Cf. Mao Tsung-kang's comment on the hopeless efforts to stop Ssu-ma Chao in chapter 111 (18:32): "The desire itself is commendable; one need not evaluate it in terms of success or failure" 志自可取, 不必以成敗論之. See also Wang Fu-chih's discussion of the causes of the fall of the empire in *Tu T'ung-chien lun* (pp. 302, 310).

[487] Chapters 84 (14:8), 85 (14:13–14), 104 (17:30, and additional poem in 1522, 21:83a–b). See n. 142.

return" 運移漢祚終難復,[488] may be interpreted as expressions of cosmic futility. But even without reference to Tu Fu's other poems, we can say that the net effect of these lines in the novel goes more in the direction of a sense of emptiness that is not accepted as a calm fact of existence, that is definitely a cause for deep regret. It is this sort of combination of grandeur and futility, as expressed in the elusive concept of *k'ang-k'ai* 慷慨 (for which Ts'ao Ts'ao's "Brief Ballad" may be the *locus classicus*), that gives the novel its sense of epic greatness.

[488] This is especially true in the subject of the Eight Trigrams maze in chapter 84, where Tu Fu's bemoaning of tragic failure, though far removed from the popular view of this as an example of Chu-ko Liang's invincibility, is fully consonant with the import of the scene in the context of the novel. For all his cynicism and scorn for the failings of the *San-kuo* heroes, the "Li Cho-wu" commentator (chapter 120, p. 16a) also signs off with a sigh of pity for the outcome of the interminable struggles of the narrative.

CHAPTER 6

Neo-Confucian
Interpretations of
the Four Masterworks

In the four principal chapters that comprise the substance of this book, I have taken up one by one in considerable detail—perhaps excessively so—each of the great works of Chinese fiction known collectively as *ssu ta ch'i-shu*, the "four masterworks of the Ming novel" as I have rendered it here. I have presented rather extensive analyses of a range of structural and rhetorical variables that I believe show a degree of common form sufficient to support the notion of a well-defined genre of prose fiction taking shape precisely during the sixteenth century. I then went on in each chapter to suggest, on the basis of this generic framework, a reinterpretation of the range of meanings in the respective works as reflections of the vital cultural and intellectual movements that characterize this particular period in Chinese history. The exercises in textual analysis of each work have, I hope, already confirmed the first half of my argument, regarding the formal side of the generic continuity linking *San-kuo yen-i*, *Shui-hu chuan*, *Hsi-yu chi*, and *Chin P'ing Mei*. At this point, it may be helpful to pull together, one final time, some of the ideas that have emerged in the interpretive discussions in this book, in order to reaffirm the common ground of meaning running through these very disparate texts.

Let us first review the formal features of the genre outlined here, which are shared to one extent or another by all four of our masterworks. Under the heading of narrative structure, I have considered such points of common form as their paradigmatic length of one hundred chapters, narrative rhythms based on division into ten-chapter units, further subdivision into building blocks of three- or four-chapter episodes, contrived symmetries between the first and second halves of the texts, special exploitation of opening and closing sections, as well as certain other schemes of spatial and temporal ordering, notably the plotting of events on seasonal or geographical grids. In my analyses, I have tried to show that three of the four—*Chin P'ing Mei, Hsi-yu chi,* and the *fan-pen* recension of *Shui-hu chuan*—show a remarkable degree of conformity to this structural model, in spite of their sharp divergence in subject matter and narrative focus. Even *San-kuo,* with its 120-chapter length and annalistic structural framework, shares enough of these features to fit the basic generic mold.

In a second area of analysis, that of narrative rhetoric, I have examined a range of devices relating to the modulation of linguistic medium and narrative voice. Here, I considered such features as the adaptation of conventionalized rhetorical techniques associated with the oral-storytelling tradition, and the use of special linguistic effects, ranging from puns and word games to innovative uses of incidental verse, among other things. Once again, we observed that *San-kuo* departs noticeably from the formal model of the other three, due to its more consistent employment of classical diction, and its unique mimesis of the voice of the official historian. But it, too, falls back squarely within the generic outlines drawn here in its exemplification of what I have isolated as the central rhetorical feature of the literati novel: the infusion of irony into its reframing of traditional narrative material.

My attempt to posit ironic revision of prior narrative sources as the core concept in the formation of this new genre of Chinese prose fiction has a number of possible implications. Not only is this meant to reaffirm the significance of the late Ming novel as a product of literati culture, as opposed to the common view of such works as direct expressions of the popular imagination; but it also provides a substantive basis for bringing these works into comparative alignment with the slightly later European novel form, to which the Chinese genre is most often—and quite fruitfully—likened. More to the point, the reading of each of these works in terms of ironic disjunctions of surface and underlying meaning has been the guiding principle of my interpretation of their literary design.

The precise nature and functioning of this ironic element, however, differ in each of the four masterworks. In *Chin P'ing Mei,* it primarily takes the form of satiric inversion, the glaring juxtaposition of abject moral bankruptcy with pious statements, even lyric expressions, of conventional ideals of behavior. This is brought out with particular force by means of the unique device of setting up a counterpoint between the base corruption acted out on center stage, and the running choric commentary, the "background noise," made up of sentimental popular songs, disingenuous quotations, and allusions to canonical wisdom. In *Shui-hu chuan*, the ironic dimension comes into play in the deflation of heroic myths and stereotypes from the popular tradition. This is accomplished for the most part through the cross-reflection of positive and negative examples of heroic mettle, which in the end succeeds in invalidating, or at least relativizing, the code of honor vaunted by the Liang-shan warriors. The ironic effect in *San-kuo* materializes in its manifest disjunction between idealized conceptions of dynastic order and the actual political and military realities of a world in chaos. Its exploration of the gap between ambition and capacity is governed by a consistent tone of implied judgment, on the order of the pointed rhetoric of the official historian (*ch'ü-pi* 曲筆). In *Hsi-yu chi*, the ironic devaluation of surface imagery and explicit didactic pronouncements is put in the service of an allegorical projection that begins with vague doubts about the high seriousness of the quest mission, and ends with a view of salvation radically different from its own professed soteriology.

Although the type of ironic discourse employed is different in each case, still all four of the works share a rhetorical ground based on the undercutting of surface texture, with the implied redirection of the reader's vision toward some unarticulated exploration of positive values. We have seen that hints of ironic erosion begin to surface to a more localized extent in lighter or humorous instances; but ultimately the mocking tone turns more serious in each case as it begins to adumbrate certain substantive patterns of meaning. Now is the time to attempt to further articulate where that common ground of meaning may lie.

Before doing so, however, I will make a slight digression to recall the degree to which our four works are linked by a web of intertextual cross-reference. In the four principal chapters of this study, we have observed at various points apparent threads of allusion binding the separate works to one another. In many cases this was simply a matter of stock narrative material taken over from the oral tradition. For example, we have seen a number of stereotyped scenes or other conventional *topoi* shared by these different texts. In certain cases these were conveniently labeled as such with set terms, as in the various scenes of "wreaking great havoc" (*ta-nao*), "honorable release of a captive enemy" (*i-shih*), formal contests of prowess, or encounters of characters with their own doubles.[1] In such examples as the parody of the Peach Garden vows of brotherhood restaged early in *Chin P'ing Mei*, or the boudoir conquest of unwilling "brides" in both *Shui-hu chuan* and *Hsi-yu chi*, however, we can probably discern some form of direct borrowing. On the level of individual characters, we have also observed

---

[1] Other examples of shared narrative *topoi* include such scenes as stylized individual combat, triumphal gathering of heroes, meetings with prophetic monks, writing of seditious poems, striking out names from lists of the damned, and many more.

the frequent appearance of stock figures: for example, innkeepers, boatmen, panderers, and the like.[2] Beyond this, there is an obvious measure of inter-textual reference at work in the framing of certain characters—Li K'uei in *Shui-hu* and Chang Fei in *San-kuo*, for example, who are clearly of a piece. In this example, the perceived commonality may simply reflect the basic stereotypes of this sort of dark, violent type within the popular imagi-nation. But when we notice the manner in which certain aspects of these shared attributes inform the characterization of P'an Chin-lien, and perhaps Sun Wu-k'ung as well, we can recognize something more on the order of a self-conscious allusion. By the same token, Sung Chiang and Liu Pei share a certain antiheroic quality that is not altogether unconnected to the hollow-ness of Hsüan-tsang and Hsi-men Ch'ing. Of course, a full elucidation of this cross-fertilization would hinge to a large extent on establishing the chronological order of composition of the texts in question.[3] For my purposes, however, the simple fact of intertextual borrowing is more im-portant than the precise direction of transfer. This is because, first, the sense of a common pool of narrative material and presentation helps to shore up the argument that these four different works constitute a single literary genre. Moreover, we also see here evidence of a very pointed reworking of material, to the point of parody in some cases, which interposes yet another layer of ironic detachment from the simple retelling of the source stories, and shifts our attention toward a more general reflection on the underlying issues.

This brings us back to my promise to elaborate the ground of potential meaning in these texts, as obliquely projected through the prism of ironic expression. In the separate discussions of the four novels in this book, I have suggested readings that lean rather heavily on a set of ideas I tried to label, in some sense, "Confucian" in nature. My frequent use of this term may well have left many readers less than convinced. After all, looking at our first two books, *Chin P'ing Mei* loudly proclaims its moral message in unambiguous Buddhist terms, while *Hsi-yu chi* is glossed by virtually all of its traditional commentators (with one lone and slightly demented exception) in terms of Buddhist or Taoist verities. *Shui-hu chuan*, on the other hand, probably gives most readers the impression that it has no systematic thought content at all. Only *San-kuo* clearly deals with issues of statecraft of the sort debated by Confucian thinkers, but any attempt to reduce the novel to this one dimension of Confucian concerns would be simplistic to the point of meaninglessness. Why, then, my repeated emphasis on Con-

---

[2] Cf. Hanan's discussion of the appearance of identically named stock figures in several parts of *Shui-hu chuan* and in *P'ing-yao chuan* (see Chapter 4, b.n. I).

[3] The deliberate borrowing involving *San-kuo* and *Shui-hu* is discussed by Chang Hsüeh-ch'eng in *Ping-ch'en cha-chi* (see Chapter 5, n. 458).

fucianism in my attempt to wring some meaning out of these apparently unwilling texts?

The principal justification for this interpretive approach goes back to my argument about the specific cultural milieu that spawned this sophisticated new literary genre built upon ironic revision of narrative materials from the popular tradition. I have insisted that the four masterworks of this genre, for all their links to earlier narrative sources, should be considered primarily as products of late Ming literati culture. In attempting to characterize the intellectual horizons of the educated elite of this period in China in my introductory chapter, I dwelled primarily on the pervasive undercurrent of syncretic thinking—a degree of syncretism that was related to, but far outstripped, that of the popular three-teachings cults of the time, with their hybrid mythologies and ritual amalgams. On the more sophisticated level, we can observe a deeper melding of ideas, one in which more often than not it is basic Four Books Confucianism—the mental baggage of all potential candidates for status in the Ming literary elite—that formed the warp of thinking into which strands of Buddhist and Taoist teachings could then be liberally interwoven. In this context, the overworked term "Neo-Confucianism" takes in all but the most sectarian of heterodox positions (so that perhaps all it means in this context is something as broad as "Chinese thought" of the later imperial period). In any event, the point here is not to deny or diminish the serious dimension of Buddhist and Taoist thought in these books, only to restore the centrality of bedrock Confucian concepts within the constellation of ideas at the heart of late Ming literati culture, despite the fashion at the time of professing distaste for stodgy Confucian moralizing and the free use of un-Confucian terms of discourse appropriated from the other "schools."

If I wish to speak of a Confucian range of meaning in these books, however, I must first distinguish between several possible frames of reference implied by that loaded term. Obviously, these four narratives are not literally about the Confucian life-style: the world of the examination system, official service, classical scholarship, and the gentlemanly arts, such as came to dominate a large segment of the fiction of the Ch'ing period. The closest of the four to such a perspective is, again, *San-kuo*, which is in a real sense a book about the art of rulership, or more accurately, the failure of dynastic rule during one period of chaos. For that matter, *Shui-hu* is obviously not unrelated to such matters; and *Chin P'ing Mei*, as we have seen, also brushes up against affairs of state by virtue of the pointed correlation it makes between the breakdown of the world of one individual and the crumbling macrocosm of the imperial world order. But we cannot really say that rulership is the central focus of this author's vision.

I have also observed the degree to which all four of our narratives intersect with actual historical fact. This applies not only to *San-kuo* and *Shui-hu*, with their extensive real and imagined encounters with historical figures and concrete political issues, but also to *Chin P'ing Mei*, with its contrived attempt to bring the fall of the northern Sung state into its tale about a purely fictional wastrel in a provincial backwater. Even in *Hsi-yu chi*, we were not allowed to forget some of the questions of perennial historical judgment regarding the reign of the T'ang founder. But all this historical consciousness only puts us back into the limited sphere of an overly narrow definition of Confucian concerns.

At a slightly more abstract level, we come closer to an explicit grappling with Confucian issues in the treatment of specific ethical values in the four works. It did not take much argumentation to show that both *San-kuo* and *Shui-hu* revolve around the redefinition of concepts of loyalty (*chung* 忠) and honor (*i* 義) in a world of conflicting obligations. This is immediately clear in the conspicuous highlighting of these two terms in the full title of the *fan-pen Shui-hu chuan*, and in chapter headings and poems in both works. *Chin P'ing Mei* also provided us with numerous instances of pointed caricatures of cardinal human relations, going hand in hand with protestations of honorable intentions using the same vocabulary of Confucian ideals. Even more crucial was the significant place accorded to the quintessential Confucian concept of filiality (*hsiao* 孝) within the spectrum of values violated in these books. In *San-kuo* and *Shui-hu*, this came out in a number of somewhat stereotyped conflicts between private and public duty, specifically between family and state loyalties. In *Chin P'ing Mei*, the negative transformation of proper filial subordination of the self—into a worship of self-gratification that denies paternity and posterity—occupies very much of the central core of the book, such that the themes of incest, childlessness, and gross unfiliality are not just symptomatic of the disorder in the house of Hsi-men Ch'ing, but come to symbolize the root of the evil that ultimately brings about the loss of both the individual and the national patrimony. Once again, *Hsi-yu chi* surprises us by reserving considerable attention for the theme of filial piety, this in a narrative otherwise restricted to the adventures of wandering monks extracted from family obligations.

But here, too, we are given in the novels very little, if anything, in the way of speculation on more academic philosophical questions. A few such points do, I believe, come close to the surface in certain scenes. For example, such archetypal situations as a descent into a well in *Shui-hu*, treading on thin ice in *Hsi-yu*, lending a hand to a sister-in-law in *Chin P'ing Mei*, and others, all suggest scriptural sources in the Confucian classics. Along these lines, one might say that the treatment of dark impulses, the seemingly congenital predisposition to violence on the part of such characters as Li K'uei and P'an Chin-lien, and to a lesser extent Chang Fei, is never far removed from the classical Confucian debate over the possibility of inherent evil in human nature 性本善, 性本惡. But admittedly, this implication is never developed to the point of explicit philosophical discussion. Also conspicuous for its absence is any specific treatment of the sort of stereotyped conflicts between individual desire (*ch'ing* 情) and moral principle (*li* 理) such as find expression in late Ming drama and short fiction.[4] Even less can we seek here any direct reflection of more technical points of Ch'eng-Chu orthodoxy or post—Wang Yang-ming "philosophy of mind," such as were debated in the sixteenth-century academies.

The dimension in which specifically Confucian issues do begin to occupy our attention emerges, I believe, in conjunction with the broad reflection in these books of the notion of self-cultivation: the central framework of all Neo-Confucian thinking extracted by the Sung masters from the Four Books and developed into the heart of the system. Once again, for want of abstract philosophizing in these novels, one can rarely look for any kind of programmatic, one-to-one correspondences between narrative configurations and discrete points of doctrine. Nevertheless, certain formulations from the Four Books have helped us get a grip on levels of meaning not far below the surface of the texts.

One of the neatest of these correspondences that I have brought to bear on my interpretations is the opening section of the *Ta-hsüeh* text, especially the passage on "failure to regulate one's household" (*pu ch'i ch'i chia* 不齊其家), which provided an easy gloss on the particular inversion of self-cultivation in the world of Hsi-men Ch'ing. Without wishing to appear to reduce complex sets of associations to a single source, I would like to return one more time to this passage, to show that all four of our masterworks reflect their own respective aspects of this canonical vision of self-cultivation. That is, in terms of the famous chain syllogism in the opening section of that text, if we can say *Chin P'ing Mei* is primarily concerned with life in the narrow sphere of the household, with failure at that level framed in such a way as to bring out corresponding failures at other levels, in the case of *Shui-hu chuan* we witness a comparable collapse of authority. But now it is on the level of law and order in the political and military arena, so that the steady escalation from small-scale disruptions to something approaching empirewide upheavals can be chalked up to a failure to maintain order in the state (*pu chih ch'i kuo* 不治其國). In *San-kuo*, of course, the clash of forces presented has already risen to the highest levels of imperial rule,

---

[4] The most obvious example of this is in T'ang Hsien-tsu's *Mu-tan t'ing* and other plays. See discussion by C. T. Hsia in "Time and the Human Condition in the plays of T'ang Hsien-tsu" (see above Chapter 1, n. 151), and his "To What Fyn Live I Thus," in *The Classic Chinese Novel*, pp. 299–321. Cf. Chang Chu-p'o's introduction of these terms in his *tu-fa* essay on *Chin P'ing Mei*, item 43 (see above, Chapter 2, nn. 289, 295).

and much of the didacticism voiced in the text is couched in the rhetoric of universal order through dynastic authority. In this light, the central issue is raised to a higher power, one that can be fairly neatly conceived as the inability to bring harmony to the entire world (*pu p'ing t'ien-hsia* 不平天下). But this by no means excludes instances of corresponding failures in the governing of separate states, and in the private spheres of individual actors, which are also relevant to this novel's exploration of the dynamics of historical change.

For my interpretation of the allegorical level in *Hsi-yu chi*, I had to look in the opposite direction, from its initial concern with national salvation and family order in the opening sections, in the direction of the internal dimension of the mind—what according to the *Ta-hsüeh* formula comes under the phases of "rectification of the mind" (*cheng ch'i hsin* 正其心) and "stabilization of the will" (*ch'eng ch'i i* 誠其意). We have seen that the principal impediments on the path of enlightenment as allegorized in this work lurk more in internal than external perils. This *psychomachia* is often presented in such seemingly un-Confucian terms as "forging the internal cinnabar" (*lien-tan* 鍊丹), the "stilling of the monkey of the mind" (*ting hsin-yüan* 定心猿), and "forming the perfect fruit" (*ch'eng cheng-kuo* 成正果), but it also draws upon a very pointed invocation of the Mencian idea of the "exile and recovery of the mind" (*ch'iu ch'i fang-hsin* 求其放心), and thereby restates the various figures of heterodox cultivation in terms of the range of ideas taken in by "philosophy of mind" (*hsin-hsüeh*) within the syncretic breadth of late Ming Neo-Confucianism.

This intellectual concern with the exploration of the inner workings of the mind is obviously of most direct relevance to *Hsi-yu chi*, but it is not entirely absent from the other three novels. For example, in *Chin P'ing Mei* we observed the manner in which the externally destructive forces unleashed in the narrative whirl around an inner core of existential emptiness. Specifically, we saw that the final phases of Hsi-men Ching's self-destruction were in a very real sense a function of his vain pursuit of images of his own hollow selfhood. Similar terms were also brought into play in *San-kuo*, where we considered instances of the disordering and destabilization of the mind (*tung-hsin*, 動心, *hsin-luan* 心亂) as primary motivating factors in many of the key scenes in the narrative. In *Shui-hu* we would have to stretch the point a bit to speak of a focus on the inner dimension, although here, too, instances of weakness of will, delusions of grandeur, and obsessive self-image proved to be just as significant as tests of physical capacity in defining the limitations of heroism.

The common denominator in all four works is an emphasis on the breakdown of order or failure of the will propelling the respective narratives forward, whether that is conceived at the level of the external social and political context, or the internal equilibrium of the self. This tendency to disequilibrium or loss of control in so many key scenes may in one sense be explained as nothing more than a stock feature of the Chinese narrative tradition (or any narrative tradition, for that matter). But within the context of Ming Confucian thought, it may be diagnosed as a reflection of a more abstract issue of disorder (*luan*) threatening the hypothetical foundations of the *t'ien-hsia* order.

Typically, this problem of disorder is reduced in the fictional context of our works to instances of excessive gratification of the ego, which may explain why the simple formula "four vices of excess" (*ssu t'an* 四貪) has accounted in my discussions for such a broad range of narrative eventualities. In *Chin P'ing Mei*, of course, the fourfold scourge of excessive indulgence in wine, women, wealth, and wrath is worked out in all its fulsome detail. The first and last of these "vices" were also quite explicitly treated in *Shui-hu*, although some readers may have been a bit surprised by the degree to which dark impulses were found to be lurking within the sexual hostility unleashed in repeated scenes involving confrontations between masculine pride and feminine provocation. In *San-kuo* as well, we reviewed a number of scenes in which sexual self-indulgence or other forms of undue gratification were held vaguely responsible for some of the momentous failures of Ts'ao Ts'ao, Liu Pei, and others. Even in *Hsi-yu chi*, we found ourselves paying considerable attention to the fact that, alongside of the various forms of excessive self-consciousness (*to-hsin* 多心) inhibiting the progress of the as yet unenlightened master—most noticeably manifested in his fear, discomfort, and wrath—a surprisingly large number of scenes highlighted sexual temptation as the most formidable obstacle on the allegorical journey to the Holy Mountain. Here, however, the issue was not so much sexuality per se as something more fundamental: questions of destructive self-indulgence and gratification of the will which apply just as well to the unbridled heroics and the drive for power in the two more action-oriented narratives. Thus, we arrive at a point in the ironic reflection on self-cultivation where this concept is turned upon itself, such that the ideal nurturing of balanced selfhood gives way to a cultivation of one's own garden—whether that takes the form of gratification or, alternatively, delusions of grandeur or premature spiritual attainment.

Up to this point, I have been dwelling exclusively on the dark side of the ironic projection of meaning in the four Ming masterworks. I have emphasized the subversion of conventional ideals that dominates their pages, and interpreted this phenomenon as a negative transformation of the Neo-Confucian concept of self-cultivation, as worked out in the fictional medium. But there is still the other edge of the cutting blade of irony to be accounted for. That is the potential ground of positive meaning that ironic discourse implies, but which it nevertheless, by the very nature of the beast, stubbornly refuses to articulate. If this theoretical understanding of narrative irony has any validity as a feature of the novel form in general, and if, moreover, it can be transferred to these works of Chinese fiction, then we must still consider in what directions the ironies elaborated here may point.

Paradoxically, the consideration of this question is inhibited by the very fact that all four of our texts, to one degree or another, ostensibly provide something of a grand design, or at least a set of didactic standards of evaluation that would seem to condition any possible interpretations. These broader patterns of significance are typically presented in terms of Buddhist conceptions of karmic retribution. In *Shui-hu chuan*, this dimension is limited to not much more than the implied message in the mythical opening section relating the release of the evil star-spirits, carrying the suggestion that the 108 heroes are to become a scourge of mankind, or at least of the corrupt imperial court, as some sort of unspecified agents of divine justice. In *San-kuo*, the retributive framework comes to the surface in the poetic justice meted out to Ts'ao Ts'ao and others through the intervention of supernatural forces and mystical characters, as punishment for their various sins of excess. Even Chu-ko Liang can be regarded in the same light, as a victim struck down by jealous gods for his own hubristic excesses. The didactic frame in *Chin P'ing Mei*, of course, is elaborated into an explicit scheme of reincarnation, which serves to lend a measure of structural coherence to this sprawling narrative despite all its loose ends and dangling inconsistencies. In the case of *Hsi-yu chi*, the framework of quest and redemption is the basic groundwork of the plot, which it informs from beginning to end.

However, in all these exercises in Buddhist apologetics, we are ultimately left with a strong sense that this is not what the books are really about. This may be because these didactic pronouncements are themselves sooner or later subjected to some of the same ironic erosion directed toward the failings of the central figures. It is temping to simply wave away these didactic frames as little more than decorative afterthoughts, or perhaps to take them as tongue-in-cheek justification for indulging in the vicarious pleasure afforded by fictional license. The inadequacy of the retribution scheme in *Shui-hu* is immediately evident, since the introductory frame tale of errant spirits remains almost entirely inconsequential in the subsequent unfolding of the body of the narrative. The same can be said of *San-kuo*, where the more impressive sense of monumental misdeeds and inexorable consequences that takes shape in that work is, in the final analysis, submerged within a drama of human strivings and failings presented according to the laws of political and psychological dynamics. In *Hsi-yu chi*, the morality play of the quest is consistently compromised by the continual debunking of its messianic earnestness, thus leading the reader not to take too seriously its preachy didacticism. This tendency is carried even further in *Chin P'ing Mei*, where the ostensible message of spiritual blindness giving way to ultimate enlightenment is undercut by the parodic treatment of a parade of oracular Buddhist and Taoist figures, not the least among which is the foreign monk whose instrument of salvation proffered to Hsi-men Ch'ing only hastens the inevitable process of his self-destruction. For this reason the entire didactic edifice of the *Chin P'ing Mei* is generally sloughed off by modern readers as a lame attempt to cover up what is at best an exploration of sordid mores, and at worst a poorly camouflaged exercise in pornography.

Some critics have been tempted to see in the didacticism in *Chin P'ing Mei*, as well as in our other three novels, schemes of essentially aesthetic rather than doctrinal significance: a kind of formal feature of the genre that can function to provide a sense of closure by tying up loose ends, and by shedding a sense of symmetry on the plots.[5] There is probably a large measure of truth in this view. But it may be more significant here to say that the *beauty* of all this poetic justice, the reason it carries aesthetic weight, is still dependent on a certain amount of conviction. In other words, the structural balance provided by frames of karmic symmetry "works" only because this reflects an underlying faith in the justice of the cosmic system. This may perhaps be too big a claim, but at the very least this sort of retributive scheme provides a good example of the assimilation of Buddhist conceptions to the Confucian core of late Ming syncretism.

One particular form in which this issue is worked out in the individual cases of our fictional heroes is in the conflicts repeatedly staged between gratification of personal or collective desire and limitations imposed by external circumstances—the way of world. In many instances this translates into something like a clash between free will and deterministic constraints, however these may be conceived. This problem exercised Neo-Confucian thinkers perhaps less literally but no less deeply than their counterparts among Western philosophers and theologians.

In all four of our masterworks, the given framework of foreordination is sooner or later brought up for serious questioning. In *Shui-hu chuan*, the prefixing of a pseudo-mythical prologue to the main structural outlines of the text is taken for granted by readers of traditional Chinese fiction, familiar with this device as a kind of formal convention of the genre. But upon closer investigation, we see that the implications of this section are ill matched to the body of the novel, in which the etiological myth of the

---

[5] For discussions of the aesthetic function of karmic schemes in the literati novel, see my "After the Fall," p. 552. See also Idema, *Chinese Vernacular Fiction*, pp. 50ff., 127f.

baneful stars is never quite reconciled with what strikes most readers as a generally sympathetic recounting of the fortunes of these lost souls in the world of men. Even if we go along with those Ming and Ch'ing critics who perceive the more problematic side of the Liang-shan heroes, or if, perhaps, we agree with those recent critics who judge the novel as a fable of dangerously misguided political behavior, we must still acknowledge that the initial pseudo-allegorical parable fails to explain or adequately motivate what takes place in the rest of the book.

Similarly, in *San-kuo* the inexorability of the alternation of union and disunion that is first set before us in the review of the dynastic cycle that starts the narrative—later codified in the opening poem added in the Mao Tsung-kang edition—eventually comes rolling around to its foregone conclusion with the ascendance of the Chin forces 120 chapters later. This would seem to present a persuasive outline of historical predetermination along the lines of traditional Chinese dynastic theory. But this can scarcely be said to diminish the primary focus of the narrative on individual pride and ambition as the principal motors of historical change. Also, as in *Shui-hu*, we find significant logical inconsistencies in the ways in which this is worked out. The very fact of tripartite division, which forms the structural core of the entire work, immediately throws off the simple scheme of cyclical inevitability, as each "kingdom" stakes its own claims to an ascending arc of the dynastic cycle. By the same token, by the time we get to the ultimate rise of Ssu-ma I, we see that the "winner's" behavior is scarcely distinguished from the repeated pattern of so many other pretenders to dynastic authority, whose short-lived "unifications" had always carried the seeds of their own rapid demise.

The same can be said for *Chin P'ing Mei*. Here, again, the simplistic scheme of karmic retribution leaves unanswered the questions of guilt and final salvation of the Hsi-men household. To be sure, the gruesome wages of Hsi-men Ch'ing's sins, just like those visited upon P'an Chin-lien, Li P'ing-erh, Ch'en Ching-chi, and P'ang Ch'un-mei, do fit the crimes committed. But what are we to make of the truncated "restoration" of the house of Hsi-men Ch'ing under the muddle-headed sway of Yüeh-niang and the wily houseboy Tai-an, themselves bearing a portion of the responsibility for Hsi-men Ch'ing's downfall? For that matter, the figure of Hsiao-ko, through whom the material and spiritual redemption of the family is effected, remains equally ambiguous. His birth at the precise moment of Hsi-men's hideous self-destruction makes him something of a reincarnation of the father, thus making the irony of his name "filial son" all the more cutting. Yet the author himself denies this neat explanation by giving Hsi-men Ch'ing another gratuitous rebirth in the final vision in chapter 100. As a result, Hsiao-ko comes across more as a faceless victim than as an

instrument of salvation. Nor does the implied analogy of the partial restoration of the Southern Sung provide a fully satisfying explanation of the
significance of the ending of the book. As I have suggested, this historical
parallel sets up an important dimension of the book's meaning, but by no
means does this fully account for the powerful immediacy of the crumbling
world of Hsi-men Ch'ing evoked in the concluding phases of the narrative
itself.

In *Hsi-yu chi*, the overall pattern of quest and attainment, solemnly
foretold at the outset by Kuan-yin and reaffirmed at frequent intervals,
sheds a strong sense of predetermination on the narrative. But at a number
of points this is undermined, particularly where the question is raised as to
the purpose of putting the pilgrims through their arduous journey in the
first place, when Sun Wu-k'ung, or any one of a number of divine pro-
tectors for that matter, could as easily somersault in a single bound to
the Holy Mountain to obtain the means of salvation originally promised.
Instead, we are frequently lectured on the theological and literary necessity
of working out the enlightenment of our pilgrims through the process of
the allegorical journey itself, a point driven home transparently enough at
the end in the anticlimactic joke about the uselessness of the long-sought
scriptures.

Thus we see in all four examples that the solutions held out by pseudo-
oracular didactic voices must be worked out on the narrative level in terms
of the dynamics of human action and consequences. In each case, the
scheme of foreordination given leaves significant leeway for the exercise
of freedom of the will. Or, paradoxically, it is the very fact of preordained
causality that shifts the weight onto the consequentiality of human action.
This, at least, is an idea underlying programmatic statements such as that
voiced by Chu-ko Liang in the famous line "The planning of great deeds
is the province of men, the fulfillment of great deeds is the province of
heaven" 謀事在人, 成事在天, which, as I have argued in the discussion of
San-kuo, carries as much the implication of individual commitment to
human striving—that which remains in man's hands—as of resignation to
that which is in the hands of Heaven. Within this context, the characteristic
use of frames of karmic predestination may likewise be reinterpreted as less
fully deterministic than insistent on a far-reaching consequentiality in the
realm of human action.

Here we can perhaps see a specific link between the world view reflected
in each of our novels and the intellectual history of the sixteenth century.
This was, as I noted in Chapter 1, a time of unaccustomed interest in matters
of individual accountability. This phenomenon was manifested across a
broad spectrum of intellectual and spiritual life, from the popular level, with
its morality books and its account sheets of merits and demerits, to exer-

cises in public confession on the part of prominent literati figures.[6] This
tendency was even more pronounced in the following century, especially
during the generation that lived through the trauma of the collapse of the
Ming state; but it is already observable in incipient form by the early Wan-
li period, in the few decades that saw the printing and circulation of versions
of all four of these fictional works. In the broadest sense, this heightened
consciousness of the autonomy of the moral self also grows out of the
revised understanding of self-cultivation gradually emerging in the intellectual ferment of the post–Wang Yang–ming era.

In all four of our masterworks, however, this apparent interest in the
positive significance of actions and consequences still leaves unexplained
the recurrent emphasis on failure and meaninglessness, the intimations of
cosmic futility, which succeed in placing the entire mimetic edifice of the
works into the status of passing dreams of vanity. In *Shui-hu chuan*, for
example, the greater part of the narrative traces the seemingly unstoppable
expansion of the Liang-shan band, followed by one or more triumphant
campaigns. But then we come to the final section in which the band, at the
height of its powers in the service of a nominally just cause, is swiftly
decimated, leaving behind a miserable remnant to act out the final throes of
self-destruction. All of this, moreover, transpires amidst a flurry of images
of futility and emptiness, providing some of the most memorable moments
in an otherwise uninspired recitation of battles in the style of the popular
"military romances." The fact that the only winners here seem to be those
whose insight enables them to extricate themselves from worldly entanglements—whether that be through the stereotyped enlightenment of a Lu
Ta or the less pretentious withdrawal of a Yen Ch'ing—casts an ironic
light on the entire heroic enterprise experienced in the course of the novel.

A very similar sense attends the concluding phases of *San-kuo*, where the
self-destructive acts of Ts'ao Ts'ao, Liu Pei, Kuan Yü, Chang Fei, and a host
of lesser figures also take place against a backdrop of imagery emphasizing
the *vanitas* theme. The most powerful example of this is seen in the
ambiguous demise of Chu-ko Liang. As a result, it took only a slight
doctoring of the text on Mao Tsung-kang's part to enable him to say that
his book both begins and ends on a note of cosmic emptiness.

In *Chin P'ing Mei*, the didactic resolution of the novel appears even more
insistent in its message of a final emptiness. This is certainly the impression
the reader gets when he experiences the deafening silence of the concluding scene, coming after a very noisy text climaxing to a din of battle just
moments before. But if anything, the problem in *Chin P'ing Mei* is that its
conclusion is not empty enough, as Chang Chu-p'o complains in a very

---

[6] See references in Chapter 1, n. 52.

telling passage in his *tu-fa* introduction.[7] Or, in the terms of my argument, the depth and complexity of ironic expression that makes up the dense rhetorical texture of this remarkable book denies us the easy resolution of a simplistic "message" of worldly vanity.

Only in *Hsi-yu chi* does the author seem to take this extra step to negate the literal protestations of emptiness that are set forth in a number of key scenes, only to be deflated by ironic reflection on the Master's literal-minded pursuit of the Void. Gradually we come to understand that it is precisely this tendency toward the reification of emptiness as a final solution that turns out to be the principal block to transcendent insight. Thus, even without the parting joke about the wordless scriptures, the reader, who has been led to expect a final revelation of the meaning of the allegorical quest, is left with only a sense of the emptiness of the notion of emptiness.

One raft we can try to cling to in order to avoid being submerged in these intimations of the Void may be provided by the yoking of the term "emptiness" (*k'ung* 空) with its sister term "perceived reality" (*se* 色) in so many of my interpretive discussions. (Here, by the way, we have another excellent example of an originally Buddhist concept accommodated within the vocabulary of both the popular three-teachings movements and serious philosophical discussion under the Neo-Confucian umbrella in Ming China.) This paired concept is most succinctly expressed in the opening formula of the Heart Sutra, "Reality is emptiness, emptiness is reality," which is cited at prominent points in both *Hsi-yu chi* and *Chin P'ing Mei*.[8] At least in the former case, I have argued that this provides an important doctrinal gloss on the message of the book—not in the sense of a simple antithesis of reality and illusion, but more in the logical identity and interpenetration of these apparently contradictory ideas. If nothing else, this has lent a bit of conceptual underpinning to my observation of the interest in the problem of sexuality that looms so large not only in *Chin P'ing Mei*, where it comprises the stuff of the plot, but also in our other narratives nominally about wandering pilgrims and unseducible warriors. In terms of the dialectics of *se* and *k'ung*, this thematic area lies close to the heart of the matter, inasmuch as sexuality, or more loosely sensuality, covers at one and the same time the most real and the most illusory ground of human experience. Within this context, the attractive pull of *k'ung* in all four of our novels is never quite presented as an ultimate answer to the problematics of *se*. Instead, each of our texts attempts to straddle the fine line between reality and illusion in its exploration of the interface of human

[7] See Chang Chu-p'o, *tu-fa*, items 75 and 76.

[8] Cf. the apparent play on these words in the name of Sun Wu-k'ung, as well as a similar development of the idea in chapter 1 of *Hung-lou meng*.

consequentiality and cosmic futility. It is this sort of conditional affirmation of the sphere of human action in the real world, tempered by a respectful awe for the abyss of emptiness this tentative acceptance merely papers over, that I have in mind when I speak of a "Confucian" range of meanings in the four Ming masterworks.

Perhaps this is making too much of what is in the end a sprinkling of pseudo-philosophical musings in these books. After all, I have admitted at the outset that our sixteenth-century authors and editors were not necessarily the most profound thinkers of their time, and often they are doing little more than mouthing ready-made formulas that happened to be in the air in their day. But at the same time, the act of fiction writing—the business of fabricating illusions of reality—gives these writers a privileged vantage point on the cutting edge of this issue. Theoretically, they are free to manipulate their texts virtually at will, to contrive beginnings and endings and arrange structural outlines to fit their own varying senses of poetic and moral justice. Yet at the same time, they remain undeniably bound by the determining limitations of logical plausibility and aesthetic expectations on the part of their audience—not to mention the additional layer of predetermination imposed by their reliance on preexisting narrative material. But if there is any pretension here to a serious level of meaning suggested by the ironic surface of these books, and I am convinced there is, it may perhaps lie in some of the directions I have attempted to outline here.

The "Li Cho-wu"
Commentary Editions

Much ink has been spilled over the vexed question of the authorship of the "Li Cho-wu" commentaries attached to three out of four of our masterworks. For discussions on the *Hsi-yu chi* and *San-kuo yen-i* examples, see Chapter 3, note 83, and Chapter 5, note 54. With respect to the case of the *Shui-hu chuan* commentaries ascribed to Li Chih, the evidence presently available does not warrant a definitive conclusion. There is, however, a more or less general consensus among scholars about a number of points regarding these materials, which can be summarized as follows.

1. There is little doubt that Li Chih did compose a textual commentary for an edition of *Shui-hu chuan*. Besides his well-known preface included in *Fen shu* (pp. 108ff.), we have certain pieces of testimony by friends and contemporaries that he was engaged in this project during the last phase of his life. Chief among these are Yüan Chung-tao's 袁中道 report in his *Yu-chü fei-lu* 游居柿錄 (alternate reading: *Yu-chü shih-lu*) that Li was working on a "word-by-word" (*chu-tzu* 逐字) commentary on the novel, and a letter to this effect from Li to Chiao Hung 焦竑 preserved in his *Hsü Fen shu*, pp. 363f. (in Ma T'i-chi, *Tzu-liao*, pp. 3ff.). See Kung Chao-chi, "Jung-pen Li-p'ing wei Yeh Chou wei-tso shuo chih-i," p. 158. We also have a preface by Lü T'ien-ch'eng 呂天成 to the play *I-hsia chi* 義俠記 by Shen Ching 沈璟 noting the same point, among other examples (see Chin Tai-t'ung, "Li Chih yü Shui-hu," p. 73). See also Nieh Kan-nu, "Shui-hu wu-lun," pp. 102f.; and Min Tse, *Chung-kuo wen-hsüeh li-lun p'i-ping shih*, pp. 718ff.

2. A number of extant editions claim to reprint the reported commentary

of Li Chih. Only in two of these, the 1610 100-chapter Jung-yü t'ang edition and the 120-chapter *Shui-hu ch'üan-chuan*, printed slightly later by Yüan Wu-yai, is the attribution taken at all seriously. Since these two commentaries sharply differ in their style and content, a heated debate has developed over the question of which one of them (if either) has a greater likelihood of deriving from Li Chih's original comments. The majority of scholars have rejected the Jung-yü t'ang version on the basis of its less sophisticated style and certain points of ideological divergence from the point of view presented in the Li Chih preface. For this opinion, see Ch'en Chin-chao, "Li Cho-wu p'i-tien Shui-hu chuan chih yen-chiu," p. 45; and Ou-yang Chien, "Shui-hu chien-pen fan-pen ti-shan kuo-ch'eng hsin-cheng," pp. 251ff. Only Wei Tzu-yün has attempted to argue for the authenticity of the Jung-yü t'ang commentary. See his "Lun Ming-tai ti Chin P'ing Mei shih-liao," p. 26. As far as the second "Li Cho-wu" commentary edition is concerned, this attribution has been rejected by many critics, but others have confirmed the relationship between Li Chih and Yang Ting-chien, as described in the latter's preface to the Yüan Wu-yai edition, as well as Yang's claim that Li Chih entrusted his manuscript commentary to him for publication. See, for example, Chin Tai-t'ung, "Li Chih," p. 75; A Ying (Ch'ien Hsing-ts'un), *Hsiao-shuo hsien-t'an*, pp. 158, 162f.; Ou-yang Chien, "Ti-shan kuo-ch'eng," p. 262; Ch'en Chin-chao, "Li Cho-wu p'i-tien," pp. 46f., plus his *Li Chih chih wen-lun*, pp. 76ff. On the other hand, even those who support this position generally admit that the Yüan Wu-yai commentary is probably not an unadulterated transmission of Li Chih's work, but rather shows traces of contributions by more than one hand. See Kung Chao-chi, "Chih-i," p. 166. This impression is immediately supported by the observation that the Yüan Wu-yai edition patently borrows a number of comments from the Jung-yü t'ang commentary. See Yeh Lang, "Yeh Chou p'i-tien Shui-hu chuan k'ao-cheng," in *Chung-kuo hsiao-shuo mei-hsüeh*, pp. 292f.; and Huang Lin, "Shui-hu ch'üan-chuan Li Chih p'ing yeh shu wei-t'o," pp. 45ff. It has also been suggested along these lines that perhaps the marginal and interlinear comments in this edition may derive from Li Chih's work, with the chapter-ending discussions (*tsung-p'i* 總批) representing the hand of a forger. This theory fits the testimony by Yüan Chung-tao that the original was a "word by word" commentary. See Yeh Lang, "Yeh Chou p'i-tien," pp. 293f. A few scholars, such as Tai Wang-shu and Ch'en Chin-chao, go as far as to assert without qualification that the Yüan Wu-yai commentary was in fact the work of Li Chih. See Tai's "Yüan-k'an Shui-hu chuan chih chen-wei," pp. 63ff. Yeh Lang ("Yeh Chou p'i-tien," pp. 289ff.) concurs, although he allows for a small contribution by Yeh Chou. The fact that Li Chih makes no mention of the T'ien Hu and Wang Ch'ing campaigns in his preface might indicate that he worked with a hundred-chapter edition; but it has also been pointed out that the comments on these twenty chapters are noticeably more sparse and could well have been interpolated by a later editor (see Ch'en Chin-chao, "Li Cho-wu p'i-tien," p.48). Fan Ning ("Shui-hu chuan pan-pen yüan-liu k'ao," p. 73) suggests that this entire commentary may have been taken over from an earlier commentary reportedly included in the nonextant Ta-ti yü-jen preface edition. For reviews of the various arguments on this issue, see Fan Ning, "Yüan-liu k'ao," pp. 72ff., and Huang Lin, "Wei-t'o," pp. 44ff. A small piece of evidence that might prove that the Yüan Wu-yai commentary as we have it could not have come from Li Chih's brush is provided by Yeh Lang ("Yeh Chou p'i-tien," p. 294), who cites a quotation in a chapter-comment on chapter 3 of the Yüan text of a line by the Wan-li literary figure Ch'en Chi-ju 陳繼儒, which was not written until after Li Chih's death.

3. Most critics have observed that the comments in the Jung-yü t'ang edition are generally superficial, whereas practically all agree that those in the Yüan Wu-yai edition are closer to the political thinking of Li Chih as expressed in his preface than those in the Jung-yü t'ang version. See Yeh Lang, "Yeh Chou p'i-tien," pp. 288, 290; Nieh Kan-nu, "Wu-lun," pp. 96ff., 119. Nieh (p. 109) also argues that the Jung-yü t'ang commentator's frequent practice of recommending the excision of certain passages (k'e-shan 可刪) betrays a critical attitude inconsistent with that of Li Chih. See also Huang Lin, "Wei-t'o," p. 46; and Kung Chao-chi, "Chih-i," p. 161.

4. Virtually all of the scholars who dismiss one or both of the commentaries as forgeries identify the principal forger as Yeh Chou 葉畫, a shadowy figure who has left a trail of questionable contributions to late Ming fiction criticism. This accusation is based on several late Ming and Ch'ing sources, including Ch'ien Hsi-yen's Hsi-hsia and Chou Liang-kung's Yin-shu-wu shu-ying, passages reprinted in Ma T'i-chi, Shui-hu tzu-liao hui-pien, pp. 375f., 360f., 377; and Chu I-hsüan and Liu Yü-ch'en, Shui hu chuan tzu-liao hui-pien, pp. 150f., 152, 351. For further discussion, see Ho Hsin, Shui-hu yen-chiu, p. 38; Shiroki Naoya, "Ippyaku nijūkai Suikozenden no kenkyū: sono Ri Takugo hyō o megutte," p. 106; and Yeh Lang, "Yeh Chou p'i-tien," pp. 280ff. There is ample evidence that Yeh Chou was involved to one degree or another in producing some of the "Li Cho-wu" commentaries. Cheng Chen-to notes that Yeh acknowledged his own contribution in a comment on the play Chü-p'u chi 橘浦記 (see his "San-kuo chih yen-i ti yen-hua," p. 216), and for this reason expresses reservations about the assumption that Yeh was nothing but an unscrupulous forger. In the parallel "Li Cho-wu" commentary on San-kuo, Yeh Chou also signs his own name in at least one point. See also Yeh Lang, "Yeh Chou p'i-tien," pp. 286, 296. Nieh Kan-nu ("Wu-lun," p. 109) notes several other "Li Cho-wu" commentaries on the plays Pai-yüeh chi and P'i-p'a chi (some printed by the

Jung-yü t'ang printing house), in which Yeh Chou uses the expression "should be excised" in a manner similar to that found in the Jung-yü t'ang commentary.

However, the information about Yeh Chou is not totally uncontested. First, there are certain textual problems about the evidence on Yeh Chou's alleged role, especially with respect to the *Hsi-hsia* passage (see Irwin, *The Evolution of a Chinese Novel*, p. 100, n. 47; and Huang Lin, "Wei-t'o," p. 48). At the very least, as Chin Tai-t'ung points out ("Li Chih," p. 74), Ch'ien Hsi-yen's attribution of the commentary to Yeh Chou would probably refer to the Jung-yü t'ang commentary, since Ch'ien's work is dated 1613, before the accepted date of publication of the Yüan Wu-yai edition. Another qualification of the attribution of the "Li Cho-wu" commentaries to Yeh Chou arises in connection with the monk Huai-lin 懷林, whose name has been attached to several prefatory essays included in the Jung-yü t'ang edition (and also reworked in the "Chung Hsing" edition), as well as in a postscript added to the prefatory piece "P'i-p'ing Shui-hu chuan shu-yü" 批評水滸傳述語 in the Jung-yü t'ang edition (also mentioned in Yüan's *fa-fan* preface) advertising one or more separate narratives entitled *Hei hsüan-feng chi* 黑旋風集 and *Ch'ing-feng shih* 清風史. See Ma T'i-chi, *Tzu-liao*, p. 6; and Chu I-hsüan, *Shui-hu tzu-liao*, p. 208. According to certain late Ming sources cited by Chin Tai-t'ung ("Li Chih," p.74) and Tai Wang-shu ("Chen-wei," pp. 59ff.), the author of these passages, and perhaps of the nonextant books as well, may actually have been Yeh Chou himself. See also Nieh Kan-nu, "Wu-lun," pp. 101ff., 109f.; Huang Lin, "Wei-t'o," p. 46; and Yeh Lang, "Yeh Chou p'i-tien," p. 284. See also Huang Lin's note suggesting that Huai-lin was a nom de plume for Yeh Chou, in *Chung-kuo li-tai hsiao-shuo lun-chu hsüan*, p. 184. Huang does, however, retain the name Huai-lin for the attribution of the piece "A Comparative Ranking" (as do Ma T'i-chi and Chu I-hsüan in their *Tzu-liao* collections). In addition, there are indications that a number of other individuals may have been involved in this commentary project, including Feng Meng-lung 馮夢龍 and Hsü Tzu-ch'ang 許自昌, along with Yeh Chou, all of whom can be shown to have been personally connected to one another. Cf. Wilt Idema's discussion of Feng Meng-lung's role in the *Shui-hu* editions in his *Chinese Vernacular Fiction*, p. 36 (although he inadvertently speaks of the T'ien-tu wai-ch'en edition rather than the Yüan edition). Wang Li-ch'i documents the collaboration between Yüan Wu-yai and Hsü Tzu-ch'ang in "Shui-hu ch'üan-chuan T'ien Wang erh-chuan shih shui so-chia," p. 388. See also Chin Tai-t'ung, "Li Chih," p. 75; and Ch'en Chin-chao, "Li Cho-wu p'i-tien," p. 48. Huang Lin ("Wei-t'o, p. 47) argues that the commentary was primarily by Yüan Wu-yai himself, with some help from Feng Meng-lung. This opinion is seconded by Ou-yang Chien ("Ti-shan kuo-ch'eng," p. 262). A final aspect of the attribution to Yeh Chou concerns whether any or all of the other commentaries attributed to Li Chih, including those on *Hsi-yu chi* and *San-kuo yen-i* plus a number of plays, and the commentary texts *Shih-kang p'ing-yao* 史綱評要, *Ssu-shu p'ing* 四書評, and others were (as suggested in a large number of contemporary references cited in Chapter 4, above) also the handiwork of Yeh Chou. For reviews of these, see Ts'ui Wen-yin, "Shih-kang p'ing-yao," in Chan Hok-lam, *Li Chih in Contemporary Chinese Historiography*, pp. 173–82; Ch'en Chin-chao, *Wen-lun*, pp. 25–30, 32f., 40; and Ts'ui Wen-yin, "Li Chih Ssu-shu p'ing chen-wei pien." The fullest review of the entire issue is printed in Yeh Lang's appendix (pp. 280–92), in which he argues for the appreciation of the contribution of Yeh Chou in his own right as a pioneering figure of late Ming fiction criticism.

5. A large number of other Ming and Ch'ing editions of *Shui-hu chuan* carry attributions to Li Chih. Even the K'ang-hsi reprint we have of the T'ien-tu wai-ch'en edition bears such an attribution on its title page. For examples of other *fan-pen* attributed to Li Chih, such as the Chieh-tzu yüan and Mukyūkai editions in Japan, see Shiroki Naoya, "Ippyaku nijūkai Suikozenden," p. 95. Interestingly, these attributions are not restricted to the *fan-pen* system alone, as for example in the Wen-hsing t'ang edition (see Cheng Chen-to, "Yen-hua," p. 149). Ōuchida Saburō notes the citation of a poem attributed to Li Chih in chapter 42 of a 115-chapter *chien-pen* edition. See his "Suikoden hanponkō," no.1, p. 61.

BIBLIOGRAPHY

Abbreviations

PERIODICALS OCCURRING MORE THAN ONE TIME

AA	*Acta Asiatica*
AM	*Asia Major*
CBH	*Chūgoku bungaku hō* 中国文学報
CHLT	*Chiang-han lun-t'an* 江漢論壇
CHWHFHYK	*Chung-hua wen-hua fu-hsing yüeh-k'an* 中華文化復興月刊
CHWSLT	*Chung-hua wen-shih lun-ts'ung* 中華文史論叢
CKSP	*Chung-kuo shih-pao* 中國時報
CLEAR	*Chinese Literature: Essays, Articles, Reviews*
CWWH	*Chung-wai wen-hsüeh* 中外文學
CYYCYLSYYYCSCK	*Chung-yang yen-chiu yüan li-shih yü-yen yen-chiu-so chi-k'an* 中央研究院歷史語言研究所集刊
FTHP	*Fu-tan hsüeh-pao* 復旦學報
HCSFHYHP	*Hsü-chou shih-fan hsüeh-yüan hsüeh-pao* 徐州師範學院學報
HCTHHP	*Hang-chou ta-hsüeh hsüeh-pao* 杭州大學學報
HDBK	*Hiroshima daigaku bungakubu kiyō* 広島大学文学部紀要
HJAS	*Harvard Journal of Asiatic Studies*
HR	*History of Religions*
HYHP	*Hsin-ya hsüeh-pao* 新亞學報
JAOS	*Journal of the American Oriental Society*
JAS	*Journal of Asian Studies*
JCP	*Journal of Chinese Philosophy*

JOS	*Journal of Oriental Studies*
JOSA	*Journal of the Oriental Society of Australia*
KGR	*Kōbe gaidai ronsō* 神戸外大論叢
KLPPTSKKK	*Kuo-li Pei-p'ing t'u-shu-kuan kuan-k'an* 國立北平圖書館館刊
MPYK	*Ming-pao yüeh-k'an* 明報月刊
NAAB	*New Asia Academic Bulletin*
NCGH	*Nihon Chūgoku gakkai hō* 日本中国学会報
OE	*Oriens Extremus*
SHKHCH	*She-hui k'e-hsüeh chan-hsien* 社會科學戰線
SMCK	*Shu-mu chi-k'an* 書目季刊
SSG	*Shoshigaku* 書誌學
STG	*Shūkan tōyōgaku* 集刊東洋学
TDGH	*Tenri daigaku gakuhō* 天理大学学報
THGH	*Tōhō gakuhō* 東方学報
THJCS	*Tsing-hua Journal of Chinese Studies*
TP	*T'oung-Pao*
TR	*Tamkang Review*
WH	*Wen-hsien* 文獻
WHIC	*Wen-hsüeh i-ch'an* 文學遺產, numbered series in *Kuang-ming jih-pao* 光明日報, or *Wen-hsüeh i-ch'an* (a separate periodical)
WS	*Wen-shih* 文史
WW	*Wen-wu* 文物
YSYK	*Yu-shih yüeh-k'an* 幼獅月刊

COLLECTIONS OF ARTICLES, PUBLICATIONS SERIES, AND COLLECTANEA

Academia Sinica Conference	*Proceedings of the International Conference on Sinology*, Academia Sinica, Taipei, August 1980 (publication 1981).
Cambridge History	*Cambridge History of China: The Ming Dynasty (1368–1644)*. Edited by Frederick W. Mote and Denis Twitchett. Vol. 7, part 1. Cambridge and New York: Cambridge University Press, 1987.
CHDS	*Chūgoku no hachi daishōsetsu* 中国の八大小説. Edited by Ōsaka shiritsu daigaku 大阪市立大学. Tokyo: Heibonsha, 1967.
Chinese Government	*Chinese Government in Ming Times*. Edited by Charles O. Hucker. New York: Columbia University Press, 1968.
Chinese Literary Genres	*Studies in Chinese Literary Genres*. Edited by Cyril Birch. Berkeley: University of California Press, 1974.
Chinese Narrative	*Chinese Narrative: Critical and Theoretical Essays*. Edited by Andrew H. Plaks. Princeton: Princeton University Press, 1977.
City	*The City in Late Imperial China*. Edited by G. William Skinner. Palo Alto: Stanford University Press, 1977.
CKBT	*Chūgoku koten bungaku taikei* series. Tokyo: Heibonsha, 1967–75.
CKHSTK	Chao Ching-shen 趙景深, *Chung-kuo hsiao-shuo ts'ung-k'ao* 中國小說叢考. Chi-nan: Ch'i-lu, 1980.
CKKTHCLCCC	*Chung-kuo ku-tien hsi-ch'ü lun-chu chi-ch'eng* 中國古典戲曲論著集成. Peking: Chung-kuo hsi-ch'ü, 1959.

CKKTHSYCCC   *Chung-kuo ku-tien hsiao-shuo yen-chiu chuan-chi* 中國古典小說研究專集. Taipei: Lien-ching, 1979 (Vol. 1), 1980 (Vol. 2), 1983 (Vol. 6).

CKKTWHYCTK   *Chung-kuo ku-tien wen-hsüeh yen-chiu ts'ung-k'an* 中國古典文學研究叢刊. Edited by K'e Ch'ing-ming 柯慶明 and Lin Ming-te 林明德. Taipei: Chü-liu, 1977.

CKWHYC   Cheng Chen-to 鄭振鐸. *Chung-kuo wen-hsüeh yen-chiu hsin-pien* 中國文學研究新編. 1930. Reprint of 1957 Peking edition. Taipei: Ming-lun, 1971.

CSSK   Ogawa Tamaki 小川環樹. *Chūgoku shōsetsu shi no kenkyū* 中国小説史の研究. Tokyo: Iwanami, 1968.

DMB   *Dictionary of Ming Biography*. Edited by L. Carrington Goodrich and Chao-ying Fang. New York: Columbia University Press, 1976.

HFTTSC   Liu Ts'un-yan 柳存仁. *Ho-feng t'ang tu-shu chi* 和風堂讀書記. Hong Kong: Lung-men, 1977.

HSISK   *Huang-shih i-shu k'ao* 黃氏逸書考. Edited by Huang Shih 黃奭. Reprint. Taipei: I-wen, 1971.

HSWT   *Hu Shih wen-ts'un* 胡適文存. 1921. Reprint. Taipei: Yüan-tung, 1953.

HYCYC   *Hsi-yu chi yen-chiu* 西遊記研究. Nan-ching: Chiang-su she-hui k'e-hsüeh yüan, 1984.

HYCYCLWC   *Hsi-yu chi yen-chiu lun-wen chi* 西遊記研究論文集. Shanghai: Tso-chia, 1957.

Indiana Conference   Conference on *Chin P'ing Mei* held at University of Indiana, May 1983. Selected papers to be published in *CLEAR*, 1987.

KHCPTS   *Kuo-hsüeh chi-pen ts'ung-shu* 國學基本叢書. General editor Wang Yün-wu 王雲五. Taipei: Shang-wu, 1968.

KTHSHCTK   Liu Hsiu-yeh 劉修業. *Ku-tien hsiao-shuo hsi-ch'ü ts'ung-k'ao* 古典小說戲曲叢考. Peking: Tso-chia, 1958.

LCPM   *Lun Chin P'ing Mei* 論金瓶梅. Edited by Hu Wen-pin 胡文彬 and Chang Ch'ing-shan 張慶善. Peking: Wen-hua i-shu, 1984.

MCHSYCLWC   *Ming-Ch'ing hsiao-shuo yen-chiu lun-wen chi* 明清小說研究論文集. Peking: Jen-min wen-hsüeh, 1959.

Ming to Ch'ing   *From Ming to Ch'ing: Conquest, Region, and Continuity in Seventeenth-century China*. Edited by J. D. Spence and John E. Wills, Jr. New Haven: Yale University Press, 1979.

Personalities   *Confucian Personalities*. Edited by Arthur F. Wright. Palo Alto: Stanford University Press, 1962.

PPTSCC   *Pai-pu ts'ung-shu chi-ch'eng* 百部叢書集成. Reprint. Taipei: I-wen.

PWCY   *P'ing-wai chih-yen* 瓶外卮言. Edited by Yao Ling-hsi 姚靈犀. 1940. Reprint. Hong Kong: Hua-hsia, 1967 (under title *Chin P'ing Mei yen-chiu lun-chi* 金瓶梅研究論集).

Self and Society   *Self and Society in Ming Thought*. Edited by W. T. deBary. New York: Columbia University Press, 1970.

SHCM   *Shui-hu cheng-ming* 水滸爭鳴. Edited by Hu-pei sheng she-hui

	k'e-hsüeh yüan, wen-hsüeh yen-chiu so 湖北省社會科學院 文學研究所, and Hu-pei sheng Shui-hu yen-chiu hui 水滸研究會. Wu-han?: Ch'ang-chiang wen-i, 1982 (Vol. 1), 1983 (Vol. 2), 1984 (Vol. 3).
SHYCLWC	*Shui-hu yen-chiu lun-wen chi* 水滸研究論文集. Peking: Tso-chia, 1957.
SKCS	*Ssu-k'u ch'üan-shu* 四庫全書.
SKYIYCC	*San-kuo yen-i yen-chiu chi* 三國演義研究集. Ch'eng-tu: Ssu-ch'uan sheng she-hui k'e-hsüeh yüan, 1983.
SLTK	Chou Shao-liang 周紹良. *Shao-liang ts'ung-kao* 紹良叢稿. Chi-nan: Ch'i-lu, 1984.
SPTK	*Ssu-pu ts'ung-k'an* 四部叢刊.
TCC	Sun K'ai-ti 孫楷第. *Ts'ang-chou chi* 滄州集. 2 vols. Peking: Chung-hua, 1965.
Thought and Institutions	*Chinese Thought and Institutions*. Edited by John K. Fairbank. Chicago: University of Chicago Press, 1957.
THT	Hsü Shuo-fang 徐朔方. *Lun T'ang Hsien-tsu chi ch'i-t'a* 論湯顯祖 及其他. Shanghai: Shang-hai ku-chi, 1983.
TTCH	*Tao-tsang ching-hua* 道藏精華. Taipei: Tzu-yu, 1957–1966.
Unfolding	*The Unfolding of Neo-Confucianism*. Edited by W. T. deBary. New York: Columbia University Press, 1975.
Ways in Warfare	*Chinese Ways in Warfare*. Edited by Frank A, Kierman, Jr., and John K. Fairbank. Cambridge: Harvard University Press, 1974.
WHICTK	*Wen-hsüeh i-ch'an tseng-k'an* 文學遺產增刊. Peking: Tso-chia, 1958.

Bibliographical Notes on Sources and Editions of the Four Masterworks

Chin P'ing Mei

I. This study is based on the following editions of the novel.

1. *Tz'u-hua* edition 詞話本

   Chin P'ing Mei tz'u-hua 金瓶梅詞話 (Tokyo: Kobayashi, 1983), a photo-reprint of the 1963 Daian offset edition of the rare text held in the Jigendō Temple library in Nikkō. Additional reprints available: Taipei, 1980, and Hong Kong, 1975, among others. See Lévy, *Fleur en Fiole d'Or*, pp. CXXXVIff.

2. Ch'ung-chen edition 崇禎本

   Hsin-k'e hsiu-hsiang p'i-p'ing Chin P'ing Mei 新刻繡像批評金瓶梅. Original in Tokyo University, Tōyō bunka kenkyūjo. Microfilm copy in Gest Oriental

Library, Princeton, New Jersey; additional microfilm courtesy of University of Chicago. Other exemplars examined at Peking University Library and Peking Metropolitan Library.

3. Chang Chu-p'o edition (Ti-i ch'i-shu 第一奇書)

Ch'i-shu ti-ssu chung 奇書第四種. Ch'ing edition, Hsieh I 謝頤 preface dated 1477, apparently equivalent to Torii Hisayasu's no.20 (see "Kinpeibai hanponkō," p. 360). In rare book collection of Gest Oriental Library. Other copies examined in Peking University Library, Metropolitan Library, and Bibliothèque nationale, Paris. An offset edition of an inferior Chang Chu-p'o text was published in Hong Kong in 1975 by Ku-i hsiao-shuo yen-chiu hui 古佚小說研究會, under the title *Liang-chung Chu-p'o p'ing-tien-pen ho-k'an t'ien-hsia ti-i ch'i-shu* 兩種竹坡評點本合刊天下第一奇書. For convenience, I will cite page references to Chang's prefaces in this more readily available edition. All other references are to Gest copy.

For descriptions of the known exemplars of the three textual systems, see Hanan, "The Text of the *Chin P'ing Mei*," pp. 2–11; Wrenn, "Textual Method in Chinese with Illustrative Examples," pp. 151–55; Torii, "Hanponkō," pp. 337–63; Wei Tzu-yün, *Chin P'ing Mei ti wen-shih yü yen-pien*, pp. 55ff. A combined commentary edition (*hui-p'ing pen* 會評本) with selected comments by all the major critics (including the newly discovered Wen Lung edition) is currently being prepared by Liu Hui (see note 52).

Hsi-yu chi

I. For the sources and antecedents of the *Hsi-yu chi*, see the following selected studies cited in my notes.

1. On the relations of the novel to folklore materials, see Hu Shih, "Hsi-yu chi k'ao-cheng," pp. 368ff.; Anthony Yu, *The Journey to the West*, pp. 11ff.; Cheng Chen-to, "Hsi-yu chi ti yen-hua," 1: 291ff.; Glen Dudbridge, *The Hsi-yu chi*, pp. 11–24; Yeh Te-chün, "Wu Chih-ch'i ch'uan-shuo k'ao," pp. 495–515; C. T. Hsia, *The Classic Chinese Novel*, pp. 117ff.; Ch'en Yü-p'i, "Ts'ung 'kuo huo-yen-shan' k'an Wu Ch'eng-en tui ch'ing-chieh ti ch'u-li"; Wang Ch'iu-kuei, "Erh-lang shen ch'uan-shuo pu-k'ao"; Cheng Ming-li, "Huo-yen shan ku-shih ti hsing-ch'eng." See also Ts'ao Shih-pang, "Hsi-yu chi chung jo-kan ch'ing-chieh pen-yüan ti t'an-t'ao"; plus follow-up articles: ". . . tsai-t'an"; ". . . ssu-t'an"; and ". . . wu-t'an."

2. On the records of the actual Hsüan-tsang's journey, see Li Shih-jen, "Lüeh-lun Wu Ch'eng-en Hsi-yu chi chung ti T'ang-seng ch'u-shih ku-shih"; Ch'en Yin-k'e, "Hsi-yu chi Hsüan-tsang ti-tzu ku-shih ti yen-pien"; Ch'ien Ching-fang, *Hsiao*

shuo ts'ung-k'ao, pp. 47f.; and Ōta Tatsuo, "Kaisetsu," pp. 431f. See also Arthur Waley, *The Real Tripitaka and Other Pieces*; and K'ung Ling-ching, *Chung-kuo hsiao-shuo shih-liao*, p. 68 (citation from Chai Hao, *T'ung-su pien*, 20: 229f.).

3. For discussions of the *Shih-hua* version, see Dudbridge, *Hsi-yu chi*, pp. 28–45; Hu Shih, "K'ao-cheng," pp. 360ff.; Anthony Yu, *Journey*, pp. 7f.; Chao Ts'ung, *Chung-kuo ssu ta hsiao-shuo chih yen-chiu*, p. 148. Li Shih-jen and Ts'ai Ching-hao, in "Ta-T'ang San-tsang ch'ü-ching shih-hua ch'eng-shu shih-tai k'ao-pien," try to push the date of this text back to the late T'ang. For original texts and modern reprints of the *Shih-hua*, see Dudbridge, *Hsi-yu chi*, pp. 25f. A copy of a related text, *Ta-T'ang San-tsang fa-shih ch'ü-ching chi*, held in Ochanomizu Library, Tokyo, is available on microfilm in the Michigan series (G-63, reel 18). See b. n. II. 1. for description of this series.

4. On treatments of the same narrative outlines in dramatic works, especially the *Hsi-yu chi tsa-chü*, see Dudbridge, *Hsi-yu chi*, pp. 75–89; Cheng Chen-to, "Yen-hua," pp. 290ff, and "Hsi-yu chi tsa-chü," pp. 615f.; Hu Shih, "K'ao-cheng," pp. 372ff. The text is available in *Yang Tung-lai p'i-p'ing Hsi-yu chi*. For rediscovery and first reprint, see Dudbridge, *Hsi-yu chi*, pp. 76f. Several sources speak of a *yüan-pen* 院本 version of the story, here perhaps a loose designation for dramatic treatment rather than the specific *yüan-pen* form. See, for example, T'ao Tsung-i's *Ch'o-keng lu*, *chüan* 25, p. 660 (also cited in Dudbridge, *Hsi-yu chi*, p. 44, n. 2). A line in Scene 6 of the *Hsi-yu chi tsa-chü* drama itself gives a similar term. On the problems of dating and authorship of the *tsa-chü*, see Sun K'ai-ti, "Wu Ch'ang-ling yü tsa-chü Hsi-yu chi"; Yen Tun-i, "Hsi-yu chi ho ku-tien hsi-ch'ü ti kuan-hsi"; Anthony Yu, *Journey*, pp. 12f.; Ogawa Tamaki, "Saiyūki genpon to sono kaisaku," pp. 84f.; Ōta Tatsuo, "Kaisetsu," p. 444; and Isobe Akira, "Saiyūki ni okeru Cho Hakkai zō no keisei," pp. 185f. Liu Ts'un-yan ("Wu Ch'eng-en," pp. 72ff.) argues against the idea of the *tsa-chü* as a direct source for the novel. On the reflections of the *Hsi-yu chi* narrative in the Ming play *Mu-lien chiu-mu ch'üan-shan hsi-wen* (reprinted in *Ku-pen hsi-ch'ü ts'ung-k'an*, 1st ser., vols. 80–82), see Ōta Tatsuo, "A New Study on the Formation of the *Hsi-yu chi*," pp. 101ff. (published in Japanese as "Saiyūki seiritsu shiryaku"), and his earlier "Saiyūki seiritsushi no shomondai"; and Dudbridge, *Hsi-yu chi*, pp. 33, 165. For references to other dramatic works on *Hsi-yu* themes, see Chao Ts'ung, *Ssu ta hsiao-shuo*, pp. 150f.; and Cheng Chen-to, "Yen-hua," p. 293. See also Isobe Akira, "Hsi-yu chi ti chieh-na yü liu-ch'uan."

5. For the popular religious narratives covering some of the same basic material, see *Hsiao-shih chen-k'ung pao-chüan*, discussed by Hu Shih in "Pa Hsiao-shih chen-k'ung pao-chüan," and Dudbridge in *Hsi-yu chi*, pp. 94ff.; and the *Hsüan-tsang San-tsang tu-t'ien yu-lai yüan-ch'i*, discussed by Dudbridge in *Hsi-yu chi*, pp. 99f. See also Hu Shih, "K'ao-cheng," p. 386, for possible sources

of the narrative in Buddhist scripture, especially the Lotus Sutra; and Isobe Akira, "Genpon Saiyūki ni okeru Son Gyōja no keisei," pp. 106ff., for possible scriptural sources of the Sun Wu-k'ung figure.

6. As for popular storytelling on *Hsi-yu* themes, evidence of the popularity of the Hsüan-tsang story cycle is found in references as early as the Sung in such texts as the *Tsui-weng t'an-lu*, the *Yu-huan chi-wen* 洫宦紀聞 by Chang Shih-nan 張世南 (see Ōta Tatsuo, "New Study," pp. 96f., etc.). See Dudbridge, *Hsi-yu chi*, p. 104; and Chao Ts'ung, *Ssu ta hsiao-shuo*, pp. 144f. In the sixteenth century, a "journey to the west" is specified as the subject of a storytelling session depicted in chapter 15 of *Chin P'ing Mei* (see Ōta Tatsuo, "Kaisetsu," p. 444). This popularity continues down to the present day, as demonstrated in the printed adaptation in Lo Yang and Shen P'eng-nien, eds., *Shuo-ch'ang Hsi-yu chi*. Cf. a sixteenth-century reference to a *tao-ch'ing* 道情 performance entitled *Hsi-yu chi* found in Li Hsü, *Chieh-an lao-jen man-pi, chüan* 5, p. 173; and an allusion to Chu Pa-chieh in the Yuan Taoist text *Chin-tan ta-yao* (*Tao-tsang ching-hua* edition, *chüan* 2, p. 25a).

II. In preparing this study, I have used the following editions.

1. Shih-te t'ang edition 世德堂

Hsin-k'e ch'u-hsiang kuan-pan ta-tzu Hsi-yu chi 新刻出像官板大字西遊記, compiled by Hua-yang tung-t'ien chu-jen 華陽洞天主人, preface by Ch'en Yüan-chih 陳元之; 20 *chüan*, 100 *hui*; full-page illustrations. Available in microfilm series of National Peiping Library rare book collection (Library of Congress), no. 971–72. For further descriptions of the Shih-te t'ang text, see Tu Te-ch'iao (Glen Dudbridge), "Hsi-yu chi tsu-pen k'ao ti tsai-shang-ch'üeh," pp. 500, 513; and Dudbridge, *Hsi-yu chi*, p. 174; Liu Ts'un-yan, "Ssu-yu chi ti Ming k'e-pen," p. 363; Cheng Chen-to, "Yen-hua," p. 268; Ōta Tatsuo, "Kaisetsu," p. 438. For the identification of Hua-yang tung-t'ien chu-jen as Li Ch'un-fang, see above, Chapter 3, n. 22. See also Ōta Tatsuo, "Saiyūki zakkō," pp. 10ff., for the same theory. For further information on the Shih-te t'ang printings, see K. T. Wu, "Ming Printing and Printers," p. 239; Liu Ts'un-yan, *Chinese Popular Fiction in Two London Libraries*, p. 39; and Nagasawa Kikuya, "Mindai gikyoku kankōsha hyō shokō." Patrick Hanan notes a Shih-te t'ang printing of *P'ing-yao chuan* in his "The Composition of the *P'ing-yao chuan*," pp. 202f.

For further information, see also Huang Su-ch'iu, "Hsi-yu Chi ti chiao-ting ho chu-shih kung-tso," p. 180; Dudbridge, "The Hundred-Chapter *Hsi-yu chi* and Its Early Versions"; and Torii Hisayasu, "Shinkoku shutsuzō kanpan daiji Saiyūki oboegaki". Additional information in Sun K'ai-ti, *Chung-kuo t'ung-su hsiao-shuo shu-mu*, p. 189; and Wang Chung-min, *Chung-kuo shan-pen shu t'i-yao*, p. 402.

—*Ting-chüan ching-pen ch'üan-hsiang Hsi-yu chi-chuan* 鼎鐫京本全相西遊記傳, compiled by Hua-yang tung-t'ien chu-jen, preface by Ch'en Yüan-chih; 20 *chüan*, 100 *hui*; Fukien-style printing (*Min-pen*) by Yang Min-chai 楊閩齋. Available in University of Michigan microfilm series (G-68, reel 21), Rare Chinese Novels in Japanese Collections (*Jih-pen so ts'ang Chung-kuo hsiao-shuo han-chien pen ch'ao-pen* 日本所藏中國小說罕見本抄本), prepared by James Crump (Tokyo, 1955), 24 reels (letter G in reel numbers apparently refers to Guggenheim Foundation, which supported the project). For complete list, see Raymond Tang and Wei-yi Ma, *A Checklist of Chinese Materials on Microfilm in the Asian Library* (Ann Arbor: University of Michigan, 1968), pp. 58f. See Sun K'ai-ti, *Shu-mu*, p. 189, and *Jih-pen Tung-ching so chien Chung-kuo hsiao-shuo shu-mu*, p. 72f. On the significance of the term *ching-pen*, see Tai Pu-fan, *Hsiao-shuo chien-wen lu*, pp. 101f.

—*Hsin-k'e ch'üan-hsiang T'ang-seng Hsi-yu chi-chuan* 新刻全像唐僧西遊記傳 (*Ting hsin-ch'ieh San-tsang Hsi-yu ch'üan-chuan* 鼎新鍥三藏西遊全傳). Attributed to Yang Chih-ho 楊致和 [sic] (see b.n.II.3 for more verifiable Yang Chih-ho edition). Printed by Che-kuei t'ang 折桂堂. In Biblioteca Apostolica Vaticana, Rome, Borgia collection.

2. Chu Ting-ch'en edition 朱鼎臣

Ting-ch'ieh ch'üan-hsiang T'ang San-tsang Hsi-yu chuan 鼎鍥全像唐三藏西遊傳 (alternate title *Hsin-ch'ieh ch'üan-hsiang T'ang San-tsang Hsi-yu shih-ni [o] chuan* 新鍥全像唐三藏西遊釋尼傳); 10 *chüan*, 67 (68) sections, unnumbered and irregularly distributed; Wan-li period, Fukien-style printing. Available in National Peiping Library microfilm series, no. 971 (*chüan* 6–10 only). For description, see Sun K'ai-ti, *Shu-mu*, p. 190, and *Jih-pen*, pp. 81f.; Dudbridge, "Early Versions," pp. 157f., Wang Chung-min, *Shan-pen*; N. Koss, "The Xiyouji in Its Formative Stages," pp. 1f.; Cheng Ming-li, "Lun Hsi-yu chi san pan-pen chien chih kuan-hsi;" and Liu Ts'un-yan, "Ssu-yu chi," pp. 354ff.

3. Yang Chih-ho edition 楊致和

Hsi-yu T'ang San-tsang ch'u-shen chuan 西遊唐三藏出身傳 (alternate title *Hsin-ch'ieh San-tsang ch'u-shen ch'üan-chuan* 新鍥三藏出身全傳); 4 *chüan*, 41 *hui*. Possible Ming edition in Bodleian Library, Oxford; see Dudbridge, "Early Versions," pp. 155f.; and Isobe Akira, "'Hsi-yu chi ti chieh-na yü liu-ch'uan," p. 165; Ch'ing edition included with three other novels in *Ssu-yu chi*, pp. 100–169. See Liu Ts'un-yan, "Ssu-yu chi," and *Two London Libraries*, pp. 138–44; Hu Shih, "Pa Ssu-yu chi pen ti Hsi-yu chi-chuan" (see Chapter 3, n. 4, of this book); Koss, "Formative Stages," p. 2.

4. "Li Cho-wu" commentary edition

Li Cho-wu hsien-sheng p'i-p'ing Hsi-yu chi 李卓吾先生批評西遊記, no *chüan* division, 100 *hui*. Preface by Man-t'ing kuo-k'e 幔亭過客 (Yüan Yü-ling 袁于令, 1599–1674). Includes *fan-li* introduction, headnotes, chapter-

commentaries, and fine illustrations. Located in Naikaku Bunko, Tokyo, available in Michigan microfilm series, G-67a–67b, reel 19. For descriptions, see Sun K'ai-ti, *Shu-mu*, p. 189, and *Jih-pen*, pp. 76ff. Liu Ts'un-yan ("Ssu-yu chi," p. 369) affirms the authenticity of the preface. Cheng Chen-to ("Yen-hua," pp. 268) dates this in the T'ien-ch'i or Ch'ung-chen period. See Appendix of this book for a discussion of the problem of the attribution of the three *Li Cho-wu hsien-sheng p'i-p'ing* commentary editions of the Ming masterworks.
—Same as above, but located in Bibliothèque nationale, Paris.
—Same as above, but located in Biblioteca Apostolica Vaticana, Rome, Borgia collection.

5. Wang Hsiang-hsü commentary edition (*Hsi-yu cheng-tao shu* 西遊證道書)

Chüan-hsiang ku-pen Hsi-yu cheng-tao shu 鐫像古本西遊證道書 (alternate title *Hsin-chüan ch'u-hsiang ku-pen Hsi-yu cheng-tao shu* 新鐫出像古本西遊證道書); no *chüan* division, 100 *hui*. Wang Hsiang-hsü 汪象旭 (Tan-i tzu 憺漪子) and Huang T'ai-hung 黃太鴻 (Hsiao-ts'ang tzu 笑蒼子). Isobe Akira ("Son Gyōja," p. 71) identifies Huang as Huang Chou-hsing 黃周星 (*chin-shih* Ch'ung-chen 13, 1640). See Liu Ts'un-yan, "Ch'üan-chen chiao ho hsiao-shuo Hsi-yu chi," pt. 1, p. 58. See also Ōta Tatsuo, "Saiyū shōdōsho kō," p. 8. For biographical information on Wang and Huang, see *Ssu-k'u ch'üan-shu tsung-mu t'i-yao, chüan* 105, pp. 51f., which lists two books on obstetrics by someone named Wang Ch'i 汪淇 (Chan-i 瞻漪), and *Kuo-ch'ao ch'i hsien lei cheng ch'u-pien* 國朝耆獻類徵初編 (rpt. Taipei: Shang-wu, 1966), *chüan* 473, and *Huang-Ming i-min chuan* 皇明遺民傳 (rpt. Peking: Peking University, 1936), *chüan* 2. "Original Preface" (*yüan-hsü* 原序) attributed to Yü Chi. Additional front matter: "Biography of Ch'ang-ch'un chen-jen" 丘長春眞君傳, and "Factual Evidence on Hsüan-tsang's Quest for Scriptures" 玄奘取經事蹟. Interlinear comments and chapter commentaries. Edition dated K'ang-hsi 8 (1662); in Naikaku Bunko, microfilm in Gest Oriental Library, Princeton, New Jersey. For fullest description and study, see Ōta Tatsuo, "Shōdōshokō," plus Sun K'ai-ti, *Shu-mu*, p. 190. Textual commentary draws on "Li Cho-wu" edition (see explicit reference to "Li Cho-wu" commentary in comment in chapter 22).
—*Tseng-p'ing Hsi-yu cheng-tao ch'i-shu* 增評西遊證道奇書 (alternate title *Hsi-yu chi ta ch'i shu*), Ts'ai Yüan-fang 蔡元放 (Yeh-yün chu-jen 野雲主人), ed. (1736–70). Preface dated Ch'ien-lung 15 (1750). Printed by Huai-te t'ang 懷德堂. Microfilm of *tu-fa* in Gest Oriental Library, courtesy of Bibliothèque nationale, Paris.

6. Chang Shu-shen commentary edition (*Hsin-shuo Hsi-yu chi* 新說西遊記)

Hsin-shuo Hsi-yu chi, Chang Shu-shen 張書紳 (Nan-hsün 南薰). Preface dated Ch'ien-lung 14 (1749); no *chüan* division, 100 *hui*. Additional front matter: "Scriptural Topic-headings" 經書題目, "General Discussion" 總論, "General Commentary" 總批, "General Conclusion" 總結 (appended to chapter 100). Interlinear comments and pre- and post-chapter commentaries. Copy in Tokyo

University, Department of Chinese, Chinese Books Corner (*Kanseki kōnā* 漢籍 コーナァ); microfilm in Gest Oriental Library, courtesy of Professor Itō Sōhei. Additional copies in Peking Library, Metropolitan Library, Peking University Library, British Library. For further description, see Sun K'ai-ti, *Shu-mu*, p. 191; Ōta Tatsuo, "Kaisetsu," p. 440; Liu Ts'un-yan, "Wu Ch'eng-en," p. 67; Chao Ts'ung, *Ssu ta hsiao-shuo*, pp. 170f. Recently reprinted in China.

7. Ch'en Shih-pin commentary edition (*Hsi-yu chen-ch'üan* 西遊眞詮)

Late Ch'ing reprint *Hui-t'u chia-p'i Hsi-yu chi* 繪圖加批西遊記. T'ien-pao shu-chü 天寶書局, n.d. Preface to original edition by Yu T'ung 尤侗, dated K'ang-hsi 35 (1696); 12 *chüan*, 100 *hui*, irregularly distributed. Ōta Tatsuo ("Kaisetsu," p. 440) dates the original edition 1694, according to another preface by the editor in a copy available to him. Headnotes and chapter commentaries. See Sun K'ai-ti (*Shu-mu*, p. 191), who dates the edition he has seen Ch'ien-lung 45 (1749). For further discussion of this commentary, see Ts'ai Kuo-liang, "Ch'en Shih-pin tui Hsi-yu chi jen-wu ho ch'ing-chieh chieh-kou ti p'i-p'ing."
—Typeset reprint published in *Kuo-hsüeh chi-pen ts'ung-shu*, vol. 256. Yu T'ung preface and extensive chapter commentaries. Commentary often follows, but far exceeds, that of Wang Hsiang-hsü, Chang Shu-shen, and "Li Cho-wu" editions.

8. Liu I-ming commentary edition (*Hsi-yu yüan-chih* 西遊原旨)

Ch'ung-k'e Hsi-yu yüan-chih 重刻. Edited by Liu I-ming 劉一明 (Wu-yüan tzu 悟元子). Microfilm in Gest Oriental Library, Princeton, Courtesy of University of Chicago. Additional copies held in Harvard-Yenching Library. Preface by editor, dated Ch'ien-lung 43 (1778); other prefaces dated Chia-ch'ing 3 (1798) and 6 (1801). Ōta Tatsuo ("Kaisetsu," p. 440) dates this edition 1810. Sun K'ai-ti (*Shu-mu*, p. 192) dates his copy Chia-ch'ing 24 (1819). Additional front matter includes *Hsi-yu yüan-chih tu-fa* 西遊原旨讀法. *Tu-fa* reprinted in *Ching-yin tao-shu shih-erh chung* 精印道書十二種 (Taipei: Hsin wen feng, 1975), vol. 1 (5). Translation of *tu-fa* by Anthony Yu, included in David Rolston, ed., *How to Read the Chinese Novel*.

9. *T'ung-i Hsi-yu cheng-chih* 通易西遊正旨

Chang Han-chang 張含章 (Feng-yüan 逢源) ed. Dated by Sun K'ai-ti (*Shu-mu*, p. 192) Tao-kuang 19 (1839); 10 *chüan*, 100 *hui*; interlinear comments and chapter-commentaries. Microfilm in Gest Oriental Library, courtesy of Peking University Library; first *han* missing.

10. *Hsi-yu chi shih-i* 西遊記釋義

Lung-men hsin-chuan 龍門心傳, 100 *hui*. Ch'en Tun-fu 陳敦甫. Preface and introductory essays, plus chapter-commentaries.

An additional commentary edition, *Hsi-yu chi p'ing-chu* 西遊記評註, by Han-ching tzu 含晶子 has been unavailable to me. See description in Liu Yin-po, "Hsi-yu chi Ming-Ch'ing liang-tai ch'u-pan shih k'ao," p. 78; and Dudbridge, "Early Versions," p. 154. Ōta Tatsuo ("Kaisetsu," p. 440) dates it 1891. A copy is listed in Cheng Chen-to's *Hsi-t'i shu-mu* 西諦書目. For more detailed information on the above editions and editors, see Sun K'ai-ti, *Shu-mu*, pp. 188–92, and *Jih-pen*, pp. 72–84; Dudbridge, "Early Versions," pp. 141–91; Cheng Chen-to, "Yen-hua," pp. 268f.; Chao Ts'ung, *Ssu ta hsiao-shuo*, pp. 161–72; Kuo Chen-i, *Chung-kuo hsiao-shuo shih*, pp. 292f.; Ogawa Tamaki, "Saiyūki genpon," pp. 86ff.; Ōta Tatsuo, "Kaisetsu," pp. 435–41, "New Study," pp. 106ff., and "Shin kanpon Saiyūki kō"; Anthony Yu, *Journey*, pp. 14f.; Saitō Akio and Itō Keiichi, "Saiyūki no kenkyū to shiryō," pp. 210ff.; Liu Ts'un-yan, "Ssu-yu chi," pp. 369ff.

III. The "Yü Chi" preface does not appear in copies of *Tao-yüan hsüeh-ku lu* held in Gest Oriental Library, in Princeton, the East Asian Library at Columbia University, or the Harvard-Yenching Library. Nor is it mentioned in Lu Chün-ling's *Yuan-jen wen-chi p'ien-mu fen-lei so-yin* (and the compiler of this index appears to rely on the *Ssu-pu ts'ung-k'an* reprint for this text). Ōta Tatsuo ("Shōdōsho," p. 4) also reports his unsuccessful attempts to locate this preface. The *Ssu-k'u ch'üan-shu tsung-mu t'i-yao* (*chüan* 267, pp. 23a–24b) notes the incomplete state of most later editions. Modern reprints are available in *Ssu-pu pei-yao* (D-71, 72), *Ssu-pu ts'ung-k'an ch'u-pien* (vol. 134), *Ssu-pu ts'ung-k'an ch'u-pien so-pen* (vol. 76), and more. An edition that appears to be the closest extant text to the original 50-*chüan* Yuan edition with the date Chih-cheng 5 (1345) is listed by Sun K'e-k'uan as held in the National Peiping Library rare book collection, but it too is apparently incomplete (anyway, I have been unable to find it in printed catalogues of that collection). See Sun's discussion of the bibliographical complexities surrounding the *Tao-yüan hsüeh-ku lu* in his *Yuan-tai Han wen-hua chih huo-tung*, pp. 471–80. Sun also cites entries in the *Pei-p'ing t'u-shu-kuan shan-pen shu-mu* 北平圖書館善本書目, *chüan* 4, indicating an incomplete Yuan printing of another collection entitled *Tao-yüan lei-kao* 道園類稿. The piece is also not found in the equally rare supplementary collection entitled *Tao-yüan i-kao* 道園遺稿, in 6 *chüan*, which contains only Yü's poetry. Copies of this *Tao-yüan i-kao* available on microfilm in the Gest Oriental Library, National Peiping Library rare book collection (Library of Congress), reel 443; and in *Ssu-k'u ch'üan-shu chen-pen, wu-chi* 五集 (Taipei: Shang-wu, 1974), vol. 292. See also Sun's bibliographical note reprinted in "T'ai-wan hsien-ts'un Yuan-jen pieh-chi hsiao-lu," Appendix 4; and in *T'u-shu-kuan hsüeh-pao* 圖書館學報 5 (August 1963): 9–17. In his *Nihon genson Gen-jin bunshū mokuroku* 日本現存元人文集目録 (Tokyo: Kyūko, 1970), Yamane Yukio 山根幸夫 lists a Ch'ing edition of *Hsüeh-ku lu* in 60 *chüan* [sic] and a "Yuan edition" of *Tao-yüan i-kao* in 6 *chüan*, both in the Seikadō collection (pp. 9ff.). Another bibliographical entry cited by Sun (*Yuan-tai*, p. 472) lists a *Tao-yüan i-kao* in 16 *chüan* (perhaps a scribal error?). See also John D. Langlois, Jr., "Yü Chi and his Mongol Sovereign," *Journal of Asian Studies* 38, no. 1 (November 1978): 99–116, esp. 99, n. 1.

The life and writings of Yü Chi are well documented, even though this has not helped to solve the mystery. See, for example, Sun K'e-k'uan's "Yuan Yü Chi yü nan-fang tao-chiao" 元虞集與南方道教, in *Ta-lu tsa-chih* 大陸雜誌 53, no. 6 (December 15, 1976): 1–12; and his expanded English version, "Yü Chi and Southern Taoism during the Yuan Period," in John D. Langlois, Jr., ed., *China under Mongol Rule* (Princeton: Princeton University Press, 1981), pp. 212–53. See also Langlois's "Yü Chi and his Mongol Sovereign," p. 100, n. 7. Yü Chi's official biography appears in the *Yuan shih* 元史, *chüan* 181 (Peking: Chung-hua, 1976), pp. 4174–82. I have been unable to obtain a copy of Yü Chi's *nien-p'u* compiled by Weng Fang-kang 翁方綱 (see Yamane Yukio, *Bunshū mokuroku*, p. 10, for description of a copy in Kyoto). A monograph on Yü Chi by Magnus Kriegeskorte of the University of Bonn was reported in progress in the *Bulletin of Sung-Yuan Studies*, no. 16 (1981): 110. I would like to acknowledge the assistance of Professors Frederick W. Mote of Princeton and Hok-lam Chan of the University of Washington, and Ma Tai-loi of the University of Chicago for assistance in this search. For a helpful but inconclusive treatment of the question of the Yü Chi preface, see Isobe Akira ("Genpon Saiyūki," pp. 60–75), who points out certain discrepancies in dates and official titles given in the piece.

Shui-hu chuan

I. For further information on the sources of the novel, see the following selected studies cited in notes.

1. On the historical sources relating to the principal *Shui-hu* figures, see Yü Chia-hsi, *Shui-hu chuan san-shih-liu jen k'ao-shih*; Wang Li-ch'i, "Shui-hu ti chen-jen chen-shih"; Nieh Kan-nu, "Shui-hu wu-lun," pp. 10f., 41f.; Mineji Utarō, "Suikoden no kenkyū to shiryō"; Hua Shan, "Shui-hu chuan ho Sung-shih." Many of the relevant sources are collected in Ma T'i-chi, *Shui-hu tzu-liao hui-pien*, pp. 444–57; and Chu I-hsüan and Liu Yü-ch'en, *Shui-hu chuan tzu-liao hui-pien*, pp. 10–19, 32–37.

2. On the treatment of *Shui-hu* materials in popular storytelling, see Nieh Kan-nu, "Wu-lun," pp. 10–22, 35–44; Irwin, *The Evolution of a Chinese Novel*, pp. 23–32; etc. The existence of northern and southern regional variants in the *Shui-hu* cycles are discussed by Lü Nai-yen in "Shui-hu ku-shih tsai nan-pei liang-ti liu-ch'uan ti ch'ing-k'uang"; Tai Pu-fan, *Chien-wen lu*, pp. 94f.; Wang Li-ch'i, "Shui-hu chung so ts'ai-yung ti hua-pen tzu-liao," pp. 312f.; and Sun Shu-yü, *Shui-hu chuan ti lai-li, hsin-t'ai, yü i-shu*, pp. 192ff. Cf. the explicit reference to the *shu-hui* 書會 story-tellers' guilds in a passage in chapter 114 of the novel (*Shui-hu ch'üan-chuan*, p. 1710). See Liu Ts'un-yan, "Sur l'authenticité des romans historiques de Lo Guanzhong," p. 284. This article appeared in Chinese in *Hsiang-kang Chung-wen ta-hsüeh Chung-kuo wen-hua yen-chiu-so hsüeh-pao* 8, no. 1 (1975), and has been reprinted in *Ho-feng t'ang tu-shu chi*, pp. 235–300. Patrick Hanan discusses the relationship between *Shui-hu chuan* and the oral tradition in *The Chinese Short Story*, pp. 203f., and notes the

appearance of certain stock figures from this tradition in "*P'ing-yao chuan,*" pp. 215f. For a general discussion of *Hsüan-ho i-shih*, see Hu Shih-ying, *Hua-pen hsiao-shuo kai-lun*, pp. 714—19. See also Chou Shao-liang, "Hsiu-keng shan-fang tzu Hsüan-ho i-shih pa"; and Kao Ming-ko, "Shui-hu chuan yü Hsüan-ho i-shih." The *Shui-hu* section of *Hsüan-ho i-shih* is found in 1955 Shanghai reprint, pp. 34—46, and is reproduced in Chu I-hsüan, *Tzu-liao*, pp. 42ff.

3. The theory of an antecedent of *Shui-hu* narrative material in the *tz'u-hua* form was advanced by Sun K'ai-ti in "Shui-hu chuan chiu-pen k'ao." See also Yeh Te-chün, *Sung-Yuan-Ming chiang-ch'ang wen-hsüeh*, pp. 48ff.; Richard Irwin, *Evolution*, pp. 38—43; and Andrew Hing-bun Lo, "*San-kuo chih yen-i* and *Shui-hu chuan* in the Context of Historiography," p. 118, etc. The basis for this speculation is a line in a preface by Hsü Wei originally noticed by Yeh Te-chün (see Chao Ching-shen, "Shui-hu chuan chien-lun," in *Shui-hu jen-wu yü Shui-hu chuan*, p. 138). The passage is printed in Ma T'i-chi, *Tzu-liao*, p. 352. Some scholars have suggested another possible trace of a mid-Ming *Shui-hu tz'u-hua* in a line by Yang Shen (see Chapter 4, n. 6). An even earlier piece of evidence indicating the prior development of the *Shui-hu* cycles is the "encomium" by Kung K'ai 龔開 (Sheng-yü 聖與) written on a series of portraits of the Liang-shan heroes, included in Chou Mi, *Kuei-hsin tsa-chih hsü-chi*. The text is available in Ma T'i-chi, *Tzu-liao*, pp. 452ff., Chu I-hsüan, *Tzu-liao*, pp. 21ff.; and K'ung Ling-ching, *Chung-kuo hsiao-shuo shih-liao*, pp. 11—14. A thorough annotation of this text is provided by Chang Kuo-kuang in *Shui-hu yü Chin Sheng-t'an yen-chiu*, pp. 44—55. Cf. a line in this passage interpreted by Hu Shih as a reference to another early text, but later shown to refer only to pictorial representations. See Cheng Chen-to, "Yen-hua," p. 103; and Chao Ching-shen, "Shui-hu chuan tsa-chih," p. 37.

4. For reviews of dramatic treatments of *Shui-hu* materials, see Cheng Chen-to, "Yen-hua," pp. 105—10; Sun K'ai-ti, "Chiu-pen k'ao," pp. 199f.; Chao Ching-shen, "Tsa-chih," pp. 38ff.; Hu Shih, "K'ao-cheng," pp. 16—30; Nieh Kan-nu, "Wu-lun," pp. 27—33; Wen Ying, "Shui-hu chuan liu-pien ssu-chang," pp. 209ff.; Tai Pu-fan, *Chien-wen lu*, p. 93; and Hsieh Pi-hsia, *Shui-hu hsi-ch'ü erh-shih chung yen-chiu*; etc. Most of these materials are collected in Fu Hsi-hua, *Shui-hu hsi-ch'ü chi*. Synopses of some of the extant plays are provided by Sun Shu-yü in *Lai-li, hsin-t'ai, i-shu*, pp. 370—72. For later treatments of *Shui-hu* themes in oral storytelling and popular drama subsequent to the appearance of the novel, see Cheng Chen-to, "Yen-hua," pp. 109—64; Liu Ching-chih, "Yuan-tai chih hou ti Shui-hu hsi," pp. 275ff; and Yang Shao-hsüan, "Lun Shui-hu chuan yü Shui-hu hsi," pp. 354ff. Cf. the Ch'ing dramatic work *Chung-i hsüan-t'u* 忠義璇圖, which covers much of the plot of the novel. See Tai Pu-fan, *Chien-wen lu*, p. 92; and Chuang I-fu, ed., *Ku-tien hsi-ch'ü ts'un-mu hui-k'ao*, p. 1304. For convenient synopses of *Shui-hu* plays in Peking Opera—style, *su-ch'ü*, and other performing art forms, see Chu I-hsüan, *Tzu-liao*, pp. 645—64, 665—80, 681—91.

II. I have read or examined the following *fan-pen* editions in the course of this study.

1. T'ien-tu wai-ch'en preface edition

   Chung-i shui-hu chuan 忠義水滸傳. K'ang-hsi reprint by Shih-ch'ü ko 石渠閣; preface by T'ien-tu wai-ch'en 天都外臣 (for possible identification, see above, Chapter 4, n. 28), tentatively dated 1589 (see n. 26); 20 *chüan*, 100 *hui*. Original copy held in Peking Library; microfilm in Gest Oriental Library, Princeton, obtained by courtesy of Peking Library and University of Chicago Library. Reprint of novel based on this text available in *Shui-hu ch'üan-chuan*, chapters 1–90 and 111–20.

2. Jung-yü t'ang "Li Cho-wu" commentary edition

   Chung-i shui-hu chuan 忠義水滸傳, "Li Cho-wu" 李卓吾 commentary edition, published by Jung-yü t'ang 容與堂 in 1610; prefatory essays attributed to Li Chih and Huai-lin 懷林; 100 *chüan*, 100 *hui*. Original in Naikaku Bunko, Tokyo; microfilm in University of Michigan series (see *Hsi-yu chi*, b.n. II.1) prepared by James Crump (reel G-59a and b) in Gest Oriental Library, Princeton. (Hereafter referred to as Jung-yü t'ang edition.) Additional copies in Peking Library, Peking University Library, and Chinese Academy of Social Sciences, Institute of Literature. Reprint. Shanghai: Chung-hua, 1966.

3. Yüan Wu-yai "Li Cho-wu" commentary edition

   Chung-i shui-hu ch'üan-chuan 忠義水滸全傳, "Li Cho-wu" commentary edition, published by Yüan Wu-yai 袁無涯 in 1614; preface by Yang Ting-chien 楊定見; 120 *hui*. Original in Academia Sinica, Taipei; microfilm in Gest Oriental Library, Princeton, courtesy of Harvard-Yenching Library. (Hereafter referred to as Yüan Wu-yai edition.) Additional copies in Peking Library, Peking University Library, Peking Metropolitan Library, Seikadō and Sonkeikaku libraries in Tokyo, Bibliothèque nationale in Paris, and Institut vostokovedenija in Leningrad.

4. "Chung Hsing" commentary edition

   Chung-i shui-hu chuan 忠義水滸傳, "Chung Po-ching" 鍾伯敬 commentary edition, published by Ssu-chih kuan 四知館; 100 *chüan*, 100 *hui*. Original in Bibliothèque nationale, Paris; microfilm in Gest Oriental Library, Princeton. (Hereafter referred to as Chung Hsing edition.)

5. "Chieh-tzu yüan" commentary edition

   Chung-i shui-hu chuan 忠義水滸傳, "Li Cho-wu" commentary edition, published by Chieh-tzu yüan 芥子園; 100 *hui*. Originally held in Nihon Teikoku

Library, Tokyo; microfilm in Michigan series (G-59b), incomplete copy includes table of contents and chapters 71–76, 97–100. (Hereafter referred to as "Chieh-tzu yüan" edition.) Additional copy in Peking University Library (chapters 61–72, 77–100). Complete reprint available in *Ming-Ch'ing shan-pen hsiao-shuo ts'ung-k'an* 明清善本小說叢刊, Taipei.

6. Chin Sheng-t'an commentary edition

Ti-wu ts'ai-tzu shu Shih Nai-an Shui-hu chuan 第五才子書施耐庵水滸傳, "Kuan-hua t'ang" 貫華堂 edition, Chin Sheng-t'an 金聖歎 commentary edition, 75 *chüan*. Reprint (8 vols.). Peking: Chung-hua, 1975. Original copies and various Ch'ing reprints available in many libraries.

7. Wang Wang-ju commentary edition

P'ing-lun ch'u-hsiang Shui-hu chuan 評論出像水滸傳, Chin Sheng-t'an commentary edition, plus additional comments by Wang Wang-ju 王望如, printed by Tsui-keng t'ang 醉耕堂, preface by T'ung-an lao-jen 桐庵老人, dated 1657; 75 *chüan*. Original in Peking Library; microfilm in Gest Oriental Library, Princeton, courtesy of University of Chicago Library.

III. In preparing this study, I have read or examined the following *chien-pen* editions.

1. *Hsin-k'an ching-pen ch'üan-hsiang ch'a-tseng T'ien Hu Wang Ch'ing Chung-i shui-hu chuan* 新刊京本全像插增田虎王慶忠義水滸傳, in Bibliothèque nationale, Paris; incomplete copy includes *chüan* 20 and half of 21 out of 24 *chüan*, 120 *hui* (hereafter *Ch'a-tseng pen*). I have also seen a related fragmentary edition entitled *Hsin-k'an ch'üan-hsiang tseng Huai-hsi Wang Ch'ing ch'u-shen Shui-hu chuan* 新刊全像增淮西王慶出身水滸傳, *chüan* 21–25, held in the Vatican Library.

2. *Ching-pen tseng-pu chiao-cheng ch'üan-hsiang Chung-i shui-hu chih-chuan p'ing-lin* 京本增補校正全像忠義水滸志傳評林, 18 *chüan* fragment (*chüan* 8–25). Published by Shuang-feng t'ang 雙峯堂 in 1594; original in Naikaku Bunko, Tokyo; microfilm in Michigan series (G-61), in Gest Oriental Library, Princeton. (Hereafter referred to as *P'ing-lin*.) Additional copies held in Vatican Library, and Peking Metropolitan Library. A facsimile reprint of this edition was reportedly published in the 1950s.

3. *Shui-hu chuan*, in *Ming-kung p'i-tien ho-k'e San-kuo Shui-hu ch'üan-chuan: Erh-k'e ying-hsing p'u* 名公批點合刻三國水滸全傳, 二刻英雄譜, printed by Hsiung-fei kuan 雄飛館; preface by Hsiung Fei-ch'ih 熊飛赤, 21 *chüan*, 110 *hui*.

Original in Naikaku Bunko, Tokyo; microfilm in Michigan Series (G-47), in Gest Oriental Library, Princeton. (Hereafter referred to as *Ying-hsiung p'u*.) Additional copies held in Sonkeikaku Library, Tokyo, and School of Oriental and African Studies, London.

4. *Chung-i shui-hu chuan* 忠義水滸傳, in *Hsiu-hsiang Han Sung ch'i-shu* 繡像漢宋奇書; 115 *hui*. Copies in British Museum, London (Ta-yu t'ang 大酉堂 ed.), Bibliothèque nationale, Paris (Yün-hsiang t'ang 芸香堂 ed.), and Tōyō bunka kenkyūjo, Tokyo University (Hui-hsien t'ang 會賢堂 ed.).

5. *Wen-hsing t'ang p'ing-tien Shui-hu chuan* 文杏堂評點水滸傳. Pao-han lou edition 寶瀚樓 (or 翰); preface by Wu-hu lao-jen 五湖老人. 30 *chüan*, 100 *hui*. Copy in Bibliothèque nationale, Paris.

I have been unable to see any of the copies of the 124-chapter *Shui-hu ch'üan-chuan* described by Sun K'ai-ti, *Shu-mu*, p. 215; and Ōuchida Saburō, "Suikoden hanponkō," no. 3, pp. 1–10; Nieh Kan-nu, "Wu-lun," p. 156; etc. Cf. an edition entitled *Hsin-k'e ch'üan-hsiang Chung-i shui-hu chih-chuan* 新刻全像忠義水滸志傳, in 150 *hui*, listed in catalogue of Mori Ōgai collection, Kyoto University Library. Other less well-known *chien-pen* texts include the "Liu Hsing-wo" 劉興我 fragment held in the Tōyō bunka kenkyūjo at Tokyo University, described by Nieh Kan-nu in "Wu-lun," p. 167; a fragment recently uncovered in the Bodleian Library at Oxford (originally acquired in the East Indies and held in Leiden), described by Y. W. Ma (Ma Yau-woon) in "Niu-chin ta-hsüeh so-ts'ang Ming-tai chien-pen Shui-hu ts'an-yeh shu-hou"; and other fragmentary and rare copies in various European libraries, introduced by Y. W. Ma in "Ying-yin liang-chung Ming-tai hsiao-shuo chen-pen hsü." (See also his "Hu-yü yen-chiu chien-pen Shui-hu i-chien shu," pp. 186ff.) According to Cheng Chen-to ("Yen-hua," pp. 140ff.), Y. W. Ma ("P'ai tso-tz'u i-hou Shui-hu chuan ti ch'ing-chieh ho jen-wu an-p'ai," p. 85), Liu Ts'un-yan ("Sur l'authenticité," pp. 262ff.), Fan Ning ("Shui-hu chuan pan-pen yüan-liu k'ao," p. 73), and others, the earliest of the extant *chien-pen* texts may have been the *Ch'a-tseng pen*. Nieh Kan-nu ("Wu-lun," p. 155) takes the *P'ing-lin* edition as the earliest, although elsewhere (p. 34) he cites the 115-chapter edition as one of the earliest. On the date of this edition, see Ōuchida Saburō, "Hanponkō," no. 1, p. 61, and no. 2, p. 1. The term "capital edition" (*ching-pen* 京本) in the titles of these two editions is explained by Nieh Kan-nu ("Wu-lun," pp. 169, 196) and Tai Pu-fan (*Chien-wen lu*, p. 101). The complete *P'ing-lin* copy held in the Jigendō Library in Nikkō, Japan was reportedly reprinted in China by Wen-hsüeh ku-chi (see III:2). (See Shiroki Naoya, in "Eiin Suiko shiden hyōrin kanpon o te ni shite," pp. 239ff.). There are several variants of the *Ying-hsiung p'u* and *Han-Sung ch'i-shu* editions. See Andrew Lo, "Historiography," pp. 209ff., 269f.; and Nieh Kan-nu, "Wu-lun," pp. 155f. The table of contents of the *Ying-hsiung p'u* published by the Hsiung-fei kuan lists only 106 chapters, although the text in fact comprises 110 chapters.

San-kuo chih yen-i

I. I have used the following editions in preparing this study.

1. *San-kuo chih t'ung-su yen-i* 三國志通俗演義

    Facsimile reprint, 8 vols. (Peking: Jen-min wen-hsüeh, 1975); 24 *chüan*, 240 *tse*.
    Original held in Shanghai Library. Prefaces dated 1494 and 1522.

2. Mao Tsung-kang 毛宗崗 commentary edition (*Ti-i ts'ai-tzu shu* 第一才子書)

    Typeset reprint, 2 vols. (Hong Kong: Shang-wu, 1962 and 1978); 19 *chüan*,
    120 *hui*. Original copies held in various libraries. Another modern reprint
    under the title *Ch'üan-t'u hsiu-hsiang San-kuo yen-i* 全圖綉像三國演義 was
    published recently in China (Hu-ho-hao-t'e: Nei-meng-ku jen-min, 1981); 3
    vols.

3. "Li Cho-wu" 李卓吾 commentary edition

    Li Cho-wu hsien-sheng p'i-p'ing San-kuo chih yen-i 李卓吾先生批評三國志演義,
    contains prefatory piece dated 1687, 120 *hui*. Original in Bibliothèque na-
    tionale, Paris; microfilm in Gest Oriental Library, Princeton (see Sun K'ai-ti,
    Shu-mu, p. 42).

4. "Li Yü" 李漁 commentary edition

    Li Li-weng p'i-yüeh San-kuo chih 李笠翁批閱三國志; 24 *chüan*, 120 *hui*. Original
    in Bibliothèque nationale, Paris; microfilm in Gest Oriental Library, Princeton
    (see Sun K'ai-ti, *Shu-mu*, pp. 43–44).

5. *Chih-chuan* 志傳 edition

    Ch'ung-k'e ching-pen t'ung-su yen-i an-chien San-kuo chih-chuan 重刻京本通俗
    演義按鑑三國志傳, printed in 1610; 20 *chüan*, 240 *tse*. Original in Naikaku
    Bunko, Tokyo; microfilm in University of Michigan microfilm series (see
    Chapter 3, b.n. II.1), no. G-48; copy in Gest Oriental Library, Princeton (see
    Sun K'ai-ti, *Shu-mu*, p. 39). Additional copy in British Library, attributed to Yü
    Hsiang-wu 余象烏 [sic].

6. *Ch'üan-chuan* 全傳 edition

    Hsin-k'e ching-pen pu-i t'ung-su yen-i San-kuo ch'üan-chuan 新刻京本補遺通俗
    演義三國全傳, 1596 printing; 20 *chüan*. Original in Peking Library; microfilm
    in National Peiping Library Rare books series, no. P-593, and in Michigan

series, no. G-52 (incomplete); copies in Gest Oriental Library, Princeton (see Sun K'ai-ti, *Shu-mu*, p. 38).

7. *P'ing-lin* 評林 edition

Hsin-k'an ching-pen chiao-cheng yen-i ch'üan-hsiang San-kuo chih-chuan p'ing-lin 新刊京本校正演義全像三國志傳評林, Wan-li printing by Yü Hsiang-tou; 20 *chüan*. Original in Waseda University Library, Tokyo; microfilm in Michigan series, no. G-49; copy in Gest Oriental Library, Princeton (see Sun K'ai-ti, *Shu-mu*, p. 38).

8. *Lien-hui t'ang* 聯輝堂 edition

Hsin-chüan ching-pen chiao-cheng t'ung-su yen-i an-chien San-kuo chih-chuan 新鐫京本校正通俗演義按鑑三國志傳, *Ch'ih-ti yü-pien* 赤帝餘編; 1605 printing by Lien-hui t'ang; 20 *chüan*. Original in Naikaku Bunko; microfilm in Gest Oriental Library, Princeton (see Sun K'ai-ti, *Shu-mu*, p. 38).

9. *Ying-hsiung p'u* edition 英雄譜

Ming-kung p'i-tien ho-k'an San-kuo Shui-hu ch'üan-chuan 名公批點合刊三國水滸全傳, *Ying-hsiung p'u* 英雄譜; Ch'ung-chen printing by Hsiung-fei kuan 雄飛館; 20 *chüan*, 240 *hui*. Original in Naikaku Bunko, Tokyo; microfilm in Michigan series, no. G-47; copy in Gest Oriental Library, Princeton (see Sun K'ai-ti, *Shu-mu*, p. 41).

10. *Chou Yüeh-chiao* edition 周曰校本

Hsin-k'an chiao-cheng ku-pen ta-tzu yin-shih San-kuo chih t'ung-su yen-i 新刊校正古本大字音釋三國志通俗演義; 1591 printing by Chou Yüeh-chiao; 12 *chüan*, 240 *tse*. Original in Peking University Library; microfilm in National Peiping Library rare books series, no. P-110, and in Michigan series, no. G-50, 51; copies in Gest Oriental Library, Princeton (see Sun K'ai-ti, *Shu-mu*, p. 36). Additional copies in National Diet Library and Naikaku Bunko, Tokyo.

II. Additional editions not available to me referred to in this chapter include the "Chung Hsing" commentary edition entitled *Chung Po-ching hsien-sheng p'i-p'ing San-kuo chih* 鍾伯敬先生批評三國志, held in Tōyō bunka kenkyūjo, Tokyo (see Sun K'ai-ti, *Shu-mu*, p. 40; and Andrew Lo, "Historiography," p. 260), and a Chia-ching edition of *San-kuo chih-chuan* (preface dated 1549), held in the Escorial Library in Madrid (see Andrew Lo, "Historiography."). I am grateful to Andrew Lo for providing me with a copy of the preface to the Escorial edition, and a transcript of some of the "Chung Hsing" commentaries. For further descriptions of the above texts, see Cheng Chen-to, "Yen-hua," pp. 210ff.

Chinese Sources

(In alphabetizing Chinese titles, I have disregarded all apostrophes and umlauts, and have considered all syllables separate words.) Known dates of premodern authors are provided where not given in text.

A Ying (Ch'ien Hsing-ts'un) 阿英 (錢杏邨). *Hsiao-shuo hsien-t'an* 小說閑談. Shanghai: Ku-tien wen-hsüeh, 1958.

Chai Hao 翟灝 (1736–88). *T'ung-su pien* 通俗編. Reprint. Taipei: Shih-chieh, 1963.

Chang Cheng-lang 張政烺. "Chiang-shih yü yung-shih shih" 講史與詠史詩. In *CYYCYLSYYYCSCK* 10 (1948): 601–44.

———. "Sung Chiang k'ao" 宋江考. In *SHYCLWC*, pp. 207–33.

Chang Ching 張敬. *Ming-Ch'ing ch'uan-ch'i tao-lun* 明清傳奇導論. Taipei: Tung-fang, 1961.

Chang Ching-erh 張靜二. *Hsi-yu chi jen-wu yen-chiu* 西遊記人物研究. Taipei: Hsüeh-sheng, 1984.

———. "Lun Hsi-yu ku-shih chung ti Wu-k'ung" 論西遊故事中的悟空. In *CWWH* 10, no. 11 (April 1982): 14–59.

Chang Ch'ou 張丑 (1577–1643). *Chen-chi jih-lu* 眞蹟日錄. In *SKCS, chen-pen*, series 3 珍本三集. Taipei: Shang-wu, 1972, *chüan* 5.

Ch'ang Ch'ung-i 常崇宜. "Shui-hu chung ti Li K'uei hsing-hsiang chih-i" 水滸中的李逵形象質疑. In *SHCM* 2: 351–59.

Chang Han-liang 張漢良. "Shih-hsi Shui-hu chuan ti chieh-kou" 試析水滸傳的結構. *CHWHFHYK* 9, no. 6 (June 1976): 45–47.

Chang Hsiao-hu 張嘯虎. "Shih Nai-an wei chiang-hu i-jen shuo" 施耐庵爲江湖藝人說. In *CHWSLT*, 1982, no. 4: 89–100.

Chang Hsüeh-ch'eng 章學誠 (1738–1801). *Ping-ch'en cha-chi* 丙辰劄記. In *Chü-hsüeh hsüan ts'ung-shu* 聚學軒叢書, compiled by Liu Shih-heng 劉世珩, Vol. 16. Reprint. Taipei: I-wen, 1970.

Chang Hung-hsün 張鴻勛. "Shih-t'an Chin P'ing Mei ti tso-che, shih-tai, ch'ü-ts'ai" 試談金瓶梅的作者時代取材. In *WHICTK* 6 (1958): 281–91.

Chang Kuo-kuang 張國光. "Lu Hsün ti Shih Nai-an wei fan-pen Shui-hu tso-che chih t'o-ming shuo wu k'e chih-i," 魯迅的施耐庵爲繁本水滸作者之托名說無可置疑. In *SHCM* 1: 49–64.

———. "P'ing Chung-i chuan ts'an-yeh fa-hsien i-i fei-ch'ang chung-ta lun" 評忠義傳殘頁發現意義非常重大論. *Wu-han shih-fan hsüeh-yüan hsüeh-pao* 武漢師範學院學報, 1984, no. 1: 107–12.

———. "San-kuo chih t'ung-su yen-i ch'eng-shu yü Ming chung-yeh pien" 三國志通俗演義成書於明中葉辨. In *SKYIYCC*, pp. 266–79.

———. "Shui-hu tsu-pen t'an-k'ao: chien lun Shih Nai-an wei Kuo Hsün men-k'e chih t'o-ming" 水滸祖本探考：兼論施耐庵爲郭勛門客之托名. In *CHLT*, no. 1 (1982): 39–44.

———. *Shui-hu yü Chin Sheng-t'an yen-chiu* 水滸與金聖歎研究. Honan, Chung-chou: Shu-hua, 1981.

———. "Tui Lo Erh-kang hsien-sheng Shui-hu chen-i k'ao i-wen chih shang-ch'üeh" 對羅爾綱先生水滸眞義考一文之商榷. In *Wu-han shih-fan hsüeh-yüan hsüeh-pao* 武漢師範學院學報, 1984, no. 4: 41–45, 51f.

Chang P'ei-heng 章培恒. "Pai-hui-pen Hsi-yu chi shih-fou Wu Ch'eng-en so-tso" 百回本西遊記是否吳承恩所作. In *SHKHCH*, 1983, no. 4: 295–305.

———. "Shih Nai-an mu-chih pien-wei chi ch'i-t'a" 施耐庵墓誌辨僞及其他. In *CHWSLT*, 1982, no. 4: 11–30.

Chang P'ei-heng and Huang Lin 黃霖. *Sung Chiang hsi* 宋江析. Shanghai: Jen-min, 1975.

Chang Po-tuan 張伯端 (Tzu-yang 紫陽) (987–1082). *Wu-chen p'ien chi-chu* 悟眞篇集註. In *TTCH* 6, no. 1. Taipei: Tzu-yu, 1962.

Chang Shu-hsiang 張淑香. "Ts'ung ching-t'ien tung-ti tao chi-t'ien mo-ti: Shui-hu ch'üan-chuan chieh-chü chih ch'üan-shih" 從驚天動地到寂天寞地：水滸全傳結局之詮釋. In *CWWH* 12, no. 11 (April 1984): 138–57.

Chang Tai 張岱 (1597–1684). *T'ao-an meng-i* 陶菴夢憶. In *Yüeh-ya t'ang ts'ung-shu* 粵雅堂叢書. 1853. Reprint. Taipei: Hua-lien, 1965, *chüan* 4.

Chang Yüan-fen 張遠芬. "Chin P'ing Mei tso-che hsin-cheng" 金瓶梅作者新證. In *HCSFHYHP*, 1982, no. 3: 7–15. Reprinted in *LCPM*, pp. 94–115.

———. "Hsin fa-hsien ti Chin P'ing Mei yen-chiu tzu-liao ch'u-t'an" 新發現的金瓶梅研究資料初探. In *LCPM*, pp. 331–38. Originally published in *HCSFH-YHP* 徐州師範學院學報, 1980, no. 4: 32–35.

Chao Ching-shen 趙景深. "Chin P'ing Mei tz'u-hua yü ch'ü-tzu" 金瓶梅詞話與曲子. In *CKHSTK*, pp. 308–12. Reprinted in *LCPM*, pp. 335–42.

———. "Hsi-yu chi tso-che Wu Ch'eng-en nien-p'u" 西遊記作者吳承恩年譜. In *CKHSTK*, pp. 251–63.

———. "Shui-hu chuan chien-lun" 水滸傳簡論. In *CKHSTK*, pp. 138–58. Reprinted in *Shui-hu jen-wu yü Shui-hu chuan* 水滸人物與水滸傳, by Yü Chia-hsi 余嘉錫, pp. 121–54. Taipei: Hsüeh-sheng, 1971.

———. "Shui-hu chuan tsa-chih" 水滸傳雜識. In *CKHSTK*, pp. 159–63. Also in *Hsiao-shuo hsi-ch'ü hsin-k'ao* 小說戲曲新考, pp. 37–42. Shanghai: Shih-chieh, 1939.

———. "T'an Ming Ch'eng-hua k'an-pen shuo-ch'ang tz'u-hua" 談明成化刊本說唱詞話. In *WW*, 1982, no. 2: 19–22.

———. "Tu Ssu-yu chi" and "Ssu-yu chi tsa-chih" 讀四遊記, 四遊記雜識. Reprinted in *CKHSTK*, pp. 221–28.

Ch'ao Li 晁瑮. *Pao-wen t'ang shu-mu* 寶文堂書目. Shanghai: Ku-tien wen-hsüeh, 1957.

Chao Ts'ung 趙聰. *Chung-kuo ssu ta hsiao-shuo chih yen-chiu* 中國四大小說之研究. Hong Kong: Yu-lien, 1964.

Ch'en Chao 陳詔. "Chin P'ing Mei hsiao-k'ao" 金瓶梅小考. In *Shang-hai shih-fan hsüeh-yüan hsüeh-pao* 上海師範學院學報, 1980, no. 3: 51–56. Reprinted in *LCPM*, pp. 397–414.

Ch'en Chien 陳建 (1497–1567). *Huang-Ming ts'ung-hsin lu* 皇明從信錄. Preface, 1620. Copy in rare book collection of Gest Oriental Library, Princeton, New Jersey.

Ch'en Chih-hsü 陳致虛 (Shang-yang tzu 上陽子). *Chin-tan ta-yao* 金丹大要. In *TTCH* 8, no. 5 (1963). T'ao Su-ssu 陶素耜, ed.

Ch'en Chin-chao 陳錦釗. *Li Chih chih wen-lun* 李贄之文論. Taipei: Chia-hsiu, 1974.

————. "Li Cho-wu p'i-tien Shui-hu chuan chih yen-chiu" 李卓吾批點水滸傳之研究. In *SMCK* 7, no. 4 (March 16, 1974): 45–65.

————. "T'an Kuan-hua t'ang Chin Sheng-t'an p'i-pen Shui-hu chuan" 談貫華堂金聖歎批本水滸傳. In *SMCK* 7, no. 2 (December 1972): 59–64.

Ch'en Chou-ch'ang 陳周昌. "Lun Shui-hu yün-wen ti i-shu tso-yung" 論水滸韻文的藝術作用. In *SHCM* 2: 278–90.

————. "Sung Chiang hsing-ko chieh-kou shih-t'an" 宋江性格結構試探. In *SHCM* 1: 149–61.

Ch'en Chung-fan 陳中凡. "Shih-lun Shui-hu chuan ti chu-che chi ch'i ch'uang-tso shih-tai" 試論水滸傳的著者及其創作時代. 1956. Reprint. In *SHYCLWC*, pp. 113–26.

Ch'en Hsi-chung 陳曦鍾. "Kuan-yü Chung Po-ching hsien-sheng p'i-p'ing Chung-i shui-hu chuan" 關於鍾伯敬先生批評忠義水滸傳. In *WH* 15 (March 1983): 42–52.

————, Hou Chung-i 侯忠義, and Lu Yü-ch'uan 魯玉川, eds. *Shui-hu chuan hui-p'ing pen* 水滸傳會評本. Peking: Peking University, 1981.

Ch'en Hsiang-hua 陳翔華. "Lun Chu-ko Liang tien-hsing chi ch'i fu-tsa-hsing" 論諸葛亮典型及其複雜性. In *WH* (1984): 252–69.

Ch'en Hsien-chang 陳獻章 (1428–1500). *Pai-sha tzu ch'üan-chi* 白沙子全集. Reprint. Taipei: Shang-wu, 1973.

Ch'en Hsin 陳新. "Ch'ung-p'ing Chu Ting-ch'en T'ang San-tsang Hsi-yu shih-o chuan ti ti-wei ho chia-chih" 重評朱鼎臣唐三藏西遊釋厄傳的地位和價值. In *Chiang-hai hsüeh-k'an* 江海學刊, 1983, no. 1: 61–66.

————. "Hsi-yu chi pan-pen yüan-liu ti i-ko chia-she" 西遊記版本原流的一個假設. In *HYCYC*, pp. 190–205.

Ch'en Kan 陳澉. "Wu Ch'eng-en ti Ching-fu chi-shan chih pu ho Hsi-yu chi ti hsieh-tso k'an-k'e" 吳承恩的荊府紀善之補和西遊記的寫作刊刻. In *HYCYC*, pp. 206–14.

Ch'en Ming-kuei 陳銘珪. *Ch'ang-ch'un tao-chiao yüan-liu* 長春道教原流. N.p., Kuang-hsü 5 (1879).

Ch'en Shao-t'ang 陳少棠. *Wan-Ming hsiao-p'in wen lun-hsi* 晚明小品文論析. Hong Kong: Po-wen, 1981.

Ch'en Shou 陳壽 (233–297). *San-kuo chih* 三國志. Reprint. Peking: Chung-hua, 1959. Additional printing (5 vols.), 1982.

Chen Te-hsiu 真德秀 (1178–1235). *Wen-chang cheng-tsung* 文章正宗. In *SKCS*, *chen-pen*, series 2, 珍本二集. Vol. 191–96. Taipei: Shang-wu, 1981.

Ch'en Tun-fu 陳敦甫. *Hsi-yu chi shih-i* 西遊記釋義. Taipei: Ch'üan-chen chiao ch'u-pan she, 1976.

Ch'en Yin-k'e 陳寅恪. "Hsi-yu chi Hsüan-tsang ti-tzu ku-shih ti yen-pien" 西遊記玄奘弟子故事的演變. In *Li-shih yü-yen yen-chiu-so chi-k'an* 歷史語言研究所集刊 2: 1 (1930): 157–60.

Ch'en Yü-p'i 陳毓羆. "Ts'ung 'kuo huo-yen-shan' k'an Wu Ch'eng-en tui ch'ing-chieh ti ch'u-li" 從過火燄山看吳承恩對情節的處理. In *WHIC*, no. 491 (May 12, 1963).

————. "Wu Ch'eng-en Hsi-yu chi ch'eng yü wan-nien shuo hsin-cheng" 吳承恩

西遊記成於晚年說新證. In *WHIC*, no. 631 (March 27, 1984).

Ch'en Yüan 陳垣. *Ch'en-shih Chung-hsi-hui shih jih-li* 陳氏中西回史日曆. Peking: Sinological Research Institute at the National University of Peking, 1926.

Cheng Chen-to 鄭振鐸. *Chieh-chung te-shu chi* 刼中得書記. 1941. Reprint. Shanghai: Ku-tien wen-hsüeh, 1956.

————. *Chung-kuo wen-hsüeh yen-chiu hsin pien* 中國文學研究新編. Peking: Tso-chia, 1957. Reprint. Taipei: Ming-lun, 1971.

————. "Hsi-yu chi ti yen-hua" 西遊記的演化. In *CKWHYC*, pp. 263–99.

————. "Hsi-yu chi tsa-chü" 西遊記雜劇. In *CKWHYC*, pp. 615–16.

————. "Lu Chih-shen ti chia-t'ing" 魯智深的家庭 and "Wu Sung yü ch'i ch'i Chia-shih" 武松與其妻賈氏. In *CKWHYC*, pp. 759–62.

————. "Lun wen-tzu ti fan chien" 論文字的繁簡. In *CKWHYC*, pp. 1174–77.

————. "San-kuo chih yen-i ti yen-hua" 三國志演義的演化. In *CKWHYC*, pp. 166–239.

————. "Shui-hu chuan ti yen-hua" 水滸傳的演化. 1929. Reprinted in *CKWHYC*, pp. 101–57.

————. "T'an Chin P'ing Mei tz'u-hua" 談金瓶梅詞話. In *CKWHYC*, pp. 242–62. Also in *PWCY*, pp. 43–60, under pseudonym Kuo Yüan-hsin 郭源新.

Cheng Kung-tun 鄭公盾. *Shui-hu chuan lun-wen chi* 水滸傳論文集. 2 vols. Yin-ch'uan: Ning-hsia jen-min, 1983.

Cheng Ming-li 鄭明娳. *Hsi-yu chi t'an-yüan* 西遊記探源. Taipei: Wen-k'ai, 1982.

————. "Huo-yen shan ku-shih ti hsing-ch'eng" 火焰山故事的形成. In *CWWH* 10, no. 11 (April 1982), pp. 4–13.

————. "Lun Hsi-yu chi san pan-pen chien chih kuan-hsi" 論西遊記三版本間之關係. In *CKKTHSYCCC*, 6: 173–234.

Cheng P'ei-k'ai 鄭培凱. "Chin P'ing Mei chung yin-chiu yü tso ma-t'ung ti wen-t'i" 金瓶梅飲酒與坐馬桶的問題. In *CKSP* (September 22, 1983), p. 8.

————. "Chin P'ing Mei tz'u-hua hsü-pa so fan-ying ti she-hui tao-te i-shih" 金瓶梅詞話序跋所反映的社會道德意識. In *Tou-sou* 抖擻 53 (July 1983): 31–39.

————. "Chin P'ing Mei tz'u-hua yü Ming-jen yin-chiu feng-shang" 金瓶梅詞話與明人飲酒風尚. In *CWWH* 12, no. 6 (November 1983): 5–44.

Chi Ch'eng 計成. *Yüan-yeh* 園冶. In *Hsi-yung hsüan ts'ung-shu* 喜咏軒叢書. Vol. 5. N.p., 1929–30.

Chi Wen-fu 嵇文甫. *Wan-Ming ssu-hsiang shih-lun* 晚明思想史論. Ch'ung-ch'ing: Shang-wu, 1944.

Chia Chung-ming 賈仲明 (ca. 1343–1422). *Hsü Lu-kuei pu* 續錄鬼簿. In *Lu-kuei pu hsin chiao-chu* 錄鬼簿新校注. Peking: Wen-hsüeh ku-chi, 1957.

Chiang Jui-tsao 蔣瑞藻. *Hsiao-shuo k'ao-cheng* 小說考證. 1920. Reprint. Shanghai: Shang-wu, 1957.

Ch'ien Chi-po 錢基博. *Ming-tai wen-hsüeh* 明代文學. Shanghai: Shang-wu, 1939.

Ch'ien Ching-fang 錢靜方. *Hsiao-shuo ts'ung-k'ao* 小說叢考. Shanghai: Ku-tien wen-hsüeh, 1957.

Ch'ien Chung-shu 錢鍾書. *T'an-i lu* 談藝錄. 1937. Reprint. Hong Kong: Lung-men, 1965.

————. *Yeh-shih chi* 也是集. Hong Kong: Kuang chiao-ching, 1984.

Chien-feng 劍鋒. "Chin-kuo pu jang hsü mei: lun San-kuo yen-i chung ti fu-nü ti i-shu hsing-hsiang" 巾幗不讓鬚眉：論三國演義中的婦女的藝術形象. In *SKYIYCC*, pp. 234–39.

Ch'ien Hsi-yen 錢希言. *Hsi-hsia* 戲瑕. Preface 1613. In *Chieh-yüeh shan-fang hui-ch'ao* 借月山房彙鈔. PPTSCC edition, no. 48. Taipei: I-wen, 1967.

Ch'ien Mu 錢穆. *Kuo-hsüeh kai-lun* 國學概論. 1931. Reprint. Taipei: Shang-wu, 1963.

————. *Li-hsüeh liu-chia shih-ch'ao* 理學六家詩鈔. Taipei: Chung-hua, 1974.

Ch'ien Nan-yang 錢南揚, ed. *Yuan-Ming-Ch'ing ch'ü hsüan* 元明清曲選. In *Kuo-wen-ts'ui hsüan ts'ung-shu* 國文粹選叢書. General editor, Yeh Ch'u-ts'ang 葉楚傖. Taipei: Cheng-chung, 1952.

Ch'ien Ta-hsin 錢大昕 (1728–1804). *Ch'ien-yen t'ang wen-chi* 潛研堂文集. KHCPTS edition, vol. 323.

Chin-kang ching chien-chu 金剛經箋註. Translated by Kumārajīva 鳩摩羅什 (d. 412?). Edited by Ting Fu-pao 丁福保. Shanghai: I-hsüeh, n.d.

Chin Sheng-t'an 金聖歎 (Chin Jen-jui 金人瑞). *Ch'ang-ching t'ang ts'ai-tzu shu hui-pien* 唱經堂才子書彙編. Shanghai: Kuo-hsüeh yen-chiu, 1936.

————. *Chin Sheng-t'an ch'i-shu shih-pa chung* 金聖歎奇書十八種. Shanghai: Kuang-i, 1936.

Chin shu 晉書. Compiled by Fang Hsüan-ling 房玄齡 (578–648), et al. Reprint. Peking: Chung-hua, 1974.

Chin Tai-t'ung 靳岱同 (Yü Sung-ch'ing 喻松青). "Li Chih yü Shui-hu" 李贄與水滸. In *Li-shih yen-chiu* 歷史研究, 1976, no. 6: 72–84.

Ch'iu Ch'u-chi 邱處機 (1148–1227). *Ch'iu-tsu ch'üan-shu chieh-chi* 邱祖全書節輯. In *TTCH* 5, no. 2 (1960).

———— (attrib.). *Lung-men mi-chih* 龍門秘旨. Edited by Kao Jen-t'ung 高仁峒. In *TTCH* 2, no. 3 (1966).

————. *P'an-hsi tz'u* 磻溪詞. In *Chiang-ts'un ts'ung-shu* 疆邨叢書. Vol. 33. N.p., 1922.

Chou Chih-p'ing 周質平. "Lun wan-Ming wen-jen tui hsiao-shuo ti t'ai-tu" 論晚明文人對小說的態度. In *CWWH* 11, no. 12 (May 1983): 100–109.

————. "P'ing Kung-an p'ai chih shih-lun" 評公安派之詩論. In *CWWH* 12, no. 10 (March 1984): 70–94.

Chou Chih-wen 周志文. "T'ai-chou hsüeh-p'ai tui wan-Ming wen-hsüeh feng-ch'i ti ying-hsiang" 泰州學派對晚明文學風氣的影響. Master's thesis, National Taiwan University, 1977.

Chou Hui 周暉. *Chin-ling so-shih* 金陵瑣事. Preface, 1610. Reprint. Peking: Wen-hsüeh ku-chi, 1955.

Chou Hung-tsu 周弘祖. *Ku-chin shu-k'e* 古今書刻. Reprint. Shanghai: Ku-tien wen-hsüeh, 1957.

Chou-i che-chung 周易折中 (1715). Arrangement and commentary by Li Kuang-ti 李光地 (1642–1718). Reprint. Taipei: Chen-shan-mei, 1971.

Chou I-pai 周貽白, ed. *Ming-jen tsa-chü hsüan* 明人雜劇選. Peking: Jen-min wen-hsüeh, 1962.

Chou Liang-kung 周亮工 (1612–1672). *Yin-shu-wu shu-ying* 印書屋書影. Reprint. Shanghai: Ku-tien wen-hsüeh, 1957.

Chou Mi 周密 (1232–1308). *Kuei-hsin tsa-chih* 癸辛雜識, 續集. In *Hsüeh-chin t'ao-yüan* 學津討原. *PPTSCC* edition, Vol. 26, no. 3, pp. 28b–34a. Taipei, 1965.

Chou Shao-liang 周紹良. "Hsiu-keng shan-fang tzu Hsüan-ho i-shih pa" 修綆山房梓宣和遺事跋. In *SHCM* 1, pp. 19–32. Reprinted in *SLTK*, pp. 190–206.

———. "Kuan So k'ao" 關索考. In *SLTK*, pp. 207–22.

———. "T'an T'ang-tai ti San-kuo ku-shih" 談唐代的三國故事. In *WHICTK* 10 (1962): 117–26. Reprinted in *SLTK*, pp. 223–33.

Chou Tso-jen 周作人. *Chung-kuo hsin wen-hsüeh ti yüan-liu* 中國新文學的源流. 1934. Reprint. Hong Kong: Hui-wen ko, 1972.

Ch'ü Chia-yüan 曲家源. "Shui-hu i-pai-tan-pa chiang ch'o-hao k'ao-shih" 水滸一百單八將綽號考釋. In *Sung-Liao hsüeh-k'an* 松遼學刊 1, no. 23 (1984): 63–70.

Chu Hsi 朱熹 (1130–1200). *Yü-p'i Tzu-chih t'ung-chien kang-mu* 御批資治通鑑綱目. In *SKCS, chen-pen*, series 6 珍本六集. Vol. 140(8). Reprint. Taipei, 1976.

Chu Hsing 朱星. *Chin P'ing Mei k'ao-cheng* 金瓶梅考證. Tientsin: Pai-hua wen-i, 1980. Originally appeared in *SHKHCH*, 1979, no. 2: 259–72.

———. "Chin P'ing Mei ti tso-che chiu-ching shih shui" 金瓶梅的作者究竟是誰. In *SHKHCH*, 1979, no. 3: 270–78. Also in *Chin P'ing Mei k'ao-cheng*, pp. 31–50.

Chu I-hsüan and Liu Yü-ch'en 朱一玄, 劉毓忱. *Hsi-yu chi tzu-liao hui-pien* 西遊記資料滙編. Cheng-chou: Chung-chou shu-hua, 1983.

———. *Shui-hu chuan tzu-liao hui-pien* 水滸傳資料滙編. Tientsin: Pai-hua wen-i, 1981. Original preface, 1965.

Chu I-tsun 朱彝尊. *Ming-shih tsung* 明詩綜. 1705. Reprint. Taipei: Shih-chieh, 1962.

Chu T'an 朱倓. "Tung-lin tien-chiang lu k'ao-i" 東林點將錄考異. In *Chung-shan ta-hsüeh wen-shih hsüeh yen-chiu-so yüeh-k'an* 中山大學文史學研究所月刊 2 (October 1933): 569–601 (33–65).

Chu T'ung 朱彤, "Lun Sun Wu-k'ung" 論孫悟空. In *An-hui shih-fan ta-hsüeh hsüeh-pao* 安徽師範大學學報, 1978, no. 1: 68–79.

Chu Tung-jun 朱東潤. *Chang Chü-cheng ta chuan* 張居正大傳. Wu-han: Hupei jen-min, 1957.

———. *Chung-kuo wen-hsüeh p'i-p'ing shih ta-kang* 中國文學批評史大綱. Shanghai: Ku-tien wen-hsüeh, 1957.

Ch'üan Yuan tsa-chü ch'u-pien 全元雜劇初編. In *Chung-kuo hsüeh-shu ming-chu* 中國學術名著. Editor of series Yang Chia-lo 楊家駱. Reprint. Taipei: Shih-chieh, 1963.

Chuang I-fu 莊一拂, ed. *Ku-tien hsi-ch'ü ts'un-mu hui-k'ao* 古典戲曲存目滙考. 3 vols. Shanghai: Ku-chi, 1982.

Chung Hsing 鍾惺 (1574–1624). *Shih-huai* 史懷. Reprint. N.p., 1891.

Chung-kuo ku-tien hsi-ch'ü lun-chu chi-ch'eng 中國古典戲曲論著集成. 10 vols. Peking: Chung-kuo hsi-ch'ü, 1959.

Chung-kuo wen-hsüeh shih 中國文學史. Edited by Chung-kuo k'e-hsüeh yüan, wen-hsüeh yen-chiu-so 中國科學院文學研究所. Peking: Jen-min wen-hsüeh, 1962.

Chung-kuo wen-hsüeh shih 中國文學史. Edited by Dept. of Chinese, Peking University. Peking: Jen-min wen-hsüeh, 1959.

Chung-li Ch'üan 鍾離權 and Lü Yen 呂嚴 (attrib.). *Chung-Lü ch'uan-tao chi* 鍾呂傳
　　道集. In *TTCH* 1, no. 3 (1965).
Chung Ssu-ch'eng 鍾嗣成 (fl. 1321). *Lu-kuei pu hsin chiao-chu* 錄鬼簿新校注. Edited
　　by Ma Lien 馬廉. Peking: Wen-hsüeh ku-chi, 1957.
Fan Ning 范寧. "Shui-hu chuan pan-pen yüan-liu k'ao" 水滸傳版本源流考. In
　　CHWSLT, 1982, no. 4: 65–77'
Fang Tsu-shen 方祖燊. "Lo Kuan-chung yü San-kuo chih yen-i" 羅貫中與三國志
　　演義. In *CHWHFHYK* 9, no. 6 (June 1976): 48–57.
Feng Meng-lung 馮夢龍 (1574?–1645?). *Shan-ko* 山歌. Peking: Chung-hua, 1962.
Feng Yüan-chün 馮沅君 (Shu-lan 淑蘭). "Chin P'ing Mei tz'u-hua chung ti wen-
　　hsüeh shih-liao" 金瓶梅詞話中的文學史料. In *Ku-chü shuo-hui* 古劇說彙,
　　pp.170–213. Peking: Tso-chia, 1956.
Fu Hsi-hua 傅惜華. *Ming-tai ch'uan-ch'i ch'üan-mu* 明代傳奇全目. Peking: Jen-min
　　wen-hsüeh, 1959.
————. *Ming-tai tsa-chü ch'üan-mu* 明代雜劇全目. Peking: Tso-chia, 1959.
————. *Ming tsa-chü k'ao* 明雜劇考. Taipei: Shih-chieh, 1961.
————. *Shui-hu hsi-ch'ü chi* 水滸戲曲集. 2 vols. Shanghai: Chung-hua, 1962.
————. *Tzu-ti shu tsung-mu* 子弟書總目. Shanghai: Wen-i lien-ho, 1954.
————. *Yuan-tai tsa-chü ch'üan-mu* 元代雜劇全目. Peking: Tso-chia, 1957.
Fu Shu-hsien 傅述先 (James S. Fu). "Hsi-yu chi chung wu-sheng ti kuan-hsi"
　　西遊記中五聖的關係. In *CHWHFHYK* 9, no. 5 (May 1976): 10–17.
Ho Hsin 何心 (Lu Tan-an 陸澹安). *Shui-hu yen-chiu* 水滸研究. Shanghai: Wen-i
　　lien-ho, 1955. Reprint. Taipei: Ho-lo, 1978.
Ho Man-tzu 何滿子. *Lun Chin Sheng-t'an p'ing-kai Shui-hu chuan* 論金聖嘆評改
　　水滸傳. Shanghai: Shanghai ch'u-pan she, 1954.
————. "Ts'ung Sung Yuan shuo-hua chia-shu t'an-so Shui-hu fan-chien-pen
　　yüan-yüan chi ch'i tso-che wen-t'i" 從宋元說話家屬探索水滸繁簡本淵源及
　　其作者問題. *CHWSLT*, 1982, no. 4: 31–44.
Hou Han shu 後漢書. Compiled by Fan Yeh 范曄 (398–445). Reprint. Peking:
　　Chung-hua, 1965.
Hou Wai-lu 侯外盧. *Chung-kuo ssu-hsiang t'ung-shih* 中國思想通史. Peking: Jen-
　　min, 1960
Hsi Tso-ch'ih 習鑿齒. *Han Chin ch'un-ch'iu* 漢晉春秋. Reprint. In *HSISK*, vol. 31.
Hsi-yu chi 西遊記. Attributed to Wu Ch'eng-en 吳承恩. Peking: Jen-min wen-
　　hsüeh, 1972.
Hsi-yu chi tsa-chü 西遊記雜劇. Attributed to Yang Ching-hsien 楊景賢. Reprinted
　　in Sui Shu-sen, *Yuan-ch'ü hsüan wai-pien.*
Hsia Ch'ung-p'u 夏崇璞. "Ming-tai fu-ku p'ai yü T'ang-Sung wen-p'ai chih ch'ao-
　　liu" 明代復古派與唐宋文派之潮流. *Hsüeh-heng* 學衡 9 (September 1922):
　　1219–28.
Hsia Hsieh 夏燮 (1799–1875?). *Ming t'ung-chien* 明通鑑 (ca. 1870). 4 vols. Reprint.
　　Peking: Chung-hua, 1959.
Hsiao Tso-ming 肖作銘. "T'an Shui-hu tso-che ti tao-chia ssu-hsiang" 談水滸作者
　　的道家思想. In *SHCM* 2: 175–81.
Hsieh Chao-che 謝肇淛 (fl. 1592–1607). *Wu tsa-tsu* 五雜組. Ca. 1600. Reprint.
　　Taipei: Hsin-hsing, 1971. *chüan* 15.
Hsieh Kuo-chen 謝國楨. *Ming-Ch'ing chih chi tang-she yün-tung k'ao* 明清之際

黨社運動考. Shanghai: Shang-wu, 1934.

Hsieh Pi-hsia 謝碧霞. *Shui-hu hsi-ch'ü erh-shih chung yen-chiu* 水滸戲曲二十種研究. Taipei: Tai-wan ta-hsüeh wen-shih ts'ung-k'an, 1981.

Hsin-ch'ou chi-wen 辛丑紀聞. Anon. Ch'ing work. Reprinted in *Ming-Ch'ing shih-liao hui-pien* 明清史料彙編. Taipei: Wen-hai, 1967. Vol. 16, pp. 1235—68.

Hsing-ming kuei-chih 性命圭旨. In *TTCH* 1, no. 5 (1965).

Hsiung Wen-ch'in 熊文欽 and Shih Lin 石麟. "Ts'ung Shui-hu hsi tao Shui-hu chuan, k'an Li K'uei hsing-hsiang ti fa-chan" 從水滸戲到水滸傳,看李逵形象的發展. In *SHCM* 1: 141—48.

Hsü Chen-chi 徐貞姬. "Hsi-yu chi pa-shih-i nan yen-chiu" 西遊記八十一難研究. Master's thesis, Fu Jen University, Taipei, 1980.

Hsü Fu-ming 徐扶明. "Ming-feng chi ch'u-t'an" 鳴鳳記初探. In *WHICTK* 12 (1963), pp. 29—38.

Hsü Meng-hsiang 徐夢湘. "Kuan-yü Chin P'ing Mei ti tso-che" 關於金瓶梅的作者. In *WHIC*, no. 50 (April 17, 1955). Reprinted in *MCHSYCLWC*, pp. 181—84.

Hsü Shuo-fang 徐朔方. "Chin P'ing Mei ch'eng-shu hsin-t'an" 金瓶梅成書新探. Unpublished manuscript.

————. "Chin P'ing Mei ch'eng-shu pu-cheng" 金瓶梅成書補證. In *HCTHHP* 11, no. 1 (March 1981): 80—84, 95. Reprinted in *THT*, pp. 148—58.

————. "Chin P'ing Mei ti hsieh-ting-che shih Li K'ai-hsien" 金瓶梅的寫定者是李開先. In *HCTHHP* 1 (March 1980): 78—85. Also reprinted in *THT*, pp. 133—47, and *Tou, sou* 42 (January 1981): 47—53.

————. "Hung-lou meng ho Chin P'ing Mei" 紅樓夢和金瓶梅. In *Hung-lou meng yen-chiu chi-k'an* 紅樓夢研究集刊. 7th series (1981), pp. 143—62.

————. "Kuan-yü Chang Feng-i ho T'ien-tu wai-ch'en ti Shui-hu chuan hsü" 關於張鳳翼和天都外臣的水滸傳序. In *WHIC*, no. 586 (March 10, 1983).

————. "T'ang Hsien-tsu ho Chin P'ing Mei" 湯顯祖和金瓶梅. In *THT*, pp. 125—32.

————, ed. *T'ang Hsien-tsu shih-wen chi* 湯顯祖詩文集. Shanghai: Ku-chi, 1982.

————. "Ts'ung Sung Chiang ch'i-i tao Shui-hu chuan ch'eng-shu" 從宋江起義到水滸傳成書. In *CHWSLT*, 1982, no. 4: 45—64. Reprinted in *THT*, pp. 179—200.

Hsü Wei 徐渭 (1521—1593). *Hsü Wen-ch'ang i-kao* 徐文長逸稿. Reprint. Taipei: Wei-wen, 1977.

————. *Nan-tz'u hsü-lu* 南詞敍錄. In *CKKTHCLCCC*, vol. 3, pp. 233—56.

Hsüan-ho i-shih 宣和遺事. Reprint. *Hsin-k'an Hsüan-ho i-shih* 新刊宣和遺事. Shanghai: Ku-tien wen-hsüeh, 1955.

Hu Chen-wu 胡振務. "T'an Wu Yung" 談吳用. In *SHCM* 2: 360—71.

Hu Kuang-chou 胡光舟. *Wu Ch'eng-en ho Hsi-yu chi* 吳承恩和西遊記. Shanghai: Shang-hai ku-chi, 1982.

Hu Pang-wei 胡邦煒. "Ts'ung ho chiu pi fen tao fen chiu pi ho, San-kuo yen-i chu-t'i pien" 從合久必分到分久必合三國演義主題辨. In *SKYIYCC*, pp. 60—75.

Hu Shih 胡適. "Hsi-yu chi k'ao-cheng" 西遊記考證. 1923. Reprinted in *HSWT* 2, no. 2, pp. 354—90. Also in *Chung-kuo chang-hui hsiao-shuo k'ao-cheng* 中國章回小說考證, pp. 315—79. 1942. Reprint. Taipei: Feng-yün, 1976.

———. "Pa Hsiao-shih chen-k'ung pao-chüan" 跋銷釋眞空寶卷. In *KLPPTSKKK* 5, no. 3 (1931): 3609–20.

———. "Pa Ssu-yu chi pen ti Hsi-yu chi-chuan" 跋四遊記本的西遊記傳. In *HSWT* 4, no. 3, pp. 408–11.

———. "Pai-erh-shih hui pen Chung-i shui-hu chuan hsü 百二十回本忠義水滸傳序. 1929. Reprinted in Hu Shih, *Chang-hui hsiao-shuo k'ao-cheng*, pp. 101–49.

———. "San-kuo chih yen-i hsü" 三國志演義序. 1922, reprinted in *HSWT* 2, no. 2: 467–75. Also in Hu Shih, *Chang-hui hsiao-shuo k'ao-cheng*, pp. 381–91.

———. "Shui-hu chuan k'ao-cheng" 水滸傳考證. 1920. Reprinted in *Chang-hui hsiao-shuo k'ao-cheng*, pp. 1–63. Also in *HSWT* 1, no. 3: 500–74 and 3, no. 5: 404–40.

———. "Ta Ch'ien Hsüan-t'ung shu" 答錢玄同書. In *HSWT* 1, no. 1, pp. 41–44.

Hu Shih-ying. 胡士瑩. *Hua-pen hsiao-shuo kai-lun* 話本小說概論. Peking: Chung-hua, 1980.

Hu Tseng 胡曾. *Hsin tiao-chu yung-shih shih* 新彫注詠史詩. In *SPTK, san-pien* 三編, Vol. 41, no. 4.

Hu Ying-lin 胡應麟. *Shao-shih shan-fang pi-ts'ung* 少室山房筆叢. Preface, 1584. Reprint. Peking: Chung-hua, 1959.

Hua Shan 華山. "Shui-hu chuan ho Sung-shih" 水滸傳和宋史. In *SHYCLWC*, pp. 232–47.

Hua Shu 華淑 (1589–1643). *Ming-shih hsüan-tsui* 明詩選最. Reprinted as *Ming-jen hsüan Ming-shih* 明人選明詩. Taipei: Ta-tung, 1974.

Huang Lin 黃霖. "Chin P'ing Mei tso-che T'u Lung k'ao" 金瓶梅作者屠隆考. In *FTHP*, 1983, no. 3: 31–39.

———. "Chung-i shui-hu chuan yü Chin P'ing Mei tz'u-hua" 忠義水滸傳與金瓶梅詞話. In *SHCM*, 1: 228–32.

———. "I-chung chih-te chu-mu ti Shui-hu ku-pen" 一種值得注目的水滸古本. In *FTHP*, 1980, no. 4: 86–89.

———. "Shui-hu ch'üan-chuan Li Chih p'ing yeh shu wei-t'o" 水滸全傳李贄評也屬偽托. In *CHLT*, 1982, no. 1: 44–49.

———. "Yu-kuan Mao-pen San-kuo yen-i ti jo-kan wen-t'i" 有關毛本三國演義的若干問題. In *SKYIYCC*, pp. 326–43.

Huang Lin and Han T'ung-wen 韓同文. *Chung-kuo li-tai hsiao-shuo lun-chu hsüan* 中國歷代小說論著選. Nan-ch'ang: Chiang-hsi jen-min, 1982.

Huang-Ming wen-chüan 皇明文雋. Attributed to Yüan Hung-tao, ed. Preface, 1620. In rare book collection of Gest Oriental Library, Princeton, New Jersey.

Huang Su-ch'iu 黃肅秋. "Hsi-yu chi ti chiao-ting ho chu-shih kung-tso" 西遊記的校訂和注釋工作. In *HYCYCLWC*, pp. 150–84.

———. "Lun Hsi-yu chi ti ti-chiu-hui wen-t'i" 論西遊記的第九回問題. In *HYCYCLWC*, pp. 172–77.

Huang Tsung-hsi 黃宗羲, ed. *Ming-ju hsüeh-an* 明儒學案. 1667. Reprint. Taipei: Shih-chieh, 1961.

———, ed. (attributed). *Ming-wen an* 明文案. Original in National Central Library, Taipei. Microfilm in Gest Oriental Library, Princeton, New Jersey.

———, ed. (attributed). *Ming-wen shou-tu*. 明文授讀. Tokyo: Kyūko, 1972.

Huang Yün-mei 黃雲眉. *Ming-shih k'ao-cheng* 明史考證. Vol. 1. Peking: Chung-hua, 1979.

Hung Pien 洪楩 (fl. 1500–1560). *Ch'ing-p'ing shan-t'ang hua-pen* 清平山堂話本. Edited by T'an Cheng-pi 譚正璧. Shanghai: Ku-tien wen-hsüeh, 1957.

Isobe Akira 磯部彰. "Hsi-yu chi ti chieh-na yü liu-ch'uan" 西遊記的接納與流傳. In *CKKTHSYCCC* 6 (1983): 141–71.

Juan K'uei-sheng 阮葵生 (1727–1789). *Ch'a-yü k'e-hua* 茶餘客話. Shanghai: Chung-hua, 1959.

Jung Chao-tsu 容肇祖. *Ming-tai ssu-hsiang shih* 明代思想史. Taipei: K'ai-ming, 1962.

K'an To 闞鐸 (Huo-ch'u 霍初). "Hung-lou meng chüeh-wei" 紅樓夢抉微. 1925. Reprinted in *PWCY*, pp. 78–86.

Kao Hsi-tseng 高熙曾. "Hsi-yu chi li ti tao-chiao ho tao-shih" 西遊記裡的道教和道士. In *HYCYCLWC*, pp. 153–59.

Kao Ju 高儒. *Pai-ch'uan shu-chih* 百川書志. Reprint. Shanghai: Ku-tien wen-hsüeh, 1957.

Kao Ming-ko 高明閣. "Ch'ü-ching shih-hua yüeh-tu cha-chi" 取經詩話閱讀札記. In *HYCYC*, pp. 149–68.

———. "Hsi-yu chi li ti shen-mo wen-t'i" 西遊記裡的神魔問題. In *WHIC*, 1981, no. 2: 118–27.

———. "Lun Shui-hu ti chien-pen hsi-t'ung" 論水滸的簡本系統. In *SHCM* 3: 222–32.

———. "Shui-hu chuan yü Hsüan-ho i-shih" 水滸傳與宣和遺事. In *SHCM* 1: 33–48.

Kao T'ang 高塘, ed. *Ming-wen ch'ao* 明文鈔. In rare book collection of Gest Oriental Library, Princeton, New Jersey.

Ko Ch'u-ying 葛楚英. "T'an Shui-hu ti chung-i" 談水滸的忠義. In *SHCM* 1: 129–40.

——— and Chin Chia-hsing 金家興. "Chin Sheng-t'an yao-chan Shui-hu ti i-shu kou-ssu" 金聖歎腰斬水滸的藝術構思. In *CHLT*, 1983, no. 4: 50–53.

Ku-pen Yuan-Ming tsa-chü 孤本元明雜劇. Edited by Wang Chi-lieh 王季烈. Reprint. Peking: Chung-kuo hsi-chü, 1958.

Ku T'ing-lung 顧廷龍, and Shen Chin 沈津. "Kuan-yü hsin fa-hsien ti Ching-pen chung-i chuan ts'an-yeh" 關於新發現的京本忠義傳殘頁. In *Hsüeh-hsi yü p'i-p'an* 學習與批判. 1975, no. 12: 34–35. Reprinted in *Shui-hu p'ing-lun chi* 水滸評論集, pp. 105f. Shanghai: Jen-min, 1976.

Ku Yen-wu 顧炎武 (1613–82). *Jih-chih lu*. 1670. Commentary edition. *Jih-chih lu chi-shih* 日知錄集釋. Edited by Huang Ju-ch'eng 黃汝成. 1872. Taipei: Shih-chieh, 1968.

Ku Ying-t'ai 谷應泰. *Ming-shih chi-shih pen-mo* 明史紀事本末. 1658. Reprint of 1956 edition. Taipei: San-min, 1968.

Ku Yu-hsiao 顧有孝, ed. *Ming-wen ying-hua* 明文英華. Original in National Central Library, Taipei. Microfilm in Gest Oriental Library, Princeton, New Jersey.

Kuan Te-tung 關德棟. *Chia Fu-hsi mu-p'i tz'u chiao-chu* 賈鳧西木皮詞校注. Chi-nan: Ch'i-lu, 1982.

———. "Feng Meng-lung chi-chi ti kua-chih-erh" 馮夢龍輯集的掛枝兒. In *Ch'ü-i lun-chi* 曲藝論集, pp. 175–81. 1960. Reprint. Shanghai: Ku-chi, 1983.

Kuei Yu-kuang 歸有光. *Wen-chang chih-nan* 文章指南. Reprint. Taipei: Kuang-wen, 1971.

Kung Chao-chi 龔兆吉. "Jung-pen Li-p'ing wei Yeh Chou wei-tso shuo chih-i" 容本李評爲葉晝僞作說質疑. In *SHCM* 2: 155–67.

K'ung Ling-ching 孔另境. *Chung-kuo hsiao-shuo shih-liao*. 中國小說史料. 1957. Reprint. Peking: Chung-hua, 1962.

Kuo Chen-i 郭箴一. *Chung-kuo hsiao-shuo shih* 中國小說史. Taipei: Shang-wu, 1965.

Kuo Hsün 郭勛. *Yung-hsi yüeh-fu* 雍熙樂府. Reprint. *SPTK hsü-pien, chi-pu* 續編集部, Vol. 48, no. 20.

Kuo Shao-yü 郭紹虞. *Chung-kuo wen-hsüeh p'i-p'ing shih* 中國文學批評史. Shanghai: Hsin wen-i, 1955.

———. "Ming-tai ti wen-jen chi-t'uan" 明代的文人集團. In *Wen-i fu-hsing* 文藝復興 4 (September 10, 1948): 86–128.

Lang Ying 郎瑛. *Ch'i-hsiu lei-kao* 七修類稿. Ca. 1566. Reprint. Peking: Chung-hua, 1959.

Li Chih 李贄. *Fen shu* 焚書. 1590. Reprint. Peking: Chung-hua, 1961.

———. *Hsü Fen shu*. 續焚書. 1611. Reprint. Peking: Chung-hua, 1959. Also in *Li shih Fen shu Hsü Fen shu* 李氏焚書續焚書. Kyoto: Chūbun, 1971.

———. *Shih-kang p'ing-yao* 史綱評要. Reprint. Peking: Chung-hua, 1974.

———. *Ts'ang shu*. 藏書. 1599, 1602. Reprint. Peking: Chung-hua, 1959.

Li Chih-ch'ang 李志常. *Ch'ang-ch'un chen-jen Hsi-yu chi chu* 長春眞人西遊記注. Edited by Wang Kuo-wei 王國維. In Yen I-p'ing 嚴一萍, ed. *Tao-chiao yen-chiu tzu-liao* 道教研究資料, no. 2. Taipei: I-wen, 1974.

Li Fang 李昉 (925–996) et al. *T'ai-p'ing kuang-chi* 太平廣記. Reprint. Peking: Jen-min wen-hsüeh, 1959.

Li Hsü 李詡. *Chieh-an lao-jen man-pi* 戒庵老人漫筆. Reprint. Wei Lien-k'e 魏連科, ed. *Yuan-Ming shih-liao pi-chi ts'ung-k'an* 元明史料筆記叢刊. Peking: Chung-hua, 1982, *chüan* 5.

Li K'ai-hsien 李開先. *I-hsiao san* 一笑散. Yeh Feng 葉楓, ed. Peking: Wen-hsüeh ku-chi, 1955.

———. *Tz'u-nüeh* 詞謔. Reprinted in *CKKTHCLCCC*, 3: 257–418.

Li Ling-nien 李靈年. "Shih Nai-an tsa-k'ao" 施耐庵雜考. In *Nan-ching shih-yüan hsüeh-pao* 南京師院學報 1982, no. 3: 61–66.

Li Shang-yin 李商隱 (813–858). *Li I-shan shih-chi* 李義山詩集. *SPTK ch'u-pien so-pen* 初編縮本. Taipei: Shang-wu, 1967.

Li Shih-jen 李時人. "Hsi-yu chi ti ch'eng-shu kuo-ch'eng ho Sun Wu-k'ung hsing-hsiang ti yüan-yüan" 西遊記的成書過程和孫悟空形象的淵源. In *HYCYC*, pp. 169–89.

———. "I-p'i yu-kuan Chang Chu-p'o ti chung-yao tzu-liao chien-chieh" 一批有關張竹坡的重要資料簡介. Unpublished paper.

———. "Lüeh-lun Wu Ch'eng-en Hsi-yu chi chung ti T'ang-seng ch'u-shih ku-shih" 略論吳承恩西遊記中的唐僧出世故事. In *WHIC*, 1983, no. 1: 86–93.

Li Shih-jen and Ts'ai Ching-hao 蔡鏡浩. "Ta-T'ang San-tsang ch'ü-ching shih-hua ch'eng-shu shih-tai k'ao-pien" 大唐三藏取經詩話成書時代考辨. In *HCSFHYHP*, 1982, no. 3: 22–30.

Li T'o-chih 李拓之. "Hu pao-i k'ao" 呼保義考. In *SHYCLWC*, pp. 248–54.

Li Tsung-t'ung 李宗侗 (Hsüan-po 玄伯). "Tu Shui-hu chi" 讀水滸記. In *Li-shih ti p'ou-mien* 歷史的剖面, pp. 9–26. Taipei: Wen-hsing, 1965.

Li Tzu 李滋. "Shui-hu ti pan-pen ho Shui-hu ti cheng-chih ch'ing-hsiang" 水滸的版本和水滸的政治傾向. In *WW*, 1975, no. 11: 31–41.

Li Yü 李漁 (1611–1680?). *Hsien-ch'ing ou-chi* 閒情偶寄. Partial reprint in *Li Li-weng ch'ü-hua*. 李笠翁曲話. Hu-nan: Jen-min, 1980. Also reprinted in Peking: Chung-kuo hsi-ch'ü,1962.

Li Yüeh-kang 李曰剛. Sheng-Ming shih t'ai-ko t'i yü chu pieh-t'i chih liu-pien" 盛明詩臺閣體與諸別體之流變. In *Chung-kuo shih chi-k'an* 中國詩季刊. 7, no. 3 (September 1976): 46–93.

Liao Nan 蓼南. "Kuo-nei fa-hsien Ming-k'an Li Cho-wu p'ing Hsi-yu chi" 國內發現明刊李卓吾評西遊記. In *WHIC*, 1980, no. 2, p. 34.

Liao Tao-nan 廖道南, ed. *Tien-ko tz'u-lin chi* 殿閣詞林記. 1545. Reprinted in *SKCS chen-pen*, series 9 珍本九集. Taipei: Shang-wu, 1979.

Lin Wen-shan 林文山. "Shui-hu ti ch'ing-chieh an-p'ai" 水滸的情節安排. In *SHCM* 1: 185–203.

Liu Chih-chien 劉知漸. "Lo Kuan-chung wei shen-mo yao fan-tui Ts'ao Ts'ao" 羅貫中爲甚麼要反對曹操. In *Ts'ao Ts'ao lun-chi* 曹操論集, pp. 322–36. Peking: San-lien, 1964.

Liu Ching-chih 劉靖之. *Kuan Han-ch'ing San-kuo ku-shih tsa-chü yen-chiu* 關漢卿三國故事雜劇研究. Hong Kong: San-lien, 1980.

———. "Yuan-tai chih hou ti Shui-hu hsi" 元代之後的水滸戲. In *SHCM* 3: 263–80.

Liu Hsiu-yeh 劉修業. *Ku-tien hsiao-shuo hsi-ch'ü ts'ung-k'ao* 古典小說戲曲叢考. Peking: Tso-chia, 1958.

———. "Wu Ch'eng-en chu-shu k'ao" 吳承恩著述考. In *Wu Ch'eng-en shih-wen chi* 吳承恩詩文集, pp. 232–40. Shanghai: Ku-tien wen-hsüeh, 1958. Reprinted in Liu Hsiu-yeh, *Ku-tien hsiao-shuo hsi-ch'ü ts'ung-k'ao*, pp. 33–39.

———. "Wu Ch'eng-en lun-chu tsa-shih k'ao" 吳承恩論著雜事考. In *Wu Ch'eng-en shih-wen chi*, pp. 240–46. Also in Liu Hsiu-yeh, *Ku-tien hsiao-shuo hsi-ch'ü ts'ung-k'ao*, pp. 40–46.

Liu Hui 劉輝. "Pei-t'u-kuan ts'ang Shan-lin ching-chi chi yü Chin P'ing Mei" 北圖館藏山林經濟籍與金瓶梅. In *WH*, no. 24 (April 1985): 10–26.

———. "Pei-t'u ts'ang Chin P'ing Mei Wen Lung p'i-pen hui-p'ing chi-lu" 北圖藏金瓶梅文龍批本會評輯錄. In *WH*, no. 26 (October 1985): 37–65; no. 27 (January 1986): 38–71; no. 28 (April 1986): 33–66.

Liu I-ch'ing 劉義慶 (403–444). *Shih-shuo hsin-yü* 世說新語. Commentary by Liu Hsiao-piao 劉孝標. *KHCPTS* edition, vol. 244.

Liu Jo-yü 劉若愚. *Cho chung chih* 酌中志. Ca. 1638. In *Hai-shan hsien-kuan ts'ung-shu* 海山仙館叢書. Reprint. Taipei: I-wen, 1967, *chüan* 18.

Liu Kuo-chün 劉國鈞. *Chung-kuo shu-shih chien-pien* 中國書史簡編. Peking: Kao-teng chiao-yü, 1958.

Liu Shih-ku 劉師古. *Hsien-hua Chin P'ing Mei* 閒話金瓶梅. Taipei: Shih-shih, 1977.

Liu Shih-te 劉世德. "T'an San-fen shih-lüeh: t'a ho San-kuo chih p'ing-hua ti i-t'ung ho hsien-hou" 談三分事略：它和三國志平話的異同和先後. Unidentified offprint, pp. 99–111.

————. "T'an Shui-hu chuan Ying-hsüeh ts'ao-t'ang k'an-pen ti kai-k'uang, hsü-wen, ho piao-mu" 談水滸傳映雪草堂刊本的概況, 序文, 和標目. In *SHCM* 3: 134–62.

Liu Ta-chieh 劉大杰. *Chung-kuo wen-hsüeh fa-ta shih* 中國文學發達史. Original title *Fa-chan shih* 發展史. Reprint. Taipei: Chung-hua, 1960.

Liu T'ing-chi 劉廷璣 (fl. 1676). *Tsai-yüan tsa-chih* 在園雜志. In *Liao-hai ts'ung shu* 遼海叢書, vol. 15. Reprint. Taipei: I-wen, 1971.

Liu Ts'ao-nan 劉操南. "Lun Wu shih-hui" 論武十回. In *SHCM* 2 (1983): 484–96.

Liu Ts'un-yan 柳存仁. "Ch'üan-chen chiao ho hsiao-shuo Hsi-yu chi" 全真教和小說西遊記. In *MPYK*, part 1 (May 1985): 55–62; part 2 (June 1985): 59–64; part 3 (July 1985): 85–90; part 4 (August 1985): 85–90; part 5 (September 1985): 70–74.

————. *Ming-Ch'ing Chung-kuo t'ung-su hsiao-shuo pan-pen yen-chiu* 明清中國通俗小說版本研究. Kowloon: Chung-shan t'u-shu kung-ssu, 1972.

————. "Ming-ju yü tao-chiao" 明儒與道教. In *HFTTSC*, 1: 233–71.

————. "Ssu-yu chi ti Ming k'e-pen" 四遊記的明刻本. In *HFTTSC*, pp. 379–432. Originally published in *HYHP* 5, no. 2 (1963): 323–75.

Liu Tung 劉冬 and Ou-yang Chien 歐陽健. "Ching-pen chung-i chuan p'ing-chia shang-tui" 京本忠義傳評價商兌. In *Kuei-chou wen-shih ts'ung-k'an* 貴州文史叢刊, 1985, no. 2: 127–33.

Liu Yin-po 劉蔭伯. "Hsi-yu chi Ming-Ch'ing liang-tai ch'u-pan shih k'ao" 西遊記明清兩代出版史考. In *Hua-tung shih-fan ta-hsüeh hsüeh-pao* 華東範師大學學報, 1983, no. 3: 76–79.

Liu Yu-chu 劉友竹. "San-kuo chih t'ung-su yen-i shih Yuan-tai tso-p'in" 三國志通俗演義是元代作品. In *SKYIYCC*, pp. 296–305.

Lo Chin-t'ang 羅錦堂. "Hua Kuan So ch'uan-shuo k'ao" 花關索傳說考. In *CWWH* 9, no. 9 (February 1981): 4–37.

————. "Kuan Yü yü Kuan So" 關羽與關索. In *Essays in Commemoration of the Golden Jubilee of the Fung Ping Shan Library*. Hong Kong: n.p., 1982.

————. *Li-tai t'u-shu pan-pen chih-yao* 歷代圖書板本志要. Taipei: Chung-hua, 1958.

Lo Lung-chih 羅龍治. "Hsi-yu chi ti yü-yen ho hsi-nüeh t'e-chih" 西遊記的寓言和戲謔特質. In *Shu-p'ing shu-mu* 書評書目. 52 (August 1977): 11–19.

Lo Te-jung 羅德榮. "Ying-hsiung ch'uan-ch'i ti k'ai-shan chih tso Shui-hu chuan" 英雄傳奇的開山之作水滸傳. In *Kuei-chou wen-shih ts'ung-k'an* 貴州文史叢刊, 1984, no. 2: 127–33.

Lo Tung-pien 羅東昇. "Man-shuo Shui-hu li ti Wang Lun" 漫說水滸裡的王倫. In *SHCM* 2: 372–78.

Lo Yang 羅揚 and Shen P'eng-nien 沈彭年, eds. *Shuo-ch'ang Hsi-yu chi* 說唱西遊記. Peking: T'ung-su wen-i, 1956.

Lo Yeh 羅燁. *Tsui-weng t'an-lu* 醉翁談錄. In *Chung-kuo pi-chi hsiao-shuo ming-chu* 中國筆記小說名著. General editor, Yang Chia-lo 楊家駱. Taipei: Shih-chieh, 1959.

Lu Chün-ling 陸峻嶺. *Yuan-jen wen-chi p'ien-mu fen-lei so-yin* 元人文集篇目分類所引. Peking: Chung-hua, 1979.

Lu Hsin 盧炘. "Chin-p'i Shui-hu ti ch'ü-pi yü Sung Chiang" 金批水滸的曲筆與

宋江. In *Che-chiang hsüeh-k'an* 浙江學刊, 1984, no. 1: 49–53.

Lü Hsing-ch'ang 呂興昌. "Shui-hu chuan ch'u-t'an: ts'ung hsing yü ch'üan-li ti kuan-nien lun Sung Chiang" 水滸傳初探, 從性與權力的觀念論宋江. In *CKKTWHYCTK* 3: 21–47.

Lu Hsün 魯迅. *Chung-kuo hsiao-shuo shih-lüeh* 中國小說史略. In *Lu Hsün ch'üan-chi* 魯迅全集, vol. 9. Peking: Jen-min, 1981. Also in *Lu Hsün san-shih-nien chi* 魯迅三十年集, vol. 3. Hong Kong: Hsin-i, 1968.

———. *Hsiao-shuo chiu-wen ch'ao* 小說舊文鈔. In *Lu Hsün ch'üan-chi* 魯迅全集, vol. 10. Peking: Jen-min, 1973. Also reprinted in Hong Kong: Ta-t'ung, 1959.

———. "Liu-mang yü pien-ch'ien" 流氓與變遷. In *Lu Hsün ch'üan-chi*, vol. 14, pp. 160–62. Peking: Jen-min, 1973.

Lu Kung 路工. *Ming-Ch'ing p'ing-hua hsiao-shuo hsüan* 明清平話小說選. Shanghai: Ku-tien wen-hsüeh, 1958.

Lu Lien-hsing 陸聯星. "Li Chih p'i-p'ing San-kuo yen-i pien-wei" 李贄批評三國演義辨偽. In *WHIC*, no. 458 (April 7, 1963).

Lü Nai-yen 呂乃岩. "Shui-hu ku-shih tsai nan-pei liang-ti liu-ch'uan ch'ing-k'uang" 水滸故事在南北兩地流傳情況. In *SHCM* 3: 119–33.

Lü Ssu-mien 呂思勉. *San-kuo shih-hua* 三國史話. Shanghai: K'ai-ming, 1934.

Lü Tsu-ch'ien 呂祖謙 (1137–1181). *Ku-wen kuan-chien* 古文關鍵. Reprint Taipei: Kuang-wen, 1970.

Lü Wen 呂溫 (772–811). "Chu-ko Liang Wu-hou miao chi" 諸葛亮武侯廟記. In *Yüeh-ya t'ang ts'ung-shu* 粵雅堂叢書, vol. 64, no. 253. *PPTSCC* edition.

Ma Lien 馬廉. "Chiu-pen San-kuo yen-i pan-pen ti tiao-ch'a" 舊本三國演義板本的調查. In *Pei-p'ing pei-hai t'u-shu-kuan yüeh-k'an* 北平北海圖書館月刊. 2, no. 5 (1929): 397–401.

Ma Tai-loi 馬泰來. "Hsieh Chao-che ti Chin P'ing Mei pa" 謝肇淛的金瓶梅跋. In *CHWSLT*, 1980, no. 4: 299–305.

———. "Ma-ch'eng Liu-chia ho Chin P'ing Mei" 麻城劉家和金瓶梅. In *CHWSLT*, 1982, no. 1: 111–20.

———. "Ming-pan Shui-hu chuan ch'a-t'u erh-chung shu hou" 明版水滸傳插圖二種書後. In *Hsiang-kang ta-hsüeh Chung-wen hsüeh-hui nien-k'an* 香港大學中文學會年刊 (1966–1967), pp. 121–26.

———. "Yu-kuan Chin P'ing Mei tsao-ch'i ch'uan-po ti i-t'iao tzu-liao" 有關金瓶梅早期傳播的一條資料. In *WHIC*, no. 650 (August 14, 1984).

Ma T'i-chi 馬蹄疾. *Shui-hu tzu-liao hui-pien* 水滸資料彙編. Peking: Chung-hua, 1980.

Ma Yau-woon 馬幼垣 (Y. W. Ma). "Hsien-ts'un tsui tsao ti chien-pen Shui-hu chuan" 現存最早的簡本水滸傳. In *CHWSLT*, 1985, no. 3: 73–121.

———. "Hu-yü yen-chiu chien-pen Shui-hu i-chien shu" 呼籲研究簡本水滸意見書. In *SHCM* 3: 183–204.

———. "Liang-shan chü-pao chi" 梁山聚寶記. In *MPYK* 20, no. 5 (May 1984): 20–25. Also in *CWWH* 13, no. 9 (February 1985): 4–25.

———. "Liang-shan po fu-ch'ou kuan-nien pien" 梁山濼復仇觀念辨. In *MPYK* 20, no. 9 (September 1985): 106–8.

———. "Lun Chin P'ing Mei Hsieh pa shu" 論金瓶梅謝跋書. In *CKKTHSYCCC*, 2: 215–19.

———. "Niu-chin ta-hsüeh so ts'ang Ming-tai chien-pen Shui-hu ts'an-yeh shu hou" 牛津大學所藏明代簡本水滸殘頁書後. In *CHWSLT*, 1981, no. 4: 47–66.

———. "P'ai tso-tz'u i-hou Shui-hu chuan ti ch'ing-chieh ho jen-wu an-p'ai" 排座次以後水滸傳的情節和人物安排. In *MPYK* 20, no. 6 (June 1985): 85–92. Also in *Ku-tien wen-hsüeh* 古典文學 7 (August 1985): 857–76.

———. "Shui-hu chuan chan-cheng ch'ang-mien ti lei-pieh ho nei-han" 水滸傳戰爭場面的類別和內涵. In *Lien-ho wen-hsüeh* 聯合文學 1:9 (July 1985): 16–22.

———. "Shui-hu chuan li ti hao-se jen-wu" 水滸傳裡的好色人物. In Ma Yau-woon. *Chung-kuo hsiao-shuo shih chi-kao* 中國小說史集稿, pp. 225–31. Taipei: Shih-pao, 1980.

———. "Yen-chiu Chin P'ing Mei ti i-t'iao hsin tzu-liao" 研究金瓶梅的一條新資料. In *CKKTHSYCCC*, 1: 151–56.

———. "Ying-yin liang-chung Ming-tai hsiao-shuo chen-pen hsü" 影印兩種明代小說珍本序. In *SHCM* 2: 132–38.

Mao Tun 茅盾. "T'an Shui-hu ti jen-wu ho chieh-kou" 談水滸的人物和結構. In *Wen-i pao* 文藝報 2, no. 2. Reprinted in *SHYCLWC*, pp. 1–5.

Meng Sen 孟森. *Ming-tai shih* 明代史. 1957. Reprint. Taipei: Chung-hua, 1967.

Min Tse 敏澤. *Chung-kuo wen-hsüeh li-lun p'i-p'ing shih* 中國文學理論批評史. Peking: Jen-min, 1981.

Ming-jen tsa-chü hsüan 明人雜劇選. Edited by Chou I-pai 周貽白. Peking: Jen-min wen-hsüeh, 1962.

Ming shih 明史. Compiled by Chang T'ing-yü 張廷玉 (1672–1755) et al. 28 vols. Reprint. Peking: Chung-hua, 1974.

Ming-wen an 明文案. Edited by Huang Tsung-hsi 黃宗羲 (attributed). Original in National Central Library, Taipei. Microfilm in Gest Oriental Library, Princeton, New Jersey.

Ming-wen ch'ao 明文鈔. Edited by Kao T'ang 高塘 (attributed). Preface, 1786. In rare book collection of Gest Oriental Library, Princeton, New Jersey.

Ming-wen shou-tu 明文授讀. Edited by Huang Tsung-hsi 黃宗羲 (attributed). Reprint. Tokyo: Kyūko, 1972.

Ming-wen ying-hua 明文英華. Edited by Ku Yu-hsiao 顧有孝. Preface, 1687. Microfilm in Gest Oriental Library, Princeton.

Mu-lien chiu-mu ch'üan-shan hsi-wen 目蓮救母勸善戲文. Reprinted in *Ku-pen hsi-ch'ü ts'ung-k'an* 古本戲曲叢刊. 1st series, vols. 80–82.

Na Tsung-hsün. 那宗訓. "Hsi-yu chi chung ti Sun Wu-k'ung" 西遊記中的孫悟空. In *CWWH* 10, no. 11 (April 1982): 66–78.

Nieh Kan-nu 聶紺弩. "Shui-hu wu-lun" 水滸五論. In *Chung-kuo ku-tien hsiao-shuo lun-chi* 中國古典小說論集, pp. 9–204. Shanghai: Shanghai ku-chi, 1981.

Ou-yang Chien 歐陽建. "Hsi-yu chi ti wan-shih chu-i ho hsien-shih ching-shen" 西遊記的玩世主義和現實精神. In *HYCYC*, pp. 54–71.

———. "Shih-lun San-kuo chih t'ung-su yen-i ti ch'eng-shu nien-tai" 試論三國志通俗演義的成書年代. In *SKYIYCC*, pp. 280–95.

———. "Shui-hu chien-pen fan-pen ti-shan kuo-ch'eng hsin cheng" 水滸簡本繁本遞續過程新證. In *WS* 18 (1983): 211–31.

P'an Ch'eng-pi 潘承弼 and Ku T'ing-lung 顧廷龍. *Ming-tai pan-pen t'u-lu ch'u-pien*

明代版本圖錄初編. Taipei: Kai-ming, 1971.

P'an K'ai-p'ei 潘開沛. "Chin P'ing Mei ti ch'an-sheng ho tso-che" 金瓶梅的產生和
作者. In *MCHSYCLWC*, pp. 173–80.

P'eng Hai 彭海. "Hsi-yu chi chung tui fo-chiao ti p'i-p'an t'ai-tu" 西遊記中對佛教
的批判態度. In *WHIC*, no. 77 (October 30, 1955). Reprinted in *HYCYCLWC*,
pp. 158–71.

San-kuo chih p'ing-hua 三國志平話. Reprinted in *Li-shih t'ung-su yen-i* 歷史通俗
演義. Taipei: National Central Library, 1971. Also in *Ch'üan-hsiang p'ing-hua
wu-chung* 全相平話五種. Peking: Wen-hsüeh ku-chi k'an-hsing-she, 1956.
Typeset edition, Shanghai: Ku-tien wen-hsüeh, 1955.

Shen Te-ch'ien 沈德潛 (1673–1769), ed. *Ming-shih pieh-ts'ai* 明詩別裁. Reprint.
Shanghai: Shang-wu, 1958.

Shen Te-fu 沈德符 (1578–1642). *Wan-li yeh-huo pien* 萬曆野獲編. Edited by
Ch'ien Fang 錢枋. 1619. Reprint. Peking: Chung-hua, 1959 and 1980.

Shih Mei-ts'en (Mei-ch'in) 史梅岑. *Chung-kuo yin-shua fa-chan shih* 中國印刷
發展史. Taipei: Shang-wu, 1966.

Shih Nai-an yen-chiu chuan-chi 施耐庵研究專輯. *Ta-feng hsien wen-shih tzu-liao*
大豐縣文史資料, no. 3 (1983).

Shui-hu ch'üan-chuan 水滸全傳. Attributed to Lo Kuan-chung 羅貫中 or Shih Nai-
an 施耐庵. Edited by Cheng Chen-to 鄭振鐸, with Wu Hsiao-ling 吳曉鈴
and Wang Li-ch'i 王利器. Peking: Jen-min wen-hsüeh, 1954. 3 vols. Reprint.
Hong Kong: Chung-hua, 1958.

Shui-hu chuan hui-p'ing pen 水滸傳會評本. Compiled by Ch'en Hsi-chung 陳曦鐘,
with Hou Chung-i 侯忠義 and Lu Yü-ch'uan 魯玉川. 2 vols. Peking: Peking
University, 1981.

Ssu-k'u ch'üan-shu tsung-mu t'i-yao 四庫全書總目提要. Compiled by Chi Yün 紀昀.
Completed 1781–83. *KHCPTS* edition. Shanghai: Shang-wu, 1931.

Ssu-ma Kuang 司馬光 (1019–1086). *Tzu-chih t'ung-chien* 資治通鑑. Reprint. Peking:
Chung-hua, 1976.

Ssu-shu chi-chu 四書集注. Reprint. Taipei: Shih-chieh, 1968.

Ssu-yu chi 四遊記. Reprint. Shanghai: Ku-tien wen-hsüeh, 1956.

Su Hsing 蘇興. "Hsi-yu chi so-t'an" 西遊記瑣談. In *WHIC*, 1980, no. 3: 54–63.

———. "Hsi-yu chi tui Ming Shih-tsung ti yin-yü p'i-p'an ho ch'ao-feng" 西遊記
對明世宗的隱寓批判和嘲諷. In *HYCYC*, pp. 33–53.

———. "Kuan-yü Hsi-yu chi ti chi-ko wen-t'i" 關於西遊記的幾個問題. In
WHICTK 10 (1962): 134–48.

———. "Wu Ch'eng-en Hsi-yu chi ti-chiu-hui wen-t'i" 吳承恩西遊記第九回
問題. In *Pei-fang lun-ts'ung*. 北方論叢, 1981, no. 4: 31–36.

———. "Yeh t'an pai-hui-pen Hsi-yu chi shih-fou Wu Ch'eng-en so-tso" 也談百
回本西遊記是否吳承恩所作. In *SHKHCH*, 1985, no. 1: 245–52.

Su Huan-chung 蘇寰中. "Ming-feng chi ti tso-che wen-t'i" 鳴鳳記的作者問題.
In *Chung-shan ta-hsüeh hsüeh-pao* 中山大學學報, 1980, no. 3: 82–85.

Su Shih 蘇軾 (1036–1101). "Chu-ko Liang lun" 諸葛亮論. In *Su Tung-p'o chi*
蘇東坡集. *KHCPTS* edition. Vol. 282, no. 4, pp. 71–72.

———. *Tung-p'o chih-lin* 東坡志林. Reprint in *Ts'ung-shu chi-ch'eng chien-pien*.
叢書集成簡編. Taipei: Shang-wu, 1965. Also printed in Wang Sung-ling
王松齡, ed. Peking: Chung-hua, 1981.

Sui Shu-sen 隋樹森. *Yuan-ch'ü hsüan wai-pien* 元曲選外編. Peking: Chung-hua, 1959.

Sun K'ai-ti 孫楷第. *Chung-kuo t'ung-su hsiao-shuo shu-mu.* 中國通俗小說書目. 1933. Reprint. Peking: Jen-min wen-hsüeh, 1982.

———. *Jih-pen Tung-ching so chien Chung-kuo hsiao-shuo shu-mu* 日本東京所見中國小說書目. 1932. Reprint. Hong Kong: Shih-yung, 1967.

———. "San-kuo chih p'ing-hua yü San-kuo chih-chuan t'ung-su yen-i" 三國志平話與三國志傳通俗演義. 1934. Reprint. In *TCC,* 1:109−20.

———. "San-yen Erh-p'ai yüan-liu k'ao" 三言二拍源流考. In *KLPPTSKKK* 5, no. 2 (1931):3481−532 (11−62). Reprinted in *TCC,* 1:149−208.

———. "Shui-hu chuan chiu-pen k'ao" 水滸傳舊本考. In *T'u-shu chi-k'an* 圖書季刊. N.s. 3, nos. 3−4 (December 1941):193−207. Reprinted in *TCC,* 1:121−43.

———. "Wu Ch'ang-ling yü tsa-chü Hsi-yu chi" 吳昌齡與雜劇西遊記. In *TCC,* 2:366−98.

Sun K'e-k'uan 孫克寬. *Sung-Yuan tao-chiao yüan-liu* 宋元道教源流. Taipei: Tung-hai ta-hsüeh, 1968.

———. "T'ai-wan hsien-ts'un Yuan-jen pieh-chi hsiao-lu" 臺灣現存元人別集小錄. In *T'u-shu-kuan hsüeh-pao* 圖書館學報. 2 (July 1960):133−35; 3 (July 1961):105−7; 4 (July 1962):107−16; 5 (August 1963):9−17.

———. *Yuan-tai Han wen-hua chih huo-tung* 元代漢文化之活動. Taipei: Chung-hua, 1968.

Sun Sheng 孫盛. *Chin yang-ch'iu* 晉陽秋. Reprint in *HSISK,* vol. 31.

Sun Shou-wei 孫壽瑋. "Man-t'an Shui-hu li ti fu-nü hsing-hsiang" 漫談水滸裡的婦女形象. In *SHCM* 3: 417−25.

Sun Shu-yü 孫述宇 (Phillip Sun). *Chin P'ing Mei ti i-shu* 金瓶梅的藝術. Taipei: Shih-pao, 1979.

———. "Chin P'ing Mei ti ming-ming" 金瓶梅的命名. In *MPYK* 12, no. 12 (December 1977):9−16. Reprinted in *I-shu,* pp. 89−94.

———. "Hsi-men-ch'ing ti hsing-hsiang yü Chin P'ing Mei ti ch'eng-chiu" 西門慶的形象與金瓶梅的成就. In *MPYK* 13, no. 2 (February 1978):17−23. Reprinted in *I-shu,* pp. 103−11.

———. "Liang-shan ying-hsiung ti i-ch'i" 梁山英雄的義氣. In *MPYK* 13, no. 10 (October 1978):17−23.

———. "Nü-tzu wu jung pien shih te" 女子無容便是德. In *MPYK* 13, no. 12 (December 1978):36−41.

———. "Shui-hu chuan: ch'iang-jen chiang kei ch'iang-jen t'ing ti ku-shih" 水滸傳：強人講給強人聽的故事. In *MPYK* 13, no. 8 (August 1978):2−7. Reprinted in Sun Shu-yü, *Shui-hu chuan ti lai-li, hsin-tai, yü i-shu,* pp. 25ff.

———. "Shui-hu chuan pei-hou ti wang-ming han" 水滸傳背後的亡命漢. In *CKKTHSYCCC,* 1:55−76. Reprinted in Sun Shu-yü, *Shui-hu chuan ti lai-li, hsin-t'ai, yü i-shu,* pp. 44ff.

———. "Shui-hu chuan ti hsüan-ch'uan i-shu: hung-yen huo-shui" 水滸傳的宣傳藝術：紅顏禍水. In *CHWHFHYK* 9, no. 6 (June 1976):28−32. Reprinted in Sun Shu-yü, *Shui-hu chuan ti lai-li, hsin-t'ai, yü i-shu,* pp. 293ff.

———. *Shui-hu chuan ti lai-li, hsin-t'ai, yü i-shu* 水滸傳的來歷、心態、與藝術. Taipei: Shih-pao, 1981.

————. "Shui-hu chuan ti t'ung-su hsiao-shuo i-shu" 水滸傳的通俗小說藝術. In *Hsin-ya shu-yüan hsüeh-shu nien-k'an* 新亞書院學術年刊 12 (1970):129–44.

Sun Yung-tu 孫永都. "Lun Liang-shan i-chün chung ti Chih-to hsing Wu Yung" 論梁山義軍中的智多星吳用. In *SHCM* 3: 376–86.

Sung P'ei-wei 宋佩偉. *Ming wen-hsüeh shih* 明文學史. Shanghai: Shang-wu, 1934.

Ta-T'ang San-tsang ch'ü-ching shih-hua 大唐三藏取經詩話. Reprint. Shanghai: Chung-kuo ku-tien wen-hsüeh, 1954.

Ta-yeh shih-i chi 大業拾遺記. Attributed to Yen Shih-ku 顏師古 (581–645). In *T'ai-p'ing kuang-chi* 太平廣記, *chüan* 226, pp. 1735–36. Reprint. Peking: Jen-min wen-hsüeh, 1959.

Tai Hung-sen 戴鴻森. "Ts'ung Chin P'ing Mei k'an Ming-jen ti yin-shih feng-mao" 從金瓶梅看明人的飲食風貌. In *LCPM*, pp. 372–78.

Tai Pu-fan 戴不凡. *Hsiao-shuo chien-wen lu* 小說見聞錄. Hang-chou: Che-chiang jen-min, 1982.

Tai Wang-shu 戴望舒. "Yüan-k'an Shui-hu chuan chih chen-wei" 袁刊水滸傳之眞僞. In *Hsiao-shuo hsi-ch'ü lun-chi* 小說戲曲論集, pp. 59–66. Peking: Tso-chia, 1958.

T'an Cheng-pi 譚正璧. *Chung-kuo hsiao-shuo fa-ta shih* 中國小說發達史. 1935. Reprint. Taipei: Ch'i-yeh, 1973.

————. *Hua-pen yü ku-chü* 話本與古劇. Shanghai: Ku-tien wen-hsüeh, 1957.

T'an Chia-chien 譚家健. "Sun Wu-k'ung san ta Pai-ku ching ku-shih t'an-yüan" 孫悟空三打白骨精故事探源. In *WHIC*, 1981, no. 3: 66.

T'an Liang-hsiao 譚艮嘯. "Hua Kuan So chuan tui San-kuo yen-i ti ch'i-shih" 花關索傳對三國演義的啓示. In *SKYIYCC*, pp. 388–97.

T'ang Chün-i 唐君毅. *Chung-kuo che-hsüeh yüan-lun* 中國哲學原論. Hong Kong: Hsin-ya yen-chiu, 1975.

T'ang Hsien-tsu 湯顯祖. *T'ang Hsien-tsu shih-wen chi* 湯顯祖詩文集. Edited by Hsü Shuo-fang. Shanghai: Shang-hai ku-chi, 1982.

T'ao Tsung-i 陶宗儀 (fl. 1360–68). *Ch'o-keng lu* 輟耕錄. Preface 1366. Reprint in *Pi-chi hsiao-shu ta-kuan* 筆記小說大觀, 7th series, 1:257–752. Reprint. Taipei: Ko-ta, 1975.

Teng Chih-ch'eng 鄧之誠. *Ku-t'ung so-chi ch'üan-pien* 骨董瑣記全編. Peking: San-lien, 1955.

————. "Sung-k'an hsiao-chi" 松堪小記, no. 2 下. In *Wen-shih* 文史 17 (1983): 123–40.

T'ien Ju-ch'eng 田汝成. *Hsi-hu yu-lan chih-yü* 西湖遊覽志餘. Preface, 1547. 1584. Reprint. Shanghai: Chung-hua, 1958.

Ting Yen 丁晏 (1794–1875). *Shih-t'ing chi-shih hsü-pien* 石亭記事續編. Preface 1848. In *I-chih chai ts'ung shu* 頤志齋叢書, vol. 6. Reprint. Taipei: I-wen, 1971.

Ts'ai I 蔡毅. "San-kuo yen-i chung ti shen-kuai miao-hsieh" 三國演義中的神怪描寫. In *She-hui k'e hsüeh yen-chiu* 社會科學研究, 1983, no. 1: 81–86.

Ts'ai Kuo-liang 蔡國樑. "Ch'en Shih-pin tui Hsi-yu chi jen-wu ho ch'ing-chieh chieh-kou ti p'i-p'ing" 陳士斌對西遊記人物和情節結構的批評. In *WH* (1984):12–24.

————. "Ming-jen, Ch'ing-jen, chin-jen p'ing Chin P'ing Mei" 明人清人今人評金瓶梅. In *SHKHCH*, 1983, no. 4: 306–12.

Ts'ai Tung-fan 蔡東藩. *Ming-shih t'ung-su yen-i* 明史通俗演義. In *Li-ch'ao t'ung-su yen-i* 歷朝通俗演義. Taipei: Tung-fang, 1963.

Ts'ao Chü-jen 曹聚仁. "Ming-tai ch'ien-hou ch'i-tzu ti fu-ku yün-tung yu-che tzen-yang ti she-hui pei-ching" 明代前後七子的復古運動有着怎樣的社會背景. In *Wen-hsüeh pai-t'i* 文學百題, pp. 381–85. Shanghai: Sheng-hua, 1935.

Ts'ao Shih-pang 曹仕邦. "Hsi-yu chi chung jo-kan ch'ing-chieh pen-yüan ti t'an-t'ao" 西遊記中若干情節本源的探討. In *Chung-kuo hsüeh-jen* 中國學人 1 (March 1970):99–104.

———. "Hsi-yu chi: jo-kan ch'ing-chieh ti pen-yüan tsai t'an" 再探. In *YSYK* 41, no. 3 (March 1975):32–37.

——— "Hsi-yu chi jo-kan ch'ing-chieh ti pen-yüan ssu-t'an" 四探. In *SMCK* 15, no. 3 (December 1981):117–26.

———. "Hsi-yu chi jo-kan ch'ing-chieh ti pen-yüan wu-t'an" 五探. In *SMCK* 16, no. 4 (March 1983):35–43.

Ts'ui Wen-yin 崔文印. "Li Chih Ssu-shu p'ing chen-wei pien" 李贄四書評真偽辨. In *WHIC*, 1979, no. 4: 31–34.

Tu Fu 杜甫. *Tu-shih yin-te* 杜詩引得. Harvard-Yenching Concordance. Taipei: Ch'eng-wen, 1966.

Tu Te-ch'iao 杜德橋 (Glen Dudbridge). "Hsi-yu chi tsu-pen k'ao ti tsai-shang-ch'üeh" 西遊記祖本考的再商榷. In *HYHP* 6, no. 2 (1964):497–519.

Tung Mei-k'an 董每戡. *San-kuo yen-i shih-lun* 三國演義試論. Shanghai: Ku-tien wen-hsüeh, 1956.

Wan-li ti-ch'ao 萬曆邸抄. Reprint. Taipei: Hsüeh-sheng, 1968.

Wang Ch'i 王圻. *Hsü wen-hsien t'ung-k'ao* 續文獻通考. 1586. Reprint. Taipei: Wen-hai, 1979, *chüan* 177.

———. *Pai-shih hui-pien* 稗史彙編. Reprint. Taipei: Hsin-hsing, 1969.

Wang Ch'i-chou 王齊洲. "Li Shih-shih hsing-hsiang ti su-tsao yü Shui-hu chuan ti ch'uang-tso ssu-hsiang" 李師師形象的塑造與水滸傳的創作思想. In *T'ien-chin she-hui k'e-hsüeh* 天津社會科學, 1984, no. 5: 73–77, 33.

Wang Chih-yüan 王致遠, ed. *Li-tai tz'u-ch'ü p'ing-hsüan* 歷代詞曲評選. Taipei: Shanghai yin-shua, 1964.

Wang Ch'iu-kuei 王秋桂. "Erh-lang shen ch'uan-shuo pu-k'ao" 二郎神傳說補考. In *Min-su ch'ü-i* 民俗曲藝. 22 (March 1983):1–26.

Wang Chung-min 王重民. *Chung-kuo shan-pen shu t'i-yao* 中國善本書題要. Shang-hai ku-chi, 1983.

Wang Fu-chih 王扶之 (1619–1692). *Tu T'ung-chien lun* 讀通鑑論. Reprint. Peking: Chung-hua, 1975.

Wang Hsiao-chia 王曉家. "Shih-t'an San-kuo yen-i ti tui-pi shou-fa" 試談三國演義的對比手法. In *SKYIYCC*, pp. 119–28.

———. "Shui-hu chuan tso-che hsi Lo Kuan-chung k'ao-pien" 水滸傳作者係羅貫中考辨. In *SHCM* 2: 139–54.

Wang Hsiao-ch'uan 王曉傳 (pseudonym of Wang Li-ch'i). *Yuan-Ming-Ch'ing san-tai chin-hui hsiao-shuo hsi-ch'ü shih-liao* 元明清三代禁毀小說戲曲史料. Peking: Tso-chia, 1958.

Wang Hsiao-i 汪效倚. "Kuan-yü T'ien-tu wai-ch'en Wang Tao-k'un" 關於天都

外臣汪道昆. In *WHIC*, no. 617 (December 20, 1983).

Wang I 王易. *Tz'u-ch'ü shih* 中國詞曲史. 1932. Reprint. Taipei: Kuang-wen, 1960. Also reprinted as *Chung-kuo tz'u-ch'ü shih*. Taipei: Hung-shih ch'u-pan she, 1981.

Wang Ken-lin 王根林. "Shui-hu tsu-pen t'an-k'ao chih-i" 水滸祖本探考質疑. In *CHWSLT*, 1982, no. 4: 79–88.

Wang Kuo-wei 王國維. *Jen-chien tz'u-hua* 人間詞話. Reprint. Peking: Chung-hua, 1955.

Wang Li-ch'i 王利器. "Kuan-yü Shui-hu ch'üan-chuan ti pan-pen chi chiao-ting" 關於水滸全傳的版本及校訂. In *SHCYCLWC*, pp. 398–402.

———. "Lo Kuan-chung yü San-kuo chih t'ung-su yen-i" 羅貫中與三國志通俗演義. In *She-hui k'e-hsüeh yen-chiu* 社會科學研究, 1983, no. 1: 68–73 and no. 2: 64–71. Reprinted in *SKYIYCC*, pp. 240–65.

———. "Shui-hu ch'üan-chuan T'ien Wang erh-chuan shih shui so chia 水滸全傳田王二傳是誰所加. In *WHICTK* 1 (1955):381–93.

———. "Shui-hu chuan shih tsen-yang tsuan-hsiu ti" 水滸傳是怎樣纂修的. In *Wen-hsüeh p'ing-lun* 文學評論, 1982, no. 3, pp. 86–101.

———. "Shui-hu chung so ts'ai-yung ti hua-pen tzu-liao" 水滸中所採用的話本資料. In *SHYCLWC*, pp. 312f.

———. "Shui-hu Li Cho-wu p'ing-pen ti chen-wei wen-t'i" 水滸李卓吾評本的真偽問題. In *Wen-hsüeh p'ing-lun ts'ung-k'an* 文學評論叢刊, no. 2. Peking: Chung-kuo she-hui k'e-hsüeh, 1979.

———. "Shui-hu ti chen-jen chen-shih" 水滸的真人真事. In *SHCM* 1: 1–18, and 2: 13–39.

———. "Shui-hu ying-hsiung ti ch'o-hao" 水滸英雄的綽號. In *SHYCLWC*, pp. 271–308.

Wang P'ei-lun 王沛綸. *Hsi-ch'ü tz'u-tien* 戲曲辭典. Taipei: Chung-hua, 1969.

Wang Shao-t'ang 王少堂. *Yang-chou p'ing-hua Shui-hu: Wu Sung* 揚州平話水滸武松. 2 vols. Nanking: Chiang-su wen-i, 1959.

Wang Shih-chen 王世貞. *K'e-shih k'ao* 科試考. In *Yen-shan t'ang pieh-chi* 弇山堂別集 (1590), *chüan* 81–84. Reprint in *Chung-kuo shih-hsüeh ts'ung-shu* 中國史學叢書. No. 16. Wu Hsiang-hsiang 吳相湘, ed. Taipei: Hsüeh-sheng, 1965.

Wang T'o 王拓. "San-kuo yen-i chung ti ting-ming kuan-nien" 三國演義中的定命觀念. In *YSYK* 40, no. 3 (September 1974):48–54.

Wang Yüan-p'ing 汪遠平. "Shui-hu ti hsing-ko k'e-hua yü ch'ing-chieh an-p'ai" 水滸的性格刻劃與情節安排. In *Hu-nan shih-yüan hsüeh-pao* 湖南師院學報, 1984, no. 2: 69–73.

Wang Yung-chien 王永健. "Ts'ung Ming-ch'u ti Shui-hu hsi k'an Shui-hu chuan tsu-pen ti ch'eng-shu nien-tai" 從明初的水滸戲看水滸傳祖本的成書年代. In *SHCM* 3: 233–41.

Wei Tzu-yün 魏子雲. "Chin P'ing Mei pien-nien shuo" 金瓶梅編年說. In *CWWH* 8, no. 11 (April 1980):42–55.

———. *Chin P'ing Mei shen-t'an* 金瓶梅審探. Taipei: Shang-wu, 1982.

———. *Chin P'ing Mei t'an-yüan* 金瓶梅探源. Taipei: Chü-liu, 1979.

———. *Chin P'ing Mei ti wen-shih yü yen-pien* 金瓶梅的問世與演變. Taipei: Shih-pao, 1981.

————. "Chin P'ing Mei t'ou-shang ti wang-kuan" 金瓶梅頭上的王冠. In *CKKTHSYCCC*, 2:221–43. Reprinted in *Wen-shih yü yen-pien*, pp. 81–92.

————. "Chin P'ing Mei tso-che hsin-t'an" 金瓶梅作者新探. In *CKSP* (September 1–3, 1983).

————. "Chin P'ing Mei tz'u-hua ti ch'eng-shu nien-tai" 金瓶梅詞話的成書年代. In *Ch'u-pan yü yen-chiu* 出版與研究 (August 16, 1977):3.

————. "Chin P'ing Mei tz'u-hua ti tso-che" 金瓶梅詞話的作者. *Chung-hua jih-pao* 中華日報 (July 28–31, 1977).

————. "Lun Ming-tai ti Chin P'ing Mei shih-liao" 論明代的金瓶梅史料. In *CWWH* 6, no. 6 (November 1977):18–39.

————. "Yüan Chung-lang yü Chin P'ing Mei" 袁中郎與金瓶梅. In *Chung-kuo ku-tien hsiao-shuo lun-chi* 中國古典小說論集, 1:255–76. Taipei: Yu-shih ch'i-k'an lun-ts'ung, 1977. Also in *Shu han jen* 書和人 224 (November 24, 1973): 1–8.

Wen Chi 文輯. "Hsi-yu chi cha-chi" 西遊記札記. In *Chung-kuo ku-tien hsiao-shuo chiang-hua* 中國古典小說講話, pp. 42–57. Hong Kong: Shang-hai shu-chü, 1958.

Wen Ying 聞鶯. "Shui-hu chuan liu-pien ssu-chang" 水滸流變四章. In *SHCM* 3: 205–21.

Weng Po-nien 翁柏年. "Ching o-meng hsin-hsi" 驚噩夢新析. In *SHCM* 2: 402–10.

Wu Ch'eng-en 吳承恩. *She-yang hsien-sheng ts'un-kao* 射陽先生存稿. Reprint. Peking: Ku-kung po-wu-yüan, 1930.

Wu Chien-li 吳堅立, "San-kuo yen-i k'ao-shu" 三國演義考述. Master's thesis, Soochow University, Taipei, 1976.

Wu Ch'ung-hsü 伍沖虛 (Shou-yang 守陽). *Wu Liu hsien-tsung ch'üan-chi* 伍柳仙踪全集. Reprint. Taipei: Chen, shan, mei, 1962.

Wu Han 吳晗. "Chin P'ing Mei ti chu-tso shih-tai chi ch'i she-hui pei-ching" 金瓶梅的著作時代及其社會背景. 1933. In *Tu-shih cha-chi* 讀史箚記, pp. 1–38. 1956. Reprint. Peking: San-lien, 1961. Also reprinted in Yao Ling-hsi, *Chin P'ing Mei yen-chiu lun-chi*, pp. 1–42.

Wu Hsiao-ling 吳曉鈴. "Man-t'an T'ien-tu wai-ch'en hsü-pen Chung-i shui-hu chuan" 漫談天都外臣序本忠義水滸傳 and "Ta k'e san nan" 答客三難. In *WHIC*, no. 597 (August 2, 1983), and no. 624 (February 7, 1984).

————. "Ta-lu wai ti Chin P'ing Mei je" 大陸外的金瓶梅熱. In *Huan-ch'iu* 環球 (August 1985):13–15, 48.

Wu Kan 吳敢. "Chang Chu-p'o sheng-nien shu-lüeh" 張竹坡生年述略. In *HCSFHYHP*, 1984, no. 3: 74–79.

Wu Mei 吳梅. *Chung-kuo hsi-ch'ü kai-lun* 中國戲曲概論. Reprint. Taipei: Kuang-wen, 1971.

Wu Pi-yung 吳璧雍. "Hsi-yu chi yen-chiu" 西遊記研究. Master's thesis, Taiwan Normal University, 1980.

Wu Ta-yün. 吳達芸. "T'ien-ti pu ch'üan: Hsi-yu chi chu-t'i shih-t'an" 天地不全：西遊記主題試探. In *CWWH* 10, no. 11 (April 1982):80–109.

Wu Ts'ung-hsien 吳從先. *Hsiao-ch'uang tzu-chi* 小窗自紀. Preface, 1614. In rare book collection of Gest Oriental Library, Princeton, New Jersey.

Yang Shao-hsüan 楊紹萱. "Lun Shui-hu chuan yü Shui-hu hsi" 論水滸傳與水滸戲. In *SHYCLWC*, pp. 336–61.

Yang Shen 楊慎. *Nien-i shih t'an-tz'u chu* 廿一史彈詞註. Edited by Chang San-i 張三異. Reprint. Kowloon: Chung-hua, 1938.

———— (attributed). *Tung-t'ien hsüan-chi* 洞天玄記. Han-fen-lou 涵芬樓 edition. Preface by Yang T'i 楊悌. Reprinted in *Ku-pen Yuan-Ming tsa-chü*. Vol. 2.

———— and Huang O 黃峨 (Hsiu-mei 秀眉). *Sheng-an fu-fu yüeh-fu* 升菴夫婦樂府. Shanghai: Chung-hua, 1940.

Yang Tung-lai p'i-p'ing Hsi-yu chi 楊東萊批評西遊記. In *Ku-pen hsi-ch'ü ts'ung-k'an* 古本戲曲叢刊, 1st Series, vol. 21. Shanghai, 1954. Also in *Yuan-ch'ü hsüan wai-pien* 元曲選外編, edited by Sui Shu-sen 隋樹森. Peking: Chung-hua, 1959.

Yao Ling-hsi 姚靈犀. "Chin-Hung ts'o-yü" 金紅脞語. In *PWCY*, pp. 87–97.

————. *P'ing-wai chih-yen* 瓶外卮言. Tientsin: T'ien-chin shu-chü, 1940. Reprinted under title *Chin P'ing Mei yen-chiu lun-chi* 金瓶梅研究論集. Hong Kong: Hua-hsia, 1967.

Yeh Ch'ing-ping 葉慶炳 (and Shao Hung 邵紅). *Chung-kuo wen-hsüeh p'i-p'ing tzu-liao hui-pien* 中國文學批評資料彙編：明代. Taipei: Ch'eng-wen, 1979.

Yeh Lang 葉朗. *Chung-kuo hsiao-shuo mei-hsüeh* 中國小說美學. Peking: Peking University, 1982.

Yeh Te-chün 葉德均. *Hsi-ch'ü hsiao-shuo ts'ung-k'ao* 戲曲小說叢考. Peking: Chung-hua, 1979.

————. "Hsi-yu chi yen-chiu ti ts'ai-liao" 西遊記研究的材料. In Yeh Te-chün, *Hsi-ch'ü hsiao-shuo ts'ung-k'ao*, pp. 556–60.

————. "Ming-tai nan-hsi wu ta ch'iang-tiao chi ch'i chih-liu" 明代南戲五大腔調及其支流. In *Hsi-ch'ü hsiao-shuo ts'ung-k'ao*, pp. 1–67.

————. *Sung, Yuan, Ming chiang-ch'ang wen-hsüeh* 宋元明講唱文學. Peking: Chung-hua, 1959.

————. "Tu Ming-tai ch'uan-ch'i wen ch'i chung" 讀明代傳奇文七種. In *Hsi-ch'ü hsiao-shuo ts'ung-k'ao*, pp. 535–41.

————. "Wu-chih-ch'i ch'uan-shuo k'ao" 無支祈傳說考. In *Hsi-ch'ü hsiao-shuo ts'ung-k'ao*, pp. 495–515.

Yen Tun-i 嚴敦易. "Hsi-yu chi ho ku-tien hsi-ch'ü ti kuan-hsi" 西遊記和古典戲曲的關係. 1954. Reprinted in *HYCYCLWC*, pp. 145–52.

————. *Shui-hu chuan ti yen-pien* 水滸傳的演變. Peking: Tso-chia, 1957.

Yü Chi 虞集. *Yü Tao-yüan chi* 道園集. Edited by Lin Shu 林紓. Shanghai: Shang-wu, 1924.

Yü Chia-hsi 余嘉錫. *Shui-hu chuan san-shih-liu jen k'ao-shih* 水滸傳三十六人考實. Peking: Tso-chia, 1955. Reprinted in Yü Chia-hsi, *Shui-hu jen-wu yü Shui-hu chuan*, pp. 1–120.

————. *Shui-hu jen-wu yü Shui-hu chuan* 水滸人物與水滸傳. Taipei: Hsüeh-sheng shu-chü, 1971.

Yü Shih-nan 虞世南. "Lun-lüeh" 論略. In *T'ang-wen shih-i* 唐文拾遺, compiled by Lu Hsin-yüan 陸心源. Reprint. Taipei: Wen-hai, 1962.

Yü Ying-shih 余英時. "Ts'ung Sung Ming ju-hsüeh ti fa-chan lun Ch'ing-tai ssu-

hsiang shih" 從宋明儒學的發展論清代思想史. In *Chung-kuo hsüeh-jen*. 中國
學人 2 (September 1970):19–42.

Yuan-ch'ü hsüan 元曲選. Edited by Tsang Mao-hsün 臧懋循 (c.s. 1580). *SPPY*
edition. Shanghai: Chung-hua, n.d.

Yüan Huang 袁黃 (1533–1606), and Wang Shih-chen 王世貞 (attrib.). *Yüan Wang
kang-chien ho-pien* 袁王綱鑑合編. Reprint. Shanghai: Shang-wu, 1904.

Yüan Hung-tao 袁宏道. *Yüan Chung-lang ch'üan-chi* 袁中郎全集. Hong Kong:
Kuang chih, n.d.

————. *Yüan Hung-tao chi-chien chiao* 袁宏道集箋校. Edited by Ch'ien Po-ch'eng
錢伯城. Shanghai: Ku-chi, 1981.

Yüan Liang 原梁. "Wen Cheng-ming hsieh-pen Shui-hu" 文徵明寫本水滸. In
Hsin-min wan-pao, August 16, 1961.

Yüan Shu 袁樞 (1131–1203). *T'ung-chien chi-shih pen-mo* 通鑑紀事本末. Reprint.
Peking: Chung-hua, 1964.

Yüan Tsung-tao 袁宗道. "Lun wen" 論文. In *Ming-Ch'ing san-wen hsüan* 清明
散文選, edited by Liu Yen-ling 劉延陵, pp. 61–70. Taipei: Cheng-chung;
1952.

Yüeh Heng-chün 樂蘅軍. "Liang-shan po ti ti-tsao ho huan-mieh" 梁山濼的締造
和幻滅. In *Ku-tien hsiao-shuo san-lun* 古典小說散論, pp. 67–99. Taipei: Ch'un
wen-hsüeh, 1976.

Yung-lo ta-tien 永樂大典. Compiled by Hsieh Chin 解縉 et al. Completed 1408.
Reprint. Taipei: Shih-chieh, 1962.

Japanese Sources

Aikawa Kayoko 相川佳予子. "Mindai no fukushoku" 明代の服飾. In *Min-Shin
jidai no kagaku gijutsushi* 明清時代の科学技術史, edited by Yabuuchi Kiyoshi
薮内清 and Yoshida Mitsukuni 吉田光邦, pp. 429–64. Kyoto: Kyōto
daigaku, 1970.

Arai Ken 荒井健. "Saiyūki no naka no Saiyūki" 西遊記の中の西遊記. In *THGH*
36 (1964):591–609.

Araki Kengo 荒木見悟. *Mindai shisō kenkyū* 明代思想研究. Tokyo: Sobunsha,
1972.

Ikemoto Yoshio 池本義男. *Kinpeibai shiwa no inshoku shishaku kō* 金瓶梅詞話の
飲食私釈稿. Nagoya: Saika shorin, 1973.

Iriya Yoshitaka 入矢義高. *Mindai shibun* 明代詩文. Tokyo: Chikuma, 1978.

Isobe Akira 磯部彰. "Genpon Saiyūki ni okeru Son Gyōja no keisei" 元本西遊記
における孫行者の形成. In *STG* 38 (November 1977):103–27.

————. "Genpon Saiyūki o meguru mondai 元本西遊記をめぐる問題. In *Bunka*
文化 42, nos. 3–4 (March 1979):60–75 (204–19).

————. "Saiyūki ni okeru Cho Hakkai zō no keisei" 西遊記における猪八戒
像の形成. In *NCGH* 31 (1979):183–96.

Itō Sōhei 伊藤漱平. "Kaisetsu" 解説. Appendix to translation of *Chiao-hung chi*
嬌紅記 printed as supplement in *Kinko kikan* 今古奇観 (*Chin-ku ch'i-kuan*),

vol. 2. *CKBT* edition (1973): 462–91.

Koyanagi Shikita 小柳司気太. "Min-matsu no sankyō kankei" 明末の三教関係. In *Takase hakushi kanreki kinen* 高瀬博士還暦紀念, pp. 349–70. Kyoto: Kōbun, 1928.

Maeno Naoaki 前野直彬. "Min shichishi no sensei: Yō I-tei no bungakukan ni tsuite" 明七子の先声：楊維楨の文学観について. In *CBH* 5 (October 1956): 41–69.

Matsushita Tadashi 松下忠. "Ō Seitei no kobunjisetsu yori no dakka ni tsuite" 王世貞の古文辞説よりの脱化について. In *CBH* 5 (October 1956): 70–85.

Mineji Utarō. 峯地右太郎 "Suikoden no kenkyū to shiryō" 水滸伝の研究と資料. In *CHDS*, pp. 157–69.

Miyakawa Hisayuki 宮川尚志. "Min no Kasei jidai no dokyō" 明の嘉靖時代の道教. In *Yoshioka hakushi kanreki kinen: Dōkyō kenkyū ronshū* 吉岡博士還暦紀念道教研究論集, pp. 631–43. Tokyo: Kokusho kankōkai, 1977.

Nagasawa Kikuya 長澤規矩也. "Genson Mindai shōsetsu-sho kankōsha hyō shohen" 現存明代小説書刊行者表初編. In *SSG* 3, no. 3 (1934): 41–48.

———. "Mindai gikyoku kankōsha hyō shokō" 明代戯曲刊行者表初稿. In *SSG* 7, no. 1 (1936): 2–9.

———. *Shoshigaku ronkō* 書誌学論考. Reprint. Tokyo: Kyūko, 1982.

———. *Wakansho no insatsu to sono rekishi* 和漢書の印刷とその歴史. 1952. Reprint. Tokyo: Kyūko, 1982.

Nakano Miyoko 中野美代子. *Saiyūki no himitsu* 西遊記の秘密. Tokyo: Fukubu shoten, 1984.

Ogawa Tamaki 小川環樹. *Chūgoku shōsetsu shi no kenkyū* 中国小説史の研究. Tokyo: Iwanami, 1968.

———. "Kan Saku no densetsu sono hoka" 関索の伝説そのほか. In *CSSK*, pp. 162–72.

———. "Saiyūki genpon to sono kaisaku" 西遊記原本とその改作. In *CSSK*, pp. 75–124.

———. "Sankoku engi no Mō Seizan hihyōbon to Ri Ryūō bon" 三国演義の毛声山批評本と李笠翁本. In *CSSK*, pp. 153–62.

Okuno Shintarō 奥野信太郎. "Mizu to honō no denshō" 水と炎の伝承. In *NCGH* 18 (1966): 225–31.

Ōta Tatsuo 太田辰夫 "Boku tsūji genkai shoin Saiyūki kō" 朴通事諺解所引西遊記考. In *KGR* 10, no. 2 (October 1959): 1–22.

———. "Kaisetsu" 解説. In *Saiyūki* 西遊記 (1971): 431–46. *CKBT* edition, Vol. 31.

———. "Saiyū shōdōsho kō" 西遊證道書考. In *KGR* 21, no. 5 (December 1970): 1–17.

———. *Saiyūki no kenkyū* 西遊記の研究. Tokyo: Kenbun, 1984.

———. "Saiyūki seiritsushi no sho-mondai" 西遊記成立史の諸問題. In *NCGH* 24 (October 1972): 153–66.

———. "Saiyūki seiritsu shiryaku" 西遊記成立史略. In *KGR* 28, no. 3 (August 1977): 19–38.

———. "Saiyūki zakkō" 西遊記雑考. In *KGR* 21, nos. 1–2 (July 1970): 1–18, and 32, no. 3 (October 1981): 33–44.

————. "Shin kanpon Saiyūki kō" 清刊本西遊記考. In *KGR* 22, no. 4 (October 1971):1–19.

Ōuchida Saburō 大内田三郎. "Eiin Suiko shiden hyōrin kanpon o te ni shite" 影印水滸志伝評林完本を手にして. In *Shinagaku kenkyū* 支那学研究 24, no. 5, pp. 239–45.

————. "Suikoden hanponkō: Hanpon to kanpon no kankei o chūshin ni" 水滸伝版本考繁本と簡本の関係を中心に (no. 1). In *TDGH* 60 (November 1968): 50–63.

————. "Suikoden hanponkō: Suiko shiden hyōrin-bon no seiritsu katei o chūshin ni" 水滸志伝評林本の成立過程を中心に (no. 2). In *TDGH* 64 (December 1969):1–13.

————. "Suikoden hanponkō: Hyaku jikkai bon ni tsuite" 百十回本について (no. 3). In *TDGH* 70 (January 1971):1–15.

————. "Suikoden hanponkō: Hyaku nijūyon kai bon ni tsuite" 百二十四回本について (no. 4). In *TDGH* 99 (September 1975):1–10.

Saitō Akio 斎藤秋男, and Itō Keiichi 伊藤敬一, "Saiyūki no kenkyū to shiryō" 西遊記の研究と資料. In *CHDS*, pp. 210–22.

Sawada Mizuho 沢田瑞穂. "Kinpeibai no kenkyū to shiryō" 金瓶梅の研究と資料. In *CHDS*, pp. 262–72.

————. "Kinpeibai shiwa shoin no hōkan ni tsuite" 金瓶梅詞話所引の宝巻について. In *CBH* 5 (1956):86–98.

————. "Kinpeibai shomoku kō 金瓶書目稿. Tenri: Tenri daigaku, 1959.

————. "Sankyō shisō to engi shōsetsu" 三教思想と演義小説. In *Bukkyō to Chūgoku bungaku* 仏教と中国文学, pp. 163–67. Tokyo: Kokusho kankōkai, 1975.

Shimada Kenji 島田虔次. *Chūgoku ni okeru kindai shii no zasetsu* 中国における近代思惟の挫折. Tokyo: Chikuma, 1949.

Shionoya On 鹽谷溫. *Shina bungaku gairon kōwa* 支那文学概論講話. Tokyo: Dai Nihon yūbenkai, 1921.

Shiroki Naoya 白木直也. "Haiin Suikozenden e no hihan to teigen" 排印水滸全伝への批判と提言. In *Tōhōgaku* 東方学 45 (January 1973):57–73 (1–17).

————. "Ippyaku nijūkai Suikozenden no kenkyū: hatsubon o tsūjite kokoromita" 一百二十回水滸全伝の研究発凡を通じて試みた. In *NCGH* 25 (1973): 125–39.

————. "Ippyaku nijūkai Suikozenden no kenkyū: sono Ri Takugo hyō o megutte" 一百二十回水滸全伝の研究:その李卓吾評をめぐって. In *NCGH* 26 (1974):95–111.

————. "Kaku Butei hon shikō" 郭武定本私考 (part 1). In *HDBK* 27, no. 1 (December 1967/January 1968):140–59.

————. "Ko-shi, Shin-shi kyōcho kanyo shinhakkenteki Kyōbon chūgiden zanya hihan" 顧氏沈氏共著関於新発現的京本忠義伝残頁批判. *Tohogaku*, no. 66 (July 1983), pp. 76–88.

————. "Shō Hakkei hihyō Shichikan kanpon no kenkyū" 鍾伯敬批評四知館刊本の研究. Part 1 in *STG* 42 (August 1971):98–113. Part 2 in *NCGH* 23 (October 1971):171–85. Part 3 in *HDBK* 31, no. 1 (January 1972):116–48.

————. "Sōzō to iu koto: Suikoden ni okeru Ryōkoku koji no mondai" 插増とい

うこと：水滸伝における遼国故事の問題. In *HDBK* 22, no. 3 (March 1963): 93–125.

Tanaka Iwao 田中巖. "Saiyūki no sakusha" 西遊記の作者. In *Shibun* 斯文, n.s. 8 (1953): 32–39.

Teramura Masao 寺村政男. "Kinpeibai shiwabon yori kaiteibon e no kaihen o megutte" 金瓶梅詞話本より改訂本への改変をめぐつて. In *Chūgoku koten kenkyū*, no. 23 (June 1978), pp. 74–88.

———. "Kinpeibai shiwa ni okeru sakusha kainyūbun" 金瓶梅詞話における作者介入文. In *Chūgoku kenkyū* 中国研究 2 (1976): 19–31.

Torii Hisayasu. 鳥居久靖. "Kinpeibai hanponkō" 金瓶梅版本考. In *TDGH* 18 (October 1955): 335–66.

———. "Kinpeibai no gengo" 金瓶梅の言語. In *CHDS*, pp. 253–61.

———. "Kinpeibai shiwa hennenkō oboegaki" 金瓶梅詞話編年考覚え書き. In *TDGH* 42 (December 1963): 58–80.

———. "Shinkoku shutsuzō kanpan daiji Saiyūki oboegaki" 新刻出像官板大字西遊記覚え書き. *Biblia* 12 (October 1958): 7–15.

Yoshikawa Kōjirō 吉川幸次郎. "Gen-Min shi gaisetsu" 元明詩概説. In *Chūgoku shijin senshū* 中国詩人選集. Edited by Yoshikawa Kōjirō and Ogawa Tamaki, vol. 2. Tokyo: Iwanami, 1962.

Yoshioka Yoshitoyo 吉岡義豊. *Dōkyō no kenkyū* 道教の研究. Kyoto: Hōzōkan, 1952.

Yoshizawa Tadashi 吉沢忠. "Nanga to bunjinga" 南画と文人画. In *Kokusui* 国粋 82, no. 9 (September 1942): 257–62; 82, no. 11 (November 1942): 345–50; 82, no. 12 (December 1942): 336–81; 83, no. 1 (January 1943): 27ff.

Western-language Sources

Amano Motosuke. "Ming Agriculture." In *Cambridge History*. Vol. 8, forthcoming.

Araki Kengo. "Confucianism and Buddhism in the Late Ming." In *Unfolding*, pp. 39–66.

Atwell, William S. "From Education to Politics: The Fu She." In *Unfolding*, pp. 333–67.

———. "International Bullion Flows and the Chinese Economy, 1550–1650." Unpublished paper.

———. "Notes on Silver, Foreign Trade, and the Late Ming Economy." Unpublished paper.

———. "Time and Money: Another Approach to the Periodization of Ming History." Unpublished paper.

Auerbach, Erich. *Mimesis.* Translated by Willard R. Trask. Princeton: Princeton University Press, 1953.

———. *Scenes from the Drama of European Literature.* New York: Meridian, 1959.

Barnhardt, Richard. "The Wild and Heterodox School in Ming Painting." In *Theories of the Arts in China*, edited by Susan Bush and Christian Murck, pp. 365–96. Princeton: Princeton University Press, 1983.

Berling, Judith. "Curing the Delusions of the Sages in the Street: The Religious and Social World-view of the Three Teachings Cult in a Popular Novel." Unpublished paper, Columbia University Regional Seminar on Neo-Confucian Thought, February 1980.

————. "Paths of Convergence: Interactions of Inner Alchemy Taoism and Neo-Confucianism." *JCP* 6, no. 2 (June 1979): 123–47.

Birch, Cyril. "Some Concerns and Methods of the Ming *Ch'uan-ch'i* Drama." In *Chinese Literary Genres*, pp. 220–58.

————. "Some Formal Characteristics of the Hua-pen Story." *Bulletin of the School of Oriental and African Studies* 17, no. 2 (1955): 346–64.

Bishop, John. "A Colloquial Short Story in the Chin P'ing Mei." In *Studies in Chinese Literature*, edited by John Bishop, pp. 226–34. Cambridge, Mass.: Harvard University Press, 1966.

Bloom, Irene. "Wang Yang-ming, Lo Ch'in-shun, and Concepts of Personal Identity in Ming Neo-Confucianism." Academia Sinica Conference, Thought and Philosophy Section, pp. 263–76.

Bol, Peter. "Culture and the Way in Eleventh-Century China." Ph. D. dissertation, Princeton University, 1982.

Booth, Wayne. *The Rhetoric of Irony*. Chicago: University of Chicago Press, 1974.

Bryant, Daniel. "Three Varied Centuries of Verse: A Brief Note on Ming Poetry." *Renditions* 8 (Autumn 1977): 82–91.

Busch, Heinrich. "The Tung-lin shu-yuan and Its Political and Philosophical Significance." *Monumenta Serica* 14 (1949–55): 1–163.

Bush, Susan. *The Chinese Literati on Painting*. Cambridge, Mass.: Harvard University Press, 1971.

Cahill, James. *The Compelling Image: Nature and Style in Seventeenth-Century Chinese Painting*. Cambridge, Mass.: Harvard University Press, 1982.

————. *Distant Mountains: Chinese Painting of the Late Ming Dynasty*. New York and Tokyo: Weatherhill, 1982.

————. *Fantastics and Eccentrics in Chinese Painting*. New York: Asia Society, 1967.

————. *Parting at the Shore: Chinese Painting of the Early and Middle Ming Dynasty*. New York and Tokyo: Weatherhill, 1978.

————. *The Restless Landscape*. Berkeley: University of California Press, 1971.

Carlitz, Katherine. "Puns and Puzzles in the *Chin P'ing Mei*." *TP* 67, nos. 3–5 (1981): 216–39.

————. *The Rhetoric of Chin P'ing Mei*. Bloomington: University of Indiana Press, 1986.

————. "The Role of Drama in the Chin P'ing Mei." Ph. D. dissertation, University of Chicago, 1978.

Cartier, Michel. "Nouvelles données sur la démographie chinoise à l'époque des Ming, 1368–1644." *Annales: Économies, Sociétés, Civilisations* 28, no. 6 (November–December 1973): 1341–60.

Cass, Victoria. "Celebrations at the Gate of Death: Symbol and Structure in Chin P'ing Mei." Ph. D. dissertation, University of California, 1979.

Chan, Albert, S. J. "Peking at the Time of the Wan-li Emperor." *Proceedings of the International Association of Historians of Asia Conference*, edited by Chiang Kuei-yung, pp. 119–48. Taipei, 1962.

Chan, Hok-lam, ed. *Li Chih in Contemporary Chinese Historiography.* White Plains, N.Y.: Sharpe, 1980.

———. "Liu Chi in the Ying-lieh chuan." *JOSA* 5, no. 12 (December 1967): 26–42.

Chan, Wing-tsit. "The Ch'eng-Chu School of Early Ming." In *Self and Society,* pp. 29–51.

———. *Instructions for Practical Living and Other Neo-Confucian Writings by Wang Yang-ming.* New York: Columbia University Press, 1963.

———. *A Source Book in Chinese Philosophy.* Princeton: Princeton University Press, 1963.

Chang Ching-erh. "The Monkey-hero in the *Hsi-yu chi* Cycle." *Chinese Studies* 1, no. 1 (June 1983): 191–217, and no. 2 (December 1983): 537–91.

———. "The Structure and Theme of the *Hsi-yu chi.*" *TR* 11, no. 2 (1980): 169–88.

Chang, K. C., ed. *Food in Chinese Culture.* New Haven: Yale University Press, 1977.

Chang, K'ang-i Sun. "Songs in the *Chin P'ing Mei tz'u-hua.*" *JOS,* nos. 1–2 (1980): 26–34.

Chaves, Jonathan. "The Panoply of Images: A Reconsideration of the Literary Theory of the Kung-an School." Unpublished paper.

Ch'en, Kenneth. *Buddhism in China: A Historical Survey.* Princeton: Princeton University Press, 1964.

Ch'ien, Edward. "Chiao Hung and the Revolt against Ch'eng-Chu Orthodoxy." In *Unfolding,* pp. 271–303.

Ching, Julia. *To Acquire Wisdom: The Way of Wang Yang-ming.* New York: Columbia University Press, 1976.

Chou Chih-p'ing. "The Poetry and Poetic Theory of Yüan Hung-tao (1568–1610)." *THJCS,* n.s. 15, nos. 1–2 (December 1983): 113–42.

Crawford, Robert B. "Chang Chü-cheng's Confucian Legalism." In *Self and Society,* pp. 367–413.

———. "Eunuch Power in the Ming Dynasty." *TP* 49, no. 3 (1961): 115–48.

Crump, James. "*P'ing-hua* and the Early History of the *San-kuo chih.*" *JAOS* 71 (1951): 249–56.

Cua, A.S. *The Unity of Knowledge and Action: A Study in Wang Yang-ming's Moral Psychology.* Honolulu: University of Hawaii Press, 1982.

deBary, W. T. "Chinese Despotism and Confucian Ideals." In *Thought and Institutions,* pp. 153–203.

———. "Individualism and Humanitarianism in Late Ming Thought." In *Self and Society,* pp. 145–247.

———. *Principle and Practicality.* New York: Columbia University Press, 1979.

de Crespigny, Rafe. "Political Protest in Imperial China: The Great Proscription of Later Han." *Papers on Far Eastern History* 1 (11 March 1975): 1–36.

———. *The Records of the Three Kingdoms.* Occasional Paper no. 9. Canberra: Australian National University, 1970.

Dimberg, Ronald G. "The Sage and Society: The Life and Thought of Ho Hsin-yin." Ph. D. dissertation, University of Hawaii, 1974.

Dudbridge, Glen. *The Hsi-yu chi: A Study of Antecedents to the Sixteenth-Century*

Chinese Novel. Cambridge, England: Cambridge University Press, 1970.

———. "The Hundred-chapter *Hsi-yu chi* and Its Early Versions." *AM*, n.s. 14, no. 2 (1969): 141–91.

Duyvendak, J. J. L. "A Chinese Divina Commedia." *TP* 41 (1952): 255–316.

Eisenstadt, S. N. *The Decline of Empires.* Englewood Cliffs, N.J.: Prentice-Hall, 1967.

———. *The Political Systems of Empires.* New York: Macmillan, 1963.

Eliot, T. S. "Tradition and the Individual Talent." In *The Sacred Wood*, pp. 47–59. London: Methuen, 1920.

Elvin, Mark. *The Pattern of the Chinese Past.* Palo Alto: Stanford University Press, 1973.

Fisher, Carney T. "The Great Ritual Controversy in Ming China." Ph. D. dissertation, University of Michigan, 1977.

Franke, Herbert. "Eine Novellensammlung der frühen Ming-Zeit: Das *Chien-teng hsin-hua* des Ch'ü Yu." *Zeitschrift der Deutschen Morgenlaendischen Gesellschaft* 108, no. 2 (1958): 338–82.

Fu, James S. *Mythic and Comic Aspects of the Quest.* Singapore: Singapore University Press, 1977.

Fu, Marilyn and Shen Fu. *Studies in Connoisseurship.* Princeton: Princeton University Press, 1973.

Fung Yu-lan. *A History of Chinese Philosophy.* Translated by Derk Bodde. Princeton: Princeton University Press, 1953.

Gedalecia, David. "Evolution and Synthesis in Neo-Confucianism." *JCP* 6 (1979): 91–102.

Geiss, James. "The Cheng-te Reign, 1506–1521." In *Cambridge History*, pp. 403–39.

———. "The Chia-ching Reign, 1522–1566." In *Cambridge History*, pp. 440–510.

———. "Peking under the Ming." Ph. D. dissertation, Princeton University, 1979.

Girardot, N. J. *Myth and Meaning in Early Taoism.* Berkeley: University of California Press, 1983.

Grimm, Tilemann. "Das Neiko der Ming-Zeit." *OE* 1 (1954): 139–77.

———. *Erziehung und Politik im Konfuzianischen China der Ming-Zeit.* Hamburg: Gesellschaft für Natur- und Völkerkunde Ostasiens, 1960.

———. "Intellectual Groups in Fifteenth and Sixteenth Century Kiangsi: A Study of Regionalism in Forming Elites." Unpublished paper.

———. "Ming Educational Intendants." In *Chinese Government*, pp. 129–47.

——— and Twitchett, Denis. "The Cheng-t'ung, Ching-t'ai, and T'ien-shun Reigns, 1436–1464." In *Cambridge History*, pp. 305–42.

Hanan, Patrick. *The Chinese Short Story.* Cambridge, Mass.: Harvard University Press, 1973.

———. *The Chinese Vernacular Story.* Cambridge, Mass.: Harvard University Press, 1981.

———. "The Composition of the *P'ing-yao chuan.*" *HJAS* 31 (1971): 201–19.

———. "The Erotic Novel: Some Early Reflections." Indiana Conference paper, May 1983.

———. "A Landmark of the Chinese Novel." *University of Toronto Quarterly* 30, no. 3 (1961): 325–35.

———. "The Nature of Ling Meng-ch'u's Fiction." In *Chinese Narrative*, pp. 85–144.

———. "Sources of the *Chin P'ing Mei*." *AM*, n.s. 10, no. 2 (1963):23–67.

———. "The Text of the *Chin P'ing Mei*." *AM*, n.s. 9, no. 1 (1962):1–57.

Handlin, Joanna. *Action in Late Ming Thought: The Reorientation of Lü K'un and Other Ming-Dynasty Scholar-Officials*. Berkeley: University of California Press, 1983.

Hawkes, David. "Reflections on Some Yuan *Tsa-chü*." *AM* 16, nos. 1–2 (1971): 69–81.

Hayden, George. "A Skeptical Note on the Early History of Shui-hu chuan." *Monumenta Serica* 32 (1976):374–99.

Hegel, Robert. *The Novel in Seventeenth-Century China*. New York: Columbia University Press, 1981.

———. "Sui-T'ang yen-i and the Seventeenth-Century Literary Elite." In *Chinese Narrative*, pp. 124–59.

Higgins, Roland C. "Piracy and Coastal Defense in the Ming Period: Government Response to Coastal Disturbances, 1523–1549." Ph. D. dissertation, University of Minnesota, 1981.

Ho Ping-ti. *The Ladder of Success in Imperial China*. New York: Columbia University Press, 1962.

———. *Studies on the Population of China, 1368–1953*. Cambridge, Mass.: Harvard University Press, 1959.

Hollander, Robert. "*Vita Nuova*: Dante's Perceptions of Beatrice." *Dante Studies* 92 (1974):1–18.

Hsia, C. T. *The Classic Chinese Novel*. New York: Columbia University Press, 1968.

———. "The Military Romance: A Genre of Chinese Fiction." In *Chinese Literary Genres*, pp. 339–90.

———. "Time and the Human Condition in the Plays of T'ang Hsien-tsu." In *Self and Society*, pp. 249–90.

Hsü Sung-peng. "The Life and Thought of Han-shan Te-ch'ing." Ph. D. dissertation, University of Pennsylvania, 1971.

Huang, Ray. *1587: A Year of No Significance*. New Haven: Yale University Press, 1981.

———. "Fiscal Administration during the Ming Dynasty." In *Chinese Government*, pp. 73–128.

———. "The Lung-ch'ing and Wan-li Reigns, 1567–1620." In *Cambridge History*, pp. 511–84.

———. *Taxation and Government Finance in Sixteenty-Century Ming China*. Cambridge, England: Cambridge University Press, 1974.

Hucker, Charles. "Chu I-chün." In *DMB*, 1:324–38.

———. *A Dictionary of Official Titles in Imperial China*. Palo Alto: Stanford University Press, 1985.

———. "Hu Tsung-hsien's Campaign against Hsü Hai, 1556." In *Ways in Warfare*, pp. 273–307.

———. *The Traditional Chinese State in Ming Times*. Tucson: University of Arizona Press, 1961.

Hughes, E. R. *The Great Learning and the Mean in Action.* New York: E. P. Dutton, 1943.

Hummell, Arthur, ed. *Eminent Chinese of the Ch'ing Period.* 1943. 2 Vols. Reprint. Taipei: Ch'eng-wen, 1970.

Hung, Josephine Huang. *Ming Drama.* Taipei: Heritage Press, 1966.

Hurvitz, Leon. "Chu-hung's One Mind of Pure Land and Ch'an Buddhism." In *Self and Society,* pp. 451–81.

Idema, Wilt. *Chinese Vernacular Fiction: The Formative Period.* Leiden: Brill, 1974.

———. "Some Remarks and Speculations Concerning P'ing-hua." *TP* 60 (1974): 121–72.

———. "Zhu Youdun's Dramatic Prefaces and Traditional Fiction." In *Ming Studies* 10 (Spring 1980): 17–21, and 11 (Fall 1980): 45.

Irwin, Richard. *The Evolution of a Chinese Novel.* Cambridge, Mass.: Harvard University Press, 1966.

———. "Water Margin Revisited." *TP* 48, nos. 4–5 (1960): 393–416.

Jen Yu-wen. "Ch'en Hsien-chang's Philosophy of the Natural." In *Self and Society,* pp. 53–92.

Kao, Karl S. Y. "An Archetypal Approach to *Hsi-yu chi.*" *TR* 5, no. 2 (October 1974): 63–98.

Keswick, Maggie. *The Chinese Garden: History, Art, and Architecture.* New York: Rizzoli, 1978.

Koss, Nicholas. "The Xiyouji in its Formative Stages: The Late Ming Editions." Ph. D. dissertation, University of Indiana, 1981.

Krafft, Barbara. "Wang Shih-chen: Abriss seines Lebens." *OE* 5 (1958): 169–201.

Ku Chieh-kang. "A Study of Literary Persecution during the Ming." Translated by L. Carrington Goodrich. *HJAS* 3 (1938): 254–311.

Legge, James. *The Four Books.* 1870, Shanghai, 1923. Reprint. New York: Paragon Books, 1966.

Lerner, Daniel. *The Passing of a Traditional Society.* Glencoe, Ill.: Free Press, 1958.

Levenson, Joseph. "The Amateur Ideal in Ming and Early Ch'ing Society." In *Thought and Institutions,* pp. 320–41.

Lévy, André. "About the Date of the First Printed Edition of the *Chin P'ing Mei.*" *CLEAR* 1, no. 1 (1979): 43–47.

———. *Le conte en langue vulgaire du XVIIe siècle.* Paris: Presses Universitaires de France, 1981.

———. "Un document sur la querelle des anciens et des modernes *more sinico.*" *TP* 54, nos. 4–5 (1968): 251–74.

———. *Études sur le conte et le roman chinois.* Paris: École française d'Extrême-Orient, 1971.

———. *Fleur en Fiole d'Or.* Paris: Gallimard, 1985.

———. "Pour une clarification de quelques aspects de la problematique du Jin Ping Mei." *TP* 66, nos. 4–5 (1980): 183–98.

———. "The Question of the *Jin Ping Mei* Authorship: A Reassessment." Paper delivered at Princeton University, May 1984.

———. "Recent Publications on the *Chin P'ing Mei.*" *CLEAR* 3, no. 1 (1981): 144–49.

————. "Une texte burlesque du 16e siècle dans le style de la chantefable." *Bulletin de l'École française d'Extrême-Orient* 56 (1969): 119–24.

Liang Fang-chung. *The Single-whip Method of Taxation in China.* Translated by Wang Yü-ch'üan. Cambridge, Mass.: Harvard University Press, 1956.

Liu, James J. Y. *The Chinese Knight-Errant.* London: Routledge and Kegan Paul, 1967.

Liu Shih-te. "An Analysis of the Historical Relics and Materials Concerning Shi Naian." In *Social Sciences in China*, pp. 185–221. Undated offprint.

Liu Ts'un-yan. *Buddhist and Taoist Influences on Chinese Novels.* Weisbaden: Harrassowitz, 1962.

————. *Chinese Popular Fiction in Two London Libraries.* Hong Kong: Lung-men, 1967.

————. "Lin Chao-en, the Master of the Three Teachings." *TP* 53, nos. 4–5 (1967): 253–78.

————. "The Penetration of Taoism into the Ming Neo-Confucian Elite." *TP* 57 (1971): 31–102.

————. "The Prototypes of Monkey." *TP* 51, no. 1 (1964): 55–71.

————. "Sur l'authenticité des romans historiques de Lo Guanzhong." In *Mélanges de Sinologie offerts à M. Paul Demiéville*, 2: 231–96. Paris: Presses universitaires de France, 1974. Also in Chinese in *HFTTSC*, 2: 235–300.

————. "Taoist Self-cultivation in Ming Thought." In *Self and Society*, pp. 291–330. Also in Chinese in *HFTTSC*, 1: 233–72. Originally published in *HYHP* 8, no. 1 (1967).

————. "Wu Ch'eng-en: His Life and Career." *TP* 53, nos. 1–3 (1967): 1–97.

————. "Yüan Huang and His Four Admonitions." *JOSA* 5, nos. 1–2 (December 1967): 108–32.

———— and Judith Berling. "The Three Teachings in the Mongol Yuan Period." In *Yuan Thought: Chinese Thought and Religion under the Mongols*, edited by Wing-tsit Chan and W. T. deBary, pp. 479–509. New York: Columbia University Press, 1982.

Lo, Andrew Hing-bun. "The *San-kuo chih yen-i*: A Study of its Overall Structure and Narrative Patterns." Unpublished paper presented at International Congress of Human Sciences in Asia and North Africa, Mexico City, August 1976.

————. "*San-kuo chih yen-i* and *Shui-hu chuan* in the Context of Historiography: An Interpretive Study." Ph. D. dissertation, Princeton University, 1981.

Lo Chin-t'ang. "Clues Leading to the Discovery of the *Hsi-yu chi P'ing-hua*." *JOS* 7, no. 2 (1969): 176–94.

Lo Jung-pang. "Policy Formulation and Decision-making on Issues Respecting Peace and War." In *Chinese Government*, pp. 41–72.

Longworth, Philip. *The Three Empresses.* London: Constable, 1972.

Lotman, Yurij. *Struktura khudožestvennogo teksta.* Moscow: Isskustvo, 1970.

Lovell, H. C. *Annotated Bibliography of Chinese Painting Catalogues and Related Texts.* Ann Arbor: University of Michigan Press, 1973.

Lung, Alice Nai-yin. "An Interpretation of the *Hsi-yu chi* Pilgrims in Terms of the Five Elements." Unpublished paper.

Lynn, Richard. "Alternate Routes to Self-realization in Ming Theories of Poetry." Unpublished paper.

———. "Orthodoxy and Enlightenment: Wang Shih-chen's Theory of Poetry and Its Antecedents." In *Unfolding*, pp. 217–69.

Ma Tai-loi. "The Early Textual History of the *Chin P'ing Mei*; A Study of Hsieh Chao-che's Postcript." Unpublished paper. Also in Chinese in *WHIC*, no. 650.

Ma, Y. W. "The Beginnings of Professional Storytelling in China: A Critique of Current Theories and Practice." In *Études d'histoire et de littérature chinoises offertes au Professeur Jaroslav Průšek*, pp. 227–46. Paris: Presses universitaires de France, 1970.

———. "The Chinese Historical Novel: An Outline of Themes and Contexts." *JAS* 34, no. 2 (February 1975):277–93.

———. "The Textual Tradition of Ming Kung-an Fiction: A Study of the *Lung-t'u kung-an*." *HJAS* 35 (1975):190–220.

McLaren, Anne E. "Chantefable and the Textual Evolution of the *San-kuo chih yen-i*." *TP* 71, nos. 4–5 (1985):1–69.

McMahon, R. K. "The Gap in the Wall: Containment and Abandon in Seventeenth-Century Chinese Fiction." Ph. D. dissertation, Princeton University, 1984.

———. "Eroticism in Late Ming Fiction." Unpublished paper.

Manukhin, Viktor. *Cveti slivy v zolotoj vaze*. Moscow: Khudožestvennaya literatura, 1977.

Marmé, Michael. "Population and Possibility in Ming Suzhou: A Quantified Model." *Ming Studies* 12 (Spring 1981):29–64.

Martinson, Paul. "*Chin P'ing Mei* as Wisdom Literature: A Methodological Essay." *Ming Studies* 5 (Fall 1977):44–56.

———. "Pao, Order, and Redemption: Perspectives on Chinese Religion and Society Based on a Study of the Chin P'ing Mei." Ph. D. dissertation, University of Chicago, 1973.

Meskill, John. "Academies and Politics in the Ming Dynasty." In *Chinese Government*, pp. 149–74.

Metzger, Thomas A. *Escape from Predicament: Neo-Confucianism and China's Evolving Political Culture*. New York: Columbia University Press, 1977.

Mote, Frederick W. "The Arts and the Theorizing Mode of the Civilization." In *Artists and Traditions*, edited by Christian Murck, pp. 3–8. Princeton: Princeton University Press, 1978.

———. "The Ch'eng-hua and Hung-chih Reigns, 1465–1505." In *Cambridge History*, pp. 343–402.

———. "A Millennium of Chinese Urban History: Form, Time, and Space Concepts in Soochow." *Rice University Studies* 59, no. 4 (Fall 1973):35–65.

———. "The Transformation of Nanking, 1350–1400." In *City*, pp. 101–52.

———. "The T'u-mu Incident of 1449." In *Ways in Warfare*, pp. 243–72.

———. "Yuan and Ming." In *Food in Chinese Culture*, edited by K. C. Chang, pp. 193–257. New Haven: Yale University Press, 1977.

Murck, Christian F. "Chu Yün-ming and Cultural Commitment in Suchou." Ph. D. dissertation, Princeton University, 1978.

Nienhauser, William. "Ming Short Fiction, Popular Culture, and the Mass Critique."
     Unpublished paper.
Nivison, David. "Protest against Convention and Conventions of Protest." In
     The Confucian Persuasion, edited by Arthur F. Wright, pp. 137–201. Palo Alto:
     Stanford University Press, 1960.
Okada Takehiko. "Wang Chi and the Rise of Existentialism." In *Self and Society*,
     pp. 121–44.
Ono Shinobu. "*Chin P'ing Mei*: A Critical Study." *AA* 5 (1963):76–89.
Ota Tatsuo. "A New Study on the Formation of the *Hsi-yu chi*." *AA* 32 (1977):
     96–113.
Overmyer, Daniel L. "Boatmen and Buddhas: The Lo Chiao in Ming Dynasty
     China." *HR* 17, nos. 3–4 (February–May 1978):284–302.
————. *Folk Buddhist Religion: Dissenting Sects in Late Traditional China*. Cambridge,
     Mass.: Harvard University Press, 1976.
Pan 'In (P'ang Ying). "K voprosu ob avtorstvje i vremeni sozdanija romana
     Recnije zavodi." In *Pis'mennije pamjatniki vostoka* (1974), pp. 200–208.
Parsons, James B. "The Ming Dynasty Bureaucracy: Aspects of Background
     Forces." In *Chinese Government*, pp. 175–227.
Pelliot, Paul. "L'édition collective des oeuvres de Wang Kuou-wei." *TP* 26 (1928):
     113–200.
Perkins, Dwight H. *Agricultural Development in China, 1368–1968*. Chicago: Aldine
     Press, 1969.
Peterson, Willard. *Bitter Gourd*. New Haven: Yale University Press, 1979.
————. "Ming Periodization: An Immodest Proposal." *Ming Studies* 3, nos. 7–8
     (Fall 1976):7–8.
Plaks, Andrew H. "After the Fall: *Hsing-shih yin-yüan chuan* and the Seventeenth-
     Century Chinese Novel." *HJAS* 45, no. 2 (December 1985):543–80.
————. "Allegory in *Hsi-yu chi* and *Hung-lou meng*." In *Chinese Narrative*,
     pp. 163–202.
————. *Archetype and Allegory in the Dream of the Red Chamber*. Princeton: Prince-
     ton University Press, 1976.
————. "The Ch'ung-chen Commentary on the *Chin P'ing Mei*: Gems Amidst the
     Dross." Indiana Conference paper.
————. "Conceptual Models in Chinese Narrative Theory." *JCP* 4 (1977):25–47.
————. "Full-Length *Hsiao-shuo* and the Western Novel: A Generic Reappraisal."
     NAAB 1 (1978):163–76.
————. "Towards a Critical Theory of Chinese Narrative." In *Chinese Narrative*,
     pp. 309–52.
Propp, Vladimir. *The Morphology of the Folktale*. Translated by Laurence Scott.
     Reprint. Austin: University of Texas Press, 1975.
Rawski, Evelyn Sakakida. *Agricultural Change and the Peasant Economy of South
     China*. Cambridge, Mass.: Harvard University Press, 1972.
————. "Economic and Social Foundations of Ming and Ch'ing Culture." *Ming
     Studies* 2 (1978):12–19.
————. *Education and Popular Literacy in Ch'ing China*. Ann Arbor: University of
     Michigan Press, 1979.

Ricci, Matteo. *Journal*. Translated by Louis J. Gallagher, S. J., as *China in the Sixteenth Century: The Journals of Matteo Ricci, 1583–1610*. 1942. Reprint. New York: Random House, 1953.

Riftin, Boris. *Istoricheskaya epopeia i fol'klornaya traditsija v kitae*. Moscow: Nauka, 1970.

———. *Ot mifa k romanu*. Moscow: Nauka, 1979.

Rolston, David, ed. *How to Read the Chinese Novel*. Forthcoming book.

Roy, David T. "The Case for T'ang Hsien-tsu's Authorship of the *Chin P'ing Mei*." Unpublished paper.

———. Chang Chu-p'o's Commentary on the *Chin P'ing Mei*." In *Chinese Narrative*, pp. 115–23.

———. "A Confucian Interpretation of the *Chin P'ing Mei*." Academia Sinica Conference, Literature Section, pp. 39–61.

———. "The Fifteenth-Century *Shuo-ch'ang tz'u-hua* as Examples of Written Formulaic Composition." Unpublished paper.

Ruhlmann, Robert. "Motives and Meanings of Suicide in the *San-kuo chih yen-i*." Unpublished paper presented at International Congress of Human Sciences in Asia and Africa, Mexico City, August 1976.

Sakai, Tadao. "Confucianism and Popular Educational Works." In *Self and Society*, pp. 331–66.

Schipper, Kristofer. *Le corps taoïste*. Paris: Fayard, 1982.

Scott, Mary E. "The Image of the Garden in *Chin P'ing Mei* and *Hung-lou meng*." Indiana Conference paper.

Shek, Richard. "Religion and Society in Late Ming: Sectarianism and Popular Thought in Sixteenth and Seventeenth Century China." Ph. D. dissertation, University of California, 1980.

Sirén, Osvald. *Gardens of China*. New York: Ronald Press, 1949.

Skinner, G. W. "Introduction: Urban Development in Imperial China." In *City*, pp. 3–31.

Šklovskij, Viktor. *O Teorii prozi*. Moscow: Federačija, 1929.

So, Francis. "Some Rhetorical Conventions of the Verse Sections of *Hsi-yu chi*." *NAAB* 1 (1978): 177–94.

So, Kwan-wai. *Japanese Piracy in Ming China during the Sixteenth Century*. East Lansing, Michigan: Michigan State University Press, 1975.

Strassberg, Richard. "The Peach-blossom Fan: Personal Cultivation in a Chinese Drama." Ph. D. dissertation, Princeton University, 1975.

Swann, Nancy Lee, "Seven Intimate Library Owners." *HJAS* 1 (1936): 363–90.

Tang Chün-i. "The Development of the Concept of Moral Mind from Wang Yang-ming to Wang Chi." In *Self and Society*, pp. 93–119.

———. "Liu Tsung-chou's Doctrine of Moral Mind and Practice and His Critique of Wang Yang-ming." In *Unfolding*, pp. 305–31.

Taylor, Rodney L. "The Centered Self: Religious Autobiography in the Neo-Confucian Tradition." *HR* 17, nos. 3–4 (February–June 1978): 266–84.

———. "Meditation in Ming Neo-Orthodoxy: Kao P'an-lung's Writings on Quiet-Sitting." *JCP* 6, no. 2 (June 1979): 149–82.

Ts'ui Wen-yin, "Problems Concerning the Authenticity of the *Shih-kang p'ing-yao*."

In *Li Chih in Contemporary Chinese Historiography*, edited by Hok-lam Chan, pp. 125–51. White Plains, N.Y.: Sharpe, 1980.

Tu Ching-i. "The Chinese Examination Essay: Some Literary Considerations." *Monumenta Serica* (1977):393–406.

Tu Wei-ming. *Neo-Confucianism Thought in Action: Wang Yang-ming's Youth (1472–1509)*. Berkeley: University of California Press, 1976.

———. "Ultimate Self-transformation as a Communal Act: Comments on Modes of Self-cultivation in Traditional China." *JCP* 6 (1979):237–46.

Van Gulik, Robert H. *Sexual Life in Ancient China*. Leiden: Brill, 1974.

Wakeman, Frederic, Jr. "The Price of Autonomy: Intellectuals in Ming and Ch'ing Politics." *Daedalus* 101 (Spring 1972):35–70.

Waley, Arthur. *Monkey*. 1943. Reprint. New York: Grove Press, 1958.

———. *The Real Tripitaka and Other Pieces*. London & New York: Allen, 1952.

———. *Travels of an Alchemist*. London: Routledge, 1931.

Wang, John C. Y. "The Chih-yen chai Commentary and the *Dream of the Red Chamber*: A Literary Study." In *Chinese Approaches to Literature*, edited by Adele Rickett, pp. 189–220. Princeton: Princeton University Press, 1978.

Watt, Ian. *The Rise of the Novel*. Berkeley: University of California Press, 1957.

West, Stephen H. "Mongol Influence on the Development of Northern Drama." In *China Under Mongol Rule*, edited by J. Langlois, pp. 434–65. Princeton: Princeton University Press, 1981.

Wilhelm, Hellmut. *The I Ching, or Book of Changes*. Translated by Cary F. Baynes. Princeton: Princeton University Press, 1967.

———. "On Ming Orthodoxy." *Monumenta Serica* 29 (1970):1–26.

Wills, John E., Jr. "Maritime China from Wang Chih to Shih Lang: Themes in Peripheral History." In *Ming to Ch'ing*, pp. 201–38.

Wivell, Charles. "The Term 'Hua-pen'." In *Transition and Permanence: Chinese History and Culture*, edited by David D. Buxbaum and Frederick W. Mote, pp. 295–305. Hong Kong: Cathay Press, 1972.

Wrenn, James J. "Textual Method in Chinese with Illustrative Examples." *THJCS*, n.s. 6, nos. 1–2 (1967):150–99.

Wright, Arthur. "Sui Yang-ti: Personality and Stereotype." In *The Confucian Persuasion*, edited by Arthur Wright, pp. 47–76. Palo Alto: Stanford University Press, 1960.

Wu, K. T. "Ming Printing and Printers." *HJAS* 7, no. 3 (1943):203–60.

Wu, Nelson. "Tung Ch'i-ch'ang: Apathy in Government and Fervor in Art." In *Personalities*, pp. 260–93.

Wu Pei-yi. "Self-examination and Confession of Sins in Traditional China." *HJAS* 39 (1979):5–38.

———. "The Spiritual Autobiography of Te-ch'ing." In *Unfolding*, pp. 67–92.

Yang, Winston L. Y. "The Literary Transformation of Historical Figures in the *San-kuo chih yen-i*." In *Critical Essays on Chinese Fiction*, edited by Winston Yang and Curtis Adkins, pp. 47–84. Hong Kong: Chinese University Press, 1980.

———. "Lo Kuan-chung." In *DMB*, 1:978–80.

———. "The Use of the San-kuo chih as a Source of the *San-kuo chih yen-i*."

Ph. D. dissertation, Stanford University, 1971.

Yao Hsin-nung. "The Rise and Fall of K'un-ch'ü Drama." *Tien-hsia Monthly* 2, no. 1 (1936):63–84.

Yu, Anthony C. "Heroic Verse and Heroic Mission: Dimensions of the Epic in the *Hsi-yu chi*." *JAS* 31, no. 4 (August 1972):879–97.

———. *The Journey to the West*. 4 vols. Chicago: Chicago University Press, 1977–83.

———. "Narrative Structure and the Problem of Chapter Nine in the *Hsi-yu chi*." *JAS* 34, no. 2 (February 1975):295–311.

———. "Two Literary Examples of Religious Pilgrimage: The *Commedia* and the *Journey to the West*." *HR* 22, no. 3 (February 1983):202–30.

Yü Chün-fang (Kristin Yü Greenblatt). "Chu-hung and Lay Buddhism in the Late Ming." In *Unfolding*, pp. 93–140.

———. *The Revival of Buddhism in China: Chu-hung and the Late-Ming Synthesis.* New York: Columbia University Press, 1981.

———. "Some Ming Buddhists' Responses to Neo-Confucianism." Unpublished paper.

Yuan Tsing. "Continuities and Discontinuities in Chinese Agriculture." *Ming Studies* 7 (Fall 1978):35–51.

———. "Urban Riots and Disturbances." In *Ming to Ch'ing*, pp. 277–320.

LIBRARY OF CONGRESS CATALOGING-
IN-PUBLICATION DATA

Plaks, Andrew H., 1945–
The four masterworks of the Ming novel.

Bibliography: p.
Includes index.
1. Chinese fiction—Ming dynasty, 1368–1644—
History and criticism.   I. Title.
PL2436.P53 1987   895.1'34'09   87-45534
ISBN 0-691-06708-2